BRITISH
MUSICAL BIOGRAPHY

Da Capo Press Music Reprint Series

GENERAL EDITOR

FREDERICK FREEDMAN

VASSAR COLLEGE

BRITISH
MUSICAL BIOGRAPHY

A Dictionary of Musical Artists, Authors and
Composers Born in Britain and Its Colonies

BY
JAMES D. BROWN
AND
STEPHEN S. STRATTON

𝄢 DA CAPO PRESS · NEW YORK · 1971

A Da Capo Press Reprint Edition

This Da Capo Press edition of
British Musical Biography
is an unabridged republication of the 1897
edition published in London.

Library of Congress Catalog Card Number 76-139197

SBN 306-70076-X

Published by Da Capo Press
A Division of Plenum Publishing Corporation
227 West 17th Street, New York, N.Y. 10011

BRITISH
MUSICAL BIOGRAPHY

BRITISH

MUSICAL BIOGRAPHY:

A DICTIONARY OF

MUSICAL ARTISTS, AUTHORS AND COMPOSERS,

BORN IN

BRITAIN AND ITS COLONIES.

BY

JAMES D. BROWN,

AUTHOR OF A "BIOGRAPHICAL DICTIONARY OF MUSICIANS," ETC.,

AND

STEPHEN S. STRATTON.

LONDON

WILLIAM REEVES Bookseller Ltd.

1a Norbury Crescent, S.W.16

1897.

TO THE INCORPORATED SOCIETY OF MUSICIANS

THIS WORK IS

DEDICATED

BY THE AUTHORS.

PREFACE.

In undertaking this work, the authors have been animated by the desire to present the true position of the British Empire in the world of music. A country is musical only by the music it produces for itself, not by what it takes from others. In this work, therefore, only what has been done by Britain's own sons and daughters is placed on record. It is probable that in no other nation is there, at the present time, greater musical activity, creative or executive, than is to be witnessed in our own; and this not only in the great centres of population and culture, but everywhere throughout the Empire. In this connection the work of provincial and colonial musicians has received its proper share of attention. The greater masters, already noticed at length in other similar publications, have been treated with brevity in order to afford space for mention of many worthy, if obscure, workers in the cause of Art, hitherto passed over by writers of biography. The very large number (probably over 40,000) of persons engaged in the musical profession at the present time will explain the apparent preponderance of notices devoted to living musicians. This part of the work, however, is intended rather to be representative than complete; and from various causes, in many cases only a bare outline could be accomplished. While some names may seem to have but slight claim to inclusion, it is hoped that no artist of eminence has been omitted. The book being written from an independent standpoint, matters of opinion have been subordinated to the presentment of facts; and its usefulness as a work of reference has been one of the main objects of the authors. Accuracy has been striven for as regards dates of birth and death; first performance of important works; and first appearances of artists, which have been carefully collated, where possible, from contemporary notices. Many of these differ from dates hitherto accepted. Still, faults and omissions may be detected, and any information in correction thereof will be gladly received. The work is issued by the authors themselves as a kind of experiment in publishing, their object being a patriotic desire to record the achievements of British workers in the field of musical art.

The authors are indebted to the following gentlemen for information or aid rendered during the progress of the work:—Mr. Reginald B. Moore, Exeter; Mr. J. A. Browne, editor of the *British Musician;* Dr. James C. Culwick, Dublin; Mr. Spencer Curwen, London; Mr. T. B. Dowling, Cape Town, South Africa; Mr. Emlyn Evans, Cemmes, Montgomery; Mr. John Glen, Edinburgh; Mr. W. J. Ions, King's Norton; Mr. E. P. Jones, Brisbane, Australia; Mr. J. A. Matthews, Cheltenham; Mr. C. F. South, Salisbury; Mr. C. J. B. Tirbutt, Reading; Mr. Herbert Thompson, Leeds; and Mr. F. H. Torrington, Toronto, Canada. Also to those artists who responded to the applications made to them for personal information. In addition to the catalogues of the British Museum and other public libraries, general newspapers, and other sources of information, the following works have been drawn upon for particular details:—Brown's Biographical Dictionary of Musicians; Grove's Dictionary of Music and Musicians; the works of Fétis and Mendel-Reissmann; Dictionary of National Biography; Love's Scottish Church Music; Baptie's Musicians of All Times, and Musical Scotland; Roll of the Union of Graduates in Music; Degrees in Music, Abdy Williams, etc. The chief authorities for dates within their period have been the *Musical World*, 1836-91; *Dramatic and Musical Review*, 1842-51; *Musical Times*, from 1844; *Musical Standard*, from 1862; besides the musical journals of more recent date. For many particulars of less-known musicians, bandmasters, and teachers, much has been gleaned from the *Orchestral Times, British Musician*, the *Musical Herald*, and other papers.

STEPHEN S. STRATTON,
247, Monument Road,
Birmingham.

JAMES D. BROWN,
Public Library,
Clerkenwell, London, E.C.

ABBREVIATIONS.

C.M. ..	..	Choirmaster.
F.C.O...	..	Fellow of the College of Organists.
G.S.M.	..	Guildhall School of Music.
I.S.M...	..	Incorporated Society of Musicians.
Mus. B.	..	Bachelor of Music.
Mus. D.	..	Doctor of Music.
R.A.M.	..	Royal Academy of Music ;

A.—Associate ; F.—Fellow ; L.—Licentiate.

R.C.M.	..	Royal College of Music.

A.—Associate of the same.

R.C.O...	..	Royal College of Organists ;

F.—Fellow of the same.

R.I.A.M.	..	Royal Irish Academy of Music.
T.C.L...	..	Trinity College, London ;

L.—Licentiate of the same.

Pf.	.. ..	Pianoforte.
Ps.	.. ..	Psalm.

Dates or words within square brackets, thus—[1846] are approximations, or have been supplied from other sources to supplement undated title-pages, etc.

BRITISH MUSICAL BIOGRAPHY

Aaron. Scottish writer, who was consecrated Abbot of St. Martin, Cologne, in 1042. He wrote a work on chanting in public worship, entitled, "De Utilitate cantus vocalis et de modo cantandi atque psallendi." He died in 1052.

Abbott, Rev. Henry. Writer. Was lecturer of the Church of St. John the Baptist, Bristol. Author of "The use and benefit of Church musick towards quick'ning our devotion. A sermon." London, 1724.

Abbott, Thomas Moreton, violinist, born at Bilston, Staffordshire, August 13, 1843. Studied under Henry Hayward, of Wolverhampton. Resident for some years at Walsall; he ultimately settled in Birmingham. His repertory is large, and he is in wide demand as a soloist. As orchestral principal violin he has been associated with Mr. Stockley's orchestral concerts since 1873, first as colleague with Henry Hayward, and then with F. Ward; also, at the concerts of the Birmingham Festival Choral Society, and societies at Oxford, Wolverhampton, and other festivals. He is an accomplished violoncellist and pianist, but in these capacities restricts himself to teaching.

Abell, John, alto singer and song collector, born, probably, about 1660. In May, 1679, he became a gentleman extraordinary of the Chapel Royal, and was shortly afterwards sent to Italy by Charles II., to study music and singing. He returned to England in 1681-2, and re-entered the Chapel Royal, where he remained till 1688. He was made a Bachelor of Music at Cambridge, in 1684. In 1688 he was dismissed on account of his being a Roman Catholic, and he went to Holland and Germany, where he became known as a lute-player and singer. He sang also in Poland, and it is related of him that on refusing to sing before the King at Warsaw, he was seized and suspended in a chair over a bear-pit, when the threat of being lowered into its midst compelled a display of his vocal powers. In 1698-9 he was Intendant at Cassel, and in 1700 he returned to England. He afterwards resided at Cambridge, and is supposed to have died there about 1724.

WORKS.—Collection of songs in several languages, London, 1701. Collection of songs in English, London, 1701 (contains To all

lovers of musick, a poem by Abell). Song on Queen Ann's coronation [1702]. Collection of . . . Scotch songs, etc. [1740], containing songs by Abell. Two songs in "Pills to purge melancholy" [1719].

Abingdon, Willoughby Bertie, Earl of, amateur composer and flute-player, was born on January 16, 1740, and died September 26, 1799. He established concerts in London, and composed "Representation of the execution of Queen Mary of Scots, in seven views, the music composed and adapted to each view by the Earl of Abingdon," "Twelve sentimental catches and glees for three voices;" Duets, songs, flute music, etc.

Abram, John, organist and composer, born at Margate, August 7, 1840; graduated Mus. Bac., Oxon., 1868; Mus. Doc., Oxon., 1874; Fellow of the Royal College of Organists. Has held appointments as organist at St. John's, Torquay, 1864; St. Peter and Paul, Wantage, 1865; St. Paul's, St. Leonards-on-Sea, 1869; and is at present organist of All Saints', Hastings. Conductor of St. Leonards and Hastings Choral Union, a society that, under his direction, has done much for the cause of music in the locality. He is also director of the Hastings Pier Summer concerts.

His compositions include an oratorio, The Widow of Nain; cantatas, Jerusalem, and a Military Ballade, 1892; anthems, services; Festival March for organ and voices, to the hymn Onward Christian Soldiers; pianoforte pieces, etc.

Abrams, Harriet, soprano vocalist and composer, was born in 1760. She studied under Dr. T. A. Arne, and made her first appearance at Drury Lane in his "May Day," in 1775. In 1776 she appeared with her sister Theodosia at the Concert of Ancient Music, and in 1784 she sang at the great Handel Commemoration. She afterwards sang at the principal London concerts during her time. She died about 1825.

WORKS.—Eight Italian and English Canzonets for one and two voices. London, 1785. Second sett of . . Canzonets . . [1805]. Collection of Scotch Airs harmonized for three voices [1790]. Collection of twelve Songs, London, 1803. Songs — Crazy Jane; The Felon [1800]; Female hardship; Friend of

ABYNGDON.

my heart; Orphan's Prayer; Smile and a tear; Tom Halliard; William and Mary. Also, Little Boy blue, glee; All nature mourns, duet [1805]; And must we part? duet [1810].

Her sisters, ELIZA and THEODOSIA (1766—1834, afterwards Mrs. Garrow) were also vocalists of some reputation, the latter possessing a fine mezzo-soprano voice.

Abyngdon, Henry (also Habyngton and Abyngton), composer, of the 15th century. He was succentor of Wells Cathedral in 1447-97; Mus. Bac., Cambridge, 1463; Master of song in the Chapel Royal, London, 1465; Master of St. Catherine's Hospital, Bristol, 1478. He was celebrated as an organist and singer. Died September 1, 1497.

Ackroyd, Thomas, musician, compiler of "An original set of 51 Psalm and Hymn tunes, for four voices, with organ or pianoforte accompaniment." Halifax, 1848.

Acland, Arthur H. D., See TROYTE, Arthur H. D.

Acland, T. G., author of "Chanting simplified." London, 1843.

Acton, John, composer and teacher of singing, born 1863. Studied music privately, Manchester; later, singing under Francesco Lamperti, of Milan. F.C.O. 1882; qualified for Mus. Bac., Oxford, 1893. Held various organ appointments 1882-93; now devoted entirely to teaching singing and directing choral societies. Professor of singing at the Manchester R.C.M. since its opening, 1893; conductor of the St. Cecilia Choral Society, Manchester, 1894. He has composed two cantatas for ladies' voices: Forest bells, [1888]; The rose and the nightingale [1893]. Was awarded the prize offered by the South London Musical Club, 1888, for Chorus, men's voices, with pf. obbligato, For home and liberty. Other works are ducts for ladies' voices: six duets; Songs on the river (six); The fairies (six); and Songs of wood and fairyland (six). He has also written pieces for pf. &c.

Adam, Alexander, printer, established in Glasgow at the end of last century. He published "The Psalms of David in metre, newly translated . . . allowed by the authority of the general assembly of the Kirk of Scotland and appointed to be sung in congregations and families, with twenty-three select psalm-tunes particularly adapted to the subject of the psalms to which they are set." Glasgow, 1773. "The Musical Repository, a collection of favourite Scotch, English, and Irish songs set to music." Glasgow, 1799, also Edinburgh, 1802, etc.

Adams, Abraham, organist and composer, who flourished at the end of the 17th and beginning of the 18th centuries. He was organist of the parish church of St. Mary-le-bone, London, in 1710, and compiled "The Psalmist's New Companion," London, n.d., of which a 6th edition appeared about 1720.

ADCOCK.

Adams, James B., musician, who flourished in the latter part of the 18th and beginning of the present century. He published a large number of songs and pianoforte pieces, among which may be named the following:— The Paphian Doves [1783], a musical play. Three sonatas for the pf. or harpsichord and flute and violin op. 4 [1790]. A collection of songs, etc., London [1770]. Select songs set to music [1803]. *Songs*: Bacchanalian; Come gentle god of soft repose; Daphne; Invocation; Myrtilla; Power of music; The request; etc.

Adams, John S., writer, author of "Five thousand musical terms." London, 1861.

Adams, Stephen, see MAYBRICK, MICHAEL).

Adams, Thomas, organist and composer, was born at [London?], on September 5, 1785. He studied under Dr. T. Busby, and became organist of Carlisle Chapel, Lambeth, 1802-14. Organist of St. Paul, Deptford, 1814; of St. George, Camberwell, 1824; and of St. Dunstan's, 1833. He died in London on September 5, 1858.

WORKS.—A grand march and quick step, composed for the regiment of loyal London volunteers [1808]. Six fugues for organ or pianoforte [1820]. Six voluntaries for the organ [1820]. Grand organ piece [1824]. Three voluntaries for the organ [1824]. Six organ pieces [1825]. Three organ pieces [1835]. Fantasias, interludes, and transcriptions for organ and pianoforte. Anthems and hymns.

An organist of much celebrity in his day, who was a very remarkable extempore player.

Adams, Thomas Julian, composer and conductor, was born at London, January 28, 1824. He studied under Moscheles and at Paris, and settled in England as a teacher and conductor. In 1851 he formed an orchestra and visited Edinburgh, Glasgow, and Greenock, giving a series of weekly concerts. In 1853 he performed at Paris, and in 1855 organised another orchestra, with which he travelled in England, giving concerts of high-class music. He afterwards resided at Scarborough, Tynemouth, and Buxton as concert-conductor. In 1877 he settled at Eastbourne as conductor of the Devonshire Park concerts. He died at Eastbourne, May 7, 1887.

He introduced Debain's harmonium into England, and wrote for it a work entitled Method for the patent harmonium (1855). He also composed fantasias, studies, marches, and concert-pieces for the orchestra.

Adcock, James, composer, born at Eton, June 29, 1778. He was a chorister in St. George's Chapel, Windsor, 1786, and a lay-clerk in 1797. Member of Trinity, St. John's, and King's Colleges, Cambridge. Schoolmaster to the choristers of King's College, Cambridge. He died at Cambridge April 30, 1860.

ADCOCK.

WORKS.—Evening sevice in B flat. Anthems. Three glees for three and four voices, dedicated to Sir Patrick Blake (1815). Hark how the bees, glee for four voices. Welcome mirth and festive song, glee for three voices. *Songs*—Lucy, Queen of pleasure's languid smile, etc. Rudiments of music, N.D.

Adcock, John, author of "The singers' guide to pronunciation, with an appendix consisting of a pronouncing dictionary of musical terms, etc.," Nottingham, [1873]. Mr. Adcock is choirmaster of Castle Gate Chapel, and conductor of the Sacred Harmonic Society, Nottingham.

Addington, Rev. Stephen, Independent clergyman and musician, born at Northampton June 9th, 1729. He was successively minister at Spalding, Market Harborough, and Miles' Lane Meeting House, Cannon Street, London, 1781. He died at London, February 6th, 1796. Compiler of "A collection of Psalm-tunes for publick worship," 1780; 6th ed., 1786; supplement, 1800. "A collection of approved anthems sellected from the most eminent masters" [1795].

Addison, John, composer and double-bass player, was born at London in 1765. He played the 'cello at Vauxhall Gardens, and was double-bass player at the Italian Opera, the Concerts of Ancient Music, and the Vocal Concerts. He married Miss Willems, the vocalist, in 1793. In the latter part of his career, he embarked in commercial speculations and was greatly reduced in circumstances. He died at London, January 30, 1844.

WORKS.—The sleeping beauty, 1805. The Russian imposter, 1809. My aunt, 1813. Two words, 1816. Free and easy, 1816. My uncle, 1817. Bobinet, the bandit, 1818 ; *Musical Dramas.* Elijah, a sacred drama. *Songs*—Songs of Almacks (with Bishop and Bayley), 1831 ; Allen-a-dale ; Clay cold dwelling ; Cupid's frolic ; Zephyr's reply ; and many others. Singing practically treated in a series of instructions, London [1836].

Addison was a successful teacher of singing and numbered Alex. Lee and Pearman among his pupils. His wife, Miss WILLEMS, who was a niece of Reinhold the vocalist, was a singer, and made her first appearance in 1796, in "Love in a village." She sang at Vauxhall, Covent Garden, and other concerts in London, and appeared also at Liverpool, Dublin, etc.

Addison, Robert Brydges, composer, born at Dorchester, Oxford. Studied at R.A.M. under G. A. Macfarren, to whom he was sub-professor for four years. A.R.A.M., 1882, and professor of harmony and composition. Professor, Trinity College, London, 1892. While at the R.A.M. he composed some works noticeable for high aim and finish, the chief being a symphony in G minor (two movements from which were performed at R.A.M. concert, De-

AGUILAR,

cember 15, 1881) ; concert allegro in G, orchestra. Sonata in A minor, pf. ; andante and variations, pf. ; cantata, "A vision," for contralto solo, chorus, orchestra, and organ (R.A.M., June 1880) ; Ps. 126, four voices ; Motet, Save me, O God ; two albums for children—"Please sing me a song," and "Children's voices." But he is more widely known by his songs, tasteful and fresh in feeling, Wandering wishes ; Two doves ; Do I love thee ? O rushing wind ; and others, also a trio for female voices, "Quiet hours."

Adlington, William, pianist, teacher, and publisher, born at Southwell, Notts., in 1838. He was educated at the R.A.M., of which he became an Associate in 1865, and a Fellow in 1882. In 1864 he settled in Edinburgh, and held various important teaching appointments. Afterwards he resided at Aberdeen, where he was conductor of the University Orchestral Society. He is now engaged in musicselling and publishing. Author of "Elementary principles of music and elements of harmony adapted for those studying the pianoforte." Edinburgh, 1881.

Adye, Willett, amateur musician, author of "Musical notes," London, 1869, a work on violinists.

Agabeg, Mrs., *see* WYNNE, Sarah Edith.

Aguilar, Emanuel A., composer and pianist, born in Clapham, London, August 23, 1824. Son of E. Aguilar, a West Indian of Spanish extraction, and brother of Miss Grace Aguilar, the novelist. Resident in London as teacher and concert-giver. Has also given concerts in Germany, where some of his most important works have been produced. His pianoforte recitals have been, for many years, a regular feature of the London musical season. Played at the Gewandhaus concerts, Leipzig, March 30th, 1848.

WORKS.—Psalm I., voices and orchestra, 1861 (MS). *Operas*—Wave king, 1855 (MS) ; The bridal wreath, 1863. Cantatas, The bridal of Triermain, Bedford, 1880 ; Summer night, 1875, Goblin market, 1880, both for treble voices. *Songs*—The stars are brightly beaming, The appeal, etc. *Symphonies*—No. 1, in C, 1844 (MS.), Frankfort on Main ; No. 2, in E minor, 1844, Frankfort, 1851, London ; No. 3, in D minor, 1854, London. *Overtures*—Alpheus, 1853, London ; St. George, 1875, London ; also at Kissingen and elsewhere on the continent. *Pianoforte works* — Allegro maestoso, pf. and orchestra, 1852, London ; Septet, pf., wind, and strings, 1883 ; Sextet, pf. and wind, 1860 ; Quartet, pf. and strings, 1888 ; Quartets in A and D minor, strings, 1884-5. These have been performed at concerts of the Musical Artists' Society, the septet excepted. Trios, pf. and strings, in G minor, 1853 ; E major, 1856 ; A minor, 1889, performed at various concerts. Fantasia for organ, two pianos, and violin, 1880 ; Duo concertante, in C, two pianos, 1878 ; Sonata, pf. duet, 1885 ; Six sonatas, many smaller pieces, and a little book, How to learn the pianoforte, 1883.

Agutter, Benjamin, organist and composer, born at St. Albans, April 2, 1844. Studied singing under Manuel Garcia ; organ and composition with E. J. Hopkins ; and harmony and counterpoint with Dr. Wylde. Graduated Mus. B., Oxon., 1870 ; Mus. D., Cantuar, 1891 ; F.R.C.O., etc. Since 1867, precentor, organist, and choirmaster, St. Peter's, Streatham. He has composed a Missa de Sancto Albans ; Missa de Sancto Petro ; and six other services for Holy Communion ; sequence, To the Paschal victim (scored for orchestra) ; anthems ; morning and evening services in D and A flat ; hymns, carols, &c., &c.

Ainley, William Clark, organist and composer, born at Kirkheaton, Yorkshire, July 13, 1834. Was a chorister at the Parish Church when ten years old ; pursued his musical studies privately. A.R.C.O., Mus. B., Cambridge, 1885. Has been organist and choirmaster successively at Kirkburton Parish Church, 1856; Kirkheaton, 1863; Mold Green Parish Church, 1865 ; and Mirfield Parish Church, 1874 to present time. Conductor of the Mirfield Choral Society. His compositions are :—Ps. 46, for soli, chorus, and organ [1885] ; cantata, The great day of the Lord, produced Mirfield, 1891. *Anthems*—O give thanks ; Behold, O God our defender (written for the Queen's jubilee, 1887) ; and others. Te Deum, communion service in G, evening service in E, introits, organ pieces, &c.

Aird, James, music publisher of the last half of the 18th century, was established in business in Glasgow, where he died in September, 1795. He issued among other works " A selection of Scots, English, Irish, and foreign airs adapted for the fife, violin, and German flute," Glasgow, 1784, etc.. 6 vols. He was succeeded in business by J. McFadyen, who published new editions or continuations of Aird's publications.

Airy, Sir George Biddell, astronomer, born at Alnwick, June 21, 1801. He was educated at Cambridge, etc., and in 1835 was appointed astronomer-royal. He died on January 1, 1892. Author of " On sound and atmospheric vibrations, with the mathematical elements of music," London, 1868 ; also many works on astronomical and mathematical subjects.

Akeroyd, Arthur Thomas, Organist and composer, born at Bradford, March 10th, 1862. Articled pupil of F. C. Atkinson, A.R.C.M. Organist and choirmaster, St. Paul's Bradford ; music master, Girls' Grammar School, Bradford ; and conductor of the

Ilkley Vocal Society. Hon. Sec. Yorkshire Section of the Incorporated Society of Musicians. He has composed an opera, " The Professor " (book by G. W. Harwin, produced Theatre Royal, Bradford, 1891) ; an operetta, " The Doctor's Dilemma " (Technical College, 1893) ; an anthem for Christmas ; songs and part-songs; minuet and trio for organ, and pieces for pf.

Akeroyde, Samuel, composer, born in Yorkshire at end of 17th century. He composed many songs in the "Theater of Musick," 1685-87 ; " Banquet of musick," 1688 ; and in other collections of the same period. Among his single songs may be mentioned, Give me kind Heaven [1700]; Thursday in the morn [1730] ; Rays of dear Clarinda's eyes [1700] ; etc. He died early in the 18th century.

Alaw, Ddu. *See* REES, William Thomas.

Alawydd. *See* ROBERTS, David.

Albani. *See* LA JEUNESSE.

Albert, Prince Francis C. A. A. E. (Prince Consort), amateur musician, born Rosenau, Coburg, August 26, 1819. Married Queen Victoria, February, 1840. Died Windsor, December 14, 1861.

He composed a number of anthems, services, songs, psalm-tunes, etc., most of which have been collected in " Songs and ballads written and set to music by their Royal Highnesses, Albert and Ernest, Princes of Saxe-Coburg and Gotha." Edited by E. J. Loder, London, 1840; and "Vocal compositions of H.R.H. the Prince Consort." London, 1862. In 1849 and 1855 his piece, entitled L'Invocazione all' Armonia was produced at the Birmingham Festival. Most of the members of his family are musical.

Albert, Eugene François Charles d', pianist and composer (son of Charles Louis Napoleon d' Albert, famous dance-music composer, who died in 1886), born at Glasgow, April 10, 1864. His mother, *neé* Annie Rowell, of Newcastle-on Tyne, was his first music teacher. After a few pf. lessons from the late G. A. Osborne, d' Albert gained the Newcastle scholarship at the National Training School of Music, in 1876, and later on was elected to the Queen's Scholarship, which he held until 1881. His teachers were Arthur Sullivan, John Stainer, E. Prout, and E. Pauer. In 1881, he was nominated to the Mendelssohn Scholarship, which he only held for one year, failing to comply with the regulations. While still a student he made his debut at the Monday Popular Concerts, November 22, 1880, playing Schumann's Etudes Symphoniques ; and at the Crystal Palace, February 5, 1881, taking the solo part in Schumann's pf. concerto in A minor. In October, 1881, he appeared at a Richter Concert as a composer, with his own Concerto in A. As a pianist he gained a high

ALBERTAZZI.

reputation. Hans Richter then took him to Vienna, but he played again in London in the spring of 1882. He now became a pupil of Liszt, and was appointed Court pianist to the Grand Duke of Weimar. During the next four years he made artistic tours through Germany; visited Russia, Italy, Spain; and twice undertook concert tours in America. He held various appointments, the last being that of Kapellmeister at Weimar, 1895, which he did not hold long. He reappeared in London, April 28, 1896, at one of the Mottl concerts; began a series of Recitals, May 1; and played Liszt's concerto in E flat at the Philharmonic concert, May 6, being most enthusiastically received.

WORKS. — Operas : Ghismonda (Dresden, 1895); Der Rubin (composed 1892); A work for chorus and orchestra, founded on Otto Ludwig's Man and Life (1893); songs, etc. Symphony in F (1885); Concerto in B minor, op. 2 (1884); in E, op. 12 (Berlin, Jan. 1893), for pf. and orchestra. Overtures : Hyperion (Berlin, 1885); Dramatic overture in A, op. 9 (Cologne, 1887); Esther (Vienna, 1888); String quartets, in A minor, op. 8; in E flat, op. 11; Suite for pf., op. 1 ; Sonata, F sharp minor, op. 10, &c.

Albertazzi, Emma (born HOWSON), contralto vocalist, born in London, May 1, 1813 [1814]. She was a daughter of Francis Howson, musician of London. In 1827 she studied under Costa, and in November, 1829 she was married to Signor Albertazzi. She first appeared in the Argyle Rooms, London, in 1829, and in 1830 she sang at the King's Theatre. In 1832 she appeared at Milan, and afterwards at Madrid and Paris. She reappeared at London in *La Cenerentola*, April, 1837, and in 1838 sang at Drury Lane in *La Gazza Ladra*. She frequently appeared as a concert vocalist, and died in London, September 27, 1847.

Alcock or **Allcock, John,** composer and organist, born at London, April 11, 1715. He was a chorister in St. Paul's Cathedral under Charles King, and afterwards studied under John Stanley, the blind organist. He held successively the appointment of organist at All Hallows Church, London, 1735; St. Andrew's, Plymouth, 1737 ; St. Lawrence's Reading, 1742-49 ; and Lichfield Cathedral, 1749-60, where he was also vicar-choral and master of the choristers. In 1755 he graduated as Mus. Bac. Oxford, and in 1761 or 1765 proceeded to Mus. Doc. Oxford. He held the appointment of organist at Sutton Coldfield parish church, 1761-86 ; and at Tamworth parish church, 1766-90. He gained a prize medal of the Catch Club in 1770. He retained the post of lay-vicar at Lichfield till his death at Lichfield on February 23, 1806.

WORKS.—Morning and Evening Service in E minor, 1753; Six-and-twenty select anthems

ALDRICH.

in score . . . to which are added a burial service for 4 voices and part of the last verse of the 150th Psalm for 8 voices and instruments, London, 21 parts, 1771. Miserere, or the 51st Psalm in Latin for 4 voices, 1771. Fifty select portions collected from the singing Psalms, Reading, 1748. The Pious Soul's heavenly exercise, or divine harmony; being a choice collection of those excellent psalm tunes which are used in the parish churches in London, etc., Lichfield, n.d. Harmony of Sion, or a collection of all the capital psalm tunes that are used in London, Derby, n d. Divine Harmony, or a collection of 55 double and single chants for 4 voices, as they are sung at the cathedral of Lichfield, 1752. Parochial Harmony, 1777. Harmony of Jerusalem, being a collection of 106 psalms and hymns in score, 1801. Harmonia Festi, or a collection of canons, cheerful and serious glees, and catches for 4 and 5 voices, Lichfield, 1791. Hail, ever-pleasing solitude! (prize glee), 1770. Twelve English songs, 1740. Eight easy voluntaries for the organ, 1760. Six suites of easy lessons for the harpsichord or spinnet, with a trumpet piece, Reading, 1742. Six easy solos for the German flute or violin, 1750. Life of Miss Fanny Brown (a novel).

Alcock, John, son of the above, was born probably at Plymouth about 1740, and studied under his father. He became organist of St. Mary Magdalene, Newark-on-Trent, in 1758, and remained there till 1768. In 1773, he became organist of the Parish Church, Walsall, and died there, March 30, 1791. In 1766 he graduated as Mus. Bac. at Oxford. He composed some anthems, songs, and harpsichord music, among which are—A cantata and six songs [1770] ; Venus and Bacchus, a two-part song ; Let me sink to regions of shade (song) ; Three sonatas for two violins and violoncello ; The chace (pianoforte piece).

Alcock, William Bennis, organist. Studied under Sir R. P. Stewart. Graduated Mus. B., Oxford, 1879. Was appointed the first organist of Christ Church, Morningside, Edinburgh, in 1876, where he worked up the musical service to a high pitch of excellence. He was a most skilful organist. In 1891 he resigned his post at Christ Church, and was appointed music master in Speir's School, Beith, Ayrshire, where he taught with much success. He died, of congestion of the lungs, October, 1892. Madrigals and glees, he made a study of, and lectured upon the subject in Morningside Athenæum.

Aldrich, Henry, divine and composer, born at Westminster in 1647. He was educated at Westminster School, and at Christ Church, Oxford, from 1662. He became B.A., 1666 ; M.A., 1669 ; Canon of Christ Church, 1681 ; D.D., 1682 ; and Dean of Christ Church, 1689, all of Oxford. He died at

ALEXANDER.

Oxford, December 14, 1710, and left his musical library to Christ Church. WORKS.—Services in G and A. *Anthems*— I am well pleased; Not unto us, O Lord; Out of the deep; O give thanks; O praise the Lord; Thy beauty, O Israel; We have heard with our ears. *Glees* — Hark, the bonny Christ Church bells, for three voices; A catch on tobacco, etc. Works on logic, etc. Another musician of this name, viz., BED-FORD ALDRICH, composed and published a number of songs in the first half of the 18th century.

Alexander, Alfred, organist and composer, born at Rochester, Kent, May 6, 1844. Chorister at the Cathedral, pupil of, and, later, assistant to, John Hopkins, the Cathedral organist. Took the Toronto degree of Mus. B. in 1889. When seventeen, succeeded J. F. Bridge as organist of Shorne Church, near Rochester; then appointed to Strood Parish Church, and afterwards offered the post of organist to the Earl of Mar and Kellie. When Dr. Colborne left St. Michael's College, Tenbury, Sir Frederick Ouseley invited Mr. Alexander to fill the vacancy. He afterwards went to Wigan Parish Church; then (1891-2) to Nice, as organist of the American Church; and is now at St. Andrew's, Southport. Has given organ recitals, and conducted concerts of the Wigan Choral Society. His compositions include a cantata; Ps. 126, for soprano solo, chorus of women's voices, and orchestra; services, anthems, songs, part-songs, etc. Triumphal march, orchestra; Sonata in B flat, for string quartet; Romances, violin; Sonata in D minor, for organ (published in Novello's original organ compositions, 1892).

Alexander, James, writer and performer, published various works, of which the following are the most important:—Alexander's Book of instructions for the accordion, London, 2 pts. [1845]. Complete instructions for the harmonicon, etc., London [1865]. Various arrangements, waltzes, etc., for accordion and pianoforte.

Alford, John, lutenist of the 16th century, published a translation of Adrian Le Roy's book on the Lute as "A Briefe and Easye Introduction to learne the tablature, to conduct and dispose the hands unto the Lute." London, 1568.

Alford, Marmaduke, vocalist and composer, was born in Somersetshire in 1647. He was a yeoman and sergeant of the vestry of the Chapel Royal, and died in May, 1715.

Allan, Archibald, violinist and composer of dance music, was born at Forfar about 1790. He was a member of Nathanial Gow's band, and played at balls and other gatherings in Scotland. He died at Forfar 1831. He composed strathspeys and other Scots dance

ALLCHIN.

tunes. His brother, THOMAS R. ALLAN (born Forfar, 1807, died Dysart, Fife, 1851), was also a violinist and composer of dance music; and JAMES ALLAN, cousin of the above (born Forfar, October 17, 1800; died there August 18, 1877), was another member of the same family of violinists which at one time was well-known all over the centre and south of Scotland.

Allan, David Skea, tonic sol-fa teacher, born at Calfsound, Island of Eday, Orkneys, March 14, 1840. Son of a crofter-fisherman, his humble home was brightened by music; and the boy worked hard at his musical studies, overcoming difficulties of no ordinary nature. In 1864 he settled in Glasgow, where he has ever since remained. After holding several appointments as Precentor, he was asked, in 1877, to take the practical classes at Anderson's College. These were transferred to the Christian Institute in 1881, and under the auspices of the Sunday School Union, continue to be popular and successful. He is also conductor of St. Andrew's Choir, and has charge of the music in many of the Glasgow board schools. He is a Fellow of the Educational Institute of Scotland, and is favourably known as a writer of delicate, tasteful verse. His publications consist of books of school songs; part-songs, the Gloaming, &c.

Allan, James, the "celebrated Northumberland piper," was born at Rothbury, March 1734, and died in Durham jail on November 13, 1810. He was well-known all over the borders as a strolling vagrant, and his biography by James Thompson was issued as the "Life of James Allan, the celebrated Northumberland Piper, detailing his surprising adventures, etc." Newcastle, 1817. This has been frequently reprinted as a chap-book.

Allan, James, baritone singer and conductor, was born near Falkirk, July 27, 1842. He became a lithographer in Glasgow and was successively precentor in Sydney Place U.P. Church and Kelvinside Free Church in that city. He held the position of conductor of the Glasgow Select Choir from 1880 to 1885, during which time it gave successful concerts in Scotland and England. He died at Glasgow, August 10, 1885. He composed various hymn tunes, of which "Vevay" was printed in the *Free Church Hymnal*, and arranged various songs and airs for choir and school use.

Allchin, William Thomas Howell, organist and composer, born 1843. He became Mus. Bac., Oxford, 1869, and conductor of the Oxford Choral Soc. in the same year. Organist of St. John's College, Oxford, 1875, and local examiner for R.A.M. in 1881. He died at Oxford, January 8, 1883.

WORKS—The Rebellion of Korah, sacred cantata, composed and produced for the degree of Mus. Bac., June 1869 (ms.). *Songs*—Christ-

ALLEN.

mas greeting, The forsaken, Lament for the Summer, O but to see her face again, Prythee why so pale, Rainy day, Sea song, A shadow, Song for November, The wrecked hope, etc.

Allen, Alfred Benjamin, pianist and composer, born at Kingsland, London, September 4, 1850. Began the study of the pianoforte at the age of five, afterwards becoming a student at the London Academy of Music. Settled in London as performer and teacher. His compositions include a cantata and a number of orchestral pieces still in MS. Among his published works are the songs, Lead, kindly light; She sang to her harp; Sweet birdie, mine, and many others. *Pianoforte music*—Minuet in C; Gavotte in D; Egyptian Court Dance, etc. Also pieces for the organ.

Allen, Edward Heron-, author, born St. John's Wood, London, December 17, 1861. Educated at Elstree and Harrow. In 1878 he began the formation of his library of works on the violin. In 1879-1881 he studied violin making under Chanot. Admitted a solicitor 1884. Special commissioner to Italy on behalf of Historic Loan Department of Music and Inventions Exhibition, 1885, for which service he was awarded a silver medal. Lectured in United States, 1886-89. Married to Marianna, daughter of Rudolph Lehmann, the artist. Elected "Socio onorario e benemerito" of the Accademia of Sta. Cecilia of Rome, for Bibliography of the Violin.

WORKS.—De Fidiculis Bibliographia: being the basis of a bibliography of the violin and all other instruments played with a bow. Lond. 1890-93, 12 parts. Violin-making as it was and is. Lond. 1884. Manual of Cheirosophy. Lond. 1885. Poems, tales, translations, etc.

Allen, George Benjamin, composer and vocalist, born in London, April 21, 1822. Chorister, St. Martin-in-the-fields, 1830; the same in Westminster Abbey, 1832. Established the "Abbey Glee Club," in 1841, and two years later was appointed to the choir of Armagh Cathedral as a bass. Conductor of Classical Harmonists' Society, Belfast, and originated and executed the scheme for building the Ulster Hall, Belfast. Graduated as Mus. Bac., Oxon., in 1852. Left Armagh, and became organist at All Saints', Kensington, and later went to Australia, where he was organist at Toorak, Melbourne, and conductor of Lyster's Opera Company. Returning to England, he established a Comedy Opera Company, and produced the Gilbert and Sullivan operas, "The Sorcerer," "H.M.S. Pinafore," and "The Pirates of Penzance." He had previously made successful tours with his pupil, Miss Alice May (died U.S.A., 1857), in Australia, New Zealand, and India, his opera company being admirably organised.

ALLISON.

Since 1890 he has been settled in Brisbane, New S. Wales

WORKS.—*Operas*— Castle Grim, two acts, London, 1865. The Viking, five acts. The Wicklow rose, Manchester, 1882. Fayette (J. Brunton Stephens), not yet (1895) produced; and others in MS. *Cantatas*—Harvest home, 1863; The Vintage of the Rhine, 1865; Ministering (female voices,) 1884. *Te Deums* in D and F. *Introits* and *Anthems*—A book of fifteen anthems, 1853, and eight others. *Concerted vocal music*—Six four-part songs [1861]; Morning; May; and others. *Songs*—A Shadow; The arrow and the song; and settings of many of Longfellow's lyrics, the total amounting to about 300. Pianoforte and organ music. The Scales in music and colours—their analogy; from the *Musical World*. New pianoforte school. London [1884].

Allen, Henry Robinson, tenor vocalist and composer, born at Cork in 1809. He studied at the R.A.M., and first appeared in Mozart's "Figaro" in 1831. Afterwards he sang in opera, chiefly in London, till about 1856, when he occupied himself as a teacher of singing. He died at Hammersmith, London, November 27, 1876. He composed many songs, of which the following are best known: Adaline; As steals the dew; Bella donna, would'st thou know; Broken spell; Dearest, wake; Dear halls of my fathers; Green are thy hills; Maid of Athens [1861]; Mine, only mine; Pilgrim's lament; Sea is calm; When first we met; When we two parted, etc.

Allen, James Vaughan, musician, published "Ten Cathedral Chants in score, with an accompaniment for the organ. London [1842].

Allen, John, organist and composer of latter part of 16th and early part of 17th centuries. He was organist of Chester Cathedral, and in 1612 he graduated Mus. Bac., Oxford.

Allen, John, violinist, born in London, and began his career as a leader in 1841. Subsequently he went to America, and for thirty years was identified with the San Francisco theatres. His four daughters, Ricca, Ray, Louise, and Anna, are well-known dancers. He died at Brooklyn, New York, about August 1892, at the age of seventy-two.

Allen, Richard, writer, who flourished at the end of the 17th and begining of the 18th centuries. Author of "An Essay to prove the singing of psalms with conjoint voices a christian duty." London, 1696. "Brief vindication of an Essay to prove the singing of psalms with conjoint voices a christian duty, from Dr. Russell's Animadversions and Mr. Marlow's remarks." London, 1696.

Allison, Horton Claridge, composer, organist, and pianist, born in London, July 25, 1846. Entered the Royal Academy of Music in 1856, and appeared as a pianist at Willis's Rooms in May 1860, as a pupil of W. H.

ALLISON.

Holmes. Studied at Leipzig Cons. 1862-65, gaining, in the last year, the first prize for general proficiency, his teachers being Plaidy, E. F. Richter, C. Reinecke, Hauptmann, and Moscheles. Commenced giving concerts in London, July, 1865, and has since appeared in various towns in the provinces. Resident as teacher in Manchester. Was elected Associate of the R.A.M., 1862, and Member in 1880. Graduated Mus. Bac., Cantab., 1877; Mus. Doc., Dublin, the same year. Appointed one of Her Majesty's Examiners in Music, Intermediate Education Board for Ireland, 1884. WORKS.—Cantatas — 1871-74. Setting of Psalms cx., cxvii., and cxxxiv., for soli, chorus, and string orchestra, 1876, all in MS. Anthems, songs, and part-songs. Symphony for Orchestra, 1875. Suite for Orchestra. Concerto in D. Pf. and Orchestra, composed in 1870, performed 1877, and at the concert of the Westminster Orchestral Society, December 9, 1891, and a second concerto, performed Manchester, February 1894, all in MS. Quartet, strings, 1865. Concert Duet for two Pianofortes, 1865. Studies and Concert Pieces. Sonata for the Organ, 1865, published 1879. Marches and various other pieces.

Allison, or Alison, Richard, composer, who flourished in the latter part of the 16th century, and died early in the 17th century. He published " The Psalmes of David in meter, the plaine song being the common tunne to be sung and plaide vpon the lute, orpharyon, citterne or base violl, severally or altogether, the singing part to be either tenor or treble to the instrument, according to the nature of the voyce, or for foure voyces, etc. Lond. 1599." " An houre's recreation in Musicke, apt for instruments and voyces . . . Lond. 1606. He was one of the composers who harmonised the tunes in Thomas Este's " Whole Booke of Psalmes," 1592.

Allitsen, Frances, vocalist and composer of the present time. Made her debut at Grosvenor Hall, July, 1882 ; and has since sung at various concerts. She has composed six songs (Tennyson) ; eight songs (Heine) ; After long years ; Mary Hamilton ; In times of old ; Warning ; False or true, and others. EMMA ALLITSEN, her sister, is a contralto vocalist, pupil of the late J. P. Goldberg. Has appeared at, and given concerts in London. Was a professor of singing at the Blackheath Conservatoire.

Allon, Rev. Henry, Congregational minister and musician, born at Welton, near Hull, October 13, 1818. He was educated at Cheshunt College, Herts., and was minister of Union Chapel, Islington, from 1844 till 1892. He also acted as editor of the *British Quarterly Review*. He died at Islington, London, April 16, 1892. WORKS.—Congregational Psalmist, edited

ALPRESS.

with Dr. Gauntlett, Lond. 1858; also 1860-79 four sections, and numerous other editions. Book of chants, 1860. Book of church anthems, 1872. Children's worship hymns, 1878. Church song in its relations to church life, Lond. 1862. The worship of the church, 1870 (In Reynolds' " Ecclesia ").

Allon, Erskine, composer, son of Dr. Henry Allon, born at Canonbury, London, 1864. Educated at Reading and Trin. Coll. Cambridge. Studied music under W. H. Birch and other masters, and later under F. Corder. Resident in London. WORKS.—Comic opera, MS. *Cantatas*— May Margaret, Op. 17, 1889 ; Annie of Lochroyan, Op. 20, 1890, produced by the Philharmonic Society, May 18, 1893 ; The Childe of Elle, Op. 23, 1891, produced Islington, Dec. 18, 1891 ; The Maid of Colonsay, Op. 25, 1894; Sir Nicholas (choral ballad), 1895 ; and The Oak of Geismar, 1895 (MS.). *Songs*—Op. 3, 5 ; Twelve songs. Op. 7 ; Albums of old English songs, Op. 15, 18, 24, 28, and 34 ; Ten love songs, Op. 13 ; Six pastorals, Op. 34 ; Albums of songs (words by Dolly Radford), Op. 9, 27, 29, and 33 ; various songs, duets, and part - songs. *Instrumental* — Chamber music ; Quintet in C, pf. and strings, Op. 35 ; Trio, Op. 22 ; Sonatas, pf. and violin, in F, Op. 19, in G, Op. 21. *Pianoforte Solo*— Sonatas, in C and G minor, Op. 11 and 12 ; The Months, twelve pieces, Op. 8 ; Three sets of European dances, Op. 16, 30, and 31 (also for orchestra) ; Suite in F minor, Op. 26 ; Ballet music, and other pieces, in dance rhythms, &c.

Allum, Charles Edward, organist and conductor, born at Great Marlow, Bucks., June 27, 1852. Studied under Mr. Yates, organist of Bisham Abbey, and afterwards was pupil and assistant of the late W. W. Ringrose. Graduated Mus. Bac., 1883, Mus. Doc., 1887, Dublin. In 1874 he was appointed organist and choirmaster of Holy Trinity Episcopal Church, Stirling, and also conductor of the Stirling Choral Society. By his energy and ability the musical services of the church were greatly improved, and the Choral Society raised to more than local importance. The first performance in Scotland of Gounod's *Mors et vita*, took place under his direction, December 11, 1885. He holds the appointments of organist of the Public Halls, Stirling, and Town Hall, Alloa. His compositions include a setting of Ps. 84, and a short oratorio, "The Deliverence of Israel "; only some church music, and transcriptions for the organ, have been published. Author of The Complete Scale and Arpeggio Manuel (Wickins). Dr. Allum holds the rank of Captain in the 4th Stirlingshire Volunteer Battalion.

Alpress H. G. Rivers, violinist, born in Bendigo, Victoria, Australia, in 1864. He

ALQUIN.

AMOTT.

founded the Sydney Orpheus Society, and for some years was conductor of the Sydney Lie-dertafel. He is now associated with the Sydney Amateur Orchestral Society, and is heard at the principal concerts. As a solo player his reputation is very high, and his repertory embraces the concertos of the great masters, and the principal works of all schools for the violin.

Alquin, Frank C. d', bass vocalist, born in London, of German parentage. Studied at Milan, under Visoni and Nava. Sang with success in Italy and Germany; and has been heard in concerts in various parts of Britain. Now resident at Brighton as teacher of singing. When a child he studied the violoncello under Piatti, and at his concerts in Brighton he frequently plays solos upon that instrument. He is well-known as a song composer, his publications including The carol singers; Romanza Pastorale; L' Aube Nait (Victor Hugo); and numerous others; also the "Preparatory Exercise for the Shake."

Alsop, John, composer of present time, of Newton Abbey, was awarded the Sir Michael Costa Prize of ten guineas, Trinity College, London, with the gold medal, 1888, for an orchestral overture in F. He is also the composer of a cantata, "The Sower" [1895].

Alston, John, educationist, was born at Glasgow in 1777. He was a merchant and magistrate of Glasgow, and identified himself with the Blind Asylum, of which he became a director and honorary treasurer. In 1837 he published specimens of printing for the blind in raised Roman type, and from that date he issued a large number of books, chiefly educational, for use among the blind. His two works on music in raised type for the blind are the earliest of the kind known to us. The first was "Musical catechism, with tunes, for the blind." Glasgow [1838]; and the second "A selection of Scottish songs, embossed for the use of the blind." Glasgow (printed in the Asylum at the Institution Press), 1844. This work is stated to be "the first book of songs, set to music, printed in relief for the instruction of the blind." In 1843 a bust of Alston from the chisel of James Fillans was unveiled in the Glasgow Asylum for the blind, the inscription on which records the fact that he printed the first bible "in raised letters for the use of the blind." He died at Glasgow, August 20, 1846, after a career of usefulness and distinction.

Ambler, Sarah, see BRERETON, Mrs.W. H.

Ames, John Carlowitz, composer and pianist, born at Westbury-on-Trym, near Bristol, January 8, 1860. His father, Geo. A. Ames (born May 10, 1827; died in London, January 3, 1893), was a talented amateur violinist, pupil of Molique, and, under an assumed name, played in the orchestra of the Birmingham Festival of 1846, when Mendelssohn's "Elijah"

was produced. He was the composer of a string quartet, and other works. J. C. Ames first studied under Sir Herbert Oakeley, who persuaded his father to let him take up music as a profession. He then went to Stuttgart, 1878, remaining there until 1881, studying the pf. under Lebert and Pruckner, and composition under Goetschius and Faisst. Afterwards he became a pupil of Franz Wüllner at Dresden. One of the early advocates of the Janko Keyboard, he exhibited its powers at a concert at the Burlington Hall, London, in December, 1888, and has given recitals at the Conferences of the Incorporated Society of Musicians in London, 1893, and Scarborough, 1894, and since in several towns in the provinces.

WORKS.—Psalm 130, for soli, chorus, and orchestra, Dresden, 1877. Consertstück, Dresden, 1888; Concerto in C minor, Op. 8, Crystal Palace (Oscar Beringer), 1889, both for pf. and orchestra. Concerto in D minor, violin and orchestra, London, 1892; Quartet in E minor, strings (Dresden); Trio in E, pf. and strings; Sonata, pf. and violin; pianoforte pieces, etc.

MARIE MILDRED AMES, sister of the preceding, was born June 20, 1867. Studied under her brother for three years, and then at the R.A.M., instrumentation with F. Corder; later at Berlin. Won the Charles Mortimer Prize for composition at R.A.M., 1894. Has written an Andante and Rondo for clarionet and pf.; Andante in G, Barcarolle, and other pieces for violin and pf., etc.

Amner, John, composer and organist, was born about the end of the 16th century. He was appointed organist and choirmaster of Ely Cathedral in 1610, and took the degree of Mus. Bac. Oxford in 1613. He died at Ely in 1641.

WORKS.—Sacred hymns of 3, 4. 5, and 6 parts for voyces and vyols. London, 1615. Some of his anthems and other music for the church service are preserved in ms. at Ely, Cambridge (Peterhouse and Christ Church), Oxford, and in the British Museum. According to Burney he published some madrigals.

RALPH AMNER, a bass singer, probably a relative of the above, was a lay clerk at Ely Cathedral in 1604, and gentleman of the Chapel Royal in 1623. He was a minor canon of St. George's Chapel, Windsor. He died at Windsor, March 3, 1664.

Amott, John, composer and organist, born at Monmouth in 1798, was organist of Abbey Church, Shrewsbury, from 1822 to 1832; and organist of Gloucester Cathedral in succession to Mutlow, 1832-65. He died at Gloucester, February 9, 1865. He composed services, anthems, etc., and acted as conductor of the Gloucester Musical Festivals. He edited a second edition of Lysons' work on the Three choirs festivals, entitled "The Annals of the Three Choirs, etc." London [1864].

AMPS.

Amps, William, organist and composer of the present time. Was conductor, for some years, of the Cambridge University Musical Society, the concerts of which he distinguished by the production of choral works—Mendelssohn's "Elijah" (1853); Antigone, and others. He was organist of St. Peter's Church, Cambridge. Of his compositions, two pf. sonatas, and two sonatinas have been published, as also six vocal quartets (1850), and six part-songs (1865).

Anchors, William, musician of early part of 18th century, published "A Choice Collection of Psalm-Tunes, Hymns, and Anthems." London [1720].

Anderson, Andrew, compiler of " Sacred Harmony . . . adapted to the version of the psalms, paraphrases, and hymns used in Presbyterian churches and chapels . . . London [1840].

Anderson, George Frederick, violinist, born London, 1793. He married Miss Lucy Philpot, the pianist, in July, 1820. He held the appointments of conductor of Royal Private Band, and hon. treasurer of Philharmonic Society and Royal Society of Musicians. He died at London, December 14, 1876. He published " Statement of Mr. G. F. Anderson, in reply to calumnious charges against him as Director of Her Majesty's Private Band." Norwich [1855]. Privately printed.

Anderson, James Smith, organist and composer, born at Crail, Fifeshire, June 30, 1853. Musical training, private. F.R.C.O. ; Mus. Bac., Oxon., 1878. Has held various organ appointments. including the Parish Church, Abbey, 1877-9, and St. Andrew's Parish Church, from 1881. He is teacher of pf. at Moray House Training College and School; and lecturer on harmony and counterpoint at St. George's Classes, Edinburgh ; both positions dating from 1892. A skilful organist, he has rendered valuable service at concerts. His compositions comprise Psalm 100, for soli, chorus, and orchestra ; operettas, " Hearts and homes " and " Land of romance," which are published ; as also some songs and pf. pieces. He also revised the harmonies of the " Blackburn tune book," and composed hymn tunes.

Anderson, John, violinist and composer, born 1737 ; died at Inverness, June 5, 1808. He published " Selection of the most approved Highland strathspeys, country dances, English and French dances, with a harpsichord or violoncello bass." Edinburgh [1790], two collections. " Budget of strathspeys, reels, and country dances for the German flute or violin," Edinburgh, n.d.

Anderson, Josephine, born BARTOLOZZI, mezzo-soprano singer, born at London in 1806. She was a younger sister of Madame Vestris, and studied under Corri, etc. In 1828 she

ANDERSON.

made her début as Rosina in the " Barber of Seville," at the Haymarket Theatre, London, and afterwards sang at London and provincial concerts. She died of consumption, on May 1, 1848, aged 42.

Anderson, Lucy, born PHILPOT, wife of G. F. Anderson, was born at Bath, December, 1790. She was instructed in music by her father and James W. Windsor, and became a pianist of great promise. She appeared at the Philharmonic Society concert in London, April 29, 1822, being the first lady pianist who ever did so, and afterwards played at many of the principal concerts. She was teacher of Queen Victoria and several other members of the royal family. Died at London, December 24, 1878.

Anderson, Robert, amateur musician, was born in Fraserburgh, Aberdeenshire, May 6, 1835, and died there on November 22, 1882. He was a solicitor in Fraserburgh and composed several part-songs of which the " Herring Song " is best known. He also composed " Songs of Zion " in 12 numbers, published by Novello.

Anderson, Rev. William, clergyman and musician, born at Kilsyth, Stirlingshire, January 6, 1799. He was a popular minister of the United Presbyterian Church in Glasgow, and for many years was pastor of John Street United Presbyterian Church. He died at Uddingston, near Glasgow, September 15, 1872.

Early in his career he edited and published anonymously, "The Sacred Choir: a collection of music adapted to the psalms, paraphrases and hymns in general use in Scotland, and specially to the collection of hymns sanctioned by the Synod of Relief," Glasgow [1841]. This contains "Thanksgiving," "Trinity," and the " Sacred Choir," tunes by himself. The harmonies were revised by Samuel Barr. He also compiled " A selection of psalm and hymn-tunes, adapted to various measures." Glasgow [1844]. For " The Choir: a collection of psalm and hymn tunes . . . selected and composed by Alex. Duncan." Glasgow, 1828, he wrote a preface. Among other literary works he wrote " Apology for the Organ as an assistance of congregational psalmody." Glasgow, 1829.

Anderson, William, writer and musician, born at Aberdeen [1817]. He was a clothier in Aberdeen and held the appointment of precentor in the South Parish Church from 1835, and in the Free South Church from 1843 to 1871. He died at Aberdeen, August 6, 1875.

Author of " Remarks on congregational Psalmody." Aberdeen, 1855. " Precentors and Musical Professors : being brief sketches of some of those more worthy of notice who flourished in Aberdeen in the course of the last hundred years." Aberdeen, 1876. This work contains 26 notices and is prefaced by a memoir of the author.

ANDERTON.

Anderton, Thomas, composer, organist, and pianist, born in Birmingham, April 15, 1836. Teacher of music in that city, and organist of Parish Church, Solihull. Mus. Bac., Cambridge, 1865. Conducted the first singing class established at the Birmingham and Midland Institute, and for some years carried on a series of high-class orchestral concerts at the Exchange Assembly Rooms. Musical critic of the *Birmingham Daily Gazette*. Becoming part proprietor and editor of the *Midland Counties' Herald*, he retired from the musical profession in 1874, but continued to compose and occasionally gave lectures on musical subjects.

WORKS.—*Cantatas :* The song of Deborah and Barak, Solihull, 1871 ; The wise and foolish virgins ; The Wreck of the Hesperus ; John Gilpin ; The three jovial huntsmen, 1881 ; The Norman Baron, 1884 ; Yule Tide, Birmingham Festival, 1885. An English requiem, 1890. Prize glee, Mat o' the Mill. *Songs :* Come to me, O ye children; The felling of the trees, and many others. *Orchestral :* Symphony in D ; Overtures ; Marches ; Allemande in F ; Quartet in F, strings, 1884. *Pianoforte :* Allemande ; Play hours, etc. *Literary :* Letters from a country house, 1891.

His brother, JOHN ANDERTON, is a librettist and dramatic author, and has furnished more than one " book " for the composer.

Andrews, F. H., Canadian (?) musician. Published " Collection of original sacred music, with organ or pianoforte accompaniment," Montreal, 1848.

Andrews, John Charles Bond-, pianist and composer, born at Birkenhead. At eleven years of age, began his musical career by giving a series of pf. recitals ; and two years afterwards was sent to Leipzig, where he studied under Reinecke and others. He also had lessons from Sterndale Bennett, at the R.A.M., and studied at Vienna. In 1876 he gave recitals at Birkenhead, and has appeared with success as a pianist in London and other cities ; he has also officiated as conductor to touring opera companies. He has composed several operas—" Herne's Oak," produced at Liverpool, October, 1887 ; " The Rose of Windsor " (both books by Walter Parke), Accrington, August, 1889 ; and an operetta, " A Pair of Lunatics " (1892). Quartet in B flat ; Trio in D minor, pf. and strings ; Sonata in G minor ; " May Pole " suite ; and many other pieces for pf., &c.

Andrews, Mrs. John Holman, born JENNY CONSTANT, a teacher of singing and composer, born in 1817. She resided in London as a teacher, and died there April 29, 1878. She published " Two part exercises " (for the voice) [1860]. *Songs*—Adieu ; Autumn's golden leaf ; Go lovely rose ; Prince Charley's farewell to Scotland, etc. Nocturne

APTOMMAS.

for pf., and other instrumental music.

Andrews, Richard Hoffmann, writer and composer, born in London, November 22, 1803. Appeared as a child actor on the stage at the Theatre Royal, Birmingham, and in 1809 played the part of Pistol's boy in Henry V., at Liverpool. At the age of nine he was apprenticed to the leader of the Manchester Theatre band, and continued to reside in that city as teacher, and later as music publisher. He gave a concert so late as February 23, 1885, when he played a violin solo. He edited and arranged a vast number of works for the pianoforte, and wrote several glees which enjoyed great popularity—" Hail fair peace " being one of the earliest. He was author of " Music as a Science," 1885 ; " Sacred music, adapted for public and private devotion ;" and edited " The Family Vocalist," " Songs of the Hearth," " Handel's Songs," " The German Choral Harmonist," etc. He died at Longsight, Manchester, June 8, 1891. His sons, RICHARD HOFFMANN (born at Manchester, May 24, 1831), and EDWARD HOFFMANN (born at Manchester, February 7, 1836), are settled in the United States as pianists and composers.

Angel, Alfred, organist and composer, was born in 1816. Held appointment of organist of Exeter Cathedral 1842-1876. He died at Exeter, May 24, 1876. Composer of " Arise my fair and come away," part song, songs, and other vocal music. A son of his was drowned in the wreck of the " London," in 1865.

Anger, Joseph Humfrey, organist and composer. Musical training private ; graduated Mus. Bac., Oxford, 1889. Organist at Bristol and, in 1891, of Ludlow parish church, and music master in King Edward VI. school there. Appointed, 1893, principal in theory department of Toronto Conservatoire of Music and organist and C.M. of the Church of the Ascension. His setting of Psalm 96, for soli, chorus, and orchestra, gained the gold medal of the Bath Philharmonic Society, and was performed by that Society, April 11, 1888. Other compositions are " Bonnie Belle," madrigal for six voices, London Madrigal Society prize, 1890 ; madrigal, " All on a summer's morning ;" Pianoforte pieces, &c.

Ansell, J. K., musician. Published " Collection of sacred music for the service of the Catholic Church . . . ." London [1818]. " Ave Regina, for four voices and chorus." Songs, Cavalry march, &c.

Anstey, Thomas, musician. Issued a collection of " Sacred music . . . in solo, duet, trio, and quartett." London [1830], 2 vols.

Aptommas, Thomas Thomas, harpist (brother of John Thomas), born at Bridgend, Glamorgan, 1829. Has made tours throughout the United Kingdom, and played at many musical centres on the continent, appearing at the celebrated Gewandhaus Concerts, Leipzig, January 18, 1872. Has a wide reputation as a brilliant performer on the harp. Author of a "History of the Harp," 1859, and many Fantasias and other pieces for that instrument.

Aquila, pseudonym, of EDWIN RANSFORD.

Archer, Frederic, composer and organist, born at Oxford, June 16, 1838. Chorister at All Saints', Margaret Street, London, and afterwards studied at Leipzig. He succeeded Dr. Chipp as organist at the Panopticon, and held similar positions at Merton College, Oxford, and the Alexandra Palace, Muswell Hill, following Mr. Weist Hill as conductor at the latter, a post he held until 1880. Conductor, 1878-80, of the Glasgow Select Choir, for which he arranged several Scotch airs as part-songs. About the same time he was also conductor of the Blanche Cole Opera Company on its provincial tours. In 1881 he was appointed organist of the Rev. H. Ward Beecher's Church, Brooklyn, U.S.A., but left the next year for the Episcopal Church of the Incarnation. Since then he has been organist of several different churches, his latest post being at Pittsburg, with an annual stipend of £800. He was organist at Mapleson's New York season of Italian Opera, 1882, and at the Toronto Festival, June, 1886. For some years he was editor of the New York Musical paper, the *Keynote*, and contributed many articles to the earlier volumes of *Musical Opinion*, London, and other papers.

WORKS.—The Organ : a theoretical and practical treatise (Novello & Co.); The college organist (Weekes); Grand fantasia in F; Concert variations ; March triomphale ; and many pieces for the organ. Duo concertante, flute and pf.; Three impromptus; Two gavottes; and other pieces for pf, Songs, part-songs, etc.

Argent, William Ignatius, organist, composer, and conductor, born at Colchester, August 26, 1844. Organist of Little Oratory, Brompton, 1859-60. Since 1868 resident in Liverpool and Birkenhead. Organist successively at St. Lawrence, Birkenhead, and St. Anne's (R.C.), Edge Hill. Conductor at different periods of musical societies at Widnes, Frodsham, Garston, and of the St. Cecilia Society, Liverpool. Musical critic of the *Liverpool Albion*, 1873-80, and *Mercury*, 1886-90. Contributor to the *Musical Times* and other papers. One of the founders of the Liverpool Sunday Society, in connection with which he has not only delivered lectures, but organised an orchestra of seventy performers, and for years given series of Sunday Concerts in St. George's Hall.

WORKS.—Mass in A (1875); Mass in B flat (1887); Tantum ergo and O Salutaris hostia, for chorus and orchestra; Motets, anthems,

etc. An opera di camera (1863), and other works in ms. Author of "Half-a-century of music in Liverpool," 1889.

Arkwright, Mrs. Robert, was a daughter of Stephen Kemble, the actor (1758-1822). She appeared as an actress at Newcastle and Edinburgh, and was married to a Captain Arkwright.

WORKS.—Set of six ancient Spanish ballads . . . London [1832], 2nd set [1835]. Set of six songs, the words from Mrs. Hemans, Mrs. Opie, Sir Walter Scott, etc., with pf. accompaniment by T. Cooke [1835]. Three other similar sets. Six sacred songs [1866]. *Ballads*— Beloved one, Beth Gelert, Repentence. Sabbath bell at sea, Sailor's grave, Pirate's farewell, Zara's ear-rings, etc.

Armes, Philip, composer and organist, born at Norwich, March 29, 1836. Chorister at Norwich Cathedral, 1846-48, and at Rochester Cathedral, 1848-50. Was articled to Dr. J. L. Hopkins in 1850, and was assistant organist at the Cathedral up to 1856. In 1855 he was appointed organist at Trinity Church, Milton, Gravesend, and two years later went to St. Andrew's, Wells Street, London. Here he remained till 1861, when he was appointed organist of Chichester Cathedral, a post he left a year later for Durham Cathedral, which position he still holds. He graduated Mus. Bac. Oxon., 1858, and Mus. Doc. 1864. In addition he has received the degrees of Mus. Bac. *ad eundem*, Durham, 1863 ; Mus. Doc., 1874 ; M.A. *Honoris causâ*, 1891 ; and was elected Fellow of the (Royal) College of Organists in 1892. Resident Examiner in Music to University of Durham, 1890; Examiner in Music to University of Oxford, 1894.

WORKS.—Hezekiah, an oratorio, produced at Newcastle-on-Tyne, 1877, and revised and enlarged at the Worcester Festival, 1878. Church oratorios : St. John the Evangelist, produced at St. Peter's Church, Bramley, Leeds, July 5, 1881, and at the Choir Festival, York Minster, July 7; St. Barnabas, produced at Durham Cathedral, July 30, 1891. Communion services, in A and B flat Anthems : The Lord preserveth (Harvest); Rejoice in the Lord, etc. Cantata and Deus for Festival in Durham Cathedral, July, 1894. Paper on English church music of Purcell's period, read at the Church Congress, Norwich, October 10, 1895.

Armitt, Mary Louisa, writer on music, born at Salford, September 24, 1851. Her father, of a musical family, was assistant overseer of Salford. Her own tastes being of an antiquarian turn in connection with music, she has spent much time in exploring the Bodleian, Cambridge University, and other libraries in England and on the continent ; and her contributions to the press have real historical value. She wrote the musical sketches, "The Choirman of Grayford" and

ARMSTRONG.

"A Stranger's visit" for the *Quarterly Musical Review* (edited by Dr. Hiles), and also papers on Anthony a' Wood, and Old English Viol Music. In the *Musical Times* (November, 1891), "A Richmond Idyll" reveals facts not generally known concerning Charles Coleman's domestic life; a paper on "Old English Fingering" (March, 1895), in the same journal, should be also mentioned. Miss Armitt has also contributed to *The Queen, Musical Standard, Musical World, Musical News,* and acted as musical critic for some time for the *Manchester City News.* She is now resident at Ambleside, Westmorland.

Armstrong, Helen Porter, born MIT-CHELL, known professionally as MADAME MELBA, soprano vocalist, born at Melbourne, Australia, 1859. Daughter of David Mitchell, contractor. Sang in the choir of St. Francis' Roman Catholic Church, Melbourne, and appeared at the Melbourne Liedertafel concerts, 1884. Made her first appearance in Europe at Emil Bach's concert, Prince's Hall, London, June 1, 1886. A pupil of Madame Marchesi, her operatic début took place at the Théâtre de la Monnaie, Brussels, as "Gilda," in "Rigoletto," October 12, 1887. She appeared at the Royal Opera, Covent Garden, May 24, 1888, as "Lucia," in the "Bride of Lammermoor," and has in subsequent seasons been heard in a variety of parts. She sang at La Scala, Milan, in 1893; at the Handel Festival, Crystal Palace, June 27, 1894 (Selection Day); in opera, New York, and elsewhere, and has established herself as a *prima donna* of the first rank. In 1882 she married Mr. Charles Armstrong, of Queensland.

Her sister, FREDERICA MITCHELL, is considered one of the most accomplished vocalists in Melbourne. In 1891 she was principal soprano in the Roman Catholic Church (St. George's) Carlton, Melbourne. She sang, November 24, 1883, in Dublin, at a concert of the University Choral Society.

Arne, Michael, composer, natural son of Thomas A. Arne, born London, 1741. He was educated for the stage by his aunt, Mrs. Cibber. In 1751 he first appeared as a vocalist. He married Elizabeth Wright, the soprano singer, in November, 1766, and in 1779 became director of music at a theatre in Dublin. He returned to London and was director of oratorios in 1784. He devoted himself latterly to the study of alchemy and lost his fortune in the pursuit. Died at Lambeth, London, January 14, 1786.

WORKS.—*Musical dramas:* The fairy tale, 1763; Almena (with Battishill) 1764; Positive man, 1764; Hymen, 1764; Cymon, 1767; The Father, 1778; The Belle's stratagem, 1780; Choice of Harlequin, 1781; Tristram Shandy, 1783. The flow'ret, a new collection of English songs. Glees, many single songs, etc.

ARNE.

His wife ELIZABETH WRIGHT (born about 1743, died?) soprano singer, sang at the principal concerts of her day.

Anne, Susanna Maria, *see* CIBBER (Susanna M.)

Arne, Thomas Augustine, composer, born in King Street, Covent Garden, London, May 28, 1710, son of an upholsterer. He was educated at Eton College, being intended for the legal profession, but his natural aptitude for music led him to study privately, and he had lessons on the spinnet, and private lessons on the violin, from Festing. In 1736 he married Cecilia Young. daughter of Charles Young, an organist, and in 1738 became composer to Drury Lane Theatre. From 1742 to 1744 he resided in Dublin, and on his return to London in 1745 he became composer to Vauxhall Gardens, Covent Garden Theatre, and the principal London theatres. Doc. Mus., Oxford, 1759. He died, London, March 5, 1778, and is buried in St. Paul's, Covent Garden.

WORKS.—*Operas and Musical Dramas:* Rosamond (Addison), Lincoln's Inn Field's Theatre, March 7, 1733; Opera of operas, or Tom Thumb, 1733; Dido and Æneas, 1734; Comus, a masque, London, 1738; Judgment of Paris, a masque, 1740; Alfred, a masque, London, 1740 [by Thomson and Mallet, in which is the celebrated national song "Rule, Britannia," written by Thomson]; Britannia, a masque, Dublin, 1743; Eliza, opera, Dublin, 1743; Artaxerxes, opera, London, 1762 [the well-known psalm-tune "Artaxerxes" is taken from the minuet at the end of the overture to this opera, and was first adapted by R. Harrison in vol. 1 of his "Sacred harmony," 1784]; The fairies, 1762; Olimpiade, 1765. *Music to Plays:* Fall of Phaeton, London, 1736; Zara, 1736; Blind beggar of Bethnall Green, 1741; Thomas and Sally, Dublin, 1743; Temple of Dulness, 1745; King Pepin's campaign, 1745; Neptune and Amphitrite, 1746; Don Saverio, 1749; The Prophetess, 1759; The Sultan, 1759; Love in a village, 1762; Birth of Hercules (never produced) 1763; Guardian outwitted, 1764; Ladies' frolic (with W. Bates), 1770; Fairy prince, 1771; The Cooper, 1772; Elfrida (by Mason) 1772; The Rose, 1773; Contest of beauty and virtue, 1773; Achilles in petticoats, 1773; May-Day, 1775; Phœbe at court, 1776; Caractacus (by Mason), 1776 (MS. lost). Music to Shakespeare's As you like it, 1740; Twelfth Night, 1741; Merchant of Venice, 1742; Tempest, 1746; Romeo and Juliet, 1750. *Oratorios:* Abel, London, March, 1755; Judith, London, February, 1764. Ode on Shakespeare, composed for the Stratford Jubilee, 1769. *Songs, etc.:* Lyric harmony, for voice, harpsichord and violin; The Syren, a collection of favourite songs; Vocal grove;

ARNE.

Summer amusement ; Winter amusement : Vocal melody, 1760 ; Glees, catches, etc., in Warren's collection and elsewhere. Overtures for orchestra. Sonatas for violin. Concertos for organ. Sonatas for harpsichord. The compleat musician, . . . being a collection of vocal and instrumental music . . . . London [1760].

Arne, Mrs. born CECILIA YOUNG (born 1711, died October 6, 1789), was a singer of much note in her day and appeared in many of her husband's works, as well as at most of the leading concerts.

Arnold, George Benjamin, composer and organist, born at Petworth, Sussex, December 22, 1832. Studied under Dr. S. Sebastian Wesley, and graduated Mus. Bac., Oxon., 1855, and Mus. Doc., 1861. Organist successively at St. Columba's College, 1852 ; St. Mary's, Torquay, 1856 ; New College, Oxford, 1860 ; and Winchester Cathedral, 1865, in which city he is resident at the present time. He has given concerts with his specially formed choir, and appeared with success as a pianist.

WORKS.—*Oratorios :* Ahab, Exeter Hall, London, by the National Choral Society, April 6, 1864 ; The second coming of our Lord (MS.) *Cantatas :* The Song of David (MS.) ; Sennacherib, Gloucester Festival, 1883 ; The Song of the redeemed, written for St. James's church, New York, and produced there, 1891. Communion Service in G ; Te Deum and Jubilate in D, etc. *Anthems :* Praise the Lord ; Let the righteous be glad ; The night is far spent, etc. *Part Songs :* Thou soft flowing Avon ; Live like the rose, etc. *Songs :* Go, sit by the summer sea. Harmony (Lancashire Choral Union Prize Glee), and others. *Pianoforte Music :* Sonata in F minor ; Sonata in D ; Prelude and Fugue, etc.

Arnold, John, "Philo Musicae," composer, of Great Warley, Essex, born [c. 1715-20] ; died in February, 1792. He issued the following collections :—The Compleat Psalmodist, or organist's parish clerk's and psalm-singer's companion, in four books, 1741 ; also London, 1750 ; 4th ed., 1756 ; 5th ed., 1761 ; 6th ed., 1769 ; 7th ed., 1779. The Psalmist's recreation . . . 1757. The Leicestershire harmony, containing a set of excellent psalm tunes and anthems composed in modern taste for 4 voices, by an eminent master of the county of Leicester, and now first published by J. Arnold, London, 1759 ; also 2nd ed., 1771. Essex Harmony : being a choice collection of the most celebrated songs, catches, canons, epigrams, canzonets and glees, for 2, 3, 4, and 5 voices . . . vol. 1., 1750 ; vol. 2, 1769 ; various editions of both volumes.

Arnold, Matthew, organist and con-

ARNOLD.

ductor. Was organist at Leeds ; in 1865 appointed to Wesleyan Chapel, Eccleshill, near Bradford ; and of Enniskillen Parish Church in 1875. He very soon established a choral society there, and for nearly twenty years conducted a series of concerts, appearing likewise as violinist and pianist, and occasionally as lecturer on musical topics. An active and useful career was closed by his death, at Enniskillen, March 24, 1894. His son, CHARLES HAYDN ARNOLD, born 1871, is a pianist and organist. He made his début at his father's concert, September 11, 1884 (with his sister Edith, two years his junior), and at the age of seventeen, in 1888, was appointed organist and choirmaster of St. Flannan's (cathedral) Church, Killaloe, near Limerick, where he is engaged as teacher, and also conductor of choral classes, &c.

Arnold, Samuel, organist and composer, born London, August 10, 1740. He was educated in the Chapel Royal, under Bernard Gates and Nares. In 1763 he was composer to Covent Garden Theatre, and he afterwards became owner of Marylebone Gardens, in 1769, at which he produced various dramatic entertainments, of which two were written by Thomas Chatterton. He retired from this enterprise in 1771, after much loss. In 1771 he married Miss Napier. He was made Mus. Bac. and Doc., Oxford, 1773. In 1783 he succeeded Dr. Nares as organist and composer to the Chapel Royal, and in the following year acted as sub-director of the Handel commemoration. He was conductor of the Academy of Ancient Music from 1789, and organist of Westminster Abbey from 1793. In conjunction with Dr. Callcott he established the Glee Club, and was connected with many of the musical enterprises of his time. He died at London, October 22, 1802, and is buried in Westminster Abbey, where a monument to his memory is placed.

WORKS.—*Musical Dramas, &c.*—Maid of the Mill, 1765 ; Rosamond, 1767 ; Portrait, 1770 ; Mother Shipton, 1770 ; Son-in-law, 1779 ; Summer amusements, 1779 ; Fire and water, 1780 ; Wedding night, 1780 ; Silver tankard, 1780 ; Dead alive, 1781 ; Castle of Andalusia, 1782 ; Harlequin Teague, 1782 ; Gretna Green, 1783 ; Hunt the slipper, 1784 ; Two to one, 1784 ; Turk and no Turk, 1785 ; Siege of Cuzzola, 1785 ; Inkle and Yarico, 1787 ; Enraged musician, 1788 ; Battle of Hexham, 1789 ; New Spain, 1790 ; Basket maker, 1790 ; Surrender of Calais, 1791 ; Harlequin and Faustus, 1793 ; Children in the wood, 1793 ; Auld Robin Grey, 1794 ; Zorinski, 1795 ; Mountaineers, 1795 ; Love and money, 1795 ; Who pays the reckoning ? 1795 ; Shipwreck, comic opera, 1796, Op. 40 ; Bannian Day, 1796 ; Italian monk, 1797 ; False and true, 1798 ; Cambro-Britains, 1798 ;

ARNOLD.

Throw physic to the dogs, 1798; Obi, 1800, The Review, 1801; Corsair, 1801; Veteran Tar, 1801; Sixty-third letter, 1802; Fairies' revels, 1802; The Revenge; Woman of spirit. *Oratorios*—Cure of Saul, 1767; Abimelech, 1768; Prodigal Son, 1773; Resurrection, 1777; Redemption (compiled from Handel's works), 1786; Elijah, 1795. Two services in A and B flat. Anthems. Cathedral music, a collection in score of the most valuable and useful compositions by the English masters of the 17th and 18th centuries. London, 1790. The Psalms of David, for the use of Parish Churches, edited with J. W. Callcott. London, 1791. O de for the anniversary of the London Hospital. Anacreontic songs for one, two, three, and four voices. London, 1785. Songs composed for Vauxhall Gardens, several sets. Concertos, overtures, lessons, and sonatas for harpsichord or pf. Edited works of Handel, in 36 vols.

Arnold, Thomas, musician. Published "The Celestial Wreath, a collection of favourite Psalms and Hymns." London [1840]. Daily Exercises for a soprano voice, etc. London [1861]. Songs. Selection of popular airs for two performers on the pianoforte, etc. London [1862]. 12 nos. "The Union," a collection of easy duets for pf. [1866].

Arnott, Archibald Davidson, composer and organist, born in Glasgow, February 25, 1870. His parents removed to London when he was ten years old, but, though passionately fond of music, he did not begin the serious study of the art until he entered his twenty-first year. He graduated Mus. Bac., Durham, 1891, being the first graduate by examination at that University. His exercise was a Gloria in four movements, for solo, chorus, and orchestra, parts of which have frequently been given since as an anthem in Durham Cathedral. Studied for a year at the R.C.M., under Drs. Parry and Stanford, and afterwards with Mr. F. Corder. Organist of St. George's, Perry Vale; Trinity Church, Forest Hill; St. Gabriel's, Pimlico; and, since 1893, organist to the Hon. Soc. of Gray's Inn.

WORKS.—*Operas*: Angelo, a Noble of Venice (two acts, composed January, 1895); Marie Ancel (four acts, music and libretto, composed July, 1895); *Cantatas*: Young Lochinvar, op. 6, for chorus and orchestra (composed 1893, produced Crystal Palace, March 16, 1895); The ballad of Carmilhan, for baritone solo, chorus, and orchestra (composed 1894, produced Queen's Hall, February 26, 1895); The Lost galleon, poem by Bret Harte, for the same combination (1896); Vita Christi, a sacred mystery (1896). *Scena*: The Stilling of the tempest, op. 8, for baritone and orchestra. 4 Cycles of songs, words by Edith M. Dunaway and others, op. 1, 2, 12, 13; various songs, etc. Two concert overtures for orch-

ASHLEY.

estra, op. 3, in D minor, op. 5, in D major; Trio in A, op. 4, for pf. and strings, produced Mus. Artists' Society, March 16, 1896.

Arthur, J., musician, author of "The modern Art of Flute Playing." London, 1827.

Ascher, Joseph, composer and pianist, born of German parents at London in 1831. He studied the pianoforte under Moscheles and at Paris, where he chiefly resided. He held the appointment of pianist to the Empress Eugenie. He died London, June 20, 1869.

WORKS. — *Pianoforte*: Op. 1 Tarentella; Valses: Op. 2, 4, 18, 46, 100, 108; Nocturnes: Op. 3, 125; Dances: Op. 6, 24, 61; Op. 7; La Fileuse, Reveries, etc.: Op. 9, 10, 42, 78, 89, 110, 124, 127; Mazurkas: Op. 11, 41, 98, 107; Impromptus: Op. 12, 26, 65, 81, 82, 99, 105; Polkas, Galops: Op. 13, 31, 49, 83, 91, 96; Op. 14, Barcarolle; Caprices: Op. 17, 22, 30, 109,111, 113; Op. 21, L'orgie; Marches: Op. 25, 43, 62, 72; Idylles: Op. 29, 39, 128; Op. 32, Le Papillon; Op. 35, Styrienne; Op. 38, 64, Souvenirs; Op. 40, Fanfare; Op. 42, Prière; Op. 48, Les Clochettes; Op. 51, La Savillana; Op. 52, La Fanchonette; Op 58, Tyrolienne; Op. 66, Ave Maria; Op. 73, La Zingara; Op. 74, La Favorite; Op. 80, La Cascade de Roses; Op. 88, Berceuse; Op. 90, Fantasia; Op. 92, Serenade; Op. 93, La Phalène; Op. 94, Le Chalet ;Op. 102, Rhapsodie: Op. 104, Ronde des Elfes; Op. 106, La Cloche du Couvent; Op. 112, I Lazzaroni; Op. 119, Les Sylphes des Bois; Op. 121, Volhynia; Op. 126, Marinifla. Transcriptions and other arrangements: Op. 16, 19, 20, 27, 28, 33-37, 44, 45, 50, 53, 55, 56, 60, 63, 67-71, 75-77, 87, 101, 103, 114-118, 122, etc. *Songs*: Alice, where art thou?; Bygone love; I'll think of thee; Mélanie: Twilight dream, etc.

Ashe, Andrew, flute-player, born Lisburn, 1758 [1756]? He was educated at Woolwich, where he learned the violin, and was afterwards adopted by General Bentinck, with whom he went to Minorca, and subsequently to Spain, Portugal, France, Germany, and Holland. At the Hague he received lessons on the flute from Wendling, and became family musician to Lord Torrington at Brussels, where he gained the post of first flute-player at the Opera House, in competition with Vanhall, 1779. He resided in Dublin, 1784-91, and appeard at London, 1792, at Saloman's second concert, where he played a flute concerto of his own. In 1799 he married Miss Comer, a vocalist. He held the position of principal flute-player at the Italian Opera, London, and was director of the Bath concerts from 1810 to 1822. He died at Dublin, April, 1838. He composed concertos, etc. for the flute.

Ashley, John, musician and conductor, born in first half of the 18th century. He was assistant-conductor under Joah Bates of the Handel commemoration, 1784, director of ora-

ASHLEY.

torio at Covent Garden Theatre, 1795, and a performer on the double-bass. He organized a band, in which his sons were performers, which gave concerts of instrumental music in various parts of England. He died March 2, 1805.

His sons, all of whom played in his band, were GENERAL CHARLES (1769—August 28, 1818), a violinist; JOHN JAMES (1771—London, January 5, 1815), an organist and teacher of singing, who numbered among his pupils Mrs. Salmon, Mrs. Vaughan, and others. He composed "Three Canzonets, Op. 5," songs, and instrumental music. CHARLES JANE (1773—August 20, 1843), violoncellist, was one of the founders of the Glee Club, and Sec. to Royal Soc. of Musicians. He was also a member of the Philharmonic Soc., and became proprietor of the Tivoli Gardens in 1843. For nearly twenty years he was a prisoner for debt in King's Bench Prison, London. His brother RICHARD (1775—1836) was a violinist, and played chiefly in provincial orchestras.

Ashley, Josiah or **John**, composer and vocalist, born Bath, 1780. He resided chiefly at Bath, where he was a teacher and concert vocalist. Died at Bath in 1830.

WORKS.—*Songs*; Honest Ben; Heart that o'erflows with good nature; Origin of old bachelors; Poor Joe, the marine; Poor orphan maid, etc. Reminiscences and observations respecting the origin of our national anthem . . . 1827. Letter to the Rev. W. L. Bowles, supplementary to the observations . . . 1827. Both tracts in answer to Richard Clark's work. In the "Bath and Bristol Magazine," October, 1834, the article on "God save the king" is reprinted.

Ashton, Algernon Bennet Langton, composer and pianist, third son of Charles Ashton (*q.v.*), born at Durham, December 9, 1859. On the death of his father, the family went to reside at Leipzig, and Moscheles took a great interest in the boy, whose talent was manifested at a very early age. His first instructors at Leipzig were Franz Heinig and Ivan Knorr. At the age of fifteen he entered the Conservatorium, his teachers being Reinecke, E. F. Richter, Jadassohn, R. Papperitz, and Coccius. On leaving, in 1879, he was awarded the Helbig prize, having on two previous occasions taken the yearly prizes for composition. He then visited England for a short time, returning to Germany for further study under Raff, at Frankfort, 1880-1. After that time he took up his residence in London, and in 1885 was appointed Professor of the pianoforte at the Royal College of Music. He has given many concerts in London and elsewhere, and has appeared as pianist at Leipzig, and in 1894 toured on the Continent with Mr. Ben Davies, the vocalist. His compositions are very numerous, the following list including the most important of them.

ASHTON.

WORKS.—*Orchestral :* Three concert overtures (one in F, produced at the Hanley Festival, 1888); Concerto, pf. and orchestra; Concerto, violin and orchestra. *Chamber Music :* Quintets in C, op. 25 ; in E minor; Quartets, F sharp minor, op. 34 ; C minor; Trios, in E flat ; in A, op. 88, all for pf. and strings ; Quartet in B flat, strings (Musical Artists' Society Prize, 1886) ; Sonatas in F, op. 6 ; in G, pf. and violoncello ; in A minor, op. 14 ; in E, op. 38 ; in C minor, op. 86, pf. and violin ; Op. 44, pf. and viola ; and many pieces in smaller form. *Pianoforte :* Suite in F, for two pianos ; Six sets of duets ; Three pieces, op. 63 ; "Aquarellen," seven pieces, op. 87, etc. *Vocal :* Salvum fac regem, for chorus, op. 27 ; Part-songs for men's voices, and for mixed choirs ; Duets ; Four songs (Geibel), op. 46 ; Six songs, op. 52 ; Nine songs, op. 89, etc. *Organ :* Interludium, op. 11 ; Minuet in C, op. 81, etc.

Ashton, Charles, tenor singer, born at Lincoln, Feb. 1, 1815. In 1822 he became a chorister in the cathedral under Benjamin Whall, the choirmaster. Appointed first tenor at Lincoln Cathedral, 1831, and held the post till 1841. He also acted as organist in the churches of St. Peter's at Gowts, and St. Peter's in Eastgate, Lincoln. He was leading tenor at Durham Cathedral from 1841 till 1862. He was a successful teacher of singing, and sang at many of the provincial festivals. Died a. London, July 11, 1862, when there seeking medical advice. He published several anthems arranged from Beethoven, Mozart, etc., and issued " Services of the church . . . consisting of the Preces, Responses, etc., as sung in Durham Cathedral . . ." London, 1844. Several of his children inherited his musical taste, among whom are Algernon and Diana, separately noticed.

Ashton, Diana Uvedale, daughter of the preceding, born at Durham, October 21, 1840. Studied at first with her father, and, shewing great ability, was sent to Leipzig, where she received instruction from Moscheles, Hauptmann, and E. F. Richter. Returning after three years' stay in Leipzig, she intended settling in London, but the unexpected death of her father necessitated a change in the plans of the family. For some time she remained in Durham, occupied in teaching ; but seeking a wider sphere for her talent she went to New York, and later to Chicago, where she married a German musician, Louis Staab. She lost all her property in the great fire at Chicago in 1871, and never recovering the shock of that terrible event, this accomplished artist died in New York, December 21, 1873. E. F. Richter dedicated his fine pf. Sonata, op. 27, to Miss Ashton.

Ashton, Frank B., *see* CRAWFORD, WILLIAM.

Ashton, Gertrude Cave-, born HOLMAN ANDREWS, soprano vocalist, born in London, April 17, 1855. Studied under her mother (Mrs. J. Holman Andrews), and Thorpe Pede. Début at Alexandra Palace Theatre, 1873 ; the Popular Concerts, 1876. Sang in the provinces with Mr. Sims Reeves ; and in opera with the Hersee Opera Company, 1877, and the Blanche Cole Company, 1879- Has also appeared at the principal concerts in many provincial towns, and in London. In 1875 she was married to Mr. Frank H. Cave.

Ashton, or **Aston, Hugh,** composer who flourished during the 16th century and held the appointment of organist to Henry VIII. He composed several masses and anthems which are preserved in the Music School at Oxford.

Ashwell, Thomas, composer who flourished during the first half of the 16th century. He composed "Twenty Songs," 1530, and various motets, etc., preserved in MS. in the Music School at Oxford.

Ashworth, Caleb, musician. born at Clough-Fold, Rossendale, Lancashire, in 1722. He was educated under Doddridge, at North-ampton, and was Baptist minister and tutor at Daventry. He died at Daventry July 18, 1775. He compiled "A Collection of Tunes, suited to the several metres commonly used in public worship, set in four parts . . . [1760], 3rd edition, 1766 ; and wrote an "Introduction to the Art of Singing," London, 1770, prefixed to the later editions of the Collection of Tunes. He also published a Hebrew Grammar, Sermons, etc.

Aspa, Edwin, composer and teacher, was born in London in May, 1835, of Italian parents. He died at Lincoln, August 17, 1883. Composer of "The Gipsies" and "Endymion," cantatas ; songs, pf. music, etc.

Aspull, George, pianist and composer, born, Manchester, June, 1813. He first appeard at a concert in 1822, and in 1823 appeared at London. Afterwards he gave concerts in England and Ireland, and in 1825 played at Paris, being everywhere hailed as a precocious genius of exceptional brilliancy. He died at Leamington, August 19, 1832. His works were published as "Posthumous Works of George Aspull," edited by his father (Thomas Aspull), Book 1. London [1837].

Aspull, Wiillam, composer, born Nottingham, 1798. Teacher and singer in London. Died in London, January 16, 1875. WORKS.—Songs for the drawing room [1840]. *Songs:* Bird of the forest ; Bright eyes ; Come, let us sing ; Eastern love-letter ; Good-night ; I think of thee ; Lonely heart ; We have met ; The wreckers, etc. Various transcriptions and other works for pf. Translations of Lemoine's harmony, Nauenburg's vocal exercises, Rink's Organ school, etc,

Asquith, John, organist and composer of the present time. Graduated Mus. Bac., Cambridge, 1878. Organist of Parish Church, Barnsley. Has published church services, anthems, pieces for pf., organ, songs, etc. Is author of a pamphlet "On Ecclesiastical Music."

Aston, Hugh, see ASHTON, HUGH.

Atkins, Robert Augustus, organist and composer, was born in 1812. He became organist of St. Asaph's Cathedral, and held the post for over 50 years. He died at St. Asaph, August 3, 1889. His compositions consist of anthems and other church music.

Atkinson, Frederick Cook, organist and composer, born at Norwich, August 21, 1841. Studied under Dr. Buck, and was assistant organist at the Cathedral until appointed to Manningham Church, Bradford. He graduated Mus. Bac., Cambridge, 1867, and in 1881 was appointed organist of Norwich Cathedral, a post he resigned in 1885. From 1886, he has been organist of St. Mary's Parish Church, Lewisham. He has composed some services and anthems ; a volume of Masonic music ; songs and part-songs ; and pianoforte pieces.

Atkinson, G. G., musician. Published "The Abbey Bell, a collection of original Psalm and hymn tunes . . ." London[1861].

Atkyns, B. K., author. Issued "A Choirmaster's Manual : containing full instructions for training a choir." n.d.

Atter, William, musician. Compiled "Collection of Sacred music, adapted to the hymns of Burder and Dr. Watts, with accompaniment for organ or pianoforte." London [1845].

Atterbury, Luffman, composer, born London, in first half of 18th century [c. 1735-40]. After being trained in music he became musician in ordinary to George III., and a teacher in London. He sang in the Handel Commemoration, 1784, and gained several prizes from the Catch Club. He died at Westminster, London, June 11, 1796, while giving a concert WORKS.—Mago and Dago (play with music) 1794. Goliath, oratorio, 1773. Collection of 12 glees, rounds, etc., Op. 2 [1788]. Collection of glees, canzonets, and rounds for 2, 3, and 4 voices, Op. 3. London [1790]. Collection of catches and glees. London, n.d. *Single Glees, &c.*—Come let us all a Maying go ; Come mount your fleet coursers ; Come ye rural nymphs ; Cottagers ; Happy we ; Lads and lasses hither come ; Lay that sullen garland by thee ; Let's banish strife and sorrow ; Will you go to the fair ; With horns and hounds, etc. *Songs*—Mark the sweet rosebud ; Say why a blush ; Undaunted Britons, etc.

Attey, John, composer, born about 1590 ; died at Ross, Hereford, about 1640. He composed "First booke of ayres of foure parts, with tableture for the lute, so made that all the parts may be plaid together with the lute, or one voyce with the lute and bass viol." London, 1622.

Attwater, John Post, pianist, organist, and composer; born at Faversham, Kent, June 26, 1862. In 1884 he went to London, and is now organist of Clapham Congrega- tional Church. Studied under Dr. C. J. Frost, Dr. C. W. Pearce, and others; is a violinist and vocalist, and F.R.C.O. His compositions include a setting of Psalm 34, for soli, chorus, and organ, and many songs and pieces for pf., reaching to Op. 79.

Attwood, Thomas, composer and organ- ist, born London, November 23, 1765. En- tered Chapel Royal as chorister 1774. He studied under Nares and Ayrton 1774-1781. In 1783 he was sent to Italy by George IV., then Prince of Wales, to continue his musical studies, and he received instruction from La- tilla at Naples, Mozart at Vienna, etc., from 1783 to 1787. On his return to England he became organist of St. George the Martyr, Holborn, 1787, and a member of the Prince of Wales' private band. From 1792 to 1795 he acted as music master to several members of the royal family. In June, 1796, he be- came organist of St. Paul's Cathedral, Lon- don, and, in the same year, composer to the Chapel Royal. He was a member of the Philharmonic Society, 1813, and held the appointments of organist to George IV. at his private chapel at Brighton, 1821, and organist of the Chapel Royal, 1836. He died at Chel- sea, London, March 24, 1838, and is buried in St. Paul's Cathedral, under the organ.

WORKS.—*Musical Dramas, &c.*—The Priso- ner, 1792; Mariners, 1793; Caernarvon Castle, 1793; Adopted child, 1795; Poor sailor, 1795; Smugglers, 1796; Devil of a lover, 1798; Mouth of the Nile, 1798; Day at Rome, 1799; Red Cross Knight, 1799; Castle of Sorrento, 1799; Magic oak, 1799; Old clothesman, 1799; Do- minion of fancy, 1800; True friends, 1800; The Escapes, or the water carrier (from Cherubini), 1801; Il Bondocani, 1801; St. David's Day, 1804; Adrian and Orilla (with M. Kelly), 1806; Curfew, 1807. Church services in F, A, D, and C. *Anthems*—Come Holy Ghost; Enter not into judgment; Grant, we beseech Thee; I was glad; Let the words of my mouth; O God, who by the leading of a star; They that go down to the sea; Turn Thee again O Lord; Turn Thy face from my sins; Withdraw not Thou Thy mercy. Nine glees for three, four, five, and six voices. London [1828]. *Songs*— Dear vale, whose green retreats; The sigh; Soldier's dream; Spacious firmament; Young Lochinvar, etc.

Audsley, George Ashdown, architect and musician, was born at Elgin September 6, 1838. Has lectured on Bach and other

musical subjects, and is author of a work on the organ. He has also produced a number of finely illustrated books on architecture and decoration.

Austen, Augusta Amherst (MRS. T. ANSTEY GUTHRIE), composer and organist, born London, August 2, 1827. She studied at the Royal Academy of Music, and was ap- pointed organist of Ealing Church in 1844. This post she held till 1848, when she re- ceived a similar appointment at Paddington Chapel. This she resigned in 1857, and soon after she married Mr. T. A. Guthrie. She died at Glasgow August 5, 1877. She com- posed various hymn-tunes, etc. Her son, F. ANSTEY, is the popular novelist, author of "Vice Versa" and other works.

Austin, John, author, born at Craigton, near Glasgow, April 17. 1752. He was a manu- facturer in Glasgow, where he died about 1830. He published "A System of Stenographic Music." London, N.D. [1820], in which the proposal is made to substitute one line and six characters for the ordinary five lines and symbols of the existing musical notation. There is a short notice of Austin, with por- trait, in Kay's "Original Portraits," vol. 2. p. 376. Edinburgh, 1838.

Austin, Walter, Amateur composer, born at Leeds. Engaged in the Civil Service. First came into notice by his Cantata, "The Fire King," accepted for the Leeds Festival of 1877. He is also the composer of an Operetta, "The Stepmother" (Arthur Sketchley), produced at St. George's Hall, London, 1880; an overture, "The Camp," performed at the Covent Gar- den Promenade Concerts, August, 1880; and some songs and pf. pieces.

Austin, William Frank, organist and composer, born at Lichfield, December 23, 1846. Began his career as a chorister, in Lich- field Cathedral, and was afterwards associated with the musical work of Rugby School, and Trinity College, London. He took up warmly the subject of "English Opera," upon which he lectured and wrote. His last organ appoint- ment was at St. Andrew's, Fulham. He died in London, February 16, 1891. His composi- tions include a chorus, The Crusaders; The Gondolier; Farewell, dear Love, and other songs; and a few pieces for pianoforte.

Avison, Charles, composer, author, and organist, born at Newcastle-upon-Tyne, 1710. He is supposed to have gone to Italy to study music, and. he certainly had lessons from Geminiani in London. In July, 1736, he be- came organist of St. John's Church, New- castle, and in October of the same year he was appointed organist of St. Nicholas' Church, Newcastle. From 1736 he gave sub- scription concerts in Newcastle, and resided there as a teacher. He died Newcastle-upon- Tyne, May 9, 1770.

AYLWARD.

WORKS.— Twenty-six concertos for four violins, Newcastle, 1758. Eight concertos in seven parts for four violins, one alto-viola, a violoncello, and a thorough-bass for the harpsichord, 1755. Twelve concertos in seven parts for four violins, one alto-violin, violoncello, and thorough-bass for the harpsichord, op. 6. Six concertos in seven parts, op. 10, London, 1769. Six sonatas for the harpsichord, with accompaniments for two violins and violoncello, op. 5, London, 1756; another set, op. 7, Newcastle, 1760; third set, op. 8, London, 1764. Concertos for organ or harpsichord, op. 9. Songs, etc. An Essay on musical expression, London, 1752. This provoked an acrimonious discussion with Dr. Philip Hayes of Oxford. He replied to Hayes in the second edition, 1753, of. his essay, and included in it "A letter to the author concerning the music of the ancients," written by Dr. Jortin. The third edition appeared in 1775, "with alterations and large additions," and in the same year a German translation was published at Leipzig. He assisted Dr. Garth, of Durham, with his edition of Marcello's Psalms, 1759, after having himself issued proposals for publishing them. His best-remembered composition is "Sound the loud timbrel," otherwise called "Miriam's song." In Robert Browning's poem, "Parleyings with certain people of importance," a part is devoted to Avison.

His eldest son, EDWARD (1747-1776) succeeded him as organist at St. Nicholas', and his second son, CHARLES (1750-1793) was organist of St. John's.

Aylward, Theodore, composer and organist, born about 1731. He was a member of the Royal Society of Musicians in 1763, and gained a prize medal from the Catch Club in 1769. In June, 1771, he was appointed Professor of Music at Gresham College. In 1784 he was assistant director of the Handel commemoration. He held the appointments of organist of St. Lawrence, Jewry, 1762; St. Michael's, Cornhill, 1768; and St. George's Chapel, Windsor, 1788. In 1791 he was Mus. Bac. and Doc., Oxford. He died London, February 27, 1801, and is buried in St. George's Chapel, Windsor.

WORKS.—*Musical dramas*: Harlequin's invasion [1787]; Midsummer night's dream; Mago and Dago, etc. Six lessons for the harpsichord, organ, or pianoforte, op. 1 [1792]; Elegies and glees [1785]; Eight canzonets for two soprano voices, London [1785]. *Songs*: Oft Oft have I seen; Sweet tyrant love, etc. Church music in ms.

Aylward. A family of musicians related to the above. WILLIAM PRICE AYLWARD, great-nephew, was born at Salisbury, *circa*, 1810. Was for about thirty years organist of St. Martin's, Salisbury, and in 1865 also appointed to St. Edmunds. Conductor of the

AYRTON.

Sarum Choral Society, and Bandmaster of First Wilts. Rifle Volunteers. He was an excellent flute player. Was elected Mayor of Salisbury, 1868-9. Died 1890. He had seven children in the musical profession:— AUGUSTUS ALBERT, born at Salisbury, organist successively of St. Edmund's and St. Thomas', Salisbury. Contrabassist and conductor of orchestral concerts. In 1889 he was appointed organist and choirmaster of St. Peter's, Ashtabula, Ohio, U.S.A., where he gained distinction by his organ recitals. He is now resident at Basingstoke, Hants.—THEODORE PRICE, organist, was born at Salisbury, 1844. Articled pupil of Dr. S. S. Wesley, at Winchester and Gloucester. Organist of St. Matthew's, Cheltenham; St. Columba's College, Rathfarnham, Dublin; St. Martin's, Salisbury (during his father's term of office as Mayor); Llandaff Cathedral; Chichester Cathedral; and since 1886, of the Park Hall, and St. Andrew's Church, Cardiff. Editor of the Sarum Hymnal, 1870.—WILLIAM HENRY, violoncellist, born at Salisbury, 1835. Educated at the R.A.M.; King's Scholar, 1850. Member of the Philharmonic and Royal Italian opera orchestras; also distinguished as a quartet player. Died at Slough, March 12, 1878.— AMY AYLWARD, soprano vocalist, educated at R.A.M., and elected an Associate. Sang at the Monday Popular Concerts, 1880; Cambridge University Society's Concerts; and elsewhere, and is now resident in London.—GERTRUDE AYLWARD, also a soprano, has sung in London, and given concerts during the last few years.—JANEITA AYLWARD. pianist, King's Scholar, R.A.M., 1852, a brilliant and highly promising student, died June 7, 1853, in her sixteenth year.—LEILA J. AYLWARD, pianist, and contralto vocalist, student, and Fellow R.A.M., has given some excellent Chamber Concerts in Salisbury; and has for years done good work in the advancement of musical education in the district.

Ayrton Edmund, composer and organist, born Ripon, Yorks., 1734. He was a pupil of Dr. Nares, at York Minster, 1744. Organist of Collegiate Church, Southwell, 1754-67. Gentleman of Chapel Royal, 1764, and vicar-choral St. Paul's Cathedral, London, 1767. Lay-Vicar, Westminster Abbey, 1780. Master of children of Chapel Royal, 1783-1805. Mus. Doc., Cambridge, 1784. Said also to have incorporated Mus. Doc., Oxford, in 1788. Assistant-director of Handel Commemoration, 1784. He died London, May 22, 1808, and is buried in the cloisters of Westminster Abbey.

WORKS.—Services for the church in C and E flat; Anthem, "Begin unto my God," degree exercise, 1784. Ode to Harmony [1790]. Canon, five in two [1790]. Songs, etc.

His son THOMAS (born 1781, died 1822), was organist of Ripon Cathedral for some years.

Ayrton, William, author and composer, son of Edmund Ayrton, born London. Feb. 24, 1777. He married a daughter of Dr. Samuel Arnold, and in 1801 unsuccessfully competed for the Gresham professorship of music. He was successively editor of the *Morning Chronicle,* 1813-26 ; *Harmonicon,* 1823-33 ; and *Examiner,* 1837-51. Member of Royal Society, Antiquarian Society, Athenæum Club, Philharmonic Society, etc. He died London, May 8, 1858.

WORKS.—Sacred Minstrelsy : a collection of sacred music by the great masters of all ages and nations . . . with biographies. London, 1835, 2 vols. Knight's Musical Library (edited), 1834, etc., 8 vols. Duets : Fair and fair ; Oh ! oh ! memory. Songs, etc., etc.

Ayton, Fanny, soprano vocalist, born Macclesfield, 1806. She studied under Manielli at Florence, and first appeared at Venice in opera, 1825, in Coccia's "Clotilda." In February, 1827, she appeared in London as Ninetta in Rossini's "La Gazza Ladra," at the King's Theatre. She afterwards sang in London, Birmingham, and elsewhere, both in opera and oratorio. The date of her death remains in doubt, but was subsequent to 1832 as she appeared in February of that year in a version of Meyerbeer's "Robert le Diable."

Babell, William, violinist and composer, born 1690. He studied under Dr. Pepusch, and became a member of the Royal Band. He was also organist of All Hallows Church, Bread Street, London. He died London, September 23, 1723.

WORKS.—XII. solos for a violin or hautboy, with a bass figur'd for the harpsichord. London [1720]. XII. solos for a violin, hoboy, or German flute, with a bass figur'd for the harpsichord. London [1723]. Twelve solos for the flute or hoboy, Op. 2. Six concertos for the piccolo, flute, and violins. Suits of harpsichord and spinnet lessons collected from the most celebrated masters' works. London [1712]. Book of the lady's entertainment, or banquet of musick, being a choice collection of aires and duets curiously set and fitted to the harpsichord or spinnet (four books with varying titles). London [1710-25].

Baber, Miss Colbourne (MRS. HARRISON WHITE); soprano vocalist of present time, born at Hobart, Tasmania. Pupil of Madame Lucy Chambers. Appeared at Melbourne Opera House ; toured through India, China, and Japan. Now settled in Sydney, N.S.W.

Bache, Constance, pianist and writer, born at Edgbaston, Birmingham, the youngest child of the Rev. Samuel Bache (1804-1876), Minister of the Church of the Messiah, Birmingham. Her musical talent was fostered by her brother, Walter Bache, and she studied at the Conservatorium, Munich, becoming,

later on, a pupil of Klindworth and Fritz Hartvigson. An accident to her right hand put a stop to the public career open to her, but she played occasionally at concerts in Birmingham, up to the year 1883, when she settled in London as a teacher, devoting, however, much of her time to musical literature and translations, of which the following are the most important :—*Liszt :* Oratorio, St. Elizabeth (see BACHE, WALTER) ; Letters, 2 vols. (Grevel, 1894) ; words of many of his songs. H. von Bulow—Letters and literary remains (Unwin, 1896), *Wagner :*—Descriptive sketch of Beethoven's Ninth Symphony (for Richter concert programmes). *Heintz :* Analyses of Wagner's "Tristan" (1891) ; Meistersinger (1891) ; "Parsifal" (1892). *Schumann :* "The Rose's Pilgrimage ;" Scenes from Goethe's "Faust." *Mozart :* Libretto of "Bastian and Bastienne" (1894). *Humperdinck :* Libretto of "Hänsel and Gretel ;" Lobe's Catechism of Music, and Von Bulow's annotated editions of Cramer, Chopin, etc. Constance Bache is the composer of the songs, "To my Love" and "The rain is falling."

Bache, Francis Edward, composer and pianist, eldest son of the Rev. Samuel Bache, born at Edgbaston, Birmingham, September 14, 1833. In early childhood he showed extraordinary aptitude for music, studying the pianoforte, organ, and violin, making such progress in the last, under Alfred Mellon, that he was given a place in the Festival Orchestra in 1846, when Mendelssohn produced "Elijah." Upon leaving school in 1849, he took lessons from Mr. James Stimpson, but soon left for London, where he studied with Sterndale Bennett. In 1853 he went to Leipzig, studying under Hauptmann and Plaidy, and took organ lessons from J. G. Schneider at Dresden, in 1854. He gave his first concert in Birmingham, at the beginning of December, 1855, but his health was already failing, and he spent the winter in Algiers. Here he gave a concert, in March, 1856, and his playing created a marked impression. From Algiers he went to Leipzig, and thence to Rome, where he spent the next winter. In 1857 he returned home, wintering in Torquay ; back in Birmingham, April, 1858, he gradually sank, and expired August 24, before he had completed his 25th year. His capacity for work knew no bounds ; he was always composing ; and only a few weeks before his death he gave a concert, chiefly of his own works, but he was unable, though present, to take his part in the performance. He was a thinker, and in a series of letters, written in 1856, advocated the establishment of a permanent orchestra in Birmingham, pointing out the great artistic results that should follow. The letters were not considered suitable for the pages of the journal to which they

BACHE.

were addressed, and have only recently been published, and that in connection with the formation of the Scottish Orchestra at Glasgow, in 1893. His compositions must be looked upon as the promise of what might have been had he lived longer; they prove, however, that in Francis Edward Bache death robbed England of a highly gifted artist.

WORKS.—*Operas :* Which is which (1851); Rubezahl (1853). *Orchestral :* Overture (performed, Adelphi Theatre, November, 1850); Concerto for pianoforte and orchestra in E; Andante, Rondo, and Polonaise; Morceau de concert in F, for pf. and orchestra. Trio in D, pf. and strings, Op. 28; Two Romances, violin and pf.; Romance in G, flute and pf.; Romance for pf. and 'cello, Op. 21. *Pianoforte :* Three Impromptus, Op. 1; Two Romances, Op. 12; Four Mazurkas, Op. 13; Five characteristic pieces, Op. 15; Deux Polkas, Op. 17; Souvenirs d'Italie, eight pieces, Op 19; Les Clochettas des traineau, Op. 20; La Penseroso e l'Allegra, Op. 24; Souvenirs de Torquay, five pieces, Op. 26; other pieces and transcriptions, more than fifty in all. Introduction and Allegro, organ. Six songs for voice and pf., Op. 16; Litany, words and music [1862]. Four songs [1859]; and single songs—the "Farewell" being worthy to stand side by side with the *lieder* of Schubert and Schumann.

Bache, Walter, pianist, born at Edgbaston, Birmingham, June 19, 1842. Fourth son of the Rev. Samuel Bache. Educated at the Proprietary School, Edgbaston. Began the study of music under James Stimpson, and at the age of 16 (August 1858) proceeded to Leipzig, studying at the Conservatorium, under Plaidy, Moscheles, Hauptmann, and Richter. At the end of three years, he left Leipzig, and visited Milan and Florence, where he began to give lessons. In 1862, he went to Rome and studying for three years with Liszt, formed a life-long friendship with the illustrious artist. In May, 1865, he settled in London as a teacher and performer. He gave his first concert, in conjunction with Mr. Gustave Garcia, in Collard's Rooms, July 4, 1865, and then began that ardent championship of the claims of Liszt as a composer that lasted to the end of his life. The concerts were gradually extended, and the services of an orchestra requisitioned in 1871, when Bache played the Concerto in E flat, and gave the symphonic poem, "Les Preludes"—introduced in 1865 for two pianos—with full orchestra. Other modern composers were not overlooked, for works by Wagner, Berlioz, and Schumann, were introduced from time to time. But his affection for Liszt was strongest and his last recital, October 22, 1887, was exclusively devoted to that master. Undaunted by hostile criticism, or financial loss, Bache went on with his propagandism, and if

BAILDON.

he did not succeed in what he felt to be his mission, he did more than any one to break down that conservatism in music that was a positive hindrance to the art in this country. Bache's reception to Liszt at the Grosvenor Gallery, April 8, 1886, was a memorable incident of the great pianist's last visit to this country. He was an active promoter of the Liszt Scholarship at the Royal Academy of Music; the Scholarship to his own memory was incorporated in that of the man he so revered. Bache died, after a few days' illness, March 26, 1888, and was interred in the cemetery at West Hampstead. He had, for some years, been a professor of the pianoforte at the R.A.M.

Among the works of Liszt brought forward at Bache's concerts, the following were performed in England for the first time :—The "Faust" Symphony, March 11, 1880; Symphonic poem, "Les Preludes," May 26, 1871; Scena, "Jeanne d'Arc au bûcher," for soprano solo and orchestra; Angelus, strings, February 5, 1885; Fantasia quasi Sonata, "Apris une Lecture du Dante," February 21, 1887. The Legend of Saint Elizabeth was first performed in England, by the New Philharmonic Society, June 15, 1870, anticipating Bache, who brought out the work, February 24, 1876.

Back, Sir George, naval officer, born Stockport, 1796; died, 1878. He issued "Canadian Airs, collected by Lieut Back, R.N, during the late Arctic expedition under Captain Franklin. With symphonies and accompaniments by E. Knight, jun., the words by George Soane." London, 1823.

Bacon, Richard Mackenzie, author and editor, born Norwich, 1776. He was editor of the "Quarterly Musical Magazine and Review." Died at Norwich, 1844.

WO KS. -Science and practice of vocal ornament, London, N.D. Elements of vocal science, being a philosophical enquiry into some of the principles of singing. London, 1824 Art of improving the voice and ear, and of increasing their musical powers on philosophical principles. London, 1825.

His daughter LOUISA MARY BACON, born at Norwich, March 4, 1800; died February 2, 1885, was also a musician She married a Mr. Barwell.

Bacon, Rev. Robert, clergyman and musician of the 18th century. He graduated B.A., Oxford, in 1738; and in 1753 became priest vicar of Salisbury Cathedral. He died in 1759. Composer of chants, etc.

Badland, Thomas, musician, published "Set of original Tunes in four parts, adapted to the Hymns of the Rev. J. Wesley, etc. London [1827].

Baildon, Joseph, composer and vocalist, born 1727. He was a Gentleman of the Chapel Royal, and Lay-Vicar of Westminster

BAILLIE.

Abbey, about the middle of the 18th century. He gained prizes given by the Catch Club in 1763 and 1766. He held the position of organist of St. Luke's, Old Street, and All Saints, Fulham, London. Died at London, May 7, 1774.

:WORKS.—Collection of glees and catches. London [1768]. The Laurel, a collection of songs. Ode to Contentment. Numerous single songs, and others in " Love in a Village," etc.

Baillie, Alexander, musician of the 18th century. He was an engraver in Edinburgh. Editor of " Airs for the Flute, with a thorough bass for the Harpsichord. Edinburgh, 1735.

Baillie, Peter, commonly called " Pate Baillie," violinist, was born at Stenhouse, in Liberton parish, Midlothian, February 25, 1774, and was a descendant of the gipsy family of Baillies of the Upper Ward of Lanarkshire, his father being Matthew Baillie of that sept. He was originally a stonemason, and worked for a time at the Edinburgh University building, but he settled as a violin-player at Loanhead and Bonnyrigg in Midlothian. He died at Liberton, Midlothian, about 1841, and is buried in the churchyard there. A selection of his compositions were published as " A Selection of Original Tunes for the pianoforte and violin." Edinburgh, 1825; for the benefit of his family. He was a talented performer of Scots music, and was widely employed "at penny weddings, kirns, and other merry ' splores,' " but seems to have been a rude, offensive fellow, much given to bouts of intemperance.

Bain, John, musician and teacher in Glasgow in the latter half of the 18th century, published " The Vocal Musician, being a collection of select Scots and English Songs, adapted to two, three, or four voices." Glasgow, 1774.

Bairstow, Thomas, musician, published "An Original set of Psalm and Hymn Tunes arranged for one or four voices, with an accompaniment for the organ or pf." Halifax [1852]. Second set of Original Psalm and Hymn Tunes . . . Halifax [1852].

Baker, George, composer, born Exeter about 1773. He studied under Jackson of Exeter and Hugh Bond. He entered the family of the Earl of Uxbridge, and received further instruction from Cramer and Dussek. Organist successively of St. Mary's, Stafford, 1794; All Saints', Derby, 1810; and Rugeley, 1824. In 1797 he took the degree of Mus. Bac., Oxford., but did not proceed to Mus. Doc. as is usually supposed. He died at Rugeley, February 19, 1847. He composed "The Caffres," a musical entertainment, London, 1802; Sonatas for the pf.; Organ voluntaries; Songs; Six Anthems for 4, 5, and 6 voices; and Glees for 3 and 4 voices.

BALFE.

Baker, Sir Henry Williams, Bart., musician and clergyman, born London, May 27, 1821. Son of vice-admiral Sir Henry Loraine Baker, C.B.. He was educated at Cambridge University, and graduated B.A., 1844, and M.A., 1847. Vicar of Monkland, near Leominster, 1851. Succeeded his father as a baronet, 1859. Died at Monkland Vicarage, February 12, 1877. He was the originator and one of the compilers of " Hymns Ancient and Modern," 1858, and numerous later editions, to which he contributed " Stephanos " and " St. Timothy." He published a volume of " Daily Prayers " and various religious works.

Baker, James Andrew, organist and composer, born Birmingham, November 8, 1824; died there November 17, 1863. He studied at Leipzig, and was organist of St. Luke's Church, Bristol Street, Birmingham, from about 1849 to 1863. His wife was a well-known and accomplished local singer. He composed a few chants and hymn tunes.

Baldwin, W——, author, published "The Science of Music." London, 1829.

Balfe, Michael William, composer and vocalist, born in Pitt Street, Dublin, May 15, 1808. He studied under C. E. Horn, Rooke, and Alex. Lee in Ireland. He accompanied Horn to England, and became a violinist at Drury Lane, 1824. In 1825 he was adopted by Count Mazzara, whom he accompanied to Italy. He sang in Italy and in Paris in 1827, and remained on the continent till 1835. There he was married to Mlle. Lina Rosen, a Hungarian vocalist. In 1835 he sang in London, and in 1839 he became manager of the Lyceum Theatre. He conducted at H.M. Theatre, 1845-52, and directed the National Concerts at Drury Lane in 1850. In 1852 he sang in Russia. From 1852 till his death he was occupied chiefly as a composer. He died at Rowney Abbey, Herts., October 20, 1870.

WORKS.—Operas: I Rivali di se Stessi, Palermo, 1829; Un Avertimento di Gelosé, Pavia, 1830; Enrico Quarto al passo della Marno, Milan, 1831; Siege of Rochelle, London, 1836; Maid of Artois, London, 1836; Catherine Grey, London, 1837; Joan of Arc, London, 1837; Diadeste, London, 1838; Falstaff, London, 1838; Keolanthe, London, 1841; Le Puits d'Amour, Paris, 1843; Bohemian Girl, London, November 27, 1843; Daughter of St. Mark, London, 1844; Quatre Fils Aymon, Paris, 1844; Enchantress, London, 1845; L'Etoile de Séville, Paris, 1845; Bondman, London, 1846; The Devil's in it, London, 1847; Maid of honour, London, 1847; Sicilian Bride, London, 1852; Pittore e Duca, London, 1856 [revived as the ' Painter of Antwerp,' 1881]; Rose of Castille, London, 1857; Satanella, London, 1858; Bianca, London, 1860; Puritan's daughter, London, 1861; Blanche

BALFE.

de Nevers, London, 1862; Armourer of Nantes, London, 1863; Sleeping Queen, London, 1863; Il Talismano, London, June 11, 1874. *Cantatas*: Mazeppa, London; The Page, etc. Six new songs and a duet (words by Longfellow), 1856. Moore's Irish melodies, harmonized 1859 (Novello). *Part-songs*: Exelsior; Hark! 'tis the hunter's jovial horn; Trust her not, etc. *Songs and ballads*: Angels call me; Annie of Tharaw; Arrow and the song; As the sunshine to the flower; Ah! would that I could love thee less; Anabel Lee; Bells; Beneath a portal; Bridal Ballad; Come into the garden, Maud; Daybreak; Defence, not defiance; Evening chime is sounding; Fortune at her wheel; Fresh as a rose; Good-night, beloved; Green trees whispered; Hidden voices; I love you; Kathleen Machree; Killarney; Lady Hildred; Long ago; Lonely Rose; Maggie's Ransom; Maureen; Merry May; Nelly Gray; Phœbe, the fair; Sea hath its pearls; Stars of the summer night; Spirit of light; There is a shadow; Three fishers; What does little birdie say; and very many more. Trio for pf., violin, and 'cello; Sonata pf. and 'cello; and other instrumental works. New universal method of singing without the use of solfeggi, London. The only opera of Balfe's which now survives is the "Bohemian Girl," which continues to draw good audiences wherever produced. This opera and a few of his songs, "Killarney" and "Come into the garden, Maud," are all that have lived out of an immense number of able productions. Two biographies of Balfe have been published—"A Memoir of Michael William Balfe," by Charles Lamb Kenney, London, 1875; and "Balfe, his life and work," by W. A. Barrett, London, 1882.

His wife, LINA ROSEN (born in Hungary, 1806; died London, June 11, 1888), was a soprano vocalist of considerable ability.

Balfe, Victoire, soprano vocalist, born Paris, September 1, 1837. Daughter of M. W. Balfe. She studied under W. Sterndale Bennett, M. Garcia, and her father. On May 28, 1857, she first appeared as "Amina," in "La Sonnambula." Afterwards she sang in Ireland and Italy, in the "Bohemian Girl," "Don Giovanni," etc. She was married to Sir John F. Crampton, but was divorced, and afterwards married to the Duke de Frias, a Spanish nobleman. She died at Madrid, January 22, 1871.

Ball, Edward, *see* FITZBALL, EDWARD.

Ball, William, author and adapter, born 1784; died London, May 14, 1869. He composed a number of songs, and wrote the verses of many more, and contributed much to the musical and periodical literature of his time. He wrote the English version of Mendelssohn's "St. Paul," and provided English versions for a number of works by Rossini, Beethoven, Mozart, Haydn, etc.

BAMBRIDGE.

Baly, William, conductor and composer, born at Warwick, June 28, 1825. Studied at first under Mr. Clayton, of Warwick, and afterwards entered the R.A.M., 1843, where his teachers were Sterndale Bennett, pianoforte, and Cipriani Potter, harmony. Elected first an Associate, then Fellow, R.A.M. Resided for some years in London, and taught harmony at the Harley Street College for Ladies. In 1853 he settled in Exeter, taking over the teaching connection of Mr. Kellow Pye. He conducted the Exeter Oratorio Society's concerts for one year, and was conductor of the Madrigal Society for fifteen years, his last concert taking place May 29, 1884. On his retirement he received a handsome testimonial from the Society. He died June 4, 1891. His compositions included a Symphony in E flat, produced at the Hanover Square Rooms, July 10, 1847, and at the City of London Institute, April, 1848; Two Concert Overtures, "Macbeth" and "As you like it," performed in 1848. These were all written while a student at the R.A.M. He likewise composed a Minuet for small orchestra; a quartet in A for strings, and pieces for pf. Some part-songs, "Sweet and Low," &c., were performed in 1885-6, by the Exeter Madrigal Society. His wife, *née* ADELAIDE C. BYRN, who survives him, is a pianist, and studied at the R.A.M. under Cipriani Potter and G. A. Macfarren. She is now living in retirement in Exeter.

Bambridge, George Edmund, organist and pianist, born at Windsor, April 19, 1842. Studied at R.A.M. under Charles Lucas, G.A., and Walter Macfarren, and Charles Steggall, 1860-65. A.R.A.M. In 1881 appointed professor and examiner at Trinity College, London, and is now Vice-Dean. Has been organist at St. Luke's, Westbourne Park, since 1864, and is widely known as a skilful pianoforte teacher. His published compositions are not numerous, and consist of an Evening Service in F, and some pieces for the pf.

Bambridge, William Samuel, organist, cousin of the preceding, born at the Waimate, New Zealand, July 18, 1842. When six years old came to England, and was, for a year, a supernumery in the choir of St. George's, Windsor. At the age of ten he was appointed organist of Clewer Church. Studied at R.A.M. under H. C. Banister, C. Steggall, W. Dorrell, and W. H. Aylward. Graduated Mus. Bac., Oxford, 1872. F.R.C.O. and A.R.A.M. Since 1864, he has been organist and music master of Marlborough College, Wilts.; and is conductor of the College and Marlborough Choral Societies. His principal composition is a setting of Psalm 144, in ten movements; and he has published Hymns, Carols and Songs. His grandfather, GEORGE WHITE BAMBRIDGE was an admirable flute-player, and considered in his day, as second only to Charles Nicholson.

BAMFORD.

Bamford, H. A., musician. Wrote "The Rudiments of the theory of Music, designed for the use of pupil-teachers and students in training colleges." Manchester, 1881.

Banestre or Banaster, Gilbert, musician and poet of latter part of 15th century. He received 40 marks in 1482 as "Master of the Song, assigned to teach the children of the King's chapel." He contributed to the Fairfax MS., and wrote various works and translations in verse.

Banister, Charles William, composer and teacher, born 1768, died 1831. He composed "Twelve Psalm and Hymn Tunes," London, 1792; "Four Moral Pieces," London [1803]; "Star of Bethlehem," song, etc. His son, Henry Joshua, edited "Complete edition of the Vocal Music of C. W. Banister," London, 1831-33, in 21 numbers.

His son, HENRY JOSHUA (born London, 1803; died London, 1847), was a violoncello player and author, who performed at most of the principal concerts in his day. He published "Tutor's Assistant for the Violoncello," N.D.; One hundred and fifty Lessons for the Violoncello," London [1846]; also "Lessons on Double-notes" and "Exercises on the use of the thumb." He also wrote "Domestic Music for the wealthy, or a plea for the art and its professors," London [1843].

Another son, JOSEPH (1812-1890), was a violinist, and for many years was a member of the Philharmonic Society.

Banister, Henry Charles, composer, pianist, and writer on music, born in London, June 13, 1831. Son of H. J. Banister (*q. v.*). Studied at first under his father, and later at the R.A.M., where he won a King's Scholarship in 1846, and again in 1848. Cipriani Potter was the master he chiefly studied with. In 1851 he became Assistant Professor, and in 1853 Professor of Harmony and Composition, R.A.M., and is now F.R.A.M. As a singing boy he was heard at concerts of the Glee Clubs, and in 1846 he sang duets in "Judas Maccabæus," with Miss Dolby and Miss Sabilla Novello, at the Reading Festival of 1846 (*vide* BINFIELD). His string quartet in F sharp minor was produced by the Society of British Musicians at Erat's Saloon, December 29, 1847; and he began concert giving November 26, 1855, at St. Martin's Hall. For many years a prominent figure in the musical world, of late he has devoted himself chiefly to tuition and to musical literature. Besides his appointment at the R.A.M., he has been a Professor at the Guildhall School of Music since 1880, and is Professor of Harmony at the Royal Normal College for the Blind. Member of the Philharmonic Society.

WORKS.—In MS.:—Symphonies: No. 1, in D (1847); No. 2, in E flat (1848); No. 3, in A minor (1850); No. 4, in A (1853). Overtures:

BANKS.

No. 1, in E flat (1849); No. 2, "Cymbeline" (1852); No. 3, in E minor (1852); No. 4, **The** Serenade, in E; No. 5, From Sorrow to Joy, in B flat (1876). Andante and Rondo in E flat (1852). Capriccio in A minor. Fantasia in D (written for the Musical Society, 1863), for pf. and orchestra. String Quartets in F sharp minor (1847); in D (1850); in E minor. Sonatas for pf. duet, in G minor (1850); in A flat; in A minor; for pf. solo, in E; B flat; F sharp minor; F minor; and F sharp minor. Sacred Cantata (1851). Cantatas for female voices and orchestra: The Sea Fairies (Tennyson — R.A.M., 1861); The Maiden's Holiday, for female voices (composed for private choir of Madame Bassano). Published compositions.—Pf. pieces, Op. 2, 4; Seven variations on an original air, Op. 5; Op. 6; Sonata in F sharp minor, duet, produced 1852, Op. 7; Op. 9, 10, 11, 13, 14, 18, 22, 26, 27, 29; Andante, with variations, pf. duet, Op. 31; Op. 34; Fantasia in F minor, Op. 35 (composed 1874); Canzonets, Op. 1, 3; Part-song, Op. 8; Three songs, Op. 16; Anthem, O satisfy us early, Op. 25; Part-songs, songs, etc. Literary and didactic, including lectures delivered before the Royal NormalCollege, The Musical Association, College of Organists, and the Incorporated Society of Musicians (Conferences), etc. Text-book of Music, London, 1872, 14 editions; Some Musical Ethics and Analogies, London, 1884; Lectures on Musical Analysis, 1887; Musical Art and Study, 1888; George Alexander Macfarren: his life, works, and influence London, Bell and Sons, 1892; Two addresses on the same subject: Helpful papers for harmony students London, Ryder, 1895; and many lectures unpublished.

Banister, John, composer and violinist, born London, 1630. He was sent by Charles II. to France, where he studied the violin, and on his return became leader of the King's band of music. He established a "Musick School" at Whitefriars, and gave concerts from 1672 till 1678. He was dismissed from the King's band for maintaining that English violinists were superior to French ones. He died London, October 3, 1679. Banister composed music for Davenant's "Circe," 1667 (with P. Humphrey); for Shakespeare's "Tempest;" and published "New Ayres and Dialogues composed for voices and viols of two, three, and four parts," London, 1678 (with Thomas Low). He also composed Lessons for viols, songs, etc.

His son JOHN (?—1735) was also a violinist and a member of the private bands of Charles II., James II., and Anne. He was also principal violinist at the Italian Opera, London. Author of "The Gentleman's Tutor for the Flute," . . . 1698, and "The Compleat Tutor for the Violin, . . 1699, etc.

Banks, Ralph, musician and organist,

BANNATYNE.

born Durham, 1762; died 1841. Pupil of Ebdon, and organist of Rochester Cathedral 52 years. Published "Selection of Psalm and Hymn Tunes from Purcell, Croft, etc., with interludes to each verse." . . London [1835]. "Te Deum, Jubilate, Sanctus, etc., in score, Rochester [1840].

Bannatyne, Rev. A. M., Scottish author, Free Church minister in Aberdeen, published "Hearts and voices the only organs for Christian praises," Edinburgh, 1868. "The Great Innovation," Aberdeen, N.D., a pamphlet on the organ question.

Banner, John, musician, published "Collection of Sacred Music used at St. Michael's, Wood Street, with an accompaniment for the organ and pianoforte," London [1840]. Second edition "with an additional hymn" by Miss Mounsey. Songs, etc.

Bannister, Charles, bass vocalist, born in Gloucestershire, 1741? He joined a travelling theatrical company, and played "Romeo" and other characters. He also appeard in London as an actor. He sang at Ranelagh and Marylebone Gardens, and at the Royalty Theatre, London, and in the English provinces. He died London, October 19, 1804. He was celebrated for his imitations of other vocalists. Shield composed his song, "The Wolf," specially for Bannister.

Bantock, Granville, composer, born in London, August 7, 1868. Intended for the Indian Civil Service, and then for a scientific career. He did not enter upon serious musical study until the year 1889, when he became a pupil of Dr. Gordon Saunders, at Trinity College, London. He entered the R.A.M. the same year, and obtained the Macfarren Scholarship. While at the Academy he was very productive as a composer, and several works were performed at the Academy concerts. He was engaged as conductor for a provincial tour of the Gaiety Company, and also for an extended tour in the United States of America and Australia. In 1893 he undertook the editorship of the new Quarterly Musical Review (R. Cocks). WORKS.—Dramatic Cantata, The Fire Worshippers (overture, R.A.M., December 12, 1890, Crystal Palace, November 11, 1893); Lyrical Drama, in five acts, Rameses II (Ballet Suite, R.A.M., December 17, 1891; Strolling Players, April, 1892); one-act Opera, Caedmar (R.A.M., July 12, 1892; Olympic Theatre, October 1892); One-act Opera, The Pearl of Iran; The Curse of Kehama, for soli, chorus, and orchestra; Thorwenda's Dream, poem for recitation with accompaniment (words and music by himself, 1891); Wulstan, scena for baritone (1892); songs, etc. Pianoforte album (three pieces); Two pieces for pf., etc.

Baptie, David, composer and writer, born in Edinburgh, November 30, 1822. Self-taught

BARDD.

in music. He has compiled a Descriptive Catalogue (commenced about 1846) of upwards of 23,000 secular part-songs, glees, madrigals, trios, quartets, etc. (ms.). Editor of Harmonium Tune Book (with William Hume), 1867-68; Harmonium Chant Book (do.), 1868-69; Union Song Garland (do.), 1874; The Scottish Book of Praise (with Lambeth), 1876; Academy Vocalist (selected), 1879; Richard Werner's Hymn Book (revised), 1881, etc. Author of A Handbook of Musical Biography, London: Morley, 1883; Musicians of All Times, a concise dictionary of Musical Biography, London, Curwen, 1889; Musical Scotland, past and present, Paisley, Parlane, 1894; Sketches of the English Glee Composers, London, W. Reeves, 1895. He is the composer of My soul truly waiteth; Sing aloud unto God, and other anthems; a number of Glees and Part-songs; A rosy gift I twine for thee; Beautiful Spring; The sun's bright orb; Wind thy horn, my hunter boy, etc. Also many songs harmonized. His son, CHARLES ROBERTSON BAPTIE, born in Glasgow, May 29, 1870, is a pianist and composer. Chorister in St. Mary's Episcopal Church, and from 1885 employed in the Mitchell Library, until, in 1888, he left to devote himself to the musical profession. Studied under John Fulcher, W. G. Martin, and William Moodie. Has published a children's operetta, "Floralia," and some part-songs and pf. pieces; and was joint editor, with his father, of a work for children, "Tiny songs for Tiny Singers" (1891).

Barber, Abraham, musician, published a "Book of Psalm Tunes, in four parts," 1686; 7th edition, 1715. He was a book-seller in Wakefield.

Barber, Robert, musician, of Castleton, published various collections of psalmody. A Book of Psalmody, containing variety of tunes, with chanting tunes, etc., London, 1723; 2nd edition, 1733. The Psalm Singer's Choice Companion, or a plain and easy introduction to Musick, etc., London, 1727. David's Harp well tuned, or a book of Psalmody, containing variety of psalm tunes, etc., London, 1753, 3rd edition. Thomson's Hymn to the Seasons, in score, Op. 4 [1780]. Some of these collections are issued as by R. and J. Barber.

Barber, Thomas, musician, published "Sacred Harmony, containing two anthems, fifteen psalm and hymn tunes, etc." Woodbridge [1814].

Barcrofte, Thomas, composer and organist, who flourished during the 16th century. He was organist of Ely Cathedral in 1535. Some of his Anthems, and a Te deum, and Benedictus in F, are contained in the Tudway collection in the British Museum. His son GEORGE was organist of Ely Cathedral from 1579, and died in 1610.

Bardd Alaw, see PARRY, JOHN.

Bardy Brenin, see JONES, EDWARD.

Barham, Thomas Foster, musician and writer, born at Bedford, October 8, 1766, died at Leskinnick, near Penzance, February 25, 1844. He wrote on theological topics; sacred dramas and poems; and Musical meditations, consisting of original compositions, vocal and instrumental, London, 1811; and edited and arranged Pergolesi's Stabat Mater, with English words (1829).

Barker, George Arthur, composer and tenor singer, was born on April 15, 1812. He sang in opera in London and the provinces, and gave concerts in various parts of the country. He died at Aylstone, near Leicester, March 2, 1876.

WORKS.—Ballad Album, twelve books, London [1853]. Songs of the army and navy [1855], issued in numbers. *Single songs and ballads*: Aline O'Neal; Dublin Bay; Ellen Astore; Emigrant's bride; Emigrant's child; Excelsior; Fare thee well, my gentle Mary; Irish emigrant ("I'm sitting by the stile," words by Lady Dufferin), London [1846]; Irish peasant; Kate Connor; Lesson of the Water mill; Mabel Gray; Mary! avourneen; Mary Blane [1846]; Mountain Flower; My native mountain home; My skiff is on the shore; Nellie and I; Return of the emigrant; Sands of gold; Scottish blue bells ("Let the proud Indian boast"); Song of the silent land; Take back the ivy leaf; White squall [1835]; Wreck of the emigrant ship, etc. Why do summer roses fade? quartet; waltzes for pf. and other instrumental music.

Barker is best remembered by his three songs, "Irish emigrant," "Scottish blue bells," and "White squall," which alone survive out of the large number he composed.

Barker, Laura W., see TAYLOR, Mrs. TOM.

Barnard, Mrs. Charles, (born CHARLOTTE ALINGTON), **"Claribel,"** amateur song-writer, born December 23, 1830; married Mr. Charles C. Barnard, 1854. She studied music under W. H. Holmes. She died at Dover, January 30, 1869.

WORKS.— *Songs* : All along the valley ; Answer to the dream; Bell's whisper; Blind Alice ; Blue Ribbon ; Broken Sixpence ; The Brook ; By the blue Alsatian mountains ; Children's voices ; Come back to Erin ; Do you remember? ; Dreamland ; Drifting ; Farewell to Erin ; Far away in bonnie Scotland ; Five o'clock in the morning ; Friends for ever ; Friendship and love ; Golden days ; Half-mast high ; Hussar's parting ; I cannot sing the old songs; I leaned out of the window ; I remember it; Jamie ; Janet's bridal ; Janet's choice ; Kathleen's answer ; The life-boat ; Lowland Mary ; Maggie's secret ; Maggie's welcome ; My brilliant and I; Norah's treasure ; Old house on the hill; Only a year ago; Out at sea; Riding thro' the Broom; Sailor Boy; Susan's

story; Tell it not; Through the Jessamine; Walter's wooing; When I was young and fair; Won't you tell me why, Robin; Vocal duets, trios, quartets. Pianoforte pieces, etc. Thoughts, verses, and songs, 1877. Of the songs composed by Mrs. Barnard, under the name of Claribel, only a few survive.

Barnard, Rev. John, divine, published a "Book of Psalms, together with Fifty Tunes to sing them, neatly engraved on copper-plates." 1727, "A New version of the Psalms of David, fitted to the Tunes used in the Churches." Boston (U.S.A.), 1752.

Barnard, Rev. John, divine, who lived during the 16th and 17th centuries. He was Minor-canon of St. Paul's Cathedral in the time of Charles I.

Barnard is famed as having been the first to issue a collection of Cathedral music. His collection of "Cathedral Music" appeared in 1641, and contains services, anthems, etc., by Tallis, Gibbons, Mundy (W.), Parsons, Bird, Morley, Tye, Bull, etc. The only perfect copy of this work is contained in the library of Hereford Cathedral. Its title is, "The First Book of Selected Church Music, consisting of Services and Anthems, such as are now used in the cathedral and collegiate churches of this kingdom; never before printed, whereby such Books as were heretofore, with much difficulty and charges, transcribed for the use of the Quire, are now, to the saving of much Labour and Expense, published for the general good of all such as shall desire them either for public or private exercise. Collected out of divers approved Authors, by J. B." London, 1641.

Barnby, Sir Joseph, Kt., composer and conductor, born in York, August 12, 1838. Chorister in York Minster at age of seven; began teaching when ten; was an organist at twelve; and music master at a school when fourteen. At the age of sixteen he went to London, and entered the R.A.M., living with his brother Robert (q.v.), a vicar-choral of Westminster Abbey. Soon after his appointment as organist of Mitcham Parish Church, he was called back to York, where he remained four years. Then he was organist at St. Michael's, Queenhithe; St. James the Less, Westminster; and, in 1863, was appointed to St. Andrew's, Wells Street. There it was he acquired and exercised the influence that was to work such developments in the Choral Services of the Church. At the Dedication Festival (St. Andrew's Day) of 1866, his adaptation of Gounod's Messe Solennelle (St. Cecilia) was performed, and the harp introduced. He conducted a performance of Bach's Passion-Music (St. Matthew) at Westminster Abbey, Maunday Thursday (April 6) 1871, with full chorus and orchestra—a memorable event in the history of church music in

BARNBY.

this country; and, in 1873, he introduced, at St. Anne's, Soho, where he was then director of the music, the St. John Passion of the same master. He resigned his position at St. Andrew's in 1871, and that of St. Anne's in 1886. "Mr. Joseph Barnby's Choir' was formed in 1867, the first rehearsal taking place in the Lower Exeter Hall, February 17, and the first concert given in St. James' Hall, May 23. From 1869 the performances were given under the title, "The Oratorio Concerts," and great works were revived, notably, Handel's "Jephtha" (February 5, 1869); Beethoven's Mass in D (March 9, 1870); and Bach's "Matthew Passion" (April 6, 1870). At the end of 1872, this choir was amalgamated with that hitherto conducted by M. Gounod; and, as the Royal Albert Hall Choral Society, commenced giving concerts February 12, 1873. Wagner's "Parsifal" was produced, in concert form, by this Society, November 10, 1884. Barnby conducted the London Musical Society, 1878-86, and produced Dvoràk's *Stabat Mater*, March 10, 1883; he was also conductor, 1886-8, of the R.A.M. Concerts. In 1875 he was appointed Precentor of Eton College, an office he resigned in 1892, on his election as Principal of the Guildhall School of Music. For fifteen years, to 1876, he was musical adviser to the firm of Novello, Ewer, and Co. In November, 1882, he conducted the annual performance of the "Messiah," by the Royal Society of Musicians; the performance of Dvoràk's "Spectre's Bride" at the Leeds Festival of 1892; conducted the Cardiff Festivals, 1892 and 1895; a Halle Concert, Manchester, November 14, 1895. Was a Fellow of R.A.M., Member of the Philharmonic Society, and, in 1887, was elected Hon. Member of Tonic Sol-fa College. In 1892 he received the honour of Knighthood from the Queen. To the grief of the whole musical world, his career, in the midst of its activities, was suddenly cut short by his death at London, on January 28, 1896.

WORKS.—Rebekah, a Sacred Idyll, produced at the Oratorio Concerts, May 11, and at the Hereford Festival, August 23, 1870; Ps. 97, The Lord is King, Leeds Festival, 1883. Service in E (Morning, Communion, and Evening, composed at the age of seventeen); Magnificat and Nunc Dimittis in E flat, for voices, orchestra, and organ, for the Festival of the Sons of the Clergy, St. Paul's Cathedral, May 18, 1881; Services, Preces, Offertory Sentences, etc. Forty-six Anthems, including the Motet, King All Glorious, for soli, six-part chorus, orchestra, and organ. 250 Hymn Tunes, of which a complete edition is in preparation (1896); Glad Christmastide, and other carols; Sweet and low; It was a lover and his lass (Norwich Festival, 1884); The haven, and other part-songs. Eton songs (A. C. Ainger).

BARNES

Songs; How fades the light; My golden ship; When the tide comes in, and others. Trios for female voices. Pieces for organ. Musical editor of The Hymnary (Novello, n.d.). Music revised for "The Home and School Hymnal" (Edinburgh, Constable). Posthumous publications: Anthems, Sing to the Lord; O Lamb of God. Part-songs, The Kiss; In laudem Amoris (1896).

Barnby, Robert, alto singer, born in York, 1821. The brother referred to in the preceding notice. He was appointed a lay vicar of Westminster Abbey about 1845, and a Gentleman of the Chapel Royal in 1847, on the death of Enoch Hawkins. These positions he retained until his death, June 1, 1875. Another member of the family was HENRY BARNBY, born 1826, who was for twenty-eight years a lay clerk of St. George's Chapel, Windsor. He was considered one of the finest basses of his time, his voice being rich in quality, and of remarkable compass. He sang at the Hereford Festivals, 1852 and 1855; at the Birmingham Festival Choral Society's "Messiah" Concert, December 26, 1856; in the quartets in "Elijah," at the Birmingham Festival, 1858; and was well known as an oratorio singer. He died at Slough, April 2, 1885. SIDNEY BARNBY, alto, was elected assistant Vicar Choral of St. Paul's Cathedral, in 1873, a position he still retains.

Barnes, Edwin, organist and teacher of music, born in the parish of St. Pancras, London, June 8, 1833. Educated as chorister at King's College, London; studied pf. under Dr. W. Rea, organ and theory under J. L. Brownsmith. For many years professor of music at the London Society for teaching the Blind, where he has done much excellent work. Member of the Philharmonic Society. Organist successively of Hornsey Parish Church; St. George the Martyr, Bloomsbury; and, since 1862, of Holy Trinity Church, Paddington. Was assistant organist to the Sacred Harmonic Society, and Conductor of the Dover Choral Society, 1856-58. His compositions include an anthem, songs, and pf. pieces.

Barnes, Frederick Edwin Lucy, organist and composer, son of the above, was born in London, in 1858. He studied under Helmore in the Chapel Royal, and at R.A.M. from 1872. Organist successively of All Saints', Norfolk Square, London, 1872; St. Margaret's, Princess Square, Liverpool, 1876; Montreal Cathedral, 1878-9; Trinity Church, New York (assistant). He was conductor of the Montreal Philharmonic Society, and was married to Miss Leonora Braham in 1878. He died at Montreal, September 21, 1880.

WORKS.—*Opera :* Libretto by Mrs. G. L. Craik (ms.) Operetta for German Reed Company. Twenty-third Psalm for soli, chorus, and

BARNETT.

orchestra. *Songs :* But you know already; May song; Mither; Path through the snow; Sun and Spring. Various pieces for organ and Pianoforte.

Barnett, Alice, see under Poole, Madame.

Barnett, Emma, pianist, sister of John Francis Barnett, and daughter of Joseph Alfred Barnett, professor of singing, was born in London. Studied entirely under her brother, and made her debut at the Crystal Palace Saturday Concerts, February 28, 1874, playing Beethoven's Pianoforte Concerto in G. December 1st of the same year she played J. F. Barnett's Pianoforte Concerto in D minor at the Royal Albert Hall Concerts. She gave her first recital at St. George's Hall, June 13, 1877, and her first appearance at the Monday Popular Concerts, St. James's Hall, took place January 28, 1882. Since that time she has given many pianoforte recitals in London and the provinces, introducing the Sonata in E, the series of pieces, "Home Scenes," and other of her brother's works to public notice. Her compositions are chiefly for the pianoforte, but include a few songs. Only the Gavotte in A is as yet published.

Barnett, John, composer, was born at Bedford, July 15, 1802, son of Bernhard Beer, a Prussian watchmaker, who settled in England and changed his name to Barnett. He was articled to S. J. Arnold, proprietor of the Lyceum Theatre, and studied under C. E. Horn, Price, and Ries. Married Miss Lindley, daughter of the violoncello player, 1837. Studied Vogler's system of harmony at Frankfort, under Schnyder von Wartensee, and returned to London in 1838. He opened St. James's Theatre for English opera in 1839. Retired to Cheltenham, where he established himself as a vocal teacher, in 1841. Resided in Leipzig and in Italy for a short time, superintending the education of his children. Died near Cheltenham, April 17, 1890.

WORKS.—*Operettas and Operas* : Before Breakfast, Musical Farce, written by Richard Peake, Lyceum, 1828; Music in Miss Mitford's Rienzi, Drury Lane, 1828; Monsieur Mallet, operetta, written by Thomas Moncrieff, Adelphi Theatre, 1828; Two Seconds, operetta, written by R. Peake, Lyceum, 1829; Carnival of Naples, opera, Covent Garden, 1830; Robert the Devil, musical drama, Covent Garden, 1830; The Picturesque, operetta, written by Thomas Haynes Bayley Lyceum, 1830; Baron Trenck, operetta, written by T. Morton, sen., destroyed in the fire at Covent Garden Theatre, 1830; Country Quarters, musical farce, Covent Garden, 1831; Court of Queen's Bench, operetta, Olympic Theatre (Vestris), 1832; Paphian Bower operetta, written by Planché and C. Dance, Olympic Theatre, December, 1832; Harlequin Pat, operetta, Covent Garden, 1832; Married

BARNETT.

Lovers, musical farce, Lyceum, 1832; Promotion, musical farce, Lyceum, 1833; Pet of the Petticoats, operetta, Sadler's Wells, August, 1832; Win Her and Wear Her, opera, Drury Lane, December, 1839; Soldier's Widow, musical drama, written by E. Fitzball, English Opera Company, Adelphi, 1833; Two songs and a march in Nell Gwynne, Covent Garden, 1833; Song in Planché's Charles the Twelfth, Drury Lane, 1833; Deuce is in her, operetta, 1833; Olympic Revels, 1833; Blanche of Jersey, 1834; Mountain Sylph, opera, written by Thackwray, Lyceum, August 25, 1834 : Fair Rosamond, opera. written by C. Z. Barnett, Drury Lane, March 30, 1837; Farinelli, opera, written by C. Z. Barnett, Drury Lane, February 8, 1837; Kathleen opera (never produced), composed in 1840; Marie, opera, composed in 1845 (unfinished). *Oratorios* : Omnipresence of the Deity, published in 1829 (never performed); Daniel, unfinished. composed in 1841. A Mass. A Symphony, unfinished, composed in 1840. Two string quartets, MS., composed in 1840. Spare Moments, three sketches for concertina [1859]. *Part-songs*: Twelve Part-songs, mostly published in 1870; Chamber Madrigals, London, 1861 : It is summer it is summer; Bend down from thy chariot; Haste not; Farewell to the Flowers; Tic-tac of the mill; Dear peaceful valley; Evening drum; Merrily, merrily sounds the horn; In the merry greenwood; Wrong not, sweet mistress (madrigal); Chamois Hunter; O Lord, our governor. *Duets* . Set of six vocal duets [1845]; A smile, a tear; A spring song; Come where the flowers are blooming; Dear maid, my heart is thine; Down in the dell; The Gleaner's Bell; Good night; The Hungarian to his bride; I'll follow thee; Moonlight, music, love, and flowers: My gondola glides; No more, no more; Oh! give to me; Oh! 'tis sweet to meet again; Spring; The twilight hour; There's not a breeze; When at night; Where are the mountains; Wilt thou tempt the wave? *Songs* : Amusement for leisure hours—seven songs and one duet [1835] ; Songs of the Minstrels [1830]. Dreams of a Persian maiden [1842] ; Twelve Russian Melodies, with words by Harry Stoe van Dyk [1822] ; Songs of the Slavonians, containing Bohemian popular airs with words by John Bowring, London, 1824; Twenty-four songs in imitation of the music of various nations, with words by Van Dyk, Leon Lee, and Mayhew, 1824; Twelve Songs from Fairy Land, written by Thomas Haynes Bayley, 1827 ; Lyric Illustrations of the Modern Poets, 1834, reprinted in 1877; Adieu to thee fair Rhine; Ask me no more; A day-dream; Banks of Broomsgrove; Break, break, break; Bride's farewell ; Chase the falling tear; Clansman's bride; Come to me. thou gentle child; Dear Napoli; Days of Chivalry; Days

BARNETT.

that ne'er return ; Flower of my life ; Fill up the wine cup ; Flowers of summer ; Gc, thou art free ; Highlander's bride ; Her heart is mine ; Highland soldier ; Highland minstrel boy ; Hark, the fairy bells ; Hope for the best ; Here's a health to merry England ; The Holly ; Hark, hark to the sound ; I have been to the woods ; Is the reign of fancy over ? Knight of the golden crest ; Light guitar ; Light of heart am I ; Lord, I believe ; List to my wild guitar ; My home beside the Quadalquiver ; Minstrel's lament ; Mermaid's song ; Maid of Athens ; My native land, good night ; Maiden of Sicily ; Now the lamp of day has fled ; Normandy maid ; Rock me to sleep ; Rose of Lucerne, 1823 ; Rise, gentle moon ; Swiss shepherd ; Sing, nightingale, sing ; Sailor boy's song ; Spirit of love ; There sits a lovely maid ; The opal ring ; The ship ; Vesper hour ; Up to the Forest ; Village bells ; Young moss rose ; Year's last hours. Systems and Singing Masters, a Comment upon the Wilhem System, and remarks upon Mr. J. Hullah's Manual, London, 1842, also, 1877. School for the Voice, a theoretical and practical treatise, London [1845] ; since reprinted several times.

Barnett's Mountain Sylph was the first English Opera cast in the dramatic form followed by Weber and other masters. It was very popular on its original production in 1834, and had a run of over 100 nights. Of the immense number of songs and other vocal pieces published by Barnett, amounting in' all to nearly 2000 items, only a few are known to the present generation of musicians. His eldest daughter married Mr. Robert E. Francillon, the well-known novelist.

Barnett, John Francis, pianist and composer, born in London, October 16, 1837 ; son of Joseph Alfred Barnett. His first pianoforte teacher was his mother. In 1849 he was placed under Dr. Wylde, and in 1850 he won a King's Scholarship at the R.A.M., and was re-elected in 1852. He appeared for the first time in public at the New Philharmonic Concert, June 29, 1853, playing the solo part in Mendelssohn's Pianoforte Concerto in D minor. In 1856 he went to Leipzig, and studied at the Conservatorium, under Hauptmann, Rietz, Plaidy, and Moscheles. He played at the Gewandhaus concerts, March 22, 1860, the D minor concerto of Mendelssohn. At his reappearance in London, New Philharmonic, April 16, 1860, he was heard in Beethoven's Concerto in E flat ; and at the Philharmonic Concert, June 10, 1861, in that composer's Concerto in C minor. He was afterwards associated with Dr. Wylde as a teacher of the pianoforte in the London Academy of Music. In 1883, was appointed a Professor R.A.M., and is F.R.A.M. and Member of the Philharmonic Society. Was

BARNETT.

for a time conductor of the Berkshire Musical Society ; and conducted a Philharmonic concert, April 23, 1884. First came into notice as a composer by a Symphony produced by the Musical Society of London, 1864 ; and receiving a commission for the Birmingham Festival of 1867, he soon attained a prominent position among the younger English composers.

WORKS.—*Cantatas* : The Ancient Mariner (Birmingham Festival, 1867) ; Paradise and the Peri (the same, 1870) ; The Raising of Lazarus (Oratorio, New Philharmonic, June 18, 1873 ; Hereford Festival, 1876) ; The Good Shepherd (Brighton Festival, 1876) ; The Building of the ship (Leeds Festival, 1880) ;. Ode, The triumph of labour (Crystal Palace, August, 1888) ; The wishing bell, Cantata for female voices (Norwich Festival, 1893). Partsongs ; Songs, The Harp of Life ; The Golden Gate, etc. *Orchestral* : Symphony in A minor (1864) ; Symphonic Overture in E (Philharmonic, 1868) ; Overture, A Winter's tale (British Orchestral Society, February 6, 1873) ; Suite, The lay of the last minstrel (Liverpool Festival, 1874) ; Symphonic Poem, The Harvest Festival (Norwich Festival, 1881 ; and revised as a Pastoral Suite, Philharmonic, May 31, 1888) ; Concerto in D minor, pf. and orchestra ; The Ebbing tide ; Liebeslied, and other smaller works for orchestra. Chamber Music : Quintet in G minor ; Quartet in D minor, strings ; Trio in C minor, pf. and strings ; Sonata in G minor, Op. 41, pf. and flute ; in E minor, pf. and violin. Pianoforte solo : Sonata in E minor, Op. 45 ; Three Impromptus ; Home scenes, nine pieces ; Seven characteristic studies ; and a large number of shorter pieces, elegant in style and widely popular. Offertoire in G and other organ pieces.

Barnett, J. Maughan, pianist and organist. For some years resident at Tunbridge Wells, where he held several organ appointments, and annually gave concerts. Delicate health caused him, in 1889. to leave England for New Zealand, where he soon established a reputation as a brilliant pianist and organist, giving performances also in Tasmania. He holds the office of conductor of the Wellington Musical Society, N.Z. He has written some pieces for pianoforte.

Barnett, Joseph Alfred, tenor vocalist and teacher of singing, brother of John Barnett, was born in London. Early in life he was articled to Mr. Reeve of the Olympic Theatre, and appeared as a juvenile vocalist. Afterwards he sang as a tenor vocalist, in London and the provinces, but gradually he retired from public life, and devoted himself to voice training. He married a daughter of William Hudson, the artist, and had a large family, among whom may be named John Francis and Emma, who are separately noticed. He was for many years principal tenor at the Church of the Spanish Embassy, and choirmaster of Warwick Street Church, and St. Aloysius, Somers Town, London. Professor of Singing at the London Academy of Music, and teacher in many large schools. Composer of " Domini Salvum," quartet and chorus ; " Ave Maria," quartet ; " Exaudi Deus," tenor solo; many duets, songs, and other vocal music.

Barnett, Neville George, organist and musical critic, born in London, March 3, 1854. Pupil of R. Limpus, E. J. Hopkins, and E. H. Turpin. F.R.C.O., 1873. Appointed organist and choirmaster St. Philip's Arlington Square, in 1872. Subsequently, he went to New Zealand, where he held several appointments, but he finally settled in Sydney, New South Wales. He was organist of St. Mary's Cathedral (Roman Catholic) ; Musical Director at the Jewish Synagogue, and instructor at the Blind Institution. For blind students he invented a type-writer, enabling them to write according to the Braille system. When he went to Sydney he was appointed musical critic of the *Sydney Morning Herald,* then of the *Evening News,* and lastly, of the *Sydney Daily Telegraph.* He composed an Opera, " Pomare," on a Tahitan legend, which was performed at Auckland ; a Mass, organ pieces, part-songs, etc. He also wrote some treatises on music, his last work, " The Art Theory of Harmony (dedicated to Sir George Grove), is still in MS. He died at Picton, N.S.W., September 26, 1895.

Barnett, Robert, pianist and composer, was born at Macclesfield, in 1818. He studied at the R.A.M., and in 1840 was appointed a professor of the pf. there. In 1842 he appeared as a pianist at the Quartet Concerts, Hanover Square Rooms, and in 1850 at the Society of British Musicians. He was elected an Associate of the Philharmonic Society in 1843. Died at Slough, Windsor, November, 1875.

WORKS.—Pianists' Companion, London, 1857 (issued in parts). Sonatas, rondos, and airs for pianoforte, 1842 (selected). Useful scale practice for the pianoforte, 1843. Rondo grazioso and rondoletto scherzando for pf. Edited Pianoforte works by Mozart, Pleyel, and Dussek.

His eldest son DOMENICO, born in London, August 25, 1846. Studied at Leipzig Conservatorium under Moscheles, E. F. Richter, Reinecke, and others. Principal professor of pianoforte at the Ladies' College, Cheltenham. Has composed some music for pf., but nothing is published hitherto.

Barnhill, James, Scottish author, who graduated M.A., at Glasgow University. He published " The Statics of Harmony, with an appendix on anticipations, suspensions, and transitions, illustrated by examples from the

great masters," London, 1865. Reprinted from the *Choir.* He published various other works.

Barr, James, musician, was born at Tarbolton, Ayr, in 1781. Employed by J. Stephen, music-publisher, Wilson Street, Glasgow, 1812, and was a music teacher in Glasgow. He resided in Canada as farmer, 1832-1855. The " blithe Jamie Barr, frae St. Barchan's toun," of Tannahill. Composer of a few melodies, of which " Thou bonnie wood o' Craigielea (words by Tannahill) is well known. He died at Govan, February 24, 1860, and is buried at Kilbarchan.

Barr, Samuel, composer and writer, was born at Glasgow, in 1807. Self-taught in music. He was a teacher in Glasgow, and precentor in Dr. Wardlaw's (Independent) Church. Professor of Music in the Mechanics' Institute, Glasgow. Died, Glasgow, May 16, 1866.

WORKS.—The Theory and Practice of Harmony and Composition, London, 1861 ; Art of Singing at sight simplified, Glasgow, 1847 and 1859 ; Anthems ; Psalms. *Songs* : Hurrah! for the Highlands ; The warning ; The land for me ; The bridal gem ; Naebody kens ye. Part-songs ; Miscellaneous writings.

Barr was well known in Glasgow and the West of Scotland as a teacher of merit, and is generally supposed to have introduced class music teaching into the West of Scotland.

Barraclough, Isaac, musician, of Sheffield. Published " Sacred music, consisting of Psalm and Hymn tunes . . . for four voices, with an accompaniment for the organ or pianoforte," London [1836]. " Sacred music, consisting of original psalm and hymn tunes . . ," Sheffield [1847].

Barratt, John, organist, born near Huddersfield, January 11, 1848. Received his musical training at York Minster. Graduated Mus. B., Oxford, 1877. Organist of Paisley Abbey, the Clark Town Hall, and Conductor of Paisley Select Choir. Has published anthems, hymn-tunes, etc. His son, WILLIAM AUGUSTUS BARRATT, born 1874, was a scholar of the R.C.M. He first came into notice by his setting of " Sir Patrick Spens," for baritone solo, chorus, and orchestra, produced at Edinburgh, December 1894. A cantata, "The Death of Cuthullin," was brought out in that city, December 1895. He has also published an Album of ten songs (Paterson), etc.

Barrett. The name of a family honourably distinguished in church music in Bristol. The father, SLATER BARRETT, was in the choir of Bristol Cathedral for nearly sixty years. JOHN BARRETT, the elder son, born at Bristol, 1812, was a chorister in the Cathedral, and for many years organist of St. Augustine's Church, and also at the Blind Asylum, the choir of which he raised to a high standard of excellence. He was one of the founders

BARRETT.

BARRETT.

of the Bristol Madrigal Society (1837), and for some time, until his last illness, was a Vice-President. He died June 24, 1886. His brother, GEORGE BARRETT, was born at Bristol, March 16, 1814. Chorister in the Cathedral, and in January, 1839, appointed organist of Holy Trinity Church, Hotwells, an office he held for fifty-two years. Was also a founder of the Madrigal Society, and the last surviving original member, and a Vice-President from 1880. He died March 5, 1891, a tablet in Holy Trinity Church commemorating his long and faithful service as organist.

Barrett, John, organist and composer, born in 1674. Pupil of Dr. Blow. Music teacher at Christ's Hospital [1710]. Organist at Church of St. Mary at Hill, 1710. He died at London, 1735 [1738].

WORKS.— Music for Love's Last Shift, 1696; Tunbridge Wells, 1703; Mary, Queen of Scots, 1703; Custom of the Manor [1715]; Wife of Bath. *Songs*: Celinda; Cruel charmer, do not grieve me; Fine lady's airs; Gloriana is engaging fair; Happy fair; In the pleasant month of May; Liberia's all my thought; Love is now become a trade; Pilgrim; Three goddessses, etc.

Barrett, John, organist, born at Bristol, March 31, 1837. Chorister at the Cathedral, 1844, and in 1853 articled for five years to J. D. Corfe, Cathedral Organist. After that time he was assistant organist at the Cathedral for two years, while holding the post of organist and choirmaster successively at All Saints', Bristol, and at Bedminster Parish Church. In 1878 he resigned the latter appointment, having been elected to Christ Church, Clifton, a post he still retains. He has been, since 1883, conductor of the Bristol Church Choral Union, which holds its annual festival in the Cathedral. He has also formed a special choir, which has produced Schubert's Mass in E flat, and other important works for the first time in Bristol. A zealous worker for the Incorporated Society of Musicians, as Hon. Sec. for the Western Section, he has made it one of the most flourishing of any. It was the first to form a special library of music, which out of compliment to him, was named the Barrett Library.

Barrett, William Alexander, writer, vocalist, and organist, born at Hackney, London, October 15, 1836, son of an architect. Chorister at St. Paul's Cathedral, 1846-49, and pupil of George Cooper, W. Bayley (one of the lay-vicars), and John Goss, for composition. First sang in public at a concert given by J. B. Stansell, at St. Philip's Schools, Stepney, November, 1847. When his voice changed he took to drawing on wood, and in 1854. illustrated Holt's "Chronicle of the Crimean War," and an edition of Shakespeare. From 1855 to '57 he was engaged in

journalistic work on the *Morning Chronicle*, book reviewing; and translating stories and poems for different publishers. Appointed principal alto at St. Andrew's, Wells Street, in 1858; and in 1861, lay-vicar, Magdalen College, Oxford. He was also organist at St. John's, Cowley, Oxford, 1863-66. Sub-editor and illustrator of the *Penny Post*, Oxford, 1861-67. Graduated Mus. B., Oxford, 1871. Appointed assistant vicar choral, St. Paul's Cathedral, 1867; vicar choral, 1876. He wrote his first musical criticisms while at Oxford, which appeared in the *Oxford Times*, 1864-66. On his return to London he was offered the post of musical critic on the *Morning Post* (1869), which he retained till his death. He also wrote for the *Whitehall Review* and the *Globe* (1874-75). Was editor of the *Monthly Musical Record* (1877); the *Orchestra* (1881); and the *Musical Times* from 1887. Other appointments were, Assistant Examiner in Music with Dr. John Hullah, 1873; Examiner to the Society of Arts, and to the Council of Military Education, 1883. Mr. Barrett was elected Fellow of the College of Organists, 1871; and Fellow of the Royal Society of Literature; Lecturer to the City of London College and London Institution; Mus. D., Trinity College, Toronto; and, in 1888, appointed by the Prince of Wales Grand Organist of the United Grand Lodge of Freemasons, in succession to Sir Arthur Sullivan. It was at Walworth, in 1856, that, with a discourse on the "History of the Gipsies," he began his career as a lecturer, his extensive knowledge enabling him to deal with a great variety of topics. Some of these lectures have been published. In the midst of an active life he was attacked by apoplexy, and to the great loss of the world of music, died October 17, 1891.

WORKS.— Oratorio, Christ before Pilate (MS.); Anthems; Madrigals: On a mossy bank (eight voices. Bristol Madrigal Society, 1839), Cynthia. Literary: Flowers and festivals, or directions for the floral decorations of churches, 1868; The Chorister's Guide (1872?); Dictionary of musical terms (with Dr. Stainer), 1875; Etymons of musical terms (1876); English glee and madrigal writers, London, 1877; Introduction to form and instrumentation for beginners in composition, 1879; English church composers ("Great Musicians" series), London, Sampson Low, 1882; Balfe, his life and work, London, Remington, 1882; Editor of English folk songs; Standard English songs (Novello), etc.

Barrett, William Lewis, flutist, born in London, January 4, 1847. His father was a violinist, and his mother came off a well-known musical family in Merionethshire. Taken to Wales when an infant, he spent his early years there, and when seven years of age commenced to play the violin, which he

BARRINGTON.

afterwards changed for the flute. Destined for a commercial career, he only took up music as a profession after the death of his father. Studied the flute under R. S. Rockstro, and harmony under W. Castell. His first work was deputising for Mr. John Radcliff, and he was soon engaged by Costa as second flute and piccolo at Her Majesty's Opera, where afterwards, for many years, he was principal flute. Similar appointments were also held at the Royal Italian Opera (five years), the Carl Rosa London season (seven years); and he has been engaged for Birmingham, Leeds, and Three Choirs Festivals, the chief orchestral concerts, and is now principal flute of the Philharmonic Society, and Professor at the R.C.M. He toured with Madame Albani in Canada and the United States, and has also appeared, with success, on the continent. He has published Flute Studies; solo and important passages; Romance and Tarentella, etc.

Barrington, Hon. Daines, English writer on Law, Music, and Natural History, was born at London, 1727. Judge on Welsh Circuit, 1757. Second Justice at Chester. Retired from the Law and resided in the Temple. He died March 11, 1800.

Barrington wrote a standard work on the Statutes, a work on the possibility of reaching the North Pole, and several papers dealing with Crotch, the Wesleys, Mornington, and Mozart. See his "Miscellanies," 1781, and the Philosophical Transactions, 1780. Also author of "Experiments and Observations on the Singing of Birds," London, 1773.

Barrington, Rutland, GEORGE RUTLAND FLEET, actor and vocalist. First appeared on the stage at the Olympic Theatre; then toured for some years with Howard Paul. In 1877, he was engaged for the Opera Comique Company, and made his *début* as the Vicar, in " The Sorcerer," on its production, November 17, 1877; and has since taken part in most of the Gilbert and Sullivan Operas, his Pooh Bah, in the "Mikado," being one of his most remarkable assumptions. In 1888, he turned theatrical manager, opening the St. James's Theatre in October; but the enterprise did not prosper, and he gave it up the January following. Since then he has re-appeared at the Savoy Theatre, his latest character being Ludwig in " The Grand Duke " (March, 1896).

Barrow, J., musician of 18th century. Published "Book of Psalmody . . . ," 1730 and 1751. "Psalm-singer's choice companion, or an imitation of heaven on earth, the beauty of Holiness, being a compleat composition of Church musick, containing variety of tunes for all the common metres of the Psalms . . . with a new and compleat introduction to the skill of musick. To which is added an alphabetical dictionary . . ." N.D.

BARRY.

Barrow, Thomas, composer and alto singer of the latter half of the 18th century. He was a choirister and gentleman of the Chapel Royal, and sang in Handel's Oratorios. He died on August 13, 1789. He composed some Church music, chants, etc.

Barry, Charles Ainslie, composer, organist and writer, born in London, June 10, 1830, Educated at Rugby, and Trinity College, Cambridge. While at Cambridge he studied music with Professor T. A. Walmisley. Graduated B.A. and M.A. By his father's wish he studied for the ministry, and passed the voluntary Theological Examination at Cambridge; but music became his ultimate choice. At the Cologne Conservatorium he studied under F. Weber, E. Frank, and F. Hiller; at Leipzig, with Moscheles and E. F. Richter (1856-7); and during his residence at Dresden received valuable hints from Carl Reissiger. Returned to London, 1858, and held an appointment as organist and choirmaster at the Forest School, Leytonstone Hill, 1860; but a year earlier began to devote his attention chiefly to musical and literary composition. Under the initials "C.A.B." he has contributed many articles to the *Guardian, Monthly Musical Record, Musical World, Athenæum,* and *The Meister* ; and to the Analytical programme books of the Crystal Palace, Philharmonic, Bache, Richter, and Birmingham Festival Concerts, etc. He was secretary to the Liszt Scholarship Fund, 1886, and is widely known as a cultured musician with sympathetic leanings to the advanced modern school of composition.

WORKS.— ymphony, for orchestra; Two Overtures; March (Festival March, played at the Crystal Palace Concerts, 1862); String Quartet; Cantatas, sacred and secular, all in MS. Choral Hymns for four voices ; The story of the Resurrection, a cycle of Hymns ; The Christmas story, ditto ; Tunes in Hymns Ancient and Modern and the New Mitre Hymnal, etc. Six Songs with English and German words ; Four Songs (C. Kingsley); Two Songs (Tennyson) ; Elizabeth's Songs from The Saint's Tragedy (Kingsley); and many others. O, holy night, five-part song. Theme with variations, pf. duet ; A Birthday March; Barcarolle ; Tarantella ; Menuetto grazioso, and other pf. pieces. Transcriptions, Overture, Beatrice and Benedict, Berlioz, pf. duet ; Andante, from Tschaïkowsky's Quartet in D, pf. solo ; Pf. score of Te Deum, Berlioz. Editor of The Child's Book of Praise (Masters), etc.

Barry, William Vipond, pianist, composer, and writer, born at Bandon, March, 1827. Appeared in Belfast as pianist, 1846, and founded the Belfast Classical Harmonist Society. He resided for a time in the Potteries, England. He studied under Liszt,

BARTHELEMON.

BARTON.

and was M.A. and Ph. D. of Göttingen University *honoris causi.* Organist of the Cathedral, Port of Spain, Trinadad, and died there March 13, 1872. He composed music for the pianoforte, and wrote a work entitled "Dissertation on the Emotional Nature of Musical Art, and its Media of Operation," London, 1863. His son, WILLIAM H. BARRY, born at Belfast, April, 1858, is a composer and concert giver in Dublin.

Barthelemon, Mrs., *see* YOUNG, MARY.

Bartholomew, Ann Sheppard, born MOUNSEY, composer, organist and pianist, born in London, April 17, 1811. Became a pupil of Logier in 1817, and came under the notice of Spohr when he visited Logier's institution in 1820, her harmonising of a melody being printed in his Autobiography (English ed., Vol. II., p. 100). She afterwards studied under Samuel Wesley and Thomas Attwood, and in 1828 was appointed organist at Clapton. The next year she went to St. Michael's, Wood Street, and in 1837 to St. Vedast's, Foster Lane, a post she held for nearly fifty years. Associate of the Philharmonic Society, 1834 ; Member Royal Society of Musicians, 1839. In 1843 she began giving series of Classical Sacred Concerts at Crosby Hall, which were continued until 1848. The first concert took place November 22, 1843, and at that given January 8, 1845, Mendelssohn's "Hear my Prayer" (composed for these concerts) was performed for the first time, Miss Rainforth singing the solo part. Several of Mendelssohn's smaller pieces were first introduced at these concerts. Miss Mounsey was married to Mr. W. Bartholomew, April 28, 1853. Her artistic career was long and distinguished. She was a fine executant, particularly upon the organ. The earliest of her known compositions, a ballad, " Mary, meet me there," was published in 1832 ; and she issued a set of hymn tunes as late as 1883. She was the possessor of the original MS. of "Hear my Prayer," which she presented to the South Kensington Museum in 1871 ; and of the pianoforte score of " Elijah." The last few years of her life she passed in retirement, and died in London, June 24, 1891.

WORKS.—Oratorio, The Nativity, produced at St. Martin's Hall (Hullah Concerts) January 17, 1855 ; Sacred Cantata, Supplication and Thanksgiving, dedicated to H.R.H. the Princess of Wales, 1864 ; Sacred Harmony, Hymns, &c. ; Hymns of Prayer and Praise, (both edited and composed in conjunction with her sister, Elizabeth Mounsey) ; Thirty-four original tunes set to favourite hymns (1883), and other sacred pieces. Six songs, composed for the Royal Society of Female Musicians (1845) ; Six songs of remembrance ; many detached songs, &c. Six duets in canon (1836) ; Six four-part songs, Op. 37 ; A wreath

for Christmas, &c. Prelude and gigue, and other pieces for pianoforte. Organ music, &c. Notes, and unpublished letters of Mendelssohn, contributed to Lady Wallace's translation of Elise Polko's " Reminiscences of Mendelssohn."

Bartholomew, William, scientist, writer, and violinist, was born in London in 1793. Married to Miss Ann S. Mounsey, April 28, 1853. Chiefly known as the adapter of the librettos of Mendelssohn's works. Died in London, August 18, 1867.

WORKS.—Toy songs for children, written and adapted to pleasing melodies . . London [1849]. English version of the words of Mendelssohn's Antigone, Athalie, Ædipus, Lauda Sion, Walpurgisnacht, Loreley, Elijah, Christus ; Spohr's Jessonda ; Costa's Eli and Naaman ; Bartholomew's The Nativity, etc.

Mr. Bartholomew is best known for his connection with Mendelssohn, with whom his intercourse was friendly and intimate. Mr. Bartholomew wrote many hymns of considerable merit, in addition to the works named above.

Bartleman, James, bass vocalist, was born at Westminster, on September 19, 1769. He studied under Dr. B. Cooke. Bass chorister at the Ancient Music Concerts, 1788-91. Principal bass at the Vocal Concerts, 1791, and at the Concert of Ancient Music, 1795. He died in London, April 15, 1821. This vocalist revived, and by his magnificent performance, created an interest in the music of Henry Purcell which lived for many years.

Bartlett, John, composer, born in latter half of the 16th century. He composed a " Booke of Ayres, with a Triplicitie of Musicke, whereof the first part is for the lute or orpharion, and the viole de Gamba, and four parts to sing ; the second part is for two trebles to sing to the lute and viole ; the third part is for the lute and one voyce, and the viole de Gamba," London, 1606. Bartlett was a Bachelor of Music, Oxford, in 1610, but his biography is unknown.

Bartolozzi, Josephine, *see* ANDERSON, JOSEPHINE.

Bartolozzi, Lucia E., *see* VESTRIS, LUCIA E.

Barton, William, musician, was born about 1598. He was vicar of Mayfield, Staffordshire, and afterwards vicar of St. Martin's, Leicester. He died at Leicester, May, 1678, aged 80. He published the "Book of Psalms in metre, close and proper to the Hebrew, smoth and pleasant for the metre ; plain and easie for the tune, with musicall notes, arguments, annotations, and index. Fitted for the ready use and understanding of all good Christians . . ." London, 1644, 2nd edition, 1645 ; also 1646, 1651, 1654, 1682, 1692, Dublin, 1706. etc.

C

BASSANTIN.

Bassantin, James, astronomer and mathematician, was born in Berwickshire in the reign of James IV. of Scotland. He studied at Glasgow and Paris, and passed his life in scientific pursuits on his estate of Bassendean. He died in 1568. His works are "Astronomia Jacobi Bassantini Scoti, opus absolutissimum . . . ," Geneva, 1599; several minor works on mathematics, and "Musica secundum Platonem," published about 1560. It was issued in French and Latin, but is of no practical value, being simply an abstract-work on music on the principles of the Platonists.

Bate, Mrs. J. D., musician. Compiler of "The North India Tune-Book, containing Bhajans and Ghazals, with native tunes." London, 1886.

Bates, Frank, organist and composer, born at March, Cambridge, in 1856. Musical training private. After acting for a short time as assistant organist at the Parish Church, Leamington, he was appointed, in 1874, to St. Baldred's, North Berwick. While there, he graduated Mus. Bac., Dublin, 1880; his Doctor's Degree being conferred in July, 1884. He was organist at St. John's, Edinburgh, from 1882 to 1885, at the end of which time he received the appointment of organist of Norwich Cathedral. In 1888 he instituted Musical Services for the people, with special choir, and has been actively engaged as teacher of music in Norwich, where he resides. His compositions include an Oratorio, Samuel (Dublin, 1884) ; a setting of Ps. 67, both in MS. He has published a Morning and Evening Service in B flat, an Evening Service in G ; God is our hope; I will sing; Hear my Prayer, and other anthems.

Bates, George, organist and composer, was born on July 6, 1802. In 1839 he became organist of Ripon Cathedral, a post he retained till his death at Ripon, on January 24, 1881. He composed "Sacred Music . . . in full score for voices with an accompaniment for the organ or pianoforte." London, [1857]. Hymns, etc.

Bates, Joah, musician, and one of the founders of the Handel Commemoration, was born at Halifax in March, 1749. Instructed in music by Hartley, organist at Rochdale ; and R. Wainwright, organist, of Manchester. He resided for a time at Eton and Cambridge, and became private secretary to the Earl of Sandwich. In 1767 he graduated M.A. at Cambridge, and in 1776 he was appointed Commissioner of the Victualling Office. He established the Concert of Ancient Music, 1776, and acted as conductor till 1793. Founded Handel Commemoration (with Sir W. W. Wynn and Viscount Fitzwilliam), 1783. He died in London, June 8, 1799.

The "Handel Commemoration" with which Bates is chiefly identified was, in its time, a

BATES.

much talked of enterprise. No such gathering of a large body of musicians had ever before taken place, and the extensive arrangements undertaken in connection with it caused sufficient stir to assure its success. The vocalists who held the principle parts on the occasion of the first public performance were— Miss Cantelo, Miss Abrams, Mdlle Mara, Miss Harwood, Signors Bartolini and Tasca; and Messrs. Harrison, Dyne, Champness, Bellamy, Corfe, Norris, Knyvett, Clerk, Reinhold, and Matthieson. Bates conducted, and the festival took enormously. The first performance was in Westminster Abbey, on May 26, 1784. Second and third performances were given on May 27 and 29. The programme included "The Messiah," The Dettingen Te Deum, a Coronation Anthem, and miscellaneous selections from Handel's works.

As regards Bates it can be said that he was a famous conductor, and in every respect a musician of great knowledge and administrative ability. He did not compose anything so far as we can learn, but appears to be widely known among musicians of every grade during his lifetime. He is somewhat roughly handled by the Scotch poet, A. Macdonald, in "Monitory Madrigals to Musical Amateurs," Nos. 3 and 4, contained in his Miscellaneous Works, 1791. He was married to SARAH HARROP, a soprano vocalist, who is noticed under her own name.

Bates, John W., compiler of "The Sacred Lyre, containing original psalm and hymn tunes . . ." London [1841].

Bates, T. C., author of a "Complete Preceptor for the flageolet," London [1840]; and "Complete Preceptor for the violin," London [1845].

Bates, William, composer of the 18th century, who flourished between 1720 and 1790. He was connected with the Marylebone and Vauxhall Gardens, for which he composed much vocal music. In 1760 he acted as singing master to Ann Cateley, the vocalist, and in 1763 he was prosecuted and fined for trying to dispose of or sell the person of his pupil for immoral purposes to Sir Francis Blake Delavel. He died, probably in London, about 1790.

WORKS.—*Operas and Musical Dramas*— Flora, or Hob in the well ; Pharmaces, an English opera altered from the Italian ; The Theatrical candidates, a prelude [1788]; The Ladies frolick (with T. A. Arne), 1770. *Songs*— Collection of songs sung at Vauxhall, London, 1771, also 1776 ; Songs sung at the Grotto Gardens, 1771 ; The buck's motto; The butterfly ; Ye famed and witty one, etc. Various glees and catches. Six sonatas for two violins, with a thorough bass for the harpsichord or violoncello, London [1750]. Eighteen duettinos for two guitars, two French horns or two clarinetts, London [1780].

BATESON.

BAYLEY.

Bateson, Thomas, composer and organist, was born in the latter half of the the 16th century. Organist of Chester Cathedral, 1599. Resided in Ireland for many years, from 1608. Organist and vicar choral of Christ Church Cathedral, Dublin, 1608. Mus. Bac., Dublin. (The first on whom the degree was conferred by the University). The date of his death is unknown.

WORKS.—First set of madrigals, 1604 (reprinted by the Musical Antiquarian Society in 1846); Second set of madrigals, 1618; Two madrigals in the Triumphs of Oriana.

Bathe, William, Irish Jesuit and writer, was born in Dublin, 1564. Studied at Louvain and Padua, and became rector of the Irish College of Salamanca. He died Madrid, June 17th, 1614. Author of "A brief introduction to the true arte of musicke, wherein are set down exact and easie rules for such as seeke to know the trueth, with arguments and there solutions, for such as seeke also to know the reason of the trueth : with rules be means whereby any by his own industrie may shortly, easily, and regularly attaine to all such things as to the arte doe belong : to which otherwise any can hardly attaine without tedious difficult practice, by means of the irregular order now used in teaching ; lately set forth by William Bathe, student at Oxenford." London, 1584. Another edition was issued under the title of "A briefe introduction to the skill of song, concerning the practice set forth by William Bathe, gent." London [1590].

Batson, Rev. Arthur Wellesley, composer. Mus. B., Oxford, 1878. Appointed Precentor, St. Anne's, Soho, 1888, and conducted Lenten performance of Bach's "St. John" Passion music in February of that year. Composer of a sacred cantata, "The Vineyard;" music to Fletcher's pastoral, "The Faithful shepherdess ;" comic operetta, "The burglar and the bishop." Has also published anthems, services, madrigals, songs, etc.

Batten, Adrian, composer and organist, was born in latter portion of 16th century [1585—90]. He studied under Holmes, of Winchester Cathedral. Became vicar-choral of Westminster Abbey, 1614, and vicar-choral of St. Paul's Cathedral, 1624. Organist, St. Paul's Cathedral, 1624. He died about the middle of the 17th century [1637].

WORKS.—*Anthems*—Hear my prayer ; O praise the Lord; Deliver us, O Lord (in Boyce's Cathedral music) ; Te Deum, Benedictus, Jubilate, Kyrie, etc., in D (Novello) ; Thirty-four anthems (words only—Clifford) ; Twenty-four anthems in Barnard's Cathedral music.

Battishill, Jonathan, composer and organist, was born in London in May, 1738. Son of Jonathan Battishill, solicitor, and

Mary Leverton, his wife. He became a chorister in St. Paul's Cathedral under W. Savage, 1748. He became deputy organist, under Boyce, of the Chapel Royal. Conductor and accompanist at Covent Garden Theatre. Married to Miss Davies (the original "Madge" in "Love in a Village"), 1763. Organist of united parishes of S. Clement, Eastcheap and S. Martin, Orgar, 1764. Organist of Christ Church, Newgate Street, 1767. Resigned post at Covent Garden. Devoted himself to teaching and composition. Presented with gold medal by the Nobleman's Catch-club, 1771. On the death of his wife in 1777, he lost taste for music and became addicted to drink. He died at Islington, December 10, 1801, and was buried in St. Paul's Cathedral.

WORKS.—Almena, an opera (with M. Arne), Drury Lane, 1764 : The Rites of Hecate, a musical entertainment, 1764. *Anthems* : Behold, how good and joyful; Call to remembrance : I will magnify Thee, O God; O Lord, look down from heaven ; Six anthems and ten chants, edited by Page, 1804 (with memoir by Dr. Busby, and portrait) ; Twelve hymns, the words by the Rev. Charles Wesley . . . . London [1765]. *Glees* : Amidst the myrtles ; Again my mournful sighs ; Here rests his head [1805]; Kate, of Aberdeen ; Come, bind my hair. A collection of songs for three and four voices, London [1783] 2 books ; Collection of catches. *Songs* : Collection of favourite songs sung at the publick gardens and theatres [1761]; At eve with the woodlark I rest ; Charms of Silvia ; Gay Damon ; Kind request; Shepherd and shepherdess ; The Wish. Select pieces for the organ or pianoforte, containing an overture and nine pieces selected from original MSS. by John Page. London [1805].

Battye, James, composer and teacher, was born at Huddersfield in 1803, and died there on October 10, 1858. He published "Twelve glees for four and five voices, with pianoforte accompaniment." London [1854]; "My soul truly waiteth," Gresham prize anthem, 1845 ; Songs, etc.

Baumer, Henry, composer and teacher, born about 1835. Head master of Watford School of Music ; retired in 1886. He died at Watford, Herts. July 29, 1888. He composed the "Triumph of Labour," a cantata, 1875 ; Part-songs ; and many single songs ; String quartet ; Three sketches for pf., etc.

Baxter, Rev. J. A., clergyman and musician, published "Harmonia Sacra, a collection of introductory sentences, chants, responses, doxologies, with 200 psalm and hymn tunes, arranged for four voices and pf. or organ. Revised by Vincent Novello." London, 1840.

Bayley, William, organist and composer, was born in [1810]. Vicar-choral St. Paul's Cathedral, and master of the choristers in succession to Hawes. Organist of St. John's,

Horsleydown, Southwark. He died at London, November 8, 1858. He composed many songs and other vocal pieces, and published "The Paneuphonon: a selection of the most popular tunes, with chants for one or four voices . . ." N.D.

Bayly, Rev. Anselm, writer and divine, born 1719. He matriculated at Exeter College, Oxford, 1740. Lay-vicar at Westminster Abbey, 1741. Gentleman of the Chapel Royal, 1741. Priest do., 1744. B.C.L., 1749. D.C.L., Oxford, 1764. Sub-dean of Chapel Royal, 1764. He died in 1792.

WORKS.—Practical Treatise on Singing and Playing with just expression and real elegance, London, 1771; The Alliance of Musick, Poetry, and Oratory, 1789; The Sacred Singer, containing an Essay on Grammar, the requisites of singing cathedral compositions, etc., London, 1771. Collection of Anthems used in His Majesty's Chapel Royal, and most cathedral churches in England and Ireland, 1769. Sermons, etc.

Bayly, Barre Dalton, violinist, born at St. Heliers, Jersey, 1850. Youngest son of the late Captain Edgar Bayly, H.M. 12th Regiment, and his wife, daughter of Lord Charles B. Kerr, second son of the fifth Lord Lothian. Pupil of M. Currie de Hauteville and Ludwig Straus. Some time violinist at the Grand Opera House and Steinway Hall, New York. Leader of the orchestra, Exeter Oratorio Society, 1870-1895; principal violin at important concerts at Barnstaple (Easter Musical Festivals), and soloist at concerts in London, &c., and a successful teacher.

Bayly, Thomas Haynes, lyrical poet and composer, born at Bath, October 13, 1797; died London, April 22, 1839. He composed the music for a large number of his own ballads, such as The bower, the Carrier dove, The Circassian, The Deserter, Fly away pretty moth, &c., but most of his more popular songs were set by Bishop, Knight, Lee, Loder, and others.

Baynham, Thomas, published a "Collection of psalm and hymn tunes, single and double chants . . . ," London, 1860. He also composed some pianoforte music.

Beale, Charles James, organist and composer, born in 1819. He was organist of St. Paul's, Covent Garden, London, for several years. Died at London, March 19, 1882. Composer of a "Laudate Dominum" and other church and vocal music.

Beale, George Galloway, organist, born in London, 1868. Chorister, Marlborough College; pupil of Dr. J. F. Bridge; Mus. Bac., Durham, 1891; F.R.C.O.; Organist and assistant master, St. John's School, Leatherhead, 1887-9; Organist, St. John's, Paddington, 1890-3, and Conductor of the Paddington Choral and Orchestral Association; in 1894,

appointed Organist and Choirmaster of Llandaff Cathedral.

Beale, John, composer and pianist, was born in London, about 1776. Pupil of J. B. Cramer, and member of Philharmonic Society, 1820. He was a professor of pianoforte at the R.A.M., and a teacher in London. He also directed the music at the Argyle Rooms. Died after 1830.

WORKS.—Lyrical specimens of German and French composers, adapted to English poetry written and selected by L. S. Costello, London [1822]. *Songs:* The kiss dear maid; Crusader's return; Russian maiden's song, etc. Rondo for pianoforte, Op. 2; Forty-seven preludes . . . for the pianoforte [1827]. Complete Guide to the art of playing the German flute, London [1820].

Beale, Thomas Willert (WALTER MAYNARD), born in London, 1828, son of Frederick Beale, of the firm of Cramer, Beale, and Addison. Studied under Edward Roeckel, G. F. Flowers, and Pugni. Was one of the founders of the New Philharmonic Society, but did not adopt music as a profession, being called to the bar at Lincoln's Inn, 1863. Besides the works mentioned below, he contributed many articles to different magazines. He died at Gipsy Hill, London, October 3, 1894.

WORKS.—The Enterprising Impresario (Bradbury, Evans, & Co.), 1867; The Light of other days (Bentley), 1890. *Operettas:* An Easter egg; Matrimonial news. Part-songs and songs, pianoforte pieces, &c.

Beale, Thurley, baritone vocalist, born at Royston, Hertfordshire, April 23, 1849. Studied under (Sir) Joseph Barnby, and was a chorister at St. Andrew's, Wells Street, London, and at St. Paul's Cathedral. A singer of repute, he has been heard at the principal London and Provincial Concerts, the Hereford Festival of 1879, &c.

Beale, William, composer, born at Landrake, Cornwall, January 1, 1784. He studied under Dr. Arnold and R. Cooke, and was gentleman of the Chapel Royal, 1816-20. He resided in London as a teacher of music, and held the appointments of organist of Wandsworth Parish Church, and St. John's, Clapham Rise. From November, 1820, to December, 1821, he was organist of Trinity College, Cambridge. In 1813, he gained the prize cup of the Madrigal Society with his madrigal, "Awake, sweet muse," and in 1840, a prize from the Adelphi Glee Club. He died in London, May 3, 1854.

WORKS.—*Madrigals and Glees:* A first book of Madrigals, Glees, etc., for three, four, and five voices, Op. 6, London, 1815; Collection of Glees and Madrigals, London, 1820; Collection of thirteen Glees, edited by E. Plater [1879]; Awake, sweet muse (1813),

BEALE.

prize madrigal ; Come let us join the rounde-lay ; This pleasant month of May ; What ho ! what ho ! (1816) ; etc. Songs. Sonata for the pianoforte, with an accompaniment for the violin [1815] ; Second Sonata for piano-forte, Op. 8 [1816].

Beale, William George Frederick, published " Congregational Psalmody : a col-lection of psalm and hymn tunes," London [1852]. He also wrote songs and pianoforte music.

Another BEALE, HENRY WOLFGANG AMA-DEUS, published a large number of Songs and Pianoforte Pieces between 1854 and 1878, and edited (with W. T. Wrighton) "Congregational Psalmody " [1858].

Beard, John, tenor vocalist, born in 1716, was a chorister in Chapel Royal, under Bernard Gates. First appeared at Covent Garden in 1736, and at Drury Lane in 1737. Married to Lady Henrietta Herbert, widow of Lord Edward Herbert, 1739, and afterwards to Miss Rich (daughter of Rich, of Covent Garden Theatre), 1759. He was one of the proprietors of Covent Garden Theatre, 1761. Retired from public life, 1768. He died at Hampton, Middlesex. February 4, 1791. He composed a few songs.

Beardmore, Mrs., see PARKE, MARIA H.

Beatson, John, musician. Published " A Complete collection of all the tunes sung by the different congregations in Hull. To which is prefixed an introduction to the art of Psalmody " [1780].

Beattie, James, poet and author, born at Laurencekirk, October 25, 1735. Professor of Moral Philosophy, Marischal College, Aberdeen, 1760. He died at Aberdeen, August 18, 1803. Author of " Essays on poetry and music as they affect the mind, etc.," London, 1776 ; second edition, 1779. " Letter to the Rev. Hugh Blair, D.D., on the improvement of psalmody in Scotland," 1778 ; another edition, Edinburgh, 1829. Poems, Ethical works, etc.

His eldest son, JAMES HAY BEATTIE (born Aberdeen, 1768—died 1790) was a violinist, and amateur musician of great promise.

Beatty=Kingston, W., see KINGSTON, WILLIAM.

Beaty, Richard William, musician, was born in Dublin about 1799. He was originally a chorister of Christ Church Cathe-dral, and became organist and teacher at the Molyneux Asylum for Blind Women in 1824. He was organist of the Free Church, Great Charles Street, from 1828 to 1877, and choir-master of Christ Church Cathedral, Dublin, from 1830 to 1872. He died at Dublin in 1883.

WORKS.—One hundred and fifty hymns . . [1844], with Weyman and I. Smith. Sequel to Melodia Sacra. Songs, etc.

Beaumont, Alexander S., composer of

BEAZLEY.

the present day. His works include a Suite for strings (produced, Norwood, 1887); Suite in D, strings and pf. ; Lullaby, pf., violin, viola, and harmonium ; Gondoliera and Marcia funèbre, for pf. and string quartet; pieces for violin and violoncello. Duets for pf., songs, etc.

Beaumont, Henry, tenor vocalist, native of Yorkshire. Studied first under Joshua Marshall, of Huddersfield, and later with Luigi Caracciolo, at Dublin. Made his debut at Huddersfield, October 22, 1881, at a con-cert of the festival in celebration of the opening of the first Town Hall in the borough. He soon made his way in public estimation, and in 1883 was offered a position in the choir of Christ Church Cathedral, Dublin. Here he remained about two years, singing at the principal Dublin concerts, when, in 1885, he joined the Carl Rosa Opera Company. He also sang in Grand Opera in Drury Lane, and joined the Burns-Crotty " Cinderella " tour, 1891-2. Has visited America three times, the first occasion being in 1888, when he was with Mr. Ludwig's party. Now resident in London, and chiefly engaged in concert-singing. Married, April 26, 1888, the Dublin soprano, ADELAIDE MULLEN (q.v.)

Beaumont, John, musician, published " The New Harmonic Magazine, or Com-pendious Repository of Sacred Music, in full Score," London, 1801.

Beazley, James Charles, pianist, vio-linist and composer, born in Ryde, I.W., 1850. Studied music privately for some years, and then entered the R.A.M., where his masters were H. C. Banister, harmony ; Dr. Steggall, counterpoint; W. Sterndale Bennett, composition; and F. B. Jewson, pianoforte. After leaving the Academy he was appointed music-master at the King's School, Sherborne, Dorset, but delicate health compelled his return to Ryde, where he has since resided as teacher and composer. During the last few weeks of Sir Sterndale Bennett's life, Beazley acted as his private secretary, the most cordial relations exist-ing between them.

WORKS.—Cantatas : Drusilda (Ryde, 1888); Josiah (1891) ; The Red dwarf ; The Golden flitch. Services of song. Part-songs, songs, The white gondola, etc. Instrumental : Sona-tinas in D minor, F, and G minor ; Six sketches ; Six bagatelles ; Six miniatures ; Deux pensées ; Elegy, and other pieces for violin and pf., with a large number still in MS. ; Thirty-five studies ; Four easy sketches ; Album of pieces, and other compositions for the pf. Pieces for flute and pf. Albums for American organ or harmonium. Author of " Aids to the violinist : a short treatise in reference to bow-marks " (Cary, London).

BECHER,

Becher, Alfred Julius, composer, of German extraction, was born at Manchester in 1803. Educated at Universities of Heidelberg, Berlin, etc. Resided at Vienna as editor of the *Radikale*, a democratic sheet, which was filled with seditious articles by Becher. Shot at Vienna for sedition, Nov. 23, 1846

WORKS.—Op. 1, Songs for solo voice and piano; op. 2, Lyrical pieces for the pf.; op. 3, Six poems for voice and pf.; op. 5, Rondo for the pf.; op. 6, Six songs for voice and pf.; op. 7, Three sonatas for pf. solo; op. 8, Original theme for pf.; op. 9, Monologue for pf.; op. 10, Six songs for voice and pf.; op. 11, Sonata for pf.; op. 18, Nine pieces for pf.; A Symphody; String quartet, and various articles on music.

Beckwith, John Christmas, composer and organist, born at Norwich, December 25, 1750. Studied under Dr. Wm. and Philip Hayes, at St. Magdalen College, Oxford. Organist of St. Peter's, Mancroft, Norwich, 1794. Organist of Norwich Cathedral in succession to Thos. Garland, 1808. Mus. Bac. and Doc. Oxon, 1803. Instructed Thomas Vaughan, the vocalist, in singing. Died at Norwich, June 3, 1809.

WORKS.—The First verse of every Psalm of David, with an ancient or modern chant in score, adapted as much as possible to the sentiment of each Psalm. London, 1808. Six Anthems in Score, for 1, 2, 3, 4, and 5 voices. London [1790]. *Glees*: Hark, o'er the waves; Chimney sweepers; Favourite concerto for the organ, harpsichord, or pianoforte, op. 4 [1795]; Sonata for the harpsichord or pf., op. 3; Six voluntaries for the organ or harpsichord, London, 1780; Songs, etc.

Beckwith was an organist of much genius, and was famous for his extempore playing. The name, "Christmas," is supposed to be a nickname given on account of his birthday. His son, JOHN CHARLES (born 1788, died October 5, 1828) was an organist of much ability, and succeeded to the post at Norwich Cathedral in 1809. His uncle, JOHN BECKWITH (born 1728, died May 14, 1800), was a layclerk in Norwich cathedral. His brother, the Rev. Edward James Beckwith (died January 7, 1833), was succentor of St. Paul's Cathedral, and the composer af some chants.

Bedford, Arthur, divine and writer, was born at Tiddenham, Gloucester, September, 1668. Studied at Oxford. Died at London, 1745.

WORKS.—The Temple Musick, or an Essay concerning the Method of Singing the Psalms of David in the Temple before the Babylonish Captivity, wherein the musick of our Cathedrals is vindicated . . . Bristol, 1706; Essay on Singing David's Psalms, 1708; The Great abuse of Musick, containing an account of the use and design of Musick among the Antient

BEESLEY.

Jews, Greeks, Romans, etc., London, 1711; The Excellency of Divine Musick . . . to which is added a specimen of easy grave tunes instead of those which are used in our profane and wanton ballads, London, 1733; Scripture Chronology demonstrated by Astronomical Calculations, London, 1730; The Present State of the Republick of Letters, London, 1730; Serious Reflections on the Scandalous Abuse and Effects of the Stage, Bristol, 1705.

Bedford, Herbert, composer, born in London, 1867, Musically educated at the Guildhall School of Music, where he was twice awarded the annual prize for composition. First came prominently into notice by a concert of his works at the Meistersinger's Club, May 30, 1892. His principal compositions are "La Belle Dame sans merci" (Keats), and "La Joie fait peur," for voice and orchestra; an opera, "Kit Marlowe," not yet produced; an Ave Maria, for contralto solo, contralto chorus, violoncello, pf., harp, and organ; a group of French songs; an Album of English songs (including a setting of Shelley's Ode to Music), etc. In 1894 he married Miss Liza Lehmann, the vocalist and composer (*q.v.*).

Bedford, Paul John, comedian and bass vocalist, born at Bath, 1792? Sang at Drury Lane, November 10, 1824, in the first proper or complete performance of Weber's "Der Freischütz," taking the part of Bernhard. From 1833 he sang in opera at Covent Garden; and later in farces at the Adelphi. He had a good, deep bass voice. He died in London, January 11, 1871.

Bedsmore, Thomas, organist and composer, was born at Lichfield in 1833. Chorister, Lichfield Cathedral, 1843; articled to Samuel Spofforth, the Cathedral organist; and after the death of his teacher, in 1864, he was appointed his successor. Died at Lichfield, June 9, 1881. Composer of Church music, songs, pianoforte music, etc.

Beecroft, George Andus Beaumont, amateur composer, was born in 1845. His father was M.P. for Leeds. He was educated at Oxford, where he graduated B.A., in 1868, and M.A., in 1872; Mus. Bac., Oxford, 1867. He died on May 3, 1873. He composed some vocal music, and contributed to the *Choir* and other musical journals. He also published a Magnificat and Nunc dimittis; a Minuet and Trio for Pianoforte; Three casts from the antique for Pianoforte, etc.

Beesley, Mrs., *see* SPINNEY, MATTIE.

Beesley, Michael, published "A Book of Psalmody, containing instructions for young beginners, after as plain and familiar a manner as any, with a collection of psalm tunes, anthems, hymns, etc. . . . engraved by M. Beesley," 17—.

Begg, Rev. James, Scottish divine, born 1809, died at Edinburgh, 1883. Author of

BELCHER.

"The Use of Organs and other instruments of music in Christian worship indefensible," Glasgow, 1866. "Instrumental Music unwarranted in the worship of God," Edinburgh, N.D. His father, the Rev. James Begg, D.D., minister of New Monkland, Lanarkshire, wrote a tract entitled "Treatise on the use of organs and other instruments of music in the worship of God," Glasgow, 1808, reprinted in his son's tract of 1866.

Belcher, John, English writer, author of "Lectures on the History of Ecclesiastical Music," London, 1872.

Belcher, William Thomas, organist and composer, born in Birmingham, March 8, 1827. Graduated Mus. B. Oxon., 1867; Mus. D. 1872. Organist of Great Barr Church, 1856, and subsequently of several churches in Birmingham, up to 1884, when he was appointed organist and choir-master at Holy Trinity, Bordesley, a position he still holds. Has given organ recitals in Birmingham and neighbouring towns. His son, W. E. Belcher, M.A., is deputy organist of the Leeds Town Hall, and teacher of music at Headingly, near Leeds.

WORKS.—Oratorio, The Sea of Galilee (MS.), Oxford, 1872; Cantata, The Fates, Oxford, 1867; Cantatas composed for the opening of Adderley and Aston Parks, Birmingham; Cantatina, Excelsior; Opera, Estelle. *Church Music :* Anthem for double choir, from Psalm 122; Anthems, Hymns, Chants, &c. Glees and part-songs, including a Jubilee Song—Fifty years glad blessings bringing—a copy of which was graciously accepted by the Queen, 1887. Pianoforte pieces, etc.

Bell, John, composer and organist, was born at Gourock, in Renfrewshire. He studied music from an early age, and became a A. Mus. T.C.L.; F.F.S.C.; and Mus. Doc., Trinity College, Toronto. Has held the appointments of organist or conductor of psalmody in Westbourne Free Church; Springburn Parish Church; Anderston Parish Church; and St. Vincent Parish Church, all in Glasgow. He also conducted a Select Choir, and acted as conductor of the Glasgow Temperance Choral Society; Cathcart Musical Association; Vale of Leven Choral Society; Carluke Choral Society; and St. Andrew's Musical Association. For four or five years he was musical critic to the *North British Daily Mail.* Composer and arranger of about 150 anthems and part-songs; the 145th Psalm for soli, double chorus, and orchestra (degree exercise), etc.

Bell, John Montgomerie, amateur composer, was born at Edinburgh, May 28, 1837. He is a writer to the signet. His compositions include anthems, songs, and hymn tunes, some of which have been published in various Scottish Church Hymnals.

Bellamy J., musician, compiled " A

BELLERBY.

System of Divine Musick," 1745.

Bellamy, Richard, bass singer and composer, was born about 1743. In 1771 he was appointed a gentleman of the Chapel Royal, and in 1773 he became a lay-vicar of Westminster Abbey. He graduated Mus. Bac., Cambridge, in 1775. He became a vicar-choral of St. Paul's Cathedral, London, in 1793, and succeeded Hudson, as almoner and master of the children, in 1793, a post he held till 1799. He died at London, September 11, 1813. Bellamy was one of the best bass singers of his day, and composed a Te Deum; A set of anthems, 1788; Six glees for three and four voices, 1789; and other works.

Bellamy, Thomas Ludford, bass vocalist, son of above, was born at Westminster, London, in 1770. He was a chorister in Westminster Abbey under Cooke. He studied singing under Tasca, and appeared as a concert vocalist in London till 1794. Stage manager of theatre in Dublin, 1794-97. He became part-proprietor of Chester, Lichfield, Manchester, and Shrewsbury theatres, 1800. Proprietor of Belfast, Londonderry, and Newry theatres, 1803. Sang in Covent Garden theatre, 1807-12, and at Drury Lane theatre, 1812-17. Choir-master at Chapel of Spanish Embassy, London, 1819. Bass Singer at Concert of Ancient Music. He died at London, January 3, 1843.

WORKS.— Songs and part-songs. Lyric poetry of glees, madrigals, catches. rounds, canons, and duets. London, 1840.

WILLIAM HENRY BELLAMY (born in 1799—died at London, March 3, 1880), probably a relative of the above, composed A lady's page; The neglected lute; The pilgrim, and other songs.

Bellasis, Edward, writer, born January 28, 1852. "Lancaster Herald." 1882. Author of Cherubini: memorials illustrative of his life, London, 1874. The Law of arms, 1880; The Machells of Crackenthorpe . . Kendal, 1886.; Memorials of Mr. Serjeant Bellasis, 1800-1873, London, 1893, etc. *Songs :* Alone I wandered; Ministering spirits; The haven; Consolation; Waiting for the morning; The two worlds; Tyre; Marionette pantomime; Pf. music, etc.

His brother, the REV. RICHARD BELLASIS of the Oratory, Edgbaston, Birmingham, is a musician, and occasionally conducts concerts.

Bellerby, Edward Johnson, organist, pianist, and composer, born March 28, 1858, at Pickering, Yorkshire. Studied under Dr. E. G. Monk, of York Minster, 1876-80, and was assistant organist during most of that time. In 1879 he graduated Mus. Bac., Oxford; and Mus. Doc., 1895. He was organist to Lord Hotham, 1877-8; of Selby Abbey Church, 1878-81; then appointed to Margate Parish Church, 1881; and in 1884 to Holy

BELVILLE.

BENNETT.

Trinity, Margate, where he remains to the present time. An able executant, both as pianist and organist; he has appeared at various concerts, and his organ recitals are very popular. He has a considerable reputation as an extempore player.

WORKS.— Psalm 46, for soli, eight-part chorus, and orchestra; Communion service in F. *Anthems*: Jesu, my Lord, and others; songs, and a volume of nursery rhymes. Festive overture (Selby Orchestral Society, 1887); Symphonic fantasia (composed 1888, and produced by Margate Philharmonic Society, 1895), for orchestra; organ and pf. pieces, etc. Author of a "Primer on Harmonising Melodies."

Belville, Edward (or **Jakobowski**), composer of the present time. At a concert given at the R.A.M., in conjunction with Mr. Sinclair Dunn, he introduced his comic opera, The Three Beggars (July 28, 1883), which has been followed by many others: Dick (Globe Theatre, April, 17, 1884); Ermine (book by Bellamy and H. Paulton, Grand Theatre, Birmingham, November 9, 1885); The Palace of pearl (joint composition with Stanislaus, Empire Theatre, June, 1886); Mynheer Jan (Comedy Theatre, February, 1887); Paola (H. Paulton); La Rosière (Shaftesbury, January, 1893); A Venetian singer (one act, Court Theatre, Nov. 1893), etc. Six songs (Sinclair Dunn), etc., etc.

Bendall, Wilfred Ellington, composer, born in London, April 22, 1850. Studied harmony and composition under Charles Lucas and E. Silas; and at the Conservatorium, Leipzig, 1872-4. Resident in London as composer and teacher of pf.

WORKS.—Sacred Cantata, Parizādeh (produced by Willing's Choir, St. James's Hall, April 22, 1884); Cantatas for female voices: The Lady of Shallott; The Rosiere; The Woman of Canaan. Operettas: Lover's knots (St. George's Hall, 1880); Quid pro quo (1880). Trios, for female voices, The fountain, etc. Six vocal duets, part-songs, songs, etc. Six pieces, violin and pf. In the Tyrol, three pieces for pf. Toccata in E flat, etc.

Bennet, John, composer, who flourished at the end of the 16th and beginning of the 17th centuries [1570-1615].

WORKS.—Madrigalls to four voyces, newly published by John Bennett, his first works at London, 1599; Madrigal, "All creatures now are merrily minded," in the Triumphs of Oriana, 1601; Songs in a collection published by Ravenscroft; O God of Gods, verse anthem, Sacred Harmonic Society's Library; Anthems and madrigals in MS.

Nothing as to his biography appears to have been chronicled. His book of madrigals was re-published in 1845 by the Musical Antiquarian Society.

Bennet, Robert, musician, published "The Psalm-singer's necessary Companion, containing above sixty choice psalm tunes," London, 1718.

Bennet, Saunders, organist, pianist, and composer, born in last quarter of the 18th century. He was organist of a church at Woodstock, and died at Woodstock, May 25, 1809. He wrote some vocal music (glees and songs), and a number of rondos, sonatas, variations, etc., for the organ and pf. Also edited "Selection of sacred music for three voices, with an accompaniment for the organ," London, 1810.

Bennett, Alfred William, son of Thomas Bennett, organist of Chichester Cathedral, was born in 1805. He studied under his father. Organist of New College, Oxford, 1825. Mus. Bac., Oxon., 1825. Killed by a fall from a coach while on his way to Worcester Festival, September 12, 1830.

WORKS.—Church Services and Anthems; Cathedral Chants, 1829, edited with W. Marshall, Mus. Bac.; Cathedral Music . . edited by T. and H. Bennett, London [1830]; Songs; Instructions for the pianoforte, with popular National Airs arranged as Lessons, London, [1825]; Instructions for the Spanish guitar, London [1828]: Vocalist's Guide, comprised in a series of instruction and solfeggi, London [1830], also [1865].

Bennett, Charles, organist and composer, was born about 1740. He was organist at Truro for 40 years, and died there on May 12, 1804. Composer of "Twelve songs and a cantata," London, 1765, etc.

Bennett, Frederick James Wentworth, flutist and composer, born at Cadbury, Somerset, 1856. Studied at R.A.M. and R.C.M., also privately under A. P. Vivian and R. S. Rockstro, L.R.A.M., 1895. Has performed in London and the provinces; and was conductor of the Castle Cary Choral Society, 1883-90, and the Cadbury Musical Society, 1887-90. Appointed Professor of the Flute at the Brighton School of Music, 1895. Author of a brochure on "Conducting, and being Conducted" (1889), and now engaged on a work "On Solo Flute-playing." Has contributed articles to the *Musical Times* and other papers.

WORKS.—Mass in C minor (1888); Sacred Cantata, *Anno Domini* (1888); Cantata, "Eurydice" (1884); Operettas: Dr. Whack'um (1880); King Richard I. (1883); King Arthur (1884); The King's Foresters (1886); and The Black Eagle (1888). Symphony in C, orchestra (1885); Rustic Idyll, orchestra (1893). Concerto in E minor, flute and orchestra (1887); Sonata, pf. Many pieces for pf. and flute. Various part-songs, and nearly 200 songs.

Bennett, George John, composer and organist, born at Andover, Hants, May 5, 1863.

BENNETT.

BENNETT.

Was a chorister at Winchester Cathedral, 1872-78, and entered the Royal Academy of Music in 1879, studying under Sir G. A. Macfarren. Here he remained until 1884, and at the R.A.M. concerts the first movement of a symphony, two overtures, a pianoforte concerto, and other works of his were produced. From 1884 to 1887 he was enabled— through the instrumentality of the firm of Novello, Ewer, and Co., who were greatly interested in the talented young musician—to study at Berlin, under Friedrich Kiel, and at Munich, under Rheinberger. Returning to England, he was (1888) created a Fellow, and appointed Professor of Harmony, R.A.M., having, six years previously, obtained the diploma, F.(R.)C.O. He graduated Mus. Bac., Cambridge, 1888; Mus. Doc., 1893. He was organist of St. John the Evangelist from 1890, until his appointment to Lincoln Cathedral in August, 1895. Other offices held by him are Conductor, London Organ School Orchestra (1893), and Church Orchestral Society (1895).

WORKS.—Mass, in B flat minor; Festival Te Deum in D, for soli, double choir, and orchestra, in MS.; Festival Evening Service in A, Dedication Festival, St. Paul's Cathedral, 1890; Easter Hymn, for soli, chorus, and orchestra, Festival of Sons of the Clergy, St. Paul's, 1895; Morning, Evening, and Communion Services; Anthems, etc. Two Albums of Songs (Novello); Trios for female voices; Part-songs, etc. Orchestral: Serenade, in Symphonic form; Overture, Jugendträume, Crystal Palace, March, October, 1887; Overture, "Leonatus and Imogen," Philharmonic Society, 1895. Trio in E, pf., vn., and 'cello, London, 1893; various pf. pieces, Voluntaries for organ, etc.

Bennett, James, composer and writer, born at Salford, 1804; died at Brighton, June, 1870. Author of "A Practical Introduction to part and sight-singing," London, 1843: "Elementary exercises for the cultivation of the voice," London, N.D. Composed songs, etc.

Bennett, Joseph, musical critic, librettist, and journalist, born at Berkeley, Gloucestershire, November 29, 1831. In his youth he studied the organ, violin, viola, and violoncello; went through a course of training for scholastic profession at the Borough Road College, London; acted as precentor at the historical Weigh House Chapel, and was sometime organist of Westminster Chapel. Finally, adopting musical criticism, he was connected successively with the *Sunday Times, Daily Telegraph, Pall Mall Gazette, and Graphic.* For many years he contributed to the *Musical World,* also to the *Musical Standard,* and *Musical Times,* devoting himself now to the last-named and the *Daily Telegraph.* He was editor of *Concordia,* 1875-6; and of the *Lute,*

1883-6. In 1885, he was engaged as annotator of the Philharmonic Society's programmes, and succeeded the late J. W. Davison as writer of the analytical programmes for the Saturday and Monday Popular Concerts. He has also done similar work for the Leeds, Birmingham, and other Festivals. He has acted as adjudicator at Eisteddfodan; is a member of the Committee of the Mendelssohn Scholarship Fund; and President of the Gloucester Choral Society. Of his innumerable contributions to the press, the most important are a series of papers on the Great Composers (*Musical Times,* 1877-91); "Elijah," a comparison of the original and revised scores (commenced in the short-lived *Concordia,* and reprinted and completed in the *Musical Times,* October, 1882, to April, 1883); and "From my study," *Musical Times,* (1892 to present time). As a librettist, Joseph Bennett has done much. His chief works, adapted or original are, The Golden Legend (Sullivan); The Rose of Sharon, The Dream of Jubal, the Story of Sayid, and Bethlehem (Meckenzie); Ruth, Thorgrim, The Transfiguration (Cowen), Jeanie Deans (MacCunn), and books for Dr. J. F. Bridge, C. Lee Williams, Barnett, Mancinelli, and others. His chief publications are: Letters from Bayreuth (Novello, 1877); The Musical Year [1883] (Novello, 1884); Primers of Musical Biography, five books, enlargements of some of the papers above-named; and History of the Leeds Musical Festivals, 1858-1889 (in conjunction with F. R. Spark,) Novello, 1892. He is also the author of a number of poetical pieces.

Bennett, Robert, musician, was born at Bakewell, Derbyshire, in January or February, 1788. He became a chorister in King's College, Cambridge, and was articled to Dr. Clarke-Whitfield. In 1811 he became organist of the Parish Church, Sheffield. He died at Sheffield, November 3, 1819. He was married to Elizabeth Don, daughter of the botanist, and his son was William Sterndale Bennett, separately noticed. He composed a number of songs and various hymn tunes.

Bennett, Thomas, organist and composer, born at Fonthill in 1779. Chorister in Salisbury Cathedral under Joseph Corfe. Organist of St. John's Chapel, Chichester, and of Chichester Cathedral, 1803-48. He died at Chichester, March 21, 1848, and was succeeded by his son Henry, who held the appointment till 1860.

WORKS.—Introduction to the Art of Singing, London, N.D.; Songs and organ pieces. Sacred Melodies: A collection of psalms and hymns, sung at the Cathedral and Chapel of St. John, Chichester, London, 1825; Cathedral selections, consisting of anthems, sanctus commandments, and chants, London; several editions.

BENNETT.

Bennett, William, organist and composer, born near Teignmouth, 1767. He studied under Jackson of Exeter, and J. C. Bach and Schroeter, London. Organist of St. Andrew's Church, Plymouth. He died about 1830.

WORKS.—Six songs and a glee, London [1799] ; anthems and organ music, etc.

Bennett, W. J. E., compiler of a "Psalter, containing a selection of psalm tunes, chants, services, and other ecclesiastical music . . . arranged for congregational singing in four parts," 1843-44.

Bennett, William Mineard, composer and painter, born at Exeter, in 1778, died there October 17, 1858. He composed a number of glees and songs, and was a portrait painter.

Bennett, Sir William Sterndale, composer and pianist, was born at Sheffield, April 13, 1816. He studied as a chorister in choir of King's College, Cambridge, under his grandfather, John Bennett, and received subsequent instruction from Charles Lucas, Dr. Crotch, Cipriani Potter, and W. H. Holmes. He studied at Leipzig Conservatorium under Moscheles, at the expense and on the suggestion of Messrs. Broadwood and Sons, during 1836-40. He appeared in England as concert-giver, 1843-1856, and was an unsuccessful candidate for Music Professorship at Edinburgh University, 1844. He married Miss Mary Ann Wood, 1844. Founded (with others) the Bach Society, 1849. Conducted the Philharmonic Society Concerts, 1856-66. Conducted the Leeds Musical Festival, 1858. Professor of Music at Cambridge, 1856. Mus. Doc., Cambridge, 1856. M.A., Cambridge, 1857. Principal of the R.A.M., 1866. D.C.L., Oxford, 1870. Knighted, 1871. Presented with testimonial, 1872. He died at London, February 1, 1875.

WORKS.—Op. 1, First Concerto for pianoforte and orchestra, in D minor, 1832 ; Op. 2, Capriccio for pianoforte, in D ; Op. 3, Overture for full orchestra, Parisina, 1834-35 ; Op. 4, Second Concerto for pianoforte and orchestra, in E flat ; Op. 8, Sestet for pianoforte and strings, 1844 ; Op. 9, Third Concerto for pianoforte and orchestra, in C minor, 1834 ; Op. 10, Three musical sketches for pianoforte ; Op. 11, Six studies for the pianoforte ; Op. 12, Three impromptus for pianoforte ; Op. 13, Sonata for pianoforte, 1842 ; Op. 14, Three romances for pianoforte ; Op. 15, Overture for full orchestra, The Naiads, 1836 ; Op. 16, Fantasia for pianoforte, 1842 ; Op. 17, Three Diversions for pianoforte duet ; Op. 18, Allegro Grazioso for pianoforte ; Op. 19, Fourth Concerto for pianoforte and orchestra, in F minor, 1836-1849 ; Op. 20, Overture for full orchestra, The Wood Nymph, 1840 ; Op. 22. Caprice in E for pianoforte and orchestra, 1840 ; Op. 23, Six

BENSON.

songs for solo voice with pianoforte accompaniment ; Op. 24, Suite de Pieces, for pianoforte, 1843 ; Op. 25, Rondo Piacevale for pianoforte ; Op. 26, Trio for pianoforte, violin, and 'cello, 1844 ; Op. 27, Scherzo for pianoforte ; Op. 28, Rondino for pianoforte, 1853 ; Op. 29, Two studies for pianoforte ; Op. 30, Four sacred duets ; Op. 31, Tema e variazione for pianoforte ; Op. 32, Sonata for pianoforte and 'cello, 1852 ; Op. 33, Sixty preludes and lessons for pianoforte, 1853 ; Op. 34, Rondo for pianoforte ; Op. 35, Six songs (second set) for voice and pianoforte ; Op. 36, Flowers of the month ; Op. 37, Rondeau à la Polonaise pour le pianoforte [1858] ; Op. 38, Toccato for pianoforte ; Op. 39, The May Queen, a pastoral, by H. F. Chorley (cantata) for solo voices, chorus, and orchestra, Leeds Musical Festival, 1858 ; Op. 40, Ode, written for the opening of the International Exhibition, 1862, by (Lord) Alfred Tennyson, 1862 ; Op. 41, Cambridge Installation Ode, 1862 ; Op. 42, Fantasie-overture, Paradise and the Peri, for full orchestra, 1862 ; Op. 43, Symphony for full orchestra, in G minor ; op. 44, The Woman of Samaria, an oratorio, for solo voices, chorus, and orchestra, Birmingham Festival, 1867 ; op. 45, Music to Sophocles' Ajax ; Op. 46, Pianoforte Sonata, The Maid of Orleans.

In addition to the above he wrote overtures, The Merry Wives of Windsor ; Marie du Bois, 1845 ; A quintet for pianoforte and wind instruments, etc., songs, part-songs, pianoforte music, and collections of chants, etc., most of which have been published.

Benson, George, composer and tenor singer, was born in 1814. He was a gentleman of the Chapel Royal, and in 1878 he graduated Mus. Bac., Cambridge. He died at London, August 9, 1884. He composed Glees : If music be the food of love (prize, 1863) ; Orpheus with his lute ; True love to win. Sleep little baby, sleep, four-part song. The Wooer, madrigal. My God look upon me ; I will arise, anthems. Songs, etc.

Benson, John, musician, compiled "Sacred Harmony, a collection of tunes composed and arranged for one, two, three and four voices." London [1840].

Benson, John Allanson, composer, organist and teacher, born near Ripley, Yorkshire, February 8, 1848. Connected with the family of the late Archbishop of Canterbury. He was intended, by his father, for an architect, but his love for music ultimately prevailed, and he adopted the art as his profession. He received his earliest instruction as a choir boy after the removal of his family to Harrogate, and afterwards became conductor of the local Philharmonic Society. As organist, teacher, lecturer, and composer, he is a prominent and busy figure in musical life at Harrogate.

BENTLEY.

WORKS.—Oratorio, King Hezekiah (composed, 1886, produced, Harrogate, 1891); Sacred cantatas, *Laudate Dominum ;* Christ at Nain (which obtained the £50 prize offered by Curwen and Sons, 1895); Cantata, Bottreaux bells (1873); Six school cantatas; The crown of roses, Summer holiday, etc., etc. Jubilee ode, Victoria! Victoria! (1887). Services of song, anthems, school songs, etc. In MS. are two comic operas, King Cophetua (produced, 1881), and Endymion (1883), and a dramatic cantata, The water nymph (1885). Organ music contributed to the " Organist's Quarterly Journal " and other publications, and hymn tunes in the "National Tune Book " (London : Patey and Willis), etc., etc.

Bentley, John Morgan, composer and organist, born at Manchester, September 3, 1837. Graduated at Cambridge, Mus. Bac., 1877 ; Mus. Doc., 1879. Was organist successively at St. Philip's, Salford, 1855 ; St. Stephen's, Manchester, 1860 ; St. Saviour's, 1866 ; and of Bowden Parish Church, and Cheadle Abbey Church. During that time he conducted choral societies in those districts, and at Blackburn, Winsford, and Eccles. In 1881 he was appointed local examiner for R.A.M., and in the same year was made Provincial Grand Organist of East Lancashire.

WORKS.—Oratorio, What is life? (1879); Dramatic cantata, Gethsemane (1877); Cantatas, Yuletide, and The Golden butterfly—the latter for female voices. Vesper canticles; Psalter pointed, and Psalter chants (Heywood, Manchester). Symphony and other orchestral works in MS. Horæ Sacræ, pieces for violin and pf. ; The Two violinists, a series of duets for violins, with pf. accompaniment ; Songs, etc., etc.

Benton, Alfred, organist and conductor, born in Leeds. Began his musical career at the age of ten as a choir boy in Leeds Parish Church. His first instructor on the organ and pianoforte was Mr. Wm. Dawson, then deputy organist of the Parish Church. Afterwards he became the pupil of R. S. Burton, and took lessons in counterpoint from W. J. Pritchard (a famous blind organist) and in composition from F. W. Hird. When fourteen years old he obtained the post of organist at All Saints', Leeds, and subsequently was appointed to Windermere Parish Church, Arthington ; St. Mark's, Manningham ; St. Martin's, Potternewtown; and finally, in 1891, succeeding Dr. Creser as organist and choirmaster of Leeds Parish Church. Here he worthily sustains the high reputation gained for the services. In 1889 he was appointed organist of the Leeds Festival, a position he still retains, with that of chorusmaster, since 1895. He has introduced many important works at the Advent and Lent

BERRY.

services, including the Requiem by Brahms, Spohr's Last Judgment, and Bach's Matthew Passion. For years past he has been noted as a skilful conductor, societies in Barnsley, Morley, Bramley, and other places being under his direction. A permanent orchestra was formed in Leeds, in 1895, and a choral union also, the conductorship of both being entrusted to Mr. Benton, who now occupies a most responsible and honoured position in Leeds. He has also a high reputation as a teacher of singing, many of his pupils now holding appointments in English cathedrals.

Berger, Francesco, pianist and composer, born June 10, 1834, in London, where his father, an Austrian, had settled as a merchant. Studied in Italy under Luigi Ricci and Carl Lickl, and at Leipzig under Hauptmann and others. Settled in London, 1855. Appeared at concerts in London and the provinces as solo pianist. In 1868 established the " Après-midi Instrumentales." Was appointed a professor of pf. at the R.A.M. in 1885, and became hon. sec. of the Philharmonic Society in 1887. In 1864 he married Miss Lascelles, contralto vocalist. His works include a mass and an opera; the music to The Frozen deep (Wilkie Collins, 1857) ; a Suite in G, and other pieces for pf. Cavatina for violoncello and pf. Part-songs : Poor and rich (Leslie's Choir, 1884), and others. Songs : Amor timido; Fair, but fleeting; Only thyself, etc., etc. Author of " First steps at the pianoforte " (Novello).

Berry, Sarah, contralto vocalist, born at Bamford, near Manchester, where, from her eighth to her seventeenth year, she was a weaver in a mill. She gained the Courtney Scholarship, R.C.M., and pursued her studies under the late Madame Goldschmidt, having lessons also in declamation from Mrs. Kendal. She made her *début* in Manchester, January 7, 1888, at a concert of M. De Jong, and at once achieved success. In October of the same year, she sung in "Elijah" at Huddersfield, and in that oratorio at the Albert Hall (Royal Choral Society), January 22, 1890. She has also appeared at concerts in Birmingham and other places ; and at the Leeds Festival of 1895, created a highly favourable impression. She sang at the Norwich Festival of 1896, and is gaining a good position among the singers of the day.

Berry, Thomas, organist and composer, born at Shepley, York, June 21, 1850. He settled in Glasgow about 1873, and has been a teacher and organist there ever since. Among his appointments may be named the organistship of Trinity Congregational Church and Bellhaven Church, Glasgow. He has also given organ recitals in Glasgow and in various parts of Scotland. Composer of various works preserved in manuscript.

BERTINI.

Bertini, Henri Jerome, composer and pianist of French parentage, born at London, October 28, 1798. Studied under his father, etc. He travelled through Germany and Holland, and in England and Scotland. Resided in Paris as teacher and concert-giver from 1821. He died at Meylan, near Grenoble, October 1, 1876. WORKS.—Studies for the pf., op. 29, 32, 66, 86, 94, 100, 133, 134, 134a, 137, 142, 147, 166, 175, 176, 177, 178, 180; Trios for pf., violin, and 'cello; Sextets for pf., 2 violins, viola, 'cello, and bass, op. 79, 85, 90, 114; Sonatas for pf. and violin, op. 152, 153, 156,; Nonetto for pf. with wind instruments.

Bervon, Inglis, organist and composer, born in Birmingham, 1837. Principal bass at St. Andrew's, Wells Street, London, 1861; organist of the Parish Church, Aberystwith, 1866; thence to Welshpool, and to St. Mary's Stafford, which last he held till about 1880. Editor of a " Collection of 201 Chants for Psalms and Canticles," and composer of organ pieces (published in the Organists' Quarterly Journal), songs, etc. He died at Shelton, near Hanley, Staffs., December 18, 1891.

Best, William Thomas, organist and composer, born at Carlisle, August 13, 1826. Took lessons from Young, the cathedral organist, but being intended for the profession of a civil engineer, he only took up the study of music seriously when in Liverpool, 1840, he decided to change his vocation. His first appointment was that of organist at Pembroke Chapel, Liverpool, 1840; then, in 1847, to the Church for the Blind; and in 1848, organist to the Liverpool Philharmonic Society. In 1852 he was in London, giving recitals on various organs, playing at the Crystal Palace (Hyde Park), April 10. He held the office of organist at Lincoln's Inn Chapel, and in October, 1853, was appointed organist and professor of the organ at the Royal Panopticon. About the beginning of 1855 he was appointed to St. Martin-in-the-Fields, and in August of that year he was elected organist of St. George's Hall, Liverpool. He conducted a grand concert, October 10, on the occasion of the visit of the Duke of Cambridge, when the organ was opened, and gave his first popular recital, October 20. For many years he officiated as organist at churches in Birkenhead and Liverpool, and in 1871 was organist at the Royal Albert Hall at Kensington. Throughout the United Kingdom he was recognised as the finest organist of his time, and his recitals were of the most important service to the art of organ-playing. His influence in promoting uniformity in organ construction has been great. He has given recitals in Paris and Rome, and in 1890 (August 9) opened the vast organ in the Town Hall, Sydney, N.S.W. In February, 1894, ill health caused him to re-

BETJEMANN.

sign his appointment at St. George's Hall, and the famous organist, after fifty odd years of artistic activity, retired into private life. A commemorative bust was unveiled in the Hall, October 20, 1896. As a composer, he was known from 1845, when his Fantasia in two movements was published: he is also a fine pianist, and some compositions for the pianoforte were issued in 1852. In 1880 he received a Civil List pension of £100 per annum. He is an Hon. R.A.M.

WORKS.—Two overtures and a march, orchestra; Morning and Evening Service in F, op. 40. composed for Leeds Parish Church; Services, Kyries, etc.; Behold, I bring you glad tidings; Praise the Lord, and other anthems and hymns; Eighty chorals, selected and newly harmonized for four voices and organ, Novello, 1852. Glee, five voices. What mournful thoughts. Tarantella, Allegretto pastorale, Notturno, op. 27, marches, and other pieces for pf. Organ works. The modern school for the organ (1853?); The art of organ playing, parts I. and II. (1870); Thirty progressive studies; Collection of pieces, expressly composed for church use, six books; Six concert pieces; Three preludes and fugues; Sonatas in G and D minor; Fantasias, etc. Arrangements from the scores of the Great Masters, five volumes; Mozart's overture, "Die Zauberflöte" (1846); Editor of "Cecilia," a collection of organ pieces in diverse styles (containing important compositions of his own, festival overture in B flat, etc., 56 books published, still in progress); Organ music by Italian composers; Handel's organ concertos; Handel album; and a bicentenary edition of the organ works of J. S. Bach, commenced in 1885.

Bestwick, Lavinia, see FENTON LAVINIA.

Betjemann, Gilbert Henry; violinist and conductor, born in London. Pupil of C. W. Doyle. In 1858 was engaged by Costa as a second violin at the Royal Italian Opera, and later played in the orchestra of the Pyne and Harrison Company. For some years connected with the Carl Rosa Opera Company as violinist, conductor, and director of the *mise-en-scène*. Conducted performances of Royal English Opera Company at Covent Garden Theatre, January, 1884, and Italian Opera at Her Majesty's Theatre in November. Gave Chamber Concerts at Highgate, 1884-5; succeeded Dr. J. F. Bridge as Conductor of the Highbury Philharmonic Society in 1886; and about two years later was chosen as director of the operatic class at the R.A.M. In 1893 he was joint conductor and principal violin at the Promenade Concerts, Covent Garden; in 1895 he succeeded the late J. T. Carrodus as principal first violin at Covent Garden Opera; and in 1896 accepted conductorship of the Oxford Orchestral Society. Hon. R.A.M.;

BETTS.

Associate of the Philharmonic Society, and musician in ordinary to Her Majesty. His son, GILBERT RICHARD, A.R.A.M., born in London, 1864, was a violinist and composer, and member of the Royal Italian Opera orchestra. His " Song of the Western Men," for chorus and orchestra, was produced by the Highbury Philharmonic, March, 1890. He has also written some songs and pieces for violin. He was killed while descending the Wetterhorn, September 9, 1896, by falling through a snow bridge.

Betts, Arthur, violinist and composer, a native of Lincolnshire, born 1774 ? Studied under Hindmarsh, Viotti, Dussek, and Steibelt. Was for 49 years a member of the Royal Society of Musicians, and celebrated as a violin connoisseur. Died in London, September, 1847, aged 73. His daughter was a popular vocalist. Composed sonatas, duets for violin and 'cello, arrangements, etc.

Betts, Edward, musician and writer of 18th century. He compiled " An introduction to the Skill of Musick, anthems, hymns, and psalm tunes, in several parts," London, 1724.

Beugo, John, musician and engraver, born in 1759; died at Edinburgh in 1841. He was a friend of Burns, the poet, whose portrait he engraved in 1787, partly from special sittings. He was an engraver of portraits and similar works in Edinburgh, and an amateur musician. Among other works he issued " The New Caliope, being a selection cf British and occasionally foreign melodies, newly arranged for the pianoforte, and engraved on copper, by John Beugo." Edinburgh, 1823-25, published in quarterly parts.

Bevan, Frederick Charles, bass vocalist and composer, born in London, July 3, 1856. Began his career as a chorister at All Saints', Margaret Street, London, and having a fine voice was, at the age of eleven, chosen as solo boy of the choir. Studied the organ under C. E. Willing, and W. S. Hoyte, and held, for a time, appointments at St. Martin's, Haverstock Hill, and St. Margaret Pattens. Sang in the Henry Leslie and Joseph Barnby choirs, and, after studying with Schira, H. Deacon, and F. Walker, obtained the post of Gentleman of the Chapel Royal, Whitehall, 1877, and succeeded the late William Winn at the Chapel Royal St. James's Palace, 1888. Now widely known as a concert-singer, and the composer of a number of songs—The silver path, The sailor's sweetheart, The flight of ages, The dream of my heart, The mighty river, Watching and waiting, My angel, The everlasting day, and others extensively popular.

Bevin, Elway, Welsh composer and organist, was born about the middle of the 16th century [1560-70]. He studied under Tallis, and was organist of Bristol Cathedral in 1589.

BIGGS.

Gentleman Extraordinary of the Chapel Royal 1605. Lost both places on its being discovered that he was a Roman Catholic, 1637. He died about 1640.

WORKS.—A Briefe and Short Introduction to the Art of Musicke, to teach how to make Discant of all Proportions that are in use: very necessary for all such as are desirous to attaine to knowledge in the Art ; and may, by Practice, if they can sing, soon be able to compose three, four, and five parts ; and also to compose all sorts of Canons that are usuall, by these directions, of two or three parts in one, upon a Plain Song, 1631. A Short Service in D minor, and Praise the Lord, anthem, in Barnard's Collection. Other anthems exist in manuscript. Bevin is usually credited with having been the first in England to systematise the rules for the composition of canons.

Bexfield, William Richard, composer and organist, was born at Norwich, April 27, 1824. He studied under Dr. Zachariah Buck. Organist of Boston Church, Lincoln, 1845. Mus. Bac., Oxon., 1846. Unsuccessful candidate for the Music Professorship of Oxford University. Organist of St. Helen's Church, Bishopsgate Street, London, 1848. Mus. Doc., Cantab., 1849. He died at London, October 29, 1853.

WORKS.—Israel Restored, oratorio, produced, Norwich, October 16, 1851 ; and at the Norwich Festival, September 22, 1852 ; reproduced, Royal Albert Hall, London, April 15, 1880. Church Anthems, in score, with portrait, London, [1849]. A set of concert fugues for the organ, London, [1845-1846.] Musica di camera [1848]. Eight Chorales for voices and organ [1845-1847 ?]. Six songs [1847], part-songs, etc.

Bickham, George, engraver and penman, flourished in the first part of the 18th century. He engraved " The Musical Entertainer," London, 2 vols. [c. 1737], a collection of songs of some value. He died in 1769.

Bicknell, John Laurence, writer and barrister-at-law, was born in 1740, and died March 27, 1787. He wrote a poem called " The dying negro," and is the reputed author of " Musical travels through England, by Joel Collier, Licentiate in Music." London, 1774 (various editions). In 1818 appeared " Redivivus, an entirely new edition of that celebrated author's Musical Travels." The work is a satire on Burney, and is an amusing production now getting very scarce. It has also been ascribed to Peter Beckford, a writer on musical and other subjects.

Biggs, Edward Smith, glee composer and pianist, was born during the latter half of the 18th century, and died about 1820. He was a teacher of music in London.

WORKS.—Six duets and three trios, London,

BIGGS.

1800; Six Sicilian airs for one voice, London, 1805; Six Welsh airs adapted to English words, and harmonized for two, three and four voices, London, two sets; Four sets of twelve Venetian airs for one voice, London, 1800; Six songs, written by Mrs. Opie, London, 1800. *Glees :* Ah! me, with that false one; A poor soul sat sighing; Bring the song; Hark! what sound; Here beneath this willow sleepeth; Here's lawn as white as driven snow; In my cot, tho' small's my store; Lost is my quiet for ever; Now ev'ning's come; O! synge unto mie Roundelaie; Under the greenwood tree; Where feeds your flock; Will you buy any tape? *Songs :* The suicide; Come, my lads, time posts away; Fox and the crow; Barbara Allan; Where are you going my pretty maid? Duets. *Pianoforte :* Twenty-eight Waltzes; Rondos and marches.

Biggs, Rev. L. C., author of "English Hymnology" (a series of articles reprinted from the "Monthly Packet.")

Biggs, Walter Lyle, organist, composer, and conductor, born at Notting Hill, London, September 16, 1857. Received his first musical instruction from his mother's uncle, the Rev. S. Lillycrop (*q.v.*), afterwards studied organ and harmony under G. F. Geaussent. Was organist of, All Saints', Child's Hill, Kilburn, 1877-81, and in 1882, elected, after competition, to St. Peter le Bailey, Oxford, since when he has founded a musical society, given oratorio services in the Church, and concerts in the Old Town Hall. He conducted the Holy Trinity Musical Society, 1887-8; and in 1895 founded the East Oxford Musical Society. He has also given organ recitals in Wadham, Worcester, and Trinity College Chapels.

WORKS.—Sacred cantata, Elihu, Op. 3 (produced, Wadham College Chapel, July, 1891); Psalms 147-8-9 and 150, Op. 5, 6, 7, 8, for soli, chorus and orchestra; Epithalamium (Spenser), Op. 4, for soprano and baritone soli, men's chorus, and small orchestra; Church compositions, Op. 2. Fairy opera, Marie (libretto by Mrs. Linsley, produced, Oxford Institute, February, 1896); Set of four songs, Op. 9; Short organ pieces, Op. 1. Of these only the Cantata and Church compositions are yet published.

Bilby, Thomas, musician, was born at Southampton, April 18, 1794. He served for some time in the army, but subsequently entered the teaching profession. For twenty-eight years he was parish clerk of St. Mary's, Islington. He died at Islington, London, September 24, 1872. He is only known as the composer of the hymn-tune called "Joyful," which is usually sung to his own words " Here we suffer grief and pain."

Billington, Elizabeth, born WEICHSEL,

BILTON.

soprano vocalist, born in Soho, London, about 1768. She studied under her father, who was a German, and Schroeter, from an early age. In 1782 she sang at Oxford, and in October, 1783 she was married to James Billington, a double-bass player of Drury Lane Theatre. She appeared on the stage at Dublin in 1783, and sang in different parts of Ireland till 1786. She sang in "Love in a Village" at London, February 13, 1786. Afterwards, she went to Paris, but in 1787 she returned to London. Owing, in part, to anonymous attacks on her character, she went to Italy with her husband in 1794, and appeared in various cities with much success, In 1799 she married a Frenchman named Felissent (Billington having died in 1794), but left him, owing to his ill-treatment, and returned to London in 1801, when she appeared at Covent Garden, King's Theatre, etc. In 1811 she retired, and in 1817 she was reconciled to her husband. She died at St. Artein, August 25, 1818. Full details of her career will be found in Hogarth's "Memoirs of the Musical Drama," and in " Memoirs of Mrs. Billington from her birth; containing a a variety of matter, ludicrous, theatrical, musical, and with copies of several original letters written by Mrs. Billington to her mother," London, 1792. A suppressed book, to which she replied in "An Answer to the Memoirs of Mrs. Billington," 1792.

Billington, Thomas, pianist, harpist, and composer, was born at Exeter in 1754. He lived in London as a teacher of the piano and harp, but died at Tunis in 1832.

WORKS.—Music to Gray's Elegies, Op. 8 ! Pope's Eloisa to Abelard; Prior's Garland; Petrarch's Laura; The Children in the Wood, Morton; Four sets of twelve canzonets for two voices, London, 1784-90; Six songs for voice and pianoforte; Shenstone's Pastorals, consisting of 24 ballads; Music to Young's Night Thoughts, 1790; Music to Pope's Elegy to the Memory of an unfortunate Lady; Numerous glees; Songs; Scotch airs, etc., harmonized, London [1785]; Six sonatas for harpsichord or pianoforte, Op. 5; Three trios for a violin, tenor, and 'cello, Op. 7 [1780].

Bilton, J. Manuel, bandmaster and composer, born at Plymouth, October 8, 1862, son of a master-at-arms in the Royal Navy. Educated at the Royal Naval School, Greenwich, and joining the school band, his playing the baritone at a concert of the band at the Crystal Palace, 1875, attracted the attention of J. Lawson, bandmaster of the Royal Artillery Brass Band, who took him into that band. He met with a friend in Colonel Hime, who helped him in every way. In 1886 he was appointed Trumpet-Major of a Brigade of Artillery at Limerick, and studied under Stanislaus Elliott, and in 1887 entered Kneller Hall. After the death of Charles Cousins

BINFIELD.

(May 1890) Bilton was made Director *pro tem,* an office which he filled until his appointment as Bandmaster of the 17th Lancers, in February, 1891. He began composition very early, and his first attempt was a Grand Overture. This, rewritten and corrected, was performed at Woolwich, in 1878. At the Military Exhibition of 1890, he was awarded prizes for a Morning Service, Concert Overture, and a work for brass, military, and string band, singly and collectively. He has also written a Wind Quintet, Cantata, "The Wreck of the Hesperus," a Symphony, and Overtures.

Binfield, a musical family of importance, for many years prominent in the town of Reading, Berks, where the first of the name, RICHARD BINFIELD, established a music business in 1799. He was organist of St Laurence Church from 1804 to the time of his death, 1839. The Berkshire Musical Festival, dating back at least to 1786, was for many years under his direction, and he conducted a performance of the "Messiah" so late as September 28, 1839, when Balfe sang some of the bass solos. He edited and compiled the Reading Psalmody, and Reading Choral Service, works much in use in the neighbourhood for a long time. His son, JOHN BILSON BINFIELD, born at Reading, 1805, was an organist, and appears to have continued the Triennial Festivals, as they were given up to the year 1846. He was the first to set Dean Milman's "Martyr of Antioch" to music (Milman being vicar of St. Mary's, Reading, 1818-35). He died at Reading, June 8, 1875. Another son, THOMAS BINFIELD, settled in London, where he was engaged as a violoncellist. He was also a good violinist and pianist. Member of the Royal Society of Musicians. Died, London, December 23, 1840.—R. L. BINFIELD, a third son, was in the business at Reading, and conducted Choral Concerts, but no particulars can be gleaned concerning him.— HANNAH RAMPTON BINFIELD, born at Reading, 1810, sister of those preceding, was in her turn proprietor of the business. She was an excellent pianist and harpist, and contributed many hymn tunes and chants to the collections edited by her father, whom she succeeded as organist of St. Laurence, a post she held for forty-five years. Her annual concerts were the chief events of the Reading musical season, and she played, at the Festival of 1839, a concerto upon the organ. Her death took place at Reading, May 2, 1887. FANNY JANE daughter of John Bilson Binfield, was a pianist and concert-giver, and an artist of repute. She died at Reading, September 3, 1881. Of other members of the family little can be ascertained, but LOUISA BINFIELD, as a performer on the concertina, was often heard at Reading and elsewhere from thirty to forty years ago. Another, Louisa

BIRCH.

Binfield, third daughter of Richard, died at Reading, November 26, 1856.

Bingley, Rev. William, writer and clergyman, was born at Doncaster in 1774. He studied at Cambridge, where he graduated M.A. He died at London, March 11, 1823. Author of "Musical Biography, or Memoirs of the lives and writings of the most eminent musical composers and writers who have flourished in the different countries of Europe during the last three centuries," London, 1814, 2 vols.; 2nd edition, London, 1834, 2 vols. Animal Biography, 1802, 3 vols., etc. He also added "Sixty of the most admired Welsh airs, collected by W. Bingley, the basses and variations arranged for the pf. by W. Russell, jun.," London, 1810.

Binney, Thomas, clergyman and author, published "The Service of Song in the House of the Lord," London, 1849. He edited Baird's Liturgies, and wrote numerous other works.

Birch, Charlotte Ann, soprano vocalist, was born at London in 1815; and died there in 1857. She sang chiefly at London and provincial concerts.

Birch, Edward, clergyman, author of "A Tract on Responding, with a postscript on Singing," Manchester, 1862.

Birch, Edward Henry, organist. Received his training in music at the Cathedrals of Gloucester and Winchester. Graduated Mus. Bac., Oxford, 1875. Has held organ appointments successively at St. Saviour's, Eastbourne (1872); St. Gabriel's, Warwick Square, London (1873); All Saints', Kensington Park (1874); St. James's, Notting Hill (1886); Choirmaster, St. Columbas', Notting Hill. His compositions include a cantata, "Vortigern and Rowena" (produced Ladbroke Hall, Notting Hill, April 12, 1891), an Evening service, and other church music, organ pieces, etc.

Birch, James Albert, alto vocalist, born at Sheffield, 1839. Sang in church choirs in Sheffield, and subsequently was in the choir of Canterbury Cathedral (1873-6); then at Westminster Abbey; and finally at the Chapel Royal, St. James's, a post he retired from in 1892, owing to ill health. Lecturer on vocal music at the Church Missionary College; founder and conductor of the Temperance Choral Society; and sometime conductor of the London Board School Festival Concerts at the Crystal Palace. Musical editor of the Standard Book of Song, for Temperance Meetings and Home Use, and author of a booklet, The Voice Trainer. A Vice-President of the Tonic Sol-fa Association, he was a zealous worker to the last. He died somewhat suddenly, at Hastings, June 22, 1895.

Birch, Samuel, composer and minor poet, was born at London, November 8, 1757. He served as a Lord Mayor of London in 1815. Died at London, December 10, 1841.

BIRCH.

WORKS.— *Musical dramas, etc.*: The Mariners, 1793 ; Packet Boat, or a peep behind the veil (a masque), 1794 ; Adopted child, 1795 ; Smugglers, 1796 ; Fast asleep, 1795 ; Albert and Adelaide, 1798. Glees, songs, etc. To some of these musical dramas, Attwood and others wrote the music.

Birch, William, organist and composer, born at Lichfield in 1775. He was an organist at Tamworth, and died November 17, 1815. Another WILLIAM BIRCH issued " Sacred Music, consisting of psalms, hymns, anthems, etc." London [1825].

Birch, William Henry, organist and composer, born at Uxbridge, May 5, 1826. He studied under Elvey, Blagrove, and R. Barnett. He became organist of St. Mary's Church, Amersham, and was a teacher of music at Caversham, near Reading. He died there July 18, 1888.

WORKS.—The Merry men of Sherwood Forest, operetta, 1872; Wreck of the Argosy, cantata, 1879 ; Twelve anthems, Reading, 1877. Choruses, glees, quartetts, trios, etc, 1856. Canticles of the Church of England [1875]; Evensong, a selection of hymns and chants [1860]; Gems of sacred harmony [1853], Sabbath Recreation, a selection of favourite sacred melodies . . . 1857; Standard Psalmist . . . [1853-4]. Comic series of juvenile songs, concertina albums, journals, pf. music, songs, etc., etc.

Bird, George, organist, was appointed to the Parish Church, Walthamstow, March 26, 1829, after playing on probation with other candidates from the previous Advent Sunday, November 30, 1828. This post he held till the time of his death, August 14, 1894, a period exceeding 65 years, during which he officiated under three vicars, and assisted at the consecration of the first three of the churches which have been added to the district. He edited " A collection of 100 chants " (Novello), and a Hymn Tune-Book, in much use in their day. His son, HENRY RICHARD BIRD, born at Walthamstow, November 14, 1842, was appointed organist of St. John's, Walthamstow, in 1851. Then for some years he studied with J. Turle, and in 1858 was elected organist of St. Mark's, Clerkenwell ; in 1860 appointed to Holy Trinity, Sloane Street ; in 1866 to St. Gabriel's, Pimlico ; and in 1872 to St. Mary Abbots, Kensington, a post he retains. He was organist at the Festivals of the London Church Choir Association, at St. Paul's Cathedral in 1880-1 ; and has for a long time given concerts at Kensington. In 1891 he was appointed accompanist at the Monday and Saturday Popular Concerts, a capacity in which he is in much request. He is a Professor of the pf. at R.C.M., and at Trinity College, London.

Bird, William, musician of Watford, issued " A Set of Psalm and Hymn Tunes with

BISHOP.

an Anthem for four voices," London, 1807, 2nd edition, 1810 ; "Original Psalmody, 57 Psalm and Hymn Tunes in score . . . revised by S. Wesley," 1827, also 1830 ; " Gems of metrical Psalmody," London, 1835.

Bird, William Hamilton, musician, published " The Oriental Miscellany, a collection of the most favourite airs of Hindoostan, adapted for the harpsichord," Calcutta, 1789.

Birde, William, *see* BYRD, WILLIAM.

Birkensha, John, Irish author and musician, who lived in London as a teacher of the viol during the first half of the 17th century. He translated the " Templum Musicum," of Alstedius, as " Templum Musicum, or the musical synopsis of the learned and famous Johannes Henricus, Alstedius : being a compendium of the rudiments both of the mathematical and practical part of musick . . " London, 1664.

Birnie, Patie, or **Patrick,** violinist and minor poet, who lived at Kinghorn, in Fife, at the end of the 17th century. He wrote " The auld man's mear's dead " and other songs, and was a famous fiddler in his day. He distinguished himself at the Battle of Bothwell Bridge, which he took part in as one of the Fife militia, by running away.

Bishenden, Charles James, bass vocalist and teacher, born at Hemel-Hempstead, Herts, in 1848. Has sung with success in his native town and other places. He was one of the early advocates for the adoption of the French pitch in this country. In 1882 he married Isabel Mary Beachey, a vocalist, who has appeared with him at various concerts. He is the author of a pamphlet, "The voice, and how to use it," and "How to sing," etc.

Bishop, Anna, born Rivière, wife of the undernoted. A French soprano vocalist, was born in London, 1812 [1814-15]. She studied under Moscheles at the R.A.M., and married Sir Henry Bishop, 1832. *Début* at London, 1837. She sang at the musical festivals of Gloucester, York, and Hereford. She left her husband and travelled with Bochsa in Europe 1839. Appeared in Copenhagen, 1839. She sang in Stockholm in 1840 ; St. Petersburg, 1840 ; in Russia, 1840-1 ; in Austria, etc., 1842 ; Italy, 1843. She went to America in 1846, and travelled there and in Australia, etc., 1853-8. She married Martin Schultz, of New York, 1858. Returned to England, 1858, and in 1859 went back to America. She travelled round the world, concert-giving, in 1865-69, and again in 1873-76. Between the years 1839 and 1843 she sang at 260 concerts. She was a cultivated vocalist and member of many musical societies. She died at New York, March 18 [20], 1884.

Bishop, Sir Henry Rowley, composer, was born at London, November 18, 1786. He studied music under F. Bianchi, and became

BISHOP.

musical director at Drury Lane Theatre, 1810-11. Founded (with others) the Philharmonic Society, 1813. Visited Dublin, 1820. Conductor at Drury Lane Theatre, 1825. Musical director of Vauxhall Gardens, 1830. He married (1st) Sarah Lyon (died 1831) and (2nd) Anna Rivière. Mus. Bac., Oxon., 1839. Musical director at Covent Garden Theatre, 1840-41. Conductor of the Ancient Concerts, 1840-48. Professor of Music at the Edinburgh University (in succession to John Thomson), 1841-3. Knighted, 1842. Professor of Music at Oxford University (in succession to Dr. Crotch), 1848. Mus. Doc., Oxon., 1853. He died at London, April 30, 1855. Buried at Finchley (or Marylebone) Cemetery.

WORKS.—*Operas and Musical Dramas*: Angelina farce, 1804; Tamerlan et Bajazet, ballet, 1806; Narcissa et les Graces, grand Anacreontic ballet, 1806; Caractacus, ballet, 1806; Love in a tub, a pastoral ballet, 1806; Mysterious bride, 1808; Circassian bride, 1809; Mora's love, ballet, 1809; Vintagers, 1809; Maniac, or Swiss banditti, 1810; Knight of Snowdoun, 1811; Virgin of the sun, 1812; Œthiop, or Child of the desert, 1812; Renegade, 1812; Haroun Alraschid (altered from Æthiop), 1813; Brazen bust, 1813; Harry Le Roy, 1813; Miller and his men, 1813; For England ho! 1813; Farmer's wife (with Reeve and Davy), 1814; Wandering boys, or the Castle of Olival, 1814; Sadak and Kalasrade, or the Waters of oblivion, 1814; Grand alliance, 1814; Forest of Bondy, or Dog of Montargus, 1814; Maid of the mill, comic opera, 1814; Noble outlaw, 1815; Telemachus, 1815; Midsummer night's dream (Shakespeare), 1816; Guy Mannering, or the Gypsey's prophecy (from Scott), (with Whittaker), 1816; Heir of Vironi, or Honesty the best policy, 1817; Don Juan, or the Libertine (compiled from Mozart), 1817; Duke of Savoy, or Wife and mistress, 1817; Barber of Seville (compiled from Rossini), 1818; Marriage of Figaro (compiled from Mozart), 1819; Heart of Midlothian (from Scott), 1819; A Rowland for an Oliver, 1819; Gnome king, or the Giant mountains, 1819; Comedy of errors (Shakespeare), 1819; Antiquary (from Scott), 1820; Battle of Bothwell Brigg, 1820; Henri Quatre, or Paris in the olden time, 1820; Twelfth night (Shakespeare), 1820; Don John, or the Two Violettas, 1820; Two gentlemen of Verona (Shakespeare), 1821; Montrose, or the Children of the mist (from Scott), 1820; Law of Java, 1822; Maid Marian, or the Huntress of Arlingford, opera, 1822; Clari, or the Maid of Milan, opera in three acts (J. H. Payne), 1823; Beacon of liberty, 1823; Cortez, or the Conquest of Mexico, 1823; Native land, or Return from slavery, 1824; Charles the Second, operetta, 1824; Fall of Algiers, opera, 3 acts, 1825: Hofer, the Tell of the Tyrol (compiled from Rossini), 1825; Edward the Black Prince,

1825; Aladdin, or the Wonderful lamp, opera (by J. R. Planché), London, 1825; Knights of the cross, opera, 1826; Under the oak, opera, 1830: Adelaide, or the Royal William, opera, 1832; Home, sweet home, operatic drama, 2 acts, 1832; Magic fan, or the Fillip on the nose, operetta, 1832; Yelva, musical drama, 2 acts, 1833; Rencontre, operatic comedy, 1833; Doom kiss, opera, 1836; Slave, opera in 3 acts (by J. R. Planché), 1816; As you like it (Shakespeare); Aurora, ballet; Brother and sister, 1814; Cymon (from M. Arne), 1815; Comus, 1815: Dr. Sangrado, ballet, 1814; December and May; Don Pedro, tragedy (2 glees); Der Freyschutz (compiled from Weber), 1824; Englishman in India, comic opera, 1827; Faustus, 1825; Fortunatus and his sons, 1819; John of Paris (from Boieldieu), 1814; John du Bart (incidental music), 1815; Ninetta, opera, 3 acts; Bottle of champagne, operetta; Czar of Muscovy, opera; Humorous lieutenant, 1817; Romance of a day, operatic drama; Zuma, or the Tree of health, comic opera, 1818. Fallen angel, oratorio; Seventh day, cantata, 1833. *Glees*: Six original English glees (poetry by Hemans, Baillie, etc.); Twelve original English glees; Complete collection of glees, 8 vols., 1839 (other collections have since appeared, one—Novello's—with orchestral accompaniments). *Songs*: Songs for the seasons, by T. H. Bayly; Select and rare Scottish melodies, poetry by Hogg; Songs of the old chateau, poetry by Bayly; Lays and legends of the Rhine, J. R. Planché; Do. of the Upper Rhine; Melodies of various nations, Bayly; Songs for leisure hours, W. Walton; Edition of Handel's trios, choruses, etc.; Grand triumphal ode, Accession of the king; Funeral ode; Jolly beggars, cantata by Robert Burns; Single songs in great numbers. Pf. music, and various pieces of instrumental music. English national melodies, poetry, edited by Chas. Mackay. Syllabus of a course of six lectures on the origin and progress of the lyric drama, or opera . . . to be delivered in the Manchester Athenæum, 8vo, 1845.

Bishop is now remembered chiefly by his songs and glees, which are among the finest specimens of the modern English School. None of his operas or musical dramas save "Guy Mannering" are now performed. Many of them were mere occasional pieces, but a number of the songs and concerted vocal pieces scattered through them are in constant use by vocalists and choral societies.

Bishop, John, composer and organist, born in 1665. Studied under Daniel Roseingrave. In 1687 he was lay-vicar at King's College, Cambridge, and in 1688 became teacher of choristers. Organist of Winchester College in succession to Jeremiah Clark in 1695; lay-vicar of Winchester Cathedral, and in 1729 succeeded Vaughan Richardson as

D

BISHOP.

organist. He died at Winchester, December 19, 1737. He published "A Sett of new Psalm Tunes, in four parts," cantus, medius, tenor and bassus, J. Walsh [1700]; "Supplement to the new Psalm-book, consisting of 6 new anthems and 6 new Psalm tunes," London, 1725; and some of his compositions in MS. are in the British Museum.

Bishop, John, organist and author, born at Cheltenham, July 31, 1818. He was successively organist of St. Paul's, Cheltenham, 1831; Blackburn, 1838-39; St. James', Cheltenham; Roman Catholic Chapel, and St. John's, Cheltenham. These appointments he resigned in 1852. He died at Cheltenham, February 3, 1890.

WORKS—Anthems, organ music, songs, etc. Two collections of Chants, 1852-57, containing "Remarks on the singing of the daily Psalms." Brief memoir of George Frederick Handel, 1856. Remarks on the causes of the present generally degraded state of music in our churches, 1860. Repertorium Musicæ Antiquæ—a miscellaneous collection of classical compositions by the greatest masters of Italy, Germany, ed. (with J. Warren) London, 1848. He edited various collections of organ music, and translated various works on musical theory by Czerny, Reicha, G. Weber, Otto, Spohr, etc.

Bisse, Thomas, clergyman and author, published "A Sermon preached at Hereford at the meeting of the choirs of Hereford, Gloucester and Worcester, in September, 1726—'I got me men-singers and women-singers and the delights of the sons of men, as musical instruments, and that of all sorts,'" 1726. Dr. Bisse was the virtual founder of the Three Choirs Festivals, which he first proposed at Gloucester in 1724.

Bisset, Catherine, pianist, born London in 1795. She was eldest daughter of Robert Bisset, LL.D., author of a "Life of Burke," and other works. She studied under J. B. Cramer, and first appeared at the New Musical Fund Concert in 1811. In 1823 she appeared at Paris, and thereafter was much engaged in London as pianist at private concerts. She died at Barnes in February, 1864. Her younger sister, ELIZABETH ANNE (born London, 1800; died —?), was a harp-player and composer, who studied under F. Dizi. She published a number of arrangements and fantasias for the harp and pianoforte.

Black, Andrew, baritone vocalist, born in Glasgow, January 15, 1859. Was for some time organist of the Anderston U. P. Church, Glasgow, but developing a fine baritone voice, he studied singing under A. Randegger, and J. B. Welch; afterwards receiving instruction from Domenico Scafati in Milan. From 1884 his singing attracted attention in Scotland; but it was at the Crystal Palace Concert,

BLAGROVE.

July 30, 1887, that he achieved his first great success. He sang there twice during the following month, and from that time his advance was rapid. He made a tour in America, and sang in opera. His first appearance at a provincial Festival was at Leeds in 1892; and in 1894 he was selected for the title part in "Elijah" at the Birmingham Festival, and was engaged for the same at Gloucester in 1895, and at Norwich, 1896. He has sung at all the most important concerts in the Kingdom. Since its opening, in 1893, he has been a professor of singing at the Manchester Royal College of Music. He is a painter of considerable ability, and his wife is an accomplished pianist.

Blackwell, Isaac, composer, flourished during latter part of 17th century. Composed "Choice Ayres, Songs, and Dialogues to the theorbo-lute and bass-violo," London, 1657.

Blackwood, Helen, see DUFFERIN, Lady.

Blagrave, Thomas, composer and musician, was born in Berkshire about 1661. He was a Gentleman of the Chapel Royal, and a member of the private band of Charles II. He died on November 21, 1688, and is buried in the north cloister of Westminster Abbey. He composed a few songs.

Blagrove, Richard, violinist and teacher. Author of "A New and Improved System to the Art of Playing the Violin." Lond., 1828. Fantasias, etc., for pf., concertina, etc. His brother WILLIAM, who died at London in 1858, was also a violinist.

Blagrove, Henry Gamble, violinist, was born at Nottingham, October 20th, 1811. Son of above. First appeared in public, 1816. Taken to London by his father, 1817. Played at Drury Lane Theatre, 1817. Studied under Spagnoletti, 1821, and became a pupil at the R.A.M., 1823. Gained silver medal, R.A.M., for violin playing, 1824. Member of Queen Adelaide's private band, 1830-1837. Studied under Spohr in Germany, 1832-34. Played at London Concerts and Provincial Festivals. He died at London, December 15th, 1872.

Blagrove, Richard Manning, viola and concertina player, brother of the preceding, was born at Nottingham. In 1837 he entered the R.A.M., studying the viola under H. Hill. He also studied the concertina, and played a solo on that instrument at the Hanover Square Rooms, March 12th, 1842. With Giulio Regondi, George Case, and A. B. Sedgwick, he formed a concertina quartet, the first concert taking place in the room just named, June 12th, 1844. The next year found him engaged at concerts as pianoforte accompanist, and viola player in his brother Henry's quartet concerts. From that time onward he was prominent in musical work. On the death of Henry Hill, in 1856, he

BLAIKIE.

BLEW.

succeeded him as principal viola in the Philharmonic orchestra, and at the Three Choirs Festivals, posts he held until 1894. For many years, up to 1890, he was a professor at the R.A.M., and a Fellow of that Institution. In 1890, he began a series of concerts at Clapham Hall, assisted by his sons STANLEY and ARTHUR, and his wife, *née* FREETH, a gifted pianist. He died in London, October 21st, 1895. Published Concertina Journal, 1853, Fantasias, etc., pf. and concertina. It was specially for him that G. A. Macfarren wrote his concertina quintet.

Blaikie, Andrew, engraver and musician, who flourished in Paisley in the first half of the present century. He noted down and engraved the tunes in "Motherwell's Minstrelsy," 1827, and was the owner of two 17th century musical manuscripts of considerable value.

Blair, Hugh, organist and composer, eldest son of the late Rev. R. H. Blair, M.A., F.R.A.S., of Ayrshire family. He was born at Worcester, May 26th, 1864, and educated in Yorkshire, and the Cathedral school, Worcester, studying music under the late Dr. Done. In 1883 he gained the Choral Scholarship at Christ College, Cambridge, where he was a pupil of Dr. Garrett, and Sir G. A. Macfarren. He graduated B.A., 1886, and Mus. Bac., 1887. Deputy organist at Worcester Cathedral, 1887, he was appointed organist-in-charge, 1889, and succeeded Dr. Done as organist in 1895. He conducted the opening service of the Worcester Festival in 1890, and the Festivals of 1893-6. He is Conductor of Musical Societies at Worcester and Redditch, and a Vice-President of the London Church Orchestral Society.

His compositions include two Cantatas:— "Harvest Tide" (Trinity Church, Barnes, 1892); "Blessed are they who watch" (Worcester, 1894); Festival Evening Service, eight voices (Worcester Festival, 1887); Evening Service in B flat (Gloucester Festival, 1892); Te Deum and Jubilate in D (Worcester Festival, 1893); Anthems, Services, etc.

Blair, William, violinist and composer, born at Crathie, Aberdeenshire, October 26th, 1793, died there November 12th, 1884. He was famous as a player of Scots dance music, and was a sort of fiddler to Queen Victoria from 1848. He composed some dance music, and is remembered by his strathspey, entitled, "The Queen's Fiddler's compliments to Mr. Troup." His sons JOHN and JAMES are also violinists.

Blake, Benjamin, composer, was born at Kingsland, London, 1751. He studied music by himself, and learned the violin, 1760. Member of orchestra of Italian opera, London, 1768. Professor of music in Public School at Kensington, 1789-1810. He died in London, 1827.

WORKS.—Three books of six duets for violin and viola. Six sonatas for pf. and violin. Collection of sacred music for voices and organ. Three solos for viola, with accompaniment for bass. Glees and songs. A musical dialogue between master and scholar. Six duets for violin and tenor (1765), 2nd sett; 3rd sett, Op. 3; Six sonatas for the pf., Op. 4. Miscellaneous collection of vocal music, Op. 6, 1814.

Blake, Rev. Edward, composer, was born at Salisbury, 1708. Fellow of Oriel College, Oxford. Prebendary of Salisbury Cathedral, and rector of Tortworth, Gloucester, 1757. Perpetual Curate of St. Thomas' Church, Salisbury. Vicar of St. Mary the Virgin, Oxford, 1754. He died on June 11, 1765. Composed anthems and instrumental duets.

Blakeley, William, organist and composer, born at Wakefield, February 12, 1852. He studied under Dr. W. Spark and Dr. J. F. Bridge. In 1868 he became organist of Thornes Church, Wakefield; Wakefield Choral Society, 1868-69; and afterwards at Croydon, Batley, Morningside U. P. Church, Edinburgh, 1881-90; Queen's Park Parish Church, Glasgow, 1890. He is a Mus. Bac. of Toronto. Composer of "Jonah," an oratorio; anthems, part-songs, songs, and music for the organ, etc. Also "Prize Psalmody," a collection of original hymn tunes.

Blancks, Edward, composer of tunes in Este's "Whole booke of Psalmes," 1592. He lived during the latter part of the 16th and and beginning of the 17th centuries.

Bland, Dora, see JORDAN, Mrs.

Bland, Maria Theresa, born Romanzini. Soprano vocalist, was born in London, of Italian parents in 1769. First appeared at Royal Circus, London, 1773. Sang at Dublin Theatre. *Début* at Drury Lane Theatre, October 24, 1786. Married Mr. Bland, brother to Mrs. Jordan. Sang at Haymarket Theatre, 1791. Sang in London till 1824. She died at Westminster, January 15, 1838, insane.

She was a magnificent ballad vocalist, and earned most of her success on the operatic stage.

Blandford, George, Marquis of, 4th Duke of Marlborough, born January 26th [1738]. He was connected with many of the musical enterprises during the end of last and beginning of the present centuries. He died on January 13, 1817. Among other works he published "Twelve Glees for three and four voices," London [1798]; a "Collection of vocal music," and various Sonatas for the pianoforte.

Blew, William Charles Arlington, barrister-at-law and musician, was born at London in 1848, and called to the bar in 1876. Author of "Organs and Organists in Parish Churches. A hand-book of the law

BLEWITT.

BLOW.

relating to the custody, control, and use of organs, and the duties, rights and disabilities of organists," London, 1878.

Blewitt, Jonas, composer and organist, born in first half of 18th century. He held the appointments of organist to St. Margaret Pattens, and St. Gabriel, Fenchurch, London, about 1795, and to St. Catherine Coleman, Fenchurch Street. He performed in public. Died at London in 1805.

WORKS.—Ten voluntaries or pieces for the organ, op. 5 ; Twelve easy and familiar movements for the organ, op. 6 ; Treatise on the organ with explanatory voluntaries, op. 4, London, n.d.

Blewitt, Jonathan, son of above, composer and organist, born London in 1782. He studied under his father and Battishill, and in 1793 became deputy to his father. He was successively organist of Haverhill, Suffolk ; Brecon ; Sheffield, and of St. Andrew's Church, Dublin, in 1811. In 1811 he became composer and conductor at the Theatre Royal, Dublin, and soon after was made grand organist to the Masonic Society of Ireland. He returned to London in 1826, and became musical director at Sadler's Wells Theatre, 1828-29. Teacher of vocal music and organist in London. He died at London, Sept. 4, 1853.

WORKS—*Music to Plays, etc.* : Harlequin, or the Man in the Moon, 1826, Talisman of the Elements ; Auld Robin Gray ; My Old Woman ; Corsair ; Magician ; Island of Saints ; Rory O'More ; Mischief Making, etc. *Instrumental :* Concerto for pf. and orch. ; Sonatas and Duets for pf. ; Caprices, fugues, and sonatas for the organ. Vocal Assistant, treatise on singing, London, n.d. *Songs* : A nice little man ; Adieu my moustachios ; Barney Brallaghan ; England, merry England ; Let us drink to old friends ; My hopes are fixed upon thee ; Emerald Isle ; The White Cliffs of England ; Good bye ; Groves of Blarney ; Hamlet ; I saw him but once : New cries of London ; O for a cot ; Our jolly stout jackets of blue ; Phillis, have you seen my love ?, Pic-nic ; When crowned with summer roses.

Bliss, Mrs. J. Worthington, *born* M. LINDSAY, composer of the present time. Has written a large number of songs, some of which attained great popularity in their day. Among them may be named—Airy, fairy Lilian ; Alone ; Arrow and the song ; The Bridge [1856] ; Danish Maid ; Excelsior [1854] ; Far away [1868] ; Home they brought her warrior dead [1858] ; Hymn of the Moravian Nuns (Pulaski's Banner) [1854] ; Songs for children, 1871-72, in numbers ; Part-songs, etc.

Blitheman, William, composer and organist, flourished in latter half of 16th century. He was master of the choristers of Christ Church, Oxford, in 1564, and one of

the organists of the Chapel Royal. Mus. Bac., Cantab., 1586. Mus. Doc., do. [15 ?]. He died at London, in 1591.

Blitheman was the preceptor of Dr. John Bull, and was succeeded by him at the Chapel Royal in 1591. His biography is unknown, but it is believed that he composed church music, and had much celebrity in his time.

Blockley, John, composer, writer, and publisher, was born in 1800. Engaged in music-publishing business in London. He died at London, December 24th, 1882.

WORKS.—The Sabbath Minstrel [collection of sacred music], London, n.d. ; The Singer's Companion, London, n.d. *Songs :* My childhood's home ; I remember thy voice ; We have been friends together ; The absent one ; A blessing on thine eyes ; The Arab's farewell to his favourite steed ; The friend of our early days ; Love not ; Love on (reply) ; The Englishman ; and numerous other songs written to words of the Hon. Mrs. Norton, etc. Selection of sacred melodies from the works of the most celebrated composers, n.d. Collection of psalm and hymn tunes for four voices, London, n.d.

Blow, John, composer and organist, was born at Westminster (not North Collingham, Nottingham, as usually stated), 1648. One of Children of Chapel Royal, 1660. He studied under Captain Cook, Hingeston, and Christopher Gibbons. Organist of Westminster Abbey, 1669-80. Gentleman of Chapel Royal, 1673-74. Master of the Children, do., July, 1674. Organist of Chapel Royal, 1676. Private Musician to King James II., 1685. Almoner and master of the choristers of St. Paul's Cathedral, 1687-93. Re-appointed organist of Westminster Abbey, 1695-1708. Married Elizabeth Braddock. Composer to Chapel Royal, 1699. He died at London, October 1st, 1708. Buried in north choir aisle, Westminster.

WORKS.—Amphion Anglicus, a work of many compositions for one, two, three, and four voices, with several accompagnements of Instrumental Musick, and a Thorow-Bass for each song, figur'd for an Organ, Harpsichord, or Theorboe-Lute, Lond. [1700]. *Odes :* A Second Musical Entertainment, performed on St. Cecilia's Day, November 22nd, 1684, words by John Oldham, London, 1684 ; Great Quire of Heaven, St. Cecilia's Day, 1691 ; Te Deum and Jubilate, composed for St. Cecilia's Day, 1695 ; Triumphant Fame, St. Cecilia's Day, 1700 ; Arise, Great Monarch, New Year's Day, 1681 ; New Year's Day Ode, 1683 ; Hail, Monarch, do., 1686 ; Is it a Dream ? do., 1687 ; Ye Sons of Phœbus, do., 1688 ; others in 1689 and 1693-94 ; Appear in all thy pomp, appear, do., 1700 ; Ode on the death of Mr. Henry Purcell, the words by Mr. Dryden, London, 1696 ; Three Elegies upon the much lamented loss of our late most Gracious Queen Mary,—sett to Musick by Dr. Blow and Mr. Henry Purcell, Lond., fol., 1695. Church Services in A, G, and E minor, one in triple measure and 10 unedited. Anthems, numbering about 100, published in Boyce's Collection, Clifford's Collection, Page's Harmonia Sacra, Novello's Series; others existing in MS. A choice Collection of Lessons for the Harpsichord, Spinnett, etc., containing four Setts, as grounds, almands, corants, sarabands, minuets, and jiggs, 1698. A choice Collection of Lessons, being excellently sett to the Harpsichord, etc., by Blow and Purcell, 1705. Catches in the "Pleasant Musical Companion," published in various editions; Do. pub. in The Catch Club, or Merry Companions; Songs in D'Urfey's collections, and in others of the same period; Organ music; Chants.

Blow, Rev. William, rector of Layer-Breton, Essex. A direct descendant of John Blow. Was esteemed one of the finest amateur violinists in Europe. He possessed the finest collection of violins in Great Britain. Died in January, 1887.

Blower, John Henry, bass vocalist, born at Wolverhampton. Studied at the National Training School for Music, under J. B. Welch. He sang in concerts in Birmingham and district from about 1878; appeared at the Crystal Palace Concerts, April 15th, 1882, and at the Leeds Festival of 1883. Afterwards he gave himself up to teaching, and is now a Professor at the R.C.M. Miss Clara Butt was for some time his pupil.

Bloxsome, Charles, author of "Elementary practice for the Vocal Student," Lond., 1857; "Elements of singing, chord and scale exercises to develop the voice," London, n.d.

Blyth, Benjamin, composer and organist, who graduated Mus. Doc., Oxford, in 1833. He composed church music, "A Sanctus, two jubilates, and eight double chants," London, 1841. Pf. music, and songs. His son, BENJAMIN BLYTH, was organist of Magdalen College, Oxford. M.A., Oxford. Died at Whitchurch, Oxford, July 20th, 1883, aged 58.

Boardman, John George. Published "Sacred Music, a selection of psalm tunes," London, 1844. THOMAS JAMES BOARDMAN issued a "Collection of psalm and hymn tunes, ancient and modern," London, 1854; "The Copious Tune Book, a collection of psalm and hymn tunes," London [1860]. Two editions. He also composed songs, etc.

Bodda, Louisa Fanny, see PYNE, Louisa Fanny.

Bogue, Christina W., see MORISON, Christina W.

Bokwe, John Knox, Kaffir composer. Secretary of the Lovedale Institution, Cape Colony. Composer of Kaffir hymn tunes, and a book of part-songs, of which the type-setting

and the whole production were the work of coloured sol-faists.

Bolton, Thomas, musician and teacher, who flourished *circa* 1760-1820. He issued "Collection of Lessons, songs, etc., for the harp, lute, or lyre," London, 1797; "Collection of airs, marches, dances, etc., adapted for the pf., with accompaniments for the lyre or lute," London, 1806; Six Rondeaus, three songs, etc., op. 3; "Select collection of songs and airs arranged for the harp, lute, etc," 1815; "Treatise on singing," London, 1810. MARY CATHERINE BOLTON (who became Lady Thurlow, in 1813), a soprano vocalist. Born, London, 1790, died, Southampton, September 28th, 1830; and ELIZA BOLTON, her sister, who was also a soprano singer, appearing at concerts about the same time, were probably daughters of Thomas Bolton.

Bond, Capel, composer and organist, lived in Coventry during middle of last century. He was organist and conductor of the first Birmingham Musical Festival, 1768, and died in 1790.

WORKS.—Six anthems in score, one of which is for Christmas Day, 1769. Six concertos for 4 violins, tenor, and 'cello, with thorough bass, 1766. Glees and songs.

Bond, Hugh, organist and composer, was born at Exeter in the beginning of the 18th century. Lay-vicar Exeter Cathedral, 1762. Organist of Church of St. Mary Arches. He died in 1792.

WORKS.—Twelve hymns and four anthems, for four voices, London, 1776; The psalms of David; also an appendix containing select hymns, London, 1780. Glees and songs.

Bond, Jessie, vocalist and actress, born in Liverpool, daughter of John Bond, pianoforte mechanician of that city. Appeared at Hope Hall as a pianist at the age of eight, and was educated as a pianist at the R.A.M. But developing a contralto voice she took to singing, and became a pupil of Manuel Garcia. She sang at the Crystal Palace, at Rivière's Concerts, and in the provinces. She was the original Hebe in "H.M.S. Pinafore"; and since then has filled a round of characters in the Gilbert and Sullivan operas at the Savoy Theatre.

Bond-Andrews, see Andrews (J. C. Bond).

Bonnyboots. English singer and dancer of much fame in the reign of Queen Elizabeth bore this nickname. He is noticed in Hawkins' "History of Music."

Booth, Josiah, organist and composer, born in Coventry, March 27, 1852. Studied under the late Edward Sims, Coventry; Dr. James Taylor, Oxford; and later, at the R.A.M. under Brinley Richards, and G. A. Macfarren. Appointed organist at Banbury, 1867, and has been since 1877, organist and choirmaster at Park Chapel, Crouch End.

BOOTH.

WORKS.—Oratorios, Nehemiah (produced 1885); Cantata, The Day of Rest, for female voices. School operettas; The Babes in the Wood; Dick Whittington; and The six Princesses. Church Services; Anthems, Grant, we beseech Thee; Thou crownest the year, and others. Hymn-tunes and chants. Part-songs; The Mighty Caravan (produced by Henry Leslie's Choir, 1883) Album of twelve songs, &c., &c. Musical editor of Parts II. and III. of the Congregational Church Hymnal, and author of Everybody's Guide to Music, London, Saxon.

Booth, Robert, organist and composer, born at St. Andrews, December 29, 1862. Studied at the Madras School there, and under different masters. Organist, Holy Trinity Church, Kilmarnock, 1880, and for some time musical director of Kilmarnock Opera House. In 1887, he was appointed organist and choirmaster of Coltness Memorial Church, Newmains.

WORKS.—Festival Service in G; Gloria in Excelsis; Anthem, The Lord is my Shepherd; Operetta, Sisters Three; or Britannia's Heroes, for principals, chorus and orchestra; Eight-part song, with solo, Lochinvar; School Song-book, in three-part harmony—symphony, and overture, orchestra; Intermezzo, Maypole dance, for strings. Waltzes, for pf. and orchestra. Author of a book on Musical Theory, and other didactic works.

Borton, Alice, pianist, and composer. Educated at R.A.M., of which she is an Associate. Has composed Sacred Choral Music, and songs; an Andante and Rondo for pf. and orchestra; Suite in the olden style, pf.; Three Scotch pieces, etc.

Borwick, W. Leonard, pianist, born at Walthamstow, Essex, February 26, 1868. Comes of an old Staffordshire family, many members of which were musical. His disposition for music was shewn at a very early age; and after some years of study under London masters, he entered the Hoch Conservatorium, Frankfort, 1884, where he was a pupil of Madame Schumann for five years. He also studied composition with Bernard Scholz and Iwan Knorr. His *debut* took place at the Museum Concerts, Frankfort, November 8, 1889, when he played the solo part in Beethoven's E flat Concerto. His success was so marked that he was engaged for the London Philharmonic Concerts, and he made his first appearance in England, May 8, 1890, playing Schumann's Concerto. He appeared at the Richter, Crystal Palace, and Popular Concerts, St. James's Hall, the same year; and has now been heard at the principal musical centres in Britain, and Germany, ranking with the great pianists of the day.

Bosanquet, R. H. M., Fellow of St. John's College, Oxford. Author of " An Ele-

BOWDLER.

mentary treatise on musical intervals and temperament, London, 1876; also of various papers read before the Musical Association (1874); the College of Organists; and the R.A.M. In 1881, he accepted the professorship of acoustics, R.A.M.

Botting, Herbert William, composer, organist and pianist, born at Brighton, March 28, 1869. Studied for two years with Dr. F. J. Sawyer, during which time he obtained the diploma of F.R.C.O.; then proceeded to Leipzig Conservatorium, and on his return was articled to Dr. J. F. Bridge, of Westminster Abbey. Graduated Mus. B., Durham, 1891. In Leipzig, he held the post of organist and choirmaster at the English Church (1888); in 1891, he was appointed to St. Luke's, Southport, and four years later to St. Nicholas, Brighton, and finally to St. Augustine's, Preston Park, Brighton, 1896. He is founder and conductor of the Preston Park Choral and Orchestral Society; and is known as a pianist, organist, and horn player. His compositions comprise an Ode, Christ's Nativity, for soprano solo, chorus and orchestra (Univ. ex.); The Chase, and The Return of Spring, for soli, chorus and orchestra; A Spring Idyll, for orchestra; pieces for pf., organ, violin, violoncello; songs, etc.

Bottomley, Joseph, composer, organist, and pianist, was born at Halifax, Yorkshire, 1786. Studied in Manchester, under Grimshaw, Watts, Yaniewicz; and at Leeds, under Lawton, to whom he was articled pupil. He afterwards studied pf. under Woelfl, at London. Organist of Parish Church of Bradford, 1807; organist of Parish Church, Sheffield, 1820. He died after 1850.

WORKS.—Dictionary of Music, London, 1816. New System of Practising and Teaching the Pianoforte, Sheffield, n.d. [1847]. Six Exercises for the pf. Rondos and airs for pf. Divertissements for pf. and flute. Twelve Sonatinas for pf. Songs, Glees, etc.

Bourne, C. E., author of "The great composers, or stories of the lives of eminent musicians," London, 1884. He has also written a number of popular works on biography, etc.

Bowdler, Cyril William, composer, of Welsh descent on the maternal side, born in Yorkshire, September 28th, 1839. As a boy, he studied music under Dr. John Camidge, of York, and subsequently with Sir R. Prescott Stewart, whose pupil he remained for a long period. Graduated Mus. B. and B.A., Dublin, 1864, and LL.D., Dublin, 1896. For two years, 1877-9, he was hon. organist at All Saints', Aldershot; but he is chiefly devoted to composition.

WORKS.—Music for the divine liturgy of St. John Chrysostom (Greek, 1864); complete church services in E, F, G, B flat, and C;

BOWIE.

numerous anthems, hymn tunes, etc.; "Imelda," three-act Italian opera; *Cantata—* The descent of spring; songs, organ and pf. pieces, etc.

Bowie, John, violinist and composer. Was born near Perth, in 1759, and died there in 1815. He published about the end of last century a " Collection of strathspey reels and country dances, with a bass for the violoncello or harpsichord. Dedicated to the Countess of Kinnoul," Edinburgh [1789]. He also published several dance tunes on single sheets. He was engaged as a music-seller in Perth, and gave balls in conjunction with his brother.

His brother PETER (1763-1846), was also a violinist, and a teacher of the pianoforte.

Bowley, Robert Kanzow, musician, was born in London, May, 1813, and died in August, 1870. Author of "Grand Handel Musical Festival at the Crystal Palace in 1857, a Letter," London, 1856. "The Sacred Harmonic Society, a thirty-five years retrospect," London, 1867. This musician was connected with the Sacred Harmonic Society, and he assisted in establishing the Great Handel Celebrations at the Crystal Palace, London.

Bowling, a family of musicians. The father, JOHN BOWLING, organist, violinist, and pianist, was born at Leeds, November 11th, 1820. At the age of eleven he was appointed organist of Heckmondwike parish church, and afterwards filled the office of organist of East Parade chapel, Leeds, for 34 years. He was conductor of musical societies in several Yorkshire towns, and of the Leeds Madrigal and Motet Society. He died at Leeds, April 16th, 1882.

His son, JOHN PEW BOWLING, born at Leeds, May 26th, 1851, was considered the finest pianist in the county. He was also an able violinist, and organist, holding an appointment at All Souls' (Hook Memorial) Church. Was the first Principal of the Yorkshire College of Music, Leeds, and conductor of the Leeds Amateur Orchestral Society, and the Huddersfield Orpheus Society. He died at Leeds, July 6th, 1886.

JAMES WHEWALL BOWLING, the youngest son, was born at Leeds, January 6th, 1860. Besides being an excellent pianist and organist, he showed much ability as a composer. He succeeded his brother as Principal of the College of Music, and was organist to Lady Mary Vyner, Skelton, near Ripon. His compositions comprised six songs; four songs for tenor, Op. 5; a second set of four songs; suite, Op. 3, for pianoforte, etc. He died December 13th, 1888, under mournful circumstances. His health being delicate, he was spending the winter in Switzerland (the Engadine). Skating on the lake near the hotel, one of the party fell through the ice, and Bowling was drowned in attempting a rescue.

BOYCE.

Bowman, Henry, composer, flourished during latter half of 17th century. Wrote "Songs for one, two, and three voyces to the Thorow-Bass. With some short Symphonies. Collected out of some of the select poems of the incomparable Mr. Cowley, and others, and composed by Henry Bowman, Philo-Musicus," Oxford. 1677.

Bowman, Rev. Thomas, amateur musician, born in 1728. He was vicar of Martham, Norfolk, and died in 1792. He composed " A collection of English odes, cantatas, songs, etc." London, 1760. Single songs, etc.

Box, Charles, author of "Church music in the Metropolis, its past and present condition, with notes critical and explanatory," London, 1884.

Boyce, Ethel Mary, composer and pianist, born at Chertsey, Surrey, October 5th, 1863. Daughter of George Boyce, J.P. Studied at R.A.M., pianoforte under Walter Macfarren, and composition under F. W. Davenport. Was Lady Goldsmid Scholar, 1885; Potter Exhibitioner, 1886; won the Sterndale Bennett Prize the same year, and the Lucas Medal for composition, 1889. Resident in Chertsey as composer and teacher. Associate, R.A.M., 1890.

WORKS.—Cantatas: The Lay of the brown rosary (Mrs. Browning), 1890; Young Lochinvar, 1891; The sands of Corriemie, female voices, 1895; March in E, orchestra, Westminster Orchestral Society, 1889; Eight pieces, violin and pianoforte (Novello's albums). Songs—" So she went drifting," and others. Part-songs: "Love has come," etc. Pianoforte pieces: "To Phyllis"; Short pieces for children, etc.

Boyce, William, composer and organist, was born in London, 1710. Chorister in St. Paul's Cathedral under Charles King. Articled pupil to Maurice Greene, organist of St. Paul's. Organist of St. Peter's, Vere Street, 1734. Studied under Dr. Pepusch. Organist (in succession to Kelway) of St. Michael's, Cornhill, 1736-68. Composer to Chapel Royal and the King, June, 1736. Conductor at meetings of choirs of Gloucester, Hereford, and Worcester, 1737. Organist of Allhallows the Great and the Less, Thames Street, 1749-69. Bac. and Doc. of Music, Cambridge, 1749. Master of Royal Band of Music, 1775. One of the organists to Chapel Royal, 1758. He died at Kensington, London, February 7th, 1779. Buried in crypt, St. Paul's Cathedral.

WORKS.—Peleus and Thetis, masque, by Lord Lansdowne, 17?; Solomon, serenata by Dr. Edward Moore, 1747; The Chaplet, a musical drama, London, 1745; David's lamentation over Saul and Jonathan, oratorio, by Lockman, 1736; Ode for St. Cecilia's Day, by Lockman; Ode for St. Cecilia's Day, by Vidal; Music to the Shepherd's Lottery, 1750;

BOYCE.

Ode for the Installation of the Duke of New-castle as Chancellor of Cambridge University, 1749 ; Fifteen anthems and a te deum and jubilate, 1780 ; Collection of twelve anthems and a service, 1790 ; Ode to charity; Pindar's first Pythian ode, 1749 ; Masque in the Tempest. Cathedral music, being a collection in score of the most valuable and useful compo-sitions for that service, etc. [containing examples of Aldrich, Batten, Bevin, Byrd, Blow, Bull, Child, Jer. Clark, Creyghton, Croft, Farrant, Gibbons, Goldwin, Humphreys, King Henry VIII., Lawes, Locke, Morley, Purcell, Rogers, Tallis, Turner, Tye, Weldon, and Wise] London, 3 vols. fol., 1760-78 ; second edition, with memoir by Sir J. Hawkins, 1778, also editions by V. Novello and J. Warren, 1849. Eight symphonies for various instru-ments ; Twelve sonatas for two violins and bass, 1749. Organ concerto. Lyra Britannica, Collection of songs, duets, and cantatas, n.d. Overtures. Songs, duets, etc., in contempo-rary collections.

Boyce, William, only son of the above, was born March 25th, 1764. He was intended for the church, and sent to Oxford ; but com-mitting some irregularity, was obliged to quit that university without obtaining a degree. He then became a double-bass player at the opera and principal concerts, and was in the orchestra at the Birmingham Festivals, 1802-5. Considerable property coming to him, he lived in retirement some years before his death, which took place early in 1824.

Boyd, Henry, musician of 18th century, was a teacher of psalmody and precentor in the Methodist Chapel, John Street, Glasgow. He died at Glasgow, November 17th, 1792.

He compiled " A select collection of psalm and hymn tunes in three parts, adapted to a great variety of measures, to which is prefixed an introduction to the art of singing." . . . . Published for the benefit of his widow, 1793.

Boyle, Frank, tenor vocalist, born at Barnstaple, August 13th, 1857. His father, William Boyle, has sung in the choir of Barn-staple Parish Church from his boyhood, and is still principal alto there. Frank, as a boy, displayed musical talent. His father taught him singing, and he had violin lessons from the late John Edwards, and organ lessons from Dr. J. H. Edwards. Was a chorister at Holy Trinity Church, and, after leaving school, entered a newspaper office, singing, at times, at local concerts. He soon decided to devote himself to music, and winning the Corporation of London Scholarship, entered the National Training School, South Ken-sington. While there he sang as principal tenor at St. Matthias, Stoke Newington. Sang in the Messiah at the Albert Hall, Good Friday, 1880, and at the promenade concerts the same year. In 1882, was engaged for the

BRADFORD.

Hereford Festival. Joined D'Oyly Carte's Opera Company ; toured in Australia, 1885-6; on his return rejoined D'Oyly Carte, and sang in George Edwards' English Opera Company. In 1891 his health broke down. He burst a blood vessel in the lungs, and died at Barn-staple, February 6th, 1892.

Boys, Henry, composer and teacher, was born about 1806, and died at Margate, Febru-ary 8th, 1851. He composed Cupid and Campaspe, a cantata, 1842, and the following glees : Friar Tuck ; The pearl divers ; Smug-gler's chaunt; War-boat song of the Crusaders, etc.

Bradberry, Gervas, amateur composer, was born about 1776, died at Pentonville, London, December 29th, 1862. He composed glees and songs, and harmonized a number of glees by other composers, as " Twenty-four select melodies of eminent composers harmon-ized for three voices," London [1825].

Bradbury, Orlando, vocalist and com-poser, was born about 1805. He was a Gen-tleman of the Chapel Royal, St. James' Palace, London ; lay-vicar of Westminster Abbey, and a bass singer of some note. He died at London, December 14th, 1872. Composer of ballads and other vocal music.

Brade, William, composer and viol-player, who flourished about beginning of 17th cen-tury, and died at Frankfort in 1647. He published Paduanen, galliarden, canzonetten, etc., 1609 ; Neue Paduanen und gagliarden mit stimmen, 1614 ; Neue Lustige Volten Couranten, Balletten, etc.

Bradford, Jacob, organist and composer, born at Bow, London, June 3, 1842. Chor-ister, St. Paul's, Walworth. To a great extent self-taught in music, but was a pupil of Sir John Goss, and Dr. Steggall. Assistant or-ganist to Scotson Clark at St. Helens, and St. Ethelburga, Bishopsgate ; and at the age of twenty, gained the appointment of organist at St. Philip's, Kennington. Graduated Mus. B., 1873 ; Mus. D., 1878, Oxford. Organist, St. James's, Hatcham, 1868-75, and conductor of orchestral services he introduced there ; and, after holding various appointments, went to St. Mary's, Newington, in 1892, holding that position to the present time. Was music master at the Royal Naval School, New Cross, 1881-90 ; and is a professor at West Kent Grammar School, and conductor of the New-ington Choral Society. From 1882 he was for some years Hon. Sec. to the Musical Artists' Society. Has contributed articles to *Musical News*, and other papers.

WORKS.—Oratorio, Judith (produced, St. James's Hall, Feb. 28, 1888) ; Cantata, The Song of Jubilee, Op. 44 ; Cantata, Praise the Lord ; Harvest Cantata ; Anthems, Church Services, etc. Sinfonia Ecclesiastica, for double choir and orchestra ; overtures, etc.,

BRADLEY.

BRAINE.

in MS. Trio in E flat, pf. and strings; organ Sonata in C minor, Op. 47, etc. Compiler of The Music Pupil's Register (Novello).

Bradley, Charles, organist and composer, born at Wakefield, October 20, 1846. Trained under R. S. Burton, Dr. P. Armes and F. W. Davenport. Organist successively of St. Michael's, Wakefield, 1856-66; St. Paul's, Middlesbrough, 1871-82; St. George's, Edinburgh, 1882-85; Abbey Parish Church, 1885-87; and South Leith Parish Church, 1887. He was organist to the Edinburgh Choral Union, from 1883 to 1890. Composer of anthems and other Church music, songs, and organ music.

Bradley, Frank H., organist and pianist, born in Birmingham. Pupil of A. Deakin, and A. R. Gaul. Organist of St. Barnabas, Birmingham, 1867; at Stoke-on-Trent; Quebec Cathedral, Canada; professor of music, and organist, Tettenhall College, Wolverhampton; St. John's, Wilton Road, London; St. Andrews, West Kensington (1884). Has given organ and pianoforte recitals in Birmingham, Paris, South Kensington International Exhibition, 1883; at the Kimberley Exhibition, South Africa, 1892-3; also in Australia, and was accompanist and conductor during Mr. Santley's tour in Australia, 1889-90.

Bradley, Joseph, pianist and conductor, born at Hyde, Cheshire, February 28, 1857. At twelve, he was organist at St. Paul's, Stalybridge; and two years later at Heaton Chapel, Manchester; F.R.C.O., 1873; Mus. B., Oxford, 1875. For six years, 1881-7, he was organist and deputy chorus-master to Sir Charles Halle at Manchester, and conductor of societies at Stockport, Stalybridge, and other places. In 1887, he was appointed chorus-master to the Glasgow Choral Union, and later, conductor of the Choral Concerts. He composed "A Song of Praise," for chorus and orchestra, expressly for performance when the Queen visited Glasgow Exhibition in August, 1888.

Bradley, Orton, pianist and conductor, born at Greenwich, December 11th, 1858. Educated at Harrow, and Hertford College, Oxford. Pupil of John Farmer; scholar and organist of his college; graduated M.A., with classical honours. Organist, King Edward's School, Bromsgrove, 1891, for one year. From 1887 to 1893, held the position of Musical Director to the People's Palace, London, and was the first conductor of the National Sunday League Choir. As a pianist, he has devoted much attention to the compositions of Brahms. In 1893 he went to New York, where he gained a distinguished position as conductor and pianist. His settings of poems by Jean Ingelow, and Rossetti (The Blessed Damosel), for recitation, have been performed at the Lyric Club [1886].

Bradshaw, Ann Maria, born TREE, soprano vocalist and actress, born at London, in August, 1801. She first appeared in the "Barber of Seville" at Covent Garden, in 1818, and continued to act and sing in public till 1825, when she married Mr. James Bradshaw, and retired. She was sister to Ellen Tree the actress.

Bradshaw, Ralph, musician and compiler, was born in Bolton about 1776. He died in 1832. Issued "Twenty-four psalm and hymn tunes, composed and arranged for four voices . . ." [1820]. A Second set of psalm or hymn tunes, London [1825].

Brady, Nicholas, divine and poet, born at Bandon, 1659, died at Richmond, Surrey, 1726. He was associated with Tate in the production of a metrical version of the Psalms of David. He also wrote "Church music vindicated; a sermon preached at St. Bride's Church on Monday, November 22nd, 1697, being St. Cæcilia's Day, the anniversary feast of the lovers of musick," London, 1697.

Braham, John, tenor vocalist and composer, born in London, of Jewish parents, 1774 [1772]. He studied under Leoni, and first appeared at the Royalty Theatre, Wellclose Square, London, 1787. He appeared at Covent Garden, April 21st, 1787, and sang at Bath in 1794, where he studied under Rauzzini. He sang at Drury Lane Theatre in 1796, and afterwards travelled in Italy, and appeared at Florence, Rome, Naples, Milan, Genoa, Venice, etc., with Mrs. Billington and others. While in Italy he studied under Isola, and in 1801 he returned to London, where he re-appeared at Covent Garden Theatre. He married Miss Bolton, of Ardwick, in 1816. He sang as Huon in Weber's Oberon, in 1826. Lost his fortune by failure of several speculations, 1851. Died at London, February 17th, 1856.

WORKS.—*Music to Dramas :* The Cabinet, 1801; Family Quarrels, 1802; The English Fleet, 1802 (containing "All's Well," duet, etc.); Thirty Thousand, 1804; Out of Place, 1805; False Alarms, 1807; Kais, or Love in a Desert, 1808 (with Reeve); The Devil's Bridge (with C. E. Horn), 1812; The Paragraph; Narensky, or The Road to Yarostaf; The Americans; The Magicians (with M. P. King). Single songs, glees, etc. Death of Nelson, song.

His sons, JOHN HAMILTON BRAHAM (London, 1818; Rochester, December 22nd, 1862), and CHARLES BAMFYLDE (London, 1822; London, June 11th, 1884), were both vocalists, the former, a baritone, who first appeared at the Hanover Square Rooms, November 2nd, 1843; and the latter, a tenor. His grandson, EDWARD B. BRAHAM, appeared as a 'cellist in 1885.

Braine, William Richard, organist and composer, born at London, November 8, 1829; died there February 19, 1865. Was for 18 years organist of St. Barnabas, Kensington. Compiler of "The St. Barnabas Music Book,"

BRANSCOMBE.

1850; "Hymns for the Church, or home circle," London, 1861. Composer of duets, songs, and pf. music.

Branscombe, Edward, tenor vocalist, born at Camberwell, London. Studied for three years at the Guildhall School of Music; at the R.C.M. for two years, under Blume, and later with Sims Reeves. When nineteen, he was appointed choirmaster and assistant organist of St. Paul's, West Brixton, and formed the Brixton Orpheus Glee Club. A concert he gave in Brixton Hall, October 19, 1885, brought him into notice as a singer. In 1887, he was appointed to the Church of St. Andrew, Wells Street; and in December, 1890, lay-vicar, Westminster Abbey. He has sung at the principal London concerts; at the Crystal Palace; and in the chief provincial centres. He married MARIE HOOTON, the contralto vocalist, who studied at the R.A.M., winning the Westmoreland Scholarship, 1888, and the Parepa Rosa Gold Medal, 1890. The artist pair now rank among the most successful of our younger singers.

Braun, Charles, composer, born in Liverpool, 1868, where his father, an accomplished amateur, was partner in a large business firm. He was educated at Clifton, and Cambridge. Studied music at Leipzig, under Hans Sitt. Resident in England, and engaged in composition. His cantata, "Sir Olaf," was produced at the Philharmonic Hall, Liverpool, March 5, 1889, and attracted much attention. In December, 1890, a second cantata, "Sigurd," was produced with success at the same place, both performances being conducted by Mr. Rodewald, an amateur, who has done much for music in Liverpool. Charles Braun has written a good many songs, and is now engaged on an opera.

Bray, Mrs. Anna Eliza (born Kempe), writer, born at St. Mary, Newington, Surrey, December 25, 1790. She died at London, January 21, 1883. Wrote a number of novels and miscellaneous works, and "Handel: his Life, Personal and Professional, with Thoughts on Sacred Music," London (Ward & Co.,) 1857.

Breakspeare, Eustace John, composer, writer and pianist, born in Birmingham, April 22, 1854. Studied under S. S. Stratton. Has appeared at concerts in Birmingham, as solo pianist and accompanist, but is better known as a writer on music. He has read papers on "Musical Aesthetics," and other subjects, at meetings of the Musical Association (1880-2-3); the College of Organists (1883), and at various institutions in Birmingham. His contributions to the *Musical Standard, Musical Record, Musical Times, Musical Opinion,* and other papers, are very numerous, and embrace a wide range of subject matter. He has written a Suite, and many pieces for pf., and a number of songs, but hitherto very little has been published.

BREMA.

Brechin, William, teacher, and inventor of "Brechin's Stave Sol-fa Notation," was born at Brechin, Forfar, 1824. He held appointments as precentor in Montrose, Forfar, Perth, Leith, and Edinburgh. The principal feature of his system is the employment of letters, as in the ordinary Tonic Sol-fa, to represent the notes, together with certain signs to mark the duration. The notes are written on the staff. In addition to the invention of the Stave Sol-fa Notation, Brechin has edited and compiled "Vocal Exercises, Rounds, etc., in the Stave Sol-fa Notation, forming a short course of Lessons in Sight Singing in the key of F." "Congregational Music, Psalms, Hymns, etc., in Stave Sol-fa Notation." "The Standard Scottish Psalmody" (compiled from the foregoing) "Exercises in Sight Singing"; "School Song Books"; "The Stave Sol-fa Journal" (publishing in parts) containing pieces by Croft, Beethoven, Mason, Stevenson, Blow, Handel, etc."; Two Books of Swedish Songs.

Breden, Owen, music master at St. Mark's College, Chelsea, was born at Norwood in 1841. He was for five years a pupil teacher at King's Somborne School, Hants.; and in 1860, gained a Queen's Scholarship at St. Mark's College, as a student. He had previously learned pianoforte and organ playing; and as the organ at the College Chapel was put up while he was a student, he has played it from the first, and continues to act as organist and choirmaster. He became successively master of the upper school, tutor, and vice-principal; and in 1883, gave up the last to undertake the musical work. For this, he had qualified himself by studying pianoforte under Dr. Wylde, organ under Dr. E. J. Hopkins, and singing under John Elwin.

Brekell, John, clergyman, author of "A Discourse on Musick, chiefly Church Musick; occasioned by the opening of the new Organ in St. Peter's Church in Liverpool . . . Sermon," London, 1766.

Brema, Marie, originally BREMER, vocalist, mezzo-soprano, a native of Liverpool. She studied under G. Henschel, and made her *début* at the Monday Popular Concerts, February 23, 1891. Later (October) in the same year, she appeared as Lola in "Cavalleria Rusticana," at the Shaftesbury Theatre. She first sang at the Philharmonic Concerts, April 20, 1893, and at the Crystal Palace, March 24, 1894. She was engaged for the Bayreuth performance of 1894, appearing as Ortrud, and in 1896, as Fricka and Kundry. Her Festival *début* took place at Birmingham, October 3, 1895, when she created a marked impression by her dramatic rendering of the part of the Evil Spirit in Hubert Parry's oratorio, "King Saul." She now ranks among the leading singers of the day.

BREMNER.

Bremner, Robert, musician and publisher, born in Scotland about 1720 [1713]. He was a pupil of Geminiani, and taught music in Edinburgh. On December 13, 1753, he gave a concert in the High School, Leith. He commenced business as a music-seller and publisher at the Golden Harp, opposite the head of Blackfriars Wynd, Edinburgh, in 1754; in 1755 he changed his sign to the Harp and Hautboy; and in 1759 he removed to another shop in the High Street. He removed to London, and opened a shop with the Harp and Hautboy sign, in the Strand, opposite Somerset House, in 1762. Both businesses were carried on till his death, the Edinburgh one being managed by John Bryson, who succeeded him. He died at Kensington Gore, London, on May 12, 1789.

WORKS.—Collection of the best Church tunes, in four parts. Published by Robert Bremner, by order of the Honourable the Committee for improving Church music in the City of Edinburgh, n.d. Thirty Scotch songs, some of which are for two voices, with a thorough bass for the harpsichord or spinnet . . . The words from Allan Ramsay, except a few never before printed. Edin. [1757] A Second Set of Scots Songs, Edin., n.d. These were re-issued in London about 1762-65. The Songs in the Gentle Shepherd, adapted to the guitar, Edin. 1759. The Vocal Harmonists' Magazine, being a collection of catches, glees, canons, and canzonets, London, n.d. The Freemasons' Songs, with choruses in 3 and 4 parts . . . to which is added some other songs proper for Lodges, London [1759]. A collection of Scots Reels, or Country dances, with a bass for the violoncello or harpsichord . . , Edin. [issued in 8 parts, 1757-61] A second collection of Scots Reels or Country dances . . . London [2 parts, 1768]. A curious collection of Scots tunes, with variations for the violin, and a bass for the violoncello or harpsichord, Edin. 759. Rudiments of Music, or a short and easy treatise on that subject, to which is added a collection of the best Church tunes, canons and anthems. Edin. 1756; 2nd ed. Edin., 1762; 3rd ed. London, 1763. Instructions for the guitar, London, n.d. Thoughts on the performance of Concert music [prefixed to Schetky's Quartets, Op. 6], London, n.d. The Harpsichord or Spinnet Miscellany, London [1760]. Select concert pieces for the Harpsichord or Pianoforte . . . London, 1780, pub. in numbers.

Brent, Charlotte, see PINTO, Mrs.

Brereton, William Henry, bass vocalist, born at Bedford, in 1860. Son of the late Rev. Canon Brereton, rector of St. Mary's, Bedford. Studied under Manuel Garcia, R.A.M., 1877-80; with Sebastian Ronconi, Milan, 1881; and had occasional lessons from the late J. B. Welch, and Alberto Randegger,

BREWSTER.

1882, and later. He made a successful *début* at the Crystal Palace Saturday Concerts, February 18th, 1882, and appeared at the Three Choirs Festivals in turn, at Gloucester, 1883, Worcester, 1884, and Hereford, 1885, and onwards. He sang at the Leeds Festival for the first time, in 1886; at the Birmingham Festival, in 1888, in which year he was also engaged for the Handel Festival at the Crystal Palace. Has sung at the principal concerts in the United Kingdom. In 1882 he was appointed principal bass at the Foundling Hospital; to St. Paul's Cathedral, 1886; and a Gentleman of the Chapel Royal, St. James's, 1887. In 1884 he married Miss SARAH AMBLER, a soprano vocalist, who has been heard in London concerts, and at the provincial festivals.

Brett, Harry, author of The Cornet, scales, exercises, etc. (Novello's primers, No. 28).

Brewer, Alfred Herbert, organist and composer, born at Gloucester, June 21st, 1865. Chorister in the Cathedral, and pupil of Dr. C. H. Lloyd. Educated at the Cathedral School, and Exeter College, Oxford. In 1882, was elected organist of St. Giles' Church, Oxford, and in 1883 gained the first organ scholarship, R.C.M., studying under Walter Parratt, and other masters. At the end of this year he was elected Organ Scholar of Exeter College, Oxford; was appointed to St. Michael's, Coventry, in 1886; in September, 1892, organist and music master at Tonbridge School; and in December, 1896, organist of Gloucester Cathedral. Beyond his organ work, he is known as a conductor, the Coventry Musical Society having been under his direction for some years.

WORKS.—Five evening services (an orchestral setting in C, composed by request, and produced at the Gloucester Festival, 1895); anthems, carols, hymn tunes, etc. An operetta, Rosamond; part-songs (Song and summer, Gloucester Festival, 1892; Sad hearts, Hereford, 1894); school song, duets, songs; three organ pieces, two Romances, violin and pf., pieces for pf. solo, and pf. duets.

Brewer, Thomas, composer, flourished during the 17th century [1610-80]. Educated at Christ's Hospital. He was a performer on the viol. Dates of birth and death unknown.

WORKS.—Seven fantasias for the viol; Rounds and catches in Hilton's "Catch that catch can"; Turn, Amaryllis, to thy Swain, part-song in Playford's Musical Companion.

The biography of this composer is obscure. "Turn, Amaryllis," is a well-known and pretty piece.

Brewster, Henry, writer. Author of a "Concise Method of playing thoroughbass," London, 1797. Composer of a Set of lessons for the harpsichord or pf., op. 4, 1785. Vauxhall and grotto songs, London, 1771.

BRIAN.

BRIDGEMAN.

Brian, *see* BRYNE (A.)

Briant, Rowland, organist. Pupil of R.A.M., also associate and professor of the organ there. F.C.O. Organist successively of Eccleston Square Church; Westbourne Park Chapel; and New Court Chapel, Tollington Park. Conductor of various choral societies. Composer of Hear my prayer; Praise ye the Lord; Come unto me; Come now, and let us reason together; and other anthems.

Bridge, Frederick Albert, organist, vocalist, lecturer and writer; born in London, 1841. Choirmaster and solo bass, St. Andrew's Undershaft; Organist, St. Martin's, Ludgate, 1873-8; Choirmaster, St. Martin-in-the-Fields, 1878-82; of St. John's, Lewisham. Commenced his Musical Monologue Lecture Entertainment in 1872. Conductor of St. John's Choral Society, Lewisham, 1885-91; and of the North West London Musical and Dramatic Society. Author of A Brief history of Mr. Henry Leslie's choir (London, 1880). Married, in 1863, Miss ELIZABETH STIRLING (*q.v.*)

Bridge, John Frederick, composer, organist, and didactic writer, born at Oldbury, Worcestershire, December 5, 1844. [His father, John Bridge, was for many years a lay-clerk at Rochester Cathedral, and an original member of the Choir Benevolent Fund. He died at Chester, September 1, 1893]. Entered Rochester Cathedral as a chorister in 1850, and after being taught for some time by his father, was articled to J. Hopkins, studying later with (Sir) John Goss. F.R.C.O., 1867; Mus. Bac., 1868; Mus. D., Oxford, 1874. Was appointed organist of Trinity Church, Windsor, 1865; Manchester Cathedral, 1869; Professor of harmony at Owen's College, 1872; permanent deputy organist at Westminster Abbey, 1875, and, after the death of James Turle (1882), organist and master of the choristers. Conductor of the Highbury Philharmonic Society, 1878-86, and of the Western Madrigal Society. Examiner in Music, Oxford University, 1885, and in London University, 1891; Vice-President, Trinity College, London, 1891. Appointed Gresham Professor of Music, May, 1890, the scope and variety of the "Gresham Lectures" being greatly extended by him. He became conductor of the Royal Choral Society in succession to Sir Joseph Barnby in 1896. During his tenure of office at Westminster Abbey he has had some very important functions to discharge. He arranged all the music and composed a special anthem ("Blessed be the Lord") for the celebration of the Queen's Jubilee, June 21, 1887; receiving the thanks of Her Majesty, and the Silver Jubilee Medal. Other notable musical arrangements were those for the funeral of Lord Tennyson (October 12, 1892), and the Purcell

Commemoration (November 21, 1895). Dr. Bridge is Professor of Harmony and Counterpoint, R.C.M.; Hon. R.A.M., and a member of the Philharmonic Society. He has lectured on musical subjects in Birmingham and other places.

WORKS.—Mount Moriah, oratorio (1874); Boadicea, cantata (Highbury Phil. Soc., May 31, 1880); Hymn to the Creator (Highbury, 1883; Worcester Festival, 1884); Rock of Ages (Mr. Gladstone's Latin translation, Birmingham Festival, 1885); Callirhoë, cantata, Birmingham, 1888; The Repentance of Nineveh, dramatic oratorio (book by Joseph Bennett, Worcester Festival, 1890); The Lord's Prayer (from Dante's Purgatorio, translated by Rev. E. H. Plumpton, Gloucester, 1892); The Cradle of Christ (Stabat Mater Speciosa, Hereford, 1894); choral ballads, The Festival (men's voices); The Inchcape bell. Church services, anthems, etc. Editor of Westminster Abbey Chant Book; Songs from Shakespeare. Partsongs. Concert overture, Morte d' Arthur (Birmingham, 1886); Minuet and trio, orchestra; Sonata in D, organ, etc. Author of Primer on Counterpoint, Double Counterpoint, Organ accompaniment, and Musical Gestures and Rudiments in Rhymes (Novello).

Bridge, Joseph Cox, composer and organist, brother of the preceding, born at Rochester, August 16, 1853. Received his musical training at the Cathedral, where he became assistant organist; afterwards acting in a similar capacity to his brother at Manchester Cathedral. In 1871 he was appointed organist of Exeter College, Oxford. Graduated B.A., 1875; Mus. B., 1876; M.A., 1878; and Mus. D., Oxford, 1884. F.C.O., 1879. Appointed Organist of Chester Cathedral, 1877, he has been Conductor of the Triennial Festivals there since their re-establishment in 1879. For some years, from 1887, he was Conductor of the Bradford Festival Choral Society, His compositions include several works produced at the Chester Festivals: Magnificat and Nunc Dimittis, for voices, orchestra, and organ (1879); Oratorio, "Daniel" (1885); Cantata, Rudel (1891); and a Symphony in F, orchestra (1894). He has also composed an operetta, "The Belle of the Area"; an anthem for Harvest Festivals; some pieces for pf.; songs; also transcriptions for the organ.

Bridgeman, Charles, organist, was born at Hertford, August 20, 1778. Studied the organ under J. Cubitt Pring, and violin under François Cramer. In 1823 he founded the Hertford Musical Society, and for many years was teacher of music at Christ's Hospital, Hertford. He was organist of Hertford Parish Church for the long period of 81 years. Died at Hertford, August 3, 1873.

Bridgeman, John Vipon, musician and writer, born in 1819. He was for upwards of

30 years foreign editor of the *Musical World.* Translated Wagner's "Oper und Drama," Judaism in music, etc. Wrote libretto of Balfe's, Armourer of Nantes, and Puritan's daughter. Also translated various novels and other works from the French and German, such as Freytag's "Soll und Haben" (Debit and Credit), and works by Gautier, Blanc, and Hugo. He died at London, September 30, 1889.

Bridgewater, Robert, composer and bass singer, born at York (?) in 1814.? Son of Thomas Bridgewater, organist of St. Saviour's, York, who died January 6, 1831. He died at Windsor, July 24, 1869. Compiler of "Sacred music, consisting of chants, etc." York, 1840. "Church psalmody . . ." London, 1850. He also composed songs, etc.

Bridgman, Frederick William, pianist, born in London, January 16, 1833. While very young went to reside with his grandfather, Mr. Eager, an esteemed teacher of music, at Edinburgh. He first appeared as a juvenile performer on the concertina, and made his *début* as a pianist in March, 1840. He continued to play, in Edinburgh and other places, as a musical prodigy, but in 1851 he went to Leipzig, and entered upon a thorough course of study, winning the favour of Moscheles whose pupil he was. In 1854 he returned to England, and appeared as soloist and conductor in London and the provinces. He was for some years manager of the Metropolitan English Opera Company. He settled in Edinburgh as a teacher in 1862, where he was highly successful. He was organist of the United Presbyterian Church, College Street, and was accompanist at the Glasgow City Hall Saturday Concerts, celebrating his artistic Jubilee at one of them, March 22, 1890. Died at Edinburgh, December 28, 1892.

Bridson, John, baritone vocalist, born in Liverpool, 1837. Engaged in business pursuits, he sang as an amateur for many years, ultimately, studying under J. B. Welch, adopting singing as a profession. One of his early successes was, as a substitute for Mr. Santley, in the first performance as an oratorio, of Rossini's "Mosè in Egitto," at a concert of the Sacred Harmonic Society, under Sir Michael Costa, May 24th, 1878. The same year he sang in "Judas Maccabæus," in Birmingham, and created a very favourable impression. He afterwards appeared at the principal London and provincial concerts. His voice, if not remarkable for power, was of admirable quality; and he was a singer of culture and refinement. He died in London, December 11th, 1895.

Bright, Dora Estella, pianist and composer, born at Sheffield, August 16th, 1863. Upon the death of her father, an excellent amateur violinist, in 1881, she entered the

R.A.M., studying the pianoforte under Walter Macfarren, and composition under Ebenezer Prout. She remained at the Academy until 1888, gaining the Potter Exhibition in 1884, and other prizes, including the Lucas Medal, for composition, in 1888, being the first woman to obtain that honour. During this time she wrote several important works. Her progress as a pianist was such that she was allowed to appear at the Promenade Concerts, Covent Garden, in October, 1882. She began her pianoforte recitals in January, 1889, and appeared at the Crystal Palace Concerts, March 28th, 1891, playing her Pianoforte Concerto in A minor. The next year (May 11th), she played her Fantasia in G, for pf. and orchestra, at the Philharmonic Concerts, the first instance of an orchestral work by a woman being admitted to the programme of the Society. She gave recitals of English music, from Byrd to Cowen, in 1892, and in October, 1895, began a series of national pianoforte recitals. Her first continental tour was undertaken in the autumn of 1889, when she appeared with success at Dresden, Cologne, and Leipzig. In 1892, she was married to Captain Knatchbull, of Bath.

WORKS.—Air with variations, orchestra, London, 1890; Concerto in A minor, pf. and orchestra, London, 1888; Concerto, No. 2, Cologne, 1892; Fantasia in G, 1892; Quartet in D, pf. and strings, 1893; Suite, violin and pf., 1890; Duo, two pianos, Musical Artists' Society, 1886. Pieces for pf. and flute, pf. solo; Twelve songs (Novello), etc.

Brind, Richard, organist and composer of 17th century. Educated at St. Paul's. Organist of St. Paul's Cathedral. Composed a thanksgiving anthem, etc., but is best known as the teacher of Greene. He died about 1718.

Britton, Thomas, musician, was born at Higham Ferrers, Northamptonshire, in 1651. He was apprenticed to a coal-dealer in London, and afterwards commenced business on his own account as a coal-dealer in Aylesbury Street, at the corner of Jerusalem Passage, Clerkenwell. He studied Music, Chemistry, and Bibliography, and established weekly concerts in his own house, and formed a musical club. He died at Clerkenwell, London, 27th September, 1714.

The musical club was formed by Britton for the practice of chamber music, and the performers consisted of Handel, Pepusch, Banister, H. Needler, Hughes (the poet), P. Hart, H. Symonds, A. Whichello, Shuttleworth, Wollaston (the painter), etc. Matthew Dubourg when a child played his first solo in Britton's house. The origin of these concerts and their continuance was due to Britton's personal love for music, together, it is believed, with the mutual love for bibliographical and

BROADHOUSE.

other studies held by many members of his audience. The admission to these concerts was originally free, but afterwards a subscription of 10s. per annum was charged. At the end of 1892 the Britton concerts were established in memory of Thomas Britton, at the Hampden Club, Phœnix Street, St. Pancras, London. Britton's books were sold after his death, and the catalogue was published as "The Library of Mr. Thomas Britton, small-coalman, deceas'd, who at his own charge kept up a consort of musick above 40 years in his little cottage, 1714-15. Being a curious Collection of Books in Divinity, History, Physick, and Chimistry, in all volumes." . . .

His portrait, by J. Wollaston, hangs in the National Portrait Gallery, London.

Broadhouse, John, organist and writer of the present day. Appointed organist of Christ Church, Barnet, 1876; St. John's, Whetstone, 1886; and St. Barnabas', Woodside Park, 1889. Editor of the *Musical Standard*, 1878-80; 1886-8; and again subsequently; and also of the *London Musical Review*, 1882-3. Author of Facts about Fiddles, Violins, Old and New; The Student's Helmholtz (1881); Henry Smart's Compositions for the Organ Analysed (reprinted, 1880, from the *Musical Standard*). Translator of Thibaut's "Purity in Music" (London, 1883); Schmitt's "Use of the Pedal in pf. playing"; Bülow's "Notes on Beethoven's Pianoforte Sonatas." Author of "Love which alters not: a story of to-day," which appeared in the *Orchestra* (new series), vols. VIII. and IX.

Broadwood, Lucy E., collector, editor, and composer, youngest child of Henry Fowler Broadwood, of the firm of John Broadwood and Sons, was born in Scotland. Especially interested in singing, she studied under W. Shakespeare, and then continued the work of her uncle, the Rev. John Broadwood (which he completed in 1840), of collecting songs from the country people of Surrey and Sussex. In 1893, collaborated with J. A. Fuller Maitland (*q.v.*) in editing and arranging "English County Songs"; also in the series of "Old World Songs"; and is now (1896) engaged in editing some of Purcell's works. Has arranged and published the old Scotch airs, "Jess Macfarlane," and "In Loyalty," and has composed and published Nae mair we'll meet; Tammy; When trees did bud; Annie's Tryst, and other songs.

Brocklesby, Richard, physician of the 18th century. Author of "Reflections on Ancient and Modern Music, with its application to the cure of Diseases," London, 1749.

Broderip, Edmund, organist and composer, who flourished in the beginning of the 18th century. He was organist of Wells Cathedral about 1720, and wrote a service, anthems, and glees. He was the son of WILLIAM BRO-

BROOKS.

DERIP, born 1683; died Wells, January 31, 1726, who was an organist and composer.

Broderip, John, composer and organist, was born about 1710, and died in 1771, was organist of Wells Cathedral, 1740. He wrote various sets of songs, psalms, and "Six Glees for three Voices," London, N.D., "The Flower Garden, a collection of songs, duets, and cantatas"; "Portions of Psalms, in one, two, three, and four parts, adapted to 50 tunes composed by John and Robert Broderip, London, 1780"; also "Psalms, hymns, and spiritual songs in score, for publick or private use," London [1765] n.d.

Broderip, Robert, organist and composer, was born about the middle of the 18th century. He was organist of St. James', Bristol, and died at Bristol, May 14, 1808. Brother of the preceding. Compiled "Miscellaneous Collection of Vocal music," n.d.; "Organist's Journal, selections from great Masters," n.d.; "Cecilian Harmony, a set of the most favourite duets, rotas, canons, catches, and glees," London, 1790; "Plain and easy instructions for young performers on the pianoforte or harpsichord, op. 6"; "Eight voluntaries for the organ, op. 5"; "Concerto for the harpsichord or pianoforte, with accompaniment for two violins and violoncello, op. 7." He also wrote songs, single glees, and edited a book of psalms with his brother.

Bromley, Robert Anthony, author and clergyman, died London, 1806. He published a tract entitled "On Opening the Church and Organ, Sermon on Psalm cxxii.," Lond., 1771.

Brookbank, Rev. Joseph, clergyman and schoolmaster, born at Halifax in 1612. He was educated at Oxford and ordained a minister. For some time he was a preacher in Wycombe, Bucks., but in 1651 he settled in London as a schoolmaster and minister. He died after 1668.

WORKS.—The Well-tun'd organ, or an exercitation wherein this question is discuss'd whether or no instrumental and organic Musick be lawful in holy publick assemblies, London, 1660; The Organ's Echo, London, 1641; The Organ's Funeral, London, 1642; The Holy Harmony, or a plea for the abolishing of Organs and other Musick in Churches, London, 1643; Gospel Musick, by N. H., London, 1644; The Compleat Schoolmaster, 1660.

Brooke, Daniel, clergyman and author. Published a Sermon preached at Worcester, at the meeting of the three western choirs, in September, 1743; a discourse on the musick of the church on the occasion of the performance of Handel's oratorio, "Athalia," 1743.

Brooks, James, musician and glee composer, who flourished in Bath between 1760 and 1812. He composed "Twelve glees for three and four voices," n.d.; "Second Sett of twelve glees for three and four voices," n.d.;

BROOKS.

"Twelve English ballads," op. 5 [1790].
Concerto for the violin, in nine parts, 1797 ;
Nocturne for the pf. and 'cello or flute ;
Thirty-six select pieces for a military band.

Brooks, Walter, organist, born at Long-
don, Worcestershire, April 1st, 1832. Recommended to the Rev. Sir J. H. Seymour, Bart.
(preacher at the Gloucester Festival of 1832),
he was accepted as a chorister at Gloucester
Cathedral, and afterwards articled to John
Amott, the organist. On leaving, he was appointed organist and choirmaster at Upton,
St. Leonard ; then to Christ Church, Hampstead ; St. Mary's, Atherstone, and, in 1857,
after competition, to St. Martin's, Birmingham, a post he holds to the present time.
Beyond conducting some concerts of the St.
Martin's Musical Society, he has not taken
part in public work, but has devoted himself
to church music and to teaching.

WALTER WILLIAM BROOKS, eldest son of
the above, composer, conductor, and writer
on music, was born at Edgbaston, Birmingham, March 19th, 1861. Received his earliest
musical education from his parents, and was
a chorister at St. Martin's Church. Educated
at King Edward's School, obtaining first place
in all England for music (theory) in the Oxford local examinations. From 1879-81, he
studied composition at the R.A.M., under
(Professor) E. Prout, after which he settled
in London as teacher and writer. He has
held, since 1889, the position of teacher of
pianoforte and singing at the William Ellis
Endowed School, Gospel Oak. He has contributed articles to *The Monthly Musical
Record* (of which he was sometime editor),
Musical Opinion, and other papers, and has
had some experience as a dramatic critic on
the *London Figaro.* His compositions include
an Allegro, for orchestra (Prize, 1891, Belfast
Philharmonic Society) ; Deux Morceaux, op.
14 ; Album Lyrique, op. 48 ; Trois Morceaux,
op. 50, all for violin and pf. Prelude and Fugue
in D minor (dedicated to Sir F. Ouseley) ; "The
family circle," twelve characteristic pieces ;
Six progressive studies, and other pieces for
pf. ; songs, and part-songs.

ARTHUR CHARLES BROOKS, the younger
brother of preceding, was born at Edgbaston,
May 4th, 1864. Chorister at St. Martin's.
Educated at King Edward's School. Early
musical training at home ; then studied at
R.C.M., under Dr. G. C. Martin, Dr. J. F.
Bridge, Franklin Taylor, and others. In 1884,
appointed organist and musicmaster at Bea-
consfield School, Bucks, and organist of the
Parish Church ; in 1890, to St. John's, Sligo,
Ireland, which office he resigned in 1896 to
return to Birmingham, where he is engaged
in general musical tuition.

Brooksbank, Hugh, organist, born at
Peterborough, September 13th, 1854. Chor-

BROOME.

ister at St. George's Chapel Royal, Windsor,
and afterwards articled to Dr. Keeton, of
Peterborough Cathedral. Organ scholar, Exeter College, Oxford, where he graduated Mus.
Bac., 1874, also taking the F.C.O. the same
year. In 1881 he was appointed organist to
the new church of St. Alban, Birmingham ;
and in 1882 to Llandaff Cathedral, a post he
held till his death, at Cardiff, April 28th, 1894.
He was organist at the first Cardiff Musical
Festival, 1892. His published works include
Evening Services in E flat, and B flat (unison) ;
a Benedicite, and songs. His brother, OLIVER
OLDHAM BROOKSBANK, was born at Peter-
borough, May 17th, 1859. Was also chorister
at St. George's, Windsor, and pupil of Dr.
Keeton. F.R.C.O., Mus. Bac., Durham, 1894.
Organist at Fletton, 1877 ; Alton Parish
Church, 1880; St. Leonard's, 1882; St. John's,
Leatherhead, 1883 ; St. Martin's, Bedford,
1893 ; and Addlestone Parish Church. Has
also held appointments as organist or music-
master at Chardstock (1880) ; Highbury and
Tonbridge Schools (1891); assistant at Trinity
College, Glenalmond (1881), and music-master,
Leamington College (1887). His compositions
are : "Story of the Cross" (1895); church
services, offertory sentences, set of hymn-tunes
(1891). Songs : If 'tis love ; The song of
Medora, etc. ; pf. and organ pieces, etc.

Broome, Edward, organist and composer,
a native of North Wales. For some time
organist and choirmaster, St. Mary's, Bangor.
Successful competitor as composer and choral
conductor at Eisteddfodan. Among his compositions is an anthem in memory of Eos
Morlais (Robert Rees, *q.v.*), which won the
prize at the Eisteddfod, Pontypridd, 1893.
Now resident as organist and professor of
music at Montreal, Canada.

Broome, Michael, musician, was born
in 1700. He was clerk of St. Philip's Church,
Birmingham, but appears to have been a
singing-master at Isleworth, Middlesex, and
also a printer or engraver in Birmingham.
According to his tombstone at St. Philip's,
Birmingham, he was "Father of the Musical
Society in this town." He died at Birmingham, September 20, 1775, aged 75.

WORKS.—"Michael Broome's Collection of
Church Musick for the use of his Scholars,"
n.d. "A Choice Collection of Psalm Tunes,
Hymns and Anthems, all in three or four parts,
with the gamut and its branches : newly done
in a fair large character ; the whole being drawn
out in schore : Collected and printed by Michael
Broom, singing-master, Isleworth, Middlesex" [1731]. Another edition [1738]. "A Choice
Collection of Twenty-four Psalm Tunes, all in
four parts ; and Fifteen Anthems, set by different authors . . . ; the whole collected, engraved
and printed by Michael Broome, Birmingham," [1738]. "A Collection of Twenty-

BROOMFIELD.

eight Psalm Tunes in four parts . . . for the use of the Churches and Chapels in and near Birmingham," Birmingham, 1753. "The Catch Club, or Pleasant Musical Companion, containing a Choice Collection of Fifty Catches, both Ancient and Modern . . . collected, printed and sold by Michael Broome, near St. Philip's Church, Birmingham, 1757."

Broomfield, William Robert, composer and writer. Born at Inverary, Argyle, 14th October, 1826. He was for a time in an accountant's office in Glasgow, where he studied music under John Turnbull. About 1850 he settled in Aberdeen as a music teacher, and while there he did much work for William Hamilton, of Glasgow. He was a confirmed dipsomaniac, and, in spite of several efforts to cure him, he became victim to his habits, and died at Aberdeen, October 16, 1888. In July, 1889, a monument to his memory was erected over his grave in Allanvale Cemetery, Aberdeen. WORKS.—*Psalm Tunes:* "St. Kilda," "Shandon," "Zion." *Songs:* Edited "National Songs, harmonised as vocal quartettes," first series, London, n.d.; second series, Glasgow, 1868. "The Principles of Ancient and Modern Music, deduced from the Harmonical Numbers of Antiquity," Aberdeen, 1863. "Manual of Harmony for the use of Students in Musical Composition," Glasgow, 1872.

Broughton, Alfred, pianist and conductor, born near Dewsbury, Yorkshire, January 12, 1853. Studied at first under his brother James (*q.v.*), and then under Lebert, Tod, and Attinger, at Stuttgart Conservatorium. In 1872 he was appointed organist to the Leeds Philharmonic Society, and in 1884, conductor. He was accompanist at the Leeds Festival of 1883, and choirmaster from 1886. Trained bodies of Leeds choristers have been under his direction, associated with the Festivals at Worcester, 1887, and Hereford, 1888; and he has taken detachments of his choir to assist at the Richter and Henschel concerts in London. He was a pianist of high attainments, as well as a conductor. He died at Leeds, June 12, 1895. His brother, JAMES BROUGHTON, born near Dewsbury, in 1833, went to Leeds at the age of thirteen, and was appointed organist of St. Ann's Roman Catholic Church, where he remained for over twenty years. He was chorus-master of the Leeds Festival from 1874 to 1883, and for a period of ten years gave series of classical chamber concerts in Leeds. He died March 12, 1887.

Brouncker, William Viscount, writer, born in 1620, died in 1684. Translated "Descarte's Musical Compendium," 1653. Published anonymously an "Excellent Compendium of Musick; with necessary and judicious animadversions thereupon, by a Person of Honour."

BROWN.

Brown, Abraham, violinist and composer. Was one of the principal performers at Ranelagh Gardens, where he succeeded Festing, about 1752, and at the aristocratic concerts in London about the middle of last century. His tone is mentioned as having been clear, but loud.

Brown, Arthur Henry, organist and composer, born at Brentwood, Essex, July 24, 1830. Organist of Brentwood Parish Church, 1841; St. Edward's, Romford, 1852-7; Brentwood, 1857-85; St. Peter's, South Weald, Brentford, 1889. Associated with the revival of Gregorian music, and member of the Committee of the London Gregorian Choral Association. WORKS.—Cantata, The First Miracle; Missa Seraphica (Communion service, in C); Missa Quinti Toni (plain chant Communion service); Missa Cœlestis; A flower service; Children's festival service (compiled by Rev. S. Childs Clarke. M.A.); Harvest Tide, a service of song for Harvest Thanksgivings; A century of Hymn tunes (1880); The Gregorian Canticles and Psalter (1874); Anglican Canticles and Psalter (1877); The Canticles of Holy Church (Gregorian); The Matin and Vesper Canticles (Anglican); Metrical Litanies; The Prayer Book noted, with plain chant for all the offices of the Church (1885); Introits for Sundays and Festivals of the year (1885); Te Deum, Magnificat, and Nunc Dimittis; Anthem for Christmas, etc.: A Christmas volume of prose and song (Barbara Wordsworth); Part-songs; Songs: Across the field of barley; Somebody's darling; Gather ye rosebuds, etc. New Pianoforte Tutor (1882). Pieces for pf.: Sarabande and Gigue; Gavotte and minuet, etc. Organ Harmonies for the Gregorian tones: select compositions from the great Masters (arranged); Select overtures from the great Masters; Twenty original voluntaries for organ or harmonium. Carols and hymn tunes, contributed to Hymns Ancient and Modern, and various collections.

Brown, Colin, musician and theoretical writer, was born at Liverpool, August 25, 1818. He was descended from an Argyleshire family. Euing lecturer on Music in Anderson's College, Glasgow, from 1868. He died at Hillhead, Glasgow, December 19, 1896. WORKS.—Music in Common Things, Part I.: Analysis of a Musical Sound, and the Production therefrom of the Musical Scale, 1874; Part 2: Mathematical and Musical Relations of the Scale, shewing the Principles, Construction, and Tuning of the Natural Fingerboard with Perfect Intonation, 1876; Part 4: Music in Speech and Speech in Music, Glasgow, 1870. Songs of Scotland (with J. Pittman) London, n.d. The Thistle, A Miscellany of Scottish Song, with Notes, Critical and Historical, Instrumental Accompaniments and Harmonies by James Merrylees, Glasgow, 1884 [originally issued in parts].

Mr. Brown constructed an instrument called the Voice Harmonium, founded upon the Monopolytone, to which the principles of perfect intonation were successfully applied. The novel character of the keyboard, fully described in "Music in Common Things," part II., will perhaps act as an obstruction to its speedy adoption. The Monopolytone above mentioned is a small instrument for striking on the keyboard of a pf., producing a perfect unison, though sounding every note and discord of the scale. His harmonium was awarded the first place at an exhibition of instruments illustrating the same principle held in London.

Brown, Edward, organist and conductor of present time. Graduated Mus. Bac., 1878; Mus. Doc., 1883, Oxford. Organist and choirmaster, St. James', Barrow-in-Furness, and St. Paul's, Grange-over-Sands; choirmaster, Furness Association of Church Choirs. Conductor of choral societies at Barrow, Ulverston and Grange. His setting of Psalm 45 (University exercise for Mus. Doc.), was performed with success, April 9th, 1883. He has published some church music, songs, etc.

Brown, H., musician and author of present time, resident in Brixton, London. Issued "Historical sketch of music from the most ancient to modern times," London [1886]; also "Sonnets by Shakspeare solved."

Brown, J. C., musician of Clerkenwell, London. Compiled "Collection of original sacred music, containing 104 psalm and hymn tunes, and four pieces harmonized for four voices, and arranged for the organ," London, 1818.

Brown, James D., tenor singer, lecturer and teacher, was born at Aberdeen in 1834. He studied music and singing under James Davie, Samuel Barr, Thomas Macfarlane, H. Kuchler, and Alex. W. Smith, and was conductor of psalmody in Free St. David's Church, Edinburgh, from 1865 till 1877. Since 1866, he has given many concerts and lectures on the ballad music of Scotland, and has done much to aid the movement in favour of thorough voice cultivation, and to foster a taste for the old and genuine ballad music of Scotland. He has composed a few songs to words by Burns, etc. His son, JAMES DUFF BROWN, was born at Edinburgh, November 6th, 1862. He was educated at the Church of Scotland Normal School, and afterwards entered the employment of publishing firms in Edinburgh and Glasgow. From 1878 till 1888 he was an assistant-librarian in the Mitchell Library, Glasgow, and in September, 1888, he was appointed librarian of Clerkenwell Public Library, London, a position he now holds. Author of "Biographical diction-

ary of musicians, with a bibliography of English writings on music," Paisley, 1886. "Handbook of library appliances: the technical equipment of libraries," London, 1892. "Guide to the formation of a music library," London, 1893. Numerous papers on library economy, and on topics connected with bibliography and literature.

Brown John, clergyman and writer, born at Rothbury, Northumberland, 1715. Educated at Cambridge. Vicar of Great Horkesley, Essex, 1754. Vicar of St. Nicholas', Newcastle, 1758. Committed suicide while insane, September 23rd, 1766.

WORKS.—Honour, a poem; Essay on satire; Sermons; Essays on Shaftesbury's Characteristics, 1751; Dissertation on the rise, union, and power, the progressions, separations, and corruptions of poetry and music, to which is prefixed The Cure of Saul, a sacred ode, London, 1763; Remarks on some observations on Dr. Brown's dissertation on poetry and musick, London, 1764; An estimate of the manners and principles of the times, 1757.

An Italian edition of the Dissertation was published in 1772.

Brown, John, artist and writer, born at Edinburgh, 1752. Resided in Italy from 1771 till 1781. He died in Scotland, 1781. Author of "Letters upon the Poetry and Music of the Italian Opera," Edinburgh, 1789.

Brown, Robert, of Rockhaven, writer and theorist, was born at Glasgow, 1789-90, and died at Rockhaven, near Fairlie, Ayrshire, 25th August, 1873. Author of The Elements of Musical Science, London, 1860. An Introduction to Musical Arithmetic, with its application to Temperament, London, 1865. Rudiments of Harmony and Counterpoint on a New Method . . . London, 1863. Also a work on Scottish Highland Psalm Tunes.

In the first work Brown advocates the adoption of a uniform clef, and illustrates this in the course of his book. He also suggests certain modifications in the method of expressing harmonical combinations, etc.

Brown, Thomas, musician of 18th century. Author of "The Compleat Musick Master, being plain, easie and familiar rules for singing and playing" . . London [1704].

Another THOMAS BROWN, styled "junior," was organist of St. Margaret Pattens and St. Gabriel, Fenchurch Street, London, in latter part of the 18th century. He published a "Collection of Songs, and a Cantata for the harpsichord or pianoforte," London, 1774.

Brown, Thomas, musician, compiled "Psalms and hymns, as sung at the Sunday evening lectures in the galilee of Durham Cathedral, arranged for four voices, with an accompaniment for the organ or pianoforte," Durham, 1842.

Brown, William, musician, issued a col-

E

BROWN.

lection of Psalm Tunes, in four parts," Glasgow, 1700.

Brown, William, musician, of 18th century, was a teacher in Glasgow, and precentor in the Wynd Church (St. George's Parish Church), which he resigned in 1807. He compiled "The Precentor, or an easy introduction to Church Music, with a choice collection of Psalm Tunes" . . . 6th ed., 1799, originally issued in 1776, by John McLachlan.

Brown-Borthwick, Rev. Robert, clergyman and amateur musician; was born at Aberdeen, May 18th, 1840. Son of William Brown, Esq., of H.M. Civil Service, Aberdeen, who was an amateur musician, well-known at the concerts of that city. Ordained deacon in 1865. Ordained priest, 1866. Curate of Sudely Manor, Gloucestershire, and Chaplain to the Winchcomb Union. Curate of Evesham, Worcestershire, and assistant-minister of Quebec Chapel, London. Mr. Brown-Borthwick assumed additional surname of Borthwick on his marriage in 1868 to Grace (D. 1884), only surviving daughter of the late, and sister of the present, John Borthwick, Esq., of Borthwick Castle, and Crookston, Midlothian. Incumbent of Holy Trinity, Grange-in-Borrowdale, Cumberland, 1869-72. Vicar of All Saints, Scarborough, 1872. Chaplain for a few years to the Bishop of Aberdeen. Vicar of St. John's, Clapham. Died March 17th, 1894. WORKS.—Supplemental hymn and tune book (Novello), containing contributions by Goss, Sullivan, Stainer, E. J. Hopkins, and J. B. Calkin, four editions. Twelve Kyries. Kyries and Sanctuses, edited. Blessed are the dead, anthem. Words of "Church hymns" (with the Bishop of Bedford (Dr. W. How), Rev. J. Ellerton, Rev. B. Compton), the hymn book issued by the S.P.C.K. Select hymns for church and home, Edin., 1871. The History of the Princes de Condé, by H.R.H. le duc d'Aumale, translated, London, 8vo, 2 vols. Life and works of Stephen Heller, by H. Barbedette, translated, London. Hymns, contributed to various collections. Sermons on various subjects, as "Art in worship," "The praise of God," etc., all published.

Browne, James A., violinist, conductor, and writer on music; born at Woolwich, May 9th, 1838. Joined the Royal Artillery Band in 1848, as a singing-boy, and received instruction on the flute and violin; was appointed solo flutist in the band in 1864, and from that date was similarly engaged in London theatres, concerts, and the Handel and other festivals. Appointed band-master, Royal Horse Artillery, in 1870, retiring on a pension in 1878, when he accepted the post of band-master to the South Metropolitan Schools, Sutton. Musical Director, Royal Court Theatre, London, 1880-1 ; Conductor of the Orchestral Festival Services, St. Agnes,

BROWNSMITH.

Kennington Park, 1881-94; teacher of the violin. Started the *Surrey Musical Journal* (which existed only for six months), in 1885 ; became sub-editor *British Musician*, 1893 ; sole editor, 1895 ; proprietor and editor, 1896. His published works include ; Military band arrangements ; a part-song, "The dragoons"; songs ; March, "Cleopatra," an oboe solo. In MS. he has a drawing-room oratorio ; an opera ; a string quartet, and some dramatic music. Author of The north-west passage [1860] ; History of the Royal Artillery [1865] ; and papers on bands and music in the *Service Advertiser* [1884] ; and the *Surrey Musical Journal*, etc., etc.

Browne, Lennox, surgeon and writer on the voice, born at London, in 1841. He was the son of a distinguished surgeon. Educated at Edinburgh and London. F.R.C.S., Edin., 1873 ; M.R.C.S., Eng., 1863. Member of numerous medical societies, and surgeon to various musical societies. Author of "The throat and its diseases," London, 1878, 4th ed., 1893. "Voice, song, and speech, a complete manual for singers and speakers," London (Low), 1883; 15th ed. 1892. Written in conjunction with E. Behnke. "The child's voice ; its treatment with regard to after development," London, 1885 (with Behnke). "Voice, use, and stimulants," 1885. "Mechanism of hearing," 1889, etc. "Science and singing," 1884.

Browne, Richard, medical writer, who was an apothecary at Oakham. Author of "Medicina musica; or a mechanical essay on the effects of singing, musick, and dancing, on human bodies; to which is annexed a new essay on the nature and cure of the spleen and vapours," London, 1729.

Browne, Thomas (Tom), violinist, born at Newcastle in 1812 ? Studied under Eliason, and theory with T. Severn, and French Flowers. In the band of Her Majesty's Theatre ; Sacred Harmonic Society, etc. Popular as a teacher, and composer of dance music, his "Helena Waltz" having had a great circulation. Of his songs, "On the swelling deep," deserves mention. Died in London, August 10, 1884.

Brownsmith, John Leman, organist, was born at Westminster, in 1809. Chorister at Westminster Abbey under Greatorex, with whom he studied the organ. Organist of St. John's Church, Waterloo Road, London, 1829, an appointment he was compelled to resign when made Lay-vicar of Westminster Abbey, in 1838, because the vestry refused to allow him to have a deputy when on duty at the Abbey. Organist to Sacred Harmonic Society, 1848 ; organist at Handel Festivals of 1857, 1859, 1862, and 1865 ; organist of St. Gabriel, Pimlico. He died at London, Sept. 14, 1866.

Bruce, John, violinist and composer, was a native of Braemar, and according to Burns, who knew him well, " a red-wud (*i.e.*, stark-mad) Highlander." He settled in Dumfries after the rebellion of 1745, in which he took part, and died there December 31. 1785. He is generally regarded as the composer of the air usually sung to " Whistle o'er the lave o't."

Bruce, John Collingwood, M.A., LL.D., D.C.L., F.S.A., historian of the Roman Wall, and author of numerous books on the Roman occupation of Britain, and mediæval life upon Tyne-side. He was a great authority on the subject of the Northumbrian Pipes, and read a paper relating to them at the Conference of Musicians, held at Newcastle-on-Tyne, in January, 1892. He died in that town, April 5, 1892, aged 86.

Bruce, Thomas, musician, of 18th century, was a schoolmaster in the Cowgate of Edinburgh. Author of " The Common tunes, or Scotland's Church Musick made plain, with a description of the antiquity, use, authors and inventors of Musick." Edinburgh, 1726; 2nd ed. n.d.

Bryan, Cornelius, organist and composer, born at Bristol, about 1775. He held the appointments of organist of St. Mark's, and St. Mary, Redcliffe, Bristol. Died at Bristol, March 18, 1840, from the effects of a fall.

WORKS.—Lundy, operetta, 1840. Collection of the most esteemed Psalm Tunes, ancient and modern . . . interspersed with a few original compositions, 1830. Effusions for the organ, containing eight voluntaries, one hundred interludes and three psalms. n.d.

Bryce, Rev. ? divine and writer who lived in Belfast. Author of " A Rational Introduction to Music, being an attempt to simplify the first principles of the science," London, 1845.

Bryne, Albert (or Albertus), composer and organist, who flourished in the 17th century, and was born about 1621, and died in 1669. He was a pupil of John Tomkins, whom he succeeded as organist of St. Paul's Cathedral in 1638. Afterwards, he became organist of Westminster Abbey. His compositions appear in Boyce, Clifford, and some are in MS. in the British Museum. They consist of services, anthems, and organ music. His name is variously spelt, Brian, Bryan, etc.

Bryson, John, musician, who flourished during latter part of 18th century. He was manager to Robert Bremner at the Harp and Hautboy, Edinburgh, from 1769, and succeeded him in the business in 1789, carrying it on till 1818. Published " A Curious selection of favourite Scots tunes, with variations; to which are added upwards of fifty favourite Irish airs for a German flute or violin; with a bass for the harpsichord or violincello," Edin. [1791].

Buchanan, Thomas, surgeon and author. Author of "Physiological Illustrations of the organ of hearing, more particularly of the secretion of cerumen and its effects in rendering auditory perceptions accurate and acute." London, 1828.

Buck, Percy Carter, organist, born at West Ham, Essex, 1871. Educated at Merchant Taylors School. Chorister at West Ham Parish Church. Pupil of Dr. C. J. Frost, and F. Davenport, at Guildhall School of Music; and later, winner of an organ scholarship, R.C.M., studying under Dr. Hubert Parry, C. H. Lloyd, and (Sir) Walter Parratt. Prize-winner for composition, Stratford Musical Festivals, 1887-8. F.R.C.O., A.R.C.M., Mus. B., Oxford, 1892, and qualified by Examination for Mus. D., 1893. Organist at Surbiton; Worcester College, Oxford; Music-master, Rugby School; and on the death of Mr. C. W. Lavington (Oct. 1895), appointed organist and choirmaster of Wells Cathedral. He has published an organ sonata in E flat, and some trios for female voices, and has written songs, and is joint author with Rev. Dr. Mee, and F. C. Woods,) of " Ten years of University music in Oxford" (Oxford : Bowden, 1894).

Buck, Zechariah, organist and composer, born at Norwich, Sept. 9, 1798. He was a chorister in Norwich Cathedral, under Garland and Beckwith. Organist and choirmaster of Norwich Cathedral, from 1828 to 1877. Mus. Doc., Cantuar, 1853. He acquired great fame as a trainer of boys' voices. Died Newport, Essex, August 5, 1879.

WORKS.—Anthems : Come hither, angel tongues invite (1849) ; I heard a voice from heaven; O Lord, give Thy holy spirit. Eight chants in Farr's collection.

Buckenham, J——, of Bramfield, musician of 18th century, issued " Psalm-singer's Devout Exercises, containing (1) new and compleat introduction to the grounds of Musick ; (2) Select collection of Church Musick ; (3) Two chanting tunes ; (4) Sixteen anthems and alphabetical glossary."

Buckland, Henry, tenor vocalist, was a vicar-choral at St. Paul's Cathedral, and master of the choristers. He conducted the annual festivals of the Charity children, at St. Paul's, 1863-7 ; also the special evening services held there. A very good concert singer. He died in London, August 13, 1867, at the age of 41.

Buckley, Mrs., born OLIVIA DUSSEK, pianist and writer, born in London in 1799. Daughter of J. L. Dussek, was taught by her mother, and appeared in public at the age of eight. Organist of Kensington Parish Church, from 1840. Died in London, in 1847. Author of " Musical Truths," London, 1843 ; two books of " Fairy songs and ballads for the

BUCKNALL.

young," 1846; pf. pieces; arrangement of "Rule Britannia," for pf. and harp, etc.

Bucknall, Cedric, organist and composer. Studied privately, and graduated Mus. Bac., Oxford, 1878. Organist of All Saints, Clifton, and of the Victoria Rooms. Has published a communion service in B flat; composed, revised, and selected tunes for "Hymns for school worship" (Novello, 1893 ?); also composed part-songs, carols, etc.

Budd, George William, partner in the publishing firm of Calkin and Budd, was born in 1806. He was the founder of the Western Madrigal Society, and secretary of the Philharmonic Society, 1847-50. Edited, for the Musical Antiquarian Society, the second set of madrigals by John Wilbye; and was the composer of some glees, etc. He died in London, August 1st, 1850.

Buddicom, Rev. Robert Pedder, clergyman, and musician, born 1,770, died July, 1846. Incumbent of Everton, Liverpool. Published "One hundred psalm and hymn tunes, with chants," edited by C. H. Wilton, London, 1827. Re-published as "Devotional Harmony," consisting of psalms and hymns, Liverpool, 1833.

Buels, William W. C., violoncellist and author, was principal of the Kensington School of Music, London. He died in London, Dec. 6th, 1890. Author of a "New and improved catechism of the rudiments of music," London, 1880.

His father, JOHN BUELS, was also a musician, as are his brothers ED. F., baritone vocalist, and LOUIS, violinist, and his sister MARIAN, pianist.

Bull, John, composer and organist, was born in Somersetshire [1563]. He studied under William Blitheman, and became organist and master of the children of Hereford Cathedral, 1582. Gentleman of the Chapel Royal, January, 1585. Bac. Mus. Oxon., 1586. Doc. Mus. Oxon., 1592. Organist to Chapel Royal, 1591. Professor of Music at Gresham College, 1596. Travelled on the continent, 1601-5. Married to Elizabeth Walter, 1607. Musician to Prince Henry, 1611. Quitted England without leave from his employer, 1613. Organist at Notre Dame Cathedral, Antwerp [1617]. He was organist in service of the Archduke of Austria. He died at Hamburg, Lübeck, or Antwerp, March 13th, 1628.

The productions of this composer are mentioned by nearly every writer as having been voluminous, but comparatively few of them appear to have been printed. Specimens of his style can be seen in Barnard's Collection, Boyce, Leighton's "Teares," the Fitzwilliam music, "Parthenia," Queen Elizabeth's Virginal Book, etc. A motet for five voices is preserved in Burney's Musical Extracts,

BUNCE.

British Museum. E. Pauer gives specimens of his virginal music in "Old English Composers." The extraordinary celebrity which this musician obtained during his lifetime must have been grounded on some uncommon degree of merit, either in his compositions or performance. A list of his works is contained in Ward's "Lives of the Gresham Professors," and in addition he wrote a great number of pieces of sacred vocal music. "The strength of this composer's talents lay in the production and execution of pieces fully harmonized, and comprising fugues, double-fugues, and the various species of canon; and fortunately, for himself, he lived in an age that listened with pleasure to music of that description. . . . . He surmounted old and invented new difficulties; and disdaining to be embarassed, aimed, in the province of polyphonic fabrication, at a species of omnipotence."—*Busby*.

The question as to the composition of the English national anthem remains undecided in a general way, though Carey appears to have been strongly accredited with the composition. See writings of Chappell, Cummings, Clark, etc. In connection with Gresham College, Dr. Bull delivered "The Oration of Maister John Bull, Doctor of Musicke, and one of the Gentlemen of hir Majesty's Royal Chappell, as he pronounced the same, before divers worshipful persons, the Aldermen and Commoners of the citie of London, with a great multitude of other people, the 6th day of October, 1597, in the new erected Colledge of Sir Thomas Gresham, Knt. deceased: made in the commendation of the founder, and the excellent science of Musicke," London, este 1597.

Bull, T., musician, wrote "New and complete modern preceptor for the royal Kent bugle," London, 1835. "New instructions for the improved flageolet, etc.," London [1845].

Bumpus, John S., writer on music of the present time. Has written a number of valuable antiquarian papers on musical subjects, among which may be named "A short history of English Cathedral Music"; "St. Patrick's and Christ Church Cathedrals, Dublin"; and "The Organists and Composers of St. Paul's Cathedral." These were originally contributed to the *Musical Standard*, 1884-8.

Bunce, John Thackray, journalist, born at Farringdon, Berkshire, 1828. Removing to Birmingham in 1839, he was educated there; and devoting himself to journalism, became editor of the *Birmingham Daily Post.* Author of "the History of the Birmingham Corporation"; "History of St. Martin's Church. Birmingham"; and other works. He originated the Corporation School of Art, and has been identified with the Educational and Scientific work of the city. Is a J.P., and

BUNCH.

F.S.S. He claims notice here as author of "A History of the Birmingham General Hospital and the Musical Festivals, 1768-1873, Birmingham, Cornish, 1873.

Bunch, James, musician, editor of "Ceciliana: a collection of favourite catches, canons, rondos, and rounds, by eminent authors, ancient and modern, in score, with biographical notes." London, 1825.

Bunn, Alfred, operatic manager and librettist, was born at London, 1798. Stage manager at Drury Lane Theatre under Elliston, 1823; Manager and Lessee of Drury Lane Theatre from 1834. He died at Boulogne Dec. 20, 1860. Bunn adapted a great number of pieces for the English stage, and produced the following among other operas;—Maid of Artois; Bohemian Girl; and Daughter of St. Mark (Balfe): Brides of Venice (Benedict); Maritana (Wallace), etc. He also wrote a work entitled "The Stage, both before and behind the curtain, from observations taken on the spot." 3 vols., London, 1840. Poems, London, 1816. For a severe skit on Bunn, see "A word with Bunn, after Burns's Address to the Deil." By J. R. Adam, the Cremorne Poet, London [1847].

Bunnett, Edward, organist and composer, born at Shipdham, Norfolk, June 26, 1834. Entered as a chorister at Norwich Cathedral, 1842; articled to Dr. Buck, 1849, and from 1855 to 1877 was his assistant organist and partner. Graduated Mus. Bac., 1857; Mus. Doc., 1869, Cambridge; F.C.O., 1870. In January, 1849, sang in the trio "Lift thine eyes," with Jenny Lind and Miss Dolby, at a concert given in Norwich. From 1871 to 1892 he was conductor of the Norwich Musical Union; has been organist of the Norwich Musical Festivals since 1872; of St. Peter's, Mancroft, from 1877; and Borough Organist since 1880, his recitals always attracting large audiences. From 1890 he has had charge of the pier concerts at Lowestoft. He celebrated his musical jubilee, April 18, 1896, when he was presented by the Mayor (John Moore, Esq.) with an address and handsome testimonial from his fellow citizens. He has occasionally lectured on Oratorio and other subjects.

WORKS.—Song of Praise (Degree Exercise, 1869); Ps. 130, *De Profundis* (Norwich, 1880); Unison Service in F; Office for the Holy Communion, in E; Services, &c. *Anthems* —Blessed be Thou; If we believe that Jesus died; If ye love me; and others. Twenty-four original tunes to favourite Hymns; Ten Christmas Carols. *Cantatas*—Rhineland, for soprano solo, chorus, and orchestra (composed for Mlle. Tietjens, but sung by Florence Lancia, and produced, Norwich Festival, 1872; Lora (W. W. Turnbull. Produced by Norwich Musical Union, June 1, 1876). Comedietta,

BURGH.

Incognita (Mrs. Edward Adams, Lowestoft, August, 1892). *Part-songs*—The Rhine Maiden (Norwich Festival, 1884); Victoria, soprano solo and chorus (1887), and others. Various Songs. Andante and rondo, pf. and orchestra; Trio, pf. and strings; Sonata, pf. and violin (MS. 1873); Duet, pf. and clarinet; Pieces for pf., etc. Eight organ pieces; Six original compositions for organ (1884); Twelve short and easy pieces for organ; Largo in E flat, for organ; Ave Maria, etc.

Bunning, Herbert, composer of the present time. Studied in France and Italy, chiefly in Milan, under Vincenzo Ferroni. Settled in London about the close of 1891. Of his compositions, a Scena, for baritone, "Ludovico il Moro," was given at the Crystal Palace Concerts, February 27, 1892, the late Eugène Oudin being the singer; and a "Village Suite," in four movements, for orchestra, was produced at the same, April 4, 1896. He has composed an opera, "The Last days of Pompeii;" Two symphonic poems, and a Rhapsody, for orchestra; a string quartet, and some songs.

Bunting, Edward, musician and editor, was born at Armagh, in February, 1773. He was articled assistant to Weir, at a church in Belfast, in 1784. Organist of St. Stephen's chapel, Belfast. Married to Miss Chapman, 1819. He died at Dublin, December 21, 1843.

WORKS.—A General Collection of the Ancient Irish Music; containing a variety of admired airs never before published, and also the compositions of Conolan and Carolan, Lond., 1796. A General Collection of the Ancient Music of Ireland, arranged for the Pianoforte; some of the most admired Melodies are adapted for the Voice, to poetry chiefly translated from the original Irish songs by Thomas Campbell, Esq., and other eminent poets; to which is prefaced an Historical and Critical Dissertation on the Egyptian, British, and Irish Harp, London, 1809. The Ancient Music of Ireland, arranged for the Pianoforte; to which is prefixed a Dissertation on the Irish Harps and Harpers, including an account of the Old Melodies of Ireland. Dublin, 1840. These collections of Irish music are among the best which have been made, and Bunting is regarded as a fairly accurate compiler.

Burgess, Alexander, the "Fife Paganini," violinist and poet, born in Fife, in 1807; drowned at Whin Quarry, Starr, Fife, August 2, 1886. He will be best remembered in Scotland, as a contributor of humorous phonetically spelt verses to the *People's Journal*, under the signature of "Poute." Some of these poems were collected as "Nettercaps, being poutery, prose, and verse," 1875. His fame as a violinist was only local.

Burgh, A . . , writer, who graduated

BURGHERSH.

M.A. at one of the Universities. He compiled "Anecdotes of Music, historical and biographical, in a series of letters from a gentleman to his daughter," London, 1814, 3 vols.

Burghersh, Lord, see WESTMORELAND, Earl of.

Burgon, William Henry, bass vocalist, born at Croydon, in 1858. Studied under Manuel Garcia, at the London Academy of Music. Made his *début* in oratorio, 1881, singing in Bach's Mass in B minor (Bach Choir), June 1st, and in Judas Maccabæus (Sacred Harmonic Society), in November. Has since sung for the principal choral societies in London, Liverpool, Glasgow, and elsewhere. Sang in opera at Covent Garden, 1884, and afterwards joined the Carl Rosa company. He was the original Ostap in Thomas's "Nadeshda" (produced at Drury Lane, April 16th, 1885), and Count des Grieux, in Massenet's "Manon," at its first performance at Drury Lane, May 7th, 1885. Of his later assumptions are Cedric, in "Ivanhoe," 1891, and Louis XII. in Messager's "La Basoche."

Burgoyne, Montagu, see HARRIS (J. Macdonald).

Burnet, Alfred, musician. Published "Instructions for the Spanish guitar, founded on the systems of Carulli, Giuliani, etc." London, 1829.

Burnet, George, amateur musician and herald, who held the office of Lyon king of arms in Edinburgh. He died at Edinburgh, January 24th, 1890. He was an authority on Scottish heraldry, and edited several antiquarian works. For many years he acted as musical critic to the Edinburgh newspapers, and was a very enthusiastic amateur musician.

Burnett, Alfred, violinist. Educated at R.A.M., where he is now professor of the violin, and viola, also hon. R.A.M. Has appeared in chamber concerts, London ; was principal violin of the Reading Philharmonic Society ; and, since 1885, has been principal violin in the Birmingham Festival orchestra. Was *ad interim* conductor of R.A.M. concerts, 1888. In 1893, succeeded Mr. J. T. Carrodus as principal violin at the Worcester Festival ; and since the death of that artist, has filled the same post at the other meetings of the Three Choirs. He has written some pieces for four violins, for the use of learners.

Burnett, Henry, tenor vocalist. Studied under Sir George Smart, upon whose recommendation he was elected a pupil of the R.A.M. There he met Fanny Dickens (eldest sister of the great novelist), whom he married. He appeared on the stage with success, and settled for some years in Manchester, singing at the Gentlemen's Concerts in 1842; at the Liverpool Philharmonic Concerts, 1844, and in many

BURNEY.

provincial towns. His wife died in 1848, and soon afterwards a delicate little boy, who was the original of Paul Dombey. Burnett appears to have retired soon afterwards. He died at his residence, Titchfield, Hampshire, in February, 1893, in his 82nd year. He composed a number of songs, published for the most part under an assumed name. His son, WALTER BURNETT, a professor of music, died at Hatcham, London, July 27th, 1887, aged 37.

Burnett, Nathan J., see SPORLE (Nathan J.)

Burney, Charles, author, organist, and composer, was born at Shrewsbury, April 7th, 1726. He was the son of James and Anne Macburney, and was baptized as such on May 5th, 1726. He never used the prefix Mac. Educated at the Free School, Shrewsbury, and at Chester Public School. He studied music under Baker, organist of Chester Cathedral, and in London under Dr. Arne, 1744-47. Organist of St. Dionis Back-Church, Fenchurch Street, London, 1749. Harpsichord player at the subscription concerts, King's Arms, Cornhill. Organist at Lynn-Regis, Norfolk, 1751-60. Bac. and Doc. of Music, Oxford, 1769. He travelled in Italy, 1770, and returned to London, 1771. He also travelled in Germany, the Netherlands, etc., during 1772. Elected Fellow of Royal Society, 1773. Organist of Chelsea College, 1783. In 1806 he received a pension of £300 from Fox, and in 1810 he was made member of the Institute of France. He died at Chelsea, April 12th, 1814.

WORKS.—Translation of Signor Tartini's Letter to Signor Lombardini, published as an important lesson to performers on the violin, London, 1771. The Present state of music in France and Italy, or the journal of a tour through those countries, undertaken to collect materials for a general history of music, London, 1771. The Present state of music in Germany, the Netherlands, and United Provinces, or the journal of a tour through those countries, undertaken to collect materials for a general history of music, London, 1773. 2 vols. A General History of music, from the earliest ages to the present period, to which is prefixed a dissertation on the music of the ancients, London, four vols., 1776-1789. An account of the musical performances in Westminster Abbey and the Pantheon, May 26th, 27th, 29th, and June the 3rd and 5th, 1784, in commemoration of Handel, London, 1785; Dublin edition, 1785. A paper on Crotch, the infant musician, presented to the Royal Society, Transactions, 1779. Striking views of Lamia, the celebrated flute-player, Massachusset's Magazine, 1786. Memoirs of the life and writings of the Abbate Metastasio, in which are incorporated trans-

BURNS.

lations of his principal letters, London, 3 vols., 1796. A plan for a music school, London, 1774. An essay towards the history of comets, London, 1769. Articles on music in Ree's Encyclopædia. Sonata for two violins and a bass, 1765. Six concert pieces, with an introduction for the diapasons and fugue proper for young organists and practitioners on the harpsichord. Twelve canzonets from Metastasio. Six duets for the German flute. Six concertos for the violin, in eight parts. Two sonatas for pf., violin, and 'cello. Six harpsichord lessons. Two sonatas for harp or pf., with accomp. for violin or 'cello. Anthems, glees, instrumental music, etc.

Burney is best known to musicians of the present day by his "History of music;" a work of much learning and ability. It is written in a pleasant style, but its historical value is somewhat destroyed by a vexatious absence of dates. He has given much space to the glorification of forgotten Italian composers, and comparatively little to the more interesting musicians of other nationalities. The "History" is less valuable than that of Hawkins, though much superior to it from a literary point of view. His most successful musical effort was an adaptation of Rousseau's "Devin du Village," produced under the title of "The cunning man." His daughter Frances was the Madame D'Arblay of English literary renown. It may further be added that Burney was one of the most esteemed organists of his time. His brother JAMES (born 1709 ; died 1789), was organist at Shrewsbury for many years.

Burns, Daniel Joseph, Irish organist and writer. Organist of St. Patrick's Church, and of St. Malachy's College, Belfast. Conductor of the Philo-Celtic Society. Author of "Practical Notes upon Harmony and Counterpoint for Junior Pupils." London [1883]. "Exercises in Figured Bass." London, n.d.

Burns, Georgina (Mrs. LESLIE CROTTY), soprano vocalist, born in London, 1860. Granddaughter of Rev. Jabez Burns. Displayed musical talent at an early age, and first appeared at the Westminster Aquarium Promenade Concerts. She made her first appearance in the Carl Rosa Opera Company at the Adelphi Theatre, February 11, 1878, when she took the part of Ann Page in " The Merry Wives of Windsor." During the time she remained with the Company she sang with success in many operas, creating the part of Filina—in English—in " Mignon," and the titular part of Goring Thomas's " Esmeralda," was written expressly for her. In 1882, she married Leslie Crotty (q.v.), the popular baritone, and when the pair quitted the Carl Rosa Company, they started a light Opera Company, and revived with much success, Rossini's " La Cenerentola," in English,

BURTON.

with which they undertook tours throughout the United Kingdom.

Burns, John, Scottish violinist and composer, of early part of 19th century, published " Strathspeys, reels, jigs, etc., for the pf., v olin and violoncello." Edinburgh, n.d.

Burrowes, John Freckleton, writer and composer, was born in London, April 23, 1787. He studied under W. Horsley, and was a Member of the Philharmonic Society. Organist of St. James's Church, Piccadilly, London. He died at London, March 31, 1852.

WORKS.—Op. 1. Six English Ballads, for voice and pf. ; Sonatas for pf. and flute, and for pf. and 'cello ; Overture for full orch., produced by Philharmonic Society ; Six Divertissements for pf. ; Three Sonatas for pf. and violin ; Sonata for pf., on Scotch airs, op. 9 ; Select airs from Mozart's operas, for pf. and flute, 18 numbers ; Mozart's overtures, arranged for pf., violin, flute, and 'cello ; Duets, for harp and pf. and other instruments. Collection of Psalm Tunes, with figured bass, n.d. Burrowes' Pianoforte Primer, containing the rudiments of Music, in question and answer, calculated either for private tuition or teaching in classes : London, 1822. The Thoroughbass Primer : London, 1818. Companion to the Thorough-bass Primer : London, 1835. Songs, part-songs, etc.

Bursfall, Frederick Hampton, organist, born in Liverpool, January 29, 1851. Studied under Dr. Röhner, and in 1870 was appointed organist of Childwall Parish Church. In 1876, he obtained the post of organist at Wallasey Church. When the new Diocese of Liverpool was formed, in 1880, he was elected organist and director of the choir at the Cathedral Church. In 1883, he formed a large special choir for oratorio services, and in 1889 undertook the parochial Sunday services, resigning his post at Wallasey. He is a clever performer, and has given organ recitals at St. George's Hall. He married, in 1875, Mintie, daughter of the late Samuel Martin, shipowner, of Liverpool. His wife is an excellent musician. Of his compositions the principal is a Festival Te Deum ; he has also written anthems, motets, songs, and pf. pieces, etc.

Burton, Avery, English composer, who flourished during the 16th century. His compositions are preserved in MS. in the Music School of Oxford.

Burton, John, English composer and harpsichord player, born in Yorkshire, in 1730. He studied under Keeble, and died in 1785.

WORKS.—Ten sonatas for the harpsichord, organ, or pianoforte ; Six trios for the harpsichord and violins. Six solos for the harpsichord. Songs, glees, organ music, etc.

Burton, Robert Senior, organist, pianist, and conductor, born at Dewsbury, Yorkshire,

BURTON.

in 1820. Studied under Cipriani Potter, and commenced his career in Leeds, in 1840, succeeding Dr. S. S. Wesley as organist of Leeds Parish Church in 1849. Was chorus-master of the first Musical Festival, Leeds, 1858, and conducted choral societies at different periods in York, Barnsley, Leeds, Wakefield, Bradford, and Halifax. He eventually settled at Harrogate, where he founded a Choral Society, 1880; he was also musical director at the Spa; and, up to his death, organist of St. Peter's Church. He was a fine performer on the organ, an admirable accompanist, and had a high reputation as a choir trainer and teacher of singing. He died at Harrogate, August 2, 1892.

Burton, T. Arthur, organist and choirmaster of St. Augustine's Church, Bournemouth, and conductor of a musical society in that town, is the composer of an oratorio, "Jonah," produced at Bournemouth, January 28, 1881. He has written a concert march for organ, etc.

Busby, Thomas, composer and author, was born at Westminster, in December, 1755. Articled to Battishill, 1769-74. Successively Organist of S. Mary's, Newington, Surrey, and at S. Mary, Woolnoth, Lombard Street, 1798. Mus. Doc. Cantab., 1800. LL.D., Cambridge. He died at Islington, London, May 28, 1838.

WORKS.—The Prophecy, oratorio, March, 1799; Ode— British Genius, from Grey; Ode to St. Cecilia's Day, Pope; Comala, a Dramatic Romance from Ossian, 1800; Thanksgiving Ode (Degree exercise), 1800; Music to Joanna, drama by R. Cumberland, 1800; Music to M. G. Lewis's Rugantino, 1805; The Divine Harmonist, a collection of Anthems, etc., 1788; Melodia Britannica, do., 1790 (unfinished). Sonatas for the pf. ' Anthem for the Funeral of Battishill. Miscellaneous anthems, glees, songs; Music to Holcroft's Tale of Mystery, 1802; Music to Porter's Fair Fugitives. Dictionary of Music, with Introduction to the First Principles of that Science, London, 8vo., 1786. A Grammar of Music: to which are prefixed Observations explanatory of the Properties and Powers of Music as a Science, and of the general scope and object of the work, London, 1818. A General history of Music, from the earliest times to the present; comprising the Lives of Eminent Composers and Musical Writers, London, 2 vols., 1819 (Whittaker). Concert Room and Orchestra, Anecdotes of Music and Musicians, Ancient and Modern, 3 vols., London, 1825. Musical Manual, or Technical Directory, with Descriptions of various Voices and Instruments, London, 1828.

Bussell, Rev. Frederick William, composer, son of the Rev. F. Bussell, vicar of Great Marlow, born at Cadmore End, Oxford-

BUTLER.

shire, April 23, 1862, of a Devonshire family. Educated at Charter House, 1876-81; Demy of Magdalen College, Oxford, 1880; Craven Scholar, and B.A., 1885 (First Class Classics, Lit. Hum., Theology); M.A., 1887; B.D., 1892: Mus. B., 1892. Musical training private. Fellow, tutor, chaplain, junior dean, Brazenose College, Oxford; Select Preacher to the University, Oxford, 1896; and Morley Lecturer at St. Margaret's, Westminster.

WORKS.—Magnificat (Latin), for five voices, small orchestra, and organ; Mass in G minor, voices, orchestra, and organ (performed at Italian Church, Hatton Garden, Sept. 1892). Incidental music to "The Merchant of Venice," composed for Oxford University Dramatic Society, and produced at the New Theatre, February, 1895. Collaborator in preparation of "Songs of the West" (Methuen), and "English Minstrelsie" (Edinburgh, Jack). Has published the "School of Plato" (Methuen, 1895), and other works.

Buswell, John, composer of the 18th century, who was connected with the Chapel Royal. He graduated Mus. Bac., Cambridge, in 1757, and Mus. Doc., Oxford, in 1759. Composer of songs and other vocal music.

Butler, Charles, musician and author, born at Wycombe, Bucks., in 1559. M.A., Oxford. Master of the Free school at Basingstoke, Hants. Vicar at Wooton, St Lawrence, Hants. He died on March 29, 1647.

WORKS.—The Feminine Monarchie; or, the Historie of Bees . . . proving that in the Bees' song are the grounds of Musicke. Oxford, 1609; other editions. The Principles of Musick in singing and setting: with the twofold use thereof, ecclesiastical and civil. London, 1636. An English Grammar, and other works. The first work is a curious production; the second a learned treatise on theory and on the abuses in sacred and secular music. His works were printed partly in characters taken from the Anglo-Saxon alphabet, partly in others of his own invention, which are described in his Grammar.

Butler, Charles, English musician, and author, of Lincoln's Inn, London, wrote "Reminisences, with a letter to a lady, on ancient and modern music." 1824, 4th ed.

Butler, Thomas Hamly, composer and pianist, was born at London, 1762. He studied under Dr. Nares at the Chapel Royal, and under Piccini in Italy. Composer to Drury Lane Theatre, under Sheridan. Teacher and pianist in Edinburgh. He died at Edinburgh, 1823.

WORKS.—The Widow of Delphi (R. Cumberland), musical drama, 1780. Rondos on the following Scotch airs:—Duncan [Gray, Flowers of Edinburgh, I'll gang nae mair to yon toun, Lewie Gordon, Roy's Wife, There's cauld kail in Aberdeen, etc. (Clementi). A

BUTT.

select collection of original Scottish airs, arranged for one and two voices, with introductory and concluding symphonies for the flute, violin, and pf., Edinburgh [1790]. Sonatas for the pf. (various). Songs, part-songs, single pieces for pf., etc.

Butt, Clara, contralto vocalist, born at Southwick, near Brighton. Studied under D. W. Rootham, Bristol, for some years, and sang at Miss Lock's concert, December, 1889, with success. Entering the R.C.M., she distinguished herself at the College concerts, and particularly in the performances of opera. She made her *début* at the Albert Hall, as Ursula in Sullivan's "Golden Legend," Dec. 7, 1892, and sang there in oratorio (Israel in Egypt) the next year. Her Festival *début* took place at Hanley, October 21, 1893, and she sang at the Bristol Festival, October 25, of the same year. She appeared at the Handel Festival of 1894, and has sung at the principal London and provincial concerts.

Butterworth, Annie, contralto vocalist. Educated at R.A.M. Westmoreland scholar, 1871 ; Nilsson prize, 1878. A.R.A.M. She won the first prize for contralto singing at the National Music Meetings at the Crystal Palace, July, 1875, and sang at the Crystal Palace concerts twice in March, 1876, in Beethoven's choral symphony, etc. She soon gained a high position as a concert singer, but her career was brief. She died at the age of 33, at Hendon, December 9th, 1885.

Button, H. Elliot, alto vocalist, and composer ; born at Clevedon, Somerset, August 8th, 1861. His father was a private schoolmaster and organist, and the whole family were musical, being able to provide both a vocal and a string quartet. In theory Mr. Button is self taught. He is a pianist, organist, and violinist, besides being solo alto at Holy Trinity, Upper Chelsea. He was awarded the gold medal for an ode "The song of the sower," performed at the National Co-operative Festival at the Crystal Palace, August 15th, 1891. His compositions include "Ivry," a dramatic ballad for baritone solo, chorus, and orchestra (1892); anthems, chants, etc. ; part-songs ; songs for children ; organ pieces, etc. Edited the third series of the Bristol Tune Book, and other collections.

Butts, Thomas, English musician of the 18th century. Compiler of "Harmonia Sacra, or a choice collection of psalm and hymn tunes . . . in 2, 3, and 4 parts . . . made use of in the principal chapels and churches in London." London, n.d. [c. 1776 or 1780].

Byrd, or Birde, William, composer and organist, was born [at Lincoln] about 1538. Senior chorister at St. Paul's Cathedral, 1554. He studied under Tallis. Organist of Lincoln Cathedral, 1563-72. Gentleman of Chapel Royal, 1569. Organist of Chapel Royal (with

BYRNE.

Tallis), 1575. He died at London, July 4th, 1623.

WORKS.—Cantiones quae ab argumento sacræ vocantur quinque et sex partium, 1575. Psalmes, sonets, and songs of sadnes and pietie, made into musicke of five partes, London, 1588. Songs of sundrie natures, some of gravitie, and others of myrth, fit for all companies and voyces, lately made and composed into musicke of three, four, five, and six parts, London, 1589. Liber primus sacrarum cantionum quartum aliæ ad quinque, aliæ uno ad sex voces aedita sunt, London, 1589 ; reprinted by Musical Antiquarian Society, edited by W. Horsley. Liber secundus sacrarum cantionum quartum aliæ ad quinque, aliæ uno ad sex voces aedita sunt, London, 1591. Gradualia, ac cantiones sacræ liber primus, 1607. Gradualia, ac cantiones sacræ liber secundus, 1610. Psalmes, songs, and sonnets, some solemne, others joyfull, etc., 1611. Parthenia, or the maidenhead of the first musick that ever was printed for the virginals, composed by the three famous masters, William Byrd, Dr. John Bull, and Orlando Gibbons, Gentlemen of Her Majestie's Chappell, London, 1655. Service in D minor (Boyce) ; Three anthems (Boyce) ; Mass for five voices (Mus. Ant. Soc., Rimbault), 1841 ; Compositions contained in the royal virginal book ; Compositions contained in Lady Neville's musick book, 1591 ; Music in Leighton's "Teares ;" Non nobis dominae, in Hilton's Catches, 1652. Madrigals in various collections ; Two other masses ; anthems, etc.

Byrd was one of the greatest composers of the 16th century. He lived at a period when the musical glory of England was supreme. Among his contemporaries were such men as Tallis, Tye, Farrant, Dowland, Bull, Morley, Hooper, Gibbons, Wilbye, Lawes, Weelkes, and Parsons. Byrd's claims to recognition rest chiefly on his sacred music, which is both dignified and grand without undue elaboration. He was one of the first in England to make use of the madrigal as an expressive musical form, though it must be admitted that his treatment of works of this class is not generally so happy as that of some of his successors. He was an organist of much ability. His compositions for the virginals are somewhat dry and elaborated exercises in counterpoint. Byrd secured with Tallis, in 1575, by patent, the supreme right to publish music in England, and under this patent they published the collection of sacred music first named in the foregoing list of Byrd's compositions.

Byrn, Adelaide C., *see sub* BALY, WILLIAM.

Byrne, C. S., musician. Published a "Selection of Scottish melodies, with words by George Linley." London, 1827.

Byrne, Patrick, Irish harpist and composer. Was born at Farney, about the end of 18th century. He died at Dundalk, 1863.

Bywater, Thomas, tenor vocalist and composer. A native of Staffordshire. For many years he was very popular in Birmingham, Wolverhampton, and the midlands. He has sung at the Crystal Palace, and other places. He is also a clever organist, and was for some time organist of St. Mark's, Wolverhampton, but is now chiefly engaged as a concert agent. He is blind. Some songs of his have been published ; and in 1876 he issued a Collection of twenty-five hymn tunes, and twelve chants (Novello).

Caerwarden, John, composer and teacher of the violin, who flourished during the 17th century. He was a member of the private band of Charles I. Hawkins mentions him as having been a noted teacher but a harsh composer.

Cæsar, Julius, physician and composer, who lived in Rochester during part of the 17th and 18th centuries. He was an amateur composer only, but Hawkins speaks of two of his catches appearing in the " Pleasant Musical Companion," 1726, as being " inferior to none in that collection."

Calah, John, organist and composer, who was born in 1758. He was organist of Peterborough Cathedral at the end of the 18th century, and died on August 4, 1798. He wrote music for the Church service, hymns, ballads, and sonatas for the pf., etc.

Caldicott, Alfred James, composer and organist, born at Worcester, November 26, 1842 Of a musical family, he, with six brothers, went through a course of training in the choir of Worcester Cathedral. At the age of fourteen he was articled to William Done, the organist, whose assistant he became. He afterwards studied at Leipzig Conservatorium, under Moscheles, Hauptmann, E. F. Richter, and others, and in 1864 settled in Worcester. Graduated Mus. Bac., Cambridge, 1878. Organist, St. Stephen's Church, and to the Corporation of Worcester ; Conductor of the Musical and Instrumental Societies. In 1882 he removed to Torquay, and the following year settled in London, and was appointed Professor of harmony at the R.C.M. In 1885 he was appointed Musical Director at the Albert Palace, Battersea, composing a Dedication Ode for the opening, June 6. Toured in America as conductor of the Agnes Huntingdon Opera Company, 1890-91 ; was appointed Principal of the Educational Department, London College of Music, 1892 ; and Musical Director, Comedy Theatre, 1893.

WORKS.—Sacred Cantata, The Widow of Nain (Worcester Festival, 1881) ; Cantatas

for female voices—A Rhine Legend ; Queen of May. *Operettas*—Treasure Trove (1883) ; A Moss Rose Rent (1883) ; Old Knockles (1884) ; In Cupid's Court (1885) ; A united Pair (1886) ; The Bo'sun's Mate (1888) ; produced at the German Reed Entertainments. Operetta, John Smith (Prince of Wales' Theatre, 1889) ; The Girton Girl and the Milkmaid (1893), etc. Winter Days, prize serious glee (1879, Huddersfield) ; Humpty Dumpty, prize humorous glee (1878, Manchester Gentleman's Glee Society) ; Part-Songs, various. Story of the Priest Philemon (Marie Corelli), special accompaniment for recitation, St. James's Hall, May 2, 1896. A number of songs ; The Dickens' series, etc. Editor of " Morley's Part-song Journal."

Calkin, George, violoncellist and teacher of singing, born St. Pancras, London, August 10, 1829. Youngest son of James Calkin. Organist for twenty-five years at St. Mark's, Regent's Park. As conductor of a Choral Society, gave concerts at the Hampstead Vestry Hall. Professor at the London Academy of Music. For many years a violoncellist in the orchestra of the Philharmonic Society, Royal Italian Opera, and the Provincial Festivals, including that of Birmingham in 1846, when " Elijah " was produced. Is the composer of sixteen books of Soft Voluntaries for the organ ; arrangements of airs from " Elijah," two books ; and organ transcriptions from Mendelssohn, in eight books (Novello), all very popular with organists.

Calkin, James, pianist and composer, was born at London, in 1786. He studied under Thomas Lyon. Associate of the Philharmonic Society, 1823. Wrote Symphony for orchestra, pf. music, string quartets, etc. He died at London in 1862.

Calkin, John Baptiste, composer, pianist, and organist, born in London, March 16, 1827. Studied under his father, James Calkin. Organist, precentor, and choirmaster, St. Columba's College, Ireland, 1846-53 ; Woburn Chapel, London, 1853-7 ; Camden Road Chapel, 1863-8 ; St. Thomas' Church, Camden Town, 1870-84. F.C.O. Member of the Philharmonic Society ; Member of the Council, Trinity College, London ; Professor at Guildhall School of Music.

WORKS.—Morning and Evening Services in B flat, Op. 43. G, Op. 96, and D ; Te Deum in D ; Communion Service in C, Op. 134 ; Magnificat and Nunc Dimittis in F. *Anthems*—Behold, now praise ye the Lord ; I will always give thanks ; I will magnify Thee ; Thou visitest the Earth ; and many others. Seven Introits. *Glees and Part-songs*—Breathe soft, ye winds ; Come, fill my boys ; My Lady is so wondrous fair ; and others. *Songs*—Coming light ; Sleep on, my heart ; Oh, lovely night ; and others. Quintet and Quartet,

CALKIN.

strings; Trio, pf. and strings; Sonata, pf. and violoncello. Duet, pf. "Overture"; Youth and Age, six pieces, pf., Op. 100; Rondo grazioso, Op. 93; Les Arpeges, Op. 94; The Pixie's Revel, Op. 95; Les trois graces (Sonata); Studies; Concert Study in double-notes; Transcriptions, etc. *Organ*—Andante con moto, Op. 101; Andante varied; Harvest Thanksgiving March; Festal March, etc., etc.

Calkin, Joseph, violinist, born London, 1781. Studied under Thos. Lyon and Spagnoletti, and was violinist at Drury Lane Theatre from 1798 till 1808. He married the widow of Mr. Budd, bookseller, and carried on the business under the name of Calkin and Budd, booksellers to the King. In 1821 he was appointed violinist in the King's band. He also played violin in the Philharmonic orchestra. Died London, December 30, 1846. Calkin assisted at the capture of Hatfield, when he fired at George III.

His son, JAMES JOSEPH, born 1813, died London, 1868, was a violinist; and another son JOSEPH, known as TENNIELLI CALKIN, born 1816, was a tenor singer; studied under Lamperti at Milan, and appeared at the Philharmonic and other concerts. He retired after a few years, and became a successful vocal teacher, and was also composer of some songs. He died in London, June 6, 1874.

Callcott, John George, pianist and composer, born in London, July 9, 1821. Was organist of Eaton Episcopal Chapel, Eaton Square; St. Stephen's, Westminster, for over thirty years, resigning in 1881; and Parish Church, Teddington, to 1895. Accompanist to Henry Leslie's Choir, 1855-82, and was awarded a Medal for his services during the visit of the choir to Paris, 1878. He contributed to the pasticcio, "Harold Glynde (1881), and composed two cantatas—Hallowe'en, and The Golden Harvest. He also wrote part-songs, "Love wakes and weeps," and others, produced by Leslie's Choir. An excellent pianist; he was almost unrivalled as an accompanist; whilst as a teacher he was in great request. He died at Teddington, January 7, 1895.

His father, JOHN CALLCOTT, entered the band of the Coldstream Guards at an early age. He was one of those who had to beat to arms in Brussels on the eve of Waterloo. He was for some years third horn in the Opera orchestra under Spagnoletti, Costa, and others. He died at Richmond, Surrey, February 16, 1882.

Callcott, John Wall, composer and writer, was born at Kensington, London, November 20, 1766. He was largely self-taught in music, but he had lessons from Henry Whitney, organist of Kensington Parish Church. Deputy organist to Reinhold, of St. George the Martyr's, Bloomsbury, 1783-5.

CALLCOTT.

Member of orchestra of Academy of Ancient Music. Unsuccessful competitor for prize offered by the Catch Club, 1784 (his first trial). Gained three prizes (medals) out of the four offered by the Catch Club, 1785. Mus. Bac. Oxon., July, 1785. Gained two medals, Catch Club, 1786; and two prizes in 1787 (he sent in about 100 compositions). Founded, with others, the "Glee Club," 1787. Gained all the prizes offered by the Catch Club, 1789. Joint organist (with C. S. Evans) of St. Paul's, Covent Garden, 1789. He studied under Haydn in 1790. Organist of Asylum for Female Orphans, 1793-1802. Gained nine medals for his glees during 1790-93. Mus. Doc. Oxon., 1800. Lecturer at the Royal Institution in succession to Crotch, 1806. He died at London, May 15, 1821.

WORKS.—Select Collection of Catches, Canons, and Glees, 3 books (D'Almaine), n.d. (edited); Five Glees for 2 Trebles and Bass in Score; Five Glees, chiefly for Treble voices, Op. 12; Six Glees in Score; Collection of Glees, Canons, and Catches, including some pieces never before published, with Memoir by W. Horsley (the editor), 2 vols., folio, Lond., 1824. Church Psalmody (selection); Services, Anthems. Ode to Fancy (Warton), degree exercise. *Titles of some of his principal Glees and Catches*—Æella; Are the white hours; Blow, Warder, blow; Desolate is the dwelling of Morna; Dull repining sons of care; Drink to me only; Father of Heroes; Forgive blest shade; Erl King; Farewell to Lochaber; Friend of fancy; The Friar; Go, idle boy; If happily we wish to live; In the lonely vale of streams; Lo! where incumbent o'er the shade; Lovely seems the morn's fair lustre: Lordly gallants; The May-fly; Mark the merry elves; Oh, share my cottage; Once upon my cheek; O, snatch me swift; O thou where'er; O fancy, friend of nature; Peace to the souls of the heroes; Queen of the valley; Red Cross Knight; Soft and safe; See with ivy chaplet; Thyrsis, when he left me; Tho' from thy bank; To all you Ladies now on land; Thalaba; Thou pride of the forest; Triumphant love; Whann battayle; When Arthur first; When time was entwining; Who comes so dark; With sighs, sweet rose; Ye Gentlemen of England. Songs, etc. Grammar of Music, Lond., 1806 (other editions); Glees, Catches, and Canons, Op. 4 (Clementi), n.d.; Explanations of the Notes, Marks, Words, etc. used in Music (Clementi), n.d.

Callcott, Maria Hutchins, English musician, born in 1799; died London, April 3, 1859. Sister of W. H. Callcott. Author of "The Singer's Alphabet, or hints on the English vowels, etc," London, 1849.

Callcott, William Hutchins, composer and pianist, son of J. W. Callcott, was born at Kensington, September 28, 1807. He died at

CALLOW.

London, August 5, 1882. Was organist of St. Barnabas', and teacher in London, for a considerable period. Among his various compositions may be named the following :— *Pianoforte*—Elegant Extracts from Mendelssohn; Favourite Marches, etc. An enormous number of arrangements of classical works for pf. solo and duet. A selection of Glees for three voices. Songs, part-songs, etc. "A Few Facts in the Life of Handel," London, 1859.

His son, WILLIAM ROBERT STUART (born in 1852; died 1886), was also a musician. Another of the name, WILLIAM CALLCOTT, a violinist, was born about 1800. He was principal violinist at H.M. Theatre for many years, and afterwards musical director of the Adelphi, Olympic, and Astley's Theatres. He died at Gravesend, November 6, 1878. aged 78. He was father of William and Albert Callcott, the scenic artists.

Callow, Mrs., see sub. Smart, Henry.

Calvert, Thomas, Scottish musician of the latter part of the 18th and beginning of the 19th centuries. Published "A Collection of marches, quicksteps, strathspeys, and reels," Edinburgh, n.d.

Cambridge, Frederick, organist and composer, born at South Runcton, Norfolk, March 29, 1841. Received his early musical training at Norwich Cathedral under Dr. Buck, subsequently studying harmony under Molique. In 1862, he was appointed organist and choirmaster to St. Columba's College, Dublin; removing to St. Mary's, Leicester, in 1866; and to the Parish Church, Croydon, in 1868, holding this position to the present time. Conductor of Croydon Vocal Union, and of Festivals of Croydon Church Choirs, 1882, etc. Is honorary local examiner for R.C.M. Graduated Mus. Bac., Durham, 1893. He won the prize of ten guineas offered by the Nottingham Anacreontic Society for the best Glee, in 1863; and among his published compositions are, a Communion Service in C (1864). *Anthems*—Not unto us; I was in the Spirit; Offertory sentences, hymn-tunes, chants, etc. Postlude in D, organ; pianoforte pieces, etc.

Cameron, Andrew Robertson, amateur musician and physician, born at Logie Coldstone, Scotland, in 1838. Educated at Aberdeen University. Settled in Australia as a medical practitioner in 1867. Died at Richmond, near Sydney, N.S.W., October 18, 1876. He composed some overtures and vocal music and acted as critic for various journals.

Camidge, John, composer and organist, was born about 1734. Chorister in York Cathedral. He studied under Greene and Handel, and was organist of York Cathedral, 1756-1803. He died at York, April 25, 1803. Buried S. Olave's Churchyard, York.

CAMPBELL.

WORKS.—Six Easy Lessons for the Harpsichord, York, n.d.; Glees; Miscellaneous works for the Harpsichord; Church music and songs, etc.

Camidge, Matthew, composer and organist, son of the above, was born at York, in 1758. He studied under Dr. Nares at the the Chapel Royal, and was organist of York Cathedral, 1803-1842. He died at York, October 23, 1844. Buried S. Olave's Churchyard.

WORKS.—Collection of Tunes adapted to Sandy's version of the Psalms, York, 1789; Sunday Hymns, the words by the Rev. W. Mason, York [1795]. Musical Companion to the Psalms used in the Church of St. Michael le Belfry, and most of the churches in York and its vicinity, n.d. [1830]. Method of instruction in music by questions and answers, n.d.; Twenty-four original psalm and hymn tunes, n.d.; Cathedral Music, [1790]; Sonatas for the pf., Op. 8-9, etc. Instructions for the pianoforte or harpsichord and eight sonatas [1795]. Marches for the pf. Glees and songs.

Camidge, John, composer and organist, son of Matthew, was born at York, in 1790. He studied under his father. Bac. Mus., Camb., 1812. Doc. Mus., Camb., 1819. Doc. Mus., Lambeth, 1855. Organist of York Cathedral, 1844-1859. He died at York, September 29, 1859.

WORKS.—Cathedral Music, consisting of a Service . . Anthems and 50 Double Chants, 1828. Six Glees for 3 and 4 voices, n.d., etc.

His son, THOMAS SIMPSON CAMIDGE, was deputy organist at York Minster from 1848 to 1859. Afterwards organist of St. Saviour's, York; Hexham Abbey, 1882; Swindon Parish Church, 1889; and Swansea. JOHN CAMIDGE, son of T. S. Camidge, is organist of Beverley Minster, and has composed "Marsyas and Apollo," a musical panorama for chorus and orchestra, Bridlington, 1896.

Campbell, Rev. A., author of "Two papers on Church music, read before the Liverpool Ecclesiastical Musical Society," Liverpool, 1854.

Campbell, Alexander, writer and musician. Was born at Tombea, on Loch Lubnaig, Callander, February 22nd, 1764. He was educated at Callander Grammar School. He studied music at Edinburgh under Tenducci, and was a teacher of pf. in Edinburgh. Organist in the non-juring chapel, Nicolson Street, Edinburgh. Was musical instructor of Sir Walter Scott. He died at Edinburgh, May 15th, 1824.

WORKS.—An introduction to the history of poetry in Scotland, ... Edinburgh, 1798. Sangs of the Lowlands of Scotland, carefully compared with the original editions, and embellished with characteristic designs com-

CAMPBELL.

CANTELO.

posed and engraved by the late David Allen, Esq., historical painter, Edinburgh, 1799. A tour from Edinburgh through parts of North Britain, London, 2 vols., 1802. Another edition, 2 vols., 1811. The Grampians desolate, a poem, 1804. Albyn's Anthology, or a select collection of the melodies and vocal poetry peculiar to Scotland and the Isles, hitherto unpublished, collected and arranged by Alex. Campbell, the modern Scottish and English verses adapted to the Highland, Hebridean, and Lowland melodies, written by Walter Scott, Esq., etc., Edinburgh, Oliver & Boyd, 2 vols., 1816-1818. Collections of Scottish songs, with violin, London, 1792. A second collection arranged for harpsichord, n.d., etc. The fine air now used with Tannahill's "Gloomy winter's now awa'," was claimed by Campbell as his composition, and it is said to have first appeared in leaflet form long before its alleged first publication by Gow as "Lord Balgonie's favourite."

Campbell, Lady Archibald, musician of present time. Author of "Rainbow music, the philosophy of harmony in colour grouping," London, 1886.

Campbell, Donald, Scottish writer and collector. Author of "A Treatise on the language, poetry, and music of the Highland clans, with illustrative traditions and anecdotes, and numerous ancient Highland airs," Edinburgh, 1862. This work contains a number of ancient Highland melodies badly set to inferior basses. The compiler describes himself as "late lieutenant of the 57th regiment," and appears to have been a resident in Port-Glasgow on the Clyde. He was a claimant to the Breadalbane Peerage.

Campbell, Gilbert James, GILBERTO GHILBERTI, bass vocalist, son of Major-General T. Hay Campbell, R.A. He sang at the Gloucester Festival, 1880, and in opera at Her Majesty's Theatre the same year. Has sung in oratorio and other concerts in various parts of the United Kingdom, and in Ireland. He married, July 31st, 1884, Miss ELLEN DE FONBLANQUE, soprano vocalist, who sang at the Gloucester Festival, 1880, and is known as an artistic vocalist at the Monday popular and other concerts.

Campbell, John, music-seller and teacher, who lived in Edinburgh in the latter half of last century. He published a collection of psalmody and other works.

Campbell, John, amateur musician, was born at Paisley in 1807; died at Glasgow, October 7th, 1860. He was a merchant in Glasgow, and issued "The Sacred psaltery in four vocal parts, consisting principally of original psalm and hymn tunes," Glasgow [1854]. He also edited "Campbell's Selection of anthem's and doxologies, with a separate piano accompaniment," Glasgow, 1848; and

wrote a few original anthems of mediocre quality, some of which were once very popular in Glasgow and neighbourhood.

Campbell, Joshua, Scottish collector, who was a music-seller and bell-ringer in Glasgow, and died there early in the present century. He issued, about 1795, "A collection of new Reels and Highland Strathspeys, with a bass for the violoncello and harpsichord," Glasgow, n.d. "Collection of favourite tunes," with variations, etc., n.d.

Campbell, Mary Maxwell, musician and poetess, born at Pitlour House, Fife, in 1812; died at St. Andrew's, January 15, 1886. Fifth daughter of Sir D. J. Campbell. Composer of the words and music of that blatant, though well-known song, "The March of the Cameron Men," and of "The mole and the bat" (1867), and other vocal pieces.

Campbell, William, Scottish collector, who flourished in London, published about 1790, and later, "Campbell's First Book of New and Favourite Country Dances and Strathspey Reels, for the harpsichord or violin." Afterwards issued a "Collection of the newest and most favourite country dances and reels," London, various dates. Of these collections at least 23 books were issued.

Campion, Thomas, poet, dramatist, composer, and physician, flourished in first part of 17th century, and died in February, 1619.

WORKS.—Observations on the art of English poesie, 1602: The first, second, third, and fourth booke of Ayres, containing divine and morrall songs; to be sung to the Lute and Viols, in two, three, and foure parts; or by one voyce to an instrument, London, 1610-12; Songs of mourning bewailing the untimely death of Prince Henry, 1613. A new way of making foure parts in Counter-point, by a most familiar and infallible rule, 1618 [and 1655 in Playford's "Introduction to the skill of Musick"); Ayres for the Mask of Flowers, 1613.

Campobello, see MARTIN, H. M.

Candlish, Rev. Robert Scott, Scottish Free Church clergyman, born Edinburgh, 1807; died 1873. He wrote "The Organ Question: Statements by Dr. Ritchie and Dr. Porteous for and against the use of the Organ in Public Worship, with an introductory notice." Edinburgh, 1856.

Cantelo, Annie, Mrs. HARRY COX, pianist, born in Nottingham. Studied at R.A.M., being Sterndale Bennett prize-holder, 1881, and Lady Goldsmid scholar, 1882. A.R.A.M., 1883. Made her first appearance in public at Mr. Walter Macfarren's concert, St. James's Hall, March 25th, 1882, playing the solo part of Schumann's pianoforte concerto. She has given concerts in Nottingham, and recitals in London with much success; and is the composer of a sonata in E minor, and other pieces for pf.

CAPEL.

Capel, J. M. Composer of the music to a comedietta, "The composer," 1892 ; also of "Six songs ; " songs, various, and pieces for pf.

Capes, Rev. John Moore, composer and writer, was born at Stroud. Was B.A., Oxford, 1836 ; M.A., 1846   Died in 1889. He composed "The Druid," a tragic opera, produced at St. George's Hall, Liverpool, February 22nd, 1879. This work attained not more than local renown. Capes has also written "An essay on the growth of the musical scale and of modern harmony," London, 1879.

Caradog, see Jones, Griffith Rhys.

Card, William, flute player and composer, born at Salisbury, in 1788 ; died at London, October 4th, 1861. He composed a large number of pieces of music for the flute, chiefly arrangements, and published a few pf. works. His son, EDWARD J. CARD, also a flute player, was a member of Her Majesty's private band, and of the Philharmonic orchestra. He died in London, May 16th, 1877, aged 60.

Cardigan, Cora, flutist, born in London. Studied under her father, and R. S. Rockstro. Appeared first at the Royal Music Hall, Holborn, then at the Oxford, and the Royal Aquarium. Her reputation as an artist being now established, she appeared with success on the concert platform, and gave a concert in Prince's Hall, February 17th, 1885. She has played at St. James's Hall ; at the Bow and Bromley recitals ; and in the provinces. Toured for two years in America, and has fulfilled engagements in Berlin and Nice. Her playing is remarkable for brilliancy of execution, and purity of tone. In 1889, she married Herr Louis Honig, a well-known pianist and composer.

Carew, Miss? English soprano vocalist, who was born in London, October 16th, 1799. She studied under Welsh, and her parents, and originally played small parts in Covent Garden Theatre. She first appeared as an operatic vocalist at Covent Garden, in July, 1815. Sang at the English Opera House, 1818, etc. She was also engaged for the Philharmonic, and principal London and provincial concerts. About 1823 she retired from the stage. Died [?]

Carey, Henry, composer and minor poet, reputed natural son of George Saville, Marquis of Halifax, was born in 1692 [1685]. Received some instruction in music from Roseingrave and Geminiani : otherwise self-taught. He was for a time a teacher of music, but was engaged chiefly in writing music for the theatres. He hanged himself in Great Warner Street, Clerkenwell, London, October 4, 1743.

WORKS.—*Musical Dramas, etc.*—The Con-

CARMICHAEL.

trivances, 1715 ; Honest Yorkshireman, 1736 ; Amelia, 1732 ; Teraminta, 1732 ; Chrononhotonthologos, 1734 ; Dragon of Wantley (words only), 1737 ; Dragoness (otherwise known as Marjery, or a worse Plague than the Dragon), 1738. Betty, 1739 ; Nancy, 1739. Poems, 1720 : Cantatas, 1732. The Musical Century, in 100 English Ballads on various Subjects and Occasions, etc., Lond., 2 vols., 1737-1740 ; Dramatic Works (Collected), 1743. *Interludes*—Thomas and Sally, etc. Melody of "God Save the Queen." (?) Carey is now known only as the composer of the fine ballad "Sally in our Alley," and of a few hymn tunes. The "Easter Hymn," usually attributed to Carey, is not his composition. His ballad "Sally in our Alley" appears to have been first published about 1715 as " (Sally in our Alley) the words and Tune by Mr. Henry Carey." It is a folio broadsheet on one side of a single leaf, and has a flute part added at the end. The melody differs considerably from more modern versions. In the 1729 edition of his "Poems on several occasions" it first appears in permanent form with an argument or note explaining the circumstances under which it was written, and referring to it as a juvenile effusion. This does not give the tune, nor is anything said about it.

His son GEORGE SAVILLE CAREY, born 1743, died 1807, was a poet and dramatist, who wrote a number of farces and other dramatic pieces.

Cargill, James, Scottish musician of present century, published "Harmonia Sacra : a collection of the most celebrated tunes and anthems, partly original and partly extracted from some of the best authors ancient and modern . . . " Aberdeen, n.d.

Carlile James, Scottish clergyman and psalmody editor, was born about 1784. He was minister of the Scottish Church, St. Mary's Abbey, Dublin, 1814-54. He died at Dublin, March 31, 1854. Compiler of a collection of psalmody issued in 1828.

Carlton, Hugh, author of "The Genesis of Harmony : an inquiry into the laws which govern musical composition," Lond., 1882.

Carlton, Rev. Richard, clergyman and composer, flourished during end of 16th and beginning of 17th centuries. He wrote "Twenty-one Madrigals for five voyces," Lond., 1601 ; and contributed "Calm was the Air," a madrigal for 5 voices, to the "Triumphs of Oriana." His biography is unknown.

Carmichael, Mary Grant, pianist and composer, born at Birkenhead. Pupil of the Academy for the higher development of pianoforte playing, where her teachers were Oscar Beringer, Walter Bache, and Fritz Hartvigson ; pupil of E. Prout for harmony and composition. As a pianist she has appeared chiefly

CARMICHAEL.

as an accompanist, at the Monday Popular Concerts, 1884-5, and elsewhere; but she is more widely known as a composer. Her works include many songs, among which may be named "Sing Song," twenty rhymes by C. Rossetti; "The Stream," a series of connected vocal pieces in the manner of a Liederkreis, produced at the Lyric Club, November, 1887; The Flower of the Vale; The Tryst, etc. Duets: A poor soul sat sighing, Who is Sylvia? Daybreak, and others. A suite for pf. Duet (1880) and smaller pf. compositions. She has also written an operetta, "The Snow Queen," and is now engaged on sacred compositions in large forms. Translator of A. Ehrlich's "Celebrated Pianists of the Past and Present," London: Grevel, 1894.

Carmichael, Peter, author of the "Science of Music Simplified," Glasgow, 1860.

Carmichael, S., author of "Dictionary of Musical Terms and Elementary Rules," London, 1878.

Carnaby, William, composer and organist, was born at London, in 1772. He studied under Nares and Ayrton as chorister in Chapel Royal. Organist at Eye, Suffolk, and at Huntingdon. Bac. Mus., 1803. Doc. Mus., Cantab., 1808. Organist at Hanover Chapel, Regent Street, London, 1823. He died at London, Nov. 13, 1839.

WORKS.—Ode, The Tears of Genius. Twelve Collects for 4 voices, in score, with organ accompaniment; Sanctus for 5 voices; Six Canzonets for voice and pf.; Six Songs for voice and pf. Glees, various. Anthems. MS. Works. The Singing Primer, or Rudiments of Solfeggi, with Exercises in the principal Major and Minor keys, London, 1827.

Carnall, Arthur, composer and organist, born at Peterborough, 1852, son of John Carnall, an amateur, who was for years choirmaster of St. Mary's, Peterborough. Pupil of Dr. Chipp, at Ely Cathedral. Graduated Mus. B., Cambridge, 1873. Organist of the Parish Church, Penge.

WORKS.—Overture, orchestra, Oxford, 1888; Quintets, in D and F, for wind instruments; Quartets, in C minor (Oxford, 1887,) and F, performed at the Conference of the Incorporated Society of Musicians, Newcastle, 1892, for strings; Nocturne, for strings, 1894. Album of duets, violin, and pf.; pieces for pf., organ, etc. Anthem for Christmas, "Hail! Thou that art highly favoured," and others; services glees and madrigals; songs, etc.

Carnie, William, writer and editor, was born at Aberdeen in November, 1824. He was originally a letter engraver, but became precentor of the Established Church, Banchory-Devenick, Aberdeen, in 1845. Inspector of Poor for same Parish, 1847. Sub-editor of the *Aberdeen Herald*, 1852. Precentor of the West, or High Church, Aberdeen, 1854. Clerk

CARRODUS.

and treasurer to the managers of Aberdeen Royal Infirmary and the Lunatic Asylum, 1861. He acted as local correspondent for a time to the *Times* and the *Scotsman*.

WORKS.—Psalmody in Scotland, a Lecture, Aberdeen, 1854; Northern Psalter, containing 402 Psalm and Hymn Tunes, Aberdeen, 1870; Anthem appendix to do.; Precentor's Companion and Teacher's Indicator; Contributions to periodical literature, etc.

Mr. Carnie's labours did much to promote good psalmody in the North of Scotland. In 1854, at the request of the local Young Men's Christian Association, he delivered a lecture on Psalmody to an audience numbering over 2000 persons, which inaugurated a very successful effort to improve the psalmody of Aberdeen churches.

Carolan, *see* O'CAROLAN.

Carr, Benjamin, English musician, born in latter part of 18th century. He settled in Philadelphia, U.S., early in the 19th century, where he was an organist and teacher. He published "The Spanish Hymn. arranged and composed for the concerts of the Musical Fund Society of Philadelphia... The air from an ancient Spanish melody... 1826." The hymn-tune called "Madrid," "Spanish melody," etc., is ascribed to Carr, but by a curious misprint, generally appears as by "B. Case."

Carstairs, *see* MOLESWORTH, Lady.

Carr, Frank Osmond, composer, born in Yorkshire. Graduated Mus. Bac., 1882; Mus. Doc., 1891, Oxford. Mus. Bac., Cambridge, 1885; M.A., 1886. He is known as the composer of music to a number of farces, burlesques, and comic operas: Joan of Arc, 1891; Blue-eyed Susan, 1892; In Town, 1892; Morocco Bound, 1893; Go Bang, 1894; His Excellency (W. S. Gilbert), produced at the Lyric Theatre, London, October 27th, 1894; Biarritz, 1896; Lord Tom Noddy, 1896; The Clergyman's Daughter, Theatre Royal, Birmingham, April, 1896; later, as My Girl, at the Gaiety, London.

Carr, John, vocal composer, who flourished at Boxford, Sussex, about the middle of last century. Among other works he issued "The Grove, or rural harmony," containing a variety of songs." London [1760].

Carr, Robert, musician of the 17th century. Issued "The delightful companion, or choice new lessons for the recorder or flute." London, 1686. Two editions.

Carrodus, John Tiplady, violinist, born at Braithwaite, near Keighley, Yorkshire, January 20th, 1836. Received his first lessons from his father, an amateur violinist, and gave a concert at the Mechanics' Institution, Keighley, in November, 1845. At the age of twelve, he was placed under Molique, with whom he studied at Stuttgart and in London.

CARROLL.

He appeared at a concert given by Mr. C. K. Salaman, at the Hanover Square Rooms, June 1st, 1849 ; and played a solo at the first Bradford Musical Festival, August 31st, 1853. He was engaged in the orchestra at Covent Garden Theatre, and ultimately became principal violinist in the Philharmonic, Three Choir Festival, and other orchestras, and was also noted as a quartet player, appearing in this capacity as early as 1850, being second violin at Molique's chamber concerts. He was leader at the Leeds festivals from 1880 to 1892, and appeared as soloist at the London Musical Society, April 22, 1863, Crystal Palace, and the leading metropolitan and provincial concerts. When the National Training School for Music was opened, in 1876, he was appointed a professor of the violin there. He commenced giving violin recitals in 1881, and toured in South Africa, 1890-1. His published compositions include fantasias, and a romance ; and he edited a collection of celebrated violin duets, and some studies. He died in London, July 13th, 1895. His son, BERNHARD MOLIQUE, violinist, was educated at home, and at the R.A.M. He has been connected with the best orchestras, and is making a reputation as a solo player, in the last capacity appearing with success at the Gloucester Festival of 1889. In 1888 he was appointed a professor at Trinity College, London. ERNEST ALEXANDER, his brother, is a contrabassist; member of the Philharmonic and other orchestras ; J. CARRODUS is a violoncellist and organist; R. CARRODUS, a violinist ; and W. O. CARRODUS, a flutist, scholar of the R.C.M. The father, with his five sons, were included in the orchestra at the Hereford Festival of 1894.

Carroll, B. Hobson, organist, pianist, and violinist. Graduated Mus. Doc., Dublin, 1884. He was for some time organist of Christ Church, Belfast, and is now organist and choirmaster of Dunfermline Abbey. Composer of a Te Deum in E flat, for soli, eight part chorus, and orchestra, Jubilate, Magnificat and Nunc dimittis, pieces for violin, etc.

Carroll, Walter, organist. Graduated Mus. Bac., Durham, 1891 ; Mus. Bac., Manchester, 1896 ; Organist and choirmaster, St. Clement's, Greenheys, Manchester, 1892 ; Music master, Day Training College, Owen's College, Manchester, 1892 ; Professor of harmony, R.C.M., Manchester, 1893. Works : Psalm 146, for soli, chorus, and orchestra ; Two sonatinas, pf., etc.

Carrott, Livesey, Organist and pianist, born at Boston, Lincolnshire. Educated at R.A.M. Was appointed organist and choirmaster at All Saints', Highgate, 1882 ; St. Matthew's, Bayswater, 1896. Resident in London as performer and teacher. Composer

CARTER.

of a sacred cantata, Martha, for female voices, 1896 ; songs, etc.

Carte, Richard, flutist and maker of musical instruments, born 1808 (?), son of Richard Cart, quartermaster of the Blues. Orginally intended as a violinist, he was placed under Griesbach, of the Queen's band ; afterwards he was a pupil, for the flute, of George Rudall. About 1828, he went to Germany, and studied composition under Hauptmann. Returning to England he resumed concert giving, and also lectured on various musical topics, enjoying a high reputation. In 1843, he adopted the Boehm flute, subsequently combining his own patent with the Boehm system. He joined the firm of Rudall and Rose in 1850, and in 1853 compiled and produced the first issue of the "Musical Directory, Register, and Almanack." He composed songs, and pieces for the flute ; and was author of "A complete course of instruction for the Boehm Flute" (1845?); and "Sketch of the successive Improvements made in the Flute" (1851?). He died at Reigate, November 26, 1891.

Carter, George, organist and composer, born in London, January 26, 1835. Studied under Sir John Goss, and was first appointed an organist in 1847. He was then successively organist at St. Thomas', Stamford Hill (1848) ; Christ Church, Camberwell (1850) ; Trinity Church, Upper Chelsea (1853) ; St. Luke's, Chelsea (1860) ; and of Montreal Cathedral (1861-70). As a performer he was known on the Continent as well as in London and America. For some years he acted as organist at the Albert Hall. His compositions include Operas—"Fair Rosamond," and "Nerone" (Italian), in MS. Operetta, "Golden Dreams." Cantatas, "Evangeline" (1873) ; "The Golden Legend" (composed 1883) ; and a Sinfonia-Cantata, Ps. 116, "I love the Lord" (1872). High Festival Communion Service (1883). Grand Festival March; Tema con variazioni, organ ; Songs and miscellaneous works.—Another GEORGE CARTER, tenor vocalist and lay vicar, Westminster Abbey, of repute as a ballad and glee singer, died at Wandsworth, November 17, 1890, at the age of fifty-six.

Carter, Henry, organist and composer, brother of the preceding, born March 6, 1837. Was some time organist of the Cathedral, Quebec, and in 1882 was appointed organist of Rev. Henry Ward Beecher's Church, New York, having previously held a similar post at Trinity Church, in that city. Has composed anthems, songs, organ music, etc. Another HENRY CARTER published a large number of waltzes and other dance pieces, songs, etc., between 1849 and 1861.

Carter, Robert, musician. Compiled "A Psalter, containing a selection of Psalm tunes,

CARTER.   CATLEY.

chants, services, and other ecclesiastical music, the Psalms selected from the new version by the Rev. W. J. E. Bennett," London, 1843.

Carter, Thomas, composer, was born in Ireland, in 1735 [1758, 1768, also given]. He studied probably in Ireland under his father, and became Organist of S. Werburgh's Church, Dublin, 1751-69. He travelled in Italy for a time [1770-1]. Conductor of Theatre in Bengal [1771-2], but settled in London as teacher and composer to the theatres, 1773. He died at London, October 12, 1804.

WORKS.—*Musical Dramas*—Rival Candidates, 1775; Milesians, 1777; Fair American, 1782; Birthday; Constant Maid; Just in Time. Lessons for the Guitar; Concerto for bassoon and pf.; Six Sonatas for the pf. Songs, detached and in collections, etc. The Soldier's farewell on the eve of a battle, song. Carter composed " O Nannie, wilt thou gang wi me," a song which owes its success to its imitation of the Scottish style. Apart from this song his merits as a composer are not great, and none of his other works are now heard.

Carter, William, organist, composer, and conductor, brother of G. and H. Carter, born in London, December 7, 1838. Studied under his father and Ernst Pauer. Chorister, St. Giles', Camberwell (1845); Chapel Royal, Whitehall; and King's College, London. Organist of Christ Church, Rotherhithe (1848); Little Stanmore, Whitchurch (1850); St. Mary, Newington (1854); and St. Helen's, Bishopsgate (1856). In 1859 he acted, for his brother Henry, as Organist of Quebec Cathedral, and conducted a grand performance of "Judas Maccabæus," April 13, the centenary of the composer's death. The next year he was organist of St. Stephen's, Westbourne Park, London; and, in 1868, of St. Paul's, Onslow Square. He established the Bayswater Musical Society in 1860, and was conductor of the London Choral Union, 1861. When the Royal Albert Hall was opened in 1871, he formed a large choir, and has for many years given choral and popular concerts in that building. In 1894 he started choral concerts in the Queen's Hall. He has also appeared with success as a performer upon the organ and pianoforte. His chief compositions are:—Placida, the Christian Martyr, a cantata produced at the Albert Hall, December 5, 1871: a Thanksgiving Anthem for recovery of H.R.H. the Prince of Wales, 1872; Victoria, an ode, 1887. He has also composed anthems, songs, and part-songs, and arranged national airs for choral-singing.

Cartledge, James, composer, organist, and singer, born at Newark [1791]; died at Manchester September 13, 1864. being the senior chorister of the Cathedral, his appointment dating from 1826. He issued "Sacred

Music, with an accompaniment for the organ or pianoforte," Lond. [1840].

Cartwright, Thomas, Puritan divine (1535-1603), who wrote against the use of music in public worship. Full particulars of what views he held will be found in Hawkins' " History of Music."

Case, George Tinkler, concertina player and writer, author of various text-books for different instruments, among which are " Instructions for performing on the Concertina, from the first Rudiments to the most difficult style of Performance," Lond. [1848]; Tutor for the Violin; Exercises for Wheatstone's patent concertina [1855]. Baritone concertina, a new method . . . Lond. [1857]; Concertina miscellany [1855]. English concertina tutor, n.d. One hundred ballads for the violin [1859].

His wife, born GRACE EGERTON, was a soprano vocalist.

Case, John, physician and writer, was born at Woodstock about the middle of the 16th century. Chorister at New College and Christ College, Oxford. Fellow of St. John's College, Oxford. Lecturer at Oxford. He died in January, 1600.

WORKS.—The Praise of Musicke, wherein its Antiquity, Dignity, Delectation, and Use, are discussed, Oxford, 1586. Apologia Musices, tem vocalis quam instrumentalis et mixtæ, Oxford, 1588. Philosophical works, etc. The " Praise of Musicke " is an exceedingly quaint work, and at the present date of great rarity. The writer was an enthusiast of the highest order.

Cassidy, James, Irish composer and bandmaster, died at Dublin, March 28, 1869. He composed and published a very large number of galops, quadrilles, and other dance music, for orchestra and pf.

Casson, Margaret, vocalist and composer, who flourished about the beginning of the present century. She wrote a number of vocal pieces of varying merit, among which may be named the songs: The Cuckoo; Attend, ye nymphs [1790]; Snowdrop; Noon [1790]; God save the Queen, etc.; The Pearl, glee. Her biography has not been preserved.

Casson, John, probably a relative of the above, composed minuets for the pf. Eight favourite airs for the pf., and other works issued between 1794-1820.

Casson, Thomas, bank manager, of Denbigh, amateur organist, and writer. Author of " The Modern Organ, London [1883]. Also papers and lectures on the organ. In 1887 he formed a company for building organs on the principle enunciated in his works.

Catley, Ann, soprano vocalist, was born at London, 1745. She was articled to Bates, the composer, in 1760, and appeared at Vauxhall Gardens in 1762. She sang at Covent

F

CAUSTON.

Garden Theatre, Oct 8, 1762. Involved in a scandalous criminal case, 1763. Sang in Ireland, 1763-70 ; Covent Garden Theatre, 1771. Made her last appearance in public in 1784. Supposed to have been latterly married to General Lascelles, with whom she lived previous to her death. She died near Brentford, Oct. 14, 1789.

The criminal case above alluded to in this singer's life was an action raised at the instance of her father against Bates, Sir Francis Delavel, and an attorney named Fraine for conspiring to prostitute her, by agreement, to the person named Delavel. Her father gained his case. She was a great favourite in London and in Ireland, and was one of the few successful vocalists who at that time made use of the staccato style. Her biography is given in "The Life and Memoirs of Miss Ann Catley, with biographical sketches of Sir F. Blake Delaval, and the Hon. Isabella Pawlet, daughter of the Earl of Thanet," by Miss Ambross, London, 1789, with portrait. Reprinted in 1888.

Causton, Thomas, composer and organist, who flourished during the 16th century. He was a Gentleman of the Chapel Royal during the reigns of Edward VI., Mary, and Elizabeth. He died on October 28, 1569. Contributed to Day's "Certain Notes set forth in four and three parts, to be sung at the Morning, Communion, and Evening Prayer." His compositions appear also in Day's "Psalms," London, 1563.

Cave, William Reginald, violinist, composer and conductor, nephew of Joseph H. Cave, many years lessee and manager of the Marylebone and other theatres. He was born in Marylebone, in 1859, and first appeared as a violinist at the Marylebone theatre in 1864, and afterwards played for three months, during the management of Nelson Lee, 1865, at the Crystal Palace. In conjunction with the late Edward Solomon and James Saunders, he gave concerts. In 1874 he founded the West London Orchestral Society, retaining the conductorship until 1887, and giving many concerts. He then formed the People's Palace Orchestra ; and, since 1876, has been a Professor of the violin at Harrow Music School. He wrote incidental music to "Mary, Queen of Scots"; two overtures, one in B flat (at the age of fourteen), for orchestra; two symphonies; a concerto for violin, and other pieces.

Cave=Ashton, Gertrude, see ASHTON, GERTRUDE CAVE-.

Cavendish, Michael, composer, who flourished during the latter portion of the 16th century. He composed "Ayres for four voices," 1599; and contributed the five-part madrigal "Come, gentle swains" to the "Triumphs of Oriana," 1601. He also aided in

CELLIER.

harmonising "The Whole Booke of Psalmes," 1592. His biography has not been preserved.

Cazalet, Rev. William Wahab, M.A., English divine and writer, was born about commencement of present century. He wrote The History of the Royal Academy of Music, compiled from authentic sources, London, 1854 ; On the right management of the voice in speaking and reading, with some remarks on phrasing and accentuation, London, 1855 (3rd edit., 1860) ; The voice, or the art of singing, London, 1861 ; On the reading of the Church liturgy, 1862 ; Exhibition lecture on the musical department of the late Exhibition, London, 1853.

Cecil, Arthur, or **Blunt,** actor and manager. Destined for the army, he played as an amateur at the Richmond Theatre, and in 1869 joined the German Reed Company, appearing as Mr. Churchmouse in Gilbert's "No Cards," and as Box in the Burnand-Sullivan burlesque, "Cox and Box." He afterwards played in the regular drama at the Globe, Gaiety, and Opera Comique. For some time he was joint manager with John Clayton, of the Court Theatre. He died at Brighton, April 16, 1896.

Cecil, Rev. Richard, clergyman and musician, was born in London, November 8, 1748. He was educated at Oxford, 1773. Deacon, 1775. Priest, 1777. Minister of St. John's Chapel, Bedford Row, London, 1780. Rector of Cobham and Bisley, Surrey, 1800. He died at Hampstead, August 15, 1810.

WORKS.—Selection of psalms and hymns for the public worship of the Church of England, London, n.d. ; 32nd edition issued, 1840 ; Sermons, lectures, etc. Best known by his anthem, "I will arise, and go to my Father." His daughter, THEOPHANIA, was born in 1782, and died in London, November 15, 1879. She was organist of St. John's Chapel; editor of "The psalm and hymn tunes, used at St. John's Chapel, Bedford Row; arranged for four voices, and adapted for the organ or pf., London, 1814.

Celli, F. H., see STANDING, FRANK.

Cellier, Alfred, composer and conductor, of French extraction, born in London (Hackney), December 1, 1844. Chorister at Chapel Royal, St. James's, 1855-60; organist of All Saints', Blackheath, 1862. In 1866 he succeeded Dr. Chipp as organist of the Ulster Hall, Belfast, and conductor of the Classical Harmonists, and two years later, was appointed organist of St. Alban's, Holborn. He now turned his attention to composition and conducting, and was engaged at the Prince's Theatre, Manchester, 1871-5 ; Opera Comique, London, 1877-9 ; and, with Sir Arthur Sullivan, joint conductor, Promenade Concerts, Covent Garden, 1878-9 ; and held other similar appointments at various times. About

CHADFIELD.

this time his health failed, and he lived much abroad, principally in Australia. He died in London, December 28, 1891, while giving the finishing touches to his opera, " The Mountebanks," the overture of which was taken from his Orchestral Suite, the intended movement never having been written. Cellier was a brilliant organist, and was credited with superior literary tastes. He wrote a trenchant little paper, " A nightmare of tradition " (*The Theatre*, October, 1878), a plea for English opera.

WORKS.—*Operettas and Operas* : Charity begins at home, 1870 ; The Sultan of Mocha (Prince's Theatre, Manchester, Nov. 16, 1874; revived, Strand Theatre, London, with a new libretto, Sept. 21, 1887) ; The Tower of London, 1875 ; Nell Gwynne, 1876 ; The Foster Brothers, London, 1876 ; Dora's Dream, 1877 ; The Spectre Knight, Feb., 1878; Bella Donna (Manchester, April, 1878) ; After All (London, 1879) ; In the Sulks, 1880 ; Pandora, grand opera (Boston, U.S., 1881) ; The Carp (Savoy Theatre, 1886) ; Dorothy (a fresh arrangement of the music of Nell Gwynne to a new libretto, Gaiety Theatre, Sept. 25, 1886) ; Mrs. Jarramie's Genie (Savoy, Feb., 1888) ; Doris (Lyric, April, 1889) ; and The Mountebanks (book by W. S. Gilbert, produced, Lyric Theatre, Jan. 1892). He also set Gray's Elegy as a cantata, produced at the Leeds Festival, 1883 ; wrote incidental music to As You Like it, 1885 ; a Suite Symphonique, for orchestra ; Barcarolle, flute and pf. ; songs, and pf. pieces.

His brother, CHARLES HERBERT CELLIER, is organist of Holy Trinity Church, Anerley ; Conductor of Lower Sydenham Choral Society, and Anerley Musical Society. He has, for many years, given concerts in that locality. FRANCIS A. CELLIER, musical director, Savoy Theatre, was joint composer of the music to " Mrs. Jarramie's Genie," and composer of an operetta, " Captain Bill," produced at the Savoy Theatre, Sept., 1891.

Chadfield, Edward, pianist, born at Derby, August 1, 1827. At the age of nine, studied under Froude Fritche (organist of All Saints' Church, Derby), but after some years, was required to take the place of a deceased brother in his father's business. From this he was released in time, and he resumed his musical studies under Henry Smart, and later, in Paris, with Henri Rosellen, and Korbach. In 1851, he returned to Derby, and established himself as a performer and teacher, founding, with Mr. A. F. Smith, a School of Music there. He held the appointment of organist at St. Werburgh's Church for eleven years, and a similar office at All Saints', which he resigned in 1887. In the early days of the Incorporated Society of Musicians, Mr. Chadfield was an active worker, and in 1885, he was induced to accept

CHAMBERLAIN.

the office of Hon. General Secretary. Since that date he has attended meetings and given addresses in all parts of the United Kingdom, and Ireland, and was chosen as a delegate to attend the annual meeting of the Music Teachers' National Association (America), held at Philadelphia, July, 1889. After the incorporation of the Society, 1893, Mr. Chadfield was presented with a handsome testimonial during the Conference held in London that year. The office being then removed to London, Mr. Chadfield left Derby for the metropolis, and as the executive officer of the Society devotes the whole of his time to its advancement. He married, in 1858, the youngest daughter of the late Alderman Madeley, some time Mayor of Derby. His eldest son, EDWARD JOSEPH CHADFIELD, was musically educated first at home, then at the Leipzig Conservatorium. He made his *début* as a pianist at Derby in 1886, and succeeded his father as teacher and joint director of the Derby School of Music.

Challoner, Neville Butler, harpist and violinist, born London, 1784. He studied in London, and first appeared as a violinist in 1793. He was violinist at Covent Garden Theatre in 1796 ; at Richmond Theatre, 1799 ; and subsequently leader at Birmingham, Sadler's Wells Theatre, etc. Harpist at Italian Opera, London, and tenor player at the Philharmonic Society. Latterly, he was a music-seller. Date of death unknown.

WORKS.—Method for the violin, London, n.d. New Guida di Musica, or instructions for beginners on the pf., n.d. Method for Guitar, n.d. ; Method for flute, n.d. ; Method for the harp, n. d. Romance and Polacca for harp, op. 14 ; Two duets on Scotch airs, op. 10 ; Three duets (trans.), op. 15 ; Duet concertante for harp, op. 22. Miscellaneous works for harp and pf. Harmonia Sacra, 4 books, London, n. d. Lays of harmony, or the musical scrap book, 1830. National airs [1830], etc.

Chalmers, James, Scottish musician and printer, son of Professor James Chalmers, of Marischal College, was born early in the 18th century ; died at Aberdeen in 1764. He compiled a collection of 20 Church tunes [*circa* 1748], containing " Observations concerning the tunes and manner of singing them," which is now exceedingly scarce. In 1736 he was appointed printer to the town council of Aberdeen, and he published the *Aberdeen Journal*, etc. His son, JAMES, born in Aberdeen, March 31, 1742 ; died June 17, 1810, succeeded him in business, and in 1774 was appointed precentor of the West Church, Aberdeen ; a position he held till 1797.

Chamberlain, Houston Stewart, writer, author of " Das Drama Richard Wagner's " (Leipzig : Breitkopf and Härtel, 1892) ;

CHAMBERLAINE.

"Richard Wagner" (Depôt for Art and Science, Munich, 1895); and occasional contributions to musical papers.

Chamberlaine, Elizabeth, *see* VON HOFF, Mrs. H.

Chamberlayne, Miss E. A., composer, of the present time. Studied under Professor Prout and H. C. Banister. Of her compositions a Scherzo for strings, harp, and flute was performed at the Crystal Palace, February 23, 1895. She has published Two Sonatas for pf., op. 16; a Suite, and smaller pieces. Also some music for organ, and songs. She has in MS. two Symphonies, overtures, an opera, and other works.

Chambers, Charles, organist and conductor. Graduated Mus. Bac., 1880 ; Mus. Doc., 1887, Cambridge. F.R.C.O., 1877. Organist successively at St. Peter's, Newcastle-on-Tyne, 1870-82; Jesmond Parish Church, 1882-90; All Saints', 1890-3; St. George's, Cullercoats, 1893. Some time conductor of Newcastle Harmonic Society. University Exercises—(Bac.) Ps. 109, for soli, chorus, strings, and organ ; (Doc.) Cantata, "The Redeemer." Composer of a Concert overture (Newcastle, 1887) ; offertory sentences, songs, etc.

Chambers, Lucy, contralto vocalist, born in Sydney, New South Wales, where her father was a lawyer. Her early studies were under Mrs. Logan, a cousin of W. Vincent Wallace; and, encouraged by Catherine Hayes, at the time in Australia, she decided to adopt the lyric stage as a profession. In January, 1862, she went to London, and studied under Garcia ; then, proceeding to Italy, became a pupil of Luigi Vannuccini, and Romani, at Florence. After a year, she made her appearance as Azucena, in *Il Trovatore*, at the Teatro Pagliano. She was then engaged for two seasons at La Scala, Milan, and while there continued her studies with Lamperti. A general tour of Europe followed, and in 1870 she returned to Australia. There she had a long career of unbroken success, her repertory being extensive and varied. She formed an Academy at Melbourne, and died in that city in 1894.

Chambers, Robert, author and publisher, a member of the well-known firm of W. and R. Chambers, Edinburgh ; born 1802, died 1871; edited "The Songs of Scotland prior to Burns, with the tunes," Edin., 1862.

Champness, Samuel, bass singer, born about 1730; died September, 1803. He was a Gentleman of the Chapel Royal, sang at the principal concerts in London during the latter half of the 18th century, and had a voice of great richness, which was much admired.

Champneys, Francis Henry, amateur composer, born at London, March 25th, 1848. Educated at Oxford, where he graduated M.A.,

CHAPPEL.

1875. He studied music under Sir John Goss. Fellow of the Royal College of Physicians. Has conducted concerts, and is the composer of hymns and other church music; "Rustic coquette," ballet for four voices, etc.

Chaplin. The name of three sisters, instrumentalists of the present day. NELLIE, the eldest, is a pianist, born in London, and musically educated at the London Academy of Music, where, among other distinctions, she was awarded the silver medal presented by the Society of Arts. Later, she studied the Deppe method with Frl. Elise Timm, at Hamburg. In 1893 she established a pianoforte school in London, and chiefly devotes herself to tuition. Miss Chaplin is known as a performer, and commenced giving concerts in 1882. She has played, with success, in London and the provinces, and, with her sisters, gained some reputation for the Chaplin trio. KATE CHAPLIN, violinist, born in London, was also trained at the London Academy, under Mr. Pollitzer, having previously received lessons from Miss Dunbar Perkins. As a very youthful performer she appeared at Mr. George Gear's concert, St. George's Hall, May 2nd, 1882; and since then has played at many concerts, in London, and the principal cities of the United Kingdom. In 1892, she went to Brussels, to study under Eugen Ysaye, and in January, 1893, had the honour, with her sister Nellie, of playing before the Queen, at Osborne, receiving the Royal compliments, and souvenirs of the event. The youngest sister, MABEL CHAPLIN, violoncellist, received her first lessons from Mr. John Boatwright, of the Philharmonic Orchestra; and entering the London Academy, became a pupil of Signor Pezze. Subsequently she studied at the Brussels Conservatoire, under Edouard Jacobs, gaining, in 1893, the first prize, with distinction, for violoncello playing, being the first English girl to carry off that honour. She had for some time taken part in the concerts given by her sisters; but gave her first concert, with Emil Sauer, in the Queen's Hall, March 28, 1895.

Chapman, Rev. James, author. Wrote "The music, or melody and rhythmus of language, with the five accidents of speech, and a musical notation." Edinburgh, 1818.

Chapman, T., musician. Published the "Young gentleman and ladies' musical companion," 1772-74. Two vols.

Chappell, William, writer and antiquary, was born in London, November 20th, 1809. Brought up in music publishing business with his father. Engaged in musical antiquarian studies. Founded (with others) the Percy Society in 1840, and the Musical Antiquarian Society in 1840. F.S.A., 1840. Partner in the firm of Cramer & Co., 1843.

CHAPPLE.

Treasurer of the Camden Society, etc. Was connected with a number of learned and antiquarian societies. He died at London, August 20, 1888.

WORKS.—A collection of national English airs, consisting of ancient song, ballad, and dance tunes, interspersed with remarks and anecdotes, and preceded by an essay on English minstrelsy ; the airs harmonized for the pianoforte by Dr. Crotch, G. A. Macfarren, and J. A. Wade. London, 4to. part I., 1838 ; II., 1839 ; III., 1840. Popular music of the olden time : a collection of ancient songs, ballads, and dance tunes, illustrative of the national music of England, etc. London, Cramer, 2 vols. [1845-59]. Old English ditties, London, 2 vols., n.d. History of music, art, and science, from the earliest records to the fall of the Roman Empire, with explanations of ancient systems of music, musical instruments, and of the true physiological basis for the science of music, whether ancient or modern, vol. I., London, 1874, all published. Edited works (collections of ancient poetry) for the Ballad, Percy, and Camden Societies. A new edition of his "Popular Music" was issued as "Old English popular music," in 1893, edited by H. Ellis Woolridge. This corrects a number of the statements concerning Scots music, which, in his anxiety to prove that England possessed an immense wealth of folk music, Chappell advanced without sufficient proof. Further proofs of Mr. Chappell's want of care in the presentation of evidence have been gathered by Mr. John Glen, and will be published soon.

Chapple, Samuel, organist and composer. Was born at Crediton, Devon, 1775. He was blind from childhood ; but after studying the pianoforte he became organist at Ashburton, 1795-1833. He died at Ashburton, October 3, 1833.

WORKS.—Five songs and a glee, op. 3 ; Six anthems in score, figured for the organ or pf., op. 4 ; A second set of six anthems in score, op. 5 ; A third set of six anthems and twelve psalm tunes in score, op. 6 ; The eighteen anthems, republished. Three sonatas for the pf. ; Six songs with pf. accompaniment ; Anthem for the coronation of George IV. ; Single pf. pieces ; Single glees, anthems, and songs.

Chard, George William, composer and organist, was born in 1765. He studied under Robert Hudson in the choir of St. Paul's. Lay-clerk at Winchester Cathedral, 1788, and organist of the Cathedral in succession to Peter Fussell, 1802. Organist of Winchester College, 1832. Doc. Mus., Cambridge, 1812. He died at Winchester, May 23, 1849.

WORKS.—Anthems : Happy is the man ; Is there not an appointed time? ; O Lord we beseech ; To celebrate Thy praise. Services.

CHERRY.

Chants in Bennett and Marshall's collection. Songs : Twelve glees for three, four, and five voices. London [1811].

Charde, John, composer of the 16th century. In 1518-19 he graduated Mus. Bac. Oxford, for which he composed a mass in five parts. This was the first composition in so many parts written by a bachelor for a degree exercise. He composed other masses.

Charke, Richard, violinist and composer of middle of 18th century. He married Charlotte Cibber, whom he illtreated, and from whom he soon separated. Notable as the first to compose *medley* overtures. He died in Jamaica of disorders brought on by dissipated habits.

Charlesworth, J. J., musician, compiler of "Fifty Select Tunes carefully adapted to the best part of the first 96 Psalms . . ." London, 1796.

Charlton, R., author, published "Reminiscences and biographical sketches of Musicians." Lincoln, 1886.

Chatfield, Mrs. Henry, see LARGE, Eliza R.

Chatterton, John Balsir, harpist and composer, was born at Portsmouth, where his father, John Chatterton, was a teacher of music, in 1802. He studied under Bochsa and Labarre, and became Professor of the harp at R.A.M. Harpist to the Queen, etc. He died at London, April, 1871.

WORKS. — Numerous transcriptions from popular operas for the harp ; Songs with harp and pf. accomp., etc.

His brother FREDERICK was also a harpist and composer. He was born in 1814, and died at London in March, 1894. His daughter JOSEPHINE made her first appearance as a harpist at Willis' Rooms on June 3, 1857. She lived for some years in America, and established a school for the harp at Chicago in 1892. In December, 1895, she appeared again in London.

Cheese, Griffith James, organist and writer, was born on May 2, 1751. He was organist at Leominster and teacher in London. Author of "Practical rules for playing and teaching the pianoforte and organ, likewise useful information to teachers and pupils born blind, op. 3," London [1806]. Songs, etc. He died on November 10, 1804.

Chell, William, writer and musician, was lay-vicar and precentor at Hereford Cathedral in 1554. Mus. Bac , Oxford, 1524. Prebendary of Eigne, 1532, and East Withington 1545. He left two treatises entitled "Musicæ Practicæ Compendium" and "De Proportionibus Musicis," which are said to be transcriptions from the works of John Dunstable, etc.

Cherry, John William, composer and teacher, born London, December 10, 1824. Self-educated in theory and on Pianoforte.

CHESHIRE.

He died in London, January, 1889. Has composed over 1,000 pieces, of which the following are the best known :—

Works.—Will-o'-the-wisp ; Shells of ocean ; Beautiful leaves ; The Blacksmith ; How beautiful is the sea ; My village home ; Monarch of the woods ; Estelle ; Gentle Spring ; Sweet Annie ; The Invitation ; Silently, silently over the sea ; Trees of the forest ; Upon the lonely shore ; Wanton breezes, whither going ; Down by the sea ; Fair Glen Lochry ; Home again to England ; Seventh day ; Spirit of the whirlpool ; Breathe soft, summer wind ; Summer twilight ; Come with me to Fairyland. *Duets*—Elfin revels ; Hark ! there's music stealing ; Let us roam away, etc. Pf. music, dances, etc.

Cheshire, John, harpist and composer, born in Birmingham, March 28, 1839. Commenced playing the harp when four years of age. Studied at R.A.M., 1852-55, and afterwards under G. A. Macfarren and J. B. Chatterton. Played at a' concert of the Society of British Musicians, February 27, 1855, after which he was presented with a fine harp by the Messrs. Erat. In that year he was appointed harpist at the Royal Italian Opera ; and, in 1865, principal harpist at Her Majesty's Theatre. Travelled in South America, 1858-61 ; Norway and Sweden, 1879. Has been heard in the principal concerts in the United Kingdom. From about 1887 resident in America ; harpist to the National Opera Company there, 1888. His compositions include an opera, "Diana," written in Brazil ; Cantatas : "The King and the Maiden" (book by Arthur Matthison), performed St. James's Hall, April 20, 1866 ; "The Buccaneers," 1886. Three overtures for orchestra. These, excepting the Buccaneers, remain in MS. He has published for the harp—Six Romances ; Album of twenty-four pieces, etc. A Duet in B flat, and a number of pieces for pf. ; Songs—Cupid the conqueror ; The withered violet, etc., etc. In 1871 he married Miss Maria Matilda Baxter, an excellent pianist, who appeared with success at many of his concerts.

Chetham, Rev. John, musician and clergyman, born about 1700. He was master of the Clerk's School, Skipton, in 1737, and curate of Skipton 1739. He died at Skipton in August, 1763. Issued "A Book of Psalmody, all set in four parts," 1718 ; 2nd ed., (?) ; 3rd, 1724 ; 4th, 1731 ; 5th, 1736 ; 8th, 1752 ; 9th, 1767 ; 10th, 1779 ; 11th, Leeds, 1787 ; of which an enlarged and revised edition by Houldsworth was published at London in 1832, and Halifax in 1868.

Chevalier, Albert Onesime Britannicus Gwathveoyd Louis, comedian, and lyric author, born at Notting Hill, London, March 21, 1862. Displayed histrionic talent at an early age, and appeared in farce at the

CHILD.

Prince of Wales' Theatre, Tottenham Street, Sept. 29, 1877, as Mr. Knight. From 1878 to 1887 he was on tour with Mr. and Mrs. Kendal, Mr. Hare, and other combinations, in "Diplomacy," and various dramas. Later, he came out as an entertainer, and in 1890 sang in comic opera at the Avenue Theatre. It was February 5, 1891, that he made his first appearance as a music-hall performer, at the New London Pavilion. His success was phenomenal, and has lasted ever since. His matinees in the provinces have attracted large and enthusiastic audiences, and "The Coster's Laureate," "The Kipling of the Music-hall," has been everywhere recognised as an artist. In 1896, he visited America. Besides his songs, he has written several pieces for the stage. His brother, Auguste, under the *nom de plume* of Charles Ingle, supplies most of his music. Assisted by Bryan Daly, he has written "Albert Chevalier ; a Record by himself," London, Macqueen, 1895. Among the best known of his songs, composed by his brother, John Crook, and others, may be named "Knocked 'em in the Old Kent Road" ; "Future Mrs. 'Awkins" ; "Coster's serenade" ; "My Old Dutch," etc.

Cheyne, Edwin, Scottish author, published "The Amateur's Vocal Guide and voice trainer . . . Glasgow, 1879.

Chilcot, Thomas, composer and organist, was born about the beginning of the 18th century. He was organist of Abbey Church, Bath, 1733, and died at Bath, in November, 1766. Chilcot is chiefly noted as having been the master of Thomas Linley. He composed six concertos for the harpsichord, with 4 violins, viola, violoncello and basso ripieno, London, 1756. two sets ; Twelve English songs, the words by Shakespeare and other celebrated poets [1745] ; single songs, glees, etc.

Child, William, composer and organist, was born at Bristol, in 1606. He studied under Elway Bevin, as chorister in Bristol Cathedral. Mus. Bac., Oxford, 1631. Organist of St. George's Chapel, Windsor, 1632. One of organists of Chapel Royal, London. Chanter of Chapel Royal, 1660. Member of King's private band, and composer to the King in 1661. Doc. Mus., Oxon., July, 1663. He died at Windsor, March 23, 1697, and is buried in St. George's Chapel.

Works.—The first set of Psalmes of 3 voyces, fitt for private chappells, with a continued bass either for the organ or theorbo, composed after the Italian way, London, 1639 (2nd edit., 1650). Divine anthems and vocal compositions to several pieces of poetry, London ; Service in D (Boyce) ; Service in E (Boyce) ; Praise the Lord, O my soul, anthem ; O Lord, grant the King, anthem ; O pray for the peace of Jerusalem, anthem ; Sing we

CHILLEY.   CHIVERS.

merrily, anthem; Services in G, F, and A minor; Court Ayres (a volume of secular vocal music); Catches and Canons, etc.

Child's compositions are very simple in general style, and approximate in character to the productions of a century later. " At times, however, as in his service in D, his harmony was rich, glowing, and closely worked. Some few of his full anthems, without any great depth of science or elevation of genius, possess a great degree of warmth, and exhibit imagination." He paved at his own expense the body of Windsor Chapel.

Chilley, Charles, tenor vocalist, born in London (Pimlico). He was educated at the Albert Memorial College, Framlingham, and then was for several years in an office, frequently singing in concerts as an amateur. Eventually he entered the Guildhall School of Music, and became a pupil of the late J. B. Welch. He sang at the Crystal Palace, in Mendelssohn's Walpurgis Nacht, 1883; at a concert of Mr. Willing's choir, 1884; and since then has been heard at the principal London and provincial concerts, having been on tour with Madame Albani, and others.

Chilmead, Edmund, scholar and musician, was born at Stow-in-the-Wold, Gloucester, 1611. Clerk of Magdalen College, Oxford. Canon of Christ Church, 1632. Resided with Este the musician, in London, 1648. He died at London in 1654. Wrote " De Musicâ Antiquâ Græcâ," printed at the end of the Oxford edition of " Aratus," 1672. He gave concerts in London, and drew up a catalogue of the Greek MSS. in the Bodleian library. " He was well versed in the old music, and was the best qualified at that time . . . . to enter upon this subject."—*Hearne.*

Chinn, Francis Farrant, composer and organist; born in 1813, died at Liverpool, April 29, 1868. Composer of glees and songs. " Harvest home, a pastoral glee." Liverpool [1844] is one of his best works.

Chipp, Edmund Thomas, composer and organist; was born at London, December 25, 1823. Son of Thomas Paul Chipp, the well-known performer on the kettledrums and harp. Chorister in Chapel Royal under William Hawes. He studied the violin under W. Thomas, J. B. Nadaud, etc., 1832-40. Organist (voluntary) of Albany Chapel, Regent's Park, London, 1843-6. Member of H. M. private band, as violinist, 1843-55. Organist St. John's Chapel, Downshire Hill, Hampstead, 1846-7; St. Olave's, Southwark (in succession to H. J. Gauntlett), 1847-52; St. Mary-at-Hill, East-Cheap, 1852-6; Royal Panopticon (in succession to W. T. Best), 1855; Holy Trinity Church, Paddington (in succession to C. E Stephens), 1856-62. Mus. Bac. Cantab., March 17th, 1859. Mus. Doc., do., June 21st, 1860. Organist Ulster Hall,

and St. George's Church, Belfast, 1862-6. Conductor of the Anacreontic, Classical Harmonists, and Vocal Union Societies, Belfast. Organist of Kinnaird Hall, Dundee, Feb.-Nov., 1866; St. Paul's, Edinburgh, May to Nov., 1866. Organist, and Master of Choristers, Ely Cathedral, November, 1866. Was also member of the Royal Italian Opera, the Philharmonic, and Sacred Harmonic Society Bands. He died at Nice, December 17, 1886.

WORKS.—Job, an Oratorio, for solo voices, chorus, and orchestra; Naomi, a Sacred Idyll, for solo voices, chorus, and orchestra. Music for the Church Service and home circle, containing 10 Sentences, 24 single and 41 double Chants, 4 Te Deums, 2 Jubilate, 2 Benedictus, 1 Te Deum in unison, 2 Sanctus, 12 Kyrie, 4 Gloria, 2 Magnificat, Nunc Dimittis, 4 Cantate Domine, Deus Misereatur, and 108 Church Melodies, in short, common, long, and irregular measures, by various authors. Te Deum, Jubilâte, Sanctus and Kyrie in D; Church Service in A; Te Deum in D; Gloria for male voices. Three Studies for the Organ, op. 7; Introduction and six variations upon Handel's Harmonious blacksmith, for organ; Do. and seven variations on God preserve the Emperor, for organ; Lord of all power and might, anthem; Part-songs; Songs, and miscellaneous Church and chamber music.

Chipp, Thomas Paul, English harpist, father of the foregoing, was born in London, May 23, 1793, and died on June 19, 1870. He was well-known as a drum player and harpist, and as a leading performer at all the principal festivals. He retired in 1866. His compositions include a string quintet in E minor, 1836; quartet, 1845; Fantasias, etc., for harp.

Chisholm, James, commonly called Marquis Chisholm, musician and entertainer, born Neilston, Renfrew, about 1837; died Toronto, Canada, December, 1877. He was a fair pianist, and travelled much in Australia, Asia, Scotland, and America with a Chinese giant named Chang. He composed the somewhat vulgar song entitled " The Battle of Stirling," which has been frequently parodied in Scotland, and published " The Adventures of a travelling musician in Australia, China, and Japan," Glasgow, 1865, reprinted from the *Glasgow Herald.* He also published " Gems of Scottish melody " [1869], and the " Chin-Chin-Chang" Galop; " Great Chang Polkas," and similar works.

Chisney, E., author of a work entitled " Concertina Instruction," London, 1853.

Chivers. G. M. S., musician and dancing-master of first half of the present century. He published a number of works, among which may be named—Recueil de danses Espagnoles, or Spanish country dances, arranged

CHOPE.

for pf., London, 1819; First set of Chiverian quadrilles [1820]; New set of contre dances; The Modern dancing-master, London, 1822, etc.

Chope, Richard Robert, clergyman and musician, born September, 1830. Vicar of St. Augustine's, South Kensington. Editor of "Hymn and Tune Book," 1857-62;" "Choir and Musical Record," 1862; Versicles, Canticles, Litany. Psalter (Gregorian), 1862. Choral Communion (Marbecke, etc.), 1863. Carols for use in Church, 1868-76. Easter and Harvest Carols, 1884.

Chorley, Henry Fothergill, musician, journalist, general writer, etc., was born at Blackley Hurst, near Billinge, Lancashire, December 15th, 1808. Brought up for mercantile life. Commenced connection with the "Athenæum," 1830. Member of the "Athenæum" staff, 1833-1871. He died at London, February 16, 1872.

WORKS.—Sketches of a sea-port town,3 vols., 1835 (novel); Conti the discarded, a novel, 3 vols., 1835; Memorials of Mrs. Hemans, 2 vols., 1836; The Lion, a tale of the coteries, 3 vols., 1839; Music and manners in France and Germany, 3 vols., London, 1841; Pomfret, a novel, 1845; Old love and new fortune, a play, 1850; Modern German music, recollections and criticisms, London, 3 vols., 1854; Roccabella, a novel, 1859; Thirty years' musical recollections, London, 2 vols., 1862; Prodigy, a tale of music, London, 3 vols., 1866; Handel studies, 2 parts, 1859; National music of the world, edited by H. G. Hewlett, 1880; Librettos for Wallace's Amber Witch; Bennett's May Queen, etc.; Translations of Mercadante's Elena da Feltre; Cimarosa's Il Matrimonio segreto; Hérold's Zampa; Auber's Haydée; Mendelssohn's Son and Stranger, etc.

Chorley was too many-sided ever to attain great distinction in any one of the numerous walks he attempted. His musical writings possess greater literary merit than most of the English work of the same period, but the judgments formed in them, especially with regard to Mendelssohn, have long since been overturned. His "Autobiography, Memoir, and Letters," edited by Henry G. Hewlett, was published in London, 2 vols., 1873, with a photograph.

Christie, William, violinist and composer, was born about 1778, and died 1849. He resided at Cuminestown, Monquhitter, Aberdeenshire, as a dancing-master and teacher. Composer of a "Collection of Reels, etc." Edinburgh.

His son WILLIAM was born at Monquhitter in 1817, and died at Bellie, near Fochabers, December 12, 1885. He studied at Aberdeen University, and was ordained in 1839 as incumbent of the Scottish Episcopal Church

CIANCHETTINI.

of Arradoul and Buckie. In 1861 he was appointed Dean of the United Diocese of Moray, Ross, and Caithness. He compiled "Traditional Ballad Airs, arranged and harmonised for the Pianoforte and Harmonium, from copies procured in the counties of Aberdeen, Banff, and Moray, by W. Christie, M.A., and the late William Christie, Monquhitter, edited by W. Christie, M.A., Dean of Moray," etc. Edinburgh, 2 vols., 1876-81. A very handsome and interesting work, containing a number of previously uncollected airs.

Church, John, composer, born at Windsor in 1675. He was a chorister of St. John's College, Oxford. Gentleman of Chapel Royal, 1696. Lay-vicar Westminster Abbey; Choirmaster, 1704-41. He died at Westminster, January 6, 1741. Author of an "Introduction to Psalmody, containing useful Instructions for young Beginners, explained in a familiar and easie manner," London, 1723. Service in F, in Ouseley's "Cathedral Services." Anthems. Four chants in Vandernan's "Divine Harmony." Songs, etc.

Churchill, William, pianist and composer, who flourished in London at the end of last and beginning of the present century. He wrote a number of works for his instrument, including Three Sonatas for pf. and violin; Six Duos for 2 violins, op. 2; Six Duos for violin and alto; Ten Progressive Lessons for pf., op. 5 and 10. Six trios, four for a violin, tenor and violoncello obligato, and two for two violins and violoncello obligato, op. 1 [1780]; Favorite Sonata for the harpsichord [1785]. Another musician of this name, probably a relative, was JOSEPH CHURCHILL, who issued "A selection of Cathedral Chants," London [1841]. Songs, dance music, etc.

Churchyard, Thomas, poet and musician, who flourished during the 16th century. Wrote "The Commendation of Musyke by Churchyarde," 1562. For other works see Hazlitt's "Handbook of Poetical Literature," 1867.

Cianchettini Pio, composer, was born at London, December 11, 1779. Son of Francesco Cianchettini. Appeared as infant prodigy, 1804. Travelled through Germany, Holland, and France. Returned to London, 1805. Accompanist and conductor to Catalani. Teacher and composer in London. He died at Cheltenham, July 20, 1851.

WORKS.—Pope's Ode to Solitude. Sixty Italian Catches, for two, three, and four voices (Martini), edited. Cantata for two voices from "Milton's Paradise Lost," "Take, O take those lips away," song. Music by Mozart, and Beethoven, edited, and a large number of fantasias, concertos, rondos, divertimentos, etc., for pf. His mother was VERONICA ROSALIE DUSSEK (1779-1833), sister

CIBBER.

CLARK.

of J. L. Dussek, and his sister, VERONICA ELISABETH CIANCHETTINI, was a composer of overtures, rondos, sonatas, waltzes, etc.

Cibber, Susanna Maria, born ARNE, soprano vocalist, born London, February, 1714. Sister of Thomas A. Arne, under whom she studied music. She first appeared in Lampe's "Amelie," in 1732. Married to Thomas Cibber in 1734. She appeared as an actress in Hill's "Zara," in 1736, and afterwards sang at concerts in London and elsewhere. Died, London, January 30, 1766.

Clagget, Charles, musician, born London, 1755. Was a violinist, and acted as leader at a theatre in Dublin. Invented various instruments, 1776-90, which he exhibited in London in 1791. He died in 1820.

WORKS.—Six duos for 2 flutes; Six duos for two violins; Six duos for violin and violoncello, op. 6. Musical Phænomena: an Organ made without pipes, strings, bells or glasses, the only instrument in the world that will never require to be retuned. A cromatic trumpet, capable of producing just intervals and regular melodies in all keys, without undergoing any change whatever. A French horn, answering the above description of the trumpet. London, 1793.

Clagget, Walter, English composer and pianist, who lived in latter half of the 18th century. He gave concerts in Norwich and London.

WORKS.—A New Medley overture, consisting entirely of Scots tunes and thirty-six of the most favourite Scots airs ... for 2 violins or 2 German flutes and a violoncello. Six solos and six Scots airs, with variations for the viola or violoncello. op. 2. Discourse on Musick, to be delivered at Clagget's Attic Consort, October 31, 1793.

Clapham, Jonathan, clergyman and author. Rector of Wramplingham, Norfolk, in the 17th century. He wrote "A short and full vindication of that sweet and comfortable ordinance of singing of Psalms," London, 1656.

Clare, Edward, organist and author, who died [London] April 9th, 1869. Issued "Analysis of practical Thorough-bass," London [1835]. A simple guide for chanting, for the use of amateurs ..., London, n.d. He composed a large number of ballads, transcriptions for pf., etc.

Claribel, see BARNARD, MRS.

Clark, Rev. Frederick Scotson, organist and composer, born in London, November 16th, 1840. He studied under his mother (a pupil of Mrs. Anderson and Chopin), and the pianoforte and harmony under Sergent, organist of Notre Dame. Organist of Regent Square Church, London, 1855. Studied organ under E. J. Hopkins; music at R.A.M., under Bennett, Goss, Engel, Pinsuti, and Pettit.

Organist successively of a number of London churches. Founded a College of Music in London, 1865. He studied for the ministry at Oxford, and became organist of Exeter College, Oxford. Bac. Mus., Oxon., 1867. Head master of St. Michael's Grammar School, Brighton, 1867. Curate of Lewes, Sussex. For a time he studied at Leipzig Conservatorium under Richter, Reinecke, etc., and was assistant in English church there. He also studied under Lebert, Pruckner, and Kruger at Stuttgart. He returned to London, 1873, and resumed his connection with the College or London Organ School, 1875. Represented English organ-playing at Paris Exhibition, 1878. He died at London, July 5, 1883.

WORKS.—Organ: Voluntaries; Pastorale; Douce Pensée; Andantes in F and D; Melodies in D, A, F, and E flat; Postlude. *Marches:* Anglaise, aux Flambeaux, des Fantômes, des Girondins, des Jacobins, Militaire, Belgian, Commemoration, Festal, Procession, Roman, Russian, Vienna, etc.; Communions in D minor, F, C minor, A minor, G and E; Offertoires in F, D, A, G, and C; Meditation, in B flat; Fantasias in F, etc.; Improvisations in B flat, C, G, F; Impromptus, prayers, romances; Gavottes; Minuets, airs. *Harmonium:* Voluntaries; Rêverie, Gavotte, Ave Maria, Songs. Meditation, in B flat, for violin, harmonium and pf. *Pianoforte:* Chinese march; Indian march; Turkish march, etc.; Mazurkas, polkas, galops, valses, and minuets; Barcarolles, studies, nocturnes, melodies. *Vocal:* Kyrie Eleison and Sanctus in E, from communion service No. 1; Do. from No. 2; Magnificat and nunc Dimittis, chant service in F. Cupid, part-song. Songs. First steps in organ-playing, London (Augener), n.d.; First steps in harmonium-playing (Do.) n.d.; First steps in pianoforte-playing, do.

Clark, J. Moir-, composer, born at Aberdeen. Studied at R.A.M. under E. Prout, and later in Germany. He gave concerts in Dresden, 1892, when several of his compositions were produced. Among his chief works are a Scotch Suite, for orchestra, performed by the Stock Exchange Orchestral Society at the Queen's Hall, April 29, 1895. Quintet in F, pf. and strings, Dresden, 1892; Princes' Hall (Miss Dora Bright's concert), April 19, 1893; and the Monday Popular Concerts, November 5th, 1894. He has also written a Suite, and other pieces for flute and pf., produced by Mr. F. Griffith, 1893; a Polonaise, violin and pf.; Variations on an original theme, pf., played by Miss Dora Bright at her recital, January 30, 1889—the first public performance of any of his works; Pf. duets; songs, etc.

Clark, Jeremiah, composer and organist, born in London, 1669 [or earlier]. He studied under Blow as a chorister in the Chapel Royal. Organist of Winchester College, 1692-

CLARK.

1695. Almoner and master of the Choristers of St. Paul's Cathedral, London, 1693. Organist and Vicar-Choral of St. Paul's, 1695 ; Gentleman of Chapel Royal, 1700. Joint organist of Chapel Royal with Croft, 1704. He committed suicide by shooting himself in St. Paul's churchyard, London, December 1, 1707.

WORKS.—*Music to the following plays*— Antony and Cleopatra (Sedley), 1677 ; Fond Husband, 1676 ; Titus Andronicus, 1687 ; World in the Moon (with D. Purcell), 1697 ; Campaigners, 1698 ; Island Princess (with D. Purcell and Leveridge), 1699 ; All for the better, 1702 ; The Committee, 1706. *Odes*— Alexander's Feast, Dryden ; Ode in Praise of the Island of Barbadoes. Services in G and C minor. *Anthems*—Praise the Lord, O Jerusalem ; How long wilt Thou forget me ? ; I will love Thee, O Lord ; O Lord God of my Salvation ; Bow down Thine Ear. Songs in D'Urfey's " Pills to Purge Melancholy." The Assumption, Cantata ; Lessons for the Harpsichord ; Ten Songs, op. 4 ; Secular music, miscellaneous.

Clark is now best remembered by a few of his anthems and the psalm-tune" St. Magnus." His dramatic music is completely forgotten, and none of his other secular works are in use.

Clark, John, Scottish collector and violinist of the 18th century. Published "Flores Musicæ, or the Scots Musician, being a general collection of the most celebrated Scots Tunes, Reels, Minuets, and Marches, adapted for the Violin, Hautboy, or German Flute, with a Bass for the violoncello or Harpsichord." Edinburgh, 1773.

A musician of the same name, probably the same individual or a relative, published at Perth " A Collection of new Strathspey reels and country dances, with a bass for the violoncello or harpsichord, dedicated to the Musical Society of Perth," 1795.

Clark, Richard, writer and singer, grandson of John Sale, was born at Datchet, Bucks., April 5, 1780. Chorister in St. George's Chapel, Windsor, under Aylward. Chorister at Eton College, under S. Heather. Lay-Clerk at St. George's Chapel, and Eton College, 1802-11. Secretary of the Glee Club. Lay-Vicar of Westminster Abbey and Vicar-Choral of St. Paul's, 1811. Gentleman of Chapel Royal, 1820. He died at London, October 8, 1856.

WORKS.—Words of the most favourite pieces performed at the Glee Club, Catch Club, and other public societies, London, 1814. First volume of poetry, revised, improved, and considerably enlarged, containing the most favourite pieces performed at the Glee Clubs, etc., London, 1824. Continuation, 1833. An account of the National Anthem entitled " God save the King," etc., London, 1822.

CLARKE.

Reminiscences of Handel, His Grace the Duke of Chandos, Powells the Harpers, The Harmonious Blacksmith, and others, London, 1836. Reading and playing from score simplified, London, 1838. An examination into the derivation, etymology, and definition of the word " Madrigale," London, 1852. On the sacred oratorio of " The Messiah " previous to the death of G. F. Handel, 1759, London, 1852. An address to the directors of the Ancient Concerts on the high pitch of the scale, London, 1845. Glees, anthems, chants, etc.

Clark, Thomas, musician, born at Canterbury, 1775 ; died there, May 30th, 1859. He was conductor of music at the Wesleyan Chapel, and latterly of the Unitarian Chapel, Canterbury. He published " The Union Harmonist, a selection of sacred music," 1841. " The Union Tune Book, a selection of tunes and chants suitable for use in congregations and Sunday schools," London [1842]. Psalm and hymn tunes, n.d. Composer of " Crediton," and other hymn tunes.

Clark, Windeyer, organist, pianist, and composer. Began his studies in a Tonic Sol-fa class. He entered the London Academy of Music, studying under Dr. Wylde, and afterwards took organ lessons from J. W. Elliott. From about 1877 he became amanuensis to Sir G. A. Macfarren, whose later oratorios he took down from dictation, and also played to the Cambridge Professor the Degree exercises sent in. Held organ appointments at St. Philip's, Paddington ; Curzon Chapel, Mayfair ; and Westbourne Grove Chapel. Gave frequent recitals, for some of which Macfarren wrote organ pieces. In 1889 he was made L.R.A.M. He composed some pieces for pf., and arranged the scores of Macfarren's " May Day," Haydn's " Creation," Mozart's First Mass, and Mendelssohn's " Lauda Zion," for pianoforte and harmonium. Joint translator, with J. T. Hutchinson, of Gounod's commentary on " Don Giovanni," London, Cocks & Co., 1895. He died of consumption, June 13, 1896, at the early age of thirty-seven.

Clarke, Charles E. J., organist and composer, born at Worcester, 1796. He was a chorister in Worcester Cathedral. Organist successively of Durham Cathedral, 1812, and Worcester Cathedral, 1814. Conductor of the Worcester Festival from 1815 (when only nineteen years of age), to 1839. Ill health compelled him to relinquish the task in 1842, when Joseph Surman was appointed conductor. Died at Worcester, April 27, 1844.

Clarke, Frederick William, composer, born in 1852 ; died in 1883. He graduated Mus. Bac. Oxford in 1880. Composer of Reveries, polonaises, gavottes, etc., for pf. ; Songs and other vocal music. An Album of his

CLARKE.

songs, edited by Rev. W. Mann, Precentor of Bristol Cathedral, and Charles South, organist of Salisbury Cathedral, was published, *In Memoriam,* by Novello and Co., 1885.

Clarke, James, writer and teacher, born at London, 1793; died at Leeds, 1859. Author of a "Catechism of Wind Instruments, containing explanations of the scale and compass of each instrument, and particular directions for writing the parts of flutes, clarinets, etc.," London, n.d. "Instruction Book for Children on the Pianoforte," London, n.d. "The Child's Alphabet of Music," London, n.d. "Exercises in Harmony, designed to facilitate the study of the Theory of Music and the Practice of Thorough Bass, London, 1832 (pub. in 24 nos). "Catechism of the Rudiments of Music," London, n.d. "New School of Music, combining the Practice of Singing with that of the Pianoforte," London, n.d.

Clarke, James Hamilton Smee, composer and conductor, born in Birmingham, January 25, 1840. His father was an amateur organist, and encouraged his son's musical studies, but did not intend him to follow the art as a profession. At twelve he was organist of St. Matthew's, Duddeston, and at fifteen was sent as pupil to an analytical chemist, but gave that up and was articled to a land surveyor, 1855-61. At the expiration of his articles he entered the musical profession, and obtained (1862) a post as organist of Parsonstown Parish Church, Ireland, changing, a year later, to Zion Church, Rathgar, Dublin. While here he joined the Dublin Philharmonic orchestra as first violin, and frequently assisted Dr. Stewart at Christchurch Cathedral. In 1864 he was appointed conductor of the Belfast Anacreontic Society, and organist of Caremony Church. This year he won the first prize offered by the then recently established College of Organists for an anthem. He was appointed organist of Queen's College, Oxford, in June, 1866, after holding office a few months at Llandaff Cathedral, and graduated Mus. Bac., 1867. During his five years' residence in this city he conducted the Queen's College Musical Society, and played the clarinet at several College concerts. He was organist of Kensington Parish Church, 1871, and succeeded (Sir) Arthur Sullivan at St. Peter's, South Kensington, in 1872. From this time he turned his attention to the theatre, and was conductor at the Opera Comique, Comedy, Toole's, Gaiety, and other houses; conductor of the D'Oyly Carte Company in the provinces, 1878, and of various concert parties. From 1878, for some years, he was musical director at the Lyceum Theatre, and composed music for several dramas produced by (Sir) Henry Irving. In 1889 he was appointed conductor of the Victorian National Orchestra, returning from Australia in 1891.

CLARKE.

While there he acted as inspector of military bands, and had the honorary rank of Captain conferred upon him. In 1893 he accepted the post of principal conductor of the Carl Rosa Company. He is now resident in London. His published works are nearly four hundred in number, and can only be outlined in the subjoined list. He contributed an important series of papers to *Musical Society,* 1886-7.

WORKS.—*Dramatic :* Incidental music to Hamlet, 1878 ; Merchant of Venice, 1879 ; Eugene Aram, 1879 ; The Iron Chest (partly from Storace), 1879 ; The Corsican Brothers, 1880 ; The Cup (Tennyson, 1881) ; King Lear, 1892 ; and Cymbeline, 1896 ; all for the Lyceum Theatre, under Henry Irving. Music to Vittoria Contanari, and other dramas. Comediettas and operettas for the German Reed Entertainments ; Martial Law ; Castle Botherem, 1880 ; A pretty Bequest, etc. School Cantatas and Operettas : Daisy Chain ; Hornpipe Harry, op. 358, etc. Sacred Cantata : Praise, op. 68 ; Ode to Industry, op. 90 ; The Lord is my Light, anthem in 8 parts, op. 44 (College of Organists' Prize, 1864) ; many anthems, Church services, songs, part-songs, etc. *Orchestral* : Symphony, No. 1, in F (Exhibition Concerts, Albert Hall, August, 1873) ; No. 2, in G minor, op. 122 (Promenade Concerts, Covent Garden, 1879) ; six overtures, and other pieces. Concerto, pf. and orchestra, op. 78 ; Quartets, strings ; Quartet, pf. and strings. Sonata and Romance, pf. and flute, etc. *Organ :* Six sonatas ; Three andantes ; Three offertories ; Three pieces, op. 348, etc., etc.

Clarke, James P., Scottish musician, who held a good teaching position in the West of Scotland. For some time he was assistant to a music-seller in Edinburgh. In 1829, he was leader of psalmody in St. George's Church, Glasgow ; and in 1834, he succeeded Thomas Macfarlane, as organist of St. Mary's Episcopal Chapel. In 1835, he emigrated to Canada, after which all trace of him seems to be lost. He edited "Parochial Psalmody, a new Collection of approved Psalm tunes, including several composed expressly for this work, to which are prefixed, Lessons in the Art of Singing," Glasgow, [c. 1830], 2nd ed., 1832. The Choir : a selection of choruses, anthems, etc., edited by J. P. Clarke, late organist of St. Mary's Chapel, and A. Thomson, organist of St. Andrew's Chapel, Glasgow [1835]. He also composed songs in Atkinson's "Chameleon," and in Hogg's "Border Garland" [1829], etc.

Clarke, Jane, musician and organist, published "Select portions of psalms and hymns, adapted to music, as sung at Oxford Chapel," London [1808].

Clarke, Jessie Murray, authoress of "How to excel in Singing and Elocution. A manual for lady students," London, 1884.

CLARKE.

CLAXTON.

Clarke, John Charles, musician of first half of the present century, who resided in Edinburgh as a conductor and vocalist. He published a "Collection of Glees and Choruses," Edinburgh [1840].

Clarke, John, or Clarke=Whitfeld, composer and organist, was born at Gloucester, December 13th, 1770. He studied under Philip Hayes, and became organist of St. Lawrence's, Ludlow, 1789-94. Mus. Bac., Oxon., 1793. Organist of Armagh Cathedral, 1794-97. Mus. Doc., Dublin, 1795. Master of choristers and organist of Christ Church and St. Patrick's Cathedral, Dublin, 1798. Organist and Choirmaster of Trinity and St. John's Colleges, Cambridge, 1799-1820. Mus. Doc., Cantab., 1799. Mus. Doc., Oxon., 1810. Organist of Hereford Cathedral, 1820-33. Professor of Music, Cambridge University, 1821. He died at Holmer, near Hereford, February 22, 1836, and is buried in Hereford Cathedral.

WORKS.—Cathedral music (consisting of services and anthems), 4 vols., 1805-1822, reprinted by Novello. Crucifixion and the Resurrection, oratorio, 1822. Twelve Glees, composed and inscribed by permission to H.R.H. the Prince Regent [1805]; Twelve vocal pieces, with original poetry, 2 vols., n.d. Glees, etc.: Alice Brand; The Carpet Weaver; Celestial Hope; Come, Ossian, come; The Coronach; Dawn of Day; Edith of Lorn; Hymn for the dead; Hymn to the morning star; It was a night of lovely June; Merrily bounds the bark; Minstrel's tale; Red Cross Knights; What tho' the Knights; When I am doom'd; Wide o'er the brim. Songs: Ah! whither, Morpheus; Blanche of Devon's song; Bonnie, bonnie blue; Days that are gone; Ellen's song; The Maid of the Moor; Here's the vow; In peace love tunes; Know ye the land; Laugh and rejoice; Minstrel's Harp; Moorland Mary; Oh! sweet is the perfume; Poor Mary; Smile of affection; Soldier, rest; Thou dear native land; Wake, Maid of Lorn; With jet black eyes; Young Lochinvar. The Beauties of Purcell. Thirty-four favourite anthems, selected from various English composers, 2 vols. The Vocal works composed by G. F. Handel, arranged for organ or pianoforte, London, 17 vols. [1809]. Selection of single and double chants, in score, 2 vols., n.d.

Clarke, Mary Cowden, born MARY VICTORIA NOVELLO, writer, daughter of Vincent Novello, was born at London, June, 1809. She was married in 1828 to Charles Cowden Clarke. She compiled the famous "Shakespeare Concordance," wrote novels and poetry, edited an edition of Shakespeare, and wrote the "Life and labours of Vincent Novello." London, 1864 (portrait). "My long life: an autobiographic sketch," London, Unwin, 1896.

Clarke, Payne, tenor vocalist, born in Manchester, December 23, 1860. He sang as a boy at the Church of the Holy Name, Manchester, and subsequently as an alto and tenor for some years. He studied under Dr. Henry Hiles, and later with Mr. William Shakespeare. After some experience in opera, he joined Mr. J. W. Turner's Company in 1886, and later in the same year was a member of the Carl Rosa Opera Company, in which he remained for three years, sustaining a number of characters. In 1890 he appeared at Denver, U.S.A., as Manrico, in *Il Trovatore*, and as Lohengrin at the National Theatre, Mexico, in 1891. He was singing in concerts in London, 1894; but he is more widely known in the north as a concert singer.

Clarke, Stephen, musician, was born at Durham about the middle of the 18th century. He was organist of the Episcopal Chapel in the Cowgate of Edinburgh, and a teacher there from about 1764. He died at Edinburgh, August 6, 1797. He composed "Two Sonatas for the Pianoforte or Harpsichord, in which are introduced favourite Scotch airs, composed and respectfully dedicated to Mr. Erskine, Jun., of Mar," op. 3. Edinburgh, 1790. He also harmonized the airs in Johnson's "Scots Musical Museum." On his death the work was continued by his son WILLIAM (born Edinburgh [c. 1780]; died Edinburgh, 1820), who was organist of St. Paul's Episcopal Chapel, and a teacher and writer of some small pieces for the pianoforte and voice. He issued "A Collection of the most favourite airs, progressively arranged and fingered for the pianoforte." Edinburgh, n.d.

Clarke, William, musician, born 1740; died December 5, 1820. He was a Vicar-Choral of St. Paul's Cathedral, and Minor Canon, 1769. He is buried in the crypt of St. Paul's. He edited "A Collection of Chaunts, Psalm Tunes, Hymns, and an Anthem in four parts," n.d.

Clarkson, John, Scottish dancing-master and violinist, who died at St. Andrews, January 20, 1812. He compiled "Clarkson's Musical Entertainment, being a selection of various Tunes and Pieces of Music adapted for the Pf. or Harpsichord," n.d.

His son JOHN was a dancing-master and violinist, and published "A Complete Collection of the much-admired Tunes, as Danced at the Balls and Publics of the late Mr. Strange, Teacher of Dancing in Edinburgh." This work appeared about the beginning of this century.

Claxton, Rev. William, organist of St. Michael's College, Tenbury, graduated B.A., 1876; Mus. B., 1882, Oxford, Curate of Hartley Wintney, 1887. Composer of a morning communion, and evening service, in G; anthems; songs; part-song, "Ye little birds

CLAY.

that sit and sing" (men's voices and orchestra), etc.

Clay, Frederick, composer, born at Paris, August 3, 1840. Son of James Clay, who was M.P. for Hull, and a famous whist player. He studied under Molique at Paris, and Hauptmann at Leipzig. For a short time he held a post in the Treasury Department. He resided in London as a teacher and composer, but latterly, owing to ill-health, retired to Great Marlow, Bucks, where he died Nov. 24, 1889.

WORKS.—*Operas and Operettas :* The Pirate's Isle, 1859; Out of Sight, 1860; Court and Cottage, 1862; Constance. 1865; Ages Ago, 1869; Gentleman in Black, 1870; Happy Arcadia, 1872; Cattarina, 1874; Princess Toto, 1875; Don Quixote, 1875; Babil and Bijou, 1872 (with others); Black Crook, 1872; Oriana; Merry Duchess, 1883; Music to Shakespeare's "Twelfth Night." *Cantatas :* Knights of the Cross, 1866; Lalla Rookh, 1877. Part-songs, songs, etc.

Clayton, Eleanor Creathorne (Mrs. NEEDHAM), novelist and musical writer, born at Dublin in 1832. Author of "Queens of Song; being memoirs of some of the most celebrated female vocalists who have appeared on the lyric stage from the earliest days of opera to the present time, with a chronological list of all the operas that have been performed in Europe." London, 1863, 2 vols.

Clayton, Thomas, English composer, born in 1670. He was a member of the Royal Band of William and Mary, 1692-1702. After residing in Italy he returned to England and introduced Italian opera. He died in 1730. He composed music for Addison's Rosamund; Arsinoe; Dryden's Alexander's Feast; The Passion of Sappho, etc., but none of it appears to possess much merit.

Clegg, David, organist of Littleborough Parish Church (1891), is the composer of a cantata, "The Daughter of Jairus," produced at Rochdale, December 8, 1891; and an opera, "Cleopatra," selections from which were given at the same place and date.

Clegg, John, violinist, born Ireland, 1714. He studied under Dubourg and Buononcini, and first appeared in London, 1723. After travelling in Italy, he was appointed principal violin at the Opera, London. He became insane towards the end of his career, and died in 1746.

Cleland, George, musician and organist of the end of 18th and first half of present century. He was organist of St. Mary's Chapel, Bath. He published "A selection of chants never before published, together with a sanctus and kyrie eleison, arranged in score," London [1824].

Clench, Leonora, violinist, native of St. Mary's, Canada. Studied at Leipzig Conserv-

CLIFTON.

atorium, and played at a concert given in that town by Miss Marie Wurm, November 7, 1886, and at other concerts in the same year. In London she made her *début* at a concert at the Lyric Club, June 24, 1892. Appeared as soloist at the Hovingham Festival, Yorks., 1896.

Cliffe, Frederick, pianist and composer, born at Low Moor, near Bradford, Yorkshire, May 2. 1857. As quite a child he had a local reputation as pianist and organist, and at sixteen (in 1873) he was appointed organist to the Bradford Festival Choral Society. In 1876 he was elected to a Scholarship in the National Training School for Music, after leaving which he was pianist and accompanist on various concert tours. He played a concerto at the Promenade Concerts, Covent Garden, in 1882; and on the opening of the Royal College of Music, in 1883, he was appointed a professor of the pianoforte. He came into notice as a composer with a symphony in C minor, produced at the Crystal Palace, April 20, 1889. In 1890 he composed an orchestra picture, "Clouds and sunshine," for the Philharmonic Society, which was produced May 22 of that year. For the Leeds Festival of 1892 he wrote a second Symphony, "A summer night," and a violin concerto for the Norwich Festival of 1896. He has also composed several songs, etc.

Clifford, Rev. James, clergyman and musician, born at Oxford, 1622. Chorister of Magdalen College, Oxford, 1632-42. Minor Canon St. Paul's Cathedral, London, 1661. Senior Cardinal, St. Paul's, London, 1682. Curate of Parish Church of St. Gregory. Chaplain to Society of Serjeant's Inn. He died at London, September, 1698.

WORKS.—A Collection of Divine Services and Anthems, usually sung in His Majesty's Chapel, and in all the cathedral and collegiate choirs of England and Ireland, by James Clifford, 1663, 2nd edition enlarged, 1664. Sermons, etc.

Clifford, Walter, baritone vocalist. Sang as a boy in the choir of Holy Trinity Church, Hull. Became a pupil of Edwin Holland, and made his *début* at Mr. Ambrose Austin's concert at St. James's Hall, 1879, appearing at the Covent Garden Promenade Concerts the same year. He sang in English Opera in the provinces, and took the part of *De Brètigny* in Massenet's "Manon," when the opera was produced by Carl Rosa at Drury Lane, May 7, 1885. After singing for some time at concerts in various places, he was engaged, in 1887, for an American tour by the Chicago Symphonic Orchestral Society.

Clifton, Henry Robert, better known as "Harry Clifton," author and composer of comic songs, born at Hoddesden, Hereford, in 1831, died, Hammersmith, London, July 15,

CLIFTON.

1872. Well-known in his day as author and composer of music-hall lyrics of the "motto" variety, among which were "Paddle your own canoe;" "Pulling hard against the stream;" "Shelling green peas;" "Work, boys, work," and many others. He also wrote "Polly Perkins of Paddington Green" [1865], and other songs of a mock-sentimental type, such as the "Agreeable young man;" "Convivial man;" "Jemima Brown;" "On board of the Kangaroo" [1865], etc. For many years he resided in Glasgow as a music-hall singer.

Clifton, John Charles, composer and pianist, born at London, 1781. Studied under R. Bellamy and Charles Wesley. Employed for a time in mercantile pursuits. Resided at Bath as teacher and conductor. Went to Dublin, 1802, and resided there as teacher and composer till 1815. Settled in London, 1816, as teacher of the pf. and advocate of Logier's system. He died at Hammersmith, London, November 18, 1841.

WORKS.— Edwin, opera, Dublin, 1815; Series of Moral Songs, by W. F. Collard, published in parts, 1823-4; Selection of British Melodies, with appropriate words, by J. F. M. Dovaston, London, n.d.; Collection of French Airs, with symphonies and accompaniments, 2 vols. As pants the hart, canon. *Glees*— Three glees for 3, 4, and 5 voices, 1823; A blossom wreath; Maid of Toro; On a rock whose haughty brow; Quick flew the gales of rosy spring; Hushed is the harp; Pray goody. *Songs*—As through life's early path; First dawn of love; Good-night, my pretty Anne; If music be the food of love (canzonet); Miller's daughter; Sensitive Plant; Soft on the violet bank; With love-fraught eyes; Nay, if you threaten; Sweet choice of my heart; A bumper of sparkling wine, etc. Theory of Harmony Simplified, 1816; Instructions for the Pianoforte; Memoir of Sir John Stevenson (in a review), etc.

Clifton was a pianist of much ability, and invented, in 1816, an instrument called the "Eidomusicon," which, on being fastened to the keyboard of the pianoforte, produced the notes and chords as they were struck, with a view to displaying them to the eye, and so facilitate sight-singing, etc.

Clinton, George Arthur, clarinettist, born at Newcastle-on-Tyne. For many years a member of the Crystal Palace Orchestra, and a soloist at the concerts there at least since 1876. Principal clarinet in Her Majesty's Private Band, and in the Philharmonic Orchestra. Professor of the Clarinet at R.A.M. Has given Chamber Concerts of music for wind instruments in various halls in London, 1892-6, and has played at the Saturday Popular Concerts, etc,

Clinton, John, flute player and writer, born in 1810; died at London in 1864. Author

COBB.

of A Treatise upon the Mechanism and general principles of the Flute, London, n.d.; Complete School for the Boehm Flute, containing everything necessary to learn that instrument, from the elements to the most advanced stage, London, n.d. (5 editions), Ashdown; A Code of Instruction for the Equisonant flute, in which the fingering and resources of that instrument are fully explained by numerous examples; First Set of three Grand Studies for the Flute; Second do.; Universal Flute Tutor (Boosey). *Flute music*—Trios for two flutes and pf., opp. 2, 3, 10; Trios for three flutes, opp. 7 and 9; Five Notturnos, flute and harp (with Oberthür); Gems of the Italian School; Cavatinas, or songs without words; The Drawing-Room Concert, written by W. Ball; Transcriptions for flute and pf., of which he published an enormous number.

Clipsham, J——, musician, compiled the "Divine Psalmist's Companion," Market Harborough, 1753,

Clive, Catherine, *born* RAFFTOR, soprano vocalist, born in London, of Irish parents, in 1711. She sang at Drury Lane Theatre from 1728. Married to George Clive, a barrister, in 1734, and separated from him in 1769. Retired from stage. She died at Twickenham, Dec. 6, 1785. See Life of Catherine Clive, with an account of her adventures on and off the stage ... by Percy Fitzgerald, London, 1888.

Clive, Franklin F., bass vocalist of the present day. He learnt the violin at nine years of age, and when seventeen entered an office in the city of London. In time his voice developed, and gaining a Scholarship at Trinity College, London, he studied for the profession. About the year 1882, he was becoming known as a singer; sang in the "Messiah," at Birmingham, Boxing Night, 1883, with success, and in other places. He was on tour with an Opera Company in 1887, and appeared as King Richard, in Sullivan's "Ivanhoe," at the Royal English Opera, in February, 1891.

Clutsam, George H——, pianist and composer, a native of Australia. He was a member of the Amy Sherwin Concert Party in Australia, 1888; and acted as accompanist during the Melba tour in England, 1893. His compositions include a Symphony (a movement from which was performed at the Covent Garden Promenade Concerts, October 3, 1890), and other works; Songs, etc.

Cobb, Gerard Francis, composer, born at Nettlestead, Kent, October 15, 1838. Educated at Marlborough College, and Trinity College, Cambridge, of which he was elected Scholar in 1860; and, after taking a double First, a Fellow, in 1863. His musical training was chiefly in Dresden. He was President of the Cambridge University Musical Society for

COBB.

COLBORNE.

some ten years, from 1874 ; and Chairman of the University Board of Musical Studies for fifteen years, from 1877. His compositions are very numerous, although, from the claims of his official work at the University, it was many years before he was able to devote his attention to creative art.

WORKS.—Psalm 62, for soli, chorus, and orchestra, composed for the Festival of the North-Eastern Choir Association, Ripon Cathedral, 1892. Seven Church services, including a full Morning, Communion, and Evening Service in C major, for men's voices, composed (by request) for the use of the Choir of St. George's Chapel, Windsor. Motet, *Surge Illuminare* (Leslie's Choir, March, 1887); Seven anthems. Prize Glee (four voices), A Message to Phyllis ; Prize Madrigal (six voices), Sleeping Beauty, etc. Six Songs (W. Fergusson); Lieder und Gesänge (six songs); Three English Ballads ; Three Sacred Songs ; Barrack Room Ballads (Rudyard Kipling); Song and Silence, with horn obligato, and many other songs. Quintet in C, op. 22, pf. and strings; Suite, violin and pf. ; Suite, Voices of the Sea, pf., etc., etc.

Cobb, Richard, English composer and organist during the 16th and 17th centuries. Was organist to Charles I., and composed some vocal music. "Smiths are good fellows," a catch, is by him.

Cobb, Richard Barker, baritone vocalist, known by the *nom de théâtre* of Richard Temple, made his *début* in opera at the Crystal Palace, 1872. Toured in the Gilbert and Sullivan operas, 1879 ; sang at the Savoy Theatre in "Princess Ida" and "The Mikado," 1884-5 ; gave performances of opera in Italian at the Gaiety Theatre, May, 1886, himself taking the title-part in "Rigoletto;" revived Gounod's "The Mock Doctor" at the Grand Theatre, London, 1890 ; and sang at the Olympic Theatre, under Signor Lago's management, October, 1892. He turned to the music halls early in that year, and appeared at the Trocadero ; sang again in the concert-room, 1893; and recited in Mendelssohn's "Athalie" at the Queen's Hall, November 13, 1895.

Cobbold, William, composer, born in Parish of St. Andrew, Norwich, January 5, 1559-60. In 1599 he became organist of Norwich Cathedral, but in 1608 he became a singing man, while the post of organist was held by Wm. Inglott. He died at Beccles in Suffolk, November 7, 1639, and was buried in the south aisle of the Parish Church, where a stone marks his grave.

He contributed to Este's "Whole Book of Psalms," 1592, and wrote the madrigal, "With wreaths of rose and laurel" in the "Triumphs of Oriana." Some of his works remain in MS., and an anthem, "In Bethlehem town," appears in Clifford's Services, 1663.

Cochran, John, musician, who issued "A Selection of Psalm and Hymn Tunes . . . with Anthems." Dublin, 1811, two editions.

Cock, Arthur, organist and composer of the 16th century. He was organist of Exeter Cathedral, and in 1593 he graduated Mus. Bac., Oxford.

Cogan, Philip, composer, organist, and pianist, born at Cork in 1750 [Doncaster 1757 ?]. Chorister and choirman of Cathedral of St. Finn Barre, Cork. Stipendiary of Christ Church, Dublin, 1772. He died in 1834.

WORKS.—Anthems, various ; Six sonatas for pf. and violin, op. 2, 1788; Sonatas for pf., op. 4 ; Concerto in E flat for 2 violins, viola, 'cello, 2 flutes, and 2 horns, op. 6, 1792 ; Sonatas for pf. (Clementi), op. 8 ; Harpsichord Lessons ; Songs.

Coggins, Joseph, composer and pianist, was born in 1780. He studied under J. W. Callcott. Teacher of pf. in London, where he died, in first half of present century.

WORKS.—The Musical Assistant, containing all that is truly useful to the theory and practice of the pianoforte, London, 1815 ; Companion to the Musical Assistant, containing all that is truly useful to the theory and practice of the pianoforte, also a complete dictionary, London, 8vo, 1824 ; Admired Hymns....adapted for the use of schools, 2 parts ; Pf. music, fantasias, etc. ; Songs ; Complete instructions for the flute, according to Drouet's system, London, 1830.

Coghlan, J. P., author of "An essay on the Church plain-chant," London, 1782.

Colbeck, William Robert, organist and conductor, born at Bebington, Cheshire, 1852. Studied under Dr. French Flowers, and F. W. Hird. Began his career as an organist at the age of eleven, at Gamston Parish Church, Notts. ; afterwards appointed to St. Peter's, Morley, Leeds ; St. Mathias, Burley, Leeds, 1869 ; and, in 1876, to the Parish Church, Folkestone. Later in that year (1876), he left for British Guiana, being appointed to St. Philip's, Georgetown. This appointment he still holds, together with that of organist of the Town Hall, from its opening in 1891. His organ recitals are popular, and an important feature in the season's music. He was conductor for twelve years of the Musical Society, now defunct ; and is president and conductor of the recently formed Orchestral Society. He composed a march for the opening of the Town Hall organ, Georgetown (1891); and has published some pf. pieces, and songs (including a prize song in Cassell's Magazine, 1884).

Colborne, Langdon, organist and composer, born at Hackney, London, September 15, 1837. Studied under George Cooper. Organist of St. Michael's College, Tenbury, 1860. Mus. Bac., Cantab., 1864. Mus. Doc., Cantuar,

COLE.

1883. Organist of Beverley Minster, 1874; Wigan Parish Church, 1875; Dorking Parish Church, 1877; Hereford Cathedral, 1877. He died at Hereford, September 16, 1889.

WORKS.—Samuel, oratorio, Hereford, 1889; Complete Service in C; Magnificat and Nunc Dimittis in D, A, and B flat; Te Deum and Benedictus in E flat. *Anthems*—I will lay me down; O Lord, our Governor; Out of the deep; Ponder my words, O Lord; Rend your hearts. *Part-songs:* If slumber sweet, Lisena; The Siesta; The bright-hair'd morn is glowing; Songs, etc.

Cole, Blanche, *see sub.* NAYLOR, SIDNEY.

Cole, Charlotte, and Susanna, vocalists, formerly known in the musical world as the Misses Cole, were born at Tarrington, Herefordshire. Their father came of a musical family, and was for many years organist of the parish church, choir trainer, and teacher of music. The children, from their infancy, were brought up in a musical atmosphere, and were familiar with the works of the great masters. At the R.A.M. they studied under Manuel Garcia, and both were elected Associates of that Institution. Charlotte, the elder, a soprano, was a leading member of the students' choir in Hanover Chapel, Regent Street; and of the semi-chorus of the Concerts of Ancient Music. She sang in the double quartet in "Elijah" at the Hereford Festival of 1849, and Mr. J. W. Davison at that time hearing the sisters sing Mendelssohn's two-part songs, advised them to appear in London as duet singers. Their *début* took place at Exeter Hall, in the Wednesday Concerts, November 14, 1849; and for years afterwards they were in great request, succeeding the Misses Williams in public favour. They sang at the Crystal Palace in 1855, and at the principal London and provincial concerts. In 1853 Charlotte Cole married Mr. ALFRED GILBERT (*q.v.*), and after singing at his concerts for some years, devoted her attention chiefly to teaching singing. She is an Associate of the Philharmonic Society, and the composer of some tasteful songs, etc. Susanna, whose voice was a mezzo-soprano of beautiful quality, continued to sing both in opera and concerts; but she also married, and now is engaged in teaching singing, both for the stage and concert room.

Cole, James Parry, composer and conductor, born at Tarrington, Herefordshire, brother of the foregoing. While a child he was taught the violin by his father, and at the age of eight became a chorister of Hereford Cathedral, and pupil of G. Townshend Smith. When fifteen he entered the R.A.M., studying under Charles Lucas, R. Blagrove, W. Dorrell, and G. A. Macfarren. On leaving the Academy he went to Arundel, Sussex, as a teacher of music, and organist of the parish church.

COLERIDGE.

There he remained five years, and returning to London, he has occupied various posts as organist, musical director, and teacher. He has composed much, chiefly devoting his attention to music for the stage. While a chorister he composed an oratorio, "Deborah and Barak," as well as some church services. Later works are—Cantata, By the waters of Babylon. *Operas and Operettas:* Vokin's Vengeance (St. George's Hall, 1877); The Golden Wedding (1883); All for nothing (1883); Black and White; a Romance of the Harem (1887); The Black Count (1890); The Pillow of Roses; Hypatia (Grand opera in four acts); Bunell's Bride; Pas Seul; Romance and reality; The Grecian Dancer; Woman's Honour; V. V.; Give him a rest; The deaf knight, etc. A book of chamber songs; songs, various; pieces for pf. and violin, pf. pieces, etc., etc.

Cole, William, musician, who was born about 1764. He was an organist and teacher at Colchester, and London. He died at Pimlico, London, August 11, 1848.

WORKS.—Morning and evening service, with six anthems in score, n.d. The Psalmodist's Exercise, or a set of psalm tunes and anthems, all entirely new, composed for the use of country choirs, London, n.d. View of modern psalmody, being an attempt to reform the practice of singing in the worship of God. Colchester, 1819.

Cole, William Henry, violinist and conductor, born at Dudley, April 7, 1847. Studied under Henry Hayward and J. T. Carrodus. He has taken a leading part in the musical life of Glasgow since 1868. He has organised various quartet parties and bands, which have performed in Glasgow, and in most of the Scottish provincial towns. Mr. Cole is well-known as a teacher of the violin.

Coleire, Richard, English clergyman. Wrote "The Antiquity and usefulness of instrumental musick in the service of God, a sermon on erecting an organ at Isleworth," London, 1738.

Coleman, Charles (or COLMAN), composer, who was born about the beginning of the 17th century [1600]. He was a member of the private band of Charles I. Doc. Mus., Cambridge, 1651. He died at London, 1664.

WORKS.—The Siege of Rhodes, Davenant (with Lawes, Cook, and Hudson), 1657; Musicall Ayres and Dialogues, 1652; Musick's Recreation on the Lyra-violl, 1656; Select Ayres, 1659; The Musical Vocabulary in Phillips' New World of Words, 1658.

Coleman, Edward, brother of above, was born in 1633. He became Gentleman of Chapel Royal, and died at Greenwich, August 29, 1669. Wrote songs in various collections, etc.

Coleridge, Arthur Duke, amateur vocalist, lecturer, and translator, was born on Feb-

COLES.

ruary 1, 1830. He is a M.A., and was called to the bar in 1860. Clerk of the Arraigns for the Midland Circuit, and nephew of the late Chief Justice, Lord Coleridge. In the days of the Amateur Musical Society, under Henry Leslie, he occasionally sang at their concerts, having a good tenor voice. He has lectured in various places upon Bach, Weber, Spohr, and Schumann; and rendered service to musical literature by his translations of K. von Hellborn's "Life of Schubert," London, Longmans, 1869, 2 vols.; and the "Life of Moscheles, with selections from his diaries and correspondence," by his wife. London : Hurst and Blackett, 1873, 2 vols. He also contributed articles to Grove's "Dictionary of Music and Musicians."

Coles, Sydney George Randolph, organist and composer, born at Bristol, 1852, Chorister at St. Paul's Church, Clifton, and pupil of the late Alfred Stone. When eighteen he was appointed organist of St. John's, Broad Street, Bristol. In 1873 he became an articled pupil of, and assistant to, the late Dr. W. H. Monk. F.C.O., 1876; Mus. Bac., Trin. Coll., Toronto, 1887. Resident in Eastbourne since 1881, as pianist, teacher; and was organist of the Parish Church for ten years, now holding a similar office at the Presbyterian Church, and being also organist to the Hadrian Lodge of Freemasons, No. 2,483, When the legality of the *in absentia* degrees was questioned, Mr. Coles strongly upheld the *bona fide* nature of the examinations. This subject is beyond the scope of the present work, and readers are referred to the musical press, 1890-93.

WORKS.—Psalm 23, for soli, chorus, and organ (performed by the Musical Artists' Society, R.A.M., 1882); Communion Service; Offertory Sentences; Carol, The Bellringers (Crystal Palace Sunday School Festival, 1895); an Imperial Hymn, etc. Triumphal march for orchestra; March and Postlude, organ; pieces for pf., etc.

Collet, Sophia Dobson, born in London, 1822, was associated with Eliza and Sarah Flower in the music at South Place Chapel, and composed some of the music still in use there. She died at Highbury Park, March 27, 1894.

Collett, John, instrumental composer, who flourished during the middle of the 18th century. He composed "Six Solos for the violin, with a thorough bass for ye harpsichord, op. 1," London [1770], and other instrumental music.

Collier, Joel, *see* BICKNELL, John L.

Collins, Isaac, violinist, born in 1797; died November 24, 1871. Was for many years principal second violin in the Crystal Palace Orchestra. In the forties he gave concerts in London, with his five children, of whom the best known were George Collins, violoncellist,

CONINGSBY.

who died in 1869, and Viotti Collins, violinist, who is still actively engaged in his profession.

Collinson, Thomas Henry, organist and conductor, born at Alnwick, April 24, 1858. Pupil of Dr. Armes', at Durham Cathedral, and later, deputy organist there. Graduated Mus. Bac., Oxford, 1877. Organist of St. Oswald's, Durham; and in 1878, appointed to St. Mary's Cathedral, Edinburgh. From 1883 he has been conductor of the Edinburgh Choral Union. At the Cathedral he has directed special Oratorio Services; and has given organ performances at the Edinburgh Exhibition, 1886, and has a high reputation as an executant. He is Church Music lecturer to the Episcopal Theological College. Of his compositions only some anthems are published.

Collisson, W. A. Houston, pianist and composer, resident in Dublin. His playing attracted attention about 1884, and he began giving Saturday Popular Concerts in 1885, in the Leinster Hall, Dublin; and in May, 1887, started a series of Saturday Evening Concerts in St. James's Hall, London. He was appointed organist of the Parish Church, Rathfarnham, 1885; and to Holy Trinity, Rathmines, Dublin, 1886. He graduated Mus. Bac. [1885?]; Mus. Doc., Dublin, 1890. Of his compositions two comic operas have been produced : The Knight of the Road, Dublin, 1891; and Strongbow, Dublin, 1892.

Colville, David, musician, born at Campbeltown, January 15, 1829. He published "Graduated course of elementary instruction in singing, on the letter-note method, in twenty-six lessons, with hints on self-instruction, etc." (with George Bentley), 1864 ; Collections of Part-songs, under the title of "Choral Harmony," "Amphion," etc.

Comon, or Cormac Dall, Irish harper, story-teller, and vocalist, was born at Woodstock, Mayo, May, 1703. He lived an itinerant life, and was famous as a composer of songs and elegies. He died about the end of the 18th century, or at least after 1786, at which date he was alive.

Compton, Mrs. A., *see* GRAY, LOUISA,

Condell, Henry, violinist and composer, was born in the latter part of the 18th century. He was a violinist at Drury Lane and Covent Garden Theatres. Gained prize at Catch Club with glee, "Loud blowe the wyndes," 1811. He died at Battersea, London, June, 1824.

WORKS.—Enchanted Island, ballet, 1804 ; Who wins? or The Widow's choice, farce, 1808; Transformation, farce, 1810; Farmer's wife, 1814; Glees; Songs, etc.

Congreve, Benjamin, composer, was born in 1836, and died at London on March 23, 1871. He composed part-songs and songs.

Coningsby, George, clergyman. Author of "A Sermon preached at the Cathedral

CONRAN.

Church of Hereford, at the anniversary meeting of the Three Choirs, September 6, 1732, Church Musick vindicated," Oxford, 1733.

Conran, D., Irish writer, author of " Musical Research, or General System of Modulation," Dublin, 1840.

Conran, Michael, probably a relative of the above. Organist of St. Patrick's Church, Manchester. Author of "The National Music of Ireland ; containing the History of the Irish bards, the national melodies, the harp, etc.," Dublin, 1846; London, 1850. Collection of admired Hymns and Gregorian Chants, with English words ; n.d.

Cook, Aynsley, bass vocalist, born near Newcastle-on-Tyne, 1836 (?). Was a chorister at St. Paul's Cathedral. Through the generosity of the Marquis of Anglesey he studied in Germany, and there made his *début* in opera. He sang at Drury Lane about 1854, but his name is not noticed. Later he joined the Pyne and Harrison Company; but he reached the full measure of his popularity as a member of the Carl Rosa Company, from 1875 to the end of his career. His repertory was extensive, but his Devilshoof in the "Bohemian Girl"—an elaboration of his own in the last act—was his favourite character with the public. His last appearance in opera was at Liverpool, February 2, 1894, and he died just a fortnight later. His wife, *née* PAYNE, was a contralto singer, and a member of the Pyne and Harrison, and Carl Rosa Companies. She also sang on tour with Mr. Sims Reeves in "The Waterman," etc. ALICE AYNSLEY COOK, his daughter, has sung in the provinces in the Gilbert and Sullivan operas, burlesques, etc.

Cook, Mrs. Dutton, *see* SCATES, LINDA.

Cook, Richard, musician of early part of the present century. Issued " Kentish Psalmodist's Companion," London, n.d.

Cooke, Benjamin, composer and organist, was born at London in 1734. He studied under Pepusch, and became deputy-organist at Westminster Abbey in 1746. Conductor of Academy of Ancient Music, 1752-1789. Master of the boys at Westminster Abbey, 1757. Lay-clerk, do., 1758. Full organist, Westminster, 1762, succeeding John Robinson. Doc. Mus., Cantab., 1775. Organist of St. Martin-in-the-Fields, 1782, Sub-director at Handel Commemoration, 1784. He died at Westminster, London, Sept.14,1793. Buried in West Cloister of Westminster Abbey.

WORKS.—Ode on Handel, for 8 voices. *Glees :* Collection of twenty glees, catches and canons, for 3, 4, 5 and 6 voices, in score, London, 1775 ; As now the shades ; Ere the beams of morning break ; Farewell ; Hand in hand ; Hark, the lark ; How sleep the brave ; In the merry month of May ; I've been young, though now grown old ; Now the bright morning star, day's harbinger ; Let Rubinelli charm the ear,

COOKE.

duet ; Thrysis, when he left me, duet ; The Dormouse, glee ; Beneath in the dust. Nine glees and two duets, op. 9 [1795]. Ode on the Passions (Collins), 1784, etc. Concertos for combinations of various instruments. Organ and harpsichord music. Anthems and Church Services. Morning and Evening Service in G. Songs, etc.

" Dr. Cooke's glees are numerous, and of great beauty. They are remarkable for natural and graceful ease of melody, great simplicity and yet much art in the disposition of parts, and fine expression."—*Hogarth.* A number of them are still in use among our singing societies ; " Hark, the lark," being one of those perennial favourites of which the English school furnishes not a few examples.

Cooke, Henry, composer and teacher, born at the beginning of the 17th century. He was educated at the Chapel Royal, and obtained a captain's commission during the Civil War, 1642. Gentleman of Chapel Royal and Master of Children, 1660. Composer to the King, 1664. He died July 13, 1672. Buried in East Cloister, Westminster Abbey.

WORKS.—Anthems and Services preserved (MS.) in the Collection formed by Dr. Aldrich in Christ Church, Oxford. Madrigals, songs, etc.

Cooke was the teacher of Blow, Wise, Purcell, and Humfrey, and for that alone is entitled to some little credit and esteem.

Cooke, John P., composer and conductor, was born at Chester, October 31, 1820. He went to America, and became conductor of various theatre orchestras in New York. He died at New York, November 4, 1865. Composed music to Shakespeare's Plays, Songs, etc.

Cooke, Miss, *see* WAYLETT, Mrs.

Cooke, Nathaniel, composer and organist, born at Bosham, near Chichester, 1773. He studied under his uncle, Matthew Cooke, of London (organist). Organist of the Parish Church of Brighton. He died sometime after 1820.

WORKS.—Collection of Psalms and Hymns sung at Brighthelmston, with several Canons, and a Te Deum, arranged for the Organ or Pianoforte, n.d. Glees and Songs. Pianoforte Music.

Cooke was a good organist, and composed the canon, "I have set God always before me."

Cooke, Robert, organist and composer, was a son of Benjamin Cooke, born in 1768. He studied under his father, and succeeded him as organist of St. Martin-in-the-Fields, 1793. Organist and choir-master at Westminster Abbey, 1802. Drowned in Thames, August 13, 1814. Buried in West Cloister of Westminster Abbey.

WORKS.—Evening Service in C ; Magnificat and Nunc Dimittis in C. Anthems. *Glees :* In the rose's fragrant shade ; Love and folly

COOKE.

were at play; Mark, where the silver queen of night; Queen of the sea; Round thy pillow; Sweet warbling bird; Why o'er the verdant banks. Collection of Eight Glees (Clementi) [1805]. Songs, etc.

Cooke, Thomas Simpson, vocalist and composer, was born at Dublin in 1782. He studied under his father and Giordani. In 1803 he acted as conductor of a theatre in Dublin, and made his *début* as a vocalist in Storace's "Siege of Belgrade." 1n 1813 he appeared in London, and in the same year was appointed conductor and vocalist at Drury Lane Theatre. He married Miss Howell. Member of the Royal Academy of Music, Philharmonic Society, Noblemans' Catch Club, Glee Club, etc. He died at London, February 26, 1848.

WORKS.—*Music to Plays:* The Count of Anjou; A Tale of the Times, 1822; The Wager, 1825; Oberon, or the Charmed Horn, 1826; Malvina, 1826; The Boy of Santillane, 1827; The Brigand, 1829; Peter the Great, 1829; The Dragon's Gift, 1830; The Ice Witch, 1831; Hyder Ali, 1831; St. Patrick's Eve, 1832; King Arthur, 1835; The King's Proxy; Frederick the Great; The Five Lovers; Numerous Farces. Adaptations of Foreign Operas. Mass in A minor. *Glees:* Six Glees for 3 and 4 voices, London, 1844; Come Spirits of Air; Fill me, boy, as deep a draught; Strike, strike the lyre; Away with gloom and care; O strike the harp; Take thou this cup. *Duets:* Love and War; Army and Navy; Songs. Singing Exemplified in a Series of Solfeggi and exercises, progressively arranged, London, n.d.; Singing in parts, containing progressive instructions, extracts, exercises, and original compositions, London, n.d. [c. 1842], etc.

Cooke, Henry Angelo Michael. GRATTAN COOKE, eldest son of the above, born in London in 1809. He studied at the R.A.M., 1822-28, of which he became a professor. In 1837 he married Miss Kiallmark. He was band-master of the 2nd life guards 1849-56. In 1845 he appeared at the Hanover Square Rooms as a tenor singer, and took part in a glee at the Norwich Festival that year. He lived for nearly twenty years in retirement at Harting, Sussex, and died there September 12, 1889. He composed a number of operettas and songs, and was a fine oboe player. Author of "Statement of facts and correspondence between the Directors of the Philharmonic Society and Mr. Grattan Cooke," London [1850].

Coombe, William Francis, organist and composer, was born at Plymouth, 1786. He studied under his father (a singing master) and W. Jackson of Exeter. Organist at Chard, Somerset, 1800; Totnes, Devon, 1802-11; and Chelmsford, 1811-22. He probably died

COOPER.

at Chelmsford about 1850. He composed a few pianoforte sonatas, and other works.

Coombs, James Morris, organist and composer, born at Salisbury, 1769. Chorister at Salisbury Cathedral, 1776-1784. He studied under Dr. Stephens and Parry. Organist at Chippenham, Wilts., 1789 to 1820. He died at Chippenham, on March 7, 1820.

WORKS.—Set of Canzonets; Te Deums; Divine amusement for churches, families, etc., being hymns, anthems and other sacred pieces, psalms, etc., from the works of Marcello, Handel, Haydn, Mason, etc., etc.; Glees and songs.

WILLIAM COOMBS, who flourished at Bristol in the latter part of last century, composed the psalm tune "Oxford," which is sometimes attributed to James Morris Coombs.

Cooney, Edward, organist and teacher. Educated at Christ Church Cathedral, Dublin. Graduated Mus. Bac., 1885; Mus. Doc., 1887, Dublin. Organist, Parish Church, Ballymena; teacher of pf. and singing in Coleraine Academic Institute. University Exercises: (Bac.) Psalm 145; (Doc.) Psalm 139, for soli, chorus, and orchestra. He has published Church Services and Anthems; Songs and part-songs.

Cooper, Alexander Samuel, organist and composer, born in London, April 30, 1835. F.R.C.O. Organist of St. John's, Putney, to 1866; St. Paul's, Covent Garden, later. Awarded a prize by the Ely Diocesan Church Music Society for a setting of the Nicene Creed, 1869. Composer of anthems, music for Holy Communion, chants, hymn tunes, songs, and part-songs. Editor of "Parochial Psalter," and "Parochial Chant Book," both of which have passed through several editions.

Cooper, George, composer and organist, born Lambeth, London, July 7, 1820. Successively organist of St. Benet's, Paul's Wharf; St. Anne and St. Agnes, 1836; St. Sepulchre, 1843; Christ's Hospital, and the Chapel Royal, all in London. He was also assistant organist for a time at St. Paul's Cathedral. He died, London, October 2, 1876.

WORKS.—The Organist's Assistant, a series of arrangements . . . London (Novello). Organist's Manual . . . select movements from the most eminent composers, London (Novello). Organ Arrangements, London. Part-songs, songs, etc.

His father, George Cooper, who died in London, in 1843, was an organist of repute. He was assistant organist of St. Paul's Cathedral, and organist of St. Sepulchre's until his death, when he was succeeded by his son.

Cooper, Henry Christopher, violinist, was born at Bath in 1819. Studied violin under Spagnoletti. Appeared as solo violinist at Drury Lane Theatre, 1830. Principal violinist at Royal Italian Opera. Leader at

Philharmonic Society. Violinist at Provincial Festivals. Conductor at various theatres. Latterly conductor at the Gaiety Theatre, Glasgow. He died at Glasgow, January 26, 1881. He was one of the foremost of the English school of violinists, and at one time well known in London. He was married to Madame Tonnellier, the vocalist.

Cooper, Isaac, violinist and composer, born at Banff about 1755. He was a teacher of music and dancing in Banff, and died there about 1820.

WORKS.—Thirty new Strathspey Reels for the violin or harpsichord, Banff, 1780. Collection of Slow airs, Strathspeys, Reels, and Jigs, 1806. New Instructions for the harpsichord or pianoforte, Banff, 1785.

Cooper, Rev. James, clergyman and writer, author of "Musicæ Sacræ, being Selections from Bowdler, Heber, etc., set to music, to which is prefixed an Essay on Church Music." London, 1860.

Cooper, John, called also COPERARIO, composer and viol-da-gamba player, was born in latter part of the 16th century. He was music-master to the children of James I., and master of Henry and William Lawes. He died early in the 17th century.

WORKS.—Funeral Tears for the death of the Right Honourable the Earle of Devonshire, figured in seaven songs, whereof sixe are soe set forth that the words may be expressed by a Treble voyce alone to the Lute and Base Voil, or else that the meane part may be added, if any shall affect more fulnesse of Parts, etc., 1606. Songs of Mourning, bewailing the untimely death of Prince Henry, London, folio, 1613; Music in Leighton's "Teares"; Music to Masque by Dr. Campion; Songs and Fancies, etc.

Cooper, John Wilbye, tenor vocalist and author. He sang at the first Leeds Festival, in 1858, and at the Worcester Festival of 1863. In the concert room he was a favourite for a good many years. He retired for some time before his death, in London, March 19, 1885. Author of "The Voice, the Music of Language, and the Soul of Song," London, 1874. Editor of "Cramer's Vocal School."

Cooper, Joseph Thomas, organist and composer, born at London, May 25, 1819. He was a pupil of Henry Holmes and Moscheles. Organist of Christ Church, Newgate Street. Organist of Christ's Hospital. He was an Associate of the Philharmonic Society, Member of the Society of British Musicians, and Fellow of the Royal Astronomical Society. He died at London, November 17, 1879.

WORKS.—Orchestral music in MS. Songs, Part-songs, Sacred music, Organ music, etc.

Cooper or **Cowper, Robert**, musician and priest of the 15th century. He was a Mus. Bac., Cambridge, and in 1504 proceeded

to the degree of Mus. Doc. He composed songs and other secular music, and is mentioned in Morley's Catalogue of Musicians.

Coote, Charles, composer and bandmaster, born 1809; died London, March 6, 1880. Composer of a large number of waltzes, galops, polkas, etc., chiefly based on popular airs.

His son CHARLES is a bandmaster and composer of popular dance music.

Cope, Samuel, bandmaster, son of a bandmaster in the West of England. As a boy he sang in a Church choir, and played in a drum and fife band, afterwards taking to the cornet, on which he became a proficient performer. After holding various appointments he was offered, and accepted, in 1888, the conductorship of the Queen's Park (West London) Military Band, a position he still holds. He founded the magazine, *The British Bandsman* (the title has since been changed to *The Orchestral Times* and *British Musician*), which he edited for some years. He was also editor of the *Champion Journal*, the pioneer of popular band journal music, founded at Hull, by the late Richard Smith, in 1853; and has composed a large number of pieces, of which only a few have been published.

Copland, Charles, baritone vocalist, born at Brightlingsea, Essex, August 20, 1861. Son of a distinguished London physician. Studied under F. Walker, at the Guildhall School, and R.A.M. Evill prizeholder, 1885. Later, he studied abroad, and took lessons from the late Eugène Oudin. During his student days, he sang in London occasionally, 1884-5; and in Otto Booth's operetta, "Traveller's Rest," 1887, gave the first evidence of his histrionic talent. He appeared at the Promenade Concerts, Her Majesty's Theatre, 1887, and also at Covent Garden Theatre. In the South of France, 1887-8, he sang, by request, to the late Dom Pedro, Emperor of Brazil. He was engaged to play Isaac of York, in "Ivanhoe," at its production, January 31, 1891, a part he sustained through the run of the opera. In December, 1894, he created the part of the Broom-maker, in "Hänsel and Gretel," when produced at Daly's Theatre. He has also appeared, with success, at the principal Concerts, Royal Albert Hall, etc.

Corbett, Felix, organist and conductor, born at Cinderford, Forest of Dean, Gloucestershire, July 3, 1861. Son of J. F. Corbett, a colliery proprietor. The family moving to Birmingham, he studied under James Stimpson, of that town. In 1882 he was appointed organist and choirmaster of the Parish Church, Middlesbrough, in which town he has for some years given a series of excellent concerts, and has played at Harrison's Concerts, Birmingham and elsewhere. He is the composer of a number of songs; of which one entitled

CORBETT.

CORFE.

"Butterflies" (Algernon Swinburne), has enjoyed great popularity.

Corbett, Samuel, organist and composer, born at Wellington, Shropshire, January 29, 1852. Pupil of James Stimpson (Birmingham), and of Sir G. A. Macfarren and James Coward. F.C.O., 1871 ; Mus. Bac., 1873 ; Mus. Doc., 1879, Cambridge. Organist of Christ Church, Wellington, 1867 ; St. Mary's, Bridgenorth, 1875 ; All Saints', Derby, 1886 ; and Holy Trinity, Bournemouth, from 1892. Mr. Corbett lost his sight when only three months old, but he has trained choirs, conducted concerts, and frequently played from memory the whole of such works as the Messiah, Israel, Elijah, etc. He committed to memory the score of Israel in Egypt in six weeks, for his Mus. D. examination, and was the first person so situated to pass. As a teacher he has been eminently successful. His compositions are : " Bethany," a cantata ; Sonata for pf. ; Evening Service in F ; Anthem ; Songs, and part-songs, etc. He has acted as press correspondent for the Birmingham and other Festivals, following by ear every note in a score.

Corbett, William, composer and violinist, born about 1669. Member of King's Band. Travelled in Italy, Burney says, on behalf of the English Government, who paid him to watch the movements of the Pretender. Returned to England, 1740, where he died, in 1748. He collected a valuable musical library. WORKS.—Op. 1, Sonata for two violins and bass, London, 1705; Op. 2, Sonata for two flutes and bass, London, 1706 ; Op. 3, Sonata for two flutes and bass, London, 1707 ; Op. 4, Six Sonatas, a 3° for two flutes or two German flutes and a bass, consisting of preludes, allemands, corants, sarabands, gavots, and jiggs, Book 1; Six Sonatas for two violins and thoro'-bass for the spinet or harpsichord, Book 2, London, n.d. ; Six Sonatas for two oboes or trumpets, two violins, and bass ; Concertos, or Universal Bizzarries, composed on all the new Gustos during many years' residence in Italy, op. 5, London, 1741 ; Twelve Concertos for various instruments ; Music to " Henry IV.," 1700 ; Music to " Love Betrayed," 1703 ; Songs in collections, etc.

Corder, Frederick, composer and conductor, born in London, January 26, 1852. Though he showed musical talent at an early age, he was intended for a business career ; and it was not until 1874 that he entered the R.A.M. as a student. The next year he gained the Mendelssohn Scholarship, and studied four years with Ferdinand Hiller at Cologne. Soon after his return to England he was appointed conductor at the Brighton Aquarium, June, 1880, an office he resigned, September,

1882. He gave many important works during that period, and greatly improved the character of the concerts. The next few years were given up to musical composition and literature. In 1890 he was appointed orchestral director at Trinity College, London ; Curator of the R.A.M. ; and conductor of the Borough of Hackney Choral Association. In 1891 he was elected a member of the managing committee, R.A.M., and in 1892, a Fellow of the Institution. He was editor of *The Overture*, a monthly paper published by students of the R.A.M., 1890-4 ; and, in 1896, lectured at the Royal Institution on Berlioz, Wagner, and Liszt. His contributions to the press have been voluminous and important, including elaborate analyses of Wagner's works, and translations of " Die Meistersinger," and " Der Ring des Nibelungen," in which he was assisted by his accomplished wife, a lady (born Walford) not unknown in literary and artistic society.

WORKS.—*Operas :* Morte d'Arthur, in four acts (1877-9) ; Nordisa (produced by Carl Rosa, Liverpool, January 26, 1887). *Operettas :* Philomel (1880) ; A storm in a tea-cup (1880); The Nabob's Pickle (Brighton, September, 1883) ; The Noble Savage (Brighton, October, 1885). *Cantatas :* The Cyclops (1880) ; The Bridal of Triermain (Wolverhampton Festival, 1886) ; The Sword of Argantyr (Leeds Festival, 1889) ; Dreamland, ode for chorus and orchestra ; The Minstrel's Curse, for declamation and orchestra; The Blind Girl of Castel, cantata, female voices ; Songs, various. *For orchestra :* Evening on the sea-shore, Idyl (1876) ; Suite, In the Black Forest (composed 1876 ; performed, Crystal Palace, March 20, 1880). *Overtures :* Ossian (Philharmonic Society, March, 1882) ; Prospero (Crystal Palace, October, 1885)) ; Nocturne (1882, Brighton Festival) ; Suite, Scenes from the Tempest (1886) ; Roumanian Suite (composed for, and produced by Philharmonic Society, 1887). Roumanian dances, violin and pf. *Literary :* Exercises in Harmony and Counterpoint (Forsyth, 1891) ; A plain and easy introduction to Music, or the new Morley (Forsyth, 1893) ; The Orchestra, and how to write for it (Robert Cocks, 1896) ; Articles in Grove's Dictionary of Music and Musicians.

Cordner, William John, organist, born at Duncannon, Wexford, Ireland, 1826. Went to Australia in 1854, and was organist at St. Patrick's, Sydney, until 1856, when he was appointed to St. Mary's R. C. Cathedral, an office he held until his death, July 15, 1870. He was held in much estimation as a teacher.

Corfe, Joseph, organist, writer, and composer, born at Salisbury in 1740. Chorister at Salisbury Cathedral. Gentleman of Chapel Royal, 1783. Organist and choir-master at

CORFE.

Salisbury Cathedral, 1792-1804. He died at Salisbury, September, 1820.

WORKS.—A Treatise on Singing, explaining in the most simple manner all the Rules for learning to Sing by Note without the assistance of an Instrument, with some Observations on Vocal Music, London, fol., 1791, another ed., 1801; Thorough-bass Simplified, London, n.d. Beauties of Handel, being 154 songs, duetts, and trios with accompaniment for pf., 3 vols., n.d.; Beauties of Purcell, 2 vols., n.d.; First Set of 12 Glees, n.d.; Second Set of 12 Glees; Third Set of 12 Glees, in score for 3 and 4 voices, from melodies of Sacchini, Paisiello, Haydn, Pleyel, Storace, etc. Sacred Music, consisting of a selection of the most admired pieces. adapted to some of the choicest music of Jomelli, Pergolesi, Perez, Martini, Biretti, etc., 2 vols., Salisbury, n.d.; Three Collections of Scottish Songs; Anthems; Nine Vocal Trios, harmonized, London, n.d.

Corfe, Arthur Thomas, composer, organist, and writer, son of above, was born at Salisbury, April 9, 1773. Chorister in Westminster Abbey, 1782. He studied under Dr. Cooke and Clementi. Organist and choirmaster of Salisbury Cathedral, 1804. He died at Salisbury, January 28, 1863. Buried in Salisbury Cathedral.

WORKS.—Anthems; Church Services; Pf. music. The Principles of Harmony and Thorough-Bass explained, London, n.d. Songs; Glees, etc. Anthems adapted from Mozart, etc.

Corfe, Charles William, organist and composer, son of the above, born at Salisbury, July 13, 1814. Studied under his father, etc. Organist of Christ Church Cathedral, Oxford, December, 1846. Mus. Bac., Oxon., March, 1847. Conductor of the Oxford University Motett and Madrigal Society, 1848. Mus. Doc., Oxon., June, 1852. Choragus of the University of Oxford, 1860. He died at Oxford, December 16, 1883.

WORKS.—Vocal music, as songs, part-songs; Anthems.

Corkine, William, lute player and composer, was born in the latter part of the 16th century, and died in the first part of the 17th century.

WORKS.—Ayres to Sing and Play to the Lute and Basse Violl, with Pavins, Galliards, Almaines, and Corantos for the Lyra Violl, 1610; the Second Booke of Ayres, some to sing and play to the Base violl alone, etc., 1612.

Cornish, William, English poet and musician, flourished about 1500. He wrote a " Parable between Information and Musike," a poem, which will be found in Hawkins. He was a member of the Chapel Royal choir, and died 1526. His compositions exist in MS. His son William was also a composer.

Cornwall, Channon, pianist and com-

COSYN.

poser, born at Aberdeen, in 1845. He was organist of St. John's Episcopal Church, Glasgow, and in 1880 he became accompanist to the Glasgow Choral Union. Composer of some part-songs, etc. He was drowned in the Forth and Clyde Canal, Glasgow, May 4, 1885.

Corri, Montague, second son of Dominico Corri (Rome, 1746, London, 1825), was born at Edinburgh in 1784. He studied under his father, Winter, and Steibelt, and became composer to the Surrey and Astley's Theatres, London. In 1816-17 he was chorus-master to the English Opera House. Afterwards, he resided successively at Edinburgh, Newcastle, Manchester, and Liverpool. He died at London, September 19, 1849. His brother, HAYDN, was born at Edinburgh, in 1785, and resided chiefly in Dublin as a conductor and teacher. He died at Dublin, February 19, 1860. His wife (born 1800; died 1867), was an operatic singer. His sister, SOPHIE (born at Edinburgh, 1775; died —— ?), was a singer and harp player. She married J. L. Dussek (1761-1812), the composer. FRANCES, or FANNY CORRI, a mezzo-soprano vocalist, was a daughter of Dominico Corri's brother Natale (1765-1822), and was born at Edinburgh in 1801. She studied under her father, and Braham, and first appeared at the King's Theatre, London. Afterwards, she appeared in Germany, Italy, Spain, and Russia, and in 1821 she married Signor Paltoni. Her sister ROSALIE (born 1803), was also a singer, who appeared in London from 1820. Other members of this musical family were EUGENE DUSSEK (1815; February 4, 1870), a bass vocalist, who married ANNIE THIRLWALL (1830; London, October 19, 1881), a soprano singer; HENRY (1822; Philadelphia, February 28, 1888) a bass singer, son of Haydn the elder; PATRICK ANTHONY (born Dublin, 1820; died Bradford, June 1, 1876), a singer, conductor, and composer, another son of Haydn the elder; and HAYDN, *Junr.* (born in 1842; died December 19, 1877), a baritone singer.

Costeley, William, Scottish composer, was born in 1531. He settled in France as organist to Henry II. and Charles IX. He was a member of the society known as " Puy de musique à honneur de Ste. Cecile." He died at Evreux in 1606. His works consist of songs in Le Roy's Collections of Chansons, etc., and a treatise entitled "Musique," Paris, 1579.

Cosyn, Benjamin, composer for, and performer on, the Virginals, who flourished in first part of 17th century. He wrote music of a difficult and complicated style for his instrument, and was one of the best performers of his day.

Cosyn, John, composer, probably a relation of above. Wrote " Musicke of six and five parts made upon the common tunes used in singing of the Psalms," 1585.

COTES.

Cotes, Digby, clergyman and writer, author of "Music a rational assistant in the duty of praise when united with charity, a Sermon," 1756.

Cotterill, Thomas, musician and editor, published "Christian Psalmody for congregational or family use, arranged and harmonized by S. Mather and other professors under the direction of Thomas Cotterill," London, 1831.

Cottman, Arthur, amateur composer, born 1842. He was a solicitor by profession, and died at Ealing on June 3, 1879. He published "Ten Original Tunes," 1872, among which is "Caterham," a hymn tune which has been used in various Church hymn-books.

Couldery, Claudius Herbert, composer and pianist, born at Lewisham, Kent, August 17, 1842. He learnt to play while a child, but some years were passed in business pursuits before he was able to devote himself to the art of music. Then he entered the R.A.M., studying harmony under Sir John Goss, composition with Sir W. S. Bennett, etc. A sacred cantata, "Christ's entry into Jerusalem," was performed at the R.A.M., and drew attention to the composer's ability. His chief works are—Overture, Richard I., performed at the Crystal Palace, February 14, 1885; Overture, To the memory of a hero (at the same) February 8, 1890; Suite in C minor, a romance from which has been given in many places in England and Scotland; and a Cradle Song, in D flat, Crystal Palace, November 18, 1893; Suite in C, composed 1893-5; Andante religioso, St. Cecilia, for organ, harp, violin, and orchestra, Crystal Palace, November 2, 1895. Twelve Reveries, op. 15; three series of studies, pf., etc.

Courteville, Raphael, musician, who was born in first part of the 17th century. He was Gentleman of the Chapel Royal in time of Charles I., and founder of the Courteville family. He died on December 28, 1675.

Courteville, Raphael, organist and composer, son of above, was born in the latter part of 17th century. Organist of St. James' Church, Westminster, 1691. He died in June, 1772.

WORKS.—Don Quixote, opera by D'Urfey (with Purcell, etc.), 1696; Six Sonatas for two violins; Sonatas for two flutes, 1685; Songs in contemporary collections; "St. James" psalm tune, etc. He was a severe political writer, and gained the nickname of *Court-evil.* He wrote "Memoirs of Lord Burleigh," 1738, and a number of political squibs.

Courteville, John, English song-writer of the 17th century, son of Raphael, the elder. His works appear in the "Theater of Music," 1685-87, etc.

Courtney, Wililam, tenor vocalist, born in Monmouthshire. Studied under F. Bodda, Sidney Naylor, and afterwards with Vannuc-

COWARD.

cini, at Florence. Toured with Louisa Pyne and F. Bodda; sang in Cellier's "Nell Gwynne," and Sullivan's "Trial by Jury," when first produced; and was, for a short time, a member of the Carl Rosa Opera Company. Subsequently went to America, singing first at Boston. Settled as a teacher, in New York, removing to Denver, Colorado, 1896.

Cousins, Charles, musician and bandmaster, was born near Portsmouth, January 2, 1830. Educated at the Royal Hospital Schools, Greenwich, from 1841. Assistant band-master of the Royal Caledonian Asylum, 1846. Member of band of the 1st Life Guards, under Mr. James Waddell. Studied at Kneller Hall, Hounslow, for a band-mastership. Band-master of 2nd Dragoon Guards, October, 1863. Served with Guards in India, 1864-70. Held appointment till 1874. Director of Music at Kneller Hall, November 1, 1874. He died in June, 1890.

Coutts, W. G. ITHURIEL. Author of "Scottish *versus* Classic Music, and the ethical and æsthetical aspect of the question," Edinburgh, 1877 (2 eds.).

Coward, Henry, composer and conductor, born in Liverpool, November 26, 1849, but a Yorkshireman by family and descent, and resident in Sheffield as conductor and teacher. He is a graduate of the Tonic Sol-fa College; Mus. Bac., 1889; Mus. Doc., 1894, Oxford. Lecturer on Music, Firth College; Teacher of Singing at the Girls' High School, Sheffield; Conductor of the Musical Union, 1880; and Amateur Instrumental Society, Sheffield, 1878. Chorus-master, Sheffield Festival, 1896. Musical critic, for the provincial and Handel Festivals, to the *Sheffield Independent :* Conductor of the festivals of the Sheffield Sunday School Union, etc.

WORKS.—*Cantatas :* Magna Charta, Sheffield, February, 1882; Queen Victoria, 1885; The Story of Bethany, 1891; The King's Error (Crystal Palace, Tonic Sol-fa Festival, July, 1894), and Heroes of Faith (Sheffield, September, 1895). The Fairy Mirror, cantata for ladies' voices, with tableaux vivants. Anthems, Sunday School pieces, Temperance choruses, School songs, Hymn tunes, Glees, etc.

Coward, Hilda, soprano vocalist, daughter of the late James Coward. Pupil of Madame Sainton-Dolby. She made her *début* at a concert given by W. Lemare, at the Crystal Palace, Monday, March 6, 1882, taking part in F. Clay's "Lalla Rookh"; and appeared at the Crystal Palace Saturday Concerts, October 27, 1883. After singing in various provincial concerts, she was engaged for the Hereford Festival of 1885, singing in the concerted music in "Elijah," and Gounod's "Redemption," and with great success at the concluding Chamber concert. Severe illness

COWARD.

compelled her to spend the winter of 1887-8 in a milder climate, and her public appearances since then have not been frequent.

Coward, James, organist and composer, born at London, January 25, 1824. Chorister in Westminster Abbey. Organist of Crystal Palace, 1857-80. He died at London, January 22, 1880. WORKS.—Full anthem, "O Lord, correct me." Ten glees, for 4 and 5 voices, London, 1857; Ten glees, London, 1871. Numerous dart-songs, songs, etc.

His brother, WILLIAM (born in London, 1826; died 1873), was an alto singer in Westminster Abbey.

Coward, James Munro, composer and performer on the Mustel organ, understood to be connected with the firm of Metzler & Co. Has given performances at the South Kensington Exhibition, 1885 (The "Inventions,") Prince's Hall, and other places, exhibiting much skill in improvisation. He has composed a cantata, "The Fishers," produced at Portman Hall, April 9, 1889; A Jubilee Hymn, for chorus and military band (Crystal Palace, 1887); and pieces for American organ, etc. Editor of *American Organ Journal* (Metzler).

Cowell, Samuel Haughton, comedian, and comic singer, born at London, April 5, 1820. Son of Joseph Leathley Cowell (1792-1863), the actor, by whom he was taken to the United States in 1822. He resided for a number of years in the States, and appeared there as an actor; afterwards he appeared in Edinburgh, where he acted under his uncle, W. H. Murray, and where he was married, in 1842, to Emilie Marguerite Ebsworth. He appeared in London as an actor and singer, and subsequently sang chiefly as a comic vocalist in various parts of Britain, laying the foundation, to a considerable extent, of the modern music-hall profession. He died at Blandford, Dorset, March 11, 1864. His songs were published in many different collections, such as "Sam Cowell's new universal illustrated pocket songster," London [1856], 4 vols., and among his most successful songs may be named "Lord Lovel," "Alonzo the Brave," "Billy Barlow," "Rat-Catcher's daughter," "Corn cobs," etc.

Cowen, Frederic Hymen, composer, conductor, and pianist, born at Kingston, Jamaica, January 29. 1852. Brought to England when four years old, and placed under the tuition of Julius Benedict, and John Goss, with whom he remained until 1865. His "Mima Waltz" was published in 1858. Studied at Leipzig and Berlin, under Hauptmann, Moscheles, Reinecke, and others, returning to London in 1868. He soon became known as a brilliant pianist and composer, giving his first concert, June 24, 1868, at Dudley House, and introducing his pianoforte

COWEN.

trio in A minor. Other works followed, and at his orchestral concert, St. James's Hall, December 9, 1869, he produced his first symphony (in C minor). Shortly after he went on tour, as pianist and accompanist, with operatic concert parties; gave a series of Saturday Evening Concerts in St. James's Hall, 1880-1; conducted at the Promenade Concerts, Covent Garden, 1880. During the next two years he appeared at various places in Germany, conducting his own compositions. Conducted concerts at the Crystal Palace (December 16, 1882; December 13, 1884, etc.;) Philharmonic Society (May 7 and 28, 1884); was given the post of Musical Director of the Melbourne Centennial Exhibition, 1888; and visited Sydney. Conductor of the Philharmonic Society, 1888-92; appointed successor to the late Sir Charles Halle as conductor of the Liverpool Philharmonic Society, and the Halle Concerts, Manchester, 1896. Conducted various compositions at the principal musical festivals, 1876-95.

WORKS.—*Operas :* Pauline (Lyceum, Carl Rosa, November 22, 1876); Thorgrim (book by Joseph Bennett, produced Drury Lane, April 20, 1890); Signa (Dal Verme Theatre, Milan, November 12, 1893); Harold (book by Sir Ed. Malet, produced at Covent Garden, in English—an unique occurrence—June 8, 1895). *Operettas:* Garibaldi (an early work); One too many (German Reed, 1874). Incidental music to Maid of Orleans (1871). *Oratorios and Cantatas :* The Rose Maiden (1870); The Corsair (Birmingham Festival, 1876: The Deluge (Brighton Festival, 1878); St. Ursula (Norwich Festival, 1881); The Sleeping Beauty (Birmingham, 1885); Ruth (Worcester, 1887); Song of Thanksgiving (Melbourne, 1888); St. John's Eve (Crystal Palace, 1889); The Water Lily (Norwich, 1893); The Transfiguration (Gloucester, 1895). *For female voices :* Summer on the river; Christmas scenes; The Rose of Life; A daughter of the sea, etc. Part-songs, trios, duets, etc. Many songs, among which may be mentioned: Two Roses; Marguerite; The better land; The unfinished song; More than all to me; The promise of life; Nine songs (Longfellow); Songs for children (1896), etc. *Orchestral:* Symphony, No. 1, in C minor (1869); No. 2, in F (1872); No. 3, in C minor, The Scandinavian, produced St. James's Hall, December 18, 1880, and since heard the world over; No. 4, in B flat minor, Philharmonic, May 28, 1884; No. 5, in F (Cambridge, 1887). Overtures, etc. D minor (1866); Festival (Norwich, 1872); Characteristic overture, Niagara; and others. *Suites :* The Language of flowers (1880); In the olden time (for strings, 1883); In Fairyland (Philharmonic, May 6, 1896); Four English dances in the olden style; Sinfonietta in A; Marches, etc.

COX.   CRAWFORD.

Concerto in A minor, pf. and orchestra; Quartet in C minor; Trio in A minor, pf. and strings; Sonata fantasia, Allegretto grazioso, Romance and scherzo, Valses, and other pieces for pf., etc.

Cox, Frank Rowland, professor of singing, born at Exeter, September, 1819. Intended to follow his father's profession, a solicitor, but deciding for music, was admitted as an out-student of the Royal Academy of Music in October, 1839, and, later, was a pupil of Domenico Crivelli. In 1849 he was appointed an Assistant Professor of Singing at the Royal Academy of Music; in 1852 was made an Associate, and in 1862 elected a Member. He joined the Committee in 1868, and was elected a Director in 1880. With the exception of a short period passed at Trentham, his whole professional life was devoted to this Institution. He died in London, April 3, 1891, at the age of 71. Translator of Crivelli's "L'Arte del Canto," last edition, 1850.

Cox, Mrs. Harry, see CANTELO ANNIE.

Cox, Rev. John Edmund, D.D., clergyman and writer, was born at Norwich, October 9, 1812. Vicar of St. Helen's, and St. Martin's, Bishopsgate, London, 1849, etc. Author of "Musical Recollections of the last Half Century," London, 2 vols., 1872. He was Hon. Chaplain of the Royal Society of Musicians. He died at Bath, October 27, 1890.

Coy, Harry, organist and composer. Became F.R.C.O., 1878; graduated Mus. Bac., 1878; Mus. Doc., 1885, Oxford. Organist and choirmaster, St. John the Divine, Brookland, near Manchester, from 1878; Conductor of Sale District Musical Society, 1892. Composer of a sacred cantata, "Esther"; a setting of Psalm 85, for tenor solo, chorus, and orchestra; anthems, etc.

Craig, Adam, Scottish violinist and collector, born in latter half of 17th century. He performed at the public concerts in Edinburgh during his lifetime. Died at Edinburgh, September 3, 1741.

WORKS.—A Collection of the choicest Scots Tunes, adapted for the Harp or Spinnet, and within the compass of the voice, violin, or German Flute, Edinburgh, 1730. A manuscript volume of original compositions by Craig was exposed for sale in 1728.

Craig, John Millar, conductor and baritone vocalist, born in Edinburgh, November 15, 1839. Was apprenticed to a printer, and during that time studied singing under A. W. Smith, and Signor Bucher. When twenty-six years of age, devoted himself to music as a profession, and began teaching. He afterwards studied at Milan and Florence, with Leoni and Romani. Held several appointments as Precentor, and in 1886, succeeded the late James Allan as conductor of the famous Glasgow Select Choir. Has sung in

many towns in Scotland, and with the Choir has made tours of the United Kingdom, giving an annual concert in London on St. Andrew's Day. He is also conductor of the Edinburgh Bach Society. As a teacher he has had many pupils who have taken high positions as singers. His wife, born ELIZABETH NOBLE, studied singing first with her husband, then under Professor Goetze, in Leipzig. She sings occasionally in concerts in Edinburgh, but is chiefly occupied in teaching, in which she has met with great success, THOMAS CRAIG, brother of J. M. Craig, is a pianist. He was born in Edinburgh, October 1, 1851. Studied at Leipzig Conservatorium. He has played at Chamber concerts in Edinburgh, and is teacher of the pf. at George Watson's College, Edinburgh.

Crament, John Maude, organist, conductor, and composer, born at Bolton-Percy, Yorkshire, April 2, 1845. Studied under (Sir) G. A. Macfarren, and at the Hoch Schule, Berlin, under Haupt, and Kiel. Graduated Mus. Bac., Oxford, 1880. Professor of Music at the Church Education Society's Training College, Dublin, 1873-5. Organist of Brompton Parish Church, and now of St. Paul's, Kensington. Secretary and conductor, People's Entertainment Society, 1879-92; Conductor of Choral Societies at Richmond, Surbiton, and Putney; Kensington Oratorio Society, and Orpheus Musical Society (men's voices), etc. His compositions comprise a setting of Psalm 145, for soli, chorus, and orchestra (Richmond, January, 1887). Cantatas: May Morn; Little Red Riding Hood; The Crystal Cup (for female voices). Anthems, carols, songs, and part-songs.

Crampton, Thomas, organist, composer and editor, born Sheerness, 1817. Has edited several collections of choral music, and composed anthems, glees, and instrumental music. He was made purchaser of music to the British Museum in 1875. Editor of *Pitman's Musical Monthly.* He died at Chiswick, April 13, 1885.

Cranford, William, composer of the 17th century. He was one of the choristers of St. Paul's Cathedral, London, in 1650. He composed rounds, catches, and songs, printed in the collections of Hilton, Playford, etc.

Craven, John Thomas, writer and teacher, born in 1796. Author of "The Child's First Singing Book," London, n.d.; "The Child's First Music Book, or Introduction to the Art of Playing the Pianoforte," London, n.d.

Crawford, Major George Arthur, M.A., writer on Music, born in Dublin, 1827. His chief work was in connection with Church music, and consisted of articles in the *Musical Times*; Grove's Dictionary of Music and Musicians; and Julian's Dictionary of

CRAWFORD.

Hymnology. He compiled the biographical index in the Irish Church Hymnal. He was a member of the Musical Association, 1874-91, and frequently spoke at the meetings, his great knowledge giving more than ordinary value to his remarks. In 1881, he issued "Succession of Organists . . . of the cathedral churches of St, Patrick, Armagh; of the Holy Trinity . . . and of St. Patrick, Dublin," etc. A small tract of 39 pages, containing brief biographical notices of the organists." He died at Sevenoaks, June 9, 1893.

Crawford, William, composer and pianist, was born in 1848; died at Glasgow, March 2, 1878. He composed a considerable number of pieces for the pianoforte, many of which were issued under the pseudonyms of "Rudolph Rookford," and "Frank B. Ashton. His father, JAMES PAUL CRAWFORD (1825-1887), is best known as a minor poet, his poem, entitled "The Drunkard's raggit wean," being a popular piece of its kind.

Creser, William, organist and composer, born in York, 1844, his father being choirmaster of St. John's Church in that city. He was a chorister in York Minster at eight, and studied for some time under (Sir) G. A. Macfarren. Graduated Mus. Bac., 1869; Mus. Doc., 1880, Oxford. F.R.C.O., and Associate of the Philharmonic Society. When fifteen, he was organist of Holy Trinity, Micklegate, York; then of St. Paul's; and (1863-75) St. Andrew's, Grinton. In 1875 he was appointed to St. Martin's, Scarborough, and to the Leeds Parish Church, 1881. Here he remained ten years, maintaining the reputation of the musical services, and producing Bach's Matthew Passion, and other great works on special occasions. In 1891 he was appointed organist of the Chapel Royal, St. James's, and composer to Her Majesty's Chapels Royal. Conductor, Western Madrigal Society, 1896. He has given concerts at Leeds, and organ recitals at the Edinburgh Exhibition, 1890; Exeter Hall, 1891; Bow and Bromley Institute, 1892, etc. His wife, born AMELIA CLARKE, is a contralto vocalist of repute, who has sung at many concerts in Yorkshire, and the Metropolis, with much success.

WORKS.—Oratorio, Micaiah; Mass in C; Psalm 46, motet for double choir; Psalm 145, for soli, chorus, and orchestra; Luther's hymn (Latin version). Cantatas, Eudora (Leeds, 1882); The Golden Legend; The Sacrifice of Freia (book by F. Hueffer, produced at the Leeds Festival, October 10, 1889); and Tegner's Drapa (Longfellow). Operetta, Naxine; various songs. Old English suite for orchestra (Queen's Hall, May, 1896); Quartet in A minor, strings; Trio in A, pf. and strings; Sonata, pf. and violin; Sonata in A minor, and other pieces for organ.

CROFT.

Creyghton, Robert, D.D., divine and composer, was born at Cambridge in 1639. He became Professor of Greek in the University of Cambridge in 1662; Canon Residentiary and Precentor of Wells Cathedral, 1674. He died at Wells, February 17, 1733.

WORKS.—Services in E flat and B flat. *Anthems*—Behold now, praise the Lord; I will arise; Praise the Lord, O my soul, etc, Music mostly in MS.

Creyghton is chiefly remarkable for a cadence which he employed at the close of his compositions, styled by some writers the "Creyghtonian seventh."

Crisp, William, musician, compiled "Divine Harmony, or the Psalm Singer instructed," London, 1755.

Croager, Edward George, organist and conductor, born in London, June 20, 1861. Chorister, St. Andrew's, Wells Street; afterwards studied at R.A.M., obtaining the Certificate of Merit, and being made an Associate. He was for some years assistant organist at St. Andrew's, and afterwards organist and choirmaster successively at Quebec Chapel, St. Mark's, North Audley Street, and St. James's, West Hampstead, which post he now holds. Conductor of the West Hampstead Choral and Orchestral Society, the London Diocesan Choral Union (II.), and Organist to the London Handel Society. His patriotic cantata, "Our Watchword," produced in 1888, has been frequently performed. His other compositions are chiefly for Church use— hymn tunes, etc.

Croal, George, composer and pianist, born at Edinburgh, February 28, 1811. Son of Mr. Croal, who was sub-editor of the *Caledonian Mercury.* He was apprenticed to Alex. Robertson, music-seller, in 1823, and remained with him till 1833. He was in business for himself as a music-seller from 1840 till 1848. Afterwards he was a teacher of music in Edinburgh.

WORKS. — The Centenary Souvenir, six songs by Sir Walter Scott. *Songs*—Away to the woods; Emigrant's dream; My grannie's pouch, etc. He also discovered and adapted the airs now known as "When the kye comes hame" (1836), and "My Nannie's awa" (1842). Under the *pseudonym* of "Carlo Zotti" Mr. Croal has published numerous arrangements, transcriptions, and dances for the pianoforte.

Croft, William, composer and organist, born at Nether-Eatington, Warwick, 1678. He studied under Dr. Blow, and was chorister in the Chapel Royal. He was organist of St. Anne's, Soho, London, from 1700 to 1711. In 1700 he became a Gentleman of the Chapel Royal; in 1704 joint organist with Jeremiah Clark; and in 1707 sole organist, In 1708 he was appointed master of the choristers and composer to the Chapel Royal, also organist

CROKER.

of Westminster Abbey. He resigned his post at St. Anne's to John Isham in 1711. Mus. Doc., Oxon., 1713. Appointed tuner of the regals, a Court office, 1716. Original member of the Academy of Vocal Music, 1725. He died at Bath, August 14, 1727, and was buried in Westminster Abbey.

WORKS. — Operas (incidental music to plays)—Courtship à la mode, 1700; The Funeral, 1702; Twin rivals, 1703; Lying lover, 1704. Divine Harmony, or a new collection of select anthems used at H.M. Chapel Royal, etc., 1712; Cathedral Music, or thirty select anthems in score, consisting of 1, 2, 3, 4, 5, 6, 7, and 8 parts . . . London, 2 vols., 1724; Musica Sacra, or select anthems in score . . . 1724. Numerous single anthems. Miscellaneous Odes for public occasions. Musicus Apparatus Academicus, being a composition of two odes, etc., 1713. Three Odes, for degree of Mus. Doc., 1715; Six sets of tunes for two violins and bass; Six Sonatas for two flutes. Six solos for the flute.

Croft introduced the printing of music from pewter plates, a practice which was generally followed afterwards.

Croker, Norris, baritone vocalist of the present time. Has given English song recitals at Steinway Hall, London, 1890, etc. Author of " Handbook for Singers," London, Augener, 1896.

Cromar, Rev. Alexander, writer and clergyman of a Presbyterian congregation in Liverpool, wrote "A Vindication of the Organ—a Review of the Rev. Dr. Candish's publication, entitled "The Organ Question," Edinburgh, 1856.

Crome, Robert, a musician who flourished during the middle of last century. He published "A Collection of Dr. Watts's divine and moral songs," London [1740]. "The Fiddle new model'd, or a useful introduction for the violin," London [1745]. A Compleat tutor for the violoncello, London [1765]. Songs, etc.

Crompton, John, musician, of Southwold, Suffolk. Edited "The Psalm Singer's Assistant, or a key to psalmody, containing a new, easy, and familiar introduction, with an astronomical account of the two fundamental keys," London, 1778.

Cromwell, Thomas, English writer, author of " Church Music ; a Sermon on the Antiquity, Excellence, and Propriety of the general adoption of the legitimate Music of the Christian Church," London, 1843.

Crook, John, conductor and composer. Sometime musical director, Theatre Royal, Manchester. Composer of music to burlesques "Robinson Crusoe," Avenue Theatre, 1887; and " Lancelot the Lovely," the same, 1889. Operetta, The Transferred Ghost. Music to some of Chevalier's songs, etc.

CROSSLEY.

Crook, Joseph, musician of the first half of the present century. Published " New Sacred Music, thirty-four psalm and hymn tunes for four voices," London [1839].

Crosdill, John, violoncellist, born at London, 1755. He was educated at Westminster School, and became a chorister in Westminster Abbey. He studied under B. Cooke and J. Robinson. Member of the Royal Society of Musicians, 1768-1825. Violinist in Chapel Royal, 1777. Chamber-musician to Queen Charlotte, 1782. Principal violoncellist at the Handel Commemoration, 1784. Principal 'cello at Ancient Concerts, etc. Married, and retired, 1790. He died at Escrick, Yorkshire, October, 1825.

Crosdill was violoncellist-in-ordinary to King George IV., and a performer on the violoncello of the greatest ability. A number of anecdotes concerning him will be found in Parke's " Musical Memoirs."

Cross, William, musician and organist. born in latter half of 18th century. He was organist of Christ Church Cathedral, St. John's College, and University Church, Oxford, 1807. He died in 1826.

WORKS.—Collection of Chants, Kyries, and Sanctuses, n.d. A Collection of Psalm Tunes for the Church of England. London [1818].

Cross, William Paterson, conductor and voice-trainer, born at Blairoaks, Caldarvan, Dunbartonshire, October 24, 1837. Studied in Birmingham, where he was choirmaster for several years of Broad Street Presbyterian Church. Settled in Greenock, 1862, as conductor and teacher. Conductor of the Choral Union, Greenock, and of other societies in the locality. Has composed many songs, part-songs, and pf. pieces, etc.; arranged Scottish melodies as part-songs, and compiled school song-books, etc.

Crosse, John, writer and musician. Author of "An account of the Grand Musical Festival held in September, 1823, in the Cathedral Church of York, to which is prefixed a Sketch of the Rise and Progress of Musical Festivals in Great Britain, with Biographical and Historical Notes," York, 1825. This is a valuable work, of more than local interest. Crosse died at York, October 20, 1833.

Crossley, Frank Herbert, violinist and conductor, born at Sheffield, May 30, 1864. Studied violin and pf. under private masters. In 1880 went to Natal, where he was appointed Conductor of the Cathedral Choir, and of the Philharmonic Society, Pietermaritzburg. Afterwards went to Berlin (1887), and studied violin under Emile Sauret, and composition with Wilhelm Tappert. In 1890 he was appointed Conductor of the Warrington Musical Society, and later of similar societies at Runcorn, and Newton-le-Willows, positions

CROSSLEY.

he still retains. He has in MS. a cantata, Adéle, for soli, chorus, and orchestra; a string quartet, etc. He has published six songs; Melody in D, violoncello and pf.; Romance in F, violin and pf.; Three sketches, pf., etc.

Crossley, Hastings, amateur composer, born at Glenburn, Antrim, August 1, 1846. Studied under Berthold Tours. Professor of Greek, Queen's College, Belfast. Composer of Reine d'amour; The cottage by the sea; Strew on her roses; Under the star, and other songs.

Crotch, William, writer, composer, and organist, was born at Norwich, July 5, 1775. He gave early evidence of great talent for music, and was taken to London in 1780. Assistant organist to Dr. Randall, at Cambridge, 1786. Studied for the Church at Oxford, 1788. Organist of Christ Church, Oxford, 1790-1807. Mus. Bac., Oxon., 1794. Organist of St. John's College, Oxford, 1797-1806. Professor of music at Oxford, March, 1797. Mus. Doc., Oxon., 1799. Lectured in Music School of Oxford, 1800-4. Lectured at the Royal Institution, London, 1820. First Principal of the Royal Academy of Music, London, 1822. He died at Taunton, December 29, 1847.

WORKS.—*Oratorios:* The Captivity of Judah, 1789; Palestine, by Bishop Heber, 1812; The Captivity of Judah, re-written, 1834. *Anthems:* Ten anthems dedicated to the Dean and Chapter of Christ Church [1798]; Thirty select anthems, ed. by V: Novello, 2 vols. Collection of seventy-two original single and double chants, 1842; Tunes adapted to the old and new versions of the psalms....1807; Be Merciful unto Me; Comfort, O Lord, the Soul of Thy Servant; Holy, Holy, Holy; How dear are Thy counsels; In God's Word will I rejoice; Lo! Star-led Chiefs; Methinks I hear the full Celestial Choir; My God, look upon me; O come hither, and hearken; O Lord God of Hosts; Sing we merrily; The Lord is King; Who is like unto Thee. Three concertos for the organ with accompts.; Fugues for the organ; Sonatas for the pf.; Handel's oratorios (portions) adapted for the organ or pf. Ode on the Accession of George IV., 1827; Ode to Fancy, Warton (Doctor's exercise), 1799. Glees, various. Elements of Musical Composition, comprehending the rules of Thorough-bass and the theory of Tuning, London, 1812; 2nd edition, 1833; 3rd edition, Novello, 1856; Practical Thorough-bass, or the art of playing from a figured bass, London, n.d.; Questions for the Examination of Pupils who are studying the work called Elements of Musical Composition and Practical Thorough-bass, London [1830]; Substance of several courses of Lectures on Music, 1831; Specimens of various styles of Music referred to in a course of Lectures read

CROUCH.

at Oxford and London, and adapted to keyed Instruments, London, 3 vols., n.d.; Preludes for the Pianoforte, Compositions in various styles, to which are prefixed the rudiments of playing the instrument [1823].

Crotty, Leslie, baritone vocalist, born at Galway in 1853. Intended for a commercial life, he entered an office after leaving school, and was then for some years in a bank in Dublin. During this time he studied music under Alessandro Cellini, and frequently sang in concerts as an amateur. As such he also sang at times in opera for Mr. Carl Rosa, during the second visit of his company to Dublin (1875?). He then went to Florence, and studied under Mabellini. Returning to England, he joined, in 1877, the Carl Rosa Opera Company, in which he remained for a little over ten years, his repertory comprising the parts of Rigoletto, Henry Ashton (Lucia di Lammermoor), Count di Luna (Il Trovatore), Danny Mann (Lily of Killarney), Escamillo (Carmen), and others. In 1889 he made his *début* at Covent Garden, in Italian Opera, as the Count, in Il Trovatore. In 1882 he married Miss GEORGINA BURNS (*q.v.*), and about 1890 started a company for the production in English of Rossini's opera, "Cinderella," which successfully toured the provinces for some years.

Crouch, Anna Maria, *born* PHILLIPS, soprano vocalist, born at London, April 20, 1763. She studied under T. Linley, to whom she was articled in 1779, and first appeared at Drury Lane Theatre in Arne's "Artaxerxes," 1780. Appeared in Ireland with great success, 1783. Married to Mr. Crouch, a lieutenant in the navy, 1785. Sang at oratorios at Drury Lane, 1787. Separated from Crouch, 1792. Resided afterwards with Michael Kelly. Retired from the stage, 1800. She died at Brighton, October 2, 1805.

"She had a remarkably sweet voice, and a naive, affecting style of singing; this, added to extraordinary personal charms, made her a great favourite of the public for many years." A most laudatory poem on her is entitled "Euphrosyné, an Ode to Beauty: addressed to Mrs. Crouch, by Silvester Otway [otherwise John Oswald], London, 1788. *See also* "Memoirs of Mrs. Crouch," by M. Young, London, 2 vols., 1806, with portrait.

Crouch, Frederick Nicholls, composer, vocalist and violoncellist, born in Warren Street, Fitzroy Square, London, July 31, 1808. Son of F. W. Crouch, violoncellist (*q.v.*). At the age of nine he played in the band of the Royal Coburg Theatre. Then he travelled in Yorkshire and Scotland, and was for two years, through necessity, a common seaman on coasting smacks plying between London and Leith. Through the interest of William Watts, then secretary of the Philharmonic

CROUCH.

Society, he entered the orchestra of Drury Lane Theatre. His voice developing, he studied under William Hawes, and was in the choir of Westminster Abbey and St. Paul's Cathedral. Then, entering the R.A.M., he was for a short time under Crotch, Attwood, Lindley, etc., and member of the Philharmonic, Ancient Concerts, and Royal Italian Opera orchestras. Travelled for a time for a firm of metal brokers, and invented the engraving process known as zincography. Afterwards musical supervisor to D'Almaine and Co., London. About 1838 he was giving an entertainment on the " Songs and Legends of Ireland," and was for years known as the Irish lecturer. The song " Kathleen Mavourneen" was one of a series, " The Echoes of the Lakes," published about 1838. In 1849 he went to America, and filled various offices, conducting at Portland, Philadelphia, Washington, Richmond, etc. He joined the Confederate army, and served through the Civil War. His last years were spent in Baltimore, where he died, August 19, 1896. He published his Autobiography in the *Boston Folio*, 1887 (?). He wrote the music of two operas—Sir Roger de Coverley, and the Fifth of November, 1670. His published songs comprised — Songs of Erin ; Echoes of the Past ; Bardic Reminiscences ; Songs of the Olden Time ; Songs of a Rambler ; Wayside Melodies, and many detached songs by various writers, which in their day had great popularity.

Crouch, Frederick William, father of the above, was born in Great Smith Street, Westminster, about the year 1783. He was the eldest son of William Crouch (*q.v.*). He received his first instruction from his father, and was afterwards placed under John Smith, a fine player, when his rapid progress soon enabled him to appear in public in concertos, etc. In 1817 he became second principal at the Italian Opera House, and was also in the orchestra of the Ancient Concerts and Philharmonic Society. For years, and up to a few months before his death, he played everywhere with Robert Lindley. He married the daughter of John Nicholls, an eminent barrister. His death took place, July, 1844. He was the author of " A Complete Treatise on the Violoncello " (London, Chapell, 1826), based largely on the authorized Methode of the Paris Conservatoire ; a Supplement, with accompanied Scales and Exercises on Double Stops ; Duets for two violoncellos ; Duets for pf. and violoncello ; Arrangements, songs, etc.

Crouch, William (father of F. W. Crouch, and grandfather of F. N. Crouch), musician and organist. He was for upwards of fifty years organist of St. Luke's Church, Old Street, London, and was also at the same time, for many years organist of Clapham

CROWE.

Parish Church. Compiler of " Selection of Psalm tunes, as sung in Clapham Church," London [1820] ; and composer of six sonatas or lessons for the harpsichord or pf., op. 1 ; six sonatas for pf., op. 7 ; two sonatas for the pf., op. 9 ; The Triumph of Innocence, an ode ; The Maid of Selma, a song, etc.

Crow, Edwin John, organist and composer, born at Sittingbourne, Kent, September 17, 1841. Chorister at Rochester Cathedral, and articled pupil of the organist, Mr. J. L. Hopkins, up to 1856, when the latter removed to Cambridge. Under his successor, John Hopkins, young Crow remained two years, receiving lessons and also teaching the choir boys. In 1858 he went to Leicester, and studied with G. A. Löhr, whom he succeeded as organist of Trinity Church, after being acting organist for three years. He was then organist successively at St. Andrew's, and St. John's, Leicester ; and in 1873 was appointed organist and choirmaster of Ripon Cathedral, entering upon his duties January 1, 1874, and still retaining those offices. In 1868, he became F.R.C.O. ; graduated Mus. Bac., 1872 ; Mus. Doc., 1882, Cambridge. He is an Examiner for the Incorporated Society of Musicians, and Royal College of Organists, and music master at Ripon Grammar School ; also conductor, in rotation, of the North-East Cathedral Choir Association.

His Compositions, besides the Degree exercises, Psalm 146, and a Harvest Oratorio, include a Communion Service in F (College of Organists' Prize, 1872), a Morning Service in C (written for the opening ot the Cathedral Organ, April 24, 1878), Evening Services in G, A, and D. Organ and pf. music. Songs, and Masonic music.

Crowdy, John, writer and editor, born at Lewknor, January 6, 1834. Editor successively of *The Musician, Musical Standard,* and *The Artist.* Sub-editor of the *Guardian* from 1854. He died, Addlestone, Surrey, January 12, 1883.

WORKS.—A Kalendar of Cadences, in the form called Free Chant, adapted for the recitation of the Psalms, London, n.d. The Free Church Canticle Book, n.d. The Psalter, n.d. The Church Choirmaster . . . London, 1864. A short Commentary on Handel's oratorio, " The Messiah," London [1875].

Crowe, Alfred Gwyllym, bandmaster and composer, born in Bermuda, November 3, 1835. Of a family of soldiers (his father, Captain Crowe, was in the 30th and 50th regiments, and was killed in the Sikh war, 1845), he joined the 30th regiment at Manchester when he was twelve years old. He entered the band, and played oboe and horn ; served in the Crimea, and was present at the battles of the Alma, Inkerman, and the siege of Sebastopol, for which he received medal

CROWEST.

and clasps. Returning to England, he raised a new band for the 30th, and afterwards studied for two years at Kueller Hall. Then he was appointed (1860) to the 14th Light Dragoons, retiring on a pension in 1874. Under the management of Mr. Freeman Thomas, he conducted the promenade concerts at Covent Garden, from 1881, having previously been engaged at the Southport Aquarium. In 1893, he was appointed conductor of the Llandudno Pier and Pavilion Concerts. He died March 8, 1894. His compositions were light, ballet music, and waltzes chiefly. The "See-Saw Waltz" (Covent Garden, 1884), was extensively popular.

Crowest, Frederick J., writer on music, organist and choirmaster, born in London, 1850. Has held several appointments in London, and elsewhere, and is now organist and precentor at Christ Church, Kilburn, and choirmaster of St. Mary's, Somers Town. He has composed some Church music and songs. For some years he was favourably known as a tenor singer, under the name of Arthur Vitton. Besides contributions to the *National Review*, and other papers, he has written the following : "The Great Tone Poets," London, Bentley, 1874; "Book of Musical Anecdotes," Bentley, 1878, 2 vols. ; "Phases of Musical England," Remington, 1881; "Musical History and Biography, in the form of Question and Answer," 1883; "Advice to Singers;" "Musical Groundwork," Warne & Co. ; "Cherubini," the Great Musicians' series, Sampson Low ; "Dictionary of British Musicians," Jarrold, 1895 ; and "The Story of British Music," Vol. I., Bentley, 1895.

Crozier, William, oboe-player, pupil of Barrett. Member of Crystal Palace orchestra from 1855-1870. He died December 20, 1870.

Cruickshank, James, Scottish musician and teacher. Author of "Flutina and Accordion Teacher," London, 1851. Cruickshank's Accordion and Flutina Teacher, Aberdeen [1853]. Also issued several books of music for the Accordion, and composed waltzes and other dance music.

Cruickshank, William, Alexander Campbell, organist and composer, son of the late William Cruickshank, M.D., Deputy General Inspector of Hospitals, and of the 52nd Regiment, born at Greenlaw, Berwickshire, June 1, 1854. Educated at Epsom College, where he received his first musical instruction, afterwards becoming a pupil of the late Thomas Hewlett. Graduated Mus. Bac., Oxford, 1885. Was resident musicmaster at Loretto School, Musselburgh, 1874-1875 ; Organist and Choirmaster, St. John's, Selkirk, and Conductor of the Selkirk Choral Union, 1875-6 ; of St. John's, Alloa, and Conductor of the Alloa Musical Association,

CULLEN.

1876-80; and of the Parish Church, Burnley, from 1880, and Conductor of Burnley Vocal Union, and of the Ruridecanal Festival Services. WORKS.—Psalm 145, "I will magnify Thee, O God," for soli, chorus, and orchestra ; Magnificat and Nunc Dimittis in G, composed for the Festival of the London Church Choir Association, and performed in St. Paul's Cathedral, May, 1889 ; Communion Service in E flat ; My heart is fixed ; Sing, O ye heavens ; Praise the Lord, composed for Annual Festival in aid of Burnley Hospital, 1896 ; and other anthems. Hymn tunes, chants, etc., contributed to various collections. Songs: An autumn wind ; Homeward bound ; Waking ; Waiting ; and others. Part-songs : Waken, lords and ladies gay ; and others. Romance for violoncello, pf. and organ pieces, and organ arrangements, etc.

Cruse, Edward, musician and writer, who died in 1879. He was an organist and teacher in London. Compiled "Psalms of the Church, adapted for four voices, containing a History of Church Music and Notation, biographical notices, etc., the whole calculated for general adoption by every sect of the Reformed Religion," London [1835] ; Te Deum, and other church music.

Cudmore, Richard, violinist, composer, and pianist, was born at Chichester, in 1787. He studied under a musician named James Fargett, Reinagle, and Salomon. Violinist at Chichester Theatre, 1799. Resided in Chichester as violinist and teacher, 1799-1808. He studied the pianoforte under Woelfl, at London. Member of Philharmonic Band, London. Resided in Manchester as leader of Gentlemen's Concerts. He died at Manchester, December 29, 1840. WORKS.—The Martyr of Antioch, oratorio ; Concertos for the violin ; Concertos for the pf. ; Songs, etc.

Cudworth, William, musician, author of "Musical Reminiscences of Bradford." Reprinted from the *Bradford Observer*. Bradford [1885].

Cuisset, Frank F., organist and writer, born at London, February 23, 1812. Studied music under Sir H. Bishop, Sir George Smart, etc. Organist of Holy Trinity Church, Coventry ; Bishop Ryder's, Birmingham ; Selly Oak Church, Birmingham ; and Busbridge Church, Godalming. Author of "The Vocalist's Indispensable Practice, a series of exercises for promoting the strength and flexibility of the voice." London [1875]. Composer also of Concerted vocal music, songs, hymn tunes, etc.

Cullen, Rose, MRS. ALBERT TENCH, vocalist and actress, born near London. Made her *début* at the Lyceum Theatre, January 22, 1870, as the Page in "Chilperic," afterwards

CULWICK

appeared at the Strand and Olympic, and in the provinces. She died, December, 1888.

Culwick, James C., composer and organist, born at West Bromwich, Staffordshire, in 1845. Chorister (articled, at fourteen, to Thomas Bedsmore), and afterwards assistant organist of Lichfield Cathedral. Organist successively at St. Chad's, Lichfield; Parsonstown, Ireland, 1866; Bray, 1868; St. Ann's, Dublin, 1870; Chapel Royal, Dublin, 1881. Professor of pianoforte and theory, Alexandra College, and Conductor of Harmonic Society, Dublin. Lecturer on Music. In 1893 the degree of Mus. Doc., *honoris causâ*, Dublin, was conferred upon him.

WORKS.—Dramatic Cantata, The Legend of Stauffenberg (Ancient Concert Rooms, Dublin, May 3, 1890); Hymn for a May morning, both in MS.; Psalm 104, for soli, chorus, and orchestra. Anthems: Bless the Lord, O my soul, for soli, four, and eight part chorus (1896); Praise the Lord; O Lord, grant the Queen a long life; and others. Church services, including a Te Deum and Benedictus, for men's voices (written by invitation for Lichfield Cathedral, 1892). Various part-songs, and an Elegy in memory of Sir Robert Stewart. Windle straws, a cycle of eight songs; To the Cuckoo, with parts for strings and flutes; duos, etc. *Instrumental*: Quartet in E flat, for pf. and strings (Dublin, 1884); Sonata in D minor, organ; Suite, op. 1; Sonatina, op. 4; Ballade, op. 2, and other pieces for pf. In MS., a concert overture, for orchestra; Quartet and suite for strings; Pieces for violoncello, violin, and pf., etc. Author of the Rudiments of Music, a text-book, Dublin, 1880; 2nd ed., 1882; Pamphlets and papers, Handel's Messiah; Discovery of the original word-book used at the first performance in Dublin, with some notes, 1891; The study of music and its place in general education, Dublin, 1882; Artistic landmarks (Musical Association), London, 1891, etc. Lectures on Folk Song, and what it has done for us. The ethics and practice of Music, etc., etc. Dr. Culwick's father was a tenor vocalist; Lay-clerk of Lichfield Cathedral, a zealous worker in the cause of music, and an oratorio singer of repute in the Midlands.

Cumming, Angus, Scottish violinist and composer who flourished during the latter half of the 18th century. He published " A Collection of Strathspey or Old Highland Reels, with a bass for the violoncello and harpsichord, by Angus Cumming, musician, at Grantown in Strathspey," Edinburgh, 1780. A second edition was published at Glasgow some time after.

Cummings, William Hayman, tenor vocalist, composer, conductor and writer, born at Sidbury, Devon, August 22, 1831. Chor-

CUMMINGS.

ister at St. Paul's Cathedral in his seventh year, he was placed under William Hawes; afterwards entering the choir of the Temple Church, he studied under E. J. Hopkins, and, on leaving, was appointed organist of Waltham Abbey. While in the Temple choir, he sang among the altos in "Elijah," April 16, 1847. After some time he resumed his vocal studies under J. W. Hobbs, whose daughter he married, and soon gained a high position in the concert room, while holding appointments at Westminster Abbey, and the Chapel Royal. He sang at the Birmingham Festival of 1864, and at later celebrations; at the Three Choir Festivals, at various times from that at Gloucester, 1865, to Hereford, 1879, frequently taking important parts for other singers at the briefest notice. In 1870, he appeared in opera at the Gaiety Theatre, and later at Drury Lane and elsewhere. Visited America in 1871, singing at the Festival of the Handel and Haydn Society, early in the year; in "Elijah," at New York, October 31; and at various places on tour. He has been heard at every important concert centre in the United Kingdom and Ireland, and has sung occasionally up to the last few years. In 1879 he became a professor of the R.A.M., of which he is now an Honorary Member; and later, joined the staff of the Guildhall School; and many years professor at the Royal Normal College for the Blind. In 1882, he was appointed chorus-master of the Sacred Harmonic Society, and afterwards conductor. He was precentor of St. Annes, Soho, 1886-88. In 1884, he was elected F.S.A. He is Hon. Treasurer, and was orchestral director of the Philharmonic Society up to 1896; Hon. Treasurer of the Royal Society of Musicians; editor for the Purcell Society's publications; and conductor of the annual festivals of the Royal Society of Musicians. In June, 1896, he was elected Principal of the Guildhall School of Music. A learned musical antiquary, he has acquired one of the finest musical libraries in private hands, especially rich in early printed works and MSS., and is the possessor of the duplicate of Handel's autograph will. He lectured on " English Schools of Composition," at the Royal Institution, 1894, and has frequently lectured and given addresses before the Musical Association; the Incorporated Society of Musicians Conferences; the R.A.M., Trinity College, London, etc. Author of The Rudiments of Music (London, Novello, 1877), which has gone through many editions, and has been translated into several languages; Purcell (Great Musicians' series), London, 1882. Biographical Dictionary of Musicians, London, Novello, 1892. Contributions to Grove's Dictionary of Music and Musicians, the Dictionary of National Biography, and musical periodicals.

CUMMINS.

His Compositions include a cantata, The Fairy Ring, produced, St. James's Hall, May 24, 1872; Morning Service in D; anthem, O Lord, give ear; Sunday part-songs (6 Nos.); part-songs; many songs: Yellow lie the corn rigs; Ask me no more; Hush thy sounds (with 'cello obligato), etc. Glees: O thou sweet bird (Abbey Glee Club Prize, 1850); with four other prize glees, etc.

His son, NORMAN PERCY CUMMINGS, born at Dulwich, September 12, 1868, musically educated at home, made his *début* as a pianist at Dulwich College, July, 1884. He then studied at Leipzig, and on his return played at the Crystal Palace Wednesday Concerts, October 24, 1888. He has assisted at his father's lectures, and is professor of pf. at the Royal Normal College, Norwood.

Cummins, Charles, composer, pianist, and violinist, born at York in 1785. He studied under Dr. Miller, of Doncaster. Leader and violinist in theatres of the West of England. Wrote an amount of music for dramatic pieces, and a pamphlet against the system of J. B. Logier. The date of his death has not been ascertained.

Cunningham, Francis, musician. Published " A Selection of Psalm Tunes, adapted to a selection of psalms and hymns extracted from various authors," London, 1826; and " A Selection of Psalm Tunes, designed to assist public worship." London, 1834.

Currie, Rev. James, LL.D., musician and educationist, born April 24, 1828. He was Rector of the Church of Scotland Training College, Edinburgh, for upwards of thirty years. He wrote The Elements of Musical Analysis, Edinburgh, 1858; A First Musical Grammar, Edinburgh, 1873. Works on Infant and Secondary Education; School Songs, etc. He died at Edinburgh, September 26, 1886. A monument to his memory was erected in Warriston Cemetery, Edinburgh, in 1890.

Currie, William, violinist and composer, born about 1828; died at Peterhead, December 1, 1881. He was blind. Composer of the " Miller of Dron," and other reels.

Curtis, Thomas, musician. Compiled " Divine Amusement, a selection of Psalms and Hymns as sung in all the principal churches, chapels, etc." London, n.d.

Curwen, John, musician and writer, was born at Heckmondwike, Yorks., November 14, 1816. Educated at Coward College and London University. Ordained minister. Assistant minister at Independent Church, Basingstoke, Hants., 1838. Co-pastor at Stowmarket, Suffolk, 1841. Pastor at Plaistow, Essex, 844. Founded Tonic Sol-Fa Associations, 1853. Established Tonic Sol-Fa College, 1862. Resigned ministry, and devoted himself to propagation of the system,

CURWEN.

1867. Established " Tonic Sol-Fa Reporter," and publishing agency in London. He died at Heaton Mersey House, near Manchester, May 26, 1880.

WORKS.—An Account of the Tonic Sol-fa Method of Teaching to Sing, London, 1854; Grammar of Vocal Music, with Lessons and Exercises founded on the Tonic Sol-fa method, and a full introduction to the art of singing at sight from the Old Notation, London, n.d.; Standard Course of Lessons on the Tonic Sol-fa method of teaching to sing, London, n.d.; Tonic Sol-fa instrumental instruction books; Harmonium and Organ; Theory of Fingering; The First Pianoforte Book; Reed Band Book; Brass Band Book; String Band Book: separate Works, all London, n.d. Musical Statics; Art of Teaching, being the Teacher's Manual of the Tonic Sol-fa, n.d.; Musical Theory, London [1879]; The Common-places of Music (Lectures), 10 parts, 1871-3; Primer of Tonic Sol-fa (Novello), n.d.; Music in Worship and other papers on the People's Psalmody, London, n.d.; The Present Crisis of Music in Schools, a Reply to Mr. Hullah, London, [1873]; The Child's own Hymn-Book; How to Observe Harmony; Construction Exercises in Elementary Composition; Arrangements, etc.

Curwen, John Spencer, son of the foregoing, was born at Plaistow in 1847. Studied at first under his father and G. Oakey; and later at R.A.M., under G. A. Macfarren, A. Sullivan, and E. Prout. A.R.A.M., 1879; F.R.A.M., 1885. Associate of the Philharmonic Society. He has composed and arranged part-songs, etc., but his life has been devoted to the Tonic Sol-fa movement, and to the promotion of music in elementary schools. He was made President of the Tonic Sol-fa College in 1880, and has taken an active part in the festivals held at Stratford-le-Bow since their establishment in 1883. He has lectured in many places in the United Kingdom; visited the Continent, examining the various methods of teaching singing in schools; and in 1887 he made an extended tour in the United States, to enquire into the condition of music there. The results of these undertakings have been embodied in pamphlets, and in papers contributed to the *Tonic Sol-fa Reporter* (now the *Musical Herald*) and other publications. He is author of Studies in Worship Music, London, 1880; a second series, London, 1885; Memorials of John Curwen, London, 1882; Musical Notes in Paris, London, 1882; The Tonic Sol-fa System; a paper read before the Society of Arts, March 22, 1882, etc.

Curwen, Mrs., born ANNIE JESSY GREGG, is a native of Dublin, where her father practised as a solicitor. Her first composition was published by friends when she was fourteen.

CUSINS.

CUTLER.

Studied at the Royal Irish Academy of Music, under Mr. and Mrs. Joseph Robinson and Sir Robert Stewart. Practiced the musical profession in Dublin for some years, and afterwards resided in Scotland, where she first came in contact with the Tonic Sol-fa system. Applying its principles to pianoforte teaching and the Staff Notation, she wrote " The Child Pianist " (London, Curwen, 1866), a work now extensively adopted. She has lectured considerably on the subject. Was an adjudicator at the singing competition of Dublin Schools, 1893.

Cusins, Sir William George, Kt., composer, pianist and conductor, born in London, October 14, 1833. Chorister in Chapel Royal, 1843. Studied at the Brussels Conservatoire, from 1844, piano, violin and harmony. In 1847, he won a King's Scholarship at R.A.M., and was re-elected 1849, studying under Potter, Bennett, Lucas, and Sainton. Played Mendelssohn's Rondo in B minor, with orchestra, at an Academy Concert at the Hanover Square Rooms, June 6, 1849, and the same year was appointed to the Queen's Private Chapel, and entered the orchestra of the Royal Italian Opera. In 1851, made assistant professor at R.A.M., and later professor. Conductor Philharmonic Society, 1867-83; Master of the Queen's Music, 1870-93; Conductor of the London Select Choir, 1885. Professor, Guildhall School of Music, 1885. He conducted the performance of Bennett's oratorio, "The Woman of Samaria," at the Birmingham Festival, 1867. As a pianist, he played at the Gewandhaus Concerts, Leipzig, October 12, 1856; Berlin; at the Philharmonic and Crystal Palace Concerts; Rome, 1883; and at his own annual concerts, London, from 1885. He was elected Hon. Member of the Academy of St. Cecilia, Rome, 1883; received the honour of Knighthood from the Queen, 1892; and the Cross of Isabella the Catholic, from the Queen of Spain, 1893. He died, suddenly, from influenza, August, 31, 1893, at Remonchamps, in the Ardennes.

WORKS.—Royal Wedding Serenata, 1863; Gideon, an oratorio (produced at the Gloucester Festival, 1871); Te Deum, for soli, chorus and orchestra (Sacred Harmonic Society, February 24, 1882); Jubilee Cantata, Grant the Queen a Long Life (State Concerts, 1887); anthems; Masonic prayers; Responses to the Commandments, &c. Editor of, and contributor to, Songs from the published writings of Alfred Tennyson; songs, and part-songs. Symphony in C, for orchestra (Sarasate Concert, St. James's Hall, June 18, 1892); two concert overtures—Les Travailleurs de la Mer (1869); and Love's Labour Lost (1875); March, in honour of Prince Albert Victor (Albert Hall, January, 1885); Concerto

in A Minor, pf. and orchestra; Concerto, violin (MS.); Septet, for wind instruments and double-bass (1891); Trio in C Minor, pf. and strings (produced at the composer's concert, June 14, 1882); Sonata in A minor, pf. and violin (1893); pf. pieces, &c. Author of a pamphlet, Handel's Messiah, an examination of the original and of some contemporary MSS. (Augener), 1874, and contributor to Grove's Dictionary of Music and Musicians.

Custard, Walter Goss, organist, pianist, and composer, born, June 9, 1841. Nephew of Sir John Goss. Articled pupil of Sir George Elvey, at Windsor, 1857. Organist of Spring Grove Church, Isleworth, 1861; Christ Church, St. Leonards-on-Sea, 1865, to the present time. Conductor, for some years, of the Hastings and St. Leonards Sacred Harmonic Society, and St. Leonards Vocal Association. Has given pianoforte recitals with much success. His works include The Office of the Holy Communion, in E flat; Communion Service in F; Te Deum and Benedictus in F; Hymns, various. The Chorister's Daily Practice, London, n.d. Pianoforte—Short studies in all the major and minor keys; Twelve studies, op. 22; Nocturne in C minor; Rondino in A, op. 17, &c. Triumphal March for organ (with chorus); Songs, &c.

Cutell, Richard, musician and writer of the fifteenth century, author of a treatise on Counterpoint, preserved in the Bodleian Library, Oxford (MS. imperfect).

Cutler, Edward, amateur composer and *litterateur*, born at Canons Park, the seat of his grandfather, Sir Thomas Plumer, Master of the Rolls, and was educated at Eton and Dresden. Well-known as a Q C. and Chancery barrister, he is still more widely recognised as a clever composer. He was for some time organist of Whitchurch, Edgeware; and in 1891 was appointed by the Prince of Wales grand organist of the Freemasons of England —the first amateur to hold that office. He gave a matinée at Erard's Rooms, February 23, 1893, with a programme of his own compositions. He has composed a Scherzetto, and other pieces for orchestra; Romance for violin; Postlude in C, &c., for organ; several pf. pieces. An Arab's Song; Child and Mother; The Rose Walk, and numerous other songs; and has contributed various articles to the musical press.

Cutler, William Henry, pianist, vocalist and composer, born at London, in 1792. He studied under Dr. Arnold and W. Russell, and made his *debut* as pianist with a concerto by Viotti, in 1800. Chorister in St. Paul's Cathedral. Mus. Bac., Oxon, 1812. Organist of St. Helen's, Bishopsgate, 1818. Taught Music by Logier's System. Organist of Quebec Chapel, Portman Square, 1823. He sang at the principal London concerts.

CUZENS.

WORKS.—Church Music; The Psalms, Te Deum, Jubilate, etc., used at Quebec Chapel, Portman Square, n.d.; Pf. music; fantasias, rondos, marches, duets, songs, etc.

Cuzens, Benjamin, composer and organist, who flourished about the end of the eighteenth century. He published "The Portsmouth Harmony," n.d. "Divine Harmony, containing six anthems and a Christmas ode." Anthems, etc.

Cympson, Edward, composer and lyric author of present time. Teacher of singing in London Board Schools, 1876. He has composed two sacred cantatas, "The Ruler's Daughter" (performed Greenock, 1888); and "The Angel of the Harvest" (London, 1892). Words for temperance songs, &c.

Czapek, *pseudonym of* HATTON, JOHN LIPTROT.

D'Albert, *see* ALBERT.

Dale, C. J., amateur organist and conductor, born at Longton, Staffordshire, in May, 1842. Educated at Belper, Derby. Studied music with Mr. R. Sharpe (organist of St. Mary's, Southampton). Went to London in 1860, where he is engaged in business. He was organist of St. John's Square (Clerkenwell) Wesleyan Church for nineteen years; of Finsbury Park Wesleyan Church for fifteen years; and is now Choirmaster of Holly Park Wesleyan Church. Up to 1894 he was conductor of the Finsbury Choral Association, which he raised from small beginnings to a position of artistic importance. In 1889 he established the Metropolitan College of Music, which has flourishing classes for Tonic Sol-fa and other students. Of this he is still the Principal, and Chairman of Corporation Committees. He has composed a Morning Service, some simple anthems, and a few hymn tunes. Musical editor of "Psalms and Canticles pointed for chanting," London, Wesleyan Book-room, 1888.

Dale, Isaac, musician and organist, compiled "The Mona Melodist, a selection of Psalm and Hymn Tunes suited to all the variations of metrical psalmody, for congregational or family worship, newly harmonised for four voices, with an accompaniment for the organ or pianoforte." Douglas [1842]. An excessively scarce book.

Dale, Joseph, composer and editor, born in 1750. He was organist of St. Anthony and St. John Baptist, Watling Street, London. He died at Edinburgh, August 21, 1821. Author of "Dale's Collection of Sixty Favourite Scotch Songs, taken from the original manuscripts of the most celebrated Scotch authors and composers, properly adapted for the German flute," Books I., II., and III., n.d. [1794]. Wrote an "Intro-

DAMIAN.

duction to the Pianoforte, Harpsichord, or Organ," op. 12, n.d. Thirty organ pieces, op. 11, n.d., and many works for pf., etc. Also a collection of English songs.

Dale, Rev. Reginald Francis, clergyman and musician, born at Sydenham, London, September 12, 1845. Educated at Oxford, and graduated B.A. and Mus. Bac. in 1866. Clerk in Holy Orders, 1870. Assistant master in Westminster School, 1870-1886. Rector of Bletchingdon, Oxford, 1885. Joint author with the Rev. John Troutbeck of "Music Primer for Schools," 1873, etc; and composer of hymn tunes, some of which appeared in "Twenty-two original Hymn Tunes, by two Oxford Graduates" [1867].

Dalglish, Robert, composer, born at Pollokshaws, Renfrewshire, July, 1806; died there, August 5, 1875. He was a weaver by trade, and self-educated in music. Composed a number of anthems, glees, and psalms, of a somewhat feeble class, which were at one time regarded with some favour in Glasgow.

D'Alquen, Frank C., *see* ALQUEN, FRANK C. D'.

Daly, William, violinist, born in Dublin, *circa* 1848. Settled in Edinburgh for many years, and teacher of the violin at Fettes' College there. Leader of the Edinburgh Quartet, which began giving chamber concerts in 1890. Author of a treatise on the violin, published in the "Musical Educator' (*see* Greig, John). His son, WILLIAM, has contributed a treatise on Musical History to the same publication. JOHN DALY, violinist, born in Dublin, August, 1851, is brother to William Daly. Studied at R.A.M., Dublin, under Sir Robert Stewart and others. Resided for a time at Glasgow; then in Manchester, where he was for some years in Halle's orchestra as a violin player; at present time in Glasgow as teacher and performer.

Dalyell, Sir John Graham, antiquary, was born in 1776, and died June 7, 1851. He was educated for the bar, and succeeded as sixth baronet of Binns, Linlithgow, in 1841. In addition to a number of valuable historical and scientific works, he wrote "Musical Memoirs of Scotland, with historical annotations, and numerous illustrative plates," Edinburgh, 1849. This is now a scarce work, and is of some value as a contribution to Scottish musical archæology.

Damian, Grace, contralto vocalist, born at Brighton. Studied under Madame Sainton-Dolby. Made her *debut* at the Monday Popular Concerts, January 12, 1880; and in the same year sang in "Elijah," and other works, at the Gloucester Festival. She also sang at the Leeds Festival, 1883, in Raff's "End of the World"; and has been heard at the principal London and provincial concerts.

DAMON.

In 1889, she was on tour with Madame Albani in the United States and Canada. She made her first appearance on the stage at Covent Garden, October 29, 1890, in " La Gioconda."

Damon, William, composer and organist, was born 1540. Organist of Queen Elizabeth's Chapel. He died early in the seventeenth century.

WORKS.—The Psalmes of David in English Meter, with notes of foure parts set unto them by Gulielmo Damon, for John Bull, to the use of Christians for recreating themselves, instede of fond and unseemly ballades, 1579 [said to have been published by Bull, a goldsmith in London, without Damon's consent or knowledge]. The Former Booke of the Musicke of Mr. William Damon, late one of Her Majesties musitions ; conteining all the Tunes of Dauids Psalmes as they are ordinarily soung in the church, most excellently by him composed into four parts, altus, cantus, tenor, bassus ; in which sett the tenor singeth the church tune. Published for the recreation of such as delight in musicke, by W. Swayne, Gent. Printed by T. Este, 1591. The Second Booke of the Musicke of Mr. William Damon, containing all the Tunes of David's Psalmes, differing from the former in respect that the highest part singeth the Church tune, London, 1591. The tunes to which Damon gave harmonies are forty in number, and are the first psalms with harmonies published in England.

Danby, John, English glee composer, was born in 1757 [1750]. He gained ten prizes from the Catch Club, for seven glees, two canons, and an ode, 1781-94. He was organist of the chapel of the Spanish Embassy, Manchester Square, London, and died at London, May 16, 1798. Very little has been preserved concerning the biography of this musician.

WORKS. —Masses ; Motets ; Catches, canons and glees, for three, four, and five voices, in Score, four books, London, n.d. [c. 1785-98]; La Guida alla Musica Vocale, Op. 2, London [1787], n.d. Glees—When Sappho tuned (Smollett), three voices ; When generous wine expands ; When floods retire to the sea ; The fairest flowers the vale prefer ; Sweet thrush ; Shepherds, I have lost my love ; Go to my Anna's breast ; Fair Flora decks ; Come, ye party jangling swains ; Awake, Æolian lyre, four voices ; Music has power ; Soft pleasing pains unknown before ; When beauty's soul ; The nightingale ; O salutaris hostia, etc.

Dance, William, violinist, pianist, and composer, born 1755. He studied under Aylward, Baumgarten, and Giardini, and was a violinist at Drury Lane Theatre, 1771-74. He was leader at King's Theatre, 1775-93, and led the band of the Handel Commemo-

DANIEL.

rations in 1790, etc. He was one of the founders of the Philharmonic Society, and acted as director and treasurer. He died at London, June 5, 1840.

Dance was a successful piano teacher in London, and composed sonatas, fantasias, variations, etc. His brother, GEORGE DANCE (1741—London, January 14, 1825), was a painter and a Royal Academician. He was a singer and vocal composer.

Dando, Joseph Haydon Bourne, violinist, born in Somers Town, London, in 1806. Studied under his uncle, Gaetano Brandi, and then for seven years under Nicolas Mori, 1819-26. In 1831, he became a member of the Philharmonic Orchestra, and remained so till 1855. He was also in all the leading orchestras, and in those of the Birmingham, Three Choirs, and other festivals. He anticipated the Concerti da Camera, started November 7, 1835, by giving a chamber concert of a similar type at the Horns Tavern, September 23 of that year. In 1836, he joined Blagrove, Gattie, and Lucas in chamber quartet concerts, at the Hanover Square Rooms, the first taking place March 17, Dando playing viola. His claim to the introduction of public performances of the string quartet cannot be maintained, as they were played from the date of the first Philharmonic Concert, March 8, 1813 ; and at the British Concerts, given in the ball-room of the Argyll Rooms in 1823. But Dando did good work in his day, up to his retirement in 1875. His appointment as music master to the Charterhouse Schools he held from 1875 almost to the time of his death, at Godalming, in May, 1894.

Daniel, Albert Edward, composer and pianist, born in Birmingham, November 9, 1862. Studied privately under several masters, but owes much to his own unaided exertions. F.R.C.O. 1885. Has appeared as pianist and organist, giving recitals in the Birmingham Town Hall and other places. Increasing deafness has put a stop to a promising public career, and his time is now chiefly devoted to teaching.

WORKS.—Two masses ; a Harvest Cantata, performed 1888-9, but remaining in MS., and other church music ; Choral song, The Summer Rain, produced by the Birmingham Festival Choral Society, April, 1891 ; A comic operatta, MS ; many songs, etc. Two concert overtures, orchestra ; Quintet and trio, pf. and strings ; Quartet, strings ; Fantasia, Clarinet and pf. ; Sonatas for organ and pianoforte, and various pieces in smaller forms.

Daniel, John, musician, was born at Aberdeen, in 1803. He studied music under John Ross, and was a music-teacher in Aberdeen for a number of years. He was also precentor of St. John's Church, Montrose,

DANIEL.

about 1833, and in 1843 he settled in New York as a teacher. He died at New York, June 21, 1881. He edited " The National Psalmody of the Church of Scotland, a collection of the most esteemed psalm and hymn tunes . . . " [1837], 2nd ed. [1843]. Composed, also, part-songs, songs, and pf. music. JAMES DANIEL (Aberdeen, July 24, 1810—February 17, 1889), probably a brother of the foregoing, was a music-engraver and editor. He issued " A Collection of Reels, Strathspeys, slow airs, etc," Aberdeen [1840].

Daniel, Rev. Richard Blackburne, curate of Tickenhall, Derby, 1878, and formerly organist of the parish churches of St. Mary Bredin and St. Mary Bredman, Canterbury. Author of " Chapters on Church Music," London : Elliot Stock, 1894.

Danneley, John Feltham, writer, pianist, and composer, born at Oakingham, Berkshire, 1786. He studied under C. Knyvett, S. Webbe, Woelfl, and C. Neate. Resided in Hampshire as teacher till 1812. Organist of Church of St. Mary of the Tower, Ipswich, 1812. Visited Paris, and studied under Reicha and Pradher, 1816. He died at London, 1836.

WORKS.—A set of twelve Italian duets; Glees and songs; Pf. music. An Introduction to the Elementary Principles of Thorough Bass and classical music, Ipswich, 1820; An Encyclopædia, or Dictionary of Music, London, 1825; A Musical Grammar, comprehending the principles and rules of the science, London, 1826.

Danyl, or Daniel, John, composer, of the latter part of the 16th and beginning of the 17th centuries. He is supposed to have been the brother of Daniel, the poet, and was a Bachelor of Music, Oxon., 1604. He published " Songs for the Lute, Viol, and Voyce," London, 1606, and others of his compositions are preserved in MS.

Darnton, Charles, organist and composer, born in London, October 10, 1836. Many years organist of Park Chapel, Camden Town. Composer of the sacred cantatas, " The Star of Bethleham " (1893) ; 'The Song of Creation;" " Abraham " (1895) ; " Spring-time and Harvest " (1895). Pastoral cantata, "Village Life," performed, London, 1891. Anthems for Church and Home; various anthems, etc.; Sacred songs. Compiler of " Comprehensive Psalmody " (London, 1866).

Dart, Henry John Baker, organist, born at Torquay, March 5, 1854. Chorister at St. Luke's Church there, 1866-8 ; organist, St. Michael's Mission Church, 1868 ; and Christ Church, Ellacombe, 1873. In 1875 he removed to London, and later on studied at the London Academy of Music, under Dr. E. J. Hopkins, J. F. Barnett, and E. H. Turpin, his earlier teachers having been Charles Fowler and T. Craddock. Conductor, 1877-80, of

DAVENPORT.

the North London Philharmonic Society, at the concerts of which more than one important work was given for the first time in London. In 1879 he was appointed organist of St. John's, Waterloo Road, where he organised the series of recitals and oratorio performances that became famous. In 1893 he resigned that post for the parish church (St. James's), of Paddington, where he is still in office. He is A.R.C.O. and Professor at the London Academy of Music. He has written a Sonata for organ and trombone, performed at St. John's, February, 1884 ; Concert allegro for organ. A setting of Psalm 84, for soli, chorus, and organ, was produced at the Church of St. John, March, 1893. A morning and evening Service in D is published.

Darwall, Rev. John, clergyman and composer, was born at Haughton, Staffordshire, in January, 1731. He was educated at Manchester and Oxford, where he graduated in 1756. In 1769 he became vicar of Walsall, and died there December 18, 1789. He composed the Psalm tune, " Darwall's " and many others not so well known.

Dauney, William, musician and antiquary, born at Aberdeen, October 27, 1800. Educated at Dulwich and Edinburgh University. Called to the Scottish Bar, 1823. Solicitor-General for British Guiana, at Demerara, 1838. He died at Georgetown, Demerara, July 28, 1843.

WORK.—Ancient Scottish Melodies from a manuscript of the reign of King James VI., with Introductory Inquiry (Skene Manuscript), Edinburgh, 1838.

In the preface to this work, Dauney covers an amount of ground previously unattempted either by Tytler, Ritson, or Stenhouse, and displays much judgment and learning in the general handling of his subject.

Davenport, Francis William, composer, born at Wilderslow, near Derby, 1847. Educated at University College, Oxford. Pupil of Sir G. A. Macfarren, whose son-in-law he afterwards became. Appointed Professor of Harmony and Composition, R.A.M., 1879, and subsequently elected an Honorary Member of the same. He is also a Professor at the Guildhall School of Music. His compositions number two Symphonies in D minor and G, the first winning the prize in the Symphony Competition at the Alexandra Palace, 1876. Also an overture, " Twelfth Night," produced at the Viard-Louis Concerts, St. James's Hall, February 18, 1879 ; and a prelude and fugue for orchestra, performed at the Crystal Palace, November 1, 1879. His other works include a trio in B flat, op. 5, for pf. and strings (Monday Popular Concerts, January 31, 1881) ; six pieces for pf. and violoncello ; French songs, for children ;

DAVENPORT.

songs and part-songs. Author of "Elements of Music" (Longman, 1884); "Elements of Harmony and Counterpoint" (Longman, 1886); "A Guide for Pianoforte Students" (jointly with Percy Baker), Longman, 1891.

Davenport, Uriah, ·composer and writer of the latter part of last century, and teacher in London, compiler of "The Psalm-Singer's Pocket Companion, containing a new introduction, with such directions for singing, as is proper and necessary for learners," London, 1755; 2nd ed. 1758; 3rd ed. 1785.

Davey, Henry, pianist and writer on music, born at Brighton, November 29, 1853. He acquired the first rudiments of music through the Tonic Sol-fa method; and studied for three years at the Conservatorium, Leipzig. Resident in Brighton as teacher. He is a Scholar, and his work is not confined to music, as he is librarian of the Brighton and Sussex Natural History Society, and active in other ways. He is author of "The Students' Musical History," Lond., Curwen [1891]; "History of English Music," 1895; and has contributed articles to the "Dictionary of National Biography," and to the musical press.

Davidson, Peter, Scottish violinist and writer, was born about 1834. Author of "The Violin: a concise exposition of the general principles of construction, theoretically and practically treated," Glasgow, 1871. Second edition, London, 1880, with lives of the most eminent artists and dictionary of violin makers, and lists of violin sales. In 1886 Davidson went to America. He is reputed to have dabbled in occult science and to have made magic mirrors.

Davidson, Thomas, Scottish musician of the 17th century, was appointed teacher in the Music (or Song) School, Aberdeen, in 1640. This position he must have held till far on in the century, as we find from the Burgh Records of Aberdeen, that on January 16, 1666, he received an augmentation of his salary, making it 250 merks. He is chiefly celebrated as the editor of "Cantus, Songs, and Fancies. To Thre, Foure, or Five partes, both apt for voices and viols. With a brief Introduction of Musick, as is taught by the Musick-Schole of Aberdene, by T. D., Mr. of Musick," Aberdeen, printed by John Forbes, 1662. Second edit., 1666. Third edit., 1682. Reprint, New Club Series, Paisley, 1879. The three editions of the "Cantus" differ slightly in respect of several omissions and insertions. It was the first secular music-book published in Scotland, and consists chiefly of English and foreign melodies, some by Gastoldi, or imitations of them, arranged. All these editions are extremely scarce and valuable.

Davie, James, violinist, flute-player, and composer, born about 1783. He resided in

DAVIES.

Aberdeen as a teacher, and member of the Aberdeen theatre orchestra. He was choir-master of St. Andrew's Church, Aberdeen, and conductor of Aberdeen Choral Society. He died at Aberdeen, November 19, 1857.

WORKS.—Music of the Church of Scotland, being a numerous selection of Psalm and Hymn Tunes, Ancient and Modern, in Four Vocal Parts, with an Instrumental Accompaniment . . . To which are prefixed Remarks on Church Music, etc., Aberdeen, 8vo., [1841]. The Chorister . . . Psalm and hymn tunes . . . arranged in four parts, Aberdeen, n.d. A Compendious Introduction to the Art of Singing, comprising the most useful scales and examples, Aberdeen, n.d. The Vocal Harmonist, a Collection of Duets, Trios, Glees, etc., n.d. Caledonian Repository of the most favourite Scottish slow airs, Marches, Strathspeys, Reels, Jigs, Hornpipes, etc., expressly adapted for the Violin. Aberdeen and Edinburgh, 8vo., about 1829-30 [six books]. Scales for the Voice. Songs, etc.

Davies, Ben, tenor vocalist, born at Pontardawe, near Swansea, in 1858. Gaining a reputation locally, he decided upon his profession, and entered the R.A.M., studying under Randegger. In 1880, he won the Evill prize for declamatory singing, and was elected an Associate. He joined the Carl Rosa Company, and made his operatic *début* at Her Majesty's Theatre, as Thaddeus, in "The Bohemian Girl;" sang for a long period in Cellier's "Dorothy;" in the title part in Sullivan's "Ivanhoe" on its production; and in Augustus Harris's Company, 1892. He first appeared at a Festival, at Cardiff, 1892, in Dvořák's *Stabat Mater;* sang at the Norwich Festivals of 1893-96; Leeds, 1895; and Bristol, 1896. Sang with great success in Chicago, 1893, and Berlin, 1894; as well as at all important concerts in the United Kingdom, standing in the first rank of artists. In 1885, he married Miss CLARA PERRY, a soprano singer, who was for some time a member of the Carl Rosa Company. She sang in the provinces at first, and appeared in London as Arline, March 27, 1883, at Drury Lane.

Davies, Cecilia, vocalist, born in 1752 [1740]. Travelled in France and Italy, and sang with success. *Début* in London, 1773, in Sacchini's "Lucio Vero." Sang in London and on Continent, till 1791. She died at London, July 3, 1836. Her sister MARIANNE (born 1736, died 1792), was a harmonica-player, and appeared with her sister in public. She was a skilful performer on her instrument.

Davies, Clara Novello, pianist, conductor and teacher, born at Cardiff, April 7, 1861. Daughter of Jacob Davies (noticed below), by whom she was principally taught. Began as accompanist and teacher of the pianoforte. About 1884 she formed a ladies'

DAVIES.

choir, and gave concerts at Cardiff for some years. The reputation of the choir rising, tours were undertaken, and performances given in London, from 1890; in Birmingham, 1892; and on tour with Madame Patti, In 1893 Madame Davies took her choir to Chicago, and won the gold medal in the competition for ladies' voices. On her return she was, with her choir, commanded to sing before the Queen, at Osborne, February, 1894. She is the head of a Music Institute at Cardiff. In 1882, she married Mr. David Davies, of Cardiff. Her father, JACOB DAVIES, born at St. Fagans, in 1840, is a well known musician and conductor. The Blue Ribbon Choir became famous under his direction, and won many prizes. He now conducts the Cardiff Glee Society, and is resident in that town.

Davies, David Ffrangcon, baritone vocalist, born at Bethesda, Carnarvonshire, December 11, 1860. He received his first musical instruction from his father, an amateur; but he was originally intended for another profession, and educated at Oxford, graduating B.A. and M.A. Deciding to become a singer, he entered the Guildhall School of Music, and studied under Richard Latter, afterwards becoming a pupil of W. Shakespeare. He made his first appearance in January, 1890, at Mr. De Jong's concerts, in Manchester; sang in the title-part, in " Elijah," at the Hovingham (Yorks.) Festival the following October ; at the Monday Popular Concerts, November 3; and in the " Messiah," at Birmingham, December 26. His Festival *début* was at Hanley, in October, 1893, where he was engaged again, 1896; and he sang at the Cardiff Festival of 1895. In opera he has appeared at times from 1890, in " Faust," " Lohengrin," &c., and created the part of Cedric in Sullivan's "Ivanhoe." In the Spring of 1896 he toured with great success in the United States; and as an oratorio singer, especially, now occupies a foremost position.

Davies, Fanny, pianist, though born in Guernsey, June 27, 1861, is connected with Birmingham by family and early residence. Her first teachers were Miss Welchman, Charles E. Flavell, and A. R. Gaul (harmony), all of Birmingham. Studied at Leipzig,1882-3, under Reinecke, Oscar Paul, and Jadassohn ; at Frankfort, 1883-5, with Madame Schumann and Bernhard Scholz. She made her first appearance, on her return to England, at the Crystal Palace Concerts, October 17, 1885, playing the solo part in Beethoven's concerto in G; on November 16, she played at the Monday Popular Concerts; at the Saturday Concerts, November 28. She then played at Manchester, Glasgow, and other places,making her Birmingham *début*, March 30, 1886, since which time she has annually given a recital, or concert, with Joachim and Piatti, in that

DAVIES.

city. She played at the Philharmonic Concerts, April 15, 1886, choosing Bennett's concerto in C minor; and has given recitals in London and many places. She has played in the old and new Gewandhaus, Leipzig, 1887-8 ; at Berlin, and Rome, 1890, and before several reigning Sovereigns ; and has achieved a high position, being regarded as a specially fine interpreter of the music of Schumann.

Davies, H. Walford, composer, studied at R.C.M., and while there produced a number of important works. He has written a Symphony, produced at the Crystal Palace, October, 1895 ; an overture, quartets, for strings, and pf. and strings ; sonata, for pf. and violin. Also a choral ballad, " Hervè Riel," poem by Browning. In 1894, he won the Bristol Orpheus Society's prize with his glee, " The Sturdy Rock," and he has written other vocal music. In 1895 he was appointed a Professor at the R.C.M.

Davies, Hugh, organist and composer of early part of the 17th century. He was organist of Hereford Cathedral, and in 1623 he graduated Mus. Bac., Oxford. He died about 1644. Composer of Church music, none of which has been preserved.

Davies, Llewela, pianist and composer, born at Brecon, South Wales. Gained admission to the R.A.M., 1887, by winning the John Thomas (Welsh) Scholarship. Pupil of Walter Macfarren* for pf., and of Stewart Macpherson for harmony and composition. Her career at the Academy was distinguished, and she took, among other prizes, the Macfarren Scholarship, 1892 ; The Lucas Medal, 1894, both for composition. In 1893 she was awarded the Medal of the Worshipful Company of Musicians. She appeared as solo pianist at the Hereford Festival chamber concerts in 1891, and 1894, and has played at concerts in St. James's Hall, Queen's Hall, and the Covent Garden Promenade Concerts. Her compositions comprise Three sketches for orchestra ; A quartet for strings ; Sonata, produced by the Musical Artists' Society, March, 1894, pf. and violin ; and a number of songs.

Davies, Miss, *see sub* BATTISHILL, JONATHAN.

Davies, Margaret, soprano vocalist, born at Dowlais, South Wales. Sang in public from ten years of age. In 1886 gained a Scholarship at R.C.M., and while a student there appeared with success at the Crystal Palace Concerts, April 5, 1890. She sang at the Cardiff Festival in 1892 ; has been heard at many of the best concerts; and was chosen for the part of Kitty O'Toole at the production of Stanford's Opera, " Shamus O'Brien," March 2, 1896.

Davies, Mary, soprano vocalist, born in London, of Welsh parents, February 27, 1855.

DAVIES.

Educated in the Home and Colonial Schools, Gray's Inn Road. Singing at Welsh concerts in London, she attracted the notice of Brinley Richards and Edith Wynne, both of whom gave her instruction. She won the Welsh Choral Union Scholarship in 1873, and studied at the R.A.M., chiefly under Randegger, winning the Parepa-Rosa Gold Medal, 1876, and the Nilsson prize, 1877. In 1878 she appeared with success at the Worcester Festival; also sang at Gloucester, 1883, and at Norwich and Chester Festivals. She sang in the first complete performances in England of Berlioz' Faust, at the Halle concerts, Manchester, March 11, 1880, and at St. James's Hall, May 21. As a ballad singer she is best known, and has sung at the principal concerts throughout the country. She has been elected, first an Associate, then a Fellow of R.A.M. In 1888, she was married to Mr. W. Cadwaladr Davies, of the Inner Temple.

Davies, Rev. Owen, Eos Llechyd, composer, born at Llanllechid, Bangor, September, 1828. In years past a successful Eisteddfodic competitor. Has devoted his attention chiefly to Church music; and his anthems are held in much esteem. He has been a zealous worker in the cause of music in Wales, and is still living.

Davis, Gabriel, composer and vocalist, was a native of Bath, where he was born, about 1770. He was choirmaster of a Baptist Chapel at Portsea early in the present century. Composer of "Sacred Music, two hymns on the nativity of Christ, and forty psalm tunes," London, 1800; Ode for Christmas Day, etc.

Davis, Mrs. Gabriel, born Marianne Davis, composer of a large number of part-songs and songs. She died at Littlemore, Oxford, July 18, 1888. Among her compositions may be named—By the river; Dame Trot; Dame Wiggins of Lee; King Carnival; Three Stars; Zingara; Four-part songs, etc.

Davis, Miss, an Irish composer of the present time, has written a large number of sacred and secular songs, duets, etc. Among her songs may be named—The arrow and the song; Better land; Old clock on the stairs; Ruth; Song of the bell, etc.

Davis, J. D., composer and pianist, born at Edgbaston, Birmingham, October 22, 1867. Was musical from childhood, but in 1882 was sent to Frankfort-on-the-Main to study German, with a view to business pursuits. While there he entered the Conservatorium, and had lessons from Hans von Bülow. In 1883, he went to Brussels, and took up the study of music in earnest, under Zarembski, Kufferath, and Arthur de Greef. Returning to Birmingham, in 1888, he gave himself up to composing and teaching. His works include an opera, "The Zaporogues," produced by amateurs at the Theatre Royal, Birmingham, May 7, 1895;

DAWBER.

Legend, "Hero and Leander," for bass solo and orchestra; songs and part songs. A suite, overture, and nocturne for orchestra—the last given at Mr. Stockley's concerts, January, 1892; Sonatas for pf. and violin, pf. and cello., and pf. solo; six pieces for pf. and violin (Novello's Album); two suites for same; pieces for pf., etc.

Davison, James William, composer and writer, born at London, October 5, 1813. He studied under W. H. Holmes and (Sir) G. A. Macfarren. Married Miss Arabella Goddard, 1860. Musical critic of the Times and Musical World. He died at Margate, March 24, 1885.

WORKS.—An Essay on the Works of Frederic Chopin, London [1849], n d. Songs—Swifter far than summer's flight; The light canoe; Poor heart, be still; Sweet village bells; The lover to his mistress; False friends, wilt thou smile or weep? Pianoforte Music—Four Bagatelles à la valse, op. 4; First Sonata, op. 6; Tarantella, op. 7; Three Sketches, op. 8; Romance, op. 11. Dramatic Overture to the fairy tale of "Fortunatus," for pf. duet. Contributions to periodical literature. Contributions to Grove's "Dictionary of Music and Musicians."

Davison, (Mrs. J. W.), See Goddard, Arabella.

Davy, John, composer, was born at Upton-Helions, Exeter, December 23, 1763. Articled to Jackson of Exeter, 1777. Resided in Exeter as teacher. He afterwards became a violinist in the orchestra of Covent Garden Theatre, and a teacher and composer in London. He died in St. Martin's Lane, London, February 22, 1824, in extreme indigence, having out-lived all his kindred.

WORKS.—Music to Plays, etc.—What a blunder! 1800; Perouse (with J. Moorhead), 1801; Brazen mask, ballet (with Mountain), 1802; Cabinet (with Braham), 1802; Caffres, 1802; Rob Roy, 1803; Miller's maid, 1804; Harlequin Quicksilver, 1804; Thirty thousand (with Reeve and Braham), 1805; Spanish dollars, 1805; Harlequin's magnet, 1805; Blind boy, 1808; Farmer's wife, 1814; Rob Roy Macgregor (new version), 1818; Woman's will, a riddle, 1820. Overture to Shakespere's Tempest. Six quartets for voices, in score, with figured basses for the pf., op. 1, n.d.; Six madrigals for four voices, op. 13 [c. 1810]. Beauties of Handel, 6 vols., n.d. Songs—Bay of Biscay, O mighty Bacchus, Beggar boy, Brave marine, Darling Sue, Harvest home, Milkmaid, Smuggler, Son of old Saturn, etc. Single and double chants, various. Anthem, Lord, who shall dwell, op. 9.

Davy, Richard, composer of the 16th century, some of whose works are in score in the British Museum, among the Fayrfax MSS.

Dawber, James, organist, born at Wigan,

DAWSON.

September 18, 1851. Received his musical training at Henshaw's Blind Asylum, Manchester, 1864-9, and then studied under (Sir) Walter Parratt for two years. Graduated Mus. Bac., Cambridge, 1878. Settled in Wigan as teacher, organist, and choirmaster, St. Paul's Congregational Church. To Mr. Dawber is due the inception of the movement which resulted in the formation of what is now known as the Incorporated Society of Musicians, and he was its first Secretary, 1882. He has given chamber concerts, and has published songs and part-songs.

Dawson, Charles, author of "Analysis of Musical Composition, showing the construction of all Musical pieces, together with a concise and comprehensive system of Harmony," London, 1845. "Elements of Music, condensed for the use of students of the pianoforte," London, 1844.

Dawson, Frederick H., pianist, born at Leeds, July 16, 1868. At the age of five he began his studies under his father, William Dawson, a pianist of repute; and when ten he was taken to (Sir) Charles Halle, who at once recognised his great ability. From Rubinstein, a few years later, he also received encouragement. As a juvenile prodigy, he played a great deal in public in the north; but his first important engagement was at Ed. Haddock's concerts, Harrogate, in October, 1885. He appeared at the Halle Concerts, Manchester, December, 1890, and made his London *début* April 18, 1891, at a chamber concert of Willy Hess. Gave recitals at St. James's Hall, 1891; appeared at the Monday Popular Concerts, January 8, 1893; at the Crystal Palace, February 23, 1895; and at the Philharmonic Concerts, March 20, of the same year. He is now recognised among the leading pianists of the day.

Dawson, W. H. C., musician, compiled "Psalm and hymn tunes, in score, for four voices," n.d.

Day, Alfred, physician and musician, born at London, in January, 1810, and died there February 11, 1849. Author of a "Treatise on Harmony," London [1845], n.d. His work on harmony advocates many alterations in theory, and a number of technical terms, most of which have been adopted by Macfarren and others.

Day, Alfred H., organist, of present time. He held an appointment at Kimberley, South Africa, and went thence to Graham's Town, where he was appointed to the Cathedral. There he established a College of Music. In 1893 he was appointed borough organist, and conductor of the Philharmonic Society at Maritzburg, Natal, where he remains.

Day, Captain C. R., writer on music. Son of the Rev. Russell Day, of Horstead, Norfolk; born in 1860. Educated at Eton,

DAY.

and studied music under the late Sir Joseph Barnby. Entered the Oxfordshire Light Infantry (the old 43rd) in 1882, and served in India until 1887. Was severely wounded in the operations against the Moplas in 1885. Married, in 1892, Katherine, daughter of Mr. Scott-Chad, of Thursford Hall, Norfolk. His principal works are: "The Music and Musical Instruments of Southern India and the Deccan," London, Novello, 1891; and "A Descriptive Catalogue of the Musical Instruments recently exhibited at the Royal Military Exhibition, London, 1890" (Eyre and Spottiswoode, 1891). These are both important and valuable books. He contributed an article on African Musical Instruments to Ferryman's "Up the Niger," 1892. Author of several papers and brochures on National and Military Music, read at meetings of the Musical Association (1894), etc. He was a Member of the English Committee of the Vienna International Musical and Dramatic Exhibition of 1892.

Day, Ellen, pianist, born in London, March 3, 1828. Studied under her father, William Day (*q.v.*), Henry Westrop, and Eduard Schulz. Her first appearance was at Drury Lane Theatre, in 1836, when she played a fantasia by Hünten, with orchestra, Mori leading. In 1838 she played at a concert given by Thomas Baker, violinist, in Windsor Town Hall; and the next evening played, by command, before the Queen at Windsor Castle. The same year she played in London with Teresa Milanollo, in June. Then, for some years, she appeared in conjunction with her brother John (*q.v.*) When Mendelssohn was in London, in 1844, she was invited to his house to play to him, and highly complimented by him. At the first concert the two young artists gave, June 16, 1846, Ellen Day played a pianoforte duet with Vincent Wallace. She continued to play in public for many years, in London and the provinces, and still retains her powers of execution. For about thirty years she has been an organist, first at St. Matthew's, and to the present time at Christ Church, Westminster. Balfe was her staunch friend, and she was instructor of his two daughters for some years.

Day, John, publisher and editor, was born in St. Peter's parish, Dunwich, Suffolk, in 1522. He was established at Holborn, London, in 1549, as printer and publisher. He died at Walden, Essex, July 23, 1584. He published Damon's Psalmes of David, in English meter, 1579, and a work bearing the title "The Whole Booke of Psalmes, collected into English metre by T. Starnhold, I. Hopkins, and others; conferred with the Ebrue, with apt notes to synge therewithal, faithfully perused and alowed according to the ordre appointed in the Quene's maiesties injunctions,"....

DAY.

London, 1562. In 1563 he issued the first English psalter with music in four parts, and in 1565 another edition was issued. The title is "The Whole Psalmes, in foure parts, whiche may be sung to al musical instrumentes, set forth for the encrease of vertue, and abolishying of other vague and triflying ballads," London, 1563.

Day, John, composer, who flourished at end of last, and beginning of the present century. Composer of "Harmonica Lyrica, selected from the poems of M. T. Scott, and adapted for organ or pianoforte," 1820.

Day, John, violinist, brother of Ellen Day (q.v.), was born in London, March 7, 1830. Studied under his father, and first appeared at the Hanover Square Rooms in 1838. With his sister, he was, early in the forties, engaged by M. Jullien, and they performed at the Lyceum, Covent Garden, and on his provincial tours. In 1843, the pair visited Brussels, and De Beriot took the young violinist to his home as a pupil, afterwards passing him into his class at the Conservatoire. On his return home he made his *début* at the Philharmonic Concerts, June 23, 1845, playing two movements of De Beriot's second concerto. He played at the Norwich Festival, in September, and at the second concert of the Birmingham Festival Choral Society, October 30, of the same year; and engagements followed at every important musical centre. He entered the Queen's private band in 1847, and is now the senior member. He was appointed organist of New Upton Church, Slough, in 1853; of Old Upton Church shortly afterwards, resigning in 1857. Two years later, he went to All Saints', Fulham, where he remained until 1869. For the last forty-five years his hobby has been the making of copies of violins by the old masters. These have been pronounced by competent judges to be equal to the originals. See "Violins, old and new," Reeves, reprinted from the *Musical Standard.*

WILLIAM DAY, father of the above, was a violinist of some reputation. He acted for many years as leader at Drury Lane Theatre. Died in London, March 3, 1851.

Day, W., musician, compiler of "Sacred Harmony," Madras, 1818.

Deacon, Harry Collings, vocalist, teacher, and writer, born London, 1822. He studied pf. under Cip. Potter, and singing under Mazzucato the elder. He lost his voice while he was studying at Milan, and he afterwards resided in London as a teacher and pianist. He trained Anna Williams, Herbert Thorndike, etc. One of the contributors to Grove's "Dictionary of Music." He died in London, February 24, 1890. He composed "Anacreon's Grave," a four-part song; Contemplation; Ethel; May-time; Only once

DEAKIN.

more; Over the crisp white snow; Sing to me; and other songs. First set of 24 studies for the pf., London, 1864; Tarantella, for the pf., etc.

Deacon, Mary Ann, pianist, organist, and teacher, born at Leicester, June 26, 1821. Began the study of music at the age of six, and in 1838 began, at Leicester, her career as a teacher, which was successfully maintained until her retirement a year or two ago. Though not conspicuously public, Miss Deacon's life has been one of consistent usefulness to the cause of music in Leicester, and the locality. For twenty years she was organist at St. Mary's Church, and officiated for ten years at two Congregational Churches. From 1842 onwards she has appeared as vocalist or pianist at many concerts; assisting at Mr. Oldershaw's lectures; training choirs for oratorio performances; and being intimately associated with the musical work of that enthusiastic amateur, the late William Gardiner. In May, 1896, a complimentary concert was given to her by all the musical societies in Leicester, on which occasion she played in a duet for pf. and flute, with Mr. Henry Nicholson, a life-long friend and colleague in art. On October 28, 1896, she was publicly presented with a portrait of herself, and a sum of money; the latter she placed in trust for founding a "Deacon prize" for students resident in Leicester.

Deakin, Andrew, organist, and critical writer, born in Birmingham, April 13, 1822. Began to study music at a very early age, and, entirely self-taught, became a creditable vocalist, organist, and violinist. Served a strict apprenticeship to the printing trade, and printed, in 1845, the *Birmingham Musical Examiner,* edited by James Stimpson. After some years service as organist at different places of worship, he was appointed to the Church of the Saviour (founded by George Dawson, the great preacher and lecturer), in 1847, a post he held until 1878. As early as 1849 he began writing musical criticisms for newspapers, and when the *Birmingham Morning News* was started in 1871, he was appointed its musical critic. In 1876 he joined the *Birmingham Daily Gazette* in a similar capacity, resigning the office towards the close of 1894. A diligent student of everything appertaining to music, he is recognised as an authority, and his services are much in request as an annotator of concert programmes. He has composed hymn tunes, chants, and anthems, and among larger works a Stabat Mater for solo voices, chorus, and organ, and a "Miserere," have been performed at the Church of the Saviour. In 1846 he compiled and published "Euphonia," one of the very earliest collections of music for nonconformist public worship; a work that exerted

DEAN.

more than a local influence. A recent publication is a "Musical Bibliography, a catalogue of historical and theoretical works published in England, from the 15th to the 18th centuries," Birmingham, Stockley and Sabin, 1892; a companion work on a large scale, dealing with the music of the same periods, is in preparation. Mr. Deakin is also known as a landscape painter and etcher, and some forty years ago his name was often seen in the catalogues of London and provincial exhibitions.

Dean, J., author of "Guide and Self-Instructor for the Violin," London, 1853.

Deane, Thomas, composer and organist, who flourished during the end of the 17th and first half of the 18th centuries. He was organist at Warwick and Coventry, and became Mus. Bac. and Doc., Oxon, 1731. He composed music for Oldmixon's "Governor of Cyprus," contributed to the "Division Violin," and was the first to introduce Corelli's Sonatas to England.

Dearle, Edward, organist and composer, born at Cambridge, March 2, 1806. As a boy he was a chorister in King's, Trinity, and St. John's Colleges, Cambridge, and having studied the organ, obtained his first appointment at St. Paul's Deptford, 1827. He was successively at Blackheath parish church, 1830; Wisbeach parish church, 1832; St. Mary's, Warwick, 1833; organist of the parish church and master of the song school, Newark, 1835-64. While at Newark he graduated Mus. Bac., 1836, and Mus. Doc., 1842, Cambridge. In 1864 he removed to Camberwell, where he continued to reside. He was one of the founders of Trinity College, London, and took an active interest in the welfare of the musical profession. An occasional contributor to the press, he wrote in 1850, a series of letters on organisation, anticipating in a remarkable manner the formation of the Incorporated Society of Musicians. He died at Camberwell, London, March 20, 1891.

WORKS.—Israel in the Wilderness, oratorio (published 1879); Morning and evening service in F (1832); Morning and evening service (1852?); A volume of church music (1838). Anthem, Turn Thee again, Thou God of Hosts (Gresham Prize, 1837); The desert shall rejoice; Rend your hearts; Four anthems (1852), etc. Thirty-six chants (1852). *Songs* —Lays of the heart (1829), etc. *Part-songs*— Sigh no more, ladies; Mountain Daisy, and others. Andante Cantabile, organ, etc.

Dearnaley, Irvine, organist and conductor, born in the village of Broadbottom, Chester, September 29, 1839. His father was a spinner in a cotton mill, and was devoted to music, helping his son as far as he could. When seventeen, young Dearnaley obtained the post of organist at Staleybridge, and

DEMPSTER.

studied under J. J. Harris, afterwards taking pianoforte lessons from Halle, and working at harmony under H. Hiles. Then he became organist of Christ Church, and of the parish church, Ashton-under-Lyne, from 1864. He was conductor of the Gentlemen's Glee Club, and Philharmonic Society in that town; and in 1883, was made musical director of the Gentlemen's Glee Club, Manchester. Gave many organ recitals in the district. Composed some anthems and pieces for the organ. He died at Ashton, September 18, 1894.

Deering, or Dering, Richard, composer and organist, born in Kent, at the end of the 16th century. He was educated in Italy, and afterwards became organist at a monastery of English nuns in Brussels, 1617. Organist to Henrietta Maria, Consort of Charles I., 1625. Mus. Bac., Oxon., 1610. He died in 1630.

WORKS.— Cantiones Sacræ quinque vocum, cum basso continuo ad organum, Antwerp, 1597; Cantica Sacræ ad melodiam madrigalium elaborata senis vocibus, Antwerp, 1618; Cantiones Sacræ, 1619; Canzonette, 1620. He also wrote motets, madrigals, etc., many of which are preserved in MS. at Oxford and London. He died in the Roman Catholic faith. It is claimed for Deering that his 1597 Cantiones were the first works issued with a figured bass.

De Fonblanque, Ellen, *See sub.* Campbell, Gilbert James.

De la Fond, John Francis, author and teacher of languages in London during the first half of last century. He issued, among other works, a "New System of Musick, both theoretical and practical, and yet not mathematical, written in a manner entirely new, that is to say, in a style plain and intelligible," London, 1724.

Delany, J. A., organist and composer, born in London, 1852. Went to Sydney, Australia, and became a pupil of W. J. Cordner, whom he succeeded as organist of St. Mary's R. C. Cathedral, a post he held 1871-6. Then he went as chorus-master and pianist to the Opera House, Melbourne (then under the management of W. S. Lyster, who died in 1880), where he remained some years. In 1882 he was appointed choir-master of St. Mary's Cathedral, Sydney, and three years later succeeded Max Vogrich as conductor of the Sydney Liedertafel, which positions he still holds. For St. Mary's Cathedral he has composed Masses in F, and A flat; and has also composed a Cantata, "Captain Cook," and other works.

Dempster, William Richardson, composer, born at Keith, Banffshire, in 1808; died at London, March 7, 1871. He composed a number of part-songs and pf. pieces; also *Songs:* Bird of the wilderness; Blind boy; Come o'er the mountain to me; Doubting.

DENNIS.

heart; May queen; My love Annie; Songs in the Idylls of the King, Tennyson [1864].

Dennis, John, writer and musician, born at London in 1657. He studied at Cambridge, and afterwards travelled in France and Italy. He died on January 6th, 1733. Author of "An Essay on the Italian Opera," London, 1706.

Derham, William, English writer, was born in 1657, and died in 1735. Author of, among other works, the following, "The Artificial Clock-maker..shewing..the way to alter clock-work, to make chimes and set them to musical notes," London, 1696 [other editions].

Dering, see DEERING.

D'Este, John, musician and writer, author of "Music made easy, the Rudiments of Music," London, 1849; "The Vocalist's Vade Mecum, or Pocket Companion, Practical Hints on Singing," etc., London, 1872.

Deval, Harry, writer and composer, author of "The Art of Vocalization, with complete instructions for the Cultivation of the Voice," London, n.d. Composer of "The Rival Clans," Opera, Newcastle, 1846, and of music to "A Midsummer night's dream," Newcastle, 1846.

Dewar, Daniel, Scottish clergyman and author of the end of last and beginning of the present century. He was professor of moral philosophy in Aberdeen University. He wrote "Observations on the character, customs, superstitions, music, poetry, and language of the Irish," London, 1812, 2 vols.

Dewar, James, composer, conductor, and violinist, born at Edinburgh, July 26, 1793. Deputy-leader in Theatre Royal, Edinburgh, 1807, and afterwards musical director. Organist of St. George's Episcopal Church, 1815-35. Conductor of Edinburgh Musical Association. He died at Edinburgh, January 4, 1846. Dewar is famous for his arrangements of Scottish airs for the orchestra, a pf. edition of which was published about 1850. His work with the title, "Popular National Melodies adapted for the Pianoforte," Edinburgh, 1826, had a large circulation. He composed also a few part-songs and other vocal pieces, and edited "The Border Garland, Poetry by Hogg," [c. 1829]. His brother JOHN was also a composer.

Dewberry, William Charles, organist and conductor, born at Cambridge, January 16, 1843. Chorister and solo boy at King's College, Cambridge, and afterwards assistant-organist. Pupil, later, of Sterndale Bennett, C. Lucas, and W. G. Cusins, and R.A.M. silver medalist and Associate. Organist of Clare College, and St. Edward's Church, Cambridge, where he is resident as performer and teacher. He graduated Mus. Bac., Cambridge, 1887. He took an active part in establishing several of the college musical societies, and under his

DIBDIN.

direction the Cambridge Musical Society attained a high position, producing such works as Macfarren's "St. John the Baptist," etc. As a Freemason he is a P.M. of Lodge 441, and P.P.G.O. for the Grand Chapter and Province of Cambridgeshire. His compositions embrace a setting of Psalm 13; An Evening Service in E flat; Anthems, chants, and part-songs, etc.

FREDERICK DEWBERRY, his younger brother, was born at Cambridge in 1848. Chorister at Trinity College, Cambridge, and articled pupil of the late J. L. Hopkins. In 1868, elected organist and choirmaster of Gonville and Caius College, retiring in 1892. Organist of St. Michael's, Cambridge, 1871; St. Andrew the Great, 1873, to the present time, with the exception of a year, 1890-1, at St. Mary's, Saffron Walden. Graduated Mus. Bac., Cambridge, 1886; F.R.C.O., L.R.A.M. In 1882 he was given the appointment of organist at the Guildhall, Cambridge, and is also organist to Dr. A. H. Mann's festival choir. Has given many recitals. Like his brother, he is a prominent Freemason, holding important offices in the Provincial Grand Chapter.

Dews, Elizabeth, contralto vocalist, born at Wolverhampton. Received her early musical training from local teachers and masters in Birmingham. Appeared in that city in "Elijah," in November, 1884, while still a young student Afterwards proceeded to London, and studied under W. Shakespeare, and Signor Randegger. She made her *debut* in St. James's Hall, November 25, 1891; sang at Boosey's ballad concerts, 1893; and at the Crystal Palace, in Berlioz' "Romeo et Juliette," December 15, 1894. She went on a tour in Germany with Madame Valleria, and is now a singer of established reputation, being engaged for such concerts as those of the Birmingham Festival Choral Society, the Liverpool Philharmonic, and societies at Leeds, Edinburgh, Glasgow, and Dublin. Madame Dews sang at the jubilee performance of "Elijah," at the Royal Albert Hall, April 23, 1896. She is married to a Scotsman, Mr. D. A. Parker.

Dibdin, Charles, composer and writer, was born at Dibden, near Southampton [baptized March 4], 1745. He studied at Winchester College, and was taught music by Kent and Fussell. Appeared as an actor at Richmond and Birmingham. Went to London, and was employed by Bickerstaff as composer and singer, 1765. Renounced stage, and commenced giving medley monodramas in London, 1788. He died at London, July 25, 1814.

WORKS.—*Musical Dramas etc.*—Shepherd's Artifice, 1763; Love in the city, 1767; Damon and Phillida, 1768; Lionel and Clarissa, 1768; Padlock, 1768; Maid the Mistress, 1769; Re-

DIBDIN.

-cruiting Sergeant, 1769; Ephesian Matron, 1769; Jubilee, 1769; Queen Mab, 1769; Captive, 1769; Pigmy Revel, 1770; Wedding Ring; Institution of the Garter, 1770; Ladle, 1772; Mischance; Brickdust Man; Widow of Abingdon; Palace of Mirth, 1772; Christmas Tale, 1773; Trip to Portsmouth; Deserter; Grenadier, 1773; Waterman, 1774; Cobbler, 1774; Quaker, 1775; Two Misers, 1775; Seraglio, 1776; Blackamoor; Metamorphoses; Razor grinder; Yo, yea, or the friendly Tars; Old Woman of eighty; Mad Doctor; She is mad for a Husband; England against Italy; Fortune Hunter: All's not gold that glitters, 1776; Poor Vulcan, 1778; Rose and Colin; Wives Revenged; Annette and Lubin; Milkmaid, 1778; Plymouth in an uproar, 1779; Chelsea Pensioners; Mirror; Touchstone, 1779; Shepherdess of the Alps, 1780; Harlequin Freemason; Islanders, 1780; Jupiter and Alcmena, 1781; None so blind as those who won't see, 1782; Barrier of Parnassus, 1783; Graces; Saloon; Mandarina; Land of simplicity; Passions; Statue; Clump and Cudden; Benevolent Tar; Regions of Accomplishment; Lancashire Witches, 1783; Cestus, 1784; Pandora; Long Odds; Liberty hall, 1785; Harvest Home, 1787; Loyal effusion, 1797. *Monodramas*—Whim of the moment, 1788; Oddities, 1789; Wags; Private Theatricals, 1791; Quizzes, 1792; Castles in the air, 1793; Great news, 1794; Will of the wisp, 1795; Christmas gambols, 1795; General Election, 1796; Sphinx, 1797; Valentine's day, 1797; King and Queen, 1798; Tour to the Land's End, 1799; Tom Wilkins, 1799; Cake house, 1800; Frisk, 1801; Most votes, 1802; New Year's Gifts; Broken Gold; Briton's Strike Home; Datchet Mead; Commodore Pennant; Heads and Tails; Frolic, etc. *Literary Musical Works*—The Harmonic Preceptor, a Didactic poem in three parts, London, 1804; The English Pythagoras, or every man his own music-master, London, 1808; Music epitomized, a School Book in which the whole science of music is clearly explained, London, n.d. Hannah Hewitt, or the female Crusoe, novel, 1792; Younger brother, novel, 1793; Musical tour, Sheffield, 1788; History of the Stage, London, 5 vols., 1795; Observations on a Tour through almost the whole of England, and a considerable part of Scotland . . . London, 2 vols., 1801; The professional life of Mr. Dibdin, written by himself, with the words of six hundred songs selected from his works, London, 4 vols., 1803. Songs, chronologically arranged, with notes, memoir, etc., by George Hogarth, 1842, 2 vols.

Dibdin, according to the biography prefixed by his son Thomas to the 1875 edition of his songs, wrote over 1300 songs. In addition to these he wrote other music in his entertain-

DICK.

ments, etc., the gross amount of music and words which he wrote being in number over 3000 pieces. Of these, very few are now used, " The Waterman " is the only large piece, and " Poor Jack " and " Tom Bowling " almost the only songs.

Dibdin, Charles, Jun., son of the above, poet and writer, born about 1769. He was for some years part-proprietor of Sadlers' Wells Theatre, London, and wrote, among other pieces, the "Farmer's wife," "My spouse and I," and a number of Burlettas, Pantomimes, Songs, etc. He died at London, January 13, 1833.

Dibdin, Henry Edward, musician and compiler, born in London, September 8, 1813. Grandson of Charles Dibdin. He studied under his sister, Mrs. Tonna, and Bochsa, the harpist. From 1833 he resided at Morningside, Edinburgh, as a teacher; and he also was hon. organist of Trinity Chapel, Edinburgh. He died at Edinburgh, May 6, 1866. WORKS.—The Standard Psalm-Tune Book, containing upwards of 600 specimens, compiled from the original editions .. London [1851]; Reid's Praise Book, 1868, harmonised; Collection of Church Music, consisting of chants, psalm and hymn tunes, etc., 1843, edited with J. T. Surenne.

His sons, EDWARD RIMBAULT VERE (Edinburgh, August 25, 1853), and JAMES ROBERT WILLIAM (Edinburgh, December 9, 1856), are both musicians. The former has composed some songs and part-songs, and the latter is perhaps best known by his " Annals of the Edinburgh stage," 1888. His wife, born ISABELLA PERKINS PALMER, was born at Southwold, Suffolk, January 19, 1828. She was married in 1846. She composed a few hymn tunes, and was a good soprano vocalist. His sister, MARY ANNE DIBDIN, born about 1800, was a harpist, and studied under Challoner and Bochsa. In 1824 she became assistant teacher of the harp at the R.A.M. She married Mr. Tonna.

Dibdin, Thomas John, dramatist and musician, son of Charles, senr., born, London, March 21, 1771. He was an actor and dramatic author, and appeared in the provinces and at Sadler's Wells Theatre, and Covent Garden Theatre, London. He was joint proprietor of Sadler's Wells Theatre from 1802, and died at Clerkenwell, London, September 16, 1841. WORKS.—Numerous dramatic pieces, produced at Sadler's Wells, and elsewhere. The Cabinet, an opera. Songs in the collection entitled " Lays of the last three Dibdins." Reminiscences of Thomas Dibdin of Covent Garden," etc., London, 1827, 2 vols.

Dick, Charles George Cotsford, composer, born in London, September 1, 1846. Educated at Oxford, and prepared for the

DICKONS.

Bar, but obliged, from ill-health, to give it up.
WORKS.—Operettas: Our doll's house (German Reed, 1876); Our new doll's house (the same, 1877); Back from India (1879); Doctor D, comic opera (Royalty Theatre, 1885); The Baroness (the same, 1892). A Children's Opera, A Fairy Wedding, in six parts, for pf. The Waif (play, adapted from the French, Haymarket Theatre, May, 1892). Songs: Dolly Varden; Olivia; Golden wedding song; Three songs, etc. Pf. pieces: Fireside fancies, six pieces; Toccata; December and May; Belinda Gavotte; Deux Melodies; etc. Author of a volume of verse: The Way of the World (London, Redway, 1896).

Dickons, Maria, born POOLE, soprano vocalist, born at London about 1770. She studied under Rauzzini, at Bath, and first appeared at Vauxhall in 1783. She appeared at Covent Garden in 1793, and sang regularly at the Ancient (from 1792) and Vocal concerts, and in the principal provincial towns. In 1800 she married Mr. Dickons, and retired for a time, but she resumed public singing again in London in 1806, and afterwards appeared at Paris, 1816, Venice, etc. She was made a member of the Instituto Filarmonico, Venice. She appeared for a short time in London in 1819, but retired soon afterwards, and died May 4, 1833.

Dickson, Ellen, "DOLORES," composer, daughter of General Sir Alex. Dickson, was born at Woolwich, in 1819. She resided during her life-time chiefly at Lyndhurst, in the New Forest, having been an invalid from youth. She became known in her district for many charitable actions. She died at Lyndhurst, July 4, 1878.

WORKS.—Songs: Clear and cool; Destiny; Goldilocks; The land of long ago; O my lost love; Pack clouds away; The racing river; She walked beside me; Tell her not when I am gone; Unchanged, etc.

These songs acquired a considerable amount of popularity in their day, and some of them are even now in vogue.

Dickson, Rev. William Edward, clergyman and writer, born at Richmond, Yorkshire, 1823. B.A., Cantab., 1846; M.A. 1851. Ordained 1846. Precentor of Ely Cathedral, 1858.

WORKS.—Singing in Parish Churches, 1858; Cathedral Choirs, 1877; Practical Organ Building, London, 1881; Fifty years of Church Music, Ely, 1895.

Diemer, Philip Henry, composer, pianist and organist, born at Bedford, July 18, 1839. Of German extraction, and cousin of the distinguished pianist, Louis Diemer, of Paris. Studied at R.A.M., pianoforte, under W. H. Holmes, and harmony with G. A. Macfarren. Elected Associate of the Philharmonic Society 1882. Has been organist and choirmaster of

DISTIN.

Holy Trinity, Bedford, for more than thirty years, and has directed musical services there when Bach's "Passion," and other oratorios have been given with orchestra. Director of Music at Bedford Grammar School for over thirty-five years. In 1866, founded the Bedford Musical Society, which gives four concerts annually; at the 100th concert he was publicly presented with a testimonial. For ten years he gave a short season of chamber concerts, at which he appeared as pianist.

WORKS. – Cantatas: Thoughts of home, treble voices (1867); Bethany, Bedford, 1881, and, later, in London, many other places, and some of the Colonies; Alcestis (written for 25th annual concert of the Grammar School). Farewell, and a Jubilee Ode (both with orchestra). Collection of original hymn-tunes; anthems; Songs and part-songs; Pf. pieces, etc.

Dignum, Charles, tenor vocalist, was born at Rotherhithe, London, in 1765. Chorister in chapel of Sardinian ambassador, London. He studied music under Samuel Webbe, and worked for a time as carver and gilder. Articled to T. Linley for seven years. Début as Meadows in "Love in a Village," 1784. Sang afterwards at Vauxhall, Haymarket Theatre, etc. He died at London, March 29, 1827.

Dignum, who was usually regarded as the successor of Beard, composed a number of songs, and published a collection of "Vocal Music, consisting of songs, duets, and glees," London [c. 1810], with portrait. He was most successful as a singer of English ballads. Among his single songs may be named Maid of the rock; Neglected Tar; Poor Recruit; Soldier's consolation; Sweet Jane; William of Allerton Green, etc.

Ding, Lawrence, musician and publisher, who was engaged in business in Edinburgh, and died there in October, 1800. He published "The Songster's Favourite, or a new collection containing 40 of the most celebrated songs, duets, trios, etc.," Edinburgh, n.d. "The Anacreontic Museum," Edinburgh, n.d., etc.

Distin, Theodore, composer and singer, born at Brighton, in 1823. Son of John Distin (1793-1863), a celebrated trumpet-player and inventor of the keyed bugle, under whom he studied. His father having organized a band, composed of members of the family, Theodore played the French horn in it, and travelled with it from 1836 to 1844. Afterwards he studied singing under T. Cooke and Negri and became a baritone singer in the Pyne and Harrison Opera Company. He was a singer in Bencher's Chapel, Lincoln's Inn, and an Associate of the R.A.M. He was latterly a teacher in London, and died on April 12, 1893.

DIXON.

DONE.

WORKS.—Services in C and G. Glees and part-songs. Two masses. Songs, etc. In 1890, he wrote a madrigalian chorus entitled The Break of Day. Tutor for the Ballad Horn [1871]. His father issued A selection of Swedish Melodies arranged for cornet, saxhorn, etc. [1847].

Dixon, Rev. E. S., writer, author of " The Piano Primer, and Instructor's Assistant," n.d.

Dixon, George, composer and organist, born at Norwich, June 5, 1820. Chorister Norwich Cathedral, 1827-34. Musically trained as a private pupil of Dr. Buck to 1835. Pupil and assistant organist of Parish Church, Grantham, 1835-45. Organist of the Parish Church, Retford, Notts., 1845-59; Parish Church, Louth, 1859-65; Parish Church, Grantham, 1865, resigned, 1886. Mus. Bac., Oxon., 1852; Mus. Doc., 1858. An Hon. Examiner for Royal College of Music, at Grantham and Lincoln. He died at Finchley, June 8, 1887.

WORKS.—121st Psalm, for voices and orchestra (MS.) Pope's Messiah, cantata for voices and orchestra (MS.) Numerous anthems, hymns, chants, etc. Songs. He also contributed to various collections of psalms and chants.

Dixon, J., musician, author of " Canto Recitativo, or a system of English Chant . . " London [1816].

Dixon, William, writer, teacher, and music-engraver, born about 1760; died London, 1825. He resided chiefly in Liverpool and London.

WORKS.—Sacred music, consisting of a Te Deum . . . anthems, psalm tunes, and hymns . . . [1790]. Euphonia . . . 62 Psalm and hymn tunes in four parts . . . for the congregation of All Saints' Church, Liverpool. Six glees for three voices. Moralities : six glees, Cambridge [1800]. Introduction to singing, containing rules for singing at sight . . . 1795.

Dixon, William Hubert, organist and composer, born at Bishopstone, Wilts., August 1, 1846. Organist of High Church, Kilmarnock, from 1869, and conductor of the Philharmonic Society there. His sacred cantata, " Jerusalem," was produced at Kilmarnock, December, 1887; he has also written some part songs and pf. pieces. He died at Kilmarnock, July 31, 1893.

Dobson, John, psalmody collector and composer, was born in 1814, died, Richmond, Surrey, May 1, 1888. He was an industrious collector of psalm and hymn books, and his library was sold in November, 1889, in 492 lots, consisting mainly of collections of psalmody. He edited "Tunes new and old," 1864, and other editions till 1877, of which some were revised by Dr. Gauntlett.

Docker, Frederick Arthur William, organist and conductor, born in London, August 14, 1852. Studied, R.A.M. Associate of the Academy. Organist and choirmaster, St. Andrew's, Wells Street, London, where he was first a chorister, then pupil of, and assistant to, the late Sir Joseph Barnby. When the Handel Society was formed, in 1882, he was appointed conductor; an office he held for ten years. He also conducts the concerts of the Kyrle Society, succeeding Malcolm Lawson in 1886. He has published a setting of the Te Deum ; O ye that love the Lord, and other church music ; part-songs, etc.

Dodds, Tom William, organist and composer, son of Thomas Dodds, tenor vocalist (died 1892), was born at Leeds, September 22, 1852. At nine years of age became a chorister at Leeds Parish Church, and a year later organist of Headingley Chapel. Educated at Bury Grammar School. Organist successively of St. Matthew's, Leeds; 1863-6 ; St. Wilfred's Collegiate Chapel, 1866-72 ; and of Queen's College, and St. Clement's Church, Oxford, since 1872. Graduated Mus. Bac., 1876 ; Mus. Doc., 1887, Oxford. Examiner for musical degrees in Oxford University, 1895. His compositions comprise an oratorio, " Hezekiah," a setting of Psalm 8 ; chants, hymn tunes and pf. pieces.

Dodwell, Rev. Henry, clergyman and writer, born at Dublin, 1641, died in 1711. In addition to many theological works, he wrote " A Treatise on the lawfulness of instrumental Musick in Holy Offices,". London, 1700 ; 2nd edition, with large additions, 1700.

Dodworth, Harvey B., bandmaster and composer, born at Sheffield in 1822. Inventor of the rotary string-valve and bell-back instruments. Settled in the United States. He wrote and published several works on band instruments and military band instrumentation. The first military band in the U.S. was organised by Mr. Dodworth. He was a musician of sterling worth, and was much esteemed in the United States. He died at New York, in April, 1891.

Dolby, Charlotte, see SAINTON-DOLBY.

" Dolores." See DICKSON (Ellen).

Donaldson, John, musician, theorist, and Professor of Music in Edinburgh University, 1845-65, was born about 1790, died at Cramond, near Edinburgh, August 12, 1865. He was for some time previous to his appointment a teacher of music in Glasgow, and had been bred to the law. He did much to promote the interests of the Chair of Music in the University, and practically did everything to establish the efficiency of the Chair, by the erection of the music room and organ, and by getting the rights of the Music Chair established by process at Law in 1851-55.

Done, Joshua, organist and writer, was

DONE.

born in London. He studied at Paris under Cherubini, and was organist successively of S. John's, Lambeth; Chelsea Old Church; Knightsbridge Chapel; and S. Augustine's, Liverpool. He died at King's Lynn, November 2, 1848, in extreme poverty. Author of "A Short Treatise on Harmony, Thorough Bass, and Modulation, including the compass and properties of Musical Instruments in general." London, Cocks, n.d. "Treatise on the Organ," London, 1837. "Tuner's Companion: a Treatise on the Construction of Pianofortes..with various methods of Tuning them," London, n.d. "Selection of the most popular, with many original Psalm and Hymn Tunes, Chants, etc.," London [1830.]

Done, William, organist and conductor, born at Worcester, 1815. Entered the Cathedral choir in 1825, and sang in the chorus at the Worcester Festival of 1827. In 1839 he was apprenticed to Charles E. J. Clarke, the Cathedral Organist, and was elected his successor, June, 1844. He conducted the Worcester Festival of 1845, and was associated with the meetings of the Three Choirs until 1890, when he resigned the *bâton*, and took upon himself the duty of orchestral steward. In 1894, he celebrated his jubilee as organist of the Cathedral, when the Archbishop of Canterbury conferred on him the honorary degree of Doctor of Music. He was for many years conductor of the Worcester Philharmonic Society, an office he resigned in 1884. He composed much Church music, but will be remembered by the reforms he instituted in the Cathedral services, the introduction of great works on special occasions, and the formation of a large voluntary choir. He died at Worcester, August 17, 1895.

Donkin, W. F., writer and musician, M.A., F.R.S., etc. Savilian Professor of Astronomy, Oxford. Author of "Acoustics, Theoretical." Part I., Oxford, 1870. All published of a work designed to cover the whole range of the science of sound.

Doorly, Martin Edward, organist and composer, born in Demerara, British Guiana, 1847. Was for many years organist of the Cathedral, Bridgetown, Barbadoes, and conductor of concerts; also music master at Queen's College, Barbadoes. In 1891, he graduated Mus. Bac., Durham, after examination held at Codrington College (affiliated to Durham University), Barbadoes. He composed an oratorio, "The Raising of Lazarus," produced at Marshall's Hall, Bridgetown, August 24, 1880, and repeated on the 27th, in St. Leonard's Church; this performance being conducted by the Lord Bishop of the diocese (Dr. Mitchinson). He also wrote an opera, "Equality;" A burlesque; and published some organ pieces and songs. He died at Barbadoes, August 22, 1895.

DORRELL.

His brother, the Rev. W. S. DOORLY, was born at Upper Park Camp, Jamaica, in 1851. Studied music under F. Jackson, of Hull; J. Whomes, of Woolwich; with Dr. Wylde, and others at the London Academy of Music; and Tonic Sol-fa with L. C. Venables. Was organist of St. Mary's, Bridgetown, Barbadoes, 1870-2; appointed organist and choirmaster of Holy Trinity Cathedral, Trinidad, in 1872. Took holy orders in 1877, and was appointed Hon. Canon and Precentor of the Cathedral in 1894. At Port-of-Spain he has been very active as a conductor of choral and orchestral societies; and in addition to the Messiah, Elijah, Hymn of Praise, and such established compositions, has brought forward "The Redemption" (Gounod); "Lazarus" (M. E. Doorly, 1883); "St. John the Evangelist" (Armes); "The Prodigal Son" (Sullivan); "The Crucifixion" (Stainer); and many other important works for the first time in Trinidad.

Doran, Rev. John Wilberforce, clergyman and author, born London, 1834. B.A., Cantab, 1857; M.A., 1861; Ordained, 1857. Vicar of Fen Stanton, Huntingdonshire, 1883. He has compiled a large number of works for the musical service of the Church of England, such as Choir Directory of Plain Song. The Psalter and Canticles arranged for Gregorian chanting. Ritual Music of the Altar. Choir Book of Ritual Music of the Altar. Hyfforddwr av y Gân Eglwysig (Welsh Plain-song Directory). Te Deums, Chants, etc.

Dorrell, William, pianist, born in London, September 5, 1810. Son of Edmund Dorrell, painter, and early member of the old Water Colour Society. William Dorrell received his first lessons from his eldest sister, and afterwards entered the R.A.M., and studied under Dr. Crotch, Cipriani Potter, and Charles Lucas. In 1844 he went to Paris, and studied with Kalkbrenner and Stephen Heller. Returning to London, he was made a Professor of the Pf. at the R.A.M., an office he retained for over forty years. Half a century ago Mr. Dorrell was known as a most skilful pianist, and he appeared occasionally in public. One noticeable concert he gave at the Hanover Square Rooms, June 2, 1842, when he played Bennett's Concerto in E flat. Mendelssohn was present at this concert. His time was afterwards mainly occupied in teaching, his pupils including members of many noble families. Of his compositions very little is known. At a *Matinée d'invitation* he gave at his residence, June 20, 1882, he introduced a movement from a Sonata for pf. and violin, which he played with M. Sainton. He was one of the founders of the Bach Society, in 1849; Member of the Royal Society of Musicians, and of the Philharmonic Society. He died in London, December 13, 1896. The sister, already mentioned, JANE

DORRINGTON.

DORRELL, was a fine pianist, pupil of Mrs. Anderson, and Cipriani Potter. In 1830, she played at the "Oratorios" at Covent Garden Theatre. She played Mendelssohn's Rondo brilliant in B minor, at the concert of June 2, 1842; and once had the honour of playing to Queen Adelaide, at St. James's Palace. She died in London, July 19, 1883

Dorrington, Theoph., clergyman of the 18th century, author of "A Discourse on Singing in the Worship of God," London, 1704.

Dougall, Neil, minor poet and composer, was born at Greenock, December 9, 1776. Apprenticed to mercantile marine service, 1791. He continued a seaman till accidentally wounded while discharging a cannon, in 1794. Became a teacher of music, 1799. Married Margaret Donaldson, 1806. Inn-keeper in Greenock, 1824. He died at Greenock, October 1, 1862.

WORKS.— Poems and Songs, Greenock, 1854. *Psalm tunes :* Naples, 1801; Kilmarnock, 1823; Patience; New East Church; etc. Also tunes contributed to Stevens' "Sacred Music," vol. 6.

His daughter, LILLY DOUGALL, was at one time a well-known contralto vocalist.

Dow, Daniel, composer, teacher, and collector of last century, was born in Perthshire in 1732, and from 1765 he resided in Edinburgh as a teacher, etc. He died at Edinburgh, January 20, 1783.

WORKS.—Twenty Minuets and sixteen Reels, or Country Dances for the Violin, Harpsichord, or German Flute, Edinburgh [1775]. Collection of Ancient Scots Music [1778]. A Collection of Ancient Scots Music for the Violin, Harpsichord, or German Flute, never before printed, consisting of Ports, Salutations, Marches or Pibrochs, etc., Edinburgh, n.d. Thirty-seven New Reels and Strathspeys, for the Violin, Harpsichord, Pianoforte, or German Flute, Edinburgh (N. Stewart), n.d. Of his dances, "Monymusk," a strathspey, is probably best known.

Dowland, John, composer and lutenist, born at Westminster, in 1562. He resided on the Continent in 1581-84, but returned to England and became Mus. Bac., Oxon., in 1588, and also Cantab., in 1592. Lutenist to Charles IV. of Denmark about 1599. Returned to England in 1605, and after another period of residence in Denmark he finally settled in England from 1609. He became lutenist to the King in 1625. He died in 1626.

WORKS.—The First booke of Songes or Ayres of foure parts, with tablature for the Lute, 1595. Second booke, do., 1600. Third booke, do., 1602. Lachrimæ, or seven teares figured in seaven passionate pavans, with divers other pavans, galiards, and almands, set forth for

DOYLE.

the lute, viols, or violins, in five parts, 1605. A Pilgrim's solace, wherein is contained musical harmony of three, four, and five parts, to be sung and plaid with lute and viols, 1612. Translation of Ornithoparcus, his Micrologus, or introduction : containing the art of singing and the perfect use of the monochord . . . London, 1609. Harmonies in Este's Psalms, etc.

The poetry and music both in Dowland's works are of an exceptionally high degree of excellence, and he is properly classed among the best musicians of his time. The poetry, indeed, is so good that Professor Arber has reprinted the three books of songs, etc. (words only), in his valuable series of classical reprints, while the Musical Antiquarian Society have done a like service for the first book of the same set. His music has that quaint, delightful flavour common to compositions of the 16th and 17th centuries. Shakespeare has shown his preference for Dowland in the sonnet commencing—

"If music and sweet poetry agree."

Dowland, Robert, composer, son of above, succeeded his father as lutenist to the King, in 1626. He edited several musical publications, and a "Varietie of Lessons," etc.

Dowling, Thomas Barrow, organist and conductor of the present time. Student and Associate, R.A.M. Some time organist of St. Philip's, Regent Street, London. In 1888, appointed organist of St. George's Cathedral, Cape Town, and conductor of a choral union. After four seasons he amalgamated this with a society in Cape Town, and began producing oratorios on a fuller scale. In 1895 he was invited to conduct the Orchestral Society in Cape Town, which dated back to 1864. The chief works of the great masters, and those of the modern school, have been presented under his direction. He has also developed the Cathedral choir, which has given performances of Mendelssohn's "St. Paul," and other great works. A new organ was erected in the Cathedral, and Mr. Barrow opened it with a recital; Nov. 4, 1890, since when he has given many public performances upon the instrument; and is a busy worker in the cause of music in South Africa.

Downes, Rev. James F., amateur composer, born in the West Riding of Yorkshire, has written the cantatas, "The Parable of the ten Virgins," Leeds, 1882; and "The Prodigal Son," 1885; and some secular pieces. He is a priest of the Roman Catholic Church, and is at present at St. Patrick's, Bradford.

Doyle, C. W., viola player, born at Scarborough. Educated at R.A.M., and elected a Fellow of that Institution. For many years Member of the Royal Italian Opera, and other orchestras. Principal viola, Birmingham Festival orchestra, 1861-82;

DRIFFIELD.

Leeds Festival, 1874-92 ; Worcester Festival, 1893. Played in chamber concerts with the Carrodus Quartet, 1877, etc. Professor in the Guildhall School of Music. ADA DOYLE, his daughter, contralto vocalist, was a pupil of Madame Dolby, and made her *début* at Buxton, in May, 1885.

Driffield, Edward Townshend, amateur organist and composer, born at Prescot, near Liverpool, December 10, 1851. Organist of Christ Church, Claughton, Birkenhead, where he has given recitals, 1883-4. He is the composer of a Cantata, " My soul doth magnify the Lord "; a Sonata in G, for organ ; and some glees, one of which, " Come follow me" was sung by the Bristol Orpheus Society at its annual concert, February 9, 1893.

Druitt, Dr. Robert, writer, author of " A Popular Tract on Church Music, with remarks on its moral and political importance, and a practical scheme for its reformation," London, 1845; "Conversations on the Choral Service, being an examination of the popular prejudices against Church Music," London, 1853.

Drummond, George, organist and composer, was born in 1798, died in 1839. Blind from infancy. He studied under Crotch, and published " Parochial Psalmody, or 70 plain psalm tunes arranged for the organ or pianoforte," n.d. O give thanks unto the Lord, Anthem.

Drummond, James, musician, was born at Cambuslang, near Glasgow, in October, 1811. He was choirmaster of St. George's Church, Glasgow, from 1852 to 1875. Well-known in Glasgow as a good musician. He died at Glasgow, November 18, 1883. His youngest son, THOMAS SMITH DRUMMOND, born, Glasgow, June 1, 1854, is a pianist and conductor. He holds various positions in Glasgow, and has composed some vocal music.

Dryden, Henry E. L., author of " On Church Music, and the Fittings of Churches for Music," London, 1854.

Drysdale, F. Learmont, composer, born in Edinburgh, 1866. Originally educated for an architect, he turned to music, and entered the R.A.M., winning, in 1890, the Lucas prize for composition. While a student he produced a ballad for orchestra, " The Spirit of the Glen " (1889) ; Orchestral prelude, "Thomas the Rhymer " (1890); and a scena, forming part of a Cantata, " The Kelpie," afterwards produced at Edinburgh (Paterson concerts), December 17, 1894. His overture, " Tam O'Shanter," was awarded a prize by the Glasgow Society of Musicians, 1891, and it was performed at the Crystal Palace, October 24, of that year. Another overture, " Herondian," was produced by the Stock Exchange Orchestral Society, April 24, 1894. He has been selected to compose the music to

DUDENEY.

the opera founded on Baring-Gould's novel, "The Red Spider." His mystic musical play, " The Plague," was produced at the Lyceum Theatre, Edinburgh, in October, 1896.

Dubourg, George, writer, grandson of Matthew, was born in 1799, died at Maidenhead, April 17, 1882. Author of "The Violin; being an account of that leading Instrument, and its most Eminent Professors," London [1832] ; 2nd edition, 1837; 4th edition, 1852; 5th edition, 1856.

Dubourg, Matthew, violinist and composer, was born at London in 1703. He studied under Geminiani. Appeared first at Britton's concerts, 1715. Composer and master of state music in Ireland, 1728. Succeeded Festing as member of King's band, 1752. Leader of band on production of Handel's " Messiah." He died at London, July 3, 1767. He composed concertos, solos, and variations for the violin; odes, songs, and other vocal music. He was the leading English violinist of his day, and one of the greatest among his contemporaries.

Duchemin, Charles Jean Batiste, pianist, composer, and conductor, born in Birmingham, May 12, 1827. His father was a French naval officer, who was taken prisoner during the war with Napoleon I. He married an English lady, and settled in Birmingham as a teacher of languages. The son was educated at King Edward's Grammar School, and his musical talent developing, he was sent to Brussels, where he studied at the Conservatoire under M. Fétis. On his return he devoted his attention to teaching, and concert work, and was for many years a foremost figure in musical life in the Midlands. He was organist successively at St. Peter's, R.C. Church, and the Oratory, Edgbaston, where he had the present Duke of Norfolk as a pupil. He conducted the German Liederkranz ; founded the Edgbaston Amateur Musical Union, an orchestral society of which he was for nearly twenty years the conductor. With two other artists he originated chamber concerts in Birmingham, which he continued for some time, introducing many famous performers to the town. He was for many years local secretary for Trinity College, London. His compositions include several operettas, and orchestral pieces, which remain in MS. Many of his pf. pieces have been published: Tarantella in F minor; Saltarello in D minor; La Velocité Etude, in octaves ; Caprice brilliante ; Idyll in E flat, etc. He has also composed songs, trios, etc.

Dudeney, Thomas James, organist, composer, and conductor, born at Mayfield, Sussex, November 29, 1854. Studied under G. A. Macfarren. Organist Dunster parish church (1876); St. James's, Taunton ; and now of St. Anne's, Eastbourne. Established

I

in 1875 the Taunton Philharmonic Association, and a similar one at Dunster, in 1877; and the Washwood Musical Society in 1880. Principal of the Taunton College of Music, 1888. He has given many concerts, noticeable for the production of important works by British composers. He has written a cantata, "Song of joy," for soli, chorus, and orchestra; "Who is Sylvia," eight-part chorus, with orchestra; songs and part-songs. Also an overture, "Cassibelan; an Elegy (In Memoriam, Sterndale Bennett), for orchestra; String quartets in D and E minor; organ pieces, etc.

Duff, Charles, Scottish collector, was a teacher in Dundee about the beginning of the present century, and a partner in the music and bookselling firm of Duff and Chalmers. His partner, James Chalmers, was the inventor of the adhesive postage stamp, which did so much to make the establishment of the penny post such a success. Duff published "A Collection of Strathspeys, Reels, Jiggs, etc., with a bass for the violincello or harpsichord, etc." Edinburgh, [1790]. Duff died at Dundee, about 1822.

ARCHIBALD DUFF, brother of the above, was a dancing-master and composer in Montrose and Aberdeen, and published "A Collection of Strathspeys, Reels, etc., for the pianoforte, violin, and violoncello," Edinburgh, 1794. "The first part of a choice selection of Minuets, Dances, etc.," Aberdeen, 1812. Duff was a teacher of dancing in Aberdeen till 1820, and is said to have been conductor of the Philharmonic Society before John Mackenzie, grandfather of Sir A. C. Mackenzie.

Dufferin, Helen Selina, Lady, was born in 1807. She was a daughter of Thomas Sheridan, and grand-daughter of R. B. Sheridan. Her sister was Caroline, the Hon. Mrs. Norton. In 1825 she married the fourth Baron Dufferin, and, in 1862, was married a second time, to the Earl of Gifford. She died on June 13, 1867. She was mother of the present Marquess of Dufferin. Composer of "A Set of ten Songs and two Duets, the words and music by two sisters" [1833]. Also sets of twelve and seven Songs [1833-39]. Ten Songs for contralto or mezzo-soprano voice, with pf. accompaniment [1861]. She also composed "Terence's farewell to Kathleen" ("So, my Kathleen! you're goin' to lave me"), and wrote many lyrics set by Barker, etc. See further, "Songs, Poems, and verses, by Helen, Lady Dufferin, edited by the Marquess of Dufferin and Ava," 1894.

Duggan, Joseph Francis, composer and pianist, born in Dublin, July 10, 1817. He went early in life to the United States, and became accompanist to the recitatives in the Italian Opera at New York. Afterwards he became musical conductor of opera under John Wilson, and of a German opera com-

pany. He became a teacher in Philadelphia. Baltimore, and Washington, and was principal of the Philadelphia Musical Institute, 1841. He resided in Paris as a pianist and teacher, 1844-45, and afterwards in Edinburgh. Afterwards he settled in London, and became musical director at the Marylebone Theatre, 1854, and later a professor of singing at the Guildhall School of Music, etc.

WORKS.—*Operas*—Pierre, London, November, 1853; Leonie, London, March, 1854; The Brides of Venice (MS.); Alfred, Philadelphia (MS.); Le Nain Noir, Paris (MS.) Overture, etc., to As you like it, 1854. Home and foreign lyrics, a set of thirteen songs. Rhythmic tentatives, six songs, Op. 1 (1879). Two symphonies in C and E flat. Six string quartets. Numerous pianoforte pieces and songs. Author of the Singing-masters assistant, a first series of vocal exercises, London, [1878]; and translator of Albrechtsberger's "Science of Music," Philadelphia, 1842; and Fétis' "Counterpoint and Fugue."

Dun, Finlay, composer and teacher, was born at Aberdeen, February 24, 1795. He studied under Baillot, and at Milan. He played first tenor in the theatre of San Carlo. Afterwards he studied singing under Crescentini, and settled in Edinburgh as violinist, composer, and teacher. He died, Edinburgh, November 28, 1853.

WORKS.—Two Symphonies for full orch. (MS.); Solfeggi and Exercises upon Scales, Intervals, etc...to which is prefixed an Introductory Discourse on Vocal Expression, London, 1829; Two prize glees; The Vocal Melodies of Scotland, edited with John Thomson (Paterson); Wood's Songs of Scotland, edited with G. F. Graham, etc.; Pf. music. *Part-songs and Glees:* June; The Parted Spirit (prize at Manchester Gentlemen's Glee Club), 1831; She is coming, trio, etc; Anthems, psalms, hymns; Lays from Strathearn, by the Baroness Nairne, Glasgow, n.d. [c. 1845-7]; The Musical Scrap Book, Edinburgh [1833], 2 vols. Orain na'h Albain, a Collection of Gaelic Songs, with English and Gaelic words, and an Appendix containing Traditionary Notes to many of the Songs Edinburgh, 1848. Analysis of Scottish Music, etc.

Duncan, Alexander, music-teacher and vocalist, born about 1796. He was precentor of the outer High Church (now St. Paul's), Glasgow, from 1829 to 1836. Died at Springburn, Glasgow, March 26, 1863. Compiler of "The Choir, a collection of psalm and hymn tunes, adapted to various measures..with copious rudimental instructions in the art of vocal music," Glasgow, 1828. For this work the Rev. Dr. Wm. Anderson wrote a preface.

Duncan, Arthur, violinist, who resided in Dumfries. Published "A Collection of

DUNCAN.

reels, strathspeys, quadrilles, waltzes, etc,'' Glasgow, 1852. Of this we have only seen one part.

Duncan, Gideon, author of the " True Presbyterian, or a brief account of the new singing, its author and progress in general.'' 1755.

Duncan, William Edmondstoune, composer, pianist, and organist, born at Sale, Cheshire, in 1866. Showed musical talent very early, and became A.R.C.O. at sixteen. At the opening of the R.C.M. in 1883, he won an open Scholarship for composition, studying under Hubert Parry, Villiers Stanford, E. Pauer, and G. C. Martin. He studied, after leaving R.C.M., with Sir G. A. Macfarren, and for ten years pursued his profession in London, during which time several of his works were performed, notably a concert overture under the direction of Hamish McCunn, at Hampstead, in June, 1888. He then returned to his native town, where he is chiefly occupied in composition; also holding a professorship at the Oldham College of Music. While in London he was musical critic to a provincial, and also to a London daily paper.

WORKS.—Ye Mariners of England, ode for chorus and orchestra, op. 4, produced by the Glasgow Choral Union, March 4, 1890; Mass in F minor, op. 13, compo-ed, 1892; Perseus, opera in two acts (libretto by Professor Marshall Hall), 1892; Ode to Music (Swinburne), soprano solo, chorus and orchestra, 1893; Sonnet to the Nightingale (Milton), soprano solo and orchestra, op. 32, 1895. Morning and Evening Service, together with the office for Holy Communion, set to music in the key of G, op. 21. Album of four Songs, op. 1; Three Songs; Four Sonnets of Shakespeare; Ye Mariners of England; Hymn to the Queen, 1897, and other songs; part-songs, etc. *Orchestral :* Concert Overture in D minor, op. 4, composed 1887, produced 1888; A Tone Poem. op. 7; Processional March; In Memoriam, meditation in D minor, op. 17; Trio in E minor, pf. and strings, op. 28, produced at Oldham, December 18, 1895; Sonatas in C minor, op. 3, D minor, op. 8, and E flat minor, op. 9; Six tone pictures; Six pieces for children, all for pf.; Six pieces for organ (Cecilia, Book 49); Meditation; Postlude; Processional March, organ, etc.

Dunkley, Ferdinand L., composer and organist, born in London, 1869, related to the family of Smart. In 1881, he was in the practising schools of St. John's, Battersea, under Edward Mills, Mus. Bac. In 1886 he obtained the F.R.C.O., and the same year gained a scholarship at the R.C.M., where he remained four years, studying composition under Dr. Hubert Parry. He gained the prize of 50 guineas offered by the directors of

DUNN.

the Promenade Concerts at Her Majesty's Theatre, 1889, for a Suite for orchestra. His setting of "The Wreck of the Hesperus," for chorus and orchestra, was produced at the Crystal Palace, April 7, 1894. He has also composed several songs. In 1893 he was appointed Professor of Music in St. Agnes' School, Albany, U.S.A., and holds the office of organist in the chief church in that place.

Dunmore, Earl of, Charles Adolphus Murray, amateur composer, born on March 24, 1841. In 1866 he married the 3rd daughter of the Earl of Leicester. He was a captain in the Scots Guards; Lord Lieutenant of Stirlingshire, etc. Composer of a Suite Symphonique, for orchestra, produced at the Brighton Festival, 1880; Pastorale, for violin and pf. (1878); Military march, for the pf.; Dance music. *Songs :* Fisher maid; For ever; Spirit of my dream; Years, years ago, duet, etc.

Dunn, John F., violinist, born at Hull, February 10, 1866. Began learning the violin when eight years old under his brother, the leader at a Hull theatre. He was soon playing at concerts, and when barely eleven was engaged as assistant leader at the Theatre Royal, Hull. In 1878 he entered the Conservatorium, Leipzig, studying under Schradieck (violin), Jadassohn, and E. F. Richter. After distinguishing himself at the Conservatorium, and playing the first movement of the Beethoven Concerto at the Hauptprüfung, in May, 1882, he gave some Chamber concerts in different towns in Saxony, and returned to England. He made his first appearance at Covent Garden Promenade Concerts, October 4, 1882, playing the Concerto in E, of Vieuxtemps. In 1885 he appeared at the Crystal Palace Concerts (Mr. Manns' benefit), and also November 13, 1886, when he played Gade's Concerto in D minor. Since then he has given concerts in many places, and gained a place among the finest violinists of the day. His repertory embraces all schools, from Paganini to Spohr; and it was as the exponent of the Ninth Concerto of the last-named that he made his first appearance at the Philharmonic Society's Concerts, February 27, 1896.

Dunn, Matthew Sinclair, tenor vocalist, lyric author, and composer, born at Glasgow, August 3, 1846. As a lad he played the cornet in a Volunteer band, and later while engaged in business, kept up his musical studies as a Tonic Sol-faist. Was precentor in Ayrshire, and choirmaster to the late Lady Elizabeth Pringle, in Berwickshire, where he wrote and gave his popular entertainments. In 1879 he won a scholarship at the Tonic Sol-fa College, and went to London. He afterwards entered the R.A.M., studying singing under Ettore Fiori, W. H. Cummings, and J. B. Welch, and harmony with Sir G. A. Macfarren. He

DUNNE.

has sung at the Crystal Palace, the Promenade Concerts, and in most of the provincial towns. His concert lectures and entertainments, and chamber concerts of Scottish song, have been given in many places. In 1888 he was appointed conductor of the Choral class, and teacher of singing in Trinity College, London. He is author of The Solo Singer; The Solo Singer's vade mecum, Curwen; The Art of Singing; The Choir-boy's Manual; and The Music Class, or Sight-singer. Editor of Auld Scotch Sangs, two collections, each of 96 Songs, Glasgow, Morison. Author of The Bride of Cambus (set by W. G. Wood), and other opera *libretti*; also many lyrics, set by himself and other composers. His compositions comprise twelve trios for ladies' voices; twelve two-part songs; Beautiful Snow, and other Services of Song; Stars of the Summer Night (with 'cello obligato); Sweetheart, come back, and many other songs. Six anthems. Matin Chimes, a collection of easy voluntaries for organ or harmonium, composed and arranged, 11 books; Fireside Fancies, pf. pieces for little players, etc.

Dunne, John, composer and organist, born at York in 1834. In 1850 he became a chorister in Worcester Cathedral, and in 1854 chorister in Cashel Cathedral, Ireland. He was a member of Christ Church, St. Patrick's Cathedral and Trinity College choirs, Dublin. In 1866 he graduated Mus. Bac., and in 1870, Mus. Doc., Dublin. He was an examiner to the Government Intermediate Educational Board of Ireland. He died at Ashton, Killiney, near Dublin, June 7, 1883. Composer of " Myra," and " The Hanging of the Crane" (Longfellow), cantatas; Church services, anthems, glees, songs, etc.

Dunstable, John, composer and mathematician, was born at Dunstable in Bedfordshire, early in the 15th century. Author of " De Mensurabilis Musice," a work quoted by Ravenscroft and others. Little is known of his biography, but he died in 1453. He was erroneously attributed with the invention of counterpoint by Tinctor, but is generally held up by succeeding musicians as a composer of much ability and a musician of universal influence.

Dunstan, Ralph, organist, writer, and teacher, born at Carnon Downs, near Truro, in 1857. In music chiefly self-taught. Pupil teacher at St. Mary's Wesleyan Day School, Truro, 1871-6. In 1877, entered Westminster Training College, as a Queen's Scholar, and received his first regular instruction in music from Mr. James Thomson, then music master there. In 1880 he was appointed organist at the College Chapel, and in 1882, music master. That year he graduated Mus. Bac., and in 1892, Mus. Doc., Cambridge. He is also a graduate and member of the Council of the

DYCE.

Tonic Sol-fa College. Since 1885 he has been music master at the Southlands Training College for Schoolmistresses; and from 1893, head of the music department at the Battersea Polytechnic Institution. Besides his degree exercises, Ps. 146, and " The Wreck of the Hesperus," cantata, he has composed services, anthems, hymn-tunes; a school cantata, "The Jester," school songs, etc. He is author of "The Teachers' Manual of Music," 1886, fourteen editions ; " Basses and Melodies " (Novello's primers), 1894, two editions; " First steps in harmony, and the harmonizing of melodies," London, Curwen, 1895.

Dupuis, Thomas Sanders, composer and organist, born at London, November 5, 1730. Son of John Dupuis, who was descended from a family of Huguenot refugees. Member of the Chapel Royal. He studied under Gates, and Travers, and became organist of Chapel Royal, in 1789. Organist of Charlotte Street Chapel, near Buckingham Palace, in 1773. Mus. Bac. and Doc., Oxon., 1790. He died at London, July 17, 1796.

WORKS.—Cathedral music, in score, composed for the use of His Majesty's Royal Chapel, by the late T. S. Dupuis, selected from the original manuscripts, and carefully revised, by John Spencer, London, n.d., 3 vols. Twenty-four double and single chants [1780]. Sixteen double and single chants, as performed at the Chapel Royal. Second set of Chants [1784]. Twenty-four double and single Chants . . . [1791]. Five Concertos for organ, with accompaniments [1768]. Concertos, sonatas and lessons for pf. Songs, six glees [1785], etc.

D'Urfey, Thomas, minor poet, playwright, and musician, was born at Exeter, of French parents, in 1649. He lived in London as a writer for the playhouses and the court, and died there on February 26, 1723. He edited " Wit and mirth, or pills to purge melancholy, being a collection of the best merry ballads and songs, old and new, fitted to all humours, having each their proper tune for either voice or instrument.".. London, 1719-20, 6 vols., and also other editions and reprints. " Musa et musica, or humour and musick, being an extraordinary collection of pleasant and merry humours, with Scotch and love songs," London, n.d. Many of the songs in " Wit and Mirth " were set to music by Purcell and other musicians of distinction.

Dussek, Olivia, *see* BUCKLEY, MRS.

Dyce, William, artist and musician, born at Aberdeen, in 1806, died at Streatham, London, February 14, 1864. The celebrated painter and Royal Academician, who did so much for art education in Britain. He was a cultured musician, and was one of the founders of the old Motett Society, for which he edited in 1844 the Book of Common Prayer, with the ancient Canto Fermo set to it at the Reformation period, with an essay on that class of music." Also editor of The Order of daily service, the Litany and order of the administration of the Holy Communion, with plain tune; according to the use of the United Church of England and Ireland, London, 1843; and author of Articles on Music in the "Encyclopædia Britannica," etc. He was an accomplished organist, and composed various pieces of music possessing merit

Dyer, Arthur Edwin, composer, organist and pianist, born at Frome, February 20, 1843. Musical training, private. Graduated Mus. Bac., 1873; Mus. Doc., 1880, Oxford. F.R. C.O. Organist of the Parish Church, Weston-super-Mare, 1865-75, and from that date has held the office of organist and director of the music at Cheltenham College. He was also, for some time, Conductor of the Cheltenham Musical Society. His compositions are: Sacred Cantata, "Salvator Mundi" (Degree Ex.; Mus. Doc., 1880); Cantata, "Harold," produced at Cheltenham, 1882; Music to Sophocles' "Electra," produced at Cheltenham College, June 28, 1888, and two following days. "I wish to tune my quivering lyre," chorus (Gloucester Festival, 1883); Psalm 97, for soli, chorus, and orchestra; Anthem, "Except the Lord build the house," composed for the College Jubilee, 1891; An Evening Service; Songs, etc. Also an Opera, "The Lady of Bayonne," produced, Cheltenham, February, 1897. His brother, WILLIAM CHINNOCK DYER, organist of St. Peter's, Norbiton, and Conductor of the Norbiton Choral Society, is the inventor of a patented attachment of pedals to the pianoforte.

Dyer, William Fear, organist and composer, not related to the foregoing. Has for some years held an appointment at St. Nicholas' Church, Bristol, and also that of conductor at the festivals of the Bristol Church Choral Union. He is the composer of a Cantata, "The Second Advent of the Redeemer," performed at St. Nicholas Church, December 22, 1889, and several anthems.

Dygon, John, composer of the 15th century, who was supposed to be prior of the convent of S. Augustine, Canterbury in 1497. He died in 1509. There is much doubt as regards the identity of this musician, the authority hitherto followed having been Hawkins, who published a three-part motet by Dygon, entitled "Ad lapidis positionem" in his "History of Music." A John Dygon graduated as bachelor of music at Oxford, in 1512. He was a Benedictine monk, but it is doubtful if he is the same as the Dygon mentioned by Hawkins.

Dykes, Rev. John Bacchus, composer and clergyman, was born at Kingston-upon-Hull, March 10, 1823. He was a son of

William Hey Dykes, bank-manager at Hull. He was educated at a proprietary school at Wakefield, and entered St. Catherine's Hall, Cambridge, in 1843. While there he was a leading member of the University Musical Society. He had previously studied music under Skelton, the organist of St. John's Church, Hull, which had been built by his grandfather, the Rev. Thomas Dykes, LL.B. Afterwards, he studied music under Dr. Walmisley. In 1847, he graduated B.A. at Cambridge, and in the same year he was appointed curate at Malton, Yorkshire. He became minor canon and precentor of Durham Cathedral, 1849. In 1850 he married Susan, daughter of George Kingston, of Malton, M.A., Cantab., 1851. Mus. Doc., Durham, 1861. Vicar of St. Oswald, Durham, 1862. He died at St. Leonards-on-Sea, January 22. 1876.

WORKS.—Service in F; The Lord is my Shepherd, 23rd Psalm; These are they which came out of great tribulation, anthem. Part-songs. *Psalms and hymns* : Alford, St. Cross, Melita, Vox Dilecti, Horbury, Hollingside, St. Cuthbert, Dies Iræ, Lux Benigna, Nicæa, St. Agnes, Durham, and a variety of others. He also published Eucharistic truth and ritual, a letter . . . London, 1874, and various sermons, etc.

The hymns of Dykes are among the finest examples of modern times. Melody and harmony are beautifully and agreeably combined in all. They are so well known, that little need be said beyond that their place in our collections will always be assured. His services and anthems are occasionally used, but their merits are not by any means so high as the genuine beauty of his hymns would lead us to expect. His son, JOHN ST. OSWALD DYKES, is a composer and pianist.

Dyne, John, composer and alto vocalist of the 18th century. He was a gentleman of the Chapel Royal in 1772; a Lay-Vicar of Westminster Abbey in 1779; and Principal at the Handel Commemoration in 1784. He committed suicide on October 30, 1788. He composed prize and other glees, songs, etc.

Eady, W. H., musician. Author of an "Introduction to the theory of Music," London [1878]. Composer of pf. music, etc.

Eager, John, composer, organist, violinist, etc., was born at Norwich, August 15, 1782. He removed with his parents to Yarmouth early in life, and in 1794 was noticed by the Duke of Dorset, who took him to Knowle, where he remained for some time. In 1800 he married Miss Barnby, of Yarmouth, and in 1803 he became town organist of Yarmouth, and organist of St. George's Chapel. He directed many concert enterprises in Yarmouth. About 1836 he settled in Edinburgh, and acted for a time as teacher to the royal children at Balmoral, He was a violinist at the principal Edinburgh and Glasgow concerts, and is remembered as an enthusiastic advocate and teacher of Logier's system. He died at Edinburgh, June 1, 1853. He had two daughters, one of whom married Joseph Lowe (*q.v.*), the reel composer, and another Mr. Bridgman, a pianist, father of F. W. Bridgman (*q.v.*) Eager wrote a tract, entitled " A brief account, with accompanying examples of what was actually done at the second examination of Mr. Eager's pupils in music, educated upon Mr. Logier's system." London, 1819.

Earnshaw, Robert Henry, organist and composer, born at Todmorden, Lancashire, September 17, 1856. Musically educated in London under various masters, returning to Lancashire in 1880. Graduated Mus. Bac., 1892, Mus. Doc., 1893, Dublin. Organist and choirmaster, Parish Church, Morecambe, 1882-5 ; St. Philip's, Southport, 1890-1 ; Christ Church, Preston, 1891, in which town he occupies a high position as an earnest worker for music. His compositions include "The Wreck of the Hesperus" (University Exercise), and a cantata, " Hail to the Lord's Anointed," for soli, eight-part chorus and orchestra (Exercise for Mus. Doc.) He has published anthems, part-songs, songs, and pf. pieces, some of which have attained considerable popularity.

Earsden, John, composer of end of 16th and beginning of the 17th centuries. He composed songs, etc., and is mentioned in Hawkins' History.

Eastcott, Richard, writer and musician, born at Exeter in 1740. Chaplain of Livery Dale, Devon. He died in 1828.

WORKS.—Sketches of the origin, progress, and effects of musick, with an account of the ancient bards and minstrels, illustrated with various historical facts, anecdotes, etc., Bath, 1793 (2 editions). The harmony of the Muses (songs), n.d. Six sonatas for pf., etc.

Eastlake, Lady, English writer, born 1816, died 1852, authoress of " Music and the Art of Dress," London, 1852. Wife of Sir Charles Eastlake the painter.

Eaton, Thomas Damant, writer and musician, at one time President of the Norwich Choral Society. He wrote Critical Notices of Bexfield's " Israel restored," and Pierson's "Jerusalem" (reprinted from the *Norfolk News*), Norwich, 1852. Musical Criticism and Biography from the published and unpublished writings of T. D. Eaton, edited by his son, London, 1872.

Eavestaff, William, writer and pianoforte-maker. Author of " Instructions for the Pianoforte," London, 1830. A selection of French Melodies, with symphonies and accompaniments, the words by W. H. Bellamy,

six books, 1825-6.

Eayres, William Henry, violinist, born in Marylebone, London, 1846. As a child, he studied the violin under Henry Blagrove, and subsequently under Sainton and Henri Wieniawski, his pupilage with the latter ripening into close intimacy and friendship. He has also made a study of the pf. and organ, and for about four years was organist of Limerick Cathedral. He heads the second violins in the orchestras of the Philharmonic Society, the Leeds and Three Choirs Festivals ; was principal violin, with T. Carrington, Bristol Festival, 1896 ; and holds important positions in London. Of his compositions, the music to Richard Davey's classical comedy, " Lesbia," was performed at the Lyceum Theatre. in September, 1888. He also wrote the music of one act of " Babil and Bijou," and has composed various anthems, Church services, and songs—Beguiling eyes, Our sister May, Ever thine, The chapel by the sea, etc. An overture, two string quartets, pieces for violin, pf , etc.

Ebdon, Thomas, composer and organist, born at Durham, 1738. He was trained in Durham Cathedral, as a chorister, and acted as organist in it from 1763 till 1811. He died at Durham, September 23, 1811.

WORKS.—Sacred music, composed for the use of the choir of Durham, 1780, two vols. Anthems. Collection of six glees, Op. 3, 1780. Songs. Two sonatas for the harpsichord, 1780.

Ebers. John, impresario and theatre manager, born at London, in 1785, of German parentage. He managed King's Theatre, from 1821-28. Was ruined, and relinquished direction, 1828. He wrote " Seven Years at the King's Theatre," London, 1828. The date of his death is unknown.

Ebsworth, Joseph, musician and dramatist, born at Islington, London, October 10, 1788. After living for a time in Cornwall and London, he settled in Edinburgh, in 1826, and became a teacher of music there, and precentor of St. Stephen's Church. He wrote and translated a number of dramas, and was for fifteen years a bookseller. Besides being leader of psalmody of St. Stephen's, he was teacher of music in many of the principal schools and colleges in Edinburgh. Died at Edinburgh, June 22, 1868. He published two collections of psalm and hymn tunes, 1834 and [1845], and issued a General index to first hundred volumes of the music in library of the Edinburgh Harmonists' Society . . . Edinburgh, 1844. Short introduction to Vocal Music, adapted either for private tuition or class singing, Edinburgh, n.d. Songs, hymns and other compositions.

Eccles, Henry, violinist and composer, son of Solomon Eccles, was born at the end of

ECCLES.

the 17th century. Member of the King's Band, 1694 to 1710. He published in Paris "Twelve excellent Solos for Violin," 1720. He was a member of the King's Band in Paris, and died about 1742. His brother THOMAS was also a violinist.

Eccles, John, composer and violinist, born 1668. Son of Solomon Eccles. He studied under his father. Member of the Queen's band of music, 1700. Master of Queen's Band, 1704. He died at Kingston, Surrey, January 12, 1735.

WORKS.—Acis and Galatea, masque, 1701; Ode for S. Cecilia's Day (Congreve), 1701; The Judgment of Paris (Congreve), masque, 2nd prize in competition with Weldon, etc.; The Mad Lover, 1701; The City Lady; The Fair Penitent, 1703; The Lancashire Witches, 1682; The Spanish Friar, 1681; Justice Busy, 1690; The Chances, 1682; The Way of the World, 1700; The Provoked Wife, 1697; The Richmond Heiress, 1693; Rinaldo and Armida (Dennis), 1699; Don Quixote; Love for Love, 1695. Collection of Songs for one, two, and three voices, etc., London [1701]. Songs in Pills to purge Melancholy, etc. Eccles was one of the most popular composers of his day, and some of his melodies are very fine, though not now in vogue.

Eccles, Solomon, composer and violinist, was born in London, 1618. Father of Henry and John Eccles. He became a quaker in 1660, and was frequently arrested for disturbing congregations at worship, and behaving with much eccentricity in the name of religion. He died at London, February 11, 1683. He contributed to the "Division Violin," 1693, and wrote a work entitled "A Musick-Lector, or the Art of Musick..discoursed of, by way of dialogue, between three men of several judgements: the one a musician..the other a Baptist..the other a Quaker (so-called), being formerly of that art, doth give his judgment and sentence against it, but yet approves of the musick that pleaseth God," London, 1667.

Edmonds, M., author of "Musical Catechism adapted to the first class of performers on the Pianoforte," Dublin, 1807.

Edwardes, Richard, poet and composer, born in Somersetshire, 1523. Scholar of Corpus Christi College, Oxford. Studied music under George Etheridge. M.A., Oxon., 1547. Master of Children, Chapel Royal, and Gentleman, do. Member of Lincoln's Inn. He died on October 31, 1566.

WORKS.—The Paradise of Dainty deuises. The Soul's Knell, poem. Damon and Pythias, comedy. Palemon and Arcite, comedy. "In going to my naked bed," madrigal. Many poems, tracts, etc.

Edwardes is not known now save by his lovely madrigal, "In going to my naked bed," which is one of the finest examples of this

EDWARDS.

species of composition extant. The titles of his other poems are set out at length in Ritson's and Hazlitt's works on Early English Poetry.

Edwards, C. A., author of "Organs and organ building, a treatise on the history and construction of the Organ, from its origin to the present day." . . London, 1881.

Edwards, Frederick George, organist and writer on music, born in London, October 11, 1853. Studied at R.A.M. Elected A.R.A.M., 1896. Organist of Surrey Chapel, Blackfriars Road, 1873; Christ Church, Westminster Road, 1876; and of St. John's Wood Presbyterian Church since 1881. Conductor of Lavender Hill Choral Society, 1883. Composer of anthems and pieces for pf. Author of "United Praise: a practical handbook of Nonconformist Church Music," 1887; Romance of Psalter and Hymnal" (jointly with Rev. R. E. Welsh, M.A.), 1889; "The Musical Haunts of London," J. Curwen and Sons, 1895; "History of Mendelsson's 'Elijah,'" Novello, 1896. Contributor to the *Musical Times* and other papers.

Edwards, Henry John, organist, pianist, and composer, born at Barnstaple, Devon, February 24, 1854. Studied at first under his father (noticed below), and later in London, under Sterndale Bennett, G. A. Macfarren, H. C. Banister, and George Cooper. Graduated Mus. Bac., 1876; Mus. Doc., 1885, Oxford. Returning to Barnstaple, he succeeded his father as organist of the parish church, and, in 1886, as conductor of the Easter Musical Festival Society. In 1896, he was appointed conductor of the Exeter Oratorio Society. As a pianist he has appeared at the most important concerts in his county.

WORKS.—Psalm 145 (Exercise for Mus. Bac.), produced in Barnstaple; Oratorio, The Ascension (Exercise for Mus. Doc.), performed at the Western Counties' Festival, Exeter, April 12, 1888; Motet, Praise to the Holiest (from Cardinal Newman's Dream of Gerontius), produced at the Hereford Festival, 1891; Cantata, the Epiphany, Barnstaple, 1891. Two oratorios in MS. Church service; Anthems; Songs; Devonia, The Vigil, The beautiful City, and others; Part-songs, etc. Triumphal March, orchestra and military band, performed at the promenade concerts, Covent Garden, 1883; pieces for pf., etc.

His father, JOHN EDWARDS, was born at Crediton, Devon, in 1808. Studied under Moxen, of Exeter, and about 1833 removed to Barnstaple. He was connected with the parish church for half a century, first as assistant to Huxtable the organist, then as organist and choirmaster; the latter office being held until about 1886. He founded the Choral Society, first known as the Barnstaple Philharmonic Society; and still in existence

EDWARDS.

under the title in the preceding notice. He was also a violinist, and for years was the leading professor of music in the district. His compositions were mostly for the Church, consisting of services, anthems, hymn-tunes, and chants. He died at Barnstaple, in April, 1894.

Edwards, Henry Sutherland, author, born at Hendon, September 5, 1829. Author of " History of the Opera in Italy, France, Germany, Russia, and England, from Monteverde to Verdi," . . . London, 1862, two vols. Life of Rossini, London, 1869. The life and artistic career of Sims Reeves, London, Tinsley, n.d. Rossini (great musicians series), London, 1881. The Lyric Drama, essays on subjects, composers, and executants of modern Opera, London, 1881, two vols. The Faust Legend, Remington, 1886; Famous first representations, Chapman and Hall, 1886 ; The Prima Donna, her history and surroundings, from the 17th to the 19th century, two vols., Remington, 1888. Mr. Edwards has written a large number of works about Russia, Poland, etc., as well as opera libretti, novels, etc.

Edwards, Rev. John David, clergyman and composer, born in 1806. He was vicar of Rosymedre, Ruabon. He died at Llanddoget Rectory, Denbighshire, November 24, 1885, aged 79.

Edwards, Julian, composer and conductor, born 1858. First came into notice through an overture, " Corinne," produced at Mr. Cowen's Concerts in St. James's Hall, November 13, 1880. For some years afterwards, he was engaged as conductor for the Royal English Opera Company, at Covent Garden, 1884, and also in the provinces. He is now resident in America. His compositions include the operas, " Corinne," " Victorian," produced at Sheffield, 1883; " Brian Boru," Broadway Theatre, New York, 1896 ; a cantata for female voices, " De Montford's Daughter;" a sonata for pf., etc.

Edwards, Robert James, organist at Banbury, Oxfordshire, in 1825. Published " Sacred music, being a large and valuable selection of the best Psalm tunes, both ancient and modern, arranged for four voices, or a single voice, with an accompaniment for the organ or pianoforte," London. Preston, 1825.

Edwin, John, singer and actor, born in London, August 10, 1749. He is mentioned by O'Keefe, and appeared in various musical pieces during the latter half of last century. Died in London, October 31, 1790. His son JOHN was married to ELIZABETH REBECCA RICHARDS, who was an actress and vocalist.

Egan, Charles, Irish writer and harpist, author of a " Harp Primer, being a familiar introduction to the Study of the Harp," London, 1822, also, 1829. The Royal Harp Director..London, 1827.

ELGAR.

Egan, F., Irish flute player. Author of " The single and double Flageolet preceptor.. Dublin [1810], and arranger of numerous airs, etc., for flageolet or flute.

Egerton, Hon. John Gray Seymour, son of the second Earl of Wilton (*q.v.*), amateur violinist and composer. He has written some good part-songs : Adieu to the Woods ; King Winter; Spring's approach ; The Rose and the Soul, etc. Also songs, and a cantata.

Eglinton, Hugh Montgomerie, Twelfth Earl of, composer, was born on November 29, 1739. He entered the army and became a colonel, and after his succession to the title, distinguished himself by initiating many public improvements in Ayrshire. He died on December 15, 1819. He was a patron of music, and composed "New Strathspey Reels, composed by a gentleman, and given with permission to be published by Nathl. Gow," Edinburgh, 1796.

Egville, John Herve d', bass vocalist, born at Worcester, 1857. Studied at R.A.M.; Parepa-Rosa prizeholder, 1879. Joined the Carl Rosa Company in 1881 ; and some years later toured with D'Oyly Carte Company in a round of the Gilbert-Sullivan operas. Well known also as a concert singer of repute.

Ehrenberg, Alexandra, *see* WARWICK, GIULIA.

Elford, Richard, alto vocalist, was born about the middle of the 17th century. He was a counter-tenor in Lincoln and Durham Cathedrals. He afterwards sang on the stage in London ; and became a Gentleman of the Chapel Royal in 1702, and Lay-vicar of St. Paul's Cathedral, and Westminster. He died October 29, 1714. It was for him Croft is supposed to have written florid solos in his anthems.

Elgar, Edward William, composer, born at Broadheath, near Worcester, June 2, 1857. Son of W. H. Elgar, organist, of Worcester. Studied the violin under Adolphe Pollitzer, and was well-known as soloist and orchestral leader in Worcester and district ; was also for a time a member of Mr. Stockley's orchestra, Birmingham, and of the North Staffordshire Festival orchestra. Conductor of the Worcester Instrumental Society, 1882 ; and organist of St. George's (Roman Catholic) Church, 1885, succeeding his father who had held the post for 37 years. Both these positions he gave up in 1889, when he removed to London. Ill-health compelled him to leave London in 1891, since which time he has resided at Malvern, devoting himself exclusively to composition.

WORKS.—*Oratorio*, The Light of Life (Lux Christi, book by Rev. E. Capel-Cure, produced at the Worcester Festival, September 7, 1896). *Cantatas :* The Black Knight (Worcester, 1893), and Scenes from the Saga of King Olaf

ELLA.

(North Staffordshire Festival, October, 1896); Choral Suite: Six scenes from the Bavarian Highlands, chorus and orchestra (Worcester, April, 1896); Spanish serenade, chorus and orchestra. Four Litanies, and other Catholic Church Music. *Part-Songs:* My love dwelt in a northern land, etc.; The snow; Fly, singing bird (for ladies' voices, with accompaniment for pf. and two violins). *Songs:* Like to the damask rose; The wind at dawn; The Poet's life, and others. *Orchestral:* Concert overture, Froissart (composed for the Worcester Festival, 1890); Sevillana; Liebesgruss; Serenade (strings only), and other pieces. Romance, violin and orchestra; pieces for violin and pf.; Etudes caracteristiques, violin solo. Sonata, for organ, composed for the visit of the American Musicians to Worcester, July, 1895. and played by Mr. Hugh Blair in Worcester Cathedral on that occasion. Cantatas and other works in MS.

Ella, John, violinist, critic, and lecturer, born at Thirsk, Yorks., December 19, 1802. He studied for the law, but became a violinist in the King's theatre in 1822; Concert of Ancient Music; Philharmonic Concerts, etc. He studied music under Attwood and Fétis, 1826-29. Established the "Musical Union," 1845-80. Established "Musical Winter Evenings," 1845-80. Lecturer on Music at London Institution, 1855. He died at London, October 2, 1888.

WORKS.—Lectures on Dramatic Music and Musical Education abroad and at home, 1872. Musical sketches abroad and at home, 1861 (3 editions), 1869-78. Records of the Musical Union, 1845-78 (analytical programmes, notes, biographies). Personal memoir of Meyerbeer, with an analysis of Les Huguenots, London, 1868. French Song and traditional Melody, *Anglice,* The Harmonious Blacksmith, London, 1865; etc.

Ellerton, John Lodge, amateur composer and poet, born at Chester (?), January 11, 1801. Son of Adam Lodge, of Liverpool. He assumed the name of Ellerton about 1845. Educated at Rugby School, and at Oxford, graduating B.A., 1821, and M.A., 1828. In this last year was published a song, "And will thy spirit view," which was very favourably reviewed in the *Harmonicon.* He had begun his musical studies early, and after leaving Oxford he went to Rome and studied under Pietro Terziani, *maestro di capella* at the Church of San Giovanni Laterano. While there he is said to have composed seven Italian operas. He resided a good deal in Germany, his symphonies having been composed at Wiesbaden, and other places. When in London he had quartet meetings at his house with the best artists. He died in London, January 3, 1873.

WORKS.—*Oratorio:* Paradise Lost, published

ELLICOTT.

1857; Stabat Mater, female voices and orchestra, op. 130; Mass in C, op. 53 (1843); in B flat, op. 106; in D, for two tenors and a bass, op. 103; Motets and anthems. *Operas:* Issiple; Berenice in Armenio; Annibale in Capua; Il Sacrifizio di Epito; Andromacca; Il Carnovale di Venezia; Il Marito a Vista (Italian); Carl Rosa; Lucinda (German); Dominica, produced Drury Lane, June 7, 1838; The Bridal of Triermain (English). Nineteen Italian duets, with orchestra; duets, songs, etc. Symphony, No. 1, in F, op. 65, performed in London, December 11, 1849; No. 2, in D, op. 66, composed 1845, performed London, 1847; No. 3, in D minor (Wald Symphonie), op. 120, published; No. 4, in E flat, op. 126; No. 5, in C, op. 123; No. 6, in E minor, op. 127, the last two composed in 1858. Overtures, La Tarantella, and others; one performed in London, 1831. Three string quintets, Forty-four string quartets, op. 60, 62, 70, 76, 101, 102, 124, etc. Three string trios; eight trios, pf. and strings, etc. Thirteen sonatas, etc. Many glees, including Catch Club prizes, 1836, and 1838. Bridal of Salerno, a romance in 6 cantos, with other poems, 1845; The Elixir of Youth, a legend in four parts, with other poems and notes, 1864.

Ellicott, Rosalind Frances, composer and pianist, born at Cambridge, November 14, 1857. Daughter of the Right Rev. Charles John Ellicott, Bishop of Gloucester and Bristol. Mrs. Ellicott, her mother, is an accomplished musician and vocalist, for whom the late Rev. Sir F. A. G. Ouseley wrote the part of Hagar, in his oratorio so named. She established the Handel Society, London, in 1882. Miss Ellicott began to compose when only six years of age, having a natural gift for harmony. When seventeen she entered the R.A.M., and afterwards studied form and orchestration for seven years with the late Thomas Wingham. Her compositions are numerous, and have secured her an honourable place among women composers.

WORKS.—Cantatas: Elysium (Gloucester Festival, 1889); The birth of Song (the same, 1892); Radiant sister of the dawn (Cheltenham Festival, 1887; Bristol and Gloucester, 1888); Henry of Navarre (men's voices, prod. Queen's College, Oxford, 1894); both for chorus and orchestra. Part-song, Bring the bright garlands, Bristol Madrigal Society, 1890, and others; Duets, songs—To the Immortals, Gloucester Festival, 1883, etc. Dramatic overture, Gloucester Festival, 1886, Crystal Palace, 1891, etc. Concert overture, Spring, St. James's Hall, 1886. Festival overture, Cheltenham Festival, 1893. Fantasia in A minor, pf. and orchestra, Gloucester Festival, 1895. Quartet in F; Trios in G, and D minor, pf. and strings; and other smaller works. A sonata for pf. and violoncello; one for pf.

ELLIOTT.

and violin, with other works, remain in MS.

Elliott, Carlotta, soprano vocalist of the present time. First came into notice at Ganz's concerts, 1880-2. Sang at the Saturday Popular Concerts, December, 1882; at the Philharmonic concerts, 1885. Has given vocal recitals, and appeared with success in many provincial towns.

Elliott, J., author of "Philosophical Observations on the Senses of Vision and Hearing; and a Treatise on Harmonic Sounds," London, 1780.

Elliott, James, composer and bass vocalist, was born in 1783, and died at London in 1856. He was a singer of reputation, and was one of the principals at the Birmingham Festival of 1802, and, it is supposed, sang some soprano solos at the Festival of 1799. Writer of a large number of glees, some of which obtained prizes. Among them may be named: A choir of bright beauties; At her fair hands; The Bee, when varying flow'rs; Chaunt we the requiem; Come, my Celia; Go, lovely rose; Invest my head with fragrant roses; Let those complain; Mild is the air, etc.

Elliott, James William, organist and composer, born at Warwick, February 13, 1833. Chorister in Leamington Parish Church, 1846-48. Studied under G. A. Macfarren, etc. Organist of Leamington Chapel, 1847-52. Private organist to the Earl of Wilton, Heaton Hall, 1859-60; of Parish Church, Banbury, 1860-62; St. Mary, Boltons, London, 1862-64; All Saints', St. John's Wood, 1864-74; and from 1874, organist and choirmaster, St. Mark's, Hamilton Terrace, London. Composer of two operettas: "Romance and Reality," produced at Charing Cross Theatre, with F. Maccabe in the principal part; and "Dan'l's Delight," German Reed, Easter, 1893. Other works are: "National Nursery Rhymes" (Novello, 1870, with sixty-five illustrations, engraved by the brothers Dalziel); "The Harmonium Treasury," 2 vols. (arrangements); Six original pieces for harmonium. "The Choral Service Book," 1892; Hymn Tunes, with varied harmonies, Phillips and Page, 1895; Anthems, services, part-songs; Song, Hybrias the Cretan, etc.,

Ellis, Alexander John, musician and author, was born of parents named Sharpe, at Hoxton, London, June 14, 1814: He was educated at Shrewsbury, Eton, and Trinity College, Cambridge, and graduated B.A. in 1837. Afterwards, he became a Fellow of the Royal Society, in 1864, and a member of the Council in 1880-81. He was also president of the Philological Society, and member of many learned societies. He died at Kensington, London, October 28, 1890.

To the proceedings of the Royal Society he contributed various papers on musical theory

ELVEY.

and its physical basis, and published "Pronounciation for Singers, with especial reference to the English, German, Italian, and French languages, with exercises for teachers and for advanced students," London, 1877. "Speech in song," 1878 (music primer). He also translated, with considerable additions, Helmholtz's "Die Lehre von den Tonempfindungen als physiologische grundlage fur die theorie der musik," as "On the sensations of tone as a physiological basis for the theory of music," London, 1875, and with appendix and notes re-written, 1885.

Ellis, Rev. David Henry, composer and writer on music. Graduated Mus. Bac., 1872; LL.D., 1880; B.D., 1886, Trinity College, Dublin. Minor Canon, Bangor Cathedral, 1872-6; Precentor, Sidney Cathedral, 1880-4; Goulburn Cathedral, and examining Chaplain to the Bishop of Goulburn, 1885-9; vicar of St. Botolph, Lincoln, 1891. *Compositions—* Psalm 104, soli and chorus; Communion service; Evening service; Christmas anthems, etc. Author of "Essay on Cathedrals and Cathedral music."

Ellis, Henry Bramley, organist and conductor, born at Newark, Notts, February 3, 1841. Studied under Dr. Dearle. F.R.C.O. Organist successively at St. Andrew's, Halstead, 1863; St. John's, Leicester, 1874; and St. Mary's, Leicester, from 1878. Conductor of Leicester Orchestral Society, Philharmonic Society, etc. He has given a series of excellent concerts, and introduced many important works to the district.

Ellis, William, composer and organist of 17th century. He was organist of Eton College, and of St. John's College, Oxford. On being expelled from St. John's at the Rebellion, he established music meetings at his house in Oxford, which were attended by many of the most distinguished musicians of the time. At the Restoration it is believed Ellis was reinstated as organist at St. John's. In 1639, he graduated Mus. Bac., Oxford, and in 1674, he died there. He composed rounds and canons in Hilton's collection.

Elvey, Sir George Job, Kt., organist and composer, born at Canterbury, March 27, 1816. Chorister, and pupil of Highmore Skeats, at Canterbury Cathedral; he also studied under his brother, Stephen Elvey, and later at R.A.M., under Cipriani Potter and Dr Crotch. In 1835, he succeeded Highmore Skeats, the younger, as organist and master of the boys at St. George's Chapel, Windsor, a post he held until 1882, when he retired. During his long period of office he had the arrangement of the music in connection with many important events in the Royal Family— the marriage of the Prince of Wales, in 1863; the Princess Louise, 1871, and of the Duke of Albany, in 1882. He graduated

ELVEY.

ESTE.

Mus. Bac., 1838; Mus. Doc., 1840, Oxford. In 1871, he received the honour of knighthood. While at Windsor he was conductor of the Glee and Madrigal Society, and of the Windsor and Eton Choral Society. As late as October 18, 1893, he conducted some of his compositions at the annual concert of the St. George's Chapel Choir. His death took place at Windlesham, Surrey, December 9, 1893. He was four times married; his widow being a sister of Sir Joseph Savory, ex-Lord Mayor of London. In 1894, she published "The Life and Reminiscences of Sir George Elvey, London, Sampson Low.

WORKS.—*Oratorios:* The Resurrection and Ascension (exercise for Mus. Bac.), 1838, performed by the Sacred Harmonic Society, Exeter Hall, December 2, 1840; Mount Carmel. A birthday ode; Victoria, an ode composed for opening of Royal Holloway College, June 30, 1886, words by Martin Holloway; An ode to the north-east wind. *Anthems:* Bow down thine ear, Gresham prize, 1834; The ways of Zion do mourn (exercise for Mus. Doc.), 1840; The Lord is King, composed for Gloucester Festival, 1853; Sing, O Heavens, (for Worcester), 1857, and many others. Morning and evening services; Thirty cathedral chants; Fifteen double chants. Tunes contributed to Hymns ancient and modern, and other collections. Glees and part-songs. Festal March for orchestra, composed for th marriage of Princess Louise; Introduction and gavotte, violin and pf.; Christm s Bells, impromptu for organ or pf., etc.

Elvey, Stephen, composer and organist, brother of above, born at Canterbury, in June, 1805. He studied, at Canterbury Cathedral, under Skeats, and became organist of New College, Oxford, 1830. Mus. Bac., Oxon., 1831. Mus. Doc., Oxon., 1838. Choragus at Oxford, 1848-60. He died at Oxford, October 6, 1860.

WORKS.—Services and Anthems. The Psalter, or Canticles and Psalms, Pointed for Chanting, upon a New Principle, London (6 editions to 1866). Hymns, etc.

Emanuel, Louis Alexander, composer, born at Plymouth, in 1819. Student and Associate, R.A.M. In 1841 was appointed bandmaster to the King's Royal Rifle Corps, and saw active service in India. For many years he has been choirmaster of the Bayswater Synagogue, London. Among his compositions are: The part-song, "Gentle winds"; the duet, "The Syren and the Friar"; and the descriptive song, "The Desert," which is still popular.

Emdin, John, amateur musician, was born at Bristol in 1784, and died April 13, 1827. He composed the duets: Ever true; Hope, his Pilot shall be, etc.; Dearest Ellen, awake; Lady, tho' thy golden hair; and other songs, and vocal music.

Emerson, William, mathematical writer, author of, among other works, "Cyclomathesis, or an easy introduction to the several branches of the Mathematics," London, 14 vols., 1763-70. [Vol. 13 contains "Music," etc].

Eos Llechyd, *see* DAVIES (Rev. Owen).

Eos Morlais, *see* REES (Robert).

Ennis, John Matthew, organist, pianist, and composer, born at Dover, August 5, 1864. Graduated Mus. Bac., 1892; Mus. Doc., 1895, London. Was organist and choirmaster of St. Philip's, Clerkenwell, 1883-7; Holy Trinity, Knightsbridge, 1887-93; and St. Mary, Brookfield, London, 1893. Has given concerts in Myddelton Hall, Islington, etc. His works are: Psalm 46, for contralto solo, chorus, and orchestra; Magnificat, for soli, chorus, strings, and organ; Songs: Beautiful maiden, etc.

Esmond, Wilfred, tenor vocalist and comedian. Was for many years a member of the Carl Rosa Opera Company, and also sang in comic opera, "Les Cloches de Corneville," etc. In 1890, he appeared as Thaddeus in the "Bohemian Girl," at Capetown, South Africa. In 1895, he acted as stage manager for the operatic performance of the Guildhall School Students at Drury Lane Theatre.

Essex, Edward Charles, composer; of the firm of Hodge and Essex, instrument dealers. He has composed an Oratorio, "David," which was performed at Deal, in December, 1893; A Trio, Ave Maria; Songs, etc.

Essex, Timothy, composer and organist, born at Coventry in 1764. He was a teacher in Coventry, and afterwards organist and choirmaster of St. George's Chapel, Albemarle Street, London, near which he also had a musical academy. Mus. Bac., Oxon., 1806. Mus. Doc., Oxon., 1812. He died at London, September 27, 1847. Composed "Sonnets" of various kinds, by various authors, and wrote Rondos, six duets for 2 flutes, and miscellaneous pf. music.

Essex, Countess of, *see* STEPHENS (Catherine).

Este, Michael, composer, born in latter part of the 16th century. Son of Thomas Este. Mus. Bac., Camb., 1606. He was master of the choristers of Lichfield Cathedral, 1618. Died about 1638.

WORKS.—First set of Madrigals, London, 1604; Second set, London, 1606; Third set of Bookes, wherein are Pastorals, Anthems, Neapolitanes, Fancies, and Madrigals, to 5 and 6 parts, London, 1610; Set of Madrigals, Anthems, etc., 1618; Anthems, 1624; Duos and Fancies for Viols, 1638; Hence, Stars, you dazzle, 5 part Madrigal in the "Triumphs of Oriana," etc.

The name of this composer is variously spelt Est, East, and Easte. He is only supposed to be the son of Thomas Este.

ESTE.

Este, Thomas, publisher and musician during latter half of 16th and beginning of the 17th centuries. He died about 1609. He published all of the more important works of his time, including among others "The whole Booke of Psalmes; with their wonted tunes as they are sung in Churches, composed into foure parts," London, 1592; Byrd's Psalms; The Triumphs of Oriana; and music by Campion, Dowland, Gibbons (Orlando), Weelkes, Kirbye, Wilbye, Mundy, etc.

Estwick, Rev. Sampson, clergyman and musician, born in 1657. One of children of the Chapel Royal. He studied at Oxford, and became Chaplain of Christ Church. Minor Canon of St. Paul's Cathedral, 1692. Vicar of St. Helen's, Bishopsgate, London, 1701. Do. of St. Michael's, Queenhithe, 1712. He died in February, 1739.
WORKS.—The usefulness of Church Music; a sermon preached at Christ Church, November 27, 1696, London, 1696. Odes, sermons, etc.

Etheridge, George, composer of the 16th century, was born at Thame, Oxfordshire. Wrote anthems, madrigals, and songs.

Euing, William, musician and collector, was born at Partick, near Glasgow, May 20, 1788. Educated at Glasgow Grammar School. Was an underwriter and insurance broker. He died at Glasgow, May 12, 1874. He founded, in connection with Anderson's College, Glasgow, a music lectureship, by deed dated 1866, and the lectures have been delivered since 1869. He left also his valuable musical library to the same institution, together with £1,000 for its maintenance. This library has never been perfectly accessible to students and the public alike, by reason of some neglect in the administration of the provisions of the bequest. The library is one of the most valuable in Britain, and contains many rare and costly books on musical theory and history, together with valuable texts. The library of the late Dr. Rimbault is included in this collection. In 1876, a very poor catalogue of this library was published, and in 1885, a notice of its contents, by Jas. D. Brown, appeared anonymously in Mason's "Public and private Libraries of Glasgow."

Evans, Charles, composer and organist. He was organist at Ludlow, Shropshire, early in the present century. Composer of six sonatas for pf. or harpsichord, op. 3, London [1790]; March, for a military band, op. 7 [1807]; Epicedium on the death of Lord Viscount Nelson [1806].

Evans, Charles Smart, composer and organist, born at London, in 1778. Chorister at Chapel Royal, under Ayrton. Gentleman of the Chapel Royal, 1808. Organist of St. Paul's, Covent Garden. Gained prizes for glees in 1817, 1818, and 1821. He died at London, January 4, 1849.

EVANS.

WORKS.—Six Glees (Clementi), [1812]. Collection of Glees, etc., London, 1825. Music to Linley's Ode to the memory of Samuel Webbe, 1817 (prize from Catch Club). Two anthems, being the collects for the first Sunday after Easter . . . [1830]. I will love Thee, anthem, etc.

Evans, David Emlyn, composer, born near Newcastle Emlyn, Cardiganshire, September 21, 1843. Is musically self-taught, with the exception of a few pianoforte and organ lessons, which he took while engaged in business in Cheltenham. More than twenty years of his life have been spent in commercial pursuits, so that his musical activity has been something extraordinary. From 1865 to 1867 he competed at the leading Eisteddfodau in composition, the number of his prize works being nearly seventy. After the Wrexham Eisteddfod of 1876, when all the prizes (four) in vocal compositions were awarded him, he retired from active competition; he has since acted, however, on many occasions, as adjudicator. He has edited various musical Journals, and is now joint-editor of *Y Cerddor* (The Musician); also edited The Biography of Welsh Musicians, for which a prize of £30 was awarded M. O. Jones (q.v.) at the London National Eisteddfod (1887). Is author of a Manual on Accompaniment, and a series of papers on orchestration—the first ever published in Wales; and has contributed various papers on musical subjects to the London Cymmrodorion, and other Welsh literary societies.

His published compositions include a sacred cantata, The Christian's Prayer (produced, Corwen, 1891); Songs of the Beatitudes, for Sunday School Choirs; a secular cantata, The Fairy tribe; twenty-six anthems and sacred choruses; thirty glees and part-songs; forty-eight hymn tunes; thirty-six songs; and he has a large number of works in MS., including a cantata, Merch y Llyn (The Maid of the Lake). He has arranged a number of old Welsh tunes, anthems, and airs,—amongst the last, The melodies of Wales, specially issued, and performed by a select choir before the Queen, at Palé, Merionethshire, during Her Majesty's visit there (1889). Chief musical editor of the Psalmist, a selection of tunes and hymns, chants and anthems, for the use of the Welsh Congregationalists—a book since merged in a much larger collection, The Congregational Singer. Editor of a collection of music for Sunday Schools; and has arranged for pf. 500 hitherto unpublished Welsh airs, Alawon Fy Ngwlad, 2 vols., Newtown, Phillips, 1896. Scored for full orchestra, the first Welsh oratorio, The Sea of Tiberias (Rev. E. Stephen, q.v.).

Evans, David Pughe, tenor vocalist and song composer, born at Conwil-in-Elvet, Car-

EVANS.

marthenshire, 1866. Played the violin, and sang in a choir in his early days. Won an open scholarship for singing at R.C.M., 1887, studying under G. Henschel, and others. On leaving, he joined the Rôusbey Opera Company, and sang in several provincial towns, but ill-health obliged him to quit the stage. He afterwards resided in Swansea as a teacher, and died there, February 3, 1897, of chest disease. He composed songs, some of which have been popular; and won prizes at various Eisteddfodau.

Evans, Edwin, organist and composer, of the present time. Has given organ recitals at the Bow and Bromley Institute, London, 1881-2; and conducted concerts at Richmond, Surrey, 1884, etc. His compositions include a symphony; pianoforte concerto (performed at the Promenade Concerts, November, 1882); suite de ballet, orchestra (the same, October, 1888); sonata, pf. duet; a series of pieces for the organ, and some vocal music.

Evans, Evan, clergyman and musician, born 20th April, 1795; died at Rhyl, January 21, 1855. He issued, among other works, "Y Seraph, sef casgliad o donau crefyddol, ar amrywiol fesurau": Caerleon, 1838. A collection of religious tunes: Chester, 1838.

Evans, Fanny, see FRICKENHAUS, MADAME

Evans, Hugh, Welsh musician, author of a catechism of music entitled "Egwyddorion peroriaeth, ar ddull holwyddoreg . . ." Llanrwst [1825].

Evans, Robert Harding, writer, author of "An Essay on the Music of the Hebrews, intended as a preliminary discourse to the Hebrew Melodies of Braham and Nathan," London, 1816.

Ewing, Alexander, amateur composer, born at Aberdeen, January 3, 1830. Nephew of Bishop Ewing. He was educated at Marischal College, Aberdeen. After being trained for the law, he entered the army, in 1855, and became a st ff paymaster, with the honorary rank of lieut.-colonel. In 1867 he married Juliana Horatia Gatty ("Aunt Judy"), the authoress of many books for the young. He died at Taunton, July 14, 1895.

He is chiefly known as composer of the hymn-tune, "Ewing," usually sung to the verses beginning "Jerusalem the Golden." This has frequently been ascribed to his uncle, Bishop Ewing.

Eyre, Alfred James, organist, born at Lambeth, October 24, 1853. Studied at R.A.M., under (Sir) G. A. Macfarren, F. Westlake, and others; and the organ with W. S. Hoyte, and G. Cooper. Organist at St. Peter's, Vauxhall, 1867-72, and again, 1874-81; St. Ethelburga's, Bishopsgate Street, 1872-74; and St. John Evangelist, Upper Norwood, from 1881. In May, 1880, he was appointed organist of the Crystal Palace, a position he

FANING.

held until ill-health compelled him to retire in 1894. He has given recitals at the Bow and Bromley Institute; Birmingham Town Hall (October, 1890), and elsewhere. In 1885, he was elected a member of the R.A.M., and is now a Fellow. His compositions include Church Services (one written for the Salisbury Diocesan Choral Association); Songs, part-songs, and pieces for pf. In MS. he has a setting of the 126th Psalm; a scena for soprano solo and orchestra; String quartet; pf. trio, etc. He married MISS MARGARET BUCKNALL, an accomplished pianist, A.R.A.M. Who has played at various concerts with success.

Facer, Thomas, organist and composer of present time. Has held various organ appointments in Birmingham, and is teacher of singing at King Edward's Grammar Schools in that city. Conductor of a Choral Union, and gives concerts in the Birmingham Town Hall. He has composed the Cantatas, Noël-Tide, 1892; The Crusaders, 1893; Maid of Lorn, produced at the Tonic Sol-fa Festival, Crystal Palace, July 11, 1896; Part-songs, school music, action songs, etc.

Fairbairn, James, writer, author of "Elements of Music: Part I., Melody, containing an explanation of the Simpler Principles of the Science. Part II., Harmony, with Appendix on the nature and causes of sound, and the consonance and dissonance of intervals, as arising from one system of vibration," Edinburgh, 1832.

Fairfax, Robert, or **Fayrfax,** composer, born at Bayford, Herts, in latter part of the fifteenth century [1470]. Mus. Doc., Cantab., 1501-2; Do., Oxford, 1511. About 1509 he was appointed one of the Gentlemen of the King's Chapel. Organist of the Abbey Church of St. Albans. He died at St. Albans in 1529-30. He composed sacred and secular music, but is chiefly known as the composer of a volume of songs in two, three, and four parts, now preserved in MS. in the British Museum. Other compositions of the same master are in the Music School of Oxford, at Cambridge, Lambeth Palace, etc.

Faning, Eaton, composer and conductor, born at Helston, Cornwall, May 20, 1850. Received his first lessons from his parents, and, in 1870, entered the R.A.M., studying under Sterndale Bennett, C. Steggall, and others. In 1873 he won the Mendelssohn Scholarship, and in 1876 the Lucas medal for composition. A.R.A.M., 1877; Professor, 1878; and later, a Fellow of the Institution. Graduated Mus. Bac., Cambridge, 1894. Held various posts at the National Training School, the Guildhall School of Music, and R.C.M., until 1885, when he was offered, and accepted, the position of Director of the

Music at Harrow School, which he still holds. His compositions include a Magnificat and Nunc Dimittis, for voices and orchestra, performed at the Festival of the Sons of the Clergy, at St. Paul's Cathedral, 1878; Anthems, part-songs; Moonlight, Song of the Vikings; Choral ballad, The Miller's Wooing; Chorus, Daybreak, with orchestra; Songs, etc. Operettas: The Two Majors, R.A.M., 1877; Mock Turtle, 1881; and The Head of the Poll, German Reed, 1882. Dramatic Cantata, Liberty, 1882; Cantata for female voices. Buttercups and Daisies. Symphony in C minor; Overture, The Holiday, Promenade Concerts, Covent Garden, 1882; Quartets; Allegro, pf. and clarinet; Pf. pieces, etc.

Fanning, Charles, Irish harp-player and collector, born about 1736. Assisted Bunting with his collections. Date of death unknown.

Farmer, Henry, violinist and composer, born at Nottingham, May 13, 1819, son of John Farmer, a vocalist. Chiefly self-taught in music, but had some lessons from J. Wade Thirlwall. A concert-giver from 1841, he led a busy life to the last in his native town. Was for many years leader of the Birmingham Festival Choral Society's concerts and member of the Festival orchestra in 1846 (but not leader), and for some time after. Organist of High Pavement Chapel, Nottingham, for over 40 years; and conductor of the Nottingham Sacred Harmonic Society up to 1880. An active volunteer, he became Captain in the Robin Hood Rifles. Engaged in a music business for fifty years, he retired on a fortune just two days before his death, which took place June 25, 1891. His works comprised a Mass in B flat, published in 1844; a violin concerto, performed at Nottingham, November 25, 1841; other concertos and violin pieces; Overture, "Calypso," Nottingham, 1845. *Glees*—Welcome joy and harmony, prize, Nottingham, 1845; The Wine Cup, and others. "Singing Quadrilles," and various pf. pieces. New Violin School; The Violin Student; New Violin Tutor; Tutor for American Organ and Harmonium; various arrangements, etc. His daughter, EMILY BARDSLEY FARMER (Mrs. Arthur W. Lambert), is a composer, her works including a quartet for pf. and strings; an operetta for children, " Nell," produced at Nottingham, 1893; pieces for harp and pf., songs, etc. Other musical artists of the name were ANNA MARIA FARMER, a vocalist, who died in London, April 11, 1846; and her sister, DINAH FARMER, a pianist of distinction (afterwards, Mrs. De Lisle Allen), who died in London, March 10, 1884.

Farmer, John, composer of the 16th century, harmonized Este's Psalms, and composed " Cantas, the first set of English Madrigals to foure Voyces, newly composed

by John Farmer, practitioner in the art of musicque, Little Saint Helen's," 1599; " Fair Nymphs," six-part Madrigal in "Triumphs of Oriana;" Divers and Saundrie waies of two parts in one, to the number of fortie upon one playn-song," etc., London, 1591. His biography is unknown.

Farmer, John, organist and composer, born at Nottingham, August 16, 1836. Nephew of Henry Farmer. Studied at Leipzig Conservatorium, and under Andreas Späth, at Coburg. Resident as music teacher for some years at Zurich. In 1862 was appointed music master at Harrow School, a position he held until 1885, when he became organist of Balliol College, Oxford. There he instituted a Musical Society, and has given much attention to concerts of an educational character. His compositions include an oratorio, " Christ and his Soldiers," produced at Harrow, March, 1878; Requiem in memory of departed Harrow friends; " Cinderella," a fairy opera, composed 1882, performed, Harrow, November, 1883; Comic cantata, " Froggy would a wooing go," Oxford, 1887; Nursery rhymes quadrilles, for chorus and orchestra. Septets in C and D, for pf., strings, and flute; Quintet, pf. and strings, Harrow, 1874. Editor of hymns and tunes for High Schools; Harrow glee book; Harrow School Songs; Harrow marches; Dulce Domum; Rhymes and songs, etc.

Farmer, Thomas, composer of the 17th century, was one of the waits of London, and Mus. Bac., Cantab., 1684. He died before 1695, and Purcell has included an elegy on him in " Orpheus Britannicus."

WORKS.—A consort of musick in four parts, containing thirty-three lessons, beginning with an overture, 1686. A second consort of musick in four parts, containing eleven Lessons, beginning with a ground, 1690. Songs in Playford's Choice Ayres, 1675, and in various collections of his time.

Farnaby, Giles, composer and spinnet player, born at Truro, Cornwall, about middle of the 16th century [1560]. Mus. Bac., Oxon., July, 1592. Date of death unknown, but he lived mostly in London, and Sevenoaks, Kent.

WORKS.—Canzonets to foure Voyces, with a Song of eight parts, London, 1598. Madrigals. Pieces contributed to Queen Elizabeth's Virginal Book (which also contains four pieces by Richard Farnaby, a son of Giles). Psalms in Ravenscroft's collection, etc.

Farnie, Henry Brougham, musician and librettist, was born in Fife about 1837. He was educated at St. Andrews and Cambridge Universities, and was for some time editor of the *Fifeshire Journal*. In 1863 he settled in London, and was editor of the *Orchestra, Sock and Buskin,* and *Paris Times.*

FARNOL.

FAWCETT.

He also was associated with Henderson in the opera bouffe productions at the Strand, Folly, Avenue, and Comedy Theatres. He compiled and wrote the librettos of a number of operettas, pantomimes, songs, etc.; and translated most of the more successful modern French comic operas. His talents as an adapter were of the highest order. Among his productions may be named "Sleeping Queen," "Rip Van Winkle," "Cloches de Corneville," by Planquette. He also wrote words for Arditi's "Stirrup Cup," and translated Gounod's "Romeo et Juliette," "La Reine de Saba," etc. He died at Paris, September 21, 1889. By his will he left £23,072 to his sister.

Farnol, Eleanor, see Moir, Mrs. F. L.

Farquharson, James, musician and teacher in Edinburgh. Published a "Selection of Sacred Music, suitable for public and private devotion," Edinburgh, 1824.

Farrant, Daniel, composer, of the 16th and 17th centuries; set lessons for the viol in what was known as lyra-way, in imitation of the lute.

Farrant, John, composer, of the 16th century, was organist of Salisbury Cathedral, about 1600. Biography unknown.

Another JOHN FARRANT, or not unlikely the same, was organist of Christ's Hospital, London, about the same time.

Farrant, Richard, composer and organist, was born about 1530. He was one of the Gentlemen of the Chapel Royal to 1564. Master of Choristers, St. George's Chapel, Windsor, 1564-69. Again Gentleman of the Chapel Royal, 1569-80. Organist and Lay-Vicar, St. George's Chapel. He died at Windsor, November 30, 1580.

WORKS.—Services in G minor, D minor, and A minor. *Anthems*: Call to Remembrance; Hide not thou thy face; Lord for Thy tender mercies sake; O Lord, Almighty, etc.

The work by which Farrant is best known is "Lord for Thy tender mercies sake," an anthem which is of disputed authorship, some attributing it to John Hilton. It has also been adapted as a psalm tune, in which form it appears in numerous collections.

Farrar, Joseph, writer and physician, who studied at Edinburgh, etc., and graduated M.D. at St. Andrews, 1884. Now in practice in Gainsborough. Author of "The Human Voice and connected parts. A practice book for orators, clergymen, vocalists, and others." London, 1881, etc.

Farren, George, author of "The Mortalities of Celebrated Musicians," London, 1834.

Faulkes, William, organist, pianist, and composer, born in Liverpool, November 4, 1863. Studied under William Dawson, and the late Henry Dillon-Newman. Organist of

St. Margaret's, Anfield, Liverpool, since 1886. Resident there as teacher and performer.

WORKS.—Concerto in C minor, pf. and orchestra, 1891; Concerto in A minor, violin and orchestra, composed 1892, performed, Art Club, Liverpool, May, 1893; Suite in C minor, for flute, oboe, trumpet, strings, and pf., 1892. Trios, for pf., violin, and 'cello, D minor, composed 1891, performed at Conference of Incorporated Society of Musicians, London, January, 1893; G minor, and C minor. Twelve pieces for organ: Sonata in D minor; Concert overture in E flat; and other organ pieces. Pianoforte pieces; three pieces awarded the prize offered by the North-Western Section, I.S.M., 1893. Pieces for violin, violoncello, etc.

Faulkner, Thomas, musician. Author of "Organ Builders' Assistant," London, 1826. "Designs for Organs," London, 1838.

Fawcett, a remarkable Yorkshire family of musicians. JOSEPH FAWCETT, the head was born about 1815, and followed his occupation as a weaver at Horsforth, and afterwards at Eccleshill, whither he was invited to assist in the choir of the New Connexion Chapel. He sang tenor, played the violin, and was choirmaster. He has five sons, musicians, JOHN, JOSEPH, SAMUEL, trombone players; TOM, pianist and organist; and HANDEL, contrabassist. John has two sons in the profession;—HARRY, a violinist; and MENDELSSOHN, a clarinettist. Joseph junior's son, CHARLES, is a violinist; and the three sons of Samuel, named CHARLESWORTH, VERDI, and WEBER, play clarinet, violin, and oboe, respectively; while FAWCETT MIDGLEY, the married sister's son, is a bassoonist. The members of this family are known all over the north of England; they have played regularly for the Carl Rosa Opera Company, and some have toured the country through, while others are known as skilled players in Chamber Concerts.

Fawcett, John, composer and writer, was born at Kendal, in 1789. He was a shoemaker for a time, but afterwards became a teacher of music in Bolton, Lancashire. He died at Bolton, October 26, 1867.

WORKS.—New set of sacred music, in three parts ... by John Fawcett, of Kendal [1830]. Miriam's timbrel, a new set of psalm and hymn tunes... London, n.d. Melodia divina, a collection of psalm and hymn tunes, London [1841]. Harp of Zion, consisting of original tunes, and pieces [1845]. The Cherub Lute ... hymns, etc., London [1845]. Voice of Devotion, containing 400 psalm and hymn tunes, Glasgow [1862-63]. Music for Thousands, or the vocalist's manual [1845]. Lancashire Vocalist, a complete guide to singing at sight, London [1854]. Chanting made easy, London [1857]. Paradise, oratorio [1865].

FAWCETT.

The Seraphic Choir, a Christmas piece, 1840. Juvenile Pianist's Companion, 1850. Etude de Salon, for pf., op. 1. Anthems, Temperance songs, etc.

Fawcett, John, composer and organist, son of above, born at Bolton, 1824. He studied under his father, and became organist of St. John's Church, Farnworth, 1835. Organist of Parish Church, Bolton, 1842. He studied at the R.A.M., London, under Bennett, from 1845. Organist of Curzon Street Chapel, London, 1845-46. Mus. Bac., Oxon., 1852. He died at Manchester, July 1, 1857.

He wrote a cantata, "Supplication and Thanksgiving," as a degree exercise, 1852 ; anthems, glees, songs, and pf. music.

Fawcett. Rev. Joshua. musician, edited "Lyra Ecclesiastica, consisting of voluntaries, introits, chants, services, anthems." Bradford, 1845. Preface by Rev. W. H. Havergal.

Fayrfax. Robert; see FAIRFAX.

Fearnside, Frederick, didactic writer, was a chorister at Norwich Cathedral in 1848, and afterwards articled to Dr. Buck. He died at Bradford, October, 1888. Author of "The Systematic and Comprehensive Singing Manual" [1887].

Fearon, see GLOSSOP.

Featherstone, Isabella, see PAUL (Mrs. HOWARD).

Felton, Rev. William, organist and composer, born in 1715. Was Vicar-Choral at Hereford in 1741, and afterwards Minor canon, He was Vicar of Norton Canon, 1751-69. He died on December 6, 1769. He wrote concertos for organ and harpsichord ; and eight sets of easy lessons for the harpsichord, ops. 3 and 8. He composed the well-known hymn tune, "Fabian." He was esteemed in his day a remarkable performer.

Fenton, Lavinia, *born* BESTWICK, soprano vocalist, who made her *début* at London in 1726. She was the original Polly Peachem in "The Beggar's Opera," January 29, 1728. Retired from the stage as mistress of the third Duke of Bolton. Married to him at Aix, Provence, 1751. She died at Greenwich, January, 1760.

This singer has interest for the present time only in her connection with that ever-famous work, "The Beggar's Opera," in which she scored an enormous success.

Fergus, John, composer, was born at Huntly, Aberdeenshire, in 1767. He was organist of St. Andrew's Episcopal Church, Glasgow, for a number of years. Died at Glasgow, June 10, 1825. He composed three glees, songs, and organ pieces.

Ferrabosco, a family of musicians. ALFONSO, son of an Italian composer of the same name, who settled in England some time before 1567, was born at Greenwich, at a date unknown, probably about 1570. He was taken

FIELD.

to Italy by his father, and studied at Bologna. Musical instructor to Prince Henry, 1605. Published "Ayres," 1609. Died in 1628. His works included lessons, and fancies, and he contributed to Sir William Leighton's "Lamentacions," 1614. His son, ALFONSO FERRABOSCO, succeeded his father in the King's band in March, 1627-8. With his brother, HENRY, he was appointed a musician-in-ordinary to the King. Some pieces for viols are to be found in the Addit. MSS., British Museum. He died in 1661. JOHN FERRABOSCO, son either of Alfonso or Henry, was Mus. Bac., Cambridge, 1671. Organist of Ely Cathedral from 1662 to 1682, when he died. Anthems by him are in the Ely Cathedral library. The history of this family is obscure, but the best account will be found in the Dictionary of National Biography, xviii., pp. 375-7.

Ferrey, George, organist of Christ Church Priory, Hampshire, from 1851, until his death, February 10, 1893. His predecessor, a Mr. Hiscock, was appointed when the organ was built, in 1788, the two holding office for more than a century.

Ffrangcon = Davies, see DAVIES, D. FFRANGCON.

Field, Henry Ibbot, composer and pianist, born at Bath, December 6, 1797. He studied under Coombs, of Cheltenham, and taught music at Bath, where he died, May 19, 1848. He wrote some unimportant music for the pianoforte. He was one of the few provincial pianists thought worthy of a hearing in London. At the Philharmonic Concerts, February 25, 1822, he played a concerto by Hummel (in A minor ?), for the first time in England ; and, June 22, 1840, he played Hummel's B minor concerto. His father, THOMAS FIELD, was organist of Bath Abbey.

Field, John, composer and pianist, born at Dublin, July 26, 1782. Apprenticed to Clementi, London, under whom he afterwards studied. Taken by Clementi to Paris, Germany and Russia. Teacher at St. Petersburg, 1804, and at Moscow, 1823. Appeared at London Philharmonic Concert, 1832. He played in Belgium, Switzerland, and Italy, and afterwards returned to Russia with a family named Raemann. He died at Moscow, January 11, 1837.

WORKS.—Op. 1. Three Sonatas for pf. in A, E flat, and C minor. Seven Concertos for pf. and orch., in E flat, A flat, E flat, E flat, C, C minor. Two Divertissements for pf., with accomp. for 2 vns., flute, alto and bass. Quintet for pf., 2 vns., alto and bass. Rondo for pf. and quartet. Variations on Russian air for pf. duet. Grand Valse for pf. duet. Three Sonatas for pf. in A, B, and C. Sonata for pf. in B. Exercise in Modulation for pf. Two Airs for pf. Fantasias for pf. Eighteen Nocturnes for pf. Rondo Ecossais for pf.

FIELD.

FISHER.

Polonaises for pf. Two Songs for Voice and pf. Romances for pf. Rondos, and miscellaneous pieces.

Field, John Thomas, organist and composer, born near Manchester, February 4, 1850. First musical studies private. Later, pupil of Sir John Stainer, and Dr. J. F. Bridge. In 1868, appointed organist and choirmaster, Parish Church, Holywell, North Wales; 1870, Christ Church, Southport; 1872, St. German's, Blackheath; and, two years later, to Christ Church, Lee Park, Kent, where he is still in office. Associate of the Philharmonic Society. WORKS.—Morning, Communion, and Evening Service in D; Benedictus and Agnus Dei, in F; Magnificat and Nunc Dimittis in G; The Canticles of the Church, Two Sets; Chant Services. *Anthems:* Send out Thy Light; Lord of our life; Hail! gladdening light; and others; Carols. *Songs:* An old story; Two children fair; Part-songs, etc. Offertoire á la Sonate, in three movements, and other organ pieces; Nocturne, pf.; Pieces for pf. and violin; Romance in A, etc., etc.

Filby, William Charles, organist and composer, born at Hammersmith, 1836. Was organist of St. Peter, Hammersmith, in 1849, afterwards spending some time in study in France. Organist and choirmaster, Parish Church, Bromley, 1853; St. Peter's, Walworth; St. Matthew's, Bayswater; St. Luke's, Westbourne Park; Holy Trinity, Margate; Holy Trinity, Stepney; and since 1884, of St. Paul's, West Greenwich. Conductor of Choral Societies at Greenwich, Chelsea, etc. Has given organ recitals in London, and in various provincial towns. Was one of the appointed organists at the International Exhibitions, 1882 and 1885. Lecturer on subjects connected with Church music, the opera, and musical education. His compositions are very numerous, and include settings in Cantata form, of Psalms 13, 23, and 65; A Mass in E flat, op. 24; Mass in E, op. 28; Salve Regina, op. 67, and other music for the Roman Catholic Service. Anthems, settings of the Canticles. Operettas, Your money or your life; Alabama claims. A number of songs, choruses, and part-songs. Sonatas in E, op. 66, and G minor, op. 76, with many other pieces for pf. Four organ voluntaries, op. 110; Three organ pieces, op. 124, etc. Revising editor of Lady V. Freke's tune-book, Song of Praise; and of J. B. Mead's, The Treasury. Contributor of hymn-tunes to Hymns Ancient and Modern; The Bristol Tune-book, etc. Author of Piccolo Tutor (London: Williams); Flute Tutor; How to write music; The Student's Copy Book (London, 1882).

His brother, STEPHEN FILBY (born 1834, died 1895), was organist of the Parish Church, Hammersmith, for over twenty years, and afterwards of Holy Trinity, Barnes, and the

Parish Church, Wealdstone, Harrow. He was an extemporaneous player of repute.

Filmer, Edward, composer of the 17th century. He published "French Court Ayres of four and five parts," 1629.

Finch, Hon. and Rev. Edward, composer and clergyman, fifth son of the 1st Earl of Nottingham, born in 1664, died at York, February 14, 1738. He composed anthems, psalms, etc.; also a "Grammar for Thoroughbass, with examples." MS. of 66 pages in the Euing Library, Glasgow.

Findlay, William, violinist and composer, born at Crofthead, Linlithgow, August 11, 1854. Resident at Broxburn, in the same county, as a music teacher. He has composed a number of reels, hornpipes, strathspeys, and other Scottish dance music,

Firth, R. A., composer, and organist of St. John's, Hampstead, compiled "Select portions of the new version of Psalms, adapted to a choice collection of Psalm tunes, for the use of the Parish Church of St. John, Hampstead," London, 1819. "Congregational and domestic praise, consisting of select portions of psalms and hymns adapted to appropriate tunes . . .," London, 1835. Six canzonets [1825]. Hymns, pf. music, etc.

Fish, William, violinist and composer, born at Norwich, in 1775. Violinist in Norwich theatre. Teacher of music at Norwich. Was musical preceptor of Edward Taylor and George Perry, and a composer of concertos; grand sonata for the pf., op. 1; glees, and songs. He died at Norwich, March 15, 1866.

Fisher, Arthur E., is a professor of harmony, counterpoint, and composition, in the Toronto College of Music. He is a Mus. Bac. (Toronto?) and A.R.C.O., England. He has composed a cantata for female voices, "The Wreck of the Hesperus." EDWARD FISHER, another Toronto musician, was musically educated in Germany. He was musical director of the Ottawa Ladies' College, and conductor of the Choral Society in that city. Organist of St. Andrew's Church, Toronto; conductor of the Toronto Choral Society for some years up to 1891. From its establishment, in 1887, he has been principal of the Toronto Conservatory of Music. Elected President of the Canadian Society of Musicians, 1888, and again in 1889.

Fisher, Henry, didactic writer, and teacher, born at Blackpool, December 21, 1845. Chiefly self-taught in music. Apprenticed to a firm of music-sellers in Manchester, he acquired a knowledge of the pianoforte, and gained further experience as assistant to a professor of music at Darlington. Graduated Mus. Bac., 1876; Mus. Doc., 1878, Cambridge. For three years was organist of Christ Church, Blackpool, in which town he is settled as a teacher of singing, pianoforte,

J

FISHER.

and harmony. He is an earnest student in every branch of knowledge, and has been elected a Fellow of the Geological Society. His compositions are two cantatas, " Ruth, the Gleauer," and " The Call of Gideon;" a romance for viola and orchestra, and some minor works. Besides contributions to the musical press, and lectures, he is author of The Musical Profession, a handbook for professors of the present and the future; The Candidate in Music, Part I., a text book of musical elements, and II., Harmony; editor and part author of E. Q. Norton's Construction, tuning, and care of the pianoforte; and also of John Curwen's The Harmony Player, for the harmonium, all published by Curwen and Sons, for which firm he has arranged a number of operas for children's voices.

Fisher, J. Churchill, a composer, born in Australia. Has written a Cantata, " The Emigrants," produced at Parramata, February 22, 1887.

Fisher, John Abraham, composer and violinist, born at Dunstable, or London, 1744. He studied under Pinto, and appeared at King's Theatre as violinist, 1763. In 1764 he became a member of the Royal Society of Musicians. Married Miss Powell, 1770. Bac. and Doc. Mus., Oxon., 1777. Travelled in Russia and Germany. Married Anne Selina Storace, 1784, but separated from her soon afterwards. He lived in Dublin as a teacher, and died in May, 1806.

WORKS.—Music to The Monster of the Wood, 1772; The Sylphs, 1774; Prometheus, 1776; The Norwood Gypsies, 1777; Macbeth. Providence, oratorio (for degree), 1777. Symphonies; Concertos for pf., and for oboe; Violin and flute music; Canzonets. A comparative view of the English, French, and Italian Schools, consisting of Airs and Glees composed as examples of their several manners, London, n.d.

Fisin, James, musician, born at Colchester, in 1755. He studied under Burney and Reinhold. Teacher in Chester. Wrote " The Seasons, or Vocal Year " ; " The Judgment of Paris," a masque (Congreve); " Sacred Songs on the most Prominent Incidents of our Saviour's Life and Death," London, n.d. Sonatas, Glees, Canzonets, Ballads, etc. He died September 8, 1847.

Fitzball, Edward, or BALL, dramatist and writer, born at Burwell, near Newmarket, 1793. He died at Chatham, October 27, 1873. He wrote the librettos of some of the most popular of English operas, Wallace's " Maritana " being perhaps his most successful production. Although something more than a mere play-wright, his poetical powers were not of a high order. He published " Thirty-five Years of a Dramatic Author's Life," London, 2 vols., 1859.

FLAVELL.

Fitzherbert, William, clergyman and musician, born 1713. He was a minor canon of St. Paul's Cathedral, London, 1744. He was successively rector of Hadlow, Kent, 1753; Hornedon-on-the-Hill, Essex, 1756-1771; and of St. Gregory by St. Paul. He died at St. Paul's College, October 2, 1797. Composer of a double chant in F, and other church music.

Fitzpatrick, W. A., musician, compiler of " Devotional Music; being a selection of nearly 100 melodies," London [1837], and composer of glees and songs.

Fitzwilliam, Edward Francis, composer and conductor, born at Deal, August 1, 1824. Music-director, Haymarket Theatre, London. Married Miss Ellen Chaplin, 1855. He died, London, January 20, 1857.

WORKS.—Music for The Green Bushes (1845); Anything for a change (1846); Love's alarms (1854); and other dramatic pieces. Queen of a day, comic opera. Set of songs [1853]; Songs for a winter night [1855]; Dramatic Songs, London [1856], 4 books; Four four-part songs, London, 1855 : Glees, etc. Te Deum, ballads, pf. music.

His father, EDWARD FRANCIS (1785-1852), was an actor and singer, and his sister, KATHLEEN MARY (born 1826), who married Mr. C. Withall, was also a singer and actress.

Fitzwilliam, Richard, 7th Viscount, English peer, and founder of the Fitzwilliam Museum, Cambridge, was born in August, 1745; and died February 5, 1816. The title is now extinct.

He bequeathed to the University of Cambridge, a collection of paintings, music, and books, the musical portion of which included a number of fine MS. compositions of early composers, principally Italian. These are housed in the fine Fitzwilliam Museum at Cambridge, The sacred music contained in this collection was edited and published by Vincent Novello, in 5 volumes, as " The Fitzwilliam Music, being a collection of sacred pieces from the MSS. of Italian composers in the Fitzwilliam Museum," n.d.

Flavell, Charles Edwin, pianist, born in Birmingham about 1817. Studied under Robert Barnett, and later at Frankfort-on-the-Main, under Aloys Schmitt. Settled in Birmingham, as teacher. About the year 1856, in conjunction with Mr. Duchemin (q.v.) he gave a series of chamber concerts, which were continued for some time, and then he started others on his own account. He removed to London about 1873 to undertake the agency for this country of the Kaps pianos; and he died there, February 1, 1879.

Flavell, Edwin Mark, pianist and composer, of present time. Educated at R.A.M. Sometime conductor of a choral society at West Hill, Wandsworth. He is the composer of a cantata, Babylon's Wave, produced at

FLEET.

Wandsworth Town Hall, October 18, 1883; cantata, "The Fairy Ring," 1883; Songs and duets; Pieces for pf. solo, and duet, etc.

Fleet, George R., *see* BARRINGTON, RUTLAND.

Fleming, Rev. Alexander. Scottish clergyman, born in 1770; died in June, 1845. He was minister at Neilston in Renfrewshire. Author of ". . . Letters . . . on the subject of the organ which . . . was introduced into St. St. Andrew's Church, Glasgow. To which are added remarks on the Rev. James Begg's Treatise on the use of Organs," Glasgow, 1808. "Answer to a statement of the proceedings of the Presbytery of Glasgow, relative to the use of an organ," Glasgow, 1808.

Another clergyman of the same name, Rev. JOHN FLEMING, was minister at Airdrie in Lanarkshire, and wrote "An inquiry into the compositions with which the praise of God should be celebrated in His public worship," Edinburgh, 1821.

Fleming, James M., writer and violinist, born at Glasgow in 1839. Studied for a time under the late Samuel D. Smythe, of Glasgow, and received some hints from Ole Bull. Contributor to various musical periodicals; Composer of Easy legato studies for the violin; and author of "Old Violins and their Makers," 1883; "The Practical Violin School," 1886; and "The Fiddle Fancier's Guide," 1892.

Fletcher, Charles, violinist and conductor, born at Wincanton, Somerset, July 11, 1846. His father was a schoolmaster and a musical amateur, and his mother was a cousin of Charles Lucas. At five years of age Charles Fletcher began his vocal studies, and at seven appeared in public as a singer and flute-player. When nine he was appointed soprano soloist and harmonium player at the Parish Church of Shepton Montague, at a salary of £50 per annum. He had studied the violin from his seventh year, and now became prominent as a performer. He was engaged by the late Lord Arundel for the private chapel and chamber concerts at Wardour Castle, where he remained three years. His voice changing, he settled as a violinist at Southampton. Failing health necessitated sea voyages, and for some time he was in Egypt and Brazil. Ultimately he took up his residence at Bournemouth, where he has established a string orchestra of ladies', mostly his pupils. He has played as soloist, and in chamber concerts in London, and many provincial towns, and at the conferences of the Incorporated Society of Musicians. He was principal professor of the violin at Winchester College for ten years. At the Bournemouth Festival of 1896 he was principal first violinist. He married, in 1869, a German lady, a pianist of repute. His daughter MAUD made her appearance as a violoncellist in Handel's Concerto

FLORENCE.

Grosso in D minor, at a concert given by the Rev. E. H. Moberly, with his ladies' orchestra, at Prince's Hall, London, December 4, 1894.

Fletcher, Thomas, double-bass player, in his day the leading professional musician in Birmingham. He was a member of the Festival Orchestra from 1808, if not earlier; and was for years in the band of the Italian Opera under Weichsel. He died in Birmingham, in June, 1845, at the age of 60. There were several other musicians of the same family. JANE FLETCHER, a contralto vocalist, was one of the principal singers at the Birmingham Festival of 1811.

Flinn, Kate, soprano vocalist. Studied under Ardellmann, and W. Shakespeare. She made her first appearance at a concert given by Mr. W. Ganz, July 1, 1884, and sang at the Ballad Concerts, St. James's Hall, the next year. Made her *début* at the Crystal Palace Concerts, March 17, 1886, and at the Saturday Popular Concerts, March 26, 1887, since which time she has sung at many important concerts in London and the provinces.

Flintoft, Rev. Luke, clergyman and musician of 18th century, who was probably a native of Worcester. B.A. Cambridge, 1700. Priest-vicar of Lincoln Cathedral, 1704-14. Gentleman of Chapel Royal, 1715. Reader in Chapel Royal, Whitehall, 1719. Minor canon, Westminster Abbey, 1719. He died at London, November 3, 1727, and is buried in Westminster Abbey. He invented the double chant, or rather adapted one of the earliest specimens yet discovered. It is in G minor, and will be found in any large collection.

Flood, Edwin, organist and composer, born early in the present century. He was organist of the Parish Church of Honiton, and died there in 1869. He compiled Psalmodia Britannica, a collection of psalms, anthems, chants, etc., London, 1847-54, 2 vols. issued in 12 books. Collection of chants for 4 voices [1846]. The Psalmodist, a collection of psalm and hymn tunes used in the Parish Church of Honiton, London, 1850. Gipsy's life is a joyous life, song. Sets of quadrilles, and other pf. music. Another EDWIN FLOOD, possibly a son or other relative of the above, died at Honiton, April 29, 1848. We have been unable to disentangle the works of these two, both being contemporary composers.

Florence, Amy, soprano vocalist, born at Edgbaston, Birmingham. Studied singing locally, and under San Giovanni at Milan. Made her *début* in opera in Malta, afterwards singing at Como and Naples. Returning to England, she joined the Carl Rosa Opera Company, singing in "Carmen," and other works. In the season 1886-7, she sang at Covent Garden in "La Favorita," etc., and a year later under the management of Augustus

FLOWER.

FORBES.

Harris. She took the stage name of Mlle. Firenze. She has given concerts at Steinway Hall, 1888, and elsewhere.

Flower, Eliza, soprano vocalist and composer. Sister of Sarah Flower (Mrs. Wm. Brydges Adams, died 1847, or August, 1848), author of " Nearer my God to Thee," and other hymns. She was born at Harlow, Essex, April 19, 1803; and died December 12, 1846. Composer of " Hymns and Anthems," composed for the services at Finsbury Chapel, South Place, London; "Musical Illustrations of the Waverley Novels," London, 1831. "Now pray we for our country," and other part-songs ; Songs of the Seasons, etc.

Flower, Sara, contralto vocalist, born February 22, 1805 ; died at Melbourne, August 16, 1865. A concert singer who sang in England and the Colonies. Her sister, ELIZA- BETH, was a soprano vocalist and sang in public. These are frequently confounded with the two Flower sisters mentioned above.

Flowers, George French, composer, organist, and writer, born at Boston, Lincoln, in 1811. He studied in Germany under Rinck and Schnyder von Wartensee. He was organist of the English Chapel, Paris, and of St. Mark's, Myddelton Square, Clerken- well, London. Mus. Bac., Oxon., 1839. Mus. Doc., Oxon., 1865. Editor of *Literary Gazette*. Flowers was an unsuccessful candidate for the Music Professorship at Oxford in 1848, and also for that of Gresham College in 1863. He was a successful teacher of singing, numbering Mrs. Howard Paul among his pupils, and established a British School of Vocalization. He died at London, June 14, 1872.

WORKS.—Anthems, songs, etc. Essay on the construction of Fugue . . , London, 1846. Poem on Muscular Vocalisation, with intro- duction,"Barton-upon-Humber, 1861. Trans- lation of Basler's Pictorial representation of the science of harmony . . . n.d., etc.

Fludd, Robert, scholar and author, born at Milgate, Bearsted, Kent, 1574 ; died at London, September 8, 1637. Author of " Ut- riusque cosmi majoris scilicet et minoris meta- physica, physica atque technica historia," Oppenheim, 1617 (*q.v.*). He was educated at Oxford, and is best known as a philosophical writer.

Foley, Allan James (SIGNOR FOLI), bass vocalist, born in Cahir, Tipperary, in 1842. His early years were spent in America. Studied in Naples, under Bisaccia, and sang in opera at Catania, Turin, Milan, and Paris, 1862-4. He made his *début* at Her Majesty's Theatre, June 17, 1865, as St. Bris in the " Huguenots," and for some years sang in many operas there, at Covent Garden, and Drury Lane. He has also appeared in opera in America, Russia, Austria, and elsewhere. His first performance in oratorio was in " Israel in Egypt," National

Choral Society's Concert, April 25, 1866, when he sang in the duet, " The Lord is a man o: war," with Mr. Santley. He sang at the Handel Festival, 1868 ; and in the provincia. Festivals successively at Norwich, 1869 ; Bir mingham, 1870; Gloucester, 1871 ; and Leeds 1877. As a concert singer he has been heard in every important musical centre. In 1892 he toured in Australia ; was in South Africa 1893 ; and singing in London again in 1896.

Folkestone, Viscountess, *see* RADNOR, COUNTESS OF.

Foote, Frank Barrington, baritone voca- list, born at Plymouth, February 2, 1855. Was intended for the army, but his voice developing while he was at school in Germany he was sent to Florence to study, his masters being Zuccardi, and Lamperti at Milan. As Signor Franceschi he made his *début* in opera at Pavia, and he sang, later, in Milan. In 1880 he was engaged at Her Majesty's Theatre, singing in Verdi's "Aïda," etc. Later he went to America with Mapleson's troupe, and afterwards again visited Italy. In 1884 he was with the Carl Rosa Company, and sang in "Colomba," and "The Canterbury Pil- grims"; and in 1885 he took part in the Handel Bi-centennial Festival, at the Crystal Palace. He now was busy with concert work, and studying oratorio with Mr. Randegger. He appeared at the Norwich Festival, 1887 ; and those of Gloucester and Leeds in 1889. In the spring of 1889, and again in 1891, he visited America, and has toured with Madame Albani, and Madame Patti. He was giving concerts in London in 1896.

Forbes, George, pianist and composer, born at Pimlico, London, July 1, 1813. He studied under his brother Henry, and Sir G. Smart. Gave concerts with his brother in London, 1831-1844. Subsequently gave sub- scription concerts on his own account. Was organist of St. Mary's, Bryanston Square, for 45 years. He died at London, September 11, 1883.

WORKS.—*Pianoforte*: Sonata in C; March des Guides ; Larghetto and Rondo Capriccioso in E ; Rappelle toi ; La Caprera ; La Castellu- cia ; Carnival de Florence ; Marziale ; La pluie des Perles ; Forbes's Valse de Concert and Valse de Sylphes ; Calliope Valse ; Pluie de Printemps ; La Rosamund, a nocturne ; Lou- ise, nocturne. Four operatic duets. Six teaching pieces for pf. Gavotte, Queen Eliza- beth. March et Finale brillant, op. 7. Italian fantasia. Espaniola. Billet-doux. Tran- scriptions, etc. Three books of easy Volun- taries for organ or harmonium. Offertoire for organ in F.

Forbes, Henry, composer and pianist, brother of the above, born at London in 1804. A pupil of Sir G. Smart, Hummel, Moscheles, and Herz. Conductor of the Societa Armonica.

FORBES.

Organist of Parish Church of S. Luke, Chelsea. Gave concerts with his brother George. He died at London, November 24, 1859. WORKS.—Fairy Oak, opera, Drury Lane, October 18, 1845. Ruth, oratorio, 1847. Pf. music. Songs. Psalms, etc. National Psalmody [1843].

Forbes, John, Scottish printer and publisher, established in business at Aberdeen in middle of 17th century, where he died, in December, 1675. He is chiefly remarkable as having published the first book of secular music in Scotland [See Davidson, Thomas]; and for the authorship of three inflated epistles dedicatory, prefixed to the "Cantus" of 1662, and changed, to the edition of 1666; and again different, to the edition of 1682.

Ford, Ann, performer on the Harmonica, who flourished during the 18th century. Married to the Hon. P. Thicknesse. Sat to Gainsborough for her portrait. Authoress of "Instructions for playing on the Musical Glasses, with a copperplate representing the order and manner of placing the glasses; with such directions for performing on them, that any person of a musical turn may learn in a few days, if not in a few hours," London, 1762.

Ford, David Everard, composer and organist, who flourished during the first half of the present century. He was organist at Lymington, Hants. He wrote "The Rudiments of Music, etc." n.d., and published "Original Psalm and Hymn Tunes," London, 7 books, 1827-36. "Progressive Exercises for the Voice..," 1829.

Ford, Ernest A. C., composer, born in London, February 17, 1858. Studied at the R.A.M. under Sir Arthur Sullivan (composition), and later at Paris with Edouard Lalo. Was the first Sir John Goss Scholar at R.A.M. (1875), F.R.C.O. the same year, and A.R.A.M., 1883. Has acted as accompanist at the Saturday Popular Concerts, and is conductor at the Empire Theatre. He was chosen by Sir Arthur Sullivan to conduct "Ivanhoe" on its production, in 1891. WORKS.—Motet, Domine Deus (performed at 250th Anniversary of Harvard University, U.S.A.). Operas; Daniel O'Rourke (1884); Nydia (Duologue, 1889, libretto by Justin-H. McCarthy); Joan (Robert Martin, 1890); Mr. Jericho (operetta, H. Greenbank, 1893); Jane Annie (opera. book by J. M. Barrie and Conan Doyle, produced Savoy Theatre, May 13, 1893, and taken on tour in the provinces). Cantata, The Eve of the Festa, female voices. Music to the Ballets produced at the Empire Theatre, 1894-5. Album of six songs; Six two-part songs; Songs, various, etc.

Ford, Henry Edmund, organist, born at Warlingham, Surrey. Chorister in Rochester Cathedral. Pupil of Ralph Banks, and later his assistant organist. In 1842 appointed

FORSTER.

organist of Carlisle Cathedral, a position he still holds. The jubilee of his office as Cathedral organist was celebrated by the public presentation of a testimonial at the County Hotel, Carlisle, April 23, 1892. In November, 1891, he received the degree of Mus. Doc. from the Archbishop of Canterbury.

Ford, Thomas, composer, who was born in the latter half of the 16th century [1580]. Musician in suite of Prince Henry (Son of James I.). Musician to Charles I., on his accession. He died in November, 1648. WORKS.—Musicke of sundrie kindes set forth in two Bookes, the first whereof are Aires for foure Voyces to the lute, orpherion, or basse viol, with a dialogue for two voices and two basse violls, in parts tunde the luteway. The second are Pavans, Galiards, Almaines Toies, Jiggs, Thumpes, and such like for two base viols the liera-way, so made as the greatest number may serve to play alone, very easy to be performed, 1607. Contributions in Leighton's "Teares." Canons, etc., in Hilton's "Catch that catch can." Ford is now chiefly remembered as the composer of the beautiful madrigal "Since first I saw your face."

Ford, Thomas, clergyman, author of "Singing of Psalmes the duty of Christians, in V Sermons," London, 1659.

Forde, William, musician, born 1796, died 1850. Author of "An Essay on the Key in Music, fully illustrated by examples," London, 1841. Encyclopedia of Melody, 3050 Airs of all Countries.., 6 vols., n.d. New Pianoforte Primer, London, n.d. New Method of Singing according to the Italian School, 87 exercises, London, n.d. Art of Singing at Sight, London [1840]. Principles of Singing, with practical examples, London [1830], 7 editions. Master's Class Book on the Scales [1841]. 300 National Melodies of the British Isles, for pf., 3 vols. [1850]. Irish national quadrilles, etc.

Formby, Rev. Henry, writer, author of ... Duties and Privileges of Congregational Singing, Sermon, 1849. The Roman Ritual and its Canto Fermo compared with the w rks of modern music, London, 1849. The Catholic Christian's guide to the right use of Christian Psalmody and the Psalter, London, 1847. Collection of Catholic hymns, 1853.

Forster, Simon Andrew, writer and violin maker, was born at London, May 13, 1801, died February 2, 1870. He was a violin and violoncello maker in London, and was a member of the celebrated Forster family of violin and double-bass players, of whom WILLIAM (Brampton, Cumberland, May 4, 1739—London, December 14, 1808); his son WILLIAM (London, January 7, 1764; June 24, 1824); and grandson, WILLIAM (London,

FORTAY.

December 14, 1788 ; October 8, 1824), were the principal members. S. A. Forster helped William Sandys with his " History of the Violin," 1864.

Fortay, James Butler, organist and composer, born in Liverpool, October 26, 1856. Studied under D. C. Browne, and G. W. Röhner. Was an organist at an early age, subsequently holding appointments at Emmanuel Church, Everton (1879-91) ; and at St. Michael's-in-the-Hamlet since 1891. Resident in Liverpool as teacher. Since 1891 he has lectured on musical topics annually for the Liverpool Corporation Library and Arts Committee ; and has also lectured in other districts. He has published Hymns of the Church, a collection of original tunes ; and contributed to The Chant Book Companion ; Church of England Hymnal ; Welsh Calvinistic Methodist Tune Book, etc. ; and is the composer of Night and Morning ; Faithful unto death ; Joy cometh in the morning, and other songs ; pf. pieces, etc.

Fortey, Mary Comber, pianist and composer. Studied at R.A.M. Married to Sir Julius Benedict ; and in 1886 to Mr. Frank Lawson. Author of " How to teach the pianoforte to young beginners," London, Hughes, 1883 ; and composer of Castles in Spain ; Going to Sleep ; Love, the Truant ; and other songs.

Foster, James, amateur musician, was born at Bristol, September 12, 1807. He was a builder in Bristol. He acted as honorary organist of the Bristol Tabernacle, and assisted Waite with his compilation called " Hallelujah." He died at Bristol, June 7, 1885. He composed a number of hymn tunes, among which " Claremont " is perhaps best known.

Foster, John, musician, of Sheffield, compiler of " Sacred Music, consisting of anthems, psalms and hymns in full orchestral score, with organ or pf. adaptation," York, n.d.

Foster, John, alto vocalist, organist, and composer, born at Staines, August, 1827. Pupil of Sir G. Elvey. Organist, St. Andrew's, Wells Street, London, 1847-56. Lay-Vicar of Westminster Abbey since 1856. His glee, " Sweet Queen of Autumn," men's voices, obtained a prize in 1852. In 1865 he published " Psalms and Hymns, adapted to the Church of England." He also issued " Tunes for the Psalms and Hymns," London, 1864. Choral Harmonist [1872]. etc.

Foster, Myles Birket, organist and composer, born in London, November 29, 1851. Eldest son of Birket Foster, the celebrated artist. Being of a Quaker family his early love of music was not encouraged, and he was placed in a stockbroker's office. This he left in 1871, and studied music under Hamilton Clarke, and at R.A.M. under Sullivan,

FOWLES.

Prout, and Westlake. He held the post of organist at Rev. H. R. Haweis' Church, 1873-4, and was organist of the Foundling Hospital, 1880-1892. At the present time he is musical editor to Messrs. Boosey. He was elected an Associate of the Philharmonic Society in 1880 ; A.R.A.M. ; and 895, F.R.A.M. Travelling Examiner for T.C., London, in which capacity he visited Australia and New Zealand in 1895.

WORKS.—Eve ing service in C (male voices); in A, Sons of the Clergy Festival, 1883 ; Communion service in B flat ; Anthems, etc. Cantatas for Children : Cinderella ; Lampblack ; Beauty and the beast ; The Angels of the bells ; The bonnie fishwife ; The snow fairies ; and The coming of the King. Songs : The children's Christmas ; A day in a child's life ; Six two-part songs ; a second set ; Songs and part-songs. Instrumental compositions in MS. : Symphony in F sharp minor, " Isle of Arran " ; Overtures ; String quartet, pf. trio, etc.

Foster, William Martin, composer and conductor, born in London about 1834. He acted as bandmaster of the 9th regiment, and was afterwards in the orchestras of Drury Lane Theatre and the Crystal Palace. He became leader of the orchestra of the Glasgow Theatre Royal about 1870. He died at Newcastle-on-Tyne, December 18, 1872. He composed incidental music to various plays, but is best known for his overture to the play of " Rob Roy," based on Scott's novel.

Fowle, Thomas Lloyd, organist, writer and editor, born at Amesbury, Wilts, October 16, 1827. His father was a clergyman, a prebendary of Salisbury. Self-taught in music, he acted for some years as organist at his father's church, Amesbury, and later at Crawley, Sussex. From 1856 to recent times he has been engaged as editor and publisher. He is Ph. Doc. of Giessen. He has published 4 vols. of anthems ; 5 cantatas ; 4 vols. of organ voluntaries ; 12 marches for special seasons ; The Church Tune Book ; 2 Services, and numerous other musical works. Handel, a memoir ; Charles Dickens, a memoir ; Gentle Edith, a novel, and miscellaneous writings.

Fowler, Chas., pianist, studied under Sir W. Sterndale Bennett, at the Royal Academy of Music, and was appointed a Professor there in 1885. At Torquay, where he resided, he was in high repute as a teacher, and gave frequent concerts. His compositions include a Sonata for pianoforte and violin, a Sonata Trio, for voice, violin, and pianoforte, and a Sonata Concertante for four violins. He was also the author of several humorous sketches, which were received with favour. He died at Torquay, in May, 1891.

Fowles, Ernest, pianist and composer,

born at Portsmouth, April 27, 1864. Gained the Chappell Scholarship at the National Training School for Music, in 1876, and studied there for six years. In 1884 he entered the R.A.M., studying composition under Sir G. A. Macfarren, distinguishing himself at the Academy Concerts, producing several pf. compositions in the larger forms, and being elected an Associate. From 1887 he has given annual concerts in the Prince's Hall, and, October 29, 1894, began a series of Concerts of British Chamber Music, introducing important works by Algernon Ashton, J. C. Ames, Walford Davies, and other young writers, besides works by Hubert Parry, Villiers Stanford, Swinnerton Heap, among more widely known composers. His own compositions comprise a Quartet for strings; A Trio in D, for pf. and strings; Two Sonatas, and other pieces for pf.

Fowles, Margaret F., pianist, organist, and conductor, born at Ryde, Isle-of-Wight, daughter of an artist. Studied pf. harmony and counterpoint under Chalmers Masters; organ under Dr. Hopkins; and voice production and singing under Emil Behnke, Alberto Randegger, and W. Shakespeare. At the age of fifteen she was appointed organist of St. James's, Ryde; and in 1878, organist and choir director at St. Michael and All Angels, which office she retains. In 1874 she founded the Ryde Choral Union, the concerts of which she conducted for twenty years, retiring in December, 1894. From the first concert, April 6, 1875, to the close of her official connection with the Society, Miss Fowles has produced many oratorios and other important works, and has done great service in the cause of music. She is the composer of a number of anthems, and hymn tunes, also of several songs.

Fox, Albert H., pianist, composer, and conductor, born at Dulwich. Studied at R.A.M., pf. under Walter Macfarren, composition under F. W. Davenport. Hine Exhibitioner, 1883; Balfe Scholar, 1884; Sterndale Bennett Scholar, and Heathcote Long Prize winner, 1886. A.R.A.M., 1890. He is musical director at the Royalty Theatre, London. His compositions include an opera, operettas; music to "Merry Monte Carlo," 1895; Romance for orchestra, 1893; March for band of harps, 1888; pf. pieces, etc.

Fox, Arthur, pupil and Associate, R.A.M., is choirmaster at Christ's Hospital, and a tenor vocalist. He has published an Album of eight songs.

Fox, George, composer and baritone vocalist. Sang at the Crystal Palace, March, 1876; on tour with Pyatt's operatic company in 1879; in Italian opera, at Her Majesty's, in October, 1880; and with the Royal English Opera Company, in the provinces, 1883. He is the composer of a number of comic can-

tatas and operettas, some of which have gained much popularity.

WORKS.—*Cantatas:* The jackdaw of Rheims; The babes in the wood; The fair Imogene, 1880; Lord Lovel; Winifred Price, 1882; Gabriel Grub (adapted from "Pickwick"), 1882; John Gilpin; Hamilton Tighe, 1884; The messenger dove. *Comedies and operas:* The captain of the guard, 1882; Welcome home, 1885; Robert Macaire, 1887; The Corsican brothers, 1888; Nydia (from Bulwer-Lytton's "Last Days of Pompeii"), 1892. The last three were produced at the Crystal Palace. *Songs:* Grandmamma's jokes for little folks; Songs for little singers, etc.

Francis, Thomas, alto singer and composer, was born in 1812. He was a vicar-choral of St. Paul's Cathedral, London. He died at Hackney, London, September 2, 1887. Composer of glees and other vocal music.

Fraser, John, author and musician, was born at Johnstone, Renfrewshire, about 1794, and died there on March 3, 1879. He was at one time well known in Scotland for the series of lectures and concerts he gave in conjunction with various members of his family, chiefly illustrative of Scots national music. He edited for a time a chartist newspaper called "The True Scotsman." His youngest son, JAMES ROY FRASER, was born at Johnstone, September 21, 1832, and since 1865 has resided in Paisley as a music-seller and teacher. Since 1875 he has been organist of the Mid Church, Paisley. He was one of the organisers and conductors of the Tannahill concerts on Gleniffer Braes, which produced the funds which were applied to the erection of a statue of that poet at Paisley. Mr. Fraser composed a cantata, "The Cottar's Saturday Night," and several songs.

Fraser, Captain Simon, collector and violinist, born at Ardachie, Inverness, in 1773; and died in 1852. Published "The Airs and Melodies peculiar to the Highlands of Scotland and the Isles, with a plain harmony for the pianoforte, harp, organ, or violoncello, acquired 1715-45," Edinburgh, 1815. Another edition, 1874; also 1884. A valuable and scarce collection, containing a number of reels and strathspeys by Fraser himself. He also issued "Thirty Highland airs, strathspeys, etc. Selected and composed by Mr. S. F .. r." n.d.

Fredericks, Charles Wigg, tenor vocalist, vicar-choral, Lichfield Cathedral, is a well-known concert singer in the Midlands and the North. He has sung at the Crystal Palace; at M. Gounod's Trocadero Concerts, Paris, 1884; and at St. James's Hall, London; also at the Hereford Festival of 1891, of which Cathedral choir he was formerly a member.

Freemantle, George, organist and musical

FRENCH.

critic, born at Ely, April 23, 1833. His father, about 1838, was appointed to the choir of Durham Cathedral, and in due time the son became a chorister there, and pupil of Dr. William Henshaw, the Cathedral organist. In the autumn of 1853, he gained the post of organist and teacher of music at the Blind Asylum, Manchester, and later held various positions in that city. He gave up music for a business life, but accepted the office of musical critic to the *Manchester Guardian*, which he held for thirty years. When the Carl Rosa Opera Company was re-organised he became one of the directors. He died at Ardwick, Manchester, May 31, 1894. His brother, WILLIAM THOMAS FREEMANTLE, many years his junior, was assistant organist of Lincoln Cathedral, and in 1871 appointed organist of Sharrow Church, Sheffield. He published in 1876-7, " A Collection of Kyries, Glorias, Chants, etc., by various Composers," in 8 books (Novello).

French, John, violinist and composer, of Ayr, in Scotland, who flourished in the latter part of last century. Composer of "A Collection of new strathspey reels, etc., dedicated to Mrs. Boswell of Auchinleck," Edinburgh, n.d.

Frere, Walter, composer of present time. He has published five songs for baritone; Three Italian songs; Six songs (Herrick's " Hesperides "), etc.

Frere, Rev. Walter Howard, amateur musician and author. Educated at Cambridge; graduated M.A.; ordained in 1887. Curate of St. Dunstan, Stepney, 1887-92. His works include the Order of the Holy Communion for men's voices; Memorials of Stepney Parish, 1891; The Marian Reaction in its relation to the English Clergy, S.P.C.K., 1897. Editor of " Eighteen well-known hymn tunes, as set in Ravenscroft's Psalter (1621)," London [1888]. Graduale Sarisburiense, 1894. Bibliotheca Musico-Liturgica, a descriptive hand-list of the musical and latin liturgical MSS. of the middle ages, London. The Sarum Gradual and the Gregorian Antiphonale Missarum : a Dissertation and an Historical Index, London, Quaritch, 1896.

Frewer, Frank, organist of St. James', Garlick Hithe. Is author of a Collection of hymn tunes, chants, and kyries, London, Salter, 1886; also composer of songs, a scherzo for pf. and violin, etc.

Frewin, Tom Harrison, violinist and composer. Educated at R.A.M.; Balfe Scholar, 1885. He has composed a Mass, performed, 1896; Orchestral pieces: " The Battle of the Flowers," 1895; Ballad, Mazeppa, 1896, both performed at the Queen's Hall Concerts. Also pieces for violin and pf., etc.

Frickenhaus, Fanny, *born* EVANS, pianist, born at Cheltenham, June 7, 1849. She

FRITH.

studied under George Mount, and later at the Brussels Conservatoire, under Auguste Dupont, also with Wm. Bohrer. She first came prominently before the public, January 11, 1879, at one of the Saturday Evening Concerts, started in St. James's Hall, in November, 1878, Her success was immediate, and she was engaged for the rest of the series. She gave a recital in the concert room of the R.A.M., March 31, 1880 ; appeared at the Crystal Palace, November 20 ; and a week later played for the first time in London the pianoforte concerto of Goetz, at Cowen's Saturday Concerts. Her first appearance at the Popular Concerts was on Saturday, January 27, 1883, and at the Philharmonic, March 4, 1886. From 1884, in conjunction with Joseph Ludwig, she has given chamber concerts at the Prince's Hall, introducing important novelties ; and has been heard at the best concerts in Birmingham and other places, ranking among the leading pianists of the day.

Frias, Duchess de, *see* BALFE (VICTOIRE).

Fricker, Anne, or MOGFORD, songwriter and poetess, who was born about 1820. Married Mr. Mogford. First song published, 1839.

WORKS.—*Songs :* A harvest hymn ; Angel of peace ; Autumn breezes ; Consolation ; Dear voices of home ; Dinna ye hear ? ; Distant bells ; Fading away ; The fancy fair ; Faithless swallow ; Flow, gentle river ; Footprints in the snow ; Gentle Clare ; Gentle Shepherd ; Heart of hearts ; Hesperus ; I cried unto Thee ; I stood beneath the chestnut trees ; Marguerite ; Memory's tears ; Nightingale ; The old man's home ; Oh, weary eyes ; Phillis, fair ; Regret ; Robin ; Ruth's gleaning song ; She is not mine ; Softly at thy window ; Sunshine ; Sweet queen of hearts ; Thirty years ago ; To Thee alone ; Village bells ; When Celia sings ; When thou art nigh ; You ask me for a song. Pf. music, etc.

Fripp, Edward Bowles, amateur organist and composer, born at Kingsdown, Bristol, January 29, 1787. He held the appointment of honorary organist successively at St. James' Church, Bristol ; Westbury, Gloucestershire ; and Hutton, near Weston-super-Mare. He died at Teignmouth, Sept. 1, 1870. He edited " Selection of Psalms and Hymns, adapted in portions for every Sunday and Festival of the Church of England " (1850) ; " Church Psalmody, a collection of tunes harmonised for four voices . " He also composed much music for the church service, including the hymn tune " Charmouth."

Frith, John, organist and composer of early part of the 17th century. He was organist of St. John's College, Oxford, and graduated Mus. Bac. in 1626. He died in

FROST.

1644. Composer of a degree exercise in seven parts and of other music.

Frost, Charles Joseph, organist and composer, born at Westbury-on-Trym, June 20, 1848. His father moved soon after to Tewkesbury, where he was schoolmaster and organist of Trinity Church. The son when quite a child played the pianoforte, organ, violin, and violoncello, and was soon actively engaged in concert work. His first organ appointment was at St. James', Cheltenham, 1865, from whence he returned to Westbury, as organist of Holy Trinity. During this time he made periodic visits to London, studying under George Cooper, John Goss, and others. He was next appointed to Holy Trinity, Weston-super-Mare, 1869 ; Holy Trinity, Lee, 1873 ; St. Mary, Haggerstone, 1876 ; Christ Church, Newgate Street, London, 1880 ; and since 1884 has been organist at St. Peter's, Brockley. He started a choral society there in 1885, and has given important concerts. In 1872 he was made F.C.O. ; graduated Mus. B., 1877 ; Mus. D., 1882, Cambridge. He has been, since 1880, a professor of the organ at the Guildhall School of Music ; is head of the Music Section in the Goldsmith's Institute, New Cross ; has given recitals at the Bow and Bromley Instute, and elsewhere. He is an examiner for the College of Organists, and I.S.M., has lectured in many places, and contributed a number of articles to *Musical Opinion,* and other papers. Of his voluminous compositions only a selection can be named. WORKS.—Oratorios, Nathan's Parable, 1878 ; Harvest Cantata, 1880 (both in MS.) ; Psalms 92 and 137, for soli, chorus, and organ ; Festival Te Deum ; services, anthems, hymn-tunes, and chants. Secular choral works : Lollipop Dick ; King John and the Abbot of Canterbury ; Sing a Song of Sixpence ; The Gipsies ; The Bell, and others. Songs : The Strawberry Girl, Paradise, and others ; Part-songs. Symphony for orchestra (MS.). *Organ:* Collection of organ pieces ; 55 hymn-tune voluntaries ; Sonata in A ; Forty preludes, 1880 ; 27 original pieces, &c. Two sets of six original pieces for harmonium ; Bouquet of Flowers, 24 pieces ; Seven sonatinas, &c., for pf.

Frost, Henry Frederick, organist and musical critic, born in London, March 15, 1848, son of THOMAS FROST (a well-known bass vocalist, died 1884), and ELIZA, his wife (contralto, born Redford). In 1856, he was appointed a chorister at St. George's Chapel, Windsor, where he soon became solo boy, and head of the school. He frequently sang in private before the Queen, and assisted at all the Royal functions there, and to the wedding of the Prince of Wales, in 1863. In 1865, began the study of the organ under Sebastian Hart, of St. Peter's, Great Windmill Street, Lon-

FRYE.

don ; became his assistant three weeks later ; and in December of the same year gained the post of organist, after competition, at the Chapel Royal, Savoy. Began his work as a critic in 1874, on the *Weekly Despatch,* being among the earliest champions of Wagner. In 1877, was associated with E. Prout on *The Academy,* and later on *The Athenœum,* taking the whole duty on this paper in 1888, and succeeding the last Desmond L. Ryan on the *Standard,* the same year. Professor of harmony and sight-singing, Madame Dolby's Academy, and professor of pf. at Guildhall School of Music, 1880. Resigned these posts in 1888, and his position at the Savoy Chapel Royal, 1891. Author of "Schubert," Great Musicians Series, Sampson Low, London, 1881. Lecturer on Wagner's Art works, at the Musical Association ; London Wagner Society, etc. Composer of Savoy Hymn-tunes and Chants, London, Novello. His daughter, BEATRICE FROST, soprano vocalist, studied under her father, and Hermann Klein, at the Guildhall School of Music, gaining the prize for soprano, 1895. Made her *début* at St. James' Hall, April 4, 1895 ; and gave her first concert at Steinway Hall, December 15, 1896. She has appeared at other concerts, and is gaining a good position.

Frost, William Alfred, alto vocalist, composer, and teacher, brother of the foregoing, born in London, November 7, 1850. Chorister at St. George's Chapel, Windsor, 1859-66. Returning to London in 1869, he was engaged as an alto in the choir of Archbishop Tenison's Chapel (afterwards consecrated as St. Thomas', Regent Street) ; in 1870, at St. Andrew's, Wells Street ; and in 1872, at All Saints', Margaret Street. He was then elected assistant vicar-choral at St. Paul's Cathedral, entering upon his duties, March, 1873. Appointed professor of pf. and assistant singing master in the Choir School, 1888, and succeeding the late W. A. Barrett as vicar-choral in 1891. Became general secretary of the Choir Benevolent Fund, 1889. As a teacher he has been specially successful in training altos. His compositions embrace a complete morning, communion, and evening service, for men's voices, written for St. Paul's Cathedral at the request of the then organist, (Sir) John Stainer ; an anthem, "I will go unto the Altar of God"; Songs, and part-songs. Author of an historical essay, "Good Friday and Easter Eve Communion, from the Days of the Apostles to the present time."

Frost, William Lane, organist and composer. He has written an opera, "Fred"; Cantatas, "Maldwyn the Crusader," produced Forest Hill, April, 1885, and "Lord of the Harvest." Pieces for pf., etc.

Frye, John Thomas, organist, was born in 1812. When only eight years old he was

FRYER.

appointed organist of St. Mary's Church, Saffron Walden, a post he held for 64 years, from 1820 to 1884, He died at Saffron Walden, October 23, 1887.

Fryer, G., compiler, issued " The poetry of various glees, songs, etc., as performed at the Harmonists," London, 1798.

Fulcher, John, musician and editor, born at London, August 18, 1830. He studied under Meyer Lutz and Alfred Mullen, and in 1855 settled in Glasgow as a teacher, where he held the appointment of choirmaster in Glasgow Cathedral, from 1868 to 1879. He died at Glasgow, July 10, 1893. Editor of " Lays and Lyrics of Scotland," with a Historical Epitome of Scottish Song by James Ballantine, etc., London, n.d. [1870]. *Songs:* Afton Water ; Bonnie, bonnie Bell ; Hurrah for the Highlands ; Where hath Scotland found her fame ? Transcriptions, etc., for pf. Part-songs (arrangements) ; Beauties of Scottish Song (with T. S. Gleadhill and Thomson). The accompaniments and arrangements of the Scottish songs in his collections are much richer than those written by Surenne, Dun, Mudie, and others, and are accordingly more acceptable to modern taste. His son, HENRY MACLEOD FULCHER, born at Glasgow, in January, 1856, is an organist and composer of ability, who has written some effective pianoforte music.

Fuller=Maitland, *see* MAITLAND, J. A. FULLER-

Fussell, Peter, or FUSSEL, organist, born about 1750. Succeeded James Kent as organist of Winchester Cathedral, in 1774, holding that appointment until his death, July, 1802. Taught Charles Dibdin, the elder, his notes, and trained other musicians who afterwards attained good positions.

Fyfe William, Wallace, Scottish writer, author of "Christmas, its customs and carols, with compressed vocal score of select choral illustrations," London [1860]; and various poetical and other works.

Gabriel, Mary Ann Virginia, composer, was born at Banstead, Surrey, February 7, 1825. She studied music under Pixis, Döhler, Thalberg, and Molique. Married to George E. March, November, 1874. She died at London, August 7, 1877, from the effects of a carriage accident.

WORKS.—*Cantatas :* Evangeline (Longfellow) ; Dreamland ; Graziella. *Operettas :* Widows Bewitched ; Grass Widows ; Shepherd of Cornouailles ; Who's the Heir ?; A Rainy Day. *Songs:* A farewell ; Ariel ; At her wheel the maiden sitting ; Across the sea ; Alone ; At rest ; A dead past ; A fisher's wife ; Alone in the twilight ; A mother's song ; Arden towers ; Asleep ; A song in the heather ; At my feet ; At the window ; Beryl ; Beside

GAFFE.

the sea ; Brighter hours ; Bye and bye ; Change upon change ; Chattering ; Calling the roll ; Corra Linn ; Dawn ; Dawn of Springtide ; Day is dying ; Dream, baby, dream ; Echo ; Eight fishers of Calais ; Emerald ; Fisherman's Widow ; Golden wedding day ; Happy days ; His work is done ; He will not come ; Hopeless ; In the gloaming ; Lady Moon ; Lost love ; Little blossom ; Little flowers ; Light in the window ; Lady of Kienast Tower ; Mountain echo ; My love ; Nightfall at sea ; Only at home ; Oh ! spare my boy at sea ; Only ; The Opal ring ; Pearl ; The Prodigal son ; Prisoner and the linnet ; Ruby ; Remembered ; Sweet seventeen ; Shadow light ; Somebody's darling ; Sacred vows ; Servian ballad ; Skipper and his boy ; The surprise ; Three roses ; Tender and true ; The ring ; Under the palm ; Wake my beloved ; Work ; Weep not for me ; When the pale moon ; Weary ; When sparrows build. Part-songs, pianoforte pieces, etc.

Gadsby, Henry Robert, composer, born at Hackney, London, December 15, 1842. Chorister at St. Paul's Cathedral, 1849-58, and self-taught in music beyond the instruction he then received from William Bayley, master of the boys. He was organist of St. Peter's, Brockley, Surrey, for some time up to 1884, in which year he succeeded John Hullah as professor of harmony at Queen's College, London, He is also a professor at the Guildhall School of Music. Member of the Philharmonic Society, and hon. F.R.C.O.

WORKS.—Psalm 130. *Cantatas :* Alice Brand, 1870 ; The Lord of the isles, Brighton Festival, 1879 ; Columbus (male voices), Crystal Palace, March, 1881 ; The Cyclops (male voices), Queen's College, Oxford, May, 1890 ; Music to Alcestis, 1876 ; to Andromache. Festal service in D, for eight voices ; Service in C, and others. *Anthems :* He is risen ; Rejoice greatly ; Sing, O daughter of Zion, etc. Part-songs. *Orchestral :* Symphonies in A, and C, movements from one performed at the Crystal Palace, February, 1871 ; Festal Symphony in D, Crystal Palace, November 3, 1888 ; Intermezzo and Scherzo, composed for the British Orchestral Society, produced, April 21, 1875. *Overtures :* Andromeda ; Golden Legend ; Witches Frolic. Orchestral scene, The Forest of Arden, produced by the Philharmonic Society, March 4, 1886. String quartet ; Andante and rondo, flute and pf. Author of Supplemental Book of Exercises for the use of those learning to sing at sight. Harmony, a treatise, and harmonisation of given melodies, London, 1884.

Gaffe, George, organist and conductor, born at Cawston, Norfolk, July 27, 1849. Chorister, Norwich Cathedral, at the age of nine, afterwards articled to Dr. Buck for seven years. In 1874 he was appointed

GALE.

organist of Oswestry Parish Church. While there he was associated with the late Henry Leslie in founding a Music school, and establishing a Choral Society, which afterwards figured in the Musical Festivals of that town. In 1880 he was appointed to St. Alban's Cathedral. He has given performances of oratorios in the Cathedral, and been active in promoting the cause of music, founding, in 1887, a School of Music, which is successfully carried on. He is a Fellow and Member of the Council of the Royal College of Organists.

Gale, Robert, musician, was born at London, August 4, 1769. He was for a time a tuner in the service of Messrs. Broadwood, and afterwards he became a music teacher in Edinburgh. Finally he settled in Ayr, where he held the appointments of precentor in the Relief Church, and afterwards in the Old Established Church, till 1843. He died at Glasgow in May, 1845.

He compiled " Psalm and Hymn Tunes, selected from the most approved composers ... to which is prefixed a clear and easy method of initiating the scholar in the rudiments of Music," Edinburgh, 1824-1840, three editions. He also composed the songs, " Scotland, I've no friend but thee," and " The Maid of Elderslie." He was an enthusiastic musician, and formed a small circle of equally earnest musicians, who all helped to improve psalmody in Ayrshire.

Gall, Rev. James, musician and clergyman, born at Edinburgh, September 27, 1808. He devoted much of his life to the Sunday School movement, and published a number of cheap musical works through the firm of James Gall & Sons, afterwards Gall and Inglis, of which he was a member. These comprised " Children's Hymn Books," " Scottish Psalm Tune Book," " English Hymn Tune Book," etc. He invented a cheap process of music printing which greatly facilitated his work. He also composed some hymn tunes.

Gamble, John, violinist and composer of 17th century. He studied under A. Beyland, and became a violinist in the private band of Charles II., etc. He died in 1657. He composed " Ayres and Dialogues," 1657. " Ayres and Dialogues for one, two, and three voyces," 1659.

Gandsey, John, a celebrated Irish piper, who was born in 1768, and died in 1857.

Gardiner, William, musician and writer, born at Leicester, March 15, 1770. He travelled much on the Continent. Died at Leicester, November 16, 1853.

WORKS.—Sacred Melodies, from Haydn, Mozart, and Beethoven, 6 vols., London, 1812, etc. Judah, an oratorio, adapted from the works of Haydn, Mozart, and Beethoven.

GARLAND.

Pope's " Universal Prayer " set to music by Haydn, Mozart, and Beethoven. The Music of Nature ; or, an attempt to prove that what is passionate and pleasing in the art of singing, speaking, and performing upon Musical Instruments, is derived from the sounds of the animated world...London, 1832. American reprint, Ditson, Boston, n d. Music and friends ; or, pleasant recollections of a Dilettante. London, 3 vols., 1838-1853. Sights in Italy ; with some account of the present state of music and the sister arts in that country. London, 1847.

Gardiner composed some songs under the pen name of W. G. Leicester. He is chiefly to be remembered as the author of " The Music of Nature," a work which contains much useful information and curious and occasionally eccentric speculations.

Gardner, Charles Graham, organist and pianist, born at Rotherhithe, Surrey, February 14, 1808. Studied under J. B. Cramer, Moscheles, W. Horsley, and Samuel Wesley. He was highly esteemed as a teacher, and numbered among his pupils H.R.H. Prince Arthur, The Duke of Connaught, who received lessons from him during the seven years he was studying in Woolwich. He was organist of St. Margaret's Church, Lee, for 36 years, and after his death, which took place October 31, 1869, the parishioners, by whom he was held in great esteem, erected a monument to his memory.

Gardner, Charles, pianist and composer, son of above, was born at Greenwich, April 1, 1836. He received his first instruction in music from his father, afterwards studying under Oliver May and Ernest Pauer (pianoforte), and J. McMurdie and G. A. Macfarren (composition). When the church of St. Michael and All Angels, Paddington, was consecrated, Charles Gardner was appointed organist and choirmaster, an office he held for some years, but he has for a long time given up organ work. For many years his Musical Matinées have been a feature of the London season. He is a member of the Philharmonic Society, and has since 1884 continuously held the office of a Director ; also professor of the pianoforte at the Guildhall School of Music, and L.R.A.M.

WORKS.—Trio for pf. and strings ; Sonata in A. Suite for pf., op. 40 ; Suite in five movements, op. 50., pf., and many smaller pieces. Educational publications : Technical Exercises for pf. students ; Diatonic and Chromatic scales, with rules of fingering ; Arpeggios of the Common Chord, and Dominant and Diminished Sevenths, &c.

Garland, Thomas, organist of latter half of 18th, and beginning of present centuries. He was organist of Norwich Cathedral till 1808, the year of his death. Chiefly remark-

GARLAND.

able as the teacher of several musicians who have attained fame.

Garland, William Henry, organist and conductor, born at York, in June, 1852. In his eighth year was placed as a chorister in the Minster, where he was distinguished as a solo boy. He was then articled to Dr. Monk. In 1878 he took the Mus. Bac. degree at Oxford, and in 1882 passed the examination for F.C.O. His first organ appointment was at St. Paul's Church, Rome, whither he went on the expiration of his articles. Here he remained for three years, when ill-health compelled his return to England. He next held the post of organist at Reading Parish Church for three years, and after a year's work as acting organist and choirmaster at York Minster (during Dr. Monk's absence through illness), was appointed to Halifax Parish Church in 1884. In 1886 he was elected conductor of the Halifax Choral Society, one famous in local musical history, established early in the century, and now flourishing. Six years later he received a similar appointment to the Bradford Festival Choral Society, and was divisional chorus master for the Leeds Musical Festival since 1892. He died at Halifax, February 13, 1897. His Degree Exercise was a setting of Psalm 23, and he published some Church music. His brother, CHARLES T. GARLAND, was a chorister, and afterwards a bass singer in the choir of York Minster. In 1874 he was appointed to Magdalen College, Oxford, where he is now the senior lay-clerk. He is also music-master at the College School.

Garrett, George Mursell, composer and organist, born at Winchester, June 8, 1834. Son of William Garrett, master of the choristers, Winchester Cathedral. Chorister of New College, Oxford, and pupil of Dr. Stephen Elvey. Studied later under S. S. Wesley. Assistant organist, Winchester Cathedral, 1851-4; organist of Madras Cathedral, 1854-6; of St. John's College, Cambridge, 1857; and organist to the University in 1873. Graduated Mus. Bac., 1857; Mus. Doc., 1867, Cambridge; and, by grace of the Senate, received the degree of M.A. *propter merita*, 1878. F.R.C.O. University lecturer in harmony and counterpoint, 1883. Examiner in Music for the University of Cambridge, for the Irish Intermediate Education Board, and other institutions. Conductor of St. John's College Musical Society, and solo pianist at its concerts, 1876, etc. Member of the Philharmonic Society.

WORKS.—Oratorio, The Shunammite, produced by the Cambridge University Musical Society, June 13, 1882, and given at the Hereford Festival of 1882. Cantatas: The Deliverance of St. Peter; Prayer and praise; Harvest Cantata; The Two Advents, com-

GASKELL.

posed for a choir festival, New York; Secular cantata, The Triumph of Love, produced by the Cambridge University Musical Society. Church Services in D, F, E flat, and E; Evening Service in B flat, written for St. James's Choir Festival, New York, and others. Anthems: Psalm 43; In humble faith and holy love; Praise ye the Lord (Harvest); Thy mercy, O Lord, written for the Festival of the London Church Choir Association, St. Paul's Cathedral, November 16, 1893, and various others. Chants, old and new, selected and arranged in order of daily use for one calendar month, with special chants for the Venite and Proper Psalms. Part-songs, songs, organ pieces, etc.

Garrow, Mrs., see sub ABRAMS, HARRIET.

Garth, John, organist and composer, born at Durham, 1722. He died in 1810. He published "The First Fifty Psalms, set to music by Benedetto Marcello," London, 8 vols., 1757. He also wrote much instrumental music, among other works, "Six sonatas for th harpsichord, two violins, and violoncello," op. 2, 1768. Six organ voluntaries, op. 3 [1780]. Thirty collects set to music, London, 1794. Avison aided Garth with the editing of Marcello's psalms.

Garth, Richard Machill, organist and composer, born at Pudsey, near Leeds, October 15, 1860. Educated at Batley Grammar School, and chorister at the Parish Church. Pupil of the late James Broughton, Leeds, for pianoforte; also studied under J. H. Collinson, Gustav Schreck, and others. After holding several appointments he became assistant organist of St. Mary's Cathedral, Edinburgh, 1882, later undertaking the duties of private organist to, among others, Sir Michael Shaw Stewart, of Ardgowan. Organist of Clark Memorial Church, Largs, 1893; Choirmaster St. Columba's Episcopal Church, Largs, at present time. Conductor of United Choir, Cumbrae, and, 1888, of the Greenock Choral Society. Elected a Fellow of the Educational Institute of Scotland, 1885. Has given organ recitals in London ("Inventions," 1885), Edinburgh, Glasgow, and Paris.

WORKS.—Ezekiel, dramatic oratorio, 1888; Choral ballads—Charge of the Light Brigade, 1889; Wild Huntsman, 1890. Full cathedral service in E flat; anthems, hymn-tunes, and chants. *Songs*: A message from the sea; Though years have lapsed; The heaving of the lead (prize), and others. Concerto in D, violin and orchestra; Six string quartets; Sonata in F, and other organ pieces; Six Lieder ohne worte, pf., &c. A number of arrangements, and a text-book on arrangements, for military bands. In MS. an opera, The brigand (libretto by Edward Oxenford).

Gaskell, James, organist and composer,

GASKIN.

born near Wigan, August 26, 1841. Studied pianoforte with C. A. Seymour, harmony with Dr. J. M. Bentley, and organ under F. H. Burstall. Organist, Parish Church, Pemberton, near Wigan; and from 1885, of St. Barnabas, Swindon, Wilts. Composer of a collection of anthems and hymn-tunes; songs, &c.

Gaskin, James J., musician, born about 1820; died at Dublin in 1876. Author of "Early History, etc., of Vocal Music." London, 1860.

Gason, Adam F., author of "A Short Treatise in Defence of Cathedral Worship," Dublin, 1846.

Gater, William Henry, organist and composer, born in Dublin, August 8, 1849. Musical training private; studied organ under Sir R. P. Stewart. Graduated Mus. Bac., Trinity College, Dublin, 1876, and B.A., 1881, with honours in English and modern literature; Mus. Doc., 1886. He also passed through the Divinity School, obtaining several prizes. Organist of Christ Church, Bray, 1871-3; to the Exhibition Palace, Dublin, 1872-3; St. Andrew's, Dublin, 1873; and since 1876, organist of St. Stephen's, Dublin. Choirmaster, for several years, to the East Meath Diocesan Choral Association. His compositions include a setting of Ps. 66, for soli, chorus, and organ; a cantata, "The Passions" (Collins), for soli, chorus, and orchestra; two services, and other Church music; hymn-tune, "From Greenland's Icy Mountains," Wrexham Eisteddfod Prize, 1888; organ pieces, etc., the greater part remaining still in MS.

Gates, Bernard, organist and composer, born in 1685. He was one of the children of the Chapel Royal, 1702; a Gentleman, 1708; and Master of the children from 1740 to 1758. He died at North Aston, near Oxford, November 15, 1773; in the Parish Church of which there is a memorial to him. His compositions, including a service in F, are mostly in MS.

Gattie, Henry, violinist. He was second violin in the Blagrove quartet, which commenced a series of chamber concerts in the Hanover Square Rooms, March 17, 1836. For years he was associated with chamber music in connection with Joseph Banister, Dando, and others; and was in repute as a teacher. He died in London, early in 1853.

Gatty, Alfred Scott, composer and writer, born at Ecclesfield, Yorks., April 25, 1847. Second son of Rev. Alfred Gatty, D.D., vicar of Ecclesfield, Sub-dean of York Cathedral, etc. Studied at Marlborough, and Christ's College, Cambridge. Rouge Dragon, Pursuivant of Arms, Herald's College, London, 1880. He has composed two operettas, "Sandford and Merton's Christmas Party," 1880; and "Not at Home," 1886. Is author

GAUNTLETT.

of "Little songs for little voices" (words and music), two books, published originally in *Aunt Judy's Magazine*; other books for children, illustrated by C. A. Doyle; and a large number of songs, True till death; O fair dove, O fond dove; Some future day; The open window; When love was a little boy, etc. Pianoforte music, etc.

Gaudry, Richard Otto, organist and composer, born at Dublin, 1800. He was chorister in the chapel of Dublin Castle, and organist of St. Anne's, Dublin. He died at Dublin, August, 1825. Composer of anthems, etc.

Gaul, Alfred Robert, organist and composer, born at Norwich, April 30, 1837. Of a musical family, he was entered as a chorister at Norwich Cathedral at the age of nine; afterwards articled pupil of Dr. Buck, and assistant or, anist. When seventeen he was appointed organist of Fakenham parish church, which he left in 1859, for St. John's, Lady Wood, Birmingham. He has been organist and choirmaster at S . Augustine's, Edgbaston, since the church was built in 1868. He graduated Mus. Bac., 1863, Cambridge. In 1887 he succeeded Mr. Stockley as conductor of Walsall Philharmonic Society, and for some years he held that and other similar offices in different places. He is now teacher of harmony and counterpoint, and conductor of the ladies' singing class at the Birmingham and Midland Institute; teacher of harmony and singing at King Edward's High School for Girls; and teacher at the Blind Asylum. He has conducted performances of his works in many towns, and played at the Bow and Bromley Institute in 1888.

WORKS.—Hezekiah, oratorio, produced by the Amateur Harmonic Association, Town Hall, Birmingham, November 29, 1861; Psalm 1 (degree ex.), 1863. Cantatas: Ruth, 1881; The holy city, produced at the Birmingham Festival, 1882; Passion music, 1883; Joan of Arc, produced by the Birmingham Festival Choral Society, 1887; The ten virgins, 1890; Israel in the wilderness, Crystal Palace, July 9, 1892; and Una, composed for the Norwich Festival, 1893. Psalm 150, performed by the London Church Choir Association, St. Paul's, 1886; The Lord is my Shepherd; Psalm 96, for eight-part chorus, and others; hymn-tunes, chants, &c. Ode, A song of life; The shipwreck, prize glee; The silent land, performed by Leslie Choir, Paris, 1878, and given at the Birmingham Festival, 1879; The singers; The day is done, and other part-songs, school cantatas, collection of trios, duets, &c. The ferry maiden; Faithful yet; The sea's love, and other songs. Sonata in B flat minor, and various pieces for pf.

Gauntlett, Henry John, organist and composer, born at Wellington, Shropshire, July

GAWLER.

9, 1805. Son of the Rev. Henry Gauntlett. Organist at Olney, Bucks., 1815. Articled for a time to a solicitor, 1826. Organist at St. Olave's, Southwark, 1827-47. Admitted as a solicitor, 1831. Commenced his labours in connection with the establishment of the C organ, 1836, which latterly took the place of the F and G instruments. Organist of Christ Church, Newgate Street, 1836. Gave up practice of the law, 1842. Mus. Doc., Lambeth, 1843. Organist of Union Chapel, Islington, 1852-61; Church of St. Bartholomew the Less, Smithfield, 1872. He died at Kensington, London, February 21, 1876.

Works.—Hymnal for Matins and Evensong, 1844 ; The Church Hymnal and Tune Book, 1844-51; Cantus Melodici, 1845 ; The Comprehensive Tune Book, 1846-7; The Hallelujah, 1848-55; The Congregational Psalmist, 1851 ; Carlyle's Manual of Psalmody, 1861 ; Tunes, New and Old, 1868; Harland's Church Psalter and Hymnal, 1868; The Encyclopædia of the Chant ; St. Mark's Tune Book ; The Choral use of the Book of Common Prayer, London, 1854. *Anthems*—I will go unto the altar of God ; This is the day the Lord hath made ; Thou wilt keep him in perfect peace, in E flat. Hymns and Christmas carols; One Hundred and Fifty-six Questions on the art of Music-making and the science of Music, London, 1864. Songs, glees, organ-music, &c. Revised, Jos. Williams' "Christmas minstrelsy, or carols, anthems," &c.

Mr. Gauntlett was in his lifetime recognised as one of the foremost organists and authorities on psalmody. His hymnals, psalms, etc., are compilations of the highest merit, the hand of the musician being always observable where too often we find the work of the officious reviser. His anthems are in frequent use, and his hymns are favourites. Among the latter may be named Alexandria, Braylesford, Bredon, Croyland, Denbigh, Gauntlett, Houghton, and Lux Alma.

Gawler, William, organist and teacher, born in Lambeth, 1750. He was organist in the Asylum for Female Orphans. He died in March, 1809. He compiled "Harmonia Sacra, or a Collection of Psalm Tunes, with interludes, and with a thorough-bass, forming a most complete work of Sacred Music," London, 1781. Dr. Watts's Divine Songs [1780]. Lessons for the harpsichord. Hymns and psalms used at the Asylum or House of Refuge for Female Orphans, London [1785]. Voluntaries, interludes, etc., for organ. Miscellaneous collection of fugitive pieces for harpsichord or pf. [1780]. Songs, etc.

Gawthorn, Nathaniel, English musician, was conductor of psalmody at the Friday lecture in Eastcheap, London, early in the 18th century. Compiler of "Harmo-

GEAR.

niæ Perfecta, a compleat collection of psalm tunes in four parts, fitted to all the various measures now in use, taken from the most eminent masters," London, 1730.

Gawthrop, James, tenor vocalist, born in York. Studied singing under J. B. Welch. Appointed in 1877 vicar-choral of Wells Cathedral ; in 1880, to St. George's Chapel, Windsor; and in 1885 made a Gentleman of Her Majesty's Chapel Royal, St. James's. As a concert singer he has been heard at the Covent Garden Promenade Concerts, in the chief provincial cities, etc.

Gay, George, stonemason and musician, born November 17, 1771, at Corsham (?), died there, July 26, 1833. Builder of Melksham Bridge, Wilts. Organ builder and verse writer. Organist of Corsham Independent Chapel, Wilts. Committed suicide by cutting through carotid artery with his own mallet and chisel. Composer of anthems and hymn tunes in 3, 5, and 8 parts. Compiler of "Sacred Music, consisting of 50 psalm and hymn tunes..to which are prefixed some original ideas calculated to improve the method of singing," London, 1827. In 1833 he revised T. Hawkes' "Collection of Tunes."

Gear, Henry Handel, tenor vocalist and composer, born at London, October 28, 1805. Son of an artist, who held the appointment of painter to the Duke of Sussex. He was a choir boy in the Chapel Royal and St. Paul's Cathedral ; but in 1822 he went to New York and became organist of Grace Church. In 1828 he proceeded to Italy, where he studied singing under Nozzari, etc., and afterwards he went to Frankfort and sang there, and in Paris. He finally settled in London as a professor of singing, and was for over 17 years organist of Quebec Chapel, Bryanston Street. Composer of church services, anthems, songs, etc. He died in London, October 16, 1884.

His third son, GEORGE FREDERICK GEAR, composer and pianist, was born at London, May 21, 1857. He studied under Dr. Wylde, and J. F. Barnett, and in 1872 gained a scholarship at the London Academy of Music. He gained medals for harmony and pianoforte playing, and was elected an associate and professor of the London Academy of Music, and an associate of the Philharmonic Society. Musical director of the German Reed Company from 1876 to 1892, and is a member of the Incorporated Society of Musicians, and the Musical Artists' Society. He has given many concerts, and has frequently appeared as a vocalist.

Works.—String quartet; Two pf. sonatas; Scena, for soprano voice and orchestra; "A water cure," and "Hobbies," 2 operettas. *Songs :* Day is done; My Lady sleeps; Sweet visions ; The rose is dead ; When night is gathering round ; White rose, etc.

GEARY.

Geary, E. M. Author of "Musical Education, with practical observations on the art of Pianoforte playing," London, 1841, 1848, and other editions.

Geary, Timothy, composer, born at Dublin, 1783 ; died in 1806. Composed glees, duets, and other vocal music. Known also as Thomas Augustine Geary.

Geaussent, George F., pianist and conductor, born in London, in 1852. Has held organ appointments at Hampstead Parish Church, and elsewhere. As a pianist he gave recitals at various times, and as conductor of a choir bearing his name, he gave high-class concerts, introducing, for the first time in London, important works, such as Dvořák's "Patriotic Hymn." Principal of the Hampstead Conservatoire of Music, and member of the Governing Council since its re-organisation in 1896. Also director for some years of a Conservatoire at Croydon ; and, 1896, Principal of Belfast Conservatoire of Music.

Gee, Samuel, organist, born at Congleton, Cheshire, May 12, 1834. Pupil and Associate, R.A.M. Organist successively at the Parish Church, Chertsey ; St. Peter and St. Paul, Wantage, 1861; Christ Church, Clapham, 1864 ; St. Mark's, Lewisham, 1870; and in his later years at Leek, Staffordshire. He read papers on various topics at meetings of the College of Organists, and was well-known as a teacher. He died suddenly of apoplexy, in his room at the Hanley Academy of Music, Staffordshire, November 15, 1892.

Geikie, James Stewart, composer and writer, born at Edinburgh, January 12, 1811. For a number of years musical representative of the *Scotsman.* Conductor of the Edinburgh Sacred Harmonic Association, and other societies of a kindred nature at Newington. He was conductor of psalmody at St. Augustine Church, Edinburgh, from 1843 till 1880. He died at Ormiston, Haddington, August 14, 1883. He composed a number of secular vocal pieces : " How beautiful is night," partsong ; " My heather hills," song, etc.: but his psalms and other sacred music will enjoy a more lasting popularity, He edited an edition of R. A. Smith's " Sacred Harmony," entitled, " Supplement to R. A. Smith's Sacred Harmony, adapted to the Psalms and Hymns used in the churches and chapels of Scotland," n.d. Also, " Songs of the Sanctuary, a collection of psalms, scripture hymns, etc.," 1863.

His sons, SIR ARCHIBALD GEIKIE, and JAMES GEIKIE, are the well-known scientists, while his brother WALTER was the famous artist and etcher.

Geoghegan, Joseph, vocalist and teacher, born at Ballinasloe, Galway, in 1830. He lived in Edinburgh, from about 1846, where he worked originally as a bookbinder. After-

GIBBONS.

wards he became choirmaster of Old Greyfriars Church, 1857-83, and teacher in various schools and colleges in Edinburgh. He died at Musselburgh, on January 27, 1892.

George, Miss, *see* OLDMIXON, LADY.

German, J. Edward, composer, violinist and conductor, born at Whitchurch, Shropshire, February 17, 1862. Entered the R.A.M. in 1880 as an organ student, i ut the next year took the violin as principal study. In 1885, he won the Charles Lucas medal for composition, his work being a setting of the *Te Deum* for chorus and organ. While at the Royal Academy he wrote many works of importance, some of which have been performed at concerts in various places. He left the Academy in 1887, and was made an Associate, and in 1895, a Fellow of that Institution. In 1889, he was appointed Musical Director at the Globe Theatre, London. He has conducted concerts at the Crystal Palace, 1893, and performances of his own music at the Leeds Festival, 1895, and elsewhere.

WORKS.—*Dramatic :* Operetta, The Rival Poets (R.A.M., July, 1886), St. George's Hall, December 21, 1886 ; Incidental Music to Richard III, Globe Theatre, 1889 ; Henry VIII, Lyceum, 1892; The Tempter (H. A. Jones), Haymarket, 1893; Romeo and Juliet, Lyceum, 1895 ; and As you like it (for Mr. Alexander), 1896. *Orchestral :* Symphony in E minor (R.A.M., July, 1886), Crystal Palace, December 13, 1890 ; in A minor, Norwich Festival, 1893. Gipsy suite, Crystal Palace, 1892; Suite in D minor, Leeds Festival, 1895; Suites arranged from music to Henry VIII., and The Tempter; Funeral March in D minor, Henschel Concerts, January 15, 1891. *Suites :* Flute and pf., 1892; in E minor, pf. Pieces for violin and pf., oboe and pf., clarinet and pf., etc. Serenade for tenor voice, with accompaniment for pf. and wind instruments; Songs, etc.

Ghilberti, Gilberto, *see* CAMPBELL, GILBERT JAMES.

Gibb, Alexander, violinist, composer, and dancing-master, who lived in Haddington and Edinburgh in the last thirty years of the 18th century. He had a dancing school in Edinburgh from 1786 to 1809, after which all trace of him disappears. He issued " A new collection of minuets, medlies, high dances, marches, strathspey and other reels, with entertaining tunes, etc., for the pianoforte, violin, and violoncello," Edinburgh, 1798.

Gibbons, Christopher, organist and composer, born in 1615. Baptised August 22. Son of Orlando Gibbons. He studied under Edward Gibbons at Exeter. Organist of Winchester Cathedral, 1638-61. Served for a time in Royalist army. Organist of Chapel Royal, 1660-76. Private organist to Charles

GIBBONS.

II., 1660. Organist of Westminster Abbey, 1660-65. Mus. Doc., Oxon., July, 1664. Died October 20, 1676. A few works by this musician exist in MS., such as his "Act-song" (a degree exercise), music to Shirley's Cupid and Death, a masque; Compositions in Playford's "Cantica sacra," etc., but it is as an organist that he was principally known.

Gibbons, Rev. Edward, organist and composer, born about 1570. Mus. Bac., Oxford, 1592, incorporated from Cambridge. Organist of Bristol Cathedral, 1592-1611. Organist of Exeter Cathedral, 1611-44. He died about 1650. Works in MS., anthems, etc.

Gibbons, Ellis, organist and composer, born at Cambridge about end of the 16th century. Brother of Edward. Organist of Salisbury Cathedral. He died about 1650. Composer of "Long live fair Oriana," madrigal for 5 voices; "Round about her chariot," for 6 voices; both contained in the "Triumphs of Oriana."

Gibbons, Orlando, organist and composer, born at Cambridge in 1583. Brother of Edward and Ellis Gibbons. Chorister in King's College, Cambridge, 1596. Organist of the Chapel Royal, March, 1604. Mus. Bac., Cantab., 1606; Bac. and Doc. Mus., Oxon., 1622. Organist of Westminster Abbey, 1623. He died at Canterbury, June 5, 1625. Buried in Canterbury Cathedral.

Works.—Morning and Evening Service, in F; Te Deum and Jubilate, in D minor; Venite exultemus, in F; Magnificat, Nunc Dimittis, in D minor and in F; Te Deum and Benedictus, in F. A collection of the sacred compositions of Orlando Gibbons (of which the scores are not contained in Boyce's collection) from the original MSS. and part books, together with a transposed organ-part to some of his published works. Edited by the Rev. Sir F. A. Gore Ouseley, 1873 (contains two services, two sets of preces, seventeen anthems, six hymn-tunes). *Single Anthems:* Hosanna; Lift up your heads; O clap your hands; Almighty and Everlasting; God is gone up (Boyce); O Lord, in Thy wrath; O Lord, in Thee; Why art thou so heavy? Blessed be the Lord; O Lord increase my faith; Deliver us, O Lord; Behold, thou hast made; This is the record of John; Behold, I bring you; I ſye is risen again (Ouseley); We praise Thee, O Father; Lord, grant grace; Glorious and powerful God See, see, the Word is incarnate; Sing unto the Lord; Blessed are all they; Great Lord of Lords; O Thou, the Central Orb. Hymns. Fantasies of III. Parts...composed for viols; London, 4to, 1610. Reprinted, edited by E. F. Rimbault (Music. Antiq. Soc.), London, fo., 1843. Lessons in "Parthenia" (with Bull and Byrd), London, 1611. First set of madrigals

GIBSON.

and motets, for five voices, London, 4to, 1612. Reprinted, edited by Sir G. Smart (Music. Antiq. Soc.), London, fo., 1841. Fancies and songs made at King James ye First's being in Scotland, London, n. d. Tunes for "Wither's Hymns " (Reprinted by the Spenser Society, 1881). Tunes in Leighton's "Teares," 1614. *Madrigal titles*—The silver swan ; I weigh not fortune's frown ; I tremble not ; I feign not friendship; Dainty fine bird ; Farewell all joys ; Oh! dear heart ; Ne'er let the Sun ; Trust not too much ; O that the learned poets ; Nay, let me weep ; Yet if that age; I see ambition ; Fair ladies that to love ; What is our life? etc, Galiards, fantasias, preludium, pavans, etc.

Gibbs, Joseph, organist and composer, born in 1699. For forty years he was organist at Ipswich. He died December 12, 1788. Composer of " Eight Solos for a violin with a thorough bass for the harpsichord or violin " [1740], etc. Some of his pieces have recently been re-published, and a sonata and other pieces performed by Mr. Otto Peiniger, 1885-7.

Gibson, Alfred, violinist, born at Nottingham, October 27, 1849. After some early lessons from his father, a good violin teacher, he studied for two years with Henry Farmer, after which time he was practically self-taught. He played with success, from the age of eleven, in differents parts of the country, and about 1868 went to London, and was engaged as first violin in the opera at Drury Lane. In 1871 he was appointed to the Royal Opera orchestra at Covent Garden, remaining there twelve years. He appeared at the Monday Popular Concerts, January 23, 1882, as a violinist in Svendsen's Octet, ultimately taking the position of principal viola, which he still retains. He succeeded Ludwig Straus as leader of the Queen's Private Band ; is professor of the violin at the R.A.M., and of the viola at the G.S.M. Among the fine instruments he possesses is a Stradivari viola formerly belonging to Charles Reade, the novelist.

Gibson, Edmund, bishop and writer, born at Brampton, Westmoreland, in 1669; died at Bath, in 1748. Wrote a number of antiquarian works, and a "Method or course of singing in Church; direction to the Clergy of the Diocese of London, 1727; etc."

Gibson, Francis, pianist and composer, born in Edinburgh, in 1861. After studying pianoforte and harmony five years with Mr. William Townsend, he entered Dr. Hoch's Conservatorium, Frankfort-on-the-Main, studying composition under Joachim Raff, and the pianoforte with Carl Faelten. Settling in Edinburgh as a teacher, he succeeded Mr. G. L. Deas as a professor of the pianoforte and theory at the Edinburgh Ladies' College, which, with other appointments, he still holds.

GIBSON.

He has played at various chamber concerts at Edinburgh, where some of his compositions have been performed. So far he has only published an Album of ten songs; a Serenade; and a Reverie for violin.

Gibson, Rev. James, D.D., clergyman and writer, was a professor in the Free Church College, Glasgow. Author of "The Public Worship of God: its authority and modes, Hymns and Hymn Books," Glasgow, 1869.

Gibson, Louisa, teacher and writer, born in London, 1833. For some years head professor of music, Plymouth High School for Girls. Authoress of "A First Book on the Theory of Music, applied to the Pianoforte," London, 6th edition, 1876; Second and third books of same; key to exercises in third book. Songs, etc.

Gibson, Mrs. Patrick, *born* ISABELLA MARY SCOTT, vocalist and composer, born at Edinburgh, in 1786. She was a daughter of William Scott, teacher of elocution, Edinburgh, and married Patrick Gibson, R.S.A., in 1818. She at one time kept a Boarding School for Young Ladies, in Inverleith Row, Edinburgh, and was an associate of many distinguished men of her time. Distantly related to Sir Walter Scott. She was consulted much by R. A. Smith in the composition of his songs and duets, and some of her psalm tunes are in Dr. Andrew Thomson's "Sacred Harmony," 1820, and in vol. 6 of Steven's "Church Music," edited by Turnbull, 1833. Her song "Loch-na-gar" is contained in the 6th vol. of R. A. Smith's "Scotish Minstrel." Mrs. Gibson was a skilful harp player. She died at Edinburgh, November 28, 1838.

Gibsone, Burford George Henry, composer of first half of present century. He is stated to have died about 1868. Composer of fantasias for the pf., songs, and glees. His "Table Book of Glees" [1840], contains original compositions.

Gibsone, Guillaume Ignace, composer and pianist, born in London, of Scottish parentage, about 1826. Studied under Moscheles. Resident in Brussels, 1845, where he gave concerts. In 1846 he was made an honorary member of the Societé de Grand Harmonie, Brussels. Toured in Germany the same year. Returned to London in 1850, where he settled as teacher and composer. His works include three Cantatas: The Wood Nymphs, The Elfin Knight, and The Three Sisters; an Opera and two Symphonies (in MS.); Sonata for violin and pf.; A large number of pf. pieces; Meditations, 24 pieces; Polonaise; Chanson à boire; Chanson d'amour: Four sketches, etc. *Songs :* My lady sleeps; Her voice; Sweet hour of eventide, etc.

Gick, Thomas, alto vocalist and composer, born in Liverpool, February 22, 1837. Musical

GILBERT.

training private. Appointed lay-clerk, York Minster, 1859; and in 1864, vicar-choral, Christ Church, and St. Patrick's Cathedral, Dublin; he is also a member of the choir of Trinity College, Dublin. He graduated Mus. Bac., 1880; Mus. Doc., 1882, Dublin; and is Examiner in Music under the Intermediate Education Board for Ireland. His compositions comprise a cantata, The Bard, for soli, chorus, and orchestra, Dublin, 1882; a morning and evening service in B flat, and an evening service in F. He has also published: O Come, let us worship; Hear, O thou Shepherd; Blessed is He, and other anthems, etc.

Gilbert, Alfred, pianist and composer, second son of Francis and Jane Gilbert, was born at Salisbury, October 21, 1828. Commenced his musical studies at the age of six, then became a pupil of Dr. Charles Corfe, and later, of Alexander Lucas, whose asssistant organist he was at St. Thomas's Church. In 1845 he entered the R.A.M., and soon after was made assistant organist of Hanover Chapel, Regent Street. He then held organ appointments successively at St. Matthew's, Spring Gardens; Chepstow; Mitcham; Kentish Town; and St. Mark's, Hamilton Terrace, but devoted himself chiefly to pianoforte playing and composition. In 1851 he commenced a series of classical chamber concerts with the sisters, Charlotte and Susanna Cole (*q.v.*), the former of whom he married in 1853. Concerts were also given by the Arion Choir, the Polyhymnian Choir, and other societies under his direction; and he has lectured on music at various institutions. A concert of his works was given in Rome in 1884, when he received the distinction of being elected *Socio onorario della Reale Accademia S. Cecilia.* He is director of the Musical Artists' Society; Society for the Encouragement of the Fine Arts; Member, and a director of the Philharmonic Society, and in 1896 elected orchestral manager in succession to Mr. W. H. Cummings; Member of the Court of Assistants of the Royal Society of Musicians; F.R.A.M. Mr. Alfred Gilbert, R.A., the distinguished sculptor, is his son.

WORKS.—Spectacular Cantatas: Abdallah; L'Amie du Drapeau. Operettas: The rival roses; Outwitted; Blonde or brunette. Quintet in E flat, for pf., strings, and four voices, performed in Rome, January 24, 1884. Trios in C, A, and B flat, pf. and strings; Sonata in F, pf. and violoncello. Suite for strings. Pieces for pf. and violin. A complete School for the pf. Classical Library, edited. Many smaller works.

Gilbert, Davies, writer and musician, compiled "Some Ancient Christmas Carols, with the tunes to which they were formerly sung in the West of England." London, 1823; 2nd ed.

K

GILBERT.

Gilbert, (Ernest) Thomas Bennett, composer and vocal teacher, born at Salisbury, October 22, 1833. Brother of Alfred Gilbert. He studied at the R.A.M. from 1847, and at Leipzig under Moscheles, Hauptmann, Richter, etc., in 1852. Organist successively of St. George's, Isle of Man, 1853; St. Barnabas, do., 1854; St. Paul, Newport, Mon., 1856; Parish Church, Abergavenny, 1857; St. Peter's, Walworth, 1861; St. George's, Southwark, 1864; and St. Matthew's, Southwark, 1867. He was afterwards a vocal trainer in London. Died at Gipsy Hill, London, May 11, 1885.

WORKS.—*Operettas* : Night in fairyland, 1861; Das Helldichein, Leipzig, 1851. Ramiro, cantata, 1879. *Orchestral :* Concert overture, 1853; Merry wives of Windsor, overture, 1854; String quartets in E flat and C; Trio for pf., violin, and 'cello, in F. *Pianoforte :* Nocturnes, scherzos, ballads, impromptus, dances, etc. Numerous part-songs and songs. Vocal exercises, for daily use, in 2 books; School harmony, London, n.d., various editions; Practical and natural method for the pianoforte, 2 books; and other works.

Gilbert, Walter Bond, composer and organist, born at Exeter, April 21, 1829. Studied under Alfred Angel, Dr. Wesley, and Sir H. Bishop. He was organist successively at Topsham, 1847; Bideford, 1849; Tunbridge, 1854; Maidstone, 1859; Lee, Kent, 1866; Boston, Lincolnshire, 1868; and in 1869 accepted a similar post at Trinity Episcopal Chapel, New York, which he still holds. He graduated Mus. Bac., Oxford, in 1854; and while in England, in 1888, took the degree of Mus. Doc., Oxford, his Exercise having been approved more than twenty-five years before. In 1886 he was made a Mus. Doc. of Trinity College, Toronto. His talent as a composer was shewn at an early age, and one of his most widely known works is a Cathedral Service written when he was seventeen. He is the composer of two oratorios: "The Restoration of Israel," and "St. John"; the last performed at Maidstone, in 1864. Also of church services, many anthems, and organ pieces, etc. Editor of Hymnal and Canticles of the Protestant Episcopal Church, New York (with Rev. A. B. Goodrich, D.D.), 1875; The Psalter, or Psalms of David, New York, 1882. The well-known hymn tune, "Maidstone," was first published in the "Parish Tune Book" of Mr. G. F. Chambers, in 1862. Author of The Antiquities of Maidstone, 1865; Memorials of All Saints' Church, Maidstone, 1864; and other historical works.

Gilbert, William Schwenck, dramatist, and opera librettist, born in London, November 18, 1836. Educated for the Bar, and graduated B.A., London. Clerk in the Privy

GILMER.

Council Office, 1857-62. Called to the Bar of the Inner Temple, 1864. In 1891 his name was added to the Commission of the Peace for the County of Middlesex. His first dramatic piece, "Dulcamara," was produced, St. James's Theatre, 1866; but here it is only necessary to name his operas and operettas. These are: Princess Toto (Clay), 1875; The Mountebanks (Cellier), 1892; Thespis, 1871; Trial by Jury, 1875; The Sorcerer, 1877; H.M.S. Pinafore, 1878; Pirates of Penzance, 1880; Patience, 1881; Iolanthe, 1882; Princess Ida, 1884; Mikado, 1885; Ruddigore, 1887; The Yeomen of the Guard, 1888; Gondoliers, 1889; Utopia, 1893; and The Grand Duke, 1896, all set by Sullivan, (*q.v.*)

Gildon, John, composer and pianist, who flourished in the latter part of last, and early part of the present century. He composed a large quantity of pf. music, including sonatas, as well as songs and other pieces.

Giles, Nathaniel, composer and organist, born near Worcester, about 1548-50. Bac. Mus., Oxon., 1585. Doc. Mus., Oxon., 1622. Organist of St. George's Chapel, Windsor, and master of choristers, do., 1595. Master of Children of Chapel Royal, 1597, and organist, 1625. He died on January 24, 1633. Buried in St. George's Chapel, Windsor. " His services and anthems announce his learning and abilities, and, by the lovers and judges of church composition, are regarded as masterly productions."—*Busby*. He composed a complete service in C, in Barnard's Collection, and other compositions by him are in Leighton's " Teares," and various MS. collections.

His father, THOMAS GILES, or Gyles, was an organist, and succeeded John Redford as organist of St. Paul's Cathedral.

Gill, William Henry, composer and writer. Author of "The Musical ladder; or Tonic sliding scale," London [1864]. Composer of "Easy Anthems for village choirs" [1888-91]; "Voluntaries from Handel, Mendelssohn, etc." *Part-songs :* Before sweet nightingale: Three merry maids; When twilight dews, etc. Songs.

Gilmer, Alfred Walker, cornet player and conductor, was born in the parish of St. Margaret, Westminster, in 1838. As a child he played the violin, but was afterwards sent to Paris to study the cornet under Joseph Arban. His first important engagement was as first violin in a Manchester theatre, and about 1858 he joined the orchestra of the Theatre Royal, Birmingham, that town from henceforth being his home. His ability as a cornet player secured him engagements at the best orchestral concerts in the locality, and for some years he was a member of the Festival orchestra. In conjunction with Henry Synyer (*q.v.*) he formed a military band, which acquired a high reputation in the

GILMORE.

GLEADHILL.

Midlands. He was also bandmaster of the Worcestershire Yeomanry Regiment, and his annual concerts in Worcester were great events. Many of his pupils obtained good positions as cornet players. He died at Birmingham, May 16, 1892.

Gilmore, Patrick Sarsfield, bandmaster and composer, born near Dublin, December 25, 1829. Joined a military band at Athlone while a youth, and went to Boston, U.S.A., when nineteen, as a cornet player. He was for several years salesman in a music store there. In 1858 he organised a band bearing his name, which gained a high reputation, and in 1863 he was appointed director of military bands in Louisiana. The musical arrangements in the Peace Jubilee at Boston in 1869 were under his direction. He toured in Europe with his band in 1878. It is stated that his was the first military band to perform the *Tannhäuser* overture. He wrote a History of the National Peace Jubilee and great Musical Festival in Boston, 1869; Diatonic and Chromatic Scales for the Cornet; much Military band music; and composed some songs that became very popular, as— Good news from home; Building castles in the air; Freedom on the old plantation, etc. He died at St. Louis, September 25, 1892.

Gilmour, Robert, musician, who was a teacher in Paisley at the end of last century. He compiled "The Psalm-Singer's Assistant, being a collection of the most approved psalm and hymn-tunes . . . with a compendious introduction, for the use of learners . . ." Paisley [1793]; second edition, Glasgow, n.d.

Gilson, Cornforth, teacher and writer. Was originally a chorister in Durham Cathedral, and latterly Master of Music in the Edinburgh city churches, 1756. He was made Music-master of Heriot's Hospital, Edinburgh, in 1757-1764, and after a residence in London for a time, was re-appointed in in 1771. He died at Edinburgh after 1774. He wrote "Lessons on the practice of Singing, with an addition of the church tunes, in four parts, and a collection of hymns, canons, airs, and catches, for the improvement of beginners," Edinburgh, 4to, 1759. "Twelve songs for the voice and harpsichord," Edinburgh, 1769. Gilson did much to improve psalmody in the Edinburgh churches.

Girvin, John, musician and writer, who was born in Edinburgh in the first half of the 18th century. He was precentor of the Tron Kirk, Glasgow, 1761-62, and a teacher in Glasgow. He afterwards went to Port-Glasgow as a teacher in 1762. Published "A New Collection of Church Tunes," Glasgow, 1761. Author of "The Vocal Musician, Part I., wherein the grounds of music are distinctly handled, the intervals explained, and their use in practice fully shown, etc.

Illustrated with plates. For the use of Schools" (preface dated Port-Glasgow, 1763), Edinburgh, 1763.

Gladstanes, Frederick, composer, who flourished during the first half of the present century. He composed "Six Glees for 3 and 4 voices," 1830, and other glees published separately. His other works consist chiefly of pf. music and songs.

J. C. GLADSTANES, probably a relative of the above, composed "The Indian," and other glees, songs, etc.

Gladstone, Francis Edward, composer and organist, born at Summertown, near Oxford, March 2, 1845. Articled pupil of Dr. S. S. Wesley, 1859-64, then appointed organist of Holy Trinity, Weston-super-Mare. In 1866 he was chosen organist of Llandaff Cathedral, and in 1870 appointed to Chichester Cathedral. This post he resigned in 1873, and went to reside at Brighton, where he remained until 1876, when he removed to London, and became organist of St. Mark's, Lewisham. He accepted the post of organist of Norwich Cathedral, December, 1877, and in 1881 returned to London, acting as organist of Christ Church, Lancaster Gate, until 1886. The next year he was received into the Roman Catholic Church, and was director of the choir at St. Mary of the Angels, Bayswater, up to 1894. He graduated Mus. Bac., 1876; Mus. Doc., 1879, Cambridge. He is an Hon. R.A.M., F.R.C.O., and a Member of the Board of Musical Studies at Cambridge. Professor of counterpoint, etc., Trinity College, London, 1881; Professor of harmony and counterpoint, R.C.M., 1883; and examiner for various institutions.

WORKS.—*Cantatas :* Nicodemus, produced by Highbury Philharmonic Society, December 13, 1880; Philippi, Newcastle Cathedral, July 26, 1883; and Constance of Calais, Highbury, May 18, 1885. Morning and Evening Service in F; Anthems. Mass in E minor, written for the Brompton Oratory; Mass in E flat, four voices and organ, 1888. Church music, various, in MS. A wet sheet and a flowing sea, chorus and orchestra, Highbury, 1880. Overture, string quartet, Trio, pf. and strings, 1876, all in MS. Sonata in A minor; Twelve original pieces; Ten pieces; Three preludes, and other organ music. The Organ Students' Guide, several editions. Editor of Select Anthems from the works of English composers.

Glasgow, James, Irish clergyman and writer. Was professor of divinity in the Irish Presbyterian Church. Author of "Heart and voice: instrumental music in christian worship not divinely authorised"...n.d.

Gleadhill, Thomas Swift, composer and teacher, born at Edinburgh, January 30, 1827. Son of Benjamin Gleadhill, a musician, who was born in Derbyshire, April, 1789;

GLEDHILL

and died at Edinburgh, October 6, 1859. He resided in Glasgow and Edinburgh as a teacher, compiler, and choirmaster, from 1857. In 1889 he was appointed organist of the Parish Church of Peterhead, and on September 21, 1890, he drowned himself in the sea. He wrote or compiled the following works:—Beauties of Scottish song (with Fulcher and Thomson), Glasgow, n.d. Harmonium Album (popular airs arranged). Harmonium Repository (do.). Children's songs (with J. Thomson). Scottish airs arranged as part-songs, and for the pf. Lyric Gems of Scotland, Glasgow, n.d. Songs of the British Isles, 2 vols. Original songs, among which may be named, " Be kind to auld Grannie " ; " Thorn-tree " ; " Farewell to the land," etc.

Gledhill, John, pianist and composer, was one of the early students at the R.A.M., a fellow-pupil being Sterndale Bennett. He was made an Associate, and afterwards studied at Leipzig. For some years he was a professor at the R.A.M. From about 1876 he settled in Brighton as a teacher. He died there in 1891, having been disabled some three years previously by a stroke of paralysis. He composed a number of pf. pieces, and several sets of songs, etc.

Glen, Alexander, bagpipe maker, was born at Inverkeithing, Fife, in 1801. He was established in business in Edinburgh, and died there in March, 1873. He issued " The Caledonian Repository of Music for the Great Highland bagpipe . . ." Edinburgh, 1870.

His son, DAVID (born at Edinburgh in 1850), who succeeded to the business, issued a " Collection of Highland bagpipe music . . ." Edinburgh, 1876-1880, 2 parts ; and a " Highland Bagpipe tutor, with a selection of quick-steps, strathspeys, reels, etc.," Edinburgh, 1866. In 1896 this firm supplied sets of bag-pipes for use in the French army.

Glen, Annie, soprano vocalist and writer, of present time. Gave her first concert at Steinway Hall, London, January 25, 1883. Is known as the author of " Music in its Social Aspect," and an elaborate treatise, " How to Accompany," London, Cocks & Co.

Glen, Thomas Macbean, musical instrument maker, brother of Alexander, was born at Inverkeithing, Fife, in May, 1804. He established a musical instrument business in Edinburgh, in 1827, and made bagpipes, flutes, and other instruments. He invented a wooden Ophicleide, called a Serpentcleide ; and the system of modern music-holders for military band instruments. He died in Edinburgh, July 12, 1873. Publisher of " A new and complete tutor for the great Highland bagpipe . . . Edinburgh, n.d., 2 vols.

His son, JOHN (born at Edinburgh in 1833), succeeded to the business in company with his brother Robert in 1866. He compiled

GLOVER.

" The Glen Collection of Scottish Dance Music . . . arranged . . . for the pianoforte. Containing an introduction on Scottish dance music, sketches of musicians, and music-sellers . . . and a chronological list of works, ' Edinburgh, book 1, 1891 ; book 2, 1895. An accurate and valuable work. This he intends to follow up with a work on " Early Scottish Melodies," designed to clear up the misconceptions regarding their origin and history which have arisen. His brother, ROBERT (born at Edinburgh in 1835), is an artist and skilful mechanic, who has acquired a collection of musical instruments of some archæological value. The firm of J. & R. Glen has issued some books of instructions for playing the Bagpipe, and various collections of bagpipe music, among which may be named " Collection for the great Highland bagpipe, containing instructions and 52 marching, dancing and slow airs, etc." Edinburgh, n.d., 3 parts.

Glencorse, Peter, choir conductor and teacher, was born at Edinburgh, April 17, 1852. He studied under James Sneddon, A. C. Mackenzie, G. C. Martin, etc. He sang in various Edinburgh choirs as a bass, and in 1883 succeeded Joseph Geoghegan as choirmaster of Old Greyfriars Church. As conductor of a choral society in Edinburgh, Mr. Glencorse has produced many good works with much acceptance.

Glossop, Mrs., born FEARON, operatic vocalist, who sang at La Scala, Milan, in 1823-25, and appeared at the King's Theatre, London, in 1834. She married Joseph Glossop, the impresario, and was the grandmother of the late Sir Augustus Harris the theatrical manager.

Glover, Charles William, composer and violinist, born, London, February, 1806. He studied under T. Cooke, and became violinist at Drury Lane and Covent Garden Theatres. He afterwards acted as musical director of the Queen's Theatre from 1832. Died, London, March 23, 1863. He published a very large number of songs and pf. pieces, very few of which now survive.

Glover, J. H. L., composer and writer, author of a " Concise Organ Tutor," London (Goddard), n.d. Te Deum, songs, pf. music.

Glover, John William, composer, organist, and teacher, born at Dublin, June 19, 1815. He studied in Dublin, and became a violinist in the Dublin orchestra in 1830. In succession to Haydn Corri he became director of the cathedral choir, and in 1848 was appointed professor of vocal music in the Normal Training School of the Irish National Education Board. In 1851 he established the Choral Institute of Dublin, and was connected with the organisation of the musical commemorations of O'Connell, Moore, and

GLOVER.

Grattan. He has lectured on Irish music in Dublin and London, and has been active in promoting the cultivation of choral music in Ireland.

WORKS.—*Operas :* Deserted Village (Goldsmith, dramatized by Edmund Falconer) London, 1880 ; Two Italian Operas by Metastasio (MS.). *Cantatas, etc. :* St. Patrick at Tara (O'Connell centenary), 1870 ; Erin's Matin Song, Patria, 1873 ; " One hundred years ago," Ode to Thomas Moore, 1879. Masses, hymns, songs, etc. Concerto for violin and orchestra in A ; Fantasias ; Concertos and other music for organ ; Pf. music, etc. He also edited Moore's Irish Melodies, 1859, and a large number of musical works for school use.

His daughter, ERMINIA (Mrs. Mackey), was a harpist. She died at Dublin, in June, 1883.

Glover, Sarah Ann, musician and teacher, daughter of the Rev. Mr. Glover, of Norwich, was born at Norwich, 1785. Died at Malvern, October 20, 1867. She invented the Tonic Sol-fa system of musical notation, which the Rev. John Curwen afterwards modified and changed till its present form was reached. To Miss Glover much credit is necessarily due for the commencement of the system now so universally used in Britain. She published " A manual of the Norwich Sol-fa System . . . . ". [1845] ; "Manual containing a Development of the Tetrachordal system," London [1850].

Glover, Stephen, composer, brother of C. W. Glover, was born at London, in 1812. He was a teacher and composer in London, and died there on December 7, 1870.

WORKS.—*Songs :* Annie on the banks o'Dee ; Mary Astore ; Oh ! give me back my childhood's dreams ; The maiden's dream ; Dreams of childhood ; I dream of thee ; The minstrel knight ; The river of song ; Woman's wiles ; Yes or no ; Abide with me ; Autumn eve ; Bonnie Teviotdale ; Beware ; Break, break, break ; Down the green lane ; Ellen Vane ; Fair rose of Killarney ; Flower of the south ; Fond memory ; Good words ; I love him, yes ; Ildegonda ; King of the ocean wave ; Lays of the London season ; Merry mountain maid ; May Queen ; Oh far the bloom o' my ain native heather ; Oh ye mountain streams ; Pearl of the east ; Songs of other years ; There once was a knight ; Underneath your window ; Winter night ; Would you remember me. *Duets :* The cuckoo ; The dove ; The fairies' serenade ; The gleaners ; Our bark is on the Rhine ; Return of the swallows ; Savoyard maids ; The skylark ; Hymn to the night ; Stars of the summer night ; The curfew bell ; The gipsy countess ; To the woods ! to the woods ; Voices of the night ; What are the wild waves saying ? Four-part songs, trios, etc. Pianoforte music, transcriptions, etc.

GODDARD.

Glover, William, organist and composer, was born at London, in 1822. He was a chorister in Trinity College, Cambridge, 1829-38, and studied under Walmisley. Organist successively of Christ Church, Cambridge, 1841-42 ; St. Matthew's, Manchester, 1842 ; St. Luke's, Cheetham, 1846.

He has composed two oratorios " Jerusalem," 1848, and " Emmanuel," 1851, both produced at Manchester ; The " Corsair," cantata, 1849 (printed 1856) ; Chamber music, pf. music, songs, etc.

Glover, William Howard, composer and violinist, born at Kilburn, London, June 6, 1819. Son of Mrs. Glover, the actress. He studied music under Wagstaff, and for a time travelle ι in Europe. Member of the staff of the *Morning Post.* Resided in U.S.A. from 1868, and died at New York, October 28, 1875.

WORKS.—*Operas and operettas :* Ruy Blas, Covent Garden, London, October, 1861 ; Aminta, Haymarket, London ; Once too often ; The Coquette ; Palomita, or the Veiled Songstress. Tam o' Shanter, cantata, London, July, 1855 ; Overture for orchestra, Manfred ; Twelve Romances for pf., in 2 books ; Vocal quartets, duets, etc. Miscellaneous pf. music ; Songs for voice and pf.

Goddard, Arabella (DAVISON), pianist, born at St. Servan, near St. Malo, Brittany, January 12, 1836. Daughter of Thomas Goddard (died at Boulogne, July 19, 1890), of a Salisbury family. When a little child of four she played in public in her native village, and two years later received instruction from Kalkbrenner, in Paris. At the age of eight she played before the Queen and Prince Consort at Buckingham Palace, and at the same age (1844), published six Waltzes for pianoforte (D'Almaine). Her instructors at this time were Mrs. Anderson, and Thalberg. She made her *début* at the Grand National Concerts at Her Majesty's Theatre, October 30, 1850. For the next three years she studied with J. W. Davison (*q.v.*), to whom she was married in 1860. She also studied harmony under G. A. Macfarren. Her reappearance took place at Willis's Rooms, April 14, 1853, at a concert of the Quartet Association, when she played Beethoven's Sonata in B flat, Op. 106. On May 11, she played at the New Philharmonic Concerts, Bennett's Concerto in C minor ; and the same work at the Philharmonic, where she played for the first time, June 9, 1856. In 1854-5 she toured in Germany, and played at the Gewandhaus Concerts, Leipzig, January 11, 1855, Mendelssohn's D minor Concerto. Returning to England she was recognised as one of the greatest pianists of the time. She appeared at the Crystal Palace, March 15, 1858 ; Leeds Festival, 1858 ; Birmingham, 1861-70 ; Gloucester, 1865 ; and

GODDARD.

at all the leading concerts throughout the country. She first appeared at the Popular Concerts, March 9, 1859, at an extra Mozart Night, on a Wednesday; and was for many years associated with that undertaking In 1873 she left for a tour in Australia, America, and all round the world, returning in 1876. About 1880 she gave up public work, and devoted herself to teaching; but reappeared at Sims Reeves's Concert, March 21, 1882. Later, her health failing, she retired to Tunbridge Wells, where she still resides. She published a ballad, and some pf. pieces, 1852-3. A concert was given for her benefit in St. James's Hall, March 9, 1890.

Goddard, Joseph, writer and composer, born in 1833. Author of "Moral Theory of Music," 1857; "Philosophy of Music: a series of essays," London, 1862; "Musical Development, or remarks on the spirit of the principal Musical Forms," London, n.d. ; "New Graduated Method for the Pianoforte," n.d.; "Time Exercises for the use of Pianoforte Students," n.d.; "A study of Gounod's sacred Trilogy, 'The Redemption,'" London [1883]. Contributions to *Musical Times*, 1885, etc. Songs, pf. music, etc.

Godding, James Henry, organist and composer, born about 1820. He was organist for nineteen years of the Parish Church of Newbury, where he died, April 20, 1884. Compiler of "Parochial Psalmodist, being a collection of psalm and hymn tunes," London, n.d., with appendix.

Godfrey, Charles, bandmaster and composer, born at Kingston. Surrey, November 22, 1790. At an early age became a drummer in the First Royal Surrey Militia; posted to the band of the Coldstream Guards, corporal, April 10, 1820 ; Sergeant, May 3, following; and Master of the band, February 5, 1825. Discharged from military engagement, July 8, 1834, but continued as civilian bandmaster until his death, December 12, 1863. Was present with the band in Paris, 1815. Musician in ordinary to the King, 1831. He arranged a good deal of music for military bands. Three of his sons became distinguished bandmasters:—

GODFREY, DANIEL, the eldest son, born at Westminster, September 4, 1831, was educated at the R.A.M., of which institution he is a Fellow, and also professor of military music. Appointed bandmaster of the Grenadier Guards, August 29, 1856. Gazetted Honorary Second Lieutenant in the army, June 21, 1887, the first English bandmaster to hold Her Majesty's Commission; Travelled with his band in the United States of America, 1872. Has arranged much music for military bands, and is the composer of the "Mabel," "Hilda," and other waltzes, etc. In 1896 he retired from the army, and formed a band of his own.

GOMEZ.

Received a testimonial from the officers of the Guards, March 8, 1897. His son, DANIEL EYERS GODFREY, L.R.A.M., was appointed conductor of the London military band, 1890. He toured in South Africa, 1891-2, and since his return has established his reputation as a bandmaster at the Crystal Palace, Bournemouth, etc. He has published some pieces for pf.

GODFREY, ADOLPHUS FREDERICK, second son of Charles Godfrey, was born in 1837. He was educated at the R.A.M., and made a Fellow. Entered the Coldstream Regiment, September 2, 1856; served with his father as sergeant of the band, and succeeded him as bandmaster, December 14, 1863. Was compelled to resign owing to ill-health, 1880, and died, August 28, 1882. He wrote a number of dance pieces, and other music of a popular character.

GODFREY, CHARLES, third son of Charles Godfrey, was born January 17, 1839. Student and Fellow, R.A.M. Bandmaster of the Scots Fusilier Guards, 1859-68, and of the Royal Horse Guards from 1868 to the present time. He is professor of military music at the R.C.M., and at the Guildhall School. His compositions and arrangements are very numerous, including the popular Princess Beatrice, Princess Louise, Blush Rose waltzes, etc., and he is editor of *The Orpheus*, a military music periodical. He has three sons who are musicians: ARTHUR E. GODFREY, student and associate, R.A.M., who was appointed musical director at the Shaftesbury Theatre, London, 1890, and is the composer of a string quartet, songs, etc. CHARLES GEORGE, also a student, R.A.M., and composer of some orchestral pieces and songs; and HERBERT A. GODFREY, who was appointed bandmaster at Christ's Hospital.

Goldwin, John, or GOLDING, organist and composer, born in 1670. He studied under Dr. W. Child. Organist St. George's Chapel, Windsor, 1697. Master of the Choristers, do., 1703. He died at Windsor, November 7, 1719. He composed a service in F; Anthems: Behold my servant; I will sing unto the Lord; O Love the Lord; O praise God in His Holiness, etc.

Gomez, Alice, vocalist (mezzo-soprano), was born at Calcutta, her father being of Spanish and her mother of Portuguese descent. She studied under Mr. T. Henry Webb, organist of the Protestant Cathedral, Calcutta, also learning the organ sufficiently well to be able to play a service. At first her voice was a high soprano, and she studied such *rôles* as Leonora in "Trovatore." Ultimately, her voice settled into a mezzo-soprano of great compass, and remarkable evenness and purity of tone. She left Calcutta in 1885, and made her first appearance in England at a concert

GOODBAN.

GOSS.

given by Mr. Webb, at the Kensington Town Hall, July 14, 1885. Her *début* at the Crystal Palace took place April 9, 1887, and she now holds a high position as a concert-singer, having appeared at the principal concerts in London and the provinces. In 1891, she was married to Mr. Webb, now resident at Torquay.

Goodban, Thomas, composer and writer, was born at Canterbury, December, 1784. Chorister Canterbury Cathedral. He studied music under S. Porter, and was afterwards articled to a solicitor. Resigned the Law in 1798. Lay-clerk Canterbury Cathedral, 1809. Leader of the Catch Club, Canterbury, 1810. He died at Canterbury, May 4, 1863.

WORKS.—Glees, songs, pf. music. New and complete guide to the art of playing the violin, London, 1810. Guide to the piano, 1811. Rudiments of music, London, 1825 ; new edition, 1836. New and complete introduction to singing, London, 1829.

His son CHARLES (1812-1881) was a Mus. Bac., Oxon., 1847, and composed some miscellaneous pieces, the "Vocal Album" (1850), etc. HENRY WILLIAM, A.R.A.M., another son, born 1816, is a violoncello player and composer, having written "Bayham Abbey ;" overture, Crystal Palace, 1885 ; pf. music and songs. THOMAS GOODBAN, a third son, born 1822, is a violinist, and JAMES FREDERICK GOODBAN, A.R.A.M , a nephew, is an organist and composer.

Goodgroome, John, composer, born in 1630. He was a chorister of St. George's Chapel, Windsor, and became a gentleman of the Chapel Royal in 1660. Musician in ordinary to the King, 1664 He died in June, 1704. Composer of concerted sacred and secular vocal music, songs, etc.

Goodhart, Arthur Murray, assistant classical master at Eton College, has composed a ballad for chorus and orchestra, "Earl Haldan's Daughter," produced, London, January 21, 1891 ; A "Dorian song" (founded on W. Jackson's Canzonets, by F. Corder), for soprano solo, chorus, and orchestra ; "Arethusa"; School songs, etc. He graduated Mus. Bac., 1892, Cambridge; B A., 1888 ; M.A., 1894.

Goodson, Richard, composer and organist, born about the middle of the 17th century. Organist Christ Church and New College, Oxford. Mus. Bac., Oxon., 1682, and Professor of Music at Oxford University, in succession to Edward Lowe, July, 1682. He died, January 13, 1718. Composer of a few odes, songs, etc., mostly in MS.

His son, RICHARD, born in latter part of 17th century, was organist of Newbury till 1709. Mus. Bac., Oxon., 1716. He succeeded his father as organist of Christ Church and New College, Oxford, and in the Professorship

of Music, 1718. He died June 9, 1741. His compositions, in MS., are preserved in the library of Christ Church, and in the Music School at Oxford.

Goodwin, Amina Beatrice, pianist, born at Manchester, daughter of John Lawrence Goodwin, violinist and conductor (died, May, 1883). Received her first lessons from her father, and appeared in public at the age of six. Studied at Leipzig Conservatorium under Reinecke and Jadassohn; and later, under Delaborde, at Paris. Gave concerts in Manchester in 1882; played at Covent Garden Promenade Concerts, November, 1883 ; and appeared at the Crystal Palace, April 12, 1884, playing Mendelssohn's Concerto in D minor. Previous to this she had enjoyed the advantage of studying under Liszt, at Weimar. Later, she studied with Madame Schumann, making her *rentrée* in London in 1892, and now ranking among the leading pianists of the day. In 1895 she founded a Pianoforte College for ladies. She is married to Mr. W. Ingram-Adams, an American, whose new national anthem she has set to music. She has composed some pieces for pf., and is author of Practical Hints on the Technique and Touch of Pianoforte Playing, Augener, 1892.

Goold, Rev. Ebenezer, writer on music. Studied privately. Graduated Mus. Bac., 1883 ; M.A., 1883, Dublin ; Mus. Bac., 1884, London. Has composed a setting of Psalm 46, for solo, chorus, and orchestra. Author of Story of the Messiah ; Descriptive programme of the great musical works.

Gordon, George, Roman Catholic minister and musician, was born at Fochabers, Elgin, March 27, 1776. He was a violinist and composer, and issued two collections of sacred music for the use of choirs. He studied at Valladolid for the Roman Catholic priesthood. He died at Dufftown, May 10, 1856.

Gordon, John, musician, born at London, March 26, 1702. Educated at Westminster School and Trinity College, Cambridge. He studied for the Law in 1718-22, and became Professor of Music at Gresham College, January 16, 1723. Called to Bar, 1725. He died at London, December 12, 1739.

Gordon, William, musician and flute-player, was born at the end of the 18th century. He studied under Drouët, and became a Captain of the Swiss Guards in Paris. Commenced improving flute mechanism, 1830. He died insane, in consequence of unsuccessful experiments, about 1839. His system of fingering was perfected by Boehm, but authorities differ both as regards the original invention and subsequent improvements.

Goss, John Jeremiah, vocalist, born at Salisbury in 1770. He was chorister in Salisbury Cathedral, and lay-vicar, do. Gentleman of Chapel Royal, 1808. Vicar-choral,

GOSS.

St. Paul's Cathedral. Lay-vicar of West-minster Abbey. Principal alto at meetings of the Three Choirs. He died in London, April 25, 1817.

Goss, Sir John, Kt., composer and organist, born at Fareham, Hants., December 27, 1800. Son of Joseph Goss, organist, of that place. Chorister in Chapel Royal, under J. S. Smith, 1811. He studied under Attwood, and became organist of Stockwell Chapel, 1821; organist of St. Luke's, Chelsea, 1824-38; organist, St. Paul's Cathedral, 1838-72. Composer to Chapel Royal, 1856-72. Knighted, 1872. Mus. Doc., Cantab., 1876. He died at Brixton, London, May 10, 1880.

WORKS.—Church Service, in A; Burial Service, in E minor; Te Deum for H.M. Thanksgiving at St. Paul's Cathedral, for the restoration to health of H.R.H. the Prince of Wales. Benedictus. Te Deums in C, D, and F; Cantate Domino and Deus misereatur, in C; Magnificat and Nunc Dimittis, in E. *Anthems:* Almighty and merciful God; And the king said to all the people (dirge); Behold I bring you good tidings; Blessed is the man; Brother, thou art gone before us; Christ, our Passover; Come, and let us return unto the Lord; Fear not, O land; Have mercy upon me; Hear, O Lord; I heard a voice from heaven; I will magnify Thee, O God; If we believe that Jesus died; In Christ dwelleth; Lift up thine eyes round about; O give thanks; O Lord God, Thou strength of my health; O praise the Lord; O praise the Lord of heaven; O Saviour of the world; O taste and see; Praise the Lord, O my soul; Stand up and bless the Lord your God; The glory of the Lord; The Lord is my strength.; These are they which follow the Lamb; The wilderness. Seven glees, and a madrigal, London, 1852; six glees, and a madrigal, 1826. Parochial Psalmody, a collection of ancient and modern tunes, London, 1827. Collection of Voluntaries by eminent composers, organ. The Organist's Companion, 4 vols. Collection of Voluntaries, various composers. The sacred minstrel . . . 1833, 3 vols. Church Psalter and Hymn Book, for the use of congregations and families, by Rev. Wm. Mercer, M.A., Incumbent of St. George's, Sheffield, London, 1862. An introduction to Harmony and Thorough-bass, London, 1833. Pianoforte Students' Catechism of the Rudiments of Music, London, 1835. Collection of chants, ancient and modern, in score . . . 1841. Overtures for orchestra, in F, Philharmonic Society, 1825; also one in E flat, and miscellaneous orchestral music. Songs, etc.

Goss, Joseph, organist, youngest brother of Sir John Goss. Born at Poole, Dorset, 1809. In 1822, went to his brother in London. Succeeded Henry Smart, at St. Philip's, Regent Street, and was well-known in London

GOW.

and Brighton (where he resided) as a pianoforte teacher. In 1876, he retired from the profession, and went to reside at Surbiton, where he died February 13, 1892.

Gostick, Joseph, author of "A Manuel of Music," Edinburgh, 1851.

Gostling, Rev. John, bass vocalist, born in [1652], died in 1733. Was the possessor of a most powerful voice of great compass, for which it is said Purcell composed some sacred and other music.

Gould, Rev. Sabine Baring-, theological writer, novelist, and song collector, born at Exeter, January 28, 1834. Educated at Clare College, Cambridge; M.A., 1856; Ordained 1864; Incumbent of Dalton, Thirsk, 1869; Rector of East Mersea, Colchester, 1871-1881. On the death of his father in 1872, he succeeded to the family property, and in 1881, to the rectory of Lew-Trenchard, Devon, of which county he is justice of the peace. Author of "Lives of the Saints," 15 vols., and other theological works; "Mehalah," "John Herring," and many other novels. In conjunction with the Rev. H. Fleetwood Sheppard, he has collected and arranged "Songs of the West," "A Garland of Country Song," both published by Methuen, London; and edited "English Minstrelsie," 8 vols., Edinburgh, Jack, 1895; and a "Book of Nursery Songs and Rhymes," Methuen, 1895. He has composed various hymns, "Eudoxia," and other pieces.

Gow, Niel, violinist and composer, born at Inver, Dunkeld, March 22, 1727. Taught violin by John Cameron, a retainer in the Grandtully family. He was twice married, and had large families. He played at the principal gatherings and balls of his time, in the large towns of Scotland. He died at Inver, March 1, 1807.

WORKS.—A collection of Strathspey Reels, with a bass for the violoncello or harpsichord, dedicated to Her Grace the Duchess of Athole, Edinburgh (Corri), [1784]. Second collection, dedicated to the noblemen and gentlemen of the Caledonian Hunt, Edinburgh (Corri), [1788]. Third collection, dedicated to the Marchioness of Tweeddale, Edinburgh, [1792]. A complete repository of original Scots slow strathspeys and dances (the dances arranged as medleys for the harp, pianoforte, violin, and violoncello), Edinburgh [1799], issued in four parts. Fifth and sixth collections of strathspey reels, 1808 and 1822.

As personal recollections can not now be brought to bear on the subject of Gow's character, we have transcribed the following passage, which, with a curious portrait, appears in T. Garnett's "Observations on a Tour through the Highlands, etc., of Scotland." Second edition, vol. 2, p. 73, London, 1811 :—

GOW.

". . . We were favoured with a visit from Niel Gow, a singular and well-known character, and a celebrated performer on the violin. When I call him a celebrated performer, I do not mean that he can execute the sweet Italian airs with the touch of a Cramer. His only music is that of his native country, which he has acquired chiefly by the ear, being entirely self-taught; but he plays the Scotch airs with a spirit and enthusiasm peculiar to himself. . . . He excels most in the Strathspeys, which are jigs played with a peculiar spirit and life, but he executes the laments, or funeral music, with a great deal of pathos."

A great deal of nonsense has been written about the Gow family, and numerous fables of all sorts have been published regarding Niel and his alleged doings. In Glen's "Collection of Scottish Dance Music, book 2, 1895, there is a very fair and impartial examination of some of these stories, and a careful sifting of his compositions, whereby many of them are rightly assigned to other composers.

Gow, Nathaniel, violinist and composer, born at Inver, near Dunkeld, May 28, 1763. Fourth son of Niel Gow. He studied under his father, R. M'Intosh, M'Glashan, and J. Reinagle. Violinist at Edinburgh under his brother William. One of H.M. trumpeters for Scotland, 1782. Succeeded his brother William as leader of the Edinburgh concerts, 1791. Established in Music-publishing business with W. Shepherd at Edinburgh, 1796-1813. Gave up business, but subsequenly resumed it in partnership with his son Niel. Continued the firm till 1827. He died at Edinburgh, January 19, 1831.

WORKS.—The Beauties of Niel Gow, being a Selection of the most favourite tunes from his first, second, and third collections of strathspey reels and jigs, chiefly comprising the compositions of Niel Gow and Sons (edited by Nathaniel). Edinburgh, 3 parts. The Vocal Melodies of Scotland, arranged for the pianoforte, or harp, violin, and violoncello, by Nath. Gow. Edin., 3 parts, n.d. The Ancient curious Collection of Scotland, consisting of genuine Scotch tunes, with their original variations, with basses throughout, for the pianoforte, or harp, violin and 'cello. Ded. to Sir Walter Scott. Edin., 1823. A Select Collection of original dances, waltzes, marches, minuets, and airs..many of which are composed, and the whole arranged for the pf. and harp by Nath. Gow, Edin. A Collection of Strathspey Reels, with a bass for the violoncello, or harpsichord, containing the most approved old and the most fashionable new reels, some of which are composed, and others with additions, by Nath. Gow. Edin.[1797]. Complete Repository of Old and New Scotch Strathspeys, Reels, and Dances. Edin., n.d.,

GRAHAM.

3 books. Nathaniel Gow is best remembered as the composer of "Caller Herrin," and "Bothwell Castle," the former being very popular.

Gow, Niel, Jun., violinist and composer, born about 1795. Son of Nathaniel Gow. He was a partner in the music-publishing business in Edinburgh with his father. He died at Edinburgh, November 7, 1823.

WORKS.—Edinburgh Collection of Glees, Catches, Duetts, etc., Edin., n.d. A Collection of Airs, Reels, and Strathspeys, being the posthumous compositions of the late Niel Gow, Junr., arranged for pf., harp, violin, or 'cello, by Nathaniel Gow. Edin., 1849.

This most promising young man died after giving convincing proofs of his capacity for musical composition. His melodies, "Bonnie Prince Charlie" and "Flora Macdonald's Lament," are well-known all over the world. He composed a number of melodies to words by Hogg, etc., but the two songs named are those by which he is best known.

Other members of this family were ANDREW [1760-1803], JOHN [1764; died, London, November 22, 1826], and WILLIAM [1751-1791], all of whom were musicians of some fame in their day, the last being especially well known as a fresh and vigorous violinist. They all composed reels and strathspeys of merit.

Goward, Mary Anne, see KEELEY, MRS.

Gower, John Henry, organist, pianist and composer, born at Rugby, May 25, 1855. Graduated Mus. Bac., 1876; Mus. Doc., 1883, Oxford. In 1876, he was appointed organist and music master at Trent College, Notts., where he remained until 1887, when he went to Denver, Colorado, U.S.A., as precentor and organist of the cathedral there. He gave organ recitals in various towns in England; was an early and enthusiastic member of the I.S.M.; conductor of the Long Eaton Philharmonic Society; and a captain in the First Derbyshire Regiment, Volunteer Battalion. His compositions comprise a cantata, "The Good Shepherd"; part-songs, songs, etc. In 1887, he read a paper, "The needs of the Musical Profession," at the annual meeting of the Music Teachers' National Association of the U.S.A.

Graddon, Miss, soprano vocalist, born at Bishop's Lydiard, near Taunton, 1804. She studied under Tom Cooke; sang at Vauxhall in 1822, and at Dublin in 1823. Afterwards she appeared at Liverpool, Manchester, London, and throughout the English provinces. On November 10, 1824, she sang in "Der Freischutz, at London. Died?

Graeme, Elliot, Author of "Beethoven: a memoir," London, 1870, two editions. Novels, etc.

Graham, George Farquhar, composer

GRAHAM.

and writer, born at Edinburgh, December 29, 1789. Son of Colonel Humphrey Graham. He was educated at the High School and University of Edinburgh, but was chiefly self-taught in music. With George Hogarth he acted as joint-secretary to the Edinburgh Musical Festival, in 1815. For a time he resided in Italy. He was an unsuccessful candidate for the Music chair of Edinburgh University. Died at Edinburgh, March 12, 1867. WORKS.—Twelve pieces of vocal music, with accompaniments for the pf.; composed, and as a small tribute of Scottish respect, inscribed to the memory of Haydn, by a Dilettante, Edinburgh, 1811. The songs of Scotland, adapted to their appropriate melodies . . . with historical, biographical, and critical notices . . . Edinburgh, 1848-49, 3 vols. Glees, hymns, songs, etc. An account of the first Edinburgh Musical Festival, held . . . 1815, Edinburgh, 1816; 2nd edition, 1835. Elements of singing . . . Edinburgh, 1817. Essay on the theory and practice of Musical Composition . . . Edinburgh, 1838. [Being a reprint, with additions, of the article "Music" in the 7th and 8th editions of the Encyclopædia Britannica]. General observations upon Music, and remarks upon Mr. Logier's system, Edinburgh, 1817. Notes and editorial work in connection with the publication of the "Skene MS." (Dauney).

Graham, James Lascelles, organist and writer, born at Edinburgh, May 22, 1854. He is music-master of the High School of Stirling, and organist of Allan Park Church there. He is author of "Music made easy," London, n.d., a pianoforte tutor.

Graham, Maria, author of "A few words on the formation of the Major and Minor Scales, in a letter to her pupils, by M. G," London, 1852.

Graham, Thomas, composer and organist, born in 1800, died in 1867. He was organist of the Parish Church, Wigan, and a composer of vocal music. His daughter, MARY ANN. is MADAME ENDERSSOHN, the soprano singer, for many years a popular favourite.

Grain, Richard Corney, entertainer. born at Teversham, Cambridgeshire, October 26, 1844. He was educated for the law, and called to the Bar in 1866. His gifts for music and mimicry soon decided his career, and he joined the German Reed Entertainment, May 16, 1870 There he continued for the rest of his life, performing in London and the provinces. He wrote an immense number of amusing sketches, of which may be mentioned Small and early, Spring's delights, Troubles of a tourist, Echoes of the opera, Back in town, That fatal menu; as well as setting music to pieces by Arthur Law and others. His experiences he embodied in a little book, "Cor-

GRAY.

ney Grain, by himself," London, Murray, 1888. He died in London, March 16, 1895, a year fatal to the whole German Reed combination.

Grant, Donald, teacher and composer, a native of Elgin, published "A collection of strathspeys, reels, jigs, etc., for the pianoforte, violin, and violoncello," Edinburgh [1790].

Grant, Sir James Hope, musician, born 1808; died 1875. He entered the army in 1826, and served in China, etc. He retired from the army a General. See "Life of General Hope Grant, by H. Knollys, London, 1894, 2 vols. His portrait, representing him playing the violoncello, painted by his brother, Sir Francis Grant, P.R.A., is in the National Portrait Gallery, London He composed Three sketches for pf. and 'cello; The sea and the lake, for pf. and 'cello; Notturno for pf. and 'cello; The three violoncello makers, for pf. and 'cello; Elegie for pf; Voluntaries for the organ; Songs, etc.

Grant, John Campbell, musician and writer, was born at Edinburgh, in 1839. He holds various teaching appointments in Edinburgh. Author of "Elements of music and singing."

Grassineau, Jacques, musician, born, London, 1715; died there, 1769. Author of "Musical Dictionary, being a collection of terms and characters.. London, 1740.

Gray, Alan, composer and organist, born at York, December 23, 1855. Educated at St. Peter's School, York, and Trinity College, Cambridge, being intended for the legal profession. Studied music under Dr. E. G. Monk. Graduated LL.B., 1877; LL.M., 1883; Mus. Bac., 1886; Mus. Doc., 1889, Cambridge. In 1883, he was appointed musical director at Wellington College, and in 1892 succeeded Professor Stanford as organist of Trinity College, Cambridge, and Conductor of the University Musical Society, positions he still holds. WORKS.—The Widow of Zarephath (a reading, with choral exposition), produced in York Minster, May, 1888. Cantatas: Arethusa (Shelley). Leeds Festival, 1892; The Legend of the Rock Buoy Bell, Hovingham Festival, 1893; The Vision of Belshazzar, the same, 1896. In MS., Milton's version of Psalm 7 (exercise for Mus. Doc); An Easter Ode, for soli, chorus, and orchestra (composed 1892); and a Festival Te Deum, with orchestra (composed 1895). Church Services in F, and A; Anthems, etc. Album of four songs; various songs. Overture for full orchestra; Quartet, pf. and strings; Quartet, strings, all in MS. Four sonatas (composed 1889); Fantasia, and other pieces for organ. Sonata in G, pf. and violin; Sonata, pf.; and various smaller works.

Gray, George, musician and vocalist, born at Eton, in June, 1815. He was a vicar-

GRAY.

choral of St. Patrick's Cathedral, Dublin, and founder of the Choir Benevolent Fund. Died at Dublin, May 8, 1888.

His father, WILLIAM HENRY GRAY, born at Eton in 1785, died November 7, 1824, was an organist and composer.

Gray, John Locke, organist, born in 1843. He was the first pupil of Ebenezer Prout when he entered the profession in 1859. He was appointed organist of Lee Chapel, Kent, 1862; then, in succession, of St. Mark's, Lewisham; St. George the Martyr, Holborn; Holy Trinity, Richmond, 1872; and of Christ Church, Kensington. In 1875 he was appointed organist of Bombay Cathedral. He died at Bombay, from sunstroke, June, 1878.

Gray, Louisa, MRS. ABINGDON COMPTON, amateur composer of the day. Her operetta, "Between two stools," has been performed in several places; and she is the composer of a number of songs, What an angel heard; The thread of the story; Evening star, etc.

Greatheed, Rev. Samuel Stephenson, clergyman and composer, born near Weston-super-Mare, February 22, 1813. B.A., Cantab., 1835. M.A., 1838. Ordained, 1838. Rector of Corringham, Sussex.

WORKS.—Enoch's Prophecy, an oratorio, words by James Montgomery, 1852. English Gradual: a book of plain song for Holy Communion, from ancient English sources. Plain song for Holy Communion on ordinary days, so far as it differs from that for feasts; with offertory sentences, the Dies Iræ (English), and the Order for the Burial of the Dead. *Anthems*: Blessed is the man; Ye that fear the Lord; Hail, gladd'ning light; O God, Thou art worthy to be praised; Let my soul bless God; O Lord Almighty, God of Israel; O Saviour of the world; The Son of man, etc.

Greatorex, Thomas, organist, conductor, and composer, born at North Wingfield, near Chesterfield, Derby, October 5, 1758. He studied under Dr. B. Cooke, 1772. Adopted by the Earl of Sandwich. Chorister at Concert of Ancient Music, 1778. Organist of Carlisle Cathedral, 1780-84. Teacher in Newcastle, 1784-85. Travelled in Holland and Italy, 1785-88; and was introduced to Prince Charles Edward Stuart. Teacher in London, 1789. Conductor of the Concert of Ancient Music, 1793. Revived the Vocal Concerts, 1801. Organist of Westminster Abbey, in succession to G. E. Williams, 1819. Conductor of Birmingham Musical Festival. Fellow of Royal and Linnean Societies. He died at Hampton, near London, July 18, 1831.

WORKS.—Twelve glees from favourite English, Irish, and Scotch melodies, London, n.d. [1832]. Psalms, chants, etc. A selection of Tunes...London, 1829. Parochial Psalmody, a collection of approved tunes for four voices,

GREEN.

in score, with organ or pf. accompaniment, London, n.d.

Greaves, Thomas, lutenist and composer, of 16th and 17th centuries. Biography unknown.

WORKS.—Songs of sundrie kindes, 1604. Reprinted madrigals: Come away, love; Lady, the melting crystal of your eye; Sweet nymphs, etc.

Green, James, organist and composer, was organist at Hull in first half of last century. He published "A Book of Psalmody, containing chanting tunes for the Canticles, etc. . . . the reading Psalms, with eighteen anthems and a variety of Psalm-tunes in four parts," 1724; 8th edition, 1734; 11th edition, 1751. He also composed hymns, etc.

Green, John, composer and teacher, of first half of the present century. Author of "Concise Instructions for performance on the Royal Seraphine and Organ," London, 1833. The seraphine is described as "a new musical instrument having the power of a large organ, in the size and shape of a chiffonier." Green also issued "A bird's-eye view of the rudiments of music," London, 1844, and adapted airs, etc., for the pf.

Another JOHN GREEN published "Hints on the Spanish Guitar, being a preparatory tutor for that instrument," London [1830]. "Little songs for little singers," issued in parts, etc.

Green, Joseph N., writer, author of "The Tritone; a method of harmony and modulation adapted to the scales of keyed instruments, with Appendix, London [1871].

Green, Richard, baritone vocalist, born April 21, 1866, in Kensington, London Educated at Margate, and began life in a city Bank. Studying singing under Edwin Holland, he was advised to enter the R.A.M. After two years' study there, he went to Milan, in 1888, and studied with Giulio Moretti. Returning to London, in 1890, he was engaged for the Royal English Opera House, and made his *début* as Prince John, in Sullivan's "Ivanhoe," January 31, 1891, afterwards taking the part of the Templar. The next season he was engaged for the Savoy, where he created the part of Sir George Vernon, in "Haddon Hall," singing it more than 200 times. He next appeared at Covent Garden, in Italian Opera, creating the part of Silvio in "I Pagliacci," on its production, May 19, 1893. He had been engaged by Sir Augustus Harris for grand opera every season since, and has achieved success in a great number of works. He is also distinguished as a concert singer, and has appeared at the Saturday Popular Concerts, and other institutions in London and the provinces.

Green, William, musician, of 4 Cumberland Street, Shoreditch, compiler of "The

GREENE.

Clerk's Companion, or the Christian's vade-mecum, containing 373 tunes of two and three parts," London [1820]. "The Ladder to Musical learning," London, 1834. Pf. music, etc.

Greene, Harry Plunket, bass vocalist, born at Old Connaught House, County Wicklow, June 24, 1865. His mother is the authoress of "Cushions and Corners," and many other popular children's books, and sister of Mr. David Plunket, First Commissioner of Works. He was educated at Clifton College, and destined for the Bar; but, gifted with a fine voice, he ultimately decided upon entering the musical profession. In 1883 he went to Stuttgart, and later, to Florence, studying under Vannuccini. On his return to London he had lessons from J. B. Welch, and Alfred Blume. He made his *début* at the People's Palace, Stepney, January 21, 1888, in Handel's "Messiah." In March following he sang at Novello's Oratorio Concerts, St. James's Hall, in Gounod's "Redemption"; at the Crystal Palace, March, 1889 ; and in Germany the same year, being everywhere successful. His operatic *début*, was at Covent Garden, June 2, 1890; and he first appeared at the Provincial Festivals at Worcester in 1890. He has given song recitals all over the country, and has twice visited America, in 1893 (Chicago Exhibition), and 1896.

Greene, Maurice, organist and composer, born, London, 1696 [1695]. Chorister in St. Paul's Cathedral. He studied music under R. Brind. Organist of S. Dunstan in the West, Fleet Street, 1716; S. Andrew's, Holborn, 1717; S. Paul's Cathedral, 1718; Chapel Royal, 1727. Professor of Music, Cambridge, 1730. Doc. Mus., Cantab., 1730. Master of the King's Band, 1735. He died at London, December 1, 1755.

WORKS.—*Oratorios:* Jephthah, 1737 ; The Force of Truth, 1744. Florimel, or Love's Revenge, dramatic pastoral, 1737; The Judgment of Hercules, masque, 1740. Phœbe, opera, 1748. Spenser's Amoretti for voice, harpsichord, and violin. Ode on S. Cecilia's Day, Pope, 1730; Odes for King's Birthday and New Year's Day, 1730; Catches and Canons, 3 and 4 voices ; The Chaplet, collection of 12 English songs ; Church Service in C, 1737 ; Te Deum in D, 1745 ; Forty select Anthems in Score for , 2, 3, 4, 5, 6, 7 and 8 voices, London, 2 vols., 1743. Songs, organ and harpsichord music, etc.

Greenish, Arthur James, organist, born at Haverfordwest, Pembrokeshire, January 26, 1860. Musical education partly at R.A.M., partly private. Graduated Mus. Bac., 1885; Mus. Doc., 1892, Cambridge. F.R.C.O., F.R.A.M. In 1880, appointed organist of St. Mary's, Battersea ; and in 1882, organist and choirmaster of St. Saviour's, South

GREGORY.

Hampstead, which offices he still retains. Was conductor of the South Hampstead Musical Society for some time, and is an Examiner for Trinity College, London. In addition to the Degree Exercises (Sing, O ye heavens ; The miracle at Bethany), he has composed songs, and pieces for violin; and has published an Evening Service, and some songs.

His brother, FREDERICK ROBERT GREENISH, is organist of St. Mary's Church, Haverfordwest. He graduated Mus. Bac., 1883, and Mus. Doc., 1891, at Oxford. Composer of "The Church Triumphant" and "Adoration" cantatas ; Church services, anthems, etc.

Greenwood, James, organist, and teacher of singing, born of a Yorkshire family, in Lancashire, in 1837. At the age of nineteen he went from Todmorden to Bristol, and gained a place as lay-clerk in the Cathedral, an office he resigned in 1877. While there, he studied under S. S. Wesley. He was organist at St. Paul's, Bedminster; Westbury-on-Trym ; and lastly, at St. Matthew's, Kingsdown. Founder and Hon. Sec. of the Lay-clerk's Choir and Mutual Aid Society, and of a choir, 1870-79. Music-master at Colston School, and the Grammar School, Bristol. A great advocate of the Lancashire Sol-fa, of which he wrote a primer, and a Set of 396 Two-part Exercises for Choirs and Schools, Novello's Primers, Nos. 19 and 23. He also composed some Church Services, anthems, and organ pieces. This earnest and unassuming worker for music died at Clifton, June 14, 1894.

Greenwood, John, musician and teacher, of Leeds. Published "Selection of antient and modern Psalm tunes . . .," Leeds [1825] ; "Modulus Sanctus, a collection of sacred music," Leeds, 1828 ; "Psalmody harmonised in score, with accompaniment for organ and pianoforte," Halifax, 1838.

Greeting, Thomas, teacher of the flageolet, in London, at the end of the 17th century, Author of "The Pleasant Companion ; or new lessons and instructions for the Flagelot," London, 1666, another edition, 1680.

Gregg, Annie Jessy, *see sub.,* CURWEN, JOHN SPENCER.

Gregory of Bridlington, musician, of 13th century. He was a canon of the Order of St. Augustine, and precentor, and latterly Prior of Bridlington, about 1217. Author of "De Arte Musices," in 3 books.

Gregory, George Herbert, organist, born at Clewer, near Windsor, December 6, 1853. Studied under Samuel Reay. F.R.C.O., 1873, and Mus. Bac., Oxford, 1874. Organist of Holy Trinity Episcopal Church, Melrose, 1872-4 ; Tamworth Parish Church, 1874-5 ; and Boston Parish Church, 1875, to present time. Conductor of Boston Choral Society

GREGORY.

for some years. He has a good tenor voice, and has occasionally sung in oratorio and concerts in Lincolnshire. Has composed services and other church music, songs, etc., and contributed to the " Church of Scotland Children's Hymnal," and the authorised " Hymnal of the Established Church of Scotland."—JAMES LIVELY GREGORY, brother of the preceding, was born at Old Windsor, March 27, 1860. F.R.C.O., 1883, and Mus. Bac., Durham, 1892. Received most of his musical training from his brother, whom he succeeded at Melrose, in 1875. From there he went to Welford Parish Church, in 1877, and to the Parish Church, Ware, in 1880. There he is actively engaged as a teacher; he is also conductor of the Ware and other Musical Societies. He has published church services, songs, part-songs, organ and pf. pieces. A third brother, ALFRED EDWARD GREGORY, was born at Clehonger, near Hereford, May 16, 1862. He also was chiefly educated in music by the eldest brother. Graduated Mus. Bac., Oxford, 1895. Organist of the Parish Church, Lanark; conductor of the Lanark Select Choir, etc. This family presents the possibly unique circumstance of three brothers holding Degrees in Music.

Gregory, Rev. John Herbert, author of a "Letter to the Bishop of Melbourne on Church Music," Melbourne, 1857.

Greig, Gavin, organist and composer, born in Aberdeenshire, February 10, 1856. He is a schoolmaster at New Deer. Composer of " Prince Charlie," a musical drama; " Mains's Wooin'," a musical drama; numerous songs, etc.

Greig, John, composer and organist, born in Edinburgh. Educated at Moray Training College, and appointed English Master in the High School, Leith. While holding this and similar appointments he pursued his musical studies, graduating Mus. Bac., 1878; Mus. Doc., 1889; Oxford; M.A, Edinburgh; and F.C.O., 1880. Organist and choirmaster St. Cuthbert's Free Church, Edinburgh. Nominated during illness of Sir Herbert Oakeley, interim professor of music at Edinburgh University, during which time he gave many lectures and organ recitals. His compositions include an oratorio, Zion (degree exercise) ; an opera, Holyrood, Glasgow, October 5, 1896; an orchestral suite, The Graces (Edinburgh, 1890). Part-songs; Herald of Spring; Month of May; Merrily row we, etc. Editor of Scots Minstrelsie, 6 vols., Edinburgh, Jack, 1892-5, and the Musical Educator, Edinburgh, Jack.

Gresham, William, composer, born at Dunstable, about the middle of the 18th century. He died early in the present century. Compiler of " Psalmody improved, containing portions of the Psalms of David

GRIEVE.

and 13 hymns . . . ,"London [1780] ; and composer of songs by Sir Walter Scott, etc.

Grey, Annie, MRS. WADE, contralto singer, born at Edinburgh, July 4, 1860. She studied at the R. A.M. as a pupil of Randegger, and afterwards she appeared in Edinburgh. In 1890, she sang before the Queen at Balmoral, and since then she has appeared at many concerts in Scotland and England.

Grey, Rev. John, compiler of " Manual of Psalm and hymn tunes," 1857, and " A Hymnal for use in the English Church, with accompanying tunes," London, 1866.

Grice, Robert, baritone vocalist, born at Leeds, 1859. Was for seven years a chorister in Durham Cathedral, and at the age of twenty was appointed to Peterborough Cathedral as bass; a year later taking the position of principal bass at New College, Oxford. In 1885 he was elected assistant vicar-choral of St. Paul's Cathedral, from which choir he retired in 1893. He has sung at the principal concerts in London and the provinces; at Chester Festival; Hereford Festival, 1894, as the narrator in Parry's "Job"; and at the Crystal Palace in the same. He also took part in the quartets in the Jubilee performance of " Elijah " at the Crystal Palace, June 27, 1896.

Grier, William, writer. Author of "An Essay on the first principle of Music." Aberdeen, 1838. This originally appeared in "The Musical Cyclopædia, being a collection of the most approved English, Scottish, and Irish songs, edited by J. W. Wilson," London, 1835; also 1852.

Griesbach, John Henry, pianist and composer, was born at Windsor, of German parents, on June 20, 1798. Violoncellist in Queen's band, 1810. He studied under Kalkbrenner, and afterwards became pianist in London, and director of Philharmonic Society. He died at London, January 9, 1875.

WORKS.—Belshazzar's feast, 1835 ; Daniel (reproduction), 1853 ; Music to the "Tempest"; James the First, or the Royal Captive, operetta ; The Goldsmith of West Cheap, opera ; Eblis, opera, unfinished ; Raby Ruins, musical drama ; Overtures for orchestra. Analysis of Musical Sounds, with illustrative figures of the ratios of vibrations of musical intervals and their compounds, harmonic vibration, temperament, etc., n.d. Elements of Musical notation, containing tables of the comparative value of the different kinds of Notes, Signatures of the different keys, etc., n.d. Pianoforte Students' Companion, containing all the Scales in four positions, etc., London [1825]. Anthems, songs, etc.

Grieve, John Charles, composer, conductor, and didactic writer, born in Edinburgh, August 29, 1842. Fellow of the Educational Institute of Scotland; lecturer on

GRIFFIN.

musical theory, Heriot-Watt College, Edinburgh. Sometime choirmaster, Lady Yester's Church, and conductor of Phœnix Musical Association, Edinburgh. Teacher of singing in various schools, and for some years editor of *The Musical Star*.

WORKS.—Benjamin, an oratorio, Edinburgh, 1877 ; Christian songs of praise, 24 hymns, for 4 voices (1873) ; The sower and the seed, scripture parable, for soli and chorus ; The good Samaritan, ditto. Cantata, Legend of St. Swithin (1891). Kinderspiels : The happy family ; Playmates ; The flowers o' the forest ; Rip Van Winkle ; Don Quixote ; Hearts and Homes ; Day of rest and gladness. Part-songs : Good-morrow to my lady bright ; Stars of the summer night, etc. Songs : The Assyrian ; Comin' hame ; Broken vows ; Earth's partings, etc. Arrangements of Scotch songs, etc. Author of the Harmonium : how to use it (Edinburgh, n.d.) ; Practical harmony.

Griffin, George, organist and composer, born at Wingrave, Buckinghamshire. April 1, 1816. Compiler of " New Sacred Music, consisting of Psalm and Hymn-tunes, with one Christmas piece," London [1840] ; " The Buckinghamshire Harmonist," comprising a new set of original Psalm and Hymn-tunes . . . London [1842].

Griffin, George Eugene, pianist and composer, was born at London, January 8, 1781. Member of Philharmonic Society, teacher, etc. He died at London, May 28, 1863.

WORKS.—Two concertos for pf. and orchestra, op. 1 and 4 ; Ode to charity, 1820 ; Four sonatas for pf., op. 2, etc. ; Three string quartets ; Rondos, marches, variations, etc., for pf. ; Songs, glees, Cynthia (1810), etc.

Griffith, Frederic, flutist, born at Swansea, November 12, 1867. His talent was displayed at an early age, and from 1881, he won several prizes at Eisteddfodau at Merthyr, and other places, playing both piccolo and flute. Attracting the notice of leading musicians, he was advised to enter the R.A.M., where he studied under the late Olaf Svendsen. Here he carried off all the Academical honours, and on leaving, in 1891, was elected an Associate. Further studies were pursued in Paris, under Taffanel. Returning to London an accomplished artist, he gave a number of recitals ; and in 1893, appeared in the provinces, with the Melba touring party. His executive powers are very great, and his tone is pure and unforced. He was appointed, in 1895, solo flute at the Royal Italian Opera, Covent Garden. Editor of Notable Welsh Musicians, London, Goodwen, 1896.

Griffiths, F. J., musician, compiler of " Psalm Tunes and Chants, original and selected, arranged for four voices," London [1846].

GRIMSON.

Griffiths. John, bass vocalist, born about the middle of the eighteenth century. He was originally a parish clerk of a village in the Vale of Clywd. Became a member of the Worcester Cathedral Choir, and was one of the principal singers at the Three Choirs' Festivals, from that at Gloucester in 1784, to the year 1799. He remained in Worcester up the time of his death, under tragical circumstances, October 7, 1821. At the Worcester Festival he sang in the chorus, and during a solo by Vaughan, fell back in a fit, on October 5, and expired two days later. He also sang in the Covent Garden oratorios, London. His voice was of great power, and of deep compass.

Griffiths, Richard, organist and composer, born about 1789 ; died at London, July 18, 1850. Composer of instrumental music, and compiler of " Psalm tunes and chants, original and selected," London, 1846.

Griffiths, Lieutenant Samuel Charles, son of a colour-sergeant in the Royal Scots (Lothian) Regiment was born in 1847. As a boy he entered the band, and ultimately became bandmaster, in 1874, of the second battalion of that regiment. In May, 1890, he was made quarter-master of Sandhurst College, and in December appointed after competition, to the directorship of Kneller Hall. He died suddenly, while out walking near the hall, October 31, 1895. Author of " The Military Band " ; and " Hints on the Management of Army Bands."

Grigor, Alexander Lockhart, musician, born Glasgow, March 28, 1853 ; died there, March 25, 1891. Author of " Hints and Maxims to players on Pianoforte, Harmonium, etc.," Glasgow, 1883. He was a teacher in Glasgow, and held the position of harmonium player at Oatlands Church there for some years.

Grimshaw, Arthur Edmund, composer and organist, born 1864, in Leeds, where he received his musical training. Since 1883 he has been organist and choirmaster of St. Anne's R. C. Cathedral, Leeds. He has composed a setting of Psalm 141, for soprano solo, and chorus, produced, January, 1885, at Leeds, and some Church music. Also two operettas, " El Escribano," and " Amaranthus," produced at Leeds in 1891 and 1892. Songs, and part-songs. Two Melodies for string orchestra, produced by the Leeds Symphony Society, December 11, 1893 ; a Romance for violin and orchestra, etc.

Grimshaw, John, organist and composer, who died on February 18, 1819. Composer of " Twenty-four hymns, in four parts," London [1810]. Songs, etc.

Grimson, Samuel Dean, violinist of the present time, has published a book of " Technical Studies for the Violin." He is the

GROOM.

father of a remarkable family of musicians. Of his children, ANNIE is a pianist, scholar of the R.C.M. She has appeared with success at various concerts since 1886, and has composed a symphony, pieces for violoncello, etc. AMY, another daughter, pianist and violoncellist, was also educated at the R.C.M. For some time she played in the Rev. E. H. Moberley's Ladies' Orchestra, and is favourably known as a soloist. JESSIE GRIMSON is a violinist of repute, and other members of the family possess musical talent. A concert was given in the Queen's (small) Hall, January 21, 1896, by the Grimson family, numbering eight, when Mendelssohn's string Octet was played under possibly unique circumstances.

Groom, William, of Ivinghoe, composer, published " Congregational Melodies, consisting of a new set of psalm and hymn tunes . . . ," Ivinghoe, 1838 ; Supplement, 1839. London edition, edited by Thomas Jordan, 1841.

Groome, W., author of a " Concise treatise on Music. Musical Harmony and Thoroughbass," London, 1870.

Grossmith, George, vocalist and actor, who has become famous for his monologues and sketches given in London and throughout the country. From 1877 he was, for some time, associated with the Gilbert-Sullivan operas, appearing in " The Sorcerer " when produced at the Opera Comique, November 17, of that year. He was also occasionally with the German Reed party in the provinces. His official position was that of Bow street police-court reporter, a post held by his father before him. Among his sketches may be named, Cups and saucers, 1878 ; Uncle Samuel, operetta, 1881 ; Drama on crutches, 1883, etc. *Songs :* Autocratic gardener ; Awful little scrub ; Cockney's life for me ; Gay photographer ; Happy fatherland ; Haste to the wedding ; Muddle puddle porter ; See me dance the polka ; Speaker's eye, etc. He has also written various books, such as his own reminiscences in " A Society Clown," and stories in conjunction with his brother, WEEDON, the popular actor. In 1888 he published the " Autobiography of a Society Clown," Bristol, Arrowsmith.

Grosvenor, Symeon, organist and composer, was born at Dudley, January 11, 1816. He was a pupil of Moscheles and Thomas Adams, and held the position of organist of St. Thomas' Parish Church, Dudley, from 1836 to 1854. He graduated Mus. Bac., Oxon. in 1852. He died at Dudley, July 8, 1866. Editor of " Hymns, Anthems, Chants, etc., as used in the services of St. Thomas's Church, Dudley," c. 1850. He wrote some music for the church service.

Grove, Sir George, Kt., writer on music, born at Clapham, Surrey, August 13, 1820.

GROVER.

Educated as a civil engineer, but quitting that profession he became Secretary to the Society of Arts, 1850 ; and in 1852, Secretary to the Crystal Palace Company, an office he held until 1873. It was here he began his long service to music, a service difficult to over-estimate. His analytical programmes gave a great impetus to musical study. In 1867, he visited Vienna, in company with Arthur Sullivan, and recovered Schubert's music to " Rosamunde," lost since its performance in December, 1823. On leaving the Crystal Palace he was associated with the publishing firm of Macmillan and Co., and edited *Macmillan's Magazine* for more than 15 years. Other details of his long and active career are beyond the scope of this work. In 1882, he was appointed, by H.R.H. the Prince of Wales, Director of the Royal College of Music, the founding of which owed much to his strenuous efforts. In 1875, the University of Durham conferred on him the degree of D.C.L. ; on the opening of the R.C.M., May, 1883, the Queen honoured him with a knighthood ; in 1885 he was made LL.D., Glasgow ; and in 1887 he was elected on the Committee of the Bach-Gesellschaft, Leipzig. He resigned his Directorship of the R.C.M., in November, 1894. His great work is the Dictionary of Music and Musicians, 4 vols., Macmillan, 1879-89, which he edited, and to which he contributed many important articles. He wrote an appendix to Hellborn's Life of Schubert, English edition, Longmans, 1869 ; published in 1896, Beethoven and his Nine Symphonies, Novello ; and was a frequent contributor to the musical press.

Grover, George F., teacher of singing, born at Clapham, August 8, 1860. Chorister, St. Paul's Cathedral, from 1870, where he was musically educated under Sir John Goss, Dr. Stainer, F. Walker, and Dr. Martin. Organist successively at St. Michael's, Poplar ; St. John's, Wapping ; and, from 1884, St. Peterle-poor, Old Broad Street. Principally engaged as a teacher of singing, many of his pupils holding good positions. He has published a sacred cantata, " The Raising of Lazarus," produced at Tottenham, in 1882 ; and is author of " Musical Hints to Clergymen," London, W. Reeves, 1894. He has contributed articles to various musical periodicals, among them a series of biographical sketches of Old English Musicians, in *Musical Opinion*, Vols. VIII. and IX.

Grover, Haydn, composer and alto singer, is a native of London. He has sung in many churches and institutions in London ; was organist of Godstone Parish Church, 1879-80 ; and is now a teacher and concert-giver in South London. Alto in the Temple Church, etc. Composer of a madrigal, " Come, nymphs and shepherds." Part-songs. Songs : " Sons

GRUNEISEN.

of the brave," "Soldier boys," "Fill the gleaming sail," "Lyric of love," "In dreamland," etc. ; numerous pieces for pf., etc. His brother, HERBERT GROVER, is a well-known tenor singer, who has appeared at concerts in London and the provinces.

Gruneisen, Charles Lewis, musician and critic, born at London, November 2, 1806 ; died there November 1, 1879. Author of "The Opera and the Press," 1869. Memoir of Meyerbeer, London, 1848.

Guenett, Thomas Harbottle, pianist, born at Fleetwood, Lancashire, June 22, 1850. Pupil of Halle and Prout. Settled in Melbourne, Australia. Professor of pianoforte ; organist of Toorah Presbyterian Church. Musical critic of the *Melbourne Argus*; lecturer on musical subjects. Founder of the Melbourne Popular Concerts of Chamber Music, 1878.

Guernsey, Wellington, lyric poet and composer, born at Mullingar, Ireland, June 8, 1817, and died at London, November 13, 1885. Author of the words of a great quantity of songs, chiefly of a sentimental kind, of which "Mary Blane," and "Alice, where art thou ?" are examples. His own productions consist chiefly of songs, such as "I'll hang my harp on a willow tree," but he has written a Mass in B flat, and other musical works. He also issued "Old Songs of Old Ireland, with symphonies and accompaniments, by W. Guernsey, and characteristic words by Jos. Fitzgerald," London [1843].

Guest, George, organist and composer, born at Bury St. Edmunds in 1771. Son of Ralph Guest. He studied under his father. Chorister in Chapel Royal. Organist at Eye, Suffolk, in 1787 ; and at Wisbeach in 1789. He died at Wisbeach, September 10, 1831. Wrote glees, hymns, songs, duets, organ music, etc.

Guest, Ralph, composer and organist, born at Basely, Shropshire, 1742. Chorister in Basely Church, and in Portland Church, London, 1763. He studied the organ under Ford of S. James' Church, Bury, and was choir-master of S. Mary's, Bury St. Edmunds, 1805-22. He died at Bury, June, 1830.

WORKS.—The Psalms of David, collection. Hymns and Psalms suited for the use of Parish Churches, n.d. Glees, songs, etc.

Guildford, Lord, *see* NORTH, FRANCIS.

Guinneth, John, *see* GWYNNETH, JOHN.

Guise, Richard, musician, born in 1740. He was a Gentleman of the Chapel Royal, and a lay-vicar and master of choristers, Westminster Abbey. He died on March 10, 1808. Composer of 3 single chants, contained in Vandernan's "Divine Harmony," 1770.

Gunn, Barnabas, organist and composer, was born at the end of the 17th century. He was organist of St. Philip's, Birmingham, till

GUTTERIDGE.

1730, when he became organist of Gloucester Cathedral, succeeding Hine. He wrote Two cantatas and six songs, Gloucester, 1736. Sonatas for harpsichord, etc. He died at Gloucester (?) in 1743.

Gunn, John, writer and violoncello player, was born in the Highlands of Scotland [Edinburgh, 1765 ?] Teacher of 'cello at Cambridge, and in London, from 1789. He afterwards returned to Edinburgh, and married Miss Anne Young, in 1804. He died about 1824.

WORKS.—An Essay, with copious examples, towards a more easy and scientific method of commencing and pursuing the study of the Pianoforte, with the principles of thorough-bass and musical science, London, n.d. Forty favourite Scotch airs, adapted for violin, German flute, or violoncello, with the phrases mark'd . . supplement to the examples in the theory and practice of fingering the violoncello, London, n.d. The theory and practice of fingering the violoncello, containing rules and progressive lessons for attaining the knowledge and command of the whole compass of the instrument, London, 1793 ; second edition, n.d. Art of playing the German flute on new principles, n.d. An essay, theoretical and practical, on the application of harmony, thorough-bass, and modulation, to the violoncello, Edinburgh, 1801. An historical enquiry respecting the performance on the harp in the Highlands of Scotland, from the earliest times until it was discontinued about the year 1734 ; to which is prefixed an account of a very ancient Caledonian harp, and of the harp of Queen Mary. Edinburgh 1807. This work he proposed to supplement by An enquiry into the antiquity of the Harp, etc., but it never appeared. School for the German flute, n.d.

Gunn, Anne, *born* YOUNG, pianist and writer, wife of John Gunn, wrote "An introduction to music ; in which the elementary parts of the science, and the principles of thorough-bass and modulation, as illustrated by the musical games and apparatus, are fully and familiarly explained, with examples and complete directions for playing the several games," Edinburgh, 1803 ; second edition, 1820.

Gunn, William, compiler of "The Caledonian Repository of Music, adapted for the bagpipes, being a collection of strathspeys, reels, jigs, etc.," Glasgow ; Four editions to 1867.

Gurney, Edmund, musician, who died at Brighton, in June, 1888. Author of "The Power of Sound," London, 1880, and several contributions to magazines on musical subjects.

Guthrie, Mrs. T. A., *see* AUSTEN, AUGUSTA A.

Gutteridge, William, organist, violinist,

GUY.

and composer, born at Chelmsford, July 16, 1798. He travelled in Belgium, etc., in 1815. Organist of Private Royal Chapel, Brighton Pavilion, under George IV., William IV., and Victoria; also organist of St. Peter's Church, Brighton, 1828-1872. Member of private band of George IV. Leader of orchestra of Brighton Theatre, and conductor for many years of Brighton Sacred Harmonic Society. He was music-master to the Duke of Cambridge. He died at Brighton, September 23, 1872. Composer of nocturnes, galops, rondos, etc., for pf., numerous songs, etc.

Guy, Henry, tenor vocalist and composer, born at Oxford, in 1847. Student and Associate, R.A.M. In 1876 he was appointed a Gentleman of the Chapel Royal, St. James's. He sang at the Worcester Festival of 1878; at the Alexander Palace in 1876; and has been heard at the chief concerts in London and the provinces. He has written a trio, "Reflection"; a serenade, with violin obbligato; and some glees and songs.

Guylott, Robert, composer, born in 1794, died at London, December 18, 1876. He wrote songs chiefly, of which the following are among the principal: All remember thee [1848]; Beggar's petition; Bells on the water; Broken vow; Days that are gone; Down the burn, Davy love; Haste to the woodlands; In the pretty spring time; Love on; Maid of Llanwellyn; Rose shall cease to blow; and a large number of comic and other songs. Glee, The orb of day, etc. He also issued a "Book of Melody, and drawing-room companion," 1847.

Gwilym, Gwent, see WILLIAMS, WM. AUBREY.

Gwilt, Joseph, architect and musician, was born in Surrey, in 1784. Architect to the Grocers' Company, London. He died at Henley-on-Thames, September 14, 1863. He published a "Collection of Madrigals and Motets, chiefly for 4 equal voices, by the most eminent composers of the 16th and 17th centuries . . . ," London, 1815; and wrote the article "Music" in the "Encyclopædia Metropolitana." He also compiled a valuable "Encyclopædia of Architecture," etc.

Gwynneth, or Guinneth, John, musician and priest of the 16th century. One of the eminent musicians mentioned in Morley's catalogue. He graduated Mus. Doc., Oxford, in 1531, and in 1533 he became rector of St. Peter, Westchepe. Composer of Masses, songs, etc.

Gyde, Margaret, pianist and composer, born in London. Studied pianoforte and composition under W. C. and Sir G. A. Macfarren; violin under F. Ralph. Sterndale Bennett Prizeholder, 1879; Potter Exhibitioner, 1880; Lady Goldsmid, and Thalberg Scholar, 1881. A.R.A.M., 1884. Made her

HADDEN.

début at W. Macfarren's concert, St. James's Hall, February 25, 1882, when she played his Concertstück in E minor. She has played several times at the Crystal Palace concerts, including the Weber centenary, December 18, 1886; and has given recitals at Steinway Hall, 1884-91. In 1895, she established the Kensington Musical Academy. The late Richard Jefferies, novelist and naturalist, was her first cousin.

WORKS.—Pf. and violin: Sonatas in G minor, and C minor (two books); Suite, Idylls of summer (two books); Scherzo; Romanza; Reverie, etc. Impromptus; Minuet; Tarantella, and other pf. pieces. Prelude and Fugue in G minor, organ. Seas apart; The bridge of tears; Love's greeting, and other songs, etc.

Habyngton, see ABYNGDON.

Hackett, Charles Danvers, composer, born in 1812. Mus. Bac., Oxon., 1850. Died London, 1858. He edited "The National Psalmist, consisting of original psalm and hymn tunes, etc., composed expressly for this work by the most eminent authors in England," London [1839]; various editions. "Zion," a sacred cantata [1853]. Original music [1840], etc.

Hackett, Maria, musician, born November 14, 1783; died Hackney, London, November 5, 1874. She interested herself greatly in the education of cathedral choir boys, and to encourage the composition of church music founded the Gresham prize medal, in 1831. Author of "A brief account of Cathedral and Collegiate Schools, with an abstract of their statutes and endowments," London, 1827. "A memoir of Sir Thomas Gresham, with an abstract of his will," 1833, anon. "Correspondence and evidences respecting the ancient Collegiate School attached to St. Paul's Cathedral." "A popular account of St. Paul's Cathedral," London, 1816. Songs, etc.

Hadden, James Cuthbert, musician and writer, born at Banchory-Ternan, near Aberdeen, in 1861. He studied under private teachers in London, and in 1882 became organist of Mannofield Parish Church, Aberdeen. He was appointed organist of St. Michael's Parish Church, Crieff, in 1884, and in 1889 went to Edinburgh as organist of St. John's Parish Church. He resides in Edinburgh, and is chiefly engaged in literary work.

WORKS.—George Frederick Handel, London, 1888. Mendelssohn, London, 1888. Lays of Caledonia, a collection of Scottish airs arranged for the harmonium, Glasgow, 1883. Contributor of musical and other articles to the Dictionary of National Biography; Love's Scottish Church Music; Scottish Review, Quiver, Cassell's Magazine, English Illustrated Magazine, etc. Editor of the Scottish

L.

HADDOCK.

Musical Monthly. Editor also of a selection from Hogg the Ettrick Shepherd, for Bryce of Glasgow ; and author of a work on Violin Collecting, to be published in Redway's Collector Series.

Haddock, George, violinist and composer, born at Killingbeck, near Leeds. His father was musical, and at his house the great instrumentalists who visited Leeds often met for chamber music. The son began his studies at an early age, under Bywater, and in 1846 went to London. There he had lessons from Henri Vieuxtemps, and afterwards from Molique. Returning to the north he was, for many years, a foremost figure in musical life in Yorkshire. He was the first to give a performance of " Elijah " at Bradford ; and as a teacher he has sent out many players, now occupying important orchestral posts. He established a Music School at Bradford, and also the Leeds College of Music, opened in 1894. He is author of " A complete Practical School for the Violin," 3 vols., Schott and Co. " Major and Minor Scales in all positions, with exercises on double notes, octaves, and staccato bowing," etc., Ashdown. Fantasias and arrangements for violin and pianoforte.

Haddock, Edgar, son of the preceding, violinist and composer, was born at Leeds, in 1862. Studied under his father, and in 1884 started a series of " Musical Evenings " at Leeds, which have been continued annually. He appeared the same year at York, Halifax, and elsewhere. In 1891, he gave a series of concerts at the Steinway Hall, London ; and at the Huddersfield Subscription Concerts of that year (March 3) was associated with Herr Joachim in the performance of Spohr's violin duo in A minor, op. 67, No. 1, a rare compliment to an English artist. In 1896, he gave a series of Historical Recitals at Leeds. At one of the daily concerts at the Crystal Palace, March, 1885, he introduced Gade's violin concerto, more than a year before it was placed in a Saturday concert programme. The composer sent Mr. Haddock an autograph score in acknowledgment. He is one of the directors of the Leeds College of Music. His works include a Practical School for the Violin ; The Students' series of Violin Solos ; Ballade Norvegienne ; Sarabande and Tambourine, and other original compositions for violin. His brother, G. PERCY HADDOCK, violoncellist, was born at Leeds. He is associated with the management of the " Musical Evenings ;" is a Director of the Leeds College of Music ; and is known as a pianist and organist. He has composed a number of songs, of which may be named " The Soul's awakening," with accompaniment for pf., violin, and organ ; " A crown of thorns ;" and " The King of Kings." He has also written

HAGUE.

pieces for violin, violoncello, and an entr'acte for orchestra. A magnificent collection of violins and violoncellos is in the possession of this artist family. THOMAS HADDOCK, violoncellist, born at Leeds, in 1812, was another member of the family. He settled in Liverpool, as teacher and performer, and was for many years principal violoncellist of the Liverpool Philharmonic Society. He died September 22, 1893.

Haden, Arthur C., conductor and violinist, born in London, in 1852. Pupil of Sir John Goss and Henry Holmes. Conductor of the Dundee Ladies' Orchestra. His compositions include several cantatas; Campsie Glen ; Bonnie Lassie ; Two Reveries (with violin obbligato), and other songs ; Studies ; Air and variations for clarinet and pf., etc.

Hadow, William Henry, composer and writer on music, born at Ebrington, Gloucestershire, December 27, 1859. Educated at Malvern College, and Worcester College, Oxford. Studied pf. at Darmstadt (1882), and composition with Dr. C. H. Lloyd, Oxford (1884-5). Graduated B.A., 1882 ; M.A., 1885 ; and Mus. Bac., 1890, Oxford. Fellow and Tutor, Worcester College, Oxford, 1888. Lecturer on Musical Form (for Sir John Stainer) 1890-2. Appointed, 1897, to edit for Clarendon Press, a forthcoming series of works on Musical History.

WORKS.—Hymn, Who are these ? for soli, chorus, strings, and organ; Cantata, The Soul's Pilgrimage (published 1886) ; Anthem (Prize, Curwen) When I was in trouble (1885) ; Songs; Quartet in E flat, strings (1885) ; Trio in G minor, pf. and strings (composed, 1887 ; produced, Musical Artists' Society, 1890) ; Sonatas in A minor (1886), and F (1891), pf. and violin ; Sonata in B minor, pf. and viola (1889) ; Andante and allegro in F, violin and pf. Sonatas in G sharp minor (1884) ; and A flat (1890), for pf. Some of these remain in MS. Author of Studies in Modern Music, London, Seeley & Co., 1892 ; Second series, 1894 ; being essays on Criticism, Method, Berlioz, Schumann, and Wagner ; Chopin, Dvorák, Brahms, and Outlines of Musical Form. Sonata Form, Novello's Primers, No. 54 [1896].

Hafrenydd, see WILLIAMS, THOMAS.

Hague, Charles, composer and organist, born at Tadcaster, May 4, 1769. He studied the violin at Cambridge under Manini, 1779-1785. Removed to London in 1785, and studied under Salomon and Dr. Cooke. Mus. Bac., Cantab., 1794. Professor of Music, Cambridge University, in succession to Randall, 1799. Mus. Doc., Cantab., 1801. He died at Cambridge, June 18, 1821.

WORKS.—Ode performed at Cambridge in June, 1811, at the installation of the Duke of Gloucester as Chancellor of the University ;

HAIGH.

HALL.

By the waters of Babylon, Psalm. *Glees :* Two Collections ; Arrangements of Haydn's 12 symphonies as pf. duets; Plumptre's Collection of Songs, moral, sentimental, instructive, and amusing, Cambridge, 1805. Pf. music, etc.

His daughter HARRIOT (born 1793, died 1816) published in 1814 " Six Songs," with pf. accomp.

Haigh, Thomas, composer and pianist, born at London, 1769. He studied music under Haydn, at London, 1791-92. Resided in Manchester, 1793-1801. Returned to London in 1801, and died there, April, 1808.

WORKS.—Sonatas for pf. and violin, op. 4, 6, 8, 9, 10, 12, 15, 16, 24, 33, 34, 36 ; Three sonatas, pf. duet, op. 5 ; Easy sonatas for pf. duet, op. 7 ; Three divertimentos, op. 18 ; Three sonatas, pf. and flute, op. 19; Three sonatas, op. 20 ; Three capriccios, pf., op. 38 ; Three serenatas, do., op. 40; Twelve preludes; Twenty-eight familiar airs, etc., pf. ; Twelve petites pièces for the pf., with introductory preludes to each, op. 32. Songs and glees.

Haite, John James, composer and writer, who died in London in October, 1874.

WORKS.—The Principles of Natural Harmony ; being a perfect system founded upon the discovery of the true semitonic scale, London [1855]. Violoncello Tutor, London, n.d. Oratorio, operettas, symphonies. Glee Garland, various numbers. Melodies arranged for flute and other instruments. Songs.

Haking, Rev. Ranulf (Richard ?), composer, born about 1830. Ordained, 1861. Mus. Bac., 1855 ; Mus. Doc., 1864, Oxford. Some time rector of Eaton Gray, Malmesbury; and of Congham, Norfolk, 1882. Composer of anthems : Doth not wisdom cry ; Lord, let me know my end, etc. Glees : Twine no more the cypress wreath ; By the mossy fountain ; Song of the old bell ; Welcome home ; and others. Songs, etc.

Hale, Thomas, of Darnhall, Cheshire, musician. Composed " Social Harmony. A collection of songs and catches, in two, three, four, and five parts. Also several choice songs on Masonry, all with the music," London, 1763 ; 3rd edition [1770].

Hale, Mrs. William (JEANNIE M. STEVENS), pianist and vocalist, born in Birmingham. Her father, Joseph Stevens, was an energetic member for years of the Festival Committee. Miss Stevens sang in the trio, "Lift thine eyes," from " Elijah," at the Birmingham Festival of 1849, with Miss A. and Miss Williams. She was, for several years, solo pianist and principal vocalist at the Town Hall Monday Concerts. She played to Mendelssohn, who gave her a copy of Chopin's studies, upon which he wrote his name. For many years she had a large teaching connection in the locality, and was frequently heard at chamber concerts, etc. Was heard as a pianist in Lon-

don, in June, 1854; and sang at Boosey's Ballad Concerts, St. James's Hall, 1869. She is now living in retirement in North Wales. William Machin, the bass singer, was her uncle.

Hales, William, writer on acoustics, author of " Sonorum doctrina rationalis et experimentalis, ex Newtoni opt. physicorum scriptes," Dublin, 1778.

Halford, George John, organist, pianist, and conductor, born at Chilvers Coton, Warwickshire, February 13, 1858. His early musical studies were under W. Chater (organist of Holy Trinity, Coventry; died, March 27, 1880). In 1875 he went to Birmingham, and studied pianoforte, composition, etc., under Dr. C. S. Heap. F.R.C.O. ; Mus. Bac., 1892, Durham. Has been organist successively of St. Mary's and St. George's, Birmingham, 1876-80 ; St. John's, Wolverhampton, 1881 ; St. Michael's, Handsworth, 1886 ; and from 1891, of Handsworth Parish Church. Conductor of the Birmingham Musical Association from 1886, now formed into a choir bearing his name; People's Concert Society, Stourbridge, 1886-91 ; Philharmonic Society, Redditch, 1890-4 ; Birmingham Amateur Orchestral Society; and the Midland Institute Madrigal Choir. He has introduced many important works to the local public, notably Schumann's " Manfred," produced in the Town Hall, April 16, 1896 ; and has probably conducted the first performance in this country of a Symphony in a parish church, introducing at a special service at Handsworth Beethoven's Symphony, No. 1, October 6, 1892 ; and Schumann's Symphony in B flat, November 1, 1893. He has composed a cantata, " The Paraclete," produced, 1891 ; Anthems, part-songs, etc. A concert overture, 1896 ; organ pieces, etc.

Hall, Charles King, organist and composer, born in London, in 1845. Was organist of St. Paul's, Camden Square ; St. Luke's, Oseney Crescent ; and up to the time of his death, at Christ Church, Brondesbury. He wrote an Evening Service in E flat, performed at St. Paul's Cathedral by the London Church Choir Association in 1891, and other church music. The Verger ; A Strange Host; The Foster Brothers, and other operettas produced at the German Reed Entertainments; also a cantata, Beauty and the Beast ; Songs, pf. pieces, etc. Author of " A School for the Harmonium, 1874 ; Estey Organ Tutor ; and a primer on the harmonium, Novello. He died in London, September 1, 1895.

Hall, Rev. Edward Vine, composer and organist, born at Maidstone, Kent, June 11, 1837. Chorister of Magdalen College, Oxford, 1845-55, and assistant organist, 1858-9. Graduated B.A., 1859 ; M.A., 1863, Oxford. Appointed Precentor of Worcester Cathedral, in 1877, and held the office till 1890, when he

HALL.

became vicar of Bromsgrove. He has been Conductor of the Worcestershire Musical Union from 1879. His voice at its best was a light tenor of sweet tone; and he has frequently sung at the concerts of the "Magdalen Vagabonds." He has also given organ recitals, and lectures on music, at Worcester, Birmingham, and other places. His compositions include a Cantata for Lent; Two settings of the Service for Holy Communion; Two of the Magnificat and Nunc dimittis (one, in C, performed at the closing service of the Worcester Festival, 1881); Praise the Lord, O Jerusalem, and other anthems; and a part-song, Waken, lords and ladies gay, sung at the Worcester Festival, 1878.

Hall, Elias, musician, compiled "The Psalm-singer's compleat Companion," London, 1708.

Hall, G. W. L. Marshall- composer, born in Edgeware Road, London, 1862, grandson of the famous physician, Dr. Marshall Hall. Educated at King's College, London, and at Oxford. Studied music at R.C.M., and in Switzerland and Germany. Was for some time master for foreign languages at Newton College, Newton Abbott. In 1888 he was conductor of the Choral and Orchestral Societies of the London Organ School, and in 1890, was elected Ormond Professor of Music, Melbourne University, Australia. He has founded a Conservatorium of Music there, and gives an annual series of orchestral concerts. Papers have been contributed by him to the musical press. His compositions are numerous, including three operas, of which he has written both *libretti* and music: Leonard; Dido and Æneas; and Harold. A study on Tennyson's "Maud"; an overture in G minor (Crystal Palace, 1893); Idyll, for orchestra; Quartets for strings (one, in C, performed at Queen's Hall, London, December 20, 1895); smaller works, songs, etc., etc.

Hall, Henry, organist and composer, born at New Windsor in 1655. Son of Capt. Henry Hall. He was a chorister in the Chapel Royal under Capt. Henry Cooke, and he studied also under Dr. Blow. Organist of Exeter Cathedral, 1674, and organist and vicar-choral, Hereford Cathedral, 1688. He took holy orders in 1698, and died at Hereford, March 30, 1707, and is buried in the cathedral. He composed anthems, Te Deum in E flat, and other church music. He also wrote songs and poems.

His son, HENRY, was organist and vicar-choral of Hereford Cathedral, and WILLIAM, another son (died 1700), was a member of the King's band and composer of songs.

Hall, H. Foley, composer and pianist, who flourished about 1820 and 1866. He wrote a large number of sentimental songs, for many of which George Linley supplied the

HAMERTON.

words. Among them may be named "Ever of Thee" (1859); "Blame not the heart" (1860); "Far from those I love"; "O, yes, thou'rt remember'd"; When I am far away": "Still in my dreams," etc. He also wrote polkas for pf., etc.

Hall, John, violinist and composer, born at Ayr, about the end of the 18th century. He studied the violin at Edinburgh, and returned to Ayr as a teacher, and formed a band, consisting of himself, his brothers, and others, which performed at all the principal gatherings and balls in Ayrshire. In 1822 he played in Niel Gow's band when it performed before George IV. at Edinburgh. He died at Glasgow, December 4, 1862. He published "A collection of quadrilles and waltzes for pf. and violin," n.d., and "A selection of strathspeys, reels, waltzes and Irish jigs," Ayr, n.d.

His brother, JAMES (died, Ayr, 1860), played second violin in his band, and was a teacher of dancing in Ayr and neighbourhood.

His youngest brother, DOUGLAS (died, Ayr, 1878), was a violoncellist, and resided in Ayr as a teacher and performer.

Hallewell, Frederick John, bass vocalist, born in Leeds, 1846. Pupil of " Joe " Wood, of Huddersfield. Appointed solo bass at Leeds Parish Church, 1866; to York Minster, 1867; and, two years later, to New College, Oxford, where he remained until 1880. He then went to Australia, and is now bass at St. Mary's Roman Catholic Cathedral, Sydney, and engaged in teaching. Was considered the finest bass singer in Australia.

Halley, T. Douglas, musician, was organist of St. John's, Wapping, and of St. Paul's, Shadwell, London. He published " Twelve hymns appropriate to charity sermons . . . ," London, n.d.

Hambois, or **Hanboys, John,** musician and writer of the 15th century. Generally believed to have been the first English musician on whom the degree of Doctor of Music was conferred. He is supposed to have received the degree in 1463, but there is no evidence to prove that he graduated either at Oxford or Cambridge. He wrote two tracts in Latin: Summum Artis Musices and Cantionum Artificialium diversi Generis, etc.

Hamerton, William Henry, composer and writer, born at Nottingham, in 1795. Chorister of Christ Church Cathedral, Dublin. He was taught music under T. Vaughan, at London, 1812. Teacher in Dublin, 1814. Master of Choristers, Christ Church Cathedral, Dublin, 1815. Gentleman of Chapel Royal, Dublin, 1823. Teacher in Calcutta, 1829. He is supposed to have died at Calcutta.

WORKS.—St. Alban, opera, Dublin, 1827. Vocal Instructions combined with the theory and practice of pianoforte accompaniment, 1824. Anthems, chants, glees, songs, etc.

HAMILTON.

Hamilton, Sir Edward Walter, Kt., composer, son of Rt. Rev. Walter Ker Hamilton, Bishop of Salisbury (1808-1869), born July 7, 1847. Educated at Eton and Christ Church, Oxford. Studied under Dr. Stainer, and graduated Mus. Bac. 1867. Appointed a clerk in the Treasury, 1870; served as private secretary to the Rt. Hon. R Lowe, 1872-3; to the Rt. Hon. W. E. Gladstone, 1873-4; appointed principal clerk of Financial Division in Treasury, 1885; Assistant Financial Secretary, 1892; and Assistant Secretary to Treasury in 1894. Created C.B. in 1885, and K.C.B. in 1894. Member of the Council and Executive Committee of the R.C.M. His published works include a Sacred Cantata, Praise the Lord, O my soul (degree ex.); sundry songs, singing quadrilles, pieces for pf., etc.

Hamilton, James Alexander, writer and composer, born at London, in 1785; died there, August 2, 1845.

WORKS. – Cathechism on the nature, invention, exposition, development, and concatenation of musical ideas, with examples from the great masters, London, 1838 (various editions); Catechism on the art of writing for an orchestra, and on playing from score, with sixty-seven examples, 1844; second edition, 1846, other editions; Dictionary, comprising an explanation of 3,500 Italian, French, German, English, and other musical terms, phrases, and abbreviations, also a copious list of musical characters, London, 1849 (numerous other editions); The same, with appendix containing John Tinctor's Terminorum Musicæ Diffinitorium, edited by John Bishop; Modern instructions for the pianoforte, London, 1290 editions said by publishers to have been issued; New musical grammar, in three parts (four editions); Catechism on double counterpoint and fugue; Practical introduction to the art of tuning the pianoforte, etc.; Catechism of the organ, with an historical introduction, and a list and description of the principal organs in Great Britain, Ireland, Germany, France, and Switzerland (five editions); Modern instructions for singing, containing a complete compendium of the rudiments of music, etc.; Easy method for the violoncello; Catechism for the violin; Harmonium instruction book; The pupil's new daily exercise, containing all the scales and chords in their respective positions; Method for the double bass, .. London, 1833; Sacred harmony, a collection of three hundred and fifty standard psalm and hymn tunes, London [1843]. Psalms and hymns, in the order they are appointed to be sung or chanted in cathedrals, churches, chapels. etc., during the morning and evening service of the Church of England, with explanatory notes; An introduction to choral singing,

HANCOCK.

etc.; Order of chanting the morning and evening services, according to the Rubric of the Church of England; Method of chanting the Psalms, as used in the service of the Church of England. Compositions, various, pf. pieces, glees, songs, etc.

Hamilton, David, organ-builder and writer, born at Edinburgh, April 2, 1803. He was organist of St. John's Episcopal Church, Edinburgh, for many years. Died at Edinburgh, December 20, 1863. Inventor of the *pneumatic lever* action for organs, and writer of musical articles in the old edition of "Chambers' Encyclopædia." He also composed a few organ pieces, and edited a collection of chants. He edited, with J. M. Müller, his partner, "Harmonia Sancta, a collection of chants, psalm tunes, sanctuses, etc., adapted to the service of the Episcopal Church of Scotland.. [1838]; Supplement 1858. His youngest brother ADAM was born in Edinburgh and is an organist and composer, who was conductor of the Edinburgh Choral Union, 1866-83, and other societies. He studied in Germany under F. Schneider, and has composed several orchestral works. Also editor of "The Scottish Orpheus, a collection of the most admired Scots songs arranged with symphonies and accompaniments," Edin., n.d. His son CARL DRECHSLER HAMILTON, born at Edinburgh in 1846, is conductor of the Edinburgh Amateur Orchestral Society, and a violoncellist of great merit. He is a member of the Edinburgh String Quartet, formed in 1890.

Hamilton, John, musician and poet, was born in 1761, and died at Edinburgh, September 23, 1814. He was a music seller in Edinburgh, and wrote several well-known Scots songs, such as "Up in the morning early," etc. He also issued "A Collection of 24 Scots songs, chiefly pastoral," Edin., n.d. "A complete repository of old and new Scotch strathspeys, reels, and jigs.." Edin., n.d. "The Caledonian Museum, containing a favourite collection of ancient and modern Scots tunes adapted to the German flute or violin," Edin., n.d., 3 books.

Hamilton, William, musician and publisher, was born at Paisley about 1812. He was established as a music publisher in Glasgow for a number of years. Died at Kirn, April 25, 1887. Among the publications issued by Hamilton may be named the "British Minstrel and musical and literary miscellany," Glasgow, 1842-44, issued in parts. "The British Harmonist," 1847-48. "Select Songs of Scotland," 1848, etc. He was a musician and poet, and wrote songs and music under the pseudonym of William McGavin.

Hancock, Charles, musician, author of "Accordion Instructions," London [1845]. "Flute Preceptor," London [1846]. "Violin

HANCOCK.

Preceptor," London [1846]; also "Improved" editions of these works in 1852 and 1853.

JAMES HANCOCK, a musician of the early part of this century, published Hymn Tunes and Sacred Odes for 3, 4, and 5 voices London [1800]. He also composed anthems, canons, etc.

Hancock, Charles, organist and conductor, born at Islington, London, January 4, 1852. Choir boy at St. Michael's, Cornhill, 1859, under R. Limpus (q v.); and in 1861 elected to the choir of St. George's Chapel Royal, Windsor. Articled to Sir G. Elvey, 1867, at the same time being organist at Datchet, and at St. Andrew's, Uxbridge. Received pianoforte lessons from (Dr.) Keeton, and remained as assistant to Sir G. Elvey until 1875. F.C.O., 1872; Mus. Bac., 1874, Oxford. In July, 1875, he was appointed organist of St. Martin's, Leicester, in which town he still resides. He is conductor of the Leicester New Musical Society; and from 1886, of the Derby Choral Union, and actively engaged as a teacher. His compositions comprise a setting of Psalm 18, for soli, chorus, and orchestra; Organ music, Andante in A flat, Wesley Prize, College of Organists, 1887; Songs, etc.

Hanforth, Thomas William, organist and composer, born at Hunslet, a suburb of Leeds, March 6, 1867. Chorister at York Minster. Articled pupil of W. H. Garland, and studied later under Dr. Naylor. Graduated Mus. Bac., 1892, Durham. Assistant organist, York Minster; Organist to the late Archbishop Thomson, 1885; St. Martins-le-Grand, York, 1888; Deputy at York Minster, part of 1891; and in 1892 succeeded E. H. Lemare at the Parish Church, Sheffield. Conductor of Viscountess Downe's Madrigal Society, 1891; Countess of Harewood's Ladies' Choir, 1892-3. His compositions are: Psalm 1 for soli, chorus, and strings; Two evening services, anthems; Pieces for pf., and for organ; and music for the Three Masonic Craft Ceremonies.

Hann, William Henry, viola player. Musician in ordinary to the Queen. Member of the Philharmonic, and other orchestras; and for many years in the band of the Three Choirs Festivals. In 1895 he succeeded Mr. Doyle as principal viola in the Leeds Festival orchestra. Since 1886 he has, with his sons, LEWIS R. HANN, violinist, A.R.A.M.; EDWARD HOPKINS, violinist; SIDNEY H., A.R.A.M., pianist; and CLEMENT, A.R.A.M., violoncellist, given series of chamber concerts at Brixton, which have had considerable educational value. WILLIAM CHARLES HANN, violoncellist, pupil of Piatti, is a player of repute, and has appeared at London concerts with success.

Hanway, Jonas, traveller and writer,

HARDIMAN.

born at Portsmouth, in 1712; and died in 1786. He was a traveller, and occupied much of his time in acts of benevolence. Author of "Thoughts on the importance of the Sabbath, also on the use and advantage of music," London, 1765.

Harcourt, James, organist and composer, born in Norwich, October 27, 1818. After some years as chorister in the cathedral, he was apprenticed to Alfred Pettet, organist of St. Peter, Mancroft; and to this church he was appointed in 1851, after holding office at some other churches. Failing health compelled him to resign in 1877. He was for thirty years organist and conductor of the Norwich Choral Society; for many years organist at the Triennial Musical Festivals, until 1872, when he became chorus master, which last office he held for about eight years. He was a fast friend of the composer, H. Hugo Pierson. He died at Norwich, May 27, 1883. He composed a Rondo in D, for orchestra; Two string quartets (one, in C, afterwards published as a Sonata for pf. and violin); Three movements for the soft stops, organ, and some arrangements of chamber music for that instrument.

J. ARTHUR HARCOURT, his son, was born at Norwich, January 2, 1852. Received his musical education from his father. Organist and choirmaster of the Roman Catholic Church (cathedral), the nave of which was opened August 29, 1894, erected at the cost of the Duke of Norfolk. He has written much, but his compositions remain in MS. They include an operetta "The science of love" (Clifford Harrison), performed, Norwich, October, 1874; Cantata, "The return of Spring" (words by the same), Norwich, May, 1884; Liturgical music; Twelve songs; Four duets, etc. A concert overture, for orchestra; organ and pianoforte pieces, and various arrangements. ERNEST HARCOURT, brother of the foregoing, was born at Norwich, January 25, 1860. Chorister and solo boy at St. Peter, Mancroft. Resident in Norwich, as composer, conductor, violinist, and violoncellist. In 1893, founded the Norwich Orchestral Union, which gives good concerts in St. Andrew's Hall every year. Among his compositions are an oratorio, "The Deluge," op. 32; Cantatas, "The Chapel bell," op. 19; "An Autumn legend" (composed, 1890); Anthem, "And in the sixth month," op. 34; and a part-song, "A song of welcome," all with orchestral accompaniment. Arabesque, for orchestra; Quintet for wood-wind (Norwich, 1896); Chanson in F, violoncello and pf., performed by the Musical Artists' Society, London, May, 1893; and pieces for violin and pf., etc.

Hardiman, James, Irish writer and M. R. I. A., was a native of Galway. He

HARDING.

HARKER.

became Librarian of Queen's College, Galway, and died there in 1855. Author of Irish Minstrelsy, or Bardic remains of Ireland; with English poetical translations, collected and edited with notes and illustrations," Loudon, 2 vols., 1831.

Harding, Henry Alfred, organist, born at Salisbury, July 25, 1855. Studied under Dr. Abram, Dr. Keeton, and Dr. C. W. Corfe. Graduated Mus. Bac. 1877; Mus. Doc. 1882, Oxford. F.R.C.O.; L.R.A.M. (organ), 1895. Examiner for the Incorporated Society of Musicians. Organist of Sidmouth Parish Church, and conductor of Sidmouth Choral Society for some years. Organist and director of the choir Bedford Parish Church, and Corporation organist. His compositions include Psalm 106, for soli, chorus, and orchestra. and an oratorio, St. Thomas (University ex. Mus. Doc.); Morning service in D, etc. He has published some songs and pf. pieces, and is author of Analysis of Form, as displayed in Beethoven's thirty-two pianoforte sonatas, Novello, 1890.

Hare, Amy, pianist, born at Taunton, Somerset. Studied at R.A.M., winning the extra Bennett Prize, 1880; and the Potter exhibition, 1881. A.R.A.M. Appeared as solo pianist at the Gloucester Festival, 1883. Toured in Germany with success, 1886-7; and visited America in 1889. Gave recitals at Taunton and other places in 1893, and settled in Washington, U.S.A., in that year. She was again in England in 1895-7, and played at St. James's and the Queen's Hall.

Harford, Rev. Frederick K., amateur musician, born at Clifton, Bristol, in 1832. Educated at Rugby School, and at Oxford. Ordained 1856. Chaplain to the Bishop of Gibraltar; appointed a Minor Canon of Westminster Abbey, 1862. He has composed several settings of the *Te Deum* and *Jubilate*; an evening service, and a number of anthems. A cantata, "Haroun al Raschid," produced 1884; Marches and other pieces for orchestra. "Schlummerlied," and various songs. He was active in the attempt to popularize the National Anthem in India, and prepared a version that was performed at the Albert Palace, on June 20, 1887. He was the projector of the "Guild of St. Cecilia," an association having for its object the employment of music as an aid in illness. An experimental concert was given in Westminster Palace Hotel. September 14, 1891.

Hargitt, Charles, pianist and composer, born in York, in 1804. First studied under his uncle (Charles Hargitt, died 1865), and played in public, a concerto, when eleven years of age. A few years later he studied pianoforte with Charles Knyvett, harmony with Dr. Crotch, and had violin lessons from Spagnoletti. He played for three years in the

band at the Ancient Concerts. His London *début* as a pianist was at C. Knyvett's concert at the Hanover Square Rooms, May 18, 1821, when he played Field's concerto, "The Storm," for the first time in England. Subsequently he studied under Moscheles. Upon the advice of his intimate friend, J. B. Cramer, he settled in Edinburgh, where for nearly fifty years he occupied the leading position as professor. He was passionately fond of pictures, and his collection was considered one of the sights of Edinburgh. His compositions were numerous, his arrangements and variations being the best known. The Musical Beauties of Scotland, and the songs "The last rose," and "My soul doth long," may be mentioned. After retiring from the profession he resided in Liverpool, where he died, in 1880.

Hargitt, Charles John, son of the preceding, was born in Edinburgh, in 1833. Studied under his father, Charles Halle, G. A. Macfarren, and Ferdinand Hiller. Was organist of St. Mary's Catholic Church, Edinburgh. Founder, and up to 1862, Conductor of the Edinburgh Choral Union. In 1862 he went to London, where he continues to reside; and has conducted oratorio and other concert performances. He organised the Royal Albert Hall Choral Society, of which he was sub-conductor to Gounod.

WORKS.—Opera, Coronet or Crown; Two operettas; Cantata, The Harvest Queen; Overtures, marches, and incidental music to plays; Church music. Song, The Mitherless Bairn; The Last Good-night; A Parting Gift, etc. Melody for trombone and organ; Pf. pieces, etc. Scotch airs harmonised; Part-songs, etc.

Hargreaves, George, musician and artist, son of Thomas Hargreaves, the famous miniature painter, born at Liverpool, 1799. He died at Liscard, Cheshire, in 1869. Best known as the composer of numerous prize glees. He wrote masses, an opera, songs, The Battle of Muta; The Breathings of Song, eight songs; Hours of Beauty, glee, 5 voices, etc., and had some little renown as a miniature painter.

Harington Henry, M.D., composer and physician, born at Kelston, Somersetshire, September 29, 1727. Entered Queen's College, Oxford, 1745; B.A., 1748. M.D. and M.A., Oxon. Member of Oxford Musical Society. Physician at Wells and Bath. He established a Musical Society there, and at one time held office as Mayor of Bath. He died at Bath, January 15, 1816.

WORKS.—Three Books of Glees, 1770, 1785, and 1797; Single Glees; Songs; Anthems; The hymn tune "Harington," or "Retirement," etc.

Harker, W., musician, author of "Practical Grammar of Music," London, 1830-36. "Elements of Vocal Music," London, 1845.

HARLAND.

Harland, Robert Holland, vocalist and writer, born in Yorkshire, about 1822. He settled in Glasgow as a teacher of music, and died there, October 7, 1889. He composed a number of songs, and wrote a "Treatise on Singing, in which the rules of sol-fa notation, or learning to sing by notes, are explained by examples calculated to render sight-singing simple and easy," Glasgow, 1881.

Harmston, John William, composer and pianist, born in London, 1823; died Lübeck, August 26, 1881. Composer of an immense number of pianoforte pieces, such as " Le jet d'eau," op. 193 ; La belle Rosiere," op. 195 ; " Danse des Sylphes," op. 196 ; Les Naiades," op. 211, etc., chiefly printed by foreign publishers.

Harper, Charles Abraham, horn player, second son of Thomas Harper, was born in London, in 1819. For many years he was the principal performer on his instrument in the leading English orchestras, occupying the post of first horn at the Royal Italian Opera for thirty years. He retired from the profession in 1886,—his last appointment being in the orchestra of the Savoy Theatre,—receiving from his colleagues a handsome token of their esteem. Charles A. Harper died in London, January 5th, 1893.

His brother, EDMUND BRYAN HARPER (born about 1817 ; died at Hillsborough, Ireland, May 18, 1869), was also a noted horn player, and had some reputation as an organist (he was organist to the Marquis of Downshire) and composer of vocal music. Among his songs may be named "A bandit's life is the life for me," 1868 ; "Love's whisper"; "Many years ago"; "Truth in absence," etc. He also composed pf. music. He married Marianne Lincoln, the vocalist (q.v.).

Harper, Rev. John, clergyman, author of "The nature and efficacy of Musick to prepare the mind for good impressions," a sermon ; London, 1830.

Harper, Thomas, trumpet player, born Worcester, May 3, 1787. Studied in London, under Elvey, 1798. Member of the East India Volunteer Band. Principal trumpet-player at Drury Lane and English Opera House. Played at Birmingham Musical Festival, 1820. Inspector of musical instruments for the East India Company. Principal trumpet-player at Royal Italian Opera, and at Concert of Ancient Music. He died at London, Jannary 20, 1853.

He wrote an Instruction Book for the Trumpet ; "School for the Cornet-á-piston," London [1865], and compiled a number of books of selections for that instrument, the Kent bugle, etc. He also arranged airs for the bugle.

His son, THOMAS JOHN, born London, 1816, entered the R.A.M. in 1830, studying violin

HARRIS.

and pf., in addition to the trumpet. He was for a time violinist in the opera band at Her Majesty's Theatre. As a trumpet-player he was early in arriving at a high position. Associated with his father in the principal orchestras and festivals, he succeeded him as the first trumpet-player of the day. His last Festival appearance was at Hereford, 1885. He was for a long time a professor at the R.A.M., of which institution he is a Fellow.

Harper, William Henry, pianist and composer, born in London, August 26, 1845. He is accompanist to the South London Choral Association, and the composer of several songs and pf. pieces; "Hunters' chorus"; "'Tis lone on the waters," and other part-songs, etc.

Harraden, R. Ethel, MRS. FRANK GLOVER, composer of the present time. Her works comprise an operetta, " His last chance"; A cantata, "Pearl," for treble voices ; Chorus, "Over the sea our galleys went," performed by the Browning Society, November 28, 1884; The lover's leap ; Waking and dreaming ; Gaydon Inn, and many other songs. Two melodies ; Gavotte ; Legende, for violin and pf., etc. Her sister, BEATRICE HARRADEN, is a skilful performer on the violoncello, but is better known as the writer of "Ships that pass in the night," "In varying moods," and other works. HERBERT HARRADEN is a composer, pianist, and lyric author. He wrote the book of the operetta named above, and has published some songs, etc.

Harrington, Henry, see HARINGTON, HENRY.

Harris, George Frederick, RUDOLF NORMANN, organist and composer, born at London in 1796. For 45 years he was organist of St. Lawrence, Jewry, London. He died at London, November 21, 1867. Under the pseudonym of *Rudolf Normann*, he published many arrangements for the pianoforte and organ.

Harris, James, M.P., author and amateur. composer, born at Salisbury, in 1709, died, December 22, 1780. Author of "Three Treatises—Music, Painting, and Poetry," etc., London, 1744. 5 editions issued to 1792.

Harris, Joseph John, organist and composer, born at London, in 1799. Chorister in Chapel Royal. Organist of S. Olave's Church, Southwark, 1823; of Blackburn Church, 1828; and choirmaster of Collegiate Church, Manchester. He became organist of the Cathedral in 1848. He died at Manchester, February 10, 1869.

WORKS.—Selection of Psalm and Hymn Tunes, adapted to the psalms and hymns used in the Church of S. Olave, Southwark, 1827 ; Four glees [1837]; Anthems ; Songs, etc. ; The Musical Exposition, a guide for parents

HARRIS.

in their choice of qualified teachers of music, 8vo, 1845.

His son, JOSEPH THORNE HARRIS (1828-1869), was also a musician.

His brother JAMES, born 1797, died at Lewisham, April 13, 1875. Graduated as Mus. Bac., Oxford, in 1833.

Harris, Joseph Macdonald, organist and composer, born at London, in 1789. He was a chorister in Westminster Abbey, and a pupil of Robert Cooke. In 1843 he had to be confined in a lunatic asylum. He died in May [1860]. Wrote songs, duets, and pf. music. Published five vocal trios [1817]; Six glees [1812]. "Select portions of the Psalms, a collection of metrical versions, with sixty psalms and fifty hymns by the most approved authors. By Montague Burgoyne. The music newly harmonised and arranged for 1, 2, or 3 voices by J. M. Harris," London, 2 vols., 1827.

Harrison, Annie Fortescue, see sub. HILL, LORD ARTHUR.

Harrison, John, watchmaker and writer, born at Foulby, Yorkshire, 1693; died at London, March 24, 1776. Author of a work entitled "A description concerning such mechanism as will afford a nice or true mensuration of Time, with an account of the discovery of the scale of music." London, 1775. He invented an improved chronometer and was a celebrated mechanician.

Harrison, John, musician and organist, was born at Canterbury, in 1808. He was a pupil of Goodban and Field, and was for eighteen years organist of St. Andrew's Church, Deal. He died at Deal, February 21, 1871. Compiler of "Sacred Music, a selection of Psalm tunes from the works of Bach, Handel, etc.," 1838. "Chants arranged for four voices, or a single voice," etc.

Another JOHN HARRISON, of Malton, Yorkshire, issued "Original Sacred Melodies," Malton, 1865

Harrison, Rev. Ralph, clergyman and musician, born at Chinley, Derbyshire, September 10, 1748. He was minister of Cross Street Unitarian Chapel, Manchester, from 1777 till 1810. He died at Manchester, November 4, 1810. Compiler of "Sacred Harmony, a collection of Psalm tunes, ancient and modern, set in four parts . . ," 1784-91, 2 vols. This contains the well-known psalmtunes, "Warrington," "Ridley," and "Peterborough," all by Harrison.

Harrison, Samuel, tenor vocalist, born at Belper, Derby, September 8, 1760. Appeared as treble singer at the Concert of Ancient Music, 1776-78. Sang at Handel Commemoration, 1784. Tenor at Concert of Ancient Music. Married Miss Cantelo, 1790. Established (with Knyvett) the Vocal Con-

HARROP.

certs, 1791-4. He died at London, June 25, 1812.

Was one of the most popular tenor singers of his time, and was particularly successful in ballad singing.

Harrison, William, tenor vocalist and composer, born at Marylebone, London, June 15, 1813. He made his first public appearance in 1836, and afterwards studied at the R.A.M., 1836-7. He sang at Sacred Harmonic Society concerts; début in opera, at Covent Garden Theatre, in Rooke's "Henrique." Established, with Miss Louisa Pyne, "The English Opera Company," 1856. Sang in tenor rôles in operas by Balfe, Wallace, Benedict, Mellon, etc. He died at London, November 9, 1868. He composed an operetta, "Les noces de Jeannette," and a number of songs, but is best remembered as an encourager and promoter of national English opera. He produced Balfe's "Bohemian Girl"; "Rose of Castille," etc., and Wallace's "Maritana" and "Lurline."

Harrison, William, organist and composer, born at Lichfield, in 1841. He was a chorister in Lichfield Cathedral, and afterwards a music teacher at Rugby School, and at Liverpool. In 1867 he was appointed organist of St. James's Church, at Leith, and he was also conductor of the Dunfermline Choral Society. He composed a Jubilee Ode, words by W. B. Baildon, 1887. He died at Edinburgh, June 21, 1889.

Harriss, Charles Albert Edwin, organist and composer, born in London, December 15, 1862. Son of EDWIN HARRISS, sometime organist of St. Mark's, Wrexham, where he was a chorister at the age of eight. Elected Ouseley Scholar, St. Michael's College, Tenbury, 1875. Was assistant organist at St. Giles Parish Church, Reading, 1880; and in 1881, appointed to the Parish Church, Welshpool, and private organist to the Earl of Powis. In 1883, father and son settled in Montreal, Canada, and soon imparted new vigour to the musical life of the place. Charles was appointed organist and rectorchori of Christ Church Cathedral, and later to the Church of St. James the Apostle, which became, by his exertions, famous for the excellence of its musical services. A glee and madrigal society was also established. His cantata, "Daniel before the King," produced by the Montreal Philharmonic Society in 1890, was the first published work of the kind by a composer resident in Canada. He has also written an opera, "Torquil," produced Montreal, 1896; a large number of anthems, songs, pf. and organ pieces. As an extempore player on the organ he has a high reputation.

Harrop, Sarah, MRS. JOAH BATES, soprano vocalist, born in Lancashire, and was originally employed in a factory at Halifax. She

HARROWAY.

studied under Sacchini and Dr. Howard. Married to Joah Bates, 1780. She sang at all the principal London concerts and festivals. Died in London, December 11, 1811.

Harroway, John, composer and conductor, born about 1809; died, January 25, 1857. He composed music for numerous comic and other songs by Sam Cowell, J. E. Carpenter, etc., such as " Alonzo the brave " ; " That's the way the money goes " ; " Who's your hatter ?" etc. He also published much dance music.

Hart, Charles, composer and organist, born May 19, 1797. Studied at the Royal Academy of Music under Crotch. Organist successively of St. Dunstan's, Stepney, 1829-33 ; Tredegar Square Church. and St. George's, Beckenham. He died at London, March 29, 1859.

WORKS. — Omnipotence, oratorio, 1839. Three anthems dedicated to Dr. Crotch. Te Deum and Jubilate in C (Gresham prize composition, 1831). Glees, songs, etc.

Hart, George, violinist and writer, born in London, March 28, 1839. He studied at the Royal Academy of Music under Sir G. A. Macfarren and M. Sainton. While a fine violinist, he was better known as a judge of the instrument and as a maker. He succeeded to his father's business, and became head of the firm of Hart and Son, Wardour Street, London. Author of two valuable works : The Violin, its famous makers, and heir imitators, London, Dulau, 1875 ; and The Violin and its music, London, Novello, 1881. The first has passed through several editions, and was published in French, in 1886. He died in London, April 25, 1891.

Hart, Joseph Binns, organist and composer, born at London, in 1794. Chorister in St. Paul's Cathedral in 1801. He studied under John Sale, S. Wesley, M. Cooke, J. B. Cramer, and Attwood. Deputy organist to Attwood at St. Paul's. 1805. Organist at Walthamstow, and at Tottenham. Chorusmaster, English Opera House, Lyceum, 1818 20. Music-seller in Hastings, 1829. Organist St. Mary's Chapel, Hastings. He died at Hastings, December 10, 1844.

WORKS.—*Dramatic Music* : Amateurs and actors, 1818; A walk for a wager, 1819 ; The Bull's head, 1819 ; The Vampire, 1820. Sets of quadrilles, waltzes, lancers, etc.; An easy mode of teaching thorough-bass and composition. Songs, pf. music.

Hart is credited with the invention of the dance form known as the Lancer's Quadrille. His music is not of much importance. With John Fawcett, he edited " Melodia divina, a sacred companion for the pf. . . . ."

Hart, Philip, composer and organist, was born about the middle of the 17th century. He was a bass singer at York Minster till

HARVEY.

1670, when he became a Gentleman of the Chapel Royal, 1670-1718. Lay-vicar Westminster, 1670-1718. Organist of St. Andrew Undershaft, London ; St. Michael's, Cornhill; St. Dionis, Blackheath, 1724. He died at London, 1749.

WORKS.—Ode in praise of musick (Hughes), 1703 ; Morning hymn from Paradise Lost, Milton, 1729 ; Anthems ; Organ fugues ; Songs in various collections. Melodies proper to be sung to any of ye versions of ye Psalms of David " [1713].

JAMES HART (1647-1718), who was a Gentleman of the Chapel Royal and a chorister of Westminster Abbey, was probably a relative.

Hartland. A family of musicians, at West Bromwich, Staffordshire. The father, TIMOTHY HARTLAND, was born in 1810. For some years he was organist of the Parish Church, and afterwards, for 50 years, organist and choirmaster of Ebenezer Church, West Bromwich. The first in the locality to adopt the Hullah system of teaching singing, he formed a large and successful class. He had a fine tenor voice, was a skilful flute player, and did much for the promotion of music in the district. He wrote a good deal of church music, and his anthems and hymn tunes have gained popularity in America and Australia. He died at West Bromwich, February 16, 1891.

His youngest son, WILLIAM HARTLAND was born at West Bromwich in 1850. Appeared in public as a pianist at a very early age. Studied first under a local teacher, Symeon Grosvenor, and later under C. E. Flavell, and Franklin Taylor, with whom he resided in London ; studied the organ with F. Archer. Returning to West Bromwich, he held office as organist at several churches, but his teaching connection extending, he gave these up. In 1877 he was elected Town Hall organist ; and in 1875 he founded the West Bromwich Choral Society. the conductorship of which he still retains. In 1891 he started a series of Sunday evening organ recitals in the Town Hall, and has frequently appeared as pianist at concerts. The Choral Society attaining its majority, a Musical Festival—the first—was held at West Bromwich, April 22, 1896, to celebrate the event, and occasion was taken to recognise the honorary work of the conductor. He is Professor of Singing at the West Bromwich Institute. His sister, LIZZIE HARTLAND, was for some time accompanist to the Choral Society, but is now occupied in teaching and composition. Her dramatic cantata, " Cœur de Lion," was performed at West Bromwich in February, 1888. She has also written a cantata for female voices, " Queen of the roses " ; many songs, part-songs, and pf. pieces.

Harvey, Richard Frederick, composer. Has published an immense number of pf.

HARVEY.

piecos, fantasies, arrangements, and a few original compositions. Also "I love but thee alone ; The golden days ; Thady and I ; Stormy. petrel, and many other songs, part-songs, etc.

Harvey, William, musician, composer of "The Melksham Harmony, containing 50 original tunes, etc," London [1800].

Harwood, Basil, organist and composer, born at Woodhouse, Olveston. Gloucestershire, April 11, 1859. Educated at Charterhouse, and Trinity College, Oxford. Studied under J. L. Roeckel, G. Riseley, C. W. Corfe ; and at Leipzig Conservatorium under Reinecke and Jadassohn. Mus. Bac., 1880 ; B.A., 1881 ; M.A., 1884, Oxford. Organist of Trinity College, Oxford, 1878-81 ; St. Barnabas, Pimlico, 1883-7 ; Ely Cathedral, 1887-92 ; and Christ Church Cathedral, Oxford, from 1892. Conductor of Oxford Orchestral Association, 1892 ; Orpheus Society, 1894. President of the University Musical Club, 1895. His published works comprise : Agnus Dei, and O Salutaris, chorus and organ, op. 2 ; Cathedral Service in A flat, op. 6 ; Six songs, op. 3 ; Trio, female voices, To Daffodils, Christmas Carols, etc. Sonata in C sharp minor, op. 5 ; and Dythyramb, op. 7, for organ. Three pieces for pf., op. 1, etc.

Harwood, Edward, composer, born at Hoddleson, near Blackburn, 1707, died in 1787. Composed "A Set of Hymns and Psalm Tunes,"..n.d. ; "A Second Set,"..Chester, 1786. Chants and anthems, a few of which are in use at the present time. The first set of hymns contains the well-known setting of Pope's "Vital spark of heavenly flame." Harwood also wrote a number of once popular songs.

Haskins, James F., musician, compiled a Concertina Preceptor, London, 1852 ; Pianoforte Preceptor, 1853 ; Singing Preceptor, n.d. ; Modern Cornopean Preceptor, 1853, and other works, for Tegg, the publisher. He was a teacher in London, and celebrated the 40th anniversary of his musical career at Shoreditch, in 1888.

Hastings, David Henry, writer on music, was born about 1809 ; and died on December 10, 1890. He was musical critic to the *Morning Herald*, and for over forty years he contributed to the *Musical World*.

Hately, Thomas Legerwood, composer, editor, and teacher, born at Greenlaw, Berwickshire, September 26, 1815. Apprenticed when a boy to Messrs. Ballantyne & Co., printers, with whom he remained 11 years. Entered employment of Thomas Constable. Self-taught in music. Precentor of North Leith Parish Church, 1836 ; do. St. Mary's Parish Church, Edinburgh. Appointed (after disruption)precentor to Free Church Assembly. Precentor in Free High Church. Established

HATHERLY.

"Annual aggregate meetings of Congregational Classes," for practice of psalmody, 1846. Director of the Scottish Vocal Music Association, founded 1856. He died at Edinburgh, March 22, 1867.

WORKS.—The National Psalmody, a selection of tunes for the use of churches, etc., Edinburgh [1847] ; The Psalmody of the Free Church of Scotland, with an accompaniment for the pianoforte. Prepared under the superintendence of George Hogarth, Esq., Edinburgh, 1845 (other editions) ; The Scottish Psalmody, 1852 ; Irish Presbyterian Psalmody ; Hymnals of the Church of Scotland ; Historical lectures on Psalmody, with illustrations ; Lecture on music of the Scottish Reformation (included in Tricentenary proceedings), 1860 ; Harmonies of Zion. *Psalm Tunes* : Glencairn, Huntingtower, Cunningham, Leuchars, Submission, Makerstoun, Nenthorn, Kilmany, Zuingle, Polwarth, Consolation, etc. ; Seann Fhuinn nan Salm Mar tha iad air an Seinn anns A'Ghaeltachd mu Thuath ; or, the old Gaelic psalm tunes as sung in the congregations of the Free Church of Scotland in the North Highlands, Edinburgh, 1845. Melodies for the young, Edinburgh, n.d.

Hately, Walter, pianist and composer, born in Edinburgh, January 29, 1843. Son of the preceding. Educated at the High School, Edinburgh. Studied music at the Conservatorium. Leipzig, under Plaidy, Moscheles, Reinecke, Hauptmann, E. F. Richter, and Dreyschock. 1861-4. Later, he studied for a short time with Schulhoff at Dresden. Resident since 1865 in Edinburgh. Teacher of pf. in the Ladies' College ; Merchant Company's Schools ; Church of Scotland Training College ; and precentor of Free St. George's Church. President of the Edinburgh Free Church Praise Union, 1892. Mr. Hately has published : Heigh-ho, daisies and buttercups ; Ellorie ; King winter ; Row, burnie row, and other songs, including two settings from Goethe. Nocturne ; Romances ; Barcarolle, etc., for pf. ; also a New Pf. Tutor. Editor of Church of Scotland Psalter and Hymnal, 1868 ; and contributor of hymn tunes to various collections. He also aided the Psalmody Committee of the Scottish Church in the preparation of their tune-book.

Hatherly, Very Rev. Stephen George-son, composer and writer on music, born at Bristol, February 14, 1827. Studied music privately, and received instruction in composition from the Rev. W. H. Havergal. Held appointments as organist at Darlaston, 1844 ; Solihull, 1847 ; St. James's, Wednesbury, 1855 ; Tettenhall, 1863-8. Musical conductor at the Greek Church, Liverpool, 1857. Graduated Mus. Bac., Oxford, 1856 ; and in 1893, received the degree of Mus. Doc., *honoris*

HATTERSLEY.

causâ, from the University of St. Andrews. Ordained deacon and priest of the Greek Church at Constantinople, 1871 ; and in 1875 became Protopresbyter of the Patriarchal Œcumenical Throne of Constantinople. Was engaged on the Mission to Greek and Slavonian Seamen at Bristol Channel ports. He has published upwards of fifty works, many of them relating to Greek music, on which subject he is an acknowledged authority. These include Specimens of Ancient Byzantine Ecclesiastical Melody, for 4 voices, Greek text, 1879 ; Hymns of the Eastern Church, translated by Dr. Neale, complete, with music from Greek and other sources, 1882 ; A treatise on Byzantine Music, London, Gardner, 1892, an elaborate and scholarly work. An oratoriette, Baptism, 1860 ; Te Deum and Jubilate, 1853 ; Benedictus and Apostles' Creed, 1856 ; Service of the Greek Church in English, 1860 ; Common Praise, an enlarged edition (the 5th) of Rev. W. H. Havergal's Old Church Psalmody, 1864 ; Appendix to 6th edition of same, 1876. Imperial Russian Air, and God save the Queen, set in canon, etc. He has lectured on Greek Church Music (Liverpool, 1889), and contributed to *Musical Opinion*, and other papers.

Hattersley, Frederick Kilvington, pianist and composer, born at Wortley Grove, Leeds, June 11, 1861. Studied at R.A.M., winning the Balfe Scholarship, 1881, and the Charles Lucas prize for composition, 1883. Studied later at Munich Conservatorium under Rheinberger. A.R.A.M.; Mus. Bac., Cambridge, 1887. Resident in Leeds as organist and choirmaster of St. John's Church, composer and teacher.

WORKS.—Cantata, Robert of Sicily, for soli, chorus, and orchestra (specially written for the Leeds Philharmonic Society, and produced March 14, 1894) ; Evening service in E flat ; songs, etc. Symphony for orchestra (Bradford, 1885) ; Concert overture in E minor (composed for, and produced at the Leeds Festival, October 15, 1886, and performed at the Crystal Palace, February 19, 1887) ; Trio in D minor, pf. and strings (Leeds, 1885) ; Sonatas for pf. and violin, in G minor (Leeds, 1889), and F major (London, 1894) ; pieces for pf., etc.

Hatton, David, bag-pipe player, born at Thornton, Yorkshire, 1769 ; died November 22, 1847. He invented an instrument something like the Irish bag-pipe, on which he performed with much skill.

Hatton, John Liptrot, composer and pianist, born at Liverpool, October 12, 1809. He was chiefly self-taught in music, and in 1832 he settled in London, where he became pianist at Drury Lane Theatre, etc. He visited the United States in 1848. Musical director of Princesses Theatre, London, under

HATTON.

management of Charles Kean. He was a teacher and pianist, and frequently travelled in the provinces as accompanist to concert parties. He died at Margate, September 20, 1886.

WORKS.— *Operettas*—Queen of the Thames, 1844 ; Pascal Bruno, 1844. Music for Macbeth, 1853 ; Sardanapalus, 1853 ; Faust and Marguerite, 1854 ; King Henry VIII , 1855 ; The Tempest ; Richard II., 1857 ; King Lear, 1858 ; Merchant of Venice, 1858 ; and Much ado about nothing, 1858. Rose, or Love's Ransom, opera, Covent Garden, London, 1864. The First printer. Robin Hood, cantata, 1856 ; Hezekiah, sacred drama, December 15, 1877. Concert overture in G. Two fantasias for pf. and orchestra. Morning and evening service in E ; Services in C and E flat. *Anthems*—Blessed be the Lord of Israel ; Come. Holy Ghost ; I will extol Thee, my God ; I will praise Thee with my whole heart ; Out of the deep ; Thou art gone up on high ; Pastor Holy ; Graduale ; Mass for four voices and organ. *Part-songs*—Absence ; All things love thee ; A song of winter ; Auburn village ; A lover's song ; Beware ; Bird of the wilderness ; Bonney blackbird ; Come, live with me ; Good night, beloved ; Hark ! the convent bells are ringing ; I loved a lass, a fair one ; I met her in the quiet lane ; King Witlaff's drinking horn ; Lo ! the peaceful shades of evening ; Love me little, love me long ; Now let us make the welkin ring ; Over hill, over dale ; Shall I wasting in despair ; Sleep, my sweet ; Song of the gipsey maidens ; Song to Pan ; Stars of the summer night ; Summer eve ; Life boat ; Pearl divers ; Rivals ; Village blacksmith ; Venetian boatmen's evening song : When evening's twilight. *Songs*— Songs for sailors, written by W. C. Bennett ; 19 songs by Herrick, Jonson, and Sedley ; Autumn ; Aftermath ; By the millstream ; Bird of song ; Cloris ; Come back, Annie ; Dream, baby, dream ; Dick Turpin ; Fair is my love ; Fair daffodils ; Fair and false ; Friar of orders grey ; Farmer at the banks ; Garl nd, the ; Gentle flower ; Good-bye, sweetheart ; Hope ; If my mistress hide her face ; I stood on the beach ; I think on thee ; Jack o' Lantern ; King and the cobbler ; King Christmas ; Kitty Carew ; Leather bottél ; Lass of Watertown ; Lady Maud ; Memory ; Maiden's rose ; Maid I love ; Ocean ; Phœbe dearest ; Sweet as the moonlight ; Simon the cellarer ; Song should breathe of scents and flowers ; Spring ; Starbeams ; Sailor's return ; Sun to his rest ; Sea song ; Show-man ; True to love and thee ; The wishing well ; The blind boy ; The goldsmith's daughter ; The last fond look ; The nun a'd the rose ; The slave's dream ; 'Tis midnight ; Uncle Jack ; Under the greenwood tree ; Weep no more ; Winter ; When

HAVERFIELD.

far from thee in distant lands ; Wilt think of me ? *Pianoforte Music*—Six impromptus ; Prelude and fugue in G minor ; Magic music ; Presto ; Arrangements ; Dances. Singing Methods for various voices ; Thirty Elementary Studies for pf. ; and many other works.

His son, GEORGE FREDERICK HATTON, appeared at a Richter concert in London, June 13, 1881, in which year he was appointed pianist to the Duke of Saxe-Meiningen. He has played in many cities of Germany. Composer of " The Golden Rose," a cantata for treble voices ; Two trios for pf. and strings ; Organ music, songs, etc. Another of his family, a daughter, was a vocalist, now married to Mr. C. G. Moore, and resident in Canada.

Haverfield, Rev. Thomas Tunstall, clergyman and writer, author of "Feriæ Sacræ, or short notes on the great festivals of the church and the services appointed for their celebration, with appropriate chants and hymns," London, 1847. Composed Collects, etc.

Havergal, Rev. William Henry, composer and divine, born at High Wycombe, January 18, 1793. Educated at Oxford. B.A., 1815; M.A., 1819. Rector of Astley, Worcestershire, 1829-42. Rector of St. Nicholas, Worcester, and hon. canon Worcester Cathedral, 1845. Rector of Shareshill, near Wolverhampton, 1860-68. He died at Leamington, April 19, 1870.

WORKS.—A History of the Old Hundredth Psalm Tune, 1854. Old Church Psalmody, 1849. One Hundred Psalm and Hymn Tunes. Ravenscroft's Psalter (1611), edited 1847. Anthems, psalms, hymns, etc., to number of about 50. Among his best known tunes may be named Havergal (1870), and Evan (1846), the latter being very popular in Britain and America, where it was introduced by Lowell Mason.

His daughter, FRANCES RIDLEY, born at Astley Rectory, Worcestershire, December 14, 1836, was a pupil of Dr. Wm. Marshall and Alberto Randegger. She died at Caswell Bay, Swansea, June 3, 1879. She was a poetess of some note, her hymns and other pieces having been very popular. She composed some hymn tunes, " Eirene," etc.

His eldest son, the REV. HENRY EAST HAVERGAL (born 1820, died January 12, 1875), was educated at Oxford. He was made rector of Cople, Bedfordshire, in 1847, and did much to promote the cultivation of good music in Bedford and Oxford. He composed much church music, chants, hymns, etc., and edited Wither's " Hymns of the Church," 1846.

His youngest son, the REV. FRANCIS T. HAVERGAL, D.D., was vicar of Upton Bishop, Hereford. Died near Ross, in July, 1890.

HAWES.

Author of " Memorials of Sir F. A. G. Ouseley," 1889.

Hawdon, Matthias, organist and composer. A celebrated performer in his day, but of whom very few particulars are known. He was organist of Beverley Minster, and of St. Nicholas (now the Cathedral), Newcastle-on-Tyne. He was appointed to the latter in 1776, and is said to have held the dual appointment for some time. He was buried, March 22, 1787, according to his expressed wish, underneath the old Renatus Harris and Snetzler organ, in St. Nicholas' Church. His works include Two Concertos in B flat, and F ; Six Conversation Sonatas for the harpsichord or pianoforte, with accompaniment for two violins and violoncello [1785]; An Ode on the King of Prussia, and six songs. First Sett of six sonatas spirituale or voluntarys, for the harpsichord, organ, or pf., op. 4. The opening of an organ, a choice set of voluntaries. The concerto in B flat is still played at organ recitals, and his hymn tune, Beverley (C.M.), has been in use at Newcastle ever since his time. He composed " Fancy," a song, and other vocal music.

Haweis, Rev. Hugh Reginald, amateur violinist, and writer on music, born at Egham, Surrey, April 3, 1838. Educated at Cambridge, graduating B.A., 1859 ; M.A., 1864. Incumbent of St. James's, Marylebone, 1866. Editor of *Cassell's Family Magazine*, 1868. Has lectured on musical topics at the London Institution, and in many provincial towns ; and in 1885 lectured in America. His contributions to various periodicals have been numerous ; and he is the author of two volumes on music : Music and Morals, London (W. H. Allen), 1873 ; and My Musical Life, London, W. H. Allen, 1884. The first of ᐧthese has reached its 16th edition.

Hawes, William, composer and writer, born at London, June 21, 1785. Chorister in Chapel Royal, 1793-1801. Violinist in Covent Garden orchestra, 1802. Deputy Lay-vicar, Westminster, 1802 ; afterwards full vicar, a post which he held till 1820. Gentleman of Chapel Royal, 1805. Master of Choristers, Almoner, and Vicar Choral, St. Paul's Cathedral, 1812. Associate Philharmonic Society, 1813. Master of Children of Chapel Royal, 1817. Lay-vicar, Westminster Abbey, 1817-20. Established Harmonic Institution in the Argyle Rooms, Strand, where Hawes was a music-publisher for a time. Music director, English opera, Lyceum, 1824-36. Produced Weber's " Der Freyschütz," July 24, 1824. He died at London, February 18, 1846. Buried in Kensal Green Cemetery. Member of Glee Club. Conductor of Madrigal Society, etc.

WORKS.—*Music for Plays:* Broken Promises, 1825 ; The Sister of Charity, 1829 ; The Irish

HAWKER.

Girl, 1830; Comfortable Lodgings, 1832; The Dilsk gatherer, 1832; The climbing boy, 1832; The Mummy, 1833; The Quartette, 1833; Yeoman's Daughter, 1833; Convent Belles (with J. A. Wade), 1833; The Muleteer's Vow, 1835. Collection of five glees and a madrigal [1814]; Six glees for 3 and 4 voices [1815]; Six Scotch airs harmonized as glees [1817]; Prize glees. Adaptations of operas by Paër, Salieri, Winter, Mozart, Ries, Marschner, etc. *Songs :* The Beacon; Father William, etc. Edited an edition of "The Triumphs of Oriana." Chants, sanctuses, and responses to the commandments, as used at St. Paul's Cathedral and Westminster Abbey. Selected from ancient and modern composers, London, 1830, 12 pts. Anthems, and other sacred music, as used at His Majesty's Chapel Royal, and the various Cathedrals throughout the kingdom, selected from ancient and modern composers, London. A collection of Spofforth's glees, and a Collection of madrigals for 3, 4, 5 and 6 voices, from the works of the most eminent composers of the 16th and 17th centuries, carefully extracted from the original works as preserved in the Madrigal Society. Service in G minor (MS.). Croft's services and anthems, 1840. Psalm and hymn tunes.. harmonised for 3 voices, edited by J. W. Hall, London [1836].

His daughter, MARIA BILLINGTON HAWES, contralto vocalist, was born at London, April, 1816. She studied under her father, and others, and sang at the Birmingham Festival of 1846. She corresponded with Mendelssohn. Married to Mr. J. D. Merest. Died at Ryde, Isle-of-Wight, April 24, 1886. She composed a large number of ballads.

Hawker, Peter, musician, Lieut-colonel in the army, and a well-known writer on sport, etc. He died in 1853. Author of "Instructions to young performers for acquiring, by means of patent hand moulds, the best position for strength and articulation on the Pianoforte," 1840, 3 editions.

Hawker, Thomas Henry, musician, issued "Collection of Psalm and Hymn tunes, chants, etc., as sung at All Saints' Church, St. John's Wood, London [1854].

Hawker, William, musician, issued "Harmonia Sacra Familiæ, containing psalms, hymns, etc.," London, 1841. 2nd ed., Exeter [1845].

Hawkes, R. W., musician, compiler of "The Worcester Tune book . . ," London, 1865.

Hawkes, Thomas, land surveyor and musician, born at Wiveliscombe, Somerset, November 3, 1786; died at Williton, Somerset, July 9, 1857. Author of "An Introduction to divine service, Watchet, 1831; and compiler of "Hawkes's Psalmody, a collection of tunes comprising the most approved

HAWKINS.

standard, with a great variety of original compositions adapted to the hymns in use by the Wesleyan Methodist Societies," Watchet, Whitehouse, 1833. The original tunes were chiefly composed by local amateurs of Somerset and Wiltshire.

Hawkes, William, musician, author of "The Theory of Music simplified, and the principle of the temperament applied to the tuning of keyed instruments explained; also the best method of Tuning," London, 1805. "A specific statement and view of the improved musical scale for organs and pianofortes," London, 1810.

Hawkins, James, composer and organist, born in latter part of the 17th century. Chorister, St. John's College, Cambridge. Organist of Ely Cathedral, 1682-1729. Mus. Bac., Cantab., 1719, He died at Ely in 1729. Composer of Services, Anthems, collection of Scotch songs. "As northern winds, song," etc. His son, JOHN, was organist of Peterborough Cathedral. 1714-1759, and composed a number of Anthems, preserved in Tudway's collection, etc.

Another JOHN HAWKINS issued a "New Set of Psalm and Hymn Tunes," London [1810].

Hawkins, Sir John, Kt., writer and lawyer, born at London, March 30, 1719. Became an Attorney. Member of Madrigal Society, and of Academy of Antient Music. Married Miss S. Storace, 1753. Retired to Twickenham. Chairman of Middlesex Quarter Sessions. Knighted, 1772. He died at Spa, May 14, 1789.

WORKS.—Twelve Cantatas (words), 1742-43, music by J. Stanley. An account of the institution and progress of the Academy of Antient Music, 1770. A General history of the Science and Practice of Music, London, 5 vols., 1776 (with portraits); new edition, Novello, 1853. Edition of Walton and Cotton's "Compleat Angler." 1760.

Hawkins was much esteemed in his day, and was one of Dr. Johnson's literary executors. He did much by the publication of his "History" to enlighten the English musical public on the past state of the art, and though its value is less owing to the lapse of time, it is still a standard text-book to the history of music. Its merits, and superiority in some respects over the history of Burney, lie in its acknowledged greater accuracy and plainness of detail. Its merits in this respect are indeed great, for, despite some few blemishes in the matter of mis-stated facts, it is a remarkably erudite and straightforward production. Hawkins was buried in Westminster Abbey. His daughter, LÆTITIA MATILDA (1758, November 22, 1835), was a novelist, and biographical writer, and his son, JOHN SIDNEY, wrote among other works "An inquiry

HAY.

into the nature and principles of thorough-bass on a new plan," London [1818].

Hay, Walter Cecil, organist, composer, and conductor, born at Shrewsbury, August 7, 1828. Studied, R.A.M. Has been bandmaster in the army, militia, yeomanry, and volunteers. F.R.A.M. Organist and professor of music at Shrewsbury School; Conductor of New Choral Society, 1865, and of Shrewsbury Orchestral Society. Author of Prize Ode to the Victor in the Wenlock Olympian Games (1857). "The Valley of St. John," cantata (from the Bridal of Triermain, 1863); "May," cantata, Shrewsbury, 1866: "Etheldred," operetta, 1887; and incidental music to "Phyllis," a pastoral play, by J. P. Douglas, 1887.

Hayden, George, organist and composer of first half of the 18th century. He was organist of St. Mary Magdalen, Bermondsey, London. Composer of Harlequin Director, cantata [1723]; three cantatas [1723]. *Songs:* Careless Companion; Mad Tom; Welcome Damon. As I saw fair Chloe, and other two-part songs. Plumstead's "Beauty's of Melody," 1827, contains some of Hayden's songs.

Haydock, Frederick W., organist and composer. Studied under Dr. Horton Allison and privately. Graduated Mus. Bac. 1880, Mus. Doc. 1891, Dublin. Was sometime organist of St. Gabriel's, Manchester; and since 1880, of Union Chapel in that city. His compositions are two cantatas, "O magnify the Lord," and "Lazarus," for soli, chorus, and orchestra. Some songs, etc., of his have been published.

Haydon, Thomas, organist and musician, born in London, in 1787. He studied under C. Neate and Crotch, and became organist and Professor of Pianoforte at R.A.M. He died about 1845. He composed songs, and many romances, waltzes, and quadrilles for pianoforte.

Hayes, Catherine, soprano vocalist, born at Limerick, Oct. 25, 1825. She studied singing under Sapio and Garcia, and at Milan under Ronconi. *Début* at Marseilles in "I Puritani," 1845, and afterwards sang in Vienna (1846), Venice, and elsewhere in Italy. Appeared in London, Covent Garden Theatre, April 10, 1849. Sang in Ireland, America (1851), India, Australia, etc. Married to Wm. Avery Bushnell of New York, October 8, 1857. She died at Sydenham, London, August 11, 1861.

Miss Hayes was a singer of remarkable powers, and in her day was a most popular and favourite vocalist. Her chief power lay in the rendering of ballads. Her biography was issued under the title of "Memoir of Miss Catherine Hayes, the 'Swan of Erin.'" 4to, n.d., with portrait.

Hayes, William, organist and composer, born at Hanbury, Worcestershire, in Decem-

HAYNE.

ber, 1706. Chorister Gloucester Cathedral, under W. Hine. Organist of St. Mary's Church, Shrewsbury, 1729-31; of Worcester Cathedral, 1731-34; Magdalen College, Oxford, 1734-77. Mus. Bac., Oxon., 1735. Professor of Music, Oxford University, 1741. Doc. Mus., Oxon., 1749. He conducted the Gloucester Musical Festival in 1763. Died at Oxford, July 27, 1777.

WORKS.—Collins' ode to the Passions, and other odes. Twelve ariettas or ballads, and two catches, 1735. Services and anthems. Circe, masque. Glees, catches, etc., first set, 1757; second set and supplement, 1763-65. Cathedral Music, in score, edited by Philip Hayes, 1795. Instrumental music. Remarks on Mr. Avison's essay on musical expression, London, 1753. Anecdotes of the five music meetings, etc. Sixteen Psalms from Merrick's new version, set to music for the use of Magdelen College Chapel, Oxford . . . , n.d.

Hayes, William, clergyman and writer, third son of the above, born at Oxford, 1742. Chorister Magdalen College, 1749-51. B.A., 1761; M.A., 1764. Minor Canon, Worcester Cathedral, 1765. Do. St. Paul's, London, 1766. Vicar of Tillingham, Essex. He died on Oct. 22, 1790. He wrote a paper entitled, "Rules necessary to be observed by all Cathedral singers in the Kingdom," in Gentleman's Magazine, 1765. Sermons, hymn tunes, and other works.

Hayes, Philip, organist and composer, was born at Oxford, 1738. Second son of William Hayes, under whom he studied. Mus. Bac., Oxon., May, 1763. Gentleman of the Chapel Royal, 1767. Organist of New College, Oxford, 1776; Magdalen College, Oxford, and Professor of Music in the University, 1777. Mus. Doc., Oxon., 1777. Organist of St. John's College, 1790. He died at London, March 19, 1797.

WORKS.—Prophecy, oratorio, 1781; Ode for St. Cecilia's Day; Ode, Begin the song; Telemachus, a Masque. Anthems, services, psalms, glees, and songs. Harmonia Wiccamica, London [1780]. Six concertos for organ, harpsichord or pianoforte, 1769. Eight anthems, Oxford [1780].

Hayne, Rev. Leighton George, clergyman and composer, was born at St. David's Hall, Exeter, February 28, 1836. He was educated at Eton and Oxford. In 1856 he graduated Mus. Bac., and in 1860 proceeded to Doc. Mus., Oxford. In 1857 he was appointed organist, and in 1860 precentor, of Queen's College, Oxford. He was ordained in 1861. In 1863 he was made coryphæus or precentor of Oxford University; and he held the livings of Helston, 1866, and Mistley-with-Bradfield in 1871. He became succentor of Eton College in 1867, and held it till 1871. He died at Bradfield, in Essex, March 3, 1883.

HAYNES.

He edited, with the Rev. H. W. Sargeant, "The Merton Tune Book," 1863, and composed the following well-known hymn tunes: "Compline," "Hayne," "Mistley," "St. Cecilia," "St. Margaret," "Chalvey," etc. While at Eton he had a huge organ of five manuals built in the music-room; it was ultimately divided between the organs of Bradfield and Mistley.

Haynes, Walter Battison, organist, pianist, and composer, born at Kempsey, Worcester, in 1859. Studied at Leipzig Conservatorium, where some of his compositions (movements from a symphony, and songs), were performed in 1882. He was appointed organist of St. Philip's, Sydenham, in 1884; and in 1891 succeeded H. F. Frost at the Chapel Royal, Savoy. In 1890 he was appointed professor of harmony and composition at the R.A.M.; and he is an Associate of the Philharmonic Society. For the Handel Festival of 1891 he wrote additional accompaniments to Handel's Chandos anthem, "O come, let us sing." His compositions include two cantatas for female voices: The Fairies' Isle, and A Sea Dream; Three settings of the Magnificat and Nunc dimittis; A Communion Service, etc. Songs and duets. An Idyl for violin and orchestra; Prelude and Fugues for two pianos; Sonata in D minor, and other pieces for organ.

His uncle, WILLIAM HAYNES, born at Worcester, September 19, 1829, was an articled pupil of Mr. W. Done, and in 1850 was appointed organist of Malvern Priory Church, a post he held for 43 years. He has composed church music, songs, and organ pieces. In 1858 he established a music business in Malvern. His wife, born ELIZABETH BROAD, a soprano, frequently sang in public under the name of Mlle. Brétet. She was educated at the R.A.M., and the Conservatoire, Paris.

Hayter, Aaron Upjohn, organist and composer, born at Gillingham, Dorset, December 16, 1799. His father, SAMUEL HAYTER, was organist at Mere, Wilts., and composer of services, anthems, etc. In 1805 Hayter became a chorister at Salisbury Cathedral, under Corfe. Afterwards he was organist at Hereford Cathedral, but in 1835 he went to New York as organist of Grace Church. He removed to Boston, Mass., as organist of the Trinity Church Society; and in 1839 was elected organist and conductor of the Handel and Haydn Society, a position he held till 1848. He died at Boston, July 28, 1873. Hayter introduced many oratorios and cantatas to the Boston public which had never been heard in America. He was succeeded by his son, GEORGE F. HAYTER, as conductor of the Handel and Haydn Society. Another son, ARTHUR UPJOHN HAYTER, is organist of St. Mary's Church, Stratford-le-Bow.

HEALE.

Hayward, Henry, violinist and composer, born at Broseley, Salop, in 1814. Received his first lessons from his father, and played a solo in public when five years old. His studies were continued under Spagnoletti, and his executive powers were so extraordinary that he became known as the English Paganini. After some years passed in the Midlands, he made his *début* in London, at one of Mr. Carter's Soirées at the Hanover Square Rooms, June 19, 1839. He appeared at the Philharmonic Concerts, March 23, 1840, playing his introduction and Polonaise. About this time he settled in Wolverhampton, where he established musical societies, and a music business. As an orchestral player he was for many years engaged at the principal festivals, and was much associated with music in Birmingham. His compositions were numerous, but remained. mostly in MS. For some years he was in poor health, and died at Wolverhampton, November 12, 1884.

Head, F. A., musician, compiler of "Choral Psalmody, a collection of tunes to be sung in 3 parts, without instruments, by all village choirs, with simple rudiments and instructions for teaching music on a short and easy plan," London [1840].

Heale, Helene, pianist and composer, born in London, February 14, 1855. Educated at Queen's College, Harley Street, obtaining the Maurice Scholarship. Studied music under John Hullah. In 1876 she obtained a Scholarship at the National Training School, and the next year won one of the four Royal Scholarships there, which she held until 1881. Her teachers were Ernest Pauer, J. F. Barnett, E. Prout, and (Sir) A. Sullivan. In 1880 she played before the Queen at Windsor Castle. Resident in London as teacher and composer.

WORKS.—Madrigal, Mourn, oh rejoicing heart, Madrigal Society's Prize, 1882; The Watersprites, cantata for female voices, 1885; Jubilee ode; chorus and orchestra. 1887; Epithalamion (from Edmund Spenser), tenor solo, chorus and orchestra, 1893. Part-songs for female voices; three-part songs; twelve two-part songs; twenty-four rounds for female voices; eight Christmas carols; Love wakes and weeps; Cradle song; Lament, and other songs. Six characteristic pieces, pf. duet; Polacca, three violins and pf., etc. Compiler of Class Singing School, 4 books; editor and arranger of songs for female voices; songs for the young, etc.

Her sister, ALICE HEALE, contralto vocalist, was born in London, December 15, 1861. Educated at the Queen's College, and holder of the Queen's Scholarship for five years. Studied under J. Hullah. Lady Freake Scholar at the National Training School, where she studied under J. B. Welch, and

HEAP.

with him later at the Guildhall School. She made her *début* at the Crystal Palace, May 9, 1885; sang at the Glasgow Choral Union, and other concerts, and before the Queen at Windsor, 1886. After further study under Mr. W. Shakespeare, she has devoted herself entirely to teaching voice production and singing.

Heap, Charles Swinnerton, composer, organist, pianist and conductor, born at Birmingham, April 10, 1847. Sang in public as a child, and in 1858 was admitted to the choir of the Birmingham Festival as a soprano. Received lessons from Mr. Walter Brooks (*q.v.*), and acted as organist at Queen's College, during his educational course at King Edward's Grammar School. He was articled to Dr. Monk, of York Minster, and in 1865, competed for, and won, the Mendelssohn Scholarship. Proceeding to Leipzig he studied under Moscheles, Hauptmann, E. F. Richter, Reinecke, and others. There he produced several compositions, and occasionally deputised for Reinecke as accompanist at the Gewandhaus concerts. In 1867, he returned to Birmingham, and by arrangement with the Scholarship Committee placed himself under W. T. Best, for further study of the organ. He graduated Mus. Bac., 1871; Mus. Doc., 1872, Cambridge. In 1870, the Birmingham Philharmonic Union was founded, and Dr. Heap appointed conductor, an office he held until 1886, when the society was dissolved. Excellent cheap oratorio concerts were given. At various times he has been conductor of societies at Stone, Stafford, Walsall, and Stoke. In 1881, he succeeded Mr. Stockley as conductor of the Wolverhampton Festival Choral Society, and conducted the Festivals in that town in 1883, and 1886. When the North Staffordshire Festival was established at Hanley, in 1888, he was appointed conductor, an office he has held since that time. In 1895 he was elected conductor of the Birmingham Festival Choral Society, and in 1897, appointed chorus-master for the Birmingham Musical Festival. He has given chamber concerts in Birmingham, 1871-3, and 1884-6; given pianoforte and organ recitals in many places; whilst as a teacher his work and influence have been wide-spread. From 1869 to 1878 he held organ appointments in Birmingham and Wolverhampton. Was appointed examiner for Musical Degrees, Cambridge, 1884. He has received many tokens of appreciation of his work, the highest compliment paid him being the selection of his cantata, "The Maid of Astolat," for performance, under his direction, on the occasion of the visit of the Prince of Wales to Hanley, January 7, 1897.

WORKS.—Psalm 3; Oratorio, The captivity, both in MS. *Cantatas :* The Voice of Spring

HEIGHINGTON.

(Hemans), chorus and orchestra, performed by the Liverpool Philharmonic Society, 1882; The Maid of Astolat, produced at the Wolverhampton Festival, 1886; Fair Rosamund, produced at Hanley Festival, 1890 (both librettos by the late D. L. Ryan). Benedictus, for soprano solo, chorus and orchestra; anthems, songs and part-songs, etc. Two concert overtures for orchestra, one, in F, composed for, and produced at the Birmingham Festival, 1879; Quintet, pf., and wind, 1882; Trio, pf. and strings; Sonatas, for pf. and clarinet, 1879; pf. and violin; and pf. solo. Pf. pieces, various; Organ music, etc.

Heather, *or* **Heyther, William,** musician, was born at Harmondsworth, Middlesex, in 1584. Lay-vicar, Westminster Abbey. Gentleman of the Chapel Royal, 1615. Doc. Mus., Oxon., 1622. He founded a music lecture at Oxford in 1626. Died, July, 1627, and is buried in Westminster Abbey. Chiefly famous as the founder of the music lectureship at Oxford, which ultimately became the present professorship.

Heather, William Edward, composer and pianist, born in 1784, son of STEPHEN HEATHER (choirmaster at Eton College; born 1748, died at Windsor Castle, November 14, 1831). He died after 1830. Composer of National airs as trios, with variations for harp, pf. and flute [1820]; Selection of German Hebrew melodies . . . poetry by J. Hogg, London [1816]; Serenade for pf. and flute. *Songs :* Brignall banks; Cypress wreath; Hygeia, and many others, by Sir Walter Scott, and others. Author of a "Treatise on Pianoforte Study," London [1820].

Hedgcock, Walter William, organist and composer, born at Brighton, January 15, 1864. Studied the organ and composition under Dr. Alfred King, and was assistant organist to him at St. Michael's, Brighton, in 1876. Afterwards he was appointed organist of Patcham Church, near Brighton, and, in 1879, went to London as organist of St. Agnes', Kennington Park, taking, later on, also the duty of choirmaster. He was now very busy with concert work, and acting as accompanist. In 1894 he succeeded Alfred J. Eyre as organist of the Crystal Palace, Sydendam, and in a little over a month after his appointment had the onerous duties of organist at the Handel Festival, which were successfully carried out. He has been solo organist at the Crystal Palace Saturday Concerts. Of his compositions a Suite de Ballet, for orchestra, was performed at the Crystal Palace, May 16, 1892. He has, besides, written a number of songs, of which " When bright eyes shine," and others, have become popular; also some pieces for pf.

Heighington, Musgrave, composer and organist, born in 1680. He was an organist at Yarmouth, 1738, and Leicester, 1739. For

M

some time he resided at Dublin. He was a Doc. Mus., but it is not known at which university he graduated. He died at Dundee in 1774.

WORKS.—Ode for the Spalding Gentlemen's Society; The Enchantress, or Harlequin Merlin. Six select odes of Anacreon in Greek, and six of Horace in Latin, London [1760]. *Songs :* When I survey that matchless face ; Song upon a lady being drowned taking pleasure on the sea with her lover, etc. Tunes in Alcock's " Harmony of Jerusalem," etc.

Hele, John, organist. Student, and associate, R.A.M. Mus. Bac., Oxford, 1871. In 1860 he was organist of Pennycross Church, Plymouth ; and has since held appointments there, and at Devonport, Christ Church, 1863; St. Mary's, 1864 ; St. Peter's, 1872; Compton Gifford, 1894. He was organist at Morden, Surrey, 1865-7; and of Bodmin Parish Church, 1868-72. He is conductor of the Plymouth Choral and Orchestral Association, Vocal Association, and other societies. In 1883 he was appointed borough organist, Plymouth, and he gave his 2000th recital in that town in October, 1896. He has published some church and organ music.

Helmore, Frederick, writer on "Church Choirs," London ; and on "Speakers, Singers, and Stammerers," London, 1874.

Helmore, Rev. Thomas, writer and composer, born at Kidderminster, May 7, 1811. Educated at Oxford. Curate of S. Michael's, Lichfield, 1840. Priest-vicar, Lichfield Cathedral. Precentor of S. Mark's College, Chelsea, 1842. Master of Choristers, and Priest in ordinary, Chapel Royal, 1846. Died at London, July 6, 1890.

WORKS.—Manual of Plain Song, 1850 (other editions, enlarged); Primer of Plain Song (Novello's Music Primers); The St. Mark's Chant Book, 2 parts ; A Hymnal Noted, or Translations of the Ancient Hymns of the Church, set to their proper melodies ; Fuller Directory of the Plain Song of Holy Communion ; Harmonies to Psalter, Canticles, etc. ; Accompanying Harmonies to the Hymnal Noted..1852; Catechism of Music, 1867 ; Papers on Church Music read at the Church Congress at Wolverhampton, 1867 ; Swansea, 1879 ; and London, 1868 and 1880. Christmas carols, hymns, etc. Trans. of " Treatise on Choir and Chorus Singing," F. J. Fétis.

Hempel, Charles Frederick, organist and composer, born at Truro, September 7, 1811. Son of C. W. Hempel (1777-1855), who was organist of St. Mary's Church, Truro, under whom he studied. He succeeded his father as organist of St. Mary's in 1844, and in 1857 he was appointed organist of St. John's Episcopal Church, Perth, where he died, on April 25, 1867. He was Mus. Bac., 1855, and

Mus. Doc., Oxon., 1862. He composed " The Seventh Seal," oratorio, 1862 (Degree exercise); Songs, and pianoforte music.

Hempson, Dennis A., or DENYS A HAMPSY, Irish harp-player and composer, born in 1695 ; died November, 1807. Supposed to have been a skilful performer, and said to have composed some of the fine national airs of Ireland. He played at the Belfast Meeting of harpers in 1792. His harp, dated 1707, was preserved in the collection of the Rev. Sir H. Harvey Bruce, at his mansion at Downhill.

Hemsley, John, organist and composer, born at Arnold, Notts., in 1838. Chorister, Lichfield Cathedral. Organist, Merivale, Warwick, 1857. Lay-clerk, Ely Cathedral, 1860. Stipendiary Choirman, Christ Church and St. Patrick's Cathedral, Dublin, 1864. Composed anthems, songs, etc.

Hemstock, Arthur, organist and writer, born at Bingham, Notts., 1845. Author of " On Tuning the Organ," London [1876] ; and composer of church music, organ and pf. music, and a setting of Psalm 145 [1885]. He is organist at Diss, Norfolk.

Hemy, Henri Frederick, composer and organist, was born of German parents at Newcastle-on-Tyne, November 12, 1818. He was organist of St. Andrew's R. C. Church at Newcastle, and latterly a professor of Music at Tynemouth, and of singing and pianoforte at St. Cuthbert's College, Ushaw, Durham. Compiler of " Crown of Jesus Music," in four parts, 1864, etc. Best known by his " Royal Modern Tutor for the Pianoforte," 1858, which has gone through numerous large editions. His son, C. NAPIER HEMY, is a well-known marine painter.

Henderson, A. G., author of " Philosophy of Music," 1856. (Appears also in Manchester Papers, a Series of Occasional Essays, v. 1, 1856.)

Henderson, Rev. Andrew, clergyman and musician, born at Kirkwall, Orkney, January 4, 1825. He was educated at St. Andrews, and ordained minister of Coldingham, 1847, and of Abbey Close, U. P. Church, Paisley, 1855. He was secretary to the Hymnal Committee of the United Presbyterian Church. He edited " Church Melodies," 1858, 1860, and 1862 ; " The New Scottish Psalter," 1870, in which several of his own tunes appear.

Henderson, J. Dalgety, tenor vocalist, born at Montrose, Forfarshire, December 23, 1856. Brought up to a business career, he is now a well-known paper agent in London ; but coming of a musical family, he inherited the gift, and studied singing at the Guildhall School of Music, under Mr. Richard Latter. His fine voice soon gained him notice, and he has sung with success in most parts of the

HENLEY.

United Kingdom. He appeared at the Monday Popular Concerts in January, 1883 ; at the Crystal Palace in May, 1885, and has gained an honourable position among the vocalists of the time.

Henley, Rev. Phocion, clergyman and composer, born at Wootton Abbots, Wilts, 1728. Rector of St. Andrew's Wardrobe, with St. Anne, Blackfriars, 1759. He died at London, August 29, 1764. He composed "The Cure of Saul ;" "Hear my prayer," and other anthems, hymns, and chants. "Divine Harmony : being a collection of Psalm and hymn tunes in score," 1798, two vols., compiled in association with Thomas Sharp.

Henniker, Henry Faulkner, organist and composer, born at Chatham, in 1839. Entered the R.A.M., and studied under Sterndale Bennett, Sainton, and others. A.R.A.M. ; Mus. Doc., Cantuar, 1889. Since 1864, he has been organist of Holy Trinity Church, Maidstone. He is conductor of a Choral Society there. His compositions include an oratorio, " St. Stephen ;" several operas ; " Who will come with me ?" and other songs ; choruses for use in public schools. A Manual for the violin, etc.

Henry, Chaplin, *otherwise* HENRY CHAS. STROUD, bass vocalist, was born in 1826. He was originally a bookseller, but became principal bass at the Foundling Chapel. He died January 12, 1888. His daughter, ELIZABETH (or BESSIE STROUD) was also a vocalist. She married Mr. Montem Smith.

Henry, John, composer, born in North Wales, has published a cantata, " Olga," for soli, chorus, and orchestra, produced, Liverpool, February 9, 1893. He has also composed a number of songs.

Henry, John Harold, violinist and composer, born at Lichfield, August 5, 1870. Appeared at concerts when thirteen, and later, entered the R.A.M., studying under A. Burnett and Prosper Sainton. Shortly after leaving the R.A.M., he went to Leipzig for further study under Hans Sitt. On his return to England he renewed his concert engagements, and in 1892 settled in Derby. There he established an Orchestral Society, and has given some excellent concerts. He has published Scales and arpeggios for the violin ; Wiegenlied ; Cavatina ; Six Feuillets d'album, for violin and pf., etc.

Henry, P. C., author of " Universal Singing Preceptor : exercises for the formation of the Voice, the production of a good tone," etc., n.d.

Henry VIII., King of England, born at Greenwich, 1491 ; died at Westminster, 1547. He is accredited with the composition of the anthem, " O Lord, the maker of all things," and a Latin motet. He was a patron of

HERBERT.

music and the fine arts generally, and is frequently mentioned as having been a musician of some skill.

Henshaw, Grace Mary Williams, pianist. Studied at the R.A.M., and was the first to obtain the Liszt Scholarship, 1887. Studied at Berlin, with extension of the scholarship, and made her *début* there in 1890, as a pupil of Klindworth. Returned to London in 1892, and is established there as a concert-giver and teacher. She is an Associate of the R.A.M.

Henshaw, Thomas W., organist and composer, born in 1780. Entered the Chapel Royal, St. James's, when eight, and afterwards acted as assistant organist there. Organist of St. Pancras Church, London ; resigned in 1864. He died at London, October 17, 1868, accidentally burnt to death. He compiled " A Selection of the most approved Psalm and Hymn Tunes adapted to the Manual of Parochial Psalmody of the Rev. T. H. Horne.." London [1829], also [1843].

His brother, WILLIAM HENSHAW (born 1791, died September 30, 1877), was organist of Durham Cathedral from 1811 to 1862, and brought the choir to a high state of efficiency, which made it celebrated throughout Britain. He was a Mus. Doc. (Durham ?).

Henslowe, Rev. W. H., author of " The Phonarthron, or Natural System of the Sounds of Speech, including the Phonodion or Elements of Music," n.d.

Henstridge, Daniel, organist and composer of 17th and 18th centuries, was organist of Canterbury Cathedral from 1700 to 1730. He composed anthems and other church music. He died at Canterbury in 1736.

Hepworth, George, organist and composer, born at Almondbury, Yorkshire. Studied at Hamburg, and was appointed organist of the Parish Church of Mecklenburg, and later, to the Cathedral at Schwerin. He has composed a Sinfonia in G minor (published in the *Organists' Quarterly Journal*) ; a Concertstück for 4 hands, performed at Chemnitz, 1884 ; a Fantasia, and other pieces for organ.

Herbert, Edward, organist, composer and author, born in 1830. He was organist at Perth, and of Sherborne Abbey Church, and Wimborne Minster. Graduated Mus. Bac., Oxford, 1862. He died at Wimborne in 1872. Author of a " Manual of the Rudiments of Music," and composer of anthems, etc.

Herbert, Victor, violoncellist of the present day, born in Ireland (?), about 1858. Grandson of Samuel Lover. Lived for some years in Vienna, where his Suite for violoncello was produced in 1885. He married FRAULEIN FÖRSTER, soprano, of the Dresden Court Theatre, and with her went to the United States in 1886.

HERON.

Heron, Henry, musician and organist. He was organist at Ewell. Author of " Parochial music corrected : plain and distinct rules for the more pleasing and correct performance of Psalmody, to which is added an easy introduction to singing," London, 1790. Composer of songs and ballads sung at Ranelagh Gardens [1765] ; ten voluntaries for the organ or harpsichord [1770], etc.

Heron-Allen, see **Allen, E. Heron.**

Hersee, Rose, soprano vocalist, born in London. Received her first instruction from her father, and studied later with Garcia, Madame Rudersdorff, and Arditi. Made her first appearance on the concert platform at the age of eleven. Her operatic *début* was at Her Majesty's Theatre, when she sang as the Mermaid in " Oberon." Went to America in 1869 to join the Carl Rosa Company, where she met with great success. Sang in opera in Australia, New Zealand, and the Cape, 1878-80. In 1881, was *prima donna* at the Lyceum, and of the Royal English Opera in London and the provinces. Has sung at the Crystal Palace, Philharmonic, and other concerts. Married Arthur Howell, contrabassist (*q.v.*). A brilliant vocalist, she long enjoyed the favour of the public.

Her father, HENRY HERSEE, was a teacher of singing, librettist, and musical critic, retiring from *The Observer* in 1894. He was secretary of the Philharmonic Society for some years, from 1880. He died at Lewisham, May 21, 1896, in his seventy-seventh year. His chief works were English adaptations of " Carmen," " Aïda," " The Merry Wives of Windsor," and an original libretto, " Pauline " (founded on " The Lady of Lyons "), for F. H. Cowen, produced in 1876.

Hervey, Arthur, composer and writer on music, born in Paris, January 26, 1855. Only son of Charles J. V. Hervey, of Killiane Castle, Wexford, Ireland. Educated at the Oratory School, Edgbaston, Birmingham. Studied harmony under Berthold Tours, and instrumentation with Edouard Marlois. He was originally intended for the Diplomatic Service, but from 1880 has devoted himself entirely to music. For some time he acted as musical critic to *Vanity Fair;* and on January 1, 1892, he entered on a similar duty on the *Morning Post*, in succession to the late W. A. Barrett. He married a daughter of the late Sir Edmund Harrison, a lady whose literary ability is shown in the words of many of the songs he has set. The translations of the three albums of songs named below are by Mr. Hervey's father, author of " The Theatres of Paris," and numerous essays contributed to leading magazines and reviews.

WORKS.—Opera in one act, The Fairy's Post Box (Palgrave Simpson), Court Theatre, 1885; Opera (in MS.). *Songs:* Sechs Liebes-

HEYTHER.

lieder (Heine) ; Herzens Stimmen, six songs (Heine) ; Neüe Liebeslieder, eight songs; Love of my life ; May song ; Once ; Mine all, and many others. Dramatic overture, Love and fate, for orchestra, produced at St. James's Hall, November 21, 1890, and at the Crystal Palace, April, 1892; Suite for orchestra (MS.). Romance, violin and orchestra; Reverie, violin and pf. ; Cantilene and Légende Espagnole, 'cello and pf. Six album leaves ; Six esquisses en forme de valses, and other pf. pieces, etc. *Literary :* Masters of French Music (one of a series of works on contemporary musicians), London, Osgood, 1894.

Heseltine, James, organist and composer, flourished during the first part of 18th century. Organist of St. Katherine's Hospital, London, in the beginning of the 18th century. Organist of Durham Cathedral, 1711-1763. He died at Durham, June 20, 1763. Composer of anthems, and other church music.

Heullan, see ROBERTS, JOHN.

Hewett, James, author of " An Introduction to Singing ; or, the rudiments of music, to which is added a complete set of practical lessons, together with a collection of the best and most useful psalm tunes, and several anthems by eminent masters, London, 1765.

Hewitt, Daniel Chandler, musician and writer, born in 1789; died at London in 1869. Author of " New Analysis of Music, in which is developed a theory of melody, harmony, and modulation," London, 1828. " The True Science of Music, being a new exposition of the laws of melody and harmony," 1860 and 1864.

Hewlett, Henry Gay, writer, died February 25, 1897. Author of " Autobiography, Memoir, and Letters of Henry Fothergill Chorley," London, 2 vols., 1873.

Hewlett, Thomas, organist and composer, was born at Oxford, March 16, 1845. He studied music under the Rev. L. G. Hayne, at Oxford, and graduated as Mus. Bac. there in 1865. In 1865 he became organist in the private chapel of the Duke of Buccleuch at Dalkeith, a post he retained till 1871 He was also organist of St. Peter's Episcopal Church, Edinburgh, from 1868 to 1869 ; of St. Mary's R. C. Church ; of the Edinburgh Choral Union ; and of Newington Parish Church, Edinburgh, 1873-1874. He died at Edinburgh, April 10, 1874, and is buried in Newington Cemetery, where a monument, erected by the Choral Union, marks his grave. He composed some very meritorious music for the organ and pianoforte ; songs and part-songs, and wrote the two well-known hymns, Angelic songs (" Hark, hark, my soul ") and Dalkeith.

Heyther, William, See HEATHER, WILLIAM.

HEYWOOD.

Heywood, John, organist and writer on music, born at Birmingham, 1841. Studied pf. and organ under John Chapman (organist of St. Thomas's, Birmingham), and afterwards at R.A.M., under C. Steggall, Walter Macfarren, and H. Regaldi. Has held appointments as organist and choirmaster at St. Jude's, Birmingham, 1863; St. Mary's, Aston Brook (and to Plain-Song Choir, Holy Trinity, Bordesley), 1864-5; St. Margaret's, Ward End, 1865; and St. Paul's, Balsall Heath, from 1866 to the present time. Organizing Choirmaster to Church Choral Association for Archdeaconry of Coventry, 1871-95; and choir inspector for the same, 1895 to present time. For some years on the staff of *The Choir and Saturday Musical Review*, and later of *The Monthly Musical Record*. Composer of Try me, O God; I am the Lord; and other anthems. Sundry Festal Chant settings, hymn tunes, songs, etc. Editor of the Anglican Psalter Noted (1864); The Choral Office of Matins and Evensong (1876). Author of Our Church Hymnody, an essay and review (1881); The Versicles and Responses, a paper (1886); and The Art of Chanting, London, Clowes, 1893.

Hicks, Rev. Edward, B.A., author of "Church Music, a Popular Sketch; being a glance at its origin, development, and present use," Manchester, 1881.

Hickson, William Edward, composer and teacher, born early in the present century; died, London, April, 1870. Compiler of "Singing Master: containing instructions for teaching singing in schools and families.." London, 1836-42, 6 vols. "Musical gift from an old friend: containing 24 new songs for the young," London, 1859.

Higgins, Edward, composer and singer. Was a vicar-choral of Dublin Cathedrals. Died in August, 1769. A composer of chants.

Higgins, William Mullinger, F.G.S., author of "The Philosophy of Sound and Musical Composition, and History of Music," London, 1838.

Higgs, H. M., composer of the present day. He has composed a Suite de ballet, for orchestra, performed at Reading, May, 1891; Six pieces for violin and pf.; Sonata in C minor; Prelude and Fugue; Offertoire in D minor, and other pieces for organ.

Higgs, James, organist and writer, graduated Mus. Bac., Oxford, 1874. F.R.C.O. Was organist of Eaton Chapel, Pimlico, 1843; St. Benet and St. Peter, Paul's Wharf, 1844; St. Mark's, Kennington, 1852; St. Michael's, Stockwell, 1864; and from 1867, organist and choirmaster of St. Andrew's, Holborn. An Examiner for College of Organists since 1867. Author of Primers on Fugue and Modulation (Novello); Editor of a Collection of Two-part Solfeggi; Joint editor (with Dr. J. F. Bridge)

HILES.

of Bach's organ works; and writer of a series of articles on "Organ arrangements," with brief sketches of authors (*Musical Standard*, 1882). He has given organ recitals at the Bow and Bromley Institute, etc., and in 1883 was appointed professor of harmony, R.C.M.

Hiles, Henry, organist, composer, and didactic writer, born at Shrewsbury, December 31, 1826. Received his early instruction from his brother John (*q.v.*), and held an organ appointment at thirteen. In 1846 he was appointed to a church at Bury, and the next year to Bishopwearmouth. From 1852 he was abroad for some time on account of ill-health. In 1859 he was appointed to St. Michael's, Wood Street, London; and later in the year to St. Thomas's, Old Trafford, and organist and teacher to the Blind Asylum, Manchester; 1861, to Bowden Parish Church; 1864, to St. Paul's, Hulme, Manchester, which he resigned in 1867. Conductor of societies at Preston, Warrington, and other places; and of the Manchester Athenæum Musical Society up to 1891. Graduated Mus. Bac., 1862; Mus. Doc., 1867, Oxford. Gained the first prize for an organ composition, College of Organists, 1864, and four others consecutively for anthems and organ music. Elected a Fellow in 1865. Gained the prize for a serious glee, 1878, Manchester Gentlemen's Glee Club; and in 1882, won the Meadowcroft prize. Appointed, in 1876, lecturer on harmony, musical composition, and history, Owens College, Manchester, and in 1879 to the Victoria University. Drew up, in 1890, a scheme for the establishment of a faculty of music in conformity with the Charter of the University, and in 1891 was appointed permanent Senior Examiner, and Lecturer, etc., as before. Professor of harmony and composition, Royal Manchester College of Music. He took an active part in promoting what is now the Incorporated Society of Musicians, from 1882, and was one of the strongest workers for it, by pen and personal effort.

WORKS.—Oratorios, David, 1860; The Patriarchs, 1872. Cantatas; Fayre Pastoral; The Crusaders; Watchfulness, female voices and orchestra. Settings of Psalms 46, 90, 96 and 100, for voices and orchestra. Anthems, services, etc. Operetta, War in the Household, 1885; Historic opera, Harold (libretto by Marian Millar), composed, 1893; Installation Ode, Come, sacred learning, Victoria University, 1892; Break, break (Tennyson), chorus and orchestra, 1892; The Wreck of the Hesperus. Part-songs, various; Songs, etc. Concert overtures, Youth, and others. Sonata in G minor, Six Impromptus, and other works for organ; Pieces for pf., etc. Educational works: Grammar of Music, 2 vols.; Harmony of Sounds, three editions, 1871-2-8; Part Writing, or Modern Counterpoint; Har-

HILES.

mony, Chordal and Contrapuntal; Harmony versus Counterpoint, 1894. First lessons in Singing, 1881; Fingers and wrists, technical exercises for pf. Editor of, and contributor to, *The Quarterly Musical Review*, 4 vols., 1885-8. Contributions to *Musical Opinion*, and other journals; Papers read at meetings of the Musical Association, and Conferences of the Incorporated Society of Musicians, etc.

Hiles, John, writer and organist, brother of the above, was born at Shrewsbury in 1810. He held various organ appointments in Shrewsbury, Portsmouth, Brighton, and London, and was organist at Shrewsbury Festival, 1840-41. He died at London, February 4, 1882.

WORKS.—A progressive introduction to playing the organ, consisting of fifty-five Preludes, Fugues, Airs, etc., in two, three, and four parts, from the works of the great composers; to which is added some account of the instrument itself; a notice of its various stops, and the manner of combining them; with directions and exercises for the use of the pedals (Novello), n.d. Handbook for the Organ (selections). Short voluntaries (selected). A Catechism for the pianoforte student, etc. Catechism for the organ, 1878. Catechism for harmony and thorough-bass, with key, 2 vols., n.d. Dictionary of 12,500 Musical Terms, 12mo, 1871. Catechism for part-singing, n.d. Juvenile library of pianoforte music. Voluntaries for organ, original and transcribed. Pianoforte pieces, songs, etc.

Hill, Alfred F., violinist and composer, resident at Wellington, New Zealand. Conductor of an orchestral society there, and a concert-giver. He has composed an opera, "The Whipping Boy"; and two cantatas, "Time's great monotonie." produced at a Festival, Wellington, in 1894; and "Hinemoa," performed at the opening of Wellington Industrial Exhibition, November, 1896. Also some compositions for orchestra, etc.

Hill, Arthur George, architect, author of "Organ cases and organs of the middle ages and renaissance, a comprehensive essay on the art archæology of the organ; containing an account of the most interesting specimens of ancient organs in the churches of Continental Europe," etc., London, 1883.

Hill, Lord Arthur William, second son of the 4th Marquess of Downshire. Amateur composer; was born July 29, 1846. He was lieutenant in the 2nd Life Guards, and comptroller of H.M. Household, 1886-92. Married first to Annie, daughter of Lieut.-Col. Cookes (she died in 1874); second, to ANNIE FORTESCUE HARRISON, third daughter of James Fortescue Harrison, late M.P. for Kilmarnock Burghs. He has composed some songs, etc. His second wife composed " The Ferry Girl," St. George's Hall, 1883; "The Lost Husband,"

HILL.

operetta, London, 1884. Holiday songs. Many single songs: In the gloaming [1877]; At noontide; Sing to me; Yesteryear; and many patriotic songs. Pf. music. "In the gloaming" became very popular when first issued.

Hill, Frederick, organist and composer, born at Louth, Lincoln, in 1760. He was organist at Loughborough, and York, and died early in the 19th century. He composed pf. music, songs, and music for flute, clarinet, etc. His brothers, JOSEPH, organist at Stockton, and THOMAS, organist at Pontefract, were composers of glees, organ, pf., and harp music, etc.

Hill, Horace, composer and conductor, born at Norwich. Graduated Mus. Bac., 1869; Mus. Doc., 1878, Cambridge. Conductor of the Norwich Festival Choir; East Dereham Choral Society; North Walsham Musical Society; and chorusmaster, Norwich Festival. Some time conductor of Lynn Philharmonic Society. Composer of a cantata, "A Song of Praise," produced at Norwich Festival, 1869; and an oratorio, "Nehemiah," produced, Norwich, 1885. Concert overture, Norwich Festival, 1880. Overtures, "May Morning," Norwich, 1886; "Yewbarrow," Norwich Festival, 1893; "Dawn to Sunset," Norwich Philharmonic Society, May, 1896, and others. Sonnet, oboe and orchestra. Quartet, Benedictus. Part-song, "The Calm," Norwich Festival, 1884, etc.

Hill, John, composer and conductor, born at Norwich, April 5, 1797. He founded, in conjunction with Edward Taylor, the Norwich Choral Society, and acted as chorus master of the musical festivals from 1826 till his death. For some years he was precentor of St. Mary's Chapel, Norwich. He died at Norwich, July 28, 1846. In conjunction with his son, James Frederick, he edited the Norwich Tune Book, a collection of tunes by the most eminent composers . . . , 1844, to which he contributed several tunes.

JAMES FREDERICK HILL, son of above, was born in the parish of St. Michael at Thorn, Norwich, May 5, 1817. He was a chorister in Norwich Cathedral, and a pupil of Dr. Z. Buck. Succeeded to his father as conductor of the Norwich Choral Society. Conductor of the Madrigal Society, the Vocal Society, etc. Sang before the Queen at Windsor in 1850 and 1859. In conjunction with R. K. Bowley, Jos. Surman, etc., he aided in founding the Crystal Palace Handel Festivals. He died at Norwich, March 9, 1877.

WORKS.—Hypatia, a cantata, Norwich. I saw fair Chloris, madrigal; Old friends met together, part-song. *Songs*—The pearly dewdrop, etc.

THEODORE SHALDERS HILL, son of J. F., was born at Norwich, October 30, 1844. He is a professor of music at Birkenhead.

HILL.

Conductor of Wallasey Musical Society; Wirral Choral Society; Birkenhead People's Concerts; Y. M. C. A. Orchestral Society; Blackburn Orchestral Society, etc.

Hill, Thomas Henry Weist, violinist and conductor, born in London (Islington), January 3, 1828. Studied at R.A.M., under Sainton; King's Scholar. 1845. F.R.A.M., and sometime professor of the violin at that institution. He soon became known as a concert performer, being taken up first by E. J. Loder, and then by Jullien. He toured in America under the management of F. Burgess, and was the first to play Mendelssohn's violin concerto in that country. Later he visited the principal cities of Europe. On his return he was engaged in the orchestras of the Opera, Philharmonic, and Sacred Harmonic Societies. He was appointed conductor at the Alexandra Palace, which was opened in May, 1873. Conducted the orchestral concerts of Madame Viard-Louis, in 1878, bringing forward many important compositions. At the Alexandra Palace he revived Handel's "Esther," November 6, 1875 ; and "Susanna," April 1, 1876. The Symphony competition was instituted at the Palace in 1876 (*vide* Davenport and Stanford). He was appointed Principal of the Guildhall School of Music, 1880, an office he held till the time of his death, at South Kensington, December 26, 1891. He was a fine artist, and an able administrator. His compositions were not numerous ; they included a civic anthem, produced at the Guildhall, December 3, 1887 ; several pieces for violin, of which "The Pompadour Gavotte" became popular ; pieces for violoncello, etc.

His son, FERDINAND WEIST HILL, a violinist, studied at the Brussels Conservatoire, and appeared in London in 1892, and the next year played Vieuxtemps' Concerto, No. 4, at a concert of the Westminster Orchestral Society, December 20. He is now (1897) a member of the Queen's Hall String Quartet. The younger son, THOMAS E. HILL, obtained a violoncello scholarship at the R.C.M., 1889, and is now resident in London as a professor of the violoncello.

Hilton, John, composer and organist, was born at the end of the 16th century. Mus. Bac., Cantab., 1626. Organist and clerk of St. Margaret's, Westminster, 1628. He died in March, 1657, and is buried in St. Margaret's, Westminster.

WORKS.—Ayres, or Fa-las for three voyces, London, 1627, also edited by Warren for Musical Antiquarian Society, 1844. Catch that catch can ; or, a choice collection of catches, rounds, and canons, for three or four voyces, .. London, 1652. Service in G minor. Anthems. Elegy on William Lawes, 1648. Fair Oriana, beauty's queen, madrigal for

HINE.

five voices, and Fair Orian, in the morn, for six voices, are in the Triumphs of Oriana. The anthem, "Lord for thy tender mercies sake," usually ascribed to Richard Farrant, has also been attributed to Hilton.

Hilton, Robert, bass vocalist, born at Preston, Lancashire, 1840. His grandfather and father were both singers in the choir of Penwortham Church, near Preston, and he himself sang bass for some years at Preston Parish Church, whilst holding a clerkship at the Railway Station. In 1869 he was appointed a lay clerk at Salisbury Cathedral, and succeeded William Machin (who died September, 1870) as Vicar Choral of Westminster Abbey, an office he still holds. His voice is a true bass, of great depth and power, and he has been a successful singer in oratorio. He appeared at the Norwich Festival of 1878 ; the Bristol Festival of 1879 ; and the Chester Festival of 1882. He has also sung for the Birmingham Festival Choral Society, and at the principal London and Provincial Concerts. Of late his chief public work has been in connection with the combination known as the Dilettante Vocal Quartette.

Hime, Edward, Laurence composer and tenor vocalist, born in Liverpool, July 26, 1823. Sang at the Princess' Theatre, London, and appeared as Tom Tug, in "The Waterman," at Manchester, in 1846. He has written a large number of songs, "Lighthouse keepers," "Leaves from Longfellow," "Coming of Age," etc., and pf. pieces, of which "Parfait Amour," and "Danse des Paysans," became popular. The latter was also arranged for orchestra. A morceau fantastique, "Phospho," for orchestra has been played in several places. He has also done much in arrangements, etc.

Hindle, John, composer, was born at Westminster in 1761. Mus. Bac., Oxon., 1791. Lay-vicar, Westminster Abbey, 1785. He died in 1796. He published a "Collection of Songs for 1 and 2 voices" [1790], and a "Set of Glees for 3, 4, and 5 voices, op. 2" [1790].

Hindmarsh, John, violinist and composer, born about 1755, died in 1796. He was a pupil of Salomon. Composer of "Favorite Grand March, as performed by the Staffordshire band," London [1795], etc.

Hine, Benjamin, music publisher and composer, born in 1796, died at Manchester, May 19, 1871. He composed songs, and other vocal music.

Hine, William, composer and organist, born at Brightwell, Oxfordshire, in 1687. He was a Chorister of Magdalen College, Oxford, from 1694 to 1705, and a Lay-clerk in 1705. He was dismissed in the same year and went to London, where he studied under Jeremiah Clark. Organist of Gloucester Cathedral,

HINGSTON.

1712. He died at Gloucester, August 28, 1730. Buried in Gloucester Cathedral. Works.—Harmonia Sacra Glocestriensis; or, Select Anthems, in score, for 1, 2, and 3 voices, and a Te Deum and Jubilate, together with a voluntary for the organ, n.d. [1730].

Hingston, John, organist and composer of 17th century, who was a pupil of Orlando Gibbons. He was musician to Charles I., and afterwards organist to Cromwell (1654), and teacher of his daughters. He died December 17, 1683. Composer of "Fancies for the Viol."

Hinton, John William, organist and composer, born at Edmonton, Middlesex, April 26, 1849. Studied at the Paris Conservatoire. Graduated at Dublin, Mus. Bac., 1871; B.A., 1872; Mus. Doc., 1874; and M.A., 1876. Organist of St. Mary's, Charingcross Road, 1876; St. Stephen's, and Holy Trinity, Guernsey, 1877-90; and of St. Michael's, Woolwich Dockyard, 1890, to present time. Resident Secretary, 1876-8, and professor of organ and singing, Trinity College, London. He has composed an oratorio, "Pharaoh," an opera, "Mazeppa" (1880), both in MS.; Church music, anthems, organ music, etc. Editor of The International Organist, two series; Author of Facts about organs; Guide to the purchase, etc., and of A Manual of Harmonies for the Gregorian Tones, 1884.

Hinton, Joseph Harold, organist and composer, born at Claydon, Bucks., January 1, 1862. Studied under Dr. J. F. Bridge, and others. In 1885 he was appointed organist of Hyndland Church, Hillhead, Glasgow. He has composed a Setting of Psalm 130, Latin text, produced at Glasgow, April 26, 1887; a requiem, "Man goeth forth," for voices and orchestra; a cantata, and other pieces.

Hipkins, Alfred James, F.S.A., writer on music and musical instruments, born at Westminster, June 17, 1826. (His father, James Hipkins, died April 25, 1882, was for many years a contributor to the *Musical World*). In business connection with John Broadwood & Sons, London. Mr. Hipkins made a special journey to Berlin and Potsdam in 1881, under the patronage of H.R.H. The Crown Princess of Prussia (now the German Empress Frederick) to identify and examine the pianofortes made by Gottfried Silbermann, which had belonged to Frederick the Great. In 1883 he was awarded the silver medal of the Society of Arts for a lecture on the technical history of the pianoforte. In 1884, at the request of H.R.H. The Prince of Wales, he was concerned in founding Division II. (Music) of the Inventions Exhibition, South Kensington, 1885, and became a member of the Music Committee. He was also chairman of the committee of the Historic Loan Collec-

HOARE.

tion shown in the Royal Albert Hall in connection with that Exhibition, and for his services was awarded a gold medal. At the request of H.R.H. The Duke of Edinburgh, he became a member of the committee of the British Section of the Musical and Dramatic Exhibition held at Vienna in 1892, and acted as one of the honorary secretaries. He is, from 1895, honorary curator of the General Museum of the R.C.M.; and a Fellow of the Society of Antiquaries, from 1886. His lectures on the old keyboard instruments, with his illustrations on the clavichord, spinet, and harpsichord, are well-known; they were given at intervals, from 1883 to 1893. One occasion was historic: at the Musical Association, June 7, 1886, when Rubinstein was present, and turned over the leaves for the accomplished player.

His writings include contributions to the Encyclopædia Britannica; Grove's Dictionary of Music and Musicians; the *Musical Times; Musical Review* (Novello, 1883); and the (now defunct) *Musical World.* Author of "Musical instruments, historic, rare and unique" (A. and C. Black, 1888); The Cantor lectures on "Musical Instruments" (1891); "The standard of Musical Pitch" (Society of Arts, February 26, 1896); and "A description and history of the Pianoforte, and the older keyboard Stringed Instruments" (Novello, 1896).

Hird, Frederick William, organist and composer, born at Leeds, in 1826. Organist of All Souls' (Hook Memorial) Church, Leeds. He was esteemed one of the finest organists in Yorkshire, and an excellent musician and teacher, many of his pupils now occupying leading positions. He was also a good pianist, and gave chamber concerts with George Haddock, 1851-2. The splendid organ in his house was partly built, and wholly voiced by Schulze. He died at Leeds, November 9, 1887. He composed several anthems, including, "O God, our Defender," performed in York Minster, Jubilee Day, 1887; a collection of introits, kyries, hymn-tunes and chants; Theme in A, and other pieces for organ; Canzonetta, scherzo, etc., for pf.

Hirst, Thomas, author of "The Music of the Church, in four parts; containing a general history of music, including an account of Hebrew music," London, 1841. "The Zephyr . . . containing a set of original common tunes," etc. [1863].

Hitchin, Rev. Edward, Dissenting minister, author of "Scripture proof for singing of scripture Psalms, Hymns, and spiritual Songs," London, 1696.

Hoare, Margaret, soprano vocalist, studied under Sims Reeves, and at the R.A.M. under W. Shakespeare, obtaining the Parepa-Rosa Prize in 1884. She made a successful appearance in London, December 19, 1882, in Gade's "Psyche," and a few months later in Gounod's "Redemption." She was heard in many provincial towns in the next year or two. Sang at the Chester Festival, 1891; at the Royal Albert Hall, 1893; and at the Tonic Sol-fa Festival at the Crystal Palace, 1895, in "St. Paul"; and is established as a singer of reputation.

Hobbs, John William, composer, and tenor vocalist, was born at Henley-on-Thames, August 1, 1799. He was a Chorister in Canterbury Cathedral, and was articled to John Jeremiah Goss. He sang at Norwich Musical Festival in 1813. Tenor singer of Trinity, King's, and St. John's Colleges, Cambridge, and St. George's Chapel, Windsor. Gentleman of Chapel Royal, 1827. Lay-vicar Westminster Abbey, 1836. He died at Croydon, January 12, 1877.

Works.—Glees. *Songs:* Brave old Temeraire; Caliban [1861]; Crier, or lost heart; Dear father, take thy gentle child; England; Jack's alive; Music of the past; Nina; Phillis is my only joy [1848]; Soldier's departure; Then you have not forgotten; When Delia sings; Oh my own native land; Captive Greek Girl; Eulalia, and many others, amounting to over 100.

Hobson, Frederick, *see* LESLIE, FRED.

Hoby, Charles, violoncellist and bandmaster, born in London. Studied at R.C.M., violoncello, organ, and pianoforte; and instrumentation for military band under Charles Godfrey. Went to India as bandmaster of the Punjab Frontier Force. His health failing, he returned to England, and became a candidate for the bandmastership of the Royal Engineers, but was disqualified on account of not having passed through Kneller Hall. He was then appointed organist to the Royal Military Asylum, Chelsea, and was engaged on the staff of the *Orchestral Times* (now the *British Musician*), to which he contributed papers on the violoncello, and other subjects. In 1891 he went to South Africa with Mr. Daniel Godfrey, junior, as pianist to his opera company. After an extended tour, he settled in Natal as bandmaster of the Royal Rifles. He has composed a Suite for orchestra, "Scenes of childhood," produced, Durban, July, 1896; a number of pieces for violin and pf.; Songs, etc.

Hodge, William, organist, born in London, in 1862. Scholar of the National Training School for Music. Appointed organist of St. Marylebone Parish Church, 1886; Suborganist, St. Paul's Cathedral, and organist to the Royal Choral Society, Albert Hall, 1888. Gave recitals at the Bow and Bromley Institute, 1884, and elsewhere; and conducted performances of "Elijah" at St. Marylebone

Church in 1892. An organist of exceptional talent, his career was all too brief. He died in London, July 15, 1895. His brother, HERBERT HODGE, also an organist, studied at the R.C.M., and was made an Associate. He was appointed organist of Hornsey Parish Church in 1888, and is now holding a similar position at St. Peter's, South Kensington. He is Musical Director at the School for the Indigent Blind, St. George's Fields, Southwark.

Hodges, Colonel C. L., published a "Collection of Peninsular melodies, with words by Mrs. Hemans, Mrs. Norton," etc., London [1830].

Hodges, Edward, organist and composer, born at Bristol, July 20, 1796. Organist successively of Clifton Church; St. James Church, Bristol, 1819; St. Nicholas Church. Mus. Doc., Cantab., 1825. He went to America, 1838, and was appointed organist of Toronto Cathedral. In 1839 he became organist of St. John's Episcopal Chapel, New York. Organist of Trinity Church, New York, 1846. He returned to England in 1863, and died at Clifton, September 1, 1867.

Works.—Church Services. Anthems. Contributions to the Musical Journals. An Apology for Church Music and Musical Festivals, in answer to the animadversions of the *Standard* and the *Record*, London, 1834. An Essay on the Cultivation of Church Music, New York, 1841.

Hodson, George Alexander, song-writer, who flourished in the first half of this century, and died in 1863. He composed a number of fine melodies, among which may be named: Tell me, Mary, how to woo thee [1863]; My pretty gazelle; Bridal wreath; Briton's home; Child's first prayer; O give me but my Arab steed [1828]; Poor Bessie; Six ballads [1830]. His son GEORGE (born, Dublin, 1822, died, 1869), was a vocalist.

Hodson, Rev. Henry Edward, of Lichfield, Staffs., is the composer of a dramatic cantata, "The Golden Legend," performed in London, May 23, 1881; in Lichfield, Birmingham, and other places, 1882-4.

Hoeck, William Thomson, composer and conductor, born at Paisley, June 14, 1859. Studied under his father, Louis Hoeck, music teacher in Paisley; also under Dr. A. L. Peace. Organist and choirmaster Renfrew Parish Church, 1874; Queen's Park U. P. Church, Glasgow, 1880. Conductor of Paisley Philharmonic Society, 1878-83; Hillside and Pollokshields Musical Associations; and Glasgow Amateur Orchestral Society.

Works—Orchestral—Undine, characteristic piece, 1884; On the water, 1885; Overture, 1890; all produced in Glasgow. Romance, 'cello and pf., Op. 3; oboe and pf.; Legend, pf. and violin, 1890 (Prize, Glasgow Society of Musicians); pf. pieces, various. Te Deum,

HOFFMANN.

op. 2 ; A love song ; How I envy the ring, and others. Hymn tunes, etc.

Hoffmann, Richard, see ANDREWS, RICHARD HOFFMANN.

Hogarth, George, writer and composer, born at Carfrae Mill, near Oxton, Berwickshire, in 1783. He was educated at Edinburgh for the law. Member of Edinburgh Choral Union. Joint Secretary, with G. F. Graham, of Edinburgh Musical Festival, 1815. Contributed to the *Harmonicon*, 1830. Sub-editor of the *Morning Chronicle*, London, 1834 ; editor of the *Musical Herald*, 1846-7, and musical critic of *Daily News*, 1846-66. Secretary to Philharmonic Society, 1850-64. He married Miss Thomson, daughter of George Thomson. Died at London, February 12, 1870.

WORKS.—Musical history, biography, and criticism, being a general survey of music from the earliest period to the present time. London, 1835 ; second edition, 1838, 2 vols. Memoirs of the musical drama, London, 1838, 2 vols, *portraits*. Memoirs of the opera in Italy, France, Germany, and England, London, 1851. The Birmingham festival of 1852, London, 1852. The Philharmonic Society of London, from its foundation in 1813 to its fiftieth year, 1862, London, 1862. How's Book of British song, illustrated by several distinguished artists, with pianoforte accompaniments and biographical and historical notes, London, 1845, 2 vols. Contributions to periodical literature. Glees and songs.

Hogarth was one of the few cultured men of letters who have written intelligibly about music. His works are all of standard value, and are still sought among musicians. One of his daughters, CATHERINE, married Charles Dickens the novelist, in 1836 ; and another, HELEN (Mrs. Roney), was a vocalist, and taught singing in London, and at the Ladies' College, Cheltenham.

Hogg, James, the "Ettrick Shepherd," poet, musician, and general writer, was born in Ettrick Forest, Selkirk, November, 1770. Engaged as farmer at Altrive, but chiefly as contributor to *Blackwood's Magazine*, and as a general writer. He died at Altrive, November 21, 1835.

WORKS.—The Mountain Bard, 1803 ; Mador of the moor ; The pilgrim of the sun ; The Queen's wake ; The Jacobite relics of Scotland, being the songs, airs, and legends of the adherents of the House of Stuart, Edinburgh, 2 vols., 1819-21, with music ; The Border garland, 1829, with music ; tales, fugitive pieces, etc. ; musical settings of his own verses.

Hohler, Tom, tenor vocalist, son of the Rev. F. W. Hohler, Rector of Winstone and Colesborne, Gloucestershire. Born in 1839. Held an appointment in the Civil Service,

HOLDEN.

and was afterwards private secretary to the Earl of Dudley, upon whose advice he went to Italy, and studied under Romani. He sang in Italy, Switzerland, and Germany ; and returning to London at the end of 1865, he was engaged for Italian Opera at Her Majesty's Theatre. He made his *début*, April, 1866, as *Arturo*, in "I Puritani," achieving great success. He sang in oratorio, "Elijah," Manchester, January, 1868, etc., and concerts in London and the provinces. In 1869, he studied further under Pierre Wartel. He married, in 1880, Henrietta, widow of the sixth Duke of Newcastle, and retired from the stage ; singing occasionally at concerts for charitable purposes, and residing chiefly in Paris. He died at Monte Carlo, May 2, 1892.

Holborne, Anthony and William, English musicians, who, in 1597, published in London, " The Cittharne Schoole, by Antony Holborne, gentleman, and servant to her most excellent Maiestie. Hereunto are added six short Aers Neapoliton like to three voyces without the Instrument, done by his brother, William Holborne."

Holcombe, Henry, composer and vocalist, born Salisbury, 1690. He was a chorister in Salisbury Cathedral, and afterwards a singer at Drury Lane Theatre, London. He was a teacher of singing and the harpsichord in London, where he died in 1750. He published "The Musical Medley, or a collection of English songs and cantatas set to music," 1745 ; "The Garland," a collection of songs and cantatas [1740] ; six solos for a violin and thorough-bass, with some pieces for the German flute and harpsichord," op. 1, London, 1745. *Songs :* Duke upon duke ; Go, happy paper ; Happy man, etc.

Holden, George, composer and organist, was born in 1800. He was organist of St. George's Church, Liverpool, and teacher of music there. For many years he acted as conductor of the Apollo Glee Club of Liverpool. He died at Liverpool, December 5, 1856. Composed Church Music, consisting of original anthems . . . psalms, hymns, etc. [1840] ; Sacred music by various authors. Dance and organ music ; anthems, songs, etc.

Holden, John, writer and composer, who lived in Glasgow during the latter half of the 18th century. He settled in Glasgow as a potter, about 1757, and was made a burgess in 1757. He acted as instructor to the band of the Glasgow College Chapel, and was in other ways connected with the musical affairs of the University. The statement in Fétis' "Biographie universelle des Musiciens," that he was a professor at the University is apparently based on Holden's connection with the music of the College chapel, or the statement on the title-page of the "Collection of Church

HOLDEN.

Music." He issued " A Collection of Church Music, consisting of new setts of the common psalm tunes, with some other pieces . . . principally designed for the use of the University of Glasgow," Glasgow, 1766. "An essay towards a rational system of music," Glasgow, 1770 ; Calcutta, 1799 ; Edinburgh, 1807. The psalm tune " Glasgow " is usually assigned to Holden.

Holden, S., Irish musician, issued " Collection of old-established Irish slow and quick tunes arranged for the harp, pf.," etc., Dublin [1800], two books. "Selection of Masonic songs," Dublin [1812].

Holder, Joseph William, organist and composer, born in Clerkenwell, London, 1764. He was a chorister in the Chapel Royal, and studied music under Nares. Assistant to Reinhold, organist of St. George the Martyr, Queen Street. Organist successively of St. Mary's Church, Bungay, and at Chelmsford. Bac. Mus., Oxon., 1792. He died in 1832. WORKS.—Collection of catches, canons and glees, op. 6 [1787] ; Collection of songs, duetts and glees, op. 14 [1800]. A mass. Anthems and Te Deums. Favourite collection of songs, op. 4 [1786]. Six sonatas for pf., op. 2 [1785] ; Sonatas for pf., opp. 20, 47, 56. Twenty-eight preludes for pf. . . . Lassie would ye love me (Oh ! gin I were a baron's heir), Scots song, etc.

Holder, Rev. William, DD., clergyman and writer, born in Northamptonshire, in 1614. Educated at Cambridge. Rector of Blechindon, Oxford, 1642. DD., 1660. Canon of Ely. Canon of St. Paul's. Sub-dean of Chapel Royal, 1674-89. He died at London, January 24, 1697. WORKS.—A treatise of the natural grounds and principles of Harmony, London, 1694 ; another edition to which is added by way of appendix, Rules for playing a Thorow-bass, by the late M. Godfrey Keller, London, 1731 ; Evening service in C ; Anthems, etc.

Holdroyd, Israel, " Philo-Musicae," an English musician of the first half of the 18th century. He published "The Spiritual Man's Companion, or the Pious Christian's Recreation, containing an historical account of music, etc. ; grounds of music and composition in all branches. . Psalm and hymn tunes," . . 3rd edition, 1733, 5th edition, 1753. Chants and anthems, 1733, etc.

Holford, William, musician of the latter part of last and early part of the present century. He was a choir-master at Manchester. He compiled " Voce di melodia, being a collection of congregational psalm and hymn tunes, from approved authors, arranged for four voices " . . n.d. [c. 1820].

Holland, Caroline, amateur composer. Daughter of Sir Henry Holland, and sister of Lord Knutsford. Miss Holland's Choir, under

HOLLINS.

her conductorship, has given concerts annually, since 1883, at which important works by Grieg, Rheinberger, Tinel ("Franciscus," 1890), and others, have been performed for the first time in England. Her compositions include a cantata, " Miss Killmansegg and her Golden Leg," produced 1883 ; ballad, " After the Skirmish " (Rohilcund, 1858), words by Sir Alfred C. Lyall, for chorus and orchestra, 1896, etc.

Holland, Edwin, baritone vocalist and teacher of singing, born in London, March 24, 1845. At first studied the violoncello under A. Guest, and played in the orchestra at Covent Garden, while Alfred Mellon was conductor. Later, he took up singing, and received instruction from Frank Romer, his uncle. He then went to Italy and studied with Victor Maurel. For some years he sang in oratorio and concerts, but has chiefly devoted his attention to vocal training. He was appointed a professor of singing at the R.A.M., in 1880, and resigned in 1892, on establishing an academy of his own. He has given annual concerts by pupils, and operatic performances, since 1875. Author of Edwin Holland's Method of Voice Production, London, R. Cocks, in which exercises are written for each individual class of voice.

Hollingsworth, A. B., comic singer, who appeared in London music halls as the "Man with the carpet bag," and in other eccentric sketches. He died at London, October 10, 1865, and is buried at Finchley.

Hollins, Alfred, organist, pianist and composer, born at Hull, September 11, 1865. Began his musical training at the age of six, at the York School for the Blind. From there he went to the Royal Normal College for the Blind, Norwood, where he studied pianoforte playing with Fritz Hartvigson, and organ under Dr. E. J. Hopkins. He played, at a concert of the students, at the Crystal Palace, July 10, 1880, and at later ones, showing remarkable powers as pianist and organist. His organ recitals in the provinces date from 1882, and he has been heard throughout the United Kingdom and Ireland. He has twice visited America, in 1886, and 1888. Appeared as a pianist at the Monday Popular Concerts, April 10, 1886 ; and at the Philharmonic, May 31, 1888. He played in Berlin in 1885, and studied with Hans von Bulow, who called him " one of the rare true musicians amongst the piano *virtuosi*." He is now a Professor at the Royal Normal College. He has composed a Concert Overture in C ; Preludes, and other organ music ; pianoforte pieces, and songs.

Hollins, George, organist, born in Birmingham, March 16, 1809. Son of William Hollins, architect and sculptor. Pupil of Thomas Munden, whom he succeeded as

HOLLOWAY.

organist of St. Paul's, Birmingham, and of the Town Hall (about 1837). He was a fine performer on the organ, and an excellent pianist; he was also a good singer, having a baritone voice of rich quality. He was frequently engaged in concert work, and was noted for his organ accompaniment to songs. Symptoms of phthisis (brought on by overwork) manifesting themselves, he was sent to the Isle-of-Wight; while away he ruptured a blood vessel, and was brought home, where he died, December 16, 1841. Very few of his compositions were published, but he wrote many hymn tunes and chants, and a setting of the Benedicite was very popular for many years, as was a song, "Sabbath Bell."

Holloway, Arthur Stephen, organist, pianist and composer of present time. Graduated Mus. Bac., 1875; Mus. Doc., 1894, Oxford. He has composed a church cantata, "The promised King," for Advent and Christmas; Songs, organ and pf. pieces, etc., and a School Board Singing Tutor.

Holloway, H. R., author of a "Manual of Chanting," London, 1850.

Holman-Andrews, see ASHTON, GERTRUDE.

Holmes, Alfred, violinist and composer, was born at London, November 9, 1837. He studied the violin under his father, Thomas Holmes, of Lincoln. Sopranist at the Oratory, King William Street, Strand. Début with Henry, his brother, at Haymarket Theatre, July, 1847. Appeared at Beethoven Rooms, London, 1853. Played in Germany, 1856; Austria, 1857; Sweden, 1857-9; Norway and Holland, 1860-1. Settled in Paris, 1864. Organised a quartet party, 1866. Travelled with it in Holland Prussia, and Germany, 1867. He died at Paris, March 4, 1876. WORKS.—*Symphonies:* Jeanne d'Arc, St. Petersburg, 1867, London, February, 1875; The Youth of Shakspere, Paris; The Siege of Paris, 1870; Charles XII.; Romeo and Juliet; The Cid, 1874; The Muses; Robin Hood, 1870. Inez de Castro, opera, 1869. Pf. music and songs.

Holmes, Edward, writer and musician, born near London, 1797. He studied music under V. Novello. Musical critic of *Atlas* newspaper. Marr.ed grand-daughter of Samuel Webbe. He died in U.S.A., August 28, 1859. WORKS.—A ramble among the musicians of Germany, giving some account of the operas of Munich, Dresden, Berlin, etc., with remarks upon the church music, singers, performers, and composers, and a sample of the pleasures and inconveniences that await the lover of art on a similar excursion; by a musical professor; London, 1828; 2nd edit., 1830; 3rd edit., 1838. Life of Mozart, including his correspondence, London, 1845; Life of Purcell; Analytical and thematic index of

HOLMES.

Mozart's pianoforte works; Contributions to periodical literature.

Holmes' "Life of Mozart" is recognised as the standard English work on that master, and is valued accordingly. His work on German musicians is now scarce, and is valued for its clever pictures of the German musical manners of his time.

Holmes, George, organist and composer, born about the middle of the 17th century. He was organist of Lincoln Cathedral from 1704, and died in 1720. Composer of odes, anthems and songs.

Holmes, W. Gordon, physician and writer. Graduated M.D., Brussels, 1882; L.R.C.P., Edinburgh, 1871. Holds various appointments in London. Author of "Treatise on vocal physiology and hygiene, with especial reference to the cultivation and preservation of the voice," London, 1879; 2nd ed. 1880. Various works on the throat and its diseases.

Holmes, Henry, violinist and composer, brother of Alfred Holmes, born in London, November 7, 1839. Studied under his father. Toured with his brother on the Continent, from 1855, and played at the Gewandhaus concerts, Leipzig, December 4, 1856. Resided in Paris, Copenhagen, and Stockholm, from 1864. Settled in London, and established the Musical Evenings, in 1868. Led quartets at the Monday Popular Concerts, February 12, 1883. Sometime professor of the violin at the R.C.M. WORKS.—Sacred cantatas, Praise ye the Lord; and Christmas Day—the last produced at the Gloucester Festival of 1880; O may I join the Choir Invisible, for baritone solo, chorus and strings; songs, etc. Symphony in A, op. 32, Crystal Palace, February 24, 1872; No. 2; No. 3, in C; No. 4. Concert overture. Concerto in F, op. 39, violin and orchestra, Crystal Palace, December 11, 1875. Octet, strings, 1886; Quintet, strings, and pf. and strings, op. 49; Octet, strings and two horns, 1889; Quartets, strings; and numerous pieces for violin and pf., etc.

Holmes, John, organist and composer of 17th century. Organist of Winchester Cathedral about end of 16th century, and of Salisbury Cathedral, 1602-10. He was the master of Adrian Batten and Edward Lowe. He composed services and anthems for the church, and madrigals, among which is "Thus Bonnyboots the birthday celebrated," contained in the "Triumphs of Oriana," 1601.

His son, THOMAS, who died at Salisbury, March 25, 1638, was a composer.

Holmes, Mary, musician, authoress of "A few words about Music, by M. H.," London, 1851. Composer of "Songs without words, for pf." [1850].

Holmes William Henry, pianist and composer, born at Sudbury, January 8, 1812.

HOMES.

He studied at the R.A.M., where he gained two medals. He afterwards became sub-professor of pf. at R.A.M. (1826), and later, principal professor. First appeared as pianist at Philharmonic Society Concert in 1851. He died in London, April 23, 1885. Among his pupils was .W. Sterndale Bennett, J. W. Davison, George A. and Walter Macfarren, etc. WORKS.—The Elfin of the lake, opera. Symphonies for orchestra. Concerto (The Jubilee) for pf. and orchestra ; Sonata for pf. and violin ; Numerous works for pf. solo ; Songs, etc.

Homes, N., D.D., author of " Gospel Musick ; or, the Singing of David's Psalms, etc., in the publick congregations, or private families asserted and vindicated," London, 1644.

Honeyman, William Crawford, violinist and author, born of Scottish parents at Wellington, New Zealand, January 30, 1845. In 1849 he was taken to Edinburgh, and he studied music and the violin. From an early age he contributed tales and sketches to various journals, and became connected with the " People's Journal " and " People's Friend," of Dundee. To these he contributed numerous detective tales, under the pseudonym of James McGovan, and wrote various novels and articles. He also issued in the " People's Friend," a series of papers on " The Violin : how to master it," 1879, which has been reprinted in book form. He has also published "The Young Violinist's Tutor and Duet Book," 1883 ; " Three easy Fantasias on Scottish Airs," 1884 ; " Hints to Violin Players," 1885 ; " The Secrets of Violin Playing."

Hook, James, composer and organist, was born at Norwich, June 3, 1746. He studied under Garland, organist of Norwich Cathedral. Settled in London, and became organist and composer at Marylebone Gardens, 1769-1773 ; and Vauxhall Gardens, 1774-1820. Organist of St. John's, Horsleydown. Gained Catch Club prizes, 1772, 1780. Married to Miss Madden. He died at Boulogne, 1827.

WORKS.—*Music for dramatic pieces :* Dido, 1771 ; The Divorce, 1771 ; Trick upon Trick, 1772 ; Double Disguise, 1784 ; Jack of Newbury, libretto by Rev. Jas. Hook, 1795 ; Diamond cut Diamond, 1797 ; Music mad, 1807, etc. *Songs :* Hours of love ; Hermit, op. 24 ; Adieu ma liberte ; Along the birks ; And where are you going ? ; Believe not youth ; Blow cheerly, ye winds ; Bonny sailor ; Brown Bess ; Can'st thou love me, Mary ? ; Come out, my love ; Dear Mary, be mine ; Death of Auld Robin Gray ; Flitch of Bacon ; Gentle as the breath ; Gipsy girl ; Hail, lovely rose ; Hook, or by crook ; Hours of love ; Hush every breeze ; Lowland Kitty ; My Nancy was the sweetest maid ; Near Glasgow

HOPEKIRK.

city ; Orphan Bess ; Should fears alarm ; Softly waft, ye southern breezes ; Sweet lass of Richmond Hill (1789) ; Thro' the braes of Kirkcaldy ; What is love ? ; Within a mile o' Edinboro town ; Ode for the opening of the New Exhibition Room, 1772. Petrarch's Sonnets set to music, op. 60. The Hours of Love, or collection of sonnets, containing morning, noon, evening, and night. Pianoforte pieces, as sonatas, op. 16, 54, etc. ; Rondos and transcriptions ; Concertos, op. 11 ; Concertos for organ, op. 20, op. 55, etc. ; Three sonatas for pf. and flute, op. 71 ; another set, op. 72 ; and another set, op. 77. Cantatas, canzonets, catches, glees (Christmas Box, 1795). The Ascension, oratorio, 1776. Guida di Musica, being an easy introduction for beginners on the pianoforte, to which are added 24 progressive lessons, in the most useful keys, composed and fingered by the author, op. 37, London, 4to, n.d.

His sons, JAMES (1772-1826), dean of Worcester, and THEODORE (1788-1841), novelist, achieved much distinction in their day. The latter was also a musician.

Hooper, Edmund, composer, born at North Halberton, Devon [1553]. Chorister Westminster Abbey, 1582. Master of Choristers, Westminster Abbey, 1588. Gentleman of the Chapel Royal, 1603. Organist of Westminster Abbey, 1606. He died at Westminster, July 19, 1621.

WORKS.—Harmonies in The whole Booke of Psalms, 1594. Anthems in Barnard's Collection. Contributions to Leighton's Teare's.

Hooper, Mrs. M., *see* PENNA, CATHERINE.

Hooper, Rev. Richard, clergyman and musician, author of " Music and musicians (especially English) to the days of Henry Purcell . . ," London, 1855.

Hope, Robert Charles, author of various works on dialect, holy wells, church plate, etc. In 1894, he issued a book entitled, " Mediaeval Music, an historical sketch with musical illustrations," London, Stock.

Hopekirk, Helen, pianist and composer, born near Edinburgh, where her early studies were pursued under G. Lichtenstein and A. C. Mackenzie. These were followed by two years at the Leipzig Conservatorium, and study under Th. Leschetitzki at Vienna. Her *début* was made at the Gewandhaus Concerts, Leipzig, November 28, 1878, and she played, for the first time in England, at the Crystal Palace, March 15, 1879, the G minor Concerto of Saint-Saëns. Then followed recitals and concerts in England and Scotland, up to the year 1883, when Madame Hopekirk paid her first visit to America. Her first appearance was at the Boston Symphony Concerts, December 8, 1883, and her first recital in New York took place December 27. She speedily became popular, and was

HOPKINS.

engaged for the Philadelphia Festival of 1884, and played in nearly every centre of musical culture. During her stay she gave upwards of twenty concerts in New York alone, her artistic performances attracting large audiences. In the spring of 1886, she was back in Edinburgh again, but the next year she went again to Vienna, for further study with Leschetizki. While there, she also studied composition, with Carl Nawratil, and orchestration with Richard Mandl. At the close of her stay she appeared at the Vienna Philharmonic, and on her return, at the Richter Concerts, London. Two more tours in America were undertaken, and since her return to Europe, composition has chiefly occupied her time. Among her works may be named a Concertstück for pf. and orchestra, produced at Henschel's Concerts, Edinburgh, November 19, 1894, the composer taking the solo part ; a Concerto and several orchestral works ; a Sonata for pf. and violin (Boston Quartet Concerts and Chicago Exhibition, 1893) ; and upwards of a hundred Songs. Some songs, and a Serenade for pf. have been published.

Hopkins, Edward, bandmaster, born about the year 1778. Formed the first regular band of the Scots Guards in 1815, after the return of the regiment from Paris. He was the first clarinet player of his day ; and, with a brother, was in the orchestra of Covent Garden Theatre, during its occupancy by Charles Kemble. He was also at one time conductor at Old Vauxhall Gardens. He retired from the army on a pension in 1838, and died in 1860, aged 82. He was the father of a family of musicians. His son EDWARD became organist of Armagh Cathedral; and JOHN LARKIN (q.v.) of Rochester Cathedral. His daughter, LOUISA, entered the R.A.M., in 1831 ; was King's Scholar, 1834 ; and afterwards an Associate. She married Richard Lloyd, a lay vicar of Westminster Abbey, and after his death settled as a teacher of music in Cheltenham, where she died in 1880. The distinguished tenor singer, Edward Lloyd, is her son.

Hopkins, Edward John, organist and composer, born at Westminster, London, June 30, 1818. Entered the choir of the Chapel Royal, St. James's, in 1826, and studied under Wm. Hawes, in 1833 becoming a pupil of T. F. Walmisley. Obtained the post of organist at Mitcham Church, Surrey, in 1834 ; St. Peter's, Islington, 1838 ; St. Luke's, Berwick Street, 1841. He played his first probationary service at the Temple Church, May 7, 1843 ; and in the following October was elected organist to the "Honourable Societies of the Temple," a position he still retains. His Jubilee as an organist was marked by the presentation of a testimonial

HOPKINS.

in 1884 ; and on the completion of fifty years' service at the Temple Church, in May, 1893, he was the recipient of a handsome testimonial from the two Honourable Societies of the Temple. In 1851, he became a member of the Royal Society of Musicians ; Associate of the Philharmonic Society, 1852, Member, 1864 ; was one of the Founders of the College of Organists ; Hon. R.A.M., 1871 ; an original member of the Musical Association, 1874 ; and identified with Trinity College, London, as Examiner, etc. In 1882, he received the degree of Mus. Doc., from the Archbishop of Canterbury ; and from Trinity College, Toronto, 1886 ; He is professor of the organ at the Royal Normal College for the Blind, Norwood. His powers as an organist have been demonstrated not only in the services of his church, but in recitals all over the country, which he continued up to his 78th birthday, June 30, 1896 ; and modern organ building has been greatly influenced by his writings.

WORKS.—*Anthems* : Out of the deep; God is gone up (Gresham prize medals, 1838 and 1840) ; The King shall rejoice (in celebration of the marriage of the Prince of Wales, 1863) ; God who commandest the light to shine (Thanksgiving for the recovery of the Prince of Wales, 1872) ; Thou shalt cause the trumpet of the Jubilee to sound (composed for Her Majesty's Jubilee, 1887, and for which the Benchers of the Temple voted Dr. Hopkins fifty guineas) ; The Lord is full of compassion (composed for his own Jubilee), performed at the Temple Church, May 7, 1893 ; O, sing unto the Lord, and many others ; Church services, hymn tunes, and chants. *Organ* : Select organ movements, from the scores of the great masters, 22 numbers ; Select movements, 15 numbers ; Allegro moderato in A ; Adagio in D, and others. Chloe and Corinna, madrigal ; songs, part-songs, etc. Author of The organ, its history and construction, London, 1855 ; second edition, 1870 ; third edition (with E. F. Rimbault) 1877, etc. Editor of madrigals by Bennett and Weelkes, for the Musical Antiquarian Society ; The Temple Psalter, pointed ; Book of responses ; Purcell's organ music (Novello). Lectures and papers, various, read before the Royal Archæological Institute, the Conferences of the Incorporated Society of Musicians, etc. Contributions to the musical press. Senior editor of *The Organist and Choirmaster*, his colleagues being Dr. C. W. Pearce, and Dr. C. Vincent. Contributor of valuable articles on accompaniment, organ, etc., to Grove's Dictionary of music and musicians.

Hopkins, John, organist and composer, brother of Edward J. Hopkins, born at Westminster, in 1822. Became a chorister at St. Paul's Cathedral in 1831, remaining there

HOPKINS.

until 1838, but was allowed, some months previously to leaving, to take the organist's duty at Mitcham Church. He was appointed to St. Stephen's, Islington, 1839 ; Trinity Church, Islington, 1843 ; St. Mark's, Jersey, 1845 ; St. Michael's, Chester Square, London, 1846 ; and to Rochester Cathedral, May, 1856, a position he still holds. Many distinguished organists have been his pupils: Drs. J. F. and J. C. Bridge, E. J. Crow, and D. J. Wood ; and Joseph Maas, the vocalist, etc. His compositions include Church services, anthems, a large number of hymn tunes (many written expressly for use at St. John's, Chatham), chants, etc, A set of twelve Sketches for pf. ; a series of movements for the organ ; a book of ten songs, etc. GEORGE, and GLANVILL HOPKINS, his sons, are organists ; the former at Gillingham Church, and the latter at Trinity Church, Old Brompton, and assistant organist at Rochester Cathedral.

Hopkins, John Larkin, organist and composer, born at Westminster, November 25, 1819. Cousin of E. J. Hopkins. Chorister in Westminster Abbey under James Turle. He was successively organist of Rochester Cathedral, 1841 ; Trinity College, Cambridge, 1856 ; and Cambridge University, 1856. Mus Bac., 1842, and Mus. Doc., Camb., 1867. He died at Ventnor, Isle of Wight, April 25, 1873.

WORKS.—Services in C and E flat ; Te Deum in G ; Twelve anthems dedicated to the Dean and Chapter of Rochester [1830]; numerous separate anthems. Five glees, and a madrigal, London, 1842. Part-songs, songs, etc.

Hopkins, Thomas, organist, brother of E. J. Hopkins, was, *circa* 1862, organist of the Edinburgh University Music Hall, in Park Place. He afterwards removed to York, and was for many years organist of St. Saviour's Church, and also had the care and tuning of the Cathedral organ. He had a rare gift as an extempore player. He died at York, March 22, 1893.

Hopkinson, Thomas, organist and writer on music, born in York, October 22, 1826. Quite early in life he had a strong predilection for drawing, and wished to become a painter, but his father decided for music, and at the age of eight he became a chorister in York Minster. There he remained for nine years, a pupil of Matthew Camidge. Two days after leaving the choir, in 1843, he became organist of the two churches of Pontefract, posts he retained until 1856, when he removed to Hull. At that time there were only three music teachers in the town, and he soon found himself fully occupied with teaching in the district. He held several organ appointments. About 1886 he retired, and took up his favourite art of water-colour

HORN.

painting. For forty years' past he has contributed to the local Press, and the musical Journals, letters on various topics, and has been a strenuous advocate of the claims of native musicians, and our own national art.

Horan, John, organist, born at Drogheda, in 1831. Organist successively at Booterstown, Sandymount, St. Andrew's, Dublin, Adare, Tuam, and Derry. Sometime member of the Choir, Limerick Cathedral ; Assistant organist and master of the choristers ; then organist and choirmaster, Christ Church Cathedral, Dublin. He has composed some anthems, and organ music. His son, GEORGE FREDERICK, was appointed organist of Trinity Church, Rathmines, in 1886. He has written church music ; "A voice in the gloaming," and many other songs, some of which are popular. JOHN HORAN, another son, is solo bass in Christ Church Cathedral Choir, Dublin.

Horn, Charles Edward, composer and conductor, born in London, June 21, 1786. Son of Carl Friedrich Horn (1762-1830), a German musician under whom he studied. He also studied under Rauzzini, in 1808, and sang at the English Opera House in 1809. He studied singing under Thomas Welsh in 1809, and re-appeared as a vocalist in 1814. Musical director at Lyceum, 1831-32. He went to America and introduced English opera, 1833, and was a music-publisher in America for a time. Returned to England in 1843, and became musical director of Princess's Theatre, London. He settled in America as director of the Händel and Haydn Society of Boston, in 1847, and died at Boston, October 21, 1849.

WORKS.—*Oratorios :* Remission of Sin ; Satan, 1845 ; Daniel's Prediction, London, 1848. *Operas, etc.:* Magic Bride, 1810 ; Tricks upon Travellers (with Reeve), 1810 ; Bee-hive, 1811 ; Boarding-house, 1811 ; Rich and Poor, 1812 ; Devil's Bridge (with Braham), 1812 ; Godolphin, 1813 ; Ninth Statue, 1814 ; Woodman's Hut, 1814 ; Charles the Bold, 1815 ; Persia Hunter, 1816 ; Election, 1817 ; Wizard, 1817 ; Circe, 1821 ; Actors al Fresco (with Cooke and Blewitt), 1823 ; Philandering, 1824 ; Peveril of the Peak, 1826 ; Honest Frauds, 1830 ; " M. P." Christmas Bells, cantata. *Songs :* Ah, flattering man ; Breaking of the day ; Brian Boru ; Chimes of Zurich ; Cherry Ripe ; Child of earth ; Deep, deep sea ; Desert isle ; Early home ; Fond heart ; He loves and rides away ; I've been where fresh flowers ; Long time ago ; Love's stolen kiss ; My bonnie barque ; Mermaid's cave ; O never say I stole the heart ; Old ocean is calm ; The sun is on the mountain ; Trafalgar ; When Mary is away ; Woman's heart is free. Duets and glees. Pianoforte music. Hindoo Melodies Harmonized, London, 1840.

HORNCASTLE.

His wife, *born* MARIA HORTON, was born at Birmingham in 1811. She sang in opera in America and elsewhere. She devoted herself to teaching after 1849, and died at Morrisania, January, 1887. She was a sister of Mrs. German Reed.

Horncastle, Frederick William, Irish composer and organist of the present century, who flourished about 1810-50. He was organist of Armagh Cathedral, 1816-23, and afterwards a Gentleman of the Chapel Royal. He composed a great number of pieces for the pf., with songs, glees, comic rounds, etc. He compiled "The Music of Ireland; as performed at Mr. Horncastle's Irish Entertainments," London, 1844, 3 parts, etc.

Horncastle, John Henry, author of "The Whole Art of Singing at Sight," London, 1829.

Horne, George, D.D., author of "The antiquity, use, and excellence of Church Music: a sermon preached at the opening of a new organ in the Cathedral Church of Christ, Canterbury . . ." Oxford, 1784.

Horne, Rev. Thomas Hartwell, scholar and biblical writer, born in London, in 1780. He was a clergyman in London, and in 1824 he became an assistant in the British Museum, where he remained till 1860. He died at London, January 27, 1862. Compiled "Manual of Parochial Psalmòdy," London, 1829; "Selection of Psalms and Hymns, arranged by Thomas Henshaw, 1829 ('1unes for No. 1)." "Historical Notices of Psalmody," London, 1847. "Introduction to the critical study and knowledge of the Holy Scriptures," 1813, 3 vols" "Introduction to Bibliography," 2 vols., and other works.

Horner, Burnham W., organist, composer, and writer, born at Luton, Beds., in 1848. Studied under Dr E. J. Hopkins, Franklin Taylor, and Signor Ciabatta. In 1863, he was appointed organist of St. Mary's, Mortlake; and in 1867 became assistant organist of the Chapel Royal, Hampton Court. Appointments followed at Holy Trinity, Richmond, 1874; St. Luke's, South Kensington, 1893. He has appeared with success as a pianist at various concerts. Of his compositions, a cantata, "Penelope," was produced at Richmond, December, 1890; and he has published a Festival March for organ, besides arrangements of the overtures to "St. Polycarp," and "Hagar" (Ouseley). Many papers on musical topics have been issued by the "Sette of Odd Volumes," and in other ways, including "Organ writers of the 18th and 19th centuries," "Musical London a Century ago," etc. He is author of "Organ Pedal Technique," Novello, 1895.

Horner, Ralph Joseph, conductor and composer, born at Newport, Monmouthshire, April 28, 1848. Educated at Leipzig

HORSLEY.

Conservatorium, under Moscheles, Reinecke, Hauptmann, and others. Graduated Mus. Bac., Durham. Some time conductor of opera at the Alexandra Palace, Muswell Hill; and for eleven years conductor of Sullivan and other opera companies in the provinces. Organist of Park Hill Church, Nottingham, 1890-94. At the present time he is conductor of the Nottingham Amateur Orchesiral Society, and the Amateur Operatic Company; and lecturer in music at Nottingham University College. He has composed a dramatic cantata, "Confucius," produced at Albert Hall, Nottingham, February 19, 1892; several operettas; and has published numerous pf. pieces, songs, etc.

Horrocks, Amy Elsie, pianist and composer, born, of British parents, at Rio-Grande-do-Sul, Brazil, February 23, 1867. Entered R.A.M., in 1882, studying pianoforte and composition under Ad. Schloesser, and F. W. Davenport. Won the Potter Exhibition, 1888, and the Bennett Prize, 1889. Elected Associate, 1890; Fellow, 1895. At the Academy Concerts, a Pf. Trio in B flat (1887); Sonata for 'cello and pf. (1889), and other compositions were performed. Resident in London, as teacher. Has given Chamber concerts in Princes' Hall, 1891.

WORKS.—Incidental music to An Idyll of New Year's Eve, Chelsea, January, 1890; The wild Swan, op. 9; The winds, op. 21; A Spring morning, op. 22; dramatic cantatas for female voices; two Fairy songs (Elfin sleep-song, and The Fairy thrall), op. 13, for soprano solo, chorus of female voices, with strings, harp, and triangle; two songs, op. 3, with orchestra; album of twelve songs, op. 6; six songs, op. 10; fourteen songs, op. 20; eight vocal canons, op. 15; ten canons, op. 18; songs, various. Sonata in G, pf. and violoncello, op. 7; variations for pf. and strings, op. 11; orchestral legend, Undine, op. 16, Queen's Hall, February 6, 1897. Various pieces for pf. solo, violin and pf., etc.

Horsley, Charles Edward, composer and organist, son of William Horsley, was born in London, December 16, 1822. He studied under his father, Moscheles, and at Leipzig under Hauptmann and Mendelssohn. Organist of St. John's, Notting Hill, London. He went to Australia in 1868; and afterwards settled in the United States. He died at New York, May 2, 1876.

WORKS. — *Oratorios :* David; Joseph; Gideon; Glasgow, 1860. Comus, cantata for solo and chorus (Milton), 1874; Impromptu for pf., op. 12; Trio, No. 2, for pf., viola and 'cello, op. 13; Sonata for pf. and 'cello (1844); Quartet for pf. and strings, 1845; six Lieder for voice and pf., op. 21. Anthems. Pf. pieces, various. Songs, part-songs, etc. Text-book of Harmony for schools and students.

HORSLEY.

HOWELL.

Horsley, William, composer, organist, and writer, born at London, November 15, 1774. Articled to T. Smith, a pianist. He studied under J. W. Callcott and Pring. Organist of Ely Chapel, Holborn. Established Concentores Sodales (society for propagating the study of concerted vocal music), 1798-1847. Assistant organist at Asylum for Female Orphans, 1798. Mus. Bac., Oxon., 1800. Chief organist of Orphan Asylum, 1802. Organist of Belgrave Chapel, Grosvenor Place, 1812; Charter-house, on death of Stevens, 1837. He married Elizabeth H. Callcott, daughter of J. W. Callcott. He was one of the founders of the Philharmonic Society. He died at London, June 12, 1858.

WORKS.—Glees, canons, etc., published in five different collections, op. 1, 1801; op. 3, 1806; op. 4, [1808]; op. 6, 1811, and 1827. Forty canons of various species for 2, 3, 4, and 6 voices in score, op. 9. Vocal harmony (edited) Loudon, 7 vols. [1830]. Elegiac odes to memory of S. Webbe and S. Harrison. A collection of Psalms, with interludes, 1828. Twenty-four Psalm tunes and eight chants, 1844. Callcott's glees, edited with memoir, London, 2 vols., 1824. Airs of the Rhine, edited 1828 Pf. music, miscellaneous. An explanation of musical intervals, and of the major and minor scales, op. 8, London, 1825. An introduction to the study of practical harmony and modulation, London, 1847. Songs and canzonets, etc.

Horton, George, oboist. Student and Associate, R.A.M. Member of the orchestras of Her Majesty's Opera; Birmingham Festival to 1888; Leeds Festival to 1889; Three Choirs Festival to 1894, as performer on the oboe and cor Anglais. He has also played the oboe d'amore in Bach's Passion Music, etc., in Westminster Abbey and elsewhere; and long held the leading position in his special department. He is a professor at the R.A.M. and R.C.M., and a member of the Queen's private band.

Horton, Maria, see sub. HORN, CHARLES EDWARD.

Horton, Priscilla, see REED, MRS. GERMAN

Houghton, William, organist and composer, born in Dublin, 1844; died there in 1871. He was a chorister and deputy-organist in Christ Church Cathedral, Dublin, and organist of St. Ann's, Dublin. Composer of anthems, songs, and organ music.

Houldsworth, John, organist, violinist, and composer, who was born in the latter part of the eighteenth century. He was appointed organist of the Parish Church of Halifax in 1819. He played first violin at the Yorkshire Festivals of 1823 and 1825. Died after 1836. He edited an edition of Chetham's Psalmody, 1832, and composed several hymn-tunes, chants, etc.

Houseley, Henry, organist and composer, born at Ashfield, Notts., September 20, 1851. F.C.O. From about 1875 resident in Derby, and organist and choirmaster of St. Luke's Church. Then, removing to Nottingham, he became organist of St. James' Church in 1882, and Lecturer in Musical Theory at Nottingham University College. In 1888 he left England for America, as sub-organist and choirmaster of the Cathedral, Denver, Colorado. He has written an opera, "Native Silver," performed at Denver, 1892; a quartet for strings; a number of pieces for pf.; and some vocal music, among which is a part-song which gained a prize given by the Glasgow Select Choir.

Houston, Allan, Scottish musician, who lived in Glasgow as a teacher of music at the end of last and beginning of the present century. He published a "Collection of Church Tunes, with a few anthems, canons, and catches," Glasgow, 1799.

Howard, Samuel, organist and composer, born in London, 1710. He was a chorister in the Chapel Royal under Croft, and he also studied under Pepusch. Organist of St. Bride's and St. Clement Danes Churches, London. Mus. Doc., Cantab., 1769. He died at London, July 13, 1782.

WORKS.—Amorous Goddess, opera, 1744. Musical Companion, a collection of English songs, London, n.d. Anthems, psalms, cantatas; large number of songs and instrumental music.

Howard, William, conductor and violinist, born at Edinburgh, March 18, 1831. He played the violin in the Theatre Royal, Edinburgh, under Alex. Mackenzie, and in 1857 he became musical director of the Edinburgh and Glasgow assemblies. Conductor of the Edinburgh Choral Union, 1863-1865. He died at Dumfries, June 2, 1877.

Howe, W. F., author of "Lecture on French Horns, ancient and modern, both historical and practical," n.d.

Howell, Arthur, double-bass player and vocalist, born in 1836. Son of James Howell. He married Miss Rose Hersee, the vocalist, in 1874, with whom he travelled in Australia, etc. For some time he was stage manager to the Carl Rosa Opera Company. He died on April 26, 1885.

Howell, Edward, violoncellist, born in London, February, 1846. F.R.A.M. Professor of the violoncello at R.A.M., and R.C.M. Musician in ordinary to the Queen. Member of the Philharmonic Society, and for many years principal violoncellist in its orchestra; holds the same position in the Leeds Festival orchestra from 1880; and at the meetings of the Three Choirs. Is widely known as soloist and quartet player. Appeared at the Crystal Palace Concerts for the first time, October 27,

N

HOWELL.

1883, as soloist in Goltermann's third violoncello Concerto. Author of a "First Book for the Violoncello" (from Romberg), etc.

Howell, Francis, composer, son of James Howell, born in 1834 ; died, October 28, 1882. He was blind from 1881. Composer of "The Land of Promise," oratorio; "Song of the Months," cantata. Songs, etc.

Howell, James, double-bass player and teacher, born at Plymouth, in 1811. He studied at the R.A.M., under T. M. Mudie, and studied the double-bass under Anfossi. Professor of double-bass at the R.A.M. Member of R.A.M., etc. He died, London, August 5, 1879. His son, ARTHUR, was also a bass-player.

Howell, Thomas, composer, writer, and pianist, was born at Bristol in 1783. He was a teacher at Bristol. Author of "Practical instructions for the Pianoforte" [1816] ; "Lessons in all major and minor keys, for the pf.," n.d. ; "Six progressive sonatinas for the pf." [1817] ; "Original instructions for the Violin," Bristol, 1825 ; "Practical elementary examples for the violin" [1829] ; "Six quartets, for 2 violins, and other instruments," etc.

Howgate, John, musician, who issued "Sacred Music: eighteen hymn and psalm tunes," etc., Manchester [1810].

Howgill, William, organist, born in the 18th century. He was organist at Whitehaven, in 1794, and afterwards in London. Composer of four Voluntaries . . . and six favourite Psalm tunes [1820] ; Purcell's, or, the Welsh ground, with one hundred variations for the grand pf., London [1810].

Howson, see ALBERTAZZI, EMMA.

Howson, George, earthenware manufacturer—a man whose work in the cause of music deserves a word of record. With the late J. W. Powell (q.v.), he was a pioneer in the work of elementary vocal teaching in North Staffordshire, and in popularizing the Sol-fa system. He gave up teaching many years ago, but was always a warm supporter of any movement for providing good music for the people. He was president of the Hanley Glee and Madrigal Society, and founded a scholarship in connection with the Tonic Sol-fa College, for the benefit of North Staffordshire students. He died at Shelton, Hanley, April 4, 1896, aged seventy-eight.

Hoyland, John, organist and composer, born at Sheffield, 1783. He studied under Mather of Sheffield, and became organist of St. James' Church, Sheffield, in 1808 ; organist of Parish Church, Louth, Lincoln, 1819. He died January 18, 1827. Composer of anthems, songs, and organ music.

His son, WILLIAM, was also an organist.

Hoyle, John, musician, who flourished about the middle of the 18th century, and

HUDSON.

died in 1797. Author of "Dictionarium Musicæ, being a complete Dictionary or Treasury of Music," 1770. Other editions, 1790 and 1791.

Hoyte, William Stevenson, organist and composer, born at Sidmouth, Devon, September 22, 1844. Received instruction from Sir J. Goss, and George Cooper. Organist of St. Paul's, Hampstead ; All Saints', Kings Lynn ; St. Paul's, Bow Common, 1862 ; St. Matthew's, City Road, 1864 ; Holy Trinity, Westminster, 1865 ; and All Saints', Margaret Street, from 1868 to the present. Has given organ recitals at the Alexandra Palace ; the Royal Albert Hall ; in Glasgow, and other places ; and has also appeared with success as a pianist. For some years examiner to College of Organists: Professor of organ at R.C.M., from 1888 ; at R.A.M., 1893 ; and of pianoforte at Guildhall School. Member of the Philharmonic Society. He has composed a "Book of Litanies, metrical and prose, with an Evening service"; "The Choral office for the solemnization of Holy Matrimony"; Church music, various. Minuet and Trio, orchestra, 1882 ; organ and pf. pieces, etc.

Hubi, Georgeanne, see NEWCOMBE, GEORGEANNE H.

Huckel, William, musician, author of "Practical instructions in the art of Singing," London, 1845. "Practical instructions for the cultivation of the Voice, with a series of rules for its adaptation to the chamber, the concert room, and the stage." London, n.d.

Huddart, Fanny, contralto vocalist, was born in the first part of the present century. She sang in Italian and English opera, and in oratorio, in London and the Provinces, and had a high reputation in her day. She was married to Mr. John Russell, of Drury Lane Theatre. She died at London, June 28, 1880.

Hudson, Arthur, violinist and composer, born at Hull. Studied at R.A.M. Resided for some time at Clifton, Bristol ; now settled as professor of his instrument at Hull. He has composed a Sonata, a Romance, and other pieces for violin and pf , which have been performed at Bristol, etc.

His brother, JOHN WILLIAM HUDSON, born at Hull, is organist of St. James's Church there, and is the composer of a string Quartet in A minor ; a Trio for pf. and strings, produced at Hull, Bristol, etc.

Hudson, Robert, composer and vocalist, born February 25, 1732. He studied under Charles King, and was originally a tenor singer in Marylebone and Ranelagh Gardens, London, but in 1755 became assistant organist of St. Mildred, Bread Street, London. He next became vicar-choral of St. Paul's Cathedral, in 1756 ; Gentleman of the Chapel Royal, 1758 ; Almoner and master of the children of St. Paul's, 1773-93; and music-master of Christ's Hospital. He died at Eton, December 19, 1815. He composed services, anthems, hymns, and glees, and edited "The Myrtle, a collection of new English Songs," in three books, 1767.

His daughter, MARY, was organist of St. Olave, Hart Street; St. Gregory, Old Fish Street, 1790-1801. She died in London, March 28, 1801. Composer of a few hymns.

Hughes, David, baritone vocalist, born at Landore, Swansea, in 1863. After singing with success at local concerts, he entered the R.A.M., studying under Manuel Garcia, and winning the Parepa-Rosa (1887), Evill (1889), Leslie Crotty (1890), and other prizes. He made his début at the Monday Popular Concerts, Bristol, March 10, 1890, and speedily won for himself an honourable position. He has been heard at the principal oratorio concerts, etc.

Hughes, Mrs. F. J., authoress of "Harmonies of Tones and Colours developed by Evolution," London, 1883, illustrated. Appendix, 1885.

Hughes, G. A., musician and teacher, author of Instruction Book for the Pianoforte or Organ for the Blind, London, 1848. Congregational Psalmody, 1843.

Hughes, J., author of "Young Student's Musical Definitions, London, 1877.

Hughes, Joseph, harpist, born in North Wales. In 1839, published a collection of Welsh airs, partly arranged, partly composed by himself. Soon afterwards, this promising young harpist and musician went to America, and was accidently drowned in the Hudson.

Hughes, Richard Samuel, pianist and composer, born at Aberystwith, July 14, 1855, Studied at R.A.M. Organist at the Independent Chapel, Bethesda, near Bangor. Published a Cantata, The Shepherds of Bethleham, anthems, part-songs, and a number of very popular songs. In this last respect he has been called "The Sullivan of Wales." He was an able executant, and well known throughout the Principality. He died at Bethesda, March 5, 1893.

Hullah, John Pyke, composer and teacher, born at Worcester, June 27, 1812. He studied under W. Horsley, 1829, and at the R.A.M., in 1832. Visited Paris, and adopted Wilhem's method of vocal instruction. Musical instructor in Sir James Kay Shuttleworth's (then Dr. Kay) Training College, Battersea, 1840. Taught music to schoolmasters in Exeter Hall, London, 1841. Established classes in St. Martin's Hall, 1847-50. Professor of vocal music, King's College, London, 1844-74; do. Queen's College, London, and Bedford College. Organist of Charterhouse, London, 1858. Conductor at R.A.M., 1870-73. Musical Inspector of Training Schools for

United Kingdom, 1872—retired 1883. LL.D., Edinburgh, 1876. Member of Society of St. Cecilia, Rome, 1877, and of Music Academy of Florence. He died at London, February 21, 1884.

WORKS.—*Operettas* : The village coquettes (Dickens); The outpost; The barbers of Barsora. Singer's library of Concerted Music—Secular and sacred series, 6 vols. Whole book of Psalms, with the canticles and hymns of the Church, for morning and evening service ... London, 1844. Fifty-eight English songs, by composers chiefly of the 17th and 18th centuries. *Songs:* Come forth from thy bower; Home of our youth; One look of love; Free companion; Joy cometh in the morning; Message from the battlefield; The storm. Motets, anthems, concerted vocal music, etc. Method of teaching singing, by Wilhem, London, 1842; do., revised and reconstructed edition, 1850. Grammar of vocal music, founded on Wilhem's method, 1843. Duty and advantages of learning to sing, London, 1846. Grammar of musical harmony, 1853; Exercises for do., 1873 ; new edit., 1873. Music in the parish church, a lecture, London, 1856. History of modern music: a course of lectures delivered at the Royal Institution of Great Britain, 1862 (2 editions). Lectures on the third or transition period of musical history, London, 1865; 2nd edit., 1876. The Song book, words and tunes from the best poets and musicians, 1866. Cultivation of the speaking voice, Oxford, 1870; another edition, 1874. Grammar of counterpoint. Rudiments of musical grammar, n.d. Notation : Brief direction concerning the choice, adjustment, etc., of the musical alphabet, 1876. Time and tune in the elementary school; new method of teaching vocal music and exercises, 1877. Music in the house (Art at Home series), 1877. Exercises for the cultivation of the voice, 2 parts, n.d. How can a sound knowledge of music be generally disseminated? London, Longman, 1878. Reports to Government on progress of musical education in schools. Contributions to periodical literature. See "Life of John Hullah, by his wife," London, 1886.

Hulley, William Frederick, organist and composer. Conductor of Choral and Orchestral Societies, Swansea, and organist of St. David's, Roman Catholic Church in that town. He is the composer of two comic operas, "The Coastguard," produced, 1886; and "The Rustic," produced, 1888, at Swansea.

Hume, Alexander, composer and minor poet, born at Edinburgh, February 7, 1811. Engaged in business and teaching in Edinburgh and Glasgow. He died at Glasgow, February 4, 1859.

WORKS.—The English Hymn Tune Book,

HUME.

containing two hundred and four of the most common hymns used in England: arranged for four voices, Edinburgh, n.d. Anthems and Sacred Songs, containing fifty-four pieces, Edinburgh, n.d. Gall's Psalm and Hymn Book, Edinburgh, 1842. Six sensible songs. *Songs :* Afton Water ; My ain dear Nell ; The Scottish emigrant's farewell, etc. Glees and duets. Poems, various. Hume's version of "Afton Water" is now the one almost universally sung to Burns' song.

Hume, J. Ord, bandmaster and composer, born in Edinburgh, September 14, 1864. He joined the Duke of Buccleugh's Dalkeith Militia when eleven years old, and became solo cornet a year later, studying under Alexander Miller. When sixteen he went to the band of the Royal Scots Greys as solo cornet, and remained with the regiment until 1887. He was then appointed organist of the Military Presbyterian Church, Aldershot, and bandmaster of Aldershot Town, and Farnham Institute bands. After holding various other appointments, he became bandmaster of the 3rd V.B., Durham Light Infantry, Sunderland. He is also professional teacher to many bands in the district ; and in a contest held at Newcastle-on-Tyne, November 16, 1895, his bands carried off the 1st, 2nd, 3rd, 5th, and divided the 6th and 7th prizes. As an adjudicator, he has had much work, and headed the list in 1895. He has written upwards of 500 pieces, and is the principal writer for A. Haigh's Brass Band Journal, and *The Cornet* Band Journal. A book of sixteen marches by him is published by Rudall Carte & Co.

Hume, Tobias, English military officer and musician, was a performer on the viol-da-gamba, and a colonel in the army. Died in the Charterhouse, London, 1645. He wrote "The First Part of Ayres, French, Pollish, and others together, some in Tabliture and some in Pricke," 1605 ; "Captain Hume's Poeticall Musicke, principally made for two Basse Violls, yet so construed that it may be plaied eight several waies, upon sundrie instruments, with much facilitie," 1607.

Hume, William, composer and editor, son of Alexander Hume, born at Edinburgh, September 25, 1830. Settled in Glasgow as teacher of violin and singing. Editor of musical publications of Mr. Hamilton, Glasgow ; Gall and Inglis, Edinburgh ; and Parlane, Paisley. For some years, from 1872, musical critic of *The Bailie*, Glasgow, and contributor to various musical journals. His compositions include the cantatas : The call to battle ; Blind Bartimeus ; and Psalm 67, for treble voices. A motet for soli and chorus, Answer me, burning stars of night (Hemans); Anthems, songs, and part-songs. Editor of Union Sacred Tune-book ; The Westminster Wesleyan Tune-book ; Psalm and Hymn

HUNT.

tunes, with supplement of anthems ; Harmonium Tune-book, etc.

Humphrey, Pelham, or HUMFREY, composer, was born in 1647. Chorister in the Chapel Royal, under Henry Cook, 1660, and a pupil of Lulli, at Paris, in 1664. Gentleman of the Chapel Royal, 1667. Master of Choristers, do., 1672. He died at Windsor, July 14, 1674.

WORKS.—Anthems and Services in collections of Clifford, Boyce, Tudway, etc. ; Haste Thee, O God ; Have mercy upon me ; Hear, O heavens ; Like as the hart ; Lord, teach us ; O Lord my God ; Rejoice in the Lord ; Thou art my King, O God. Odes on the King's Birthday, and on New Year's Day. Songs in various collections, etc.

Humphries, John, composer and violinist of the 18th century ; died in 1730. WORKS.—12 Concertos in seven parts, for 2 violins and violoncello obligato, etc., op. 2. 12 Concertos in seven parts, for the following instruments : one for 2 trumpets and kettledrums ; two for 2 hautboys and violins, etc., op. 3.

Hunnis, William, musician and author of the 16th century. He was a Gentleman of the Chapel Royal in the time of Edward VI., but was dismissed by Mary for his part in plots against the Roman Catholics. On the accession of Elizabeth, he was reinstated at the Chapel Royal, and became custodian of gardens and orchards at Greenwich, 1562 ; and master of the children of the Chapel Royal, in succession to Edwardes, 1566. He died on June 6, 1597.

WORKS.—Certayne Psalms chosen out of the Psalter of David and drawen furth into English meter, London, 1549. A hyve full hunnye, containing the first booke of Moses, called Genesis, turned into Englishe meetre, London, 1578. Seven sobs of a sorrowful soule for sinne, . . whereunto are annexed his handfull of honisuckles, London, 1583 ; also 1585, 1587, 1621, etc. Hunnies' recreations, containing foure Godlie and compendious discourses, London, 1588. Music in MS., preserved in the Music School of Oxford.

Hunt, Anna, *see* THILLON, ANNA.

Hunt, Arabella, vocalist and lutenist of the 17th century. She was attached to the family of Queen Mary, as a teacher, and was much esteemed as a performer. Blow, Purcell, and other musicians were among her friends, and poems on her were written by Congreve and H ·ghes. She died on December 26, 1705. Kneller painted her portrait.

Hunt, Rev. Henry George Bonavia, writer on music, born at Malta, June 30, 1847. Privately educated in music. Graduated Mus. Bac., 1876, Oxford ; Mus. Bac. and Mus. Doc., Dublin, 1887. F.R.S.E., L.T.C L. Choirmaster, South Hackney Parish Church,

HUNT.

1872-5. Warden of Trinity College, London, 1872-92; Professor of Musical History, 1876-87 ; and Professor Emeritus, 1892. Appointed Curate and evening preacher, St. James's, Piccadilly. 1884 ; Incumbent of St. Paul's, Kilburn, 1887. His compositions are, "The Angels' Song," and Psalm 133, for soli, chorus and orchestra (degree exercises) ; an Evening Service, and anthems. Author of Concise History of Music for the use of Students, Cambridge, Deighton, Bell, and Co., 1878, now in its 13th edition. Also, of many papers read at Trinity College, London ; at the Social Science Congress, 1883, etc.

Hunt, John, organist and composer, born at Marnhull, Dorset, December 30, 1806. Chorister of Salisbury Cathedral from 1813, and afterwards articled to A. T. Corfe. He was educated at Salisbury Grammar School till 1827, and in that year he became lay-vicar of Lichfield Cathedral, where he remained till 1835. He became organist of Hareford cathedral in succession to S. Wesley in 1835. Died at Hareford, November 17, 1842, from the results of an accident at an audit dinner.

A collection of his songs, with a memoir, was issued in 1843.

Hunt, Thomas, composer of the 16th century, who wrote the madrigal, "Hark! did you ever heare so sweet a singing," for six voices, in the "Triumphs of Oriana." Beyond this there is nothing known about him, though it is stated he was a bachelor of music.

Hunt, T., musician, compiler of a "Selection of 40 Sacred Melodies, adapted to the Psalms . . . n.d.

Hunt, William Henry, composer and teacher of singing, born in London, in 1852. Educated at the Cooper's School, Ratcliffe, and was for years teacher of general subjects in different schools. About 1875, he went to Birkenhead as school master, and gradually drifted into the profession of music, an art he had studied since his twelfth year. He was mostly self-taught. In 1880, he graduated Mus. Bac., London, being with H. K. Moore (*q.v.*), the first recipient of that degree; and took the Mus. Doc. in 1886. He was a busy worker up to the spring of 1894, when he was smitten with paralysis. He rallied for a time, but died at Birkenhead, December 6, 1894. His works include a *Stabat Mater* for soli, eight-part chorus, and orchestra ; Church services and anthems. Two comic Operas, "Rumtifoo, or wrecked on a Princess," and "Utopia, or the finger of fate," produced, Birkenhad, May 4, 1891 ; a number of songs ; studies and exercises for pf., etc.

Hunter, Thomas Munro, vocal teacher and tenor singer. was born at Alloa, N B., in 1820. He settled as a teacher and concert-

HUTCHESON.

giver in Edinburgh, and became precentor of various churches. He was well-known in Edinburgh as a teacher of singing in schools, for which he wrote various elementary collections of exercises and songs. He died at Edinburgh, July 16, 1886, from the effects of a gig accident.

Huntley, George Frederic, organist and composer, born at Datchet, Bucks, May 31, 1859. Studied under Dr. Keeton, C. Hancock, and Sir G. Elvey, at St. George's Chapel, Windsor. Graduated Mus. Bac., Cambridge, 1887 ; Mus. Doc., 1894. Organist and Choirmaster successively at St. George's, Kensington, 1880 ; St. Andrew's, Westminster, 1890 ; Newcastle Cathedral, 1894 ; and St. Peter's, Eaton Square, London, 1895. Conducted Annual Festivals of Association of Kensington Church Choirs, and was also conductor of Staines Choral Society, Twickenham Symphony Society ; holding at present the conductorship of the Church Orchestral Society. While at Newcastle-on-Tyne he revived the orchestral services in the Cathedral, in 1894, and produced, for the first time there, Bach's Matthew Passion, in Holy Week, 1895. He is A.R.C.M., L.R.A.M., and F.R.C.O. His compositions comprise an Oratorio, Dies Domini ; Cantatas, "O Lord I will praise Thee," "Saint George for England" (produced, Crystal Palace). Festival Te Deum. Anthems, services, and hymns. Operettas— "The white Cat," "The wild Swans." Cantata, "Victoria, or the Bard's Prophecy, 1897.

Husband, Rev. Edward, amateur organist and composer, vicar of St. Michael's, Folkestone. He has given many organ recitals in his church ; also lectures on Church music ; and is the composer of an evening service, anthem, etc. Editor of "Supplemental tunes to popular hymns," Novello [1882].

Husk, William Henry, musician and writer, was born at London, November 4, 1814, and died at London, August 12, 1887. He was librarian to the late Sacred Harmonic Society. Author of "An account of the Musical Celebrations on St. Cecilia's Day, in the 16th, 17th, and 18th centuries, to which is appended a collection of Odes on St. Cecilia's Day," London, 1857 ; "Songs of the Nativity, being Christmas carols, ancient and modern, several of which appear for the first time in a collection, edited with notes," London, n.d. [1866] ; "Catalogues of the library of the Sacred Harmonic Society," 1853, 1862, and 1872 ; Contributions to Sir G. Grove's "Dictionary of Musicians." Numerous prefaces to Word Books of oratorios, and other pieces, etc.,

Hutcheson, Charles, composer, born at Glasgow, 1792. He was a merchant in Glasgow, where he died in 1858. He published "Christian Vespers," Glasgow, 1832, containing hymn-tunes harmonized, in 3 and 4

HUTCHESON.

parts, with an introductory essay on church music. He was one of the founders of the Glasgow Dilletanti Society.

Hutcheson, Francis, Francis Ireland, composer, born at Glasgow, in 1720. Son of Professor Hutcheson. He was educated at Glasgow and Dublin, and graduated B.A., 1745; M.A., 1748, and M.D., Dublin, 1762. He died in 1780. Composer of glees and catches, under the pseudonym of Francis Ireland, of which a number appeared in Warren's "Vocal Harmony." He gained prizes from the Catch Club, in 1772 and 1773. His best remembered glees are "How sleep the brave," "Where weeping yews," "Jolly Bacchus," etc.

Hutchinson, Cecilia Mary, soprano vocalist, born in India. Studied in France, and Italy, and under Joseph Robinson, Dublin, and Alfred Blume, London. She made her *début* at a special Saturday Concert at the Crystal Palace, May 21, 1881; at the Monday Popular Concerts, January 9, 1882; and appeared at the principal provincial concerts. Her Festival *début* was at Worcester, 1884; and she created the soprano part in Cowen's "Sleeping Beauty," at the Birmingham Festival of 1885; and sang at the Leeds Festival, 1886. She has done much to popularise the delicate songs of Berlioz, "Les Nuits d'Eté."

Hutchinson, Joseph T., baritone vocalist, born in London, July 12, 1849. Began his musical career as lay-vicar of Salisbury Cathedral, to which he was appointed when twenty-one years of age. At the end of a year he returned to London, and entered the R.A.M., studying singing under Manuel Garcia, and elocution with Walter Lacy. Appointed successively sub-professor, assistant-professor, and professor; and elected A.R.A.M. Gave concerts, and sang in cantatas and oratorio in various parts of the country, his most conspicuous successes being in Barnett's Ancient Mariner, and Macfarren's Lady of the Lake, and oratorios. He is co-translator, with Windeyer Clark, of Gounod's Commentary on Mozart's "Don Giovanni" (R. Cocks, 1895).

Hutchinson, Thomas, organist and composer. Musically educated at Durham Cathedral. Graduated Mus. Bac., 1879; Mus. Doc., 1894, Oxford. Organist at Silksworth Church, Sunderland, up to 1896, when he was appointed to Darlington Parish Church. His compositions include cantatas, "The Redeemer," and, "The Children of the Captivity"; Anthems; Te Deum and Jubilate in E flat; Services, various; Pieces for organ, and pf. Songs: Lovelight; Silver shadows; Fetters of gold, etc.

Hutchison, G. B., author of "Shorthand Music; an easy and rapid method of writing music," London, n.d.

HYDE.

Hutchison, M. J., author of a "Treatise on Music," London [1847].

Hutchison, William Marshall, composer, born at Glasgow, May 28, 1854. His works include: "The Story of Elaine," and "Story of Naomi and Ruth," cantatas; "H.R.H.," and "Glamour," comic operas. Also songs: Dream faces; Ehren on the Rhine; Pierrot; Mine again; Little Mandarin; Part-songs, pf. pieces, etc.

Hutt, William, organist and teacher, was a chorister at Westminster Abbey, under J. Turle. Since 1865, he has been organist of Winchester College, master of the choristers, and music master. In this retired sphere he has done much valuable work in the cause of musical education.

Huxtable, Anthony, Christopher, and William, a family of English musicians who flourished about the middle of this century. Anthony, born in 1818, was a violinist and teacher; Christopher, his son, an organist and violinist, composed much dance music; and William, a harpist, pianist, etc.

Hyam, Lottie, pianist, born in Sydney, New South Wales, 1864. At the Sydney International Exhibition, opened September 17, 1879, she was engaged by Messrs. Steinway to give a series of recitals upon their pianofortes. Resident in Sydney, she has become known as one of the best pianists in that city.

Hyde. Four generations of musicians. The first of the name, James, was a trumpet-player of some renown. Trumpeter to the Duke of York, and author of works for the trumpet; and probably the Hyde who introduced an improvement in the instrument by a small slide, sometime before 1812. His name appeared in the Birmingham Festival orchestra several times from 1802. His son, James Hyde, was also a clever performer on the trumpet, and a composer of popular ballads, one of which, "Edwy and Sue," was sung by Braham. He settled in Manchester, and his name figured in the Birmingham Festival band list from 1811. His son, James Hyde, was a violinist and teacher of the pianoforte, for many years resident in Birmingham. His son, James Hyde, born in Birmingham, 1849, is a violinist, conductor, and composer. Pupil of his father, and then of Henry Hayward, for violin, and Andrew Deakin for organ and harmony. Up to 1870 he was actively engaged as teacher, soloist, and musical director in his native town. In 1870 he removed to London, and was conductor at the Royalty Theatre. He went to South Africa in 1875 as conductor of the Turner Opera Company. For some time he resided at King William's Town, and is now settled at Johannesburg, where he is musical director of the Wanderer's Club, which has a concert room and opera house. He has com-

IEUAN.

posed cantatas, many songs (The Land of Good Hope, etc.), and pf. pieces, beside a vast number of arrangements. His wife, *née* KATE LEIPOLD, is an excellent pianist, and frequently assists at recitals, etc. FLORENCE HYDE, a sister, was drowned at Bath, in June, 1879, through the capsizing of a boat. She was a member of the Carl Rosa and D'Oyly Carte companies, and a very promising young singer.

Ieuan, Glan Alarch, *see* MILLS, REV. JOHN.

Ieuan, Gwyllt, *see* ROBERTS, REV. JOHN.

Ieuan, Dhu, *see* THOMAS, JOHN L.

Iliffe, Frederick, composer, organist, and conductor, born at Smeeton-Westerby, Leicester, February 21, 1847. Was privately educated in music, and filled his first appointment as organist at St. Wilfred's, Kibworth. In 1883 he was appointed organist and choirmaster of St. John's College, Oxford, an office he still holds. He was also, for some time, from 1878, organist of St. Barnabas', Oxford. He graduated Mus. Bac., 1873; Mus. Doc., 1879, Oxford; also M.A. Since 1883 he has been conductor of the Queen's College (Eglesfield) Musical Society. For this Society important works have been expressly composed by Dr. Bridge, Professor Prout, Dr. Mee, the subject of this notice, and others; and it has a musical record, since 1871, unequalled by any other college society.

WORKS.—Oratorio, The Visions of St. John the Divine, composed 1879, published 1880; Evening Service in D, for men's voices; Anglican chant settings for the whole of the Canticles; Short and easy anthems for parish choirs, etc. Lara, cantata for men's voices and orchestra, produced, Queen's College Musical Society, May, 1885; Sweet Echo (Milton) for eight-part chorus and orchestra, Cheltenham Festival, 1893; Morning, a Pastoral (Rev. Canon Bell) for soprano solo, chorus, and orchestra, the same, 1896. Concert overture in E; Festal overture in D, Oxford, May, 1894, Birmingham (Stockley), 1895; Serenade in G, strings, Queen's College, 1884. Prelude and fugue for organ; Sonata, and other pieces for pf., etc. Author of a Critical Analysis of Bach's Das Wohltemperirte Clavier, in four parts, Novello, 1896.

Immyns, John, attorney and lutenist, born early in the 18th century. Member of Academy of Ancient Music. Amanuensis to Dr. Pepusch. Established the Madrigal Society, 1741. Lutenist to Chapel Royal, 1752. He died at London, April 15, 1764. His son JOHN was organist of Surrey Chapel, London, and died in 1794.

Incledon, Charles, tenor vocalist, born at St. Keverne, Cornwall, 1763; baptized Benjamin on February 5th. Son of a physician.

IONS.

Articled pupil to W. Jackson, Exeter, under whom he was a Chorister in the Cathedral. Sailor on board H.M.S. "Formidable," 1779-83. Recommended as singer to Colman by Lord Admiral Hervey, but services declined. Member of Collins' Dramatic Company at Southampton, 1784. Appeared at Bath, 1785. Pupil for a time of Rauzzini, at Bath. Sang in Vauxhall Gardens, 1788. *Début* in "The Poor Soldier" at Covent Garden Theatre, London, 1790. Travelled much in the Provinces. Retired from Covent Garden, 1815. Appeared in North America, 1817. Resided at Brighton. He died at Worcester, Feb. 11, 1826, and is buried at Hampstead, London.

His son Charles (1791-1865) was also a tenor singer.

Ingham, James, musician, compiled "National Chant Book," London, 1848, also 1849; "Psalter, pointed for Chanting," London, 1856, 3rd. ed.

Ingham, Richard, composer and organist, was born in 1804. He was organist of Parish Church, Gateshead; Carlisle Cathedral, 1833; and died in June, 1841. Composer of some vocal music; "Titania's Lullaby," round [1840], etc.

Inglott, William, organist and composer, was born in 1554. He was organist of Norwich Cathedral, 1608. Died in December, 1621. Mentioned as one of the greatest of early English organists. Biography obscure.

Ingram, Thomas, musician, who was organist of Chapel Royal at Brighton. He flourished 1810-51. Author of "Choral Class Book, or Singer's Manual, containing easy and progressive exercises," London, 1851; and compiler of "Twenty-five Select Psalm Tunes, ancient and modern...., as used in Brighton College, London, 1848; "Select Chants arranged for four voices," London, 1851.

Inverarity, Eliza, Mrs. MARTYN, soprano vocalist, born Edinburgh, March 23, 1813. Grand-niece of Robert Fergusson, the poet. She studied under Mr. Thorne, of Edinburgh, then under Mr. Alex. Murray, at whose concert in 1829 she first appeared. On December 14, 1830, she sang in London in "Cinderella," and in 1836 she married Charles Martyn, a bass singer and composer. With him she appeared in opera in the United States and in England. In 1839 she sang in New York in Beethoven's "Fidelio." She died at Newcastle-on-Tyne, December 27, 1846. She composed some ballads.

Ions, Thomas, organist and composer, eldest son of James Ions, plate-glass manufacturer, of Newcastle-on-Tyne, born August 19, 1817. Displayed musical talent very early, and studied locally under Munro, Marr, Ingham, and Thompson; and later, under Moscheles. In 1833, was appointed Ingham's successor at St. Mary's Parish Church, Gates-

IONS.

head, after competition. His youthful appearance, when presented to the judges, caused them to think a mistake had been made, and he was required to repeat a fugue by Bach, and a Handel chorus, while they looked on in admiration. The next year he was elected, by the Mayor and Corporation, organist of St. Nicholas', Newcastle, on the death of his teacher, Thomas Thompson. This post he retained till his death. He was conductor of Newcastle and Gateshead Choral Society; and in 1835 established the Amateur Glee Club, and Subscription Concerts. Chorus-master, and assistant conductor (under Sir Geo. Smart), Newcastle Festival, 1842. Graduated Mus. Bac., 1848; Mus. Doc., 1854, Oxford. Conductor of Newcastle Sacred Harmonic Society, founded 1848. Public testimonial, 1855. Died suddenly, while driving home after teaching at Gateshead, September 25, 1857. In 1860, as a memorial to him, the great east window of St. Nicholas' Church was restored, and filled with stained glass at a cost of £1,000, subscribed by his admiring townspeople.

WORKS.—Cantata, Prayer and thanksgiving, eight-part chorus and orchestra; Ps. 137, six voices and orchestra; Services in C, A, and E flat; anthems, motets, etc. A Christmas madrigal, *Musical Times*, January, 1849; part-songs, songs, pf. music, etc. Editor of Cantica Ecclesiastica: a complete volume of congregational music, 1849, to which he contributed many tunes, chants, etc.

Ions, William Jamson, brother of the preceding, born at Newcastle-on-Tyne, November 3, 1833. Entered the choir of St. Nicholas' at age of nine; articled to his brother in 1849, and appointed assistant organist, 1850. Studied in Germany, 1852-4, including matters relating to the construction and voicing of large organs. Returning to Newcastle, he devoted himself chiefly to the improvement of Church music and Church organs. On the death of his brother, he was appointed organist of St. Nicholas' Church. He worked with Rev. Dr. J. B. Dykes in compiling and improving the service books for use at the Festivals of Choirs in the Northern diocese; was made a Life Governor of the Northern Counties' Orphanage, 1864, for his improvements in the music there. Was active in promoting the Festival held in St. Nicholas' (now the Cathedral) Church, July, 1883, when Dr. Gladstone's oratorio, "Philippi," was produced. Designed the new organ, opened in 1891; was publicly presented with a Testimonial, 1893; and retired from active duty, 1894, after more than half-a-century spent in the service of the Church. This step was caused by the affliction of deafness. Mr. Ions has composed anthems, services, and other Church music.

ISIDOR.

Ireland, Edmund, musician, compiled "Tunes of the Psalms, in two parts," York, 1699; 2nd edition, issued as ".The most useful Tunes of the Psalms," York, 1713.

Ireland, Francis, *see* HUTCHESON, FRANCIS.

Irons, Herbert Stephen, organist and composer, born at Canterbury, January 19, 1834. His father was a lay-vicar at the Cathedral; and Sir George and Stephen Elvey were his uncles. Chorister in Canterbury Cathedral, 1844-49; Precentor and master of choristers, St. Columba College, Ireland, 1856-57; organist of Southwell Minster, 1857-72. In 1872 he became assistant organist of Chester Cathedral. Now resident in Nottingham, and organist of St. Andrew's Church, since 1876. He has published a Te Deum and Jubilate; several anthems, an evening hymn, and edited a collection of chants.

Isaac, Benjamin Ralph, pianist, born at Liverpool (1818?) Pupil of a Mr. Molineux in that city, and in 1836, of Cipriani Potter, at R.A.M. A brilliant performer. He settled in his native place, and was shortly afterwards elected an Associate, and then Fellow of the R.A.M. He died, suddenly, at Southport, January 9, 1881.

Isaacs, Rebecca, actress and vocalist, born in London, 1828. She made her appearance 1834. *Début* in opera, at Olympic Theatre, London, in December 1836. Married Thomas Roberts, acting manager. Sang with much success in London and the provinces. She died at London, April 21, 1877.

Isham, John, or **Isum,** organist and composer, born in 1685. Deputy-organist to Dr. Croft. Organist of St. Anne's, Soho, in succession to Croft, in 1711. Mus. Bac., Oxon., 1713. Organist of St. Andrew's, Holborn, 1718; also St. Margaret's, Westminster. He died in June, 1726.

WORKS.—Church Services and Anthems; Songs, single and in collections; Catches]1710]. etc.

Isherwood, James Wright, tenor vocalist and composer, born at Manchester, March 2, 1812. He was organist of St. Anne's, Manchester. Died at Manchester, October 30, 1854. He composed "The Soldier's Dream" and "A Violet Blossomed"; Glees, produced by the gentleman's glee club, Manchester. His father, JOHN ISHERWOOD, was a bass vocalist, and sang at the York Festival of 1823. He was a member of the Manchester Philharmonic Concerts, and frequently sang in oratorio. Died at Manchester, October 29, 1849.

Isidor, Rosina, soprano vocalist, of Jewish family. Made her *début* at Her Majesty's Theatre, October 23, 1880, in the title-part of "Lucia di Lammermoor." Gave concerts in 1882. Illness, resulting in loss of sight, com-

ITHURIEL.

JACKSON.

pelled her retirement for some time; but she returned to the stage in 1885, at Modena. She gave a concert at St. James's Hall, in December, 1886; and appeard in Italian Opera at Covent Garden in 1887.

Ithuriel. See COUTTS, W. G.

Ive, Simon, composer of the 17th century, born 1600, died London, 1662. Lay-vicar of St. Paul's Cathedral, and singing master in London. Composed "The Triumph of Peace," a masque by Shirley, 1633 (with H. and W. Lawes). "Lamentation and Mourning, Elegy on the death of William Lawes." Various compositions in Hilton's Catches, Playford's Collection, etc.

Ivery, John, composer, born at Northam, Hertford, in the second part of the 18th century. Published "The Hertfordshire Melody, or Psalm Singers Recreation, being a valuable collection of Psalms, Hymns, Anthems, etc., on various occasions, to which is prefixed a new, concise, and easy introduction to the art of singing, and a copious Dictionary of the terms made use of in Music." London, 1773.

Ives, Joshua, organist and composer, born at Hyde, Cheshire, 1854. Studied under Dr. J. F. Bridge, and Dr. Chipp; graduated Mus. Bac., Cambridge, 1884. Organist, Anderston Parish Church Glasgow, and Lecturer on Music at the Glasgow Athenæum. In 1884, he was selected by Sir G. A. Macfarren and Dr. Stainer to be Professor of Music in the University of Adelaide, and was also appointed city organist. Before leaving to take up his duties in Australia, he was the recipient of a handsome testimonial from his pupils at the Glasgow Athenæum. He is the author of a work on Harmony, has given lectures on music, and composed church music, pieces for organ, etc.

Ivimey. A family of musicians. GEORGE IVIMEY, organist, born at Southampton, 1856. Studied privately. F.R.C.O. Organist and choirmaster, Holyrood Church, and Greenside Parish Church, Southampton. His daughter, ALICE IVIMEY, born at Southampton, is a pianist, and was educated musically at the Conservatorium, Stuttgart. She made her *début* at Princes' Hall, London, 1894. JOHN WILLIAM IVIMEY, cousin of George, was born at West Ham, Essex, September 12, 1868. Pupil of Henry Gadsby, and Corporation Exhibitioner, Guildhall School of Music. F.R.C.O. and A.R.C.M. (for composition). In 1888 was appointed Assistant Music Master at Wellington College, and in 1890 to a similar post at Harrow School, which he resigned in 1893. From 1891 he has been organist and choirmaster at St. Paul's, Onslow Square, Kensington; is head of the Music Section of the South-West London Polytechnic Institution; and conductor of the London County Council Musical Society, and South Kensing-

ton Choral Society. His compositions comprise five comic operas: "Fairy Genesta" (produced, Surbiton, 1892); "Y'lang Y'lang" (Surbiton, 1893); "The Red Rider" (MS., produced, St. George's Hall, London, 1894); and "Marie Tanner" (MS., Cardiff, December, 1895); "The Lady Lawyer," Garrick Theatre, London, March, 1897. He has also written a Trio for Pf. and Strings (1889); a Rondo Pastorale for Violoncello and Pf., and some Pf. pieces, etc. His brother, JOSEPH IVIMEY, is a violinist. He was born at West Ham, 1867. Studied under Alfred Gibson, and was also a Corporation Exhibitioner at the Guildhall School. In 1888 he founded the Surbiton Chamber Concerts, in connection with which he has done valuable artistic work. He is also conductor of Weybridge Orchestral Society.

Jack, David, vocalist and publisher, was born at Edinburgh, February 16, 1824. He edited and published the "Lyric Gems of Scotland" (1854-58) and "The Casquet of Lyric Gems" (1857), both collections of vocal music. He gave many concerts in various parts of Scotland.

Jackson, Arthur Herbert, composer and pianist, born in 1852. He studied at the R.A.M.; Associate; Professor of Harmony and Composition at R.A.M. He died, London, September 27, 1881.

WORKS. — Choral ballad, Lord Ullin's daughter; Jason and the golden fleece, cantata (MS.); The bride of Abydos, overture; Intermezzo for orch.; Violin concerto; Ballet suite for orch.; Concerto for pf. and orch.; Magnificat for chorus and orch; Two masses for male voices; Pf. music; Songs and partsongs.

Jackson, Frederick J., author of "The Construction of the Musical Scale, as determined by the arithmetical evolution of its measures or ratios." London [1869].

Jackson, G. K., musician, author of "First principles, or a treatise on practical Thorough-bass, with general rules for its composition and modulation," op. 5. London [1795]. Other musical works, as "Three songs and duets," op. 3; Sonatas for pf., etc.

Jackson, Jane, see sub. ROECKEL, J. L.

Jackson, John, organist and composer, born early in the 17th century. He was choirmaster of Ely Cathedral in 1669, and organist of Wells Cathedral in 1676. He died after 1688. Wrote services, anthems, etc.

Jackson, John P., musician and writer, author of "Album of the Passion Play at Ober-Ammergau . . . 1873," and other works on the same subject; Richard Wagner's "Ring of the Nibelung," an illustrated handbook, London, 1882; and an English version of "Die Meistersinger," 1892; "Parsifal," 1890; etc.

JACKSON.

Jackson, Miss, see LACY, MRS. JOHN.

Jackson, Seymour, tenor vocalist, attracted attention by his singing in Manchester and neighbourhood about 1882. Made his *début* on the stage, March 18, 1886, with the Carl Rosa Opera Company, taking the part of *Thaddeus* in Balfe's opera, "The Bohemian Girl." Toured with the same company, and gave concerts in various towns. At present resident at Blackpool as vocalist and concert agent.

Jackson, Thomas, psalm composer, born about 1715. He was organist of the Parish Church of Newark, and master of the Song School there. He died at Newark-on-Trent, November 11, 1781. Composer of the psalmtune, "Jackson's," and of Twelve Psalm tunes and eighteen double and single chants . . , composed for four voices, 1780.

Jackson, William, author of "A Preliminary Discourse to a scheme demonstrating and shewing the perfection and harmony of Sounds," Westminster, 1726.

Jackson, William, composer, organist, and writer, born at Exeter, May 28, 1730. He studied under Sylvester, the organist of Exeter Cathedral, and under J. Travers. Teacher in Exeter. Organist and choir-master Exeter Cathedral, 1777. He died at Exeter, July 12, 1803.

WORKS.—*Operas* – Lord of the Manor, London, 1780; Metamorphoses, London, 1783. *Odes*—Ode to fancy (Warton), op. 8; Lycidas, 1767; Dying Christian to his soul (Pope). *Songs*—Twelve songs, op. 1, 1755; Twelve songs, op. 4; Third set of twelve songs, op. 7; Fourth set of twelve songs. Six elegies for three male voices, op. 3 [1767]; Twelve canzonets for two voices, on. 9; Second set, op. 13; Twelve pastorals. Six vocal quartets, op. 11, 1780; Six Madrigals, op. 18, 1786; Twelve hymns, in three parts, op. 6. Six sonatas for harpsichord; Eight ditto. Six epigrams for 2, 3, and 4 voices and pf., Op. 17 [1786]; Anthems and Church services, by the late William Jackson, of Exeter, edited by James Paddon, 3 vols., London, n.d. Selection from his works, sacred and secular, London, 4 vols., n.d. Thirty letters on various subjects, London, 1782 Observations on the present state of music in London, 1791. The four ages, together with essays on various subjects, London, 1798.

Jackson was a man of varied accomplishments; an essayist, musician, organist, and painter. "He was a friend of Gainsborough, had a good taste for art, and was known in his day by his clever landscapes. In 1771 he was an honorary exhibitor at the Academy. He copied Gainsborough's work and wrote a sketch of his life."—*Redgrave*.

Jackson, William, organist and composer, born at Masham, Yorkshire, January

JACOX.

9, 1815. Self-taught in music. Organist at Masham in 1832. He was for a time a tallow chandler in Masham. Gained Huddersfield Glee Club first prize in 1840. Music-seller in Bradford, with W. Winn, vocalist, 1852. Organist of St. John's Church, Bradford; Horton Chapel, 1856. Conductor of Bradford Choral Union. Chorus-master at Bradford Festivals of 1853, '56, '59. He died at Bradford, April 15, 1866.

WORKS.—*Oratorios*—Deliverance of Israel from Babylon, 1845; Isaiah. *Cantatas*—The Year, 1859; The praise of music. 103rd Psalm for solo voice, chorus, and orchestra, 1841. Church services, a mass and anthems. The Bradford tune book (with Samuel Smith). Congregational Psalmody, 1863. A singing class manual, n.d. Glees, part-songs, and songs.

His son, WILLIAM, born at Bradford in 1853, was instructed by his father. He became organist of Morningside Parish Church, Edinburgh, but falling into bad health, died at Ripon, September 10, 1877, at the early age of 24. He published four part-songs, to words by Burns, in 1875, and left a few other works.

Jackson, William, composer and pianist, born in 1828; died at Girvan, August 19, 1876. He was a pianist in connection with various Glasgow music halls, but is now only remembered as the composer of a once popular song called " The dear little Shamrock."

Jacob, Benjamin, composer and organist, born at London, in 1778. He studied under his father, R. Willoughby, Shrubsole, and Arnold, 1796. Chorister in Portland Chapel, 1786. Organist of Salem Chapel, Soho Sq., 1788; Carlisle Chapel, Kennington Lane, 1790; Bentinck Chapel, Lisson Green, 1790-4; Surrey Chapel (Rowland Hill's), 1794-1825; St. John's, 1823. Treble singer, Westminster Abbey, at Festival, 1790-91. Member Royal Society of Musicians, 1799. Conductor of a series of oratorios, 1800. Gave organ recitals in conjunction with S. Wesley, and W. Crotch, to great audiences, 1808-14. Conductor of the Lenten Oratorios at Covent Garden Theatre, 1818. Associate, Philharmonic Society, 1818. One of Court of Assistants, Royal Society of Musicians, 1823. He died in London, Aug. 24, 1829. Buried in Bunhill Fields. In 1892, Mr. F. G. Edwards, organist of Surrey Chapel, restored the tombstones of Jacob and Shrubsole, for which he obtained subscriptions.

WORKS.—National Psalmody, a collection of Tunes for every Sunday throughout the year, London [1819]. Tunes for the use of Surrey Chapel. Dr. Watts' divine and moral songs, as solos, duets and trios. Glees, songs, and an arrangement of the "Macbeth" music.

Jacox, Rev. Francis, writer of present

time. Was curate of Wellingborough, 1847-48. Author of "Bible music, being variations in many keys on musical themes from Scripture," London, 1871 ; 2nd edition, 1874. Also writer of works on Bible history, "Traits of Character," "Aspects of Authorship," etc.

Jacques, Edgar Frederick, musical critic and lecturer, born in London, March 27. 1850, of French parentage. Educated for a commercial career, but in 1869 decided upon music as a profession. Had studied music from his eleventh year, and leaving Manchester, where he had been engaged in business, he returned to London, and began teaching. acting also as organist. In 1874 he became director of the orchestral services at St. Andrew's, Tavistock Place, an office he held for two years. Began musical Journalism in 1885, and in 1888 succeeded Dr. Hueffer as editor of the *Musical World*. This journal ceased in 1891, and the next year Mr. Jacques was appointed editor of the *Musical Times* (retiring in 1897), and in 1894, musical critic of *The Observer*. He has lectured several times at the R.A.M., and read papers before the Musical Association ; also given explanatory discourses at Mr. Bonawitz's Historical Recitals (1892), and on Kuhnau's "Biblical Sonatas," at the R.A.M. (Feb., 1896). He has composed an opera, an operetta, and part-songs, etc., which remain in MS.

Jakobowski, *see* BELVILLE, EDWARD.

James I., King of Scotland, poet and musician, born in 1394 ; died in 1437. Noticed here as the alleged inventor of the Scottish style of music. Founding on what has been regarded as a wrong reading of a passage in a work of Tassoni, the Italian poet (1565-1635), William Tytler has endeavoured to show in his "Essay on Scottish Music" that James I. not only invented the "plaintive style of melody, called Scottish," but likewise greatly influenced the style of several Italian composers, among whom are Gesualda and Palestrina. The researches of Dauney, Graham, Burney, and others, have proved this theory to be quite absurd.

James, John, organist and composer, of the 18th century. He was organist of St. Olave, Southwark ; and St. George's-in-the-East, 1738. He died in 1745. Composer of songs, organ voluntaries, and other pieces ; "Celinda," a two-part song, etc.

James, W. N., flute-player and writer, author of "A word or two on the Flute," Edinburgh, 1826. The Flutist's Catechism, in which are explained the First Principles in Music, London, 1829. The German Flute Magazine, or plain practical instructions for the flute, London [1835].

Jameson, D. D., author of "Colour-Music," London, 1844.

Jamieson, Augustus Grant, organist

and composer, was born at Edinburgh, December 20, 1844. He studied under J. C. Kieser, J. T. Surenne, Professor Donaldson, and at Stuttgart. He held the position of organist to St. Paul's Episcopal Church, Edinburgh, from 1872 till 1888, and was conductor of the Orpheus Orchestral Society. He held other appointments. Died at Edinburgh, January 21, 1888. Composer of various hymn tunes, "Brierley," "St. Sulpice," etc., and a number of pianoforte pieces.

Janes, Robert, organist and composer, was born Feb. 3, 1806. He was educated at Dulwich College, and in 1824 was articled pupil to Dr. Z. Buck of Norwich Cathedral. In 1831 he was appointed organist of Ely Cathedral, and held the post for 35 years. He died at Ely, June 10, 1866. He is said to have composed the "Ely Confession" (1864). Editor of a Psalter, and composer of vocal music. He was an amateur printer, and part-books, composed and worked off at his own press, were in use up to 1866.

Jarman, Thomas, musician, of Clipston, was born about 1788 ; died in January, 1862. Compiled the "Devotional Melodist, original set of psalm and hymn tunes, short anthems and set pieces, particularly designed for public worship," n.d. "The Sacred Harmonicon : containing upwards of 200 original tunes to all the metres now in use," n.d. "The Northamptonshire Harmony : containing a greater variety of tunes, anthems, and set pieces than has hitherto appeared in any other publication," n.d.

Jarvis, John, musician, compiled "Zion's Harmonist : comprising a new set of original psalm and hymn tunes.." London [1844].

Jarvis, Samuel, organist and composer of 18th century. He was blind. After receiving lessons from Dr. Worgan, he became organist of the Foundling Hospital, and later, of St. Sepulchre's, London. He was master of Wm. Russell, organist of the Foundling Hospital. He composed "An Ode in honour of the Albion's Society," London [1780] ; "Twelve songs, to which is added an epitaph " ; " Six songs and a cantata," etc.

Jarvis, Stephen, composer, born in 1834 ; died at Lewisham, London, November 27, 1880. He composed a quintet for strings, songs, and music for the pianoforte.

Jay, John George Henry, pianist, violinist and composer, born in Essex. November 27, 1770. He studied under Hindmarsh and Phillips, and on the continent. Settled in London, 1800, as teacher. Mus. Bac., Oxon., 1809. Mus. Doc., Cantab., 1811. Member of the R.A.M. He died at London, September 17, 1849. Wrote pf. and vocal music. His son JOHN (born 1812 ; died May 31, 1889), was also a violinist.

Jebb, Rev. John D. D., clergyman and

JEFFERSON.

musician, was born at Dublin in 1805; died at Peterstow, January 8, 1886. He was Canon of Hereford and Rector of Peterstow, Herefordshire. Author of Choral Service of the United Church of England and Ireland, being an Inquiry into the Liturgical System of the Cathedral and Collegiate Foundations of the Anglican Communion, London, 1843; Three lectures on the Cathedral Service of the United Church of England and Ireland, 1841; 2nd edit., 1845; The Choral Responses and Litanies of the United Church of England and Ireland, collected from authentic sources, London, 2 vols., 1847-57.

Jefferson, Joseph, author of "Lyra Evangelica; or an Essay on the use of instrumental music in Christian Worship," London, 1805.

Another musician of this name, WILLIAM ARTHUR JEFFREYS, organist of Leeds, issued "The National Book of hymn-tunes, chants, and kyries," 1885.

Jefferys, Charles, composer and music publisher, was born January 11, 1807. He carried on business in London, and died there June 9, 1865. He wrote the words of a number of popular songs, "Rose of Allandale," "Mary of Argyle," etc., and himself composed "Rose Atherton," "Oh Erin, my country," and other songs.

Jeffreys, George, organist and composer of 17th century. He was a son of MATTHEW JEFFREYS, Mus. Bac., Oxon., 1593, who was vicar choral of Wells Cathedral. In 1643 George became organist to Charles I. at Oxford, and from 1648 he was steward to the Hatton's of Kirby, Northamptonshire. He died in July, 1685. He composed anthems and other sacred music mostly preserved in MS. His son, CHRISTOPHER, who graduated M.A. at Oxford in 1666 was also a musician. He died in 1693.

Jeffries, John Edward, organist and composer, born at Walsall, Staffordshire, October 18, 1863. Chorister, and afterwards assistant organist at St. Paul's Church. Walsall, where his father, an amateur, held the post of organist for many years. Studied at the R.C.M., under Drs. G. C. Martin, J. F. Bridge, and F. E. Gladstone, for organ, counterpoint, and harmony, and pf. with Franklin Taylor, and is F.R.C.O. He was appointed organist of Walsall Parish Church when seventeen, and afterwards choirmaster. At the Annual Dedication Services he introduced oratorios and cantatas, with full orchestral accompaniment, and gave frequent organ recitals, also appearing as solo pianist at concerts. He was several times conductor and choral inspector for the Lichfield Diocesan Festivals. In November, 1895, he was appointed organist and choirmaster to the Cathedral, Newcastle-on-Tyne, and conducted special Advent services the next month. His

JENKINS.

first organ recital was given in the Cathedral, February 8, 1896. Conductor of Jarrow Philharmonic Society. He is the composer of an oratorio, The Life and Death of Christ; the sections, "The Annunciation," and "The Redemption" were performed in the Cathedral, in March and April (Good Friday), 1896. He has also written several works for church use.

Jeffries, Stephen, organist and composer, was born in 1660. He became a chorister in Salisbury Cathedral, under Wise, and organist of Gloucester Cathedral in 680. He died in 1712.

Jekyll, Charles Sherwood, organist and composer, born at Westminster, November 29, 1842. Chorister at Westminster Abbey. Studied under James Coward and G. A. Macfarren Organist of St. Paul's temporary church, Kensington, 1857; assistant organist Westminster Abbey, 1860-75; organist parish church, Acton, 1860; St. George's, Hanover Square, 1861-77; organist and composer to Her Majesty's Chapels Royal, St. James's Palace and Whitehall, November, 1876; retired October, 1891. Grand organist to the United Grand Lodge of England (Freemasons) 1880-2 Mr. Jekyll was the recipient of the silver Jubilee medal, presented by Her Majesty the Queen.

WORKS. — *Services*: Communion in C; Morning and evening in F (MS.); Morning and evening in C, for male voices, composed for St. Paul's Cathedral (MS.); Benedictus and Agnus Dei. *Anthems*: O, send out Thy light (eight voices); Save me, O God; Arise, O Lord; Go forth, ye daughters of Zion (Jubilee anthem, 1887); The righteous live for evermore; and others; hymns, chants, etc. Twelve kyries. *Part-Songs*: On the sea; When twilight dews; Night after the battle, etc. *Songs*: Pro Patria Mori; Now; Go, forget me; In memoriam, etc. *Organ*: Jubilee march, played by the composer, Westminster Abbey, on the Queen's Jubilee, June 21, 1887; Marche Nuptiale, played by the composer at the wedding of H.R.H. the Duchess of Fife; Grand march; Andante in A. Pieces for pf. Editor of *Musical Sunday at Home*, a series of twelve numbers.

Jenkins, David, composer, born at Trecastell, Brecon, January 1, 1849. Self-taught at first, but afterwards studied under Dr. Joseph Parry, at the University College of Wales, Aberystwith. Graduated Mus. Bac., Cambridge, 1878. Often acts as conductor of Psalmody festivals, and adjudicator at the National and other Eisteddfodau. In 1885, went to America, where he conducted at several festivals, besides being adjudicator at competitions. Is joint-editor of *The Musician*; Professor of music at the University College of Wales; Member of the Council and Examiner Tonic Sol-fa College, and Examiner

JENKINS.

R.C.M. Invited to conduct his "Psalm of Life," and Welsh airs at the Tonic Sol-fa Festival, Crystal Palace, July 11, 1896.

WORKS.—*Cantatas :* The ark of the covenant (prize of £20, Eisteddfod) ; David and Goliath ; A Psalm of life (composed for, and produced at the Cardiff Festival, 1895). *Oratorios :* David and Saul ; The Legend of St. David (Carnarvon Eisteddfod, 1894). Operetta, The village children. Anthems, part-songs, songs, etc. A collection of tunes, chants, and anthems (English and Welsh texts) ; Gems of praise, etc.

Jenkins, George, composer and teacher of dancing in Edinburgh and London, in the latter part of the 18th century. He died at London about 1806. Composer of Eighteen airs for two violins and a bass, Edinburgh [1789] ; Jenkins' thirty Highland airs, London, 1791 ; New Scotch music, consisting of slow airs, strathspeys, quick reels, country dances, and a medley on a new plan, with a bass for a violoncello or harpsichord, London [1793].

Jenkins, John, composer, born at Maidstone, in 1592. Musician to Charles I. and Charles II. Resided during the greater part of his life with H. L'Estrange of Norfolk. He died at Kimberley, October 27, 1678.

WORKS.—Elegy on the death of William Lawes, 1648. Theophila, or love's sacrifice, poem by E. Benlowes, 1652. Twelve sonatas for two violins and a bass, with a thorough-bass for the organ or theorbo, 1660. Fantasias in five or six parts for viols. Anthems, rounds. Compendium of practical music, London, 1667.

Jeremiah, John, author of "On Eisteddvodau : their antiquity and history," London, 1876. " Notes on Shakespeare and memorials of the Urban Club," London, 1876.

Jervis, St. Vincent, musician and composer, pupil of Molique. At a concert of the Amateur Musical Society of London, March 27, 1854, an adagio and rondo for pf. and orchestra, of his composition, was produced. Five sonatas for pf., by this composer, have been published at different times up to 1887, as well as other pieces.

Jeunesse, *see* La Jeunesse.

Jewell, E. Ellice, musician of present time, author of " Catechism of the rudiments of music and pianoforte-playing," London [1882] ; " Elementary exercises " [1883] for the same book.

Jewson, Frederick Bowen, pianist and composer, born in Edinburgh, July 26, 1823. Studied at R.A.M., under Cipriani Potter, and was King's Scholar, 1837. In 1835, he gave a concert at Edinburgh, and played a composition of his own. Elected in turn a member, professor, and director of the R.A.M. He was appointed a life member of the Court

JOHNSON.

of Assistants of the Royal Society of Musicians in 1849 ; and in 1866 became one of Musicians in Ordinary to the Queen. Member of the Philharmonic Society. For half a century he occupied an important position as a teacher of the pianoforte ; retired from professional life in 1889, and died in London, May 29, 1891.

WORKS.—Overture, Killicrankie, orchestra, R.A.M., May 16, 1840 ; Five overtures. Two concertos for pf. and orchestra, No. 2, in E, op. 33, performed St. James's Hall (Miss Dinah Shapley), June 28, 1882. Trio, pianoforte and strings. Six grand studies, op. 16 ; Douze Etudes, op. 23 ; Chanson d'Amour, and other pieces for pf. Songs, etc.

His wife, formerly MISS KIRKMAN, was a niece and pupil of Mrs. Anderson, and a pianist of recognised talent, who frequently took part in the musical matinées and concerts given at various times. She died in London, December 24, 1896. Two sons are in the musical profession—FREDERICK AUGUSTUS JEWSON, born in London, February 12, 1856, who is organist to the Strolling Players' Orchestral Society, and conductor of the Regent's Park Sacred Harmonic Society. He married Miss DUNBAR PERKINS, a violinist who is favourably known in musical circles. WILLIAM A. JEWSON is a violinist of repute, and conductor of musical societies.

Johnson, Basil, B. A., was appointed director of the music, and organist at Rugby School, in 1886. He is a son of the late Dean of Wells, and was musically educated at R.C.M. He has published Technical Exercises for pf.

Johnson, Edmund Charles, physician and writer, vice-president of the School for the Indigent Blind, Southwark, London. Author of " An Inquiry into the ·Musical Instruction for the Blind in France, Spain, and America," London, 1855, and other works on the Blind.

Johnson, Edward, composer of the 16th century. He graduated Mus. Bac., Cantab., 1594. Contributed to Este's Psalms. He composed the madrigal, " Come, Blessed Bird," in the " Triumphs of Oriana," 1601. His biography is unknown.

Johnson, James, engraver and publisher, was a native of the Ettrick district of Scotland. He was established in business in Edinburgh, and printed and engraved most of the collections of music published during his time. He was the first to print music from pewter plates. He died at Edinburgh, February 26, 1811. He is chiefly noted for his connection with Robert Burns, and the publication of "The Scots Musical Museum, with proper Basses for the pf...," Edinburgh, 6 vols., n.d. [1787]-[1803]. This work was re-edited by David Laing and Stenhouse, and

JOHNSON.

reprinted by Messrs. Blackwood, Edinburgh, 4 vols., 1853. The success of this venture was entirely due to the fine lyrics which Burns contributed, and which have since become world-wide favourites. The arrangements of the melodies in Johnson's Collection were by Stephen Clarke.

Johnson, Robert, clergyman and composer, who flourished about the middle of the 16th century. He composed part-songs, etc., one of which appears in the "History" of Sir John Hawkins, and others in contemporary collections.

Johnson, Robert, composer and lutenist, was born in the latter half of the 16th century. Musician in service of Sir T. Kytson of Hengrave Hall, Suffolk. Resided latterly in London as teacher, and musician in service of Prince Henry. He died after 1625.

WORKS.—*Music to Dramas :* "The Witch" (Middleton); "The Tempest" (Shakespere); "Masque of the Gipsies" (Jonson); Contributions to Leighton's "Teares." Songs, madrigals, etc.

Johnson, William, amateur organist and composer, born at Warrington, September 23, 1853. Studied pf. under the late T. Standish ; organ under T. Mee Pattison ; and, later, harmony under Dr. Horton Allison. Appointed organist of St. Anne's, Warrington, 1868, and introduced the first Choral Communion Service known in the district. Hon. organist, 1885-7, to the Warrington Musical Society (conducted by H. Hiles), which, in 1886, produced his cantata, *Ecce Homo.* Another cantata, "May Morn at Magdalen College, Oxford," remains in MS. He has composed anthems and other pieces. His grandfather, THOMAS KINGTON, was for thirty-five years organist of the Parish Church of Kingswood, Gloucester, and was reputed to be an excellent performer on every then known instrument. He died about the year 1850, aged seventy-six.

Johnson, W. Noel, violoncellist and composer, born at Repton, Derby, May 22, 1863. Educated at Emmanuel College, Cambridge. Studied violoncello at R.A.M. under W. E. Whitehouse, and afterwards proceeded to Leipzig and studied with Alwin Schröder, Oscar Paul, and Paul Klengel. He first appeared in London, in 1893, and is settled there as performer and composer. He has made several provincial tours, and met with much success. As a composer he has been very active, his works comprising Three pieces for violoncello and pf. ; Caprice, Nocturne, Serenade, Idylle, Reverie, for the same. Songs: I love thee (prize, Incorporated Society of Musicians, North-Midland Section, 1890); Four songs ; Six Songs (Heine) ; If thou wert blind ; Good-night, pretty stars; and many others. Part-songs: Where shall the lover

JONES.

rest ; When Flora decks (male voices), etc., etc. He has also written the music to several plays, one of which, "The Tournament of love," was performed in Paris (Theatre d'Application, La Bodinière), in May, 1894, with success.

Johnston, Rev. David, author of "Instrumental in the Church of Scotland, by the Minister of the United Parishes of Harray and Birsay." 1872 (privately printed).

Jolly, John, composer and organist, uncle of the undernoted, born at Knutsford, Cheshire, 1794. Was organist of St. Phillip's Chapel, London. Died at London, April, 1838. He composed "Glees, in score, for 3 and 4 voices," n.d. ; Songs, etc. ; and "Devotional Melodies, consisting of psalms, hymns, collects, and short anthems," London, 1832.

Jolly, John Marks, nephew of above, composer and conductor, was born in 1790. He was conductor at the Surrey Theatre, London, and at the Strand Theatre, in 1853. He died on July 1, 1864. Wrote a large number of songs, part-songs, etc., among which may be named Set of six songs of the wild flowers of spring [1834]; Gipsy sisters, duet ; Love is still a little boy, song : Queen of the starry night, song ; Polkas, galops, etc., for pf.

Jonas, Elizabeth G., pianist, born at Southwark, London, about 1825. Began learning the pianoforte under Mr. Platt when four years old ; then under John Field, at whose concert, in 1832, she made her *début.* She also played at the Paganini concerts, and frequently before royalty, in London and at Windsor ; at the "Oratorios" at Drury Lane, etc. She then studied under Moscheles, and in 1836 won the King's Scholarship, R.A.M., and again in 1838. In 1841 she was made an Associate, and appointed Professor of pf. and harmony. About 1852 Miss Jonas retired from the profession, her health not being good ; and enjoying an independency, she exercised her musical gifts in private circles.

Jones, Arthur Barclay, pianist and composer, born in London, December 16, 1869. Entered the choir of the Brompton Oratory when nine years old, and remained there as a singer until 1893, when, upon the death of his friend Thomas Wingham, he was appointed musical director, an office he still holds. By the advice of Wingham, whose pupil he was, he entered the Guildhall School of Music when fifteen, and gained a Scholarship. In 1889 he was made Associate, with honours, and became a Professor of pf. there in 1892, and of harmony in 1896. L.R.A.M. (pf.), 1891. His other master was H. C. Banister, who taught him harmony. His compositions include a symphony in C minor (dedicated to the memory of Thomas Wingham, and produced by the Westminster

JONES.

Orchestral Society, June 3, 1896); a Concert Overture in C minor (Crystal Palace, October 22, 1892); Sonata, violin and pf.; Pieces for violoncello, for pf., and organ. An Ave Maria, for soprano, and Hymns for children, etc.

Jones, Daniel C., organist, born at Tamworth, Staffordshire, November 20, 1857. Received his musical education at Lichfield Cathedral, under the late Thomas Bedsmore. Became F.R.C.O. at the age of nineteen, and took the degree of Mus. Bac., Trinity College, Toronto, in 1887, and Mus. Doc., of the same, 1891. In 1877 he was appointed organist and choirmaster of Londonderry Cathedral, a post he still holds. He has composed several anthems, and other church music. "Thus saith the Lord concerning the King of Assyria," was specially written for and performed at the celebration of the Bi-centenary of the closing of the Gates of Derry, in the Cathedral, December 18, 1888.

Jones, Edward, BARDY BRENIN, writer and musician, born at Llanderfel, Merionethshire, April 18, 1752. He studied the Welsh harp under his father. Appeared in London as harper, 1775. Welsh bard to Prince of Wales, 1783. He died at London, April 18, 1824.

WORKS.—Musical and poetical relicks of the Welsh bards, preserved by tradition and authentic manuscripts from very remote antiquity. with a collection of the Pennillion and Englynion epigrammatic stanzas or native pastoral sonnets of Wales, a history of the bards from the earliest period, and an account of their music, poetry, and musical instruments, London, 1784, two parts. Musical and poetical relicks of the Welsh bards, preserved by tradition and authentic manuscripts from very remote antiquity, with a select collection of the Pennillion and Englynion, with English translations, likewise a general history of the bards and druids, from the earliest period to the present time; with an account of their Music and poetry; to which is prefixed a dissertation on the musical instruments of the aboriginal Britons, London, 1794. The Bardic Museum of Primitive British Literature and other admirable rarities, forming the second volume of the Musical, Poetical, and Historical Relicks of the Welsh Bards and Druids . . . 1802. Lyric Airs, consisting of specimens of Greek, Albanian, Walachian, Turkish, Arabian, Persian, Chinese, and Moorish songs and melodies, with a short dissertation on the origin of ancient Greek music, London, 1804. Cheshire melodies; provincial airs of Cheshire, London [1803]. The musical miscellany, n.d. Terpsichore's Banquet (National airs), n.d. The minstrel's serenades, n.d. Collections from works of Handel, etc. The Musical Bouquet, or popular songs and ballads . . . London, 1799.

JONES.

Maltese Melodies, or national airs and dances usually performed by the Maltese musicians . . . London, n.d.

Jones, Edward, composer and conductor. Was for some years a first violin in Sir Michael Costa's opera orchestra; has been in America with the Mapleson Opera Company; musical director at the Court, Adelphi, and Duke of York's Theatres, London; and is at present musical director at the Lyric Theatre, London. He is the composer of incidental music to "Claudian"; "Hoodman Blind," produced, Princess's Theatre, 1885; "The Fay O'Fire," Opera Comique, November, 1885; "Pharoah," Leeds, 1892; "A Near shave," farce, Court Theatre, 1895; "The Sign of the Cross," Liverpool, 1895; etc.

Jones, Edward Stanton, writer and bandmaster, author of "Universal Cornopean Tutor . . . ," London, 1855; "Boosey's Universal Cornet Tutor," n.d.; Shilling Cornet Tutor. Songs, etc. He died in 1886.

Jones, George, author of "History of the rise and progress of Music, theoretical and practical," London, 1818. German edition, Vienna, 1821.

Jones, Griffith Rhys, or **Caradog**, a noted Welsh conductor, was born at Trecynon, December 21, 1834. His first study was the violin; but when quite a youth he became conductor of a choir known by the name of "Côr Carodog." This choir being victorious at a local Eisteddfod, the name was attached to the conductor. In 1872 he was appointed conductor of the Welsh choir which competed at the Crystal Palace contests in 1872-3, winning the challenge prize cup on each occasion. Afterwards he conducted choirs in Cardiganshire, at Cardiff, and now at Pontypridd, his male voice choir dividing the first prize at the Llandudno Eisteddfod of 1896.

Jones, Hannah, contralto vocalist, born at Skewen, near Swansea. At the age of fourteen was first prize winner at the National Eisteddfod. Entered the R.A.M., and studied under Garcia, and others, winning Llewelyn Thomas Prize, 1887, and Sainton-Dolby Prize, 1888; A.R.A.M. Sang in "Elijah" at the Royal Albert Hall, February, 1888, with success, and has since gained a good position among contralto vocalists of the day.

Jones, Henry Festing, amateur composer. In conjunction with Samuel Butler, brought out, in 1884, a collection of original gavottes, minuets, etc., in the style of Handel; and some years later, a dramatic cantata, "Narcissus." Mr. Jones is also the composer of My silks and fine array; Upbraid me not; Go, lovely rose; Six songs, op. 5; a second set of six songs, etc.

Jones, Hirwen, tenor vocalist, born near Cardigan, March 9, 1857. As a youth, attended Tonic Sol-fa classes, and was a

JONES.

successful competitor at Eisteddfodau. In 1879 he entered the R.A.M., and studied under A. Randegger, and W. Shakespeare. One of his earliest appearances in London was in Carter's "Placida," at Brixton Hall, March, 1882 ; he also sang at the Popular Concerts, and at the Crystal Palace, October 17, 1885, in the quintet from the Meistersinger. He made his festival *début* at Brighton, in 1882, and sang at the Worcester Festival, 1890 ; Hereford, 1894 ; and Leeds, 1895. He was one of the artists in Madame Patey's farewell tour, 1894, and in the Patti tour, 1895. Is now well established as a concert singer. He has had some experience in light opera, having been principal tenor in the D'Oyly Carte Continental Opera Company, in "Patience," and other works, at Berlin, Hamburg, etc., 1887-8.

Jones, Rev. James, author of "A Manual of Instructions on Plain-chant or Gregorian music, with the chants as used in Rome," London, 1845.

Jones, John, organist and composer, was born in 1728. He became organist of the Temple Church in 1749 ; Charterhouse, 1753 ; St. Paul's Cathedral in 1755. He acted as one of the directors of the Handel Commemoration in 1784. He died at London, February 17, 1796.

WORKS.—Sixty Chants, single and double, 1785. Lessons for the harpsichord, 1761 ; Eight setts of Lessons for the harpsichord, 1754. Songs, etc.

Jones, Joseph David, Welsh musician, born at Bryncrugog, Montgomery, in 1827. He was a teacher of singing at Ruthin, and taught also in the British School there. He died at Ruthin, September 17, 1870. Compiler of " Y cerub yn cynwys tonau, anthemau, a darnau gosodedig cymhwys i'w harferyd yn y gwasanalth dwyfol," Llanidloes, 1855. "Caniadau Bethlehem," Ruthin, 1857 (Welsh carols for Christmas). " Perganiedydd," Llanidloes, 1847. " Tonau ac Emynau," Wrexham, 1868. " Llys Arthur," cantata, 1864. Hymns, etc.

Jones, Moses Owen, composer, conductor, and adjudicator, born in Carnarvonshire, November 13, 1842. One of the editors of "The Congregational Singer" (see D. Emlyn Evans.) Was awarded the prize of £30 at the London National Eisteddfod, 1887, for a Biography of Welsh Musicians, since published in Welsh (see D. E. Evans); also a prize of £20 at the Carnarvon National Eisteddfod of 1894, for a Critical and Historical Essay on Welsh National Melodies.

Jones, Richard, author of "The most New and Easy Method of Singing the Psalms," London, 1705.

Jones, Richard, musician. Issued "The Cornubian Tune Book ; or Manual of hymn-

JONES.

tunes, carols, sanctuses, etc.," Penzance, 1870.

Jones, Robert, composer and lutenist, who flourished at the end of the 16th and beginning of the 17th centuries. Biography unknown, but he graduated Mus. Bac., Oxford, in 1597.

WORKS.—The First Booke of Ayres, 1601. The Second Booke of Ayres, set out to the Lute, the Base Violl the playne way, or the Base by tableture after the leero fashion. Ultimum Vale, or the Third Booke of Ayres of 1, 2, and 4 voyces, 1608. A Musicall Dreame, or the Fourth Booke of Ayres, the first part for the lute, 2 voices, and the viol da gamba ; the second part is for the lute, the viol, and four voices to sing; the third part is for one voice alone to the lute, the base-viol, or to both if you please, whereof two are Italian Ayres, London, fo., 1619. The Muse's Gardin for Delights, or the Fifth Booke of Ayres, only for the Lute, the Bass Violl, and the Voyce, n.d. The First Set of Madrigals of 3, 4, 5, 6, 7, and 8 parts for viols and for voices alone, or as you please, 1607. "Fair Oriana, seeming to wink," madrigal for 6 voices, in Triumphs of Oriana. Contributions in Leighton's Teares. Songs in Smith's Musica Antiqua.

Jones, Sidney, composer, of present time. Has written the music to "An Artist's Model," produced, February, 1895 ; and the Japanese musical play, " The Geisha," produced, April 25, 1896, both at Daly's Theatre, London.

Jones, T. H., organist of the Congregational Church, Adelaide, South Australia [1884], is known as an able executant, and has given recitals in the Town Hall, Adelaide, etc. He was the first upon whom was conferred the Degree of Mus. Bac. by the University of Adelaide, 1890.

Jones, Thomas, of Gaddesdon, musician. Composed " Ten new country dances for the Harp," 1788. " Music purposely composed for the Harp," London, 1800.

Jones, Thomas Evance, organist, born in 1805. In 1813 he entered Canterbury Cathedral as a chorister, and in 1822 became lay clerk. He was appointed singing-master to the choristers in 1830, and in 1831 he succeeded Skeats as organist. He died at Canterbury in December, 1873.

Jones, William, author of "A Discourse on the Philosophy of Musical Sounds," n.d.

Jones, Rev. William, of Nayland, composer and writer, born at Lowick, Northamptonshire, July 30, 1726. Educated at the Charterhouse, London, and at Oxford. He was successively vicar of Bethersden, Kent, 1764 ; Pluckley; Paston, Northampton, and rector of Hollingbourne, Kent, 1798. He died at Nayland, Suffolk, February 6, 1800, where he was perpetual curate from 1776.

WORKS.—Ten Church Pieces for the organ,

with four anthems in score, composed for the use of the church of Nayland, in Suffolk, op. 2, 1789. A treatise on the art of musick, in which the elements of harmony and air are practically considered and illustrated by 150 examples in notes . . the whole intended as a course of lectures preparatory to the practice of Thorough-Bass and Musical Composition, Colchester, 1784 ; Second edition, Sudbury, 1827. Church music, miscellaneous. Collected Works, published in 12 vols., 1802, and again in 6 vols., 1810.

Jones, Sir William, orientalist and scholar, born in London, 1746; died at Calcutta, 1794. Author of "Commentaries on Asiatic Poetry," 1744 ; "The Musical Modes of the Hindus," 1784 ; References to Oriental Music in Collected Works, etc.

Joran, Pauline, soprano vocalist and violinist, born in Australia. Appeared, with two sisters, as a party of juvenile artists at San Francisco in 1885. Joined the Carl Rosa Opera Company, and as *Beppi,* in "L'Amico Fritz," achieved much success, 1893. Sang in Gounod's "Faust," and other operas, at Drury Lane, 1894 ; at Covent Garden, 1895 ; and in various places in Italy, 1895-6. Played Mendelssohn's Violin Concerto at Liverpool, 1893, and also appeared as a vocalist. Gave a Concert at St. James's Hall, London, December 10, 1896, appearing as vocalist and violinist. Her sister, ELISE JORAN, is a pianist, and played Mendelssohn's G minor Concerto at Liverpool, 1893 ; and also appeared with success in London, in December, 1896. She was a pupil of E. d'Albert.

Jordan, Charles Warwick, organist and composer, born at Clifton, Bristol, December 28, 1840. Chorister at Bristol Cathedral and St. Paul's Cathedral. Appointed organist of St. Paul's, Bunhill Row, 1857 ; St. Luke's, West Holloway, 1860 ; and St. Stephen's, Lewisham, 1866 to present time. Mus. Bac., Oxford, 1869 ; Mus. Doc., *Cantuar,* 1886. F.R.C.O. Honorary organist London Gregorian Choral Association. Examiner College of Organists and Trinity College, London ; and Professor of organ and harmony Guildhall School of Music.
WORKS.—Cantata, Blow ye the trumpet in Zion, for soli, chorus, and orchestra ; Festival Te Deum, voices, organ, trumpets, and drums, Crystal Palace, 4000 voices, June 19, 1895 ; Festival Jubilate in C, the same, February 20, 1897. Communion Service in E ; anthems, etc. Overture, Pray and praise, for organ, trumpet, and three trombones, Lewisham Church, October 1, 1882 ; Duo concertante, organ and trumpet, Exeter Hall recitals, January 31, 1891, etc. Author of A short paper on the construction of the Gregorian tones, 1874 ; 150 harmonies for the same.

Jordan, Mrs., born Dora or Dorothea

BLAND, actress, singer, and composer, born near Waterford, in 1762. She was daughter of a Captain Bland. After being trained as a milliner she appeared on the stage at Dublin in 1777. She adopted the name of Mrs. Jordan in 1782, but was never married though mother of various children. She died at St. Cloud, near Paris, July 3, 1816. Her biography belongs more to theatrical than musical history, and her chief claim to notice here, apart from her slight merits as a singer, is as the composer of the "Blue Bells of Scotland." This was issued as the "Blue Bells of Scotland, a ballad as composed and sung by Mrs. Jordan," London [1800].

Jortin, Rev. John, clergyman and author, born in 1698 ; died in 1770. Vicar of Kensington. Author of "A Letter concerning the music of the Ancients," in 2nd edition of Avison's "Musical Expression."

Joseph, Kinsell, organist, born in Essequibo, British Guiana, December, 1845. For many years organist of St. George's Cathedral, Georgetown, and master of St. George's Parish School. He died May 26, 1892, and left a legacy to the choir of the Cathedral ; and this being invested, forms an endowment, probably the first of the kind in a West Indian Colony. Joseph was by race a negro, and a man of singular charm of character, winning the esteem and respect of his Bishop (Dr. Austin), and all with whom he was associated.

Joule, Benjamin St. John Baptist, organist, composer, and editor, born at Salford, November 8, 1817. Studied violin under Richard Cudmore, and organ, etc., under J. J. Harris. He was honorary organist of Holy Trinity, Hulme, 1846-53 ; St. Margaret's, Whalley Range, Manchester, 1849-52 ; and of St. Peter's, Manchester, from 1853. President of the Manchester Vocal Society ; Fellow of the Genealogical Society of Great Britain ; F.C.O. ; and J.P. for the County of Lancaster. Contributor to various periodicals, and music critic, 1850-70, to the *Manchester Courier.* He died at Manchester, May 21, 1895.
WORKS.—The hymns and canticles, pointed for chanting, 1847. Directorium Chori Anglicanum, London, 1849, which has passed through many editions. A collection of words of 2,270 Anthems, with 452 biographical notices, London, 1859. The Psalter, or Psalms of David, after the translation of the great Bible, pointed as they are to be sung or said in Churches, London, 1865. Collection of chants, London, 1860, 18 editions. The Order for Holy Communion, harmonized on a monotone ; Organ and pf. music, etc.

Jowett, Rev. Joseph, clergyman and musician, was born in 1784, and died May 13, 1856. He was rector of Silk-Willoughby. Compiler of "Lyra Sacra, select extracts

O

JOYCE.

from the Cathedral music of the Church of England, for 1, 2, 3, and 4 voices . . . ," London, 1825. "A manual of Parochial Psalmody, containing 142 Psalm and Hymn tunes, by various authors, London, 1832.

Joyce, Patrick Weston, LL.D., Irish writer, born at Ballyorgan, Limerick, in 1827. Compiler of "Ancient Irish Music, comprising one hundred airs hitherto unpublished, many of the old popular songs, and several new songs, etc., Dublin, 1873. Irish Names of Places, 2 vols., 1869-70. Old Celtic Romances, 1879. Irish music and song, a collection of songs in the Irish language set to music, London, 1888.

Joze, Thomas Richard Gonzalvez, composer and organist, born at Dublin, September 26, 1853. Entered as chorister in Christ Church Cathedral, 1861; and was deputy organist, 1869. Organist of St. Paul's, Glengarry, 1870; at present time organist of Christ Church, Leeson Park, Dublin. Graduated Mus. Doc., 1877, Dublin. Is professor of organ and harmony, R.I.A.M.; Examiner to Commissioners of Intermediate Education in Ireland, and to the Royal University of Ireland. . Conductor of the Strollers' Club; The Sackville Hall Choral Society, and Grand organist of the Grand Lodge of Freemasons, Ireland. His compositions include two cantatas, "The Prophecy of Capys," and "A Dream of the Fairies"; Prize Festival Hymn, "St. Patrick's Breastplate"; Hibernian Catch Club first prize Glee, 1871, "The dead Soldier"; Part-songs, pf. pieces, etc.

Jude, William Herbert, organist and composer, born at Westleton, Suffolk, 1851. Sometime organist of the Blue Coat Hospital, Liverpool; founder of the Purcell Society, Liverpool; Editor of the "Monthly Hymnal"; Organist, 1889, of Stretford Town Hall, near Manchester. He has given recitals in various places; lectured on musical subjects in Great Britain, and in Australia. An operetta, "Innocents Abroad," was produced at Liverpool in 1882; and he has written a number of songs, etc.

Karn, Frederick James, organist and composer, born at Leatherhead, August 29, 1862. Organist at Cobham, Surrey; now of St. John's, Downshire-hill, Hampstead. Graduated Mus. Bac., 1885, Cambridge. Has given concerts at St. John's College, Hurstpierpoint; and was appointed conductor, 1889, of the Science and Art School Orchestral Society, South Kensington. He has composed church music, songs, etc.

Keach, Benjamin, clergyman and musician, was pastor of the Baptist Church in Goatyard Passage, Horsleydown, Southwark, in latter part of 17th century. Author of "The Breach repaired in God's worship, or

KEELEY.

singing of psalms, hymns, and spiritual songs proved to be an holy ordinance of Jesus Christ," London, 1691. "Spiritual Melody," 1691; a collection of psalms, etc., the publication of which, and of the pamphlet named, led to a secession in his congregation

Kearns, William Henry, Irish musician, born in 1794. He was an instrumentalist and teacher in London. Died in London, December 28, 1846. Composer of "Bachelors' Wives, or the British at Brussels," operetta, 1817; Songs of Christmas for family choirs.. 1847; Songs, pf. music, etc. With H. J. Gauntlett, he edited "The Comprehensive Tune Book."

Kearton, Joseph Harper, tenor vocalist and composer, born at Knaresborough, October 25, 1848. At the age of seven he joined the choir of Trinity Church there, and was appointed, when fourteen, organist of the Congregational Church. Three years later he became a tenor singer at York Minster. There he studied with Mr. Howard Herring, and had some assistance from Dr. E. G. Monk. In 1867 he was oppointed a vicar choral at Wells Cathedral, and held other offices in the locality. He studied there with Edward Herbert, with a view to the profession of organist and teacher, and passed his exercise for the degree of Mus. Bac. His singing attracting attention, he devoted himself to that art exclusively, and studied for a time at the R.A.M., and in 1877 was made a vicar choral of Westminster Abbey. He sang at the Chester and Bristol Festivals, 1882, and Hereford, 1885; at the Crystal Palace, Monday Popular Concerts, and has taken part in many notable performances. He has composed anthems; Six organ voluntaries; Songs and duets; and contributed to the pasticcio, "Harold Glynde." His daughter, ANNIE KEARTON, made her *début* as a soprano vocalist, in London, June, 1893.

Keddie, Henrietta, SARAH TYTLER, Scottish novelist and writer, born at Cupar Fife, March 4, 1827. Authoress of "Musical Composers and their Works," London, 1875; 2nd ed., 1877. Also writer of other biographical works, and many novels.

Keeble, John, organist and composer, born in Chichester, 1711. Chorister in Chichester Cathedral, under Kelway. He studied music under Pepusch, and became organist of S. George's, Hanover Square, London, in 1737. Organist of Ranelagh Gardens. He died at London, December 24, 1786.

WORKS.—Five Books of Organ Pieces. Songs, etc. The Theory of Harmonics, or an Illustration of the Grecian Harmonies, London, 1784.

Keeley, Mary Anne, *born* GOWARD, vocalist and actress, born at Ipswich, November 22, 1805. Studied singing under Mrs.

KEETON.

KELLY.

Henry Smart (sister-in-law of Sir George Smart), and made her *début* in Dublin in 1824. She sang in "Rosina" at the Lyceum Theatre, London, July 2, 1825; and was the original *Mermaid* in the production of Weber's "Oberon," Covent Garden, April 12, 1826. After her marriage with Mr. Robert Keeley (died, 1860), she was seen only in comedy, in which she acquired a high reputation. When she retired from public life, her interest in the stage continued. She was present at the benefit to Ada Swanborough, Strand Theatre, December, 1884; and opened the new Theatre at Ipswich, March 28, 1891, with an address. Her 90th birthday was celebrated by a grand reception at the Lyceum Theatre, November 22, 1895.

Keeton, Haydn, organist and composer, born at Mosborough, near Chesterfield, October 26, 1847. Received his musical training at St. George's Chapel Royal, Windsor. Graduated Mus. Bac., 1869; Mus. Doc., 1877, Oxford. Was appointed organist of Datchet Parish Church, 1867; and of Peterborough Cathedral, 1870. Sometime Examiner, College of Organists; Conductor and organist, Peterborough and Lincoln Cathedral Festivals; Conductor, Peterborough Choral Union, etc. He has composed an Orchestral Symphony; Give ear, Lord, unto my prayer (Meadowcroft Prize); I will alway give thanks, and other anthems; Church Services; Offertory Sentences (College of Organists' Prize); Pf. pieces, songs, etc. Author of Church and Cathedral Choristers' Singing Method, London, Cocks, 1892.

His father, EDWIN KEETON, has been organist of Eckington Parish Church since 1848, and has taken an active part in the Festivals of the Derby Archidiaconal Choral Association, etc.

Keith, Robert William, pianist and writer, was born at Stepney, London, in 1787; died, London, June 19, 1846. Author of "A Musical Vade Mecum, being a compendious introduction to the whole Art of Music," London, 1820, 2 vols. "Instructions for the Pianoforte.." London [1833]. "Tutor for the German Flute"; "Britannia, mourn: elegiac verses on the death of Princess Charlotte," 1817, etc.

Kellie, Lawrence, tenor vocalist and composer, of Scottish descent, born in London, April 3, 1862. He was musical from childhood, but was articled to a solicitor, and did not adopt the profession of music until 1884. Studied for a time at R.A.M., but chiefly under Mr. Randegger as a private pupil. Made his *début* at the Covent Garden Promenade Concerts, in November, 1886; and commenced giving vocal recitals at Steinway Hall, May 23, 1887. He has sung in the provinces, and has made a reputation; but is

more widely known as a song composer. His works in this direction are already very numerous, and include: All for thee; My fairest child; This heart of mine; Douglas Gordon; A winter love song; The city of night, and many others. It is understood that Mr. Kellie has an opera in course of completion.

Kellie, Thomas Alexander Erskine, sixth Earl of, Scottish amateur musician, was born September 1, 1732. He studied music in Germany, under Stamitz. Succeeded his father, as sixth Earl of Kellie in 1756, but afterwards sold most of the Kellie property. He died at Brussels (unmarried), October 9, 1781. He composed a number of overtures (The Maid of the Mill, 1761, etc.); Symphonies and other works, some of which were produced at Ranelagh and Vauxhall. A collection of some of his compositions was issued as "Minuets and Songs now for the first time published, with an introductory notice by C. K. Sharpe," Edinburgh, 1839. Songs, etc. He was reckoned among the most respectable amateur violinists of his time, and was a composer of some ability.

Kelly, Charles W., baritone vocalist, member of the choirs of St. Patrick and Christ Church Cathedral, Dublin, and professor of singing in the R.I.A.M. He has a reputation in the concert room, and ranks among the best singers in Ireland. His brother, THOMAS GRATTAN KELLY, is a bass; vicar choral of St. Patrick's and Christ Church Cathedrals, Dublin, and member of the choir of Trinity College. He is also recognised in the concert-room as an artist, both as regards voice and style.

Kelly, Michael, composer and vocalist, born in Dublin, 1762. He studied singing under Rauzzini, and also at Naples under Aprile, etc., 1779. *Début* as vocalist at Dublin, 1779. Travelled in Italy, and became acquainted with Mozart. *Début* at Drury Lane, as Lionel in "Lionel and Clarissa." Sang at Concerts of Ancient Music, Handel Commemoration, in English Provinces, Ireland, etc. Manager of King's Theatre, 1793. He died at Margate, October 9, 1826.

WORKS.—Musical Dramas, for which the music was chiefly compiled, as—Adelmon the outlaw, M. G. Lewis, 1801; The Africans, 1808; Blind bargain, 1805; Blue beard, 1798; Bride of Abydos, 1818; Castle spectre, 1798; Cinderella, 1804; Conquest of Taranto, 1817; Counterfeit, 1804; False appearances, 1789; Friend in need, 1797; Hero of the north, 1803; Of age to-morrow; Pizarro, 1799; Wood demon, 1807, etc. Six English airs and six Italian duetts, 1790; The woodpecker, ballad, and other songs and glees. Elegant extracts for the German flute, 1805. Reminiscences, during a period of nearly half a century, with

KELWAY.

original anecdotes of many distinguished persons, London, 2 vols., 1826; 2nd edition, 1826.

His niece, FRANCES MARIA KELLY, a singer and actress, was born at Brighton, October 15, 1790. First appeared in Blue Beard in 1798, and sang at Drury Lane and other Theatres. She died at Feltham, Middlesex, December 6, 1882, after a life partly spent in trying to elevate the stage in public estimation.

Kelway, Joseph, organist and composer, was born about the beginning of the 18th century [1702]. He studied under Geminiani, and was organist of St. Michael's, Cornhill, London, till 1736. Organist St. Martin-in-the-Fields, 1736. Instructor on harpsichord to Queen Charlotte. He died in 1782. He composed Six sonatas and lessons for the harpsichord, London [1764]. Songs, etc.

Kelway, Thomas, organist and composer, was born about the end of the 17th century. Brother of Joseph. Organist of Chichester Cathedral, 1720. He died at Chichester May 21, 1749.

WORKS.—Evening services in B minor, A minor, G minor; Seven services and nine anthems in MS. at Chichester Cathedral.

Kemble, Adelaide, Mrs. SARTORIS, singer and actress, born in 1814. Daughter of Charles Kemble. Appeared first in London as singer. Sang at York Festival, 1835. Travelled in France and Germany. Sang in Italy, 1840. Married Mr. F. Sartoris, 1843. Author of "Past Hours," London, Bentley, 1881. She died August 4, 1879.

Kemble, see also ARKWRIGHT, Mrs. R.

Kemble, Rev. Charles, compiler of "Church Psalmody: a selection of Tunes and Chaunts in four parts," 1840. Also of various works on duties of clergymen, sermons, etc.

Kemble, Gertrude, see sub. SANTLEY CHARLES.

Kemp, Joseph, composer, born at Exeter, in 1778. He studied under W. Jackson, and became organist of Bristol Cathedral, 1802. Mus. Bac., Cantab., 1808. Music teacher in London, 1809. Mus. Doc., Cantab., 1809. He died at London, May 22, 1824.

WORKS.—The Jubilee, 1809; The siege of Isca, 1810; The Crucifixion; Musical illustrations of the Lady of the lake, 1810; Musical illustrations of the beauties of Shakespear; The vocal magazine, Edinburgh, 3 vols., 1798, 1800 [edited], also Bristol, 1807; Glees, 2 sets, London [1800-1803]; Twelve songs, op. 1, 1799, and others; chants, duets, anthems, etc. Upwards of one hundred cards containing more than 500 points in music [1810]. New system of twelve Psalmodical melodies, 1818; Sonatas or lessons for the pf. [1810]; Musical education, London [1819].

KENNEDY.

His son, JOHN, born at Exeter, 1801; Died there, January 14, 1885; was lay vicar of Exeter Cathedral.

Kemp, R., author of "Directions for tuning the Alexandre Harmonium," London, 1874.

Kemp, Stephen, pianist, born at Yarmouth, Norfolk, November 8, 1849. Educated at R.A.M. Fellow, and Professor of pf., R.A.M. Has given concerts in London, and is known as the composer of some tasteful pf. pieces; songs, "The Cavalier," etc; trio for female voices, "O, lady, leave thy silken thread," etc. He is also professor of the pf. at R.C.M., and the Guildhall School.

Kempson, James, parish clerk of St. George's, Birmingham, was an active participator in musical doings in that town from the middle of the last century. He started, in 1766, the Birmingham Choral Society that gave annual performances in St. Bartholomew's Chapel for the "Distressed Housekeepers' Charity"; and his aid was sought for the First Musical Festival held in Birmingham, in 1768. It is said that he was assistant conductor of those Festivals to the year 1817. He was called the "Father of the Oratorio Choral Society." He died at a great age, March 10, 1822.

Kempton, Thomas, organist and composer, who died in 1762, was organist of Ely Cathedral from 1729.

Kennedy, Arnold, pianist and teacher, born in London, in 1852. Educated at Edinburgh High School, and University, where he graduated M.A. His musical studies began with the Tonic Sol-fa system when he was a boy. After leaving Edinburgh, he entered the R.A.M., and was elected an Associate. He took his Mus. Bac. degree at Oxford, 1893. Resident in London as teacher and lecturer. He has published a few songs, and is part composer of children's operetta, "Prince Ferdinand."

Kennedy, David, tenor vocalist, was born at Perth, on April 15, 1825. He received no regular instruction in singing, but was a precentor and teacher for some time in Edinburgh. He was precentor of Nicolson Street U. P. Church, Edinburgh, for a number of years. He first made himself known through popular concerts which he gave originally in Edinburgh, but afterwards in most of the larger towns in Scotland. Latterly Mr. Kennedy sung in Africa, New Zealand, America, and London, in all of which places he has met with extraordinary success, giving concerts of Scottish song along with his family. He died at Stratford, Ontario, Canada, October 12, 1886.

He had a large family, most of whom were musicians. DAVID (born at Perth, 1849; died, Pietermaritzburg, December 5, 1885),

KENNEDY.

was a tenor singer and journalist, and wrote
"Singing round the World," which is incorporated in his sister's book mentioned below.
JAMES (born 1856; died March 23, 1881), was
a baritone singer, and perished in the fire at
the Opera House, Nice, where he had been
studying under Lamperti along with his
sisters, KATE (born 1861; died March 23,
1881), who was a contralto, and LIZZIE (1863-
1881), who was a soprano. Other members
of the family are ROBERT, a tenor singer, who
studied at Milan, and gives Scots concerts on
lines similar to his father; now in Australia.
HELEN (Mrs. Campbell), a soprano; MARJORY
(Mrs. Fraser), a contralto, who wrote a book
called "David Kennedy, the Scottish singer,"
Paisley, 1887; and MARGARET, who was, to
1890, sub-professor in the Royal Academy of
Music, London.

Kennedy, Rev. Rann, clergyman and
musician, born in 1773. Incumbent of St.
Paul's Chapel, Birmingham. Died at Birmingham, January 2, 1851. Author of
"Thoughts on the music and words of
Psalmody as at present in use among the
members of the Church of England," London, 1821. "Church of England Psalm
Book," 1821. Poems and other literary works.

Kenney, Charles Lamb, playwright and
writer, born in 1823; died at London, August
25, 1881. Author of "Memoir of Michael
William Balfe," London, 1876. He was also
a musical critic and barrister-at-law.

Kenningham, Alfred, tenor vocalist.
A member of the choir of St. Andrew's, Wells
Street, London. In 1872 he was elected
assistant vicar choral; and in 1888, vicar
choral, St. Paul's Cathedral. He has been
heard in concerts in London and the provinces,
and is the composer of "The hour of love,"
and other songs.

Kenningham, Charles, tenor vocalist, is
a native of Yorkshire. In 1886 he was
appointed to the Choir of Canterbury Cathedral, where he remained about four years.
He made his stage *début*, January 31, 1891,
in Sullivan's "Ivanhoe," as *De Bracy*, and
afterwards sang in "La Basoche." He then
went on tour with the D'Oyly Carte Company
in the "Nautch Girl," "Vicar of Bray,"
"Jane Annie," and other light operas; and
sang at the Savoy Theatre in "Haddon Hall,"
etc.

Kent, James, organist and composer,
born at Winchester, March 13, 1700. He was
a chorister in Winchester Cathedral under
Vaughan Richardson [1711-1714], and in the
Chapel Royal under Dr. Croft. Successively
organist of Parish Church of Finedon, Northampton, till 1731; Trinity College, Cambridge,
till 1737; and Winchester Cathedral, 1737-74.
He died at Winchester, May 6, 1776. He
composed Services in C and D, and "Twelve

KERR.

Anthems "1773,vol. 1; and "Eight Anthems,"
vol. 2, edited by Corfe. Kent's Anthems,
edited by T. Graham, London, 1844, 2 vols.;
An edition edited by Vincent Novello; also
many single anthems.

Kenward, William Daniel, composer
and vocalist, born at Lewes, March 21, 1797.
He studied under the Ashleys, and he was a
chorister in Durham Cathedral under Dr.
Camidge, and from there was appointed precentor of the West Church, Aberdeen, 1824-28.
In 1828 he became precentor of the High
Church, Edinburgh, and he acted as singing
master at Heriot's Hospital from 1837, and
conductor of the Harmonists' Society from
1829 till 1860. He died at Edinburgh, May 1,
1860.

WORKS.—Sacred Harmony [1839] also
[1848]. The Psalmody of Scotland, 1855.
The Scottish Psalm and Tune Book, 1855.
Collection of the Sacred Music of the Church
of Scotland..to which is prefixed the rudiments of Music, and scales and exercises for
the voice, Edinburgh, n.d.

Kenway, Helen, a teacher of music at
Bath, desirous of extending the means of aid-
ing musicians disabled by ill-health, or other
causes, and to provide a school for orphan
girls, has devoted herself entirely to the
realisation of these benevolent objects. Beginning, about 1877, by taking one girl into
her sister's school at Bath, she gradually
extended her operations; and in 1883 took a
house in London. Since 1894 the Orphan
School has been located at 16, Norland Square,
Notting Hill, and there Miss Kenway gives
her time and means entirely to this institution,
the only one of its kind connected with the
musical profession, and dependent upon the
voluntary pecuniary aid of those interested
in her philanthropic work.

Kerfoot, Joseph, blind organist, was born
at the end of last century. For over 53 years
he was organist of the Parish Church, Leigh,
Lancashire. He died at Leigh, in August,
1884.

His son, JOSEPH, was born in 1819, and was
organist of Winwick Parish Church from
1837 to 1890, when he retired. He died at
Leigh, in May, 1894.

THOMAS, brother of the first named, was a
native of Chester, and for over 50 years was
organist of Warrington Parish Church. He
published a book entitled "Parochial Psalmody," 1838.

Kerr, Mrs. Alexander, *born* LOUISA
HAY, song-writer and authoress of the present
century. She wrote a number of sentimental
ballads, and a few part-songs, words and music.
Among the former may be named, "Melodies,
the Words written and the Music composed
by Mrs. Alexander Kerr," London, D'Almaine
[1835]; Evening hymn, etc.

KETTLE.

Kettle, Charles Edward, organist and composer, born at Bury St. Edmunds, March 28, 1833. Organist successively at St. Margaret's, Plumstead; St. Nicholas, Plumstead; Holy Trinity, Woolwich; Hove Parish Church; Queen's Square Congregational Church, Brighton. He died, March 2, 1895. WORKS.—Sunday School Hymns, London, Weekes; Songs of the Church; Northern Psalter; Chants, ancient and modern; Kettle's Tune Book: containing 700 original tunes and chants; Hymn Tunes in various collections; Service of song. Three operas: Amelie; Hermina; The water cure (MS.). In the dawning; The voice of music, and other songs. Postlude in C; Marche Solennelle; Offertoire, etc., for organ. Pf. pieces, various. His daughter, LIZZIE KETTLE, was educated at the London Academy of Music; and is now a teacher of pf., violin, etc., at Brighton.

Key, Joseph, of Nuneaton, church composer, who flourished in the first half of the present century. He wrote a number of marches for organ, etc., and Eleven Anthems on general and particular occasions, for four voices, n.d. Five anthems, four collects, twenty psalm tunes, etc., London [1790]. Collected anthems, in 4 books, etc.

Kiallmark, George, composer and violinist, born at King's Lynn, February, 1781; baptized in March. He studied under Barthelemon, Spagnoletti, and Logier. Violinist in various orchestras, and teacher. Leader at Sadler's Wells, London. Died, Islington, March, 1835. WORKS.—*Songs*: All alone; Autumn noons; Banks of the Rhine; Bound where thou wilt; Cupid and Hymen; Fair Haidee; Fare thee well; Farewell, bright star; Helen's Farewell; Him I love; ·Maid of Athens; Now each tie; O come, my love; etc., etc. Part-songs: An immense number of divertimentos, fantasias, marches, fanfares, etc., for pf. His eldest son, GEORGE FREDERICK, was born in Islington, London, November 7, 1804. He studied at home under his father, Logier, and Moscheles, and at Paris, under Kalkbrenner, and others. He resided in London as a teacher and concert-giver, and died December 13, 1887. Celebrated as a pianoforte player.

Kidd, William James Pasley, musician and editor of first half of the present century. He compiled "The Chorister's Text-book, containing nearly 200 psalm and hymn-tunes, preceded by a comprehensive Grammar of Music," 1856. One of the contributors to the "British Minstrel."

Kidson, Frank, musician, of Leeds, compiler of "Old English Country Dances . . . with notes, and a bibliography of English country dance music," London, 1890. "Traditional Tunes, a collection of ballad airs,

KING.

chiefly obtained in Yorkshire and the South of Scotland . . . ," Oxford, 1891.

Kilburn, Nicholas, composer and conductor, born at Bishop Auckland, February 7, 1843. Was privately educated in music. Graduated Mus. Bac., Cambridge, 1880. Since 1875 he has been conductor of the Auckland Musical Society; from 1882 of the Middlesborough Musical Union; and of the Sunderland Philharmonic, from 1885. He has conducted concerts at Newcastle-on-Tyne; lectured on music; and as a zealous amateur, done much to promote musical culture in the north. His compositions include a sacred cantata, "Grant us Thy peace"; an oratorio, "St. Thomas," both for soli, chorus, and orchestra, the latter produced at Bishop Auckland, December, 1886. Psalms 23, and 137, for chorus and orchestra; Anthems, and Church services. The Golden River; The Silver Star, cantatas for female voices. Suite for orchestra (1894); Songs and part-songs. Duologue for pf. and violin. Author of pamphlets: How to manage a Choral Society; Notes and notions on Music; Wagner, a sketch of his life and works; and·Parsifal, a pilgrimage to Bayreuth.

Killen, Rev. William D., clergyman and writer. President of the Presbyterian College, Belfast, and professor of ecclesiastical history. Author of "The Westminster Divines and the use of instrumental music in the worship of God," Belfast. 1882. "A Catechism of the scriptural authority for the use of instrumental music in the Christian Church," Belfast, 1885. "Ecclesiastical history of Ireland," London, 1876, 2 vols.

Killick, Thomas, musician of early part of present century, who resided at Gravesend as an organist and teacher. Among other works he issued "Original set of Quadrilles and a waltz for the pf.," London [1829]. Also Handel's Overtures, arranged for the organ and pf., Clementi [1823].

Kilner, Thomas, organist and author, who died at London, September 30, 1876. Author of "Manual of Psalmody and Chanting," 1850; "Pocket Chant Book," 1850; Jottings about choral and congregational services, organs and organists, Gregorians, benches, and chairs, etc.," London, 8vo, 1872; second ed., 1873. Numerous pieces of organ music, etc.

King, Alfred, organist and composer, born at Shelley, Essex, April 24, 1837. He studied for the Church, but was a pupil for organ of Dr. Steggall. Became F.C.O., 1868; graduated Mus. Bac., 1872; Mus. Doc., 1890, Oxford. Held organ appointments at Cuddeston Theological College, 1856; Eastnor Castle (Earl Somers), 1857-64; St. Michael and All Angels, Brighton, 1865-77; Brighton Parish Church, 1877-87. Appointed organist to Brighton Corporation, 1878 ; and from that date to 1883, was chorus-master and part conductor of the Brighton Musical Festivals. Principal of the Brighton School of Music. His works include a cantata, "Deliverance"; an oratorio, "The Epiphany," produced at Brighton, April 9, 1891 ; Mass in B flat; an Evening Service in B flat. Madrigal; Music, when sweet voices die, for six voices, Brighton, December, 1886 ; Part-songs, hymns, etc.

King, Charles, composer and organist, born at Bury-St.-Edmunds, in 1687. Chorister in St. Paul's under Dr. Blow and Jeremiah Clark. Married to sister of J. Clark. Almoner and Master of Choristers, St. Paul's Cathedral, 1707. Mus. Bac., Oxford, 1707. Organist of St. Benet Fink, London, 1708. Vicar-choral of St. Paul's, 1730. He died at London, March 17, 1748.
WORKS.—Services in F, C, D. and B flat. *Anthems*—Rejoice in the Lord ; Hear, O Lord ; O pray for the peace of Jerusalem ; Unto Thee, O Lord ; Wherewithal shall a young man learn.

King, Donald William, tenor vocalist, was born in 1812. Was appointed principal tenor, Foundling Hospital, 1845. He sang in Opera at Drury Lane, and with the English Opera Company at the Strand Theatre, in 1848. He was a successful ballad singer. Died at Kilburn, London, August 7, 1886.

King, Frederick, baritone vocalist, born at Lichfield, January 3, 1853. Chorister at St. Mary's, Lichfield, and afterwards studied under John Pearce, Birmingham. Gained a Scholarship at the National Training School for Music, in 1876. Made his *début* at one of Harrison's Concerts, Birmingham, January 30, 1879, and sang at the Birmingham Festival the same year. In 1880 he sang at the Gloucester Festival, and in succession at the other Three Choirs' Meetings ; also at Leeds, in 1880, in the title part in "Elijah ;" and again in 1883-86, creating the part of *Lucifer* in Sullivan's "Golden Legend." He sang at the Handel Fes'ivals, 1880-82, and 1885 ; Chester Festival, 1882 ; and at the principal Metropolitan and provincial concerts. He was appointed a professor of singing at R.A.M. in 1890 ; and in 1895 made Hon. R.A.M.

King, Henry John, organist and composer, born in Australia. Composed a cantata "Ceutennial Ode " (Rev. W. Allen). performed at the opening of the Melbourne Exhibition, August 1888. He has also written a choral ballad, "Trafalgar," for men's voices, without accompaniment ; a Morning and Evening Service, with the Communion Office in F, etc.

King, James, musician, born about 1788. He was a singing master in London. Died, London, August 6, 1855. Author of "An Introduction to the theory and practice of Singing," London [1823]. "Collection of Glees, Madrigals, etc." London [1839]. Psalms of David arranged to chants. London [1840]. Songs, etc.

King, James, composer and bandmaster of the 5th Dragoons, was born about 1809. When only six years old he was present at the battle of Waterloo with his father, who was a trumpet major. He died at Derby, September 22, 1888. Composer of music for military bands.

King, Jessie, contralto vocalist. Studied in London, and appeared at the Crystal Palace June 22, 1889, taking part in the concerted music in "Elijah," performed on Festival scale in the Handel Orchestra. She was engaged for the Gloucester Festival of 1892, at Worcester the next year, and at Hereford in 1894 ; singing with much success. Since then she has gained a good position among vocalists of the day. She sang at the Gloucester Festival, 1895 ; at Tewkesbury Festival and at the Jubilee performance of "Elijah," Crystal Palace, June 27, 1896.

King, Matthew Peter, composer, born at London, 1773. He studied music under C. F. Horn, and was a teacher and musical director in London. He died at London, January, 1823.
WORKS.—Sonatas for pf., op. 1, 2, 5, 14 ; Rondos, op. 13, 22 ; Quintet for pf., flute, vn., tenor, and 'cello., op. 16 ; Divertissement for pf., op. 24. The Intercession, oratorio, 1817. (This contains the celebrated song, Eve's Lamentation.) *Music to Dramas*— Matrimony, 1804 ; The invisible girl, 1806 ; False alarms (with Braham), 1807 ; One o'clock, or the wood demon (with Kelly), 1807 ; Ella Rosenberg, 1807 ; Up all night, or the smugglers' cave, 1809 ; Plots, 1810 ; Oh, this love, 1810 ; The Americans (with Braham), 1811 ; Timour the Tartar, 1811 ; The fisherman's hut (with Davy), 1819 ; The magicians (with Braham). The Harmonist, a collection of glees and madrigals, from the classic poets [1814]. A general treatise on music, particularly on harmony or thorough-bass, and its application in composition, London, 1800. Introduction to the theory and practice of singing at first sight, 1806. Part-songs ; duets, as The minute gun at sea ; songs, etc.
His son, C. M. KING, composed songs and pf. music.

King, Oliver A., composer and pianist, born in London, in 1855. Chorister at St. Andrew's, Wells Street. Articled pupil of J. Barnby, and afterwards assistant organist at St. Anne's, Soho. Studied pf. under W. H. Holmes ; and at Leipzig Conservatorium under Reinecke, and others, 1874-7. Appointed pianist to H.R.H. the Princess Louise, 1879, and was in Canada in that capacity, 1880-3. While there, he gave recitals in

KING.

various towns, and visited New York. He has also given concerts on the continent of Europe. Sometime musical director of St. Marylebone Parish Church; he is now a professor of pf. at R.A.M. His compositions are very numerous, the principal being named below.

WORKS.—Psalm 137, for soli, chorus, and orchestra, produced, Chester Festival, 1888. Cantatas: The Romance of the Roses, op. 80; Proserpina, op. 93, female voices, both with orchestra; The Naiades, female voices; Morning and Evening Service in D; Te Deum and Jubilate in D, with free organ accompaniment. Album of duets; songs, and part-songs, Soldier, rest; The Curfew (6 voices), etc. *Orchestral:* Symphony, Night; Concert overture, Among the Pines (Prize, Philharmonic Society, 1883); Concert overture in D minor, produced at Novello Concerts, 1888; Concerto, pf. (1885, Brinsmead Prize); Concerto in G minor, violin, Henschel Concerts (Emil Mahr), January 20, 1887. Sonata in D minor; Twelve pieces, violin and pf. Legende; Miniatures, 3 books, and other pieces, pf. Twelve original voluntaries; Suite, op. 6; Sonata, op. 71, and other compositions for organ, etc.

King, Robert, composer, was born about the middle of the 17th century. Musician in band of William and Mary, and Queen Anne. Mus. Bac., Cambridge, 1696. He died after 1711.

WORKS.—Music in The Banquet of Musick, 1688; Choice Ayres, Songs, and Dialogues, 1684; Comes Amoris, 1687-93. Music to Shadwell's Ode on St. Cecilia's Day, 1690. "Once more 'tis born," Ode on Earl of Exeter, 1693. Songs for 1, 2, and 3 voices, composed to a Thorough Basse, for ye organ or harpsichord," London, n.d.

King, William, organist and composer, born in 1624. Chorister in Magdalen College, Oxford, 1648. B.A., 1649. Chaplain of Magdalen College, 1650-4. Probationer-fellow of All Soul's College, 1654. Organist of New College, Oxford, 1664. He died at Oxford, November 17, 1680. He wrote a Service in B flat, Anthems, etc., and "Poems of Mr. Cowley, and others, composed into Songs and Ayres," Oxford, 1668.

His father, GEORGE KING, was organist of Winchester Cathedral.

Kingsbury, Frederick, pianist, conductor, and teacher, born at Taunton, 1815 (?). Gave his first concerts in his native place, in January, 1841, playing pf. pieces by Hünten and Thalberg, and also appearing as a vocalist. In 1844 he became a student at the R.A.M. He conducted oratorio concerts at Holborn Theatre; was director of the London Vocal Academy; and about 1863, formed the West London Choral Union, giving concerts in St.

KINROSS.

James's Hall, and assisting, with his choir, at the Crystal Palace concerts. In 1868 he conducted the Promenade Concerts at the Agricultural Hall; and up to 1882 was engaged in concert work. In that year he was appointed a professor of singing at the Blackheath Conservatoire, and was also a professor of pf. at the Guildhall School. He died in London, February 26, 1892, at the age of seventy-seven.

Author of "The Voice and the structure and management of the vocal organ" . . . London, 1858.

Kingston, William Beatty-, journalist and writer on music, born at London in 1837. He was in the Public Record Office in 1852, and in 1856, became attached to the Austrian Consular service. Has acted as special correspondent to various newspapers, and travelled much in various parts of Europe. Author of "Music and Manners," London, 1887, Chapman and Hall, 2 vols.; "Monarchs I have met," 1887, 2 vols.; "Wanderer's Notes," 1888, 2 vols.; the English libretto of "The Beggar Student," produced by Carl Rosa, 1884; and contributions to *The Lute,* and other musical journals. In 1884, he received the Order of the Crown of Roumania, being the first Englishman so decorated; and in 1885, the Order of the Redeemer, from the King of Greece. He has also composed some pieces for pf.

His daughter, MARIE ANTOINETTE KINGSTON (now Baroness von Zedlitz), has composed a number of songs: Tell her; Sweetheart, say?; For lack of thee; When leaves are green, and others. Also some compositions for pf. Editor of Luigi Arditi's "My Reminiscences," London, Skeffington, 1896.

Kinloch, George R., Scottish ballad collector, published "Ancient Scottish Ballads recovered from tradition, and never before published, with notes and an appendix containing the airs," Edinburgh, 1827. The dance tune "Kinloch of Kinloch," usually adapted to Conolly's song, "Mary Macneil," and also to Andrew Park's "Hurrah for the Highlands," was composed by George Kinloch of Kinloch. It first appeared in Watlen's "Circus Tunes," afterwards in collections of Gow.

Kinlock, Eliza, *born* TRAUBNER, soprano singer, born at London, March 7, 1796. She appeared very early as a ballad singer, and married Mr. Lane, an actor, who died soon after. In 1827 she appeared in the United States, and in the same year married Mr. Kinlock, an actor. She died at Long Branch, New Jersey, August 11, 1887.

Kinross, John, pianist and composer, born in Edinburgh, October 16, 1848. Apprenticed to a music seller, and in early youth mostly self-taught. Was in a telegraph office in Ireland for a short time, and about 1865

KINSEY. KLEIN.

settled in Dundee, studying under G. A. Macfarren, and others, in London, during his
holidays. Settled in London, 1883. Died,
December 30, 1890. He was a successful
teacher, but devoted most of his time to composition. His works consist of a Cantata,
" Songs in a vineyard," for female voices ;
Psalm of life, part-song ; Two-part song
(Merry Songsters) ; Song, Bessie Bell and
Mary Gray ; Scotch and English songs, etc.
Twelve Scandinavian Sketches, op. 16 ; Suite,
for small hands, op. 18 ; Three Rondolettos,
and other pieces for pf. Twenty-four sketches,
in two books, for harmonium, etc.

Kinsey, Thomas Hague, pianist and
composer, born at Liverpool, December 15,
1858. ▸Pursued his early studies in private,
and went to Leipzig in 1877. There he
remained until 1880, studying under Oscar
Paul, E. F. Richter, and Jadassohn. Resident
in Liverpool as professor of pf. ; organist of
Sefton Park Church, and conductor of Sefton
Park Musical Society, etc. He has composed
several orchestral works ;. a trio in A, for pf.
and strings, produced, Liverpool, 1889 ; pieces
for pf. ; songs, part-songs, and some church
music.

Kirbye, George, composer, who flourished
in the latter half of the 16th century. He
was a native of Suffolk. He resided mostly
in Bury St. Edmunds, where he died in 1634,
and is buried in St. Mary's Church. One of
the ten composers who harmonized Este's
Psalms, 1592, and he composed the madrigal
for six voices in the "Triumphs of Oriana,"
entitled "Bright Phœbus," and published
"The First Set of English Madrigalls, to 4,
5, and 6 voyces," London, Este, 1597. Of
this a new edition, edited by G. E. P. Arkwright, was published in 1891-92.

Kirk, Helen Drysdale, Scottish contralto
vocalist, was born about 1844. She sang in
various parts of Scotland, particularly in
Edinburgh and Glasgow, along with Mr. Tom
Maclagan and others, and was well-known as
a successful singer of Scots songs. She died
at Glasgow, January 30, 1871.

Kirkhope, John, amateur musician and
conductor, born at Edinburgh, November,
1844. In 1881 he established a choir which
has performed works of a very high class,
chiefly in Edinburgh. The choir is one of
the best in Scotland, both as regards the
finish of its performances and the quality of
the works performed.

Kirkman, Mrs. Joseph, musician and
teacher, author of " A practical analysis of the
Elementary principles of Harmony," London, 1845 ; "Pianoforte Instructor for the
million . . . ," London [1854] ; "Three easy
lessons for the Spanish guitar," London
[1840] ; Pf. exercises, etc.

Kitchin, George, organist and conductor,

nephew of the Dean of Winchester. Was
organist of St. Saviour's, Brockley, 1871 ;
Holy Trinity, Sydenham, 1874. Has been
conductor of the Stock Exchange Orchestral
Society since its formation in 1885. In April,
1893, he conducted a Festival held in Winchester Cathedral.

Kitchiner, William, physician and musician, born London, 1775. Educated at
Eton, and graduated M.D., Glasgow. Having
inherited his father's fortune, he never practised, but lived mostly in London, devoting
his time to scientific and other pursuits. He
died at London, February 27, 1827.

WORKS.—The cook's oracle (1817) ; Art of
invigorating and prolonging life (1822) ; The
economy of the eyes (1824) ; The traveller's
oracle, 1827. Ivanhoe : or, the Knight Tem-
plars, musical drama. The loyal and national
songs of England, for one, two, and three
voices, selected from original manuscripts
and early printed copies in the library of
William Kitchiner, M.D., London, 1823. The
sea songs of England, etc., London, 1823.
Amatory and anacreontic songs set to music,
London, n.d. The sea songs of Charles Dibdin, with a memoir of his life and writings,
London, 1824. Observations on vocal music,
London, 1821. Glees, songs, etc.

Kiver, Ernest, pianist and organist, born
in London, September 22, 1864. Studied at
R.A.M., under the late Thomas Wingham;
A.R.A.M., and F.R.C.O. Some time organist
of St. Bride's, London, and later of The
Oratory, Brompton, which position he resigned in 1893. Has appeared as solo pianist,
and, since 1886, given high-class concerts at
Princes' Hall and Queen's Hall, bringing
forward, especially, important works by
English composers. He introduced, for the
first time in public, Sterndale Bennett's String
Quartet in G (May 14, 1886), Thomas Wingham's Quartet (May 8, 1889), and works by
other composers. He is a professor of the pf.
at the R.A.M.

Klein, Hermann, musical critic, and
teacher of singing, born at Norwich, July 23,
1856. Studied singing under Manuel Garcia,
1874-7. Appointed professor of singing, Guildhall School of Music, 1887 ; and director of
the opera class, after the death of Mr. Weist
Hill, December, 1891. He gave a performance of "Fra Diavolo," at the Lyric Theatre,
March 19, 1892. He is the composer of "The
Cavalier's Farewell " ; "The Empty Saddle " ;
"The Voice," and other songs. Among the
undertakings successfully organized by him
were the reception held in London in honour
of the Jubilee of Dr. Joachim, 1894, and the
celebration of the 70th birthday of Mr. August
Manns, 1895. In 1879-80, he was musical
critic of *The Examiner:* and has filled a
similar post on the *Sunday Times,* from 1881.

KLITZ.

Compiler of "Musical Notes," 1886-7-8-9. Lectured on the "Progress of Opera during the Queen's Reign," 1897.

Klitz, Philip, organist and composer, born at Lymington, Hampshire, January 7, 1805. He was the son of a German musician, George P. Klitz, under whom he studied. Teacher and organist in Southampton, where he held appointments at St. Lawrence and St. Joseph's Churches ; afterwards at All Saints'. He died at Southampton, January 12, 1854. Composer of "Songs of the Mid-Watch," 1838, and numerous single songs. Author of "Sketches of life, character and scenery in the New Forest," 1850.

His son, GEORGE, was also a composer, and his brothers WILLIAM (died 1857), CHARLES (died 1864), JAMES FREDERICK (died 1870), ROBERT JOHN and JOHN HENRY (died 1880), were all musicians.

Klose, Francis Joseph, composer and writer, born at London, in 1784. He was a member of the orchestra of King's Theatre, and of the Concert of Ancient Music. Teacher of the pf. in London. He died at Maryle-bone, London, March 8, 1830.

Composer of a large quantity of pf. music, and author of "Practical hints for acquiring thorough-bass," London, 1822. His songs, "My native land," "The Rose," etc., were popular in their day.

Knapp, William, composer, was born at Wareham, 1698. Was parish clerk of Poole. He died at Poole, Dorset, September, 1768. He published "A Sett of New Psalms and Anthems, in four parts, and an Introduction to Psalmody," London, 1738 ; 2nd ed. 1741 ; 4th ed., 1750 ; 7th ed. 1762. "New Church Melody, being a Set of Anthems, Psalms. Hymns, etc., in four parts ; with an Imploration wrote by Charles I., during his captivity in Carisbrook Castle," London, 1753, 5th ed., 1764.

Knapton, Philip, pianist and composer, born at York, in 1788. He studied under Hague, at Cambridge. Teacher in York. He died on June 20, 1833. He composed over-tures for orchestra, concertos for pf. and orchestra, sonatas for pf., arrangements for pf., songs, part-songs etc. His song "There be none of beauty's daughter," issued about 1818, was well known. He also published a "Collection of Tunes for Psalms and hymns, selected as a supplement to those now used in several churches in York," York [1810].

Knight, Edward, musician and composer, son of Edward Knight, comic song-writer and vocalist (1774-1826), who composed the "Sailor and Soldier," a musical farce, 1805. Young Knight edited "Canadian airs, collected by Lieut. Back, R.N., during the late Arctic Expedition under Captain Franklin, with symphonies and accompaniments," London, 1823. He also edited his father's "Comic

KNOWLES.

Songs and Recitations," London, 1827. His brother was J. Prescott Knight, the painter.

Knight, Joseph Philip, song-writer, born at Bradford-on-Avon, July 26, 1812. He studied under Corfe of Bristol Cathedral. Vicar of S. Agnes in the Scilly Isles. Retired latterly from the ministry. He died at Great Yarmouth, on June 2, 1887.

WORKS.—*Songs*—A little bird told me ; All on the summer sea ; Beautiful Venice ; Bells of Venice ; Breathe not her name ; Beautiful spirit ; Come roam to the greenwood ; Down beneath the waves ; Days gone bye ; Ellen and Patrick ; Farewell to thee, sweet Venice ; Farewell my native land ; Gentle words ; I would I were a child again ; I love the bright and smiling Spring ; Love that blooms for ever ; Music, sweet music ; Merry hearts ; May time ; My mother's song ; Old green lane ; Pale rose the moon ; Parting song ; Rocked in the cradle of the deep ; Say, what shall my song be ; She would not know me ; Spring's first violet ; Sleep and the past ; St. David's bells ; She wore a wreath of roses ; There was a time ; Though thou art cold ; Thou wert not there ; Tree of the forest ; The merry muleteer ; The old songs we sang ; The veteran ; What pleasant sounds ; World is a fairy ring ; Why chime the bells ? Duets, etc.

Knight, Thomas, musician and organist, born 1789 ; died November 21, 1811. He was organist of Peterborough Cathedral for a short time.

Knott, John, musician, son of a Baptist minister of Sevenoaks, Kent. He was a chorister in Durham Cathedral, and in 1811 became precentor in the West Church, Aber-deen. In 1824 he was appointed precentor of the New North Church, Edinburgh, and music-master at Heriot's Hospital, 1827-37. He died at Edinburgh in 1837. Compiler of "Sacred harmony, being a collection of psalm and hymn tunes . . ," Aberdeen, 1814 ; 2nd edition 1815. "Selection of tunes, in four parts, adapted to the psalms and paraphases of the Church of Scotland," Edinburgh, [1824]. Two of his sons, PHELIM and TAVER-NOR, attained some distinction in Scotland, the first as a poet and the other as a painter.

Knowles, George, amateur musician, was born in 1749. He was educated at Mar-ischal College, Aberdeen, and was licensed to preach in 1771. He became minister of Birse in Aberdeen, 1778-89. He died at Birse on March 29, 1789. Composer of "Birse," or "Balfour," a psalm tune, which appears in Smith's "People's Tune Book," etc, and other pieces of sacred music. There is a reference to Knowles in Peacock's "Travels in Scotland." He is perhaps best known as author of a descriptive poem on Deeside, which originally appeared in the "Scots' Magazine," 1814.

KNYVETT.

Another GEORGE KNOWLES published "Sacred Music, consisting of thirty-two hymn tunes, etc.," London, Goulding [1815].

Knyvett, Charles, organist and vocalist, was born on February 22, 1752. He sang at the Handel Commemoration, in 1784, and at the Concerts of Ancient Music. Gentleman of the Chapel Royal, 1786. Established, with S. Harrison, the Vocal Concerts, 1791-94. Organist of Chapel Royal, 1796. He died at London, January 19, 1822. Composed Collection of favourite glees, catches, and rounds, London, 1800. Six airs harmonized for three and four voices, London, 1815.

Knyvett, Charles, organist and composer, eldest son of above, was born in 1773. He studied under Parsons and Webbe. Revived the Vocal Concerts with W. Knyvett, Greatorex, and Bartleman. Organist of St. George's, Hanover Square, 1802. He died on November 2, 1852.

Wrote glees, etc., for "Re-Unions" of the Prince of Wales, London, 1800. Selection of Psalm tunes sung at St. George's Hanover Square, 1823; 2nd ed., 1825; 4th ed., 1850. Epitaph in Brading Church Yard, set to music for three voices, September 26, 1831. Collection of favourite glees, catches, rounds, etc.; Eight effusions for the pf., London [1847].

Knyvett, Deborah, born TRAVIS, singer, second wife of William Knyvett, was born at Shaw, near Oldham. She studied under Greatorex, and sang at the concerts of Ancient Music in 1813. Sang at principal London concerts, 1815-43. Married W. Knyvett, 1826. She died on February 10, 1876.

Knyvett, William, singer and composer, born April 21, 1779. Youngest son of Charles Knyvett, the elder. Sang at concerts of Ancient Music, 1788. Principal alto, ditto, 1795. Gentleman of Chapel Royal, 1797. Lay-Vicar of Westminster Abbey. Composer to the Chapel Royal. He sang at London and Provincial concerts, and was conductor of Concerts of Ancient Music, 1832-40. He died at Ryde, November 17, 1856. He composed anthems, glees, songs, etc., but was best known in his day as a vocalist.

Kollmann, George August, organist and composer, born in London, 1780. Son of Aug. F. C. Kollmann (1756-1829), musician and author. He succeeded his father as organist of the German Chapel Royal, St. James's, 1829. Teacher in London, where he died March 19, 1845. Composer of Three Grand Sonatas for pf., op. 1, 1808; Six waltzes for the pf. . . , London [1814], etc. He also invented a railway carriage, which had the property of traversing the base of hills, so as to avoid the need for tunnels; and a new mode of stringing and tuning pianofortes. His sister, JOHANNA SOPHIA

LACY.

(died, London, in May, 1849), succeeded him as organist of the German Chapel Royal in 1845.

Kyte, Francis, author of "Memoir relating to the Portrait of Händel . . ," 1829.

Lablache, Fanny Wyndham, born WILTON, contralto vocalist, who studied at the R.A.M., 1836-7. Début at the Lyceum. Sang at H.M. Theatre, etc. Married Frederic Lablache, son of Luigi, and retired from the stage. She died at Paris, September 23, 1877.

Lacy, Frederick St. John, composer and teacher of singing, born at Blackrock, County Cork, Ireland, March 27, 1862. Son of Lieutenant John Francis Lacy, J.P. Educated at Dublin, and intended for the Bar. Deciding for music, he became a student at the Cork School of Music, 1880-3; then a private pupil of H. C. Swertz; finally entering the R.A.M., in 1886, and studying under Sir G. A. Macfarren, E. Prout, W. H. Cummings and others. A.R.A.M. 1888, and Associate of the Philharmonic Society. Has held various appointments, and was director of the choir at St. Augustine's Ramsgate, 1893-4. His lectures and recitals, "Notes on Irish music," and "Song and Ballad music," have been given in London and the country; and he has contributed to the "Musical Standard" and other papers.

WORKS.—Four songs, op. 1; Annabel Lee, for tenor solo, chorus, and orchestra, op. 2; Three songs, op. 3; Three songs, op. 5; Four songs, op. 6; Six four-part songs, op. 7; Chastelâr, a cycle of songs from the Whyte-Melville Tableaux music, op. 8. Two sketches for violin and pf., op. 4; all published. In MS.: Bethlehem, sacred cantata; Mass in C; Benediction service, in B flat; Part-songs, etc. Incidental music to A fairy fantasy (1889); Whyte-Melville Tableaux (1890); Comic opera, Matrimony (1893); Musical farce, Chaos; The Indian serenade, tenor solo, chorus, and orchestra (1888). Overtures —Celtic, in A minor (1891); Herman and Dorothea. Orchestral serenade, in E; String quartet, in E, etc., etc.

Lacy, John, bass vocalist, was born about the end of the 18th century. He studied under Rauzzini at Bath. Appeared in London, Italy, etc., at oratorios and concerts. Married Miss Jackson, vocalist, widow of F. Bianchi, 1812. Received appointment in Calcutta, 1818, but returned to England about 1826. Resided on the continent for some time. Died while on a visit to Devonshire, 1865?

Lacy, Mrs., born JACKSON, wife of above, soprano vocalist. Appeared in London, April 25, 1798. She married F. Bianchi in 1800, and after his death, in 1810, married Lacy, 1812. She went with her husband to Calcutta, where she probably died.

LAHEE.

Lahee, Henry, composer and organist, born at Chelsea, April 11, 1826. Studied under Sterndale Bennett, John Goss, and Cipriani Potter. Organist, from 1847 to 1874, of Holy Trinity Church, Brompton. Resident in Croydon, as professor and composer. Member of the Philharmonic Society; and for years a successful pianist and concert-giver. WORKS.—*Cantatas*—The building of the ship (produced, Finsbury Chapel, Moorfields, December 27, 1869, and publicly performed at the Hanover Square Rooms, May 30, 1870); The blessing of the children, (1870); The sleeping beauty, and The blind girl of Costel Cuillé, both for female voices (the latter still in MS.); The jolly beggars (MS.) *Anthems*—Grant, we beseech Thee; Praise the Lord, and others . . . *Prize Glees*—Now the bright morning star (1855); Hark! how the birds (Bristol, 1869); Hence! loathed melancholy (Manchester, 1878); Away to the hunt (Glasgow, 1879); Love in my bosom (London, 1880); Ah! woe is me (London, 1884). These, with other glees and part-songs have enjoyed great popularity. Instrumental compositions include a suite for violoncello and pf. and pf. pieces.

Laidlaw, Anna Robena, Mrs. THOMSON, pianist, born at Bretton, Yorkshire, April 30, 1819. Pupil of Robert Müller, Edinburgh. Taken to Germany in 1830, where she pursued her studies; and took further lessons from Henri Herz in London, 1834. In 1836 she returned to Germany, and played at the Leipzig Gewandhaus concerts, July 2, 1837. While there she made the acquaintance of Robert Schumann, who dedicated to her his Phantasiestücke, op. 12. She remained in Germany until 1840, and was appointed pianist to the Queen of Hanover. Her career was continued with much success until the year 1852, when she married Mr. Thomson, a Scotsman, and has since lived in retirement.

Laing, David, LL.D., antiquary and scholar, born at Edinburgh, 1790; died at Portobello, October, 1878. WORKS.—Select remains of the ancient poetry of Scotland, 1822. Early metrical tales, 1826. An account of the Scottish Psalter of A.D. 1566, containing the psalms, canticles, and hymns, set to music in four parts, in the MSS. of Thomas Wode or Wood, Vicar of Sanct Androus, Edinburgh, 4to, 1871. See also STENHOUSE, WILLIAM.

La Jeunesse, Marie Louise Cecilia Emma, or ALBANI, soprano vocalist, born of French-Canadian parentage, at Chambly, near Montreal, in 1850. Received her first instruction in music from her father, an accomplished harpist, and studied at Albany, New York, whither the family removed, in 1864. While there she decided to adopt the profession of singing; and when she made

LAMBERT.

her *début* at Messina, in 1870, she appeared under the name of Albani. Previously she had studied at Paris, under Duprez, and at Milan under Lamperti. After singing in various places in Italy, she went to London, and made her first appearance at Covent Garden Opera House, April 2, 1872, as *Amina*, in "La Sonnambula," and, with few exceptions, has sung there every year since that time. Her repertory is very extensive, embracing the principal soprano parts in Lucia di Lammermoor, Faust, Mignon, Rigoletto, Flying Dutchman, Lohengrin, Tannhäuser, Tristan, and others, her latest addition being the part of *Donna Anna* in "Don Giovanni." July 23, 1896. She has sung in opera at Paris, Brussels, Berlin, etc. Her Festival *début* was made at Norwich, in 1872. The next year she sang at Birmingham, and at every succeeding Festival; at the Three Choirs, since 1877, at Gloucester (with two exceptions); at Bristol, from 1876; and at Leeds, 1877. She has been heard at all the principal concerts; has made several tours in Canada, and the United States, and alike in oratorio, opera, and ballad, has held a commanding position. From 1885 onward, she has frequently sung before the Queen, who has more than once visited her at Old Mar Lodge. In 1878, she married Mr. Ernest Gye.

Lake, George Handy, composer and writer, born at Uxbridge, June, 1827. Editor of the *Musical Gazette*. Held various London organ appointments. He died at London, December 24, 1865. Composer of "Daniel," oratorio, 1852, and a number of part-songs, ballads, pieces of dance music, etc.

Lake, George Ernest, organist and composer, son of George Handy Lake, born in London, May 29, 1854. Organist and music-master, St. George's School, Brampton, Hunts., 1876; St. John's Episcopal Church, Edinburgh; Weybridge Church; All Saints', North Kensington, from 1885. Of repute as an organ player, he was also known as a scholar; and the papers read before the College of Organists, and other bodies, were varied and able. He was an Examiner for Trinity College, London, and a member of the *Musical News* Syndicate. He died in London, March 15, 1893. His compositions consisted of anthems, hymn tunes, chants, etc.; some organ pieces, and part-songs. Also a musical comedy, "Sweepstakes," produced at Terry's Theatre, May 21, 1891.

Lamb, Benjamin, organist and composer, who flourished about the beginning of the 18th century. Organist of Eton College. Composed organ and church music, songs, etc.

Lambert, George Jackson, organist and composer, born at Beverley, November 16, 1794. He studied under his father, S. T. Lyon, and Dr. Crotch. Organist of Beverley Minster,

LAMBERT.

1818-1875. He died at Beverley, January 24, 1880. Wrote sonatas, trios, overtures, septet for strings, British concerts, 1823; Dance music for pf., etc.

His father, GEORGE LAMBERT, who died at Beverley on July 15, 1818, was organist of Beverley Minster for 41 years.

Lambert, James, musician and painter, was born at Jevington, Sussex, in 1725. He resided at Lewes as a painter, music teacher and organist of St. Thomas-at-Cliffe. Died at Lewes, December 7, 1788. We have not found any published works of this musician.

Lambert, Sir John, distinguished civil servant, and first Permanent Secretary to the Local Government Board, demands mention here on account of his services to Roman Catholic Church music. He was born at Bridzor, Tisbury, Wiltshire, February 4, 1815, and died at Milford House, Clapham Common, January 27, 1892. He was a member of the St. Cecilia Academy, Rome, and the recipient of a gold medal from Pius IX. for his arrangements of the Psalms and Antiphons of the Roman Liturgy. His public and political life is dealt with in the memoir in Vol. XXXII. of the Dictionary of National Biography (London : Smith, Elder & Co., 1892).

WORKS.—Totum Antiphonarium Vesperale Organistrum in Ecclesiis accommodatum, 1849; Hymnarium Vesperale, Hymnos Vesperales totius anni complectens; Ordinarium Missæ e Graduale Romano in usum organistrarum adaptatum, 1851 ; The true mode of accompanying the Gregorian Chant, 1848 ; Harmonising and singing the Ritual song ; Grammar of Plain Chant; Music of the Middle Ages, 1857, etc. He also collaborated in the preparation of other works on Liturgical Music.

Lambeth, Henry Albert, organist and conductor, born at Hardway, near Gosport, January 16, 1822. Studied the organ under Thomas Adams and Henry Smart, upon whose recommendation he was appointed Glasgow City Organist in 1853. He was conductor of the Glasgow Choral Union, 1859-80; of the new West of Scotland Choral Union, 1885. Formed a choir, which gave its first concert in 1874, and was then called by his name ; afterwards known as the " Balmoral Choir " ; and now the famed Glasgow Select Choir. This he left in 1878. He was organist at St. Mary's Episcopal Church, Glasgow, and later, at Park Church. He died at Glasgow, June 27, 1895. His compositions were settings of Psalms 86, and 137, both performed by the Glasgow Choral Union; various songs and pf. pieces. He edited (with D. Baptie) The Scottish Book of Praise, 1876; and arranged a number of Scotch songs for choral singing.

Lamond, Frederick A., pianist and composer, born at Glasgow, January 28, 1868.

LANCIA.

Studied at first with his brother, David Lamond. In 1880 he was organist of Laurieston Parish Church, and gave organ recitals. He studied the violin, while in Glasgow, with H. C. Cooper, and with Heerman when he went to Frankfort, in 1882. While at the Raff Conservatorium in that town, his master for pf. was Max Schwarz, and for composition, Anton Urspruch. Later, he had lessons from Hans von Bülow, and Liszt. He made an appearance at a concert at Berlin, November 17, 1885, and achieved a great success ; he also played at Vienna shortly after. He gave his first recital on his return to Glasgow, March 8, 1886, and was heard in London the same month, at the Princes' Hall; but he removed to St. James's Hall for the fourth recital, April 15, when he was honoured by the presence of the Abbé Liszt, then on his last visit to London. The next few years he was chiefly in Germany; but he played at the Crystal Palace (Saint-Saëns Concerto, No. 4, in C minor), April 5, 1890 ; and at the Philharmonic (Brahms' Concerto, No. 2, in B flat), May 14, 1891. Since then he has still further advanced his claim to be placed among the leading pianists of the day. He plays frequently in Germany, and was in Berlin in February, 1896, and visited Russia later in the year. His compositions are not yet very numerous, but they include a Symphony in A, produced by the Glasgow Choral Union, December 23, 1889 ; An overture, " Aus dem Schottischen Hochlande," performed by the Philharmonic Society, March 7, 1895 ; A pf. trio; Sonata, pf. and violoncello, op. 2; Eight pieces for pf., op. 1, etc.

Lampe, Mrs., see YOUNG ISABELLA.

Lancaster, Joseph, organist and composer, editor of the " Leeds Tune Book," London, 1868 ; London, 1875, etc. Composer of ballads, dance music, etc.

Lancia, Florence, soprano vocalist, born in London, March 20, 1840. Of Irish descent on her father's side. In 1856 she was taken to Milan and received lessons for a few months from Antonio Sangiovanni; and, returning to London, was instructed by Signor Brizzi, through whose aid she secured an engagement at Turin, making her *début*, early in 1858, as *Rosina* in " Il Barbiere." She then toured in opera and concerts in Ireland and Scotland, and sang in the first series of Monday Popular Concerts, January 3, 1859. In 1861 she was articled for five years to Frank Mori, but continued her public career. She first sang in oratorio at Exeter Hall, January 22, 1862, in Haydn's " Creation " ; and from that time until 1874 was constantly before the public, in opera and on the concert platform. She appeared as *prima donna* in at least thirty operas, including the chief works of Donizetti, Bellini, Verdi, Balfe, Wallace, Benedict, Auber,

LAND.

etc., and also in "Don Giovanni," "Der Freis-chütz," and "L'Africaine." She toured in the provinces with her own opera company in 1867, etc. ; sang in opera at the Crystal Palace, 1872 ; at the Gaiety Theatre, etc. One of her greatest triumphs was at the Norwich Festival of 1872, when, at shortest notice, she added to her own work, that allotted to Mlle. Titiens, in "Elijah," and Benedict's "St. Peter," the audience rising *en masse* to cheer her. After her retirement in 1874, she sang for a few years at Mr. Samuel Brandram's Shaksperean recitals ; and now teaches the art in which she had been so successful.

Land, Edward, pianist and composer, born at London, 1815. One of the children of the Chapel Royal. Accompanist to John Wilson, the Glee and Madrigal Union, etc. Secretary of the Noblemen and Gentlemen's Catch Club. He died at London, November 29, 1876.

WORKS.—Scottish melodies arranged as songs without words, pf. ; Lady Nairn's Lays from Strathearn, do. ; Miscellaneous pf. works. *Songs :* A loving heart ; Birds of the Sea ; You know not how I've missed you ; My Gentle Elodie ; Mine, love ? yes or no ; Bird of beauty, wing your flight ; Sighs that only love can share ; So sweet is love's young spring ; What can the heart want more ; Angel's watch ; Dreaming and waking ; Italian flower girl's song ; etc. Part-songs, arrangements, etc. Nine four-part Songs, harmonized, London, 1862.

Lane, E. Burritt, organist and composer, born at Christchurch, Hants, in 1849. Studied at Trinity College, London ; now Examiner there. Graduated Mus. Bac., Durham, 1891. Organist of Bromley Parish Church to 1896 ; then appointed to New Weighhouse Congregational Church, Duke Street, Grosvenor Square, London. Is professor of organ, etc., at Bromley School of Music. Has published a Te Deum, and other Church music ; also songs. Contributed articles to *Cassell's Magazine*, *Academic Gazette*, and *Musical News*.

Lane, George William Brand, conductor, and choir-trainer, born in London, August 13, 1854, but from infancy to the age of twenty lived in Brighton. Tonic Sol-fa student, and choir-trainer, Brighton. In 1875, removed to Manchester, where he conducted large Tonic Sol-fa classes, and formed a "Temperance Choir," which took the first prize in competitions at the Crystal Palace, in 1884-6, and 1889. In 1880, he founded the Manchester Philharmonic Society, which has a great reputation for refined unaccompanied singing. The Society also gave oratorios, cantatas, and operas in connection with Mr. De Jong's concerts ; and was invited by (Sir) Charles Halle to co-operate with his choir in the opening and closing ceremonies of the

LARA.

Manchester Jubilee Exhibition of 1887. Mr. Lane has been very successful as a voice-trainer, many of the leading local singers having been under his tuition.

Lane, Gerald M., is the composer of a number of songs : Only dreaming ; Dawn at last ; Lovers ; Sleeping and waking ; Love's vigil ; Tatters, etc., some of which have become popular.

Lang, John, musician, born at Paisley, October 17, 1829 ; died at Glasgow, April, 1892. Inventor of the "Union Notation." In this system the notes are indicated to Sol-fa musicians by having the initial letter of the various notes in the Sol-fa scale placed within the head of the ordinary musical characters, and so presenting a combination of both old and new notations. A considerable amount of music has been printed on this system.

Langdon, Richard, composer and organist, born at Exeter about 1729. Mus. Bac., Oxon., 1761. Organist of Exeter Cathedral, 1753-77. Organist, Bristol Cathedral, 1777-81. Organist of Ely Cathedral for a few months in 1777. Organist, Armagh Cathedral, 1782-94. He died at Exeter, September 8, 1803, aged 74.

WORKS.—Twelve Songs and two Cantatas, op. 4, London, n.d. Divine Harmony, being a collection in score of Psalms and Anthems, 1774. Anthems. Twelve Glees for 3 and 4 voices, London, 1770, etc.

Langran, James, organist, born in London, November 10, 1835. Pupil of J. B. Calkin. Graduated Mus. Bac., Oxford, 1884. Organist of St. Michael's, Wood Green, 1856 ; Holy Trinity, Tottenham, 1859 ; and from 1870 to the present time, organist of All Hallows (Parish Church), Tottenham. Musical Instructor, since 1878, at St. Katherine's Training College, Tottenham. He has published a Morning and Evening Service ; contributed tunes to Hymns Ancient and Modern ; and is Musical Editor of the New Mitre Hymnal, 1875. His hymns, "Deerhurst," and "St. Agnes," are well known.

Langshaw, John, organist and composer, born in 1718. He was organist of the Parish Church of Lancaster, and died, 1798.

His son, JOHN, born, London, 1763, studied under Charles Wesley, and succeeded his father at Lancaster, in 1798. He composed hymns, chants, songs, pf. concertos, and organ music.

Lara, Adelina de, *born* PRESTON, pianist, born at Carlisle, January 23, 1872. Her parents were musical, and were her first instructors. She played, as a juvenile prodigy, at Liverpool, Newcastle-on-Tyne, and other places ; and was afterwards placed under the care of Miss Fanny Davies, who secured her the notice of Madame Schumann. She studied with that lady at Frankfort, 1885-90, and made her *début* at the Saturday Popular Con-

LARGE.

certs, March 21, 1891, with success. She appeared at the Crystal Palace, April 25, of the same year, taking the solo part in Rubinstein's Concerto in D minor; and has since been heard at concerts in Birmingham, and other places. At the Queen's Hall, in 1895, she gave a series of concerts of Early, Mediæval, and Modern Music.

Large, Eliza, Rebecca, MRS. HENRY CHATFIELD, vocalist, was born in 1815. She studied under Sir G. Smart, and Sir Henry Bishop, and was well known as a singer at the Ancient and other London concerts. She died at Brixton, London, July 30, 1881.

Larkcom, Charlotte Agnes, soprano vocalist, born near Reading. Studied at R.A.M., winning the Westmorland Scholarship, 1874. Awarded First Prize for sopranos at the National Music Meetings, Crystal Palace, July 1, 1875; and sang at the Saturday Concerts there, January, 1876. Elected an Associate, R.A.M., she was afterwards appointed a professor of singing. Sang at concerts in the provinces; toured with success in Holland, 1886. In 1888 she married Mr. Herbert Jacobs, barrister, but still pursues her professional duties.

Larkin, Edmund, organist, born in 1785. For some time he was organist of Peterborough Cathedral; afterwards he was organist of the Parish Church of Stamford, where he died, December 9, 1838.

Larrington, Rev. George, author of "The Influence of Church Music. Sermon preach'd in the Cathedral Church of Worcester," London, 1726.

Lates, Charles, composer, who flourished about the end of the 18th century. He studied under P. Hayes; and was a candidate for an organist's appointment at Whitchurch in 1805. Composed sonatas, songs, etc. His father, JOHN JAMES, was a violinist of some local fame in Oxford, where he was a teacher. He wrote chamber music. He died in 1777.

Latham, Morton, writer on music, and composer. Educated at Cambridge University, graduating B.A., 1865; M.A., and Mus. Bac., 1882. Has lectured before the College of Organists, 1884-7, on Common Principles of Art; The effect of the Renaissance on Musical Art, etc. He has published a Te Deum, and a number of songs.

Latrobe, Rev. Christian Ignatius, writer and composer, born at Fulneck, near Leeds, February 12, 1758. He was educated at Niesky, and Barby, in Prussia. Secretary to the United (Moravian) Brethren in England. He died at Fairfield, near Liverpool, May 6, 1836.

WORKS.—Original Anthems, with organ or pf. accompaniment, 2 vols., n.d. Jubilee Anthem for George III., October 25, 1809. "Dies Irae," for 4 voices, 1799. Hymns.

LEVALLEE.

Selection of Sacred Music from the works of Eminent Composers of Germany and Italy, 6 vols., 1806-1825. Three sonatas for pf., op. 3 (dedicated to Mr. Haydn). Instrumental and miscellaneous music. Hymn Tunes of the United Brethren [1814].

Latrobe, John Antes, M.A., writer and organist, son of the above, born 1799. Vicar of St. Thomas's Kendal. He died at Gloucester, November 19, 1878.

WORKS.—Music of the Church considered in its various branches, Congregational and Choral, London, 1831. Instructions of Chenaniah: plain directions for accompanying the chant or the psalm tune, London, 1832.

His brother, the Rev. PETER LATROBE (born London, February 15, 1795; died at Bertheldorf, near Herrnhut, Germany, September 24, 1863), composed some hymn tunes and chants, and wrote an introduction to C. I. Latrobe's Hymns.

Latter, Richard, bass vocalist, born at Bromley, Kent, July 22, 1823. Received his first instruction from his brother William, and entered the R.A.M., in 1841, intending to become a pianist; but his voice developing power, he took to singing, studying under Crivelli. A.R.A.M., 1849. He sang at various concerts in London and the provinces, and made his stage *début* at the Princess's Theatre, as Malatesta in "Don Pasquale." He also played in opera at Bath, Birmingham, Manchester, and other places up to 1851, when he settled in Aberdeen as teacher, remaining there till 1871. He is now a professor of singing at the Guildhall School of Music, and F.R.A.M.

WILLIAM LATTER, his elder brother, a pianist, entered the R.A.M., in 1831. His life was spent chiefly in teaching, and he died at Lee, Kent, November 15, 1884, in his 69th year. He was also a Fellow of the R.A.M.

Lauder, W. Waugh, pianist, born in Canada. Studied at Leipzig, and was also a pupil of Liszt. Toured in Europe, and about 1885 settled in London, Ontario. In Canada and the United States he has a great reputation as an executant.

Lavallee, Calixa, pianist and composer, born at Verchères, Canada, in 1842. Studied in Paris under Marmontel, and Adrian Boieldieu the younger. Settled in Boston, Mass., where he was a professor at the Petersilea Academy of Music. He was a foremost worker for the Music Teachers' National Association, U.S.A.; and as a delegate therefrom attended the Conference of what is now the Incorporated Society of Musicians, held in London, January, 1888. He died at Boston, in January, 1891. He wrote a cantata for the reception of the Princess Louise at Quebec, in 1878; several operas; an oratorio; songs, etc.; also a symphony; string quartets, pf. pieces, etc.

LAVENU.

Lavenu, Louis Henry, composer and violoncellist, was born at London, in 1818. He studied at the R.A.M., under Potter and Bochsa. 'Cellist at the opera, London. Music-seller in partnership with N. Mori. Music director of Sydney Theatre. He died at Sydney, August 1, 1859.

WORKS.—Loretta, a tale of Seville (Bunn), opera, November 9, 1846. *Songs :* Cottage rose; Deserted; Harvest queen; Memory's dream. Come, wander with me, duet. Pf. music, etc.

Lavington, Charles Williams, organist, born at Wells, Somerset, February, 1819. Chorister, Wells Cathedral, and studied under Perkins, the Cathedral organist, and later with James Turle at Westminster Abbey. Returning to Wells, he became assistant organist at the Cathedral; in 1842 was appointed acting organist; and on the death of Perkins was made organist and master of the choristers, and organist of the Theological College. At a special service in Wells Cathedral, August 4, 1892, the Choirs of Bristol and Exeter Cathedrals assisted; indirectly marking Lavington's Jubilee. He died at Wells, October 27, 1895, and with him almost the last of the old school of organ playing, and accompanying.

Lawes, Henry, composer, born at Dinton, near Salisbury, Wiltshire, December, 1595. Son of Thomas Lawes, died 1640, Vicar-choral. He studied under John Cooper (Coperario). Epistler and Gentleman of Chapel Royal, 1625. Clerk do. Member of private band of Charles I. Music master in family of the Earl of Bridgewater. Stripped of appointments during the Protectorate, but reinstated at the Restoration, in 1660. He died at London, October 21, 1662, and is buried in the cloisters of Westminster Abbey.

WORKS.—The Triumphs of Peace, masque (with W. Lawes and S. Ives), 1633. Cœlum Britannicum, masque (Carew), 1633. Comus, masque (Milton), 1634. A Paraphrase upon the Psalmes of David, set to New Tunes for Private Devotion, and a thorow base, for voice or instrument, 1637 (Sandys' version). Choice Psalmes put into Musick for Three Voyces, 1648. Ayres and Dialogues for one, two, and three voices, 1653 ; Do., 2nd book, 1655 ; Do., 3rd book, 1658. Music to poetry by W. Cartwright, Herrick, Davenant, Milton, Waller, etc. Songs in Contemporary Collections, as The Treasury of Musick, 1669 ; Anthems in Clifford's and other collections ; Music in Select Ayres and Dialogues.

Lawes, William, composer, brother of above, born at Salisbury, 1582. He studied under Coperario. Member of Chichester Cathedral choir till 1602. Gentleman of Chapel Royal, 1602. Musician in ordinary to Charles I. Killed at siege of Chester, during the Civil War, 1645.

LAWRENCE.

WORKS.—Music to Shirley's "Peace." The Royal Consort for Viols. Songs in various collections, etc. Fantasias for various instruments, etc.

Lawler, Thomas, bass vocalist, born in 1818. Studied under Bianchi Taylor. Established the City Glee Club in 1853 ; and on his retirement in 1886, was presented with a testimonial. He was for many years a Gentleman of the Chapel Royal, resigning on a pension early in 1887. He sang in oratorio in London and the provinces, and appeared on the stage ; but it was in glee-singing, and in old English songs that he was most celebrated. He died in London, May 16, 1893.

Lawrance, Edward, organist and composer, born at Weymouth, 1836. Studied in that town under Ricardo Linter, and 1856-8, at Leipzig Conservatorium, under Moscheles, Plaidy, E. F. Richter, Hauptmann, and others. In 1859 he was appointed organist of Sidmouth Parish Church, and a year later to St. David's, Merthyr Tydfil. This appointment he held until the beginning of 1891, when he resigned in consequence of the introduction of ritualism he could not conscientiously assist in. Since 1893 he has been organist at Christ Church, Merthyr Tydfil. He is conductor of the Merthyr Musical Union. His compositions comprise an opera, "Conradine " ; a cantata, "The Siege of Harlech " (which gained the prize at the National Eisteddfod, Swansea, 1863) ; anthems, services, chants, hymn-tunes, songs, etc. Also a Trio for pf. and strings ; pieces for pf., etc.

Lawrence, Charles, organist and composer, graduated Mus. Bac., Oxford, 1875. He has held organ appointments at Bearwood, Wokingham, 1870 ; St. John's, East Dulwich, 1873 ; Christ Church, Eastbourne, 1883 ; St. Alban's, Streatham Park, 1884 ; St. Stephen's, South Dulwich, 1894. Conductor of Choral Society, East Dulwich (1883). His compositions comprise Psalm 118, for soli, chorus, and orchestra ; Quartet in A ; Trio in C minor, for pf. and strings, performed by the Musical Artists' Society. Pf. duets. Three Scotch songs ; part-songs, etc.

Lawrence, Emily M., pianist and composer, born at Rugby, in 1854. Studied under her mother, and afterwards in London under Sterndale Bennett, Manuel Garcia, and Dr. Steggall. She subsequently entered the R.A.M. remaining there three years. Madame Lawrence is the conductor of a Ladies' Choral Society at Rugby, and a Society at Wembley, near Harrow, and has given performances in both places, at the R.A.M., and elsewhere. She has been organist of St. John's Church, Wembley, since 1889. Her compositions comprise two cantatas for ladies' voices : Bonny Kilmeny, Kensington, 1890 ; and The Ten Virgins, Wembley, 1893 ; a Sonata in F

LAWRIE.

sharp minor, violin and pf., produced by the Musical Artists' Society, July, 1882; an Album of pf. pieces; Romance, op. 16, etc. The Book of Songs for Girls and Boys; A number of songs; Part-songs; Duets, and some anthems.

Her mother, MRS. ELIZABETH S. LAWRENCE, was organist of Rugby Parish Church, 1842-77. She compiled a book of psalmody, and composed some hymn tunes and chants.

Lawrie, Alexander, composer and pianist, was born at Edinburgh, June 26, 1818. Organist of S. James' Episcopal Chapel, Edinburgh, and in the Rev. John Kirk's Church in the same city. He died at Edinburgh, December 9, 1880. A blind musician of great local fame. He arranged some music for the pf., and composed some hymns and songs. He also wrote accompaniments for a few of the songs in Wood's " Songs of Scotland."

Lawson, Malcolm Leonard, composer and conductor, born at Wellington, Shropshire, in 1849. Studied under various masters in London, and in France, Italy, and Germany. Was organist and choirmaster of the Catholic Apostolic Church, London, 1876; Conductor of the Gluck Society, 1877; of the St. Cecilia Society; and for some time, from 1878, director of the musical branch of the Kyrle Society. Under his direction, important works by Gluck, Pergolesi, Leo, Purcell, and others, have been revived.

WORKS.—Festival Services, op. 1, in F; Op. 2, in D; Op. 16; all composed for the Catholic Apostolic Church. Six anthems, op. 24, for 4 voices. Music to the play, Olivia, London, 1877; Opera, The Three Princesses; Airs and interludes to the play, England, London, 1876. Six part-songs, op. 3; Three songs, op. 4; Seventeen People's songs, op. 8; Twelve love songs, op. 14; Six Motets for ladies' voices, written for the St. Cecilia Society, op. 18; Twelve Scotch songs, words by Burns, etc., op. 20; Six songs, words by the old dramatists, op. 21; Three songs, with violin obligato, op. 22; Cupid's Curse, duet; Last words, song, etc. Symphonies in D, Pan, op. 12; in G minor, Mahomet, op. 19; Overture, Savonarola, op. 23; Andante, Scherzo, and Minuet, op. 6, pf., etc.

Lawson, R. E., musical director, Theatre Royal, Manchester (1888), is the composer of the music to a comedy, " Silver Fortune," produced at Ramsgate, 1888; also of pantomime music for the Theatre Royal, Manchester.

Lazarus, Henry, clarinet player, born in London, January 1, 1815. Studied under Charles Godfrey, sen., and made his *début* as a solo player at Madame Dulcken's concert, Hanover Square Rooms, May 2, 1838. In that year he was appointed second to Willman at the Sacred Harmonic Concerts; and on the death of Willman, in 1840, succeeded him as principal clarinet at the opera, and chief

LEE.

concerts and festivals. At the Birmingham Festivals, he was engaged from 1840 to 1885; and played for the last time at a Festival at Gloucester, 1886. He was the last surviving member of the late Duke of Devonshire's private band. For many years, from 1854, a professor at R.A.M., he was made an Hon. Member of that Institution; and was, from 1858, professor at Kneller Hall. He retired from the concert platform in 1891; was given a testimonial concert at St. James's Hall, May 31, 1892; and on March 6, 1895, he died in London. He wrote fantasias and other pieces for his instrument, but will be longer remembered as the greatest player of his day.

Leach, James, composer, was born at Wardle, near Rochdale, in 1762. He received no musical instruction, and was employed as a hand-loom weaver in Rochdale. Member of the King's band, and tenor vocalist in London. Tenor singer and teacher in Rochdale, 1789, and latterly in Salford, 1796. He died from the effects of injuries received in a coach accident, Blackley, near Manchester, February 8, 1798, and is buried in Rochdale.

WORKS.—New Sett of Hymn and Psalm Tunes, adapted for the use of churches, chapels, and Sunday schools . . . London, 1789; Second. Sett of Hymn and Psalm Tunes, London [1797]; Collection of Hymn Tunes and Anthems, composed and adapted for a full choir, London [1798]; Anthems, etc.; Psalmody, by James Leach . . . Harmonised in compressed score by John Butterworth, with a sketch of the composer's life and work by Thomas Newbigging, London [1884].

Leaver, William John, organist and composer of present time. Studied at R.A.M. Graduated Mus. Bac., 1884, Cambridge. Organist and choirmaster, St. John's, Blackheath, and conductor of a choral society there. Has composed a setting of Ps. 146, for soli, chorus and orchestra; and published anthems, songs, part-songs, pf. pieces, etc.

Leburn, Alexander, violinist, who was born at Auchtermuchty, Fife, in 1767, and was a teacher of music there. He was a self-taught mathematician. He died at Auchtermuchty, in March, 1836. He published " A Collection of New Strathspey Reels, etc., with a bass for the violoncello, or harpsichord," Edinburgh, 1793.

Lee, David, organist. He held the appointment of City organist, Melbourne, Australia, for a number of years; also conductor of Melbourne Philharmonic Society, which has produced Handel's oratorios, among them " Jephtha " in 1884, for the first time in Australia. In 1887 he visited England, and played at the Crystal and Alexandra Palaces, also in the provinces. He was made an honorary member of the College of Organists that year.

P

LEE.

Lee, Ernest Markham, composer and organist, born at Cambridge, June, 1874. Entered the choir of Clare College at the age of nine, receiving instruction from W. C. Dewberry, the college organist. Graduated Mus. Bac. and B.A., Cambridge, 1894, and became F.R.C.O. the same year. In 1890, was appointed organist of St. Matthew's, Cambridge; in 1894, organist of Emmanuel College, holding, 1896, likewise a similar post at All Saints', Woodford Green. Began composition when fourteen, his first publication being a carol, *Musical Herald* Prize. His compositions comprise, Psalm 98, for soprano solo, chorus, strings, and organ; Cantatas: A stormy night at sea (produced, 1893); "Jael," an ode in honour of the birth of Prince Edward of York (published 1896). A Comedy Opera, "Alicia"; Songs, part-songs, etc.

Lee, G., author of "The Voice, its artistic production, development and preservation," 1870, 2 editions.

Lee, George Alexander, composer and conductor, born at London, 1802. Tenor singer in theatre at Dublin, 1825; Haymarket Theatre, London, 1826. Music-seller in London for a time. Opened Tottenham Street Theatre for English opera (with Chapman and Melrose). Lessee of Drury Lane Theatre, 1830. Manager of Lenten oratorios at Covent Garden and Drury Lane, 1831. Married Mrs. Waylett, the singer. Conductor of Strand Theatre, 1832; Olympic Theatre, 1845. He died at London, October 8, 1851.

WORKS.—*Music to Dramas:* Invincibles, 1828; Sublime and beautiful; Nymph of the grotto, 1829; Witness, 1829; Legion of honour, 1831; Love in a cottage; Auld Robin Gray; Fairy lake, and other operettas and musical dramas. Beauties of Byron, 8 songs; Loves of the butterflies (T. H. Bayly), 8 songs. *Songs and Ballads:* Away, away, to the mountain's brow; Annie Bell; Believe me not false; Bells upon the wind; Bells at sunset; Come, dwell with me; Come, merry fays; Cora; Come Flower of Lammermoor; Fairest flower; Fairyland; Garden of Roses; Gipsy's wild chant; Gondolier's lay; Good night, love; He comes not; I'll not beguile thee; I sigh for the woods; I'll be a fairy; I love all that thou lovest; Kate Kearney; Lad who wears the pladdy; Macgregor's gathering; Maid of Kildare; My native bells; Mermaid's invitation; Meet me in the willow glen; My cottage and my mill; Old Irish Gentleman; Rover's bride; Rose of Killarney; Sweetly sound the Village bells; She walks in beauty; Thou art not false but fickle; The wild white rose; 'Tis love's hallowed hour; When the moon is brightly beaming; Why should we sigh; Wild mandoline. A Vocal Tutor. Duets and part-songs, etc.

LEEVES.

His brother, DAVID, who died at London, in November, 1849, was a pianist and had studied under Dussek.

Lee, J., author of "Musical Education, a treatise on melody and harmony in conjunction with pianoforte playing and singing.." 1850.

Lee, J. H., musician, published "Sight-singing made easy, a progressive manual," London [1889].

Lee, J. S., composer and bandmaster, was born on February 14, 1831. He was one of the oldest military bandmasters in the British army, and for many years held the post of bandmaster of the 20th Hussars. He composed church music for military choirs; a fantasia for the cornet; Dance music for military bands; Gavottes, marches, and songs.

Leechman, John, musician, edited "The Choral Book: a selection of sacred music," London [1855].

Lees, John, musician of early part of present century, compiled "The Hymn Tunes of the Church of the Brethren..arranged for four voices, in score," London, 1824.

Lees, John Kenyon, composer, teacher, and conductor, born October 6, 1853. He studied under his father and T. S. Hill, of Norwich. He has held various organ appointments in Edinburgh, among them being that of St. Matthew's Church, Morningside, 1885-1895. In 1891 he instituted the Morningside Choral Society, which has performed a number of important works. Composer of some dance music, and editor of "The Songs of Burns, with symphonies and accompaniments by John Kenyon Lees, and introduction and historical notes by H. C. Shelley," Glasgow, 1896. "The Balmoral Reel Book," 1894, etc. He is also musical editor of a collection of 100 Scotch songs, about to be published.

Leeson, Joseph Frederick, composer and organist, was born at Armagh about 1806. He was an organist and teacher in Arbroath, and afterwards in Dunfermline, where he died, on January 1, 1862. He composed a number of glees, and some songs, among which is "Oh sing to me the auld Scotch songs" [1856], a popular but somewhat vulgar effusion.

Leete, Robert, bass singer and conductor, born in latter part of last century. He was a celebrated glee singer, and succeeded Sale as Secretary of the Catch Club. For many years he acted as conductor at the Glee Club. He died on December 25, 1835.

Leeves, Rev. William, clergyman and composer, born on June 11, 1748. He was Rector of Wrington, Somerset, from 1779. He died at Wrington, May 25, 1828. Composer of "Auld Robin Gray," 1770, a song known throughout the world. The words by Lady Anne Barnard (1750-1825) are so natural

LEFFLER.

and true to life that the musical aid afforded by Leeves' setting is not, as some suppose, the chief reason for its popularity. Leeves wrote much church music, now completely forgotten, among it being " Six Sacred Songs. . with a corrected copy in its original simplicity of the well-known ballad, " Auld Robin Gray," London, 1812. *See* " In Memoriam, with a few notices of other members of his family, printed for private circulation," 1873, ports.

Leffler, Adam, bass singer, was born in 1808. He was a chorister in Westminster Abbey, and sang in opera and at concerts. He died in London, March 28, 1857.

Legge, Robin Humphrey, writer on music, and composer, born near Liverpool, June 28, 1862. Of a Shropshire family, of Bishop's Castle, he was intended for the Bar, and entered at Trinity Hall, Cambridge ; but giving that up for music, he went to Leipzig in 1885, studying at the Conservatorium, and privately, under Gustav Schreck, Paul Klengel, Richard Hofmann, and others, and later, at Frankfort, under Anton Urspruch. Returning to England in 1890, he settled in London, and devoted himself chiefly to musical literature, contributing articles to various papers. " An appreciation of Smetana," which appeared in the New Quarterly *Musical Review,* seems to have had some influence. While in Germany he wrote a great deal of music, but his published works are few : Two books of carols ; A set of five part-songs (poems by Charles Kingsley) ; some pieces for violin and pf., etc. His most important works are : Articles in the Dictionary of National Biography (from Vol. XXXV., G. A. Macfarren) ; Translation of Wallaschek's " Die Musik der Naturvolker (Primitive Music, Longmans, 1893) ; History of the Norwich Musical Festivals, 1824-1893 (with W. L. Hansell), London, Jarrold, 1896.

Lehmann, Liza, soprano vocalist and composer, born in London. Studied singing with her mother (a daughter of Robert Chambers, LL.D.), and afterwards under Randegger ; composition with Raunkilde (Rome), Freudenberg (Wiesbaden), and Hamish MacCunn. Her *début* as a vocalist took place at the Monday Popular Concerts, November 23, 1885. She sang at the Norwich Festival, 1887 ; and has appeared at the principal concerts in the United Kingdom, also in Germany. A feature of her repertory was the inclusion of many fine old and forgotten songs, to which her artistic singing gave a new life. She was also an interpreter of her own compositions. In July, 1894, she gave a farewell concert, retiring from the profession of vocalist on her marriage with Mr. Herbert Bedford (*q.v.*). Her compositions include Two Albums of German songs ; Album of English songs ; A Musical Duologue, The

LEMARE.

Secrets of the Heart (MS.) ; A song cycle for four voices, In a Persian Garden (from Omar Khayyam), Popular Concerts, December 14, 1896 ; Songs, Mirage ; Titania's Cradle, etc. Album of Ten Sketches, and other pieces for pf. Romance for violin, etc.

Leicester, W. G., *see* GARDINER, WILLIAM.

Leigh, Arthur George, organist and composer, born at Ashton-in-Makerfield, Lancashire, August 22, 1846. Studied music, 1860-6, under the late Thomas Graham, Wigan. In 1866 he was appointed organist and choirmaster of the Parish Church, Chorley, which post he resigned in 1868. In 1877 he accepted a similar position at St. George's, Chorley, which he held until 1896. He was elected a Town Councillor when Chorley was incorporated ; and elected Alderman, and Mayor of Chorley in 1887-8-9. He has a fine library of early music and musical literature, valuable collections from which have been exhibited in London (1892-4-5), and elsewhere. His compositions are mainly for the church, and include Ten responses, Thirty-three chants, Thirty-three hymn tunes, later, merged in a work, " Sacred Music," and a portion contributed to the Church of England Hymnal, the Sacred Melodist, and other collections. The Story of the Cross. Pf. : Violet, Snowdrop, Fairies' Revel, and other pieces. He has also edited Stepping Stones to the Classics, 12 numbers.

Leighton, G. A., musician of first half of the present century. Author of " New and Improved Preceptor for the Pianoforte," London [1845].

Leighton, Sir William, musician, gentleman - pensioner, and knight, who flourished during the 16th and 17th centuries. He published " The Teares or Lamentations of a Sorrowful Soule ; composed with Musicall Ayres and Songs both for Voyces and Divers Instruments," 1614. [Psalms, Hymns, etc.]. Byrd, Bull, Dowland, Ford, O. Gibbons, Giles, Hooper, Wilbye, Weelkes, and Milton, are among the contributors to this now extremely scarce and valuable publication.

Le Jeune, Arthur, organist and pianist. With his brother CHARLES, gave organ performances from about 1866, exciting much attention by their juvenile talent. Arthur Le Jeune is resident in London as pianist and composer. He has published a number of pieces for pf. ; Liebeslied, for violin and pf., etc.

Lely, Durward, *see* LYLE, JAMES.

Lemare, Edwin H., organist and composer, born at Ventnor, Isle-of-Wight, September 9, 1865. He was elected Sir John Goss Scholar, R.A.M., in 1878 ; and on the completion of his studies made an Associate, and later, a Fellow. F.R.C.O., 1884. Organist of St. John the Evangelist's, Brownswood Park ; St. Andrew's, Cardiff ; Parish Church, Sheffield, 1886 ; Holy Trinity, Sloane Square, Pimlico ; and now of St. Margaret's, Westminster. He has given organ recitals at the Bow and Bromley Institute, 1886 ; St. George's Hall, Liverpool, etc., and ranks among the most brilliant of the younger organists of the day. Editor of The Recital Series of original organ compositions, R. Cocks, to which he has contributed several pieces.

Lemare, William, organist, conductor, and composer, born at Godalming, Surrey, in 1839. Studied under Dr. Gauntlett. Organist successively at St. Jude's, East London, 1860 ; St. Andrew's, Stockwell, 1865 ; Brixton Parish Church, 1872 ; St. Saviour's, Hernehill, 1876 ; St. Mary's, Newington, 1880 ; St. Mary's, Longfleet, 1888 ; St. Nathanael, Westbourne, 1894. In 1888 he received the degree of Mus. Doc., Cantuar. For a number of years he gave important concerts at Gresham Hall, Brixton ; and later, was conductor of choral societies at Bournemouth and locality, and conductor of the Bournemouth Festivals. In 1896 he was appointed conductor of the Nottingham Sacred Harmonic Society, and is now resident in that town, He has composed two operettas : "A Calm Sea," Brixton, 1882 ; and "Pride and Policy," Poole, 1889. His compositions also include church services, anthems, songs, etc.

Lemmens=Sherrington, see SHERRINGTON.

Lemmoné, John, flutist and composer, born at Ballarat, Victoria, Australia, June 22, 1862. His father is an Ionian, born a British subject, and his mother is English. He had to depend much upon his own efforts in the way of musical education ; but learnt much from artists visiting the country. He has toured through Australia, New Zealand, India, China, and Japan. Was associated with Madame Amy Sherwin, 1889 ; with Madame Patey, 1891, on their tours almost round the world. He visited London in 1894, and made a successful *début* at the Erard Rooms, October 25. Since then he has been heard in the principal concerts in London and the provinces ; has toured with Madame Patti, etc., and established himself as an artist of the first rank. In March, 1897, he returned to Australia. He has composed many romances, fantasias, etc., for his instrument, and has some reputation as a violoncellist.

Lemon, John, amateur composer, born at Truro in 1754. He entered the army and became a lieutenant-colonel, and also entered Parliament as member for Cornish constituencies. He died at Polvellen, near Looe, April 5, 1814. Composer of chants and other sacred music.

Leng, Robert, musician of first half of

present century, who lived at Malton in Yorkshire, issued "Original Sacred Melodies, containing several psalm tunes of various metres, together with an anthem and Hallelujah chorus set to the words ' Behold what manner of Love, etc.,' . . . The whole is arranged for four voices . . . The composer who labours under a great deprivation, namely, the loss of sight, is self-taught," Leeds, etc, 4 parts, 1847-49. Title-pages vary.

Lenton, John, composer, who flourished in the latter half of the 18th century. He was a member of the private bands of William and Mary, and Queen Anne. He died in 1719.

WORKS.—The Gentleman's Diversion, or the Violin explained, 1693 ; A Consort of Musick, in three parts, 1694. *Music for* Venice preserved, 1685 ; The Ambitious Stepmother, 1700 ; Tamburlain, 1702 ; The fair Penitent, 1703, etc. Songs in contemporary collections.

Leo, Rosa, vocalist, mezzo-soprano, born in London, of English parents ; studied singing at the London Academy of Music, and elocution under the late Mrs. Stirling. While yet a student, was engaged by Mrs. German Reed for her entertainment at St. George's Hall. Then went to Florence, and studied for some time under Luigi Vannuccini, and on her return was engaged to create the title-role in Lecocq's opera, "Manola," at the Strand Theatre, 1882. She made her *début* in concerts at the Covent Garden Promenade Concerts, and appeared at the Ballad Concerts in 1884. Since these she has been engaged for many concerts in London and the provinces, and latterly has been distinguished for her artistic vocal recitals, making a speciality of the best modern songs by French and English composers, and being supported by instrumentalists of high standing.

Leonard, William A., author of " Music in the Western Church, a lecture on psalmody . . . London, 1872 : " The Christmas Festival, with a selection of carols," London, n.d.

Leslie, Fred, professional name of FREDERICK HOBSON, baritone singer and burlesque actor, was born at Woolwich, April 1, 1855. Son of Charles Hobson, military outfitter there. He was originally engaged in commercial pursuits in London, but frequently took part in amateur theatricals. In February, 1878, he adopted the stage as a profession, and obtained his first engagement from Miss Kate Santley, at the Royalty Theatre, London. He afterwards appeared in operatic and burlesque pieces at the Alhambra, Globe, Comedy, and Gaiety Theatres in London. In 1881, he appeared in America, and in 1888 went to Australia. He also played in the English provinces, and in Scotland. Among the pieces in which he took a leading part may be named :—Mefistofele II. ; Rip Van Winkle

LESLIE.

(1882); Madame Favart (1882); Manteaux Noirs (1882); Beggar Student (1884); Little Jack Sheppard (1886-88); Monte Cristo (1888); Miss Esmeralda (1888); Cinder-Ellen (1891); Ruy Blas (1891), etc. For the text of some of these, Leslie was responsible. He died at London, December 7, 1892.

Besides writing some dramatic works he wrote a few songs and other pieces. *See* "Reminiscences of Fred Leslie, by W. T. Vincent," London, 2 vols., 1894.

Leslie, Henry David, conductor and composer, born in London, June 18, 1822. Studied under Charles Lucas, from 1838, and for some time played as an amateur violoncellist in the band of the Sacred Harmonic Society. When the Amateur Musical Society was formed, in 1847, he was appointed Hon. Sec., and from 1855 to 1861, when the Society was dissolved, he was its conductor. The famous choir, with which his name was so intimately associated, originated with Joseph Heming, who for many years acted as chorusmaster. The first concert was given in the Hanover Square Rooms, May 22, 1856. Mr. Leslie continued to conduct the concerts up to July 12, 1880, when the choir was disbanded. He went with the choir to Paris, in 1878, and gained the first prize in the International competition. The choir was resuscitated in 1882, with Mr. Randegger as conductor, and Leslie as president. The latter again assumed the direction in 1885, and gave concerts to May, 1887. In 1863 he undertook the conductorship of the Hereford Philharmonic Society, an office he retained until 1889. He was also connected with the short-lived National College of Music, 1864; and the Guild of Amateur Musicians, 1874. Retiring to an estate which he possessed at Bryn Tanat, near Oswestry, he did much to promote musical culture in the locality, and originated the Oswestry Festivals in 1879. He died, February 4, 1896.

WORKS. — *Oratorios :* Immanuel, 1853; Judith, Birmingham Festival, 1858. *Cantatas :* Holyrood, 1860; Daughter of the Isles, 1861; Biblical Pastoral, The First Christian Morn, Brighton Festival, 1880. Festival anthem, Let God arise, for soli, chorus, and orchestra, 1849; Morning service in D, etc. *Operas :* Romance, or Bold Dick Turpin, 1857; Ida, 1864. How sweet the moonlight sleeps; My soul to God, my heart to thee; The Pilgrims, and other part-songs. Editor of Choral Music, Novello; Little Songs for Little Folks, Cassell. Trio, Memory. My darling. Hush!; Flower girl; Mountain Maid, and other songs. Symphony in F, London, March 24, 1848; Symphony, Chivalry, Crystal Palace, December 17, 1881; Dramatic overture, The Templar, 1852. Quintet, pf. and wind; pieces for pf., etc.

LEVEY.

Leslie, James, Scottish musician, was an itinerating teacher of psalmody in Morayshire at the end of last and beginning of the present century. He compiled "A Collection of Psalm and Hymn Tunes selected from the best authors, by James Leslie, teacher of church music, Fochabers," Elgin, 1810. Engraved by Johnson, Edinburgh, 42 pp.

Levenston, P. M., violinist, and musical director at the Queen's Theatre, Dublin, is the composer of a Burlesque Opera, "Doctor Faust," produced at that theatre, May, 1892.

Leveridge, Richard, bass vocalist and composer, was born in 1670. He sang in opera at Drury Lane and Queen's Theatres, 1705-12; at Lincoln's Inn Fields and Covent Garden, 1713-30. He died at London, March 22, 1758.

WORKS.—Music for the Island Princess, or the Generous Portuguese, 1699; Pyramus and Thisbe, 1716; Collection of Songs, with the music, London, 1727, 2 vols., with frontispiece engraved by Hogarth. New Book of Songs, engraven, printed, and published for Richard Leveridge, London, n.d.

Leveridge is known only as a song-writer, though he has been credited with the composition of the much-discussed "Macbeth" music, on the authority of a notice in Rowe's edition of Shakespeare. The well-known songs "All in the downs" and the "Roast Beef of Old England" very fairly illustrate the style of his works.

Levesque, P., musician, was organist of St. Andrew's, Enfield. Compiled "Sacred Harmony, a new collection of psalmody in three parts.." London [1810].

Levett, English writer and composer, who flourished in London during the latter part of the 18th century. He wrote "Introductory Lessons in Singing, particularly on psalmody, to which are annexed several psalm tunes," London, n.d. Hymns for Easter, Christmas, etc.

Levey, William Charles, composer and conductor, born in Dublin, April 25, 1837. Studied under his father (noticed below), and from 1852, in Paris, under Auber, Thalberg, and Prudent. While there he was elected a member of the Societé des Auteurs et Compositeurs. On his return to London he held positions as conductor at Covent Garden; Drury Lane, 1868-74; and again, later; Haymarket, Princess's, and Adelphi, etc. He died in London, August 18, 1894.

WORKS.—Operas, etc.: Fanchette, Covent Garden, January 4, 1864; Claude; Nazarille; Punchinello, Her Majesty's, December 28, 1864; Fashion; Wanted a Parlour Maid; Music to Antony and Cleopatra; Amy Robsart; Rebecca; King o' Scots; Lady of the Lake; Esmeralda; Jack in the Box, etc. Music to various pantomimes. *Cantatas :*

LEVY.

The Man of War; Robin Hood (for boys voices); The Ride to Ware (humorous). Many songs: Esmeralda; Here stands a post; Unfading beauty; King and the beggar maid; Maritana, gay Gitana; Lullaby, etc. Pieces for pf., etc. Irish overture for orchestra.

His father, RICHARD MICHAEL LEVEY, born in Dublin, October 2, 1811, violinist, was apprenticed to James Barton, leader at the Theatre Royal, Dublin, in 1826. In 1830 he succeeded to the post, and was afterwards musical director. On his fiftieth anniversary of office he received a handsome testimonial. As a violinist he was well known at the Crystal Palace Handel Festivals, etc. He was also professor of the violin at the Royal Irish Academy of Music, and is still living. The violinist known as " Paganini Redivivus " is his son, RICHARD M. LEVEY. He first appeared in Paris, in 1850, and was for some time principal violin at Muzard's Concerts at the Hôtel d' Osmond. Then he came to London, and at the Royal Polytechnic Institution, gave a weird impersonation entitled " Paganini's Ghost." He has given recitals in the provinces and on the continent, but no particulars are available concerning his biography.

Levy, Isaac, cornet player, for many years a favourite at the Promenade concerts at Covent Garden and elsewhere. He has resided in America at different times. but reappeared at the Westminster Aquarium in 1887. Later it was stated that he had been naturalized as a citizen of the United States of America. He is author of a Popular Cornet Tutor.

Lewis, Eric, vocalist and composer of present time. He has appeared on the stage as the Duke in Osmond Carr's musical farce, " In Town," 1892, etc. His sketches, " A Round of Visits," produced at Brighton Aquarium, 1882; and " A Water Pic-nic," German Reed, 1884; with an operetta, are his principal works. He has also written a glee, etc.

Lewis, James Henry, organist and didactic writer, born at Great Malvern, February 23, 1856. Chorister, St. Peter's, Malvern; organist at St. Cuthbert's Episcopal Church, Hawick, N.B.; Parish Church, West Hartlepool; St. Peter's, Staines, Middlesex; and of Parish Church, Twickenham, from •1889. Conductor of Hartlepool Philharmonic; Staines Orchestral Society. Warden of the Church Choir Guild, London, the proceedings of which lie beyond the scope of this work. He is author of Elements of Music; Counterpoint in Catechetical Form; Double Counterpoint and Fugue, all published by Novello. He has published some Church music, etc.

Lewis, Thomas, author of " Organ building and bell founding," London, 1878.

Lewis, Thomas C., musician, who flour-

LIDDLE.

ished about 1840-60. He edited " Lewis' Times," a periodical, from 1852, and issued " The Cornopeanist," being a selection of airs . . . London [1854], and on a similar plan, works entitled " The Flautist," and " The Violinist."

Lewys, Dyved, tenor vocalist, born, March 28, 1865, at Llanerwys, Carmarthen, of musical parentage. His talent was manifest at an early age, and while yet a boy he carried off prizes for singing, and as conductor, at local Eisteddfodau. When eighteen, as a member of the Orpheus Glee Club, he sang before Adelina Patti, at Craig-y-nos, and, upon that distinguished artists' advice, decided upon adopting the profession of music, and entered the R.A.M. He soon became one of the leading Welsh tenors, and besides winning innumerable prizes at Eisteddfodau, sang in many important concerts in London and the provinces. He conducted the Welsh Festivals at St. Paul's Cathedral on several occasions; toured in the U.S.A., in 1893, appearing at the Chicago Exhibition, where he was the recipient of many tokens of success.

Leybourne, George, comic singer, who was well-known in London and provincial music-halls as a delineator of the heavy swell variety of character. He called himself the " Lion Comique," and introduced or sang such songs as " Champagne Charlie," " Up in a balloon," " She danced like a fairy," and " Lancashire Lass," etc. He died in London, September 15, 1884.

Lichfield, Henry, composer of the 16th and 17th centuries, who published " The First Set of Madrigals of Five Parts, apt both for viols and voyces." London, 1613.

An edition of his madrigal, " All ye that sleepe in pleasure," was issued in 1893, under the care of W. B. Squire.

Liddle, John Shepherd, organist and conductor. Graduated Mus. Bac., 1876, Cambridge. Organist successively of Clewer Parish Church, 1872; Halifax Parish Church, 1883; Newbury Parish Church, 1884, to present time, Conductor of Newbury Choral Society, and Orchestral Union; Avon Vale Musical Society; English Ladies' Orchestral Society; Wallingford Philharmonic. In 1896 he succeeded August Manns, as conductor of the Handel Society, London. He has given many concerts, but hitherto has not published any compositions.

JOHN S. LIDDLE, was organist at Newcastle-on-Tyne, first at St. Andrew's, for 8 years; then at St. Peter's, for 9 years. From 1863 to 1884 he was organist of the Parish Church, St. Neots, Hunts, where he died, March 30, 1884, aged 60 years.

Liddle, Robert William, organist, born at Durham, March 14, 1864. Chorister at St. Oswald's, Durham; then at the Cathedral.

LIDDLE.

Studied under Dr. Armes. Appointed organist of St. Baldred's, North Berwick, December, 1885; and organist and choirmaster, Southwell Minster, 1888. He has composed some church music.

Liddle, William Henry, organist and composer. Graduated Mus. Bac., 1891, Durham. Appointed organist to the Chapel Royal, Windsor Great Park, 1876; Parish Church, Basingstoke, 1883. Organist to H.R.H. Prince Christian, 1875. Conductor of Basingstoke Harmonic Society. His compositions include Psalm 96, for soli, chorus, and orchestra; a cantata, "Horsa," produced, Basingstoke, April 30, 1889, etc.

Lidgey, C. A., pianist and composer of present time. Has given concerts in London. His works include a setting of Browning's "Women and Roses," for chorus and orchestra, produced at the Crystal Palace, October 31, 1891; an orchestral ballade, "A Day Dream," the same, October 15, 1892; a number of songs (from Shelley, Heine, etc.); and a ballade, op. 3, for two pianofortes.

Light, Edward, musician of end of last and beginning of present century. Author of "The Art of playing the Guitar, to which is annexed a selection of the most familiar lessons, divertissements, songs, airs, etc.," 1795. "Concise Instructions for playing on the English Lute," London. "Introduction to the art of playing on the Harp-lute, and Apollo Lyre." "A First Book, or master and scholar's assistant, being a treatise on..Music, London [1785]. Various collections of arrangements for guitar; Songs, etc.

Lilley, G. Herbert, author of "The Therapeutics of Music," London, 1880, and composer of hymns, etc.

Lillycrop, Rev. Samuel, musician and writer, was originally a music teacher in Exeter early in the present century, but afterwards became a Baptist minister at Windsor, where he lived from about 1850 to 1870. He died in 1870, and is buried in the Spital cemetery at Windsor. Author of "Theoretical and practical Thorough-bass, exemplified in a plain and easy ma ner," London, n.d.

Limpus, Richard D., organist and musician, born on September 10, 1824. Son of Richard Limpus, organist of Isleworth Old Church, who died on November 1, 1868. Founded, with others, the College of Organists, 1864. Secretary to College of Organists, 1864-75. Died on March 15, 1875. Composer of songs and pf. music. His wife, who died, London, January 29, 1889, was a concert vocalist. His brother, the Rev. F. HENRY LIMPUS, was some time minor canon of St. George's Chapel, Windsor, and composer of an oratorio, "The Prodigal Son," London, May 10, 1870; Songs, etc. He died in 1893.

Lincoln, Henry John, lecturer on music,

LINCOLN.

critic, pianist and organist, born in London, October 15, 1814. Son of the organ-builder, H. C. Lincoln. Began his musical studies at an early age with the pianoforte, and was an organ pupil of Thomas Adams, for whom he frequently acted as deputy at St. Dunstan's, Fleet Street. He was appointed to Christ Church, Woburn Square, and in 1817, elected a member of the Royal Society of Musicians. He did not retain his post at Christ Church many years, owing to other claims upon his time. In 1846 he became associated with the *Daily News*, as secretary; and on the retirement of Mr. George Hogarth, in 1866, succeeded to the position of musical critic, retaining this office until 1886. The last Festival he attended was that held in Birmingham, in 1882, when Gounod's "Redemption" was produced. He began his career as a lecturer at Crosby Hall, in 1843, where he gave an annual series for some years. He also lectured at the London Institution; the Philsophical Institution, Edinburgh; Glasgow; Manchester; Liverpool, etc. His subjects included Bach, Handel, Haydn, Mozart, Cherubini, Cimarosa, Rossini, Spohr, Weber, Mendelssohn; also German song; German and French opera; the Operatic overture, etc. Vocal and instrumental illustrations were given by the Misses Lincoln, Miss Orger, and many eminent artists. In the lecture on Mendelssohn, at the Western Literary Institution, December 23, 1845, his Violin Concerto was played, for the first time in England, by Herr Kreutzer (a relative of Rodolphe Kreutzer), with Mr. Lincoln at the pianoforte. For the last few years he has lived in complete retirement. He edited "The Practical Organist" (six numbers of organ music, by Adolph Hesse); and arranged "The Organist's Anthology," a series of movements from classical compositions, in twelve numbers, published in 1839. He also contributed a few articles to Grove's Dictionary of Music and Musicians.

His eldest sister, MARIANNE LINCOLN, soprano vocalist, was born in London, in 1822. Her early progress in music led to her entering the R.A.M., in 1840, where she studied under Crivelli, Benedict, and G. A. Macfarren. Immediately on leaving she made a tour in Germany, and sang at the Leipzig Gewandhaus, December 12, 1844, and again the following month. On her return she was made an Associate of the R.A.M. She there continued her profession until her marriage with Mr. Edmund Harper (*q.v.*), when she removed to Hillsborough in Ireland. She took the leading parts in the private operatic performances organised by the Duchess of Downshire. She died at Sydenham, October 6, 1885. Her younger sister was married to Mr. H. C. Lunn (*q.v.*).

Lind, William, author of "A popular account of Ancient Musical Instruments," London, Clarke, 1897.

Lindley, Robert, violoncellist and composer, born at Rotheram, March 4, 1777. He studied the violin and 'cello, and became 'cellist at Brighton Theatre. He was principal 'cellist at the Opera, London, 1794-1851. He played at all the principal provincial and other festivals, generally in company with Dragonetti, the double-bass player. He died at London, June 13, 1855.

WORKS.—Three duetts for violin and violoncello, [1802] ; another set, op. 12 [1806]. Five sets of duets, for 2 violoncellos, op. 1 [1795] ; Op. 3 ; Op. 4 ; Op. 8, and Op. 14. Trio for bassoon, tenor, and 'cello, op. 7. Six easy solos for a 'cello and bass, op. 9. Fantasia for violoncello, first string, op. 18. Handbook for the Violoncello, London [1855]. Songs, etc.

His son, WILLIAM (born, 1802 ; died, Manchester, August 12, 1869), was a violinist of some repute in his day, and his brother, CHARLES, who died in December, 1842, was also a violoncellist, and played at the Philharmonic and Ancient Concerts.

Lindsay, Christopher, Scottish musician and writer. Brother of Lady Anne Barnard, Member of the Choir of St. Paul's Cathedral. Author of "A Scheme showing the Distance of Intervals," London, 1793.

Lindsay, Miss, see BLISS, MRS. J. W.

Lindsay, Thomas, author of "Elements of Flute-playing, according to the most approved principles of Modern Fingering," London, 1828. Mélanges for the flute and pf., and other arrangements.

Ling, William, composer, pianist, and teacher, who flourished about the end of .last and beginning of present century. Composer of op. 1, Three sonatas for harpsichord or pf. [1790] ; Op. 2, Duets for two flutes ; Divertimentos for pf., opp. 6, 7, 8 ; Sonatas for pf., opp. 12, 13 ; Serenade, op. 17, etc.

Lingard, Frederick, organist and composer, born at Manchester, in 1811. He studied music under Harris, of Manchester, and became organist of St. George's Church, Hulme. In 1835 he was lay-vicar of Durham Cathedral, a post he held till his death, at Durham, on July 4, 1847. He issued "Antiphonal Chants for the Psalter," 1843, and composed anthems, chants, etc.

Linley, Francis, composer and organist, was born at Doncaster in 1774. Blind from birth. He studied under Mather, of Doncaster, and became organist of Pentonville Chapel, London. Married to a blind lady of fortune. Opened music-selling business. Became bankrupt, and was deserted by his wife. He went to America as an organist, but returned to England in 1799, and died at Doncaster, September 15, 1800.

WORKS.—Sonatas for pf. and flute, op. 1 ; Practical Introduction to the Organ, in five parts, London [1800]. Collection of Interludes, fugues, etc., for organ, op. 6 ; Thirty-two familiar airs for 2 flutes [1790], and other music for the flute ; Songs.

Linley, George, poet and composer, born at Leeds in 1798. Died at London, Sept. 10, 1865.

WORKS.—*Operas and Operettas :* La Poupée de Nuremberg, Covent Garden, 1861 ; Law versus Love, comedietta, 1862 ; The Toy Makers, 1861 ; Francesca Doria. 1849. The Jolly Beggars, cantata (Burns). Songs of the Camp, 12 pieces. Selection of Scottish Melodies (with C. G. Byrne), 1840. Songs of the Troubadours, London, 1830 ; Selection of original hymn tunes. *Songs and Ballads :* Alice ; Bonnie New Moon ; Bird of Beauty ; Beautiful Brunette ; Ballad Singer ; By the spangled starlight ; Clara ; Chide no more ; Constance ; Dream no more of that sweet time ; Gipsy mother ; Hetty ; Hear me but once ; Ianthe ; I cannot mind my wheel ; I'm the little flower girl ; Jeanie ; Love me little, love me long ; My own happy home ; Mariner's wife ; Maid of the Rhine ; Minnie ; Queen of the fairy dance ; Some one to love ; Sweet village rose ; Star and water-lily ; Thou art gone from my gaze ; Under the vine tree. Part-songs, trios, duets.

Linley also wrote the words of a large number of songs, and published two satirical poems, "The Musical Cynics of London," London, 1862, an attack on Chorley, the musical critic, and "Modern Hudibras," London, 1864. His son GEORGE (died 1869), published some poetical works.

Linley, Thomas, composer, born at Bath, 1725. He studied under Chilcot and Paradies. Conductor of oratorios and concerts at Bath. Went to London and purchased Garrick's share in Drury Lane Theatre, with Sheridan, 1776. He died at London, November 19, 1795. Buried in Wells Cathedral.

WORKS.—*Operas and musical dramas :* Duenna (Sheridan), 1775 : Camp, 1776 ; Carnival of Venice, 1781 ; Gentle Shepherd, 1781 ; Triumph of Mirth, 1782 ; Spanish Maid, 1783 ; Selima and Azor (from Grétry), 1784 ; Spanish Rivals, 1785 ; Tom Jones, 1785 ; Strangers at home, 1786 ; Love in the East, 1788 ; Robinson Crusoe ; Beggar's opera (new accompaniments, etc.); Songs in "The School for Scandal." Six Elegies for three voices and pf., London, 1770 ; Twelve Ballads ; Canzonets. Numerous glees. single songs, and anthems. "The Posthumous Vocal Works of Thomas and T. Linley, junr," 1800, 2 vols.

Linley, Thomas, composer, son of the above, born at Bath, 1756. He studied under Boyce and his father ; also at Florence under

Nardini. He was acquainted with Mozart. Leader of Bath concerts, and at Drury Lane, London. Drowned at Grimsthorpe, Lincolnshire, August 7, 1778.

WORKS.—Music to the Tempest; Ode on the Witches and Fairies of Shakespeare, 1776; The Song of Moses, oratorio; Accompaniments for wind instruments to "Macbeth" music; Anthems, glees, and songs. The popular setting of the song, "O bid your faithful Ariel fly," in the "Tempest," is by him. His brother, the Rev. OZIAS THURSTON LINLEY (born 1765; died, London, March 6, 1831), was a composer of songs, and other vocal music.

Linley, William, composer, son of Thomas Linley, senior, born at Bath, 1767 (1771). Educated at Harrow. He studied under Abel and his father. Appointed to post in East India Company's Service, by Fox. Resided in India for a time. He died at London, May 6, 1835.

WORKS.—Shakespeare's Dramatic Songs, consisting of all the songs, duets, and choruses, in character, as introduced in his Dramas.. with an Introduction, London, 2 vols., 1815-16. Two operas. Glees, etc. He also wrote novels and other literary works.

Linley, Eliza Ann, the "MAID OF BATH," soprano vocalist, daughter of Thomas Linley, senior, born at Bath, in 1754. She was trained by her father, and sang at the Bath concerts, and in London, Worcester, Hereford, and Gloucester Festivals. She eloped with and married R. B. Sheridan in 1773. She died at Bristol, June 28, 1792.

Linley, Maria, soprano vocalist, third daughter of T. Linley, born at Bath, about 1764. Sang at Bath, etc. She died at Bath, September 5, 1784.

Linley, Mary, soprano vocalist, second daughter of T. Linley, born at Bath, in 1756, 1759 (?). Sang at Bath, Hereford Festival, 1771, etc. Married Richard Tickell in 1780. She died at Clifton, July 27, 1787.

Linter, Ricardo, pianist and composer, was born in Devonshire about 1815. In 1862 he went to Cheltenham, and became a successful teacher and pianist. He held the position of organist of St. James' and St. Luke's Churches, Cheltenham. Died at Cheltenham, February 6, 1886. Composer of a large number of polkas, quadrilles, variations on airs, and other works for pf. Songs, and other vocal music.

Linwood, Mary, composer, born in Birmingham in 1755, died at Leicester, March 2, 1845. Composed "David's First Victory," oratorio, London [1840]. The Kellerin, and The White Wreath, MS. operas. Songs, and other vocal music. She was celebrated for her fine needlework, of which she gave exhibitions in 1770, 1778, and 1798.

Lisley, John, composer, known only as the composer of a 6-part madrigal, "Faire Citharea presents hir doves," in the "Triumphs of Oriana," 1601.

Liston, Rev. Henry, writer and inventor, born in 1771. Minister of Ecclesmachan, Linlithgow, from 1793. He died at Merchistonhall, February 24, 1836. Author of "An Essay on Perfect Intonation," London, 1812. He invented an Enharmonic Organ, which was performed on in Edinburgh, and his system was applied to several other instruments, though unsuccessfully, owing to the great number of pedals, and the difficulties consequently attending manipulation. His son, ROBERT, was the famous surgeon.

Lithgow, William Hume, composer, teacher, and conductor, was born at Leith, on February 15, 1806. He studied in Edinburgh and London, and became precentor of St. Enoch's Parish Church, Glasgow, and music-master at the High School, in 1842. He died at Glasgow, August 22, 1874. Compiler of "Parochial Sacred Music, being a selection of the best ancient and modern psalm and hymn-tunes, etc. . . . Intended for the use of St. Enoch's Church, Glasgow," . . . Glasgow, n.d. [c. 1845]. "A Selection of Sacred Music, with accompaniments for the organ or pianoforte," Glasgow, n.d. He also composed a number of songs, "Old Scotland, I love thee," etc., and about 50 psalm and hymn-tunes.

Litolff, Henry Charles, composer and pianist, born in London, February 6, 1818. His father was a native of Alsace, taken prisoner by the English in the Peninsular war, who settled in London as a violinist. His mother was Irish. Litolff studied the pianoforte under Moscheles, and made his *début* at his master's concert, Covent Garden Theatre, July 24, 1832. In 1835 he married, against his parents' wish, and went to reside in France. He gave concerts in various places, toured in Germany, 1845-6, gaining the title of "The English Liszt." He played at the Leipzig Gewandhaus several times from November 28, 1844, to February 7, 1856. In 1851 he entered upon the music business of Meyer, of Brunswick, which he transferred to his son, Theodor, in 1860. From 1861 he resided chiefly in Paris; and died at Colombe, near that city, August 5, 1891. In 1882, a Festival in his honour was held at Angers.

WORKS.—*Operas :* Der Braut vom Kynast, 1847; Rodrique de Tolède; Les Templiers, written about 1865; produced, Brussels, January, 1886; The Flying Squadron of the Queen, Paris, 1888; and King Lear, finished in 1890, and found among his papers after his death. Five Symphony-concertos, for pf. and orchestra. Overtures, Robespierre; Les Girondins; Das Welfenlied; Chant des Belges.

LITTLE.

Quartet, strings ; Three Trios, pf. and strings ; and a number of pieces for pf. He was a man of genius, and his works abound with beautiful ideas ; but the workmanship is frequently faulty, and in value his compositions are very unequal.

Little, Edgar E., tenor vocalist and composer, resident in Dublin. Was for some time in the Chapel Royal Choir, Dublin Castle. He is the composer of a comedy opera, "The Warlock," produced, Dublin, February, 1892 ; also "Victoire," a military comedy (both books by Alfred Smythe), produced at Leinster Hall, Dublin, April 17, 1893, with much success. Mr. Little is an amateur of considerable attainments, and holds an appointment in the Bank of Ireland.

Little, Henry Walmsley, organist and composer, born in London, September 12, 1853. Studied at R.A.M., under G. A. Macfarren, C. Steggall, H. C. Banister, and F. B. Jewson, 1872-8. F.C.O., 1875 ; Mus. Bac., 1877 ; Mus. Doc., 1885, Oxford ; F.R.A.M., 1884. Organist of Church of the Annunciation, Chislehurst, 1871 ; Christ Church, Woburn Square, 1874 ; St. Matthew's, Denmark Hill, 1880 ; St. Giles-in-the-Fields, 1881 ; and of Holy Trinity, Tulse Hill, from 1886. Examiner for R.C.O. ; Trinity College, London ; and the Incorporated Society of Musicians. Associate of the Philharmonic Society. Has given concerts and organ recitals at Gresham Hall, etc. His compositions include cantatas, "The Rock of Israel," produced, February, 1887 ; and "Great is the Lord" (both in MS.). Church services, anthems. Part-songs, etc. He has also composed some pieces for orchestra (in MS.) ; and published a Suite de Pièces, and other works for pf.

Livingston, James R., writer and composer, native of Aberdeenshire. Resided in Glasgow from 1844. Author of "The Organ Defended : being an essay on the use of that instrument in Public Worship, with strictures on ' Phinehas Vocal's ' attack on the Organ and Dr. Anderson." Glasgow, n.d. [c. 1857]. Reply to a pamphlet entitled "Dr. Anderson as an Organist," by Phinehas Vocal, Glasgow, n.d. Composer of anthems, songs, etc.

Livingston, Rev. Neil, clergyman, was Free Church minister of Stair, in Ayrshire, from 1844 to 1886. Editor of a reprint of "The Scottish Metrical Psalter, of A.D. 1635, with copious dissertations and Notes," Glasgow, 1864.

Llanover, Lady, art patroness, daughter of Benjamin Waddington, Esq., of Llanover, was born March 21, 1802. Married, December 24, 1823, to Mr. Hall, of Hensal Castle, subsequently Sir Benjamin Hall, and Lord Llanover (died April 27, 1867). Lady Llanover revived the ancient glory of the Eisteddfod,

LLOYD.

and was a prize winner herself, for an essay, at Cardiff, in 1834. In 1838, she brought out, in conjunction with Miss Jane Williams, of Aberpergwym. a collection of Welsh Airs. Further, to promote the national music, she invited a meeting of Welsh harpers in 1869, to compete for a triple harp. She died at Llanover, January 17, 1896.

Llinos, see WILLIAMS, MARIA JANE.

Lloyd, Charles Francis, composer, born in Chester, October 7, 1852. Son of John Ambrose Lloyd (q.v.). Graduated Mus. Bac., Oxford, 1878. Appointed organist of Parish Church, Beaumaris, at the age of sixteen, and four years later, organist and director of the choir of Tynemouth Parish Church. Conductor of Tynemouth Philharmonic Society, 1879-91, and South Shields Choral Society, 1883-91. In the latter year he resigned these appointments, and has since devoted himself to composition. Adjudicator at Royal National Eisteddfod of Wales, and some time musical critic of the *Newcastle Daily Chronicle.* Composer of a Concert overture in F (National Eisteddfod, 1893) ; Orchestral suite in F (1894). Church services, anthems, part-songs. Prize Cycling Song (1891), and numerous songs, "Dearie" ; "Were I the streamlet" ; "The Chords of Life," etc., many of which have met with wide acceptance.

Lloyd, Charles Harford, organist and composer, born at Thornbury, Gloucestershire, October 16, 1849. Educated at Thornbury Grammar School, and Rossall School. Thence to Magdalen Hall (now Hertford College), Oxford, where he held an open classical scholarship. Graduated Mus. Bac., 1871 ; B.A., 1872 ; M.A., 1875 ; and Mus. Doc., 1891, Oxford. In 1876, he was appointed organist of Gloucester Cathedral ; in 1882, of Christ Church Cathedral, Oxford ; and in 1892, succeeded Joseph Barnby as precentor and musical instructor at Eton College. He was a founder, and first president of the Oxford University Musical Club ; conductor of the Gloucester Festivals of 1877 and 1880 ; and is still conductor of the Oxford Symphony Concerts.

WORKS.—*Cantatas :* Hero and Leander, produced, Worcester Festival, 1884 ; The Song of Balder, Hereford, 1885 ; Andromeda, Gloucester, 1886 ; A Song of Judgment, Hereford, 1891 ; Sir Ogie and the Lady Elsie, Hereford, 1894. Music to Alcestis, Oxford, 1887. The Gleaner's Harvest, cantata for female voices. Full Cathedral Service in E flat ; anthems, etc. Pastoral, The Rosy Dawn, Leeds Festival, 1889 ; 8-part chorus, To Morning, Worcester, 1890 ; part-songs, songs, etc. Sonata in D minor, organ ; pieces for clarinet and pf., etc.

Lloyd, Edward, tenor vocalist, born in London, March 7, 1845. Son of Richard Lloyd (noticed later), and Louisa, his wife,

LLOYD.

born Hopkins (*q.v.*). Chorister at Westminster Abbey under James Turle, leaving at fifteen, and after a year passed at a school at Southwark, joined his mother at Cheltenham, where he remained until 1865. He then sang at a church in Belsize Park, London, for a short time, obtaining an appointment at Trinity College, Cambridge in 1866. A year later he went to St. Andrew's, Wells Street, London, and shortly afterwards was appointed a Gentleman of the Chapel Royal, St James's, an office he resigned in a few years. He was now becoming known as a concert singer, taking part in the performance of Beethoven's Choral Fantasia at the Oratorio Concerts, March 9, 1870. His first great opportunity came with the Gloucester Festival of 1871, when he distinguished himself in Bach's Matthew Passion. He has sung at every meeting of the Three Choirs since that time save the years 1875, 6, and 9, while his connection with the Norwich Festivals dates from 1872. He has been principal tenor at the Leeds Festivals since 1874 ; and has sung at every Birmingham Festival from 1876. At other Festivals and Concerts he has been constantly heard, and has created the tenor part in most of the great works of recent times. As a singer of Wagner's music he is unsurpassed. He has visited America on several occasions, from the Cincinnati Festival of 1888, and has sung in Brussels and Paris.

His father, RICHARD LLOYD, born at Vauxhall, March 12, 1813, was a tenor singer of repute, and became a vicar choral of Westminster Abbey. He died, June 28, 1853. HENRY LLOYD, a younger brother of Edward, appeared as a tenor singer for a short time 1889-90; and E. TURNER LLOYD, son of Edward Lloyd, studied pianoforte under Madame Schumann, and singing under F. Walker; appeared as a vocalist ; toured in America, 1892-3 ; and is now a professor of singing at the R.A.M.

Lloyd, George, musician, who published "Peninsular Melodies," London, 1830, 2 vols.

Lloyd, John Ambrose, composer, born at Mold, Flintshire, June 14, 1815. Father of Charles Francis Lloyd (*q.v.*). Though in the main self-taught, he gained the reputation of being the most refined Welsh composer of his day. His cantata, " The Prayer of Habakkuk " (1851), was the first work of its class produced in Wales ; his anthem, " The Kingdom of the Earth " (Eisteddfod Prize, 1852), is still the most popular anthem in Wales; and his part-song, " The Last Flower," is looked upon as a Welsh classic. In 1843 he published a collection of Hymntunes ; and a second, " The Praise Offering," in 1873. Several of his hymn-tunes were awarded prizes. He often acted as adjudicator at the National Eisteddfodau. Died at Liverpool, September 14, 1874.

LOCKEY.

Lloyd, John, Frederick, musician, compiler of "The Parochial Psalmist, or a selection of Psalms and Hymns," Dublin [1845]; 2nd ed., 1848 ; 3rd ed., 1850.

Locke, Matthew, composer and writer, was born at Exeter in 1632 or 1633. He became a chorister in Exeter Cathedral, and studied music under Edward Gibbons and W. Wake. Composer in Ordinary to Charles II., 1661. Afterwards he became a Roman Catholic, and was appointed organist to the Queen. He died at London, August, 1677.

WORKS.—Cupid and Death, masque (Shirley), with C. Gibbons, 1653. Little Consort of three parts for viols, 1656. Music for The Stepmother (Stapylton), 1664 ; Davenant's alteration of " Macbeth," 1672 ; Shadwell's " Psyche," 1673 ; and the " Tempest," 1673. Anthems, various, for Chapel Royal. Kyrie and Credo, 1666 (preface defending the work against the opposition which its novel form raised, entitled, " Modern Church Music : Preaccused, censur'd, and obstructed in its performance before his Majesty," April 1, 1666). Reply to Thomas Salmon's " Essay to the Advancement of Music," entitled, " Observations upon a late book entitled, An Essay to the Advancement of Musick, by casting away the perplexity of different clifts and writing all sorts of musick in an Universal character." London, 1672. Reply to Salmon's " Vindication," entitled, " The Present practice of Musick, vindicated against the exception and new way of attaining Musick, lately published by Thomas Salmon, London, 1672. " Melothesia, or certain general Rules for playing upon a continued bass, with a choice collection of Lessons for the Harpsichord or Organ of all sorts," London, 1673. Songs in contemporary collections, as the Theater of Music; The Treasury of Music ; etc.

Lockett, William, organist and composer, was born at Manchester in 1835. He has held the appointments of deputy assistant organist of Manchester Cathedral ; organist of St. John's, Higher Broughton, 1855-61 ; St. Mark's, Cheetham ; Union Chapel, 1877 ; Cross Street Chapel, Manchester ; and conductor of Moston Choral Society. He has composed anthems; Evening, four part song; Merry mountain maid ; Mother's prayer, and other songs.

Lockey, Charles, tenor vocalist, born at Newbury, Berks, 1820. Son of Angel Lockey. Chorister, Magdalen College, Oxford, 1828-36, in which last year he went to Bath to study under Edmund Harris. In 1842, became a pupil of Sir George Smart, and lay-clerk of St. George's, Windsor. Appointed vicarchoral of St. Paul's Cathedral, 1843, but in October, 1842, made his first appearance as an oratorio singer in Rossini's " Stabat Mater," at Store Street Rooms. Was en-

LOCKHART.

gaged for the Ancient Concerts in 1846, and sang at the Birmingham Festival the same year, at the production of Mendelssohn's "Elijah." Also sang at the Three. Choirs Festivals, 1846-56, and at the concerts of the Sacred Harmonic Society. In 1848 was made a Gentleman of the Chapel Royal. Married Miss Martha Williams, contralto singer, May, 1853. An affection of the throat compelled his retirement in 1859. One of the most eminent and popular singers of his day, his early retirement was a public loss. He is now resident at Hastings, and retains, officially, his Cathedral and Chapel Royal appointments.

Lockhart, Charles, organist and composer, born in London, in 1745. He was blind from his infancy, but became organist of the Lock Chapel in 1772 ; St. Katharine Cree ; St. Mary's, Lambeth ; Orange Street Chapel ; and Lock Chapel again in 1790-97. He died at London, February 9, 1815. Composer of " A set of hymn tunes and anthems for three voices," London [1810] ; " An Epithalamium, or nuptial ode " [1770] ; Select and original vocal pieces ; March, in honour of the Lambeth Loyal Association, London [1795] ; Sonatas for harpsichord. Female advice, Rural gift, and other songs. His hymn tune " Carlisle " is included in many modern collections.

Lockwood, Adolphus Raven, harpist, born in London, 1840? Appeared, with his brother and sister, at a concert at the Hanover Square Rooms, February 18, 1848, the three then being pupils of Gerhard Taylor. He soon rose to a high position, but spent the later years of his life in Germany. He played at the Gewandhaus Concerts, Leipzig, December 14, 1876. In 1884 he was created a Royal Chamber Musician, Munich, in which place he died, January 23, 1885, aged 45. His younger brother, ERNEST LOCKWOOD, harpist, was a member of the orchestras of the Philharmonic Society, the Royal Italian Opera, and the Crystal Palace. He played Handel's Concerto for harp at the Crystal Palace, November 28, 1885, and was known as one of the foremost professors of the harp in London. He died, April 21, 1897. MISS LOCKWOOD (the sister ?) was for years harpist to the Carl Rosa Opera Company. She died suddenly at Hanley, Staffs., while on tour, February, 1897.

Loder, Edward James, composer, born at Bath, in 1813. Son of John David Loder. He studied under his father, and at Frankfort, under F. Ries, 1826-28. Returned to England, 1828. Again went to Germany and studied under Ries. Conductor at Princess's Theatre, London ; also at Manchester. He died at London, April 5, 1865.

WORKS.—*Operas :* Nourjahed, July, 1834 ;

LODER.

Dice of Death (Oxenford), 1835 ; Night Dancers, Princess Theatre, 1846 ; Puck, a ballad opera ; Sultan, dramatic piece; Young Guard, 1848 ; Island of Calypso, a masque, 1851 ; Raymond and Agnes, Manchester, 1855 ; Francis the First, 1838 (compilation); Foresters ; or, Twenty-five years since; Deer Stalkers, Scottish opera; Beggar's Opera, revised. Selection of Songs, in 3 books. Dr. Watt's Divine and Moral Songs. Sacred Songs and Ballads, Poetry by D. Ryan. Improved and Select Psalmody. Divine Harmony. Twelve Sacred Songs. Instructions and Exercises on the principles and practice of the art of Singing (Ashdown), n.d. *Songs and Ballads :* Afloat on the Ocean ; Arnold the Armourer ; Bare-footed Friar ; Brave old oak ; Come to the glen ; Columbus ; Come blushing May ; Deep-sea Fisher ; Forester's Bride ; Hermit ; Ivy tree ; I love these merry festive times ; I'll weave a sweet garland; My harp is strung for thee ; My own loved home ; Martin, the man of arms ; O here's to the holly ; Oh, the merry days ; Outlaw ; O speed my bark ; Philip the Falconer ; Rhine song ; Sweet girls of Erin ; Stars of the flowers ; Thou art gone to the grave ; The song of the water king ; The village mill ; Wake, my love ; Where is my loved one ? Part-songs, hymns, and pf. music.

Loder, George, cousin of E. J. Loder, composer and singer, born at Bath, in 1816 ; died at Adelaide, Australia, July 15, 1868. Compiled " The Old House at Home," musical entertainment ; numerous songs ; symphonies ; pf. music, etc.

Loder, John David, violinist and writer, born 1788 ; died February 13, 1846. Author of the " The Modern Art of Bowing exemplified, with exercises in the major and minor scales," London, n.d. ; Violin School, n.d. ; Works for Violin.

Loder's violin school is one of the most popular among recent productions of that nature.

Loder, John Fawcett, violinist and composer, son of above, born at Bath, 1812. Teacher and concert-director at Bath. Leader of orchestra and teacher in London. He died in London, April 16, 1853.

Loder, Kate Fanny, pianist and composer, born at Bath, August 21, 1826, only daughter of George and Fanny Loder. Her musical talent was manifest at a very early age, and when six years old she was placed under a Miss Batterbury. She was then placed with Henry Field, and in 1838 entered the R.A.M. Her teachers were Mrs. Anderson and Charles Lucas. Elected King's Scholar, 1839 ; re-elected 1841. On leaving the Academy in 1844, she was elected Professor of Harmony. She appeared at concerts, Bath, in 1840 ; played at Mrs. Anderson's

LODGE.

LONGHURST.

concert, at Her Majesty's Theatre, May 31, 1844, when Mendelssohn was present to hear her rendering of two movements from his first concerto. First appeared at the Philharmonic Concerts, March 15, 1847, as soloist in Weber's concerto in E flat; and played for the last time in public at the same, March 6, 1854, Mendelssohn's concerto in D minor. On December 16, 1851, she was married to the eminent surgeon (Sir) Henry Thompson. She continued her connection with the R.A.M. for some years after her retirement from the concert platform. Her works include an opera, L'Elisir d' Amore; an overture; two string quartets; a trio for pf. and strings; sonatas for pf., and pf. and violin; pieces for violin; pf. pieces, etc.

Lodge, John, see ELLERTON, JOHN LODGE.

Logan, Edmond, amateur musician and flute player, born about 1804; died Edinburgh January 24, 1865. He was a writer to the Signet in Edinburgh, and acted as musical critic to the *Scotsman* for many years.

Logan, William, amateur violinist and composer, was born in Ayrshire, about 1745. He was a major in the army, and is chiefly notable as a friend of Burns the poet, who addressed an "Epistle" to him beginning "Hail, thairim-inspirin' rattlin' Willie." He composed various dances, etc., contained in John Hall's collection, and elsewhere.

Löhr, Frederick Nicholls, composer, pianist, and conductor, was born at Norwich, in January, 1844. He was a pupil of Dr. Z. Buck. He settled in Plymouth as a teacher and concert-giver, and became organist of Sherwell Chapel, and conductor of the Plymouth Vocal Association. He died at Plymouth, December 18th, 1888. He composed Fairy Music, a cantata for treble voices; Country songs for the children's hour; School songs; Orchestral and pf. music, etc.

Löhr, Richard Harvey, composer, pianist, and organist, born at Leicester, June 13, 1856. Son of Geo. Aug. Löhr, many years organist of St. Margaret's, Leicester. Educated at home, and later at the R.A.M., under Sullivan, Prout, and W. H. Holmes. Won the Lucas medal for composition twice—1877-8. Potter Exhibitioner and Santley Prizeholder, 1879. A.R.A.M. Associate Philharmonic Society and Member of the Royal Society of Musicians. Has acted as organist since the age of ten, and at present holds office at St. James's, Marylebone (Rev. H. R. Haweis). In 1882, began giving concerts in London, and chamber concerts in Leicester; and is in great request as accompanist and as a teacher.

WORKS.—Oratorio, The Queen of Sheba, selection performed St. James', Marylebone, Dec. 13, 1896. Anthems: They that go down (for soprano solo, chorus, and orchestra, 1885);

God, who madest earth and heaven; Watching, praying, waiting, and others. Morning and evening service in C, op. 12; Communion service in A minor. A Border raid, chorus with orchestra (1883), and other part-songs. Album of ten songs, op. 16, etc., etc. Quartet in E minor, op. 15, pf. and strings (produced at a concert given by the composer, June, 1882; published 1889); Ballade in G, op. 3, violoncello and pf.; Duo concertanti, op. 13, pf. and violoncello; Caprice in G, op. 11, Cavatina in B flat, op. 14, violin and pf. The Window, twelve pieces, op. 7, and other compositions for pf. Scales and arpeggios, specially adapted for examinations. Author of Lohr's Primer, catechism of the Rudiments of music, London, Lucas, Weber, and Co., 1882; Principia of music, a complete explanation of the rudiments of music, etc., London, Forsyth, 1890. Editor of London chant Book, 1885.

Lomas, George, organist and composer, born at Birch Hull, Bolton, November 30, 1834. He studied under Steggall, Sterndale Bennett, and J. F. Bridge. He acted as voluntary organist of Didsbury Parish Church, and at Emmanuel Church, Barlow Moor. He graduated Mus. Bac. in 1876. He died October, 18, 1884. Composer of music for the church, the hymn tune "Submission," etc. Song, "Take me to thy heart, dear maiden" (Professor Blackie), composed expressly for Madame Marie Roze.

Long, Samuel, organist and composer of latter part of last century. Among other works he published "Four lessons and two voluntaries for the harpsichord or organ," London [1770]; "Where'er you tread," prize glee, 1764; "Hush the god of love," glee; Psalms in Riley's collection, etc.

Longbottom, T. K., composer, born at Burley, Yorkshire, 1832. He was a teacher and conductor. Died at Bradford, August 15, 1882. Composer of a number of stories with music, such as Alfred the Great, Daniel, David, Elijah, St. Paul; and other vocal music.

Longhurst, John Alexander, vocalist, born in 1809. He studied under John Watson, and first appeared in Bishop's opera, "Henri Quatre," in 1820. He sang at numerous concerts. Died in 1855.

Longhurst, William Henry, organist and composer, born at Lambeth, October 6, 1819. When he was two years old his parents went to reside at Canterbury, and in 1828 he was admitted a chorister in the Cathedral. In 1836 he was appointed assistant organist, master of the choristers, and lay-clerk; and in 1873 succeeded T. E. Jones as cathedral organist. F.C.O., 1865; Mus. Doc., Cantuar, 1875; Toronto, 1886. Musical Lecturer at St. Augustine's College, Canterbury.

LOOSEMORE.

WORKS.—Oratorio, David and Absolom, produced, Canterbury, January 10, 1872; The Village Fair, an Alpine Idyll (words by Jetty Vogel), Canterbury, February 6, 1882. Cathedral service in E; Benedicite in E; chants, etc. Anthems: Blessed is he; Grant to us, Lord; Great is the Lord; The Lord is my strength, and others. Editor of A Collection of Anthems, as performed at Canterbury Cathedral [1845]. Andante piacevole and Tarantella, violin and pf., songs, etc.

Loosemore, George, organist and composer, who flourished in the 17th century. Mus. Bac., Cantab. Chorister in King's College, Cambridge, 1660. Organist of Trinity College, 1660. Doc. Mus., Cantab., 1665. Composed Anthems, mostly preserved in MS.

Loosemore, Henry, organist and composer, father of the above, was a chorister at Cambridge. Organist of King's College, Cambridge. Mus. Bac., Cantab., 1640. Organist of Exeter Cathedral, 1660. He died in 1670. Composer of service and anthems.

His brother, JOHN (1613—April 8, 1681), was an organ-builder, and built the organ of Exeter Cathedral, etc.

Lorimer, John, amateur composer and artist, was born at Paisley, on June 9, 1812. He was an artist and poet, and resided chiefly in Paisley, where he died, on October 13, 1878. He composed a number of psalm tunes, "Crookston," etc., and several humorous songs, the best known being " I'm ower auld to marry noo."

Lott, Edwin Matthew, organist and composer, born at St. Helier, Jersey, January 31, 1836. When ten years of age he was organist of St. Matthew's Church, and held in succession several similar appointments in Jersey. Studied under W. T. Best, 1851-2; F.C.O., 1865. Organist of St. Clement Danes, and other churches in London, 1860-4; returned to Jersey in 1865, and was professor of music in Victoria College, and bandmaster of three regiments. Re-appointed organist of St. Peter's, Bayswater, 1870; organist of St. Ethelburga, Bishopsgate, 1880; and of St. Sepulchre's, Holborn, 1883 to the present time. Mr. Lott has been professor and examiner, Trinity College, London; principal of Musical International College; was made Mus. Doc., *honoris causâ,* Trinity College, Toronto; examiner for the same; and in 1891 appointed to the chair of music. He has written a cantata, "Thus saith the Lord, heaven is my throne"; church services, anthems, etc. "Into the silent land"; "The Fairy wedding," and other songs. Sonata in F; Bourrée; Minuet; Fifty-five finger inventions in all keys, for pf., with about 300 pieces for that instrument. Organ pieces in various styles. He is author of a Pianoforte Catechism; Harmony Catechism; and a Dictionary of Musical Terms, all of which have passed through several editions.

LOWE.

Lott, John Browning, organist and conductor, was a chorister at Canterbury Cathedral under Dr. Longhurst, and afterwards organist successively at the churches of St. Dunstan and St. Paul in that city. The last he left to become assistant organist at the cathedral. He went next to the parish Church, Margate, and while there graduated Mus. Bac., Oxford, 1876. In 1881 he was appointed organist and master of the choristers at Lichfield Cathedral. He conducts the Diocesan Choral Festivals, and is the founder and conductor of the Lichfield Musical Society, which has done important service to music in the locality.

Love, James, conductor, organist, and author, born at Dundee, January 1, 1858. He has been organist of High Church, Falkirk since 1878, and has for many years acted as conductor of the Falkirk and Vale of Leven Choral Societies. Author of "Scottish Church Music, its composers and sources," Edinburgh, 1891, a work of much value and accuracy which is particularly strong in its biographical details.

Lover, Samuel, poet, painter, novelist, and composer, was born at Dublin, February 24, 1797; died at Jersey, July 6, 1868.

WORKS.—Various Novels. Songs and Ballads, London, 1859. *Music to the following plays:* Rory O'More (based on his novel) 1837; White Horse of the Peppers, 1838; Happy man, 1839; Green Boy, 1840; Il Paddy Whack in Italia, 1841; MacCarthy More, 1861. *Songs:* A leaf that reminds me of thee; Angel's whisper; Birth of St. Patrick; Bowld Soger Boy; Fairy Boy; Fairy Tempter; Fisherman; Forgive but don't forget; Four leaved Shamrock; Hour before day; I leave you to guess; Irish mule driver; Land of the west; Letter (the); Low backed car; May dew; Molly Bawn; Molly Carew; My Mother dear; Rory O'More; Saint Kevin; True love can ne'er forget; 'Twas the day of the feast; Can you ever forget; Dove song; Fisherman's daughter; I can ne'er forget thee; Kathleen and the Swallows; Lady mine; Macarthy's grave; O watch you well; Rose, zephyr, and dewdrop; Sally; Say not my heart is cold; That rogue Riley; Voice within; Whistling thief; Widow Machree.

Many of Lover's songs have passed into the Irish national repertory, the "Angel's Whisper," "The Letter," "What will you do love?" and "The Fairy Tempter," being among the best known.

Lowe, C. Egerton, pianist and writer of present time. Studied at Leipzig Conservatorium. Has published Six Album leaves for violin and pf., and is author of a Chronological Cyclopædia of Musicians and Musical Events, London, Weekes, 1896.

Lowe or **Low, Edward,** organist and composer, was born at Salisbury [1615]. He

LOWE.

was a chorister in Salisbury Cathedral, under Holmes. Organist of Christ Church, Oxford, 1630. Organist of Chapel Royal, 1660. Choragus and professor of music, Oxford, 1661-82. He died at Oxford, July 11, 1682.

WORKS.—A short direction for the performance of Cathedrale service, etc., Oxford, 1661. Anthems, etc.

Lowe, Joseph, composer and dancing-master, born at Marykirk, Kincardineshire, in 1797. Son of John Lowe, a dancing-master and composer there. He resided at Brechin, Inverness, etc., and finally settled in Edinburgh, where he died on July 12, 1866. He issued a "Collection of reels, strathspeys, jigs, etc.," Edinburgh, n.d. [c. 1845], and "Royal collection of reels, strathspeys, etc.," Edinburgh, n.d.

Lowe, Thomas, tenor singer, was born early in the 18th century. *Début,* Drury Lane Theatre, September 11, 1748. Sang in Arne's "As you like it"; Handel's oratorios, etc. Appeared at Vauxhall, 1745. Manager of Marylebone Gardens, 1763-68. Sang at Sadler's Wells, 1772. He died on March 1, 1783.

Lowthian, Caroline, MRS. CYRIL A. PRESCOTT, is the composer of a number of songs, Sunshine, etc. Also a Bourrée ; Dance de Ballet, and other pieces for pf.

Luard-Selby, see SELBY.

Lucas, Charles, composer, organist, and conductor, was born at Salisbury, July 28, 1808. Chorister in Salisbury Cathedral, under Corfe, 1815-23. Pupil at R.A.M., under Lindley and Crotch. 1823-30. Member of Queen Adelaide's private band. Conductor at R.A.M., 1832. Organist of Hanover Chapel, Regent Street, 1839. He was occasionally conductor of the Ancient Concerts in 1840-43. Principal 'cello at opera, and provincial Festivals, etc. Member of firm of Addison, Hollier, and Lucas, music-publishers, 1856-65. Principal of R.A.M., 1859-66. He was married to Miss Helen Taylor, the soprano vocalist; who died at London, March 8, 1866. He died at London, March 23, 1869.

WORKS.—The Regicide, opera ; Three symphonies ; Overtures ; Violoncello concerto, etc. *Anthems :* Blessed be the Lord ; Sing, O heavens ; Hosanna ; O Lord, open thou ; O God, the strength ; O thou that dwellest. Magnificat, four voices, in canon, Gresham prize, 1836. Hail to the new-born Spring, glee. Ah, fading joy, madrigal. *Songs :* Clouds from out the sky are driven ; Homeward thoughts ; Poet's consolation. String quartets, unfinished operas, etc.

Lucas, Clarence, composer, born in Canada, 1866, studied at the Conservatoire, Paris, under Theodore Dubois. He has published a number of pieces for pf., and is the composer of the operas, " Anne Hathaway "

LUNN.

and " The Money Spider," the last produced at the Matinée Theatre, Easter Monday, 1897.

Lucome, Emma, *see sub.* REEVES, J. SIMS.

Ludwig, William, bass vocalist, born in Dublin. For many years associated with English opera companies. Toured with Carl Rosa's company in the spring of 1876 ; with the Blanche Cole company in 1879 ; and took the part of *Vanderdecken* in the "Flying Dutchman" in Mr. J. W. Turner's company in Birmingham. He was in America for some time from 1886, joining the American Opera Company in New York, Chicago, etc. He has sung in concérts and operatic recitals at the Crystal Palace and elsewhere ; and in 1896 rejoined the Carl Rosa company, creating the part of *Hans Sachs* in "The Meistersingers," at Manchester, April 16. Also appearing at the Garrick Theatre, London, January, 1897.

Lukis, Rev. William C., author of "An Account of Church Bells," London, 1857.

Lumley, Benjamin, writer and operatic manager, was born in 1812. He was brought up to law, and became solicitor in 1832. Manager of Drury Lane Theatre, 1841-52 and 1856-58. He died at London, March 17, 1875. Lumley produced a number of operas by Donizetti, Verdi, Costa, Halévy, etc., and among the singers who appeared under his management may be named Lind, Cruvelli, Johanna Wagner, Piccolomini, Tietjens, Giuglini, Ronconi, etc. He wrote a work entitled, "Reminiscences of the Opera," Lond., 1864, with portrait.

Lunn, Charles, writer and teacher of singing, born at Birmingham, January 5, 1838. Brother of Rev. J. R. Lunn (*q.v.*). Studied in Italy under Cattaneo, Sangiovanni and Vizone, from 1860. In 1864-5, sang, with success, at Worcester, Cheltenham, etc. In 1867, gave up public singing and devoted himself to voice training, settling in Birmingham. The result of his work was shown in the concerts given for many years in the Town Hall and other places, when large numbers of pupils sang. He began about this time a series of articles in *The Orchestra ;* and, in 1873, contributed to *The Medical Press and Circular.* His principal work, "The Philosophy of Voice," appeared in 1874, and reached its 8th edition in 1896. In 1880, he published a sequel to it, "Vox Populi." He has frequently lectured on the voice, in Birmingham, London, etc., and published a number of pamphlets—Roots of Musical Art ; Vocal Expression ; Conservation and Restoration.; The Artistic Voice ; The Voice and its Training ; The Ascent of Parnassus: or the Teaching of the Future, etc. In 1895 Mr. Lunn removed to London, where he continues his teaching. He is a frequent contributer to the musical press.

LUNN.

Lunn, Henry Charles, critic, pianist and composer, born in London, in 1817. Son of Joseph Lunn, Assistant-Commissary of the Field Train Department of the Ordnance. He entered the R.A.M. in 1835, remaining until 1843, studying under Mudie, W. S. Bennett, and Cipriani Potter. Elected Associate, then Fellow. Was also professor, member of the Committee of Management, and Director, retiring in 1887. From 1863 to 1887 he was editor of the *Musical Times*, to which he contributed many articles, besides notices of the provincial festivals. He married, December 28, 1848, Miss Mary Anne Lincoln, younger sister of Henry J. Lincoln (*q.v.*). From 1887 he lived in retirement, and died. January 23, 1894.

WORKS.—A descriptive essay on the patent Clavic attachment, invented by Robert Brooks, junior, showing its importance in facilitating performance on the violin, 1845 ; Musings of a musician, a series of popular sketches (appeared in the *Musical World*, 1845), London, Simpkin, Marshall & Co., 1846, several editions ; The elements of Music systematically explained, Jefferys, 1849. Compositions for orchestra ; songs, and pf. pieces.

Lunn, Rev. John Robert, clergyman and composer, born at Cleeve Prior, Worcester, March 8, 1831. His father removing to Birmingham in 1834, the son began receiving instruction in organ playing from G. Hollins in 1835, and piano lessons from W. H. Sharman in 1836. He opened an organ at Cleeve Prior in 1838, and generally displayed remarkable musical talent. Educated at King Edward VI. Grammar School; was organist of Edgbaston Parish Church, 1846-7. Heard first performance of " Elijah," and that given in April, 1847, when he wrote down the music of " Cast thy burden " as it was being sung, and received a letter of commendation from Mendelssohn, perhaps the last he penned in England. Entered Cambridge University, 1849, gaining various scholarships. Graduated B.A. (fourth wrangler) 1853 ; M.A., 1856. Ordained Deacon, 1855; Priest, 1856. Was Fellow, and Sadlerian Lecturer, St. John's College ; Sometime President of the University Musical Society, and frequently appearing as pianist at the concerts, introducing Schumann's Concerto, March, 1862, its first performance by an Englishman. Appointed vicar of Marton-cum-Grafton, Yorks., 1863. At the consecration of the new church, January 11, 1876, Schubert's Mass in F was performed, probably for the first time in an Anglican church (*vide* Joseph Short). Has given lectures on musical subjects in several places, and also pianoforte recitals, doing much to make known the works of J. S. Bach.

WORKS.—Oratorio, St. Paulinus of York

LYLE.

(1892, MS.) ; Two Motets, for two choirs and organ ; Motet, Heaven is my throne, eight-part chorus (MS.) ; Service in E, for Holy Eucharist, King's Chapel, Cambridge, November 1, 1861, published. Te Deum and Benedictus in E, for two choirs and organ, Cambridge, 1862. Priest's part for Aylward's Responses; Hymn tunes, etc. Arrangements for pf., 4 hands and harmonium, of Bennett's Woman of Samaria, and other works ; Organ arrangements, etc. Contributions to Smith's Dictionary of Christian Antiquity, *Church Times*, etc. Memoir of Caleb Parnham, Rector of Ufford, Surtees Society, 1880.

Lunn, William Arthur Brown, musician, author of " The Sequential System of Musical Notation," London, 1844. Five editions to 1871. This was published under the pseudonym of *Arthur Wallbridge*. He died in London, April 4, 1879.

Lupo, Thomas, violinist and composer, who flourished in the reign of James I. He composed masques, anthems, madrigals, songs in contemporary collections, and contributed to Leighton's " Teares." His father, THOMAS LUPO, was a member of Queen Elizabeth's Band, 1579, and was also a composer.

Lupton, Rev. James, composer and tenor vocalist, was born in York, 1799, and died at London, December 21, 1873. Chorister, York Minster. Ordained, 1824 ; and in 1829 appointed minor canon of St. Paul's, and of Westminster Abbey. He did much to improve the status of the vicars-choral. He composed church and secular vocal music.

Lyall, Charles, tenor vocalist, was a member of the Carl Rosa Opera Company, from 1875, for a number of years, taking light comedy parts. He also sang in the Royal English Opera Company, 1883, etc. He is, perhaps, better known as a caricaturist, and his cartoons in the *Musical World, Musical Herald*, and other papers, have afforded much amusement.

Lyle, George Edwin, organist of Sherborne Abbey, is the composer of the cantatas, " Nina," Sherborne, 1884 ; " Enoch," Sherborne Abbey, November, 1884 ; and " St. Philip," Sherborne Abbey, May 10, 1888. Also of a Festival Te Deum, for chorus, organ, and military band, performed at the re-opening of the Abbey organ, November 9, 1887. He is conductor of the Abbey Choral Society, and the Sherborne Philharmonic Society.

Lyle, James, DURWARD LELY, tenor vocalist, born at Arbroath, Forfarshire, in 1857. As a boy he entered a lawyer's office at Blairgowrie, and learnt the Tonic Sol-fa method from a Mr. Robertson. Gaining some reputation as a singer, he was, by the aid of Mr. Patrick Allan Fraser, of Hospitalfield, enabled

LYON.

McBURNEY.

to study in Milan, under Sangiovanni, Lamperti, and others. On his return to England he sang much in opera. He was the original *Don Jose* in " Carmen," when Miss Emily Soldene produced the work in 1879, in English. He also sang at Her Majesty's, and elsewhere, with the Carl Rosa Company, 1879-90. A few years later he started, with his wife, recitals cf " Scottish Song and Story," which met with great success in the United Kingdom, Canada, and the United States. In 1896 he was on tour with his own opera company, and produced Dr. Greig's opera, " Holyrood," at Glasgow, in October of that year.

Lyon, Thomas, organist and composer, who was a relative of Bernard Gates. He was organist of St. George's Church, Ratcliffe Highway, London, for more than 50 years. Died at London, in January, 1837, from the first known epidemic of virulent influenza. He composed " Six canzonets, and a glee for 4 voices," London [1795].

SAMUEL THOMAS LYON, probably a relative of the above, composed some pianoforte music, about 1808-1815.

Lysons, Rev. Daniel, clergyman and writer, was born about 1760; died January 3, 1834. Author of " History of the origin and progress of the meeting of the Three Choirs of Gloucester, Worcester, and Hereford," Gloucester, 1819. Second edition continued by John Amott [see that name], London, n.d. [1864] ; continued to 1894 by C. Lee Williams (*q.v.*), and H. Goodwin Chance, M.A., Gloucester, Chance and Bland, 1895.

Maas, Joseph, tenor vocalist, born at Dartford, Kent, January 30, 1847. Of Dutch descent, his father, Joseph Maas, died November 6, 1888, being also a singer. Chorister in Rochester Cathedral from 1856, studying under J. L. Hopkins and later under Madame Bodda-Pyne. When his voice broke he became a clerk at Chatham dockyard. In 1869 he went to Milan, and studied under Sangiovanni. Made his *début* at St. James's Hall, February 9, 1871, at one of Henry Leslie's concerts; sang in " Babil and Bijou " at Covent Garden, September, 1872. He then went to America and joined the Kellogg Opera Company. Joined the Carl Rosa Company in 1878, remaining with it some years, and appearing in a variety of parts. First sang in Italian Opera at Her Majesty's, May 15, 1880, in " Faust " ; and took the part of *Lohengrin* at Covent Garden, June 7, 1883. In the concert room he speedily became popular; and was engaged at the Birmingham Festivals, 1879 (Messiah), to 1885 ; Gloucester and Leeds, 1880, etc. His last public appe rance was at Nottingham, December 31, 1885, and he died in London, January 16, 1886. He was buried at West Hampstead Cemetery. A monument

over his grave was unveiled February 20, 1887 ; and a " Maas Memorial Prize" was instituted the same year, for the encouragement of tenor vocalists.

M'Allister, Robert, musician and teacher of singing, was born in Glasgow, February, 1822. Author of " The Art of Singing at Sight Simplified," 1844; " The Art of Singing at Sight ; or, a Complete Theoretical and Practical Vocal Music Instruction Book," etc. Glasgow, 1848. " Easy Introduction to the Key Board of the Pianoforte or Harmonium." Inventor of the Tonic Sliding Scale or Musical Ladder ; Initial Note Notation ; Stave Sol-fa Notation, etc.

Macbeth, Allan, composer, pianist, and conductor, born at Greenock, March 13, 1856. Son of Norman Macbeth, A.R.S.A. Educated in Germany. Studied music first under Robert Davidson, and Otto Schweitzer, Edinburgh ; and later, at Leipzig Conservatorium, under E. F. Richter, Reinecke, and Jadassohn, 1875-6. Has held organ appointments at Albany Street Congregational Chapel, Edinburgh, 1871 ; Woodside Established Church, 1882 ; and St. George's in the Fields, Glasgow, 1884. He was choirmaster of the Glasgow Choral Union, 1880-7; conductor of the Greenock Select Choir, 1881 ; and the Glasgow Kyrle Choir 1884. On the establishment of a school of music at the Glasgow Athenæum in 1890, he was appointed Principal, an office he retains.

WORKS.—Operetta, The Duke's Doctor (MS.); Cantata, The Land of Glory (Prize, Glasgow Society of Musicians), produced Glasgow, May, 1890 ; Silver Bells, cantata ; Jubilee Chorus, Glasgow Academy Choir, 1896. Three four-part songs, op. 26 ; The Steerman's song ; Near thee, still near thee ; Queen Dagmar's Cross; The Waif; My heart, its sorrows; and other songs. Arrangements of Scotch songs for four voices, etc. *In memoriam* for orchestra ; Forget me not, Gavotte, orchestra, Glasgow Choral Union, 1883 ; Intermezzo, strings; Serenata; Danse Pizzicati ; Ballet de la Cour, orchestra. Trios, pf. and strings ; Suite, 'cello, and pf. Barcarolle, op. 25 ; Berceuse; Scherzino, and other pieces for pf. Overture and incidental music to a drama, not yet produced.

Macburney, Charles, *see* BURNEY, CHAS.

McBurney, S., teacher of Tonic Sol-fa, was born at Glasgow. Son of the late Isaac McBurney, LL.D. Studied at Glasgow University, 1864-6 ; opened a school at Bathgate, near Edinburgh ; but, in 1870, for his health's sake, went to Australia, where he has made his home. For some years held various positions in schools ; but, having studied Tonic Sol-fa in his youth with John McLellan, he began to devote himself more to music. He spent some months in Germany, and attended the summer session of the Tonic Sol-fa College, London   After his return to Australia he founded the Victorian Tonic Sol-fa Association, and was its first president. In 1890 he graduated Mus. Bac. and Mus. Doc., Dublin. He holds the office of Inspector of Music to the Melbourne Educational Department. He has composed Ps. 103 for soprano solo, double chorus, and orchestra; school cantatas, Christmas Greeting; Victoria; Children's Festival; Ode for Melbourne Sunday School Union, etc.

Maccabe, Frederick, tenor vocalist, ventriloquist and entertainer, who has travelled all over Britain and the colonies with a monologue entertainment, partly musical, partly ventriloquial. He also sang in comic opera, and appeared on the stage. About 1860, his entertainment entitled "Begone dull care," was produced at Dublin, London, and other towns. He has composed the following songs —Cease thy reposing, Fluttering on the line, Lady rise, Obstinate man, Oh happy days of youth, Radiant stars, Sailing of the ship, Whisperings of hope, etc. Also author of "Art of Ventriloquism, including directions to learners," London, 1875. "Voice production," Wolverhampton, 1893.

MacCalla, James, composer and teacher, was born about the end of last century. He was a musician in London, and a member of the Royal Society of Musicians. Died London, April 3, 1847. He composed "Life, a cantata," 1840; Songs, pf. music, etc., and edited "The Choir and Congregational Part Book . . ," London, [1844].

MacCann, J. H., concertina player, in business as a concertina maker, at Plymouth. Has appeared at many concerts in the locality. Author of "New method of instructions for the new Chromatic Duet English Concertina . . . ," London [1885].

MacCunn, Hamish, composer, born at Greenock, March 22, 1868. Son of James MacCunn, shipowner, of Greenock. Commenced the study of music at an early age, and on the opening of the R.C.M., in 1883, won a Scholarship for composition. His principal teacher was Dr. Hubert Parry. The Scholarship he resigned in 1886. He became known as a composer the next year, through the instrumentality of Mr. August Manns, and in 1888, received a commission to compose a cantata for the Glasgow Choral Union. In May, 1888, he gave a series of Orchestral Concerts in the studio of Mr. John Pettie, R.A., whose daughter he married in June, 1889. He was appointed a Professor of Harmony at the R.A.M., in 1888, a post he held until 1894. In 1892 he was conductor of the Hampstead Conservatoire Orchestral Society. He has conducted performances of his compositions in different places.

WORKS.—*Operas*: Jeanie Deans (Jos. Ben-

nett), produced, Carl Rosa Company, Edinburgh, November 15, 1894; and Diarmid and Ghriné (Marquis of Lorne), composed 1896. *Cantatas*, etc.: Bonny Kilmeny, op. 2, 1888; Lord Ullin's Daughter, op. 4, Crystal Palace, February 18, 1888; The Lay of the Last Minstrel, Glasgow Choral Union, December 18, 1888; The Cameronian's Dream, op. 10, Edinburgh, January 27, 1890; Psalm 8, composed for opening of Edinburgh Exhibition, May 1, 1890; Queen Hynde of Caledon, Glasgow, January 28, 1892; The death of Parry Reed, men's chorus and orchestra. *Orchestral*: Overture, Cior Mhor, Greenock, January 22, 1887; Concert overture, Land of the mountain and the flood, Crystal Palace, November 5, 1887; Orchestral ballad, The Ship o' the fiend, Henschel Concerts, February 21, 1888; Ballad overture, The Dowie Dens o' Yarrow, Crystal Palace, October 13, 1888; Highland memories, 3 pieces. *Songs*: To Julia, weeping; Pour forth the wine; Ave Maria (The Lady of the lake); Six love lyrics; Six songs (Lady Lindsay); Six songs (Robert Bridge); Album of seven songs (George Macdonald); Part-songs, etc. Pieces for 'cello and pf. Set of six Scotch dances for pf., etc.

Macdonald, Alexander, musician of last half of 18th and early part of present centuries. He was joint music-master of Heriot's Hospital, Edinburgh, 1807-10, with Archibald Macdonald, his father, or other relative; and held the post of precentor of Old Greyfriar's Church, Edinburgh, from 1804 to 1817. He compiled "A new collection of Vocal Music, containing Church tunes, anthems, and songs for the use of the several hospitals of this city," Edinburgh, 1807. He is also, in all probability, the author of "The Notation of Music simplified, or the development of a system in which the characters employed in the notation of language are applied to the notation of music," Glasgow, 1826.

Macdonald, Donald, musician, who flourished at the end of last and beginning of the present century. Compiler of a "Collection of the ancient martial music of Caledonia, called Piobaireachd, as performed on the great Highland bagpipe, adapted to the pianoforte and violoncello, with some old Highland lilts, etc," Edinburgh. n.d. This work includes a tutor for the bagpipe. A collection of Macdonald's quicksteps, strathspeys, reels, and jigs was issued by Messrs. J. & R. Glen, of Edinburgh.

Macdonald, John Denis, M.D. and F.R.S. Held various public appointments, and was inspector-general of hospitals and fleets, 1880-6. Author of "Sound and colour, their relations, analogies and harmonies," London, 1869. "Naval Hygiene," 1881, etc.

Macdonald, Lieutenant-Col. John, musician and writer, born in 1759. Son of

MACDONALD.

Flora Macdonald, the Scottish heroine, and Macdonald of Kingsburgh, Skye. He entered the service of the East India Company, and held various other military and scientific appointments. Fellow of Royal Society in 1800. He died at Exeter, August 16, 1831. He published a number of works on military tactics, telegraphy, and a "Treatise explanatory of the principles constituting the Practice and Theory of the Violoncello," 1811. Also a "Treatise on the Harmonic System, arising from the Vibrations of the aliquot division of strings," 1822.

Macdonald, Joseph, musician, born Strathnaver, February 26, 1739; died in India, 1762. Author of "A Collection of Bagpipe Music," Edinburgh, 1803. He assisted his brother Patrick in the compilation of his collection. His "Treatise on the theory of the Scots Highland bagpipe" is published in the collection of 1803, which was edited by Patrick—see below.

Macdonald, Keith Norman, amateur musician and violinist, was born in Skye, November 23, 1834. He is a doctor by profession. Editor of "The Skye Collection of the best Reels, Strathspeys, etc., arranged for the violin and pianoforte," 1887; 2 editions in the same year.

McDonald, Malcolm, composer and violoncello player, who lived in the latter part of the 18th century. He resided at Inver, in Dunkeld Parish, and played the violoncello in Niel Gow's band. He is said to have died at Inver. He published "A collection of Strathspey reels, with a bass for the violoncello or harpsichord," Edinburgh, 1788. He also issued three other collections of the same kind; 1789, 1792, etc.

Macdonald, Patrick, musician and clergyman, was born at Durness in Strathnaver, April 22, 1729. He was educated at Aberdeen University, and licensed as minister in 1756. Presented to the living of Kilmore, in Argyleshire, 1756. He died at Kilmore, September 25, 1824. With the assistance of Joseph Macdonald, his brother, he compiled "A Collection of Highland Vocal Airs, never hitherto published, to which are added a few of the most lively Country Dances, or Reels, of the North Highlands and Western Isles; and some specimens of Bagpipe Music," Edinburgh, 1784.

Macdonald, Robert Houston, organist. Educated at R.A.M. Won Henry Smart Scholarship, 1890. In 1893 he was appointed organist and choirmaster, Presbyterian Church, Kimberley, S. Africa; and in 1895, Borough organist, Durban, Natal.

Mace, Thomas, writer and musician, born in 1619. Clerk of Trinity College, Cambridge. Married, 1636. He died in 1709, aged 90.

MACFARLANE.

WORKS.—Musick's Monument; or, a Remembrancer of the Best Practical Musick, both Divine and Civil, that has ever been known to have been in the World. Divided into Three Parts. The First Part shows a necessity of Singing Psalms well in Parochial Churches, or not to sing at all. . . . The Second Part treats of the Noble Lute (the Best of Instruments). In the Third Part, the generous Viol in its Rightest use, is treated upon. Lond., 1676 [portrait]. Mace invented a Dyphone or Double Lute of 50 strings, and a table-organ.

M'Fadyen, John, musician and publisher in Wilson Street, Glasgow, in succession to Aird, in early part of the present century. He died at Glasgow, March 8, 1837. Published collections entitled, The Repository of Scots and Irish Airs, Strathspeys, Reels, etc., Glasgow, n.d.; Miscellaneous Collection of the best English and Irish Songs, Glasgow, n.d.; Selection of Scotch, English, Irish, and Foreign Airs, adapted for the Fife, Violin, or German Flute, 6 vols. Dedicated to the Volunteers and defensive bands of Great Britain and Ireland (c., 1800); Collection of Highland Strathspey Reels... Glas., n.d., etc. He kept a music circulating library in Glasgow.

His son, JOSEPH TAYLOR M'FADYEN (1807 —Dec. 25, 1856) was also a publisher in Glasgow, and another son, JAMES (c. 1805-1850), a distinguished botanist, poet and musician, was curator of the Botanical Gardens, Kingston, Jamaica, and died there during the cholera epidemic of 1850.

Macfarlane, George, band-master and writer, was a member of the Duke of Devonshire's private band. Author of "Cornopœon Instructor, containing the elementary Principles of Music, together with Exercises, Preludes, Airs, and Duetts in every key in which the Instrument is playable with effect," Lond., n.d.; Two Fantasias for cornet and pf. [1860]; Waltzes and other dance music.

Macfarlane, John Reid, Scottish composer, was born in 1800. Precentor in the Outer High Church, Glasgow, 1824-28. Afterwards settled in London as a teacher. He died in the Middlesex Hospital, London, June 10, 1841. Composed a number of glees, psalm tunes, etc. Brother of Thomas Macfarlane noted below. He edited "Harmonia Sacra, a Selection of Sacred Music, Ancient and Modern, in four parts," Glasgow, n.d. [1835].

Macfarlane, Thomas, organist and composer, born at Horsham, Sussex, about November, 1808. Son of Duncan Macfarlane, a fine bass singer, who played the French horn in the Ayrshire Militia. Pupil of Andrew Thomson, music-teacher, Glasgow, and afterwards under J. B. Cramer, Herz, Bergotti, and M. Garcia. Organist of the Old Episcopal Chapel, Glasgow, 1827, where he remained five or six years; of St. Mary's Episcopal Church till 1834; and of St. Jude's Episcopal Church till about 1857. Precentor of Park Church, 1859-1866. He was conductor of the Glasgow Amateur Musical Society, and it was under him the first performance of Handel's "Messiah" was given in Glasgow, on April 2, 1844. He removed to London about 1869-70, and was harmoniumist in Camden Road Presbyterian Church, 1871-1882; and conductor of the Camden Road Choral Society for a time. He retired from all professional work in 1882. He compiled Congregational Psalmody of St. Jude's Church, Glasgow, n.d.; Selection of Sacred Music, containing a Selection of Psalm and Hymn Tunes, Chaunts, Te Deums, etc.; Park Church Psalmody, Glasgow, 1860; The Chorale and Supplementary Psalmody, a Selection of Ancient German and other Chorales . . Glasgow, n.d.; The Scripture Chant Book . . Glasgow, n.d. Songs in "Lyric Gems of Scotland," etc.

Macfarren, Sir George Alexander, composer, author, and professor, born in London, March 2, 1813. He studied under his father, George Macfarren (1788-1843), the dramatist, and under Charles Lucas in 1827, and Cipriani Potter at the R.A.M., 1829. In 1834 he became a professor at the R.A.M., and on March 16, 1875, was appointed Professor of Music at Cambridge University. He was Mus. Bac. and Doc. Mus., Cantab., in April, 1876. He became Principal of R.A.M. in 1876, and was knighted in 1883. He died in London, October 31, 1887. For many years he was blind.

WORKS.—*Operas:* Devil's opera (libretto by Geo. Macfarren), English Opera House, London, August 13, 1838; Don Quixote (G. Macfarren), Drury Lane, 1846; King Charles the Second (D. Ryan), Princess' Theatre, October 27, 1849; The sleeper awakened (J. Oxenford), H.M. Theatre, 1850; Robin Hood (J. Oxenford), H.M. Theatre, 1860; Jessy Lea (J. Oxenford), Gallery of Illustration, 1863; She stoops to conquer (E. Fitzball), Covent Garden, 1864; Soldier's Legacy (J. Oxenford), Gallery cf Illustration, 1864; Helvellyn (J. Oxenford), Covent Garden, 1864; Prince of Modena (MS.); Caractacus (MS.); El Malhechor (MS.); Allan of Aberfeldy (MS.). *Masques:* Emblematical tribute, on Her Majesty's marriage (G. Macfarren), Drury Lane, 1840; Freya's Gift (J. Oxenford), on marriage of the Prince of Wales, Covent Garden, 1863. *Farces and Melodramas:* Mrs. G., Queen's Theatre, 1831; Maid of Switzerland, Queen's Theatre, 1832; Genevieve, 1834; I and my Double, 1835; Old oak tree, 1835 (English Opera House); If the cap fit ye, wear it, 1836; Innocent sins, 1836; Love among the roses, 1839; Agnes

Bernduer, 1839. *Oratorios:* St. John the Baptist, Bristol Festival, October 23, 1873; Resurrection, Birmingham Festival, 1876; Joseph, Leeds Festival, 1877; King David, Leeds Festival, 1883. *Cantatas:* Lenora (Bürger-Oxenford), Harmonic Union, 1853; May Day (Oxenford), Bradford Festival, 1856; Christmas (Oxenford), London, 1860; Songs in a cornfield (Christina Rossetti), 1868; Outward Bound (Oxenford), Norwich Festival, 1872; Lady of the Lake (Scott adapted), Glasgow Festival, November 15, 1877; St. George's Te Deum, Crystal Palace, 1884. *Church Music:* Choral Service in E flat; Unison Service in G; Fifty-two Introits or short anthems for holy days and seasons of the church; Two-part anthems for female and male voices, and for female voices alone; Numerous single anthems; Hymns in Anglican Hymn Book, etc.; Chants, etc. *Secular Vocal Music:* Six convivial glees for 3 voices; Fifteen Shakspere Songs for 4 voices (1860-64); Three four-part songs for male voices; Six four-part songs (by Chas. Kingsley); Six four-part songs (by Herrick); Three madrigals; Numerous detached four-part songs, trios, duets, etc. *Songs and ballads:* Four songs from Lane's "Arabian Nights"; Two songs with clarionet accomp.; Three songs with flute accomp.; Four songs from Tennyson's "Idylls"; Three songs from Heine; Six songs from Lewis Morris' "Gwen"; Numerous detached songs. *Symphonies:* No. 1 in C (1828); No. 2 in D minor; No. 3 in F minor; No. 4 in A minor (1834); No 5 in B flat; No. 6 in C sharp minor; No. 7 in D; No. 8 in E minor. *Concert Overtures:* E flat; Merchant of Venice; Romeo and Juliet; Chevy Chase (1836); Don Carlos; Hamlet; Festival; Idyll in memory of Sir Sterndale Bennett; Concerto for pf. and orchestra, in C minor; Concerto for flute and orchestra, in G; Concerto for violin and orchestra, in G minor. *Concerted Music, Instrumental:* Quintet for pf. and strings in G minor; Quintet for concertina and strings in A; Six Quartets for strings in G minor, C, A, F, G minor and G; Trio for pf., violin, and 'cello, in E; Trio for pf., flute, and 'cello, in A; Sonatas for violin and pf. in A and C; Sonata for flute and pf. in B flat. *Organ:* Sonata in C. *Pianoforte:* Sonatas in E flat, A, G minor, D, F minor, B flat, E, and C minor, pf., etc. *Violin:* Five romances for violin and pf., etc. *Literary and Theoretical Works:* Little Clarina's Lesson Book, 1853-55; Rudiments of Harmony . . London, 1860 (14 eds.); Six Lectures on Harmony . . London, 1867, 3rd ed., 1880; On the Structure of a Sonata, London, 1871; Eighty musical sentences to illustrate chromatic chords, London, 1875; Counterpoint, a practical course of study, London, 1879; Musical history briefly narrated

MACFARREN.

and technically discussed, London, 1885 (from the " Encyclopaedia Britannica," 9th ed.) ; Analyses of oratorios, etc., for concert programs ; Addresses and lectures at R.A.M. ; Musical biographies in " Imperial Dictionary of Biography " ; Grove's " Dictionary of Music," etc. *Collections, or Edited Works :* Old English Ditties, 2 vols. ; Songs of England (Chappell) ; Old Scottish Ditties ; Moore's Irish Melodies ; British Vocal Album ; Editions of Purcell's " Dido and Eneas," Handel's " Belshazzar," " Judas Maccabeus," " Jephtha," and " Messiah." *See* " George A. Macfarren, his life, works, and influence," by H. C. Banister, London, 1891.

Macfarren, Natalia, *born* ANDREAE, vocalist and teacher, wife of the foregoing, was born at Lübeck. She has translated a number of opera libretti, and written a Vocal School, and an " Elementary Course of Vocalising and Pronouncing the English Language," London, n.d.

Macfarren, Mrs. John, *born* EMMA MARIE BENNETT, pianist, composer, and lecturer, born in London, June 19, 1824. Began her musical studies at an early age, her teachers being W. H. Kearns, and later, Madame Dulcken. Composition she studied under (Sir) G. A. Macfarren. In 1846 she married Mr. John Macfarren, a brother of Sir George, and the couple went to New York, remaining in the United States three years. Her talent was duly recognised there, but home associations drew her back to London. She gave her first concert at the New Beethoven Rooms, April 12, 1851, playing in W. H. Holmes's quartet for four pianists " Une Romance de Deux Minutes," with the composer, Arabella Goddard, and William Dorrell. Cipriani Potter and Sterndale Bennett also played at this concert—a remarkable gathering of pianists. Musical matinées were then given annually, and also concerts in the suburbs, up to the year 1883. In 1860 Mrs. Macfarren first appeared as a lecturer at St. James's Hall. These lectures were virtually pianoforte recitals, with remarks on the works performed, written expressly for her by G. A. Macfarren. They were extended over many years, and also given in the provinces. Under the *nom-de-plume* of JULES BRISSAC she produced a great number of pf. pieces, amongst the most popular being " Bonnie Scotland," and a " Valse de Bravoure." From 1883 her time was devoted exclusively to teaching and writing, and she died in London, after a brief but painful illness, on November 9, 1895.

Macfarren, Walter Cecil, pianist and composer, brother of Sir George, was born in London, August 28, 1826. Chorister at Westminster Abbey, 1836-41, under James Turle ; and pupil of R.A.M., 1842-6, studying piano-

McGIBBON.

forte under W. H. Holmes, and composition under his brother, and Cipriani Potter. During his student days he played a duet with W. H. Holmes at one of H. J. Banister's quartet concerts, March 30, 1844 ; and on the 26th of April following was introduced as a composer by a Pf. trio, at the G. A. Macfarren and Davidson concerts. In 1845 other works were produced by the Society of British Musicians. In 1846, he was appointed a professor at the R.A.M., and his 50th year in that office was marked, in 1896, by a presentation from past and present pupils. He conducted the Academy concerts, 1873-80. F.R.A.M. For many years he was connected with the Philharmonic Society as director and treasurer, having been elected an Associate in 1849. He gave a series of orchestral concerts in 1882, conducting the whole from memory. His pianoforte recitals and lectures have been numerous, and have been given in London, Bristol, and other places ; and many of his pupils have attained high positions.

WORKS.—Symphony in B flat, composed, 1879, produced, Brighton Festival, 1880. *Overtures:* A Winter's Tale (1844) ; Taming of the Shrew (1845) ; Beppo (1847) ; Pastoral (1878) ; Hero and Leander, composed, 1878, produced, Brighton Festival, 1879, Crystal Palace and Philharmonic, 1880 ; Henry V., Norwich Festival, 1881 ; Othello, composed, 1895, performed, Queen's Hall, February 16, and at Bristol Festival, October 14, 1896. Concertstück in E, pf. and orchestra, Brighton Festival, 1881. Three trios, pf., violin and 'cello ; Two sonatas, pf. and violin ; Sonata, pf. and 'cello ; four Romances, pf. and violin. *Pianoforte :* 24 Studies in Style and Technique ; 40 Preludes, in all keys, as studies in the art of Improvisation ; two sets, 12 studies. Comprehensive Scale and Arpeggio manual, Ashdown ; Pf. Method, R. Cocks. Three Suites de Pièces, in D minor, E flat, and C. Allegro appassionato ; Toccata in C minor ; and an immense number of pieces as Tarantellas. Mazurkas, Valses, Nocturnes, Impromptus, etc. *Vocal :* Cantata for female voices, The Song of the Sunbeam. Morning and Evening service in A ; Evening Service in C ; anthem, Praise ye the Lord ; Tunes in Hymns Ancient and Modern, and other Collections. Daybreak ; An emigrant's song ; Autumn ; You stole my love ; Bells across the sea ; Who is Sylvia ? ; and other part-songs. Six sacred songs ; A widow bird sat mourning ; Awake, O heart ; Ah ! sweet, thou little knowest ; and other songs. Editor of Mozart's Pf. Works ; Beethoven's Sonatas ; Popular Classics ; Morceaux Classiques, etc.

McGibbon, William, violinist and composer, was born about the beginning of the 18th century. Son of Matthew McGibbon, oboe player, who performed at the St. Cecilia

McGILL.

concert, Edinburgh, in 1695. He studied the violin under Corbet, of London. Leader of Gentlemen's Concerts at Edinburgh, and teacher there. He died at Edinburgh, October 3, 1756.

WORKS.—Six Sonatos or Solos for a German Flute or Violin, Edinburgh, 1740; A Collection of Scots Tunes, some with variations for a violin, hautbois, or German flute, with a bass for a violoncello or harpsichord—Book 1, 1742; Book 2, 1746; Book 3, 1755. Original dances, and some flute music.

McGill, John, composer, born in Ayrshire, in 1707. He was an associate of John Riddell, of Ayr, but is supposed to have been an itinerant musician in some of the towns of Ayrshire. He composed the tune now associated with the song called "Come under my plaidie."

M'Glashan, Alexander, violinist, who flourished in Edinburgh about the end of last century. He was the leader of a fashionable band, in Edinburgh, and gave concerts. He was nicknamed "King M'Glashan," on account of his fine personal appearance. He died at Edinburgh, in May, 1797. He published "A Collection of Strathspey Reels, with a bass for the violoncello or harpsichord," 1778; A Collection of Scots Measures, Hornpipes, Jigs, Allemands, Cotillons, and the fashionable Country Dances, with the bass for the violoncello or harpsichord, Edinburgh [1778].

MacGlashan, John, a teacher of the piano, and collector, who flourished in Edinburgh, about 1798-1812, was probably a relative of the above. He published "A Collection of Strathspey Reels for the pianoforte, violin, or German flute," Edinburgh, 1798.

M'Guckin, Barton, tenor vocalist, born at Dublin, July 28, 1853. At the age of ten he became a choir boy at Armagh Cathedral, and Robert Turle taught him singing, pianoforte, and organ. In 1871, he gained the post of first tenor at St. Patrick's Cathedral, Dublin, and also at Trinity College. He then studied under Joseph Robinson. After singing at concerts in Dublin, and at the Crystal Palace, 1874-5, he went to Milan, and studied under Trevulsi. On his return he sang at the Crystal Palace, October 28, 1876; and at the Ancient Concert Room, Dublin, November 28. Then followed engagements in many places. His Festival work dates from 1879, at Hereford; he sang at Bristol Festival the same year; Norwich, 1881; Leeds, 1886, etc. He made his *début* in opera, at the Theatre Royal, September 10, 1880, as *Thaddeus*, in Balfe's "The Bohemian Girl," and since that time up to 1896, as a member of the Carl Rosa Company, has appeared in a variety of parts. He also sang in opera in New York, 1887-8. His brother, ALBERT M'GUCKIN, is a baritone singer, and has been heard in opera and concerts. He married, in 1892, Miss

MACINTYRE.

Lucille Saunders, an American mezzo-soprano; and in 1893, with his wife, went to America.

Machardy, James M. P., musician and teacher, is a native of Edinburgh. Brother of the undernoted. Author of "The Rudiments of Music, as it ought to be studied, vocal and instrumental," n.d.

Machardy, Robert, composer and teacher, born at Edinburgh, September 10, 1848. Has composed "The Woodland Witch," a dramatic cantata; "Hymn of the Seasons," cantatina; some songs and pf. pieces; and edited for some time *The Scottish Musical Times,* now defunct. Author of "Progressive Pianoforte Playing," n.d.; "Progressive Sight-Singing." n.d.

Machin, William, bass singer, born at Birmingham in 1798. He was a chorister in Lichfield Cathedral, and on the recommendation of Sir Robert Peel was appointed to the Chapel Royal, London; and he afterwards sang at the Temple Church and St. Paul's Cathedral. He sang at the Birmingham Festivals from 1834 to 1849. Died at Handsworth, in September, 1870.

Machray, Alexander, amateur musician, born at Aberdeen, June 7, 1837. He studied music under Richard Latter and W. R. Broomfield. From 1855 to 1876 he was leader of psalmody in the East Church, Aberdeen, and was Secretary of the Aberdeen Choral Union, etc. He is an advocate in Aberdeen. Compiler of "The Scottish Psalmist, a manual of standard and choice psalm and hymn tunes for christian worship," Aberdeen, 1876.

McIntyre, Duncan, musician and dancing master, born about 1765. He was a teacher of dancing in London in latter part of last century. He died at London or Calcutta about 1806-7. Compiled a "Collection of slow airs, Reels and Strathspeys, etc.," London, 1795. He lived at 22, Great Marlborough Street, London, as a teacher of Scotch dancing. According to Mr. John Glen this McIntyre went to India, probably as master of ceremonies to the Governor-General's court at Calcutta.

Macintyre, Margaret, soprano vocalist, of Scottish descent, born in India. Daughter of General John Mackenzie Macintyre, R.A. Studied as an amateur at the Brighton branch of the London Academy of Music, and occasionally sang at the Academy concerts, notably when Liszt attended the performance of his oratorio, "St. Elizabeth," by the students, at St. James's Hall, April 7, 1886. She studied under Manuel Garcia, and Madame Della Valle, and declamation with Miss Carlotta Leclercq. She made her *début* at Covent Garden, May 14, 1888, as *Micaela* in "Carmen," and has since sung in a variety of parts there. She appeared with success at Milan, 1893;

MACIRONE.

toured in South Africa; and was engaged for the grand opera, St. Petersburg, 1896-7. Her first important concert appearance was at Edinburgh, December, 1888, since when she has been heard at all the chief concerts. She sang at the Leeds Festival, 1889; Birmingham, 1891, in "Elijah"; at the Handel Festival, 1891, etc., and is recognised as an artist of high attainments.

Macirone, Clara Angela, composer, pianist, and teacher, born in London, in 1821. Descended from an ancient and noble Roman family. Her grandfather, who settled in England, served in the American war of Independence. Her father was a skilled amateur tenor singer, and her mother a cultivated pianist, pupil of Charles Neate. Her musical talent developed early with such home surroundings, and her sister (who died in 1888) became a water-colour painter of note. Miss Macirone entered the R.A.M. in 1839, studying under Cipriani Potter, W. H. Holmes, Charles Lucas, and others. On leaving, in 1842, she received a testimonial from the committee, a circumstance quite unique. She was made a professor of the pf. there, and elected an Associate of the Philharmonic Society, and F.R.A.M. Her first concert was given in the Hanover Square Rooms, June 26, 1846, when Pischek sang a Benedictus of her composition. This work, later, received praise from Mendelssohn. The concerts were continued until 1864, and then her chief work was in teaching and composing. She was head music mistress at Aske's School for Girls, Hatcham, 1872-8; and at the Church of England High School for Girls, Baker Street, London, she systematised the music teaching with the best results. The last few years have been passed in comparative retirement. In addition to composition, she has contributed many articles to the *Girls Own Paper*, the *Argosy*, and other periodicals.

WORKS.—Te Deum and Jubilate, sung at Hanover Chapel, the first service by a woman ever used in the Church; Anthem, By the waters of Babylon, sung at Canterbury, Ely, and other cathedrals, etc. Sacred songs, and duets. *Songs :* Cavalier's song; Henri de Lagardere; My child; Golden grain; Dreams; The Recall; Hesperus; Oh, hush thee my babie; Sweet and Low; The Balaclava charge; There is dew for the flow'ret; Montrose's Love Song, and many others. *Part-songs :* The Battle of the Baltic; Sir Knight (sung at the composer's concert by four artists of repute, May 20, 1862); Autolycus' song; Jog on, jog on the footpath way; The Avon to the Severn runs; Old Daddy Longlegs (in the programme of the Tonic Sol-fa Festival, Exeter Hall, May 15, 1882, but the words were objected to by the authorities of the Hall, and another piece had to be substituted);

MACKENZIE.

Humptie Dumptie; Echoes; When summer's come at last; A Christmas welcome; etc. Children's songs: I had a little castle; Little Boy Blue; Little grey pussy cat. Suite de pieces in E minor, violin and pf.; Summer serenade; Cantilena; Nacht Reise Lied; Rondino in G, and other pieces for pf. Several works in MS.

Mackay, Alexander, violinist and musician, was a native of Islay. He issued a "Collection of Reels, Strathspeys, and slow tunes," Glasgow, n.d. [1805].

Mackay, Angus, Scottish collector, and piper, born about 1813. He was piper to Queen Victoria. Accidentally drowned in the river Nith, near Dumfries, March 21, 1859. Compiler of "A Collection of Ancient Piobaireachd, or Highland Pipe Music . . . To which are prefixed some sketches of the principal hereditary pipers and their establishments," Edinburgh, 1838; "The Piper's Assistant, a collection of marches, quicksteps, strathspeys, reels and jigs . ." Edinburgh, n.d.

McKay, Iver, tenor vocalist, born in Dublin. At the age of six he was a chorister at the Chapel Royal, Dublin Castle, and in the chapel of Dublin University; and also sang tenor at St. Patrick's Cathedral. After some years spent in commercial pursuits, he went to Italy. Not gaining instruction suitable for an English career, he returned to London, and placed himself under T. A. Wallworth, and W. Shakespeare, to whose training he attributes much of his success. He has been heard at the principal London and provincial concerts; sang at the Leeds Festivals of 1886, and 1889; created the tenor part in Dvořák's Requiem, at the Birmingham Festival, 1891, etc. In opera he appeared as *Lenski*, in Tschaïkowsky's "Eugene Onegin," at the New Olympic, October, 1892. He has toured with Mr. Sims Reeves (1884), and has gained an honourable position among singers of the day.

Mackay, William, musician, published "The complete Tutor for the great Highland bagpipe," Edinburgh, 1840.

Mackenzie, John, Scottish musician, born at Durham, in 1797. Son of a member of the Forfarshire militia band. He was a violinist and teacher in Aberdeen, and leader in the Theatre Royal there. At the request of James Dewar he removed to Edinburgh in 1831. He died at Edinburgh, October 28, 1852.

His son, ALEXANDER MACKENZIE, was a violinist and composer, born at Montrose, in 1819. In 1831 he accompanied his father to Edinburgh, and became a violinist in the Theatre Royal, under Dewar. He afterwards studied under Sainton, at London, and at Dresden, under Lipinski. He was leader of the orchestra of the Theatre Royal, Edin-

MACKENZIE.

burgh, under the successive management of Murray, Glover and Wyndham. He died at Edinburgh, October 2, 1857. He edited "National Dance Music of Scotland," Edinburgh, n.d.; new edition, with additions, by A. C. Mackenzie, London, 1889, 3 books. "Six Scotch Airs for Violin." "One hundred Scotch Airs for Violin." *Songs:* Grey hill plaid; Nameless lassie; Linton Lowrie, etc.

Mackenzie, Sir Alexander Campbell, Kt., son of Alexander Mackenzie, composer, violinist, and conductor, born at Edinburgh, August 22, 1847. Studied under his father, and at the age of ten was sent to Germany, where he studied at Schwarzburg-Sondershausen, under W. Uhlrich, violin, and Eduard Stein, composition. In 1861 he was a member of the Ducal orchestra. The next year he went to London, and entered the R.A.M., gaining the King's Scholarship that year, 1862. He studied under Sainton, Jewson, and Charles Lucas. In 1865 he returned to Edinburgh, and was engaged in tuition and composition. He was a professor at Queen Street Ladies' College; Choirmaster at St. George's Church; and conductor of the Scottish Vocal Association. Also member of the Festival orchestra, Birmingham, 1867-73; Concert-giver in Edinburgh, and Quartet-player. About this time his compositions began to attract attention, and in order to devote himself to this work, he went to live at Florence in 1879. He visited England occasionally to conduct compositions at the Worcester Festival, 1881; Bristol Festival, 1882, etc. Returned to London in 1885, as conductor of the Novello Oratorio Concerts; left London again in 1887, but after the death of Sir G. A. Macfarren that year, he became a candidate for the post of Principal of the R.A.M., and was elected, February 22, 1888. In 1892, he was elected conductor of the Philharmonic Society, the first concert under his direction taking place, March 9, 1893. He has conducted concerts at the Crystal Palace (October 20, 1894); Manchester (Halle concert, December 5, 1895); Royal Choral Society (February 19, 1896), etc.; and has given addresses on music in Manchester and other places; lectured at the Royal Institution, 1893, and 1895, etc.; and taken an active interest in the proceedings of the Incorporated Society of Musicians. He was elected Hon. Vice-President of the Edinburgh Choral Union, 1884; Glasgow Choral Union, 1888; received the Gold Medal for Art and Science, from the Grand Duke of Hesse, 1884; elected Corresponding Member, Istituto Reale di Firenze [1888]; received the honorary degree of Mus. Doc., St. Andrews, 1886; Cambridge, 1888; and Edinburgh, 1896; and in 1895, the honour of Knighthood from the Queen.

WORKS. — *Cantatas and Oratorios:* The

MACKENZIE.

Bride, Worcester Festival, 1881; Jason, Bristol, 1882; The Rose of Sharon, Norwich, 1884; The Story of Sayid, Leeds, 1886; Jubilee Ode, Crystal Palace, June 22, 1887; The New Covenant, Glasgow, 1888; The Dream of Jubal, composed for Jubilee of Liverpool Philharmonic Society, performed, February 5, 1889; The Cottar's Saturday Night, Edinburgh, December, 1892; Veni, Creator Spiritus, Birmingham Festival, 1891; Bethlehem, composed, 1892, produced, Royal Albert Hall, April 12, 1894. *Operas:* Colomba, produced, Drury Lane (Carl Rosa), April 9, 1883; The Troubadour, Drury Lane, June 8, 1886; His Majesty, comic opera, Savoy, February 20, 1897. Incidental music to Ravenswood, Lyceum, 1890; Marmion, 1891; Choral odes for female voices for The Bride of Love (Buchanan), Adelphi, 1890. *Orchestral:* Scherzo, Glasgow, 1878; Scottish Rhapsodies, No. 1, op. 21; No. 2, op. 24 (Burns); La Belle Dame sans Merci, Philharmonic Society, 1883. Overtures: Cervantes; To a Comedy; Tempo di Ballo; Twelfth Night, composed in Italy, 1887-88, produced, Richter concerts, June 4, 1888; Britannia, Queen's Hall, May 17, 1894. Concerto, op. 32, Birmingham Festival (Sarasate), 1885; Pibroch, Leeds (Sarasate), 1886, both for violin and orchestra. Scottish Concerto, pf. and orchestra. Quartet in E flat, op. 11, pf. and strings; Six pieces for violin, op. 37; Highland ballad, violin, op. 47; Larghetto and allegro. pf. and 'cello, op. 10; From the North, 9 violin pieces. Rustic scenes, op. 9; Five pieces, op. 13; Six pieces, op. 20, and other compositions for pf. Three short pieces, organ. Seven anthems. Song of Love and Death (Tennyson), op. 7; Two songs, op. 12; Three songs (Christina Rossetti), op. 17; Eighteen songs, op. 31; Spring songs (7); Three Shakespeare sonnets, etc. The Empire Flag, solo and chorus; part-songs, various. Vocal Melodies of Scotland, arranged for pf.

Mackenzie, Marian, contralto vocalist, born at Plymouth. Studied there under Samuel Weekes, and later at R.A.M. under A. Randegger. Westmoreland, and Parepa-Rosa Scholar; A.R.A.M.; Associate of the Philharmonic Society. She made her *début* at the London Ballad Concerts; sang at the Crystal Palace; Monday and Saturday Popular Concerts; and in the provinces. Her first Festival engagement was at Norwich, in 1890; then followed appearances at Leeds, 1892; Birmingham, 1894, etc. She also sang at the Handel Festivals, 1891-94. For a short time she sang in comic opera, making her first appearance on the stage at the Grand Theatre, Birmingham, Oct. 10, 1887. In 1885, she was married to Mr. Richard Smith Williams, a brother of Miss Anna Williams the soprano vocalist. In 1896 she made a successful tour in Australia,

MACKENZIE.

singing at festivals at Sydney, Melbourne, Adelaide, etc.

Mackenzie, Sir Morell, surgeon and musician, born at Leytonstone, Essex, July 7, 1837 ; died at London, February 3, 1892. Author of "Treatment of hoarseness and loss of voice," London, 1863; new edits., 1868, 1871. "Use of the Laryngoscope in diseases of the throat," London, 1865, also 1871. "Hygiene of the vocal organs ; a practical handbook for singers and speakers," London, 1886 ; 5th edit., 1888. "Fatal illness of Frederick the Noble," London, 1888.

M'Kercher, Duncan, violinist and composer, born at Inver, Dunkeld, N.B., in 1796. He resided chiefly in Edinburgh, and died at Colinton, near that city, on December 14, 1873. He composed a number of strathspeys, most of which were published in two collections of dance music which were issued about 1830. Many of the dances in these collections were by Captain Daniel Menzies.

Mac Kerrell, John, musician and writer, author of "Familiar Introduction to the first principles of music" . . . Op. 2., London, [1800] ; Songs and other compositions.

Mackeson, Rev. Charles, clergyman, editor, and literary musician, born May 15, 1842. Compiler of "Guide to the Churches of London and its Suburbs," published annually for some time. Editor of *The Choir*, new series, 1879-80; and of the *Churchman's Shilling Magazine.* Contributor to Grove's Dictionary of Music and Musicians. Author of biographical notices of living musicians, published in *The Choir*, 1879-80. Lecturer on Church music ; Hymn writers ; Christmas carols, etc. Ordained by Bishop of London, 1885. Curate of Church of the Good Shepherd, Hampstead, 1885-89 ; Minister, 1889-94.

MacKewan, Joseph, musician, compiled "Select Psalm Tunes, metrical hymns, chorales, chants, etc.,' London [1857]. Composer of Songs, scenas, duets and other vocal music.

Mackinlay, Thomas, music publisher, compiled "A Catalogue of Original Letters and Manuscripts in the Autograph of Distinguished Musicians, Composers, Performers, and Vocalists," London, 1846.

Mackintosh James, author of "The Musicmaster for Schools and Families," London, 1862.

Mackintosh, John, Scottish bassoon player, born in 1767. He played in the principal orchestras between 1821-1835. He died at London, March 23, 1844. Famous as one of the finest performers of his day, and celebrated all over Europe for the excellent tone and style of his playing.

Another MACKINTOSH, GEORGE, issued a "New and improved Bassoon Tutor, etc.," London [1840].

Mackintosh, Robert, Scottish composer

McLACHLAN.

and violinist, was born about the middle of the 18th century [Tullymet, 1745]. He resided in Edinburgh as a teacher and performer till about 1803, when he removed to London. Teacher in London at Little Vine Street, Piccadilly. He died at London, February, 1807.

WORKS.—Op. 1. Airs, Minuets, Gavotts, and Reels, mostly for two Violins, and a bass for the Violoncello or Harpsichord, 1783 ; op. 2. Sixty-eight new Reels, Strathspeys, and Quick Steps; also some slow pieces, with variations for the Violin or Pianoforte, with a Bass for the Violoncello or Harpsichord, 1792 ; 2nd Book, 1793 ; 3rd Book, 1793 ; 4th Book of Strathspeys, n.d.

This composer was well known in his time as *Red Rob* Mackintosh. He was a good performer, and wrote music for the song "A cogie of ale and a pickle ait-meal."

His son, ABRAHAM (born, Edinburgh, June 15, 1769 ; died, Newcastle, about 1807), was also a violinist, and issued a collection of dance music, entitled, "Thirty new Strathspey reels, etc., with a bass for the violoncello or harpsichord," Edinburgh, 1792. A Collection of Strathspeys, Reels, jigs, etc. . for the harp, pianoforte, violin, and violoncello, Newcastle [1805], 2 Nos.

McKorkell, Charles, organist and composer, was born in 1809. He studied at the R.A.M., London, and for 40 years was organist of All Saints', Northampton. He died at Northampton, January 10, 1879. Compiler of "The Sacred Music Book, a selection of 100 standard tunes with chants," n.d. ; and composer of anthems, and of many pieces of minor importance for the pf.

McLachlan, Jessie Niven, MRS. ROBERT BUCHANAN, soprano singer, born at Oban, June 18, 1866. Celebrated as a singer of Highland songs in the original Gaelic. In 1892 she sang before the Queen at Balmoral, and she has frequently appeared at concerts in Glasgow, London, and other parts of the country. Her husband, ROBERT BUCHANAN, was born at Glasgow in December, 1858, and has held various posts as church organist and pianist.

M'Lachlan, John, musician, who was a teacher in Glasgow, and precentor of the North West Church from 1774. He died in Glasgow in 1791. Compiler of "The Precentor, or an easy introduction to church music, with a choice collection of psalm tunes," Glasgow, 1776 (with Finlay); The Precentor, or an easy introduction to church music, Glasgow, 1779 ; another edition, Glasgow, 1782.

McLachlan, John, musician and piper, compiler of "The Piper's Assistant : a new collection of marches, quicksteps, strathspeys, reels and jigs. Edited by John

McLAREN.

McLachlan, late piper to Neill Malcolm, Esq., of Poltalloch," Edinburgh, n.d.

McLaren, Daniel, violinist and composer, who was born in Perthshire in the latter part of last century. He resided in Edinburgh as a teacher and performer, and probably died there about 1820. He published " A collection of strathspey reels, etc., with a bass for violoncello or harpsichord," Edinburgh [1794].

Maclean, or **Macklean, Charles,** Scottish musician, who flourished in latter part of last century. He published " Twelve solos or sonatas for a violin, op. 1," Edinburgh, 1737 ; and a " Selection of favourite Scots Tunes, with variations for the violin. . . ." Edinburgh [1770].

Maclean, Charles Donald, organist and composer, born at Cambridge, March 27, 1843. Studied under Ferd. Hiller at Cologne. Graduated Mus. Bac., Oxon., 1862 ; Mus. Doc., 1865 ; M.A., Oxon., 1875. Organist of Exeter College, Oxford, 1862, and 1872-5, music director at Eton College. From this time he spent many years in India, and is now resident in London.

WORKS.—Noah, dramatic oratorio ; Requiem Mass ; Sulmala, cantata from the Gaelic. *Orchestral:* Symphony in G ; Cynthia's Revels, concert overture ; Concert overture in C ; Ballet, without dance ; Trio in B, pf. and strings ; Music for pf., songs, etc.

Maclean, Alick, composer, son of preceding, born at Eton, July 20, 1872. His works include an opera in three acts, " Quentin Durward," and " Petruccio " (libretto by his sister), opera in one act, which won the Moody-Manners prize of £100, and was produced at Covent Garden, June 29, 1895. He has also written some songs.

Maclean, William, minor poet and amateur musician, born at Glasgow, March 22, 1805. Educated at Glasgow University. He was a manufacturer and merchant in Glasgow ; J.P. for Counties of Renfrew and Lanark, etc. He died at Glasgow, November 28, 1892. Published " Maclean's Sacred Music, arranged for four voices, with organ or pf. accompaniment," London, 2 parts, 1854-5. Also composer of a large volume of " Sacred Melodies " in manuscript, now deposited in the Mitchell Library, Glasgow.

Maclennan, William, piper and dancer, was born in Scotland in the first part of the present century. He was regarded as one of the best performers of Highland bagpipe music, and was four times commanded to pipe and dance before the Queen. He died at Montreal, Canada, in October, 1892, while on a tour with a company in America.

Macleod, Captain Neil, Scottish collector, published a " Collection of Piobaireachd or Pipe Tunes, as verbally taught by the

McMURDIE.

M'Crummin Pipers in the Isle of Skye, to their Apprentices," Edinburgh, 1828. A reprint of this scarce work was issued by Messrs. J. & R. Glen, of Edinburgh. It is distinguished by the use of an extraordinary notation, consisting of syllables, which has not yet been deciphered.

Macleod, Peter, amateur composer, son of James Macleod of Polbeth, West Calder, Midlothian, was born on May 8, 1797. Well known in Edinburgh musical and other circles during his lifetime. He associated with the leading men of the time, and was an early friend of R. A. Smith, the composer. With the profits of the work named second below he completed the Burns Monument at Edinburgh by enclosing it within an iron rail. He was a Justice of the Peace for Midlothian, and succeeded to the property of Polbeth. He died at Bonnington, near Edinburgh, February 10, 1859, and is buried at Rosebank Cemetery there.

WORKS.— Original melodies, consisting of songs, duets, and glees, the symphonies and accompaniments by Mr. Mather, the poetry written expressly for this work, Edinburgh [1828] ; Original Scottish melodies, Edinburgh, n.d., dedicated to the Duchess of Buccleuch ; Original national melodies of Scotland, London and Edinburgh [1838], dedicated to Queen Victoria ; New national songs, the melodies never before published, Edinburgh, n.d. Among Macleod's best-known songs may be named Scotland yet ; My bonnie wife ; Oh, why left I my hame ; Our's is the land o' gallant hearts ; Dowie dens o' Yarrow ; Yellow locks o' Charlie ; Land o' cakes ; Emigrant's complaint ; My Highland vale ; I had a hame ; More dear art thou to me ; I have loved thee only ; Flora's lament ; and many others, chiefly to verses of good poets.

Macmeeken, J. W., clergyman and amateur musician, was minister of Lesmahagow, in Lanarkshire. Author of a " History of the Scottish Metrical Psalms, with an account of the paraphrases and hymns, and of the music of the old psalter. Illustrated with twelve plates of MS. music of 1566," Glasgow, 1872, privately printed.

McMurdie, Joseph, composer and writer, was born at London in 1792. He studied music under Dr. Crotch. Mus. Bac., Oxon., 1814. Director of Philharmonic Society. He died at Merton, Surrey, December 23, 1878.

WORKS.—Glees. Canons, etc., London, 1828, 1836, 1840, etc. ; Trios for Female Voices, 1859 ; Glees, etc., London [1824] ; Arrangements for pf. ; Sacred Music, a collection of tunes adapted to the new version of Psalms, as sung at the Philanthropic Society's Chapel, London, 1827 ; The Elements of Music, with the Art of Playing from a Figured Bass, and

M'NABB.

an introduction to Composition, London [1845]; A Juvenile Preceptor for the Pianoforte, London, 1828; A Collection of Psalm and Hymn Tunes, London [1853]; De Profundis Clamavi, motet; Ode to Spring, glee. Handbook for Vocal Classes, Part-songs, etc., London [1859].

M'Nabb, Hugh, writer and conductor, born in Ayrshire about 1842. He is conductor of the Ayr Choral Union, and of a vocal association in connection with the 1st Lanarkshire Rifle Volunteers. From 1867 he has been choirmaster of the United Presbyterian Church, St. Vincent Street, Glasgow. Author of " Morley's New Singing Tutor," London, 1883, etc.

McNaught, William Gray, teacher, conductor, and editor, born of Scottish parentage, at Stepney, London, March 30, 1849. Began his musical studies with the Tonic Sol-fa method, and continued them after he had entered a merchant's office. Was awarded the Society of Arts' prize for composition, 1871, and, giving up business, entered the R.A.M. that year. Associate, 1878; Fellow, 1895; Mus. Doc., Cantuar, 1896. In 1872, at the National Music Meetings, Crystal Palace, the Ashcroft-Evans Choir, under his direction, won the prize of £100 in Class II. This choir, in 1874, was transferred to Bow, and formed the nucleus of the excellent choir of the Institute, conducted by him ever since. He was appointed Assistant Inspector of Music for the Educational Department in 1883, and Examiner in Music to the Society of Arts in 1893. Author of " Hints on choir training for competitions," Novello, 1896; Editor of *The School Music Review* from its commencement, in 1892; of Novello's School Songs; and translator of a number of works into the Tonic Sol-fa Notation. Adjudicator at school singing competitions, lecturer, etc.

Macphee, Donald, author and bagpipe maker, born at Coatbridge in 1841, died near Glasgow, December 9, 1880. He worked in Glasgow at his trade. Author of A Selection of Music for the Highland Bagpipe, with a complete tutor, Glasgow, 1876. Marches, quicksteps, reels, and strathspeys, and collections of Pibrochs, 1879, for the bagpipes, etc.

Macpherson, Charles, organist and composer, born in Edinburgh. In 1879 he entered the choir school of St. Paul's Cathedral, and was a chorister for about eight years, under Dr. G. C. Martin. Sometime choirmaster, St. Clement's, Eastcheap. Private organist to Sir Robert Menzies, Weem, Perthshire, 1887; at Madame de Falba's chapel, Luton Hoo Park, Beds., 1889. Entered R.A.M., 1890; Won the Charles Lucas Prize, 1892; A.R.A.M., 1896. In 1895 he was appointed assistant organist at St. Paul's Cathedral.

McSWINEY.

WORKS.—Ps. 137, chorus and orchestra, R.A.M., 1895; Three Gaelic melodies, with accompaniment for strings and harp; Glee for 5 voices, There sits a bird (awarded the prize of 10 guineas offered by the Bristol Orpheus Glee Society, for the best composition by a student of R.A.M., 1893). Overture, Cridhe an Ghaidhil (The Heart of the Gael), Crystal Palace, March 2, 1895; Highland Suite in A, orchestra; Sextet, for wind instruments, etc.

Macpherson, Charles Stewart, composer and conductor, of Scotch descent, born at Liverpool, March 29, 1865. Educated at the City of London School. In 1880 he won the Sterndale Bennett Scholarship, and entered the R.A.M. Studied pianoforte under W. Macfarren, and composition with Sir G. A. Macfarren. Balfe Scholar, 1882-3; Lucas Prize, 1884; Potter Exhibitioner, 1885. While a student he wrote a large number of works, orchestral and chamber music, etc. Elected an Associate, 1887; Fellow, 1892. In 1889 he was appointed a professor of harmony and composition at the Academy. He became organist and choirmaster of Immanuel Church, Streatham Common, 1885; was appointed conductor of the Westminster Orchestral Society the same year; and in 1886, founded the Streatham Choral Society. Has given Chamber concerts, and pianoforte recitals, and contributed occasionally to the musical press.

WORKS.—*Orchestral:* Symphony in C, 1888; Overture, The Student of Salamanca, 1887; Festal overture, 1891; Ballade, 1890; Notturno in E flat, 1892; all produced by the Westminster Society. Idyl, A Summer daydream, orchestra, Crystal Palace, December 8, 1894. Concertstück, pf. and orchestra, 1893; Romance in D, violin and orchestra, 1896, both at Westminster. Sonata in E flat, pf. and violin; Suite de Valses, pf. Church music. Songs, duets, etc. Author of " Practical Harmony, a concise treatise, 1894; and Appendix to the same.

Macpherson, D., author of " Catechism of Music, adapted for learners on the Piano, etc.," Edinburgh, n.d.

A D. MACPHERSON composed music for the pf., some of which was issued at Liverpool about 1820.

Macrory, Edmund, author of " A Few Notes on the Temple Organ," London [1859], anon.; second edit., 1861; 3rd edit., 1875.

McSwiney, Paul, composer, born at Cork, Ireland. In Cork, February 23, 1881, was produced an opera, " Amergin," of which he wrote the libretto and music. He then went to the United States of America, and became musical director of the New York branch of The Society for the Preservation of the Irish Language. He produced at Steinway

MADAN.

Hall, New York, December 28, 1884, a Gaelic Idyll, "Au Bard 'gus au Fo" (The Bard and the Knight), for solo voices, chorus and orchestra, the book and music his own. Both works were highly spoken of.

Madan, Rev. Martin, musician and clergyman, born in 1726; died on May 2, 1790. He founded the Lock Hospital, in London, and acted as chaplain. He edited "Psalms and hymns extracted from various authors," 1760; "Lock Hospital Tunes" [1769]; and composed the well-known hymntune "Huddersfield." Author of "Thelyphthora: a treatise on female ruin," 3 v., etc.

Mahaffy, Rev. John Pentland, Professor of Ancient History, Trinity College, Dublin, was born at Chapponnaire, near Vevay, on the Lake of Geneva, February 26, 1839. Educated in Germany, and Trinity College, Dublin. Received the degree of D.D., 1886; and is Mus. Doc., *honoris causâ*, Trinity College, Dublin. He is an Examiner in Music for Dublin University; has arranged some Irish melodies; and has contributed articles referring to music to *Cosmopolis* (September, 1896), and other papers.

Mahon, John, clarinet player, was born in 1755. He played in Dublin and at the Birmingham Festivals, 1802-11. Died at Dublin in 1834.

Mahon, Mary, *see* SECOND, MARY.

Mainwaring, Rev. John, clergyman and author, born 1735; died at Cambridge, April, 1807. He published anonymously, "Memoirs of the Life of the late George Frederick Handel, to which is added a catalogue of his works and observations upon them." London, 1760.

Mainwaring, Townshend, Welsh musician and author, born about 1809. He was M.P. for the Denbigh boroughs from 1841 to 1847, and again from 1857 to 1868. He died at Galltfaenan, near Denbigh, in December, 1883, aged 74. Composer of Advent hymn, Emyn ail ddyfodiad Crist; Dafydd and Myfanwry, Hanes Cymraeg, London [1880]; a Welsh romance for treble voices; Hymns, etc.

Maitland, John Alexander Fuller, writer on music, born in London, April 7, 1856. Graduated at Trinity College, Cambridge, B.A., 1879; M.A., 1882. Became F.S.A., 1886. Wrote for the *Pall Mall Gazette*, 1882-4; for the *Guardian*, 1884-9; and, after the death of Dr. Hueffer, in 1889, was appointed musical critic of *The Times*. Contributed articles to the Dictionary of National Biography; Grove's Dictionary of Music and Musicians (and editor of the Appendix to that work); the Nineteenth Century; National Review, etc. Lectured on The History of English Music, two series, 1887; and on Purcell, 1895. Has appeared as a pianist at concerts of the Bach Choir,

MAKER.

etc., and played the harpsichord at concerts of ancient music.

WORKS.—Schumann ("Great Musicians" series, Sampson Low, 1884); Life of J. S. Bach (joint translator, with Clara Bell, of Spitta's work, Novello, 3 vols., 1884); Carols of the 15th century, edited from a roll in Trinity College library, Cambridge, 1891; English county songs (joint editor, with Miss Lucy E. Broadwood), 1893; Catalogue of the music in the Fitzwilliam Museum, Cambridge, 1893; Masters of German Music (Osgood), 1894; Editor of Purcell's Twelve sonatas of three parts (1683), and Ode on St. Cecilia's Day (1692), for Purcell's Society, 1893-6; and Fitzwilliam Virginal book (with W. Barclay Squire, B.A., F.S.A.), in course of publication.

Maitland, William, musician, was born about 1796. He was originally a shoemaker, but was appointed precentor of the East Church, Aberdeen, in 1821, and held the appointment till 1827, when he emigrated to Canada and became a Congregational minister. Died in Canada, December, 1873. Compiler of "The Aberdeen Psalmody, being a collection of tunes in four parts, adapted to the Psalms and Pharaphrases of the Church of Scotland..." Aberdeen, 1823. Has view of St. Nicholas' Church. "Supplement to the Aberdeen Psalmody, being a collection of hymn tunes adapted to particular metres used in the Congregational Chapels," Edinburgh, n.d.

Major, Joseph, musician of the first half of the present century, issued "A collection of psalm and hymn tunes," London [1825]; "A collection of sacred music, consisting of fifty-two psalm and hymn tunes for four voices.." London [c. 1826]. He also composed songs, etc.

Major, S. D., musician and author, compiled "Tunes and chants for home and school," Bath, 1870; "Tunes for the family and congregation," Bristol [1877]; "Tunes for supplement to new congregational tune book" [1874]; "Notabilia of Bath," 1879, and other works.

Makepeace, William, bass vocalist, born about 1820. Chorister at St. Paul's Cathedral under Hawes. Appointed lay-clerk, Rochester Cathedral, in 1845. He was also choir schoolmaster and librarian. Many eminent musicians passed under him as pupils. He resigned the office of schoolmaster about 1886, and retired from the choir on a pension a few months only before his death, which took place at Rochester, September 11, 1896, in the 76th year of his age. He was an original member of the Choir Benevolent Fund.

Maker, Frederick Charles, organist and composer, born at Bristol. Chorister in Bristol Cathedral, and pupil of Alfred Stone.

MALCOLM.

Organist of Milk Street Methodist Free Church ; Clifton Downs Congregational Church ; and from 1882 of Redland Park Congregational Church. Has composed a cantata " Moses in the bullrushes" ; contributed tunes to the Bristol Tune Book ; Issued a collection of original tunes ; Anthems, etc.

Malcolm, Alexander, musician and author, born at Edinburgh in 1687. The particulars of his life and date of his death are unknown. Author of " A Treatise of Music, Speculative, Practical, and Historical," Edinburgh, 1721 ; also London, 1730. This work, from its scientific basis, achieved much success, and was reprinted in an abridged form by an " Eminent Musician," in 1776.

Mallandaine, John E., composer and pianist of present time. Composer of Countess Rosa, opera (1865); The Two Orphans, opera (1874); Love's Limit, comic opera (1875) ; Ali Baba, comic opera ; Uncle Tom's Cabin, songs and choruses (1879). Six songs, the words by J. Ellison, Liverpool (1871). Dance music and arrangements for pf.; Single songs, etc. In 1881 Mallandaine went to the United States.

Mallett, Louis Balfour, violinist and composer, died in London, December 12, 1891, at the early age of 24. He was an able executant, and showed much promise as a composer. His works were not numerous, consisting of a few pieces for the pianoforte, a Gavotte in F for violin and pianoforte, and a set of seven pieces for the same instruments.

Mann, Arthur Henry, organist, editor, and composer, born at Norwich, May 16, 1850. Chorister at Norwich Cathedral under Dr. Buck. F.C.O., 1871 ; Mus. Bac., 1874; Mus. Doc., 1882, Oxford. Hon. R.A.M., 1896. Organist successively at St. Peter's, Wolverhampton, 1870 ; Tettenhall Parish Church, 1871; Beverley Minster, 1875; and from 1876 organist and director of the choir, King's College, Cambridge. He is known as a Handelian Scholar, and was the discoverer, with E. Prout, of the original wind parts of " Messiah," in 1894, at the Foundling Hospital. A performance of the oratorio, with the re-constructed score, was given in King's College, Cambridge, June 13, 1894. He has composed " Ecce Homo " for soli, chorus, and orchestra, 1882; an Evening Service in E, for chorus, orchestra, and organ ; one in E for double choir, unaccompanied ; a Te Deum, for chorus, orchestra, and organ, 1887. Anthems, organ pieces, part-songs, etc. Editor (with J. A. F. Maitland) of the Catalogue of Music in the Fitzwilliam Museum, Cambridge; of Tallis's Motet for 40 voices, London, Weekes, 1888 ; and Musical Editor of the Church of England Hymnal, Hodder and Stoughton, 1895.

Mann, John A., Scottish violinist and

MANSFIELD.

violin maker, born, Forfar, May 13, 1810. Lived in Glasgow as an artist, machinist, and violin maker. He died at Glasgow, April 30, 1889.

Mann, Richard, organist and composer, was born in 1837. He was organist and teacher at Chichester, where he died in 1869. He wrote " A Manual of Singing for the use of choir trainers and school masters," London, 1866, and composed anthems, etc.

Mann, Thomas Edward, hornist. When a boy he was in the Duke of York's School, Chelsea. He became one of the finest horn players of his day, and was also a performer on the cornet. For many years he was principal in the leading orchestras, and up to 1896 was in the band of the Philharmonic Society, the Three Choirs, and other provincial Festivals, playing at the Worcester Festival of September, 1896. He died at Kilburn, London, January 17, 1897. He was professor of the horn at the Kneller Hall Military School of Music ; at the R.A.M., and R.C.M.

Manners, Charles, properly SOUTHCOTE MANSERGH, bass vocalist, born in London. Fourth son of Colonel J. C. Mansergh, R.H.A., and J.P. for Cork and Tipperary. He studied at the Royal Irish Academy of Music, and obtained the Albert Scholarship. Later he went to the R.A.M., London, and afterwards studied in Italy. In 1887, he joined the Carl Rosa Opera Company, touring in the provinces for two years. In 1890, he appeared at Covent Garden, as *Bertram*, in "Robert le Diable " ; and has sung there and at Drury Lane since that time. He made his first appearance in America at the Seidl orchestral concerts, New York, January 8, 1893. Toured in opera, Cape Town, with great success, 1896-7. He married, July 5, 1890, Miss Fanny Moody (*q.v.*), with whom he has since been associated in artistic enterprises, forming a company for concerts and opera recitals. In 1895 he offered a prize of £100 for an opera in one act. *See sub.* MACLEAN.

Mansfeldt, Edgar, see PIERSON, HENRY HUGO.

Mansfield, Orlando Augustus, organist and composer, born at Horningsham, Wilts., November 29, 1863. Son of the Rev. James Pearse Mansfield. Studied music privately, and in 1883 was appointed organist at the Manvers Street Wesleyan Chapel, Trowbridge. Thence he went in 1885 to Torquay, as organist of Holy Trinity Church, an appointment he resigned in 1895. F.R.C.O., 1885 ; Mus. Bac., 1887 ; Mus. Doc., 1890, Trinity College, Toronto. Member of the Society of Authors. Has given lectures on musical subjects, and contributed a number of articles to the *Musical Standard*, and other papers. His compositions include a number of anthems,

MANSON.

one of which obtained the prize offered in 1896 by the Nonconformist Choir Union; hymn tunes, etc. Postlude in C; Finale Fugato, op. 23 (prize voluntary); Andante piacevole; and other organ pieces. Scherzino, pf.; Romance in B flat, op. 28, pf. and violin, etc. Author of The Student's Harmony, London, Weekes, 1896; The Student's Manual of Pedal Scales and Arpeggi.

In 1886, he married Mlle. LOUISE CHRISTINE JUTZ, of Geneva. She is a pianist, medalist of the Geneva Conservatoire, and, in conjunction with her husband, has given recitals of music for two pianos.

Manson, James, musician, and minor poet, was born at Kilwinning, in Ayrshire, about 1812. His father was a tailor, and for some time James followed the same occupation. He went to Glasgow and engaged in literary pursuits, but became blind in 1858, He died at Glasgow, September 3, 1863. He edited the *British Minstrel*, 1842-44, and issued a volume of poetry, and a collection of music, in three volumes.

Marbeck, John, or MERBECKE, writer, composer, and organist, born in 1523. Chorister in St, George's Chapel, Windsor, 1531. Embraced Protestant faith, and narrowly escaped being burned for heresy, 1544. Taken under the patronage of the Bishop of Winchester. Mus. Bac., Oxon., 1550. He died about 1585.

WORKS.—The Book of Common Praier, Noted, London, 1550. A Concordance, that is to saie, a worke wherein by the ordre of the letters of A, B, C, ye maye redelye finde any worde contayned in the whole, so often as it is there expressed or mentioned, London, 1550; The Lyves of the Holy Sainctes, Prophets, Patriarchs, and others, contained in Holye Scripture, 1574; The Holie Historie of King David, etc., 1579; Book of Notes and Common Places, gathered out of divers writers, 1581.

Marbeck re-set the English Church Service almost in its entirety, and is said to have influenced later composers in the style of ecclesiastical composition. His setting continued in use during the many fluctuations in musical taste, which have been witnessed since his time, and is still in use, though not wholly.

March, Mrs., see GABRIEL, MARY ANN VIRGINIA.

Marchant, Arthur William, organist and composer, born in London, October 18, 1850. He was privately educated in music, and took the diploma of F.C.O., 1878; and graduated Mus. Bac., Oxford, 1879. Organist of St. John's, Mansfield, 1870; Streatham Parish Church, 1876; St. Luke's, Kentish Town, 1877. In 1880, he went to America as organist and choirmaster of St. John's

MARKS.

Cathedral, Denver, Colorado. While there, a fine organ was built from his specification, and a large choir formed. He returned to England in 1882, and was appointed to the Parish Church, Sevenoaks; in 1889, to All Saints', Huntingdon; and in 1895, to St. John's Episcopal Church, Dumfries, where he is doing good work. He has composed a setting of Ps. 48, for soli, chorus and orchestra; a Morning Service; Evening Service; This is the Day; Hail to the Lord; I will magnify Thee; and other anthems. Album of six songs; Vocal trios and duets; vocal music for children; part songs, etc. Suite de pièces, violin and pf.; four duets, violin and pf. Six pieces in old dance form; six Songs without words; and other pf. pieces. Preludes and Fugues; 18 original pieces in different styles; and organ pieces, various. Author of Primer, 500 Fugue Subjects and Answers, Ancient and Modern, Novello's Primers; Editor of Twelve Trios for organ, by Albrechtsberger; Pamphlet, Voice Culture, reprinted from *Dumfries and Galloway Standard*, 1896.

Marchant, Charles G., organist and conductor, resident in Dublin. For a number of years he has been organist and choirmaster of St. Patrick's Cathedral; conductor of St. Patrick's Choral Society, and director of Oratorio Services; conductor of Dublin Diocesan Choral Association; and, since the death of Sir R. P. Stewart, conductor of the Dublin University Musical Society. He has given many important oratorio and other concerts; and is Mus Bac., Trinity College, Dublin. Another musician of the name, T. FREDERICK MARCHANT, was for some time a member of the St. Patrick's Cathedral Choir; he is known as a bass vocalist of repute.

Marks, Godfrey. See SWIFT, J. F.

Marks, James Christopher, organist and composer, born at Armagh, Ireland, May 4, 1835. Chorister at Armagh Cathedral, under Robert Turle, 1842-51; deputy organist, 1852. Pupil of F. Hart for violin. Appointed organist and choirmaster, St. Finnbarre's Cathedral, Cork, in 1860, an office he still holds. Graduated Mus. Bac., 1863; Mus. Doc., 1868, Oxford. Conductor of Cork Musical Society, and has given many highclass concerts. He has composed an oratorio, " Gideon "; an anthem, " If we believe," for soli, chorus and orchestra; and has published songs and pf. pieces, etc.

His son, JAMES CHRISTOPHER MARKS, born at Cork, July 29, 1863, is an organist and composer. He was a chorister at Cork Cathedral from 1871; and in 1883 was appointed organist and choirmaster of St. Luke's Church, Cork, where he remains. His compositions comprise anthems, The day is past and over ; The souls of the righteous; and

MARKS.

others ; Evening Services in B flat, A and D. A number of songs, including My loved one, sleep secure, which won the prize offered by Methven & Co., Edinburgh, 1893; part-songs, Blow, ye gentle breezes ; I'll think of thee, etc. Vocal duets ; pf. pieces, etc.

Marks, Thomas Osborne, organist and composer, step-brother of the preceding, born at Armagh, February 6, 1845. Chorister at age of six in' Armagh Cathedral, and deputy organist to Robert Turle when fifteen. Graduated Mus. Bac., Oxford, 1870 ; Mus. Doc., Dublin, 1874. In 1872, he was appointed organist and choirmaster at the Cathedral in succession to R. Turle, a position he retains to the present time. He is conductor of the Armagh Philharmonic Society. His compositions are : Ps. 95, for soli, chorus and orchestra ; cantata, St. John Baptist (MS.) ; church music, and songs, etc.

Marlow, Isaac, clergyman and author, wrote the following tracts : — " Prelimited forms of praising God vocally sung by all the church together, proved to be no Gospel ordinance," London, 1691. " Truth solemnly defended, in a reply to Benjamin Keach, concerning Psalm - singing," 1692. " The controversie of singing brought to an end," etc., London, 1696.

Marriott, Annie Augusta, soprano vocalist, born at Nottingham, May 26, 1859. Studied under J. B. Welch at the National Training School for Music, Kensington. In 1880 she sang at the Saturday Popular Concerts, January 17 ; in Haydn's " Creation," Sacred Harmonic, April 16 ; Promenade Concerts, Covent Garden, August 4, etc. She was engaged for the Worcester Festival, 1881 ; and Leeds, 1883. A proof of her good musicianship was given at Birmingham, November 26, 1885, when at a moment's notice she sang the soprano solos in " The Spectre's Bride," without a rehearsal, and without having ever heard the work. She sang at the Handel Festival, 1885 ; and at Buckingham Palace, before the Queen, in Stanford's " Jubilee Ode," May 11, 1887. . She married, July 20, 1882, PERCY PALMER, a tenor vocalist. He was born at Flaxton, Yorks, December 17, 1861. Studied under James Broughton, Leeds ; and J. B. Welch on going to London. He was just entering upon a career of promise, when he died August 10, 1893.

Marriott, Charles Handel Rand, composer and violinist, born at London, November 3, 1831. He was a violinist, and acted as musical director at Highbury Barn, London, from 1860 till 1865. Afterwards he held the same position at the Cremorne Gardens, and at the Pier Pavilion, Hastings. He was musical editor of the *Young Ladies' Journal.* He died at Hastings, December 3, 1889.

WORKS.—*Songs :* England's trust ; Land

MARSH.

ahead; Lily of the West; Lost friends ; There grew in the forest a mighty oak. Songs for children. Numerous light pieces and arrangements for the pianoforte.

Marriott, Frederick, alto vocalist, lay-clerk in St. George's Chapel, Windsor, from about 1845, and also for some time in the choir of Eton College. He assisted at many of the Royal functions during the Queen's reign, and was the oldest lay-clerk in the Chapel. He died at Windsor, March 19, 1895, aged 82.

Marsden, George, organist, composer, and conductor, born at Stalybridge, Cheshire, April 11, 1843. Studied at the Conservatorium, Cologne, under Ferdinand Hiller, and others. Graduated Mus. Bac., 1876 ; Mus. Doc., 1882, Cambridge. He is resident in Manchester as a teacher, and is organist at St. Thomas', Werneth, near Oldham. He holds an appointment now probably unique in this country, that of conductor of a private orchestra, giving weekly concerts in the winter (*see* S. R. PLATTS), and is Principal of the Oldham School of Music. His compositions comprise settings of Psalm 23, and Psalm 46, for soli, chorus, and orchestra, and other church music. Romance for oboe and orchestra ; pieces for oboe and pf. Dorothy, a rustic dance, and other pf. pieces ; Part-songs, etc.

His brother, JOHN MARSDEN, born May 31, 1835, died at Manchester, November, 1889, was an able organist, and teacher of the pf. His pupils came out first in all England at the local examinations of Oxford, 1868, and Cambridge, 1874. The brothers were early and active workers for the Incorporated Society of Musicians.

Marsh, Alec, baritone vocalist, born at Stratford, near Salisbury, Wilts. Studied under Boyton Smith. Articled to a solicitor, but deciding to become a singer, entered the R.A.M. While a student he sang in Randegger's " The Rival Beauties," at St. George's Hall, May, 1885. Was Evill prizeholder, 1887. He made his festival *début* at Norwich in 1887, and sang in light opera the same year. In 1890 he joined the Carl Rosa Company, and has appeared in a round of characters with success. He married MISS ALICE ESTY, the American soprano, and has appeared with her on the stage, and in the concert room. These artists had a successful tour in Australia.

Marsh, Alphonso, composer, born in 1627, died in April, 1681. He was a Gentleman of the Chapel Royal in 1661, and composed songs and other vocal music in Playford's Collections.

His son, ALPHONSO, born about 1648, was also a Gentleman of the Chapel Royal in 1676. He died April 5, 1692, and is buried in

MARSH.

the west cloister of Westminster Abbey. Composer of songs, which were published in various collections.

Marsh, John, writer and composer, born at Dorking, 1752. Articled to a solicitor at Romsey, 1768. Married, 1774. Leader of Subscription Concerts at Salisbury, 1780. Resided at Chichester from 1787, and died there in 1828.

WORKS.—Six Anthems, 1790; Favorite Symphony in 13 parts, for a grand orchestra; Overture, and 8 sonatinas for the pf.; Overture and six pieces for the organ [1791]; Quartette for 2 violins, tenor and bass. Two sets of organ voluntaries. Glees, songs, etc. A Short Introduction to the theory of harmonics, or the philosophy of musical sounds, Chichester, 1809. Rudiments of Thorough-bass, London, 1805. Hints to Young Composers of instrumental music, London [1800]. Collection of the most popular and approved Psalm Tunes, with a few Hymns and easy Anthems, the whole in 3 parts..principally for the use of country choirs, to which is added a selection of 20 favourite tunes set for barrel organs, n.d. Cathedral Chant Book, London [1800].

Marsh, J., musician of present time, published "Introduction and progressive lessons for the Tenor," London [1881].

Marsh, Narcissus, amateur musician and archbishop, was born in Wiltshire in 1638. In 1703 he was consecrated Archbishop of Armagh. He died at Dublin in 1713. Now best remembered as founder of Marsh's Library, St. Patrick's Cathedral, Dublin, 1707. He wrote an "Essay touching the sympathy between lute or viol strings," 1677, published in Plot's Natural History of Oxfordshire, and an Introductory essay to the doctrine of sounds, 1683, etc.

Marshall, Frederick, composer, and teacher of music, born at Northampton about 1790. He was successively organist at Rugby School; Christ Church, Leamington; and Parish Church of Banbury, Oxford. He died near Olney, Bucks., July, 1857. He composed hymn tunes, etc.

Marshall, Julian, amateur musician, and collector, born at Headingly, Leeds, June 24, 1836. Author of the "Annals of Tennis." Contributor to the *Musical Times*, and other periodicals; and writer of a number of articles in Grove's Dictionary of Music and Musicians. He was a member of the committee of the first Leeds Festival, 1858. His large and valuable musical library was dispersed by auction, July, 1884. His wife, *born* FLORENCE A. THOMAS, born at Rome, March 30, 1843, is a composer and writer on music. She studied at the R.A.M. Conducts the concerts of the South Hampstead orchestra, and is the composer of a fairy operetta, "Prince Sprite"; a Nocturne

MARSHALL.

for clarinet and orchestra. Has contributed articles to Grove, and to various periodicals. Author of "Handel," Great Musicians' Series, London, Sampson Low, 1883; Solfeggi, Novello's Primers, 1885; Interval Exercises for Singing Classes, Novello. She is an Associate of the Philharmonic Society.

Marshall, Oldfield Sherwin, organist and pianist. In 1883 he was appointed to the Anglo-American Church, Rome; and in 1890 succeeded Dr. Mark J. Monk as organist of the Parish Church, Banbury. He has appeared as pianist at various concerts; and an orchestral Suite of his composition was performed at Abingdon in 1889. In 1884 he was elected Associate of Merit of the Academy of St. Cecilia, Rome, the only Englishman thus distinguished.

Marshall, William, violinist and composer, born at Fochabers, December 27, 1748. House steward and butler to the Duke of Gordon till 1790. In 1773 he married Jane Giles, by whom he had a family of five sons and a daughter. Farmer at Keithmore, and factor to the Duke of Gordon, 1790-1817. He died at Newfield Cottage, Dandaleith, Rothes, Elginshire, May 29, 1833, and is buried in Bellie Churchyard.

WORKS.—A Collection of Strathspey Reels, with a bass for the Violoncello or Harpsichord, Edinburgh, Neil Stewart [1781]. A second collection appeared later. Marshall's Scottish Airs, Melodies, Strathspeys, Reels, etc., for the pianoforte, violin, and violoncello, with appropriate basses. Dedicated to the Marchioness of Huntly, Edin., 1822 [containing 170 airs]. Collection of Scottish Melodies, Reels, Strathspeys, Jigs, Slow Airs, etc., for the pianoforte, violin, and violoncello, being the genuine and posthumous works of William Marshall, Edinburgh, 1847. Choice Selection of Reels and Strathspeys, Edinburgh, n.d. (with Gow).

Marshall is best known as a composer by his melodies "Of a' the airts the wind can blaw" ("Miss Admiral Gordon's Strathspey"), "This is no my ain house," "The wind blew the bonnie lassie's plaidie awa," and several others, all of which were dance tunes which have been adapted to poetry.

Marshall, William, organist and composer, was born in 1806. He became a chorister in the Chapel Royal, under J. S. Smith and W. Hawes, and in Christ Church, and St. John's College, Oxford, 1823. Organist of All Saints', Oxford. Mus. Bac., Oxon., 1826, Mus. Doc., Oxon., January, 1840. Organist of St. Mary's Church, Kidderminster, 1846. He died at Handsworth, August 17, 1875.

WORKS.—Anthems used in the Cathedral and Collegiate Churches of England and Wales, 1840. Art of Reading Church Music, and Exercises intended to accompany the

MARSHALL.

MASON.

same. Oxford, 1842-43. Miscellaneous church music. Three canzonets [1830]. Cathedral Services, arranged for organ and pf., Oxford, 1847. Cathedral Chants, edited with Alfred W. Bennett [1829].

A MRS. WILLIAM MARSHALL (wife of above?), composed a number of songs and ballads, about 1830-40.

Marshall - Hall, see HALL, W. L. MARSHALL.

Marson, George, composer of the 16th century, who wrote anthems, and a 5-part madrigal, " The Nimphes and Shepheards," in the " Triumphs of Oriana," 1601. He is said to have been a Bac. Mus., but it is not known at what university he graduated.

Martin, Amy Florence, contralto vocalist of present time. Was educated at the London Academy of Music, studying singing with Manuel Garcia; and distinguishing herself also in harmony. She won two scholarships while there, was made an Associate in 1885, receiving her diploma from the hands of Madame Patti, and was appointed a professor of singing. Her concert engagements included tours with Mr. Sims Reeves, appearances at the Crystal Palace and other concerts. She then turned her attention to opera, and assisted at the first production of several light operas, finally becoming a member of Mr. J. W. Turner's company about 1892. In the tours of this company she has appeared with success in a variety of parts, ranging from *Azucena*, in " Il Trovatore," to *Siebel*, in " Faust."

Martin, George Clement, organist and composer, born at Lambourne, Berks, September 11, 1844. Studied under J. Pearson, and Dr. Stainer. Graduated Mus Bac., Oxford, 1868; F.C.O., 1875; and received the Canterbury degree of Mus. Doc., 1883. Private organist to the Duke of Buccleuch, Dalkeith, 1871; Master of Song at the Choir School, 1874, and deputy organist, St. Paul's Cathedral, 1876; and elected organist, on the retirement of Dr. Stainer, 1888. Professor of the Organ, at R.C.M., for a few years from 1883. His compositions are chiefly for the church, and comprise a Morning, Communion, and Evening Service in C, for voices and orchestra; Evening Services for the same, and for military Band; setting of the Benedicite, and Offertory sentences. Te Deum for the Queen's Diamond Jubilee service, St. Paul's, June 22, 1897. Come my soul; Ho every one that thirsteth; Rejoice in the Lord; Veni, Creator Spiritus; and other anthems. Editor of Responses to the Commandments. Evening; Cold blows the wind; Let maids be false (men's voices), and other part-songs. Arrangements for the organ, of movements from St. Ludmila; Redemption; and Mors et Vita. Editor of

Organ Arrangements, Novello. Author of The Art of Training Choir Boys, Novello's Primers, No. 39.

Martin, George William, composer and conductor, was born on March 8, 1828. He was a chorister in St. Paul's Cathedral under W. Hawes. Professor of music at the Normal College for Army Schoolmasters; Music master at St. John's Training College, Battersea, 1845-53; Organist of Christ Church, Battersea, 1849. He conducted the concerts of the National Choral Society, the Metropolitan Schools Choral Society, etc. Editor of the "Journal of Part Music," 1861-62, and of other musical journals. He died at Bolingbroke House Hospital, Wandsworth, April 16, 1881. Martin composed several prize glees, anthems, songs, the hymn tune, " Leominster," etc.

Martin, Henry Maclean, ENRICO CAMPOBELLO, baritone vocalist, born in 1839. Sang in opera in Colonel Mapleson's company, and toured in the provinces with the same in 1872, etc. He is also well known as a concert singer. In 1874 he married the soprano vocalist, known as Madame Sinico, whose maiden name was Clarice Marini.

Martin, Jonathan, organist and composer, born in 1715. Chorister in the Chapel Royal under Croft. He studied the organ under Rosingrave, and became deputy of St. George's, Hanover Square, London, and organist of the Chapel Royal in 1736. He died at London, April 4, 1737.

Martyn, Mrs. See INVERARITY, ELIZA.

Mason, Edward, composer and teacher of singing, born at Newcastle-under-Lyme, July 4, 1864. Descended from an old Staffordshire family settled in that town from the sixteenth century. Received his musical training at St. John's College, Battersea, under Edward Mills, 1883-4; and at the Tonic Sol-Fa College, under McNaught, Venables, and others. Became a Fellow of the College in 1889, and graduated Mus. Bac., Durham, 1892. Is singing instructor to the Arbroath School Board; choirmaster, St. Mary's Episcopal Church, and conductor of several choral societies. He has composed a Good Friday Service, " The Man of Sorrows " (1896); Wee Folks' Songs; and is author of Old Notation Reader (5 Nos.), and Standard Music Charts for Schools. He executed the Tonic Sol-fa translation of Sullivan's " Light of the World," and has contributed to the Scottish Musical Review, and other papers.

Mason, John, author of " An Essay on the power of numbers and the principles of Harmony," London, 1749; and composer of songs, " The Admiring Lover," etc.

Mason, John, clergyman and musician, of the early part of the 16th century. One of the famous musicians mentioned by

R

MASON.

Morley. In 1508, he was instructor of the choristers at Magdalen College, Oxford, and in the same year he graduated Mus. Bac. He died in 1547-48.

Mason, William, poet, musician, and writer, born at Hull in 1725. Ordained minister, 1755. Prebendary and Preceptor, York Cathedral, 1763. He died at Aston, April 5, 1797. Wrote various papers on ecclesiastical music, collected under the title of "Essays, historical and critical, on English Church Music," York, 1795, and composer of "Lord of all power and might," anthem, and other vocal music. His works are chiefly literary, and he takes rank among the minor poets of England.

Massey, Richard, musician, born in 1798, was organist at the Chapel Royal, Whitehall, for 40 years [1837-77]. He died at London, April 21, 1883.

Another RICHARD MASSEY, probably the father of the foregoing, issued a work entitled "Sacred Music: twenty-six psalm tunes and three anthems," Manchester [1810].

Masson, Elizabeth, contralto singer and composer, was born in Scotland early in the present century. She was a pupil of Madame Pasta, and made her *début* at the Ancient Concerts on March 16, 1831. She founded the Royal Society of Female Musicians in 1838 along with MARY SARAH STEELE (who was a professor of singing at the R.A.M., and died at London, March 26, 1881, aged 65). Died at London, in January, 1865.

WORKS.—Original Jacobite Songs, London [1839]; Twelve songs for the classical vocalist [1845-61], 24 parts; Twelve songs by Byron [1843]; Vocal sketches. *Songs:* Oh! love was never yet without the pang [1837]; Balmoral rant [1840]; Come off to the moors; Here's a health unto Her Majesty; Is my lover on the sea? Mary, adieu; Scotland, etc. Vocal Exercises, London [1855]. Numerous arrangements, etc.

Masters, William J. Chalmers, pianist and composer, born in London, 1818. Sometime musical director, St. George's Hall, London. For many years resident as a teacher at Southsea. He was the composer of two operettas, "The Forester's Daughters," produced at St. George's Hall, November 19, 1867, and "The Rose of Salency"; of songs, pf. pieces, etc. He died at Southsea, November 28, 1893.

Masterton, Allan, Scottish musician and writing-master in the High School of Edinburgh. An associate of Robert Burns, the poet, to whose song, "Willie brew'd a peck o' maut," he wrote music. He died about 1799.

Mather, George, musician and teacher, compiled "The Calcutta Melodies, comprising thirty-six original psalm and hymn tunes, London [1844]. The Freehay Singing Class

MATHEWS.

Manual, London [1883]. Also composed songs, etc.

Mather, Samuel, organist and composer, son of William Mather, was born at Sheffield in 1783. Organist of St. James' Church, Sheffield, 1799; St. Paul's, Sheffield, 1808. Bandmaster of the Sheffield Volunteers, 1805. He died at Edinburgh, May 26, 1824. Compiled a Book of Psalm Tunes, and assisted Cotterill in the compilation of his "Christian Psalmody." He also composed glees, songs, Te Deum, numerous hymns, etc.

Mather, William, organist and composer, born in 1756. He was organist of St. Paul's, and St. James', Sheffield, and died at Sheffield, in 1808. Compiler of "Sacred Music, consisting of Twenty-six Psalm and Hymn Tunes . . ." London [1805] ; and composer of the Psalm-tune "Sheffield," known also as "Attercliffe." His son, JOHN MATHER, born in Sheffield, March 31, 1781, was organist of Sheffield Parish Church, 1805, but settled in Edinburgh about 1810. He was organist at the Musical Festival of 1815, and from 1815 till 1818, was conductor of the Edinburgh Institution for the encouragement of Sacred Music. He was pianist at the Glasgow Festival in 1821, and chorus-master at the Edinburgh Festival of 1843. He also sang at various musical festivals. Died at Edinburgh, January 20, 1850. He composed "Hail to the Chief," a glee; songs; and wrote accompaniments for Peter Macleod's "Original Melodies."

Mathews, James, amateur flutist and composer, born at Stourbridge, June 2, 1827. His father was a talented amateur both in music and painting, and gave his son such musical instruction as he received, but would not consent to his entering the musical profession. The son devoted all his spare time to the cultivation of the flute, and like his father, became a fine performer. He played his first solo in public in 1843; and up to 1878, was frequently heard in the district, and nearly every year playing in Birmingham, his services being given to every call of charity. On October 7, 1868, he was publicly presented with a gold flute, in the Union Hall, Stourbridge, a gift from his friends and admirers. The instrument was designed from his own plan of fingering, and has 32 keys, and his execution on it could not be excelled. His friendship with Mr. Walter Broadwood, an excellent amateur flutist, brought him into contact with many eminent musicians, and he has enjoyed the rare experience, in private circles, of playing to the pianoforte accompaniment of Joseph Joachim. He has composed nearly 100 songs, a few of which are published; some pieces for flute; and has arranged many movements from the great masters for his instrument.

MATT.

Retired from business, he still devotes himself to Music at his home, at Clent, in Worcestershire.

Matt, Albert E., trombonist, of the Philharmonic and other orchestras. He is the composer of an orchestral suite, " An Evening Ramble " ; " Rural Scenes," in three movements ; " Angelus " ; Idyl, " Sunset," performed by the Strolling Players' orchestra, Queen's Hall, 1895 ; Norwegian Suite, 1897 ; Idyl, " Dawn," etc., all for orchestra.

Matthay, Tobias Augustus, composer, pianist, and teacher, born at Clapham, London, February 19, 1858. Entered the R.A.M. in 1871 ; studied composition under Sterndale Bennett, Sullivan, and Prout ; and pf. under W. Dorrell, and W. Macfarren. First Sterndale Bennett Scholar, 1872 ; and awarded the first of the two Read Prizes for a pf. quartet, 1879. Made a Professor, and Associate, of the R.A.M., 1880 ; and elected a Fellow in 1895. While a student, an overture and other compositions of his were performed at the Academy concerts. He gave his first concert in Clapham Hall, May 14, 1880, when his prize quartet was performed ; and since 1884 has given annual recitals at Prince's Hall, Queen's Hall, etc. He has contributed articles on music generally, and pf. tone-production particularly, to *The Overture, The Keyboard*, and other papers. As a teacher he has done excellent work at the R.A.M., several of the most promising recent students having been his pupils. His compositions are already very numerous, and are outlined in the subjoined list.

WORKS. — *Orchestral :* Two Symphonic movements ; Four Concert overtures (one produced at Promenade Concerts, 1879) ; Scherzi, etc. Concerto ; Concert allegro in A minor, another in D minor, for pf. and orchestra. Scena, Hero and Leander, contralto solo and orchestra. Psalm 126, for chorus. Bright be the place of thy soul ; There be none of Beauty's daughter's ; The gentle eventide ; A Lament (Shelley), and other songs. Fairies' serenade, part-song. String quartet (1872) ; Quartet in F, pf. and strings (Read prize) ; Trio, pf. and strings ; Idyll, in D flat, violin and pf., Musical Artists' Society, 1884 ; Ballade, 'cello and pf., the same, 1886. About 70 pieces for pf., of which may be mentioned, Four Novelletten ; 17 variations on an original Theme, etc. ; Moods of a moment, 10 numbers ; Sonata in B minor ; 35 variations and evolvements on an original theme, in A minor ; Scottish dances ; Lyrics, etc.

In August, 1892, he married MISS JESSIE KENNEDY, a daughter of David Kennedy (*q.v.*) ; an excellent vocalist, who has sung in Scotland, 1885 ; London, 1892 ; and assisted at her husband's recitals, etc.

MATTMEWS.

Matthew, James E., writer, of present time. Author of " A popular History of Music, Musical Instruments, Ballet, and Opera, from St. Ambrose to Mozart," London, Grevel, 1888 ; " Manual of Musical History," an enlargement of the preceding, 1892 ; " The Literature of Music," London, Stock, 1896.

Matthews, H., author of " Observations on Sound : showing the causes of its indistinctness in churches," etc. London, 1826.

Matthews, John, organist, violinist and composer, born at Liskeard, Cornwall, March 27, 1856. Studied at the Conservatorium, Dresden, under Merkel, and Draeseke. Has held organ appointments at St. James's, Swansea ; Parish Church, St. Austell, Cornwall ; and, since 1889, has been organist at St. Stephen's, Guernsey. There he is actively engaged as a teacher and concert giver. His wife is a clever violoncellist, and takes part in the chamber concerts given by him. His compositions include an Evening Service in D, composed for the St. Austell Deanery Choir Festival, 1888 ; Te Deum in F ; anthem. Song of the Streamlet ; The Mother to her Child ; and other songs. Part-songs, How soft the shades, etc. Sonata in C minor ; six pieces, organ ; pieces for violin ; and for pf., etc. Editor and translator of Carl Schroeder's Catechism of Violin playing, and of Violoncello playing, Augener. Other works in MS.

Matthews, John Alexander, organist and conductor, born at Gloucester, June 17, 1841. Educated at King's College School, having entered the Cathedral Choir in 1850. Articled pupil of, and assistant organist to, John Amott, and after his death, 1865, acting organist at the Cathedral, until the appointment of Dr. S. S. Wesley. In 1866 he went to Cheltenham, and has been organist and choirmaster of the parish church of St. Matthew since that time. He started a choral society which is now known as the Festival Society, and in 1887 organised a Musical Festival, which is celebrated triennially, and at which several works of importance have been produced. This is under his own management. In 1893 he founded the County of Gloucester Musical Festival Association, numbering more than 2,000 members. He was for 15 years connected with the Gloucester Choral Society, as choirmaster, organist, and conductor. In 1876 he received a public testimonial from this society at the hands of the then Mayor of Gloucester, Anthony Jones, Esq., and in 1890, a similar token of regard through the Mayor of Cheltenham, Colonel Thoytes, at the close of the Festival. He has had a busy life as a teacher ; is hon. local representative of R.A.M., and hon. examiner for R.C.M. ; and

MATTHEWS.

prominent in the work of the Incorporated Society of Musicians. Hon. life member of Trinity College, London. Of his compositions, the songs, The Language of the Heart ; God is Love ; Church Bells ; and The Merry May, are the best known.

Matthews, Julia, soprano vocalist and actress, born in Australia. She sang principally in *opéra bouffe*, and appeared in the title - part of Offenbach's " La Grande Duchesse," on its first production in English, Covent Garden, November 16, 1867. She was also the original *Madame Lange*, in the English version of Lecocq's " La Fille de Madame Angot," produced at the Philharmonic Theatre, London, November? 1873. She died at New York, May, 1876, at the early age of 34.

Matthews, Rev. Timothy Richard, clergyman and musician, born at Colmworth Rectory, near Bedford, November 4, 1826. Educated at Bedford Grammar School and graduated B.A., Cambridge, in 1853. He studied the organ under Sir George Elvey. Rector of North Coates, near Grimsby, from 1869.

WORKS.—Tunes for holy worship, London, 1859, 2nd edit., 1860. The village-church tune-book, London, 1859. Congregational melodies ; a collection of tunes, chants and responses, London [1862]. Hymn tunes, London [1867]. North Coates supplemental tune book, London, [1878], 1883, etc. Anglican chants (Hatchards). The village organist, London [1877]. His hymn tunes, Ludborough, Chenies, and Winthorpe, have been often printed.

Matthison, Arthur, vocalist, actor and author, born in Birmingham, January 31, 1826. He studied singing in Italy as a tenor, but his voice afterwards changed to a baritone of rich quality ; and he had the rare experience of singing, at different periods, the tenor and the bass solos in the " Messiah." On the stage he took singing parts, but acted in melodrama at Drury Lane and elsewhere. For several years he was at Booth's Theatre, New York. He was a man of versatile ability, his dramatic works, including " Harold," a five-act drama, and a most successful skit on the hysterical drama, " More than ever " (1882), exceeding twenty in number ; and he also wrote the English versions of Balfe's " Talismano," Rossini's " Mosé in Egitto " (for the Sacred Harmonic production of the work as an oratorio, May, 1878), " Mignon," and " La Dame Blanche," for Carl Rosa, the libretto of " Rebekah " for Joseph Barnby, and other pieces. His poem, " The little Hero," was set by Michael Maybrick. A volume of Sketches and Essays was published by J. Camden Hotten, London, n.d. He died in London, May 21, 1883. His

MAXWELL.

younger brother, HENRY MATTHISON, too much engaged in official life in Birmingham to enter the musical profession, was for many years in request as a concert singer, having a sweet tenor voice. He married the Welsh contralto, Kate Wynne (*q.v.*), sister of Edith Wynne.

Maunder, John, organist and composer, born in Chelsea, London, 1858 Musically educated at the R.A.M. Organist St. Matthew's, Sydenham, 1876-7 ; St. Paul's Forest Hill, 1878-9. Conductor of the Civil Service Vocal Union, from 1881. Has done much work as accompanist, and in that capacity has been especially connected with Mr. Sims Reeves, playing for him at his farewell concert, at the Albert Hall, May 11 1891. He trained the choir for Henry Irving's original production of " Faust " at the Lyceum Theatre, December, 1887. His compositions include an operetta, " Daisy Dingle " (Forest Hill, 1885) ; a cantata for men's voices, " The Martyrs," composed for the Queen's College, Oxford, Concerts, and produced, May 25, 1894 ; he has also published several anthems, settings of the Te Deum, and Benedicite, two Evening Services carols, a chorus, " Thor's War Song," songs etc.

Maurice, Rev. Peter, D.D., writer and clergyman, born in 1804. Vicar of Yarnton Woodstock, and Chaplain of New College, Oxford. He died at Yarnton vicarage, March 30, 1878. Author of " What shall we do with Music ? a letter to the Earl of Derby," London, 1856. " Choral Harmony, a collection of tunes in short score for four voices," 1854. He composed an evening service, hymn tunes, etc.

Maxfield, William Henry, composer and organist, born April 27, 1849, at North Somercotes, Lincolnshire. Chorister, St. Philip's, Hulme, Manchester, 1860-5, and pupil of F. Pugh and Dr. Hiles. F.R.C.O., 1888. Took the Toronto Mus. Bac., 1889. Has held appointments as organist and choirmaster at St. Peter's, Levenshulme, 1866 ; St. Thomas', Norbury, 1872 ; St. George's, Altrincham, 1879 ; and has been, from 1884, at St. John's, Altrincham. Conductor of Choral Societies at Altrincham, Bowden, and other places ; and lecturer on subjects connected with music.

WORKS.—Cantatas: Jacob and Esau (1888); Star of the East (1889) ; The Lord is risen (1890); and The old, old story (1892). Choral Ballad, Delphi, men's voices and orchestra ; The Silver Lily, cantata for female voices. Anthems, and compositions for pf., organ, etc. Edited Collection of Fifty Minstrel Songs ; Fifty Favourite Songs, etc.

Maxwell, Francis Kelly, author of " An Essay upon Tune, being an attempt to

MAY.

free the scale of Music and the tune of instruments from imperfection," Edinburgh, 1781 ; London, 1794. Maxwell died in 1782.

May, Edward Collett, organist and composer, was born at Greenwich, October 29, 1806. He studied music and the organ under Adams, Potter, and Crivelli. Organist of Greenwich Hospital, 1837-69. Professor of Vocal Music in Queen's College, London. He died at London, January 2, 1887. Author of "Progressive Vocal Exercises for daily practice," London [1853], and composer of songs, etc. He was celebrated as an organist and teacher.

May, Florence, pianist and composer, daughter of the foregoing, born in London. Her musical talent showed itself very early, and was fostered by her father and uncle ; but it was not until some years later, after receiving some lessons from Madame Schumann, that the young pianist devoted herself to music as a profession. Through Madame Schumann's influence, Johannes Brahms accepted Florence May as a pupil, and to that happy circumstance is due her great success as an interpreter of his music. After some years spent in Germany, she returned to London about 1873, and continuing her studies for a further period, she gave her first recital in the Beethoven Rooms, February 3, 1875. At the Bennett Memorial Concert, March 10, at St. James's Hall, she played the deceased Master's F minor Concerto. Then followed engagements in London, Liverpool, and other places. Further study in harmony, etc., with her father and Sir G. A. Macfarren was followed by another visit to Germany, and she studied under Bargiel, in Berlin. Two compositions of hers, Benedictus and Osanna, were performed in Berlin at that time. In 1885 she returned to London, but has since made several tours in Germany, giving recitals in Vienna, 1890-96, etc., and has taken her place among the leading pianists of the time, giving annual recitals in London. Her published compositions include Three Mazurkas, Bourrée ; Waltzes, op. 4 ; and other pf. pieces. Three choruses for female voices ; Six songs with German and English words (her own translation). She has also edited a collection of pieces by Old Masters, from works written for harpsichord, including some by Henry Symonds (q.v.).

May, John, musician, of early part of the present century, composed "A selection of songs, duetts, glees, waltzes, etc., arranged for 1, 2, or 3 German flutes or patent flageolets," Edinburgh, 1809. "The Royal Marine Quadrilles, for pf.," London [1825].

May, Oliver, pianist, born at Greenwich, January 27, 1814. His first instruction in music was received from his brother, Edward Collett, noticed above. At the R.A.M. he

MAYBRICK.

studied for over five years, under Cipriani Potter, and on leaving was appointed organist at a chapel on Blackheath. Later he officiated for some years at a church in Bermondsey, and was for a short time, previous to 1857, organist at St. Martin-in-the-Fields. He was appointed a professor of the pf. at Queen's College, London, at its foundation. A member of the original committee of the Bach Society, London, he was an active worker while the society existed ; and was for many years a member, and occasionally a director of the Philharmonic Society ; also a Fellow, R.A.M. His retiring disposition militated against a public life, but as a teacher he was in great request and highly valued. He died at St. Albans, April 12, 1894. A fellow student at the R.A.M. with Sterndale Bennett, the closest intimacy existed between them. Many interesting mementos of Bennett and others at his death came into the possession of his niece, Florence May (q.v.). His published works were few ; an overture, Don Sebastian, op. 1, arranged for pf. duet ; I seek the haunts ; The Moon's pale beam, and other songs. In MS. remain a quartet for pf. and strings ; songs, madrigals, and pf. pieces.

Maybrick, Michael, STEPHEN ADAMS, baritone vocalist and composer, born at Liverpool, 1844. Studied under W. T. Best, and was organist of St. Peter's Church. Liverpool, 1858. In 1866 he went to Leipzig, and studied at the Conservatorium under Moscheles, Plaidy, and Richter ; but later turned his attention to singing, and studied with Gaetano Nava. He sang at the Oratorio Concerts, London, February 25, 1869, and in the provinces that year ; at the New Philharmonic Concerts, 1870 ; at the Bristol Festival, 1876 ; at the principal London and provincial concerts ; and in 1884, toured in the United States and Canada. As the interpreter of his own songs he has been a great favourite. Of these songs may be mentioned, A warrior bold ; Nancy Lee ; The Tar's farewell ; Garonne ; Good Company ; Blue Alsatian mountains ; Star of Bethlehem ; Children of the City ; Valley by the Sea ; Genevieve ; Little Hero ; Holy City ; Sweet Kildare ; Mona ; Romany Lass ; Fiona, etc. Many of these, particularly "Nancy Lee," enjoyed extraordinary popularity.

Other musicians of the name, and presumably of the same family, were WILLIAM MAYBRICK, born 1773 ; died, 1843, a composer of whom nothing appears to be known ; and MICHAEL MAYBRICK, his son, born 1799 ; died at Liverpool, May, 1846. He was a pupil of Richard Wainwright. Organist of St. Peter's, Liverpool, and organist and conductor of the Liverpool Choral Society. He published "Twelve Voluntaries for the Organ ; composed in a free style, and founded on

MAYCOCK.

Church melodies" (W. Blackman, 1844 ?), 2 books. Also two sets of original chants; arrangements for pf.; Mozart's favourite air, "Life let us cherish," with new variations for pf., etc.

Maycock, John Henry, clarinet player, was for 35 years in the orchestra of the Royal Italian Opera, and of Drury Lane. During his time many English operas were produced, and it was for him that Balfe wrote the corno di bassetto introduction to "The heart bowed down," and the bass clarinet solo in "The Daughter of St. Mark." For over fifty years Maycock occupied a high position as a performer. He retired from public life in 1892, at the age of 75.

Maynard, John, lute-player and composer, of the 16th and 17th centuries, published "The xii. Wonders of the World, set and composed for the Violl de Gambo, the lute, and the voyce, to sing the verse, all three jointly, and none severall; also Lessons for the Lute and Basse violl to play alone; with some Lessons to play lyra-wayes alone, or if you will, to fill up the parts with another violl set lute-way," London, 1611.

Maynard, John, musician, of Ponder's End, Essex, wrote "Forty-eight original hymn tunes, and two pieces," London [1830].

Maynard, Walter, see BEALE, THOMAS WILLERT.

Mayo, Charles, surgeon and amateur musician, born at Winchester in 1837; died on a voyage to Sydney in 1877. Author of a pamphlet on the "Organ in New College Chapel" [Oxford], 1875.

Mayo. Rev. Charles Herbert, author and musician. Vicar of Long Burton with Holnest, Dorset, since 1872. He has published a number of antiquarian works, family histories, and has issued "Traditional Carols for Christmas-Tide, sung at Long Burton, Dorset....harmonies arranged by E. C. Howarth," Sherborne [1893]. He also edited "Bibliotheca Dorsetiensis," 1885.

Mazzinghi, Joseph, composer, was born at London, December 25, 1765. He belonged to a Corsican family, from which he derived the title of Count. Pupil of J C. Bach, Anfossi, and Sacchini. Musical director of King's Theatre, 1784. Music teacher to Princess of Wales. He died at Bath, January 15, 1844.

WORKS.—*Musical dramas:* A day in Turkey, 1791; Paul and Virginia, 1800; Blind Girl, 1801; Exile, 1808; La belle Arsene; Sappho et Phaon; Magician no conjuror; Free Knights; Ramah Droog (with Reeve); Turnpike Gate (Reeve); Chains of the Heart (with Reeve); Wife of two Husbands. *Glees, trios, songs, etc.*: And whither would you lead me; Ava Maria; O Brignal banks; The captive to his bird; Cypress wreath; Each throbbing heart; For tenderness formed; Had I a heart; Harril the

MEEN.

brave; Hart and hind are in their lair; Haste, O haste, glorious light; Hope told a flattering tale; Huntsman rest; I seek my shepherd gone astray; If the treasured gold; John of Brent; Lady beware; Lillo Lee; Lochgyle; The Minstrel's summons; Mirth and beauty; The negro's glee; Nocturnal besiegers; O young Lochinvar; Pastoral Rondo; Roderick Vich Alpine; Soldier rest; Wake maid of Lorn; When order in this land commenced; When Phœbus rays no more appear; When tell-tale echoes; and, Where shall the lover rest. Songs, ballads, etc. He also composed Admiral Lord Nelson's victory, a sonata in commemoration of the glorious 1st of August. Twelve airs for the pf., with accompaniments for a flute and tambourine. A large number of sonatas and other pf. pieces. Selection of German national melodies....London [1815].

Meadowcroft, John, organist and composer, was born in 1827, He was a chorister in Manchester Cathedral, and for ten years honorary organist at the cathedral evening services. He died at Scarborough, August 28, 1873. Composer of chants and editor of a psalter.

Mee, Rev. John Henry, composer and writer on music, born at Riddings Vicarage, Derbyshire, August 16, 1852. Scholar and Taberdar, Queen's College, Oxford, 1871; first-class in Classical Moderations, 1873; first-class in Literæ Humaniores, 1875; B.A., and Fellow, Merton's College, 1875; Succentor, Queen's College, 1876; M.A. and classical lecturer, Worcester College, 1878; Mus. Bac., 1882; Mus. Doc., 1888, Oxford. Ordained Deacon, 1876; Priest, 1877, by Bishop of Oxford. Public Examiner in University of Oxford three times; Hon. Fellow, St. Michael's College, Tenbury, 1886; Precentor of Chichester Cathedral, 1889; County Councillor for West Sussex, 1890; and Coryphæus of Oxford University, 1890. Dr. Mee has done much for chamber music in Oxford, and has lectured at the Musical Association, etc. He has also contributed the articles Steibelt, Vogler, and others to Grove's Dictionary.

WORKS.—Dies Ascensionis for soli, chorus, and orchestra; Missa Solennis in B flat, for soli, double-chorus, and orchestra, Oxford, November 9, 1888. Ballads for men's chorus and orchestra: Horatius, London, April 21, 1891; Delphi, Oxford, 1895. Christmas Carols set to music; God who at sundry times, anthem. Madrigals, Chloris' singing, Madrigal Society's prize, 1887; The lesson of Love. Motet. Quartet in G, strings; Fantasia, organ, etc.

Meen, Fountain, pianist and organist, born at Hackney, London, September 14, 1846. Not being originally brought up to the musical profession, his studies were private, and he is for the most part self-taught. Has

MEGONE.

been organist successively at Clapton Wesleyan Chapel ; St. Mary's, Stoke Newington ; and, since 1880, at Union Chapel, Islington. Was organist to the Sacred Harmonic Society for the last seven years of its existence, and has played organ solos at the Annual Festivals of the Royal Society of Musicians, of which he is a member. In 1886 he succeeded the late Josiah Pittman as professor of the organ at the Guildhall School of Music. He is also Local Examiner for R.C.M., and an Associate of the Philharmonic Society. As a pianist he is chiefly known as a skilful accompanist.

Megone, Norfolk, conductor, born in London, March 15, 1860. Studied as an amateur under Otto Standke, at Bonn ; and also Leipzig and Frankfort. On his return to London he became connected with several musical societies, and founded the Belsize Amateur Orchestral Society. In 1882 he organised the orchestra of the Strolling Players' Amateur Dramatic Club, and gave a number of excellent concerts. He joined the profession in 1889, and was appointed conductor of the Devonshire Park Concerts, Eastbourne ; also of the Private Banks Musical Society in 1890. He has composed "Œnone," and other valses, for orchestra, etc.

Melba, Madame, see ARMSTRONG, HELEN PORTER.

Mell, Davis, violinist, and clock-maker, born at Wilton, near Salisbury, Nov. 15, 1604. He was esteemed the finest violin player in England prior to the arrival of Baltzar. Some of his compositions are to be found in Christopher Simpson's "Division Violin," 1684. The date of his death is unknown, but he was a musician in the service of Charles II.

Meller, Clara, pianist, born at Clifton, Bristol, February 3, 1856. Studied there, and in London, proceeding to Leipzig in 1871. There she entered the Conservatorium, studying under Oscar Paul, and Reinecke. She returned to England, and appeared in concerts in London and the provinces, but was back again in Germany in 1876. In 1880 she was married to Dr. Hermann Kretzschmar, now University Musical Director, Leipzig. Her professional career was not abandoned, and she occupies a high position as a pianist in Germany.

Mellon, Alfred, composer and violinist, born in London, April 7, 1820. His earlier years were spent in Birmingham, of which place his parents were natives. He was a violinist at the Royal Italian Opera, London, and conductor at Haymarket Theatre ; the Adelphi ; and of Pyne and Harrison Opera Company ; the Musical Society ; Promenade Concerts, Covent Garden ; Liverpool Philharmonic Society, 1865. Married to Miss Woolgar, the actress. He died at Chelsea, London, March 27, 1867.

MERRIOTT.

WORKS.—Irish Dragoon, opera, 1845 ; Mysterious stranger, 1846 ; Victorine, opera, Covent Garden, 1859. Crown'd with clusters of the vine, glee (1850) ; Thou soft-flowing Avon ; Good night ; Let concord tune the strain, etc. Cupid's eyes, song, and numerous other songs and pf. pieces.

Mellor, Richard, organist, born at Huddersfield, March 23, 1816. Was appointed organist at Zion Chapel, Lindley, when just eighteen ; and later held similar posts at Linthwaite Church ; Honley Wesleyan Chapel. (where he played the æolophon, a precursor of the harmonium) ; St. Patrick's Roman Catholic Church, Huddersfield ; and Ramsden Street Independent Chapel, where he remained.33 years. He retired from active duty about 1874, but played the organ at the Huddersfield Exhibition of 1883. For some years he undertook concert arrangements, and introduced Sims Reeves and other great artists to Huddersfield, and was a notable figure in the musical life of that town.

Melton, William, writer, Chancellor of the Duchy of York, flourished during the early part of the 16th century. Author of a treatise entitled, " De Musicæ Ecclesiasticæ," preserved in MS.

Menzies, Archibald, violinist and famous reel player, was born at Dull, Perthshire, in 1806, and died at Edinburgh on July 16, 1856. He was in the orchestra of the Theatre Royal, Edinburgh, and took part in many competition concerts organised by Jullien and others.

Menzies, Daniel, amateur composer and violinist, was born about 1790, and died about 1828. He was a captain in the army. He composed a number of good strathspeys, which are contained in the collections of Duncan M'Kercher.

Merbeck, John. See MARBECK, JOHN.

Meredith, Edward, bass singer, born near Wrexham in 1741. He was discovered by Sir W. Wynn singing in a cooper's workshop, and was by that baronet put with singing masters and properly trained. He had a very fine voice and sang at the Ancient Concerts in London, but was chiefly identified with Liverpool, where he sang at all the principal concerts. He died at Wrexham, December 26, 1809.

Merriott, Edwin, composer, of first half of the present century. He compiled " Select portions of the Psalms of David, with original melodies....sung at Farnham and Basingstoke " [1826]. Composer of a large number of marches for military band or pf., among which may be mentioned a once popular one in imitation of a band in the distance [1835]. The success of this led to the composition of many other marches—Circassian, Coronation, etc., issued between 1835 and 1840. He also

MERRYLEES.

published Drawing Room Melodies, London, [1838] ; Progressive Exercises for the pf. [1838] ; Progressive Lessons for the pf. [1826-1836]. Songs, etc.

Merrylees, James, amateur composer, born at Paisley, April 10, 1824. He studied music under John Curwen and Colin Brown, and gained the Euing silver and gold medals for the best hymn tune and anthem, in competition, in 1871-72. He died at Dullatur, Dumbartonshire (detached), October 31, 1891. Editor of the accompaniments in " The Thistle," a collection of Scots music compiled by Colin Brown. He also arranged for four voices, Stewart's " Killin Collection of Gaelic Melodies." His compositions were chiefly part-songs, anthems, and hymn tunes, such as "Atlantic," "Formosa," etc.

Metcalfe, Rev. Joseph Powell, musician and clergyman, born at Canterbury in 1824. He was educated at Cambridge, and graduated B.A., 1847 ; M.A., 1850. Ordained in 1847. Rector of Bilbrough, Yorkshire, 1856.

WORKS.—School Round Book. Rules in Rhymes and Rounds. Metrical Anthems. Rounds, Catches, and Canons of England (with E. F. Rimbault), London, 1873. Contributions to Musical Literature, etc.

Middleton, Edward Hulton, organist, born at Failsworth, near Manchester, February 26, 1858. Articled pupil of J. Kendrick Pyne ; also studied under James Pattinson, Dr. H. Watson, and Henry Wilson. F.R.C.O. Graduated Mus. Bac., 1884 ; Mus. Doc., 1887, Cambridge. Organist of St. Mary's, Higher Crumpsall, Manchester, 1880 ; Professor of Music, Wesley College, Sheffield, 1883 ; and from 1889 organist and choirmaster, Kelvinside Free Church, Glasgow. Has given organ recitals at Edinburgh Exhibition, 1890, etc., and has composed a Cantate Domino, and Te Deum, for soli, chorus, and orchestra.

Midgley, Samuel, pianist, born at Bierley, near Bradford, Yorkshire, December 22, 1849. His father played the violin, and was sometime choirmaster at Bethel Chapel, Bierley. The son had his first organ appointment at this chapel, and held the like at Salem Chapel, and Tong Street Church. He studied for a time under James Broughton, and afterwards proceeded to Leipzig, where he studied under Reinecke, Papperitz, Oscar Paul, and others. At the public examination, Easter, 1874, he distinguished himself in the performance of Bennett's F minor Concerto. On his return he settled at Bradford, and gave his first chamber concert, September 23, 1874. He has given annual series of these ever since, and brought forward many important works by Parry, Stanford, Mackenzie, Prout, Ashton, and others, besides compositions of Bennett, Westrop, etc. He is conductor of Cleckheaton

MILLAR.

Philharmonic Society ; pianist at the Ilkley subscription concerts ; and accompanist at the Bradford subscription concerts, and writer of the analytical programmes for the same. Examiner for the Incorporated Society of Musicians ; and local representative, R.A.M., and R.C.M. In 1888 he married HENRIETTA TOMLINSON, a soprano vocalist, who has sung in oratorio and ballad concerts throughout Yorkshire and adjoining counties, and has also been heard in London, with her sister, MARION TOMLINSON, an excellent contralto.

Miles, P. Napier, amateur composer of present time. Pupil of Dr. Hubert Parry. His setting cf Coleridge's '' Hymn before sunrise," for baritone solo, chorus, and orchestra, was produced at the Bristol Festival, October 15, 1896. He has also composed a Symphonic Suite for orchestra, produced at Riseley's concerts, Bristol ; and a Sonata in B minor, for violin and pf., Bristol, 1892.

Miles, R. E., bass vocalist, born in Rochester, May 24, 1857. At the age of nine, entered the Cathedral as a chorister, remaining there five years. Then for a time was tutor and musical instructor in the family of Captain Malcolm, R.E. Afterwards entered R.A.M., as a pupil of Alberto Randegger. In 1881, appointed choirmaster of St. Mark's, Lewisham ; and in 1886, elected to the choir of St. Paul's Cathedral, both of which positions he still retains. Appointed by Sir G. A. Macfarren, professor of singing, R.A.M., 1884. Professor, Guildhall School, 1896. Has sung in oratorio at the principal concerts ; at the Crystal Palace, and Royal Albert Hall, etc., and is a successful teacher of singing. Of his compositions, church services, and many songs are in MS., but he has published a few songs, The Stars are with the voyager, The language of the heart, etc. ; also a leaflet, " How to Sing a Song."

Milgrove, Benjamin, composer, born probably at Bath about 1731. He was precentor of the Countess of Huntingdon's chapel, Bath, and died in 1810. Composer of Church music, and of " Sixteen hymns as they are sung at the Right Honourable the Countess of Huntingdon's Chapel in Bath " [1769].

Millar, Marian, pianist and writer, born in Manchester. Studied under Dr. Hiles, and gained First Class honours, with distinction, in Cambridge University higher local examinations in music, 1884 ; and the Professional Diploma (in pf. playing) of the Incorporated Society of Musicians, with First Class honours, 1886. Though not the first of her sex to pass the Examination for a Degree in Music at an English University—vide Elizabeth Stirling, 1856 ; Adelaide Thomas, and Emilie B. Grant, 1892,—Miss Millar has the distinction of being the first woman to obtain the degree of Mus. Bac.,—at Victoria

MILLAR.

University, Manchester, June, 1894. She is professor of harmony and pf. at the Manchester High School for Girls, an appointment held from 1884. Her degree exercise was "A Song of Praise," for soli, chorus, and small orchestra. She wrote the libretto of "The Crusaders" (Dr. Hiles), and "The Armada" (G. J. Miller); and contributed many articles and translations to *The Quarterly Musical Review* (Manchester, Heywood, 1885-8), with some lyrical pieces.

Millar, Samuel, trombonist of present time. He has made a special feature of music for trombone and organ, and has frequently played at the recitals given by H. J. B. Dart (*q.v.*). He is also known as a trombone soloist at concerts, and he played Ferdinand David's Concerto for trombone at the College Hall, Richmond Green, November 20, 1884. He is professor of the trombone at the R.C.M.

Millard, Rev. James Elwin, headmaster of Magdalene College School, Oxford. Vicar of Basingstoke; Canon of Winchester. Author of "Historical Notices of the Office of Choristers," London, 1848. Account of Basingstoke and other works.

Millard, Mrs. Philip, vocal composer, of first part of the present century. She wrote a number of songs, of which "Alice Gray" (1835) was perhaps the most popular. Other songs were Dinna forget; Forget thee my Susie; Happy New Year; Lament of the Scotch fisherman's widow; Soldier's return, etc.

Millard, William, musician, of early part of this century, issued "The Branch," comprising Forty Psalm and Hymn tunes," London [1810].

Miller, Agnes Elizabeth, pianist, born at Brierley Hill, Staffs., April 20, 1857. From the age of eleven she studied under Mrs. W. P. Marshall, of Birmingham (a pupil of Moscheles). In 1873, she went to Mainz, studying under Beyschlag; and in 1876, was admitted to the Royal High School for Music, Berlin, where her teachers were Rudorff, Bargiel, Franz Schutz, and, for history, Spitta. She played at the semi-public concerts, and had the privilege of teaching two daughters of Dr. Joachim. In 1879 she returned to England, and established herself as a pf. teacher in London, giving some time to pupils in Birmingham. At the Saturday Popular Concerts, 1884, and in the provinces, she was associated with Joachim. Made her *début* at the Crystal Palace, March 7, 1885, playing Beethoven's C Minor Concerto. Gave annual series of chamber concerts in Birmingham, 1883-91, and gained an honourable position among pianists of the day. Married Herr Schauenburg, a German engineer, and in 1891 went to reside at Berlin.

Miller, Alexander, military bandmaster,

MILLER.

entered the service in 1833, in the First Battalion, Rifle Brigade. Served in Kaffir wars of 1846 and 1850; in the Crimea, 1854-5. Afterwards bugle-major and bandmaster, Edinburgh Queen's Light Infantry; appointed Queen's trumpeter, 1862; bandmaster First Midlothian Artillery Volunteers, 1878. This band, under his skill and zealous labours became one of the foremost in Edinburgh. Owing to ill-health he resigned this appointment in April, 1891, and died early in the winter of 1892-3.

Miller, Edward, Scottish musician, of the early part of the 17th century, who was a teacher at Edinburgh. He graduated M.A. at Edinburgh University in 1624, and has been identified as a teacher who taught children in Blackfriars Wynd, Edinburgh. He is best remembered as editor of "The Psalmes of David, in prose and meeter, with their whole tunes in foure or mo parts, and some psalmes in reports . . . ," Edinburgh: heirs of Andrew Hart, 1635. The preface to this work is signed "E.M.," and Miller has been proved to have been the editor.

Miller, Edward, composer and writer, was born at Norwich in 1735. He was apprenticed to a paviour, but absconded and studied music under Burney at Lynn. Organist of Church of Doncaster, 1756-1807. Mus. Doc., Cantab., 1786. He died at Doncaster, September 12, 1807.

WORKS.—Six solos for German flute; Six sonatas for the harpsichord, with an accompaniment to three of them for a violin or German flute; Elegies, songs, and an ode, with instrumental parts; Twelve songs, 1773; Psalms of David, for the use of Parish Churches, London [1790], edited by G. H. Drummond; Sacred music, containing 250 of the most favourite tunes . . the music selected and adapted for two, three, and four voices, and intended as an appendix to Dr. Watts' Psalms and Hymns, 1802; Psalms and hymns set to new music, 1801. Institutes of Music or Easy Instructions for the Harpsichord, London, n.d. [1771]; Elements of Thorough-bass and Composition, London, op. 5, 1787; The Psalms of David set to music, and arranged for every Sunday in the year, 1774; Treatise of Thorough-bass and Composition, Dublin, n.d.; History of Doncaster, Doncaster, 1804.

Miller, George John, bandmaster and composer, born at Pimlico, London, November 26, 1853. He comes of a military family, his grandfather fought at Salamanca, and his father was bandmaster of the 63rd (Manchester) Regiment. In this corps young Miller began his musical career. He afterwards became assistant in Alfred Mapleson's Music Library, and then enlisting in the 16th Regiment, he was sent to Kneller Hall to study.

MILLER.

While there he trained the choir at St. Stephen's Mission Church, Hounslow, and was organist at Whitton Parish Church. In 1875 he was appointed bandmaster of the 16th (Bedfordshire) Regiment, and went to India. Returning, he was made bandmaster and organist of the Royal Military College, Sandhurst, 1880; and in 1884 became bandmaster of the Portsmouth Division. Royal Marines. L.R.A.M., 1882; Mus. Bac., Cambridge, 1892. His band is famed all over the Empire, and he frequently has to conduct at Osborne, etc. He also conducts an amateur operatic society, and the Minnesingers glee club. His compositions comprise a cantata, The Armada; concert overture, Evangeline; Nautical fantasia, and many original pieces and arrangements for military and string bands; an operetta, etc. He also composed the funeral march for the obsequies of Prince Henry of Battenberg, 1896. Editor (with François Cellier) of The Soldier's Song Book, London, Clowes, 1897.

Miller, Henry Walter, composer, organist, and writer on music, born in London, June 15, 1843, son of the late Rev. Dr. Miller, Vicar of Greenwich. Educated at Oxford, where he graduated Mus. Bac., 1865; B.A., 1868; M.A., 1875. Musical training private. Organist of Hobart Cathedral, and Examiner to the Government of Tasmania, 1885; Conductor to the Brisbane Musical Union, and Ipswich (Queensland) Choral Society, 1887. Organist of the American Episcopal Church, Nice, 1894. In 1874 he initiated the Tallis Memorial Fund, for placing a Brass in Greenwich Parish Church, which was accomplished in 1876. Works.—The Seasons, for soli, chorus, and orchestra; Cantata, Paradise and the Peri; Jubilee Prize Ode (Queensland), for soli, chorus, and orchestra. Duo Concertante, organ and trombone. Anthems, songs, organ, and pf. pieces. Author of "Notes on Old English Music," London, 1875, and magazine articles; Editor of the "Gregorian Quarterly Magazine," 1883.

Miller, James, friend of Burns the poet, and reputed composer of the air usually sung to "Ye Banks and Braes o' Bonnie Doon." He was a writer in Edinburgh, and a friend of Stephen Clarke (q.v.), who put the tune into shape. Burns' account of the origin of the air will be found in his correspondence with George Thomas. See also Chappell's "Popular Music of the olden time," and Glen's "Scottish Dance Music," 1891. The tune was first published in Gow's second collection as "The Caledonian Hunt's delight." in 1788.

Miller, William, organist and author, was born in 1809. He was the first organist of the Sacred Harmonic Society, London, and held the post for 14 years. From 1832

MILLS.

till 1873 he was organist of St. Giles', Cripplegate, London, in which he took much interest and was active in raising funds for its restoration. He died at London, June 25, 1873. Author of a history of St. Giles' Church; a little brochure, entitled, "Jottings in Kent," etc.

Miller, William Mackie, teacher and conductor, was born at Glasgow, October 21, 1831. Conductor of Tonic Sol-fa Society, and late principal of a College of Music. He was Precentor of Free St. Matthew's Church, Glasgow, and superintendent of music in the Glasgow Board Schools from 1873. He died at Glasgow, February 3, 1894. He edited a few works by Handel, in the tonic sol-fa notation, and wrote a "Tonic Sol-fa Flute Instructor," Edinburgh, n.d., and other works designed for instruction in the tonic sol-fa notation.

Mills, Edward, organist and teacher, was a choir boy at Portman Chapel, Marylebone, and played the organ at the afternoon services at St. James's, Marylebone. Student, teacher, and eventually organist and music master, St. John's College, Battersea; Whiteland's College, Chelsea; and Home and Colonial College, Gray's Inn Road. Graduated Mus. Bac., Oxford, 1881 his exercise being a setting of Psalm 32. He has published a Course of Sight Singing.

Mills, Rev. John, Ieuan Glan Alarch, musician and clergyman, born at Llanidloes, December 12, 1812; died July 28, 1873. Author of "Gramadeg cerddoriaeth yn nghyda geirlyfr enwedigaethol yn cynwys eglurhad ar y geiriau annghynefin a arferir yn y Gwaith," Llanidloes, 1838.

Richard Mills, born near Llanidloes in March, 1809; died in September, 1844, wrote "Caniadan Seion, sef casgliad a donau addas i'w canu'yn yr addoliad dwyfol. . ." Llanidloes, 1840-42, 2 parts.

Mills, John Henry, musician, published "A Selection of Sacred Poetry, set to music," London, 1860. "A Selection of Sacred Poetry for private and congregational use, set to music," London, 1862.

Mills, Robert Watkin, baritone vocalist, born at Painswick, Gloucestershire, March 4, 1856. Sang in the church choir there as a boy. A baritone voice developing, he was in request at local concerts. He then went to London, and studied under Edwin Holland, afterwards proceeding to Milan, he studied with S. Blasco; and on his return to London had some lessons from Alfred Blume. He made a successful début at the Crystal Palace, May 17, 1884, and a still greater impression in the "Messiah," at the Royal Albert Hall, January 1, 1885. He then sang at the Monday and Saturday Popular Concerts, and made his first Festival appearance

MILLS.

MITCHISON.

at Birmingham, in August of the same year. In 1886 he was heard at the Gloucester and Leeds Festivals, and took his place among the first singers of the day, singing at every important centre in the Kingdom. From 1894, he has made annual tours in Canada and the United States, singing at Festivals, and giving vocal recitals. He made one appearance in opera, at Birmingham Theatre Royal, as *Baldassare*, in "La Favorita," May 21, 1884, but declined Mr. Carl Rosa's offer of an extended engagement, devoting himself to concert work, and oratorio singing.

Mills, Sebastian Bach, pianist, composer, and teacher, born at Cirencester, March 13, 1839. He studied music at Leipzig, and settled in New York, 1858. He played in London as an infant prodigy in 1845, and at the Gewandhaus Concerts, Leipzig, December 2, 1858. Teacher and composer in New York. He has published numerous pieces for the pf., and is regarded as one of the leading pianists in America.

Milne, Peter, violinist and composer, was born at Kincardine O'Neil, Aberdeenshire, September 30, 1824. He was a violinist in Aberdeen and Edinburgh. Compiler of a "Selection of strathspeys, reels, etc....," Keith, n.d. This work has reached at least 5 editions.

Milner, Abraham, musician of the 18th century. Compiler of "The Psalm Singer's Companion, being a collection of psalm tunes, hymns, canons, and anthems..with an introduction to psalmody..," 1751. "The Psalm Singer's Pocket Amusement, being a collection of psalm tunes..," London [1750]. A Collection, Revival and Refining (from the more gross and obscene songs) of the old catch books, together with a variety of two and three-part songs from the most eminent masters," London [1750]. Sacred Melody, being a choice collection of anthems....," London [1780].

Milnes, George, alto vocalist, born at York (?) about 1815. Sang in the chorus at the York Festivals of 1823-5-8, and 1835, in the last year removing to Huddersfield. Member of several church choirs in that town; one of the founders of the Huddersfield Choral Society; and principal alto at the George Glee Club in its best days. He died at Huddersffeld, November 25, 1883.

Milton, John, musician, who was born about the end of the 16th century. Scrivener in Bread Street, Cheapside, London, where he died in 1646. Composed "Fayre Oriana in the Morne," madrigal, and numerous songs and motets in the principal collections of the period. His merits as a musician are celebrated in a short poem, "Ad patrem," by his son, the great poet, whose works have been set by numerous composers, like Handel, Lawes, King, Nelson, and others.

Minns, George, tenor vocalist, lay-clerk of Ely Cathedral, won the Molineux Prize of £10 offered by the Madrigal Society, in 1882, for the best madrigal. He has published a Rustic Dance; Tarantella; and other pieces for pf.

Minshall, Ebenezer, organist and conductor, born at Oswestry, Salop, in 1845. Intended for the law, but, adopting music, became organist, when 16, at Leatherhead Congregational Church; then took a similar appointment in Oswestry; and removing to London in 1874, was organist at Uxbridge Road Chapel. In 1876 he was appointed organist and director of the music at the City Temple, where he remained until 1893. In 1881 he started the Thursday Popular Concerts in that building. He is Chairman of the Nonconformist Choir Union, formed in 1888, and conductor of its annual festivals at the Crystal Palace; has lectured on musical subjects; and is the composer of anthems, hymn tunes, etc. Editor of *The Nonconformist Musical Journal;* Organists' Magazine of Voluntaries; and Modern Organ Music. Author of "Organs, Organists, and Choirs," London, Curwen.

Mitchell, C. H., author of "How to hold a violin and bow," 1882.

Mitchell, Helen Porter, *see* ARMSTRONG, HELEN PORTER.

Mitchell, James, author and inventor, born at Kilmarnock, April 19, 1834. Resident at Coatbridge. Inventor of an improved metronome, and author of a work on Musical Theory, illustrated by diagrams, 1878.

Mitchell, John, bass vocalist. Entered the choir at St. George's Chapel, Windsor, in 1815, when six years of age. Sang at the Coronation of George IV., William IV., and Queen Victoria; also sang at the Jubilee Service, Westminster Abbey, June 21, 1887. In that year Her Majesty presented him with an engraved portrait of herself in recognition of his long musical service. He completed his 75th year with the chapel choir, May 1890; and died in the Horseshoe Cloisters, Windsor Castle. January 6, 1892, aged 82. He was organist of Eton College for about 40 years.

Mitchison, William, musician and publisher, was born about 1809. He was a music publisher in Glasgow till about 1854, when he went to America. He died at Brooklyn, July 1, 1867. He issued The Psalmist's Companion, a collection of devotional harmony for the use of Presbyterian Churches, selected from the works of Steven, Robertson, R. A. Smith, etc., Glasgow, n.d. [c. 1843]. A few Remarks on the Pianoforte, giving details of the mechanical construction of that instrument, etc., Glasgow, 1845. Selection of Sacred Music, n.d. R. A.

MOBERLY.

Smith's anthems, edited Glasgow, n.d. The Garland of Scotia, 1841. Handbook of the Songs of Scotland, with music and descriptive historical notes . . . to which is added a biographical sketch of the life of the late John Wilson, the celebrated Scottish vocalist, Glasgow, n.d.

Moberly, Rev. E. H., amateur conductor, born at Winchester, October 20, 1849. Son of the late Bishop of Salisbury. Self-educated in music. Brought up for the church, and took orders; but gave up clerical work about 1887. and devoted himself entirely to music. In 1885, he formed a musical society in Hampshire, the Test Valley; and later, a similar one in North Wilts. From about 1885 he has given concerts for charitable purposes with a Ladies' String Orchestra, which has now attained a high reputation. He visited London with the orchestra in 1892, and gave a concert in Princes' Hall, May 19; and again at St. James's Hall, in 1893, and later. The orchestra has been heard in Oxford, Birmingham, and other places.

Moffat, Alfred Edward, composer, born in Edinburgh, December 4, 1866. From 1882 to 1888 studied composition with Ludwig Bussler in Berlin. Since 1889, he has resided partly in Germany and partly in Britain, devoting himself entirely to composttion and arrangements of various kinds, many of his works being published in Germany. WORKS.—Cantatas: The Passing Year ; The Dressing of the Well; The Children of Samuel; A Christmas Dream; all for female or children's voices. Album of ten trios for female voices; Pastoral album, two books, duets; Twelve duets; Six duettinos; Three duets, with female chorus; Twelve sacred rounds; Eight books of school songs, etc. Two songs, with violoncello obligato; Four songs, etc., etc. Arrangements: The Minstrelsie of Scotland (200 Scottish songs, Augener); Twelve Scottish songs, in three parts; Folksongs of England, eight books (Paterson); Songs of the British Empire, etc., etc. Instrumental: Quartet, pf. and strings (Berlin, 1886); Twenty-four pieces (Simrock); Album of twelve pieces (Augener); Album of six pieces, etc., all for violin' and pf. Twelve salon pieces, Twelve pieces, Sonata, for violoncello and pf., etc. Arrangements for pf. and strings: Golden Sonata, Purcell; Thirty-two classical pieces (Schott); Nine pieces (Breitkopf and Härtel), etc. For pf. and violin : Three sonatas (oboe and figured bass), Handel ; Album of twelve pieces, etc. For pf. and violoncello : Two albums, twenty-four pieces; Lyrische stücke, ten pieces ; and a large number of pieces by Handel and Marcello. Thirty Highland reels and strathspeys, arranged for pf., etc.

MOLINEUX.

Mogford, Mrs. *See* FRICKER, ANNE.

Moir, Frank Lewis, composer, born at Market Harborough, April 22, 1852. Originally intended to follow his father's art, that of painting, but began composing music while an art student at South Kensington. He gained a scholarship when the National Training School for Music was opened in 1876, and soon acquired a reputation as a song composer. His works include a comic opera, "The Royal Watchman," Exeter, 1877 ; Church Services, etc. One Summer night; The wish of my heart; The story of years; The Golden Meadow; Only once more; Best of all; and an immense number of other songs; Duets, Over the Heather; Love shall never die; and others. Madrigal Society's Prize, 1881, When at Chloe's eyes I gaze; Melody in A, violin and pf., etc. He married, April 5, 1886, Miss ELEANOR FARNOL, of Birmingham. She is a soprano vocalist, and studied under W. C. Stockley, and at the National Training School. She has sung in London and the provinces, and has taken part in the vocal recitals given by her husband.

Moir-Clark, *see* CLARK, J. MOIR.

Molesworth, Lady, *born* CARSTAIRS, a soprano singer who was born about 1810. Her father was Bruce Carstairs. She studied at the R.A.M., and first appeard at a singer under the professional name of Miss Grant. In 1831 she married Mr. Temple West, the virtuoso, who died in 1839. She next married Sir William Molesworth in 1844, and retired from public life. She died on May 16, 1888.

Molineux, John, musician and author, of latter part of last and first-half of present century, who resided for a time in Liverpool, where he had a music academy at Newington Bridge. Author of "The Singer's Systematic Guide to the Science of Music," London, 1831; "Concise Collection of the rudiments of Vocal Music, intended to assist persons who practice glees or church music, in the art of singing at sight," London [1830]. "English Psalmody, domestic, choral, and congregational, being a collection of sacred music," [1829]. "The Venite, Te Deum, Benedicite, etc., properly accented and adapted to favourite chants," Liverpool. An Essay towards an elucidation of the principles of musical harmory, London [1841]. Principles of the notation and science of music....London [1844]. Songs, etc.

Molineux, Thomas, born in Manchester, September 16, 1802. Before he became known as a pf. maker, was a practical musician. While a youth he studied the flute, and later acquired skill on the violin, 'cello, and double-bass. He was still more accomplished as a performer on the bassoon, and played at the Gentleman's, Professional, and other concerts in Manchester up to about 1850. He was

MOLLESON.

officially connected with St. James's Hall, and the Polytechnic Institution, London; and will be remembered for his munificent gifts to the Royal Society of Musicians. He died in London, January, 31, 1891.

Molleson, Alexander, Scottish minor poet, was a bookseller in Glasgow at the end of last and beginning of the present century. Author of "Melody the soul of Music, an essay towards the improvement of the Musical Art," Glasgow, 1798; reprinted in his "Miscellanies in Prose and Verse," Glasgow, 1806.

Molloy, James Lyman, amateur composer and writer, born in 1837. Eldest son of Kedo Molloy, Esq., of Cornolore, King's County, Ireland. M.A., of the Roman Catholic University of Ireland. Called to the English bar, 1864. Married Florence, youngest daughter of Henry Baskerville, Esq., of Crowsley Park, Lord of the Manor of Shiplake, and deputy-lieutenant for the County of Oxford. Secretary to the late Sir John Holker, attorney-general. Member of the South-Eastern Circuit, and Brighton Sessions, and of the Middle Temple, etc.

WORKS.—*Operettas:* Student's frolic; My Aunt's secret; Very catching. *Songs:* Blue eyes; Because I do; By the river; Bird and the cross; Child's vision; Clang of the wooden shoon; Love's old sweet song; Darby and Joan; Home, dearie, home; Rosemarie; Old Sailor wife; Irish piper; Thady O'Flinn; The carnival; Kerry dance; A race for life; Vagabond; and many others. Six Song Stories for children. Irish melodies (Boosey), edited with new accompaniments. Prose work: Our Autumn Holiday on French Rivers.

Monk, Edwin George, organist and composer, born at Frome, Somerset, December 13, 1819. Pupil of Henry and George Field; later, in London, joined Hullah's classes, and studied singing with Henry Phillips. Held organ appointments at Midsomer Norton; Christ Church, Frome; and, 1844-46, at St. Columba's College, Rathfarnham, near Dublin, Then studied composition under G. A. Macfarren. In 1847 he was in Oxford; and the next year was appointed organist and music master at St. Peter's College, Radley. Graduated Mus. Bac., 1848; Mus. Doc., 1856, Oxford. In 1859 he was appointed organist of York Minster, in succession to John Camidge, an office he resigned in 1883. Examiner for musical degrees, Oxford, 1871-83. Now resident at Radley, near Abingdon.

WORKS.—Milton's Ode to the Nativity; Ode, The Bard. Unison service in A; Evening service; God so loved the world, and other anthems; hymn-tunes, etc. Boating song; Football song; The jolly cricket ball; and other part-songs. Editor of the Anglican

MONK.

Chant Book; Anglican Choral Service Book; with Rev. R. Corbett Singleton, Anglican Hymn Book; and, with Rev. Sir F. A. G. Ouseley, The Psalter and Canticles pointed for chanting; and Anglican Psalter Chants. Compiler of the libretti of G. A. Macfarren's oratorios, St. John the Baptist; The Resurrection; and Joseph.

His youngest brother, HENRY THEOPHILUS MONK, born at Frome, March 6, 1831, studied under his brother, and afterwards under C. W. Lavington and (Sir) G. A. Macfarren. He was successively organist at Wells; Radley, Berks.; and St. Philip's Church, Sheffield. Music master and organist at Forest Schools, Walthamstow. He was unfortunately drowned while bathing in North Wales, July 23, 1857, at the outset of a promising career. He composed some chants and other vocal music.

Monk, James Jonathan, organist, composer, and teacher, born at Bolton-le-Moors, February 20, 1846. Studied under James Thomson, and Dr. Westbrook. Has held various organ appointments in the neighbourhood of Liverpool, where he resides as teacher. Gave organ recitals at the Liverpool Exhibition, 1887; and annual concerts of his pupils. Has acted as musical critic for the *Liverpool Courier*, and *Liverpool Evening Express*; has been for many years the local correspondent for the *Musical Standard*; and has contributed to *The Choir* articles on the St. George's Hall organ, and other local matters. His compositions include a Te Deum; Festival anthem, O be joyful in God. Ah! thou pale moon; True for aye; Primrose lane; Oh, give me back those kisses; and other songs. I met my love, part-song. The Water Mill, pf. piece, etc. A paper read at Liverpool, in 1883, led to the Compilation of a Musical Directory on more distinctly professional lines, in 1884; but the experiment was not repeated.

Monk, Mark James, organist and composer, born at Hunmanby, Yorkshire, March 16, 1858. Musically educated at York Minster, 1867-78, under Dr. E. G. Monk. Organist of various churches in York; St. John's, Ladywood, Birmingham, 1879; Parish Church, Ashby-de-la-Zouch, 1880; Banbury, 1883; and of Truro Cathedral from 1890. Diocesan choirmaster, and conductor, Choral festivals; Precentor of Deanery of Powder Choral Association; conductor of Truro Philharmonic, 1890. Graduated Mus. Bac., 1878; Mus. Doc., 1888, Oxford. F.R.C.O. Composer of an Elegiac Ode (Coplas di Manrique), for soli, five-part chorus, strings and organ; Festival Te Deum; Quintet for wind; Madrigal for five voices; pf. and organ pieces, etc.

Monk, William Henry, composer and organist, born in London, March 16, 1823. He studied under T. Adams, J. A. Hamilton,

MONRO.

and G. A. Griesbach. Organist of Eaton Chapel, Pimlico, London, 1841-43; St. George's Chapel, Albemarle Street, 1843-45; Portman Chapel, Marylebone, 1845-47. Choir-master, 1847; organist, 1849; and Professor of vocal music in King's College, London, 1874. Professor of music at School for Indigent Blind, 1851. Organist of St. Matthias, Stoke Newington, 1852. Professor in National Training College for Music, 1876; Professor in Bedford College, London, 1878; Mus. Doc., Durham, *honoris causâ*, 1882. He died at Stoke Newington, London, March 18, 1889.

WORKS.—Te Deums, Kyries, and other works for the church service. *Anthems :* And the angel Gabriel; Blessed are they that alway keep judgment; If ye love me keep my commandments; In God's word will I rejoice; Like as the hart; The Lord is my strength; They shall come and sing, etc. Hymns, psalms, etc. Hymns of the Church, London, n.d.; The Holy Year, or hymns for Sundays, holidays, and other occasions throughout the year. . with appropriate tunes, London, 1865; Fifty-two simple chants; The Canticles arranged for chanting to the ecclesiastical tones; The Book of Psalms in Metre (Church of Scotland); Scottish Hymnal (edited); The Psalter (Church of Scotland); Book of Anthems (Church of Scotland), etc.

Dr. Monk composed many popular hymn tunes, of which "Eventide" is perhaps best known. ' He also acted as 'musical editor of "Hymns, Ancient and Modern." His daughter FLORENCE is a soprano vocalist of repute.

Monro, George, composer and organist, was born about the end of the 17th century. He competed unsuccessfully against T. Rosingrave for the post of organist of St. George, Hanover Square, London, 1725. Afterwards he became organist of St. Peter, Cornhill, and harpsichord player at Goodman's Fields Theatre. He died at London in 1731.

WORKS.—Temple Beau, an opera. *Songs :* Amorous swain's complaint; Charm of wine; Complaining maid; Gold, a receipt for love; Happy Dick; Passionate lover; Song in praise of Polly, etc. Songs in the "Musical Miscellany," 1731.

Monro, Henry, composer and organist, was born at Lincoln in 1774. He was a chorister in Lincoln Cathedral, and studied afterwards under Dussek, D. Corri, and others. In 1796 he became organist of St. Andrew, Newcastle-on-Tyne. Composer of songs, sonatas, and other pf. music.

Monro, John, composer and pianist, was born at Edinburgh in 1786. He was a music-seller and musician in London, where he died, on March 3, 1851.

WORKS.—Selection of English Melodies, the words by J. W. Lake, London [1825]; Border Ballads, a set of six songs, the poetry by

MOODY.

J. E. Carpenter. *Songs :* Barefooted Friar [1840]; Come now we are met; Ellen Aureen [1817]; Mary, the maid of the green; My mother's grave; My Nora; Sir Hubert's bride; Wert thou like me [1847], etc. Selection of Country Dances, issued annually, 1817-1834. The Gleaner, or select flute miscellany, 2 vols., n.d. Flute Music, 3 vols. A New and Complete Introduction to the art of playing on the Pianoforte [1819]. Also various pf. pieces.

Montgomery, R., author of "The Voice and vocalisation," London, 1879.

Montgomery, William Henry, musician, born about 1811; died at London, September 13, 1886. He produced an immense number of teaching pieces for the pianoforte, and wrote "The Royal Standard Tutor for the Harmonium," London, n.d. Composer of songs and other vocal music, and editor of an edition of Moore's Irish Melodies.

Moodie, William, musician and conductor, born at Bonhill, Dumbarton, April 19, 1833. He was successively conductor of the psalmody in Dumbarton Episcopal Church; Lansdowne United Presbyterian Church, Glasgow, 1864-77; Barony Church, 1877-89; East Pollokshields Free Church, 1889-92. He also acted as conductor of the Dumbarton Choral Union; and of the St. George's Choral Union, Glasgow, 1873-81, a society which he founded. He has composed various anthems, songs and part songs, of which last "Willie Wastle" is best known, as well as music for the pf. and various cantatas, etc., in MS.

Moody, Fanny, soprano vocalist, born at Redruth, Cornwall; daughter of Mr. J. Hawke Moody, of that town. Studied under Madame Sainton-Dolby, and sang at the concerts of her vocal academy; and at the In Memoriam concert, April 25, 1885. Made her *début* in opera at Liverpool, in February, 1887, as *Arline,* in "The Bohemian Girl," with the Carl Rosa company. Sang in London and the provinces for some time with that company, appearing in a variety of characters. From 1890 she has sung in Italian opera at Covent Garden, and Drury Lane with much success. With her own concert party has given costume recitals of operas at Crystal Palace (1894), and other places; and has sung at the principal concerts in Great Britain; also in Canada, and in South Africa, 1896-7. In 1890, she was married to Mr. Charles Manners (*q.v.*). The artist pair offered, in 1895, a prize of £100 for the best one-act opera, without chorus. This was won by a young composer, Aliek Maclean (*q.v.*), and the opera was produced at Covent Garden, June 29, 1895.

Moody, Marie, composer of present time. Her published works comprise over-

MOONIE.

tures, King Lear; Hamlet; Othello; Der Sterbende Krieger; Concert overtures in E minor, and C major. Adagio and allegretto in D; allegro moderato in D minor, for string quartet. Studies for pf. Anthem, Great Lord of Lords, etc.

Moonie, James Anderson, conductor and composer, was born at Edinburgh in 1853. He studied under Randegger, Welch and Cottell, and has held various church appointments in Edinburgh. Conductor of the Hope Park Musical Association, and of a male voice choir which have performed with great success in Edinburgh. Mr. Moonie holds various appointments in the large public schools of Edinburgh as a teacher of singing Composer of a short cantata, Jerusalem, my Happy Home.

Moore, Bertha, soprano vocalist, born at Brighton, January 19, 1862. Studied at the R.A.M. under W. H. Cummings, then took lessons from Madame Florence Lancia. Sang at Dublin and other places, but made her first great success in "Elijah," at St. James's Hall, London, May 28, 1885. The next year she sang at the Crystal Palace Concerts; has also appeared at Kuhe's Brighton Festival, 1888, and at the Monday Popular Concerts, 1891; and is now a popular and admired singer. Fond of acting, she has occasionally sung in operetta performances.

Moore, Graham Ponsonby, composer and pianist, born at Ballarat, Australia, April 14, 1859. Studied at Berlin Conservatorium under Theodor Kullak, and later with Scharwenka and Moszkowski. Making his home in London, he was appointed a professor of pf. at the R.C.M., and is an examiner under the Associated Board of the R.A.M., and R.C.M. His compositions are chiefly for the pf., and many of them have been played by the leading pianists in this country and in Germany. The principal are: Concertstücke (after Longfellow's poem, "Seaweed"); Hochzeit im Dorfe, six pieces; Fünf Klavierstücke, op. 22; Chromatische Etüden; Lyrische Tonbilder, op. 25 (10 pieces); Ten short and melodious studies, op. 30; Twelve poetical studies, op. 31; Three nocturnes, op. 32; Three archaic dances, op. 33, etc. Author of The Candidates' Practical Scale and Arpeggio Handbooks, London, R. Cocks.

Moore, Henry Keatley, didactic writer, born at London, in 1846. Studied under Dr. Westbrook. Graduated B.A., 1871; Mus. Bac., 1880, London, being, with the late Dr. W. H. Hunt *(q.v.)*, the first to receive a musical degree at London University. Has been honorary choirmaster of South Place Chapel, Finsbury, and of the Free Christian Church, Croydon; also trainer, since 1891, of a choir for unaccompanied part-singing. Hon. Treasurer of the Froebel Society, and some-

MOORE.

time Examiner in Music to the same. Co-translator and editor of Froebel's Autobiography, and Letters. Author of The Child's Pianoforte Book; The Child's Song and Game Book, in four parts, London, Swan Sonnenschein. He has composed some pieces and studies for pf.; Songs, etc.

Moore, Reginald Bowerman, organist and conductor, born, October, 1850, at Lyme Regis, Dorsetshire, where his father, an excellent musician, was for many years organist of the Parish Church. After receiving some pianoforte lessons from a lady (pupil of Dr. Wesley), Moore was sent at the age of ten to Dr. Mark, of Manchester, where he remained a year. When fourteen, he became organist of the Parish Church, Uplyme, Devon. In 1870 he was appointed to the Congregational Church, Exeter, and three years later to St. Mary Major in that city. During this time he studied with Mr. D. J. Wood, the Cathedral organist, and Dr. H. A. Harding. Became F.C.O., 1879, and graduated Mus. Bac., Oxford, 1885. Was conductor of the Historic Madrigal Society, 1884-7, and from 1886 to the present time has conducted the concerts of the Exeter Orchestral Society. Music-master to the Grammar School, and is honorary local Examiner for R.A.M., and R.C.M. His compositions comprise Psalm 145, for soli, chorus, and orchestra. Duets, and pieces for pf., organ, etc.

Moore, Thomas, music teacher, who resided in Manchester about 1740-50. He became resident in Glasgow in latter half of the 18th century, and in June, 1755, became precentor of Blackfriars Church. On November 22, 1756, he was appointed by the magistrates teacher of the free music classes in Hutcheson's Hospital. He was also a bookseller in Princes Street and Stockwell Street, and died in Glasgow about 1792. He compiled "The Psalm-Singer's Divine Companion," Manchester, 1750, 2 vols., of which another edition was issued in the same year as "Psalm-Singer's Compleat Tutor and Divine Companion," Manchester, 2 vols. "The Psalm-Singer's Pocket Companion, containing great variety of the best English Psalm-Tunes, suited to the different metres in the Scotch Version of the Psalms of David, set in three and four parts; likewise all the tunes that are usually sung in most parts of Scotland; with a plain and easy introduction to Musick..," Glasgow, 1756. "The Psalm-Singer's Delightful Pocket Companion. Containing a Plain and Easy Introduction to Psalmody, and an Introduction explaining more at large the grounds of Music in general. Illustrated with great variety of Tables, Scales, and Initial Lessons..," Glasgow, n.d. [1762]. The Vocal Concert Glasgow, 1761.

Moore, Thomas, poet and musician,

MOORE.

born at Dublin, May 28, 1779; died at Sloperton Cottage, near Devizes, February 25, 1852. Best known as author of "Lalla Rookh," and other poems, and by his "Irish Melodies," which were issued in 1807-34, with accompaniments by Sir John Stevenson. Of this collection many editions have appeared, among which may be mentioned those edited by Balfe, Bishop, Glover, Macfarren, Montgomery, Rimbault, Romer, and Shrivall. Moore composed a "Collection of Vocal Music," London [1820], among which is the Canadian boat-song "Row, brothers, row," originally published in 1805. He wrote the words of "A Selection of Popular National Airs," 1818, 6 parts, and compiled "Evenings in Greece," London, 1831, 2 vols.; a work of poetry and music. See his "Memoirs and Correspondence," by Lord John Russell.

Moore, William H., cornet player, composer, and conductor, born in Birmingham, May 7, 1852. Sometime solo cornet in the band of the Theatre Royal, Birmingham. Conductor of the orchestra at the Moseley Botanical Gardens, 1892-5; and engaged in principal local orchestral concerts. He has composed an opera, "Rudolph"; cantatas, "Torfrida," produced, Birmingham, January, 1885; "Daniel," 1886. Also a Suite, and Romance for orchestra; Fair Marguerite; Queen of my dream; and other songs, etc.

Moorehead, John, Irish violinist and composer, who was born about the middle of the 18th century. He was a violinist at the Worcester Festival of 1794, and afterwards played the viola in the orchestra of Sadler's Wells Theatre, London. In 1798 he was violinist at Covent Garden Theatre, and composed music for Sadler's Wells, Covent Garden, and other theatres. About 1802 he became insane, and was confined in Northampton House, Clerkenwell. Afterwards he was in the navy for a short time, but in March, 1804, he hanged himself near Deal in a fit of insanity.

WORKS.—*Music to Plays*: Philosopher's stone, 1795; Birds of a feather, 1796; Naval Pillar, 1799; Volcano, 1799; Speed the plough, 1799; Il Bondocani (with Attwood), 1801; Perouse (with Davy), 1801; Cabinet (with Davy), 1802; Family quarrels, 1802; Harlequin Habeas, 1802. *Songs:* Absence; Ben and Mary; Gallant Forty-second; Traveller's joys; Troubadour, etc. Duo concertante for violin (1800), etc.

His brother, ALEXANDER, was a violinist, and for a time acted as leader at Sadler's Wells Theatre. He died in a lunatic asylum at Liverpool, in 1803.

Moran, Charles, organist, born December 10, 1805. His professional life was spent at Holyhead, where he held office as organist, first at the Church of St. Cybi; and then, for

MORGAN.

nearly 60 years, at the Church of St. Seiriol. On his retirement in December, 1891, he was publicly presented with an address.

Moreton, John, musician and composer, was born at Birmingham in 1764; died in 1804. Compiler of "Sacred Melody, being 50 psalm and hymn tunes in four parts," London [1796].

Another MORETON, JAMES, issued a "Selection of Sacred Music," Longport [1856].

Morgan, Edward, musician and writer, author of "New and improved instructor for the German or Anglo-German Concertina," London [1858]; "Method of learning the Accordion," London [1852]; "Instructor for the Flutina or Accordion," London [1860].

Morgan George Washbourne, organist, born at Gloucester, April 9. 1823. He was a chorus singer in the Gloucester Philharmonic Society in 1834. Articled pupil of John Amott. Held organ appointments in Cheltenham, 1844; at Christ Church, and St. James's, Gloucester; at South Hackney, 1851; and St. Olave's, Southwark. Was an unsuccessful candidate for the Worcester Cathedral appointment, in 1845, about which time he was conductor of the Gloucester Philharmonic. In 1853 he settled in America, and was organist successively of St. Thomas's Episcopal Church, New York; Grace Church; St. Stephen's; and Brooklyn Tabernacle (Dr. Talmage's Church). The last office he held about twelve years. He died at Tacoma, Washington, July, 1892. His compositions included church music, vocal music, miscellaneous pieces for pf. and orchestra, etc.

Morgan, J. Wilford, tenor vocalist and composer. He has sung in opera in London and the provinces; in the "Old Guard," and other comic operas, at various times from 1872 to 1887. In 1888 he was appointed a professor of singing at the Guildhall School of Music. He is the composer of a cantata, "Christian the Pilgrim"; and of a number of songs, some of which, as "My Sweetheart when a Boy," have been very popular.

Morgan, Lady, *born* SYDNEY OWENSON, was born in Dublin about 1783. Best known as a novelist, but was distinguished in her day as a harp player and musician. In 1802 she published a number of Irish airs to which she had written words, and this was the forerunner of Moore's better known Irish melodies. Apart from her novels she wrote "The First Attempt," an opera, Dublin, 1807, and "The Lay of the Irish Harp," poems, 1809. In 1812 she married Sir Thomas Charles Morgan, and on April 14, 1859, she died at London.

Morgan, Robert Orlando, pianist and composer, born at Manchester, March 16, 1865. Studied at the Guildhall School of Music, where he gained the Merchant Taylors'

MORGAN.

Scholarship, for pf. playing and composition, 1883; and was awarded the Webster Prize, 1884, for a sonata for violin and pf. Appointed professor of harmony, composition and pf. at the school in 1887. In 1893 he won the prize, valued at 65 guineas, offered by the proprietors of *The Lute*, for the best anthem. At the Grand Concours International de Composition Musicale, held at Brussels in 1894, he was awarded the first prize and medal, and two diplomas of honour, for a sonata for pf., and a chorus for mixed voices, with organ accompaniment. He has also composed two cantatas for female voices, "Zitella," performed at the Guildhall School, July, 1889; and "The Legend of Eloïsa," both extensively popular; a church cantata, "The Crown of Thorns." Pieces for orchestra; Sonatas for violin and pf.; many pf. pieces; songs, part-songs, etc.

Morgan, Tom Westlake, organist and writer, born at Congnesbury, Somersetshire, August 6, 1869. Chorister, King's College, Cambridge, 1879; then pupil of Boyton Smith, at Dorchester. In 1886, organist of St. Catherine's College, Cambridge, and pupil-assistant of Dr. A. H. Mann, at King's College. Organist for a time at St. George's Anglican Church, Paris. Studied at R.C.M. under Sir Walter Parratt, and Dr. F. E. Gladstone, 1890. Organist at St. David's, Merthyr-Tydvil, 1891; founder and conductor of Philharmonic Society there. In 1892 he was appointed organist and master of the choristers, Bangor Cathedral. He has given recitals at St. George's Hall, Liverpool; at the Bow and Bromley Institute, etc. Has composed some Welsh anthems, etc.; is a contributer to periodical literature, and musical editor of *St. David's Weekly.* Has acted as adjudicator at Eisteddfodau; and is Provincial Grand Organist for North Wales in Royal Arch Freemasonry.

Mori, Nicholas, violinist and composer, born at London, January 24, 1796. Son of an Italian wig maker in the New Road, London. Pupil of Viotti. Principal violinist in London orchestras. Music publisher in Bond Street, London. He died on June 14, 1839.

Mori, Frank, composer, son of the above, born at London, March 21, 1820. Studied under Forbes and Sterndale Bennett, and in 1836 under Zimmerman at Paris. He died at Chaumont, France, August 2, 1873.

WORKS. — Fridolin, cantata, Worcester Festival, 1851. The River Sprite, operetta, words by G. Linley, Covent Garden, February 9, 1865. Songs: Twelve songs, by Mackay, Longfellow, Oxenford, etc.; Six songs, by Moore, Shelley, Tennyson, Hunt, etc.; Breathe, oh! breathe that simple strain; I love my love in the springtime; Whither art thou roaming. Vocal exercises, etc.

MORLEY.

Mori, Nicholas, the second son, was born January 14, 1822. Studied under his father, and Charles Lucas, and also in Paris. Played in public from 1838. Composer of descriptive music to Gilbert's "The Wicked World"; a setting of Psalm 137, and other works.

Morine, Charles Harland, composer and organist, was born in 1828; died at Elgin, February 19, 1879. He edited the collections of Scottish and Irish Melodies published by Maver, 1877, and composed pianoforte music. He also issued "Beauties of Scotland, airs for pianoforte," 1869. *Songs:* Burd Ailie; Golden days, etc.

Morison, Christina W., *born* BOGUE, composer, born in Dublin, 1840. She studied under Glover and John Blockley. Composer of "The Uhlans," opera, in 3 acts, Dublin, 1884, and Glasgow, 1885. Songs, and pianoforte music.

Morison, John, "musician and copier of music," born in 1772; died at Peterhead in 1848. He lived in Rose Street, Peterhead, and was precentor in St. Peter's Church there. Editor of a "Collection of New Strathspey Reels, with a few favourite marches....," Edinburgh [1801]. A Select Collection of Favourite Tunes adapted for the pianoforte, German flute, violin, and violoncello, dedicated, by permission, to General Gordon Cuming Skene," n.d.

Morison, Roderick, or RORY DALL O'CAHEN, poet, harper, and composer, was born in the Island of Lewis in 1646. He was the son of an episcopal clergyman, and was educated at Inverness. He lost his sight after an attack of small-pox, and became harper to the family of Macleod, of Lewis. He died near Stornoway early in the 18th century. He composed some Gaelic airs, but is best known as a poet.

Morley, Felix Wilson, organist and composer, born at Bassingbourne, Cambridge, November 20, 1855. From 1868 to 1873, he acted as honorary organist at the Parish Church, and in the latter year was elected Organ Scholar of Pembroke College, Cambridge, an office he was allowed to hold for a year before entering as an undergraduate. After taking the B.A. degree, he remained in residence as organist, and proceeded to M.A., 1883; and Mus. Bac., 1885. Since 1878 he has acted as hon. inspector of Choirs for the Ely Diocesan Church Music Society (now the Council of Church Music); and from 1891 has been annually elected hon. sec. In 1892, and 1895, appointed Diocesan inspector of the Choirs taking part in the Triennial Festivals at Ely Cathedral. Conductor of Royston Amateur Musical Society, 1888-94. Of his compositions there are, in MS., a setting of Psalm 150, for solo, chorus, orchestra, and organ; a Magnificat and Nunc Dimittis in

S

MORLEY.

E flat, for chorus, orchestra, and organ; his published works include church services; songs, and part-songs; pieces for violoncello, and pf.

Morley, Thomas, composer and writer, was born about 1557. He studied under Byrd, and was a chorister in St. Paul's Cathedral. Mus. Bac., Oxon., 1588; organist of St. Paul's Cathedral, London, 1591; Gentleman of the Chapel Royal, 1592-1602. Obtained patent for exclusive right to print music books, 1598. He died in 1604.

WORKS.—Canzonets, or little short songs to three voyces, 1593; Madrigalls to foure voyces, 1594; First booke of ballets to five voyces, 1595; First booke of Canzonets to two voyces, 1595; Canzonets, or little short aers to five and sixe voyces, 1597; The first booke of Consort Lessons, made by divers exquisite Authors for sixe instruments to play together, etc., 1599; The Triumphs of Oriana, to five and six voices, composed by divers several authors, newly published by Thomas Morley, London, Este, 1601 [contains madrigals by M. Este, J. Bennet, J. Hilton, J. Holmes, Wilbye, Morley, E. Johnson, T. Weelkes, Kirbye, Carlton, Cavendish, Lisley, Farmer, Milton, Jones, Croce, Hunt, Bateson, Mundy, E. Gibbons, R. Nicholson, Tomkins, Marson, F. Pilkington, Norcome, and Cobbold‡]; Services in D minor; Evening service in G minor (in Barnard's collection); Burial service (in Boyce); A Preces, Psalms, etc., in Barnard's MS. collection; Five sets of Lessons in Queen Elizabeth's Virginal Book; A plaine and easie introduction to Practicall Musicke, set downe in forme of a dialogue. Divided into three partes. The first teacheth to sing with all things necessary for the knowledge of prickt song. The second treateth of descante and to sing two parts in one upon a plain song or ground, with other things necessary for a descanter. The third and last part entreateth of composition of three, foure, five or more parts, with many profitable rules to that effect, with new songs of 2, 3, 4, and 5 parts, London, 1597, various editions. This was translated into German.

Morley, William, composer of the 18th century. Mus. Bac., 1713. Gentleman of the Chapel Royal, 1715. He died on October 29, 1731. Supposed to be the composer of the oldest double chant known, published in Boyce's Collection in D minor.

Mornington, Garrett Colley Wellesley, Earl of, Irish peer and composer, born at Dangan, Ireland, July 19, 1735. Father of the Duke of Wellington, and of the Marquis of Wellesley. Mus. Doc., Dublin, 1764, where he was the first Professor of Music in the University from 1764 to 1774. He succeeded to the title in 1758. Created Viscount Wellesley, 1760. Gained prizes from Catch Club

MORROW.

in 1776, 1777, 1779. He died at Kensington, London, May 22, 1781.

WORKS.—Glees and Madrigals composed by the Earl of Mornington, edited by Sir H. R. Bishop, London, 1846. Among them the following are famous:—As it fell upon a day; Beneath this rural shade; By greenwood tree; Come, fairest nymph; Gently hear me, charming maid; Go, happy shade; Hail, hallowed fane; Here in cool grot; O bird of eve; Rest, warrior, rest; and, Soft sleep profoundly. To these may be added the catch, "'Twas you sir." The collection of glees, etc., made by Bishop, is the only complete one extant; though all the glees, madrigals, and catches can be had as originally published in single parts. He also composed chants and other church music.

Morris, Margaret, MRS. ALFRED MORRIS, soprano vocalist, organist, and conductor, born at Caerleon, Monmouthshire. Showed musical talent from childhood, but her desire to adopt the art as a profession was not gratified until after her marriage, when monetary reverses turned her talent to practical account. She is to a great extent self-taught, but studied harmony with Dr. Bradford, and voice production with Emil Behnke. As a vocalist she is favourably known, and the Gwent Ladies' Choir, under her leadership, has a good reputation. She has conducted many concerts, including a performance of Gounod's, Mors et Vita, with full chorus and orchestra. She is organist of Christ Church, Caerleon, principal of a music school in that town, and has given lectures on musical topics at Newport, and other places.

Morrison, James, musician, author of "A New System of Music, applicable to all musical instruments," London [1852].

Morrison, William, composer and violinist, compiler of "A Collection of Highland music, consisting of strathspeys, reels, marches, waltzes, and airs, with variations original and selected, for the pf., violin, and violoncello," Inverness, n.d. [1813].

Morrow, Walter, trumpet player, born in Liverpool, June 15, 1850. Studied his instrument under Dan Godfrey, and at the R.A.M. He obtained high repute by his playing of the various parts for trumpet obligato in Handel's works, and did much to restore the Trumpet to its legitimate place in the orchestra. He developed a special trumpet for the performance of Bach's high trumpet parts, so long considered unplayable. This instrument he employed for the first time in Bach's "Ein feste Burg," at a concert of the Cambridge University Musical Society, June 11, 1885; and at the Leeds Festival of 1886 the same straight trumpet was introduced in Bach's High Mass in B Minor. Mr. Morrow is teacher of the trumpet at the R.C.M., and

MORTEN.

Guildhall School, and is now principal trumpet in the orchestras of the Philharmonic Society, Royal Choral Society, the Symphony Concerts, Handel Festival, and at most of the provincial festivals.

Morten, A., author of "Hints on the purchase of an organ," London, 1877.

Moseley, Caroline Carr, composer, daughter of the late Mr. Moseley, of Leighton Hall, Staffordshire. Studied at R.A.M. under Sir G. A. Macfarren. A.R.C.M. Composer of a number of part-songs for ladies' voices; The Child of the South; The Carol of Hope, and other songs; "Ten minutes in the country," two pieces for pf., violin, 'cello, and toy instruments, performed in London, 1882-1883, etc.

Moseley, Rev. W. Willis, author of "The quantity and Music of the Greek chorus discovered," Oxford, 1847.

Moss, Edwin, composer and tenor vocalist, born in London, January 4, 1838. He was for many years a teacher at Cardiff and Wantage. In 1866-75 he was precentor of Poultry Chapel, and from 1877 tenor in the Foundling Chapel. Editor of "The London Tune Book," 1877, and composer of a number of hymn tunes, etc.

Moss, Sydney, pianist, violinist, and conductor, born at Sydney, New South Wales, January 9, 1854. Studied at Leipzig, under Reinecke, David, and E. F. Richter, 1865-74. Returned to Sydney in 1874, and was conductor of the Musical Union in that city to the year 1881. Mr. Moss has been most disinterested in his service to music in Australia, and in many ways has done much for the advancement of the art.

Motley, Richard, composer of the early part of the 18th century. He composed a number of songs, "Draw, Cupid, draw" [1705], and issued a collection of "Ayres" in 1701.

Moul, Alfred, journalist and musician, has been resident in England and Australia. He is the composer of several songs, one of which, "'Mid Rapture" (Rossetti), was sung at the first Melbourne Festival, December, 1882. On leaving Melbourne, in 1883, he was publicly presented with an address. He has also written some pf. music. In 1888 he was appointed representative for the British Empire of the copyright interest of the Societé des Auteurs, Compositeurs et Editeurs de Musique.

Moulds, John, composer of latter part of the 18th century. He was a composer to Ranelagh Gardens, London, and to the theatres he contributed The Phisiognomist, 1795, and The Sultan, 1796, operas. Among his other works may be named Collection of Favourite Songs sung at Ranelagh, 1787; The Retrospector: a collection of sonnets [1790]. His

MOUNTAIN.

single songs include Caledonian maid [1790]; Cowslips of the valley; Description of London [1796]; Edwin and Emma (by Mallet); Deserted village (Goldsmith); Eleanor of Exeter (by G. S. Carey); Link boy; Nutbrown maid, etc.

Mounsey, Ann S., see BARTHOLOMEW, MRS.

Mounsey, Elizabeth, organist and composer, born in London, October 8, 1819. Sister of Mrs. W. Bartholomew (q.v.). As a pianist she had a good reputation, and frequently took part in the chamber concerts given at Crosby Hall by Mr. Dando (q.v.). It was chiefly as an organist that Miss Mounsey was known. She was appointed to St. Peter's, Cornhill, in 1834, and retained the office of organist until 1882, when she retired. In that church the first CC organ in England was erected, under the superintendence of Dr. Gauntlett. That was in 1840, in which year, and again in 1842, Mendelssohn performed upon it. Miss Mounsey possessed many interesting mementos of Mendelssohn, and greatly aided Mr. F. G. Edwards (q.v.) in his history of the oratorio "Elijah." She has published some vocal music, and pieces for guitar, organ, pf., etc. Since 1842 Miss Mounsey has been an Associate of the Philharmonic Society.

Mount, George, composer, contrabassist, and conductor. On the formation of the British Orchestral Society, in 1872, Mr. Mount was appointed conductor, an office he held till the dissolution of the Society a few years later. The first concert was given in St. James's Hall, December 5, 1872. He was deputy conductor, Sir Arthur Sullivan being chief, and afterwards conductor of the Royal Amateur Orchestral Society, from 1871 to the present time. Appointed assistant conductor at the Royal Aquarium, Westminster, 1876; conductor, Alexandra Palace, in 1885; and occasional conductor of the Philharmonic Concerts, 1884-7. His compositions include an overture, composed in celebration of the twenty-fifth anniversary of the Royal Amateur Orchestral Society; a "Pizzicato," for strings, 1894; and various smaller works. Mr. Mount is a professor at Trinity College, London.

Mount Edgcumbe, RICHARD EDGCUMBE, 2ND EARL, amateur composer and writer, was born September 13, 1764. Married Lady Sophia Hobart, daughter of the 2nd Earl of Buckinghamshire. He died at Richmond, Surrey, September 26, 1839. Composer of "Zenobia," an opera, King's Theatre, London, 1800. Author of "Musical Reminiscences of an Amateur, chiefly respecting the Italian Opera in England, for fifty years, 1773 to 1823, London, 1823; 2nd edition, 1827; 3rd edition, 1828; 4th edition, 1834.

Mountain, Sarah or **Sophia,** *born*

WILKINSON, soprano vocalist, was born in 1768. She made an appearance in 1782, but afterwards sang with Tate Wilkinson's Company, at Hull, and there made her *début* in 1786. In the same year she sang in Leeds and in Liverpool. She married Mr. Mountain, a violinist, in 1786. She afterwards sang at Covent Garden, and also in Dublin. In 1814 she retired, and died at Hammersmith, London, July 1, 1841.

Mudaliyar, A. M. Chinnaswami, editor of a treatise on Indian music, "Oriental Music in European Notation." Ave Maria Press, Pudupet, Madras, 1893.

Mudie, Thomas Molleson, composer and organist, born at Chelsea, London, November 30, 1809. He studied music under Crotch, Potter, etc., at R.A.M., 1823-32. Professor of Pf. at R.A.M., 1832-44. Organist at Galton, Surrey, 1834-44. Teacher in Edinburgh for a time, but returned to London in 1863. He died at London, July 24, 1876.

WORKS.—Symphonies in C, B flat, F, D; Quintets, quartets, trios, etc., for strings, etc.; Pf. music, consisting of duets, solos, fantasias, nocturnes, etc.; Anthems and sacred songs; Songs: Dying Gladiator; Evening song; Fisherman; To Memory; Six songs and two duets; Sacred songs [1840]; Three sacred duets [1842]. Accompaniments in Wood's "Songs of Scotland," edited by Graham.

Mullhollan, John Macpherson, Irish musician, who flourished in Ireland and Edinburgh about the end of last and the beginning of the present century. He issued a volume of Irish Melodies about 1800, with titles in Irish and English, based on a collection begun by his father, who died in 1770. He also issued "A Selection of Irish and Scots tunes, consisting of airs, marches, strathspeys, country dances, etc., adapted for the pianoforte, Edinburgh, n.d. [1804].

Mullen, Adelaide, soprano vocalist, born in Dublin. Daughter of Benjamin Mullen, Lay-vicar of St. Patrick's Cathedral. Studied at the Alexandra College, Dublin, and with J. B. Welch. Was first introduced to public notice by the late Sir Robert Stewart, at a concert of the University Choral Society. In March, 1882, she sang at a State Concert, and at the musical inauguration of the National Exhibition, Dublin, in August, being then an amateur. In May, 1883, she gave her first concert in Dublin, and since then has pursued a successful career, appearing in Edinburgh, 1885; Glasgow, 1886; and at the Crystal Palace Concerts, March 19, 1887. In 1888 she was engaged by Mr. William Ludwig for his concerts of Irish music in the United States, and has since twice visited America. Toured with the Burns-Crotty Company in 1891-2. Married, April 26, 1888, Henry Beaumont, the tenor vocalist *(q.v.)*.

Mullen, Alfred Frederick, musician, who died in 1881. Author of "Harmonium Tutor, with a series of easy lessons progressively arranged," London, n.d.; Easy and Complete Instructions for the Pianoforte, London, n.d.; Catechism of Music, n.d. Composer of numerous transcriptions for pf., and songs.

Mullen, Joseph, composer and organist, born at Dublin in 1826. Chorister in Christ Church Cathedral, Dublin. Organist at Tuam Cathedral; Succentor of Limerick Cathedral; Organist of St. Mary's Church, St. Catherine's Church, and of Christ Church, Leeson Park, Dublin.

Mullineux, William, organist, born at Worsley, Lancaster, April 4, 1858. Studied under his father, Dr. J. F. Bridge, and Dr. Hiles. Was organist of Worsley Wesleyan Chapel at the age of ten, and in 1876 was appointed organist of Bolton Town Hall, an office he still holds. F.R.C.O. He is the composer of a cantata, "Harvest Home," produced at Bolton, 1887.

Mullinger=Higgins, William, *see* HIGGINS, WM. MULLINGER.

Mullinex, Henry, composer and vocalist, born about 1793. He was a Gentleman of the Chapel Royal. Died at London, December 15, 1838. He composed waltzes, marches, etc., for the pf., and some vocal music.

Munday, Eliza, *see* SALMON, ELIZA.

Mundella, Emma, pianist, teacher, and composer, born at Nottingham in 1858. Daughter of the late John Mundella, of Leicester, and niece of the Right Hon. A. J. Mundella. Received her first musical instruction at home, and studied under Arthur Page, 1873-6. Won the Nottingham Scholarship on the opening of the National Training School for Music in 1876, and afterwards took the diploma, A.R.C.M. Was director of the music at St. Elphin's Clergy Daughters' School, Warrington; and from 1880 at Wimbledon High School. A career of much usefulness was cut short by death, February 20, 1896. Of her compositions the principal was "The Victory of Song" (Lewis Morris), for female chorus, three violins, pf. and band. She also published two anthems; Twelve elementary duets; Three sketches; and other pieces for pf. Editor of The Day School Hymn Book, Novello, the enlarged edition of which was in the press at the time of her death.

Munden, Thomas, organist and conductor, was a chorister of Westminster Abbey, and pupil of Greatorex. He was one of the conductors of the Birmingham Festivals from 1826 to 1846, and first organist of the Town Hall. He was also organist of Christ Church and St. Paul's, Birmingham. He died in North Wales about 1879.

MUNDY.

Mundy, John, organist and composer, was born in latter half of the 16th century. He studied under his father, and became organist of Eton College. Organist, St. George's Chapel, Windsor, 1585. Mus. Bac., Oxon., 1586; Mus. Doc., do., 1624. He died in 1630.

WORKS.—Songs and Psalms, composed into three, four, and five parts, for the use and delight of all such as either love or learne musicke, 1594; Anthems, and other sacred music; "Lightly she tripped," madrigal for 5 voices, in "Triumphs of Oriana."

Mundy, William, composer of the 16th century, father of the above. Vicar-choral, St. Paul's. Gentleman of the Chapel Royal, 1563. He died in 1591. Composer of anthems in Clifford's collection, etc.

Murby, Thomas, composer, violinist, and writer, born at Leicester, March 27, 1834. Educated at the Hill Street British School there, and in 1849 became amanuensis to William Gardiner (q.v.). In 1853 he entered the Borough Road Training College, London, and the next year was appointed its musical professor, a post he held for ten years. Beyond violin lessons from a French professor, Fémy, he was self-educated in music. He was a member of the Philharmonic orchestra for eight years; and of the Royal Amateur Society for about sixteen years; and is now the head of an educational publishing business.

WORKS.—New Tunes to choice words, 2 books; Merry-go-round, a collection of rhymes, jingles, and songs [1874]; The Golden Wreath, a collection of songs, original and adapted; The Devonshire Melodist, original settings of 12 songs by Edward Capern, the poet-postman; Merry Songs for little voices (in conjunction with Thomas Hood the younger, and his sister, Mrs. Broderip), London, Griffith & Farran. Children's cantatas, Five o'clock tea, 1887; Elsa, or the imprisoned fairy, 1888; Shakespeare's merrie meeting; and Lost Dimplechin, 1889, all performed at Gresham Hall, Brixton. Author of The Musical Student's Manual, London, 1862, now in its 8th edition.

Murdoch, Alexander Gregor, minor poet and author, born at Glasgow, April, 1843; died there, February 13, 1891. He published several volumes of poetry, and wrote a series of papers on Scots violinists and violin makers, which originally appeared in the *Glasgow Weekly Mail,* and were afterwards issued as "The Fiddle in Scotland: comprising Scotch Fiddlers and Fiddle makers," London, 1888. His son, WILLIAM, is a violinist of much promise.

Muris, John, English writer and musician, who flourished during the 14th century. Doctor and Canon of the Sorbonne, or a Chanter in the Church of Notre Dame of

NARES.

Paris. Author of a number of musical works, preserved in MS.; among which are treatises on counterpoint, and notices, the earliest of the kind of the time table. His nationality has been variously stated as Norman, or French, but a concensus of opinion seems to fix his nationality as English.

Murphy, John, musician and piper, published "A collection of Irish airs and jiggs with variations, by John Murphy, performer on the union pipes at Eglinton Castle," London, n.d. [1820].

Murray, James Robertson, composer and organist, born in 1836. Organist of St. Botolph's, Aldersgate, London. Founder of the London Church Choir Association, and conducted the annual services at St. Paul's Cathedral, 1880, etc. He died at London, September 3, 1885.

Musgrave, Frank, composer and conductor. He was musical director of the Strand Theatre, London. In 1887 he was an inmate of Bethnal Green Lunatic Asylum, and in May, 1888, he died. Composer of "Windsor Castle," burlesque opera by Burnand, Strand Theatre, 1865; and a burlesque on "L'Africaine," also by Burnand, in 1865. Songs: Early love; I'll forgive thee; Nellie Lee; She haunts me like a happy dream. A large number of polkas, valses, galops, etc., for pf.

Mutlow, William, organist, was born in 1761. He became organist of Gloucester Cathedral in 1782, and held the appointment till 1832, when he was succeeded by John Amott. He died at Gloucester in 1832. He conducted the Gloucester Festivals from 1790 to 1829. Composer of "Unto Thee, O God," anthem, etc.

Napier, William, musician and publisher, born in Scotland in 1740. He established himself in London as a music-seller, and in this capacity served the Royal family. Member of the King's band till he was forced to retire because of gout in his hands. He also played the violin at the Professional concerts. He died in Somers Town, London, June, 1812. He published A Selection of the most favourite Scots Songs, chiefly Pastoral, adapted for the harpsichord, with an accompaniment for the violin, by eminent Masters, London [1790]; A Selection of Original Scots Songs, in three parts, the harmony by Haydn, London [1792]; Napier's Selection of Dances and Strathspeys, with new and appropriate Basses, adapted for the pianoforte, harp, etc., n.d. The "eminent masters" mentioned in the first work were S. Arnold, W. Shield, Carter, and Barthelemon. This work also contains a "Dissertation on Scottish Music," by William Tytler (q.v.)

Nares, James, composer and organist, born at Stanwell, Middlesex, about April, 1715. He was a chorister in the Chapel

NASH.

Royal, under Gates, and also studied under Pepusch. Deputy-organist of St. George's Chapel, Windsor. Organist of York Cathedral, 1734. Organist and composer to the Chapel Royal, 1756. Mus. Doc., Cantab., 1757. Master of children of Chapel Royal in 1757-80. He died at London, February 10, 1783.

· WORKS.—Eight Setts of Lessons for the harpsichord, 1747; Five harpsichord lessons, 1758; Three easy do.; The Royal Pastoral, a dramatic ode; Collection of catches, canons, and glees, London [1772]; Twenty Anthems in score, for the use of H.M. Chapel Royal, London, 1778; Morning and Evening Service, with six anthems in score, 1788; Six organ fugues. A Treatise on Singing, n.d. Il Principio, or, a regular introduction to playing on the harpsichord or organ, n.d.; Concise and easy treatise on Singing . . with a set of English duets for beginners; Songs, and miscellaneous instrumental music; Six grand choruses from Handel's oratorios, adapted for the organ or harpsichord, n.d.

Nash, or Naish, F., bass vocalist, known as SIGNOR FRANCO NOVARA, born in the West of England. Made his *début* at Her Majesty's Theatre, May 28, 1881, as *Mephistopheles*, in "Faust." He sang with the Carl Rosa Company in 1883; at Covent Garden, 1889, etc. He has been on tour with Madame Patti, and has sung in many parts of the kingdom. In 1896 he was appointed a professor of singing at the R.A.M. He has composed some songs: Earl Douglas; The bold, bad Baron; Vieni con me, etc.; The plighting kiss, duet.

Nathan, Isaac, composer and writer, was born at Canterbury of Jewish parents, 1792. He was educated at Cambridge, and studied music under D. Corri. He sang at Covent Garden Theatre, and afterwards emigrated to Melbourne, Australia, in February, 1841. He was killed in Sydney, January 15, 1864.

WORKS.—*Operas:* Sweethearts and Wives, 1823; The Alcaid, opera, 1824; The Illustrious Stranger, musical farce, 1827; Merry freaks in troublous times, Sydney, 1851; Musurgia-Vocalis, an Essay on the History and Theory of Music, and on the qualities, capabilities, and management of the human voice [1823], illustrated; 2nd edition, 1836; Life of Madame Malibran de Beriot, interspersed with original anecdotes, and critical remarks on her musical powers, London, 1836. The King's Fool, drama. The Southern Euphrosyne and Australian Miscellany, containing Oriental moral tales, original anecdotes, poetry and music; an historical sketch, with examples, of the native aboriginal melodies, etc., Sydney [1846]. Hebrew Melodies (from Byron), with Braham, 1822; also 1861. Let's bow to Solomon, glee, Bristol [1819]. *Songs:* Beauty's bower; Come kiss me, said Colin; Fair

NAYLOR.

Haidée; Lady-bird; Long live our monarch (with chorus); When I roved a young Highlander, etc. Six new dances [1812].

Naylor, John, organist and composer, born at Stanningley, near Leeds, June 8, 1838. Chorister at Leeds Parish Church, pupil of R. S. Burton, and afterwards his assistant organist. Graduated Mus. Bac., 1863; Mus. Doc., 1872, Oxford. In 1856 he was appointed organist of St. Mary's, Scarborough; and in 1873 to St. Michael's Church in the same town. There, in conjunction with the Rev. R. Brown-Borthwick (*q.v.*), he raised the musical services to a high degree of excellence, and gave frequent organ recitals. On the retirement of Dr. Monk from York Minster, in 1883, Dr. Naylor gained the post of organist there. A special feature at the cathedral, since 1885, has been the annual Military service, for which he has composed anthems for choir and military band. He was conductor of the York Musical Society, retiring in June, 1896. His chief works are four cantatas : Jeremiah ; The Brazen Serpent ; Meribah, and Manna; produced at Festivals in York Minster in 1884-87-90, and 1893. He has also composed a service in G ; anthems, " O ye that love the Lord," etc. Songs and part-songs. Owing to ill-health he resigned his organ appointment in April, 1897, and died while on the voyage to Australia, May, 15, 1897.

His son, EDWARD WOODALL NAYLOR, was educated at the R.C.M., and at Emanuel College, Cambridge, graduating Mus. Bac., and M.A., 1891. He has composed a scena, "Merlin and the Gleam," for baritone solo and orchestra. Author of " Shakespeare and Music," London, Dent, 1896.

Naylor, Sidney, pianist and organist, born at Kensington, London, July 24, 1841. Chorister at the Temple Church, and pupil of Dr. E. J. Hopkins. He was organist successively at St. George's, Bloomsbury; St. Michael's, Bassishaw; St. Mary's, Newington; and St. Michael's, North Kensington. But he was more widely known as an able accompanist, officiating for many years at Boosey's Ballad Concerts; occasionally at the Monday Popular Concerts; and for many touring parties, particularly those of Mr. Sims Reeves. He was Carl Rosa's partner in the English Opera Season of 1874. He died at Shepherd's Bush, March 4, 1893. In 1868 he married MISS BLANCHE COLE, the soprano vocalist. She was born at Portsmouth, in 1851, and began her stage career very early. From 1871, she sang for a few years in concerts; but was mostly heard in opera. At various times, up to 1887, she was a member of the Carl Rosa Company; in 1879, toured with a company of her own ; and in 1882 sang in the Royal English Opera Company. She appeared in a

NEALE.

round of characters, and was very popular. Her death occurred in London, August 31, 1888.

Neale, Rev. John Mason, hymn writer, amateur musician, and clergyman, was born at London, January 24, 1818. Educated at Cambridge. Curate of St. Michael's, Guildford, 1841. Warden of Sackville College, East Grinstead. He died at East Grinstead, August 6, 1866. He composed " An Easter Carol " [1849], and some Church music, but is chiefly remembered by his works on the Eastern Church, and various popular hymns, published in such collections as Hymns for the Sick, 1843 ; Hymns for Children, 1843 ; Hymns chiefly mediæval, 1865 ; Hymnal noted, 1851-54, 2 vols. Carols for Christmas-tide, 1853 ; Carols for Easter-tide, 1854, both edited by Helmore.

Neale, Richard, compiler of " A Pocket Companion for gentlemen and ladies : being a collection of the finest opera songs and airs in English and Italian ... figured for ye organ, harpsichord, and spinet," London, 1725.

Neate, Charles, composer and pianist, born at London, March 28, 1784. He studied the Pf. under J. Field, and Woelfl. Appeared as pianist, at Covent Garden, 1800. Member of Philharmonic Society, 1813 ; afterwards a director and conductor. He became acquainted with Beethoven in 1815. He took lessons from Winter, and played in England at the principal concerts. He died at Brighton, March 30, 1877.

WORKS.—Grand Sonata for pf., op. 1, 1808 ; Sonata for pf., in D minor, op. 2, 1822 ; Les Caractères, a set of original quadrilles, op. 19 ; Fantasias, op. 4, 35 ; A Hundred impromptus, or short preludes ; Serenade, op. 15 ; Toccatas, op. 5 ; Kinloch, a Scotch air arranged for pf. [1827] ; Pf. rondos, and other instrumental works. Fantasia for pf. and 'cello, op. 9 ; Quintet, pf., wind, and double bass ; Trios for pf., violin, and 'cello, op. 21 and op. 22 [1831]. Essay on fingering, chiefly as connected with expression, together with some general observations on Pianoforte Playing, London, n.d. [1855]. Songs, etc.

Needham, Mrs., see CLAYTON, ELEANOR CREATHORNE.

Needler, Henry, musician and violinist, born, London, 1685 ; died, August, 1760. One of the original founders of the Academy of Ancient Music, and a performer of merit.

Neilson, L. C., see NIELSON, L. C.

Nelson, Sidney, composer and writer, born in 1800. He was a teacher in London, and died there on April 7, 1862.

WORKS.—Middle Temple, operetta [1829]. Cadi's Daughter, opera [1851]. Songs of the Gipsies, London, 1832 ; Mountain Lays, six sacred songs ; Six vocal trios [1852]. *Songs :* Away to the mountains [1858] ; Better land

NEWELL.

[1840] ; Gipsy fortune teller ; Highland widow ; Hunter's horn ; Life is a river ; Mary of Argyle [1860] ; Oh ! Steer my bark to Erin's Isle [1840] ; Pilot [1835] ; Rose of Allandale [1836] ; By the gentle Guadalquiver, and other vocal duets. Instructions in the art of Singing, London [1835]. Vocalist's daily practice, London, 1852. Vocal School, a series of scales, exercises, etc., London, n.d., also 1879.

Nesbitt, A. M., head-master of Toowoomba Grammar School, Queensland, Australia, was awarded the prize of fifty guineas, offered by the Brisbane Musical Union, in 1887, for a " Jubilee Ode," for chorus and orchestra.

Newark, William, composer of the 15th and 16th centuries, who contributed to the Fayrfax MS. A madrigal of his, entitled, " Thus musing," was printed by Novello in 1894.

Newbury, Philip, tenor vocalist, born in Jersey. Most of his early life was spent in Australia, where he studied under the best available teachers. In 1888 he came to England, and sang at various concerts in Sheffield, Birmingham, London, etc. He appeared in opera at the Shaftesbury Theatre, October, 1891, as the Pilot in " The Flying Dutchman." In 1896 he was back again in Australia, and after touring in different parts was reported as settling in Tasmania as a teacher of singing.

Newcombe, Georgeanne Hubi- *born* HUBI, soprano vocalist, composer, and lyric author, born in London, December 18, 1843. Studied under R. Glenn Wesley and Dr. Hiles. Organist for some years at Latchford Parish Church. Now resident at Warrington. Has written many lyrics set by Gerard Cobb, Denza, Pontet (Whisper and I shall hear), Wellings, and others. Her own compositions include such popular songs as " Ever faithful," " The miner and his boy " (*Orchestra*, prize song), " Irish Potheen," and many others. Her pf. piece, " Ye Fancye Fayre March," has met with great popularity. Her daughter, ETHEL HUBI-NEWCOMBE, gold medallist (Llewelyn Thomas), R.A.M., is a soprano vocalist of much promise.

Newell, Joseph Edward, composer and organist, born at Hunslet, near Leeds, October 11, 1843. Studied under F. W. Hird, and when about sixteen was appointed organist of St. Philip's, Leeds. In 1866 he went to St. Michael's, Headingly, where he remained until 1885, when he took over the duties of organist and singing-master at Leeds Grammar School, and its Collegiate Chapel, St. Wilfred. He removed to London in 1892, where he is chiefly engaged in composition, and arranging, etc., for some of the leading publishing firms. Of the large number of his publications the most important are : The

NEWMAN.

Christian Pilgrim, sacred cantata, produced at Trinity Church, Leeds, March 24, 1889; Spring, cantata for female voices; Stella, operetta for the same. The Song-Bird Album. Six four-part songs; Twelve two-part songs; Anthems, etc. Six Diversions, for two violins and pf.; Six musical poems, pf.; Pf. School in three grades, 1895; Tutor for harmonium and American organ; Rudiments of Music, with historical notes, 1895. He has also published much music for Mandoline and Guitar under the *noms de plume* of Carlo Murretti and Nicola Podesta.

Newman, R. A., musician and author, published "Description and use of the Harmonimetre," Weymouth, 1845.

Newson, George Lincoln, violinist, born at Diss, Norfolk. His talent was exhibited very early, and while yet a schoolboy he was engaged in the band at the festivals of Bury St. Edmunds and Norwich. Studied at R.A.M., under Mori, and was in the orchestra of the Royal Italian Opera, and played at the principal London concerts, and provincial festivals. He appears to have retired from the profession since 1890. He is an A.R.A.M.

Newth, Robert Boulcott, tenor vocalist, born at Worcester. Chorister at the Cathedral. Studied under W. Done. Was appointed organist of St. Paul's, Worcester; later, assistant to Dr. Monk, King's College, London; then to St. John's, Angell Town, Brixton, 1881. About that time, his singing attracted attention, and he appeared at various concerts in London. He sang at the Gloucester Festival, 1883; and at Worcester Festival, 1884. He is a professor at the Guildhall School of Music.

Newton, Mrs. Alexander, *born* ADELAIDE WARD, singer and composer, born at London, 1821, sister of J. C. Ward. She was one of Jenny Lind's concert party during her first tour in England. Sang at the Wednesday Concerts, Exeter Hall, 1849. She died at London, December 22, 1881. Composer of songs and pf. music; and was a bravura singer of exceptional ability.

Newton, James William, musician of end of last and first half of the present century. Compiler of "Psalmody improved, in a collection of Psalm tunes and anthems for 2, 3, and 4 voices . . . designed for the use of country choirs," Ipswich, 1775. "Companion to the Pilgrim, containing 30 psalm tunes, etc," London [1839].

Nichol, Henry Ernest, composer, pianist and organist, born at Hull, December 10, 1862. Apprenticed to civil engineering in 1877, but abandoned that for the serious study of music in 1885. Musical training private. Graduated Mus. Bac., Oxford, 1888. Settled in Hull as performer and teacher.

NICHOLSON.

Music master, Hull Grammar School; Organist, St. Andrew's, Kirk Ella; Conductor, North Cave Choral Society, and Newport Harmonic Society. WORKS.—Cantatas: Day and Night (Hull, 1892); Ode to Music, for chorus and orchestra (composed, 1894; produced at Crystal Palace, July 13, 1895, at the Tonic Sol-fa Festival); Will o' the Wisp (1896). An Evening Service in F, anthems, carols, hymns, etc. Part-songs. Sonata in A minor, pf. (MS.); pieces for pf., songs, etc. Author of a book on Choral Technics (Curwen), for choir-training, and a primer on Transposition at Sight.

Nicholds, Joseph, composer and conductor, was born at Sedgley. For some time he acted as director of Wombwell's band, but was afterwards a teacher of music. He died a pauper in Dudley Union, February 18, 1860. Composer of Babylon, oratorio; The Triumph of Zion, oratorio, Wolverhampton, September 17, 1844. Sacred Music, a selection of psalm and hymn tunes, London [1820], songs, etc.

Nicholl, Horace Wadham, composer, born at West Bromwich, Staffordshire, March 17, 1848. Son of a musician of some local repute. He has been for many years resident in New York. Of his works, a "Romance Antique" for orchestra was produced at New York in 1885; and "Cloister Scene," for soli, chorus, and orchestra, at the Pittsburgh Festival, 1889. He is said to have written a Tetralogy, "The Fall of Man; Abraham; Isaac; and Jacob."

Nicholl, William, tenor vocalist and teacher, was born at Glasgow, June 30, 1851, and originally worked as an engineer in Glasgow and India. He studied at the Royal Academy of Music, under Fiori, from January, 1884, to July, 1885, and gained the Parepa-Rosa gold medal, and the Academy bronze medal. He afterwards studied at Florence under Vannucini. He made his *début* at Glasgow, in November, 1884, with Madame Georgina Burns' party. Since 1886 he has given an annual series of classical concerts in London, and has sung at Chester (1888), Gloucester (1889), and other festivals and concerts throughout the kingdom, such as the London Ballad Concerts, Crystal Palace, Richter Concerts, etc. He has appeared twice before the Queen, by command, and in 1895 he accompanied Mr. Gladstone in the "Tantallon Castle" when Sir Donald Currie was cruising in the North Sea. He is A.R.A.M. and has been a professor of singing at the Royal Academy of Music since 1891. Joint author with George Thorpe of "Text-Book on the natural use of the Voice," London, 1895, and has lectured on "Voice Production" at the Society of Arts, January 27, 1897.

Nicholson, Alfred, oboist, born at Leicester, June 30, 1822, for many years in

NICHOLSON.

the band of the Royal Italian Opera, and also in the different festival orchestras. Appeared as soloist at the Wednesday Concerts, Exeter Hall, 1849, etc. Was in the orchestra at production of "Elijah," Birmingham, 1846. He died, August 29, 1870. His brother, HENRY NICHOLSON, flutist, was born at Leicester. He has played at the principal concerts in the provinces, in chamber music, etc. Was for nearly 30 years a member of the Birmingham Festival orchestra. In 1853 he started Concerts for the People, at Leicester, and has done much for music in that town. In May, 1886, three testimonial concerts were given in his honour by a number of artists, and a cheque for £800, the result, publicly presented to him by the Mayor of Leicester. He is still actively engaged in his profession, and took part in the complimentary concert given to Miss Deacon (q.v.) in May, 1896. Author of "Instructions for the Flute," and arranger of music for that instrument.

Nicholson Charles, flute-player and composer, born at Liverpool in 1795. Flute-player at Covent Garden, Drury Lane, Philharmonic Society, etc. He died at London, March 26, 1837. Wrote "Preceptive Lessons for the Flute," with Portrait and Appendix, London (10 numbers), 1821; "Complete Preceptor for the German Flute, in a style perfectly simple and easy," London, 2 parts [1816]; "Studies in the sharp and flat keys, composed with marks of expression and articulation for the Flute "; "Le Bouquet, or Flowers of Melody, a choice collection of airs.. for 1 or 2 flutes.."; School for the Flute, London [1836], new edition by Radcliff, London [1873]; Bolero [1825]; Collection of waltzes for the flute; Four concertinos for the flute and pf.; Admired Tyrolese melodies sung by the Rainer family (with Bochsa), 1830. Numerous fantasias, selections, etc., for flute and pf.

Nicholson, Rev. Henry D., M.A., author of "The Organ: its mechanism, stops, etc., explained, London, n.d. (2 editions). Boston edition published under the title of "Organ Manual."

Nicholson, James, musician, author of "A Concise Treatise on Thorough-bass, with practical lessons selected from the most eminent composers," London [1796]. Another JAMES NICHOLSON, probably the same, was a performer on the pipe and tabor at York, and died on August 30, 1807.

Nicholson, or Nicolson, Richard, organist and composer, was born in the second half of the 16th century. Organist and chorus-master, Magdalen College, Oxford, 1595. Mus. Bac., Oxon., 1596. He was the first choragus or professor of music in Oxford University on Heather's Foundation, in 1626. He died at Oxford, 1639. Composer of madrigals in the " Triumphs of Oriana," etc.

NIELSON.

Nicks, George, viola player and composer, was born about 1775. He was viola player in the orchestras of the Italian Opera and Covent Garden, and at the Ancient and Philharmonic concerts. For many years he acted as manager of the Subscription Concerts in the Music Rooms at Oxford. He died at London, January 8, 1841. Composer of much vocal music, among which may be named the following songs:—Adieu, Ben Cable, Kaleidoscope (1828), O Memory (1810), Pleasures of lovers (1797), Poor Harry (1806). The Robin (1825), Since truth has left the shepherd's tongue, The Tear, etc.

Nicolson, Ludovick, composer and violinist, who was a weaver to trade. He was born in Paisley about 1770, and died there August 3, 1852. He was an associate of R. A. Smith, Tannahill the poet, and other worthies of his time. Compiler of "A collection of psalm and hymn tunes in four parts, adapted to various metres and may be used in the principal churches, chapels, and dissenting congregations in Scotland," Paisley (Glasgow engraved), about 1852. The tunes "Paisley" and "Low Church" are by him.

Nield, Jonathan, tenor vocalist, born in 1769. In 1795 he was appointed a gentleman of the Chapel Royal in succession to J. Soaper. He was also in the choirs of Westminster Abbey and St. Paul's. For many years he was principal tenor at the Ancient Concerts, and a member of the Noblemen and Gentlemen's Glee Club; Royal Society of Musicians, etc. He also sang at the Gloucester Musical Festival in 1793, and afterwards at other festivals. He died at London on March 6, 1843.

WILLIAM ASHTON NIELD, probably a relative of the foregoing, composed "The Juvenile Musical Library . . ." London, 1854, illustrated by George Cruikshank, and now very scarce. "Collection of Psalms and Hymns as sung at All Sculs' Church, St. Mary-le-Bow . . ." London [1827]. *Songs:* Days of yore, Harbour of peace. Rounds; Pf. music, etc.

Nielson, Lawrence Cornelius, composer, organist and pianist, was born at London in 1760. He was taken to America in 1767, but afterwards returned and became organist at Dudley and Chesterfield. He died at Chesterfield about 1830.

WORKS.—Sonatas, duets, divertissements, etc., for pf.; Twelve favourite airs for two German Flutes [1800]; Marches for pf. [1810]. *Songs:* Balmy pledge of love, Happy the youth, When absent, etc.

His son, EDWIN JOHN NIELSON, born in 1812, was one of the foundation students of the R.A.M. He composed a number of songs between 1833—1840, of which may be named —Better land, Happy home, I hae naebody

NIGHTINGALE.

now, Mary, Queen of Scots' adieu, Norwegian love song, Remember me, etc. He was a harpist and composed some music for harp and pf. The surname of these musicians is spelt variously Neilson and Nielson.

Nightingale, John Charles, composer and organist, was born about 1785. Organist of the Foundling Hospital, London. He died about 1837. He issued a " Collection of psalm and hymn tunes, odes, etc., in 3 and 4 parts," London [1824], and composed rondos, waltzes, and arrangements for the pf. Also arranged " The celebrated choruses from Handel's oratorios for the organ " ; " A selection of overtures from Handel's most celebrated oratorios, arranged for the organ and pf." He wrote some Familiar voluntaries for the organ, which were issued in a collected form as a Series of voluntaries, about 1855; and composed Battle songs ; Indian lover's song ; Man to man, and other songs and vocal music.

JOSEPH C. NIGHTINGALE, born 1822, was an organist in Liverpool.

Nimmo, Robert Hamilton, tenor vocalist, born at Catrine, September 10, 1836. He was a music seller and gave concerts, chiefly of Scot's music, in various parts of Scotland. He died at Glasgow, March 20, 1893. He wrote the song, " Creep before ye gang," and others of a like nature.

Nisbet, James, tenor vocalist and writer, born 1817 ; died at Liverpool, February 29, 1884. Author of a " Vocal Primer, or student's singing manual," Glasgow [1860], and other works.

Nixon, Henry George, composer and organist, was born at Winchester, February 20, 1796. He was organist of St. George's Chapel, London Road, from 1817 to 1820 ; next of Warwick Street Chapel, 1820-36 ; then of St. Andrew's Roman Catholic Chapel, Glasgow, 1836-39 ; and finally of St. George's Roman Catholic Cathedral, London, 1839-49. He died in London of cholera, in 1849.

WORKS.—Five Masses and other music for the Roman Catholic Church service. Numerous airs arranged for the pf. There came to the lady's gate a knight, and other songs, etc.

He was a nephew of HENRY NIXON, born at Liverpool, 1787 ; died July 25, 1834, who was a writer on music and inventor of a musical instrument called the Eolina. H. G. Nixon was married, in 1818, to CAROLINE MELISSA DANBY (died 1857), a daughter of Danby the glee composer. They had a large family, among whom may be named JAMES CASSANA (1828-42), a violinist, and Henry Cotter, noticed below.

Nixon, Henry Cotter, fourth son of H. G. Nixon, was born in London in 1842. Studied under H. Deval, Henry Smart, Dr.

NODES.

Steggall, and G. A. Macfarren. Became F.C.O., 1867 ; graduated Mus. Bac., 1876, Cambridge. Organist of St. Peter's, Woolwich, 1864-8 ; St. James's, Spanish Place, 1870 ; St. Mary Magdalene's, St. Leonard's-on-Sea, 1872-7. Conductor of an orchestral society there. Now resident in London. He won the Trinity College, London, prize, 1880, for Pf. trio ; 1881, for Sonata, pf. and 'cello ; also prizes for six-part madrigal, Brighton Sacred Harmonic, 1889, and that of £25 offered by Methven, Simpson, Edinburgh, 1893, for the best set of two-part songs. His other works include Psalm 95, for soli, chorus and orchestra ; Overture, " Titania " ; Symphonic poem, " Palamon and Arcite," both for orchestra ; pf. pieces ; songs, etc.

Noble, Charles, organist, born at Southwell, Notts, September 17, 1812. He was organist of St. Martin's, Stamford ; of St. Mary's Nottingham, for 38 years ; and lastly of Southwell Minster. He died at Southwell, September 10, 1885. As a teacher he was very successful, and highly esteemed.

SAMUEL JOHN NOBLE, organist and pianist, was King's Scholar, R.A.M., 1839. Pupil of W. H. Holmes. He played at the Wednesday Concerts, Exeter Hall, London, 1849 ; and was organist of Spitalsfield Parish Church ; and of St. Mary-at-Hill, 1861. Another SAMUEL NOBLE, an alto singer, is a Gentleman of the Chapel Royal, St. James's.

Noble, Thomas Tertius, organist and composer, born at Bath, May 5, 1867. Educated at R.C.M., where he was exhibitioner and scholar, under Walter Parratt, Villiers Stanford, and J. F. Bridge. A.R.C.M. When fourteen was organist of All Saints', Colchester ; and after leaving the R.C.M., was appointed successively to St. John's, Wilton Road, S.W., 1889 ; Assistant organist, Trinity College, Cambridge, 1890 ; and organist and choirmaster, Ely Cathedral, 1892. There he has been active in promoting special services, introducing Haydn's "Passion," and other works of importance. He has a number of compositions, including an organ sonata, in MS. Of his published works the principal is a setting of the Communion Office, scored for voices, organ, horns, trumpets, trombones, and drums (1891). A Solemn March, and other pieces for organ, are also published. He has also composed music to the A.D.C. burlesque, Jupiter, at Cambridge.

Nodes, O., musician of early part of present century, edited with J. Bowcher " A Selection of Psalm and Hymn Tunes, adapted to the various metres now in use in all churches, chapels, and dissenting congregations throughout Great Britain," London [1803]. He also issued " A Selection of Psalm and Hymn Tunes," London [1806], published in numbers.

NORBURY.

Norbury, John, author of "The Box of Whistles, an illustrated book on organ cases ; with notes on organs at home and abroad," London, 1877.

Norcome, Daniel, musician and composer, was born at Windsor in 1576. He was a son of one of the lay-clerks at Windsor, and was probably a singer in the Chapel Royal there. He is stated to have left England on account of his religion, and he became a member of the band in the Arch-ducal Chapel at Brussels, where he was in 1647. He composed "With angel's face and brightness," a madrigal in the "Triumphs of Oriana," 1601.

Norledge, Annie E., soprano vocalist, born at Newark, Nottingham. At first she studied the violin, being a scholar of R.C.M., and later, a student at the Leipzig Conservatorium. She played the viola in the first Ladies' Quartet in Leipzig. After her return she studied singing under W. Shakespeare. For some short time she played violin in various concerts, but is now favourably known as an accomplished vocalist, having appeared with success in many parts of the United Kingdom.

Norman, Helen S., *see sub.*, STANDING, F. H.

Normann, Rudolf, *see* HARRIS, GEORGE FREDERICK.

Norris, Thomas, composer, and tenor vocalist, born at Mere, near Salisbury, about August, 1741. He became a chorister in Salisbury Cathedral under Stephens. Sang at Worcester and Hereford Festivals, 1761-62; and at Drury Lane Theatre, 1762. Organist of Christ Church, Oxford, 1765. Mus. Bac., Oxon., 1765. Organist of St. John's College, Oxford, 1765. Lay-clerk of Magdalen College, Oxford, 1771. Sang at Handel Commemoration, 1784. He died at Himley Hall, near Stourbridge, September 3, 1790.

WORKS.—Six Symphonies for 2 violins, 2 hautboys, 2 French horns, a tenor and bass, op. 1, London [1770]. Eight solo songs for voice and harpsichord, Oxford [1775]. Songs in "Amusement for Ladies." Four glees. Anthems, etc.

North, Francis, LORD GUILDFORD, writer, born in 1637, died in 1685. Held several important legal appointments, but has interest in a musical sense only as the author of "A Philosophical Essay on Music," 1677. His brother ROGER (1650-1733), was a miscellaneous writer, who left in MS. "Memoirs of Musick,...now first printed from the original MS. and edited, with copious notes, by E. F. Rimbault," London, 1846. This is an interesting work, containing a fund of information on events in the musical history of the author's period.

North, James M., vocal teacher and

NOVELLO.

composer, born at Huddersfield in 1835. He was taken to the United States in 1842, and was a pupil of Lowell Mason, G. F. Root, and G. J. Webb. He was successively a teacher in St. Louis, and in the New York State Normal School, Albany, from 1859 to 1860. Afterwards director of music in the public schools. Editor of Vocal exercises and various collections of music for church and choral society use.

North, John, conductor, and teacher of singing, born at Huddersfield in 1852. In 1862 he entered the business of Wood and Marshall, Huddersfield, and afterwards became a partner. Learnt to play pf. and violin ; was in the theatre orchestra, and ultimately leader. Conductor of the Huddersfield Glee and Madrigal Society; Philharmonic Society; and Festival Choral Society, the last one of the finest in existence ; also conducted other societies in the district. Was for some years organist of New North Road Baptist Chapel, but resigned in 1887. He died at Huddersfield, October 12, 1891.

North, Robert Augustus, Examiner in Music to the New Zealand Government, published in London, 1896, a work, entitled, "Voxometric Revelation."

Norton, Hon. Mrs., *born* CAROLINE ELIZABETH SARAH SHERIDAN, daughter of Thomas Sheridan, grand-daughter of R. B. Sheridan, and sister of Helen Lady Dufferin (*q.v.*). She was born in 1809. Best known as a novelist and poetess. In February, 1877, she was married for the second time to Sir William Stirling-Maxwell, Bart. She died at London, June 15, 1877. Joint composer of "A Set of Ten Songs, etc., by two sisters " [1833]. Composer of Set of Seven Songs and a duet, 3 sets [c. 1840]; Songs of affection ; Avenge the wrong of Adam Leslie ; Blind girls' lament ; Love of Helen Douglas; Mother's lament, and other songs. Health to the outward bound, glee. Words of a number of popular songs, like Blockley's "Love not," "Arab's farewell to his steed," etc.

Novello, Clara Anastasia, soprano vocalist, born at London, June 10, 1818. Daughter of Vincent Novello. She studied at Paris Conservatory, and under John Robinson of York. On January 7, 1833, she sang at the first concert of the Vocal Society, Hanover Square Rooms, London, and appeared at Windsor in the same year. Sang at Ancient and Philharmonic Concerts, and at all the important Provincial Festivals, and at the Gewandhaus Concerts, Leipzig, in Italy, etc. She married Count Gigliucci, 1843, and retired in 1860.

Novello, Joseph Alfred, publisher and musician, born at London in 1810. Eldest son of Vincent Novello. Choir-master of Lincoln's Inn Chapel. Bass vocalist at

NOVELLO.

various concerts. Publisher under title of Novello & Co. in succession to the business founded by his father. Retired to Genoa in 1856, and died there, July 16, 1896. He wrote "Analysis of Vocal Rudiments by Question and Answer," London, n.d.; "Concise Explanations of the Gregorian Note," London, 1842, etc. Wrote English version of Mendelssohn's "Lobgesang." He invented a form of vessel that was claimed to prevent sea-sickness.

Novello, Mary Sabilla, writer, and soprano vocalist, daughter of Vincent Novello. Appeared as singer at various places, but now known only as writer of a "Vocal School, etc..," London, n.d.; "Voice, and Vocal Art," n.d.

Novello, Vincent, organist, composer, and publisher, born, London, September 6, 1781. Chorister in the Sardinian Chapel, Duke Street, under S. Webbe. Deputy organist to Webbe and Danby. Organist of the Portuguese Chapel, 1797-1822. Founded the firm of Novello & Co., in 1811. Pianist to Italian Opera, London, 1812. Organist of Roman Catholic Chapel, in Moorfields, 1840-43. Member of Philharmonic Society, and founder of the Classical Harmonists Society. He retired to Nice, and died there August 9, 1861.

WORKS.—Collections of church music, consisting of selections from the writings of composers of all times. Anthems, kyries, hymns, and other church music. Cathedral voluntaries for organ, eight books of selections. Short melodies for organ, in six books. Select organ pieces, in 18 books containing numerous original pieces. Rosalba, cantata. Masses, various. Collection of motets for the Offertory. Convent music, collection of sacred pieces. Studies in vocal counterpoint, consisting of rounds, etc. Surrey Chapel music. Glees, songs, etc. The works of Purcell (sacred). The Fitzwilliam music. Madrigalian studies, London, eight parts, 1841. A Biographical Sketch of Henry Purcell, from the best authorities, London [1832].

Nunn, Edward Cuthbert, composer and pianist, of present time. Studied at R.A.M. Won the Lucas Medal for Composition, 1887; Bennett Scholarship, 1888. A.R.A.M. Resident at Leytonstone, Essex. He has given pf. recitals, but is better known by his compositions. The chief are: Psalm 100, for baritone solo and chorus, performed, Leytonstone, 1891; Cantatas and operettas, William Tell, or A n(arrow) escape; Sir Rupert the Fear'ess; Prince Kamar-al-Zaman, 1894; Sappho, etc. Pieces for pf., organ; an Evening Service, songs, etc.

Nunn, Elizabeth Annie, composer, died at Fallowfield, Manchester, January 7, 1894, at the age of 33. She published a Mass in C, for soli, chorus and orchestra, op. 4; and other liturgical music.

OAKELEY.

Nunn, John Hopkins, organist and conductor, born at Bury St. Edmunds, November 10, 1827. Studied at R.A.M., of which Institution he is a Fellow. Organist at Sherborne in 1852, removing to Penzance in 1854, where he has been organist of St. Mary's Church since 1859. Conductor of Penzance Choral Society, which has given many good concerts. He has composed a Te Deum, anthems, etc. His daugters, GERTRUDE and HENRIETTA, have been heard as vocalists in the Western counties, and in March, 1885, sang at the Monday Popular Concerts. The first-named is a violoncellist of some distinction. JOHN NUNN, possibly related, was at one time living at Bury St. Edmunds; and for many years was organist of St. Paul's Church, Bedford. From about 1840 to 1860, he took an active part in concert giving, and was principal violin of the Bedford Sacred Harmonic Society.

Nunn, Robert Lindley, organist and pianist, born at Bury St. Edmunds, July 15, 1826. Brother of John H. Nunn. Student, Associate, and Fellow, R.A.M. Graduated Mus. Bac., Cambridge, 1867. Organist of St. Mary-le-Tower, Ipswich, 1856-81; and sometime organist of Queen Elizabeth School. Has been a concert giver and performer at Ipswich. Colchester, and other places, from 1853. Resident at Ipswich as teacher, etc. He has two daughters, talented musicians, the one a violinist, the other a pianist, pupil of the Paris Conservatoire. EDWIN NUNN, F.C.O., of Ipswich, is the musical editor of "Hymns and chants for female voices," Novello, 1884, compiled for the use of the Ipswich High School. He also gave concerts at Ipswich, 1882-4.

Nusum, G., was, 1884, organist of the Roman Catholic Cathedral, Demerara, British Guiana, and accompanist to the Demerara Musical Society. In 1892, G. W. Nusum was appointed organist of the New Cathedral, Demerara, and opened the new organ therein, March 22, 1893, with a recital.

Oakeley, Sir Herbert Stanley, Kt., composer, organist, and conductor, born at Ealing, Middlesex, July 22, 1830. Second son of Sir Herbert Oakeley, Bart., of Athole Murray, niece of the fourth Duke of Athole. Educated at Rugby School, and Christ Church, Oxford, graduating B.A., 1853, and M.A., 1856. He had at an early age shown decided taste and talent for music, and at Oxford studied harmony under Stephen Elvey. On leaving the University he went to Leipzig and studied with Plaidy, Moscheles, and Papperitz; then under Johann Schneider, Dresden; and finally with Professor H. Karl Breidenstein, at Bonn. Though intended for another profession, he now determined to

OAKELEY.

devote himself to music ; and in 1865 became a candidate for the Reid Chair at Edinburgh. He was elected, and the position of the Professorship, so much improved by his predecessor, John Donaldson (q.v.), was much enhanced by his work. The annual "Reid Concert" became a three-days' Festival, and the fine performances of the Halle orchestra gave a great impulse to the study and appreciation of orchestral music in Scotland. His organ recitals, and the concerts of the Edinburgh University Musical Society helped forward the cause of musical education in the district. In 1864 he was elected member of a society called "Quirites," at Rome, and after his Edinburgh appointments many distinctions were awarded him : Mus. Doc., Cantuar, 1871 ; Mus. Doc., Cambridge, honoris causâ, 1871 ; the same, Oxford, 1879 ; LL.D., Aberdeen, 1881 ; D.C.L., Toronto, 1886 ; Mus. Doc., Dublin, 1887 ; St. Andrew's, 1888 ; Adelaide, 1895 ; LL.D., Edinburgh, 1891 ; and on his resignation of the Chair of Music in May of that year, he was made Emeritus Professor, 1892. He was also elected an Hon. Member of Institutions at Bologna, and Rome.

In 1876, at the inauguration of the Scottish National Monument to the late Prince Consort, the music was directed and composed by the Professor, who received the honour of knighthood from the Queen, at Holyrood. He was appointed composer to the Queen, in Scotland ; President of the Cheltenham Musical Festival, from 1887. Besides his professional work, he has lectured and given organ performances in various places ; and was for some years musical correspondent of The Guardian, and contributor to other journals.

WORKS.—Vocal : Jubilee Lyric, a short cantata, Cheltenham Festival, 1887 ; Who is this that cometh from Edom ? Six short anthems ; The Glory of Lebanon, composed for 800th anniversary of consecration of Winchester Cathedral, and performed there, April 9, 1893 ; Behold, now praise the Lord ; Seek Him that maketh the seven stars ; and other anthems. Service in E flat ; Psalms and Hymns for men's voices ; Six hymns, with orchestra ; Hymn tunes in Hymns Ancient and Modern, and other collections ; Bible Psalter ; Prayer Book Psalter, edited. Twenty songs ; Album of 26 songs, dedicated to Her Majesty ; Six songs, op. 2 ; Tears, idle tears, with orchestra, sung by Mlle. Titiens at the Birmingham Festival, 1873 ; To Mary ; and many other songs. Three duets, German words, op. 8. Quartets, op. 7, 8 ; Students' songs ; Six part-songs for men's voices, op. 17 ; Four memorial choruses ; Choral songs, op. 25. National melodies (Scottish), op. 18. Forty choruses, with orchestral accompaniment, for Edinburgh University Musical Society,

O'CAROLAN.

etc. *Instrumental :* Suite in Olden Style, Cheltenham Festival, 1893 ; Edinburgh Festal March, Liverpool, 1874 ; Funeral March, op. 23 ; Minuet, Chester Festival, 1885 ; Pastorale, Manchester, 1891, all for orchestra. Sonata in A, op. 20 ; Rondo Capriccioso ; Romance, op. 21 ; Three romances, pf. Gavotte and musette, organ. Arrangements, etc.

Oakey, George, composer, writer, and teacher, born at St. Pancras, London, October 14, 1841. Self taught in music. Gained first prizes in Society of Arts Examination under Hullah, 1869, and under Macfarren, 1873. Graduated Mus. Bac., Cambridge, 1877. Examiner in harmony and composition, Tonic Sol-fa College ; professor of the same, City of London College. He has composed Psalm 100, for soli, chorus and orchestra. Anthems : Blessed be the Lord ; Praise the Lord of Hosts. Part-songs : The Daisies peep ; Pack clouds away ; The Beacon Light, etc. Hymns, chants, and arrangements of national airs, madrigals, glees, etc., for mixed and for equal voices, published in various collections. Author of Construction Exercises in Harmony, 1877 ; Text Book of Counterpoint, 1878, eight editions, rewritten and enlarged, 1890 ; Text Book of Harmony, 1884, seven editions ; Text Book of Musical Elements, 1886, five editions ; Compendium of Harmony, 1889 ; Figured Bass, 1891, two editions ; and New Graded Exercises in Harmony, 1894. All published by Curwen, London.

O'Cahen, Rory Dall. *See* MORISON, RODERICK.

O'Carolan, or Carolan, Turlough, composer and harp-player, born at Baile-Nusah, or Newton, West Meath, in 1670. He became blind when about 16 years old, but married and settled on a farm at Mosshill, Leitrim, where his extravagant manner of living caused his ruin and he was forced to become an itinerent harper. He travelled much about the country, and became widely known as a minstrel and boon companion. He died at Alderford House, March 25, 1738. He was a poet and composed a large number of popular Irish tunes, such as "Bumper Squire Jones," "Bridget Cruise," "Liquor of Life," and "Savourna Deelish." His musical works were published in 1747, and again about 1785 as "A Favourite Collection of the so much admired old Irish tunes, the original and genuine compositions of Carolan, the celebrated Irish bard. Set for the harpsichord, violin and German flute," Dublin, John Lee, n.d. ; but it is understood that only a very small number of his tunes have been preserved or identified. Specimens of his works will be found in Hardiman, Bunting, and Walker.

O'Carroll, Patrick, author of " A Royal Road to Pianoforte Playing, 1888.

O'Daly, Gerald, Irish harpist and composer, of last century. The supposed composer of " Eileén a Roon," now adapted to the song, " Robin Adair."

Odier, Ludovic, author of " Epistola Physiologica Inauguralis de Elementariis Musicæ Sensationibus," Edinburgh, 1770. Treatise on the connection between Music and Medicine.

O'Donnely, T. J., Abbe, author of " The Academy of elementary music, containing a lucid exposition of the theory and basis of the practice from its primary notions to those of composition," etc., London, 1841 ; Paris, 1842.

O'Kelly, Joseph, violinist and composer, born at Boulogne-sur-Mer in 1829. He studied under Osborne, Kalkbrenner, etc., and resided at Paris as a musician. He died at Paris, January, 1885.

WORKS.—Paraguassü, Poem Lyrique in 3 parts, 1855 ; Ruse contre Ruse, operetta. Cantata for centenary of O'Connell, Dublin, 1878. Luten de Galway, opera, 1878 ; La Zingarella, opera, 1879. Songs. Pf. music.

Okeover, John, organist and composer of the 17th century. He was organist and vicar-choral of Wells Cathedral. In 1633 he graduated Mus. Bac., Oxford.

Okey, Maggie, pianist, studied at the London Academy of Music, and appeared with success at the Promenade Concerts, Covent Garden, August, 1882. She gave concerts from that year, and has played at Vienna, in 1883 ; Berlin, 1887 ; Paris, 1889 ; in America, 1890-1, etc. She has also played at the Monday and Saturday Popular Concerts ; the Crystal Palace ; and the Philharmonic, 1891. In 1884 she was married to Vladimir de Pachmann, and was divorced some years later. She has composed a sonata for pf. and violin ; Romance in E, do. ; Theme, with variations, pf., etc.

Old, John, composer and conductor, born at Totness, South Devon, May 28, 1827. Descended from an ancient family that occupied Rowton Hall for more than four centuries. He studied first under John and Edwin Loder, 1842 ; then at R.A.M. under Bennett and Goss ; and later with Thalberg and Molique. Resident for some time at Torquay as teacher and conductor of a choral society. He afterwards settled at Reading, founding the Layston College of Music. He composed a sacred drama,. " The Seventh Seal " ; an opera, " Herne the Hunter," performed in Reading Town Hall, December 14, 1887 ; and an overture, " Tenth of March " (on the marriage of the Prince of Wales). He also wrote a number of pieces for pf. : Etude de Concert ; Reveries ; Impromptus, etc. ; Part-songs ; Songs : I have

a home in fairyland ; Meet me at morn ; My native vale, etc. He died at Reading, February 4, 1892 ; and at his request a copy of his opera, Herne the Hunter, and two other compositions, were buried with him.

Oldham, S. Emily, composer, of present time. Has given concerts in London, and is the composer of a number of songs, among which may be mentioned His ship ; Her voice ; Fair is the dawn ; Guardami ; Loyal and true, etc. Minuet for pf.

Another Miss E. OLDHAM is an Associate of R.C.M., and professor of the pianoforte at the Royal Irish Academy of Music, Dublin.

Oldmixon, Lady, born GEORGE, soprano vocalist, was born in 1768. She sang in opposition to Mrs. Billington at Dublin, and appeared at Drury Lane Theatre, the Oratorio, and other London concerts. Biography unknown.

O'Leary, Arthur, composer and pianist, born at Tralee, County Kerry, Ireland, March 15, 1834. He came of a musical family, his grandfather having been a teacher of music, his father (died, 1846), organist of the parish church, Tralee, and his uncle (died, 1893, aged 100 or 102), organist of Killarney Cathedral. When quite a child, Arthur O'Leary's playing attracted the attention of Mr. Wyndham Goold, and through his friendship the boy was sent to the Conservatorium, in Leipzig, in 1847, and studied under Plaidy, Moscheles, Richter, etc. Returning to England, he entered the R.A.M., 1852, and studied under Potter and Bennett. Several compositions from his pen date from his student days. In 1856, he was appointed a professor at the R.A.M., and, later, elected a Fellow. Commenced concert giving about 1858. He has lectured on music, and contributed to the musical press ; and held appointments at the National Training School for Music, 1876 ; Guildhall School, from its opening ; and at the Crystal Palace School of Science and Art, 1886, etc. Member of the Philharmonic Society. Edited Sterndale Bennett's Pf. works. In 1860 he married Miss Rosetta Vinning, noticed below.

WORKS.—Overture and incidental music to Longfellow's Spanish Student (1854) ; Symphony in C ; Suite, orchestra. Concerto, pf. and orchestra. Theme in C, with variations ; Toccata in F, performed at the Monday Popular Concerts, December 14, 1885 ; Wayside sketches ; and many other pieces for pf. Six songs : Ask not why I love ; and others. Mass of St. John (unison) ; Ode to the Victor, part-song. Edited Masses by Hummel, Sechter, and Schubert.

MRS. O'LEARY, daughter of W. S. Vinning, of Newton Abbott, Devon, showed remarkable talent as a child, singing and playing at concerts when seven. Entered the R.A.M.,

OLIPHANT.

and won a King's Scholarship, December, 1851, and again in 1853. Studied under John Thomas, harp; W. H. Holmes, pf.; and Steggall and G. A. Macfarren, composition. She is a Fellow of the R.A.M., and Associate of the Philharmonic Society. She now devotes chiefly to voice training, and for some years conducted the South Kensington Ladies' Choir. Her compositions include, I am the Angel; My Song is Love; How faithful are thy branches; My Angel Lassie; and other songs.

Oliphant, Thomas, writer and musician, born at Condie, Perthshire, December 25, 1799. Member of London Madrigal Society, 1830, and acted as its hon. secretary for nearly 40 years. President of the Madrigal Society. He died at London, March 9, 1873.

WORKS.—A brief account of the Madrigal Society....London, 1835. Short account of Madrigals from their commencement to the present time, London, 1836. La Musa Madrigalesca, or a collection of madrigals, ballets, roundelays, etc., chiefly of the Elizabethan age; with remarks and annotations, London, 1837. Catalogue of MS. Music in the British Museum, London, 1842. Ten Favourite Madrigals, arranged from the original part books, with an accompaniment for the pf., London [1836]. Collection of Glees, Madrigals, etc. (Novello), n.d. Catches and Rounds, by old composers, London [1835]. Ditties of the Olden Time, London [1835]. Arrangement of Songs, etc. Tallis' Song of forty parts; Responses (edited). Stay one moment, gentle river, madrigal. Poetry for various pieces of vocal music. Swedish part-songs (1860); German songs....London, 1838-49, issued in numbers. Six ancient part-songs for five voices, London, [1845]. Songs.

Olive, Joseph, organist and composer, who was organist of St. Botolph's, Aldersgate Street, London, about the middle of last century. He died at London, October 8, 1786.

WORKS.—All for Scarlet, an interlude, 1785; India Hoa, interlude [1770]. Six songs for a voice and harpsichord. Bacchus, god of joys divine, duet [1775]. Songs: Farewell, Fox hunters, Lover's declaration, etc.

Another OLIVE, EDMUND, was probably the son or other relative of the above. He was organist of the parish church of Warrington, and is said to have held a similar office at Bangor Cathedral. Died at Warrington, November 18, 1824. He compiled " Sixteen Psalm Tunes, adapted for three voices....as sung in the parish church of Warrington," Warrington, Booth [1820], 2nd. edit.

Oliver, Frederick, bandmaster, born about 1812. He was bandmaster of the 20th Regiment for 31 years, and served in India, Burmah, and in the Crimean War; was also

ONSLOW.

bandmaster in the Donegal Militia, and the 3rd Battalion of the 60th Rifles. In 1863 he went to Kelso as bandmaster to the seventh Duke of Roxburgh, whose band he brought to a high state of efficiency. He conducted a performance before the Queen on the occasion of her visit to Floors Castle in 1867. Up to his eightieth year he played solos on the saxophone. He died at Croydon, Surrey, in February, 1892, aged 82.

O'Mara, Joseph, tenor vocalist, born in Limerick, July 16, 1866, son of James O'Mara, J.P., late High Sherriff for Limerick City. Educated at the Jesuit College there, and was trained in the Tonic Sol-fa method of singing. For some time was manager of his father's business, and, for two years, sang in the choir of Limerick Cathedral. In 1889 he gave up business, and went to Milan to study singing under Perini, and Moretti. At the end of 1890 he returned to England, and was at once engaged for the Royal English Opera House, where he appeared, February 4, 1891, in the title-part of " Ivanhoe." He then took lessons from Edwin Holland. In 1892, he sang at the Monday Popular Concerts, and has since appeared at the principal London and provincial concerts. Has been in Sir Augustus Harris's Grand Opera at Drury Lane, and Covent Garden, since 1893, in a variety of characters, and created the part of *Mike Murphy* in Stanford's " Shamus O'Brien," produced March 2, 1896. He is now in the front rank of opera singers.

O'Neil, Henry John, bandmaster and cornet player, born, Dublin, March 25, 1841. He studied under H. König, and acted as bandmaster in the Navy, 1859-62. He settled in Edinburgh, and became a member of the leading orchestras, and about 1879 was appointed Queen's trumpeter. Bandmaster of the Royal Scots Fusiliers, and of the 3rd battalion of the Volunteer Highland Light Infantry.

O'Neill, Arthur, Irish harper and collector, born in 1726; died near Armagh, in October, 1816. He was possessed of great stores of traditional melodies, etc., and was referred to by Bunting when preparing the first portion of his Irish Melodies.

Onslow, George, composer, born at Clermont-Ferrand, France, July 27, 1784. Grandson of the first Lord Onslow. He studied under Hüllmandel, Dussek, Cramer, and Reicha. Resided for a time in Vienna, 1802, but returned to Paris, and received the Cross of the Legion of Honour. Member of the Institut (in succession to Cherubini), 1842. He died at Clermont-Ferrand, October 3, 1853.

WORKS.—L'Alcade de la Vega, opera, 1824; Le Colporteur, opera, 1827; Le Duc de Guise, opera, 1837. Symphonies for orchestra, op.

ORCHARD.

41, 42. Quintets for 2 violins, viola, and 2 'cellos, or 'cello and bass, opp. 17, 18, 19, 23, 24, 25, 32, 33, 34, 35, 37, 38, 39, 40, 43, 44, 45, 51, 57, 58, 59, 61, 67, 68, 72, 73, 74, 78, 80, 82. Quartets for strings, opp. 4, 8, 9, 21, 36, 44, 46, 47, 48, 49, 50, 52, 53, 54, 55, 56, 62, 63, 64, 65, 66, 69. Trios for pf., violin, and 'cello, opp. 3, 14, 20, 24, 26, 27. Duets for pf. and violin, op. 11, 15, 21, 29, 31. Sextet, op. 30. Sonata for pf. and 'cello, op. 16. Sonatas for pf. solo, op. 1, 2. Sonatas for pf. duet, op. 7, 22.

Orchard, W. Arundel, pianist and composer, of present time. Went to Australia, 1892 (?), and then to Tasmania, where he was appointed organist and choirmaster of St. David's Cathedral, Hobart, 1897. He has written an oratorio, "Easter Morn," produced at Bloomsbury Hall, April 19, 1892; also an Andante and Scherzo for pf. and string orchestra, 1891, etc.

Orger, Caroline, pianist and composer, daughter of Mary Ann Orger, actress and dramatic author (London, 1788, Brighton, 1849). Born in London, 1818. Appeared at various concerts from the year 1840. Gave her first concert at the Hanover Square Rooms, May 3, 1843, when she introduced her Concerto for the pf.; and produced a Pf. Trio the next year at a concert given in conjunction with Miss Dolby. The Society of British Musicians brought forward her Pf. Quartet, in 1844; in E flat, 1847; and a Sonata in G, for 'cello and pf., 1846. In 1846, she married Alexander R. Reinagle (*q.v.*), and under that name afterwards published a pamphlet, "A few words on Pianoforte playing, with rules for fingering passages of frequent occurrence [1855]; Novello. She published Tarantellas and other works for the Pf.; Sonata for the Pf., op. 6. Three songs by R. Browning (1868), etc. Died at Tiverton, Devon, March 11, 1892, aged 74.

Orridge, Ellen Amelia, contralto vocalist, born at London, August 14, 1856. She studied at the R.A.M. under Garcia, and gained the Thomas (1877), Nilsson (1878), and Parepa-Rosa (1878), prizes. She was well-known at most of the London and provincial concerts, and was a special favourite in oratorio music. She died at Guernsey, September 16, 1883.

Osborne, George Alexander, pianist and composer, born at Limerick (where his father was lay-vicar and organist of the Cathedral). September 24, 1806. He was intended for the church, but having a strong bias toward music, he taught himself pianoforte playing, assisted his father at the organ, and finally decided upon music as a profession. In 1825 he went to Brussels, finding a home with the Prince de Chimay. There he studied and gave concerts, and was musical instructor

OSTLERE.

to the Prince of Orange (the late King of Holland). After the revolution of 1830 he went to Paris (Fétis says in 1826), where he studied under Pixis, Fétis, and Kalkbrenner. He remained there until 1843, occupying a prominent position as performer, teacher, and composer. In 1843 he is said to have settled in London, but he kept up his house in Paris to the end of 1847. He was in London in 1844, 1845, and also played at a concert in 1848, in which year he seems to have made London his home. From 1849 his concerts were important features of the musical season.

He was a Member, and sometime Director, of the Philharmonic Society; also Director, R.A.M., and associated with other institutions. He retired from active life about 1880, but played occasionally in performances of chamber music up to November, 1889. Personally acquainted with the greatest musicians of the century, he has penned his memories of them in papers read before the Musical Association, 1878-83. He died at London, November 16, 1893.

His compositions comprise two operas; several vocal scenas; Three overtures: The Forest Maiden, performed at Alexandra Palace, February, 1876, etc.; and Marches for orchestra. A Septet, Sestet (performed, London, 1849), and Quintet for pf., wind, and double bass; Three Trios in A (1844), G, and E (1845), for pf. and strings; Sonata, pf. and 'cello; pieces for violin, etc. A large number of pieces for pf.: La Pluie des Perles; Romance sans paroles; La Tenerezza; Valses, etc., many of them exceedingly popular. With De Beriot he wrote a number of duets for violin and pf.

Osman, Fanny Wilson, soprano vocalist, born at Reading. Studied at the R.A.M., and later under Vannuccini. She has sung in oratorio and ballad concerts in London and the provinces with success, and is favourably known as an accomplished artist.

Osmond, Harold Bartrum, organist and composer, born at Southampton, January 19, 1869. Studied at the Guildhall School of Music under D. Beardwell, Henry Gadsby, and other Masters. F.R.C.O., 1888. He was appointed organist of St. Peter's, Bethnal Green, 1884; St. Barnabas, Homerton, 1886; and, since 1889, has been organist and director of the choir of St. Peter's, Thanet. He is conductor of the Broadstairs and St. Peter's Choral Societies, and of the St. Peter's Church Oratorio Society. His chief compositions are a Sacred Cantata, The Ascension (1886); Psalm 23, for baritone solo, chorus, and orchestra (1886); Communion Service in E; Anthems, etc. Symphonic Suite for small orchestra, Margate Philharmonic, 1896, etc.

Ostlere, May, composer of dance music of present time. Her pieces include waltzes:

OSWALD.

Hypatia, Clytie, Ariadne, Idalia, Isis, Only once more, Spirit of the stars, etc. Polkas: Genesta, Thistledown, Dutch Doll, etc. Marches and songs.

Oswald, Arthur Louis, baritone vocalist, born at Brighton, July 14, 1858. At first studied as a pianist, at Paris, 1871-2, and at Mayence, with Beyschlag, 1873. Entered R.A.M., 1873, studied with Manuel Garcia until 1877, when he went to Milan for two years. Made his *début* in opera at Varese, appearing in Figaro, Il Barbiere, Faust, etc. In 1879 returned to London. Sang at the Monday Popular Concerts, Crystal Palace, and Philharmonic Concerts in 1880, achieving a high position at once. He has also sung in oratorio. In 1886 he was appointed a professor of singing at the R.A.M., and elected a Fellow in 1891. He was appointed a professor of the Guildhall School of Music in 1896.

Oswald, James, musician and editor, born in Scotland about 1710-1711. He was a dancing-master in Dunfermline, and afterwards a teacher of music and dancing in Edinburgh. He settled in London in 1742, and was engaged in business as a music-seller at the Pavement, St. Martin's Churchyard. He became chamber composer to George III. in 1761. He died at Knebworth, Herts., in 1769, aged 58.

WORKS.—A Curious Collection of Scots tunes for a violin, bass viol, or German flute, with a thorough-bass for the harpsichord, Edinburgh, n.d. [c. 1740]. Collection of curious Scots tunes for a violin, German flute, or harpsichord, London, n.d. [c. 1742]. The Caledonian Pocket Companion, containing a favourite collection of Scotch tunes, with variations for the German flute or violin, London [c. 1742-1759], issued in 12 books, forming 2 volumes of 6 books each. Six pastoral solos for a violin and violoncello, with a thorough-bass for the organ or harpsichord, London, n.d. Six Songs compos'd in the Scotch taste, for a person of distinction. Humbly inscribed to Her Grace the Dutchess of Hamilton, London, n.d. [1750]. Airs for the Spring, Summer, Autumn, and Winter, London, n.d., issued in 4 parts. Collection of Scots tunes, with variations... London, n.d. Ten Favourite Songs, sung by Miss Formantel, at Ranelagh, London, n.d. Fifty-five marches for the Militia... London, n.d. Collection of the best old Scotch and English songs set for the voice, with accompaniments and thorough bass for the harpsichord, London, n.d.

Ould, Charles, violoncellist, born at Romford, Essex, July 19, 1835. Has played in the principal orchestras in London and the provincial festivals, and appeared as soloist in Birmingham, at the Harrison and Stockley concerts, etc. He has played at the Monday Popular Concerts, and is a member of the

OUSELEY.

Gompertz string quartet, giving concerts in the Queen's Hall, London, and in the provinces. Member of Her Majesty's Private Band. His son, CHARLES HOPKINS OULD, is an excellent pianist, and has acted as accompanist at the Monday Popular Concerts (1885), etc.; and his daughter, KATE OULD, is a violoncellist who has appeared with success at various chamber concerts in London.

Ould, Edwin, contrabassist, a member of the Philharmonic and other orchestras, is the composer of a concert overture, produced, 1885; "L'Esperance," for violin and orchestra, etc. His son, PERCY OULD, violinist, was appointed to St. Andrew's College, Grahams-Town, South Africa, in 1893, and is doing good work in Cape Colony.

Ouseley, Rev. Sir Frederick Arthur Gore, Bart., composer, organist and writer, was born at London, August 12, 1825. Son of Sir William Ouseley, Bart., whom he succeeded in 1844. He was educated at Oxford, and graduated B.A., 1846; M.A., 1849. Ordained 1849. Curate of St. Paul's, Knightsbridge, 1849-50. Mus. Bac., Oxon., 1850. Mus. Doc., Oxon., 1854. Professor of Music in Oxford University (in succession to Sir Henry Bishop), 1855. Precentor of Hereford Cathedral, 1855. M.A. and Mus. Doc., Durham, 1856. Warden of St. Michael's College, and Vicar of St. Michael, Tenbury, 1856. Mus. Doc., Cantab., 1862. Hon. LL.D., Cantab., 1883. Hon. LL.D., Edinburgh, 1885. He died at Hereford, April 6, 1889.

WORKS.—The Martyrdom of St. Polycarp, oratorio, 1855; Hagar, oratorio, Hereford Festival, 1873. Church Services in D, B minor, A, G, E, E flat, and D, etc. *Anthems:* And there was a pure river; Awake, thou that sleepest; Behold now praise the Lord; Christ is risen from the dead; Great is the Lord; I will give thanks; I waited patiently for the Lord; I will magnify Thee, O Lord; It came even to pass; In God's Word will I rejoice; Love not the world; O love the Lord; O sing unto God; Sing unto the Lord; The Lord is King; The Lord is my Shepherd; Thus saith the Lord; Unto Thee will I cry; Why standest Thou so far off? etc. The Psalter, arranged for chanting, with appropriate English chants (with E. G. Monk), London, various editions and dates. Anglican Psalter Chants, London [1872]. Eighteen Preludes and Fugues for organ; Sonata for the opening of the new organ in the Sheldonian Theatre, Oxford; Three Andantes for organ; Preludes and Fugues, various. Cathedral Services by English masters [Farrant, Creyghton, Kempton, Child, Kelway, Aldrich, etc.], London, n.d. [1853]; Collection of Anthems for certain seasons and festivals (edited), 2 vols., 1861-66; Glees; Six songs, etc. Treatise on Harmony, Oxford, 1868; 2nd edition, 1876; 3rd edition,

T

OVEREND.

1883. Treatise on Counterpoint, Canon, and Fugue, based upon that of Cherubini, Oxford, 1868; 2nd edition, 1884. Treatise on Musical Form and General Composition, Oxford, 1875; 2nd edition, 1886. Naumann's History of Music, trans. by F. Praeger (edited). Sermons, etc. *See* Memorials of Sir Frederick A. G. Ouseley, Bart., by Francis T. Havergal, 1889. By his will he left his musical library to St. Michael's College, Tenbury. The value of his personal estate exceeded £54,000.

Overend, Marmaduke, organist and writer, who was born in the first half of the 18th century. He studied under Boyce, and was organist of Isleworth, Middlesex. He died in 1790.

WORKS.—A brief account of, and an introduction to, eight lectures on the science of music, London, 1781 ; Twelve sonatas for two violins and violoncello, 1779 ; The Epithalamium made on the marriage of King George III. and Queen Charlotte [London, 1761]. Vocal music, etc.

Owen, Alexander, bandmaster and cornet player, born in 1851. He has been connected for many years with brass bands in Lancashire, and has won many prizes in contests. He was conductor of the Staly-bridge Band ; solo cornet player in the Meltham Mills Band, 1875 ; conductor of the Boarhurst Band, 1877-84 ; of the Black Dyke, 1879-88 ; and of the Besses o' th' Barn Band, 1884 to the present time. With these fine bands he has given concerts in many places, and has arranged much music for their use.

Owen, David, *surnamed* DAVYDD Y GAREG - WEN, harpist and composer, who flourished in Wales about 1722—1751. He is said to have composed the " Rising of the Lark," and other Welsh airs.

Owen, David, bandmaster and conductor. He was bandmaster of a Highland regiment for some time, and in 1835 succeeded his father as bandmaster of the 2nd Dragoon Guards (Scots Greys). He died in 1867.

His younger brother, JAMES ARTHUR OWEN, was a pianist and clarionet player. He was born in 1829, and died at Brighton, November 5, 1881. Composer of a Romance for cornet and pf. (1855), and a large number of polkas, valses, marches, galops, etc., for pf. and orchestra. He also composed some songs.

Owen, John, OWAIN ALAW, composer, teacher, and baritone singer, born at Chester of Welsh parents, November 14, 1821. He was brought up to trade till 1844, when he adopted the musical profession. Organist of various churches in Chester, and a prominent advocate of musical education. He died at Chester, January 30, 1883.

WORKS.—Jeremiah, oratorio, 1878. Habakkuk's Prayer, prize cantata (with Ambrose Lloyd), 1851 ; Prince of Wales, cantata, Car-

PAGE.

narvon Eisteddfod, 1862. This was the first Welsh secular cantata. Gwalia's Holiday, cantata, Chester, 1866. Anthems, glees, songs, etc. He also edited Gems of Welsh melody, a selection of popular Welsh songs, Ruthin, 1860. The Welsh Harp, airs arranged for four voices ; a collection of tunes for Sunday schools ; a collection of English airs, etc.

His son, WILLIAM HENRY, was born at Chester in 1845. He was an organist in Dublin, and was killed in a railway accident at Abergele, on August 20, 1868, when returning to his post. Some of his anthems were published in Welsh by his father, and a Magnificat by him is in Novello's list.

Packer, Charles Sandys, organist and composer, born in 1810 ; died at Reading in September, 1883. Student, Associate, and Hon. Member, R.A.M. In 1839 he was tried and condemned for forgery. While a student he wrote an Italian sacred drama, " La Morte d'Abele," and some vocal scenas. He was a composer of much ability, and his lamentable fall put an end to a career of more than ordinary promise.

Packwood, Charles, musician, composed " Original Sacred Music, consisting of psalm and hymn tunes, etc," London, 1845.

Paddon, James, organist and composer, was born at Exeter about 1768. Educated in the Cathedral there, and was organist of the Cathedral from 1803. Died at Exeter, June 14, 1835. He composed some sacred music.

JOHN PADDON, probably the son of the foregoing, composed " Sacred Music, used at Quebec Chapel," London [1810] ; Ballads, dance music, etc. Author of " System of Musical Education," London, 1818.

Page, Arthur James, organist and composer, born at Ipswich, March 3, 1846. Entered Norwich Cathedral as a chorister at the age of seven, and when fourteen was articled for seven years to Dr. Buck. He was taught harmony and counterpoint by Dr. Bunnett. At the end of his time he was offered a partnership by Dr. Buck. This he did not accept, but obtained the appointment of organist and choirmaster at St. Mary's, Nottingham, in 1867, where he still holds office. He started and maintains a surpliced choir of some 80 voices at that church. F.C.O., 1875. Sometime music master at Trent College. An active worker from the early days of the Incorporated Society of Musicians, he has been Hon. Gen. Treasurer since 1885. At the Cardiff Conference, 1897, he was presented with a testimonial. Has contributed to the musical press, and is the composer of the following works :—Cantatas and operettas for treble voices : Red Riding

PAGE.

Hood; Meadowsweet; Nymphs and Goblins; Sea King's Daughter; Snow Queen; Spirit of the Year; Amabel; The Three Bears. Anthems and Services. Three-part, and two-part songs; Album of six songs, etc. 100 original rounds, composed and collected, Forsyth. Pieces for organ or harmonium, four books; organ pieces, various. Spring Song, Berceuse, etc., for pf. Madrigal, I dare not ask, performed by Nottingham Philharmonic Society, 1891, etc. His son, ARTHUR BERNARD PAGE, is a music teacher in Nottingham, and a lyric author of ability, having supplied the books for most of the cantatas named above.

Page, Edward Osmund, organist and composer, who resided in Manchester as an organist and teacher. He died December 23, 1883. Composer of a Mass and other vocal music.

Page, John, editor and tenor singer, was born about the middle of the 18th century. Lay-clerk, St. George's, Windsor, 1790. Gentleman of Chapel Royal. Vicar-choral, St. Paul's, 1801. He died at London, August, 1812.

WORKS.—Harmonia Sacra: a collection of anthems in score, selected for cathedral and parochial churches from the most eminent masters of the 16th, 17th, and 18th centuries, London, 3 vols., 1800; 2nd edit., by E. F. Rimbault. Festive Harmony: a collection of the most favourite madrigals, glees, and elegies, selected from the works of the most eminent composers, London, 4 vols., 1804. Collection of Hymns, London, 1804. Divine Harmony....by P. Henley, to which are added four psalm tunes, by T. Sharp, London, 1798. Burial Service, Evening Service, Anthems, etc., performed at the Funeral of Lord Nelson, January 9, 1806. Four anthems (festival), etc. Anthems and Psalms, as performed at St. Paul's Cathedral on the day of the Anniversary Meeting of the Charity Children, London [1785].

Page, William, musician, issued "The Golden Lyre, containing 130 original psalm and hymn tunes...." London [1856].

Paige, Kate, authoress of "Exercises on General Elementary Music." Part I., 1880; Part II., 1881, London. Daily Exercises for the Pf. [1883].

Paine, Robert Parker, composer, born at Sandgate, Kent, November 15, 1823. Musical from childhood, he had to pursue his studies under difficulties, and is practically self taught in composition. His friend, C. H. Purday (q.v.), then of Sandgate, was one of the first to encourage his talent, and Paine contributed to his collection of 100 rounds. When he went to Windsor he was encouraged in his work by Sir George Elvey. His principal compositions are a cantata, "The

PALMER.

Prodigal Son," performed at Eton, January, 1884; a Te Deum, brought out at the same time; and a setting of Psalm 93, for bass solo, chorus and orchestra, produced at Windsor, May 23, 1887. He has also composed, When the soft light, The wind and the waves, The Fisherman, and other songs; and has in MS. anthems, hymn-tunes, chants, songs, etc.

Palmer, Edward Davidson, organist and writer. Graduated Mus. Bac., Oxford, 1878. Organist of Upper Holloway Baptist Chapel, from 1885; professor of harmony, counterpoint and solo singing, Metropolitan College of Music. He has composed a setting of Psalm 146, for soli, chorus and orchestra; and published some pieces for organ, and arrangements for violin and pf. Author of "A Manual of Voice Training," London, Jos. Williams, 1891; and contributor of papers to the *Nineteenth Century* magazine, and the musical press.

Palmer, Isabella Perkins. See sub. DIBDIN, HENRY E.

Palmer, James, musician and editor, born at Southwold, Suffolk, December 7, 1796. He was a teacher of music in Edinburgh, and was precentor in Broughton Place United Presbyterian Church, from 1830 till 1851. He died at Edinburgh on July 23, 1861. Compiler of "Sacred Harmony, original and selected, in four vocal parts, suited to the psalms, paraphrases, and hymns used in all the congregations in Scotland," Edinburgh, n.d. "Christian Harmony, a collection of sacred music, adapted to the various metres in general use...." Edinburgh, n.d., issued in parts. "The Sacred Minstrel, a collection of original church tunes and anthems, containing also several celebrated pieces by eminent composers," Edinburgh, n.d. "Collection of Psalm and Hymn Tunes used at the Relief Church, Broughton Street, Edinburgh, 1828."

Palmer, Lucas Shelton, writer and organist, author of "First Studies in Sight-Singing, for the use of schools, choirs, and choral societies," London, Novello [1875]. "A Short Catechism on Singing," London. Part-songs, Sunset; The white rose sighed; Phyllis.

Palmer, Percy. See sub. MARRIOTT, ANNIE.

Palmer, Thomas, organist and composer, graduated Mus. Bac., Oxford, 1879. Organist of All Saints', Londonderry, 1873; parish church, Alton, Hants, 1876; Omagh, County Tyrone, 1877; and St. Matthew's, Ipswich, from 1880. Conductor of Felixstowe Choral Society. Composer of Psalm 108, for soli, chorus and orchestra; Evening Service in F; O sing unto the Lord, anthem; part-songs, songs, pf. pieces, etc.

PALTONI.

Paltoni-Corri. *See sub.* CORRI, FANNY.

Panchari Banerjea, author of a "History of Hindu Music," a lecture delivered at the Hooghly Institute, Bhowanipore, 1880. It contains a notice of many native musicians of Southern India, and valuable information concerning the musical systems of that country.

Parepa-Rosa, Euphrosyne Parepa de Boyesku, soprano vocalist, born at Edinburgh, May 7, 1836. Daughter of a native of Wallachia. Educated by her mother, Elizabeth Seguin. *Début* at Malta, 1852. Sang at Naples, Genoa, Rome, Florence, Madrid, Lisbon, etc. Appeared in London, May, 1857. Married Captain de Wolfe Carvell. Sang at Handel Festival, London, 1862-65. Married Carl Rosa (after death of her first husband, 1865), 1867. Visited America, 1867-1871. Re-visited America, autumn of 1871. She died at London, January 21, 1874. She appeared in operas by Bellini, Mellon, Macfarren, Balfe, Meyerbeer, Auber, and Mozart, and did much to establish the Carl Rosa Opera Company.

Parish-Alvars, Elias, harpist and composer, born at Teignmouth, February 28, 1810. Jewish by parentage. He studied under Dizi, Labarre, and Bochsa. Played in Germany, 1831; Italy, 1834. Appeared in London, 1836-7. Travelled in the East, 1838-42. Appeared in Germany and Italy again, 1842-44. Settled in Vienna, 1847. Chamber harpist to Emperor. He died at Vienna, January 25, 1849.

WORKS.—Voyage d'un Harpiste en Orient, Recueils d' airs et de melodies populaires en Turquie et dans l'Asie Mineure, Harp solo, op. 62 ; Concerto for harp and orchestra, in G minor, op. 81; Concerto for 2 harps and orchestra, ; Concerto for harp and orchestra in E flat, op. 98; March for harp, op. 67 ; Fantasias, transcriptions, romances, and melodies, for harp and orchestra, and harp and pf., etc.

Park, Rev. John, D.D., poet, composer, and clergyman, born at Greenock in 1804. Educated at Greenock and Paisley, and at Glasgow and Aberdeen Universities, and was licensed to preach. Assistant to Dr. Steele, West Church, Greenock, and afterwards to Dr. Grigor of Bonhill. Minister at Liverpool. Minister at Glencairn, in Dumfriesshire, and afterwards of Collegiate Parish Church of St. Andrews, first charge. He died at St. Andrews, April 8, 1865. His compositions were issued as " Songs composed and, in part, written by the late Rev. John Park, D.D., St. Andrews, with introductory notice by Principal Shairp," Leeds, 1876, with portrait.

Parke, John, oboe player and composer, was born in 1745. He studied under Simpson and Baumgarten. Oboist at the opera, 1768.

PARKER.

Concerto player at Vauxhall, 1771. Principal oboist at Drury Lane, 1771. Member of King's Private Band. Chamber Musician to Prince of Wales, 1783. Principal oboe at the Concerts of Ancient Music, etc. He died at London, August 2, 1829.

Parke, Maria Hester, BEARDMORE, pianist, composer, and singer, born in 1775. Daughter of John Parke. She studied under her father, and made her *début* as a vocalist at Gloucester Festival in 1790. Sang afterwards at London, and provincial concerts. Married Mr. Beardmore. She died on August 15, 1822.

WORKS.—Three grand Sonatas for pf., op. 1 ; Two do., op. 2 ; Two Sonatas for pf., op. 4 ; Sonata for pf., op. 7. Concerto for pf. or harpsichord, op. 6 [1800]. Two Sonatas for pf. and violin, op. 13. Set of Glees, London [1790]. Songs, etc.

Parke, William Thomas, writer, oboe player, and composer, born at London in 1762. He studied under Dance, Baumgarten, and his brother, John. Chorister at Drury Lane Theatre, 1775. Oboist at Vauxhall, 1776. Principal oboist at Covent Garden, 1783. Employed at principal concerts, Vauxhall, etc., as oboist, after 1800. He died at London, August 26, 1847.

WORKS.—Overtures to "Netley Abbey," 1794 ; " Lock and Key," 1796. Concertos for oboe. Three duetts for two German flutes [1793] ; Second set, op. 8 [1794]. Tutor for the hautboy : being a familiar introduction to the art of playing this instrument. With sixteen duets for two hautboys, n.d. *Songs* : Blue bonnets; Cupid is a wanton boy; Donald Macleod ; Lad of the moor; Maid of the village; Merry tambourine. He also adapted Dalayrac's "Nina" for the English stage. Musical Memoirs: comprising an account of the general state of Music in England from the first Commemoration of Handel in 1784 to the year 1830, interspersed with numerous anecdotes, musical, histrionic, etc., London, 2 vols., 1830.

Parke is now best remembered by his useful " Musical Memoirs," or annals of music from 1784 to 1830. It contains, among much gossippy matter and anecdotes, a very considerable proportion of historical and biographical data.

Parker, Henry, composer, conductor, and teacher of singing, born in London, August 4, 1845. Studied at Leipzig under Moscheles, Richter, and Plaidy; and at Paris under Lefort. Has given concerts in St. James's Hall, London, etc. Composer of a romantic comic opera, "Mignonette," Royalty Theatre, May, 1889 ; " Jerusalem," for bass solo and chorus, Albert Hall, 1884 ; and other songs that have become popular. Gavottes, and other short pieces for orchestra; pf. pieces, etc. Author of " The Voice : its Production and Improvement, with Practical Exercises," London, various editions.

Parker, Louis Napoleon, composer and dramatist, born in the Department of Calvados, France, October 21, 1852. Educated on the continent. Studied at R.A.M., 1870, under Sterndale Bennett, Banister, Steggall, and others. A.R.A.M., 1874. Member of Committee of the United Wagner Society, and English representative of the *Revue Wagnérienne*, 1885. In 1877 he was appointed organist and music master at Sherborne School, Dorsetshire, and he made the school concerts famous, also conducting various societies in the locality. In 1892 he left Sherborne for London, to devote himself to dramatic authorship. He was for a long time a contributor to the musical press, principally upon Wagnerian topics. His compositions comprise the cantatas, The Wreck of the Hesperus, Silvia, Young Tamerlane ; Psalm 23, for equal voices ; Orchestral overtures (MS.), violin and pf. pieces ; Songs, and part-songs, etc. Dramatic works : A buried talent ; The love knot ; Love in a mist ; The sequel ; and others written in conjunction with Murray Carson, etc.

Parker, Robert, organist and conductor, studied under W. S. Hoyte, Scotson Clark, and G. Cooper ; also violin and pf. under Lehmeyer, and singing under F. Walker. Was for some time assistant to W. H. Monk at King's College, London. About the end of 1878 he was appointed organist at the Cathedral, Wellington, New Zealand. There he established orchestral concerts, and conducted the first Musical Festival given in New Zealand, November, 1888. He has introduced many important compositions, and has exercised great influence in the musical development of the country. He is singing instructor to the Board of Education, and represents the R.A.M., and other London institutions.

Parker, Septimus, composer and organist, born at London, June 10, 1824. He was successively organist of Ashtead Parish Church, 1844-59 ; Epsom, 1859-61 ; Godalming, 1864-74 ; Ashtead, 1874-77 ; St. Paul's Episcopal Church, Aberdeen, 1877-79 ; St. John's, Longside ; St. Paul's, Aberdeen, again, 1880-82 ; and St. Mary's, Aberdeen, 1885-86. He died at Aberdeen, April 27, 1886. He composed church services, anthems, hymn-tunes, part-songs, etc. Edited a " Selection of Church Tunes and Cathedral Chants, arranged in 4 parts," Novello [1850].

Parker, William Frye, violinist, born at Dunmow, Essex, in 1855. Entered the R.A.M. in 1867, studying under the late M. Sainton. At the age of sixteen he was engaged by Costa as a first violinist in the orchestra of Her Majesty's Theatre. Professor of the violin, R.A.M. and Guildhall School of Music,

1881. F.R.A.M. Principal violin at the Promenade Concerts at Her Majesty's Theatre, 1887, and at the Queen's Hall, 1895. After the death of Mr. Carrodus, Mr. Parker was appointed principal violin at the Leeds Festival of 1885, and of the Philharmonic Society, 1896.

Parkinson, William, musician of the latter part of the 18th century. Author of " New book of Instructions for beginners on the Pianoforte," London [1790].

Parkinson, William Wignall, musician and writer, born at Catterall, Garstang, Lancashire, 1812. Author of " The natural and universal Principles of Harmony and Modulation, with illustrative and analyzed extracts from the Works of Classical Composers," London, 1873. He died at Catterall, June 3, 1878.

Parkyns, Beatrice, Mrs., *born* CRAWFORD, composer, born at Bombay, India. Her works include : A Posy of Proverbs, six songs ; A Posy of Flowers, words of both by May Gillington ; Shepherd's love song, etc. A romance for violin, " Songe d'autrefois " ; Pf. pieces, etc.

Parr, Rev. Henry, clergyman and musician, born at Lythwood Hall, Shropshire, August 16, 1815. He was educated at Oxford, and ordained in 1845. Vicar of Taunton, 1849-1858 ; Curate of Tunbridge, 1859-1861 ; Perpetual curate of Ash Church, Gloucestershire, 1861-62 ; Curate-in-Charge of Yoxford, Suffolk, 1867 ; and vicar at Yoxford, Suffolk, 1872. Compiler of " Church of England Psalmody : Psalm tunes, Chants, with responses, etc., with memoirs of the composers and histories of the pieces," London, 8 editions to 1880 ; and composer of chants.

Parratt, Sir Walter, Kt., organist and composer, born at Huddersfield, February 10, 1841. Studied under his father (noticed below), and when seven took a service at Armitage Bridge, near Huddersfield, succeeding his elder brother as organist there in 1852. Two years later he was appointed to St. Paul's, Huddersfield ; in 1861 to Witley Court, as organist to Lord Dudley ; Parish Church, Wigan, 1868 ; Magdalen College, Oxford, 1872 ; and in 1882 succeeded Sir George Elvey at St. George's Chapel, Windsor. Graduated Mus. Bac., Oxford, 1873. Appointed professor of the organ at R.C.M., 1883 ; in 1892 received the honour of Knighthood ; and in 1893 was appointed Master of the Music in Ordinary to the Queen. He is a remarkable performer on the organ, and has given recitals in many places, and also lectured and written on the organ and kindred topics. Contributor to Grove's Dictionary. He has composed music " Agamemnon," Oxford, 1880 ; set the Elegy to Patroclus, in the " Tale of Troy," London, 1883 ; Music to " Story of Orestes," London,

1886. Anthems, songs, organ and pf. pieces. Also a March for the Royal Wedding at Windsor, July 6, 1891.

His father, THOMAS PARRATT, born January 30, 1793, was an articled pupil of Brailsford, the then organist of Doncaster Parish Church. In 1812 Gray built a new organ in Huddersfield Parish Church, and Parratt was appointed organist. His first service was played on Christmas Day, 1812, and he never missed playing on the anniversary of that day till his death, March 27, 1862. He was the first organist and resident professor in Huddersfield; a fine player of the old school, and celebrated for his accompaniments.

The elder son, HENRY L. PARRATT, trained by his father, was organist first at Armitage Bridge Church; in 1852, of St. Paul's, Huddersfield; then, after some time spent in London, succeeded his father at Huddersfield Parish Church in 1862. For 85 Christmas Days in succession father and son have presided at the organ.

Parry, Charles Hubert Hastings, composer and writer, born at Bournemouth, February 27, 1848, second son of the late Gambier Parry, of Higham Court, Gloucester. Went to Eton in 1861, and while there had lessons from Dr. G. Elvey, composed a Church Service in D, and passed the examination for Mus. Bac. Proceeded to Oxford in 1866, graduated Mus. Bac., 1867; B.A., 1870; and M.A., 1874. While at Oxford he worked at music with Sir W. S. Bennett, and (Sir) G. A. Macfarren; and, making it his profession, studied further with H. H. Pierson at Stuttgart, and with E. Dannreuther. It was not until 1880 that he was generally known as a composer, though an orchestral Intermezzo Religioso from his pen was produced at the Gloucester Festival of 1868. In February, 1880, Mr. Dannreuther, at Orme Square, brought out some of his chamber music; and his "Prometheus Unbound" was produced at Gloucester Festival that year. Since then he has contributed more works to the provincial festivals than any other composer. He was appointed Choragus of the University of Oxford, in 1883; and professor of composition and musical history in the R.C.M., on its opening the same year. Examiner for Degrees in Music, London University, 1891; and on the retirement of Sir George Grove in 1894, he was elected Director of R.C.M. He was created Mus. Doc. by Decree of Convocation, Oxford, 1884; and received the same degree, *honoris causâ*, at Cambridge, 1883, and Dublin, 1891. He has lectured on music at the Royal Institution, 1891-3; at the Midland Institute, Birmingham, 1884, etc., and in other places; and has contributed to the *Academy*, 1876, and written many elaborate articles for Grove's "Dictionary of Music."

WORKS.—*Cantatas, oratorios, etc. :* Scenes from Prometheus Unbound (Shelley), Gloucester Festival, 1880; The Glories of our Blood and State, the same, 1883; Choral Ode, Blest Pair of Syrens (Milton), Bach Choir, May 17, 1887; Judith, Birmingham, 1888; St. Cecilia's Day, Leeds, 1889; L'Allegro ed il Pensieroso, Norwich, 1890; Psalm 130, for soprano solo, three choirs, and orchestra, Hereford, 1891; Choric song, The Lotos Eaters, Cambridge, May week, 1892; Oratorio, Job, Gloucester, 1892, and repeated at Worcester and Hereford, 1893-4; King Saul, Birmingham, 1894; Ode, Invocation to Music, Leeds, 1895. Ode for 450th anniversary of Eton; Music to Aristophanes' Birds (Cambridge, November, 1883); Frogs (Oxford, February 17, 1892); and to Hypatia, Haymarket, January, 1893. Anthems and Services. English Lyrics, 4 sets; Three Odes of Anacreon; Six Shakesperean and other songs, etc. *Orchestral :* Symphony No. 1, in G, Birmingham Festival, 1882; No. 2, in F, Cambridge University Musical Society, June 12, 1883; No. 3, in C, Philharmonic, May 23, 1889; No. 4, in E minor, Richter, July 1, 1889. Suite Moderne, in A minor, Gloucester, 1886; Overture, Guillem de Cabestanh, Crystal Palace, March 15, 1879; Symphonic overture, On an unwritten Tragedy, Worcester, 1893; Suite for strings, 1894. Concerto, in F sharp minor, pf. and orchestra, Crystal Palace (Dannreuther), April 3, 1880. *Chamber Music :* Nonet in B flat, Wind; Quintet in E flat; Quartet in G, strings; in A flat, pf. and strings; Trios in E minor (1880), B minor, and G, pf. and strings; Sonata in A, pf. and 'cello; Fantaisie-Sonata in B; Sonata in D; Partita in D minor; 12 short pieces for violin and pf. Duo in E minor, two pf.; sonatas in B flat and D minor; Variations; Miniatures; Sonnets and songs without words, etc., for pf. Characteristic popular tunes of the British Isles, pf. duet. Fantasia and Fugue, organ. *Literary :* Studies of Great Composers, Routledge, 1886; The Art of Music, 1893, enlarged as The Evolution of the Art of Music, 1896, Kegan Paul; Summary of Musical History, Novello's Primers, 1893.

Parry, John, Welsh harper and collector, of Ruabon, North Wales. He was bard or harper to Sir W. W. Wynne, of Wynnstay, during the middle of the 18th century. He appeared in London as a player. He died at Ruabon, October 7, 1782.

WORKS.—Antient British Music : or a collection of tunes never before published, which are retained by the Cambro Britons, more particularly in North Wales. An historical account of the rise and progress of Music among the Antient Britons, London, 1742 [with Williams]; only 1 part published. British Harmony; being a collection of Antient

Welsh airs, the traditional remains of those originally sung by the bards of Wales.... London, 1781. Music for the harpsichord.

Parry, John, "BARDD ALAW," composer and writer, born at Denbigh, February 18, 1776. Member of band of Denbigh Militia, 1795. Bandmaster of same, 1797 - 1807. Teacher of flageolet in London, 1807. Composer for Vauxhall from 1809. Conducted an Eisteddfod in Wales. Received degree of Master of Song (Bard Alaw), 1821. Musical critic of *Morning Post,* 1834-48. Treasurer of Royal Society of Musicians, 1831-49. He died at London, April 8, 1851.

WORKS.—Incidental Music to "Harlequin Hoax," 1814; Oberon's Oath, 1816; High Notions, 1817; Ivanhoe, 1820; Fair Cheating, 1814; Helpless Animals, 1818; Two Wives, 1821; My Uncle Gabriel; Caswallon, etc. The Welsh Harper, being an extensive collection of Welsh music, to which are prefixed observations on the character and antiquity of the Welsh Music, London [1839-48], 2 vols.; An account of the Royal Musical Festival held in Westminster Abbey, 1834, drawn up from official documents, n.d.; Beauties of Caledonia, or flowers of Scottish Song . . . with symphonies and accompaniments for the Pf., London, 4 vols. [1840]; Selection of six Brazillian melodies; Cambrian Harmony, being a collection of antient Welsh airs [1810], 2 books; Collection of Welsh airs . . . for the harp [1825]; The Vocal Companion; British Minstrelsy [1830]; Flowers of Song; London collection of Glees, etc.; Sonatas for the harp; Complete scales for Wheatstone's Patent Symphonium [1850]; Glees, part-songs, etc. *Songs:* Jenny Jones; Apollo and the Muses; Oh, merry row the bonny bark; Maid of Toro, etc.

Parry, John Orlando, composer, pianist, and baritone vocalist, son of above, was born at London, January 3, 1810. He studied under Bochsa and his father. *Début* as harpist in 1825. Appeared as a ballad vocalist in 1831. Sang in operettas and entertainments by himself and others. Organist of St. Jude's, Southsea, 1853. Reappeared in the German Reed Entertainments, 1860-69. Retired, 1877. He died at East Molesey, February 20, 1879.

WORKS.—Songs, of which the following is a selection:—Bridal Bells; Blue Beard; Cinderella; Country Commissions; Crotchet; Norah, the pride of Kildare; Take a bumper and try; A heart to let; Wanted a wife; Fayre Rosamunde. The A B C duet, and numerous comic and sentimental pieces. Ridiculous things, or scraps and oddities, London, 1854. Series of humerous sketches in various colours of ink.

Parry, Joseph, composer, born at Merthyr Tydvil, May 21, 1841. Picked up some know-

ledge of music when a child, but had, when ten years old, to work at a puddling furnace. In 1854 the family followed the father to America. Joseph Parry paid one visit to Wales before he finally returned home. He still continued his studies, and won Eisteddfodic prizes in 1862-3. Through the influence of Brinley Richards he entered the R.A.M. in 1868, and studied under Bennett, Garcia, and Steggall. Graduated Mus. Bac., 1871; Mus. Doc., 1878, Cambridge. F.R.A.M. Appointed Professor of Music, University College, Aberystwith, 1871; and in 1888 to the Musical Lectureship of University College of South Wales, Cardiff. He has lectured on Music, and contributed articles on Welsh musicians, etc., to the press. At the National Eisteddfod, Llandudno, July 1, 1896, he was publicly presented with a cheque for £600 for services rendered to Welsh music.

WORKS.—*Oratorios:* Emmanuel, London, 1880; Saul of Tarsus, produced at Rhyl, September 8, and Cardiff Festival, September 23, 1892. *Cantatas:* The Prodigal Son (prize); Nebuchadnezzar; and Cambria, Llandudno, 1896. *Operas:* Blodwen, Aberdare, 1878; Virginia, completed in 1883; Arianwen, produced at Cardiff, June 5, 1890; Sylvia, Cardiff, August 12, 1895; and King Arthur, completed 1897. The Druids' chorus. Many anthems, hymn tunes, songs, etc. Orchestral Ballad, Cardiff, 1892; Overtures; String quartet. Sonatas, and other pieces for pf. Editor of Cambrian Minstrelsie, 6 vols., Edinburgh, Jack.

His son, JOSEPH HAYDN PARRY, born at Pennsylvania, U.S.A., in 1864, studied under him, and at Aberystwith. In 1884 he won a prize for a pf. sonata. His comic opera, "Cigarette," was produced with success at Cardiff in 1892; and another, "Miami," in London, October 16, 1893. He finished a third, "Marigold Farm," the same year, and was the composer of a cantata for female voices, "Gwen." He was appointed a professor at the Guildhall School in 1890. Died at Hampstead, March 29, 1894.

Another son, D. MENDELSSOHN PARRY, is a pianist, and was for a time at the Harrow Music School. He is now a concert and operatic agent.

Parsons, Alfred William, organist, born at Salisbury, December 31, 1853. Chorister at Salisbury Cathedral. Organist of St. John's, Leicester, 1878; Parish Church, Aberystwith, 1889. Mus. Bac., Durham, 1891; F.R.C.O. Lecturer in music, St. David's College, Lampeter. Composer of a setting of Psalm 18; Two settings of the Te Deum; Sacred songs, etc.

Parsons, John, musician, edited "The Hindustani Choral Book, or Swar Sangrah: containing the tunes of those hymns in the Gít Sangrah which are in native metres," Benares, 1861.

PARSONS.

Another JOHN PARSONS, who lived at the end of last and beginning of this century, composed an " Ode to Liberty, composed for the centenary jubilee of the Revolution Club," Edinburgh, 1788. Author also of " Elements of Music, with progressive practical lessons," London [1800].

Parsons, Robert, composer, was born at Exeter in the first half of the 16th century. Composed services, anthems, and madrigals. Drowned in the Trent at Newark, January 25, 1570 (1569 ?). His son JOHN (?) was organist of St. Margaret's, Westminster, in 1616. Organist, etc., of Westminster Abbey, 1621. He died in 1623.

Parsons, Sir William, musician, born in 1746. Chorister under Dr. Cooke, Westminster Abbey. He studied in Italy, 1768, and became Master of the King's Music, 1786. Mus. Bac. and Mus. Doc. Oxon, 1790 (?). Knighted, 1795. Teacher of the Royal Princesses, 1796. Magistrate of Middlesex He died at London July, 19, 1817, aged 71. Composer of Six English Ballads -dedicated to the Princess Mary. *Songs :* Dear is my little native vale ; Dear to my Delia's peaceful heart ; Fair Daphne ; A scholar first my love implored, etc. The Court Minuets for His Majesty's Birthday, 1794. It was the knighthood bestowed on Parsons which gave rise to the remark that he was knighted more on the score of his merits than because of the merits of his scores.

Partridge, James, pianist and teacher, born in Staffordshire in 1850. Like many other musicians he was originally intended for the scholastic profession, and passed two years in training at Saltley College, near Birmingham. During that time he acted as organist, an unusual position for a student. After holding various organ appointments in the country, he went to London, and entered the R.A.M. in 1875, studying under Dr. Steggall and Brinley Richards. Elected A.R.A.M. Brinley Richards and he became warm friends, and on the death of the former in 1885, Partridge was appointed to his class at the Guildhall School of Music, having acted as his deputy for some years. That position he still holds, and he is also reader to one of the largest publishing houses in London. He was for some time organist at St. Andrew's, Hammersmith. His compositions consist chiefly of songs and church music ; and he has published various organ arrangements. He edited 2 vols. of Brinley Richards's original works for pf., published by R. Cocks.

Pascal, Florian. *See* WILLIAMS, JOSEPH.

Paterson, Robert Roy, composer and music publisher, a member of the Edinburgh firm of Paterson, Sons, & Co., which was founded in 1827 as Paterson & Roy. Under

PATON.

the pseudonym of " Alfred Stella " he has written a number of songs and pf. pieces.

Patey, C. A., author of " An Elementary Treatise on the Art of Playing the Violin, with Scales, Exercises, etc.," London, n.d.

Patey, Janet Monach, *born* WHYTOCK, contralto vocalist, born in London, May 1, 1842, her father being a native of Glasgow. Studied singing first with John Wass, and on August 20, 1860, made her first public appearance at James Stimpson's Monday Evening Concerts, Town Hall, Birmingham, as Miss Ellen Andrews. Became a member of Henry Leslie's Choir, and studied under Mrs. Sims Reeves and Pinsuti. In 1865 she toured with the Lemmens' Concert Party, and in 1866 married Mr. Patey (noticed below). That year she made her Festival *début* at Worcester, and sang at the Birmingham Festival, 1867 ; Norwich, 1869 ; and Leeds, 1874. On the retirement of Madame Sainton-Dolby, in 1870, she succeeded to the position of first English contralto. Toured in America, singing in " Elijah," New York, October 31, 1871. Sang in Paris, in 1875, in performance of the " Messiah," and at the Conservatoire, being presented with a medal by the Directors in commemoration of the event. Sang at all the important concerts in the United Kingdom, and was identified with the greatest compositions produced at the different festivals, etc. In 1890 she undertook a long tour in Australia, commencing with a concert at Sydney. Re-appeared at the Crystal Palace, October 11, 1891. Decided to retire in 1893, an began a farewell tour in the winter, but it was brought to a tragic close by her sudden death, February 28, 1894. She had sung at a concert at the Albert Hall, Sheffield, the previous evening, and after singing " The Banks of Allan Water " in response to the encore, fainted as she left the platform, and died at her hotel early next morning, without regaining consciousness.

Patey, John George, husband of the above, bass vocalist, born at Stonehouse, Devonshire, in 1835. Intended for the medical profession, but gave it up for music. Studied at Paris and Milan, and made his *début* at Drury Lane, as *Plunket,* in Flotow's opera " Martha," 1858. Sang for several seasons in English opera at Covent Garden, etc., and visited New York in 1871, taking part in a performance of " Elijah," October 31. Toured in the English provinces up to 1876. Was for some time a member of the choir at Lincoln's Inn Chapel. From 1888 a music publisher in London.

Paton, James Crooks, organist, composer, and violoncellist, was born at Edinburgh, March 28, 1855. He was organist of St. Leonard's Parish Church, and of Dalkeith Parish Church, and from 1881 was conductor

PATON.

of the St. Andrew's Amateur Orchestral Society; Member of Waddel's Quartet Party. He died at Edinburgh, August 27, 1886. Composer of an overture, " The Pursuit of Pleasure " (1886) ; a quartet, for strings, in G minor; Marches, gavottes, muzurkas; "Lena" (1886), etc., for orchestra; all of which are in manuscript.

Paton, Mary Ann, born WOOD, soprano vocalist, was born at Edinburgh, in October, 1802. Daughter of George Paton, writing-master at Edinburgh High School. She sang at the Edinburgh Concerts in 1810. Studied the harp and pf. under S. Webbe, Jun., and sang in London in 1811; and Bath, 1820-1. Sang at Covent Garden Theatre, London, as Susannah in Mozart's " Figaro," 1822. Appeared in Weber's " Der Frieschutz," July, 1824. Married Lord William Pitt Lennox, 1824. Created part of *Reiza* in Weber's "Oberon," April 12, 1826. Divorced from her husband (Lennox), 1830. Married Mr. Joseph Wood, tenor vocalist, 1831. Resided chiefly at Woolley Moor, Yorks., 1833-54. Visited United States, 1834-36. Appeared in London again in 1837-1844. Embraced Roman Catholic Religion, 1843, and retired from the stage in 1844. Lived abroad, 1854-63. She died at Bulcliffe Hall, near Chapelthorpe, Wakefield, July 21, 1864.

Patten, William, organist and composer, was born at Fareham in 1804. He was organist at Winchester. Died in 1863. Compiler of " Congregational Melodies, original and selected . . . " 6 parts. " Six Anthems for large or small choirs," Fareham [1860]. Collection of Sacred Music . . . London [1850] ; second collection. Six original hymns [1845]. Three sanctuses for four voices. Single anthems, songs, etc.

Patterson, Ada, soprano vocalist, born at Plymouth. Studied at R.A.M. under Manuel Garcia. She has a voice of extraordinary compass in the high register, and has sung with success at the Crystal Palace (1891, etc.), and in many parts of the country.

Patterson (Alexander), composer and baritone vocalist, was born at Glasgow, December 26, 1847. He holds various appointments as a teacher of vocal music in schools and since 1887 has been conductor of the Cathcart Musical Association. He has composed " Hohenlinden," and " Sennacherib," cantatas ; numerous original part-songs and songs; but is perhaps best known as the arranger of various Scots song for mixed voices, which have been sung all over the country by the Glasgow Select Choir, in which Mr. Patterson sings and acts as deputy conductor. He has edited a collection of 83 " Scottish Songs" n.d.

Patterson, Annie Wilson, pianist, organist, and composer, born at Lurgan,

PAUL.

County Armagh, Ireland, October 27, 1868. Of French Huguenot descent. Educated at Alexandra College, and Royal Irish Academy of Music, Dublin. Graduated Mus. Bac., and B.A., 1887, Mus. Doc., 1889, Royal University of Ireland. Examiner in music for the same, 1892-5. Conductor of Dublin Choral Union, 1891-3. Has lectured on Irish Music in Dublin, Cork, London (November 30, 1895 and 1897), etc. She has written the libretti of her own compositions, and has some name as a painter. Her compositions are : " Finola," Irish cantata, for soli, chorus and orchestra, 1888; Psalm 93, 1889; " Meta Tauta " (St. John's Vision of Heaven), for soli chorus and orchestra, produced, Dublin, February 25, 1893; cantata, " The Raising of Lazarus," Dublin, April 10, 1891. Six original Gaelic songs ; Uladh, or the Northern Star, patriotic song, with chorus and orchestra; At Parting, etc.

Pattinson (James), composer, organist, pianist and conductor, born, October 30, 1847, at Carlisle. Studied under Abraham Young, and Dr. Ford, of Carlisle Cathedral. Mus. Bac. Cambridge, 1879. Settled in Paisley, in 1874, as first organist of the Abbey. Appointed to St. Silas' Episcopal Church, Glasgow, 1880; Maxwell Parish Church, Glasgow, 1883 ; Thread Street U. P. Church, Paisley, 1890. Succeeded G. Taggart as conductor of Uddington Society, Glasgow, 1886. Conductor of Paisley Philharmonic (orchestral), and other Societies. Organ recitalist, and oratorio accompanist, at Glasgow, Edinburgh, Paisley, Carlisle, etc.

WORKS.—The Magnificat, for soli, chorus, strings and organ ; Cantata, The Ten Virgins. Songs : Becalmed ; A last Rose ; Kitty of Carlisle, and others; part-songs, Softly, oh softly glide, etc. Arrangements of Scotch and other songs. Minuet for strings ; Fantasia, and other pieces for organ. The major, minor and chromatic scales, in single and double notes, and arpeggios of common, dominant and diminished chords, in all keys, pf.

Pattison, Thomas Mee, composer and organist, born at Warrington, January 27, 1845. Organist of Paul's Church, Warrington, 1869 ; and conductor of a choral society. About 1886 he removed to London.

WORKS.—*Cantatas* : The Ancient Mariner; Lay of the Last Minstrel, 1885 ; Sherwood's Queen; John Bull and his Trades, 1886; May Day, 1887; Les Francs Chasseurs, female voices. Sacred : A Day with our Lord ; The Mother of Jesus. *Anthems:* There were Shepherds ; Truly God is loving ; O praise the Lord ; and others. Organ and pf. music. The Happy Valley, comic opera. Author of Rudiments of Vocal Music, with Preparatory Exercises.

Paul, Mrs. Howard, born ISABELLA

PAXTON.

FEATHERSTONE, actress and contralto vocalist, born at Dartford, Kent, in 1833. She appeared in the Beggar's Opera, in 1853, and in many musical and dramatic pieces. Married Mr. Henry Howard Paul, and in 1854 appeared with him in a large number of different entertainments. She had a voice of much beauty, but as she turned her attention chiefly to comedy, she never attained a great position as a vocalist. She died at London, June 6, 1879.

Paxton, Stephen, glee composer and bass singer, was born in 1735. He was a pupil of W. Savage and gained prizes from the Catch Club in 1779, 1781, 1783, 1784, and 1785. He died at London, August 18, 1787. Composer of numerous glees and catches, some of which were republished in " Collection of Glees, Catches, etc., for 3 or 4 voices," op. 5. London [1780], and in other collections. He also composed six solos for the violoncello, op. 1 ; Eight duetts for a violin or violoncello, op. 2 ; Six easy sclos for a violoncello or bassoon, op. 3 ; Twelve easy lessons for a violoncello or bass, op. 6. Masses, Kyries, songs, etc. His brother WILLIAM (born 1737, died 1781), was a violoncellist, and composed " Breathe soft, ye winds," a well-known glee for 3 voices, besides other pieces contained in the collections above noted.

Payne, Miss, See sub. Cook, Aynsley.

Payne, Richard, amateur organist and conductor, born at Birmingham in 1843. He had great talent for music, but adopted a business career, which led him to reside in London for some years. In 1874, he was appointed organist and conductor of the Psalmody class at Union Chapel, Islington, and was also conductor of the Borough of Hackney Choral Society, which gave the first performance in England of Bach's " Magnificat," May 19, 1874. Returning to Birmingham, he became organist of St. Luke's Church, 1876, and later of the Church of the Redeemer, Edgbaston. He was hon. conductor of the Birmingham Kyrle Choir from its formation until his death, at Birmingham, July 10, 1884. He was self-taught in music, and composed a Pf. Trio and some vocal music ; also contributed articles to the *Musical Record* (1874) and *Musical Standard* (1882). He was succeeded in his organ appointment by his son, a clever amateur.

Peace, Albert Lister, organist and composer, born at Huddersfield, January 26, 1844. Showed musical talent at a very early age, and was placed under Henry Horn and Henry Parratt, and in 1853 received his first organ appointment, at Holmfirth Parish Church. After being organist at Dewsbury, Huddersfield, and Cleckheaton (1858-65), he went to Glasgow as organist of Trinity Congregational Church. In 1870 he was appointed organist

PEARCE.

to the University of Glasgow ; St. John's Episcopal Church, 1873 ; Maxwell Parish Church, 1875 ; Hillhead Parish Church, 1876 ; St. Andrew's Hall, 1877 ; and in 1879 to the Cathedral. Graduated Mus. Bac., 1870 ; Mus. Doc., 1875, Oxford. F.C.O., 1886, *honoris causâ.* He has given recitals in all parts of the kingdom, and opened the organ at Canterbury Cathedral (1886), Victoria Hall, Hanley (1888), and represented Scotland in the gathering of great players at the opening of the organ in Newcastle Cathedral (St. Nicholas'), 1891. In January, 1897, he was elected organist of St. George's Hall, Liverpool, in succession to W. T. Best, and now occupies the foremost position in the country.

WORKS.—Psalm 138, for soli, chorus, and orchestra ; Cantata, St. John the Baptist, 1875. Morning, Evening, and Communion Services. Awake up, my glory ; The night is far spent (eight voices) ; God be merciful ; and other anthems. Sonata da Camera, No. 1, in D minor ; No. 2, in C minor ; No. 3, in G minor ; Concert Fantasia on Scottish melodies ; Fantasia in B flat ; two Andantes—all for organ ; and organ arrangements of Overtures, William Tell, Oberon, etc. Musical editor of Scottish Hymnal, 1885 ; Psalms and Paraphrases ; Psalter ; and Anthem Book, for Psalmody Committee of the Church of Scotland.

Peacock, Francis, musician and miniature painter, born at Aberdeen, in 1723. He was a dancing-master in Aberdeen, and a violinist who frequently led the weekly subscription concerts given by the Musical Society. He taught dancing, under the patronage of the Town Council, in a hall in Drum's Lane. He died at Aberdeen, June 26, 1807. Editor of " Fifty Favourite Scotch Airs, for a violin, German flute, and violoncello, with a thorough-bass for the harpsichord," London, n.d. [1762]. Author of " Sketches relative to the History and theory, but more especially to the practice of Dancing," Aberdeen, 1805. The publication cf this called forth a satirical poem, entitled, " On the Magistrates of the city having purchased twenty copies of ' Peacock on Dancing.' "

Peacock, Matthew, musician of first half of the present century, who was a native of Chesham, issued " A Set of Psalm and Hymn Tunes, composed in a familiar style," London [1837].

Pearce, Charles William, organist and composer, born at Salisbury, December 5, 1856. Studied the organ under Theodore E. Aylward, W. S. Hoyte, and Dr. E. J. Hopkins ; pianoforte, harmony, and composition with C. J. Read, Dr. Hopkins, and (Professor) E. Prout. Graduated Mus. Bac., 1881 ; Mus.

PEARCE.

Doc., 1884, Cambridge. Was organist of St. Martin's, Salisbury, 1871-3, and accompanist to Sarum Choral Society, 1872-3. In 1874 he was appointed to St. Luke's, Old Street, London, accepting, in 1885, the office of organist and choirmaster of St. Clement's, Eastcheap, which he still holds. Professor of Organ, Harmony, Counterpoint and Composition, Trinity College, London, 1882; Dean of the College, 1892. Examiner for degree of Mus. Bac., Cambridge, 1888-91; and for Mus. Doc., 1895. Co-editor of *The Organist and Choirmaster*, and hon. treasurer of London Section of the Incorporated Society of Musicians from 1892. Has lectured on Plain Song Melodies; The Compositions of Samuel Wesley; Organists in relation to the Clergy (Dublin, 1895), and kindred subjects.

WORKS.—Church Cantatas: All Saints (1880), The Man of Sorrows (1893), Our Risen and Ascended Lord (1895). Oratorio (Univ. Ex. Mus. Doc.) Lux benigna (1884), Enceladus, choral scena, men's voices, op. 43, produced at Bristol, 1889. Services, Anthems, Hymns, in Anglican Choir Series; Songs, etc. ; Quartet in C, for organ, pf., violin, and violoncello; Trio, "Nocte Surgentes," for pf., violin, and violoncello; Three Idylls for violin and pf. Organ music: Symphonic poem, "Corde natus;" two Sonatas (all, 1885); Preludes and fugues, fantasias, postludes, and introductory voluntaries. Educational works: Voice Training Exercises (with Behnke, 1884); Voice Training Studies (1892); Voice Training Primer (1893); Three Text-books of Musical Knowledge, Junior, Intermediate, and Senior (Hammond and Co., 1889-91); Complete Pedal Scales, organ (1892); Three books of Organ Studies (1893-4); Organ School (1895).

Pearce, Joseph, author of "Violins, and Violin-makers: biographical dictionary of the great Italian artistes, their followers and imitators to the present time. With essays on important subjects connected with the Violin," London, 1866.

Pearce, Stephen Austen, organist and composer, born near London. Pupil of Dr. J. L. Hopkins. Graduated Mus. Bac., 1859; Mus. Doc., 1864, Oxford. Held organ appointments at St. John's, Oxford Square, London; St. Saviour's, Paddington; St. Paul's, Onslow Square, and elsewhere. Visited the United States and Canada; returned to London, and gave recitals at Hanover Square Rooms, etc. Again went to America, and was appointed Instructor in vocal music at Columbia College. Organist successively at St. Mark's, Philadelphia; St. Andrew's; St. George's; New Cathedral, 5th Avenue; and St. Stephen's R. C. Church in New York. His latest appointments were, Lecturer, and professor of harmony and composition at New York

PEARSALL.

College of Music. He has given concerts and lectures in many parts of the United States, and contributed to the press of Chicago, Boston, etc., and to the principal musical journals. His compositions comprise a comedy-opera, "La Belle Americaine"; orchestral music, performed by the Thomas orchestra, etc.; many pf. pieces, songs, etc., as well as arrangements. His Degree Exercises were The Psalm of Praise, cantata ; and Celestial Visions, a dramatic oratorio. Author of A Musical Dictionary; and editor and translator of various elaborate works for American publishers.

Pearman, William, tenor vocalist, was born at Manchester in 1792. He went to sea as a cabin-boy, and was engaged at the Battle of Copenhagen, and wounded. Appeared unsuccessfully as an actor, and sang at Sadler's Wells Theatre, London. Afterwards he studied for a short time under Addison. Sang at Newcastle, Bath, Bristol, etc. *Début* as operatic vocalist at English Opera House, July 7, 1817, in "The Cabinet." Sang at Drury Lane, Covent Garden, and principal concerts. Died (?).

Pearman, James, probably a relative of the above, was born at Winchester about 1818. He studied under Dr. Chard, and was an organist and teacher of music in Dundee, where he died, on April 3, 1880. Composer of a Mass, some pf. music, songs, etc.

Pearsall, Robert Lucas de, composer, born at Clifton, March 14, 1795. Educated for Law. Called to the Bar, 1821, and practised till 1825. He then studied music under Panny, at Mayence. Re-visited England, 1829. Settled at Carlsruhe, 1830. Lived at Wartensee Castle on Lake of Constance from 1832. He died at Wartensee, August 5, 1856.

WORKS.—Madrigals for 4, 5, 6 and 8 voices, London [1840]. Eight Glees and Madrigals, London [1863]. Twenty-four Choral Songs, etc., edited by J. Hullah [1863]. Ballet Opera Choruses [1878]. Sacred Compositions, edited by Trimnell, n.d. Edited a Catholic Hymn Book, 1863, and composed psalms and anthems. *Part-songs :* A king there was in Thule; Let us all a-Maying go; O who will o'er the downs so free; Purple glow the forest mountains; Sing we and chaunt it; Sir Patrick Spens (10 parts); Bishop of Mentz; Hardy Norseman's house of yore; Red wine flows; Watchman's song; Winter song; Who shall win my lady fair? etc. Essay on Consecutive Fifths and Octaves in Counterpoint, London, n.d., etc.

Pearsall, Samuel, tenor vocalist, who sang at the Gloucester Festival of 1832, and at Worcester and Hereford at times up to 1845, and was a tenor in the choir of Lichfield Cathedral for many years. He sang at most of the provincial festivals, and gave lectures

PEARSON.

on musical subjects, illustrated by the members of Lichfield Cathedral choir. Died at Lichfield in July, 1883, at an advanced age.

Pearson Arthur, organist and composer, born at Stanningley, near Leeds, April 22, 1866. He is organist at St. Paul's Church, Huddersfield; and also Borough organist. His cantata, "The Promised Land," was produced at New Wortley, November 29, 1885. He has composed other vocal music, and was editor of *The Yorkshire Musician.*

Pearson, Henry Hugo. See PIERSON, Henry Hugo.

Pearson, Martin, composer, was born in the latter half of the 16th century. Master of the children of St. Paul's Cathedral, 1604. Mus. Bac., Oxon., 1613. He died in 1650, and left £100 to the poor of March, in the Isle of Ely.

WORKS.—Private Musicke, or the first Booke of Ayres and Dialogues, containing Songs of 4. 5, and 6 parts of severall sorts, etc., 1604. "Mottects, or grave chamber musicke, for voices and vials, with an organ part which may be performed on virginals, bass-lute, bandora, or Irish harp," 1630. Compositions in Leighton's "Teares," etc.

Pearson, William Webster, composer and organist, born at Bishop Auckland, September 27, 1839. Chorister at York Minster, under Dr. Camidge. For many years he has been organist of the Parish Church of Elmham, Norfolk, and teacher of the violin at the Norfolk County School, Dereham; also conductor of Dereham Orchestral Society. He has composed church music, organ and pf. pieces, songs, etc., a cantata, "Voices of the Flowers," for ladies' voices, and a great number of part-songs, among which may be named, Blow, Western Wind, Stars of the Night, The Lake, 'Tis Morn, Coral Grove, Woods in Winter, The Anglers, and Autumn; also a set with orchestral accompaniment: The Iron Horse, Off to Sea, Lifeboat, Ocean, Ironfounders, etc. *Humorous:* A Ryghte Merrie Geste, Ben Bowley, Carrion Crow, etc. Songs for the Little Ones, Nursery Rhymes; many contributions to Novello's School Songs. Author of Notation of Vocal Music on the principle of the substitution of Pitch; and the National Method of Vocal Music for Elementary Schools, Manchester, 1874.

Peattie, William, musician, compiler of "Selection of Psalm and Hymn Tunes, adapted to the various metres used in the principal churches, chapels, and dissenting congregations in Scotland; to which is prefixed a compendious introduction, with some useful scales and examples, calculated to promote the improvement of Sacred Music." Edinburgh, Oliver & Boyd, 1824, 6th edit.

Peck, James, music publisher and

PENNA.

engraver, established in London. He edited "Two Hundred and Fifty Psalm Tunes in Three Parts," 1798; collection of Hymn Tunes, Fugues, and Odes, 1799, 3 books; Miscellaneous Collection of Sacred Music, 1809; Beauties of Sacred Harmony, 1824; and composed glees, etc. He was succeeded in business by his son JOHN, organist of St. Faith's, who issued in conjunction with his brother JAMES, jun. (born at London, 1773). "Peck's Pocket Arrangement or general collection of Psalm and Hymn Tunes," London, 1833, 3 vols. The Union Tune Book being a collection of psalm and hymn tunes adapted for use in Sunday schools and congregations; to which is prefixed a short introduction to singing. London, 1837.

Pede, or **Peed, Thomas Thorpe,** composer, pianist, and singer, born about 1825. Was a lecturer and teacher. Died at Margate, November 9, 1888, aged 63. Composed Waltzes for pf., op. 2 [1846]; Quadrilles, etc. *Songs:* Faith is over; I have not gold; Last request; Loving for aye; Old Hall clock.

Peel, Rev. Frederick. Graduated Mus. Bac., Oxford, 1872. He was organist and music master at Reading School, Berks., 1871-5; and is now vicar of Heslington, near York. Composer of Psalm 145, for soli, chorus and orchestra; Anthems, services, hymn tunes; songs; organ and pf. pieces.

Pegler, Daniel, amateur composer and pianist, was well-known in the early part of the present century as a performer of ability. He died at Colchester, December 29, 1876. Thalberg considered Pegler one of the finest semi-professional pianists in England. He had a very wonderful memory.

Penna, Frederic, baritone vocalist and writer, born in London, July 15, 1831. Pupil of Sir George Smart. He was solo-baritone at the Oratory, Brompton, for ten years; favourably known in the concert room; and appeared in opera for one season at Her Majesty's Theatre. He is professor of singing at the London Academy of Music, and widely known as a teacher and lecturer on voice training, etc. Author of an Essay on Singing, London, 1878; Vocal Exercises, to illustrate his method, 1888; Lecture, Mendelssohn's portrait of "Elijah," musically painted: his moral qualities, etc. His wife, CATHERINE LOUISA SMITH (died, London, December 27, 1880), was an excellent soprano vocalist, who with her sister JULIA, gained much reputation for duet singing. These ladies were nieces of Catherine Stephens. His daughter, CATHERINE (Mrs. M. Hooper), was also a soprano. She sang at the Saturday Popular and Philharmonic Concerts, 1876; the Norwich Festival, etc., and was in much favour as a vocalist, Composed some songs, and organ music. She died June 6, 1894. WILLIAM

PERCIVAL.

PETERSON.

PENNA, his son, baritone, toured with success in the United States, in 1885. He died, January, 1889.

Percival, Samuel, organist, flute-player, and composer, born in 1824. He studied at the R.A.M., London, and became organist at the School for the Blind, Liverpool. Organist of Wallasey Parish Church, and teacher in Liverpool. He died at Liverpool, November 7, 1876. He composed a Magnificat and Nunc Dimittis; a cantata, entitled "The Lyre," op. 7; Sonata for pf. and flute, op. 2: original melodies for flute and pf.; Pf. music, songs, etc.

Percy, John, composer, organist, and tenor vocalist, was born in 1749. He died at London, January 24, 1797. Little is known of this musician, and he is only remembered as the composer of the ballad, "Wapping Old Stairs." He also composed some other works, many of them possessing merit, among which may be named:—Eight songs, with an accompaniment for the violin, op. 1 [1781]; Garden Scene from "Romeo and Juliet," duet, op. 2 [1785]; Six Arietts, op. 5 [1786]. *Songs:* Bonny Seaman; Captive; Gaffer Gray; Hark the horn calls away; Soft as yon silver ray; Sophrosyne; Sweet smells the brier; When Cloe tried her virgin fires; and others.

Perkins, Charles William, organist, born at Birmingham, October 4, 1855. Studied the organ under Andrew Deakin; and pianoforte and composition under Dr. Heap. Held the appointment of organist at Wretham Road Church, Handsworth, until 1884, when he went to London as assistant to Dr. Bridge, at Westminster Abbey. He studied with Dr. Bridge for some time, and held appointments successively at Immanuel Church, Streatham Common, and St. Michael's, Paddington. In June, 1888, he was elected organist of Birmingham Town Hall, an office he still holds. He is widely known as an organ player, and and has given recitals at the Crystal Palace, St. George's Hall, Liverpool, etc.; while his services are in great request at organ openings. He gives weekly free recitals in the Birmingham Town Hall, and has introduced many famous organists to the Birmingham public. He has officiated as organist at the Birmingham Festivals since 1888.

Perkins, Dodd, organist and composer, was born about 1750. For many years he was organist of Wells Cathedral, and numbered among his pupils James Turle. He died on April 9, 1820. Composer of "Ten Songs, written by the Hon. F. Seymour" [1797]. "Music, the soul of melody," glee, etc.

Another PERKINS (a son ?), was organist of Wells Cathedral, as late as 1849, but particulars concerning him are wanting.

Perren, George, tenor vocalist, born at

Camberwell, 1827. Sang in concerts in London and the provinces, afterwards going to Milan to study under Lamperti. On his return he made his *début* at the Surrey Theatre, May 28, 1855, in the "Faust" of Meyer Lutz. He appeared at the Sacred Harmonic Society, January 30, 1856, in "Elijah;" and was heard at various concerts in the principal musical centres, being very popular as a ballad singer. He took part in the first performance of Macfarren's "She Stoops to Conquer," at Drury Lane, February 11, 1864; and at times, up to 1878, sang in Italian Opera, at Her Majesty's Theatre. It is now some time since he retired from the concert platform. He composed a number of songs and ballads.

Perry, Clara, see sub. DAVIES, BEN.

Perronet, Rev. Edward, hymn-writer and composer, was born in 1721. He was a colleague of John Wesley, and afterwards preached to the Countess of Huntingdon's congregation at Canterbury Died at Canterbury, January 8, 1792. Author of "All hail the power of Jesu's name," the well-known hymn, and composer of various hymn tunes.

Perrot, Robert, see Porret.

Perry, George, organist and composer, was born at Norwich, in 1793. Chorister in Norwich Cathedral under Beckwith. Settled in London, 1822. Director of music in Haymarket Theatre, 1822. Organist of Quebec Chapel. Leader of band of Sacred Harmonic Society, 1832-47, and conductor in 1848. Organist of Trinity Church, Gray's Inn Road, 1846; He died at London, March 4, 1862. WORKS.—Overture to the Persian Hunters, 1817; Family Quarrels, opera [1830]; Morning, Noon, and Night, opera, 1822; Elijah and the Priests of Baal, oratorio; 1818; The Fall of Jerusalem, oratorio, 1830; The Death of Abel, oratorio [1846]; Belshazzar's Feast, cantata, 1836; Hezekiah, oratorio, 1847; Anthems, etc. *Songs :* I will remember thee; Spirit of the storm. Rondos and other works for pf.

Peterborough, Countess of, see ROBINSON, ANASTASIA.

Peterson, Franklin Sievewright, organist and writer on music, born in Edinburgh, February 24, 1861. Studied at Dresden and Edinburgh; organ pupil of Carl Aug. Fischer, Dresden, 1884. Graduated Mus. Bac., Oxford, 1892. Organist and choirmaster, Palmerston Place Church, Edinburgh, from 1884. Music master, Edinburgh Ladies' College, 1893, and Fettes College, 1894. Lecturer on Musical History at Dundee University College, and in Edinburgh and St. Andrews University Extension centres. Appointed, 1896, to act with Professor Niecks as additional examiner for Music Scholarships at Edinburgh University, founded by

PETRIE.

the late Signor Theophile Bucher, whose legacy is now at the disposal of the Senatus. Mr. Peterson is author of the articles on musical matters in the new edition of Chambers's Encyclopædia, and has contributed important papers to the *Musical Times*, *The Monthly Musical Record*, and the *Magazine of Music*, etc. His "Elements of Music" (Augener, 1896) reached a second edition in less than three months. He has also published An Introduction to the Study of Theory (Augener, 1897), some anthems, songs, and part-songs, etc.

Petrie, George, antiquary and author, born at Dublin in 1789. He was a painter in Ireland, and was librarian to the Hibernian Academy. Attached to the Irish Ordnance Survey, and held other appointments. Died at Dublin, January 17, 1866. Compiler of the Petrie Collection of the ancient music of Ireland, Dublin, 1855, vol. 1 and pp. 1-48 of vol. 2 all published ; and author of an "Essay on Music" in the *Dublin Examiner* of 1816. His collection of Irish music is very valuable.

Petrie, Robert, musician and violinist, born at Kirkmichael, Perth, February, 1767. He was a teacher, and played at many concerts, balls, etc. Drowned when returning home from a party, in August, 1830. He composed four "Collections of Strathspey Reels and country dances, with a bass for the violoncello," etc., London and Edinburgh [1790]. The other collections differ but slightly in the titles. Some of these collections had a large circulation, being issued in editions of over 1,000 to subscribers. In his third collection the well-known air "Comin' through the Rye" appears in its original form as the "Miller's daughter," Strathspey, and as altered by John Watlen now forms the melody usually sung with Burns's song.

Pettet, Alfred, English musician, born about 1785 ; died about 1845. Compiler of Original Sacred Music, consisting of psalms, hymns, and anthems composed expressly for this work by Attwood, Bishop, Cramer, Crotch, Goss, Horsley, Shield, Wesley, etc..." London [1815]. Duettinos and Trios, selected [1840]. Waltzes, etc., for pf. ; songs and other vocal music.

Pettit, Walter, violoncello player, born at London, March 14, 1835. He studied at the R.A.M., and was principal 'cello at Philharmonic Society, H.M. Theatre, etc. He died at London, Dec. 11, 1882. His son, WILLIAM H. PETTIT, is a violoncellist of repute.

Pettman, Edgar, organist and composer, born at Dunkirk, near Faversham, April 20, 1866. Educated at R.A.M. Organist of St. Matthew's, New Kent Road, London ; St. James's, Piccadilly. He has composed a cantata, "The Nativity," produced, 1885, at St. Matthew's Church, and some church music.

PHILLIPS.

Pew, John, violinist and conductor, was born in the first half of the present century. Appeared as violinist at concerts, Leeds, 1854, etc. He was for many years associated with the Carl Rosa Opera Company as chorus master and assistant conductor, and he acted as conductor of the English Opera Company, 1877 ; Valentine Smith's Opera Company, 1890, etc. He died at Manchester, February 22, 1890. Composer of dance music and songs.

Phasey, Alfred James, euphonium player. He was originally an ophicleide and bass trombone player in the band of the Coldstream Guards, and afterwards a member of the Queen's private band. For nearly 25 years he was a member of the Crystal Palace orchestra. He was also bandmaster of the St. George's Rifle Volunteers. He died at Chester, August 17, 1888. He introduced many improvements on, and was practically inventor of, the euphonium. Author of Instruction Book for the Euphonium [1858] ; Popular Instruction Book for the Trombone [1860] ; and composer of fantasias on operas for euphonium, cornet, etc. His son ALFRED is also a good euphonium player.

Philipps, Arthur, organist and composer, born in 1605. Clerk of New College, Oxford, 1622. Organist of Bristol Cathedral, 1638 ; Magdalen College, Oxford, 1639. Choragus or Professor of Music in Oxford University, 1639. Mus. Bac., Oxon., 1640. Organist to Queen Henrietta Maria of France, and, after his return to England, organist to Mr. Caryll, an Essex gentleman. Composed "The Requiem, or liberty of an imprisoned Royalist," 1641 ; "The Resurrection," 1649 ; etc.

Philipps, Peter, PETRUS PHILIPPUS, composer, who was born in England about [1560]. Canon of Bethune in Flanders. Organist of vice-regal chapel of the Governor of the Low Countries. Canon of Collegiate Church of St. Vincent, Soignies. He died in April, 1625.

WORKS.—Melodia Olympica di diversi eccellentissimi Musici a 4, 5, 6, e 8 voci, 1591 (and other editions). Il Primo libro de' Madrigali a sei voci, 1596. Madrigali a otto voci, 1598. Il Secondo libro di Madrigali a sei voci, 1604. Cantiones Sacræ, 5 vocum, 1612. Gemmulæ Sacræ, 2 e 3 voci, 1613. Cantiones Sacræ octi vocum, 1613. Litaniæ, 1623.

Phillips, Adelaide, contralto vocalist, born at Stratford-on-Avon in 1833. She sang in Boston and Philadelphia, and studied in London under Garcia and W. C. Masters, 1852 ; also in Italy. Appeared in London, Paris, and in United States of America. She died at Carlsbad, October 3, 1882.

Phillips, Anna Maria, *see* CROUCH, ANNA MARIA.

Phillips, Henry, baritone vocalist and

PHILLIPS.

writer, born at Bristol, August 13, 1801. He sang in chorus at Drury Lane Theatre, and studied under Broadhurst, and Sir G. Smart. Sang at the English Opera House; at the Lenten Oratorios; in Arne's "Artaxerxes," 1824; "Der Freischutz," 1824; at the Provincial Festivals, etc. He appeared in America, in 1844. Retired, in 1863. He died at Dalston, London, November 8, 1876. His daughters ALICE and FLORENCE were vocalists.

WORKS.—Adventures in America, an entertainment [1845]. The True Enjoyment of Angling, 1843. Hints on Musical Declamation. London, 1848; Birmingham edit., n.d. Musical and Personal Recollections during Half-a-Century. London, 1864, 2 vols. *Songs:* Best of all good company; Emigrant ship; Farmer's daughter of Berkshire; Terence Macarthy; Voyage through life; Woman, etc. He also issued an edition of Dibdin's Songs, 1859.

Phillips, Louisa, soprano vocalist, born at Bath. Studied at the Conservatoire, Paris, under Eugéne Crosti and Jules Barbot. Made her *début* at Colston Hall, Bristol, at Mr. Riseley's Concerts, December 4, 1882; sung at the Monday Popular Concerts, London, 1884; and has given concerts at Princes' Hall, and appeared with success at the principal concerts up to the present time.

Phillips, Thomas, tenor vocalist, lecturer and composer, born in London, 1774. Member of a Monmouthshire family. Lectured and sang at concerts during his lifetime. Made his *début* at Covent Garden, as Philip in the "Castle of Andalusia," 1796. Author of "Elementary Principles and Practices for Singing," London [1830]. Composer of a few songs, part-songs and glees, Crows in a cornfield; Faded wreath; Why tarries my love, etc. He also composed "The Mentor's Harp," moral ballads by T. H. Bayly; "Improved Psalmody for the Church and the Chamber." Also an arrangement of Linley's "Duenna." He was accidentally killed at Hartford, Cheshire, while leaving or entering a train in motion, October 27, 1841.

Phillips, William Lovell, composer and pianist, born at Bristol, December 26, 1816. Chorister in Bristol Cathedral. He studied under C. Potter at R.A.M., and became Professor of composition there. He studied the violoncello under Lindley. Member of orchestra of H. M. Theatre, Philharmonic Society, and Sacred Harmonic Society. Conductor at Olympic Theatre; Princess' Theatre. Organist of St. Catherine's Church, Regent Park, etc. He died at London, March 19, 1860.

WORKS.—Borrowing a husband, farce [1844]. Offertory Sentences set to music. Symphony in F minor; Cantata. *Songs:* Lady mine; Ivy green; The sleeping beauty; Longings; The old ballad; Pearls of the

PHIPPS.

ocean; Voice of songs; Christmas rose; England's hope and pride; One word; Sentry; What must I sing you?; Songs of summer. New and complete instructions for the violoncello. London, n.d

Phillipson, Wentworth, author of "Guide to Young Pianoforte teachers and students, with analysis of examples, etc., London [1872], 2 editions.

Philp, Elizabeth, vocal composer, born at Falmouth, in 1827. She studied music under Garcia, Marchesi, and F. Hiller. She died at London, November 26, 1885. Composer of a number of meritorious songs, etc., of which the following is a select list :—

WORKS.—*Songs :* Bye and Bye; Dolly; Fisherman's story; Forgiven; Golden past; Hop-pickers; I love him more than I can say; Love that's never told; My head is like to rend; Oh! why not be happy; Poacher's Widow; River ran between them; 'Tis all that I can say; 'Tis wine; Violets of the Spring; Wrecked hope. Part-songs, various. How to sing an English Ballad, London, 1883 [Reprint], etc.

Philpot, John, double-bass player, was born in 1759. He was for more than fifty years a member of the orchestra of Bath, and as a double-bass player was considered second only to Dragonetti. He died at Bath, January 26, 1843. He was the father of Mrs. Anderson, the pianist.

Philpot, Lucy, *See* ANDERSON, Lucy.

Philpot Stephen, musician and author, wrote "An Introduction to the art of playing on the violin on an entirely new plan." London, [1767]; "Six capital lessons for the Harpsichord or Pianoforte." [1784].

Philpot, Stephen Rowland, composer. Studied at R.A.M., under Sir G. A. Macfarren. His works include the operas, "Dante and Beatrice," produced November 25, 1889; "Zelica," December 17, 1890, in concert form, both at Gresham Hall, Brixton; Also "La Gitana," one act opera, 1896. He has also written pieces for pf. and strings; songs, etc.

Phipps, Alexander James, composer and conductor, of Liverpool. Studied under W. H. Holmes and C. Steggall, at R.A.M. Has given chamber concerts in that city, and is conductor of Opera and Oratorio Societies. Organist of St. James', Swansea, 1866; now of St. John's, Bootle, in which Church was produced his "Meditation on the Passion," for chorus and organ, 1893. He has composed an oratorio, "The Ten Virgins"; an opera, "Thea, or Solomon's Treasure '; songs, and other works. Author of "Comprehensive Guide to the study of Music," London [1874].

Phipps, Thomas Blomer, musician and author, born London, January 30, 1796; died London, February 17, 1849. Son of one of the partners of the firm of Goulding, Phipps,

PHIPSON.

and D'Almaine. He wrote "Guida de Chitarra, or complete book of instructions for the Spanish Guitar .. London, n.d. ; Shakespeare musical wreath [1840]; Pleasures of Harmony, airs for pf. ; Six Royal Scotch Polkas ; numerous " recollections," arrangements, etc., for pf. ; Songs, and other vocal music.

Phipson, T. L., amateur musician and physician in London, author of " Biographical sketches and anecdotes of celebrated Violinists," London, 1877. " Bellini and the Opera of La Sonnambula," London, 1880. " Famous Violinists and fine Violins : historical notes, anecdotes and reminiscences," London, 1896. Dr. Phipson was at one time president and solo violinist of the Bohemian Orchestral Society. He translated De Beriot's " Méthode de Violon," and wrote " Some mysteries of nature," London, 1876 ; The storm and its portents, 1878 ; Meteors, aerolites and falling stars, 1866 ; and other works.

Pickard, J., author of " Modulation exemplified by a grand tabular view of the preparations of all the notes of the octaves," London [1835]. Composer of " Thirty approved and fashionable airs for the violoncello," London [1825], 2 books.

Pickering, John, pianist and composer, born at London, May 23, 1792. He studied with Domenico Corri, and in 1812 settled as a teacher in Preston. Afterwards, in 1817, he settled in Manchester, where he attained a high position as a teacher and pianist. He died at Manchester, November 6, 1843. Composer of much pianoforte music and of music for the church.

Pickering, Thomas, musician and author, born at London, July 4, 1796. He was an associate of the Novellos, Horsleys, and other musical families, and a man of remarkable literary and musical attainments. One of the founders of the Royston Mechanics' Institute, where Charles Cowden Clarke delivered his first lecture. He formed classes for the study of music, and was president and conductor of the Royston Choral Society. He died at Royston, May 1, 1876.

Piercy, Henry Ralph, tenor vocalist, born at Birmingham. Came into notice locally about 1879. Went to London and studied under J. B. Welch, and from 1882 attracted favourable notice. He sang at the Bristol Festival, 1885 ; Wolverhampton Festival, 1886 ; Birmingham, 1888, in Dvorak's *Stabat Mater*, etc. ; and Leeds, 1889. He has been heard at the principal concerts in the United Kingdom, and has won an honourable position among singers of the day. He is a member of the Temple Church Choir.

Piercy, Rosetta, violinist and soprano vocalist, born at Birmingham, November 29, 1838. Received her first lessons on the violin from James Hyde, a local professor, and was

PIERSON.

afterwards for some years a pupil of Henry Hayward, of Wolverhampton, at one of whose concerts she made her *début*. As solo violinist and vocalist she was frequently heard at concerts in the principal Midland towns ; and was a regular contributor to the Monday Popular Concerts given in the Town Hall by the late James Stimpson, and was one of the party engaged when Madame Patey made her *début*. She retired from the profession on her marriage, in 1861, with Mr. Alfred Feeny, a journalist, formerly of London ; for some time musical critic, and later an assistant editor of the *Birmingham Daily Post*.

Pierpoint, Bantock, baritone vocalist, born at Runcorn, Cheshire, August 8, 1856. Sang in Prescot Parish Church when a boy. Was organist for some time at the Independent Chapel, Runcorn, and sang at concerts as an amateur tenor, being occupied in business. His first vocal instructor was Mr. W. I. Argent, of Liverpool, and he afterwards studied at the R.A.M., and Guildhall School of Music, under M. Visetti, eventually becoming a private pupil of Mr. W. Shakespeare, his voice settling to a baritone of exceptional compass. He sang at various concerts in London, Birmingham, and other places, but his first great opportunity was at a concert of the Sacred Harmonic Society, December 8, 1887, when (owing to the illness of Mr. Watkin Mills) he took the part of *Lucifer* in the " Golden Legend " at a few hours' notice. He first sang at the Bristol Festival in 1890, in Parry's " Judith," and has fulfilled engagements at the Norwich, Chester, and Cheltenham Festivals. He is a member of the Royal Society of Musicians, and an Associate of the Philharmonic Society.

JOSEPH PIERPOINT, no relation, was a tenor singer, and a member of several English Opera Companies. He died at Preston, June 17, 1887, aged forty.

Pierson, Henry, Hugo, or PEARSON, composer, born at Oxford, April 12, 1816. Educated at Harrow and Trinity College, Cambridge. He studied music under Attwood and Corfe, in England ; Rink, Tomaschek, and Reissiger in Germany. Professor of Music in Edinburgh University, 1844. Married to Caroline Leonhardt. Resided mostly in Germany. He died at Leipzig, January 28, 1873, and is buried at the family burying place at Sonning, Berks.

WORKS.—*Oratorios :* Jerusalem, Norwich Festival, 1852 ; London, 1853. Hezekiah, Norwich. 1869. Music to Second Part of Goethe's " Faust," Hamburg, 1854. *Operas :* Contarini, Hamburg, 1872 ; Leila, Hamburg, 1848 ; Symphony, Macbeth, op. 54. *Overtures :* " As you like it " ; " Romeo and Juliet," op. 86 ; " Julius Cæsar " ; Romantique. Salve Æternum, a Roman dirge, op. 30, 1853 ; Der

PIGGOTT.

Elfensieg. Six romances for voice and pf.; Six songs for voice and pf.; Elegies, do.; Lieder, various; Ye Mariners of England, part-song; Hurrah for Merry England; Now the bright morning star. Blessed are the dead, anthem; Ave Maria. Office of the Holy Communion set to music [1870]. Thirty Hymn Tunes, 1870; 2nd series, 1872. Te Deums, etc.

Piggott, Francis, organist and composer, born about the middle of the 17th century. He was organist of Magdalen College, Oxford, 1686-87; of Temple Church, London, 1688; and of Chapel Royal in 1697. In 1695 he was appointed Gentleman of the Chapel Royal, and in 1698 he was Mus. Bac., Cantab. He died in May, 1704. Composer of anthems; "Choice Collection of Ayres for the harpsichord, by Blow, F. Piggott, etc.," 1700.

Pilkington, Francis, composer and lutenist of the 16th and 17th centuries. He was a chorister in Chester Cathedral, and Mus. Bac., Oxon , 1595. He published First Booke of Songs or Ayres of 4 Parts, with tablature for the lute or orpharion, with the violl da gamba, 1605; First Set of Madrigals and Pastorals of 3, 4, and 5 Parts, 1613 ; Second Set of Madrigals and Pastorals of 3, 4, 5, and 6 Parts, apt for Violl and Voyce, 1624.

Pilling, Samuel Wilkinson, amateur organist and authority on organ construction, born at Bolton-le-Moors, 1856. Educated at Victoria College, Manchester; received his musical training under S. B. Whiteley, and J. Dobson, of Southport, and later under J. Kendrick Pyne, of Manchester. Has given many organ recitals in different parts of the country, and appeared at the Bow and Bromley Institute, December 2, 1882, and is also known as an occasional lecturer upon matters referring to the organ. Many improvements in organ construction have been initiated by him, and he has designed and opened upwards of one hundred-and-thirty organs in various localities. He has an exceptionally fine four-manual organ in the music-room of his residence, The Hagg, Mirfield, which was opened by Jules Grison, of Rheims, November 30, 1887, and upon which many distinguished organists have given recitals. Mr. Pilling is by profession a Civil Engineer and Railway Contractor, succeeding to the business of his father, Abraham Pilling, J.P., late of Bolton.

Pillow, John William Davis, conductor and organist, born at Chichester, in 1851. Chorister at Chichester Cathedral, and organist of St. Pancras, Chichester, when 13. Articled pupil of E. H. Thorne. In 1869 he was appointed to All Saints', Portsmouth, and in 1880 founded the Portsmouth Philharmonic Society, which has given many excellent concerts. In 1889 he accepted the post of organist at the new Parish Church of

PITTMAN.

St. Mary, Portsea He is a leading member of the local Masonic brotherhood.

Pinto, George Frederick, or SAUNDERS, violinist and composer, born in Lambeth, London, September, 25, 1786. Grandson of Thomas Pinto. He studied under Salomon, and performed at the principal London and provincial concerts; and appeared in Scotland with great success, 1802. He died at Chelsea, London, March 23, 1806.

WORKS.—Six Canzonets for voice and pf., Birmingham [1805]; Four Canzonets and a sonata, edited, with preface, by S. Wesley, Edinburgh [1807]; Canzonets, edited by T. Oliphant [1846]; Three Duets for two violins obligato, op. 5 ; Three Sonatas for pf., op. 4 ; Three Sonatas for pf. and violin [1805]; other vocal and instrumental works.

Pinto, Thomas, violinist, born in England, of Italian parents, early in the eighteenth century. He performed at provincial festivals, and at King's Theatre, London. Resided successively in Edinburgh and Ireland. Married to Miss Brent, the vocalist. He died in Ireland, in 1773.

His second wife, Miss CHARLOTTE BRENT, whom he married in 1766, was a famous soprano vocalist, and appeared as a concert vocalist for many years in London and elsewhere, from 1758. She died in London, April 10, 1802.

Pitman, Ambrose, musician and minor poet, born 1763. Musician in London. Died, London, in 1817.

WORKS.—Three favourite Amorosos for voice and pf., op. 6 [1795]; Laura, a sonnet from Petrarch (? Metastasio), 1795. Songs : Gaffer Gray; Io! Triumphe; Marian's complaint; The Robin, etc. Beauties of D. Scarlatti, selected by Ambrose Pitman [1780]; Eugenio, or the man of sorrow, by a young gentleman of seventeen, London, 1780; The Miseries of Musick Masters, a serio-comick dramatick poem, London, 1815.

Pitt, Percy, composer, of present time. Studied in Germany under Reineeke, Jadassohn, and Rheinberger. Composer of a Coronation March ; Suite, "Fêtes Galante," both performed at the Queen's Hall, 1896; and other pieces for orchestra. Three Romantic pieces, op. 18, 'cello and pf. ; Bagatelle, violin and pf. ; Modern Suite, pf. Songs, etc.

Pitt, Thomas, musician, of latter part of 18th century, who was appointed organist of Worcester Cathedral in 1793. Composer of "Church Music, consisting of Te Deum and jubilate, etc." Worcester, 1788-89, 2 vols.

Pittman, Josiah, organist and composer, born in London, September 3, 1816. He studied under S. S. Wesley, Moscheles and Schnyder von Wartensee. Organist successively at Sydenham, 1831 ; Spitalfields, 1835-47; Lincoln's Inn, 1852-64. He was

U

accompanist at Her Majesty's Theatre from 1865 to 1868, and at the Royal Italian Opera, Covent Garden, 1868-1880. He died at London, April 23, 1886.

WORKS.—The People in the Church, their Rights and Duties in connection with the Poetry and Music of the Book of Common Prayer, London, 1858. The People in the Cathedral; a letter to the very Rev. Henry Hart Milman, D.D., London, 1857. Songs of Scotland, edited (with Colin Brown). Songs from the Operas, 2 vols. (edited). Royal Edition of Operas, edited with Sir A. Sullivan (Boosey). Callcott's Grammar of Music (edited), London, n.d.

Pitts, William John, organist, born at Tansor, near Oundle, April 17, 1829. Organist at Elton, Huntingdonshire when fourteen; and when the Oratory at Kensington, London, was founded he was appointed organist, and has been actively engaged in his duties for 55 years. Composer of the hymn tune known as "Princethorpe," and some other vocal music. His father was an organ builder, and he had two brothers organists, JAMES PITTS, formerly of the R. C. Church at Brook Green, Hammersmith; and JOHN PITTS, formerly organist to the Duke of Norfolk, Arundel. Both are now deceased. JOHN and ERNEST PITTS, sons of the last named, are pianists, and have gained some reputation on the concert platform, from 1887 onwards.

Place, Gertrude, author of "A Catechism of Music for the use of young children," London, 1856.

Plaisted, Philip, organist, born at Muswell Hill, Middlesex, 1837. Went with his parents to Australia in 1857. Returned to London and became a pupil of George Cooper, E. J. Hopkins, and W. H. Monk, 1863-5. Held the post of organist at St. Stephen's, Richmond, and other churches in Melbourne. Was organist of the Melbourne Philharmonic Society, and gave Saturday Evening Concerts. In May, 1889, he became insane, and is living still in that unhappy condition. A MISS GRACE PLAISTED sang in English opera, in Melbourne, 1883-4.

Plant, Arthur Blurton, organist and composer, born at Lichfield, May 12, 1853. Was a chorister at the Cathedral for seven years, and then articled pupil of the organist, Thomas Bedsmore. Passed examination for F.R.C.O., 1875; graduated Mus. Bac., 1882; Mus. Doc., 1896, Oxford. In 1874, he was appointed organist and choirmaster of St. Paul's, Burton-on-Trent, and, in 1895, Borough organist, both of which positions he still holds. An able executant, he has given organ recitals at the Bow and Bromley Institute, and elsewhere. His compositions include a setting of Psalm 13, for soli, chorus, and orchestra; Sonata in C; six Sonatinas;

Concert Fugue; and other pieces for the organ, etc., etc.

Platt, Edward, composer and horn-player, was born on June 11, 1793; died at Stirling, June 27, 1861. For many years a member of the Philharmonic, Opera, and other orchestras; and played at the Three Choirs' Festivals for twenty years. Retired from the profession in 1849, owing to loss of teeth. The late Sir Michael Costa considered him without an equal for tone and " singing" on the horn. Author of an Instruction Book for the Pianoforte, and composer of songs, " My Bonnie, Blythesome Mary," etc., and pf. music.

Platt, Robert, musician. Author of a " New, Easy, and Correct System of Vocal Music: a Practical Manual of Singing at Sight." London, 1847.

Platt, Samuel Radcliffe, a wealthy and distinguished amateur musician, of Werneth Park, near Oldham. He maintains a complete orchestra of 45 performers, he himself playing first oboe. Concerts are given under the direction of Dr. Marsden (q.v.), and a choir has at times been employed. His library of classical and modern orchestral music, numbers over 1,000 works. The organ in St. Thomas' Church, Werneth, was his gift. It has four manuals, and cost £3,000. He is a member and trustee of the Manchester Royal College of Music; and founder and President of the Oldham School of Music. Deputy Lieutenant, J.P. for the County, and High Sheriff, 1897.

Platts, James, composer, of latter part of last and early part of present century. He composed a large number of country dances, cotillons, strathspeys, reels, quadrilles, medleys, waltzes, etc., for pf. or harp, between 1785 and 1815; also six Rondos for the harp or pf., with accompaniment for the tamborino; songs, etc.

Playford, John, composer and music-publisher, was born in London, in 1623. Established a music-selling and publishing business, in the Inner Temple, London. Clerk of the Temple Church, 1653. He died at London, in 1693.

WORKS.—An Introduction to the Skill of Musick, in two books. To which is added the Art of Descant, by Dr. Thomas Campion, and Annotations thereon by Mr. Chr. Simpson . . . (? 2nd edit.), London, 1655. (An earlier edition [1654] is noted in Grove's " Dictionary of Music," as having been in the possession of Dr. Rimbault, and the only known copy). 3rd edit., 1660; an unnumbered edit., 1662; 4th edit., with portrait, 1664; unnumbered editions in 1667, 1670; 6th edit., portrait, 1672; 7th edit., with the Order of Performing the Divine Service in Cathedrals and Collegeate Chapels, portrait, 1674; 8th

PLAYFORD.

edit., portrait, 1679 ; 9th edit. (?) ; 10th edit. (to which is added as a third book in place of Campion's treatise, " A brief Introduction to the Art of Descant, or Composing Music in Parts," ascribed in future editions to Henry Purcell), portrait, 1683 ; 11th edit., port, 1687 ; 12th edit., port, 1694 ; 13th edit., port, 1697 ; 14th edit., port, 1700 ; 15th edit., port, 1703 ; 16th edit., port, 1713 ; 17th edit., port, 1718 ; 18th edit., port, 1724 ; 19th edit., port, 1730. Psalms and hymns in Solemn Musick of foure parts on the Common Tunes to the Psalms in Metre . . . London, 1671. The Whole Book of Psalms, with the usual Hymns and Spiritual Songs, etc., composed in three p rts, London (?); other editions, 2nd, 1695, 1697 ; 6th, 1700 ; 7th, 1701 ; 8th, 1702 ; 9th, 1707 ; 10th, 1709 ; 13th, 1715 ;, 19th, 1738 ; 20th, 1757. A Paraphrase upon the Psalms of David, by George Sandys. Set to new tunes, for private devotion, by Henry Lawes. Revised and corrected by John Playford, London, 1676. The Musical Companion, in two books. The first book containing catches and rounds for three voyces, the second containing dialogues, glees, ayres, and songs for two, three, and four voyces, London, 1673. A Booke of New Lessons, for the Cythern and Gittern, London, 1652. Musick's Recreation on the Viol, Lyra-way ; being a choice collection of Lessons . . . etc., London, 2nd edit., 1682. In Locke's "Present Practice of Musick Vindicated," 1673, is " A Letter from John Playford to Mr. T. Salmon," in which he espouses Locke's cause to the disadvantage of Salmon. *Publications, various :* Hilton's Catch that catch can ; or a choice collection of catches, rounds, and canons for three and four voyces, 1652 ; Select Musical Ayres and Dialogues, in three books, for one, two, and three voyces . . . by sundry composers (composed by Wilson, Colman, Lawes, etc.), 1653 ; another edition, 1659 ; Choice Ayres, Songs, and dialogues to be sung to the theorbo . . . 5 books, 1676-84 ; The English Dancing Master : or Plaine and Easie Rules for the Dancing of Country Dances, London, 1651 ; 2nd edit., 1657 ; 3rd edit., 1665 ; and numerous other editions to 1728 ; Musick's delight on the Cithern, 1666 ; also published works of Lawes ; Court Ayres ; and most of the important music books of the period.

Playford, Henry, publisher, second son of the foregoing, born in London, May 5, 1657. Succeeded to his father's business in 1685, which he carried on for a time in company with Robert Carr, but afterwards alone at the Temple Change, Fleet Street. He died at London [1710]. His principal publications consist of the Theater of Music ; or a choice collection of the newest and best songs sung at the Court, etc. The words composed

PLUMSTEAD.

by the most ingenious wits of the age, and set to music by the greatest masters...Lond., 4 books, 1685-87. Banquet of Musick: a collection of the newest and best songs sung at Court, 6 books, 1688-92. Pleasant Musical Companion, being a choice collection of catches for three and four voices ; published chiefly for the encouragement of the Musical Societies, which will be speedily set up in all the chief cities and towns in England, 1701 ; 5th edit., 1709. A Collection of Original Scotch Tunes (full of the Highland Humours) for the Violin : being the first of this kind yet printed : most of them being in the compass of the Flute, London, 1700. He also published Purcell's " Ten Sonatas," in four parts." 4 vols., 1697 ; Purcell's " Orpheus Britannicus," 1698-1702 ; Blow's " Amphion Anglicus," 1700, etc. He also published a work which went through a number of editions, viz., " Harmonia Sacra ; or Divine Hymns and Dialogues, with a Thorow-bass, etc.," London, 1687-93 ; 3rd edit., with " four excellent hymns of the late Mr. Henry Purcell, never before printed," 1726.

His younger brother, JOHN (b. 1665, d. 1686), carried on the business of music printer, and reprinted some of his father's works. For some years he was in partnership with the widow of William Godbid, a well-known London music-printer, who executed much work for John Playford, senior.

Pleasants, Thomas, organist and composer of the 17th century. In 1676 he became organist of Norwich Cathedral. He composed some sacred and secular vocal music.

Plumridge, Henry, organist and composer, graduated Mus. Bac., 1871 ; Mus. Doc., 1888, Oxford. He is organist of University College, and the City Church, Oxford ; and the composer of an oratorio, " Daniel," 1888 ; " God came from Teman," soli, chorus, and orchestra ; anthems, etc.

Plumpton, Alfred, composer and conductor of present time. About 1875 he was conducting an opera company in India, and afterwards went to Australia. He was some time director of the choir at the Roman Catholic Cathedral, Melbourne, and produced a Mass in G there, 1881 (?) His cantata, " Endymion," was composed for the first Musical Festival at Melbourne, and performed December 26, 1882. " The Apotheosis of Hercules," for men's voices, was produced at Melbourne, September 17, 1883. In 1892 he was in London, conducting at the Prince of Wales' Theatre. For some time he was musical critic for the Melbourne *Age*, and *Leader*. He has composed some songs, etc.

Plumstead, W. H., published " Beauties of Melody, a collection of popular airs . . . also Irish and Scotch melodies," London, 1827.

POLE.

"Church of England Music," London, 1846. "Nursery Recreations for the Young," 1854-56, etc

Pole, William, civil engineer, writer on science, and amateur musician, born at Birmingham, April 22, 1814. Professor of Civil Engineering at University College, London, 1859-76, and also held appointments in India, and has done much scientific work for Government. F.R.S. of London, 1861, and Edinburgh, 1877. Cultivated his early taste for music, and graduated at Oxford, Mus. Bac., 1860; Mus. Doc., 1867. Was organist of St. Mark's, North Audley Street, London, 1836-66; Examiner in Music, London University, 1878-90. Hon. F.C.O., 1889. His contributions to musical literature date from 1836, when he contributed his first papers to the *Musical World*, on the Construction of Organ pipes; on the Horn, etc. He wrote on the Musical Instruments in the International Exhibition of 1851; and the Official Report of the Jury, on the same subject, in 1862; on the Music at the Crystal Palace—Report to the Shareholders, 1875; on the proposed Regulations for Musical Degrees, University of London, 1877; and many papers for the *Musical Times, Athenæum, Nature,* etc.; also for the programmes of the New Philharmonic Concerts; and articles in Grove's Dictionary of Music. His " Philosophy of Music," 1879, was reprinted by K. Paul, 1895; and " The Story of Mozart's Requiem," which appeared in the *Musical Times* in 1869, was issued by Novello in 1879, as a pamphlet. These are two extremely valuable works. Dr. Pole's musical compositions include a setting of Psalm 100 in cantata form, which was given at a Festival at Tenbury by Sir F. A. G. Ouseley, October 3, 1861; and the 8-part motet from it, performed at the Chester Festival, 1882. He has also done some four-handed pf. accompaniments to classical songs, and composed some organ music.

Poole, Clement William, amateur musician, born at Ealing, June 7, 1828. Studied music under Jos. T. Cooper, and has acted as honorary organist at the Parish Church, Kingston-on-Thames; and Christ Church, Ealing. Composer of vocal music, among which is the hymn tune "Westenhanger," etc.

Poole, Elizabeth, mezzo-soprano vocalist, born in London, April 5, 1820. Made her *début* in opera at Drury Lane, 1834. Sang in the United States, 1839. Was with the English Opera Company at the Strand Theatre, 1848; and, until 1870, was prominent both as a ballad singer and an actress. She married a Mr. Bacon.

Poole, Fanny Kemble, *born* BARNETT, contralto vocalist, born, 1845, in London. She did not begin her public career until after her marriage; but from about 1870 until 1891 she sang in concerts, chiefly in oratorio,

PORTER.

in all the large towns in England, Scotland, and Wales. After the death of Mr. Poole, in 1891, she retired from the platform, and gave herself up to teaching, having a large connection in the neighbourhood of Surbiton. Her sister, ALICE BARNETT (Mrs. Dickens), sang for some years at the Savoy Theatre, creating the contralto parts in many of the Gilbert-Sullivan operas; also sang in the Carl Rosa, and other companies. Toured in Australia, 1886. The sisters are connections of the celebrated Kemble family.

Poole, Maria, *see* DICKONS, MRS.

Poole, Reginald Lane-, amateur musician and author, was educated at Oxford, where he graduated, in 1878. Lecturer on modern history at Jesus College, Oxford, since 1886. Author of " Bach " (Great Musicians), London, Low, 1882.

Pope, Henry, bass vocalist, born at Bristol. Sang at the Bristol Festival of 1876, in Spohr's "Fall of Babylon." Was a member of the Carl Rosa Company for about ten years, from 1878; and sang at the principal London and provincial concerts. Now living in London as a teacher of singing.

Porret, or **Perrot, Robert,** organist and composer of the 16th century. He was born at Hackness, in Yorkshire, and in 1507 graduated Mus. Bac., Cambridge, and in 1515 became Mus. Doc., Oxford. He was organist and instructor of the choristers in Magdalen College, Oxford, 1519, and was also for a time principal of Trinity Hall, Oxford. He died in 1550.

Porteous, James, violinist and composer, was born in the latter half of the 18th century. He lived at Meinfoot, near Ecclefechan, Dumfriesshire, and was a miller on the Hoddom Estate. He died at Annan, July 17, 1847. He issued a " collection of Strathspeys, Reels and Jigs; respectfully dedicated to Lady Jardine of Applegarth. Arranged for the pianoforte, violin and violoncello," Edinburgh [1820]; 2nd edition, 1821, in parts.

Porteous, Richard, author of the " Bandmaster's Atlas, displaying at one view the scale compass and notation of every wind instrument employed in military and brass bands.." London, [1854]. " Composer's Musical Atlas, displaying the scale, compass, etc., of every instrument employed in orchestral bands.." London, 1854.

Porter, John, organist of the 17th century. Was organist at Eton College and teacher of John Weldon.

Porter, Prince Walsh, amateur composer and social leader. Composed a " Collection of melodies, duets and glees," London [1827].

Porter, Richard, author of a small tract entitled, " Rudiments of Music, abridged for the use of Choirs," Oxford [1868], 2 editions. " Rudiments of vocal music," Oxford, 1879.

PORTER.

Porter, Samuel, organist and composer, born at Norwich, in 1733. He studied under Maurice Greene, and was organist of Canterbury Cathedral, 1757-1803. He died at Canterbury, December 11, 1810. He composed Four Anthems and Two Psalm Tunes," London [1800]. "Cathedral Music in Score," edited by Rev. W. Jas. Porter, London [1815]. Twenty-five Odes, hymn tunes, etc. in four parts, London, 1800. Songs, glees, marches, etc. His Service in D has been reprinted by Novello.

WILLIAM JAMES PORTER his son, was vicar of Himbleton, and composed a " Selection of 15 Psalms from the new version.." London [1840] ; as well as anthems, etc. SAMUEL PORTER, probably another son, who died on July 14, 1823, held the position of organist of Faversham Parish Church for 37 years, and was a member of the King's Band for the same period.

Porter, Thomas, author of " How to choose a violin," London [1879].

Another THOMAS PORTER, published about 1839, a " Fantasia for the organ or pianoforte, modulating twice through all the major and minor keys," op. 1.

Porter, Walter, composer, was born about the end of the 17th century. Son of Henry Porter, who was Mus. Bac., Oxford, 1600, and musician to James I. in 1603. Gentleman of the Chapel Royal, 1616. Master of Choristers, Westminster Abbey, 1639, but was dismissed at the Rebellion. He died at London. October, 1659.

WORKS.—Madrigales and Ayres of two, three, foure, and five voyces . . . 1632. Ayres and Madrigales for two, three, four, and five voices, with a thorough-bass base for the Organ or Theorbo-lute in the Italian way, 1639. Motetts of two Voices-treble, tenor and bass, with continued bass or score, to be performed on an organ, harpsychor, lute, or bass viol, 3 parts, London, 1657. Divine Hymns (1664). Psalms of Mr. George Sandys composed into Music for two Voyces, with a Thorough-bass for the Organ [1670.]

Porter, Walter, organist and composer, born at Boston, Lincolnshire, May, 1856. Entered the choir of the Parish Church when eight, and in 1868 took lessons from W. B. Gilbert, and later became a pupil of D. J. Wood. Passed examination for F.C.O Appointed organist and choirmaster of Bourne Abbey Church, 1874 ; and to St. Mary's Parish Church, Hull, 1875, a position he retains. Conductor of Grimsby Philharmonic Society, 1884, and a similar society in Hull, since 1885. Honorary Local Examiner for R.C.M. Scholarships. Composer of a string quartet (performed at Scarborough Conference of I.S.M., 1894) ; a setting of the Office of Holy Communion, Te Deum. etc.,

POULTER.

fugue, two andantes, and other organ music ; a number of pieces for pf.

Postans, Mary, *see* SHAW, MRS. ALFRED.

Potter, John, writer and composer of last century, author of " Observations on the present state of music and musicians, with general rules for studying Music, to which is added a scheme for erecting and supporting a musical academy in this kingdom," London, 1762. He also composed for Vauxhall Gardens, and published a collection entitled, " Collection of New Songs and Ballads sung at Vauxhall Gardens," London, 1767, 1771-1772, etc.

Potter, Philip Cipriani Hambly, pianist and composer, born at London, October 2, 1792. He studied under his father, Callcott, Attwood, Crotch, and Woelfl. *Début* as pianist at Philharmonic Society Concert, in 1816. He afterwards studied at Vienna under Förster, and while there came in contact with Beethoven, 1817-18. Professor of pf. at R.A.M., London, 1822. Principal of R.A.M. in succession to Crotch, 1832-59. He died at London, September 26, 187 .

WORKS.—Medora e Corrado, cantata [1828]; Op. 1, Sonata for pf. [1817]; Op. 2, Sonata for pf. in D ; Op. 3, Sonata in E minor ; Op. 6, Grand duo for two pfs. ; Op. 7, Duet for two pfs. ; Introduction and rondo, pf., four hands ; Op. 11, Sextet for pf., flute, violin, viola, 'cello and bass ; Op. 12, Three trios for pf , violin, and 'cello, or clarinet and bassoon [1835] ; Op. 13, Sonata di bravura for pf. and horn or bassoon ; Op. 19, Studies for the pf. in all the major and minor keys, London [1827]; Op. 20, Introduction and rondo for pf. ; Op. 21, Second Rondeau brilliant for pf. ; Nine Symphonies for orchestra in A, G minor, etc. ; four overtures for orchestra ; Three concertos for pf. and orchestra ; Several string quartets ; The Enigma, variations in the style of five eminent masters, pf. [1826]; Octave lessons ; Allegro brilliant in E ; Toccattas, rondos, etc., for pf. ; Canzonets and songs. A musician and teacher of great influence in his time, who directed the studies of a large number of the best modern English musicians. His father and grandfather were both musicians.

Potter, S., musician and author, who was in the band of the Coldstream Guards. He published " Art of playing the Fife, with camp, garrison, and street duty," n.d. ; " Art of beating the Drum, with camp, garrison, and street duty," n.d.

Poulter, George Thomas, composer and organist, born at London, in September, 1838. Studied under J. W. Elliott, etc., and himself acted as one of the teachers of Hamish MacCunn (*q.v.*). Successively organist at Warperton, Warwickshire, 1854 ;

POUNDS.

Ardgowan House (Sir M. R. Shaw Stewart), private, 1857; Town Hall, Greenock, 1861; Mid Parish Church, 1868; and St. Paul's Church, Greenock, 1886. Conductor for a time of the Greenock Choral Society, etc. Composer of songs; "The Bridge of Duty," a cantata; pf. music, etc.

Pounds, Charles Courtice, vocalist and actor, was born in London, May 30, 1869. For some years he was a treble singer in church choirs, but he afterwards studied at the R.A.M. Travelled in the English provinces with concert parties, and sang in oratorio, but was most successful in the Gilbert and Sullivan operas. He sang in Australia in 1895, with the Williamson and Musgrove Opera Company.

Povey, Miss, soprano vocalist, was born in Birmingham in 1804. She made her *début* on June 3, 1817. Pupil of T. Cooke and Bartleman. She sang at Drury Lane, 1819; English Opera House, etc. She was married to a Mr. E. Knight.

Powell, Josiah W., town-clerk of Burslem, Staffordshire. He and the late George Howson (*q.v.*) were the fathers of elementary vocal music in the Potteries. Half a century ago there was scarcely a singer in the district who could read music, and if an oratorio was to be performed singers had to be imported from Birmingham. Now, through the efforts of these two men, the Potteries are vocal with song. Powell translated Mendelssohn's "Elijah" into the Tonic Sol-fa Notation, one of the first great oratorios so treated. He formed the Burslem Choir, which soon achieved a great reputation. His memory will long be affectionately cherished in North Staffordshire. He died at Wolstanton, May 22, 1891, in his 72nd year.

Powell, Thomas, violinist and composer, born in London in 1776. He studied the harp, violin, and pf. Member of the Royal Society of Musicians. He was married in 1811, and resided in Dublin as a teacher. Performed a violin concerto in Haymarket Theatre, London. He died after 1860. Composed 15 concertos for violin and orchestra; Three duets for violin and 'cello, op. 1; Three duets for 2 'cellos, op. 2; Capriccio for 'cello, op. 24; Introduction and Fugue for organ; Three grand Sonatas for pf. and violin [1825]; Overtures for orchestra, pf. arrangements, etc.

Powell, Walter, tenor vocalist, was born at Oxford in 1697. Chorister and clerk to Magdalen College, Oxford. Sang in Handel's oratorios. He died at Oxford, November 6, 1744.

Power, Lionel, composer and writer, of the 15th century, was author of various works on Musical theory, of which "Lionel Power of the Cordis of Musike" is contained in the Lansdowne MS. in the British Museum. He

PRENDERGAST.

also composed some church music, which is preserved in MS. at Bologna, the British Museum, etc.

Prat, Daniel, clergyman of 18th century, was rector of Harrixham, in Kent, and chaplain to George III. He wrote "An Ode to Mr. Handel, on his playing on the organ," London, 1722; reprinted as "An Ode on the late celebrated Handel, on his playing on the organ," Cambridge, 1791.

Pratt, John, organist and composer, born at Cambridge, 1772 [1779]; son of Jonas Pratt, music-seller. He was chorister in King's College, Cambridge, and studied under Dr. Randall, whom he succeeded as organist of King's College, 1799. Organist of Cambridge University, 1800; organist of St. Peter's College, 1813. He died at Cambridge, March 9, 1855.

WORKS.—Collection of Anthems in score, selected from the works of Handel, Haydn, Mozart, Clari, Leo, and Carissimi, with organ or pianoforte accompaniment, 2 vols. [1825]. Selection of Ancient and Modern Psalm Tunes, arranged and adapted for two trebles, or tenors, and a bass, for the use of parish churches [1810]. Psalmodia Cantabrigiensis; a selection of ancient and modern psalm tunes . . for the use of the University church, 1805; also, 1817, with an appendix of later date. Four double Chants, and the Responses to the Commandments, as performed at the King's College, Cambridge, n.d.

Pratten, Robert Sidney, flute player and composer, born at Bristol, January 23, 1824. Performed when a boy at concerts in Bath, Bristol, etc. First flute in orchestra of Theatre Royal, Dublin; at Royal Italian Opera, London, 1846; Sacred Harmonic Society; Philharmonic Society, etc. He studied for a time in Germany. He died at Ramsgate, February 10, 1868.

WORKS.—Fantasias, arrangements, studies, solos, etc. for flute, in combination with other instruments. Complete Series of Exercises for the Siccama Flute. Complete Series of Scales and Exercises, carefully fingered for Pratten's Perfected Flute, n.d. Flute Tutors (one published by Boosey & Co., and another by Edwin Ashdown).

His wife, MADAM SIDNEY PRATTEN, is a well-known guitar-player, and writer for that instrument. She has issued Solos for the Guitar, a series of about 250 original and selected pieces; Numerous Divertimentos on original and selected themes; Guitar School, being complete Instructions for Modern Guitar Playing in the common key; Learning the Guitar Simplified . . Also a book of Instructions for the Gigliera (wood and straw instrument).

Prendergast, Arthur Hugh Dalrymple, composer and conductor, born in London,

PRENTICE.

June 28, 1833. Studied under James Turle. Conductor of Lombard Amateur Musical Society, and of the Bar Musical Society's Choir. Sometime Secretary of the Bach Choir. Has lectured to the College of Organists, etc.

WORKS.—The Second Advent, Sacred Cantata ; Festival Te Deum, Church Choir Association prize, 1882 ; Communion Service in C; Cantata and Deus in F, etc. *Anthems:* O Lord our Governour ; Show me Thy ways (male voices) ; O God, thou hast cast us out. Hymn tunes. Music to The Maske of Flowers (with Birch Reynardson), performed at Gray's Inn Hall, July, 1887, in celebration of the Queen's Jubilee. Madrigal, When as she smiles, Madrigal Society's prize and medal, 1889 ; Sweet western wind; Sunshine; Hark ! how the cheerful birds, Madrigal Society's prize, 1880, and other part-songs. For men's voices: When for the world's repose ; O mistress mine, madrigal ; Song of the Silent Land ; Imbuta ; The Robin ; The Pixies' welcome, madrigal ; In this fair vale, etc, Songs : A birdie's life ; A shady nook ; Sleep, wake, live; and others.

Prentice, Thomas Ridley, pianist and composer, born at Paslow Hall, Ongar, Essex, July 6, 1842. Studied at R.A.M. under G. A. and Walter Macfarren. Potter Exhibitioner, 1863, and elected Associate on leaving. In 1869 he began a series of Monthly Popular Concerts at Brixton, which he carried on for some years ; also gave occasional concerts at the Hanover Square Rooms, St. George's Hall, and played at the Crystal Palace. In 1872 he was appointed organist of Christ Church, Lee, but this, as well as concert work, ill-health compelled him to resign. He gave a set of twelve "Twopenny Concerts " in Kensington Town Hall, 1880-1. In 1880 he was appointed a professor at the Guildhall School of Music, and was Principal of the Beckenham School of Music, established in 1883. As a teacher he was most successful and esteemed. He died at Hampstead, July 15, 1895.

WORKS.—Linda, cantata, ladies' voices; The Mermaid's Invitation, and other trios for the same. Christmas ; Ye little birds, part-songs. Break forth into joy; I love the Lord, anthems. The God of love my Shepherd is ; Evensong; Echoes, and other songs. Gavottes; Elegie ; Reverie ; By the sea; Sunday musings, etc., for the pf. Editor of Six Cantatas by Carissimi. Author of The Musician, a guide for pianoforte students, in 6 grades, London, Sonnenschein, 1883-6. Hand Gymnastics, Novello's Primers, No. 36.

Prescot, Mrs. Cyril A., see LOWTHIAN, CAROLINE.

Prescott, Oliveria Louisa, composer and writer, born in London, September 3,

PRESTON.

1842. Studied under Lindsay Sloper, and then for seven years at R.A.M., under (Sir) G. A. Macfarren, Jewson, Folkes, and Ralph. A.R.A.M. Teacher of harmony at the Church of England High School for Girls, Upper Baker Street, London, 1879-93, and lecturer in harmony and composition, for about the same period, to the correspondence system in connection with Newnham College, Cambridge. Sometime musical amanuensis to Professor Sir G. A. Macfarren.

WORKS.—Psalm 13, for soprano solo, chorus and orchestra ; Psalm 126, for voices alone (sung in St. Paul's Cathedral.) Our conversation is in heaven; The righteous live for evermore, anthems. Lord Ullin's Daughter, chorus and orchestra. Ballad of Young John ; Douglas Raid ; Cryer ; Border ballad ; and other part-songs. The Fisherwife ; Queen of my heart ; songs. *Orchestral :* Two Symphonies, in B flat, and D minor ; Overture (R.A.M., 1876) ; Concert Finale, D minor ; Concert piece, Bright October ; Concert overtures : Tithonus; Golden Supper ; Œdipus and Antigone ; Woodland. Concerto in A, pf. and orchestra. Hero watching for Leander; Love and laughter ; for soprano solo and orchastra. Bohemian song, for 4 voices and strings. Quartets in A minor and C minor, strings ; in G, pf. and strings, etc. Author of Form or Design in Music : Part I., Instrumental ; Part II., Vocal, London, 1882. Enlarged edition, prepared with the assistance of Professor Macfarren, 1894. Contributions to *Musical World*, etc. Six Lectures about Music, and what it is made of, Church of England High School, Baker Street, 1893.

Preston, James M., organist and conductor, born at Gateshead-on-Tyne, July 14, 1860. At an early age he studied violin and pf. under his father, Stephen E. Preston, a musician of repute, and when thirteen was placed under Lindsay Sloper, in London. In 1875, he was appointed organist of St. Joseph's Roman Catholic Church, Gateshead, where he remained six years, diligently working at the organ. Entered the Guildhall School of Music in 1881, and studied under Dr. Stainer. In 1883, succeeded the late Mr. Robert Potts, as organist of St. Thomas', Newcastle-on-Tyne, and in 1888 was appointed to St. George's, Jesmond, a post he still holds. In 1891 he began to give organ recitals there, on Sunday evenings ; he has also played at St. George's Hall, Liverpool, and elsewhere, and ranks among the foremost organists of the day. He is also a pianist, and has been connected with the Newcastle Chamber Music Society for years. He is conductor of the Newcastle and Gateshead Choral Union, which has more than a local reputation, and has given many important concerts. Of his compositions, but few are yet published. A

PRICE.

Festival Chorus was performed in Newcastle Town Hall, October, 1895.

Price, Daniel, baritone vocalist, born at Dowlais, Glamorgan, 1863. Was one of the first fifty scholars of the R.C.M. when it opened in 1883. Studied singing under Albert Visetti; Counterpoint, under Dr. J. F. Bridge; and composition with Dr. Stanford. Distinguished himself, especially in the operatic performances given by the students. A.R.C.M., 1888, and in the same year appointed a member of the choir, Westminster Abbey. Is a professor of singing at R.C.M., and has appeared with success at concerts in London, Birmingham, and other places; and on the occasion of the Jubilee celebrations in 1887, had the honour of singing before Her Majesty the Queen, at Windsor. While at the R.C.M. he composed some pf. pieces, which were performed at the College concerts.

Price, Tom, composer, born at Rhymney, Monmouthshire, in 1857. Worked as a boy in the coal mines. Self-taught in music, and learned much by joining different Welsh choirs. Won a prize offered by Wrexham Festival Committee, 1886, for a part-song, "Hands all round" (Tennyson); other prizes in America, etc. He has composed a dramatic cantata, anthems, part-song, songs, etc.

Pridham, John, pianist and composer, born at Popsham, Devon, October 1, 1818. He studied at the R.A.M., and when still a young man, played frequently before the Queen and Prince Consort. He died at Taunton, in August, 1896. He wrote a "Method for the Piano," London, Brewer, n.d.; and issued an immense number of easy pieces for the pf. Composer also of a few songs and duets.

Pring, Jacob Cubitt, organist and composer, was born at Lewisham, near London, in 1771. Organist of St. Botolph, Aldgate, London. Mus. Bac., Oxon., 1797. He died in 1799.

WORKS.—First book of Glees, Canons, etc. [1790]; Eight Glees, Catches, etc., London [c. 1795]; Eight anthems, as performed in St. Paul's Cathedral, London [1792]; Magnificat, in two parts; Dying Christian to his soul, ode [1794]. Easy progressive lessons, with the fingering marked for young beginners on the pf. or harpsichord, London [1800]. Six progressive sonatinas for the harpsichord or pf. Songs, sonnets, etc.

Pring, Joseph, organist and composer, brother of above, born at Kensington, London, January 15, 1776. Organist of Bangor Cathedral, 1793. Mus. Bac. and Doc., Oxon., 1808. He died at Bangor, February 13, 1842.

WORKS.—Twenty Anthems, in score, for 1, 2, 3, 4, and 5 voices, London, 1805. Magnificats, and other church music.

Pring, Isaac, organist and composer,

PRINGLE.

brother of above, born at Kensington, London, in 1777. Assistant to Dr. Philip Hayes, at New College, Oxford, and his successor in 1797. Mus. Bac., Oxon., 1799. He died at Oxford, October 18, 1799. Composer of chants, anthems, etc.

Pringle, George Robert Grant, organist and conductor, born in London, May 26, 1833. Chorister, St. Paul's Cathedral, 1841-51, and pupil of John Goss and George Cooper. Went to Victoria. Australia, in 1858. Appointed organist and conductor of Melbourne Philharmonic Society. Founded and conducted the Musical Union, which brought forward many promising singers, and produced, for the first time in Australia, Mendelssohn's Psalm 42; Spohr's "God, Thou art Great"; Leslie's "Judith," and other works. As organist of St. Peter's, Melbourne, Pringle, in 1863, trained and introduced the first surpliced choir in the colonies. He died, January, 1873, when on a visit to Leipzig.

Pringle, Godfrey, composer, of Scotch descent on his father's side, his mother being Hungarian, was born November 30, 1867, while his parents were travelling on the Continent. Much of his early life was passed in Italy, and in 1882 he was at Bayreuth when "Parsifal" was produced, and had the happiness of personal acquaintance with Wagner. The influence of that time decided him to make music his profession, and he studied at the R.C.M. under Villiers Stanford, producing part of an Italian opera, "Messalina," in 1890, which he finished after leaving the College in 1891. His orchestral ballad, "Durand" (based on Uhland), was produced at the Crystal Palace, October 14, 1893; and a rhapsody, "Lo Zingaro," for baritone solo and orchestra, November 10, 1894. He has also written an orchestral suite, "Bella Milano," and is engaged on an English opera. His other works include a Romance, for violin and orchestra; Fantasia, 'cello and pf.; pieces for pf., songs, etc.

Pringle, John, musician, resided in Edinburgh at the end of last and beginning of present century. Published "A Collection of Reels, Strathspeys, and Jigs, with a Bass for the Violoncello or Pianoforte," Edinburgh, n.d.

Pringle, Lempriere, bass vocalist, born at Hobart, Tasmania, 1869. At the age of 18 he came to England, and was admitted a student at the R.C.M. He sang in the operatic performance given in July, 1889, and later in that year went to Frankfort and studied singing under Stockhausen, and harmony and counterpoint under Humperdinck. Returning to England in 1891, he was engaged by the directors of the Carl Rosa Company, and made his first appearance in the following autumn tour. His success was such that on the death of Aynsley Cook, in February, 1894, he was called upon to undertake the most important parts filled by that artist. His repertory is large, and embraces such widely different assumptions as that of *Caspar* in " Der Frieschutz " and the *Landgrave* in "Tannhäuser." Mr. Pringle is understood to be a clever composer, but he has not yet published anything.

Pringuer, Henry Thomas, composer and conductor, of present time. Privately educated in music, F.R.C.O., 1876 ; Mus. Bac., 1877 ; Mus. Doc., 1885, Oxford. Organist of St. Matthew's, Redhill, 1870 ; St. Mary's, Stoke Newington, 1881. Conductor of Insurance Musical Society ; and of Trinity College Choir, London. Has given organ recitals at the Bow and Bromley Institute, 1884, etc. Composer of Psalm 107 and Psalm 48, for soli, chorus, and orchestra ; a comedy opera, "Guinevere," 1890 ; pf. pieces, songs, etc.

Pritchard, Rev. Rowland Hugh, musician and minister, was born at Bala, about 1813. He was a minister, and acted as precentor at the annual Sasiwns y Bala. Died at Holywell, January 25, 1887, aged 74. Composer of Welsh hymn tunes, "Hyfrydol," "Elizabeth," "Hiraeth y Cristion," etc.

Pritchard, Thomas, surnamed TWM-BACH, celebrated Welsh harper of the time of Queen Elizabeth. He died at London in 1597, and is buried in St. Sepulchre's Church.

Probin. The name of a notable Birmingham family of horn players. MOSES PROBIN, born about 1782, was the first to acquire a reputation, though his father was a horn player before him. He took part in all the principal concerts in the Midlands, from Shrewsbury to Cheltenham, and was a virtuoso on the hand horn. With two of his sons he would, commencing at five in the morning, diligently practice trios for horns. He was a man of devout mind, and regular in attendance at church. On one occasion his rector, with whom he was very intimate, expressed a wish that he would give up horn-playing and earn an *honest* living. He died August 8, 1857, in his 75th year. His son, HENRY PROBIN, was born June 10, 1812. He became famous as a horn player, and to the last used the old hand horn, as he could never reconcile himself to the valve horn. He played in the Birmingham festival orchestra for a long time, including the "Elijah" year, 1846. He was the intimate friend and companion of Alfred Mellon, and during his conductorship played in the Theatre Royal band. He retired from the profession in 1879, and died June 30, 1885. His brother SAMUEL was also a horn player, but in no way remarkable. ALFRED PROBIN, son of Henry, was born April 29, 1852, and at the age of eight began his study of the instru-

ment. Mr. Stockley gave him his first opportunity, and when sixteen he was first horn in an opera company. His first festival engagement was at Nottingham in 1873, under Costa. He was first horn at the revived Chester Festival, 1879, and since then has been in the orchestras of the Three Choirs, and Birmingham Festivals, and the principal concerts in the country. As a solo player he has been heard in chamber concerts in Birmingham, and he played Mozart's Third Concerto for horn at Leicester, February, 1887. A young son is preparing to continue the artistic career of the family.

Proudman, Joseph, conductor and teacher of singing, born in London, November 10, 1833. He sang in choirs as a boy ; was a member of the Sacred Harmonic Society in 1857 ; Conductor of the City Choral Union, 1862, and a year later applied himself to the Tonic Sol-fa method. He conducted concerts at the Crystal Palace from 1864, and won a prize at Paris in 1867. Some thousands of singers passed under his hands. For years he had acted as precentor at several churches, and he was teacher of singing to the children in Dr. Barnardo's Homes for more than twenty years, and was an indefatigable worker in the cause of popular music. He published Musical Lectures and Sketches, 1869 ; and Musical Jottings, 1872 ; and was a specialist on the staff of the *Musical Herald*. He died in London, April 21, 1891. J. FRANK PROUDMAN, his son, conductor, and sometime organist of St. Michael's, Stoke Newington, took up the work of his father in 1891, and made a reputation as a conductor and teacher. Delicate health decided him to leave England for South Africa, and in February, 1897, he sailed for the Cape, having obtained an appointment at Maritzburg.

Prout, Ebenezer, composer and didactic writer, born at Oundle, Northamptonshire, March 1, 1835. The son of a Congregational Minister, he was intended for another profession than music ; and after leaving Denmark Hill Grammar School he was engaged as a teacher in private schools in London, and Leatherhead, and when nineteen graduated B.A., London University. Musical from childhood, he had a few pianoforte lessons when a boy, and afterwards a course from Charles Salaman ; for the rest he is self-educated. It was in 1859 that he gave himself up entirely to music, and his first pupil was John Locke Gray (*q.v.*). After acting as organist at St. Thomas's Square Chapel, Hackney, and other places, he accepted the appointment at Union Chapel, Islington, which he held for 12 years, 1861-73. During the Royal Wedding Musical Fetes at the Crystal Palace, March, 1863, he on one occasion gave an organ performance in lieu of

James Coward. In 1861 he was appointed a professor of the pf. at the Crystal Palace School of Art, resigning in 1885; professor of harmony and composition at the National Training School for Music from its opening in 1876; succeeded to Sir Arthur Sullivan's class at R.A.M., 1879; and in 1884 professor of pf. at Guildhall School of Music. Conductor of Hackney Choral Association, 1876-90, during which time a high reputation was gained by the Society, and many important works produced, some for the first time in England. As a composer he was brought into notice by gaining the first prize of the Society of British Musicians in 1862, and again in 1865; and the performance of his first Organ Concerto by (Sir) John Stainer at the Crystal Palace, 1872, increased his reputation. His literary career has been equally striking. He was editor of the *Monthly Musical Record*, 1871-4; musical critic of the *Academy*, 1874-9; and of the *Athenæum*, 1879-89. On retiring from the last, he devoted himself to writing those educational works which will rank among the most masterly and comprehensive examples English musical literature can boast of. He has lectured in London and the provinces; contributed valuable papers to the Musical Association, the Conferences of the Incorporated Society of Musicians, Grove's Dictionary of Music, *Monthly Musical Record*, etc.; and has conducted performances of his works at the Crystal Palace, Birmingham and Bristol Festivals, and elsewhere. In 1894 he was elected Professor of Music in Dublin University, the degree of Mus. Doc., *honoris causâ*, being conferred upon him at the beginning of 1895, and later in the same year he was honoured by being the first to receive the degree of Mus. Doc. from the University of Edinburgh.

WORKS.—*Choral*: Magnificat in C, op. 7, for soli, chorus, and orchestra, composed 1873, produced. Crystal Palace, January 15, 1876; Chorus, Hail to the Chief, op. 10, composed for re-opening of Alexandra Palace, 1877; Cantata, Hereward, op. 12, Hackney Choral Association. 1878; Cantata, Alfred, op. 16, the same, May 1, 1882; Ode, Freedom, op. 20, the same, April 20, 1885; Psalm 100, op. 23, for soprano solo, chorus, and orchestra, 1886; Red Cross Knight, Cantata, op. 24, composed for the Jubilee of the Huddersfield Choral Society, produced October 7, 1887; Damon and Phintias (male voices), op. 25, Oxford, May 31, 1889; Queen Aimée (female voices), op. 21, 1885; Psalm 126, for soli, chorus, and orchestra, St. Paul's Cathedral, May 28. 1891; Church services and anthems, We give Thee thanks (8 voices), and others. Scena, contralto voice and orchestra, Norwich, 1887. *Orchestral*: Symphony No. 1, in C, Crystal Palace, February 28, 1874; No. 2, in G minor,

the same, December, 1877; No. 3, in F, op. 23, Birmingham Festival, 1885; No. 4, in D, Oxford, June, 1886; Minuet and Trio, St. James's Hall, March 5, 1878. Overtures: Twelfth Night, Bristol, February 14, 1881; Rokeby, Crystal Palace, March 23, 1889; Suite de Ballet, op. 28, 1891. Organ Concerto in E minor, Crystal Palace (Stainer), October 19, 1872; in E flat, Bristol (Riseley), April 6, 1885. Quartets: Op. 1, strings (prize), 1862; Op. 3, pf. and strings (prize), 1865; Op. 15, in B flat, strings; Op. 18, in F, pf. and strings. Quintet, Op. 3, pf. and strings. Sonata in D, op. 26, pf. and clarinet; Sonata, op. 4, organ; Duo Concertante, op. 6, pf. and harmonium. Organ arrangements, 44 Nos. Pf. pieces. Editor, with J. Curwen, of the Harmonium and Organ Book. Author of a primer on Instrumentation, Novello, 1876; Harmony, its Theory and Practice (with key, additional exercises and key) nine editions to 1896; Counterpoint, Strict and Free (with additional exercises), 5 editions; Double Counterpoint and Canon, 2 editions; Fugue, 3 editions; Fugal Analysis, 2 editions; Musical Form, 2 editions; and Applied Forms, 2 editions, all published by Augener. It is understood that Professor Prout has two comic operas in MS. His son, LOUIS BEETHOVEN PROUT, born in London, September 14, 1864, is a pianist and teacher. In 1888 he was appointed professor of harmony at the Crystal Palace School. He has set Psalm 93 for voices and organ, and is author of a work on Harmonic Analysis, London, Augener, and a pamphlet, Time, Rhythm, and Expression, London, Cocks.

Prys, Edmund, clergyman and musician, who was born in 1541. He was educated at Cambridge and became rector of Festiniog in 1572, and canon of St. Asaph's in 1602. He died in 1624. Editor of "Llyfr y Psalmau wedi eu cyfiethu, ai cyfansodi ar fesur cerdd yn gymraeg," 16 1, a collection of psalms in Welsh.

Pullen, H. W., author of "Our Choral Services," London, 1865; and "The real work of a Cathedral," London, 1869.

Purcell, Daniel, organist and composer, born in London, 1660. Younger son of Henry Purcell, the elder. He was the organist of Magdalen College, Oxford, 1688-95. Settled in London, 1695. Composer for various theatres. Organist of St. Andrew's Church, Holborn, 1713-17. He died at London, December 12, 17 8.

WORKS.—*Music to Dramas*: Love's Last Shift (Cibber), 1696; Indian Queen, 1696; Brutus of Alba, or Augusta's Triumph, 1697; Cynthia and Endymion (D'Urfey), 1697; Phaeton, or, the Fatal Divorce, 1698; The Island Princess (Motteaux), with Clark and Leveridge, 1699; The Grove, or Love's

PURCELL.

Paradise, 1700; The Unhappy Penitent, 1701; The Inconstant (Farquhar), 1702; The Judgement of Paris, a Pastoral (Congreve). [This masque gained the third prize in competition with Weldon, Eccles, etc.], 1700. Odes, numerous; iucluding several for "St. Cecilia's Day," by Addison and others; Songs in contemporary collections; the Psalms, set full for the organ or harpsichord, as they are plaid in churches and chappels in the maner given out; as also with their interludes in great variety, London, n.d.; Instrumental music, church music, etc.

Purcell, Edward, organist, youngest son of Henry Purcell the younger, was born at London, in 1689. Organist of St. Clement, Eastcheap, London; and of St. Margaret's, Westminster, 1726. He died at London, in 1740.

Purcell, Henry, the elder, musician, father of the celebrated Henry Purcell of musical history, was born in the first half of the 17th century. He was a Gentleman of the Chapel Royal, in 1660, and Master of the Choristers in Westminster Abbey. Member of Royal Band of Music, 1663. He died at London, August 11, 1664. Composed a three-part song in Playford's Musical Companion, 1667, etc.

Purcell, Henry, organist and composer, was born in St. Ann's Lane, Old Pye Street, Westminster, London, in 1658. Second son of Henry Purcell, the elder. He studied as a chorister in the Chapel Royal, under Cooke and Humphrey, 1664, and under Blow. Copyist in Westminster Abbey, 1676-78; Organist of Westminster Abbey, 1680. Organist of Chapel Royal, 1682. Composer in Ordinary to the King, 1683. He died at Westminster, London, November 21, 1695, and is buried in Westminster Abbey. In 1895 various commemorative concerts, etc., were given in London on the centenary of his death.

WORKS.—*Dramatic music :* Epsom Wells (Shadwell), 1676; Aurenge-Zebe (Dryden), 1676; The Libertine (Shadwell), 1676; Abdelazor (Behn), 1677; Timon of Athens (Shakspere), 1678; The virtuous wife (D'Urfey), 1680; Theodosius (Lee), 1680; Dido and Æneas (Tate), 1680 [published by the Musical Antiquarian Society, 1840]; Circe, 1685; Tyrannic love (Dryden), 1686; A fool's preferment (D'Urfey), 1688; The Tempest (Shakspere), 1690; Dioclesian, 1690; Massacre of Paris (Lee), 1690; Amphitryon, 1690; Distressed innocence (Settle), 1691; King Arthur (Dryden), 1691 [published by the Musical Antiquarian Society, 1843]; The Gordian knot untyed, 1691; Sir Anthony Low (Southerne), 1691; The fairy queen (Shakspere's Midsummer Night's Dream), 1692; The wife's excuse (Southerne), 1692; The Indian queen (Dryden), 1692; The Indian Emperour (Dry-

PURCELL.

den), 1692; Œdipus, 1692; Cleomenes, 1692; The marriage-hater match'd (D'Urfey), 1692; The old bachelor (Congreve), 1693; The Richmond heiress (D'Urfey), 1693; The maid's last prayer (Southerne), 1693; Henry the Second (Bancroft), 1693: Don Quixote (D'Urfey), 1694-95; The married beau (Crowne), 1694; The Double dealer (Congreve), 1694; The fatal marriage (Southerne), 1694; Love triumphant (Dryden), 1694; The Canterbury guests (Ravenscroft), 1695; The mock marriage (Scott), 1695; The rival sisters (Gould), 1695; Oroonoko (Southerne), 1695; The knight of Malta (Beaumont and Fletcher), 1695; Bonduca (Beaumont and Fletcher), 1695. *Odes and large Vocal Works :* Elegy on death of Matthew Locke, 1677; A Welcome Song for His Royal Highness' return from Scotland, 1680; A song to welcome His Majesty home from Windsor, 1680; Swifter, Isis, swifter flow (ode), 1681; Ode for the King on his return from Newmarket, 1682; Three odes for St. Cecilia's Day, 1683; From Hardy climes and dangerous toils of War, ode on marriage of Prince George of Denmark with Princess Anne, 1683; Welcome to all the Pleasures, ode, published, 1684; Why are all the Muses mute? ode for James I.; Ye tuneful Muses, ode, 1686; Sound the trumpet, beat the drum, ode, 1687; Celestial Music, 1689; The Yorkshire feast song, D'Urfery, 1689 [reprinted by the Purcell Society, edited by W. H. Cummings, 1878]; Arise, my Muse, ode for the Queen's birthday, 1689; Sound the trumpet, ode, 1689; Welcome, glorious morn, Birthday ode, 1691; Love's Goddess sure was blind, ode, 1692; Hail! great Cecilia, ode, 1692; Celebrate this festival, 1693; Come, come, ye sons of art, ode, 1694; Who can from joy refrain, ode, 1695. *Church Music :* Purcell's Sacred Music, edited by Vincent Novello, London, 6 vols. [1829-32], contains most of the master's church music, with portrait and biography, including the Te Deum and Jubilate in D (1694). Other collections in which his church music will be found are Boyce's; Tudway's; Smith's Harmonica Sacra; Page's Harmonia Sacra; and in nearly every other important general selection. The names of the anthems in current use in our churches and cathedrals will be found in Novello's catalogue of sacred music. *Instrumental music :* Three sonatas, for two violins, violoncello, and basso-continuo, London, 4 vols., 1683. Lessons for the harpsichord or spinnet, London, 1696. Ten sonatas, in four parts, 1st and 2nd violins, bassus and organ, London, 4 vols., 1697. Collection of Ayres compos'd for the Theatre, and on other occasions, London, 1697. Orpheus Britannicus: a collection of the choicest songs, for 1, 2, and 3 voices, with such Symphonies for violins or flutes as were by

PURCELL.

him designed for any of them, and a thorough-bass to each song figured for the organ, harpsichord, or theorbo-lute..book I., London, 1698, with portrait engraved by White. Book II., 1702; second edition (enlarged), 2 vols., 1706-1711, third edition, 1721. The Catch Club, or Merry Companion. By Purcell, Blow, etc., 2 books, n.d. "The art of Descant," contributed to the 10th edition of Playford's "Introduction to the skill of Musick," 1683. *Selections from Purcell's works:* The beauties of Purcell: a selection of the favourite songs, duets, trios and choruses from his different works, arranged with pf. accompaniments by Dr. John Clarke, 2 vols., n.d. Beauties of Purcell..edited by Joseph Corfe, n.d. The words of Henry Purcell's Vocal Music, n.d. (privately printed). A selection of his Harpsichord pieces has been edited by Herr Ernst Pauer (Augener, London).

Purcell, Thomas, composer, uncle of preceding, was born in the first half of the 17th century. He was a gentleman of the Chapel Royal in 1660, and Lay-vicar and copyist, Westminster Abbey, 1661. Composer in ordinary to the King, with Humphrey, in 1662; and master of the royal band of music (also with Humphrey), 1672. He died at London, July 31, 1682. He composed some chants, some of which are now in common use.

Purchas, Arthur Guyon, musician and composer, author of "First Lessons for Singing Classes," London, 1849. Compiler of "The New Zealand Hymnal . . . with tunes," London, 1871.

Purday, Charles Henry, composer and writer, born at Folkestone, January 11, 1799. He was a publisher of music in London, and lecturer on musical topics in London and the English provinces, and at one time a vocalist of some repute. Chiefly celebrated as a reformer of the laws relating to musical copyright. He acted for some years as conductor of Psalmody to the Scotch Church, in Crown Court, Covent Garden, London. He died at London, April 23, 1885. WORKS.—The Sacred Musical Offering, London, 1833. Copyright, a sketch of its rise and progress . . . , London, 1877; Crown Court Psalmody, one hundred Psalm tunes and chants . . . , 1854; Church and Home Tune Book . . . , London [1857]. Songs of Peace and Joy, 1879 (F. R. Havergal). Writer and composer of a considerable number of songs— Down among the barley, Home of my fathers, Maid of Llanwellyn, Old Yew tree, Real ould Irish Gintleman, etc. Joint editor with John Thomas of a large volume of Welsh airs. Trios for female voices; two volumes of children's songs, etc. He composed "Sandon," "Notting Hill," and other well-known hymns; Elementary exercises in the art of Singing, London [1851].

PYNE.

Purdie, Robert, Scots musician, who flourished in Edinburgh as a music-seller early in the present century. He issued "A Complete Repository of Strathspeys, reels, jigs, favourite airs and waltzes for the flute or violin," Edinburgh, n.d. The firm existed in Edinburgh till about 1887.

Purkis, John, organist and composer, born, London, 1781; died there in 1849. When twelve months old he became blind. He was a performer on the apollonicon and an organist. He composed some organ music. Fantasias for pf. on popular airs, marches, etc. *Songs:* Magpie and the maid, Pale the moonbeam shone, The Reprieve, Song for British Volunteers [1805].

Pye, Kellow John, pianist and composer, born at Exeter, February 9, 1812. Entered R.A.M. 1823, receiving from Cipriani Potter the first pianoforte lesson given there. Studied composition under Dr. Crotch. Won the Gresham Prize, 1832, with his anthem for five voices, "Turn Thee again, O Lord." Graduated Mus. Bac., Oxford, 1842; elected F.R.A.M. Resided in Exeter after leaving the R.A.M. in 1829; but later entered into business in London, where he also connected himself with the management of the R.A.M., and other institutions. He is now living in retirement at Exmouth. His compositions include a five-part anthem (Degree Exercise), O Lord, Thou art my God; Three Short Full Anthems; Children of Fancy, and other glees, songs, and pf. pieces. His latest publications were a Melody and Farewell, for clarinet and pf., 1889.

Pyne, James Kendrick, organist and composer, born in London, August 21, 1810. His father, JAMES KENDRICK PYNE—born, 1785; died, 1857—was a noted tenor singer in his day. Pyne was one of the early pupils of the Royal Academy of Music, studying under Dr. Crotch. In 1828 he was appointed organist of St. Mark's, Clerkenwell; and in 1839 was chosen organist of Bath Abbey, an office he held for half-a-century. He was awarded the Gresham Prize in 1840, and his compositions included Church Services, anthems, part-songs, etc. In February, 1890, he was publicly presented with testimonials from his professional friends, and from the Abbey congregation and citizens of Bath, in commemoration of his Jubilee as organist. He died while on a visit to his son, J. K. Pyne (notice below), March 2, 1893. His sister, LOUISA AUBERT PYNE (MRS. WILLMORE), was organist at St John's District Church, in the parish of St. Pancras, *circa* 1857. She composed songs and pf. pieces.

Pyne, James Kendrick, organist and composer, son of the preceding, born at Bath, February 5, 1852. Studied under his father and Dr. S. S. Wesley. Was organist of All

PYNE.

Saints', Bath, when eleven ; and assistant to Dr. Wesley at Winchester and Gloucester Cathedrals. After holding appointments at Cheltenham and other places, he was made organist of Chichester Cathedral, in 1874 ; and in 1875, he went to America, where he remained about a year. He was then appointed to Manchester Cathedral, and later, organist of the Town Hall. Professor of Manchester Royal College of Music, 1893. F.R.A M. He has given recitals in all parts of the Kingdom, and is one of the most brilliant organ players of the day. His lectures on music, and on antique musical instruments, of which he has a fine collection, have been of educational value. He has also contributed occasional articles to the musical press. He is the composer of a Festival Communion Service, with orchestra; Morning and Evening Services ; songs ; pf. pieces ; etc. MINTON PYNE, his brother, was sometime assistant-organist at Manchester Cathedral, and, in 1881, appointed to St. Mark's, Philadelphia, U.S.A. He also was a pupil of Dr. S. S. Wesley. His recitals in America gained him a high reputation. In 1888, he was in England, and gave a recital at Bath Abbey Church. Miss ZOE PYNE, a sister, is a violinist, and studied at R.C.M. She has given successful concerts at Bath (1888), and London, etc.

Pyne, Louisa Fanny, or BODDA, soprano vocalist, was born on August 27, 1832, daughter of George Pyne (1790-1877), an alto singer. Studied under Sir George Smart. First appeared in public, with her sister (Mrs. F. H. Standing), 1842. Sang in Paris, 1847. Appeared at Boulogne in "La Sonnambula," 1849. Début on London stage as Zerlina in "Don Juan," October, 1849 Sang afterwards at the principal theatres and concerts in London. Appeared in America, with her sister and Wm. Harrison, 1854-56. Established, with Wm. Harrison, the "Harrison-Pyne" English opera company, which performed with much success in Britain, and produced a number of famous English operas, 1856-62. Married Frank Bodda, a baritone vocalist, 1868, and retired from the stage. Teacher of singing in London. Her voice was a clear soprano of great compass, and possessed of much expressive power. She excelled in such works as Wallace's "Maritana" and "Lurline"; Balfe's "Bohemian Girl" and "Rose of Castile " ; and it is due to her no less than to Harrison, that the English opera flourished so successfully under their management. In 1896, she received an allowance from the Civil List. Her husband, FRANK BODDA, born about 1823, was a pupil of the R.A.M. Sang in opera in London and Boulogne, 1848-9; and was also heard in the concert-room. He died March 14, 1892, aged 69.

RADIGER.

Quarles, Charles, organist and composer of the early part of the 18th century. He was organist of Trinity College, Cambridge, and in 1698 he graduated Mus. Bac., Cambridge. In 1722 he was made organist of York Minster. He died at York, in 1727. He composed lessons for the harpsichord, etc.

Quatremayne, Frank, or SMILES, bass vocalist, born at Devonport, November 19, 1848. Studied pianoforte and theory under Charles Noble ; and singing, first with the late H. C. Deacon, then with Campana and Caravoglia. After singing in public for about three years, from 1880, he went to Milan, and studied under Antonio Sangiovanni. Since then he has sung at the principal concerts in London and the provinces, devoting himself, the last few years, chiefly to teaching, and numbers among his pupils several successful singers of the day. He is the author of a treatise, "Correct voice production" (Weekes), etc. His father is William Smiles, C.B., and he is nephew of Samuel Smiles, LL.D., author of "Self-Help," etc.

Quin, Francis Stainstreet, organist of Monkstown Church, Dublin. Was a prominent Freemason, having risen to the 32nd degree. He died, June 14, 1882, aged 54.

Quinton, Mrs. H. A., see ROSSE, JEANIE.

Radcliff, John, flutist, born in Liverpool. Studied under S. Percival, Liverpool, and at R.A.M., of which institution he is a Fellow. Became principal flutist in the orchestra of the Royal Italian Opera, after the death of Pratten ; also in the orchestras of the Three Choirs Festivals ; Leeds Festivals, 1874, 1880, and 1883 ; Handel Festivals, 1868, etc Lectured on the Flute, Ancient and Modern, at the London Institution, 1882. Toured in Australia, 1883-4, and was presented by the Melbourne Liedertafel with their Golden Lyre, only conferred on artists of the highest distinction. Re-appeared at the Promenade Concerts, London, in 1886; and began a concert-lecture entertainment, entitled "From Pan to Pinafore," in 1888. In 1896-7 he was on tour in South Africa with Madame Fanny Moody's party. His wife is the esteemed vocalist known as Madame PAULINE RITA, who has appeared at the London and Provincial concerts.

Radiger, Anton, composer and organist, born at Chatham in 1749, of German parents. He died in 1817. Composer of a number of psalm tunes, such as "Praise," "Compassion," "Denton's Green," etc. "Four setts of new Psalm and Hymn Tunes in 3 and 4 parts," London, n.d. Four new Hymn Tunes, London [1810]. Three duetts for 2 violins, op. 4 [1796]. Two favourite sonatas for pf. or harpsichord, op. 5. Miscellaneous music for pf., songs, etc.

RADNOR.

Radnor, Countess of, formerly Viscountess Folkestone, amateur musician. Assisted the establishment of the R.C.M., by organizing concerts with an orchestra of ladies. One, given at Stafford House, under her conductorship, June 29, 1882, realizing more than £850 towards the funds of the College. She has conducted concerts in the country, at St. James' Hall, etc., from that time onwards; also appeared as vocalist at the People's Entertainment Society's Concerts, etc. Some songs of hers have been published, and she is the musical editor of "An Order of Service for Children," Novello.

Rafftor, Catherine, see CLIVE, CATHERINE.

Rainforth, Elizabeth, soprano vocalist, born November 23, 1814. She studied under T. Cooke, and George Perry. Appeared in Arne's "Artaxerxes," at St. James's Theatre, 1836. Afterwards she studied under Crivelli, and sang at the Philharmonic Concerts, Concert of Ancient Music, provincial concerts, etc. She was the original Arline in Balfe's "Bohemian Girl," 1843, and sang in dramatic pieces in Dublin, etc. She resided in Edinburgh, 1852-56. Retired, and lived as a teacher at Old Windsor, from about 1858. After 1871, resided at Bristol. She died at Redland, Bristol, September 22, 1877.

Ralph, Francis, violinist, was born in 1847. He studied at the R.A.M., and was a professor of the violin there. He gave many good and interesting chamber concerts, in which, latterly, he was assisted by his wife, KATE ROBERTS, a pianist. He died at London, September 8, 1887. His wife, daughter of Ellis Roberts (q.v.), was born in London, and studied at the London Academy of Music, where she was presented with a Scholarship by Madame Schumann. Played at a National Eisteddfod when sixteen, and received the bardic name of *Morfida*. Appeared with success at the New Philharmonic, Crystal Palace, and other concerts, and has continued to give chamber concerts at the Queen's Hall, etc. Her compositions are numerous, but only a few pieces for violin and pf. have been published.

Ramage, Adam, music teacher and compiler, was born at Edinburgh, October 10, 1788. He was precentor of St. Andrew's Parish Church, Edinburgh, from 1838, and in 1846 he became singing-master at Heriot's Hospital Schools. He died in Edinburgh, April 5, 1863. He edited "The Sacred Harmony of St. Andrew's Church, Edinburgh, in four vocal parts, with accompaniment for the organ or pianoforte," Edinburgh, 1843.

Ramsay, Dugald Carmichael, musician, who was born at Rothesay in 1818, and died at Glasgow, August 12, 1891. He was author of "Four Diagrams illustrative of

RANSFORD.

intervals, scales, and chords." Glasgow, 1860.

Ramsay, Edward Bannerman Burnett, Scottish Episcopal clergyman and writer, born at Aberdeen, January 31, 1793. Dean of Diocese of Edinburgh, 1846. He died at Edinburgh, December 27, 1872. Author of "Two Lectures on the Genius of Handel, and the distinctive character of his sacred compositions," Edinburgh, 1862; "Proposals for providing a peal of bells for Edinburgh," 1863; "The Use of Organs in Christian Worship," Edinburgh, 1865, etc. Ramsay is best known by his "Reminiscences of Scottish life and character," an interesting and valuable collection of anecdotes.

Ramsay, James, musician, born at Kilwinning, in 1812, died September 10, 1888. He composed tunes in the "Universal Tune Book," songs, etc.

Ramsey, Robert, organist and composer, of latter part of the 16th and beginning of 17th centuries. He graduated Mus. Bac., Cambridge, in 1616, and was organist of Trinity College. He composed a Service in F, and various anthems.

Randall, John, organist and composer, was born in 1715. Chorister in Chapel Royal under B. Gates. Mus. Bac., Cantab., 1744. Organist of Trinity College, St. John's College, King's College, 1775, and Pembroke Hall, Cambridge. Professor of Music Cambridge University, in succession to M. Greene, 1755. Mus. Doc., Cantab., 1756. He died at Cambridge, March 18, 1799, aged 83. Composer of odes, anthems, psalms, and chants, and a "Collection of Psalm and Hymn Tunes, some of which are new, others by permission of the authors." Cambridge, 1794. *Songs:* Happy Swain, Hopeless Love, Shepherd's Wedding.

Randall, Richard, tenor vocalist, was born on September 1, 1736. He studied under B. Gates, and sang principally in the works of Handel. He died on April 15, 1828.

Randles, Elizabeth, pianist, born at Wrexham, August 1, 1800. Known as the "little Cambrian prodigy." Gave very early indications of a talent for music, which was encouraged by her father [1760-1823], a blind harper and organist in Wrexham. She studied under John Parry, and appeared in London and the English provinces. She was a teacher for a time in Liverpool, and died in 1829.

Ransford, Edwin, baritone vocalist and composer, born at Bourton-on-the-Water, Gloucester, March 13, 1805. He sang in London theatres in opera, and also as a concert vocalist. Latterly he engaged in music publishing. He died at London, July 11, 1876. Composer of a number of ballads, many of which were issued under the

RATCLIFFE.

pseudonym of "Aquila." Among them may be named—I eautiful Sea, Friar Tuck's chaunt, Harvest Home, Oak and the Ivy, Winter Night, etc. ; Gipsy life and character [1845], a collection of songs written in conjunction with Glover. His son, WILLIAM EDWIN, was also a publisher, pianist, and tenor singer, who composed some vocal music. He died at London, September 21, 1890, aged 64.

Ratcliffe, James, composer, born in 1751. He was a lay-vicar in Durham Cathedral, and died in 1818. Composer of church music, including anthems, psalms, and chants.

Ravenscroft, John, violinist and composer, was one of the Waits of the Tower Hamlets, and a violinist in Goodman's Fields Theatre. He died in 1745. He published a collection of hornpipes, also sonatas for stringed instruments ; also songs, such as Foolish woman, fly men's charms [1740], etc.

Ravenscroft, Thomas, composer and editor, was born in 1592 [1582]. He became a chorister in St. Paul's Cathedral, London, under Edward Pearce. Mus. Bac., Cantab., 1607. He died at London in 1635.

WORKS.—Pammelia, Musicke's Miscellanie, or Mixed varietie of pleasant Roudelayes and delightful Catches of 3, 4, 5, 6, 7, 8, 9, 10 parts in one. London, 1609. 2nd edition, 1618. Deuteromelia: or the Second part of Musick s Melodie, or melodious Musicke of pleasant Roundelais, K. H. mirth, or Freemen's Songs, and such delightful Catches. London, 1609. Melismata; musical Phansies, fitting the Court, Citie, and Country humours, to three, four, and five voyces. London, 1611. The Whole Booke of the Psalmes, with Hymnes Evangelicall and Songs Spiritual, composed into 4 parts by sundry authors, to such severall tunes as have been and are usually sung in England, Scotland, Wales, Germany, Italy, France, and the Netherlands. London, 1621. 2nd edition, 1633. Selections from the works of Thomas Ravenscroft, a musical composer in the time of King James I. (Roxburghe Club). London, n.d. A briefe Discourse of the True but neglected use of Charact'ring the Degrees by their Perfection, Imperfection, and Diminution in Mensurable Musicke, against the common practise and custome of these times. London, 1614.

Ravenscroft is best known by his "Booke of Psalmes," a work of much importance, containing contributions by Tallis, Dowland, Morley, Farnaby, Tomkins, Pearson, Parsons, Hooper, Kirbye, Allison, Farmer, Bennet, Milton, Cranford, Harrison, and the editor. It has been drawn upon by nearly every succeeding compiler of psalmody, and is now a somewhat rare work. It is worthy of notice that his "Pammelia" is the earliest collection of rounds and canons published in Britain.

Rawlings, Thomas, violinist, born about

RAYMOND.

1703. He studied under Pepusch, and performed at Handel's oratorios when they were originally produced. Organist of Chelsea Hospital, 1753. He died in 1767.

Rawlings, Robert, violinist, son of above, was born in London, in 1742. He studied under his father and Barsanti. Organist of Chelsea College, 1759. Musical page to the Duke of York, till 1767. Member of private band of George III. He died in 1814.

Rawlings, Thomas A., composer and violinist, son of Robert, above-noted, was born at London, in 1775. He studied under R. Rawlings and Dittenhofer, and became a violinist at the Opera, the Ancient, Vocal, and Professional Concerts, etc. Teacher in London. He died about middle of present century.

WORKS.—Concerti di Camera, for pf., flute, violins, viola, and 'cello. *Instrumental :* Three sonatas for harpsichord and violin, op. 1 [1793] ; Six new waltzes for pf., op. 2 [1794] ; Duet for harp and pf. ; and a large number of divertimentos, marches, arrangements, etc. *Songs :* Bee's wing; Evergreen leaf ; Hither, love, hither ; Home of youth ; Lila's a lady ; O 'twas sad ; Oh come to me ; Oh what a pity ; Sabbath bells ; Strike the guitar ; Weep not, thou lovely one ; When spring time was gay. Also in collected form, " Selection of Foreign Melodies " [1825], and " Songs to Rosa " [1826], with endless contributions to the musical annuals. Rawlings is usually identified with the well-known song, " Isle of Beauty," which, however, was only arranged, not composed, by him, but a Major C. S. Whitmore (q.v.) [1830].

Rawlins, Rev. John, clergyman, was rector of Leigh. Author of " The Power of Musick, and the particular influence of Church Musick: a sermon preached in the Cathedral Church of Worcester . ," 1773.

Rayleigh, Lord, John William Strutt, D.C.L., LL.D., F.R.S., Third Baron, born November 12, 1842, and succeeded to the title on the death of his father in 1873. Educated at Trinity College, Cambridge. Senior Wrangler, 1865. Author of a work on " The Theory of Sound," 2 vols. Second edition, 1896. Papers read before the Musical Association, etc.

Raymond, Fanny, Mrs. RAYMOND-RITTER, English poetess and musician, who married Frederick Louis Ritter (born 1834 ; died 1891). French-American author and musician. She has written " Woman as a musician, an art historical study," London, 1877 ; " Some Famous Songs, an art historical sketch," London, 1878 ; " Songs and Ballads," New York, 1888, etc. Translator of Ehlert's Letters on Music to a Lady, 1877, and Schumann's Music and Musicians, 1877-80, 2 vols. According to a statement on page 49 of her " Songs and Ballads," she is a native of

England, having been born " By Avon water and Arden wood."

Rea, William, organist, conductor, and composer, born in London, March 25, 1827. Articled pupil of Josiah Pittman, and later studied pf. under Sterndale Bennett, and in 1849 for a short time was at Leipzig and Prague, studying under Moscheles, Richter, and Dreyschock. Deputised as organist for Pittman ; was appointed to Christ Church, Watling Street, 1843 ; St. Andrew's Undershaft to 1858, when he went to St. Michael's, Stockwell. Played at concerts of the Society of British Musicians ; gave chamber concerts ; acted as accompanist for the Harmonic Union ; established and conducted the Polhymnia Choir of Men's Voices, 1856, and was brought into contact with Mendelssohn and other eminent composers. In 1860 he was appointed organist to the Corporation of Newcastle-on-Tyne. His church appointments were at St. Thomas's, St. Andrew's, St. Mary's, North Shields, 1864-78 ; and St. Hilda's, South Shelas, to present time. He has been a hard worker for musical culture in the North ; besides giving his recitals, he formed several societies, giving many important concerts, and introducing great works to the locality. His orchestral concerts, started in 1867, were carried on for nine years. He still conducts the Newcastle Amateur Vocal Society. His Corporation appointment he resigned in 1888. He was elected an Hon. Fellow of the College of Organists, and in 1886 the honorary degree of Mus. Doc. was conferred upon him by the University of Durham. His compositions include " Sing, O daughter of Zion," " O, give thanks," and other anthems ; a Jubilee Ode, composed for the Newcastle Exhibition, 1887 ; various songs, and pieces for organ and pf. EMMA MARY REA, his wife, was a daughter of W. S. B. Woolhouse (q.v.), and an accomplished pianist, L.R.A.M. and A.R.C.M. She was closely identified with the musical life of Newcastle for over thirty years. She died suddenly, of apoplexy, May 6, 1893.

Read, Charles John, organist and composer. Compiled " Parochial Psalmist : a manual of psalm and hymn tunes for congregational singing, for four voices," Salisbury, 1854 ; " The Te Deum, the Jubilate, etc., of the Catholic Church, performed at Stratford and at Hanover Chapel, Regent Street . . ." London, 1855 ; songs, pf. music, etc.

Read, Frederick John, organist and composer, born at Faversham, Kent. Studied under Drs. Sloman, C. W. Corfe, and J. F. Bridge. Appointed organist of Christ Church, Reading, 1876, where he remained ten years, during which time he founded the Reading Orpheus Society (1882), and gave concerts.

Graduated Mus. Bac., 1876 ; Mus. Doc., 1891, Oxford. In 1887 he took up his duties as organist of Chichester Cathedral, where he is still in office. Conductor of Chichester Musical Society.

WORKS.—*Cantatas :* Sigurd, men's voices, produced Oxford, 1892 ; The Song of Hannah, produced Cardiff, 1895. Scena, The Eve of the Battle, baritone solo and men's chorus, Reading, 1889. Meadowcroft prize anthem, " Let my complaint," 1879 ; anthems, services, etc. *Madrigals :* Love wakes and weeps (six voices) ; My dearest love (seven voices) ; Daffodils (eight voices) ; part songs, etc. ; organ pieces.

Read, John Francis Holcombe, musical amateur and composer, born at Port Royal, Kingston, Jamaica, October 29, 1821. Sent to his grandparents at Woolwich when four months old. Began to learn the violin when about twelve from a member of the Royal Artillery Band, subsequently studying composition with G. A. Macfarren. Was appointed to the War Office, afterwards entering the Stock Exchange. Resided at Walthamstow for nearly forty years ; now resident in London. Was County Magistrate for Essex, and for some years a Vice-President, and member of the Committee of Management of R.A.M. In 1867 the Walthamstow Musical Society was formed, and Mr. Read was elected President and Conductor. For twenty-five years he gave his time to it, and wrote for it many of his choral works, besides producing the standard compositions of all masters. He raised Walthamstow to an important musical centre, and to him the town is indebted for the Victoria Hall, and the Festival which inaugurated it in 1887. Mr. Read was also President of the Stock Exchange Orchestral Society for some years from its foundation in 1885.

WORKS.—*Cantatas, etc. :* Homeward Bound, produced, Walthamstow, 1868 ; Consecration of the Banner ; Psyche, 1873 ; Carastacus, 1882 ; Bartimeus, 1885 ; Harold, composed for the Walthamstow Festival, November 24, 1887 ; In the Forest, 1890 ; The Death of Young Romilly, 1891 ; both for men's voices, and produced by the Stock Exchange Society at St. James's Hall. The Hesperus, cantata, 1896. *Orchestral :* Concert Overture, composed for the first concert of the Stock Exchange Society, December 18, 1885 ; Symphony, Evangeline, the same, February 20, 1889 ; Funeral March (In Memoriam, the late Duke of Clarence) 1892. Chamber music, operettas, and orchestral works in MS Woodland Waltzes, for voices and pf. duet ; a large number of songs and part-songs, etc. Of these works many have enjoyed much popularity, and have been given in various parts of the kingdom, and in America.

BRITISH MUSICAL BIOGRAPHY.

READE.

Reade, Charles, novelist, was born in 1814; died, London, April 11, 1884. Author of "Cremona Violins, four letters descriptive of those Exhibited in 1873 at the South Kensington Museum, also giving the data for producing the True varnishes used by the great Cremona makers, reprinted from the *Pall Mall Gazette* by George H. M. Muntz," Gloucester, 1873; also reprinted in Reade's miscellaneous works entitled "Readiana." Reade is best known by his novels "Hard Cash," "It is never too late to mend," etc.

Reading, John, organist and composer, born probably some time before the middle of the 17th century. Lay-vicar of Lincoln Cathedral, 1667, and Master of the choristers there, 1670. Organist of Winchester Cathedral, 1675-81; and of Winchester College, 1681. He died at Winchester in 1692. Composed an "Election Grace" for the scholars of Winchester College; "Dulce Domum," a hymn, printed in Harmonia Wiccamica; and is stated to have composed the well-known hymn, "Adeste Fideles," otherwise the Portuguese Hymn."

Reading, John, organist and composer, son of above, was born in 1677. Chorister in Chapel Royal, where he studied under Dr. Blow. Organist of Dulwich College, London, 1700-1702. Lay-vicar. 1702, and Master of choristers, Lincoln Cathedral, 1703. Organist of St. John's, Hackney, London; St. Mary, Woolnoth; St. Dunstan in the West; St. Mary, Woolchurchhaw. He died at London, September 2, 1764.

He composed "A Book of New Anthems, containing a hundred plates fairly engraved with a thorough-bass figur'd for the Organ or Harpsichord, with proper Ritornels," London [1715]; "A Book of New Songs (after the Italian manner), with symphonies, a thorough-bass fitted to the harpsichord, etc., all within ye compass of the flute."..London [1720]. Sold by the author at his house in Arundel Street, Strand. To him has also been attributed the composition of "Adeste Fideles." Another JOHN READING was organist of Chichester Cathedral from 1674 to 1720.

Reading, Rev. John, clergyman, was prebendary of Canterbury Cathedral. Author of "A Sermon lately delivered in the Cathedral Church of Canterbury, concerning church musick." London, 1663.

Reakes, Albert, bass vocalist and conductor. Studied at the London Academy of Music; also a R.C.M. Conductor of West London Male Voice Union, and was assistant-conductor of the Bath Philharmonic Society, 1887; conductor of New Swindon Choral and Orchestral Union. Composer of glees: To the Rose; Love's a thing as I do hear (men's voices), etc.

Reay, Samuel, organist and composer,

REDDIE.

born at Hexham, March 17, 1822. Son of GEORGE AGNEW REAY, organist of Hexham Abbey Church. Showed early aptitude for music, and when eight years of age, his father having removed to Ryton-on-Tyne, he was admitted a chorister at Durham Cathedral. Studied under W. Henshaw, the Cathedral organist, and received valuable instruction from the Rev. Peter Penson, then precentor. On leaving Durham, he was placed under James Stimpson, organist of St. Andrew's, Newcastle, whom he succeeded in 1841, after holding appointments at North Shields and Houghton-le-Spring. In 1845, he became organist of St Thomas', Barras Bridge, Newcastle; St. Peter's, Tiverton, 1847; while there, giving lectures on the History of Keyed Instruments. Appointed to St. John's, Hampstead, 1854; St. Saviour's, Warwick Road, 1856; St. Stephen's, Paddington; and, in 1859, succeeding Dr. E. G. Monk as organist and precentor of St. Peter's College, Radley. In 1861, he was appointed to the Parish Church, Bury, Lancashire, famous for its choir; and in 1864, succeeded Dr. Dearle in the ancient and important office of Song Schoolmaster of the Parish Church, Newark, which he still retains. Graduated Mus. Bac., Oxford, 1871. Has given organ recitals at the Bow and Bromley Institute, at the Royal Albert Hall, and at other places. On October 27, 1879, he produced, at the Institute just named, Bach's "Coffee" and "Peasant" cantatas, for the first time in England; the English text prepared by himself and Mrs. Newton. In 1891, he was invited to take part in the inauguration of the new organ in Newcastle Cathedral. He is conductor of the Newark Philharmonic Society.

WORKS.—Psalm 102, for solo, chorus, and strings; Morning, Evening, and Communion Service in F. *Anthems:* I will go to the Altar; O Lord, why sleepest Thou? O sing unto the Lord; Rejoice in the Lord; and others. Hymn tunes contributed to the Hymnary, Bristol Tune Book, and other collections; chants, etc. Joint editor, with Drs. Gauntlett and Bridge, of Dobson's Tunes New and Old. *Part-songs:* As it fell upon a day; Fairest daughter of the day, composed for the Jubilee of the Bristol Madrigal Society, 1887; Dawn of Day; Here let's join in harmony; Huntsman, rest; English hunting song; I lov'd a lass; In an arbour green; Sweet is the breath of early morn; The clouds that wrap the setting sun; and many others, all of which have been extensively popular. Edited and arranged Songs and Ballads of Northern England (collect d by John Stoke), London, Scott, 1892.

Reddie, a family of musicians. JOSIAH FERDINAND REDDIE, of Scotch extraction, was born in London, in 1797. He was apprenticed to John Purkis, and afterwards to S. S. Wesley, who pronounced him, while a youth of eighteen, to be the best extempore player in London. Years afterwards he presented himself in rustic guise to James Turle at Westminster Abbey, and gaining his permission to touch the organ, so surprised him with his performance that the two became close friends. Reddie also studied under Thomas Adams. When sixteen, he was appointed organist of Denmark Hill Chapel; three years later to Rotherhithe Church; to St. Botolph, Boston, Lincolnshire, 1822; St. Margaret's, King's Lynn, 1826, a post he held until his death, on February 20, 1860. His reputation as an executant was very great.

JOSIAH HENRY REDDIE, son of the preceding, was born at Boston, Lincolnshire, April 2, 1822. Studied under his father, and was organist for some years at All Saints', Lynn, and succeeded his father at St. Margaret's Church, resigning about 1893. He is still living at Lynn.

CHARLES F. REDDIE, son of the preceding, is a pianist, and made his first appearance at King's Lynn at the age of ten. Studied at R.A.M. under F. Westlake and E. Prout, receiving the certificate of merit in 1884. Played at a concert of the St. George's Glee Union, October, 1885, with great success. On leaving R.A.M., 1886, was elected an Associate. Has given recitals and concerts in London and the provinces. In 1896 he was appointed a professor of pf. at the R.A.M.

Redford, John, organist and composer of the 16th century. He was organist and almoner, and master of choristers, St. Paul's Cathedral, in 1543. He died about 1546-7. Composed the well-known anthem, "Rejoice in the Lord," as well as several similar pieces in various collections.

Redhead, the name of two composers of the present time. ALFRED REDHEAD was appointed organist of St. Augustine's, Kilburn, 1878. He is the composer of two cantatas for female voices, "The Flower Pilgrims"; and "Twelfth Night"; also of Christmas carols for children; two-part songs for children, songs, various, etc.

EDWARD REDHEAD, graduated Mus. Bac., Oxford, 1845. He has published "Short Voluntaries for the organ, four books; pieces for pf., etc.

Redhead, Richard, organist and composer, born at Harrow, March 1, 1820. Chorister at Magdalene College, Oxford, and pupil of the organist, Walter Vicary. He was appointed organist at Margaret Chapel (now All Saints' Church), Margaret Street, London, in 1839, an office he held until 1864. He officiated for a short time as organist at St. Andrew's, Wells Street, in 1847. From

1864 he has been organist at St. Mary Magdalene's, Paddington.

WORKS.—Church Music: a selection of chants, sanctuses, and responses, London, 1840; Laudes Diurnæ, the Psalter and Canticles in the Morning and Evening Service, 1843; The Order for Morning and Evening Prayer, with Litany and proper Psalms; Proper Psalms, together with the Gospel Canticles, set to ancient psalm tunes; Metrical Litanies, 2 parts; Hymns for Holy Seasons; The Celebrant's Office Book; Parish Tune Book, compiled by G. F. Chambers . . . London, 1868; Ancient Hymn Melodies and other Church tunes, as used at All Saints', Margaret Street; Canticles at Matins and Evensong, adapted to the ancient Psalm chants; Music to the Divine Liturgy; The Cathedral and Church Choir Book, chiefly adaptations from the Latin works of the great masters; Parochial Church Tune Book and Appendix; Universal Organist, 5 books; Masses, Te Deum in D, anthems, etc.

Rée, Louis, English pianist and composer, pupil of the Stuttgart Conservatorium, and of Leschetitzky at Vienna, in which city he resides. Played at concerts, Stuttgart, 1886, and in February, 1888, gave what was claimed to be the first concert of English music in Vienna. His compositions embrace a suite, Fête Champêtre, for pf.; variations and fugue, for two pianos; pieces for violin and pf., etc.

Reed, Thomas German, composer and actor, born at Bristol, June 27, 1817. Organist of Catholic Chapel, Sloane street, London. Musical director of Haymarket Theatre, 1838-51, and of the Olympic Theatre, 1853. Chapel-master of Royal Bavarian Chapel, 1838. Married Miss Priscilla Horton, 1844. Established "Mr. and Mrs. German Reed's Entertainments," 1855, and produced pieces by Brough, Parry, Gilbert and Sullivan, Burnand, Clay, Cellier, Reed, and Macfarren. He died at Upper East Sheen, Surrey, March 21, 1888.

WORKS.—Drama at home (Planché), 1845; Golden Fleece; Match for a king (C. Matthews); Who's the composer? (J. M. Morton); Miss P. Horton's Illustrative Gatherings (1856), and other entertainments. *Songs:* Jock o' the mill; I would be a violet; Love makes the home; Sweet Erin; Vixen! Young man from the country; adaptations from Auber's "La Part du Diable," etc.

His wife, *born* PRISCILLA HORTON (born at Birmingham, January 1, 1818) a contralto singer and actress of great repute, who appeared in Macready's revivals of Shakespere's plays, and afterwards in Planché's pieces at the Haymarket Theatre, and in her husband's entertainments. She retired in 1879. Died at Bexley Heath, March 18, 1895.

REES.

Their son, ALFRED GERMAN REED, who continued the entertainments, died at London, March 10, 1895.

Rees, David, author of "Reasons for and against singing of Psalms in private or public worship," London, 1737.

Rees, Eleanor, contralto vocalist, born at Neath, Glamorganshire. Studied at R.A.M. under W. Shakespeare; Westmorland Scholar, 1883. Was associated with Mr. Sinclair Dunn in his recitals of Scottish songs, 1882. Toured in the provinces, 1885, with the Valleria-Foli party. Made her festival *début* at Worcester, 1887, singing in the first part of Mendelssohn's "Elijah" with much success. She sang at the Philharmonic Concerts, March 22, 1888, and is known as a refined exponent of the better class of English songs, etc.

Rees, Robert, EOS MORLAIS, tenor vocalist, born at Dowlais, Glamorganshire, April 5, 1841 Originally a working man, his great natural ability led him to follow music as a profession. His fine voice and artistic feeling soon won for him an extended fame and great popularity, and he was a special favourite at the Eisteddfodau. He sang at the Crystal Palace, the Promenade Concerts at Covent Garden, in many provincial towns, and also toured in America. He died at Swansea, June 5, 1892.

Rees, William Thomas, ALAW DDU, composer, born near Bridgend, Glamorganshire, September 29, 1838. Self-taught. Has won a number of prizes at the Eisteddfodau, and also acted as adjudicator. Conductor of Psalmody Festivals. Editor of *The Musical School*, and *The Musician of Wales*, the latter started in 1885, but neither now in existence. Published a small collection of tunes, anthems, etc.; composer of some cantatas, anthems, choruses, glees, part-songs, and songs; also of an opera for children, Llewelyn Ein Llyw Olaf, performed at Treherbert, 1891.

Reeve, Cotton, violinist and composer, who was born about 1777. He was a theatrical manager, and died at London about October, 1845. Composer of some instrumental music.

Reeve, Percy, composer, of present time. His works comprise a sketch " A condensed opera,'" produced at Steinway Hall, May 4, 1882; " A private wire," vaudeville, Savoy Theatre, April, 1883; Operetta, "The Crusader and the Craven," Globe Theatre, October, 1890. He has also composed a Symphony and Suite for orchestra; Songs, etc.

Reeve, William, composer and organist, born in 1757. He studied under Richardson, and became organist of Totness, Devon, 1781-1783. Composer to Astley's Circus, London, and to Covent Garden Theatre, 1791. Organist of Church of St. Martin, Ludgate Hill, 1792. Joint-proprietor of Sadler's Wells Theatre. He died at London, June 22, 1815.

REEVES.

WORKS.—*Music to Plays, etc.* : Oscar and Malvina, 1791; Orpheus and Eurydice, 1792; Apparition, 1794; British Fortitude, 1794; Hercules and Omphale, 1794; The Purse, 1794; Merry Sherwood, 1795; Charity Boy, 1796; Harlequin and Oberon, 1796; Bantry Bay, 1797; Raymond and Agnes, 1797; Harlequin Quixote, 1797; Round Tower, 1797; Joan of Arc, 1798; Ramah Droog (with Mazzinghi), 1798; Turnpike Gate (do.), 1799; Embarkation, 1799; Thomas and Susan 1799; Paul and Virginia (with Mazzinghi), 1800; Harlequin's Almanac, 1801; Blind Girl (with Mazzinghi), 1801; Cabinet (with Braham, Moorhead, and Davy), 1802; Family Quarrels (with Braham), 1802; Caravan, 1803; Dash, 1804; Thirty Thousand (with Davy and Braham), 1804; Out of Place, or the Lake of Lausanne (with Braham), 1805; Corsair 1805; White Plume, 1806; Rokeby Castle, 1806; An Bratach, 1806; Kais, or Love in the Deserts (with Braham), 1808; Tricks upon Travellers, 1810; Outside Passenger, 1811; Chains of the Heart (with Mazzinghi); Jamie and Anna, Scots pastoral, 1800. Glees. *Songs:* Cherry-cheeked Patty; Bird in the hand; Enamoured shepherdess; Little haymaker; Live and be jolly; Margery Grinder; Rose of the valley; Tippetywitchet, clown's songs for Grimaldi; etc. The Juvenile Preceptor, or Entertaining Instructor: a complete and concise Introduction to the Pianoforte, with 24 lessons and 4 easy duets, London, n.d. The well-known song "I am a friar of orders grey" appears in " Merry Sherwood," 1795. By this Reeve is best known.

Reeves, Daniel M. G. S., amateur musician, author of " A Treatise on the Science of Music," London, 1853; 2nd edition, 1861.

Reeves, John Sims, tenor vocalist, born at the Artillery Barracks, Woolwich, September 26, 1818; baptized in Woolwich Church, October 25, 1818. His father, JOHN REEVES, was born at West Bromwich, Staffordshire. He enlisted first in the Marines, and then in the Royal Artillery. His superior musical attainments brought him into notice, and he became a corporal in the band. He is said to have been a splendid bass singer, and a good instrumentalist. He was discharged in 1843, and died at Foots Cray, Kent, November 30, 1860. From his father young Reeves received his first instruction, and when fourteen was made organist of North Cray Church. During the next few years he became a performer on the violin, 'cello, oboe, and bassoon; studied harmony with W. H. Callcott, and pf. with J. B. Cramer. His adult voice developing, he decided on becoming a singer, and as a baritone, made his *début* as Count Rodolpho in " La Sonnambula," at the Newcastle-on-Tyne Theatre, June, 1839. The same year he sang at the Grecian Theatre, London, as Mr.

REEVES.

Johnson. He then studied as a tenor, under Hobbs, and T. Cooke, and appeared in minor parts in " King Arthur," " Der Freischütz," and other operas, at Drury Lane, 1842-3. For further study he went to Paris, and had lessons from Bordogni, and at Milan, from Mazzucato. At La Scala, Milan, he appeared in 1846, as Edgardo in " Lucia di Lammermoor," with Catherine Hayes in the title-part. Reappeared at Drury Lane, December 6, 1847, in the same part, and achieved the greatest success witnessed for many years. Then for the first time called Mr. Sims Reeves. On the 20th of the same month he appeared in his first original part, as *Lyonnel* in Balfe's " Maid of Honour," also at Drury Lane. On May 20, 1848, he made his first appearance in Italian opera, at Her Majesty's, taking the part of *Carlo* in " Linda." His operatic career extended over many years, and he was equally great in works of all kinds, down to the simple ballad-opera. He sang in " Rob Roy," at Edinburgh, so late as July, 1887. In oratorio he achieved a great success at the Worcester and Norwich Festivals of 1848, and at the Sacred Harmonic Society's performance of the " Messiah," November 24, of that year He was engaged for the Birmingham Festivals from 1849 to 1873, and it was for him that Costa wrote the tenor parts in " Eli," and " Naaman." He sang at the Crystal Palace Handel Festivals, 1857-74, his last festival performance being in " Israel in Egypt," June 26, 1874. In the concert room he reigned supreme, and was matchless in his rendering of the artistic song, and the Dibdin ballad. From 1881 his public appearances were less frequent; and in 1890 he commenced a farewell tour at Southsea, in August; and gave his final concert at the Albert Hall, May 11, 1891. He commenced teaching about this time, and was on the staff of the Guildhall School of Music. Reverses and misfortune compelled a return to public life, and after singing at Covent Garden Promenade Concerts, Queen's Hall, and other places, 1893-5, he appeared at the Empire Theatre, November 4, 1895, and made a round of the provincial Variety theatres during the winter following. Sailed for South Africa, July 25, 1896, and had a most successful tour, returning in October. In 1888 he published his " Life and Recollections," London, Simpkin, Marshall.

His wife, *born* EMMA LUCOMBE, was the daughter of Thomas Lucombe, a clever amateur actor, who died February 13, 1855. She was a pupil of Mrs. Blane Hunt, and first appeared at a concert of the Sacred Harmonic Society, in Handel's " Joshua," June 19, 1839; and sang in London and the provinces up to 1845, when she went to study in Italy; sang in opera in Milan, and made her *début*

REID.

on the English stage at Covent Garden, November 4, 1848, in the titular part of Auber's " Haydée." Appeared at the Philharmonic concerts, April 16, 1849, singing a duet with Sims Reeves, to whom she was married, at North Cray Church, November 3, 1850. For some time she continued to sing in public, and then gave her attention to teaching. She died at Upper Norwood, June 10, 1895, in her 75th year. HERBERT SIMS REEVES, their son, educated by his father, and at Milan, made his *début* at W. Ganz's concert, St. James's Hall, June 12, 1880; sang with success at the Crystal Palace, February 12, 1881, and in the provinces. Made his first appearance on the stage at Brighton, in " Guy Mannering," February 13, 1884. Has sung in " The Waterman," and taken other parts made famous by his father. He has also sung in comic opera, " Falka," etc. He has published one or two songs. His sister, CONSTANCE SIMS REEVES, made her *début* on the stage in " Guy Mannering," with her brother, singing under the name of Miss Lester. She appeared at the Strand Theatre in July, 1884; sang in " The Waterman " at the Crystal Palace, 1892; and has been heard at various concerts. Mr. Sims Reeves married again in 1895, his second wife, Miss MAUD RENE, having been his pupil. She sang with him at the Queen's Hall, Christmas Day, 1895; accompanied him on his provincial tour, 1895-6; and also on his visit to Africa. EDWIN REEVES, a brother, was a member of the Seguin troupe in their American tour, 1848-9; and sometime professor of singing at the Viceregal Court, Dublin. He died at Liverpool, in May, 1882.

Reid, Alan Stewart Bell, composer and editor, born at Arbroath, Forfarshire, February 6, 1853. Brought up at Forfar, and originally apprenticed to a cabinet-maker. His talent for music showed itself early, and he is entirely self-taught. Elected choirmaster in the Barclay Church, Edinburgh, in 1877, which appointment he still holds; also instructor in singing in three Board Schools in that city. He has composed many educational works for schools, operettas, cantatas (Round the Clock; The School Holiday; Red, White, and Blue, etc.), and action songs; Ruth, a sacred cantata (1882); Friendship's Circle, a Scottish cantata; and lyrics and melodies in " Scots Minstrelsie." A volume entitled " Music for Pupil Teachers" was recently completed, and he has a poetical authology, " The Bards of Angus and the Mearns," in course of preparation. He is, further, editor of the *National Choir*, a monthly publication of glees and harmonised songs, and author of various poetical works.

Reid, General John (born ROBERTSON), musician, and founder of the Edinburgh

REINAGLE.

Professorship of music, was born at Straloch, Perthshire, February 13, 1721 [1720]. Son of Alexander Robertson of Straloch. He studied at Edinburgh University. Lieutenant in the Earl of Loudon's Regiment, 1745; afterwards became a General in the Army. He died at London, February 6, 1807.

WORKS.—A Set of Minuets and Marches, inscribed to the Right Hon. Lady Catherine Murray, by J— R—, Esq., London [1770]. (Bremner). [Contains the well-known air, "The Garb of Old Gaul," to verses of Sir H. Erskine, of Alva.] Six Solos for a German Flute or Violin, with a Thorough-bass for the Harpsichord, by J— R—, Esq., a Member of the Temple of Apollo, London, n.d. (Oswald). There have also been ascribed to him "Three Grand Marches, and Three Quicksteps for a Full Military Band, by an Eminent Master," London, n.d.

General Reid directed in his will that, subject to the life-rent of his daughter, the sum of £52,000 should be applied to founding a Chair of Music in Edinburgh University, and that an annual concert (to include a full military band) should be given on his birthday, at which was to be performed some specimens of his own composition, to show the style of music that prevailed about the middle of last century. The chair was instituted in 1839, when a sum of between £70,000 and £80,000 became available. The succession of Professors has been John Thomson, 1839; Sir Henry Bishop, 1842; Henry Hugo Pierson, 1844; John Donaldson, 1845; Sir Herbert Stanley Oakeley, 1865; Friedrich Niecks, 1889.

Reinagle, Caroline, See ORGER, Caroline.

Reinagle, Joseph, violoncellist, composer, and writer, born at Portsmouth, of Austrian parents, in 1762. Intended for the navy, but afterwards apprenticed to an Edinburgh jeweller. He studied the 'cello under Schetkey, who married his sister, and the violin under Aragoni and Pinto, and became leader at the Edinburgh Theatre. Performed as a violoncellist in London, etc. Resided in Dublin, 1784-6. Played at Salomon's Concerts in London, and in Oxford, where he latterly resided. He died at Oxford, 1836.

WORKS.—Twenty-four Progressive Lessons for the Pianoforte, London, 1796. Twelve Duets for the violoncello, op. 2; 3 sets of six do., op., 3, 4, 5. Six Quartets for strings. Slow March for orchestra [1800]. Concertos for violin and violoncello, with accompaniment. Concise Introduction to the Art of Playing on the Violoncello, London, 1830. This work has reached 4 editions.

His son, ALEXANDER ROBERT, born at Brighton, August 21, 1799, was organist of St. Peter's-in-the-East, Oxford, 1822-53. He

RELFE.

died at Kidlington, near Oxford, April 6, 1877. Composed Preparatory Exercises for the Violin; Selection of Popular Airs, varied, for Violin; A Collection of the most favourite Scotch Tunes....London, n.d.; Violinist's Portfolio, for Amateurs; Allegro Maestoso, for Violin; Twelve Studies for the Violin [1851]; Seven Easy Studies for Violoncello; First Lessons for Beginners on Violoncello, to which are added a Selection of Psalm Tunes and Chants [1841]; Ten Airs for Organ or Harmonium; Ten original Melodies, and a Fugue for the Organ; Four Introits for Organ; Processional March, do; Twelve songs without words, pf.; Two Sets of Bagatelles, pf.; Psalm tunes for the voice and pf. [1830]; Collection of Psalm and Hymn tunes, chants, and other music, London [1839]. The well-known Psalm tune, "St. Peter," is by A. R. Reinagle.

Reinhold, Charles Frederick, bass singer and organist, born in London, of German parents, in 1737. He was a chorister in St. Paul's Cathedral and the Chapel Royal. In 1755 he appeared at Drury Lane Theatre in J. C. Smith's "Fairies." He was organist of St. George the Martyr, Bloomsbury, and sang at Marylebone Gardens, in the provinces, and at the Handel Commemoration in 1784. He died in London, September 29, 1815. Composer of galops, valses, and other music for the pf.

Relfe, John, composer and writer, born at Greenwich in 1763. Son of Lupton Relfe, who was organist of Greenwich Hospital, under whom he studied. He also studied under Keeble. Member of King's Band of Music, 1810. Teacher of harmony and pf. in London, where he died, about 1837.

WORKS.—Select set of airs for harpsichord [1787]; Progressive sonatas for the harpsichord or pf.; Lessons, songs, and duetts for pf.; Six divertimentos for pf., op. 8. *Songs:* Come thou laughter-loving power; Edwin and Angelina; Gardener; Laplander's song; Mary's dream. Editor of M. Sharp's collection of original melodies [1827]. Guida Armonica, or introduction to the general knowledge of music, theoretical and practical, London, 3 parts [1798]; reprinted as " The Principles of Harmony, containing a complete and compendious illustration of the theory of music," London, 1817. A Muschedule, or music scroll, exhibiting an epitome of the whole science of music," Camberwell [1800]. Remarks on the present state of musical instruction, with a prospectus of a new order of thoroughbass designation, and a demonstrative view of the defective nature of the customary mode.., London, 1819. Lucidus ordo: comprising an analytical course of studies on the several branches of musical science.., London, 1821.

RENDALL.

Relfe's "Guida Armonica" anticipated in a large measure the method of Logier in regard to instruction by exercises. His father issued "Hymns for the use of the Chapel of the Royal Hospital, Greenwich," London, 1789; and "Greenwich Hospital hymns and music," 1796.

Rendall, Edward Davey, composer, educated at the Hoch Schule, Berlin. Graduated M.A., 1887; Mus. Bac., 1894, Cambridge. Music master, Dulwich College. His compositions are : Psalm 137, for soli, strings, and organ; "The Compleat Angler," Idyl for soli, chorus, and orchestra, Princes' Hall, May 5, 1894; Quintet for pf. and wind, 1890; Five vocal duets; Songs, part-songs, etc.

Reynolds, Charles, oboe player, born at Stockport, Cheshire, May 30, 1850. His father, THOMAS REYNOLDS, was bandmaster of the 52nd Light Infantry (now 2nd Oxford-shire), and afterwards of the 6th Lancashire Militia. Charles Reynolds passed his boyhood in India, and while there the great mutiny broke out. On his return to England he studied the oboe under Lavigne, and joined the Hallé orchestra in 1871 as second oboe, becoming principal in 1890. Was connected with the Gentlemen's Concerts, Manchester, from 1870; Liverpool Philharmonic, 1874; joined the orchestra of the Royal Italian Opera, 1876; and the New Philharmonic Concerts, London, same year. Has played at the Bristol Festivals since 1873; Birmingham, 1885; Hanley, 1888; Handel, 1888; and at the Reid Festival, Edinburgh, 1893, he played for the first time in Great Britain Bach's Suite for oboe d'amore; and is also known as a fine performer on the Cor Anglais. He has conducted orchestras at Derby Castle, Douglas, Isle-of-Man, 1886-7; Falcon Cliff, 1889; and Rhyl, 1893. Is professor of the oboe, Royal Manchester College of Music.

Reynolds, Charles Tom, organist, composer, and conductor, born at Ross, Herefordshire, October 1, 1865. Chorister at Hereford Cathedral. Graduated Mus. Bac., 1890; Mus. Doc., 1895, Oxford. F.R.C.O. Appointed organist of Denstone College, 1883; of Oswestry Parish Church, 1885, an office he retains. Conductor of Oswestry Choral Society, which has given good concerts; of the Claughton and Oxton Choral Society; and, in 1896, appointed conductor of the Birkenhead Cambrian Choral Society. His compositions include a cantata, "The Child-hood of Samuel," produced at Birkenhead, 1896; a setting of Psalm 130; and he has published church services, anthems, and part-songs.

Reynolds, John, composer of the 18th century. Was Gentleman of Chapel Royal, 1765-1770. He died at Lambeth, London, 1770 [November, 1778?]. Composed the well-

RICHARDSON.

known anthem, "My God, my God, look upon me."

Reynolds, Williamson John, organist and composer, born in London, October 22, 1861. Graduated Mus. Bac., 1886; Mus. Doc., 1889, London. Organist of Parish Church, Barnet; St. Michael's, Cornhill, London, from 1891. He has lectured on "Music and Evolution," in Birmingham, 1895, etc. His works are a Magnificat for soli, chorus, strings and organ; Festival Te Deum, for soli, eight-part chorus and orchestra, produced at Highbury Athenæum, April 19, 1891; "Crossing the Bar," four voices, etc.

Rhodes, Alfred, organist of Brixton Independent Church, is author of a work on "Curiosities of the Key-board and the Staff; or the Staff-notation shown to be upon a scientific basis ...," London, Augener, 1896.

Richards, Henry Brinley, composer, pianist, and teacher, born at Carmarthen, November 13, 1817. Son of H. Richards, organist of St. Peter's, Carmarthen. Intended for medical profession, but abandoned it in favour of music. Entered R.A.M. as student, with assistance of the Duke of Newcastle. Gained King's Scholarship, 1835 and 1837. Member of R.A.M. Resided in London as teacher and pianist. He died at London, May 1, 1885.

WORKS.—*Orchestral :* Symphony; Overtures in F minor, Paris, 1840, London, 1841, and another; Concerto for pf, and orchestra; The "Albert Edward" march (military band), 1862; The Carmarthen march. *Pianoforte :* Andante Pastorale; The angel's song; Picciola Estelle; Fête de la Reine (1849); La Reine Blanche, scherzo; Recollections of Wales (1852); Warblings at eve (1856); Marie, nocturne (1857); Book of Octave Studies; Andante cantabile (1858); Fantasias on Welsh airs (1861); Tarantelle (1864); Evening, nocturne (1877); Autrefois (1880). *Part-songs :* Up, quit thy bower, trio (1846); In the hour of my distress, solo and choir (1856); There's not a heath (1857) ; The boat song; Ye little birds, madrigal (1863); Sun of my soul (1868) ; The Cambrian plume (1869); Let the hills resound (1873); The men of Wales (1877); Nobody cares for thee (1878). *Duets :* How beautiful is night; The old church chimes; Home, etc. *Songs :* In the hour of my distress; Cambrian war-song (1859); The harp of Wales (1862); God bless the Prince of Wales (December, 1862); As o'er the past (1868); The harper's grave (1869); The Black Watch (1874); Men of Wales (1877), etc. Songs of Wales, edited, London, 1873 (other editions).

Richardson, Alfred Madeley, organist, studied under William Haynes, of Malvern, and at R.C.M. Organ Scholar, Keble Col-

RICHARDSON.

lege, Oxford, 1885-9. Graduated Mus. Bac., and B.A., 1888; M.A., 1892, Oxford. F.R.C.O. Obtained diploma of A.C.O. when sixteen, and was then organist of Emmanuel Church, Malvern. Gave recitals in the Priory Church there, 1884. Organist of Hindlip Church, Worcester, 1889; Holy Trinity, Sloane Street, London; St. Jude's, Gray's Inn Road; All Saints', Scarborough, 1892; St. Saviour's Cathedral, Southwark, 1897. He has published church services, part-songs, etc.

Richardson, John, composer and organist, born at Preston, December 14, 1816. He was appointed organist of St. Mary's Catholic Church, Liverpool, in 1835, and from 1837 to 1857 was organist of St. Nicholas Church in the same city. He was celebrated as a teacher, and was the instructor, in counterpoint, of W. T. Best. He died at Preston, April 13, 1879. He composed music for Collins' "Ode to the Passions," masses, glees, hymn-tunes, etc.

Richardson, John Elliott, organist and composer, born at Salisbury. Studied at Salisbury Cathedral, under A. T. Corfe, whose assistant organist he was for eighteen years. Appointed organist and master of the choristers, in 1863, after the death of A. T. Corfe. Conductor of Sarum Choral Society, 1849-69. Resigned Cathedral appointment, 1881, owing to ill-health. He composed a service in F; I will give thanks; Turn Thee, O Lord; and other anthems. Author of "Salisbury Chant Book," Salisbury, 1859; "The Tour of a Cathedral Organist," Salisbury, 1870. Editor of anthems by Greene, etc.

His brother, THOMAS BENTINCK RICHARDSON, chorister, and assistant organist at Salisbury Cathedral, was organist, for nearly thirty years, of St. Mary's Church, Bury St. Edmunds. He was a good musician, and exerted great influence in his locality. He died at Bury St. Edmunds, April, 1893, aged 62.

Richardson, Joseph, flute player and composer, born in 1814. Member of Jullien's orchestra, and was principal flutist in Queen's private band. He died at London, March 22, 1862. Composer of fantasias, variations, original pieces and arrangements for flute; Set of studies for the flute, exemplifying the different modes of fingering particular notes and passages, London [1844]; Waltzes for pf., songs, and other music.

Richardson, Vaughan, organist and composer, was born in the latter half of the 17th century. He studied under Blow in the Chapel Royal. Organist of Winchester Cathedral, 1695. He died in 1729.

WORKS.—A Collection of new Songs for 1, 2, and 3 voices, accompany'd with Instruments, London, 1701. Odes, cantatas, etc. Anthems and songs. The well-known anthem

RICKARD.

"O how amiable are Thy dwellings" is by this composer.

Richardson, William, organist and composer, was a chorister in the Chapel Royal, and organist of St. Nicholas' Church, Deptford, London, 1697. He died about 1731-32. He composed "Lessons for the harpsichord or spinet," London, 1708; and "The Pious Recreation, containing a new sett of psalm tunes...," London, 1729. This contains "Greenwich," a popular psalm tune.

His brother, PELHAM RICHARDSON, was also an organist.

Richmond, Rev. Legh, clergyman and musician, born at Liverpool, January 29, 1772. He was chaplain of the Lock Hospital, and afterwards rector of Turvey, Bedfordshire. Died at Turvey, May 8, 1827. Author of "The Dairyman's Daughter" in the "Annals of the Poor," and other religious works. Known to musicians by some good glees, contained in Hague's collections. He also wrote songs, among which may be named Christian's rest [1825]; Gypsies petition; Happy cottager; Negro's prayer. Richmond founded, about 1820, the Legh Richmond Library at Iona, in Argyleshire.

Richmond, William Henry, organist and composer. Studied under James Rhodes and T. A. Marsh. Organist of Holy Trinity, Knaresborough; appointed to St. Paul's Pro-Cathedral, Dundee, 1870; and later to St. Michael's, Exeter, which he resigned through illness in 1886. He composed church services, anthems, organ music, pf. music and songs.

Rickard, Richard Henry, pianist and composer, born at Birmingham, November 12, 1858. When a child he showed much talent for music, and as a juvenile pianist frequently played at concerts. At eight years of age he was placed under Dr. C. S. Heap, with whom he studied for some years. He gave his first recital in Birmingham, March 30, 1876, and afterwards went to study at the Leipzig Conservatorium, where his teachers were Reinecke, Louis Maas, and E. F. Richter. After completing his course, he played at the Gewandhaus concerts, December 12, 1878, Reinecke's Concerto in F minor, and was favourably noticed by the press. He reappeared at Birmingham in April, 1879, and gave recitals at different times. Residing in London, he took a good position as a teacher there, and at Brighton. Played at the Crystal Palace concerts, for the first time, April 7, 1883; gave a series of recitals there, 1884; at the "Inventions" Exhibition, South Kensington, 1885; and played at concerts in various places. He also has played, with marked success, at Paris, and Dresden and other places in Germany. Visited Liszt at Weimar, and played to Rubinstein, to whom he dedicated a Ballade

RIDDELL.

and Gavotte. For upwards of ten years he has been principal professor of pf. at the Sydenham and Forest Hill Academy of Music. His compositions include a Concerto in B flat, for pf. and orchestra; six duets, six characteristic pieces, and a number of other works for pf.; Twilight Music, The Lotus Flower, and other songs, etc.

RICHARD RICKARD, his father, was mathematical master at King Edward's School, Birmingham, from 1854. He was an excellent amateur flute player, and did much to popularise music in the Midlands. In 1864 he started a penny singing class at the Birmingham and Midland Institute, and in 1882 he began a penny violin class. On the third night 525 students presented themselves! Many soon dropped off, but from these classes the Institute School of Music was developed. Mr. Rickard died at Birmingham, June 4, 1890.

Riddell, John, musician, born at Ayr, September 2, 1718. He was a music teacher, and is believed to have been blind from infancy. He died at Ayr, April 5, 1795. Composer of a "Collection of Scots Reels or country dances and minuets, with two particular slow tunes, with a bass for the violin, violincello or harpsichord . . ." Edinburgh [1766]. "Collection of Scots Reels, minuets, etc., for the violin, harpsichord, or German flute. The second edition greatly improved." Glasgow, J. Aird [1782]. Riddell composed the air of "Jenny's Bawbee" and several well-known dances.

Riddell, Captain Robert, of Glenriddell, Dumfriesshire, Scottish antiquary and musician, best known as the friend of Burns the poet. He published "A Collection of Scotch, Galwegian, and Border Tunes, for the Violin and Pianoforte, with a Bass for the Violoncello or Harpsichord," Edinburgh, 1794. "New Music for the Pianoforte or Harpsichord, composed by a Gentleman. Consisting of a Collection of Reels, Minuets, Hornpipes, Marches, and two Songs in the old Scotch taste, with variations to five favourite tunes," Edinburgh, n.d. Also music to some of Burns' songs. He died at Friar's Carse, near Dumfries, April 21, 1794.

Ridding, John A., baritone vocalist, born in Birmingham, December 5, 1862. Intended for a schoolmaster, he served as a pupil teacher at St. Mark's School, Birmingham, afterwards studying at St. Paul's Training School, Cheltenham. Having a voice that promised well, he became a candidate for admission to the Royal College of Music, and was one of the fifty scholars elected in April, 1883. He distinguished himself at the College concerts, and in March, 1887, joined Mr. J. W. Turner's Opera Company, of which he still remains a member. His repertory includes

RIDSDALE.

upwards of thirty operas, and the versatility of his talent is displayed in such widely differing impersonations as those of *Mephistopheles,* (Faust), *Lord Allcash* (Fra Diavolo), and *Alfio* (Cavalleria Rusticana). Mr. Ridding is occasionally heard in oratorio, and general concert work in Birmingham and elsewhere.

Rideout, Percy Rodney, pianist and composer. Studied at R.C.M., and privately. A.R.C.M. Graduated Mus. Bac., London, 1895. Teacher of pf. at London Organ School, etc. Composer of a setting of Psalm 115; an orchestral Symphonic poem (on Shelley's Epipsychidion), produced at Henschel concerts, January 29, 1891; an Evening Service in A, etc.

Rider, Charles, compiler of "Psalmodia Britannica, or a collection of psalm tunes selected from various composers, and adapted to the different metres used in English psalmody," London [1800], 2 vols. "Set of original Psalm Tunes," 1821-23.

Ridley, William, organist, born at Newark, Nottingham, 1820. Articled pupil of Dr. Dearle. F.C.O. Organist of Swaffham Parish Church; Kington Parish Church; and, 1853-78, of West Derby Parish Church, Liverpool. In 1878 he succeeded his son, S. Claude Ridley (q.v.), at St. John the Baptists', Tue Brook. He was for some time private organist to the Earl of Oxford, and conductor of the Kington Choral Society. During his thirty-three years' residence in Liverpool, he did much to raise the standard of church services. His compilation of 301 chants, ancient and modern, went through eight editions; and he was the composer of many hymn tunes. He died at Liverpool, October 5, 1886. His son,

Ridley, Sebastian Claude, organist, pianist, and composer, was born at West Derby, near Liverpool, December 31, 1853. Studied under his father. Was assistant organist at West Derby Parish Church from 1865 to 1870, in which last year he was appointed organist of St. John's, Tue Brook; in 1878 to the Liverpool Seaman's Orphanage; in 1892 to Renshaw Street Unitarian Chapel; and in 1894 to Great George Street Congregational Chapel. Has also acted as choirmaster at St. Cuthbert's (1883), and St. Chad's (1887). Conductor of Banner's Oratorio Choir, 1883. As an organ player he is well known, having given recitals at the Royal Albert Hall, Kensington, St. George's Hall, Liverpool, and at various provincial exhibitions. His compositions include a Church Service in G (unison); Prize hymn tunes, etc.; many songs, of which "The Wrecker" is a favourable example; Pf. pieces, "Clymene," "Fairy wings," etc.

Ridsdale, Rev. C. J., B.A., Incumbent

RIGBY.

of St. Peter's, Folkestone, is the composer of a Communion Service, with orchestra, entitled "Cantio Dominica," produced at Grosvenor Hall, London, March 17, 1882. He is also the composer of three Magnificats à faux bourdons, in the 1st and 2nd Ecclesiastical Tones, with varied organ accompaniments; a Benedicite, omnia opera, with Antiphon; Te Deum, for festal use; a second Communion Service, etc.

Rigby, George Vernon, tenor vocalist, born at Birmingham, January 21, 1840. Chorister at St Chad's R.C. Cathedral when nine. When his voice changed to a tenor, he decided upon his profession, and having made a local reputation in 1861 he went to London, singing first at the Alhambra, Leicester Square, and appearing at the Covent Garden Promenade Concerts (Alfred Mellon, conductor), September 18. In 1865 he toured in opera with H. Corri's company. He then went to Milan, studying with Sangiovanni, and appeared in opera there; also at Berlin in 1867, and later in Denmark. On returning to England he at once took a high position, singing at the Festivals of the Three Choirs, 1868-72; Norwich Festival, 1869; Birmingham, 1870-79. He sang at the Crystal Palace, Sacred Harmonic, and other London concerts, and at the chief provincial oratorio concerts. Of late years he has been seldom heard, one of his most recent performances being in Costa's "Eli," at Brighton, in November, 1887.

Riley, William, musician and writer, was "principal teacher of psalmody to the Charity Schools in London, Westminster, and parts adjacent," and singing master, St. John's, Bedford Row, London. Author of "Parochial Musick Corrected, containing Remarks on Psalmody in Country Churches; on the ridiculous and profane manner of singing by Methodists; on the bad performance of Psalmody in London and Westminster, with hints for its Improvement.. To which is added a scarce and valuable collection of Psalm Tunes,.." London, 1762. Compiler of Psalms and Hymns for the use of the chapel of the Asylum or House of Refuge for Female Orphans. London [1750]. "Parochial Harmony, consisting of a collection of Psalm Tunes in three and four parts, by some of the most eminent Ancient and Modern Composers, and others." London, 1762. Divine Harmonist's Assistant, being a collection of Psalm Tunes. London [1790]. Also tunes in Alcock's "Harmony of Jerusalem," 1801.

Rimbault, Stephen Francis, organist, pianist, and composer, born at London, in 1773. He studied under Dittenhofer, Hook, and Possin. Organist of St. Giles-in-the-Fields. He died at London, August, 1837. Published numerous adaptations for pf. from Haydn, Mozart, Beethoven, Rossini, Winter,

RIMBAULT.

etc. Composed three grand sonatas for pf., with flute accompaniment, etc.

Rimbault, Edward Francis, writer and composer, son of preceding, was born in Soho, London, June 13, 1816. He studied under his father, Samuel Wesley, and Dr. Crotch. Organist of the Swiss Church, Soho, 1832, and subsequently of several other London churches. Lectured at the Royal Institution and elsewhere on English musical history. One of the founders of the Percy and Musical Antiquarian Societies. Editor to Motett Society, 1841. F.S.A., 1842; Member of Academy of Music, and Ph. D., Stockholm, 1842. Hon. degree of LL.D.,,Harvard University, U.S.A., 1848. He died, London, September 26, 1876.

WORKS.—Who was Jack Wilson, the singer of Shakespeare's stage? an attempt to prove the identity of this person with John Wilson, Doctor of Music in the University of Oxford, A.D. 1644, London, 1846. Bibliotheca Madrigaliana; a bibliographical account of Musical and Poetical works published in England during the reigns of Elizabeth and James I... London, 1847. The first book of the pianoforte, being a plain and easy introduction to the study of Music, London, 1848. The Organ: its history and construction (with E. J. Hopkins), London, 1855 (various editions). The Pianoforte: its origin, progress, and construction; with some account of instruments of the same class which preceded it, viz.: the clavichord, the virginals, the spinet, the harpsichord, etc., London, 1860. The early English Organ-builders and their works, from the fifteenth century to the period of the great Rebellion,....London [1864]. J. S. Bach: his life and writings, compiled from Hilgenfeldt and Forkel, London, 1869. A Guide to the use of the new Alexandre Church Harmonium, with two rows of keys,....London, n.d. The Harmonium: its uses and capabilities for the drawing-room as well as the church, 1857. Rimbault's Harmonium Tutor, a concise and easy book of instruction, London, n.d. Rimbault's New Singing Tutor, adapted from the valuable work of Lablache, London, n.d. Edited, secular: Little book of Songs and Ballads, gathered from ancient musick books, MS. and printed ....London. 1840 (2nd edition, 1851). The Ancient Vocal Music of England, London, 2 vols. [1846-49]. Little lays for little learners, set to easy songs, London, n.d. Nursery Rhymes, with the tunes to which they are sung in the Nursery of England, obtained principally from oral tradition, London, 1847; 2nd edit., 1868; 3rd edit., 1857 (other edits.). Musical illustrations of Bishop Percy's Reliques of Ancient English Poetry, a collection of old ballad tunes, etc.....London, 1850. The rounds, catches, and canons of

RIMBAULT.

England....16th, 17th, and 18th centuries (with the Rev. J. Powell Metcalfe), London, n.d. The Old Cheque-book, or Book of Remembrance of the Chapel Royal, from 1561 to 1744, London (Camden Society), 1872. Memoirs of Musick by the Hon. Roger North, Attorney-General to James II..... Edited, with copious notes, London, 1846. Thomas Morley's First book of Ballets for 5 voices (Musical Antiquarian Society). Thomas Bateson's First set of Madrigals (Musical Antiquarian Society). Orlando Gibbons' Fantasias of 3 parts for viols (Musical Antiquarian Society). Purcell's Bonduca, a tragedy..to which is added a history of the rise and progress of Dramatic Music in England (Musical Antiquarian Society). Byrd, Bull and Gibbons' "Parthenia" (Musical Antiquarian Society). Purcell's ode for St. Cecilia's Day (Musical Antiquarian Society). *Edited, sacred*: Cathedral Chants of the 16th, 17th, and 18th centuries....Biographical notices of the composers, London, 1844. The Order of Daily Service..as used in the Abbey Church of Saint Peter, Westminster..London, 1844. A collection of anthems by composers of the Madrigalian era, London (Musical Antiquarian Society), 1845. Cathedral music, consisting of services and anthems..London, n.d. [Vol. 1., all published]. Collection of services and anthems, chiefly adapted from the works of Palestrina, Orlando di Lasso, Vittoria, Colonna, etc., London (Motett Society), 3 vols. The Hand-book for the Parish Choir, a collection of Psalm-tunes, services, anthems, chants, etc., London, n.d. The Order of Morning and Evening Prayer, with the harmony in 4 parts..London, n.d. Vocal Part Music, sacred and secular, a collection of anthems, motetti, madrigals, part-songs, etc., London, n.d. A little book of Christmas Carols, with the ancient melodies to which they are sung in various parts of the country ..London [1847]. Old English Carols, and two hymns, London, 1865. The full Cathedral Service, composed by Thomas Tallis.. with an historical preface, and a biography of the composer, London, n.d. The Order of Daily Service with the musical notation as adapted and composed by Thomas Tallis, London, n.d. Edward Lowe's Order of Chanting the Cathedral Service, London, n.d. The Whole Book of Psalms, with the tunes in four parts by Thomas Este, 1592..historical and biographical notice, London (Musical Antiquarian Society), n.d. The Booke of Common Prayer with musical notes, as used in the Chapel Royal of Edward VI., 1550. Compiled by John Merbecke.. reprinted in facsimile, London, n.d. *Vocal:* Country life, cantata ; Fair maid of Islington, operetta, 1838. Part-songs and numerous single songs. *Organ :* Organist's Handbook,

RISELEY.

a collection of voluntaries..arranged from composers of the German school, London, n.d. The Organist's Portfolio, a series of voluntaries from the works of ancient and modern composers, London, 1866 (Boston edition, 1867). Some original pieces. *Pianoforte:* An enormous quantity of albums, arrangements, selections, transcriptions, and other pieces for solo and duet, with a few original pieces. In addition to all the foregoing it should be mentioned that Rimbault edited many works for the Percy Society; an edition of Sir Thomas Overbury's works; several of Handel's oratorios; Operas by various composers; and contributed many articles, biographical, and otherwise, to the "Imperial Dictionary of Biography," Grove's "Dictionary of Music," and to periodical literature.

Ring, John, amateur musician, surgeon and poet, born at Wincanton, Somerset, August 21, 1752. Distinguished as an advocate of vaccination. He died at London, December 7, 1821. In addition to some poetry and professional books, he published "The Commemoration of Handel: a poem," London, 1786; 2nd edition, 1819. This was issued anonymously.

Rippon, John, clergyman and musician, born at Tiverton, April 29, 1751 ; died London, December 17, 1836. Compiler of "Selection of Psalm and Hymn tunes, in three or four parts," London [1795] ; "Selection of Psalm and Hymn Tunes from the best authors, in three and four parts . . ." London, 2nd edition, 1806; 13th edition, 1820. "Selection of Tunes in miniature," London, 1806-8. A "Companion" to this was issued in 1820, edited by Walker. About 1837 an oratorio by Rippon, entitled the "Crucifixion," was published. A selection from his tune book was issued as "Sacred Music," etc , by J. Tomlins, in 1810.

Riseley, George, organist and conductor, born at Bristol, August 28, 1845. Chorister in Bristol Cathedral when seven, and in 1862 articled to J. D. Corfe, the Cathedral organist. After holding several organ appointments he officiated at All Saints', Clifton, until 1876, when he succeeded Mr. Corfe at the Cathedral. In 1870 he was appointed organist of Colston Hall, and his recitals gained a high reputation. As a performer on the organ he has also been heard at the Royal Albert Hall, where he gave a series of recitals in 1885. In 1877 he started the Bristol Monday Popular Concerts of orchestral music, which have had a wide educational influence in the West of England. These he has carried on at great personal sacrifice, and has introduced the most important works of all schools, including upwards of a hundred examples, orchestral and

RITSON.

ROBERTS.

choral, by British composers. From 1878 he has been conductor of the Bristol Orpheus Society, the fame of which he has extended. The Society, under his direction, has given concerts in London, 1894 and 1896 ; has sung at the Gloucester Festival, 1895 ; and before the Queen, at Windsor Castle, 1895, when Her Majesty authorised the choir to use the prefix "Royal," and presented Mr. Riseley with an inscribed bâton. He is also conductor of the Bristol Society of Instrumentalists, and a busy teacher. Many tokens of the appreciation of his fellow citizens have been bestowed upon him. He was elected conductor of the Bristol Festival in 1896, gaining further distinction in that important office. In 1893 he was appointed a professor of the organ at the R.A.M., of which Institution he is an honorary member. Of his compositions mention may be made of a Jubilee Ode, performed at Bristol, 1887 ; a Jubilee March for organ ; Where'er my footsteps stray, and The Old Church Bells, part songs for men's voices ; a Christmas Carol, etc.

Ritson, Joseph, antiquary and writer, born at Stockton in 1752, died at London in 1803. Compiled, among other valuable and interesting works, "Ancient Songs, from the time of King Henry the Third to the Revolution. Prefixed are observations on the Ancient English Minstrels, and Dissertation on Ancient Songs and Music," London, 1790. "Scottish Songs, with the Music, and Historical Essay . . ." London, 2 vols., 1794. Reprinted, Glasgow, 2 vols., 1869. Also an English Anthology, Ballad Collections, and a Bibliographia Poetica, etc.

Riviere, Anna, see BISHOP, ANNA.

Roberts, Arthur, vocalist and comedian of the present time, who was born on September 21, 1852. He was a legal clerk in a financial office, and first began singing as an amateur. Made his mark in the Music Halls, and then appeared in pantomime at Oxford in 1878. Quitted the Music Halls and sang in "The Grand Mogul" at the Comedy Theatre, London, 1884. Toured in the provinces in comic opera, etc. Latterly has been giving entertainments with a party of his own. Among his best recent impersonations may be named "Gentleman Joe," which had a long and successful run at the Prince of Wales' Theatre, London. A memoir is published by Arrowsmith, Bristol, as "Adventures of Arthur Roberts, by rail, road, and river, told by himself, and chronicled by Richard Morton." [1895]. He has composed a few songs, "If I were to do such a thing;" "Keeping up the old girl's birthday," etc.

Roberts, David Alawydd, musician, was born in Carnarvonshire, June 16, 1820. He was self-taught in music, and for three years

in succession, 1851-53, won the chief prize for anthem at the Bethesda Eisteddfodau. He also conducted performances of the "Messiah," "Israel in Egypt," "Samson," etc., at Bethesda. He died on May 26, 1872. Author of a grammar of music, "Gramadeg cerddoriaeth, mewn tair rhan, sef nodiant," etc. Gwrecsam, 1848; 2nd edition, Wrexham, 1862, a small but concise work which has proved very valuable to monoglot Welsh musicians. In 1867 he issued a Psalm Tune book, also in Welsh.

Roberts, Eleazar, musician, published "Hymnau a Thonau..," Wrexham, 1870, Llawlyfr Caniadaeth," Wrexham, and other works.

Roberts, Ellis, harpist and composer, born Dolgelly in 1819. He was harpist to the Prince of Wales. Died, London, December 6, 1873. His son, ELLIS ROBERTS, born in London, 1850, was a chorister at St. Paul's Cathedral. Studied at R.A.M. as a violinist, and is a member of the Philharmonic orchestra, and principal second violin, Royal Italian Opera, since 1895.

Roberts, Frederic Egbert, bass vocalist, born at Newtown, Montgomery, September 26, 1847. Was brought up to the printing and bookselling business, but having a fine bass voice, studied singing afterwards under Chevalier Lemmens, F. Kingsbury, J. C. Beuthen, and Alfred Blume. Has sung at the principal concerts in London and the provinces. Made his *début* at the Crystal Palace Concerts, April 21, 1883. Was for some time a member of the Carl Rosa Opera Company, and sang at Drury Lane, as well as on tour in the provinces. Principal bass at the Italian Church, Hatton Garden, and, since 1894, musical director there.

Roberts, John, HEULLAN, musician, born at Heullan, March 30, 1807 ; died, April 4, 1876. Published "Caniadau y cyssegr, neu gassglaid o donau hen a diveddar gan mwyaf o gyfansoddiad Gymmreig," 1839. Selection of 55 Psalm Tunes in Welsh. "Casgliad o donau y diweddar," London, 1876.

Roberts, John Henry, composer and conductor, born at Bethesda, near Bangor, March 31, 1848. Had lessons from a local teacher, and became an organist at twelve. Removing to Towyn he started a choral society. Entered R.A.M. in 1870, and studied under Sterndale Bennett and C. Steggall. A.R.A.M. Graduated Mus. Bac., Cambridge, 1882. He is also a Fellow of the Tonic Sol Fa College. Resident at Carnarvon as organist of Castle Square Church, and teacher and composer. In 1885, at the Aberdare Eisteddfod, he won prizes for an anthem, six-part madrigal, and tenor song. He has composed an overture, "Caractacus," a cantata, and other pieces. Author of handbooks on Ele-

ROBERTS.

ments of Music and Harmony; and editor of Anthem Book for the use of Welsh Churches (Novello); musical editor of Handbook of Praise, and Congregational Tune Book.

Roberts, John Varley, organist and composer, born at Stanningley, near Leeds, September 25, 1841. His musical talent was developed at an early age, and when twelve he was appointed organist of St. John's, Farsley, near Leeds; in 1862 he was organist at St. Bartholomew's, Armley, and in 1868 organist and choirmaster of Halifax Parish Church. Graduated Mus. Bac. 1871, Mus. Doc. 1876, Oxford; F.C.O., 1876. In 1882 he was appointed to Magdalen College, Oxford, as organist and magister choristarum, also holding office, 1885-93, at St. Giles' Church, Oxford. Conductor of the Oxford Choral and Philharmonic Society, 1885-93; Madrigal Society of Magdalen College; and of the Magdalen Vagabonds. Lecturer in harmony and counterpoint for the Oxford Professor of Music; Examiner for Musical Degrees, 1883-86-89-90. He has given many high-class concerts at Oxford.

WORKS.—Jonah, sacred cantata, 1876, performed at Oxford and many other places; Psalm 103, for chorus and orchestra; A full Morning, Communion, and Evening Service in D; Full Communion Service in D; Magnificat and Nunc Dimittis in C, composed for the Festival of the London Church Choir Association, St. Paul's Cathedral, 1894; Evening Services in F, E, and G; Four settings of the Benedictus; The Lord's Prayer and Apostles' Creed in harmonised monotone; Benedicite, Omnia Opera, etc. *Anthems :* Lord, we pray Thee; Seek ye the Lord; Lord, who shall dwell; Peace I leave with you; I will sing unto the Lord, composed for the Jubilee Service in Magdalen Chapel, 1887; The whole earth is at rest; and others. *Part Songs :* Cupid once upon a bed of roses; Come, my dear one; The shades of night; A red, red rose. *Songs :* The old Parish Church; The Far-off Land; Happy Moments; My World; Maiden with the merry eye; A Farewell, etc. Andante in G, Postlude in F, Larghetto and Allegro in F, and other pieces for organ. Editor of The Parish Church Chant Book, Novello; Supplement to Cheetham's Psalmody; The Victoria Book of Hymns.

Roberts, Kate, see sub. RALPH, FRANCIS.

Roberts, Richard, harpist, known as the "blind Minstrel of Carnarvon," born 1796; died June, 1855. He was a performer of great skill, and played before Princess Victoria at Beaumaris in 1832. He compiled "Cambrian Harmony, being a collection of Welsh airs," Dublin [1840].

Roberts, Mrs. T., see ISAACS, REBECCA.

Roberts, W. Jarrett, composer and

ROBERTSON.

teacher, was born at Liverpool in 1846. He studied at the R.A.M., and afterwards became principal of the North Wales Academy of Music. He died at Bangor in November, 1886. Composer of "The Inundation of Cantrir Gwaelod," a dramatic cantata, Merthyr, 1881; Music for pf. and violin, songs, etc.

Robertson, a Scottish family of violinists, who flourished early in the present century. It consisted of HENRY, JAMES, and WILLIAM, who mostly resided at Alloa, and performed at gatherings in the surrounding country.

Robertson, Alexander, musician and teacher of first part of present century. He taught the pf. on the Logierian system, and was, in company with Penson, a violinist, as musicseller in Edinburgh. He afterwards carried on a music-publishing business in partnership with his brother John. Robertson published Marshall's Reels and Strathspeys, and many other Scottish musical works.

Robertson, Daniel, musician, who was born in the latter part of the 18th century, and died about 1857. He issued "a collection of new reels, strathspeys, jigs, waltzes, etc." Edinburgh, n.d. [1802]. "A selection of Scots, English, and Irish songs with accompaniments for the piano." Edinburgh, n.d., 2 vols. "A collection of Psalm and Hymn Tunes in miniature, arranged in three parts for voice and pf." Edinburgh, 1800.

Robertson, James Stewart, of Edradynate. Collector, was born May 15, 1823. He published "The Athole Collection of the Dance Music of Scotland,"....Edinburgh, 1884, 2 vols.

Robertson, John, musician and publisher, born about 1777. He was precentor of the Barony Church in Glasgow, and had a music-selling business in the same city. He died at Glasgow, March 11, 1827. Compiler of "a selection of the best Psalm and Hymn Tunes, some of which are printed, in four parts.." Glasgow, 1814. "The Seraph: a selection of Psalm and Hymn Tunes.." [1827]; also Glasgow [1840]. These collections were afterwards issued in oblong volumes as "Brown's Robertson's Selection of Sacred Music."

Robertson, John, organist and composer, born in Edinburgh, February 16, 1838. While attending the University Music Classes he gained one of the scholarships offered by the U. P. denomination, but deciding to make music his profession, he resigned it. After studying with Professor Donaldson, he went to Berlin, and worked with Franz Schulz. In 1884, he graduated Mus. Doc., Cambridge, the first Scotsman to take the degree at that University. F.E.I.S. Organist and director of the choir, New Greyfriars' Church, 1876-1895; St. Andrew's Episcopal Church, 1872

ROBERTSON.

to present time. Conductor of Carubbers Close Choir. Has composed a setting of Psalm 122, for soli, chorus, orchestra, and organ; anthems, Pray for the Peace of Jerusalem, and others; Te Deum in F. Part songs: Lull ye my Love asleep (prize); Awake! ye midnight mariners (sung at Crystal Palace); Victoria Pæan, etc. Is author of a Treatise on Harmony and Counterpoint, in "The Musical Educator," edited by John Greig, (q.v.)

Robertson, Sophie Maria, soprano vocalist, born at Valparaiso, Chili, July 31, 1854. Her father was a merchant who had settled there, and her mother a daughter of Lieutenant Worthington who fought under Nelson at Trafalgar. In 1864 the family returned to England, the father dying the same year. As a child Miss Robertson's singing attracted attention, and later she was placed under Randegger, and Benedict. She first appeared at the concerts of the Royal Amateur Orchestral Society, 1875-6; was heard in the provinces, 1877, and the extraordinary range of her voice contributed much to her early success. In 1884 she married Mr. Stanley Stubbs, and retired from the platform; but up to 1888 occasionally sang at the Royal Albert Hall, and in the country. Her sister, FANNY ROBERTSON, is a contralto vocalist, who has appeared at the Crystal Palace and other concerts. The duet singing of the two sisters was very artistic, recalling the similar performances of the Misses Williams, and other singers.

Robertson, Rev. Thomas, D.D., clergyman and writer, was minister at Dalmeny, Linlithgowshire, and died, Edinburgh, November 15, 1799. Author of "An Inquiry into the Fine Arts...," vol. 1, London, 1784. This volume, all that was published of the work, contains the "History and Theory of Ancient and Modern Music."

Robinson, Anastasia, COUNTESS OF PETERBOROUGH, contralto vocalist, born at London about end of 17th century [1698]. Daughter of a portrait painter. She studied under Croft and Sandoni. *Début* in "Creso," 1714. Appeared afterwards in operas by Handel, Scarlatti, and Buononcini. Privately married to the Earl of Peterborough, 1724, at which time she quitted the stage. She is supposed to have lived with him, and to have been considered as his "mistress" till 1735, when, a short time previous to his death in that year, the Earl acknowledged the marriage. She died at Bevis Mount, Southampton, 1750.

Robinson, Daniel, musician, author of "An Essay upon vocal musick," Nottingham, 1715.

Robinson, George Herbert, organist and teacher. Graduated Mus. Bac., Cambridge, 1885. Organist of St. Mary's, Abchurch,

ROBINSON.

London, 1858; St. Bartholomew's Hospital, 1864; organist and choirmaster, Charterhouse School, Godalming, from 1872. Member, and sometime Director, of the Philharmonic Society. Composer of a cantata, "Praise the Lord"; Church services, pf. pieces, etc.

Robinson, Hamilton, pianist, organist, and composer, born at Brighton, December 6, 1861. Studied at R.A.M. Mus. Bac., Durham, 1891; F.R.C.O. In 1879 appointed organist and choirmaster, Brunswick Chapel, Hyde Park, London; and in 1885 to St. Stephen's, South Kensington. Lecturer on harmony, King's College, London, and some time conductor of Burlington Choral Association. His wife, a contralto vocalist, was educated at the R.A.M., and in 1895 was appointed a professor of singing at King's College, ladies' department.

WORKS. — Sacred Cantata; Cantata for ladies' voices; Overture orchestra, and Postlude for orchestra and organ, in MS. Morning, Evening, and Communion Service; Benedictus and Agnus Dei in E flat; Three Christmas Carols. The Fisherman; In Absence; Love's Challenge; and other songs. Phantasiescenen; Impromptu; Valse Caprice; Tarantella; Gavotte and Musette; Three Sketches, etc., for pf.; andante, organ, etc.

Robinson, John, organist and composer, born in 1682. He studied in the Chapel Royal under Dr. Blow. Organist of St. Lawrence Jewry, 1710, and St. Magnus, 1713. Organist of Westminster Abbey, 1727. He died at London, April 30, 1762. Composer of chants, psalms, etc. His wife, ANN TURNER ROBERTSON, whom he married in 1716, was a vocalist of some fame in her day, and sang in the works of Handel. She died on January 5, 1741.

Robinson, Joseph, the most distinguished of a remarkable family of musicians. The father, FRANCIS ROBINSON, was vestry clerk at St. Peter's Parish Church, Dublin; a professor of music, and baritone singer. He founded, in 1810, a society called the "Sons of Handel." Of his seven children, six—four sons and two daughters—became professional musicians. FRANCIS, the eldest son, born in Dublin, 1799 (?), was a chorister in Christ Church Cathedral; organist, St. Patrick's, 1828-30; Vicar-choral, tenor, Christ Church, 1833, till his death, October 31, 1872. He was a Mus. Doc., *honoris causâ*, Dublin, and was the composer of some church music and songs. He also edited Irish Melodies, with an introduction on Irish Music, by George Farquhar Graham. Dublin, Bussell [1866]. WILLIAM, the second son, had a bass voice of exceptional quality and range. He was a member of the St. Patrick's choir as late as 1845, and also of the choirs of Christ Church and Trinity College. JOHN, the third son,

ROBINSON.

born, 1812 (?), was also in the Cathedral Choirs. He had a tenor voice ranging to the high D. He was organist of St. Patrick's, 1828; Trinity College, 1834; and of Christ Church, 1841. He died in 1844. JOSEPH, the youngest son, was born in Dublin, August 20, 1816. Entered the choir of St. Patrick's, 1824, and when his voice broke became organist of Sandford Church. When a youth, visited Paris and London, gaining valuable experience, and becoming acquainted with leading musicians. In 1834 established in Dublin, the "Antient Society," which he conducted for nearly thirty years, introducing many important works for the first time to Dublin. Became conductor of the University Choral Society in 1837. Conducted at the opening of the Exhibitions at Cork, 1852 and 1883; Dublin, 1853. Professor of singing at Royal Irish Academy of Music from 1856, into which institution he infused new life; and in 1876 established the Dublin Musical Society, which gave its last concert, December 6, 1888, but was afterwards revived under Dr. Joseph Smith (q.v.) In August, 1896, on attaining his eightieth year, Mr. Robinson retired from active work. As a baritone vocalist he long held a foremost position; while as a conductor and teacher he was in the front rank. His compositions include anthems, services, and songs; and he wrote a March for the opening of the Dublin Exhibition, 1882. It was for Joseph Robinson that Mendelssohn scored for orchestra his setting of "Hear my Prayer," originally written with an accompaniment for organ alone. He married, in 1849, Miss FANNY ARTHUR, a pianist and composer, born, September, 1831. Studied at first at Southampton, and later under Sterndale Bennett and Thalberg. She played at Dublin in February, 1849; appeared at the matinées of the Musical Union, London, June 26, 1855; and at the New Philharmonic Concerts, June 18, 1856. That year she became a professor at the R.I.A.M. She composed a sacred cantata, "God is Love," still occasionally performed; a number of pf. pieces, and some songs. She died at Dublin, October 31, 1879.

Robinson, Thomas, musician of latter part of 16th and beginning of 17th centuries. Author of "The Schoole of Musicke; wherein is taught the perfect method of true fingering of the lute, pandora, orpharion, and viol-de-gamba, with most infallible general rules both easie and delightful: also a method how you may be your own instructor for prick-song, etc.," London, 1603. New Citharen Lessons, with perfect tunings of the same, London, 1609.

Robinson, Sir William Cleaver F., amateur composer, born in 1839. Fourth son of the late Admiral Sir H. Robinson, of

ROCKSTRO.

Rosmead, County Meath, and brother of Lord Rosmead (Sir Hercules Robinson). Private Secretary to his brother; Governor of West Australia, 1880; South Australia, 1882; Victoria, 1889; and West Australia, 1890-5, when he retired, and settled in London. He died there, May 2, 1897. He composed the operas, "The Handsome Ransom, or the Brigand's Bride," produced at Perth, Western Australia, and at Melbourne, 1893; and "The Nut-brown Maid," completed 1896. His "Unfurl the Flag" was the first national song the Australians possessed. Other of his songs are: Remember me no more; Imperfectus; Severed; I love thee so; Thou art my soul, etc. He was also an accomplished violinist.

Robinson, Winifred, violinist, born at Boston, Lincolnshire. Studied at R.A.M. under Sainton. Kelsall prize holder, 1885. A.R.A.M. As a youthful performer was heard at the Birmingham Saturday Concerts in February, 1880, and in other provincial towns. In 1887 she made a successful appearance at Brunswick; and since 1888 has given concerts in London. In 1895 she organised a ladies' string quartet, which has acquired a good reputation in chamber music.

Roby, Arthur, organist and composer. Organist and choirmaster at Stamford Hill Church, London. He has composed a sacred cantata, "Blind Bartimæus," produced, October 13, 1892; and two operettas, " 1990," and "Won by wit," performed at Myddleton Hall, London, October 16, 1895.

Rock, Michael, composer and organist, born in latter part of 18th century. He studied under Dr. B. Cooke, and in 1802 became organist of St. Margaret's, Westminster. He died in London, March, 1809. Composer of glees, "Beneath a churchyard yew," "Let the sparkling wine go round" (prize, 1794), etc.

Another musician named WILLIAM ROCK, a relative of the foregoing, was organist of St. Margaret's Westminster, from 1774 to 1802. He composed glees, "Alone thro' unfrequented wilds" [1790], etc.; songs and instrumental music.

Rockstro, William Smyth, originally RACKSTRAW, organist, composer, and writer, born at North Cheam, Surrey, January 5, 1823. Studied under John Purkis, and later with Sterndale Bennett. At the farewell concert of François Cramer, Hanover Square Rooms, June 27, 1844, Staudigl sang a song, "Soon shall chilling fear," composed by Rackstraw. An overture for orchestra,, "Twelfth Night," was rehearsed by the Society of British Musicians, September 21 following; and a duet from an opera, "Die Weldon," was given at a concert of that society, March 27, 1845. After that time to the middle of

RODDIE.

1846 he studied at Leipzig Conservatorium, and was one of the few who enjoyed the direct tuition of Mendelssohn. On his return he became known as Mr. Rockstro, this being an older form of the family name. He appeared at times as a pianist, and was accompanist at the British, and "Wednesday Concerts" at Exeter Hall, etc. In 1847, in conjunction with J. Wrey Mould, he began to edit, for Boosey and Co., a series of operas in vocal score, with memoirs, and indications of the instrumentation. They were the first operas published in monthly parts, at a cheap rate. Lived for many years at Torquay, and was, from 1867, organist and honorary precentor at All Saints', Babbicombe. In 1876 he was received into the Church of Rome. He conducted concerts of Italian and English sacred music of 16th and 17th centuries at the "Inventions" Exhibition, 1885, and, returning to London in 1891, gave lectures at the R.A.M. and R.C.M., at the latter taking a class for plain song. In ancient ecclesiastical music he was a high authority. He died in London, July 2, 1895.

WORKS.—Sacred cantata, The Good Shepherd, produced at Gloucester Festival, 1886; O, too cruel fair, madrigal, five voices, Bach Choir, 1884; ballet, Flora's Path, Bristol Madrigal Society, 1891; Queen and Huntress, A Jewel for my Lady's Ear, and other songs; overture, Nieser, orchestra, 1848; numerous light pieces for pf.; Festival Psalter, adapted to the Gregorian Tones; Accompanying Harmonies to the Ferial Psalter; Harmonies for Additional Chants and the Ambrosial Te Deum. *Literary*: A History of Music for Young Students, 1879; Practical Harmony, 1881; The Rules of Counterpoint, 1882; Life of George Frederic Handel, London, Macmillan, 1883; Mendelssohn (Great Musicians Series), 1884; A General History of Music, Sampson Low, 1886; Jenny Lind, the Artist (with Canon Scott Holland), Murray, 1891; Jenny Lind, her Vocal Art and Culture (with Otto Goldschmidt), Novello, 1894; a long series of valuable papers in Grove's Dictionary; contributions to the *Musical Times*, *Musical Society*, and other journals.

RICHARD SHEPHERD ROCKSTRO, his brother, is a professor of the flute at the Guildhall School of Music. He was for years in orchestras under Costa, and principal flute in British Orchestral Society, 1872. Author of a Treatise on the Construction, History, and Practice of the Flute, London, Rudall, 1891? Also of the section relating to flutes in the descriptive catalogue of instruments at the Military Exhibition, London, 1890, compiled by Captain Day (*q.v.*)

Roddie, William Stewart, composer and teacher, born in Glasgow, September 11, 1845. Brought up to the business of an

RODWELL.

engraver; after some years abandoned it for music, for which he had a strong predilection. Received most of his musical training at the Andersonian University, Glasgow, and began his professional career at Perth, in 1871. In 1873, he removed to Inverness, where he is now settled. He is choirmaster in the Free High Church, conductor of the Choral Union, and superintendent singing-master to the School Board. He is also professor, Art of Teaching, in the Tonic Sol-Fa College, London.

WORKS.—*Operettas for Children:* Queen of the Seasons; Hermit's Cell; The little old Woman; Sir Christus the Good; Little Folks at Play; Norseman and Saxon. *School Cantatas:* The Spring-tide Holiday; The Forest Rovers; The Sleeping Beauty; The House that Jack Built; Valentine and Orson; Aladdin; Ali Babu, and others. School song books, action songs, part songs, etc. Translator of The Bohemian Girl and Maritana into Tonic Sol-fa notation.

Rodney, Paul, composer, of present time. He has published a number of songs, among which may be named A Dream of Bethlehem; A Dream of golden days; As once in May; Alone on the raft; Emmanuel; Thy King; On Carmel's Hill; Calvary; Fisher's Goodbye; In a garden of roses; Time and Tide; Venezia, etc.

Rodwell, Anne, authoress of "The Juvenile Pianist, or a mirror of music for infant minds," London, 1835; 2nd edition, 1843.

Rodwell, George Herbert Bonaparte, composer and dramatist, was born at London, November 15, 1800. Son of Thomas Rodwell, part-proprietor of the Adelphi Theatre, on whose death, in March, 1825, he succeeded to his share in the theatre. Music-director of Covent Garden, 1836. Married to Miss Liston, daughter of John Liston, the comedian. He died at Pimlico, London, January 22, 1852.

WORKS.—*Operettas, etc.:* Bottle Imp, 1828; Mason of Buda, 1828; Spring Lock, 1829; Earthquake, 1829; Devil's Elixir, 1829; My own lover, 1832; Evil eye, 1832; Lord of the Isles, 1834; Paul Clifford, 1835; Sexton of Cologne, 1836; Jack Sheppard, 1839; Grace Darling; Die Hexen am Rhien; Sathanus; Don Quixote; Bronze Horse; Quasimodo (from Weber's "Preciosa"); Last days of Pompeii. Songs of the Sabbath Eve, poetry by E. Fitzball. Songs of the Birds, by Fitzball; Six rounds, 2 books, London, n.d. Royal Serenades, 3 part-songs. *Songs:* A cup of nectar; Awake, ye gallant sons of Greece; Banks of the blue Moselle; Beautiful blue violets; Blind flower-girl's song; Flower of Ellerslie; Hurrah! for the road; Here's a health to thee, Mary; Land of the free; Muleteer; Nix, my dolly, pals fake away;

ROE.

ROGERS.

Poor Louise; Song of night; Up, brothers, up; Who cares, etc. The First Rudiments of Harmony, with an account of all instruments employed in an orchestra, London, 1830. A Catechism on Harmony, London, n.d. The Guitar, London, n.d. Edited Whittaker's hand-books of musical instruction [1845]. A Letter to the Musicians of Great Britain, London, 1833. Also a few novels, of which "Old London Bridge" ran through several editions, and was reprinted in America. "The Memoirs of an Umbrella," and "Woman's Love," are two others. He also wrote farces and dramatic pieces.

Roe, John W., bass singer, who wrote a number of songs for John Parry and others, and did much to foster the cultivation of Glees. He died at Hove, Brighton, March 2, 1853.

Roe, Richard, clergyman, vocalist, and writer, who died at London, April, 1853. He wrote "The Principles of Rhythm, both in Speech and Music, especially as exhibited in the mechanism of English verse," Dublin, 1823.

Roe, Samuel, musician, issued "Bedfordshire Harmony, a set of original tunes," London, 1825.

Roebuck, Alfred, compiler of "Old Methodist Tunes, intended to illustrate a lecture entitled "Stories of old Methodist hymns," Manchester, Heywood, 1887.

Roeckel, Joseph Leopold, pianist and composer, born in London, April 11, 1838. Youngest son of Professor JOSEPH AUGUSTUS ROECKEL, vocalist and operatic director (1783-1870), who, in 1832, produced for the first time in England, German opera in the original language, Beethoven's "Fidelio," May 10, etc. J. L. Roeckel studied under his father; at Würzburg, with Eisenhofer; and with Johann Götze, at Weimar. Settled at Clifton, as teacher and composer. Has been often heard as a pianist; played at the first of Mr. Riseley's Popular Concerts, October 6, 1877; in Birmingham the same year, on tour with Pyatt's concert party, etc. He has composed a great number of vocal and instrumental pieces, outlined in the subjoined list:—Cantatas: Fair Rosamund, produced at the Crystal Palace, 1871; Westward Ho!; The Ten Virgins; Ruth; Father Christmas; The Sea Maidens; Heather Bells; Mary Stuart; La Gitana; The Minstrel Prince; Jubilee Cantata, The Victorian Age, 1887; Miriam; Yule-tide chimes; A summer Sunday morning; The crystal slipper; The woodland sylphs; The angel's gift; Merrie old England; Mountain rose; William Tell (for boys). The Christian's Armour, service of song. The hours; The silver penny, operettas for children. Glees: Twilight; Airs of summer; Madeline; In Memoriam (Mlle. Tict-

jens), etc. Dramatic scena, "Siddartha," for baritone solo and orchestra, Bristol Festival, 1896. Songs of Nature, 12 two-part songs; Two sets of five songs, op. 12, 13; Lieder-album, six songs; The scent of the limes; Can you forget; Angus Macdonald; Won by a rose; Storm fiend; Sun dial; and many other songs. Suite for orchestra; pieces for violin and pf.; Abend-Traum; Air du Dauphin; Fête Roumaine; Impromptu caprices, 2 books; Three Musical Sketches, etc., for pf.

In 1864 he married Miss JANE JACKSON, pianist and composer, born at Clifton. Her father—the late S. Jackson, of the old Water Colour Society, and an excellent amateur musician—was her first teacher; and she studied later under Pauer, Halle, Madame Schumann, Blumenthal, and Molique. Appeared as solo pianist at concerts given by Ernst Pauer in London; and from 1862 gave concerts at Clifton, playing concertos by Hummel, etc., with orchestral accompaniments. Later, devoted herself chiefly to teaching and composition, but playing occasionally in public. On April 4, 1885, she gave a concert of compositions by women. Under the name of JULES DE SIVRAI, she has published Balmoral, Reverie Mazurka, Première Tarantella, Danse Russe, and other pieces for pf., several of which have been played by Arabella Goddard. She has also composed A Village Story, Drifting on, and numerous other songs; and is the inventor of the "Pamphonia," an appliance for learning the stave and clefs. She founded, in 1889, the Teachers' Provident Association, an excellent local institution.

Roffe, Alfred Thomas, author of "The Handbook of Shakespeare Music, being an account of three hundred and fifty pieces of music set to words taken from the plays and poems of Shakespeare, the compositions ranging from the Elizabethan Age to the present time," London, 1878. "Ghost Belief of Shakespeare," London, 1851, privately printed, etc. "A musical trial from Shakespeare.... to which is added old English singers, and Mr. Bowman, actor, singer, etc.," London, 1872.

Rogers, Benjamin, composer and organist, born at Windsor in 1614. Son of Peter Rogers, lay-clerk of St. George's Chapel. Chorister under Dr. Giles, and lay-clerk, St. George's Chapel, Windsor. Organist, Christ Church Cathedral, Dublin, 1639. Gentleman of St. George's Chapel, Windsor, 1641. Music-teacher in Windsor. Mus. Bac., Cantab., 1658. Organist of Eton College, circa 1662. Reappointed lay-clerk, Windsor, 1662. Organist of Magdalen College, Oxford, 1664-85. Mus. Doc., Oxon., 1669. He died at Oxford, June, 1698.

ROGERS.

WORKS.—A set of airs in four parts, for violins, 1653. Hymnus Eucharisticus, 1660. Evening Service in G. Services in D, A minor, E minor, and F. *Anthems :* Behold now, praise the Lord; Lord, who shall dwell; O pray for the peace of Jerusalem ; Teach me, O Lord ; etc., contained in the collections of Boyce, Page, Ouseley, and Rimbault. Hymns, songs, and instrumental pieces.

Rogers, Edmund, organist and composer, born at Salisbury, October 9, 1851. Chorister, Salisbury Cathedral, 1860-5. Appointed organist of Holy Trinity, Windsor, 1869 ; St. Alban's, Holborn, London, 1870 ; St. Thomas', Portman Square, 1871 ; and St. Michael's, Paddington, 1888, to present time. Conductor of Merchant Taylors' School Choral Society since 1886. His compositions are well known in America and Australia as well as in this country.

WORKS.—*Cantatas :* Sacred: The Pilgrim's Progress, 1883 ; Footprints of the Saviour, 1886 ; The Lord of Gold, 1890 ; Gathered Grain, 1890 ; From Cross to Crown, 1891 ; A Song of Praise, 1894 ; The King of Love, 1896. Secular : The Bridal Lay, 1871 ; Jack and the Beanstalk, 1879 ; Blue Beard, 1881 ; Beauty and the Beast, 1882 ; John Gilpin, 1883 ; Forty Thieves, 1884 ; Bells of Elsinore, female voices, 1888 ; Golden Fleece, -1890 ; Golden Flower, 1892 ; Evangeline, equal voices, 1895. *Operettas :* Elinore, or. the Border Bride, 1887 ; Daisy Dell, 1888 ; Princess Tiny Tot, 1889 ; The Florikins, 1892 ; and Woodland Fairies, 1896. Mass in D ; Offertory sentences; Hymn tunes. Anthems, songs, and part-songs. Chorus, The Crusader, written for a club at Philadelphia, 1887. Organ and pf. pieces, etc.

Rogers, Frederick F., organist and composer, born at Cheltenham in 1846. Organist and choirmaster, Highworth Parish Church, 1863 ; Assistant organist, Parish Church, Great Malvern ; and organist at the College Chapel, 1865 ; St. Peter's, Malvern Wells, 1869. Appointed manager of Steinway Hall, London, 1893.

WORKS.—Deborah, sacred cantata, for soli, chorus, and orchestra ; Psalm 69 ; Festival Te Deum in F; Offertory Sentences, and other church music. Cantatas for female voices : The Fairy Flower, 1884 ; Silver Sails, 1885 ; Elfin Chimes, 1886 ; Beautiful Land, 1887 ; In the hayfields, 1888 ; The Elfin Well, 1889. The Old Abbey; Old Church Tower; Pardon ; At set of sun ; Old England's Flag ; For ever ; and other songs. Pf. pieces : Minuet in A ; Six Morceaux de Salon ; Garland of favourites, 6 Nos., for young players ; Albumblatt, etc.

Rogers, Jeremiah, organist and author, born about 1818. He was appointed organist of Doncaster Parish Church in 1835, and held

ROMAINE.

that office until his death at Doncaster, January 22, 1879, aged 60. Author of a History of Doncaster.

Rogers, Sir John Leman, Bart., amateur composer, born April 18, 1780. Succeeded to the baronetcy, 1797. Member of the Madrigal Society, 1819. President of Madrigal Society, 1820-41. He died December 10, 1847.

WORKS.—Sixteen glees, for three, four, five, and six voices (edited by T. Oliphant), London [1842] Church Service in F ; anthems, chants, and other sacred music.

Rogers, Roland, organist, conductor, and composer, born at West Bromwich, Staffordshire, November 17, 1847. Studied under his father, a good violinist, and a local teacher. In 1858 he was organist of St. Peter's, West Bromwich, and when only fifteen secured a similar appointment at St. John's, Wolverhampton. He moved to Tettenhall Parish Church, in 1868, and in 1871 was appointed to Bangor Cathedral. There he raised the musical services to a high position. He resigned at the end of 1891. Graduated Mus. Bac. 1870, Mus. Doc. 1875, Oxford. A fine executant, he has given recitals at St. George's Hall, Liverpool (a series in 1890), and in other places, besides annual series in Bangor Cathedral. Conducted the Penrhyn and Arvonic Choirs, winning many Eisteddfodic prizes. Is now chiefly devoted to teaching, holding a leading position in Wales. His compositions comprise Psalm 130, for soli, chorus, and strings ; Prayer and Praise, cantata, soli, eight-part chorus and orchestra ; anthems and services; prize cantata, The Garden, produced at Llandudno, June 30, 1896 ; Florabel, cantata for female voices; school songs, part-songs, and songs; symphony for orchestra; string quintet; organ pieces, etc.

Rogers, Rev. Thomas, clergyman and author. Was Choral Scholar, New College, Oxford, 1859-63. Graduated M.A., Oxford, 1864 ; M.A., Durham, 1882 ; Mus. Doc., *honoris causâ,* Durham, 1882. Minor Canon, 1864-84 ; Precentor, 1872-84, Durham Cathedral. Occasionally conducted concerts at Durham, to 1884. Precentor, Chelmsford Association of Church Choirs, 1884. Vicar of Roxwell, Essex. Has published church music, hymn tunes, introits, etc. ; also songs and part songs. Author of " Musical Art : its Influence on Religious Life and Thought, 1883 ; " Church music in rural districts," 1886.

Rollinson, Matthew, violinist, teacher and conductor, born about 1806. He was well known in Yorkshire as a performer, and in Huddersfield as a teacher. He died October 6, 1874, aged 68.

Romaine, Rev. William, clergyman

w

ROMANZINI.

and writer, 1714-1795. Author of "An Essay on Psalmody, by W. R.," London, 1775.

Romanzini, Maria T., *see* BLAND, MARIA T.

Romer, Emma, soprano vocalist, born in 1814. She studied under Sir George Smart, and made her *début* at Covent Garden Theatre, London, in 1830. Sang in English Opera House, etc. Appeared chiefly in English operas, which she produced at the Surrey Theatre, London. She was married to a Mr. Almond. She died at Margate, April 11, 1868.

Romer, Francis, writer and composer, born in London, August 5, 1810. Member of the music-publishing firm of Hutchings and Romer. He died at Malvern, July 1, 1889. Father of Mr. Justice Romer. Composed Fridolin, opera, 1840; The Pacha's Bridal, opera, 1836; Mountain maidens, cantata; Musical Readings of H. W. Longfellow's Poetry, 1852-61, issued in parts. *Songs:* Six songs [1853]; Day dreams, Fair Chloris, I joyfully carol, I've watched with thee, Maiden of the sunny clime, Now smiling comes the joyous spring, O, mother, hear thy poor blind child, The lay of the chimes; Part-music for three and four voices, etc. "The Physiology of the Human Voice," London, 1845 and 1850. School of Singing, London [1861].

Romer, Thomas, tenor singer, who sang under the name of T. R. Travers, was born at Liverpool in 1817; died at London, May 20, 1855, aged 38.

His sister ANNIE (Mrs. William Brough) was a soprano singer. She was born in 1829, and died at London, February 1, 1852, aged 23. Made her stage *début* at the Adelphi Theatre, Liverpool, September 30, 1846.

CHARLES ROMER (a relative?) was singing in London at concerts in 1844, and was well spoken of.

Ronald, Landon, pianist and composer, born in London, June 7, 1873. When a child studied pianoforte under Ad. Schloesser and Carlo Albanesi. Scholar, R.C.M., studying under Franklin Taylor, Dr. Hubert Parry, R. Gompertz, and Dr. Bridge. Shewed extraordinary talent as a pianist, and appeared in public in 1887; but turned later to composition and conducting. Was pianist on tour with "L'Enfant Prodigue" company, 1891. Engaged as conductor at Drury Lane, in opera, April, 1896. He has composed an operetta, "Did you ring?" produced by the Grosvenor Club, November 29, 1892, and is understood to have in hand an opera on a large scale. His published songs include: The Future (composed at the age of eight); I love Thee; When the Lamp is shattered; Love in absence; and others. Pf. pieces: Une Idée; Ballade, etc. Part composer of music to "The Little Genius," Shaftesbury Theatre, 1896.

ROOTSEY.

Rooke, William Michael, or ROURKE, composer, born at Dublin, September 29, 1794. He was self-taught in music, with the exception of a few lessons from Dr. Cogan. Chorus-master and deputy-leader at Crow Street Theatre, Dublin, 1817. He settled in England, and became chorus-master at Drury Lane Theatre, London; leader at Vauxhall, under Bishop, and teacher of singing. He died at London, October 14, 1847.

WORKS.— *Operas:* Amilie, or the Love Test, London, 1837; Henrique, or the Love Pilgrim, London, 1839; Cagliostro, opera (MS.); The Valkyrie, opera (MS.); Overture for orchestra; Polonaise for violin; Farewell merry maids (chorus). *Songs:* Little Cupid once tapped at a maiden's heart; Hark the echo. Pf. music, etc.

Rookford, Rudolph, *see* CRAWFORD, WILLIAM.

Rootham, Daniel Wilberforce, baritone vocalist and conductor, born at Cambridge, August 15, 1837. His father, DANIEL ROOTHAM, was a bass singer in the choir of Trinity College, Cambridge, from 1815, until his death in 1852. At eight years of age the son was admitted a chorister at Trinity and St. John's Colleges. Studied under his father, and for five years with Dr. T. A. Walmisley. On the death of his father he removed to Bristol, and was appointed a lay-clerk at the Cathedral. After this time he studied singing under Schira. In 1865 he succeeded J. D. Corfe, the cathedral organist, as conductor of the celebrated Bristol Madrigal Society, and in 1878 was appointed conductor of the Bristol Festival Choir, retaining these positions to the present time, with that of chorus-master at the Bristol Festivals. Was engaged in concert singing to about 1870; and was organist at St. Peter's, Clifton Wood, 1866, giving up his cathedral appointment in 1877. His time is now chiefly devoted to voice training, and being an accomplished linguist and elocutionist, he has been engaged for lectures on voice management at Wells Theological College, and elsewhere.

His daughter, MABEL MARGARET ROOTHAM, was the first Bristol Scholar at the R.C.M., where she studied pf. under Franklin Taylor, and violin with R. Gompertz. She made a successful *début* at Victoria Rooms, Clifton, October 9, 1891, and is now pianist of the Popular Chamber Concert Society, Bristol, and engaged in teaching pf. and violin.

SAMUEL ROOTHAM, brother of D. F., tenor vocalist, was in the choir of Bristol Cathedral for many years from 1851. He is musical instructor at the Blind Asylum, Bristol, and conductor of the Redland Park Hall Band. In a quiet unobtrusive way he has done much good work.

Rootsey, S., author of "An attempt to

ROSA.

simplify the Notation of Music, together with an account of that now in use....," London, 1811.

Rosa, see PAREPA-ROSA.

Rose, Algernon S., writer on music, and composer, born in London, January 27, 1859. Educated at Broadstairs, Kent, and at Stuttgart and Yverdon, Switzerland. Studied pf. under Buttschardt, and Carl Hause, and violin under Kettenus. In business connection with the house of Broadwood & Sons, he has twice travelled round the world. F.R.G.S.; Fellow of the Philharmonic Society; and Liveryman of the Musicians' Company. Hon. Sec., Westminster Orchestral Society. Author of "Talks with Bandsmen: a popular handbook for brass instrumentalists," London, Rider; "Greater Britain, musically considered," a paper read at the Dublin Conference (1895) of the Incorporated Society of Musicians; Contributions to the musical press. Composer of the "Queen's March Past," the regimental march of the Queen's Westminster Volunteers; Waltzes, "C'est Moi," and "Chimes," for pf., and also for orchestra.

Rose, Henry Robert, organist, born at Bedford, May 6, 1855. Son of Robert Rose, many years organist of St. Paul's, Bedford, Studied at R.A.M., under G. A. Macfarren, Dr. Steggall, and others, from 1872. Second Read Prizeholder, 1879, for a quartet for pf. and strings. In 1880 he was appointed organist of St. Pancras Church, in succession to Henry Smart, a position he still holds. He has given organ recitals at Bow and Bromley Institute, from 1883, etc. Is a Fellow of R.A.M., and professor of the organ at that Institution. In 1880 he married Miss CLARA SAMUELL, the soprano vocalist. She was born at Manchester, August 29, 1857. Studied in that city under Henry Wilson; later at Milan; and in 1876 gained the Parepa-Rosa Scholarship at R.A.M., and the Parepa-Rosa Prize in 1880. Elected an Associate, 1881. She has sung at the principal London and provincial concerts; at the Crystal Palace; and is an Associate of the Philharmonic Society.

Rosen, Lina, see sub., BALFE, MICHAEL W.

Rosingrave, Daniel, or **Roseingrave,** organist, who was a chorister in the Chapel Royal, and a pupil of Purcell, and Blow. He was successively organist of Winchester Cathedral, 1681; Salisbury Cathedral, 1693-98; organist and vicar-choral, St. Patrick's Cathedral, Dublin, June 9, 1698-1727; organist and stipendiary of Christ Church, Dublin, November 11, 1698. He died at Dublin, in May, 1727. His son, RALPH, became vicar-choral of St. Patrick's Cathedral, 1719; organist there, and of Christ Church, 1727, which post he held till his death at Dublin,

ROSS.

in October, 1747. THOMAS, another son, was born at Dublin, and was educated by his father. He studied at Rome, at the expense of the Dean and Chapter of St. Patrick's Cathedral, 1710. Composer at the King's Theatre, London, 1720. Organist of St. George's, Hanover Square, 1725-37. He died insane, at London [1750]. He published "Voluntarys and Fugues, made on purpose for the organ or harpsichord," London [1730]. "Twelve solos for the German flute, with a thorough-bass for the harpsichord," n.d.; "Eight suites of lessons for the harpsichord or spinnet in most of the keys," London [1720]; Concerto for harpsichord; Six double Fugues for organ or harpsichord [1750]; Twelve solos for a German flute [1730]; Six Cantatas, with accompaniments....London, n.d.; "Narcissus," opera by D. Scarlatti, adapted for the English stage, with additional songs, 1720; A collection of forty-two suites of Lessons, by D. Scarlatti, with an introduction. Also some anthems, Italian songs, etc.

Ross, John, organist and composer, born at Newcastle-upon-Tyne, October 12, 1763. He studied music under Hawdon. In 1783 he became organist of St. Paul's Church, Aberdeen. He died at Craigie Park, Aberdeen, July 28, 1837.

WORKS.—Six concertos, for pf. and orchestra; Seven sets of 3 sonatas, for pf., op. 5, 31, 45, etc.; Three sonatas, for pf. and flute or violin, op. 16; Four sets of six waltzes, for pf., op. 9, etc.; Duets for pf., op. 26, etc. Ode to Charity, for solo, chorus, and organ; Six hymns, for 3 voices and organ; Two books of 6 canzonets, for voice and pf., op. 18, etc.; A select collection of ancient and modern Scottish airs, adapted for the voice, with introductory and concluding symphonies and accompaniments for the pianoforte, Edinburgh, 1792, 3 vols. Fifteen songs, written by Burns and Rannie, composed with accompaniments for the pf., violin or German flute, op. 11, London, n.d. Sacred Music, consisting of chants, psalms, and hymns, London, n.d. A complete Book of Instructions for beginners on the harpsichord or pianoforte, to which is added a select set of airs, Scots songs, and lessons, London, 1820. Songs: Aberdeen volunteers (Ewen); Ance I was as blythe; Braes of Ballochmyle; Come, Cynthia; The Coronach; Ellen of the Dee; Maid of Seaton Vale; Valley of Clyde, etc.

Ross, Roger Rowson, amateur musician, born at Montrose, August 25, 1817. Resident in Manchester, and has taken an active interest in music by founding two scholarships at the Royal Academy of Music, one for the study of sacred vocal music, and the other for performers on wind instruments. Composer and adapter of various hymns, etc., for the Church service.

ROSS.

Ross, Robert, musician, born in 1748. He was a music-seller in Edinburgh, and carried on business at the back of the Fountain Well, and afterwards at the head of Carrubbers' Close. He gave public concerts in Edinburgh, and retired about 1805. He died at Edinburgh in 1808, aged 60. Compiler of " A Choice Collection of Scots Reels, or country dances and strathspeys, with a bass for the violincello or harpsichord," Edinburgh, 1780.

Ross, William, piper, was born in Rossshire, about 1815, and died at Windsor, in August, 1891. In 1839 he joined the 42nd Highland Regiment, and remained in it till 1854, when he was appointed piper to the Queen. He issued a " Collection of Pipe Music," 1869, and another edition, " with an essay on the Bagpipes and its music, by the Rev. Dr. Norman Macleod " [1876] ; 3rd edition, 1885.

Rosse, Jeanie, MRS. H. A. QUINTON, contralto vocalist, born at Notting Hill, London, July 29, 1860. Received her first musical training at Madame Sainton-Dolby's Academy, afterwards studying under Randegger and W. Shakespeare ; also studied opera under Tramezzani, of the Naples Conservatoire, and declamation and acting under Edmund Russell. While still a pupil of Madame Dolby, she made her *début* at the Crystal Palace Concerts, and later had many engagements in London and the chief provincial cities. In June, 1888, she made her first appearance on the stage at St. George's Hall, London, as *Nancy,* in " Martha." The next year she joined the Carl Rosa Opera Company, but remained only a short time ; on her marriage settling in Dublin, where, 1891, she was appointed a professor of the Royal Irish Academy of Music. There she successfully conducts a declamation class, and also holds appointments at Loretto Abbey and other institutions.

Rossetor, Philip, lute-player and composer of the first part of the 17th century. Published " A Booke of Ayres, set foorth to be song to the Lute, Orpherian, and Base Violl," London, 1601 ; " Lessons for Consort, made by sundry excellent authors, and set to sixe several instruments, namely the Treble lute, Treble violl, Bass violl, Bandora, Citterne, and the Flute," London, 1609.

Rothwell, Alexander, flute player and writer, of latter part of the 17th century. Author of " The Compleat Instructor for the Flute, containing very plain and easie directions for beginners, with variety of newest tunes. .and flourishes in every key." London, [1698].

Rousbey, Arthur, baritone vocalist, studied in Italy under Sangiovanni, and in London under T. A. Wallworth. First sang

ROWLAND.

in opera in Charles Durand's Company, then from 1878 appeared in a round of characters in the Gilbert-Sullivan operas, in London, the provinces, and America. In 1884 he sang in Nessler's " Piper of Hamelin," at Covent Garden ; and subsequently in Italian opera, in " Rigoletto," etc. He has also been heard in concerts in various places. About 1888 he organised an opera company of his own, which has appeared in every important town in the United Kingdom, and has had several successful seasons in London. He produced, for the first time on any stage, Daniele Pellegrini's opera, " Mercedes," at Dublin, January 11, 1896 ; and has given, with excellent *ensemble,* a large number of standard works.

Rowbotham, John Frederick, author and composer, born in Edinburgh, April 18, 1854. Only son of the late Rev. Frederick Rowbotham, Incumbent of St. James's, Edinburgh. Educated at Edinburgh Academy, and Rossall School. Proceeding to Oxford, he gained the Balliol Scholarship when eighteen, and also took a first class in classics, and the Taylorian Scholarship for Italian. Travelled on the continent to collect materials for his History of Music. Studied music while at Oxford, and afterwards at Berlin, at the Stern Conservatorium for three years, with further study at Paris, Dresden, and Vienna. He has composed a Mass for double-chorus and orchestra ; three songs to words by Alfred Musset ; songs, various, etc. Author of " A History of Music," 3 vols. London, Trübner, 1885-7 ; " How to write Music correctly," London, Upcott Gill, 1889 ; " Private Life of Great Composers," Isbister, 1892 ; " The Troubadours, and the Courts of Love," Swan Sonnenschein, 1895. Contributed the musical articles to Chambers's Encyclopædia, and many papers to the *Nineteenth Century, National Review, Blackwood's Magazine,* and others, and also to the musical press. Author of poetical works, " The Death of Roland," 1886 ; and " The Human Epic," 1890, both published by Trübner.

Rowden, George Croke, amateur musician and clergyman, born in 1820. He was hon. precentor of Chichester Cathedral from 1859. Died, April 17, 1863. Founder of Chichester Choir Association. Composer of a magnificat and nunc dimittis, and other church music ; " Return of May," " Sweet evening hour," and various other glees, songs, etc.

Rowland, Alexander Campbell, double-bass player, violinist, and composer, born at Trinidad, January 1, 1826. His father was a fine clarinet player, and a band-master who served through the Peninsular campaign. The son, while an infant, was brought to Bath, and, when about six years old, received violin lessons from John Loder. Before he was seven, he entered the orchestra of the Queen's Theatre, London ; and also played the side-drum at the Promenade and other concerts. He learnt scoring from Waetzig, bandmaster of the Life Guards, and in 1846, began the study of the double-bass under Casolani, becoming one of the most remarkable performers on that instrument. Played cornet, drum, or viola in Jullien's band, 1842-6. Joined the Philharmonic orchestra in 1849, and was also in Royal Italian Opera, Sacred Harmonic, and principal Festival bands. In 1854, he went to reside at Southampton as music teacher, but continued his work in the Philharmonic Society until 1866, when Sterndale Bennett resigned the conductorship. At the Philharmonic concert, April 29, 1861, he played Mayseder's Violin Concerto, op. 40, on the double-bass. At Southampton, he conducted choral and orchestral societies, and did much valuable work. When sixty years old, he entered the examination for A.R.C.M., and passed with honours in seven subjects. He retired from active work in 1893, and died at Southampton, August, 1896.

WORKS.—Ps. 70, for voices and orchestra ; Overture, orchestra ; Set of Waltzes, for pf. and orchestra ; original air in C, double-bass and pf. Various works in MS. Blessed be the Lord ; Moonrise ; Morning thoughts ; and other songs. Course of Exercises in part-singing, Stanley Lucas. Author of a Method for the Double-Bass, in Two Parts, originally published by Lamborn Cock.

Rowley, Christopher Edward, composer and organist, born in Manchester, January 5, 1840. Studied pf. and organ under George Grundy, of Manchester ; harmony and counterpoint with H. C. Banister. Appointed, when nineteen, organist and choirmaster, Christ Church, Harpurhey ; since 1885, has held a similar post at St. Augustine's, Pendlebury. Has formed and trained many of the voluntary choirs in Manchester and district, and in 1879, founded the Musical Union bearing his name, a Society that has produced many operas, with stage accessories, as well as the principal oratorios and cantatas. Is now chiefly engaged as a voice trainer.

WORKS.– Operas: The Dragon of Wantley (1881); Eulalie (1887); The Early English Ring, now called Robinson's Craze (1890, produced, Manchester, 1891); Tilburina, or, The Spanish Armada (1894). Cantata, Doldrum, the Manager (1885). Anthems, Communion Service in F, Twelve Songs (1891), songs, duets, glees, and part-songs. Romance and Scherzo, wind quintet. Contributions on musical topics to the local press ; now engaged on an important work on voice-training.

Rowton, Rev. Samuel James, clergyman and musician, born in London, July 3, 1844. Musical training private. M.A., 1874, University College, Durham ; Mus. Bac., 1889 ; Mus. Doc., 1890, Dublin ; Mus. Doc., 1891, ad eundem, Durham. Organist and director of the music at Royal Medical College, Epsom, from 1872. He has set Cardinal Newman's "Dream of Gerontius," for soli, eight and twelve-part chorus, and orchestra ; and has published some hymns, songs, and pf. pieces.

Rudd, Henry William Kingston, pianist and organist, born at Norwich, May 27, 1850. Began his studies at the age of six, under his father, HENRY RUDD, a musician of repute in the Eastern Counties. Later he received instruction from Charles Halle. When ten years old he was appointed organist of Intwood Church, near Norwich ; then of Thorpe Parish Church ; and in 1870, organist and director of the choir of St. Andrew's, Norwich, offices he still holds. As a pianist he appeared with great success at the Norwich Festivals of 1872, and 1878, playing in each portions of concertos by Benedict. In 1882 he was heard at the Wednesday Concerts at the Crystal Palace. He has conducted the Norwich Gate House Choir, since 1872, and given important concerts, the first artists being associated with him in classical works.

Rush, George, composer of last half of the 18th century. He composed music for The capricious lovers [1764] ; and the Royal Shepherd. Also, Concertos for the harpsichord [1785] ; Six easy lessons for the harpsichord, calculated for the improvement of young practicioners, London [1770] ; Sonatas for pf. or harpsichord ; Concertos for pf., violin, and 'cello ; Sonatas for the guitar.

Russell, George, pianist, who was a man of mark and promise in his earlier years. When eight years old he appeared at a concert with Liszt, at H.M. Theatre, London, and afterwards appeared at a concert of Alfred Mellon's, in the Floral Hall. He died at Croydon, November 12, 1889.

Russell, Henry, vocalist and composer, born at Sheerness, Kent, December 24, 1812. Began his musical studies before he was six, and was then placed under M. O. King. Sang at the Surrey Theatre in "The Nightingale and the Raven," and "The Swiss Family," when eight years old, in a children's opera company formed by Elliston. Went to Italy in 1825, becoming an out-door student at the Conservatorio, Bologna, and afterwards studied for four months with Rossini at Naples. Was Maestro de piano in opera at Varesi, with Balfe in the company. Returning to England, he was for a time chorus master at Her Majesty's Theatre. In 1833

RUSSELL.

went to Canada, and also toured through the United States. While there he composed his first song, Mackay's "Wind of the Winter Night." On his return to England in 1841 he first went on a tour with Beale for six months, and March 8, 1842, commenced his own vocal entertainment at the Hanover Square Rooms. The Gambler's Wife, The Ship on Fire, The Maniac, and other of his songs soon became as familiar as household words. Then followed provincial tours, the success of which was unprecedented. Later, with Dr. Mackay, he formulated the entertainment, "The Far West; or, the Emigrant's Progress from the Old World to the New," with scenery painted by Mills. This was also universally popular. He retired from public life about 1865. His songs reached the number of about 800, and Longfellow, Dickens, Eliza Cook, and Charles Mackay were the principal writers whose lyrics he set. A few may be named : Wreck of the Hesperus; Chieftain's Daughter; Canadian Song; Ivy Green ; Old Sexton ; Old arm chair; Cheer, boys, cheer; To the West ; Far, far upon the Sea; Song of the Raft ; Signal Gun ; Woodman, spare that tree. To these may be added A Series of Songs from Scott's "Lady of the Lake ;" Scripture Melodies; Dramatic Scenes; Cantatas, etc., with a Memoir, London, 1846; Copyright Songs, 2 vols., 1860 ; L'Amico dei Cantanti ; The Singer's Friend, a Treatise on the art of Singing. His last composition was a Jubilee song, " Our Empress Queen," for 1887. In 1889, by authority of the Admiralty, " A Life on the Ocean Wave" was to be used by the Royal Marines as their regimental march. A " Henry Russell " night took place at Covent Garden Theatre, October 12, 1891, under the late Sir Augustus Harris's management. His songs were sung, and the venerable composer was called upon for a speech. " Truly a remarkable occasion, and one not unworthy of a remarkable man." In 1895 Mr. Russell published Cheer, boys, cheer; Memories of Men and Music, London, Macqueen.

WILLIAM CLARK RUSSELL, born at New York, February 24, 1844, whose novels of the sea have obtained great popularity, is his son. "The Wreck of the Grosvenor," "My Shipmate Louise," " Marooned," and "Convict Ship" are among some of his most popular tales. He has composed and published a few songs.

Russell, Mrs. J., see HUDDART, FANNY.

Russell, William, organist and composer, born at London, October 6, 1777. Son of an organ-builder. He studied under Shrubsole, Arnold, etc. Deputy organist of St. Mary, Aldermanbury, 1789-93 ; Chapel of Great Queen Street, Lincoln's Inn Fields,

SAFFERY.

1793-98 ; St. Ann's, Limehouse, 1798 ; Foundling Hospital, 1801. Pianist at Sadler's Wells Theatre, 1800, and he held a similar post at Covent Garden, 1801. Mus. Bac., Oxon., 1808. He died at London, November 21, 1813.

WORKS.—*Oratorios :* Job, with organ accompaniments, by S. Wesley (1826) ; The Deliverance of Israel; The Redemption. Mass in C minor, for four voices. *Operas :* Adrian and Orilla, 1806 ; False Friend, 1809 ; Harlequin and Time; Highland Camp; Loa; Rugantino; St. George; Wild Islanders, 1807 ; Wizard's Wake, 1801. *Odes :* To music; Genius of Handel; St. Cecilia's Day (Smart) ; To Harmony. Glees and Songs. Psalms, Hymns, and Anthems for the Foundling Chapel, London, 1809. Six Anthems, adapted from the works of Haydn, etc.,.... and a morning and evening service composed by the late William Russell,....arranged by William Patten. Services and anthems. March, composed for the Guildford Volunteers [1795] ; Twelve voluntaries for the organ or pf. [1810.] He arranged Bingley's Welsh Airs, 1810, etc.

Rutherford, David, musician of the 18th century. Author of "Art of Playing on the Violin, showing how to stop every note exactly.." London, n.d.; "Gentleman's Pocket Guide for the German Flute, with some agreeable Lessons.." "Ladies' Pocket Guide for the Guitar.." " Compleat collection of 112 of the most celebrated minuets with their basses..proper for German flute, violin, or harpsichord." London [1775-80], 2 vols. Compleat collection of 200 country dances." London, 1765, 2 vols.

Ryan, Michael Desmond, dramatic and musical writer, born at Kilkenny, March 3, 1816. Educated at Edinburgh University. Engaged as musical and dramatic critic on staff of *The Morning Post, Morning Herald,* and *Standard.* Sub-editor of *Musical World.* He died at London, December 8, 1868. Author of the libretto of Macfarren's " Charles II.," and words for various musical works by Crouch, Loder, Mori, etc. His son, DESMOND LUMLEY RYAN, born at London in 1851, was for a time musical critic of the *Standard ;* editor of *The Gem,* until 1885, etc. He died at London, November 29, 1888. Composed a toy symphony for pf. strings and 15 toy instruments, 1885; pf. music and songs. Librettist of Heap's " Maid of Astolat " [1886], " Fair Rosamond,"; etc.

Saffery, Eliza, MRS. HENRY SHELTON, composer of early part of the present century. Composer of Reminiscences of a Minstrel, ten songs by E. Ryan [1832] ; Hours of melody, songs [1836]. *Songs :* Broken vow; I love thee, native land ; Old yew tree;

SAHASRABADHE.

Rover's return; Sailor's grave. Arrangements and other works for pf.

OSMOND SAFFERY, probably a brother or other relative of the above, issued " An introduction to Music, with a variety of progressive lessons.. on the pf.," London [1800]. "A select collection of Psalms, as sung at Ramsgate Chapel," London, 1836. College hornpipe for pf.; Reels, dance music, etc.

Sahasrabadhe, B. T., author of " Hindu Music and the Gayan Samaj," containing notes on the recent revival of Indian music, Poona, 1888.

St. George, C., musician, editor of " Mona Melodies, a collection of ancient and original airs of the Isle of Man, arranged for the voice with a pianoforte accompaniment by an Amateur, the words by Mr. J. Barrow. edited by C. St. George," London, 1820.

Saint-George, George, violinist, composer, and performer on the viola d'amore, born at Leipzig, of English parents, November 6, 1841. Studied at Dresden, and under Moritz Mildner, at Prague. He finally settled in London, and devoted himself to teaching and composition. Taking a great interest in antique stringed instruments, he has, with his son (noticed below), given concerts, the two performing on the viola d'amore and viola da gamba, not only ancient music, but modern works as showing the true capacity of those instruments. At a concert given in Steinway Hall, London, November 14, 1895, Bach's Concerto for two violas, with strings and pf. (No. 6, of the Brandenburg *Concerti Grossi*), was performed for the first time in England. Mr. Saint-George is an enthusiastic violin maker, and devotes his leisure to that art with great success. In 1896 he finished a Viola da Gamba, with dolphin head and inlaid finger board and tail-piece, probably the first made in this century. His compositions include an overture, " Spring's Awakening "; Suite in D, op. 20; Suite in B flat, " Rose, Shamrock and Thistle," in which British National dance forms are employed; and other works for orchestra. A large number of pieces for violin; Romanesca, dedicated to Joachim; L'Ancien Regime, petite suite; Elegy; Pieces, op. 24, 25, 26, etc. Also songs.

HENRY SAINT-GEORGE, son of the preceding, was born in London, September 26, 1866. He was chiefly educated in music by his father, and is a violinist and performer on the viola da gamba, showing equal skill on both instruments. He has composed an opera, a pf. concerto, sonatas for violin and pf., songs, etc., but nearly all are as yet in MS. An artist of culture he has contributed many articles to *The Strad*, and other journals.

Saint-John, Florence, the stage name

SALAMAN.

of Miss Maggie Greig, vocalist and actress, born at Kirkcaldy. Taught by her father, she began by singing suitable songs at dioramic entertainments. Appeared as a vocalist and pianist at a concert at Plymouth. Toured with the " Cloches de Corneville " company, 1878; made her first London appearance in " Madame Favart," Strand Theatre, 1879; sang in a round of Offenbach, and other operas. Has visited America several times. Joined the Gaiety, 1888, in " Faust up to date." Has also sung in concerts. Her latest character is that of *Paolo* in " The Little Genius."

Sainton - Dolby, Charlotte Helen, *born* DOLBY, composer and contralto vocalist, born at London, May 17, 1821. She studied at the R.A.M. from 1832 under J. Bennett, Elliott, and Crivelli, and gained the King's Scholarship in 1837. Member of R.A.M. She first appeared as a public singer about 1840, and sang at a Philharmonic Concert in 1841. She also sang in oratorio and ballad music till 1846, when she appeared at a Gewandhaus concert in Leipzig, in Mendelssohn's " Elijah," the contralto part of which was specially written for her voice. She afterwards made concert tours in France and Holland. In 1860 she married M. Prosper Sainton. From thence onwards to 1870, when she retired, she appeared at all the most important concerts in Britain, and became one of the most popular and successful contraltos of her period. She established in London a Vocal Academy, 1872, in which many promising vocalists have been trained. Her last public appearance as a vocalist was made at her husband's farewell concert, in June, 1883. She died at London, February 18, 1885.

WORKS.—*Cantatas:* Legend of St. Dorothea, London, 1876; Story of the Faithful Soul, 1879; Florimel, female voices, 1885. *Songs:* A stream of golden sunshine; A-sailing we will go; Bonnie Dundee; Coming home; Charlie yet; Come forth, my love; Drummer's song; The G.L.O.V.E.; Heigho! Janet; In August; Is it for ever?; I love her; Lady's yes; My Donald; Marjorie's almanack: My love he stands upon the quay; Never again; Watching and waiting; While I listen to thy voice. Tutor for English Singers, a complete course of practical instructions in singing, London, n.d.

Saintwix, Thomas, musician of the 15th century, who was one of the earliest doctors of music. In 1463 he was made Master of King's Hall, Cambridge, by Edward IV. He had been previously made Mus. Doc., Cambridge, and he also held the appointment of chaplain to the king. Saintwix died in 1467.

Salaman, Charles Kensington, pianist, composer, lecturer, and writer, born in London,

SALAMAN.

March 3, 1814. Showed musical talent very early, and began to learn the violin when seven, but after a year left it for the pianoforte. His first lessons were from his mother, an excellent amateur pianist, and by her he was placed under S. F. Rimbault. In 1824 he was elected a student of the R.A.M., but returning to school he lost the chances thereby afforded. Studied under Charles Neate, 1826-31. Made his first appearance in public at G. Lanza's concert, Blackheath, in the summer of 1828, when his song " Oh, come, dear Louisa," his first published work, was sung. The same year he went to Paris, had lessons from Henri Herz, and played his Rondeau brilliant in D, with orchestra, for the first time in London, March 10, 1830. Produced an Ode at Stratford-on-Avon, April 23, 1830, at the Jubilee Festival in memory of Shakespeare. In 1831 began his professional career as teacher; gave annual orchestral concerts at the Hanover Square Rooms, 1833-7, introducing, among other artists, Madame Grisi, 1834, to concert audiences. Instituted, with H. Blagrove, C. Lucas, and others, the Concerti da Camera, the first taking place November 7, 1835. Elected a member of the Royal Society of Musicians, and an Associate of the Philharmonic Society, 1837, withdrawing from the latter in 1855. Visited the continent in 1836, playing at Munich, Vienna, and other places, and becoming acquainted with Schumann, Czerny, Mozart's son, Thalberg, and other artists. Resided in Rome, 1846-8, and in 1847 was made an Hon. Member of the Academy of St. Cecilia, and of the Philharmonic Society of Rome. Founded an Amateur Choral Society in London, 1849; played at the Philharmonic Concert, March 18, 1850, Beethoven's Concerto in C minor. Commenced a series of lectures on musical subjects in 1855, which were continued for some years in London and the country. In 1858 he helped to establish the Musical Society of London, and was Hon. Secretary until 1865. Assumed the name Kensington on the death of his father in 1867. (His father was born at Kensington in 1789). Was one of the founders of the Musical Association in 1874, and acted as Hon. Sec. till 1877, when he retired, and was elected a vice-president. All this time he was busy as a teacher and composer, producing a large number of works (summarised below), besides contributing papers to various musical journals, *Concordia*, *The Musical Times*, etc. He was musical critic to the *Circle* while it lasted. He played the accompaniments to his songs at Miss C. Penna's concert, June 10, 1886; and his last compositions, two songs, " The resigned lover," and " Concealed love," were issued on the completion of his 82nd year, March 3, 1896.

WORKS.—Jubilee Ode to Shakespeare, 1830.

SALE.

Psalm 84; Psalm 29, for double choir; Have mercy upon me; Preserve me, O God; and other anthems. A voiceless sigh; Fair is the swan; April, part-songs. Nearly 100 Hebrew choral works for the service of the synagogue. *Songs :* I arise from dreams of thee, 1836; A leave-taking; Al salir (Spanish); Are other eyes; A toi, toujours á toi (Hugo); Du Süsses mädchen; Farewell! if ever fondest prayer; My sweetheart; No, I never was in love; Murmured music; My star; St. Patrick's Parliament; The voice of my love (March 3, 1893); Can'st thou be true? and many others, including settings of odes, etc., by Horace, Catullus, and Anacreon. *Orchestral :* Overture in D; Fantasia in G minor; Grand Funeral March, in honour of Victor Hugo, 1885. Parade March, for military band. Rondo al capriccio, pf. and orchestra. Twelve voluntaries for organ or harmonium; Six original pieces in Morley's voluntaries. *Pianoforte :* Atalanta; Birthday valse; La vivacita, op. 13; La Notta serena, op. 17; Il Mulino, op. 18; Syrian march; Toccata, op. 44; Zephyrus, op. 54; Tranquility, op. 62; Spring, duet, etc. *Lectures :* History of the Pianoforte, and the ancient keyed instruments, 1855-6; Handel; Beethoven; Weber; Music in connection with the dance; History of Italian, German, and English opera. Papers in Proceedings of Musical Association, 1875-1877-80. Author of Jews as they are, London, Simpkin, Marshall, 1882.

His son, MALCOLM CHARLES, lyric poet and dramatist, was born in London, September 6, 1855. He is author of Ivan's love-quest, and other poems, London, 1879; and the verses of many of his father's best songs; also words for compositions by Sir G. A. Macfarren, G. A. Osborne, etc. As a dramatic author and librettist he has produced Deceivers ever, a farcical comedy, Strand Theatre, November 26, 1883; Boycotted, one act comedietta, with music by Eugene Barnett; Dimity's dilemma, farce, Gaiety Theatre; Both sides of the question, comedietta; A modern Eve, three-act drama, Haymarket Theatre. Known as a critic of the drama and of painting; Editor of the published plays of A. W. Pinero; and author of the popular book, Woman—through a man's eyeglass.

Sale, John, bass vocalist and composer, born at London in 1758. Son of John Sale (born at Gainsborough, 1734; died at Windsor in 1802), who was a lay-clerk of St. George's Chapel, Windsor. He was a chorister of St. George's Chapel, Windsor, and at Eton College from 1767 to 1775, under W. Webb, and lay-vicar from 1777 to 1796. In 1788 he became a gentleman of the Chapel Royal, London; vicar-choral, St. Paul's Cathedral, 1794; Lay-vicar, Westminster Abbey, 1796; and almoner and master of choristers of St.

SALE.

Paul's Cathedral, 1800-12. He became secretary of the Catch Club in 1812, and acted as conductor of the Glee Club, and bass at the Concert of Ancient Music, the Ladies' concerts, and at London and provincial musical festivals. He died at London, November 11, 1827, and is buried in the crypt of St. Paul's.

WORKS.—A Collection of New Glees, composed by John Sale..London [1800]. Also some others issued in a collection, with others composed by Lord Mornington, Callcott, etc.

Sale, John Bernard, composer and bass vocalist, brother of the above, born at Windsor in 1779. He was a chorister in St. George's Chapel, Windsor, and in Eton College, 1785. Lay-vicar, Westminster Abbey, 1800. Gentleman of Chapel Royal, 1803. Organist of St. Margaret's, Westminster, 1809. Musical instructor to Queen Victoria. Organist of the Chapel Royal, 1838. He died at London, September 16, 1856.

WORKS.—Psalms and Hymns for the Service of the Church, London, 1837. S. Webbe's Solfegios as Exercising Duetts, newly arranged by J. B. Sale, London, n.d. *Glees:* O listen to the voice of love; You ask the reason why I love; The Butterfly; Little Piggy, and other duets. *Songs:* The Robin, etc. Marches for pf.

His daughters, MARY ANNE, and SOPHIA, (died May 3, 1869), were also musicians. Another daughter, LAURA, married W. J. Thoms, the author. His brother, GEORGE CHARLES, born at Windsor in 1796, was a chorister in St. Paul's Cathedral, 1803. Organist, St. Mary's, Newington, in succession to Dr. T. Busby, 1817; and St. George's, Hanover Square, 1826. He died at London, January 23, 1869.

Salmon, Eliza, *born* MUNDAY, soprano vocalist, was born at Oxford about 1787. She studied under John Ashley, and made her *début* at the Lenten Oratorio Concerts, Covent Garden, London, in 1803. In 1805 she married James Salmon, a singer, and sang at the principal London and provincial concerts till 1824, when her voice was lost, through a break down of her nervous system, caused by intemperance; she married the Rev. Mr. Hinde, after Salmon's death. On the death of her second husband she became destitute, and after various ineffectual attempts to regain a position she died at Chelsea, June 5, 1849. Her husband, JAMES SALMON, was organist of St. Peter's, Liverpool, 1805. He was latterly in very embarrassed circumstances, and went to the West Indies as a soldier, where he died. His brother WILLIAM (born, 1789; died, Windsor, January 26, 1858), was a singer and teacher.

Salmon, Rev. Thomas, clergyman and author, was born in 1648. He was educated at Oxford University, of which he was M.A.,

SAMPSON.

and became Rector of Mepsall, Bedfordshire. He died in 1677. He wrote "An Essay to the Advancement of Musick by casting away the perplexity of different cleffs, and uniting all sorts of Musick, lute, viol, violins, organ, harpsichord, voice, etc. in one universal character." London, 1672. "Vindication of an Essay to the advancement of Musick, from Mr. Matthew Lock's Observations.." London, 1673. "Proposal to perform Music in perfect and mathematical proportions" London, 1688. "Theory of Music reduced to arithmetical and geometrical proportions " (In Philosophical Transactions, 1705).

Salmond, Norman, bass vocalist, born at Bradford, Yorkshire, August 27, 1858. Studied locally, and first came into notice about 1886. He sung in the "Messiah" at Leeds Philharmonic Concert, December 19, 1888; and made a still more important appearance at the Saturday Popular Concerts, London, January 18, 1890, his success being immediate. He was engaged for the part of Richard Coeur de Lion in Sullivan's "Ivanhoe," February, 1891; made his festival *début* in "Elijah," at Leeds, 1892, and has been heard at Norwich and Handel Festivals. Sang at the Philharmonic Concerts, March 23, 1893; Crystal Palace, December 15, 1894; and in the chief provincial centres. Toured in South Africa, 1895, and in America, 1896; and is now established as an artist of rank. He married an American lady, who in concerts in London and the provinces has gained a reputation as pianist.

Salter, Humphrey, composer and instrumentalist of the last half of the 17th century. Wrote "The Genteel companion, being exact directions for the Recorder, with a collection of the best and newest tunes and grounds extant." London, 1683.

Sampson, Brook, organist, born in Leeds, January 5, 1848. Choristor, as a boy, at St. Saviour's Episcopal Church, Bridge of Allan. Pupil of Dr. Spark. F.R.C.O. 1870; Mus. Bac. Oxford, 1875. After a short residence at Bradford, he was appointed, in 1868, organist and chorister of Kettering Parish Church; removing to Northampton, he held similar offices at St. Catherine's, St. Edmund's, and since 1891, All Saints' Church. Conductor of Church Choir Festivals, and of Northampton Choral Society. Has composed church music, and is author of a Harmony Primer, and "Notes, Staves, Clefs," a method of learning the rudiments of Music.

Sampson, George, organist and composer, born at Clifton, 1861. Organist at St. James's, Bristol, 1879; F.R.C.O., 1882. In 1884, he was appointed organist and director of the music at St. Alban's, Holborn, London; and in 1888, music master and precentor, Brighton College, which offices he retains.

SAMUELL.

He has composed a setting of Communion Service in D for men's voices; an Evening Service in D; O Salutaris in E flat; Ave Verum in D flat, for baritone solo, and men's chorus. Part-songs; School songs for Brighton College. Author of A Text Book of the Elements of Music; and a Text Book of the Pianoforte, for use in Schools, London, Swan and Co.

Samuell, Clara, *see sub.* ROSE, H. R.

Sanders, Alma, composer and pianist of present time. Studied at Trinity College, London; sometime professor of pf. there. She appeared as pianist at concerts, London, 1880, etc. Gained the Sir Michael Costa Prize, Trinity College, 1880, for Trio, pf. and strings; and 1883, for Quartet, pf. and strings. She has also written a Sonata for pf. and violin; four pieces, violin and pf.; pieces for pf. solo, etc.

Sanders, James, conductor and teacher, was a clarinet player at Portsmouth. About 1844, he went to Liverpool, where he was a double-bass player, music teacher, and sometime organist at St. Mary's, and St. Francis Xavier's churches. Trained the chorus at the Theatre Royal; was conductor of the Liverpool Musical Society; chorusmaster, Liverpool Festival, 1874; and filled a like office for the Liverpool Philharmonic Society, 1870-80. He died at Liverpool, October 20, 1891, aged 75. ELLEN SANDERS, his wife, was associated with him in the direction of a private choir, which did excellent work; and was a teacher of repute. She died at Liverpool, May 10, 1891, at the age of 65.

Sanders, George Frederick, *see* PINTO, George Frederick.

Sanderson, Edgar, composer and teacher, published "Harmonia Sacra, for private and congregational use," London, 1838-39, two series; and wrote part-songs and other vocal music.

Sanderson, James, violinist and composer, born at Workington, Cumberland, in 1769. Self-taught in music and on the violin. Violinist in Sunderland Theatre. Teacher in South Shields, 1784-87. Leader of theatre orchestra, Newcastle-on-Tyne, 1787. Violinist in the orchestra of Astley's Amphitheatre, 1788. Music-director at the Surrey Theatre. He was a violinist in the Philharmonic Orchestra, and composer for Vauxhall Gardens. He died at London, in 1841.

WORKS.—*Music to Operas, Pantomimes, and Dramas:* Algerine corsair, 1800; Almoran and Hamet, 1800; Blackbeard, 1797; Brave Cossack; Cora, 1799; Don Giovanni, 1820; Fair Slave; Friar Bacon; Harlequin Mariner, 1796; Harper's Son; Jew and the Gentile; John Bull and Buonaparte; Iron Tower, 1801; Laugh, and lay down, 1803; London Apprentice, 1804; Louisa of Lombardy,

SANT.

1805; Magic Pipe; The Mine; Niobe, 1798; Seasons, 1799; Sir Francis Drake, 1800; Successful Cruise, 1815; Talisman, 1810; Vicar of Wakefield, 1812; and many others. Collins' Ode on the Passions, 1789. Three duetts for 2 violins, op. 6; Six original German waltzes for pf.; Airs arranged for violin; Broadside hornpipe, for pf.; many songs, among which "Bound 'Prentice to a Waterman," is best known. It first appeared in "Sir Francis Drake," 1800. He wrote music to burlettas, pantomimes, and plays, to the number of over 150.

Sandys, William, writer, was born in 1792. He was a member of the legal profession in London; an F.S.A., etc. He died at London, February 18, 1874.

WORKS.—Christmas Carols, ancient and modern, including the most popular in the West of England, and the airs to which they are sung, also specimens of French Provincial Carols, with an introduction and notes, London, 1833. Christmas-tide, its history, festivities, and carols, with their music, London, 1852 (various editions); History of the Violin and other instruments played on with the bow, from the remotest times to the present. Also an account of the principal makers, English and foreign," London, 1864.

Sangster, Walter Hay, organist and composer, born in London, September 17, 1835. Educated at City of London School. Chorister, Temple Church. Studied under E. J. Hopkins and W. R a; also at Berlin, 1855. Graduated Mus. Bac., 1870; Mus. Doc., 1877, Oxford. F.C.O. Organist of Christ Church, Ealing; English Ambassador's Chapel, Berlin, 1855; St. Michael's, Chester Square, London; All Saints', St. John's Wood; St. James's, Weybridge; St. Michael's, Paddington, 1872; St. Saviour's, Eastbourne. Conductor of Eastbourne Musical Society, which has done excellent work. Composer of Cantatas: The Lord is my Light; The Knight of Elli; Elysium, produced, Eastbourne, May 31, 1892; Dramatic cantata, The Scottish Chief, the same. May 11, 1897. Anthems, part-songs, etc. Overture, prelude and fugue, and other organ music; pf. pieces, etc.

Sant Angelo, Pauline, pianist, born in Manchester, of Italian descent. Played in public when ten years of age, and at thirteen was appointed by Sir Charles Halle pianist to the Beethoven Society, Manchester. She made her *début* at the Cryst l Palace, June 1, 1892, playing Weber's Concertstück, and some solo pieces. This was at a Wednesday Concert, the pianist being about fourteen years of age. In 1893 she was heard at Edgar Haddock's concerts in London and Leeds; and gave her first recital at St. James's Hall, May 21, 1895. Since then she has played at

SANTLEY.

important concerts in Birmingham, and many other places.

Santley, Charles, baritone vocalist, and composer, son of WILLIAM SANTLEY (teacher of pianoforte and singing at Liverpool; died, October 22, 1891), born at Liverpool, February 28, 1834. Was a chorister at several churches in Liverpool, and sang as an amateur. Deciding upon his profession, he gave a farewell concert at Liverpool, September 15, 1855, and the next month started for Italy. He studied at Milan under Gaetano Nava, and returned to England in October, 1857. Had further lessons from Manuel Garcia, and made his *début* at St. Martin's Hall, London, November 16, 1857, as *Adam*, in Haydn's "Creation." His success was immense, and every one was struck with his magnificent voice. He sang in the "Messiah" at the same place, December 16. The next year he sang for the Sacred Harmonic Society. His first festival appearance was at Leeds in 1858, and he sang there until 1886, with the exception of the festival of 1880. With the Norwich Festival he was identified from 1860; and he sang in "Elijah" at the Birmingham Festivals from 1861 to 1891, 1867 excepted, when Weiss took the part of the Prophet. He sang at the festivals of the Three Choirs, from 1863 to 1894, with few intermissions. In concerts throughout the country he has long held the foremost position as a baritone singer. He toured in America in 1871 and 1891; and was in Australia, 1889-90. At the Handel Festivals, Crystal Palace, he has been frequently heard from 1862; and he took part in the Jubilee performance there of Mendelssohn's "Elijah," June 27, 1896. His career in opera has been almost as remarkable as in oratorio. He was first heard on the English stage at Covent Garden, October 1, 1859, as Hoel, in Dinorah; sang at the same house in Italian opera, April 15, 1862, as the Count in "Il Trovatore," and took the same part at Her Majesty's, May 31. Sang as Ford, at the production of Nicolai's "Merry Wives of Windsor," then entitled "Falstaff," at Her Majesty's, May 3, 1864; appeared in a round of characters at the same house. Sang in "Zampa," at the Gaiety, 1870; and joined the Carl Rosa Company in 1875, taking the title part in Mozart's "Figaro," at the opening performance at the Princess' Theatre, September 11, and also toured with the Company, remaining with it for some years. Mr. Santley has also gained some fame as a composer. His principal work is a Mass in A flat, for soli, chorus and orchestra (he joined the Roman Church about 1880), produced at the Pro-Cathedral, Kensington, December 25, 1892. He has also composed an Offertorium, Ave Maria, and other church

SAVAGE.

music; a berceuse for orchestra, performed at Sydney, Australia, 1890; a madrigal, and songs, some of which have been published under the name of Ralph Betterton. He is an Hon. R.A.M., and in 1887 was created by Pope Leo XIII., a Knight Commander of St. Gregory the Great. In 1859, he married Miss GERTRUDE KEMBLE, a granddaughter of Charles Kemble. She made her first appearance as a soprano vocalist in the "Messiah," at St. Martin's Hall, December 16, 1857. After her marriage she retired from public life. She died, September 1, 1882. EDITH SANTLEY, their daughter, a soprano, made her stage *début* when very young in Cherubini's "Water Carrier," at the Theatre Royal, Birmingham, May 19, 1876. She sang at the Philharmonic Concerts, May 11, 1882, and in Birmingham, etc. She married, July 14, 1884, the Hon. R. H. Lyttelton, and now resides in Warwickshire, but sings occasionally at concerts for charitable purposes.

Santley, Kate, actress and singer, appeared at the Strand Theatre, 1870, in "St. George and the Dragon." Sang in London and the provinces in comic opera, from about 1876. Began a series of entertainments, with drawing-room sketches, at Ipswich, in October, 1890. Was at Berlin, 1891, in "Faust up to Date, and has now for some years been lessee of the Royalty Theatre, London.

Sapio, Antonio, tenor vocalist, was born at London, in 1792. He was a son of an Italian vocalist (born 1751, died London, June 30, 1827), under whom he studied singing. For a time he held a commission in the army, but afterwards became a public singer, and first appeared in the "Messiah," in 1822. He sang at York, Edinburgh, and other provincial concerts, and in 1824 he appeared on the stage. He died in London, November 27, 1851, completely destitute, having occupied a garret in Queen Street, Edgeware Road, under conditions of great distress, some time previous to his death.

Sartoris, Mrs., see KEMBLE, ADELAIDE.

Saunders, Joseph Gordon, pianist and composer, graduated Mus. Bac., 1872, Mus. Doc. 1878, Oxford. Some time conductor of Clapton Philharmonic Society, from 1884. Professor of harmony and pf., Trinity College, London. Associate of the Philharmonic Society.

WORKS.—Domine, Dominus noster; Benedic, anima mea, for soli, chorus, and orchestra; anthem, The Lord in His holy temple; Evening Service, chants, etc.; vocal trio in canon, Like the gale that sighs; pf. pieces, etc. Author of a primer, Examples in Strict Counterpoint, old and new, Novello; A Practical Treatise on the Art of Phrasing, Hammond.

Savage, William, organist, composer, and bass vocalist, was born about 1720. He

SAVILE.

studied under Dr. Pepusch, and became a Gentleman of the Chapel Royal, 1744. Almoner, vicar-choral, and master of choristers, St. Paul's Cathedral, 1748. He died at London, July 27, 1789. He composed chants and other church music.

JANE SAVAGE, probably a daughter or other relative of the above, composed Six rondos for harpsichord or pf., op. 3 ; Duett for pf. or harpsichord, op. 6 [1790] ; Two duetts for voices, op. 7 [1791] ; Strephon and Flavia, cantata, op. 4 ; Hall the woodman, song, op. 5.

Savile, Jeremy or **Jeremiah,** composer of the 17th century. Now known chiefly as composer of "The Waits," a four-part song sung at the meetings of Glee societies. "Here's a health unto his majesty," "O by rivers," and other songs and part-songs contained in Playford's "Select musicall Ayres," 1653, and other contemporary collections.

Sawyer, Frank Joseph, organist, composer and conductor, born at Brighton, June 19, 1857. Studied at Leipzig Conservatorium under E. F. Richter, and others ; pupil of, and assistant organist to Dr. J. F. Bridge. F.R.C.O. ; Mus. Bac., 1877 ; Mus. Doc., 1884, Oxford. Organist and choirmaster, St. Patrick's, Hove, Brighton ; conductor of Brighton and Hove Choral and Orchestral Association up to 1896, when he resigned. Professor of sight singing, R.C.M. He has given many important concerts ; and organ recitals at Bow and Bromley Institue, etc. Lectured on organ music ; the history of the dance ; and other topics, at the College of Organists, Musical Association, London Institution, and elsewhere.

WORKS.—Oratorio, Mary the Virgin, 1884; recast as Star of the East, and produced Brighton, December 12, 1889 ; Sacred cantatas, Jerusalem, 1880 ; The Soul's Forgiveness, Chester Festival, 1894 ; Widow of Nain (female voice). Dramatic cantata, Orpheus. Methuen prize of £100, 1893 ; Cantata, The Pageant (female voice). Two Sclavish Dances, orchestra ; Concertstück in D, organ and orchestra, 1890 ; Romance, violin and pf. ; Technical exercises, and pieces various, pf. ; Anthems, part songs ; Songs of a Summer day, four vocal duets, etc. Author of a primer on Extemporisation, Novello.

Scarisbrick, Thomas, organist and composer, born at Prescot, Lancashire, March 24, 1805 ; died at Kendal, February 26, 1869, where he was organist. Composed anthems and other church music. His wife, *born* WHITNALL (born, 1829 ; died, 1874), was a contralto singer.

Scates, Linda, MRS. DUTTON COOK, pianist, second daughter of Joseph Scates. Born at Dublin, November 16, 1855. Pupil of Sir R. P. Stewart and of R.A.M. ; elected Associate,

SCOTT.

R.A.M. An accomplished pianist, she retired from public life on her marriage with Mr. E. Dutton Cook, dramatic critic, August 20, 1874. After his death (September 11, 1883), she resumed her profession in 1884, and was appointed a professor at the Guildhall School, and the same year was granted an annual pension of £150 from the Civil List. She gave concerts at the Princes' Hall, and elsewhere. On January 6, 1885, she married Charles Dickens, second son of Edmund Yates.

Schirmacher, Dora, pianist, born at Liverpool, September 1, 1857. Daughter of a professor of music in that city, who was her first instructor. Studied at Leipzig Conservatorium under Ernst F. Wenzel and Reinecke. Played at the Gewandhaus Concerts, February 1, 1877, and made her *début* at the Crystal Palace March 31 following, her selection being the D minor concerto of Mendelssohn. She appeared at the Monday Popular Concerts December 3 of the same year, and has played at concerts in Liverpool, Manchester, and other places, and also in many towns in Germany. She has published a sonata, suite, and some other pieces for pf.

Scholefield, Rev. Clement Cotterill, clergyman and amateur musician, born at Edgbaston, Birmingham, June 22, 1839. Graduated at Cambridge. Held livings of Parish Church, Hove, Brighton, in 1867-69 ; and St. Peter's South Kensington, 1869-77. Chaplain of Eton College, Windsor, since 1880. Composer of "A Wedding Hymn" [1889] ; Hymn tunes, "Fides," "Irene," "St. Clement," "St. Nicholas," etc.

Schultz, Madame, *see* BISHOP, ANNA.

Scott, Lady John Douglas, *born* ALICIA ANN SPOTTISWOODE, amateur composer. Edest daughter of John Spottiswoode, of Spottiswoode, Berwickshire. She was married on March 16, 1836, to John Douglas Scott, third son of the fourth Duke of Buccleuch, who died on January 3, 1860. In 1870 she succeeded to the estate of Spottiswoode, and, under terms of her father's will, resumed her maiden name. Composer of a number of Scots songs, among which may be named Maxwelton braes are bonny.... Annie Laurie, London [1847] ; Douglas ; Durisdeer (arranged by Eliz. Masson) ; Ettrick ; Foul fords ; Lammermoor ; Mother, oh, sing me to rest ; Shame on ye, gallants, etc. The first-named is by far the best known, and is, indeed, one of the most popular of modern Scottish melodies. It was first published anonymously about 1846-47, and appeared soon after in Wood's "Songs of Scotland," edited by G. F. Graham. The words used are the more modern of two sets. The well-known song, "By yon bonnie banks," or the

SCOTT.

" Bonnie banks o' Loch Lomond," was noted by Lady Scott from the singing of a boy in the streets of Edinburgh, and was first printed by Paterson and Sons about 1844, with an accompaniment by Finlay Dun.

Scott, Walter, pianist, violinist, and conductor, born at Long Sutton, Lincolnshire, October 10, 1842. Studied pf. under Benedict, and violin with H. Holmes. Resident in Cardiff; hon. local examiner for R.C.O.; organist of St. Margaret's Church. Has played organ solos at Eisteddfodau, Cardiff, and trained the Cardiff contingent of the choirs of the Gloucester and Worcester Festivals up to 1890, when those counties drew more from their own resources. With this Cardiff choir Mr. Scott has given some fine concerts; he has also acted as chorus-master for the Cardiff Musical Festivals. He has written a Communion Service, Te Deum and Benedictus, songs, violin and pf. pieces, etc.

Searelle, Luscombe, theatrical manager and composer. In 1884, he was conducting opera in London and the provinces; afterwards, up to 1890, he was manager of the Queen's Theatre, Kimberley, and the Theatre Royal, Johannesburg, South Africa. Since then he has again been in England. He has composed the operas " Estrella " (Walter Parke), produced at the Gaiety Theatre, London, May 24, 1883 ; and " The Black Rover " (his own libretto), produced at the Globe Theatre, September 23, 1890. Also a cantata, " Australia," produced at Lyttleton, New Zealand, April 16, 1891. Author of a series of humorous sketches, "Tales of the Transvaal," London, Fisher Unwin, 1896.

Second, Mary, *born* MAHON, soprano vocalist. Was born at Oxford, about 1771. She was a daughter of Mahon, a celebrated clarinet player. *Début* in "The Woodman," Covent Garden, London, September 17, 1796. Married to a Mr. Second, 1800. Afterwards retired from the stage. She appeared at the principal concerts of her time.

Sedding, Edmund, architect and amateur musician, was born in 1835. Pupil of the eminent architect, Mr. Street. He was sometime organist at St. Mary the Virgin, Crown Street, Soho, London. Cantor, St. Ralph, Bristol. Edited and composed a " Collection of English Carols, French Nöels, etc." ; " Collection of Ancient Christmas Carols, arranged for 4 voices." London, 1860. Third Collection of Nine Ancient and Goodly Carols for Christmas-tide, Novello. " Dives and Lazarus, a christmas carol." [1867]. Hymns of ye Holy Eastern Church, set to Musicke for 4 voices. London, 1864. He was learned in all that appertained to Ecclesiastical Plain-Song. His last years were spent at Penzance, where he died of consumption, June 11, 1868, aged 33.

SELBY.

His brother, JOHN D. SEDDING, architect, was also an organist and church musician. He assisted for years at the services at St. Mary's, both in the choir and at the organ ; and was sometime organist at Beddington, Surrey. He died, April 7, 1891, in London.

Sedgwick, Alfred B., musician and writer, author of the following works : Complete System of instruction for the Concertina, London [1854] ; Complete Method for the French Accordeon ; Complete Method for the German Accordeon ; also for German Concertina, Boston [1865]; Complete Method for the Cornet, etc. He published a large number of arrangements of popular airs for the Concertina.

Seeley, L. B., compiler of " Devotional Harmony, containing Psalms and Hymns from various authors, adapted to favourite tunes..the whole for 3 and 4 voices." London, 1806, 2 vols., 3rd edition, 1830.

Seguin, Arthur Edward Shelden, bass singer, was born at London, April 7, 1809. He was a pupil of the R.A.M., and in 1829, he sang at a musical festival at Exeter ; and in 1831, he appeared in opera in London. Afterwards he sang chiefly in opera, and at the Concert of Ancient Music (first appearance there, March 28, 1832), till 1838, when he went to the United States. He gave Rooke's " Amilie " in New York, in October, 1838, and travelled in the States with an operatic company called after himself. He died at New York, December 9, 1852. His wife, *born* ANN CHILDE, was a soprano vocalist, and appeared with her husband in all his principal concerts and operatic productions. She died at New York, in 1888. ELIZABETH SEGUIN, his sister (born London, 1815 ; died there, 1870), also a singer, was the mother of Madame Parepa-Rosa ; and WILLIAM HENRY SEGUIN (born 1814 ; died December 29, 1850), was a well-known bass singer in London.

Selby, Bertram Luard, composer and organist, born in Kent, February 12, 1853. Was organist of Salisbury Cathedral, 1881-3 ; now organist of St. Barnabas, Pimlico, London. Gave concerts in London, 1880, etc.

WORKS.—*Operas :* The Ring (1886) ; and Adela, produced at Nottingham, February, 1888. Music to Helena in Troas, London, May 17, 1886. Weather or No, musical duologue, Savoy, August 10,1896. School cantata, The Waits of Bremen. Songs and part-songs. Morning and Evening Service, with Communion office, in C. Idyl for orchestra, Henschel concerts, March 11, 1897. Two quintets, pf. and strings. Sonata and suite, violin and pf. Sonata in D, Sonata on Dies Iræ, and other pieces for organ. Suite for pf., etc.

Selby, Thomas Leeson, violinist and composer, was born near Nottingham in

SEMPLE.

1827. Studied under Henry Farmer. Conductor and teacher in Nottingham. Composer of some glees, songs, etc.

Semple, Charles Edward Armand, physician and writer, who was educated at Cambridge and London; B.A., 1867; M.B., 1872, etc. Holds a number of appointments, such as physician to Royal Society of Musicians, and examiner in vocal and aural physiology and elementary acoustics to Trinity College, London. Author of "The Voice musically and medically considered," London, 1884; other editions, 1886, etc., and a large number of professional works, chiefly on diseases of children and pharmacy.

Senior, John Edwin Ryder, organist, born at Batley, Yorkshire, March 23, 1856. Studied under Dr. Peace, James Broughton, and Hans von Bülow. F.C.O., L.R.A.M. Organist of Govan Parish Church, 1881; St. George's in the Fields, Glasgow, to present time. Has a high reputation as a performer, and has given recitals at Exeter Hall, London; Bow and Bromley Institute; Crystal Palace; East End Exhibition, Glasgow, 1891; St. George's Hall, Liverpool, November, 1895, etc. He has published some pieces for the organ.

Severn, Charles, organist, contrabassist and violoncellist, born in London, 1805. He was a Court musician at the Queen's accession, and played at her coronation. For many years a member of the principal orchestras in London, and of the provincial Festivals. He was in the orchestra at Birmingham on the production of "Elijah," 1846. He was also organist for forty-six years of Islington Parish Church. A fire broke out at his residence, Liverpool Road, Islington, April 14, 1885, in which his wife was burnt to death. He was then still organist at the church. He died at the end of December, 1894, having almost attained his ninetieth year. He wrote a glee, The Sunset, and a few other part-songs, motets, songs, etc., and edited "Psalm and Hymn Tunes, Chants, etc., for the use of the Parish Church of St. Mary, Islington." London [1853].

Severn, Thomas Henry, composer and vocalist, elder brother of above, was born at London, November 5, 1801. Son of a music master at Hoxton, and brother of Joseph Severn, the painter. He was a teacher in London, and died at Wandsworth, April 15, 1881.

WORKS.—Te Deum, vocal duets. The Lay, a collection of songs by C. V. Incledon [1845]. Songs of the Days of Chivalry, by T. H. Bayly, 1831. *Single Songs :* Dear scenes of my home; Fill the goblet; Friendship; Goe, happy rose; Her eyes the glow-worme lend thee; Jamie; Rose of Ellesmere, etc. Pf. music.

SEYMOUR.

Sewell, John, organist and composer. Has been organist for many years at St. Leonard's Church, Bridgenorth, Shropshire, where he is a music-seller. Composer of anthems, Break forth into joy; Blessed are the undefiled; This is the day; etc. The Order of Service, with choral responses, London, Skeffington, 1892.

Another JOHN SEWELL graduated Mus. Bac., 1848; Mus. Doc., 1856, Oxford. Of him no particulars can be gleaned.

WILLIAM SEWELL, son of the first-named, was born at Bridgenorth. Educated at R.A.M. Balfe Scholar, 1876; Novello Scholar, 1879, A.R.A.M. Organist of Christ Church, Clapham, 1882; the Oratory, Edgbaston, 1886 to present time. Has given organ recitals, Bridgenorth, 1882-5, etc. He has composed a Mass of St. Philip Neri; Magnificat; O Salutaris Hostia; Tantum Ergo, performed at the Brompton Oratory; Ave Maria, and other church music. Eclogue, orchestra; Quartet and trio, pf. and strings; Sonata, pf. and violoncello; pieces for pf., etc.

Sexton, William, composer and organist, born in 1764. Chorister in St. George's Chapel, Windsor, and Eton College, 1773. He studied under Edward Webb. Organist, sub-precentor, and master of choristers, St. George's Chapel, Windsor, 1801. He died about 1824. Composer of anthems, glees, and songs; and edited Handel's Chandos Anthem, 1808.

Sexton, William, alto vocalist, born at Norwich. Chorister, Norwich Cathedral, and pupil of Dr. Buck. Sometime member of the choirs of York Minster, and St. George's Chapel, Windsor. Appointed vicar choral of Westminster Abbey, 1875. Sometime conductor of Brixton Choral and other societies. The Meister Glee Singers, consisting of Messrs. Sexton, G. Hast, W. G. Torington, and W. Norcross, have gained a high reputation for finished part-singing. They have been heard at many concerts in London and the provinces from 1890.

Seymour, Charles A., violinist, born at Edinburgh in 1810. He studied at the R.A.M., and in 1830 became principal violinist in Queen Adelaide's private band. Leader of Manchester Concert-Hall orchestra, 1838; and leader of Halle's band from 1858. For some years he gave annual series of chamber concerts in Manchester. He died at Manchester, November 1, 1875.

Seymour, Joseph, organist, composer and writer, born at Cork, May 14, 1854. Studied at Malines under Lemmens, and at Ratisbon under Dr. Haberl. Succeeded his father as organist at St. Peter and St. Paul's Church, Cork, 1878; and has been organist at St. Andrew's, Westland Row, Dublin, from 1881 to present time. Graduated Mus. Bac.,

SHAKESPEARE.

Trinity College, Dublin, 1892. Professor of Music in Board of Education Training College, Drumcondra; Examiner, Royal Irish Academy of Music, etc. Editor of *Lyra Ecclesiastica*, Dublin, 1884-91; correspondent to several musical journals.

WORKS.—Mass Adeste Fideles, 1886; Mass in A flat (prize), 1888; Missa Trinitatis; Te Deum (prize), 1895; Six Motets (Archbishop of Dublin prize), 1889; other church compositions. An Irish May-Day, children's operetta on Irish Airs; Seven Irish Airs, arranged. Part-song, Bells of Shandon; Lodore (prize), etc. Editor of Curwen's Latin Series of church compositions; and other collections.

Shakespeare, William, tenor vocalist and composer, born at Croydon, June 16, 1849. After singing in a choir he became an organist at thirteen, and pupil of Molique. In 1866 gained a King's Scholarship, R.A.M. Won the Mendelssohn Scholarship, 1871, and studied at Leipzig. A tenor voice of promise developing, he was sent to Milan to study singing under Lamperti. Returning to England in 1875, he sang at the Monday Popular, Crystal Palace, and other metropolitan concerts for some years, as also in the provinces, and at the Leeds Festival, 1877. He was appointed a professor of singing at the R.A.M. in 1878; and Conductor of the Concerts in 1880, resigning this office in 1886. F.R.A.M. He is now chiefly known as a teacher, but sings occasionally at concerts. His chief compositions are a Dramatic Overture, 1874; Pf. Concerto, Brighton Festival, 1879; with a Symphony, overtures, and string quartets in MS. Also songs, and pf. pieces, etc.

Sharman, Percy Victor, violinist, born at Norwood, Surrey, in 1870. In his thirteenth year he gained a Scholarship at the R.C.M., for three years, which was extended for two years more, as he showed conspicuous talent. He also obtained the Exhibition of £60 per annum, for four years, the gift of the Worshipful Company of Skinners. This was for the purpose of enabling him to continue his studies abroad. Accordingly he entered the Royal High School of Music, at Berlin, as a pupil of Dr. Joachim. Since 1897 he has appeared with success on the concert platform, and was the violinist of Mr. Sims Reeves' touring party, 1890-1; but he is chiefly devoted to tuition, and since 1890, has been professor of the violin at the Charterhouse School, Godalming. Of his compositions only a Romance for Violin, and one or two songs, have been published.

Sharp, Edward, pianist and composer, born at Acton, Middlesex, December 27, 1831. Studied at R.A.M. under Cipriani Potter, and subsequently came under the notice of Thalberg from whom he obtained valuable instruc-

SHARPE.

tions and advice. He was organist at All Souls, St. John's Wood, for some time from 1875, but has devoted his time chiefly to composition. As a painter he has also acquired some repute. His compositions comprise a Trio for pf. and strings; Two Sonatas for pf. and 'cello; Sonata, pf. and violin; Sonata in E minor; Six Songs without words; Rondo grazioso in G, op. 19; Twenty-four Characteristic Pieces, etc., for pf.; Various Songs.

Sharp, Francis, composer and pianist, of last half of the 18th century. Author of " New Guida di Musica, being a complete book of instructions for beginners on the Pianoforte," op. 6, London [1790]. Composer of Six Sonatas for the Harpsichord [1785]; Poor Mary, a ballad.

RICHARD SHARP, probably a relative of the foregoing, composed a number of arrangements for the pf., and songs.

MARY and L. SHARP, harp-players who played at the Birmingham Festival of 1811, are probably members of the same family. Mary Sharp issued a " Collection of original melodies, edited by J. Relfe," London [1827]. A THOMAS SHARP, who lived about the same time, contributed to Henley's " Divine Harmony," 1798, and to the publications of John Page.

Sharp, Granville, writer, born at Durham in 1734; died London, July 6, 1813. Author of " A Short Introduction to Vocal Music, London, 1767; another edition, 1777. Chiefly noted for his philanthropic efforts, and his work on behalf of freeing negroes from slavery. His memoirs were written by Prince Hoare. His brothers WILLIAM and JAMES, with whom he chiefly lived, were musical, and gave concerts. The brothers apparently possessed a large musical library, as a book-plate exists, showing a view of an organ in a church, with part of a choir-screen, designed by Granville Sharp, and inscribed, " Messrs. Sharp, London." The border of this plate is surrounded by Scripture texts.

Sharp, Simeon, author of " Music, a Satire," London, 1824.

Sharp, Mrs. William, authoress, wife of William Sharp (born Glasgow, 1855), the poet and author, wrote " Great Composers," London, 1887, in the Camelot Classics series; " Sea Music, an anthology of poems and passages descriptive of the Sea," London, 1887; " Women's voices:. poems by English, Scotch, and Irish women," London, 1887.

Sharpe, Charles Kirkpatrick, amateur musician, poet, etc., born at Hoddom Castle, Dumfriesshire, May 15, 1781; died at Edinburgh, March 18, 1851. He composed music, and contributed to Stenhouse's Lyric Poetry of Scotland. He also edited and published the Earl of Kellie's " Minuets and Songs," 1839.

SHARPE.

Sharpe, Ethel, pianist, born in Dublin, 1872. Pupil of the R.I.A.M., playing at a concert, June 10, 1884, when twelve, with great success. Scholar at R.C.M., studying under Franklin Taylor, distinguishing herself at the students' concerts. Was presented with the silver medal of the Musicians' Company, 1891, in which year she gave her first chamber concert, November 12, at the Princes' Hall. She played at the Crystal Palace, March 26, 1892 ; and receiving a grant from the R.C.M., proceeded to the continent for travel and study. Gave a recital at Vienna early in 1894, creating an excellent impression. Resumed her chamber concerts, London, 1895, and played at the Crystal Palace, April 13, Eugene d' Albert's Concerto in E, op. 12. She is married to Mr. Alfred Hobday, a violinist.

Sharpe, Herbert Francis, pianist and composer, born at Halifax, Yorkshire, March 1, 1861. Gained a Pianoforte Scholarship at the opening of the National Training School for Music at South Kensington, and succeeded Eugene d' Albert as Queen's Scholar at the same institution. From 1882 he played frequently at concerts in London, Bradford, and throughout the North, as well as in other places, with much success. He was appointed a professor at the R.C.M. in 1884 ; and an Examiner under the Associated Board of R.A.M. and R.C.M. in 1890. His compositions are already very numerous, the principal being indicated in the subjoined list.

WORKS.—Comic opera in three acts (MS.) ; Three four-part songs, with orchestra, op. 52, also for female voices with pf. Songs of the Year, 12 two-part songs, op. 16 ; 12 two-part songs, op. 18 ; Songs of Moor and Mountain, 12 two-part songs, op. 19 ; Songs by the Sea, 12 trios, op. 25 ; Songs and duets, various. Concert overture, orchestra ; Romance for two pianos (both in MS.) ; Variations, op. 46, for two pianos ; Suite, op. 62, flute and pf. ; Suite, op. 65, violin and pf. ; Four duets, op. 29, two violins and pf. ; Idylle, op. 38, flute and pf. Pf. duet ; Five character pieces, op. 24 ; Three symphonic pieces, op. 59. Pf. solo : Op. 1-10, pieces various ; Five pieces, op. 23 ; Two musical sketches, op. 28 ; Suite, op. 58 ; Pantomime suite, op. 61 ; Six English fantasias, op. 71, etc. Pianoforte School, op. 60, Stanley Lucas. Arrangements of Grieg's Norwegian songs and dances, etc., for pf. duet.

Shaw, Mrs. Alfred, *born* MARY POSTANS, contralto vocalist, born at Lee, Kent, in 1814. She studied at R.A.M., and under Sir George Smart, and appeared in 1834-5 at the Concert of Ancient Music, and at York Festival. She married Alfred Shaw, artist, in 1835. Sang afterwards at all the principal festivals, and sang the contralto part in Mendelssohn's "St. Paul," on its first production in England. Sang at Leipzig, 1838 ; in Italy, 1839, and

SHAW.

afterwards in England. She was married a second time to J. F. Robinson. Her voice failed owing to the shock caused by the appearance of insanity in her first husband, who died in a private asylum, Hoxton, November 23, 1847, and she retired from public life soon after. She died at Hadleigh Hall, Suffolk, September 9, 1876.

Shaw, George Bernard, journalist, musical critic, and dramatic author, born at Dublin, 26 July, 1856. Acted as musical critic for *The Star*, and succeeded Louis Engel on *The World*, 1891-94. Lately he has devoted himself chiefly to dramatic authorship. Well-known as an active socialist and leading member of the Fabian Society. Author of " Widowers' Houses " (Independent Theatre), 1892; "Arms and the Man " (Avenue Theatre), 1894 ; and other plays. Several novels, essays on Socialism, and a series of articles on the drama in the *Saturday Review*, etc.

Shaw, James, organist and composer, born at Leeds in 1842. Studied under R. S. Burton. Organist of St. John's Episcopal Chapel, Edinburgh ; St. Paul's, Edinburgh. Conductor of Edinburgh Choral Union, 1862-1863. Organist. Hampstead Parish Church, London ; Collegiate Chapel of St. John, Clapham. Gave concerts, St. James' Hall, 1891-2. Formed the Middlesex Choral Union, 1892. Compositions : " A Thanksgiving Ode," for soli, chorus, and orchestra, 1880 ; Evening Service, composed for London Church Choir Association, 1874 ; Services and anthems. *Songs :* Break, break ; Angel's Welcome ; Morning Greeting, etc. Part-songs. Three Sketches ; Introduction and Fugue ; Two grand Studies ; and other pf. pieces. Minuet; March ; Meditation, etc., organ.

Shaw, Sidney, composer, born at Farnworth, Lancashire. Began his musical studies with the violin, and then placed himself under Dr. W. Röhner, of Liverpool, for five years, for composition. During that time he composed and produced, at Liverpool, an operetta, " Love's Trial," 1882, and another work of the same kind. He went to Leipzig, and studied at the Conservatorium, and there wrote the oratorio, " Gethsemane," which was produced at St. James' Hall, London, November 26, 1886. His other works include a Romance for violin ; a Bolero, and other pf. pieces. *Songs :* Suspense ; The Angel and the Child ; Three songs (Byron), etc. In 1892-3, he was conductor of the Georgina Burns " Cinderella " company.

Shaw, Thomas, violinist and composer, of latter part of the 18th and early part of the 19th centuries. Composer of The Stranger (opera), 1798 ; The Island of Marguerite (opera), 1789 ; anthem on the death of Princess Charlotte [1817] ; Trio for 2 violins and 'cello ; four sets of Sonatas for pf., op. 9,

SHAW.

etc. [1795-98] ; Concertos for violin and pf. ; Solo for flute, op. 8 ; Songs, etc.

Shaw, William Maxwell, musician and editor, born at Aberdeen about the middle of last century. He studied under Urbani, and was precentor successively of the High Church, Inverness, and West Church, Aberdeen, 1797-1805. He was a successful teacher of vocal music, and sang at concerts in Edinburgh. In 1805 he went to Boston, U.S., where he died in July of the same year. He compiled "A Collection of Church Tunes, compiled and composed for the improvement of those who may not have the opportunity of teachers to instruct them, with the simple graces the author rises in singing.." Aberdeen, n.d.

Shedlock, John South, pianist, critic, and author, born at Reading, 1843. Graduated B.A., London University, 1864. Studied pf. under E. Lübeck, and composition under Ed. Lalo, at Paris. On his return to London he was principally engaged in teaching, occasionally giving some excellent chamber concerts, up to 1879, when he became musical critic of the *Academy*, and from that time he devoted himself chiefly to musical literature. In 1875, however, he had contributed articles on Raff's Symphonies to the *Monthly Musical Record*. Other papers followed : and in 1892 he began an elaborate series of articles on Beethoven's Sketch Books in the *Musical Times*. In 1893 he discovered, at Berlin, a copy of Cramer's Studies, with comments by Beethoven. An account of this he published with a preface, and explanatory notes. He edited Kuhnau's "Biblical Sonatas," 1895 ; and played them at the R.A.M., 1896, to illustrative lectures by E. F. Jacques ; also edited a Selection of Harpsichord pieces by Bernardo Pasquini. He has lectured at the R.A.M., and been a busy worker for music in many ways. Author of "The Pianoforte Sonata, its origin and development, London, Methuen, 1895. His most important composition is a Quartet for pf. and strings, 1886 ; he has also written a Romance and Scherzino, etc., for pf.

Shelmerdine, William, organist and conductor, born at Salford, Manchester. Chorister in the Collegiate Church (now the Cathedral). Studied in London, under Robert Barnett, and Sterndale Bennett. Settled in Melton Mowbray as a teacher. About 1850 he obtained the post of organist at the Mechanics' Institute, Nottingham, and formed a large vocal class in connection with it. This afterwards became the Nottingham Sacred Harmonic Society, Shelmerdine being at first organist, and then conductor. He was also organist at the Baptist Chapel, Derby Road, soon after taking up his abode at Nottingham. He was active as a teacher, and exerted great influence in the town. In 1878 he retired, and went to reside at Pwllheli, North Wales,

SHEPLEY.

where he died, February 20, 1893. He edited a Collection of Psalms and Chants from the old masters, London [1857] ; "180 Chants, ancient and modern," London, Virtue, 1861, also 1864 ; The Amateur Pedalist, an introduction to the use of the pedal organ [1853] ; and composed some church music and songs.

Shenton, Rev. Robert, clergyman and musician, was B.A., Oxford, 1750 ; M.A., Cantab., 1757. He became vicar-choral, Hereford Cathedral ; Dean's vicar at Christ Church, 1757, and vicar of St. Patrick's Cathedral, Dublin, 1758. Dean's vicar at St. Patrick's, 1783. He died at Dublin in 1798. Composer of anthems and other church music.

Shepherd, Charles Henry, organist and composer, was born in 1847. Student and Associate, R.A.M. After holding appointments in London, he became organist of St. Thomas's Church, Newcastle-on-Tyne, 1876, and died there, April 29, 1886. He composed a Te Deum, anthems ; The lass I left ashore ; Do or die ; The moon shines o'er the lake, love ; and other songs ; pf. pieces, etc. His wife was a soprano vocalist, favourably known in the North.

Shepherd, William, violinist and composer, was born at Edinburgh about 1760. He was a partner with Nathaniel Gow in the firm of Gow and Shepherd, 16, Princes Street, Edinburgh, and he performed at concerts. He died at Edinburgh, January 19, 1812. He edited two collections of Strathspey reels ; "A collection of Strathspey reels ..with a bass for the violoncello or harpsichord," Edinburgh, n.d. ; "A second collection of Strathspey reels..for the pianoforte, violin and violoncello," Edinburgh, n.d.

Shepherdson, William, organist and author, born 1817 ; died, October 12, 1884. Wrote "The Organ, hints on its construction, purchase, and preservation," London, 1873.

Shepley, Daniel Sutton, bass vocalist, born at Macclesfield, 1853. As a boy he had no singing voice, but played several instruments. In 1866 his parents removed to Halifax, and he was apprenticed to a firm of engineers. His voice developing, he took lessons from Mr. W. R. Eckersley, of Halifax, and soon became a popular oratorio singer in the North. Later on he studied under Dr. Varley Roberts, Alfred Blume, and the late J. B. Welch. In 1879 came an offer to join the Carl Rosa Opera Company ; but a vacancy occurring in the choir of Lincoln Cathedral at the same time, Mr. Shepley, by the advice of friends, chose the latter, and obtained the post. A year later he was promoted to St. George's Chapel, Windsor, taking up his duties January, 1881. While there he was a member of Her Majesty's private choir. In 1887 he was appointed a

SHEPPARD.

Gentleman of the Chapel Royal, St. James's. He has done much useful work as a concert singer, and also as a teacher. His wife was a contralto vocalist, and, as Miss SARAH RILEY, was widely known in the North as a concert singer. She died at Brixton, July 12, 1894, at the early age of thirty-three.

Sheppard, Elizabeth Sara, novelist, born at Blackheath, London, in 1830; died at Brixton, London, March 13, 1862. She wrote a number of novels, of which " Charles Auchester," 1853, 3 vols., and " Rumour," 1858, 3 vols., deal with music and musicians. The character of Seraphael in " Charles Auchester " is intended for Mendelssohn.

Sheppard, Rev. Henry Fleetwood, clergyman and musician. Minor canon of Gloucester and Windsor; sub-dean, Chapel Royal, Savoy, 1884. Composer of anthems, O Lord, the very heavens; If the Lord Himself; and arranger of settings of Te Deum, Benedictus, Magnificat, and Nunc Dimittis to ancient melodies, Gregorian Tones; Series of Church Songs, 1884, 2 sets, etc. Collaborator with Rev. S. Baring-Gould (q.v.) in collecting and arranging " Songs and ballads of the West " [1891] ; " A Garland of Country Song," Methuen, 1895; English Minstrelsie, Edinburgh, Jack, 1895-96.

Sheppard, or **Shepherd, John,** organist and composer of the 16th century. He was a chorister in St. Paul's Cathedral, London, and afterwards became instructor of choristers and organist of Magdalen College, Oxford, 1542-47. He graduated Mus. Doc., Oxford, in 1554. He composed, masses, motets, and other Church music, mostly preserved in MS.

Sheringham, J. W., clergyman, and author of " Our Choir Festivals : can they be reformed without abolition ? " Gloucester, 1874.

Sherrington, Hellen, MADAME LEMMENS SHERRINGTON, soprano vocalist, born at Preston, Lancashire, October 4, 1834. The family migrated to Rotterdam in 1838. There the daughter studied under Verhulst; in 1852 entered the Brussels Conservatoire, taking first prize for singing and declamation. Made her first appearance in London, April 7, 1856, at the Amateur Musical Society's Concert, Hanover Square Rooms. She soon obtained a leading position, and was heard at the Birmingham Festivals from 1861 ; the Three Choirs, Worcester, 1863-72. In 1880 she was nominated a professor of singing at the Brussels Conservatoire, but undertook a tour in the provinces, 1883-4. She made a special visit to London in 1889, to sing in Benoit's " Lucifer " at the Albert Hall, April 3. In 1891 she resigned her professorship at Brussels, and accepted one at the R.A.M., London, the same year, which she still retains, and was

SHIELD.

elected an Hon. Member of the Institution. In opera she made her *début* at Her Majesty's Theatre, October 10, 1860, as *Maid Marian,* in Macfarren's " Robin Hood," and " took the audience by storm." She first sang in Italian Opera at the same theatre in May, 1866, as *Adalgisa* in " Norma," appearing later in many operas, English, French, and Italian. She married, in 1857, Nicolas Lemmens, the eminent Belgian organist and composer, who died January 30, 1881. Two daughters, MARY and ELLA, made successful first appearances at the Royal Academy of Music, Louvain, November 6, 1881 ; and both have been heard in London and the provinces, at times from 1882. Madame Sherrington is the composer of some songs.

Sherrington, Jose, soprano vocalist, younger sister of Madame Lemmens-Sherrington, was born at Rotterdam, October 27, 1850. Studied at Brussels under Madame Meyer-Boulard, and Signor Chiriamonte. Made her appearance in England in 1871, and sung at her sister's concerts in London, 1872, and in the provinces. Toured in Holland in 1873, but has resided chiefly in England since.

Sherwin, Amy, soprano vocalist, born in Tasmania. Received her first instruction from her mother, then joined an Italian operatic troupe, and made her *début* at Melbourne in " Lucia di Lammermoor." In 1879 went to America; sang in New York; at the Cincinnati Festival, and principal concerts, 1880-1. Studied under Theodore Thomas, Dr. Damrosch and others ; and returning to Europe, studied at Frankfort with Stockhausen ; Madame Hustache at Paris ; and also Vannuccini and Ronconi. Made her *début* at Drury Lane, April 7, 1883, in the title part of " Maritana," with Carl Rosa Company ; sang at the Promenade, Richter, Crystal Palace, and provincial concerts, 1884-5. Again went to America; and in 1888 undertook a tour through Australia, India, China, etc., singing once more in London, July, 1890. In 1896 she took her own opera company to South Africa.

Sherwood, Percy, pianist and composer, born May 23, 1866. Nephew of Edward Lawrance (q.v.). Educated at Dresden Conservatorium, 1885-8. In 1889 he won the Mendelssohn German State Prize, for a Grand Requiem for soli, chorus and orchestra. He was appointed a professor at the Dresden Conservatorium in 1893. His works comprise a Concerto for pf. and orchestra; a Symphony; Overture to Goethe's "Götz von Berlichingen"; Sonata for pf. ; chorus and songs, etc. Also chamber music, organ pieces, etc. As a pianist he has been heard at many concerts in Germany, and he has a high reputation.

Shield, William, composer and writer, born at Whickham, Durham, March 5, 1748.

SHIELD.

He studied under his father, a singing-master, and practised the violin and harpsichord. Apprenticed to a boat-builder at North Shields, on the death of his father, but afterwards became leader of the Newcastle Subscription Concerts, and studied music under Avison, who befriended him. He went to Scarborough as leader of the theatre orchestra, and the subscription concerts. Violin-player in orchestra of the opera, London, 1772; and in 1773 he was made principal viola-player. Composer to Covent Garden Theatre, 1778-91 and 1792-97. Visited France and Italy with Ritson, the antiquary, 1791. Master of the Royal Music on death of Parsons, 1817. Original member of the Philharmonic Society. He died at 31, Berners Street, London, January 25, 1829. Buried, February 4, in south cloister of Westminster Abbey. A new stone was placed over his grave in 1892. On October 19, 1891, a memorial cross was unveiled by Dr. Hodgkin in Whickham churchyard.

WORKS.—*Music to Dramas, Operas, etc.:* Flitch of Bacon, 1778; Lord Mayor's Day, 1782; Rosina, 1782; Poor soldier, 1783; Harlequin Friar Bacon, 1783; Robin Hood, 1784; Noble peasant, 1784; Fontainbleau, 1784; Magic cavern, 1784; Nunnery, 1785; Love in a camp, 1785; Choleric fathers, 1785; Omai, 1785; Richard Cœur de Lion, 1786; Enchanted castle, 1786; Marian, 1788; Prophet, 1788; Highland reel, 1788; Aladdin, 1788; Crusade, 1790; Picture of Paris, 1790; Oscar and Malvina (with Reeve), 1791; Woodman, 1792; Hartford bridge, 1792; Harlequin's Museum, 1793; Deaf lover, 1793; Midnight wanderers, 1793; Sprigs of laurel, 1793; Travellers in Switzerland, 1794; Arrived at Portsmouth, 1794; Netley Abbey, 1794; Mysteries of the Castle, 1795; Lock and key, 1796; Abroad and at home, 1796; Italian villagers, 1797; The farmer, 1798; Two faces under a hood, 1807; Wicklow mountains. A Cento, consisting of ballads, rounds, glees, and a roundelay; Cavatinas, canzonettas, etc., London [1809]. Collection of six canzonets and an elegy, London, n.d. Collection of favourite songs, etc., London, n.d. Six trios for violin, tenor, and violoncello, London, n.d., 3 vols. Six duos for two violins. Six quartettos, 5 for 2 violins, tenor and 'cello, and 1 for flute, violin, tenor, and 'cello, op. 3. An introduction to Harmony, London, 1800; 2nd edition, 1817, Rudiments of thorough-bass for young harmonists, London, 1815. Numerous songs, of which the best known are, The wolf; The thorn; Old Towler; The heaving of the lead; The Post Captain; The plough-boy; Death of Tom Moody; The Arethusa; Last whistle; Lovely Jane; My own native village; The bud of the rose; Sailor's epitaph; On by the spur of valour goaded; and Violet nurs'd in woodlands wild.

SHIRREFF.

Shinn, George, organist and composer, born at Clerkenwell, London, March 6, 1837, Privately trained in music. Graduated Mus. Bac., Cambridge, 1880. Appointed organist of St. Peter's, Hackney Road, December, 1858; St. Jude's, Whitechapel, June, 1863; St. Paul's, Canonbury, 1866; St. Matthew's, Brixton, 1872; and Christ Church, Upper Norwood, 1887, a position he still holds. Published compositions—Oratorios: The Captives of Babylon (1887); Lazarus of Bethany (1892). Cantatas, with readings: The Reformation (1880); The Victories of Judah (1881); The Life of Samuel (1884). Harvest Thanksgiving Cantata (1895). School Cantatas: The Four Seasons; The Bell Tower; The Queen of Merry May. Morning and Evening Services; Anthems; Kyries, and Hymn Tunes. Twelve School songs; songs and part-songs. Original Compositions for the Organ; Six books of Transcriptions. Six violin and pf. duets; pf. pieces, etc.

His son, FREDERICK GEORGE, organist, was born in London in 1867. He was educated at the R.C.M. Graduated Mus. Bac., Durham, 1892. F.R.C.O.; A.R.C.M. Organist and choirmaster, All Saint's, Clapham Park, 1888-1892; St. James's, Marylebone, 1892-3; Parish Church, Sydenham, 1893. Conductor of Reigate Rural Deanery Choral Union, 1893; Sydenham Choral Society. Has given organ recitals in various places. Author of a brochure; "Forty Seasons of Saturday Concerts at the Crystal Palace" (1896).

Shinner, Emily, violinist, born at Cheltenham, July 7, 1862. Began the violin at an early age, and in 1874 went to Berlin and studied under Jacobsen. When female violinists were admitted to the High School in 1876, Miss Shinner entered as a pupil of Joachim. Played in several towns in Germany, returning to England in 1881. She made a successful *début*, June 3, 1882, at Mr. H. R. Bird's Concert, Kensington Town Hall; was heard in the provinces soon after; at the Monday Popular Concerts, February 9, 1884; Crystal Palace, March 8, rapidly attaining a high position. In 1887 she organised a string quartet of ladies, the first concert taking place at King's College, London, April 2 of that year. The Shinner Quartet have played in London and the provinces each year since, with increasing success. In January, 1889, Miss Shinner married Captain A. L. Liddell, of the Artillery, the Queen sending a diamond bracelet to the bride.

Shirreff, Jane, soprano vocalist, born 1811. She studied under Thomas Welsh. *Début* at Covent Garden Theatre, London, in Arne's "Artaxerxes," 1831. She sang at the Philharmonic Concerts, the Concerts of Ancient Music, and at the Provincial Festivals; also at Drury Lane Theatre, and in 1838,

SHIRREFS.

SHRUBSOLE.

she appeared in America with Seguin's company. Married Mr. J. Walcott, secretary of the Army and Navy Club, and retired. She died at Kensington, London, December 23, 1883.

Shirrefs, Andrew, poet and musician, was born at Aberdeen in 1762. He was educated at the Grammar School and Marischal College, Aberdeen, and graduated M.A. in 1783. He was a stationer and publisher in Aberdeen and Edinburgh, and edited the *Aberdeen Chronicle* and the *Caledonian Magazine*. In 1798, he went to London and seems to have died there about 1801. His only known contributions to music were, " Forty Pieces of original music, inscribed to the Earl of Buchan," Aberdeen, n.d. [1788], and " The overture, airs, songs, and duetts in the Scots pastoral comedy of 'Jamie and Bess,' " Edinburgh, n.d. He is best remembered as the author of " Jamie and Bess."

Shoel, Thomas, composer, born at Montacute, Somerset, in 1759 ; died 1823. Compiler of Thirty Psalm Tunes, first sett ; Twenty-four Psalm Tunes, 2 hymns and 3 easy anthems, London [1801]; Book of Psalm Tunes, Hymns, and Anthems, London, 1800-6, 6 vols.; The Chearful Psalmodist, a new set of tunes, London [1809] ; Ode for Christmas Day, 1804 ; Peace, a two-part song; Shipwrecked Boy, duet ; and songs.

Shore, John, trumpeter, was born in the latter part of the 17th century. He succeeded his brother WILLIAM in office of sergeant trumpeter. Trumpeter in the Queen's band. He died November 20, 1750. He is credited with the invention of the tuning-fork. The most celebrated trumpet-player of his time. He was succeeded in his office by Valentine Snow. His sister CATHERINE, born in 1668, was a pupil of H. Purcell. Married Colley Cibber in 1693. Appeared as a singer in operas by Purcell and others. She died in 1730, The founder of the Shore family was MATTHIAS (died 1700), who was King's trumpeter in 1685, and was succeeded by his son WILLIAM (died 1707).

Shore, William, amateur composer, born at Manchester, November 21, 1791. Was founder and musical director of the Manchester Madrigal Society, and hon. secretary of the Gentlemen's Glee Club. He died at Buxton, January 16, 1877. He edited " Sacred Music, selected and arranged from the works of the most eminent composers....," London [1835], and composed glees, and the well-known trio, " O Willie brew'd a peck o' maut " [1840]; anthems, songs, and pf. music.

Short, Joseph, composer and organist, born at Caldmore, Walsall, Staffordshire, May 22, 1831. Received his early training in the local Roman Catholic Church choir,

and became acquainted with much of the finest ecclesiastical music. Self-instructed in harmony and composition. Appointed organist of the Roman Catholic Church at Wednesbury in 1853, and later of St. Mary's Walsall, where he began to produce the masses of the great composers with full orchestra. He went to Birmingham in 1861 and, having a good bass voice, was appointed cantor of St. Chad's Roman Catholic Cathedral, moving in 1867 to St. Joseph's, Nechells About this time he published a " Salve Regina," which became popular. In October 1872, he accepted the office of choir-master at St. Michael's, Moor Street, Birmingham which he still holds, and has made famous by the production of great works. He conducted a performance in this church of Schubert's Mass in F, in 1873, and gave the same at a concert in the Masonic Hall, Birmingham, September 7, 1875, with full orchestra, being the first performances of the mass in England. For some years he gave concerts in the Birmingham Town Hall. He was chosen as the English representative to give information to the Sacred Congregation of Rites in the revision of the Liturgical rules for the guidance of composers of Roman Catholic Church music, a great mark of distinction. His devotion to music has been his recreation, he being occupied in business as a merchant.

WORKS.—*Masses :* St. Joseph (dedicated to Cardinal Newman), produced Birmingham Town Hall, December 9, 1880; St. George, 1886, both for soli, chorus, organ and orchestra. *Offertoriums :* Ave Maria; Beata es Virgo Maria ; Benedic Anima Mea Domino, Benedicite Dominum ; Deus Israel, quartet and chorus; De Profundis, baritone solo, with strings; Adoramus Te, for strings. Marche Cardinale, for orchestra. In MS. two masses; a cantata, The Nativity; motets, etc.

Shoubridge, James, musician and tenor singer, born at Canterbury, in 1804. He was a teacher there for a time, but died in London, December, 1872. He was appointed conductor of the Cecilian Society, London, 1852. Composer of " Twenty-four original Psalm and Hymn tunes, for 4 voices," n.d.

Shrubsole, William, organist and composer, born at Canterbury in 1760. He was a chorister in Canterbury Cathedral from 1770 till 1777. In September, 1782, he was appointed organist of Bangor Cathedral at a salary of forty guineas a year. In December, 1783, he was dismissed for being too closely connected " with one Abbott late of this place," and for " frequenting conventicles." He therefore next became organist of Spa Fields Chapel, Clerkenwell, in 1784, and held the post till his death, at London, January 18,

SHUTTLEWORTH.

1806. He was buried in Bunhill Fields, London, where a monument marks his grave. This was restored by public subscriptions collected by Mr. F. G. Edwards, in 1892. Benjamin Jacob and William Russell were among his pupils. Shrubsole is now chiefly remembered as the composer of the once popular hymn tune called "Miles Lane," or sometimes "Scarborough."

Shuttleworth, Obadiah, organist, violinist, and composer, born at Spitalfields, London, 1675. Violinist at the Swan Tavern Concerts, Cornhill, 1728. Organist successively of St. Michael's, Cornhill, and of the Temple Church. Composer of concertos and sonatas for violin. He died in 1735.

Sibbald, James, publisher and bookseller in Edinburgh, who was born about 1747, and died at Edinburgh, April 8, 1803. He edited " The Vocal Magazine, containing a selection of the most esteemed English, Scots, and Irish Songs, ancient and modern, adapted for the harpsichord and violin," Edinburgh, 1797-99. 3 vols., issued in 19 parts. A second series only reached a few parts. " Collection of catches, canons, glees, etc., in score, from the works of the most eminent composers, ancient and modern," Edinburgh, 3 vols., n.d.

Sibly, Stephen, organist, born in 1766. He was organist of St. Thomas', Portsmouth, and of St. John's Chapel, Portsea, for 52 years. He died at Portsmouth, September 23, 1842.

Sime, David, musician and teacher, born about the middle of last century. He was a teacher in Edinburgh, where he died on July 7, 1807. He edited " The Edinburgh Musical Miscellany, a collection of the most approved Scotch, English, and Irish songs, set to music," Edinburgh, 1792-3, 2 vols ; 2nd edition, 1808, 2 vols.

Simms. A remarkable family of organists. JOHN SIMMS, the founder, was born in Staffordshire about the middle of the eighteenth century. He was brought up to the counting-house, but continued in his father's business, the iron trade, for some years. Cultivating his passion for music, he became a fair player on the organ and violin. Afterwards he devoted himself to the construction of instruments, and made, among others, an upright harpsichord, which was publicly exhibited. The date of his death is not known. He had a family of eight sons and two daughters, who were all musical, as was his wife. Of his sons, BISHOP SIMMS succeeded Joseph Harris, Mus. Bac., as organist of St. Philip's, Birmingham, and was also organist of St. Mary's Chapel in that town. He was a violinist, and one of the orchestra at the Birmingham Festivals from 1805. Date of death unknown. JAMES SIMMS was organist of Bromsgrove Parish Church, and also at Chaddesley, Worcester, but nothing is known

SIMMS.

of him after 1826. SAMUEL SIMMS, was esteemed one of the finest players of his time. In 1805 he was a candidate for the post of organist at Whitchurch, Salop, but the conditions were so unsatisfactory that only three of those assembled would compete. A curious letter on the subject appeared in *Aris's Gazette*, Birmingham, April 15, 1805. He was organist of St. Thomas's, Stourbridge, for half a century, and died sometime before 1860. EDWARD SIMMS was organist of Asburn and Oakover, Staffs., but no details can be obtained about him. HENRY SIMMS was an organist at Stourbridge, and another son, JESSE, was a musician.

Simms, Edward, son of Edward Simms named in the preceding article, was born at Oldswinford, Worcestershire, February 10, 1800. At the age of six he commenced his studies under his uncles at Stourbridge ; and when ten assisted his uncle James at Bromsgrove. He was appointed organist at Wombourne, near Wolverhampton, in 1813. Went to London in 1816, and studied under Thomas Adams, and Kalkbrenner. In 1818 he removed to Coventry, and was organist successively of Holy Trinity, 1821 ; St. John's, 1825 (having meantime held an appointment for three years in Birmingham) ; and St. Michael's, 1828, holding this last office for the period of 58 years, resigning in 1886. Established the Coventry Choral Society about 1836, and did much to disseminate a taste for music in the district. He had many pupils of distinction, including the novelist George Eliot, and it is to him that reference is made in "Middlemarch." He composed numerous pieces, but published very little. His death took place at Coventry, January 15, 1893.

Simms, Henry, organist and pianist, born in 1804. Son of Jesse Simms. He was a pupil of Moscheles for pf., to whom he dedicated a Polacca. Appointed organist of Holy Trinity, Bordesley, in 1825, he held that office until 1875 ; whilst he was also organist at St. Philip's, Birmingham, 1829-71. He was famous as an extempore player, and widely known as a teacher of pf. and singing. His compositions were chiefly teaching pieces for pf. and songs ; but he also wrote a Communion Service which remained in MS. He died, May 1, 1872.

ROBERT HENRY, his eldest son, was born at Highgate, Birmingham, in 1829. Pupil of his father, and later of R.A.M. In 1851 he was appointed Music Master at Chester College ; and organist at Wrexham Parish Church in 1853. Up to June 29, 1856, he occupied his usual post at the organ, but the next Sunday he expired as the bells were ringing for morning Service. His brother arrived from Birmingham the previous evening, to take his place, but on the Sunday, by

SIMMS.

the Vicar's desire, the organ remained silent as a mark of respect to the artist so suddenly passed away.

EDWARD BISHOP SIMMS, the second son of Henry Simms, was also the pupil of his father. He studied pf. under Cipriani Potter. Succeeded his brother as organist of Wrexham Parish Church, August, 1856; and resigned in December, 1894. He was Music Master at Chester College, 1856-86 ; and is still resident at Wrexham as a teacher.

Simms, Samuel, organist and composer, born at Stourbridge in 1836. Eldest son and pupil of Samuel Simms, previously noticed. He succeeded his father as organist of St. Thomas's Church, Stourbridge, and remained there for some years. Afterwards he took an appointment at St. John's, Ladywood, Birmingham ; and was lastly organist of St. Cyprian's, Hay Mills, Birmingham, a church distinguished for its ornate musical services. (His brother, the Rev. G. Handel Simms, became vicar of that church). He was conductor of the Brierley Hill Choral Society from its formation ; was a skilful organist and pianist. His compositions included Services, anthems, and organ pieces. He died at Stourbridge, February 22, 1885. His eldest son, SAMUEL, succeeded him as organist of St. Cyprian's, and retains that position to the present time.

Simms, Arthur, organist and composer, born at Birmingham, June 11, 1839. Son of the first-named Samuel Simms. Pupil of his uncle, Henry Simms. Was assistant organist of St. Philip's and Holy Trinity, Birmingham, 1856-65. Appointed organist of Shifnall Parish Church, 1866 ; Wilmslow, Cheshire, 1870; St. Mary's Episcopal Church, Glasgow, 1875 ; Organist and music master, Forest School, Walthamstow, 1880; Hythe Parish Church, 1893, to present time. Graduated Mus. Bac., Oxford, 1874. At Shifnall he was conductor of the Philharmonic Society; and while at Glasgow he directed a performance of Bach's Passion Music, in 1877. He is correspondence tutor of Queen Margaret College, Glasgow. His compositions are : Lazarus, an oratorio; Psalm 33, for voices and orchestra, both in MS. Anthems published for Christmas, Easter, Ascension, Annunciation, and Harvest. Service for Holy Communion. Impromptu for organ, etc.

Simper, Caleb, organist and composer, born at Barford St. Martin, Wilts., September 12, 1856. Fourteen years organist at St. Mary Magdalene, Worcester, and manager to E. J. Spark. Now resident at Barnstaple, devoting himself exclusively to composition. He has composed a large number of simple anthems—I will feed my flock ; He is risen ; Fear not, O land ; Break forth into joy, etc. ; also prize hymn tunes, Manchester Sunday School Union, etc.

SIMPSON.

Simpson, Christopher, or SYMPSON violinist and writer, born [about 1610]. He was originally a soldier in the army raised by the Duke of Newcastle for service of Charles I. Being a Roman Catholic, he was patronized by Sir Robert Bolles of Leicestershire whose son he taught the viol. He died at Turnstile, Holborn, London, about 1677.

WORKS.—The Division-Violist, or an Introduction to the playing upon a Ground, divided in two parts, the first directing the hand with other preparative instructions; the second laying open the method and manner of playing, or composing divisions to a ground London, 1659; 2nd edition as "Chelys Minuritionum artificio exornata, sive Minuritione ad Basin, etiam extempore modulandi ratio. or the Division Viol, etc., London, 1667 ; 3rd edition, with portrait, 1712. The Principles of Practical Musick, London, 1665 ; 2nd edition, A Compendium of Practical Music, in 5 parts : 1. The Rudiments of Song ; 2. The Principles of Composition ; 3. The Use of Discords ; 4. The form of Figurate Descant 5. The Contrivance of Canon..London, 1667 Of this work there are many editions dated and undated to about 1760. Art of Discant or Composing Musick in Parts, by Dr Thomas Campion, with Annotations thereon by Mr. Christopher Simpson, London, 1655 Also contained in Playford's "Introduction."

Simpson, Frederick James, composer born at Portobello, near Edinburgh, December 12, 1856. Educated at the Edinburgh Academy, and later in England and Switzerland. Entered the Leipzig Conservatorium 1887, studying under Alfred Richter ; in 1879-80 studied at the National Training School for Music, London, under E. Prout F. Taylor, and J. F. Bridge. Graduated Mus Bac., Oxford, 1886 ; and further studied composition with Ludwig Bussler, Berlin, 1887-8 He has given concerts at Edinburgh and elsewhere. His compositions include Symphony in C; overture "Robert Bruce" (produced at the Crystal Palace, November 2, 1889); which, with a sonata for pf. and violin, and two pf. sonatas, remain in MS He has also composed a cantata, "The Departure of Summer," for soli, chorus, and orchestra ; "Coronach" (from Scott's "Lady of the Lake," produced at Edinburgh, April 8, 1891); "Come to the Woods," song, with violin obligato ; A Message to Phyllis, and other songs, duets, part-songs, etc. Four sketches ; Tone pictures for the young; and other pf. pieces ; Cavatina in F, violin Allegro giocoso, two violins, etc.

Simpson, James F., composer and pianist, born in 1845; died in London October 11, 1882. In addition to a large number of album sketches, galops, and transcriptions for the pf. he composed incidenta

SIMPSON.

music to The Miller and his man, 1875, and wrote "Nursery rhymes and children's songs" London [1881]; "Six Scottish songs, the poetry selected from R. Burns" [1872]; part-songs, songs, and other works.

Simpson, John, musician of first half of the 18th century, wrote "Delightful pocket companion for the German flute," London [1740]. Another JOHN SIMPSON, who flour-ished later in the century, composed "Twelve voluntaries..for the organ or pf. to which are prefixed some remarks on stringed musical instruments." London [1800].

Simpson, John, member of a music pub-lishing firm in London, wrote "Easy method of learning the Concertina," London [1855]; "Easy method of playing the Accordion, German Accordion, or Flutina, London [1876]; Complete book of Instructions for the Flute; Arrangements for the Accordion, etc. These instruction books are issued in various editions.

Simpson, Palgrave, amateur musician and writer, born about 1815. Solicitor prac-tising in Liverpool, where he died, January 22, 1891, at the age of 75. Author of " The Bandmaster's Guide," 2 vols., London, Boosey, 1885.

Simpson, Robert, composer, was born at Glasgow, November 4, 1790. He was a weaver by trade, and led the singing in Dr. Wardlaw's church, Glasgow, for a time. Afterwards he was precentor and session clerk of the East Parish Church, Greenock, from 1823. He died at Greenock in July or August, 1832. He composed or adapted the tune well known in Scotland as " Ballerma," which was first published in Turnbull's " Selection of Original Sacred Music " (form-ing vol. 6 of Steven's Collection), 1833, from a MS. found after Simpson's death. On the strength of a by no means close resemblance, the tune " Ballerma " has been assumed to be a copy or adaptation of a melody composed or arranged by Barthélémon (1741-1808), a French violinist and composer.

Simpson, Thomas, English composer and violinist, who in 1615 was violinist in the chapel of the Prince of Holstein-Schaumberg. Composer of " Opusculum neuer Pavanen, Galliarden, Couranten, und Volten..." Frank-fort, 1610; " Pavanen, Volten und Galli-arden," Frankfort, 1611; " Tafel-Consort, allerhand lustige Lieder von 4 Instrumenten und Generalbass," Hamburg, 1621.

Simpson, T., author of " The Norma Virium, or Musical Accentuator, a disquisitory essay on the obstructions students meet with in becoming good timeists...," London, n.d.

Simpson, Thomas, organist and compo-ser, was born April 25, 1833. Compiler of the Burnley Tune Book; Part-songs; Dance music for pf., etc.

Sims, Thomas, composer and organist,

SINCLAIR.

issued " Fifty original psalm and hymn tunes, figured for the organ," London [1816].

Sinclair, George Robertson, organist and conductor, born at Croydon, October 28, 1863. Son of the late R. S. Sinclair, LL.D., of Dublin. When eight he began his studies at the R.I.A.M., Dublin, and a year later entered St. Michael's College, Tenbury, where he remained six years. In 1879 he became a pupil of Dr. Harford Lloyd, of Gloucester Cathedral, and was his assistant organist, as well as officiating at St. Mary de Crypt Church. At the close of 1881 he was appointed by the Chapter organist of Truro Cathedral, where he worked up the choir to a high efficiency, and presided over a gathering of 700 performers at the consecration service in November, 1887. He originated, and was Diocesan Choirmaster of, the Deanery of Powder Choir Association, and conductor of other societies. In 1889 he succeeded the late Dr. Colborne as organist and master of the choristers at Hereford. Conducted the Hereford Festivals of 1891 and 1894 with conspicuous ability. He is a brilliant organ player, and has given many recitals. He conducts societies at Hereford and Ross. Elected Hon. R.A.M., 1895.

Sinclair, John, tenor vocalist, was born near Edinburgh, in 1790. He became a clarinet player in the band of Campbell of Shawfield's Regiment, and afterwards a teacher of music in Aberdeen. First appear-ance as a singer in London at Haymarket Theatre, as *Cheerly* in "Lock and Key," 1880. He studied singing for a time under Thomas Welsh. Engaged for Covent Garden Theatre, and appeared in Linley's " Duenna," 1811. Married Miss Norton, daughter of Captain Norton, 1816. Appeared in London, and in English Provinces till 1819 ; when he visited Paris, and studied for a time under Pellegrini, and under Banderali at Milan. Visited Rossini at Naples, 1821. Sang in Pisa, Bologna (where he was made a member of the Phil-harmonic Academy), Modena, Florence, Venice (where Rossini wrote for him the part of *Idreno* in " Semiramide "), and Genoa, 1822-23. Re-appeared in London, Covent Garden, November 19, 1823, and at other theatres till 1830. Sang in America, and appeared in opera, 1830, and retired soon after. He died at Margate, September 23, 1857. Sinclair was one of the most popular singers of his day, and was the creator of the tenor *roles* in Bishop's "Guy Mannering," " The Slave," " Noble Outlaw," and Davy's " Roy Roy." He composed the well-known songs " Beneath the wave," " Betty Sands," " Dunbarton's bonnie dell," " Hey the bonnie breast-knots " [1828], " The Mountain Maid " [1830], " Come sit thee down," " Johnnie Sands " [1830], and others in the Scots style.

SINKINS.

Sinkins, Farley, bass vocalist, sometime lay-vicar of Exeter Cathedral. Gave subscription concerts at Exeter up to 1888; and orchestral concerts at St. James' Hall, London, 1891, introducing eminent artists for the first time in London.

Sivewright, John, musician, who was well-known in the north-east of Scotland as an itinerating teacher of psalmody. He held the office of precentor in the Parish Church of Old Meldrum till 1835, and died there about 1846, a very old man. He travelled all over the counties of Aberdeen, Banff, and Kincardine as a teacher of church choirs. He published "A Collection of Psalm Tunes, Hymns and Anthems, in three parts, by John Sivewright, teacher of music, Old Deer. The 4th edition ... Edinburgh, printed for the author ... " n.d. In the 5th edition, Edinburgh about 1815, he describes himself as "teacher of music, Turriff"; and in yet another he figures as "teacher of music, Fordoun." It is therefore probable he had an edition printed for each of his centres of operations. They are all little oblong books of about 64 to 70 pages, and are exceedingly rare.

Sivrai, Jules de, *see* ROECKEL, Mrs. J. L.

Skeaf, Joseph, composer and pianist, born at Liverpool, November 10, 1836. Studied under George Holden, and was a teacher in Liverpool, and conducted the Apollo Glee Club there. He was also Grand Organist to the Freemasons of West Lancashire. He died at Liverpool, November 1, 1884. Composer of "Harlech," a cantata, Liverpool, November 15, 1888, published by his widow; some glees. Pf. pieces: Battle of Trafalgar, The Camp, Fantasias, Sabbath evening chimes. Songs, etc.

Skeats, Highmore, organist and composer, was organist of Canterbury Cathedral. He died at Canterbury in 1831. Compiler of "A Collection of Songs," London, 1784, and edited Stephens' Cathedral Music, 1805. Also composed All gracious freedom, glee [1790]; Cease thy carols, and Victory of Fishguard, songs.

His son, HIGHMORE SKEATS, composer and organist, was born at Canterbury, in 1785. He became organist of Ely Cathedral, and afterwards of St. George's Chapel, Windsor, in 1830, and died at Windsor, February 24, 1835.

Skeffington, Hon. and Rev. T. C., author of a "Handy-Book of musical art, with some practical hints to students," London, 1858; "The Flute in its transition state, a review of its changes during the past fifty years," London, 1862; "Oh! fair and bright is the Irish girl," and other songs.

Skene, John, of Halyards, a Scottish collector of the 16th and 17th centuries, who died in 1644. He is supposed to have compiled the "Skene Manuscript," 1614-1620, a

SLATTER.

collection of vocal and dance music which was edited and published by Dauney and Graham for the Bannatyne Club, in 1838. It contains, among other melodies, the fine old setting of the tune usually sung to Jane Elliott's version of the "Flowers of the Forest."

Skinner, Florence Marian, MRS. STUART STRESA, composer, daughter of Alan Skinner, late Recorder of Windsor. Resident for many years in Italy. Her opera, "Suocera," was produced at Naples, April 15, 1877; and a second, "Maria Regina di Scozia," at San Remo in 1883, and also at Turin and London the same year.

Skinner, James Scott, violinist and composer, born at Banchory, Aberdeenshire, August 5, 1843. Son of William Skinner, who was known in the district as a good amateur violinist. He studied the violin under Dr. Mark (died 1868), a German musician of Manchester, and has performed much in Scotland, Canada, and the United States. Composer of a large number of reels, strathspeys, and songs, most of which have been issued in "The Miller O'Hirn"; "The Logie Collection of original music for voice, violin, and pf., comprising songs, slow airs, etc.," London, 1888, and other collections. Reputed one of the best players of Scottish dance music.

Slater, Ernest, organist and composer, born at Taunton, 1860. Son of Rev. W. P. Slater, formerly Governor and Chaplain of Queen's College, Taunton. Educated there, and entered R.A.M., studying under Dr. Steggall, T. A. Matthay, and Harold Thomas. Also pupil of Sir Julius Benedict, and Dr. D. J. Wood. Assistant organist of Exeter Cathedral, 1881. F.R.C.O., 1884. Organist of Lambeth Parish Church, 1883, also officiating occasionally at the Archbishop of Canterbury's private chapel. Selected by Sir John Stainer for the post of organist and choirmaster at St. John's Cathedral, Calcutta, 1885. Gave his first concert at Calcutta, September 7, 1886. Professor of Music at La Martinière College, and his private practice has included the families of three Viceroys of India. Of his compositions a festival overture for orchestra was performed at Taunton, 1885; and his Jubilee Anthem was sung at the State Service in Calcutta Cathedral, 1887, a copy being accepted by Her Majesty the Queen.

Slatter, Rev. George Maximilian, clergyman and composer, born in 1790. He was rector of West Anstey, Devon. Died on April 27, 1868. Composer of "Three anthems, a Te Deum, etc., three psalm tunes and eight chants," London [1854]; "Ten Collects, a set of chants, etc." [1835]; "Six canzonets, a trio, and a glee" [1815]. The Watcher, and other songs.

SLATYER.

Slatyer, William, musician of 17th century, issued the Psalms of David in four languages, and in four parts, set to ye Tunes of our church..1643.

Slaughter, A. Walter, composer and conductor, born in London. Educated at City of London School. Chorister, St. Andrew's, Wells Street. Studied under Alfred Cellier and Jacobi. Wrote some ballet music, etc., for the South London Palace of Varieties; afterwards appointed conductor at Royalty Theatre; later at the Olympic; Drury Lane; and St. James's Theatre. His works include An Adamless Eden, 1882; Marie's Honeymoon; The Casting Vote, 1885; Music to lyric drama, Sappho, Olympic, 1886; Comic opera, Marjorie, Prince of Wales' Theatre, July 18, 1889; The Rose and the Ring (Thackeray), the same, December, 1890. Incidental music to various pieces. Musical comedy, The French Maid, Terry's Theatre, April 24, 1897.

Sloman, Charles, composer and comic singer, born about 1808; died, London, July 21, 1870. Composed "Sacred Strains, hymns, etc." London [1860]. *Songs:* Charming Sue, Daughter of Israel, Daughters of Salem, Maiden of sunny Cachmere, Maid of Judah, Pilgrim of Erin, Promised land, Social bricks; a number of comic songs, etc.

Sloman, Robert, organist and composer, born at Gloucester (1830?). Studied under Amott, S. S. Wesley, and C. Lucas. Was private organist to Earl Powis, 1852; of the Parish Church, Welshpool; St. Martin's, Scarborough, 1869; Parish Church, Lower Norwood, 1877. Graduated Mus. Bac., 1861; Mus. Doc., 1867, Oxford. He composed a Cantata, "Supplication and Praise," which has been performed several times; and a second, "Constantin," not produced until February, 1896, some months after his death. He also composed songs, part-songs, pf. pieces, etc. For some years he contributed to the *Musical Standard* notices of the Crystal Palace Concerts. He died at West Norwood, July 2, 1895, aged 65.

Sloper, Edward Hugh Lindsay, pianist and composer, born at London, June 14, 1826. He studied under Moscheles; at Frankfort under A. Schmitt; at Heidelberg under Vollweiler; and at Paris under Rousselot, 1841-46. Appeared in London at Musical Union, 1846. Played at a Philharmonic Concert, May 6, 1850. Lectured on Music in England, at Alexandra Palace, in May, 1876. Teacher and pianist in London. He died at London, July 3, 1887.

WORKS.—Op. 1, Czartoryska, 3 mazurkas, pf. [1846]; Op. 2, Henriette, valse, pf.; Op. 3, 24 studies, pf.; Op. 4, caprice, pf.; Op. 6, capriccio, pf.; Op. 7, serenade, pf.; Op. 8, six songs; Op. 9, grand duet; Op. 11, Tarantella;

SMART.

Op. 12, serenade and canzonette, pf.; Op. 13, twelve studies, pf.; Sonata for pf. and violin; Op. 15, Pensée fugitive, pf.; Op. 39, ballad fantasia [1867]; Op. 42, By the lake, pf.; Transcriptions and arrangements for pf.; Suite for orchestra, Brighton Festival, 1879; Duo, for two pfs., in E minor [1847]. Scena, Joan of Arc in prison (by Chorley), 1853. *Songs :* Fairy's reproach; John O'Grady; Medora; Prentice lad; Rover's adieu; Siesta; Violet, etc. Pianoforte instructions, exercises and lessons, London [1854]; Technical guide to touch, fingering, and execution, London, 1877. Tutor and technical guide for the pf. Editions of pf. works of eminent composers.

Smallwood, William, pianist, organist, and composer, born at Kendal, December 31, 1831. Studied under Dr. Camidge and Henry Phillips, and has been organist of Kendal Parish Church from 1847. Composer of an immense number of pf. pieces, chiefly for use in teaching, such as Home Treasures; Flowers of Melody; Youthful Pleasures, etc.; also of anthems, hymns, and songs. Author of a Pianoforte Tutor that has had a large circulation. Another musician of the name, F. W. SMALLWOOD, was appointed organist to the Earl of Breadalbane, Taymouth Castle, in 1885; and in 1890, organist of the Town Hall, Alloa, N.B.

Smart, Christopher, writer, who died on May 18, 1770. He published a "Collection of Melodies for the Psalms of David, according to the version of Christopher Smart, A.M. By the most eminent composers of church music," London, Walsh, 1765.

Smart, Sir George Thomas, conductor and teacher, born at London, May 10, 1776. He was a chorister in the Chapel Royal under Ayrton, and studied the organ under Dupuis, and composition under Arnold. Organist of St. James' Chapel, Hampstead Road, London. Knighted at Dublin by Lord Lieutenant, after conducting a successful series of concerts. 1811. Original member of the Philharmonic Society, 1813. Conductor of concerts of Philharmonic Society, 1813-44. Conductor of the Lenten oratorios. One of the organists of the Chapel Royal, 1822. Connected with Weber, who died at his house in 1826. Conducted Mendelssohn's "St. Paul," at Liverpool in 1836. Composer to the Chapel Royal, 1838. Conducted all the principal provincial festivals of his time, and arranged and conducted the music at the coronations of William IV. and Victoria. He died at Bedford Square, London, February 23, 1867. One of the greatest English conductors. He was a successful vocal teacher, and gave instruction to Jenny Lind and Sontag.

WORKS.—A collection of glees and canons, London [1863]; Collection of sacred music, 2 vols.; Three sonatinas for pf. [1800]; An acrostic

SMART.

elegy on...Viscount Horatio Nelson [1805]; The Œolus Frigate, a favourite dance as performed at Weymouth, 1804. *Glees :* Merry Gypsies, Peace at home, Sighs, Squirrel, Butterfly's Ball (canzonnettina), Garland, The Wreck (on the loss of the Forfarshire), 1839, etc. He edited Gibbons' "First set of Madrigals," for the Musical Antiquarian Society, 1841 ; works by Beethoven, etc.

Smart, Henry, violinist, was born at London in 1778. Brother of Sir George Smart. He studied under W. Cramer, and became leader in various theatre orchestras, the Philharmonic Society, English Opera House, etc. He became part-proprietor of a brewery, which did not succeed, and afterwards established a pianoforte manufactory. He died at Dublin, November 23, 1823.

Smart, Henry, organist and composer, son of above, born at London, October 26, 1813. He studied under his father and W. H. Kearns, but was partly self-taught. Articled to a solicitor. Organist of Parish Church of Blackburn, 1831-36. Organist of St. Philip's, Regent Street, London, 1836. Married, July, 1840. Organist, St. Luke's, Old Street, London, 1844-64 ; of St. Pancras, Euston Road, 1864. His sight failed him in 1864. Granted pension of £100 per annum by the Government, in 1879. He died at London, July 6, 1879, and is buried in Hampstead Cemetery, Finchley Road, London.

WORKS.—*Operas :* Bertha, or the Gnome of Hartzberg, Haymarket Theatre, London, 1855 ; Undine (unfinished) ; Surrender of Calais, by Planchè (unfinished). *Cantatas :* The Bride of Dunkerron, Birmingham Festival, 1864 ; King René's Daughter (by F. Enoch), 1871 ; The Fishermaidens, 1871 ; Jacob, sacred, Glasgow Choral Union, November 10, 1873. Full Morning and Evening Services in F and G, 1871. *Anthems :* O God, the King of Glory ; Sing to the Lord ; The Angel Gabriel ; Be glad, O ye righteous ; The Lord is my strength ; The Lord hath done great things ; Lord thou hast been our refuge ; *Part-Songs :* Ave Maria (1859) ; Behold where laughing Spring (1859) ; Cradle Song ; Evening Hymn ; Queen of the night ; The shepherd's farewell ; The waves' reproof ; Stars of the Summer night ; Lady, rise, sweet Morn's awaking ; Six 4-part songs (1869) ; 4-part songs composed for Leslie's choir. Trios for female voices, and many vocal duets. *Songs :* The Lady of the Lea ; Soft and bright the gems of night ; The Spinning Wheel ; Near thee, still near thee ; Vineta ; The Lady Isoline ; Autumn song ; Come again Spring ; I dream of thee at morn ; Rose of May ; The gleaner maiden ; The midnight ride ; The talisman ; The fairy's whisper ; Blue eyes ; Go, whispering breeze ; Wake, Mary, wake ; Echo of the lake ; Sir Roland ; The bird's love song ; The lark's

SMIETON.

song ; etc. *Organ :* Fifty Preludes and Interludes (1862) ; Andantes in G, A, and E minor ; Eighteen short easy pieces ; Postludes in C, D, E flat, etc. ; Twelve short interludes ; Grand solemn march ; March in G ; Festive march in D ; Minuet in C ; Choral, with variations ; The Organ Student, 12 pieces. Chamber Duets and Trios, by G. F. Handel, edited by Smart for the English Handel Society, 1852. The Presbyterian Hymnal, 1877 (edited). Report on Organ of Christ Church Cathedral, Dublin, 1878.

Smart was an authority on the organ, and the very large and beautiful instruments at Leeds Town Hall, and in St. Andrew's Hall, Glasgow, were erected from his specifications. Some books on him are "Henry Smart : His Life and Works," by Wm. Spark, London, 1881, 8vo, with portrait. "Henry Smart," by W. D. Seymour [Leeds, 1881]. "Henry Smart's Compositions for the Organ, analysed by John Broadhouse," London, 1880.

His sister, HARRIET ANNE SMART, *Mrs. Callow,* was born at London, October 20, 1817 ; died, London, June 30, 1883. She married William Callow, water painter, and was an amateur composer of hymns and other vocal music.

Smart, Thomas, organist and composer of the 18th century, who was organist of St. Clement Danes, London, in 1783. He composed " Five new songs and a cantata ;" The Air balloon [1784] ; Camps, or the royal review [1780] ; Cupid's kisses ; Squire's christening ; Time and care, and many other songs ; also some pf. music, and a glee, " Happy fellow."

Smethergell, William, organist and composer, who flourished in the latter half of last century. He was organist of St. Margaret-on-the-Hill, Southwark, and of All Hallows, Barking. He composed "A Treatise on Thoroughbass," London, 1794, and "Rules for Thoroughbass, to which are annexed three sonatas for the harpsichord and violin," op. 7 [1795] ; Six concertos for harpsichord or pf., two violins and 'cello [1785] ; Six duetts for two violins, op. 12 [1800] ; Six easy solos for a violin [1790] ; Six lessons for the harpsichord or pf., op. 1 ; Six overtures in eight parts, and a Second Sett, op. 5. He also issued various adaptations from Jommelli and other composers, and a few songs.

Smieton, John More, composer, born at Dundee, 1857. Pupil of Sir H. S. Oakeley, Dr. J. F. Bridge, and others. Some time engaged in musical work at Broughty Ferry, near Dundee. His compositions comprise Psalm 121, for tenor solo, chorus and orchestra. *Cantatas :* Pearl ; Ariadne, Dundee, 1883 ; King Arthur, Broughty Ferry, December, 1889 ; The Song of the Sower, chorus and orchestra, prize, National Co-operative

SMILES.

Festival, London, 1891; The Jolly Beggars (Burns), prize, Glasgow Select Choir, 1893; Belinda (composed with Basil Hood), 1896; Corinla, cantata; school music, etc.; orchestral overture; The Princess of Thule, sketch for orchestra; string quartet, etc.

Smiles, Frank, see QUATREMAINE, FRANK.

Smith, Alexander, musician of early part of the present century, issued "A Collection of Church tunes, hymns, and canons, in two, three, and four parts," Edinburgh, J. Johnson, sculpt., n.d. Dedicated to the ladies and gentlemen of Borrowstowness or Bo'ness, where Smith was a teacher of music.

Smith, Alexander William, teacher of singing, was born at Edinburgh on November 29, 1829. He studied under Bucher, Randegger, Schira, and under Romano at Florence. He was conductor of psalmody at Broughton Place United Presbyterian Church, Edinburgh from 1849 to 1864. He has chiefly devoted himself to the teaching of singing, and as a voice trainer has been one of the most successful in Scotland.

Smith, Alfred Montem, tenor vocalist, born at Windsor, May 13, 1828, the old "Montem" day at Eton College, hence his second name. Brother of George Townshend and Samuel Smith. Chorister at St. George's Chapel, Windsor, and Eton College. About 1850 was, for a time, tenor in the Choir of St. Andrew's, Wells Street, London. Succeeded J.W. Hobbs as lay-vicar at Westminster Abbey; and was a Gentleman of the Chapel Royal, St. James's, from 1858 to the time of his death. Sang at the Concerts of the Sacred Harmonic Society; for many years at the Three Choirs Festivals, from Hereford, 1855; in the quartets in "Elijah," Birmingham, 1858-61, etc. Member of the London Glee and Madrigal Union; a fine ballad singer, and popular lecturer. Professor of singing at R.A.M., and Guildhall School of Music. He died in London, May 2, 1891. His compositions consisted of songs and glees; one of the latter, "At the dawn of Life's day," was awarded the prize of the Noblemen's Catch Club, 1881. He married Miss Elizabeth Stroud, daughter of Henry Chaplin (q.v.), a soprano vocalist, now a professor at the Guildhall School of Music.

Smith, Alice Mary, MRS. MEADOWS WHITE, composer, born at London, May 19, 1839. She was a pupil of Sir W. Sterndale Bennett and Sir G. A. Macfarren. In 1867 she was married to Mr. Frederick Meadows White, Q.C., now a judge of the County of Middlesex, and in the same year she was elected an associate of the Philharmonic Society. She died at London, December 4, 1884.

WORKS. — Cantatas: Rüdesheim, Cambridge, 1865; Ode to the North-east wind,

SMITH.

London, 1880; The Passions, ode by Collins, Hereford, 1882; Song of the Little Baltung (Kingsley), 1883; The Red King (Kingsley). Symphony in C minor, 1863. Endymion, overture, 1864 (re-written for Crystal Palace, 1871); Lalla Rookh, overture, 1865; Masque of Pandora, overture, 1878; Jason, or the Argonauts and Sirens, overture, 1879. Quartets for pf. and strings: B flat, 1861; D 1864. Quartets for strings in D, 1862 and 1870. Concerto for clarinet and orchestra, 1872. Introduction and allegro, for pf. and orchestra, 1865. Two intermezzi from "The Masque of Pandora, 1879. Part-songs, songs, etc.

Smith, Arthur Francis, organist, pianist, and conductor. Articled pupil of Edward Chadfield (q.v.), he was joint founder and director of the Derby School of Music, work in connection with which he still carries on. F.C.O., 1874; Mus. Bac., Cambridge, 1883. Organist at Tickenhall, 1869; St. Werburgh's, Derby, 1872 to present time. Conductor, Derby Archidiaconal Choral Association; and Derby Orpheus and Madrigal Society. An early member of the Incorporated Society of Musicians, he has done valuable work for it, and is editor of its *Monthly Journal*. Examiner for that Society, and local representative of R.A.M. and R.C.M. He has composed a setting of Ps. 103; and has published songs and pf. pieces.

Smith, B., musician of early part of last century, published the Psalm Singer's Magazine, 1729; Harmonious Companion, a psalm singer's magazine," 1732.

Smith, Boyton, pianist and composer, born at Dorchester, February 23, 1837. Brother of E. Sydney Smith. Educated at Hereford and Winchester Cathedrals, under Dr. S. S. Wesley. Organist of Dorchester Parish Church. He has composed Church Services in D, E flat, F, and G; Anthems, songs, etc. Organ pieces for church use, six sets; Allegretto grazioso in A; Andante con moto, etc. Also many pf. pieces of a popular kind, such as Echo of the waves; Nightingale and Zephyr; Dew pearls; Woodland echoes; Song of the sylph; La fée coquette, op. 64; Sur le lac; and numerous transcriptions.

Smith, Charles, composer and bass vocalist, born at London in 1786. He was a chorister in the Chapel Royal under Ayrton, and studied also under Costellow and John Ashley. From 1799 he sang as a soprano at Ranelagh and in Scotland, till his voice broke in 1803. He then became organist of Croydon Church, and afterwards of Welbeck Chapel in 1807. In 1813 he sang in oratorio as a bass. He was married to a Miss Both, of Norwich, and resided in Liverpool from 1816. He died at Crediton, Devon, November 22, 1856.

WORKS.—*Music to Dramas:* Yes or No,

SMITH.

1809; Hit or miss, 1810; Anything new; Knapschou, or the forest fiend, Lyceum, 1830. Glees; Songs and canzonets: Battle of Hohenlinden; Far o'er the sea; Sea boy's dream. Fantasias for harpsichord or pf. Ancient Psalmody from the publications of T. Est, Ravenscroft, Morley,, etc., arranged for 2, 3, and 4 voices, London [1844].

Smith, Clement, organist and composer, was born at Richmond, Surrey, in 1760. He graduated Mus. Bac., 1791, and Mus. Doc., Oxford, in 1800. Teacher at Richmond, where he died, November 16, 1826. He composed church music, glees, and songs. Sonata cappriciosa for pf. or harpsichord [1790]. Duets for pf., etc.

Smith, David, musician and teacher in Staffordshire. Compiler of "The Sacred Harmonist, or leader's guide, being a new selection of psalm and hymn tunes.." London, 1833, 2 vols. He also edited the 1811 edition of Thomas Walker's Companion to Rippon's Tune Book.

Smith, Edward Sydney, pianist and composer (brother of Boyton Smith), born at Dorchester, July 14, 1839. He studied at Leipzig Conservatorium, under Moscheles, Plaidy, Hauptmann, Richter, Papperitz, and Reitz, from 1855. Settled in London as pianist and composer, 1859. He died at London, March 3, 1889.

WORKS.—*Pianoforte:* Arcadia; Barcarolle; Bolero; Chant des oiseaux; Chant der savoyard; Coquetterie; Danse Napolitaine; Etudes de concert; Eventide; Fairy realms; Fairy whispers: Fandango; Fête champêtre; Fête Hongroise; Fête militaire; Gavotte; La harpe Eolienne; Le jet d'eau; Les trompettes de la guerre; Marche Hongroise; Maypole dance; Pas de sabots; Rêve angélique; Rhapsodie; Saltarello; Tarantelles; The spinning wheel; Titania; Tyrolienne; Fantasias on operas, and transcriptions, numerous.

Smith, Rev. George, author of "Church Music, two lectures," London, 1860.

Smith, George Montague, organist and composer, born at Norwich, July, 1843. Organist, Glasgow University, and conductor of the University Choral Society. Organist of St. Silas' Episcopal Church; Coats' Memorial Church, Paisley. Local examiner in music, Glasgow University; Professor of harmony, Queen Margaret's College, Glasgow. Composer of cantatas, Blessed is the man; and Psalm 137; an opera, The Killabag Shootings; Festival setting of Te Deum; Songs, part-songs, etc. Also Concert overture in E flat, Gloucester Festival, 1877; Bourrée, orchestra, Glasgow, 1887, etc.

Smith, George Townshend, organist and composer (brother of Alfred Montem and Samuel Smith), born at Windsor, November 14, 1813. Son of Edward Woodley Smith,

SMITH.

lay-clerk of St. George's Chapel, Windsor. He was a chorister in St. George's Chapel, Windsor, under Highmore Skeats, and he also studied music under S. Wesley. Organist successively of the old Parish Church, Eastbourne; of St. Margaret's, Lynn; of Hereford Cathedral, 1843. He acted as conductor and honorary secretary of the Three Choirs Festivals. Died at Hereford, August 3, 1877. He composed anthems, songs, and other vocal music, also quadrilles and other light music for the pf.

Smith, Isaac, composer, was born about the middle of the 18th century. He was clerk of Alie Street Meeting House, London. He died at London, about 1800. Published "A Collection of Psalm Tunes in Three Parts, adapted to each measure as now sung in several churches, chapels, and meeting-houses in and about London "...London [1770]; 5th edition, by S. Major, 1788. The well-known tune "Irish" appears in this collection, and has been attributed to Smith.

Smith, J. Whitehead, organist, pianist, and violinist, born at Wells, Somersetshire, 1827? Took lessons of a Mr. Dix, and of Mr. Angel. Entered the R.A.M., 1843, and distinguished himself as a pianist at the Academy concerts, and played the violin in the students' orchestra. A.R.A.M., and F.R.A.M. Assistant organist, St. Mary's, Paddington Green; librarian and organist, Marlborough College; and for more than thirty years organist of Wimborne Minster. Local examiner for R.C.M.

Smith, John, organist and composer, born at Cambridge in 1795. Stipendiary choirman of Christ Church Cathedral, Dublin, 1815. Vicar-choral of St. Patrick's Cathedral, 1816. Organist of the Chapel, Dublin Castle, 1833-35. Professor of Music in the University of Dublin. Mus. Doc., Dublin. He died near Dublin, November 12, 1861.

WORKS.—The Revelation, oratorio; Cathedral Music, in vocal score, with organ or pf. accompaniment [1837]; Lyra Masonica, collection of masonic songs, London, 1847; Selection of Mr. Kelly's Hymns on various passages of Scripture, Dublin [1850]; Seventy of the Psalms of David..the music by the best composers..Dublin [1835]. He also edited Weyman's Melodia Sacra. *Glees:* Christmas Morning, Isles of Greece, King Alfred's hymn, etc. *Songs:* Absent, Fairy gold, Rememb'rest thou, Volunteer's song, etc. Treatise on the theory and practice of Music, with the principles of harmony and composition, Dublin, 1853, 2 vols.; Irish Minstrelsy, a selection of original melodies of Erin, with characteristic words by Edward Fitzsimons; symphonies by J. Smith, Dublin 1814. His son, J. S. SMITH, succeeded him as organist of the Chapel Royal, Dublin Castle, in 1835.

Smith, John Stafford, organist and composer, born at Gloucester about March, 1750. He was the son of Martin Smith, organist of Gloucester Cathedral from 1743 to 1782. He studied music under his father and Dr. Boyce, and became a gentleman of the Chapel Royal in 1784. In 1795, he was made lay-vicar of Westminster Abbey, and in 1802, he succeeded Dr. Arnold as organist of the Chapel Royal. From 1805 to 1817, he held the position of master of the children of the Chapel Royal. He died at London, September 21, 1836.

WORKS.— Anthems, composed for the choir service of the Church of England, London, n.d. Twelve chants, composed for the use of the choirs of the Church of England, London, n.d. Collection of songs of various kinds for different voices, London, 1785. Collection of glees for 3, 4, 5, and 6 voices, London, n.d. With some of these he gained prizes between 1773 and 1780. *Edited :* Musica Antiqua, a selection of music of this and other countries, from the commencement of the twelfth to the beginning of the eighteenth century, comprising some of the earliest and most curious motettes, madrigals, etc., London, 1812, 2 vols. ; Collection of English songs, in score, for 3 and 4 voices, composed about the year 1500, taken from MSS. of the same age, London, 1779. Smith aided Hawkins with his " History of Music."

Smith, Joseph, organist, composer, and conductor, born at Dudley, Worcestershire, 1856, of Irish parents. Educated on the Continent, and chiefly self-taught in music. Graduated Mus. Bac. 1880, Mus. Doc. 1881, Dublin. Began his career at seventeen as organist of a church at Galway. In 1877 appointed to Limerick Cathedral, where he remained till 1882, founding a choral society and giving concerts. Went to Dublin in 1882 as organist of the church of the Three Patrons, Rathgar, and professor of music at the Convent school of the Sacré Cœur at Mount Annville, holding both appointments to present time. In 1883 he was appointed, in conjunction with Sir R. P. Stewart, professor of music in the Royal University of Ireland. Musical director, Dublin Artizans' Exhibition, 1885 ; conductor of Dublin Musical Society from 1889. His works include three masses ; a cantata, " St. Kevin," produced at Hereford Festival, 1885 ; an Inaugural Ode, for the Dublin exhibition just named ; motet, God be merciful, prize, National Welsh Eisteddfod, 1880 ; anthems, part-songs, etc.; Triumphal march, orchestra, 1885. Editor of Catholic Choir Music, Pohlmann, Dublin, 1891. Compiler of a Catholic Hymn-book, with tunes.

Smith, Laura Alexandrine, author of " Music of the Waters, a collection of the

Sailors' Chanties, or working songs of the sea of all maritime nations, Boatmen's, Fishermen's, and Rowing Songs and Water Legends," London, Kegan Paul, 1888. She is also the composer of some songs, My Castle in Spain, etc.

Smith, Robert, writer, was born at Cambridge, in 1689. He was Plumian Professor of Astronomy at Cambridge, and became Master of Trinity College in 1742. He died at Cambridge in 1768. He wrote " Harmonics, or the philosophy of musical sounds," Cambridge, 1749 ; 2nd edition, enlarged, London, 1759. A Postscript upon the changeable harpsichord, a perfect instrument, London, 1762.

Smith, Robert Archibald, composer, born at Reading, Berks., November 16, 1780. Son of Robert Smith, silk weaver, a native of East Kilbride, who settled at Reading in 1774, during a heavy depression of trade in Paisley. He very early gave indications of his possession of musical ability, but was apprenticed to the weaving trade, which he followed in Reading, and in Paisley, from 1800, where he became intimate with Tannahill, Motherwell, etc. He married Mary MacNicol in 1802. Teacher of music, and precentor in the Abbey Church, Paisley, 1807. Musical director of S. George's, Edinburgh, August, 1823. He died at Edinburgh, January 3, 1829, and is buried in S. Cuthbert's churchyard.

WORKS.—The Scotish Minstrel, a selection from the vocal melodies of Scotland, ancient and modern, arranged for the pianoforte, Edinburgh [c. 1821-24], 6 vols. The Irish minstrel, a selection from the vocal melodies of Ireland, ancient and modern, Edinburgh, n.d. [1825]. Flowers of Scottish Song, Glasgow, n.d. Select Melodies, with appropriate words, chiefly original, collected and arranged with symphonies and accompaniments for the pianoforte, Edinburgh, n.d. [1827.] Devotional Music, original and selected, arranged mostly in four parts, with a Thorough-bass for the Organ or Pianoforte, 1810 ; New edition by John Turnbull, Glasgow, n.d. Anthems in four vocal parts, with an accompaniment for the Organ or Pianoforte......1819. Sacred Harmony, for the use of S. George's Church, Edinburgh, being a collection of Psalm and Hymn tunes...... Edinburgh [1820] (with Rev. A. Thomson) ; other editions, and a modern one edited by Jas. S. Geikie, Edinburgh, n.d. Sacred Music, consisting of the tunes, sanctuses, doxologies, thanksgivings, etc., sung in St. George's, Church, Edinburgh, Edinburgh, 1825. Edinburgh Sacred Harmony for the use of churches and families, arranged for four voices, Edinburgh, 1829, 2 vols. The Sacred Harmony of the Church of Scotland,

SMITH.

SMITH.

n.d. [1828]. *Songs:* Jessie, the Flow'r o' Dunblane (1808); Bonnie Mary Hay; O wha's at the window?; The lass o' Arranteenie; The Harper of Mull; Loudon's bonnie woods and braes; On wi' the tartan; Maid of the sea; Highlander's farewell; The willow. *Duets:* Row weel, my boatie, row weel; etc. *Psalm tunes:* Morven, St. Mirren, Invocation, St. Lawrence, Kelburn, Selma, Paisley Abbey, and many others, all published in his collections. *Anthems:* How beautiful upon the mountains; The earth is the Lord's; etc. An Introduction to Singing, comprising various examples, with scales, exercises, and songs, etc., Edinburgh [1826].

Smith was one of the best musicians whom Scotland produced in the first part of this century. His works are now as much used as ever they were, and his songs and psalms are in constant use in Scotland. He composed many fine Scottish melodies, and did not scruple occasionally to pass a number of them off as antiques. He performed on the viola and violoncello, and played the former instrument at the Glasgow Musical Festival of 1821. His violoncello, together with some manuscripts, is preserved in the Public Museum of Paisley.

Smith, Samuel, musician and promoter of the Tonic Sol-fa, was born in 1806. He was a pioneer in the movement for promoting the chanting of psalms in nonconformist churches. He identified himself with musical affairs in Bradford, and was the chief founder of St. George's Hall and the Bradford Festival Choral Society. He died at Bradford, July 5, 1873.

Smith, Samuel, organist and composer, was born at Eton, August 29, 1821. Son of Edward Woodley Smith, and brother of Alfred Montem and George Townshend Smith. Studied in Chapel Royal under Hawes, and also under Sir Geo. J. Elvey. Organist successively at Hayes, Eton, and Egham; Trinity Church, Windsor, 1858-61; Parish Church, Windsor, 1861. Composer of Psalms and chants," London [1860]; "Selection of chants and responses used at the Parish Church..Windsor," Windsor [1865], privately printed. Psalms, hymns, and anthems [1870]. Songs, etc.

Smith, T. G., musician, issued "Original Maltese melodies, selected and purchased at Malta," London [1812]; also [1825].

Smith, T. R., author of "The Violoncello Preceptor, containing the rudiments of music, with scales," London, n.d.

Smith, Theodore, composer and pianist of latter half of the 18th and early part of 19th centuries. Composer of Six Sonatas for harpsichord, op. 5 [1770]; Six Sonatas, op. 6 [1780]; Three Sonatas and a favorite march, for pf. or harpsichord [1790]; Three Sonatas

and an overture; Three Sonatas, pf., op. 36; Sacro Divertimento..London [1810]. Songs, Welsh harper, etc.

Smith, Thomas, organist composer, and didactic writer, born at Arnold, Nottingham, February 20, 1832. Studied pf. under Henry Farmer, and organ under Charles Noble. At the age of fifteen he was organist of St. Stephen's, Snenton, Nottingham, of St. John's, Bury St. Edmunds, 1873, and since 1880 at Hozzinger, the seat of the Marquis of Bristol. Composer of O worship the Lord; Thou crownest the year; and other popular anthems. Author of "A Concise and practical explanation of the rules of simple Harmony and Thorough Bass," London, n.d.; Short practical method for teaching Singing, etc., London, n.d.

Smith, Thomas Roylands, Diocesan choirmaster and organist, born at Highgate, Middlesex, October 28, 1847. Studied under Joseph Thomas Cooper, and Scotson Clark. Held the appointment of Music Master at Abingdon Grammar School, but has now been for many years resident in Torquay. He was organist of St. John's, and St. Mary's, Torquay, resigning the former in 1876, and the latter in 1892. His principal work has been the promotion and improvement of Church music. Since 1875 he has been conductor of the Plympton Deanery Choral Union, and Exeter Diocesan Choirmaster, from 1886. In these capacities he has conducted as many as twelve choral festivals in the year, in which about 3,000 singers take part, including one in Exeter Cathedral. As a teacher he has been very successful, and in choral music his societies at Chudleigh, Teignmouth, and Torquay, have done good work. He has published a Te Deum, Pater Noster, and five Evening Services to various forms of the Gregorian and Ambrosian melodies; and has contributed many articles on church and choral music to different papers.

Smith, Thomas Sydney, composer and organist of the present time. Deputy organist and choirmaster, St. George's Cathedral, Southwark, and organist of St. Mary's South Kensington, London. Author of "Vade Mecum, a practical hand-book for the pf.," London [1879]; New Scale Practice for the pf. [1882]; Ianthe and Haidee, two melodies for pf., op. 1 [1884]. Sacred music, songs, and pf. music.

Smith, Valentine, tenor vocalist, born at Barnard Castle, Durham. Sang for some time under the name of Signor Fabrini. Joined the Carl Rosa Opera Company in 1885, after a successful operatic career in America. In 1889 he organized an opera company, which opened in London. The next year the company met with success at Hamburg and other places. He brought out an English version of Adolphe Adam's "Si j'étais Roi," for the first time, at Newcastle-on-Tyne, February 22, 1893.

Smith, Rev. William, Scottish clergyman and amateur musician, was born in 1754. He settled in New York in 1783, and died there, April 6, 1821. He published "Chants for publick worship," 1814; and "The Reasonableness of setting forth the praises of God according to the use of the primitive church, with historical views of metre psalmody," New York, 1814.

Smith, William, amateur musician, born at Chapel of Garioch, Aberdeenshire, where his father was minister, December 6, 1803. He was a merchant in Aberdeen, and died at Newtyle, Forfarshire, August 31, 1878. He issued "The People's Tune Book: a manual of Psalmody for Scotland. Selected by express permission from the copyright arrangements of Novello, Horsley, Greatorex, Havergal, Jacob, and other eminent professors." Aberdeen, 1844.

Smith, William, musician, of Chesham, issued "Musical Devotions, consisting of 20 Psalm and Hymn tunes." Chesham [1830]. Another WILLIAM SMITH edited "Sacred Harmony, containing an easy introduction to the art of Singing." Dublin, 1810.

Smith, William Braxton, tenor vocalist. Educated as an architect, but gave that up for singing. Studied at the Guildhall School under F. Walker. Made his *début* at the Crystal Palace Concerts, October 20, 1888, with success. Sang at the Popular Concerts in 1891; and has been heard in many parts of the country, and at the Bristol Festival, 1896. Toured with Madame Albani in Canada, 1896-7. Married, in October, 1896, Miss MABEL BERREY, soprano vocalist, who has sung with acceptance at the Popular Concerts (1895), Crystal Palace (1896), and in various provincial towns.

Smith, William Seymour, composer, baritone vocalist, and organist, born at Marlow, Bucks., August 20, 1836. Studied singing under Balfe, and organ, pf., and composition with C. E. Horsley. Was organist of Hampstead Parish Church, some time from 1862; Musical lecturer at the Royal Polytechnic, London. At present time Professor of Singing, R.C.M. His entertainment, "Musical Sketches," was given in London and the provinces with much success.

WORKS.— *Cantatas:* Joshua, 1887; The Fairies' Festival, and May Time, female voices. The Moon, ode for female voices. *Songs:* The Rovers; Loving Hands; I am thine, etc. Cavatina, violin and pf. Three Illustrations of Shakespeare; Six pieces in classic form; Dorothy; and other pieces for pf.; Andante for organ, etc.

Smyth, Ethel M., composer, born in London. Daughter of General J. H. Smyth,

late of the Royal Artillery. Studied a short time at the Leipzig Conservatorium; then with H. von Herzogenberg. First came into notice with a quintet for strings, performed at Leipzig, about January, 1884. Then came a Sonata in A minor, op. 7, for pf. and violin, 1887. In 1890 two of her compositions were performed at the Crystal Palace; Serenade in D, for orchestra, April 26; and overture "Antony and Cleopatra," October 18. Her most important work, a Solemn Mass in D, was performed by the Royal Choral Society at the Albert Hall, January 18, 1893. She has also published sets of songs, op. 3, and 4.

Snazelle, George Harry, bass vocalist. Was a member of the Carl Rosa Opera Company at the first season in London, Princess's Theatre, 1875; on tour with the same, 1876, etc. Also sang in concerts in the provinces. Began, as a single-handed entertainer, in Liverpool, October, 1885, and later visited other places, extending the scope of his work by engaging the assistance of other vocalists. In 1887 he was selected to give his entertainment, "Music, Song, and Story," in Australia and New Zealand.

Sneddon, James, composer and teacher, born near Dunfermline. Studied under J. Fulcher, and others. Licentiate, Tonic Sol-fa College; Mus. Bac., Cambridge, 1885. Precentor of Lauriston Place United Presbyterian Church, Edinburgh, 1870-86. Teacher of singing under Edinburgh School Board. Compositions: Psalm 130, for soli, chorus, and strings; Bright feet of May, and other part-songs. Author of The Musical Self-Instructor; Musical Training; Series of School Song-books, and articles in the "Musical Educator," edited by John Greig.

JANET C. SNEDDON, contralto vocalist, has sung with acceptance in London, 1885; Glasgow, and Edinburgh, etc., from 1887.

Snow, J., organist and composer, was organist at St. John's College, Oxford. Composer of "Variations for the harpsichord to a minuet of Corelli's, etc.," London [1790].

Snow, Valentine, trumpet-player, who was born about the beginning of the 18th century. He succeeded John Shore as serjeant-trumpeter to the King, in 1753. He played the trumpet parts in Handel's oratorios, which were specially written for him. He died in December, 1770.

MOSES SNOW, father of above, was a Gentleman of the Chapel Royal, and lay-vicar of Westminster Abbey. He graduated Mus. Bac., Cambridge, in 1696, and died in 1700.

Snowdon, J., musician, edited "The Euterpean, being a collection of glees, catches, canons, etc.," London [1825].

Soaper, John, composer, born in 1743. He was a lay-vicar of Westminster Abbey, Gentleman of the Chapel Royal, and vicar-choral of St. Paul's Cathedral. He died at London, June 5, 1794, aged 51, and is buried in the crypt of St. Paul's. Composer of psalms and chants.

Soldene, Emily, soprano vocalist and actress, born at Islington, London. Articled to Howard Glover. Made her *début* at a concert, St. James's Hall, in 1864; and in January, 1865, sang for the first time on any stage at a morning concert given by Howard Glover at Drury Lane Theatre, when she took the part of *Azucena* in the second act of "Il Trovatore." Afterwards sang at the Oxford Music Hall as Miss Fitz-Henry, also at concerts of the Sacred Harmonic Society, etc., and in the provinces. First appeared in comic opera at the Standard Theatre in 1869, in the "Grande Duchesse de Gérolstein." Visited the United States of America, 1874, and 1876-7; also Australia and New Zealand. Reappeared in London at the Alhambra, September, 1878. Securing the provincial rights of "Carmen," she produced it at Leicester, May, 1879. From 1880, again chiefly in America and Australia. Author of "My Theatrical and Musical Recollections," London, Downey, 1897; also of "Young Mrs. Staples," 1896, and other stories. At present time she is understood to be preparing, while living at San Francisco, another book of reminiscences.

Solomon, Edward, composer and conductor, born in 1855, of Jewish race. Chiefly self-taught in music. Conducted comic opera touring companies, 1878, etc. Composer of a number of comic operas: Billee Taylor, produced at Imperial Theatre, London, October 30, 1880; Claude Duval, Olympic, August 20, 1881; Vicar of Bray, Globe, July 22, 1882; Virginia, New York, January 9, 1883; Pocahontas, Empire, December 26, 1884; Maid and Moonshiner, New York, 1886; Pickwick, Comedy, February 7, 1889; The Red Hussar, Lyric, November 23, 1889; Nautch Girl, Savoy, June 30, 1891. Killicrumper, and other pieces for German Reed, etc. Also some pieces for pf. He died January 25, 1895.

His brother, FRED SOLOMON, sang in Billee Taylor, in the provinces, 1883; and is the composer of the comic opera, Captain Kidd, or the bold buccaneer, produced at the Prince of Wales Theatre, Liverpool, September 10, 1883.

Somerset, Lord Henry Richard Charles, amateur musician, second son of 8th Duke of Beaufort, was born December 7, 1849. He was M.P. for Monmouthshire, 1871-80, and comptroller of Her Majesty's Household, 1874-79. In 1872 he married Isabella Caroline, daughter of Charles, 3rd Earl Somers, who has distinguished herself in the cause of temperance. Lord Henry Somerset has composed anthems, pf. music, polkas

for orchestra, and the following among other Songs: Across the sea, All through the night, Along the sands, Dawn, Far away, First Spring day, Good-bye, Love's flight, Once more, Song of night, Song of sleep, Where'er you go, etc.

Somervell, Arthur, composer, born at Windermere. Educated at Uppingham School, and Cambridge. Studied music at Berlin High School, and at R.C.M. with Drs. Stanford and Parry.

WORKS.—Mass in C, for soli, chorus and orchestra, produced by Bach Choir, March 10, 1891; A song of praise, Exhibition, Kendal, 1891; The forsaken merman (Matthew Arnold), Leeds Festival, 1895; The Power of sound, Kendal, 1895; Elegy (Robert Bridges), alto solo, chorus and orchestra, Hovingham Festival, 1896; Charge of the Light Brigade, chorus and orchestra; Ode to the sea, soprano solo, chorus and orchestra, accepted for Birmingham Festival, 1897. The enchanted palace, operetta for schools. Orchestral ballad, Helen of Kirkconnel, Philharmonic Society, March 23, 1893; Bristol Festival, 1896; In Arcady, suite for small orchestra, Brighton, March 23, 1897. Album of seven songs; Six songs; songs, various; arrangements of old Scotch songs. Studies in pf. technique; By the sea, six sketches; On the river, five sketches; pf. pieces, various.

South, Charles Frederick, organist born in London, February 6, 1850. Received his first lessons on the organ from his brother, Henry J. South, afterwards studying under George Cooper. When sixteen years of age he obtained his first organ appointment at Aske's Hospital, Hoxton. In 1868 he was appointed to St. Augustine and St. Faith's, Watling Street, City. Here he remained until 1883, his ability as a choir-trainer being shown in the high reputation the choral services acquired. While there the organ was enlarged, in 1881. Upon leaving for Salisbury Cathedral, where he was appointed in 1883, the parishioners and choir of his church presented him with handsome testimonials. He was for some time conductor of the Sarum Choral Society. His compositions are not numerous, and are confined to church music, services, and introits, etc.

Southgate, Rev. Frederic, clergyman and composer, born at Gravesend, October 7, 1824. He was educated at Ramsgate and Cambridge, where he graduated B.A. in 1848. Curate at Castle Headingham, Suffolk; and afterwards minister of St. Mark's, Rosherville, and Northfleet, 1858. He died at Northfleet, January 30, 1885. He issued "Favourite hymn tunes . . . used at St. Botolph's Church, Northfleet." London, 1873, and composed other church music.

Southgate, Thomas Lea, organist, musical scientist, and writer, born at Highgate,

SOUTHGATE.

London, August 22, 1836. Son of Thomas Bishop Southgate, noticed below. Foundation scholar of the old Grammar School, Highgate; and musically educated under his father, John Hullah, G. W. Martin, and James Coward. Organist successively at Christ Church, Hornsey, 1862; St. Saviour's, Fitzroy Square, London, 1865; St. Saviour's, Clapham, 1867; St. Margaret's, Dulwich, 1873; and Emmanuel Church, Dulwich, 1875. In 1862, he joined W. Hammond in starting the *Musical Standard*, and became editor in 1871, carrying on the paper himself for several years. Up to 1891, he kept up his connection with that journal, writing many articles on different subjects. In 1891, a syndicate was formed to found the paper, *Musical News*, and Mr. Southgate was joint-editor with Dr. Turpin until 1895. Besides his work on these papers, he has written articles for the *Musical Times, Orchestra, Musical Record, Choir*, etc., and for Grove's " Dictionary." He has lectured before the College of Organists, Musical Association, R.A.M., and Fine Arts Society on various subjects. He took an active part in the protest against the Degrees *in absentiâ* of Trinity College, Toronto, and was publicly presented with a testimonial in recognition of his services, July 29, 1891. For the Union of Graduates in Music, he has done valuable work, and his " History of Degrees in Music," for the Roll and Kalendar, was the first essay of its kind. From the formation of the Union, 1893, he has acted as Hon. Secretary. He is a member of the Council of the Musical Association, and of the Plain-Song and Mediæval Music Society; and in 1891, was made an Hon. Member of the Royal College of Organists. His researches into the subject of Egyptian Music, as exemplified in his description of the double flutes discovered by Professor Flinders, Petrie, are of high historic and scientific value. It is understood that he has more to say on this subject. He has composed some vocal, instrumental, and orchestral music, but little has been published. Author of " Rudiments of Music for Choir-boys "; and, in conjunction with F. T. Piggott, of a portion of the work on The Music and Musical Instruments of Japan.

His father, THOMAS BISHOP SOUTHGATE, was born at Hornsey, June 8, 1814. Chorister at the Chapel Royal, St. James', and, when twelve, occasionally acted as deputy-organist for Sir George Smart. Studied harmony under Attwood and Goss, and organ under Samuel Wesley. Was organist of Leyton Church, Essex; Hornsey Parish Church for nineteen years; and of St. Anne's, Highgate Rise. An excellent violinist, he played first violin with F. Cramer for some time at the Opera House, He died at Highgate,

SPARK.

November 3, 1868. Composer of Exercises and Scales intended to facilitate the study of the pf., London [1858]; The Seasons, 4 romances for 'cello and pf. [1861]; anthems, pf. music, songs, and the hymns Nearer to Thee, Thy will be done, and others, in many collections.

Spark, William, organist and composer, the most prominent member of a family of musicians, was born at Exeter, October 28, 1823. Chorister at Exeter Cathedral, and articled pupil of Dr. S. S. Wesley. Organist of St. Lawrence's, Exeter, 1840. Removing to Leeds with Dr. Wesley, in 1842, he became deputy-organist at Leeds Parish Church, and organist at Chapeltown and St. Paul's, Leeds, successively. Afterwards he was appointed to Tiverton Parish Church, and Daventry, returning to Leeds, 1850, as organist to St. George's, an appointment he held for thirty years. Founded the Leeds Madrigal Society, 1851; and, later, the People's Concerts. Was associated with Henry Smart in designing the organ in the Leeds Town Hall; and, in 1860, was elected organist. Played his organ sonata at the Leeds Festival, 1858; and solos in 1874-7; and gave two afternoon recitals during the Festival of 1880. Has given organ recitals in many parts of the country, and has lectured on various musical topics. Contributed many articles to the *Yorkshire Post*, 1883, and the musical press. He graduated Mus. Doc., Dublin, 1861. Died at Leeds, June 16, 1897.

WORKS.—Oratorio, Immanuel, Leeds, May 17, 1887; cantata, Trust and Triumph, Dublin, 1861; Ode to Labour; The Birthday Festival. Magnificat and Nunc Dimittis in D; All we like sheep; O God, have mercy; Christ being raised from the dead; O Lord our Governour; and other anthems. Church music, various. Glees, songs, etc. Grand Sonata, op. 21. Ten original compositions. Patriotic March, composed for the visit of the Duke and Duchess of York to Leeds, 1894. Various organ pieces. Author of Lecture on Church Music, 1851; Choirs and Organs, 1852; A few words to Musical Conductors, 1853; Memoir of Dr. S. S. Wesley; Musical Tour in North Germany, 1871; Handy Book of Choral Singing. Henry Smart, his life and works, London, Reeves, 1881; Musical Memories, 1888; Musical Reminiscences, 1892, both published by Reeves. Editor of the *Organist's Quarterly Journal*, commenced in 1869, and still in progress; The Practical Choirmaster, twelve parts, contributing original compositions to each work; Sacred Harmony, selected and arranged; Batiste's organ compositions, adapted to English instruments, etc.

His father, WILLIAM SPARK, born in 1797, was a chorister and lay vicar, connected with Exeter Cathedral for nearly 60 years. He

SPEECHLEY.

was a good musician, and had sung with
Catalani. He died at Exeter, September (?),
1865, at the age of 68. EDWARD J. SPARK,
the second son, was born at Exeter, August 7,
1829. He was organist of St. Lawrence's,
Exeter, and after holding other appointments,
became, in 1852, organist of Bury Parish
Church. He then entered the railway service, and eventually settled at Worcester,
where, in 1870, he established a music business. He was organist of Holy Trinity
Church, Worcester, for 15 years, and resumed
the appointment in 1888, after officiating for
some time at St. Martin's Church. Conductor
for many years of the Worcester Amateur Vocal
Union. He has given many concerts, and done
much for music in Worcester. FREDERICK
R. SPARK, the youngest of the three brothers,
is settled in business in Leeds. He is the
proprietor of the *Leeds Express*; has been
hon. secretary of the Leeds Festival from
1877; and, in conjunction with Joseph
Bennett, wrote a "History of the Leeds
Musical Festivals, 1858-1889." Leeds: F. R.
Spark and Son, 1892.

Speechley, John, organist, was born at
Peterborough in 1811. He was organist of
the Cathedral there, and at the church of St.
John, for 33 years, and died in August, 1869.
He was considered a skilful player, and a
successful teacher.

Speer, Charlton Templeman, pianist
and composer, born at Cheltenham, November 21, 1859. Entered the R.A.M., 1873, and
obtained the Sterndale Bennett Scholarship,
1874. A.R.A.M., and Professor of Pf., 1885-
1893. Associate, Philharmonic Society. Appointed organist, All Soul's, South Hampstead,
1876; St. Paul's, Bow Common, 1880. Has
appeared in public as a pianist, and given
recitals with success. His compositions
include two cantatas, "The Arsenal," and
"The Day Dream" (Tennyson), to the latter
being awarded the Jubilee Gold Medal of the
Bath Philharmonic Society. The work was
produced at Bath, June 20, 1887, and at the
Crystal Palace, February 18, 1888. He has
also written songs, etc. His instrumental
works consist of a concert overture for
orchestra; an organ Sonata in D flat (Bow
and Bromley Institute, April, 1883); many
pieces for pf., songs, etc. Editor (with J. R.
C. Gale) of an English series of original songs,
Weekes, 1897.

Speer, William Henry, composer and
conductor, cousin of the preceding, born in
London, 1863. Studied under W. Haynes,
Malvern, Dr. C. H. Lloyd; and at Cambridge,
under Drs. Stanford and Garrett; also for
three years at R.C.M. Graduated Mus. Bac.,
1890; M.A., 1890, Cambridge. F.R.C.O. Hon.
conductor, since 1893, of St. Albans Oratorio
Society, and occasional organ recitalist. He

SPINNEY.

has published "The Jackdaw of Rheims,"
for chorus and small orchestra, op. 8; Album
of six songs, op. 1; Three Elizabethan Love
Songs, op. 7; Vocal quartet (Ladies' voices)
"To Music," op. 3; Part-songs, op. 5. String
quartet, in B flat, op. 6; Sonata in B flat,
pf., and violin, op. 4; Sonata in D, op. 2, pf.
Some of these have been performed by the
Musical Artists' Society, 1885-7. In MS. he
has songs, pieces for violin, etc.

Spence, Mrs. Sarah, authoress of "An
Introduction to the Science of Harmony,"
London, 1810.

Spencer, Charles Child, writer and composer, born at London, in 1797. He was
organist and choirmaster of St. James' Chapel,
Clapton, London. He died at London, June
4, 1869. Author of "Elements of practical
music," London, 1829; "Elements of musical
composition," London, 1840; "The Pianoforte, the rudiments of the art of playing,"
London, n.d.; "Rudimentary and practical
treatise on Music," London, 1850, 2 vols.;
"A concise explanation of the church modes,
with remarks on the mutations they have
undergone since the inventions of the hexa-
chord and the modern tonal system of Music
..," London, 1846. Some of the foregoing
works have gone through several editions.
He composed many glees: Beauteous rosebud;
Oh, merry goes the time; Now April (madrigal); Sweet flowers; When the shadows of
evening fall. Songs. Short anthems or introits, London, 1847.

Spencer, John, composer and organist,
who was a pupil of Dr. Dupuis, and afterwards his son-in-law. He composed "Again
the balmy zephyr"; "O turn to Hebe," and
other glees. Songs, carols, pf. music, etc.
Edited the "Cathedral Music" of Dr. T. S.
Dupuis, 3 vols.

Spinney—a family of musicians. THOMAS
EDWARD SPINNEY, organist and composer,
born, June 24, 1824, was a pupil of Sir Henry
Bishop. Was for many years organist of
Wilton Parish Church, and is now organist
and choirmaster of St. Edmund's, Salisbury,
and conductor of the Salisbury Orpheus
Society. A successful teacher; he was some
time musical tutor to H.R.H. the late Duke
of Albany. He has composed a cantata,
Village Belles; Church music, and songs;
"The Organist's Assistant"; nine new organ
Voluntaries; three Musical Sketches (two
sets); Novelette; Melodies Gracieuses, and
other pieces for pf., etc. MATTIE SPINNEY
(Mrs. Beesley), daughter of the above, studied
under Benedict, and Sterndale Bennett, and
later with Hans von Bülow. Held an organ
appointment at St. Paul's, Salisbury, and was
afterwards for a time organist of the Parish
Church, Banbury. She made her *début* as a
pianist at a concert of the New Philharmonic

SPINNEY.

Society, London, May 8, 1875, taking part, with Dr. von Bülow, in Bach's Concerto in C minor, for two pianos and orchestra. In 1876, she appeared at the Crystal Palace Concerts (November 25); and has since then given many performances at which she has been assisted by her pupils. EUGENE SPINNEY, the eldest son, was born in 1845. When seventeen he was appointed organist of Banbury Parish Church (1862), and in 1865, graduated Mus. Bac., Oxford. He gave good concerts, and improved the church choir; but his artistic career was short, as he was removed by death, December 4, 1867, at the early age of twenty-two. A stained glass window was placed in the Parish Church as a tribute of affection from pupils and friends. FRANK SPINNEY, brother of the preceding, was born March 20, 1850. He was articled to the Rev. Dr. Hayne, Oxford, and became F.R.C.O. His first organ appointment was to St. Denys, Warminster, 1869; from there he went to All Saints', Emscote, Warwick, 1873; and in 1878 was appointed to Leamington Parish Church. The present organ and organ gallery were built during his period of office, and largely the result of his exertions. From 1882 a number of excellent orchestral, choral, and chamber concerts were given by the Leamington Musical Society, under his direction; and he gave frequent organ recitals, being a fine executant.' He worked with great zeal for the cause of the best in musical art, but overtaxed his strength; his death, taking place, June 5, 1888. He wrote a number of hymn-tunes, an anthem for harvest, and some organ music. His memory is perpetuated by a stained glass window in the vestry of Leamington Parish Church. WALTER SPINNEY, the next brother, was born March 26, 1852. He was articled to J. E. Richardson, the cathedral organist, whose assistant he afterwards became. Then followed appointments to St. Edmund's, Salisbury; Dudley Parish Church; Christ Church, Doncaster; and finally, in 1888, on the death of his brother Frank, to Leamington Parish Church. In this town he laboured as performer, teacher, composer, and editor, until his death, June 21, 1894. He composed some church services, a number of anthems, and other vocal works; edited the " Organ library "; and the " Vesper bell " series of organ pieces, his own contributions to which enjoy wide popularity. Rev. T. HERBERT SPINNEY, youngest of the four brothers, was born January 13, 1857. Studied under Drs. G. B. Arnold, and J. F. Bridge. Harmony Prizeman, Trinity College, London, 1876. F.R.C.O. From the age of sixteen was organist at Salisbury; later, organist, and assistant chaplin, Exeter College, Oxford, having been ordained Deacon in 1881, and Priest, 1882, by the Bishop of Oxford. M.A.,

SPRAY.

Oxford, 1884. Curate of South Hinksey, Berks., 1881-2; of Wallasey, Cheshire, 1883-5; vicar of Newborough, Burton-on-Trent, to present time. Composer of Christ the first fruits; Now thank we all our God, and other anthems; Church services: Christmas carols (three series); six hymns for a flower service; organ pieces, etc., etc. He was formerly known as an able pianist, and still gives occasional organ recitals.

Spofforth, Reginald, composer, born at Southwell, Nottingham, in 1770. He studied under his uncle, Thomas Spofforth, organist of Southwell Collegiate Church, and under Dr. B. Cooke. He gained two prizes given by Nobleman's Catch Club. He died at Kensington, London, September 8, 1827, aged 57, and is buried in Kensington Parish Church, where a monument bearing the following inscription is placed : " In Memoriam. Under this church are deposited the remains of Reginald Spofforth, professor of music, born at Southwell, Nottinghamshire. He died at Brompton, on the 8th September, 1827, aged 57 years. Laus Deo."

WORKS.—Set of six glees, London [1799]; A Collection of Glees, compiled from the unpublished manuscripts of the late Mr. Spofforth, carefully collated with the originals, by W. Hawes, London, n.d.; The Christmas Box, a variety of Bagatelles for 1, 2, and 3 voices, with pf. accompaniment, 2 books, London, n.d. *Single Glees :* Hail, smiling morn (in No. 1), 1799; Come bounteous May; How calm the evening; Fill high the grape's exulting stream (prize), 1810; Health to my dear; My dear mistress; The Spring, the pleasant spring; While the madly raging nations; Where are those hours; See, smiling from the rosy east; Lightly o'er the village green. Canzonets.

A composer whose name is kept in remembrance by his ever fresh glee, " Hail, smiling morn." His brother, SAMUEL, born in 1780, studied under his uncle, and in 1798 became organist of Peterborough Cathedral, and in 1807 organist of Lichfield Cathedral. He died at Lichfield, June 6, 1864. Composer of chants and other church music.

Sporle, Nathan James, who was born BURNETT, tenor vocalist and composer, born at Ipswich, 1812. He studied under Thomas Welsh. Died March 2, 1853. Some of the best of his many songs are : A calm is o'er the sea; Draw round the fire; Country life; Heart that's true; In the days when we went gipsying [1840]; I dwell among the beautiful; Lugger; Merrie England; Old winter [1853]; The place where I was born; Sweet is the vale, etc.

Spottiswoode, Alicia Ann, *see* SCOTT, LADY JOHN D.

Spray, John, composer and singer, was

SQUIRE.

a chorister in Southwell Minster. Afterwards vicar-choral of St. Patrick's Cathedral, Dublin. Doc. Mus., Dublin. He died in Dublin, in January, 1827. Composer of some unimportant vocal pieces.

Squire, Emily, soprano vocalist of present time. Studied at R.C.M. and R.A.M. Sang at Bath early in the year 1888, but made a more important *début* at Exeter in April, at the festival of the Western Counties' Musical Association. Made her first appearance at the Crystal Palace, March 21, 1891; and at the Monday Popular Concerts, January 15, 1894. Has sung at the Birmingham Festival Choral Society's Concerts, and in the principal musical centres, attaining a good position among vocalists of the time.

Squire, William Barclay, musician and author, who is one of the staff of the British Museum, and a contributor of biographies of musicians to the Dictionary of National Biography, Grove's Dictionary of Music, etc. With J. A. Fuller Maitland he edited "The Fitzwilliam Virginal Book," 1894, and has edited a number of important works by Byrd, Gibbons, Farnaby, Weelkes, and other old English and foreign composers. He has also composed some pieces for the pf.

Squire, William Henry, violoncellist and composer, born at Ross, Herefordshire, August 8, 1871. Studied at first under his father, a cultivated amateur violinist, and played in public when seven years old. Gained a scholarship at R.C.M., 1883, which was extended for a second period of three years. Studied under Edward Howell, and was occasionally heard by Piatti, also receiving lessons in composition from Dr. Hubert Parry. Made his *début* at the Albeniz concerts, St. James's Hall, February 12, 1891. Since then has been heard at various concerts in London and the provinces. Was associated with the concerts of British Chamber Music, Queen's Hall, 1894; made his first appearance at the Crystal Palace, April 20, 1895, playing the Concerto in A of Saint-Saëns, and in the same year was appointed principal 'cello at the Royal Italian Opera, Covent Garden. He was elected an Associate of R.C.M., 1889. His compositions include a concerto for violoncello, performed R.C.M. Concert; serenade; pastorale; gavotte; tarantelle, op. 23; four sets of pieces; twelve easy exercises; and other pieces for violoncello; reverie, etc., for violin; pieces for pf. solo and duet; songs, etc.; also music for mandoline. He has two operettas in MS.

Sreeve, John, musician and organist of first half of the 18th century. Compiled "The Divine Musick Scholar's Guide, being a....collection of psalm tunes, hymns and anthems," London, 1740. "The Oxford-

STAINER.

shire Harmony, containing a select number of hymns, anthems, and chants, etc.," London, 1741, 3 vols.

Stafford, William Cooke, musician and author, born at York in 1793. He died at Norwich, December 23, 1876. Author of "A History of Music," Edinburgh, 1830 (Constable's Miscellany, vol. 52). Translated into French, Paris, 1832, and into German, Weimar, 1835.

Staggins, Nicholas, composer, was made master of the Royal music in 1682, and graduated Mus. Doc., Cantab., in the same year. He was the first professor of music in Cambridge University, 1684. He died in 1705. Composer of Odes for the birthdays of William III. and Queen Anne; Songs in Choice "Ayres, Songs, and Dialogues," 1763; music for Dryden's " Conquest of Granada," etc.

Stainer, Sir John, Kt., composer, organist, and writer, born in London, June 6, 1840. Chorister, St. Paul's Cathedral, 1847-56, during the later years often acting as organist. Studied under W. Bayley, Dr. Steggall, and George Cooper. Organist of St. Benedict and St. Peter, Paul's Wharf, 1854; and in 1856 was appointed, by Sir F. Ouseley, organist of St. Michael's College, Tenbury. In 1859 he matriculated at Christ Church, Oxford, and was appointed organist of Magdalen College the same year, and organist to the University of Oxford, 1860. Graduated Mus. Bac., 1859; B.A., 1863; Mus. Doc., 1865; and M.A., 1866, Oxford. Conductor of College Musical Societies. In 1872 he was appointed organist of St. Paul's Cathedral, in succession to (Sir) John Goss, resigning in 1888 owing to failing sight. In 1876 he was appointed professor of the organ at the National Training School for Music, and in 1881 succeeded (Sir) Arthur Sullivan as Principal. Organist to the Royal Choral Society, 1873-88; Juror at the Paris Exhibition, 1878; Government Inspector of Music in Training Schools, in succession to Mr. Hullah, 1882; and has held other important positions, his last appointment being to the Professorship of Music at Oxford University, 1889. He is an Honorary Member of R.A.M.; President of the Musical Association; Member of Council, R.C.M.; Honorary Fellow of Magdalen College, Oxford; and member of the Philharmonic Society. In 1878 he was created Chevalier of the Legion of Honour of France; received the hon. degree of Mus. Doc., Durham, 1885; Hon. D.C.L., Durham, 1895; and in 1888 was Knighted by Her Majesty the Queen.

WORKS.—Oratorio, Gideon; Cantatas, The Daughter of Jairus, Worcester Festival, 1878; St. Mary Magdalene, Gloucester, 1883; The Crucifixion, London, 1887. Church Services in E flat, A, D, and B flat; Canticles, various.

STAINS.

Awake, put on thy strength; Deliver me, O Lord; And all the people saw the thunderings, London Church Choir Association, St. Paul's Cathedral, November 8, 1883; Ye shall dwell in the land; and many other anthems. Madrigal, The Triumph of Victoria, 1887; Album of Seven Songs, with English and German words; Loyal Death; My little Pet; Slumber Song (with violoncello *ad lib.*); and other songs. Arrangements for the organ, 5 Nos. Editor of St. Paul's Cathedral Chant Book; The Cathedral Psalter; Choir-book of the Holy Communion; Marbecke's Office of the Burial of the Dead. Joint editor (with Dr. Martin) of the Ferial Responses; with W. A. Barrett, of A Dictionary of Musical Terms, Novello, 1876; with Rev. H. R. Bramley, of Carols, Old and New; with Rev. W. Russell, The Cathedral Prayer Book, Novello, 1891; and with Dr. Hubert Parry, of Novello's Music Primers. Author of Primers on The Organ; Harmony; Composition; Choral Society Vocalisation; A Treatise on Harmony (which has gone through several editions), Novello; The Music of the Bible, 1879. A Few Words to Candidates for the Degree of Mus. Bac., Oxon., Novello, 1897. Lectures and addresses, Musical Association; Conferences of I.S.M., etc. His son, C. STAINER, is author of a work on Violin Makers, Novello, 1896.

Stains, V. D. de, author of "Phonography, or the writing of sounds, in two parts, viz., logography and musicography." London, 1842.

Standing, Frank H, baritone vocalist, known as F. H. CELLI. He was a member of the Carl Rosa Opera Company from 1875, and was also known as a concert singer, 1878-82. One of his most recent assumptions was that of the Toreador in Bizet's "Carmen," at Covent Garden, April 9, 1891. He married Susan (or Susanna), sister of Louisa Pyne (she died, 1886).

His sister, Madame Helen S. Norman, known as HELEN STANDISH, was a contralto vocalist. She sang in English and Italian opera companies under Carl Rosa and Mapleson, and had also been heard in concerts. She died suddenly, in January, 1891.

Standish, Orlando, author of "Elementi di Contrappunto," Florence, 1836, with folding tables and plates of examples.

Stanford, Charles Villiers, composer and conductor, born at Dublin, September 30, 1852. Son of the late John Stanford, Esq., Examiner in the Court of Chancery, Dublin, and an accomplished amateur. He was educated in music under Arthur O'Leary and Sir R. P. Stewart; and afterwards studied, 1874-76, at Leipzig, with Reinecke, and at Berlin with F. Kiel. Matriculated at Cambridge as a choral scholar, graduating with

STANFORD.

Classical Honours, B.A., 1874; M.A., 1877. In 1873 he succeeded Dr. J. L. Hopkins as organist of Trinity College, Cambridge, an appointment he held until 1892. He was conductor of the Cambridge Amateur Vocal Guild, and directed the first performance in England of Sir R. P. Stewart's cantata "The Eve of St. John," November 19, 1872. The Cambridge University Musical Society, of which he was conductor for twenty years from 1873, attained a high position, many important compositions being heard at its concerts for the first time in England, such as Schumann's "Paradise and the Peri," the First Symphony of Brahms, etc. It was at a concert of this society that Mr. Stanford first appeared as a pianist, November 30, 1870. A few compositions date from the Cambridge period to 1875, but he came into greater prominence by winning the second prize at the symphony competition at the Alexandra Palace, 1876. From that time to the present he has been actively engaged in composition. At the opening of the R.C.M., in 1883, he was appointed professor of composition and orchestral playing, and has given distinction to the College concerts and operatic performances by his enterprise in bringing forward new or neglected works. In 1885 he became conductor of the Bach Choir; and in 1887 was appointed Professor of Music at Cambridge University. He is a member of the Philharmonic Society; in 1883 received the Hon. degree of Mus. Doc., Oxford; in 1888, by Grace of the Senate, the same degree was conferred upon him at Cambridge; and in 1892 was elected Corresponding Member of the Société dés Compositeurs de Musique, Paris. He has conducted concerts at the Crystal Palace (1883), Philharmonic Society (1884, etc.); at Berlin, Dresden, etc.; performances of his works at the chief provincial festivals, and of his operas at Hanover and Hamburg. In June, 1897, he was appointed Conductor of the Leeds Philharmonic Society.

WORKS.—*Oratorios and Cantatas :* The Resurrection (Klopstock), op. 5, for tenor solo, chorus and orchestra, Cambridge, May, 1875 ; Psalm 46, op. 8, Cambridge, 1877 ; Elegiac Ode (Walt Whitman), op. 21, Norwich Festival, 1884 ; The Three Holy Children, oratorio, Birmingham Festival, 1885 ; The Revenge, choral ballad (Tennyson), op. 24, Leeds, 1886 ; Carmen Sæculare, Jubilee Ode, op. 26 (Tennyson), performed at a State Concert, 1887.; The Voyage of Maeldune (Tennyson), Leeds Festival, 1889 ; The Battle of the Baltic (Campbell), Hereford, 1891 ; Eden, dramatic oratorio (Robert Bridges), Birmingham, 1891 ; Installation Ode, Cambridge, May week, 1892 ; Ode, East to West (Swinburne), London, 1893 ; The Bard, cantata, Cardiff Festival, 1895; Phaudrig Crohoore,

STANHOPE.

choral ballad, Norwich, 1896. *Operas :* The Veiled Prophet of Khorassan, composed, 1877, produced at Hanover, February 6, 1881 (libretto by W. Barclay Squire) ; Savonarola, produced, Hamburg, April 18, 1884 ; The Canterbury Pilgrims, produced, Covent Garden Carl Rosa), April 28, 1884 (libretto by G. A. A'Beckett) ; and Shamus O'Brien, Opera Comique, London, March 2, 1896 (text by G. H. Jessop from Le Fanu).   Incidental music to Tennyson's Queen Mary, Lyceum, April 18, 1876 ; Tennyson's Becket, Lyceum, February 6, 1893 ; Æschylus' Eumenides, Cambridge, 1885 ; Sophocles' Œdipus, Cambridge, 1887. Mass in G, op. 46 (in memoriam, Thomas Wingham), Brompton Oratory, May 26, 1893; Psalm 150, Manchester, 1887 ; Awake, my heart (Klopstock), choral hymn, op. 16, St. Paul's Cathedral, November 3, 1881; Morning, Evening, and Communion Services in B flat, F, and A ; Anthems, etc.   Elizabethan Pastorals, 4 voices; Three Cavalier songs, op. 18 ; Day is dying; To the rose ; Eight songs (George Eliot), op. 1 ; two sets of 6 songs (Heine), op. 4, 7 ; and other songs. Editor of fifty Irish melodies, 1883 ; Song book for schools, 1884 ; Irish songs and ballads, Novello, 1893 (?) ; The Irish melodies of Thomas Moore, Boosey, 1896. *Orchestral :* Symphony No. 1, in B flat (prize), 1876 ; No. 2, in D minor (Elegiac), Cambridge, March 7, 1882 ; No. 3, in F minor (Irish), Richter, June 27, 1887 ; No. 4, in F (Thro' youth to strife; thro' death to life), Berlin Philharmonic Society, January 14, 1889 ; No. 5, in D (L'Allegro ed il Pensieroso), op. 56, Philharmonic Society, London, March 20, 1895.   Serenade, op. 17, Birmingham Festival, 1882.   Overtures, Festival, in B flat, Gloucester Festival, 1877 ; Queen of the Seas (Armada Tercentenary), 1888.   Concerto. 'cello and orchestra (MS.); Concerto in G, op. 59, pf. and orchestra, Richter, May 27, 1895 ; Suite in D, violin and orchestra, Berlin, January 14, 1889. *Chamber Music :* Sonata in A, op. 9, pf. and 'cello ; in D, op. 11, pf. and violin ; Three intermezzi, pf. and clarinet, op. 13 ; Quartet in F, op. 15, pf. and strings; Quartet in D minor, op. 25 (Dannreuther), 1886 ; Trio in E flat, op. 35 ; Sonata in D minor, op. 39, pf. and 'cello, Popular Concerts, November 18, 1889; String Quartets in G, op. 44 ; A minor, op. 54 ; D minor, op. 64. Four Irish pieces, violin and pf.   Sonata in D flat, op. 20 ; Three pieces, op. 42 ; Toccata in C, etc., for pf.   Prelude and Fugue, organ, Professor Stanford's latest work is a Requiem Mass, accepted for performance at the Birmingham Festival of 1897.

Stanhope, Charles, Third Earl of, peer and scientist, born 1753, succeeded 1786, died 1816.   Author of "Principles of the science of tuning instruments with fixed tones," London, 1806.

STANLEY.

Stanislaus, Frederick, composer, and conductor, born at Kidderminster, December 27, 1844.   Studied the violin at an early age, and was one of the " Little men " taken on tour by Dr. Mark, of Manchester.   Organist of Kidderminster Parish Church, and at Hartlebury.   Conductor of several opera companies in London and the provinces. Went to America, and on his return was musical director at the Prince's Theatre, and later at the Theatre Royal, Manchester.   He then went to the Prince of Wales' Theatre, London, and subsequently spent some time in Australia.   He conducted the touring companies with the Gilbert-Sullivan operas, and was much in request as an accompanist, acting in that capacity for Sims Reeves and others. He died at Hammersmith, November 22, 1891. His compositions include an opera, " The Lancashire Witches," produced at the Theatre Royal, Manchester; music to several pantomimes ; part of the music to " The Palace of Pearl," Empire Theatre, London, 1886; songs, part-songs, etc,   His wife, as Miss FANNY ROBINA, sang with much success in comic opera.

Stanistreet, Henry Dawson, organist and composer, was a chorister in York Cathedral.   Mus. Bac., Oxon., 1862.   Mus. Doc., Dublin, 1878.   Organist at Bandon, Cork, 1862, of Taum Cathedral, 1864, and of Trinity College, Dublin.   Composer of Psalms 16 and 69, anthems, and other Church music.   He died at Dublin, August 1, 1883.

Stanley, Charles John, organist and composer, born at London, January 17, 1713. He was accidentally made blind when about two years of age.   Studied music under J. Reading and M. Greene, and became organist of All Hallows' Church, Bread Street, 1724 ; St. Andrew's, Holborn, 1726 ; and of the Temple Church, 1739.   He graduated Mus. Bac., Oxford, 1729.   In 1779 he was made master of the Royal band of music, in succession to Boyce.   He died at London, May 19, 1786.

WORKS.—*Oratorios :* Jephthah, 1757 ; Zimri, 1760 ; Fall of Egypt, 1774 ; Arcadia, or the shepherd's wedding, 1761 (dramatic pastoral to celebrate marriage of George III.)   Six cantatas for a voice and instruments, London [1742] ; Second set [1750]. *Songs :* Dull unanimated wretch ; Heigh, ho ! ; I feel new passions rise ; Leave me shepherd ; Power of musick and beauty; The red breast. *Instrumental :* Op. 1, eight solos for a German flute, violin, or harpsichord [1745], etc. ; Op. 2, six concertos in seven parts for four violins, a tenor violin, and violoncello, with a thorough-bass for the harpsichord ; Op. 4, six solos for a German flute, violin, or harpsichord [1770]; Opp. 5, 6, 7, ten voluntaries for the organ or pf. ; Six concertos set for the harpsichord or organ [1760].

STANLEY.

Stanley, Samuel, composer, born at Birmingham in 1767. He was Precentor in Carr's Lane Congregational Chapel Birmingham, and afterwards in connection with the same congregation on its removal to a new chapel in Steelhouse Lane, in 1818. He played the violoncello in the Birmingham Theatre orchestra, and in the Festival Choral Society, 1802-1818. He died at Birmingham in October, 1822. Now best remembered by his hymn tunes " Doversdale " and " Warwick." He issued " Twenty-four tunes in four parts," Birmingham, n.d. ; Two psalm tunes in four parts, Birmingham, n.d. ; Nineteen psalm, hymn, and charity hymn tunes, Birmingham [1800]; Sacred music, comprising two new psalm and hymn tunes [1825] ; Psalm and hymn tunes, 3 books [1830], collected.

Stansbury, George Frederick, composer, tenor singer, and flutist, was born at Bristol in 1800. He was trained by his father, Joseph Stansbury, and in 1819, travelled as accompanist with Catalani during a concert tour. For some time he acted as conductor at the Theatre Royal, Dublin, but in 1828 he sang at the Haymarket Theatre, London, in the " Beggar's Opera," afterwards appearing at the London theatres. He was conductor at St. James' Theatre, Surrey Theatre, and other places in London. Died at Lambeth, London, June 3, 1845.

WORKS.—Operas or musical dramas: Waverley (with Lee); Puss in Boots, 1832; Elfin Sprite, 1833, etc. The Passions, being six songs, London [1833], containing also songs by Cooke, etc. Oak and the Rose, song, and others.

Stapleton, Mrs., *born* ANNA ISABELLA MATTHEWS, is notable as having been the first professional teacher of the Tonic Sol-fa system. She died at London, March 23, 1885.

Stark, Humphrey John, organist and composer, born May 22, 1854. Graduated Mus. Bac., Oxford, 1875. One of the founders of Trinity College, London. Organist of Holy Trinity, Tulse Hill, 1875. Composer of an Evening service, with orchestra ; Church services, anthems, etc. Cantata, The Rival Seasons, performed, Trinity College, London, 1885. Twelve pieces for organ, etc. Author of various papers read before the College of Organists, and other institutions.

Statham, Francis Reginald, composer and author, settled in South Africa. He was at one time minister of a Scotch congregation. His cantata, " Prosperity and Praise," was composed for the exhibition at Kimberley, 1892; and he has also composed a cantata, " Vasco de Gama," for soli, chorus, and orchestra. Author of various volumes of poems ; " Blacks, Boers, and British," 1881 ; " Mr. Magnus," and other novels.

STEELE.

Statham, H. Heathcote, architect, author, and amateur musician. He is a Fellow of the Institute of British Architects, and editor of *The Builder.* Author of " Form and design in Music : æsthetic condition of the Art," London, Chapman and Hall, 1893 ; " Architecture for general readers. . .," London, Chapman, 1895 ; 2nd edition, 1896.

Statham, Rev. William, clergyman and musician, born at Tarporley Rectory, Cheshire, September 26, 1832. Educated at Marlborough College, and University College, Durham. B.A., 1856 ; Mus. Doc., 1876, Durham. Vicar of Ellesmere-Port from 1866, and organist of the parish church. Organising choirmaster, Fordsham Deaneries Choral Association, 1869-79. Composer of an oratorio, " The Beauty of Holiness," Liverpool, 1888 ; Church Service in F (1869), songs, etc.. Contributed to Hymns Ancient and Modern ; Hymnal Companion ; Primitive Methodist Hymnal ; and Chants Ancient and Modern. Organ arrangements, etc.

Stead, J. H., comic singer, who appeared in London and other music halls with an eccentric song, called the " Perfect Cure," which was once widely known and popular. He lost his savings in a bank failure, and died in London of consumption, January 24, 1886.

Steane, Bruce Harry Dennis, composer and organist, born at Champion Hill, Camberwell, London, June 22, 1866. Chorister at the age of eight at St. Augustine's, Forest Hill, and assistant-organist when twelve. Musical training private. Has held the posts of organist and choirmaster successively at St. Bartholomew's, Swanley ; Seal Parish Church, Sevenoaks ; and Parish Church, Whitechapel ; and is also organist and choir trainer for the Rural Deanery of Spitalfields. His compositions, chiefly in the smaller forms, are very numerous, reaching to op. 89, and include a sacred cantata, " The Ascension," op. 18 (published 1895); church services; many anthems, published in Novello's octavo series ; songs, part-songs, etc. Organ pieces, including two Albums for American organ ; pianoforte pieces, etc., etc.

Steed, Albert Orlando, composer and author, born in 1839. Studied under Sterndale Bennett. Professor of music, Totteridge Park School, Herts., about 1860-2. Organist of Parish Church, Long Melford, Suffolk, 1865 ; and at Holy Trinity, Penge, for some years up to the time of his death, October 25, 1881. Author of " Music in play and music in earnest," London, 1873 ; Favourite lessons for the pf. [1858] ; Four songs from the " Idylls of the King " [1861] ; Seven tunes to popular hymns, and two kyries, London [1878] ; duets, songs, etc.

Steele, Joshua, musician and writer,

STEELE.

author of "A short treatise on harmony," London, 1730. "Prosodia Rationalis, or an essay towards establishing the melody and measures of speech to be expressed and perpetuated by symbols," London, 1775. Two papers on musical instruments brought from the South Pacific Islands.

Steele, Mary Sarah, see sub. MASSON, ELIZABETH.

Steggall, Charles, organist and composer, born in London, June 3, 1826. After a year's private tuition on the organ, he entered the R.A.M., 1847, and studied under Sterndale Bennett, afterwards his life-long friend. In 1851 he accumulated the degrees of Mus. Bac. and Mus. Doc., Cambridge, and was appointed professor of harmony and organ at the R.A.M., of which Institution he is a Fellow. In 1848 he was appointed organist of Christ Chapel, Maida Vale; in 1855 of Christ Church, Paddington; and in 1864 the organistship of Lincoln's Inn Chapel was conferred upon him, which position he still retains. While a student at the R.A.M., in 1849, he was consulted by Bennett on the subject of the Bach Society, and from its formation, October 27, 1849, to its dissolution, 1870, he held the office of Hon. Sec. At Crosby Hall, in 1852, he gave two lectures on "Music as applied to Religion"; and October 18, 1864, delivered the inaugural lecture of the College of Organists, of which institution he was one of the founders. He has occasionally lectured at other places, but his life's work is at the R.A.M.

WORKS.—Psalm 105, O give thanks, soli, eight-part chorus, and orchestra; Psalm 33, Rejoice in the Lord (performed at R.A.M., and, 1864, Cambridge); Magnificat and Nunc dimittis in C, and Cantate Domino and Deus misereatur in C, for voices and orchestra; Morning and Evening Service in F, and various service settings. Harvest anthem, Praised be the Lord; He was as the morning star; Hear ye, and give ear; and others. Instruction Book, and various compositions for the organ. Editor of Church Psalmody (1848); Six motets of J. S. Bach; Musical Editor (1889) of Hymns, Ancient and Modern; Contributor to various collections.

His youngest son, REGINALD STEGGALL, born in London, April 17, 1867, was educated at the R.A.M., of which he is an Associate, and, since 1895, professor of the organ. In 1886 he was appointed to St. Anne's, Soho, but he now acts as his father's assistant at Lincoln's Inn Chapel. He has composed a Festival Evening Service for voices and orchestra; various anthems; Dramatic Scena, "Alcestis"; Songs, etc.; a symphony; Two overtures; a concert piece for organ and orchestra; various organ pieces; a Mass for voices, orchestra, and organ, etc.

STEPHENS.

Steil, William Henry, harpist and composer, was born about 1787; died at Poole, Dorset, February 3, 1851. Author of "An Elementary Treatise for the Harp," London, 1830. Composer of rondos, fantasias, divertimentos, duets, etc., for harp and pf., and arranger of a large number of celebrated compositions for the harp.

Stein, Grace, see WALLACE, LADY MAXWELL.

Stella, Alfred, see PATERSON, ROBERT ROY.

Stenhouse, William, writer and collector, born in Roxburghshire in 1773. He was by profession an accountant in Edinburgh. He died at Edinburgh, November 10, 1827. Published "Illustrations of the Lyric Poetry and Music of Scotland.." Edinburgh, 1839. Second edition by David Laing, LL.D., Edinburgh, 1853. This was intended as a series of annotations for Johnson's "Scots Musical Museum," and has proved a quarry for all subsequent students of Scots music. Many of Stenhouse's alleged inaccuracies, which Chappell and others have mentioned in contemptuous terms, turn out, on investigation by later and more painstaking students, to be perfectly correct statements. The work generally is not commendable on the score of correctness.

Stephen, Rev. Edward, surnamed TANYMARIAN, composer, was born near Festiniog in 1822; died at Tanymarian, near Bangor, May 10, 1885. Composed the first Welsh oratorio, "The Sea of Tiberius"; Llyfr Tonau ac Emynau [1870]; and various collections of Welsh music issued principally from Wrexham.

Stephens, Catherine, Countess of Essex, soprano vocalist, born at London, December 18, 1791. She studied under Lanza and Thos. Welsh, and appeared in Italian opera in 1812, and in Arne's "Artaxerxes," 1813. From then till 1835 she appeared at all the principal concerts in London, and at the provincial concerts. She also appeared in English opera at Covent Garden and Drury Lane Theatres. In 1835 she retired, and in 1838 was married to the Earl of Essex. She died at London, February 22, 1882. Well-known in her day as "Kitty Stephens," and was famed as an admirable exponent of English ballad music.

Stephens, Charles Edward, composer, pianist, and organist, born in London, March 18, 1821. Nephew of the preceding. Began his studies at an early age, his masters being Cipriani Potter for pf., J. A. Hamilton for harmony, etc., and Henry Blagrove for violin. He first came into notice as a member of the Society of British Musicians, an overture of his being rehearsed in January, 1842. He played second violin in the quartets, and had string quartets of his own produced, one in

STEPHENS.

G, in 1843, and one in F, 1844. He became a member of the Royal Society of Musicians in 1843, and the same year was appointed organist of St. Mark's, Myddelton Square. In 1846 he was elected organist of Holy Trinity, Paddington ; St. Marks, Hamilton Terrace, 1862; St. Clement Danes, Strand, 1864 ; St. Saviour's, Paddington, 1872, resigning in 1875. He occasionally played in public as a pianist, but was chiefly occupied in teaching. Elected an Associate, 1850, and Member, 1857, of the Philharmonic Society; and afterwards frequently chosen as a Director ; and from 1880 acted as Treasurer. F.C.O., 1865; Hon. R.A.M., 1870. An original member of the Musical Association (1874), he read several papers at its meetings. In 1885 he was appointed one of the Examiners for musical degrees at Cambridge University. He took an active interest in the I.S.M., played in his pf. duos at the Conferences of 1888 and 1890; and conducted a performance of his Symphony in G minor, at Mr. Stockley's Birmingham Concerts, April 24, 1890, and at the Philharmonic Concerts, March 19, 1891, He died in London, July 13, 1892.

WORKS.—*Orchestral*: Two symphonies; Five overtures—A Dream of Happiness, No. 4, performed at the Royal Albert Hall, October, 1873 ; A Recollection of the Past, Philharmonic, April 28, 1880. Other orchestral pieces in MS. String quartets in G, op. 21 ; in F, op. 22 (Trinity College, London, Prize Compositions), 1879 ; Quartet in B minor, op. 2 ; Trio in F, op. 1, pf. and strings; Allegro and andante varié, for flute, oboe, clarinet, horn, and bassoon, 1892 ; Sonata piacevole, op. 25, pf. and flute. *Pianoforte:* Duo brillant in E, op. 19 ; Duo concertante in G, op. 4, and in C, op. 26, two pianos. Sonata in A flat, op. 8, Musical Artists' Society, 1882 ; Romance ; Impromptu, etc. Transcriptions, various. *Organ:* Two movements, op. 3; a second set, op. 7 ; a third set, op. 15; Fantasia, Offertoire, etc. Church services and anthems. Partsong, men's voices, Come, fill ye right merrily, Prize, Leslie's Choir, 1858 ; Glees, songs, etc. Author of article, Philharmonic Society, in Grove's Dictionary. Editor of The Choir Chant Book, containing 513 chants, with Biographical Notices of the Composers, London, Bemrose, 1882.

SAMUEL JOHN STEPHENS, his brother, born in London, September 4, 1819, studied under Potter, Hamilton, and H. Blagrove. Appeared as pianist with C. E. Stephens at concerts in 1845. Associate, 1859 ; Member, 1888, Philharmonic Society. Engaged in teaching, and esteemed as an excellent pianist. Died at Hammersmith, June 29, 1889.

Stephens, John, organist and composer, was born probably at Gloucester about 1720. He was a chorister in Gloucester Cathedral,

STEVEN.

and in 1746 he succeeded Edward Thomson as organist there. In 1763 he graduated Mus. Doc., Cambridge, and in 1766 he conducted the Gloucester Festival. He died at Salisbury, December 15, 1780. A volume of his compositions for the church was issued at London in 1805, as Cathedral music, corrected and published by Highmore Skeats. One of his pieces called the Chimes of Gloucester Cathedral, was edited by C. L. Williams.

Stephenson, Joseph, musician of the 18th century, who resided at Poole, in Dorset. He published " Church Harmony sacred to devotion, being a choice set of new anthems and psalm tunes on various subjects, having the energy of our English words particularly expressed, with an air to each different subject," London [1770]. " The Musical Companion, containing te deum, jubilate in 4 parts....also 2 anthems for a club feast day....the whole for the use of country choirs...." London, n.d. Songs: The Pipe, etc., and other vocal music.

Stephenson, R. J., author of " Elementary elucidations of the major and minor of Music, exemplifying the diatonic scale...." London [1817].

Stephenson or **Stevenson, Robert,** musician of the 16th century, who graduated Mus. Bac., Oxford, in 1587, and Mus. Doc., Oxford, in 1596.

Stern, Leo, violoncellist, born at Brighton. His father, Leopold Stern, was born at Düsseldorf, but is a naturalised Englishman, and a well-known professor of the violin and conductor, at Brighton. His mother, as Miss Annie Laurence, was regarded as one of the best amateur pianists in the district. He has appeared with success at concerts in London and the provinces since about 1886. At the Philharmonic Society's concert, March 19, 1896, he played, for the first time, Dvorák's concerto for the violoncello, op. 104, and with such success that he was invited by the composer to play it at Prague, which he did on April 9. In the early part of 1897 he was in New York. He has two sisters in the musical profession. His compositions are chiefly for his special instrument, and consist of a Mazurka Fantastique, Melodie Romantique, gavotte, serenade, etc. ; also songs.

Steven, James, music publisher and collector, who lived in Glasgow as a music-seller. He was leader of psalmody at the University Hall. He died previous to 1833. Compiler of " A Selection of psalm and hymn tunes in four parts....to which is added a compendious introduction...." Glasgow, 1801, vol. 1 ; Selection of Sacred music.... vols. 2, 3, 4, and 5. The sixth volume of this collection was edited by John Turnbull as a " Selection of original sacred music,"

STEVENS.

Glasgow, 1833 ; 2nd edition, 1840. " Harmonia Sacra, a selection of the most approved psalm and hymn tunes," Glasgow, n.d., 2 vols. He also published some music for the flute, etc.

Stevens, Alfred Peck, known as ALFRED GLENVILLE VANCE, or even better as the " GREAT VANCE," a comic singer, who was born in London, in 1840. He first appeared on the stage and made his *début* as a comic singer at the Sun Music Hall, Knightsbridge. He also organised an annual concert party, and introduced the music-hall style to the higher classes of society. While singing " Are you Guilty" at the Sun Music Hall, Knightsbridge, on the night of December 26, 1888, he fell at the wings after the third verse. He was conveyed to St. George's Hospital, but died before the cab reached the institution.

Stevens, Rev. Arthur Henry, organist, graduated Mus. Bac., Oxford, 1883. B.A., 1881 ; M.A., 1884. Organist, choir-master, and conductor, Worcester College, Oxford ; Holy Trinity, Roehampton ; St. John's, Hammersmith; director of the music, organist, and precentor, Dover College, Kent. Has given organ recitals in Canterbury Cathedral (1887), etc. Compositions : Sacred cantata, " The Song of Tobit " (MS.) ; anthems, carols, evening service ; scherzo for organ, etc.

Stevens, Charles Isaac, author of " An Essay on the Theory of Music," Göttingen, 1863.

Stevens, Jeannie M., *see* HALE, MRS. WILLIAM.

Stevens, Richard John Samuel, composer and organist, born at London, 1757. He was trained as a chorister in St. Paul's Cathedral under Savage, and became organist of the Temple Church in 1786 ; and of the Charter House, 1796. Gained prizes from Catch Club, 1782 and 1786. Professor of Music, Gresham College, 1801. He died at Peckham, London, September 23, 1837.

WORKS.—Eight Glees for 4 and 5 voices, op. 3, London [1790] ; Eight Glees, op. 4, London [1792]; Ten Glees for 3, 4, 5 and 6 voices, op. 5, London [1800] ; Seven Glees, op. 6, London [1808]. Eight Glees, expressly composed for Ladies. Sacred Music for 1, 2, 3 and 4 voices, consisting of Selections from the works of the most esteemed composers, Italian and English, London, n.d., 3 vols. Ten Songs, with an accompaniment for two violins, London, n.d.

One of the most popular of English glee composers. Some of his works are in constant use at the present time. Among his best known glees are " From Oberon in Fairy Land," " Sigh no more, Ladies," " Ye spotted snakes," " The cloud-capt towers," " Crabbed

STEWART.

age and Youth," etc. Many of his glees still remain in manuscript.

Stevens, William Seaman, pianist and composer, born at Westminster in 1778. He studied under R. J. S. Stevens, Dr. Cooke, and T. Smart. Author of " Treatise on Pianoforte Expression, containing the Principles of Fine Playing on that Instrument,". . London, 1811. Composer of Lyric recitation of the garden scene in Romeo and Juliet [1815]; Ladies canzonets, 1795. Songs : Mary, or the beauty of Buttermere, The Naiad, etc.

Stevenson, Sir John Andrew, composer, born at Dublin, 1761-62, son of John Stevenson, a Scottish violinist from Glasgow, who settled in Dublin. He studied under Dr. Murphy, and was a Chorister in St. Patrick's Cathedral, 1775-80, and Vicar-choral, 1783. Mus. Doc., Dublin, 1791. Vicar-choral, Christ Church Cathedral, Dublin, 1800 ; and Chorister in Trinity College, Dublin. Married to daughter of Mr. Morton, of the Custom House, Dublin. Knighted, 1803. His daughter was married to the Earl of Headfort. He died at his daughter's house in Meath, September 14, 1833.

WORKS.—*Music to* The Son-in-Law ; The Patriot ; Border Feuds ; Bedouins ; Spanish Patriots; Agreeable surprise ; Contract, 1783 ; and Love in a blaze, 1800, etc. Thanksgiving, an oratorio. Morning and Evening Services and Anthems for the use of the church of England,. . London, 2 vols. [1825]. *Glees :* See our oars with feathered spray ; Welcome friends of harmony ; To thy lover, dear, discover ; Hail! to the mighty pow'r of song ;. Dublin Cries (round), etc. Canons, catches, and glees (collected), London. Duets and songs. Moore's Irish Melodies, with symphonies and accompaniments by Sir John Stevenson and Henry R. Bishop 10 parts and supplement, 1807-34 ; re-issued, harmonized, 1858. A series of sacred songs, duets, and trios, the words by Thomas Moore. . London, n.d. A selection of Popular National Airs, with symphonies and accompaniments by Sir John Stevenson,. . London, 1818, 2 vols., illustrated.

Stewart, Charles, composer and violinist, who flourished in the latter part of last and early in the present century. He was a musician and teacher of dancing in Leith and Edinburgh, and died in June, 1818. He issued two collections of Reels, Strathspeys, etc., entitled " Collection of Strathspey, reels, giggs, etc., with a bass for the violoncello or harpsichord." Edinburgh, 1799. " First Book of Minuets, high dances, etc." [1805]. His son, ROBERT BARCLAY STEWART, violinist, was born on October 19, 1804. In 1858 he was leader at the Theatre Royal, Edinburgh, and was mostly engaged as a

STEWART.

performer at concerts, balls, etc., in Edinburgh and its neighbourhood. He died at Edinburgh, May 16, 1885. Compiler of " A new set of military quadrilles arranged for the pianoforte," 1826; and a large collection of Scots dance music, also composer of the Jolly volunteer, song; Scott centenary quadrille, etc.

Stewart, Charles, collector, born at Glenlyon House, Fortingall, December 24, 1823, He is a lieut.-colonel in the army. Published "The Killin Collection of Gaelic Songs, with music and translations," Edinburgh, 1884.

Stewart, Mrs.Colonel, see WAINWRIGHT, HARRIET.

Stewart, Neil, Scottish music-seller, publisher, and editor, flourished in Edinburgh in latter half of last and beginning of present century. He carried on business between 1759-1805, at the sign of the Violin and German Flute, and Violin and Guitar, in various parts of Edinburgh, and in partnership with his son Malcolm. In 1805 the whole stock of the firm was sold by auction. Published, A new collection of Scots and English tunes, adapted to the guitar . . Edinburgh [1760]. A collection of the newest and best reels or country dances, adapted for the violin or German flute, with a bass for the violoncello or harpsichord, Edinburgh [1761-62], issued in 9 parts. A collection of the newest and best Minuets. . [1770]. A second collection of airs and marches for two violins, German flutes, and hautboys, all of which have basses for the violoncello or harpsichord, Edinburgh. A collection of Scots songs adapted for a voice or harpsichord, Edinburgh [1790]. A collection of catches, canons, glees, duettos, etc., selected from the works of the most eminent composers, ancient and modern, Edinburgh [1780].

Stewart, Nellie, soprano vocalist, born in Australia. Created on the Australian stage the heroines in the later Gilbert-Sullivan operas, being particularly successful in the " Mikado." Organised and directed a company with success, and being advised to visit England, took her farewell at Melbourne, in " Paul Jones," January 22, 1891. Made her first appearance at the Prince of Wales' Theatre, London, February 6, 1892, in " Blue-eyed Susan," with much success.

Stewart, Sir Robert Prescott, Kt., organist, composer, and writer, born at Dublin, December 16, 1825. Son of Charles F. Stewart, librarian of the King's Inns, Dublin. Received his musical education in the school of Christ Church Cathedral, Dublin, and was appointed cathedral organist in 1844, as well as at St. Patrick's, and Trinity College. In 1846 he became conductor of the University Choral Society; graduated Mus. Bac., and

STIDOLPH.

Mus. Doc., Dublin, 1851; and in 1861 was appointed professor of music in Dublin University. There was no fund from which to pay an organist at St. Patrick's Cathedral, so in 1852 he was made a vicar-choral, with the understanding that he would continue to play the organ as he had previously done. In 1872 he was invited to represent Ireland at the Peace Festival held at Boston, U.S.A. ; he did not go, but sent an Ode, in which Irish and American airs were worked up. About that time he began his connection with the Royal Irish Academy of Music, as professor of harmony, organ, etc. In 1873 he was appointed conductor of the Dublin Philharmonic. He was a remarkably fine organ player, and gave performances in many parts of England, his extemporisations being masterly. He travelled a good deal, and had great literary powers, as shown in his numerous lectures; and he was an authority on bagpipes of all kinds. In 1872 he was knighted by Earl Spencer, and received many public tokens of admiration at the same time. He died at Dublin, March 25, 1894.

WORKS.—Ode to Industry, Cork Exhibition, 1852; A Winter night's wake (1858), and The eve of St. John, cantatas ; Ode to Shakespeare, Birmingham Festival, 1870; " Committee " cantata, University Choral Society, 1889; Ode for Tercentenary Festival of Trinity College, Dublin, July 5, 1892. Ten other cantatas and odes in MS. Church service in E flat, for double choir; Services, various ; Motets and anthems, twelve published, others in MS. Musical editor of Church Hymnal. Glee, O Nightingale (Milton), Hibernian Catch Club Prize, 1848; five other prize glees. The bells of St. Michael's tower ; Fairest flower ; The dream ; Haymakers' song ; and other part-songs. Song, The Reefer, Orchestra prize, 1865 ; many songs, published and in MS. Suite in G, violins, Dublin, 1891. Orchestral music, MS. Concert fantasia in D minor, and other pieces for organ. *Lectures :* Ancient Irish music ; Irish composers ; Bagpipes ; Eastern music ; Musical epochs, etc. Essays in Cassell's Biographical Dictionary; and articles in Grove's Dictionary.

Stidolph, Harold Edward, Organist, born at Tunbridge, Kent, 1845. Articled pupil of Walter Bond Gilbert. When eight years old, played the services in Tunbridge Parish Church, and acted as organist at the Chapel of the Grammar School, while a pupil there. In 1863 he was appointed organist and choirmaster of Speen Parish Church, Berkshire, and, a year later, to the Parish Church, Chelmsford ; and also choirmaster of the Diocesan Music Association. There he founded a Vocal and Instrumental Association. In 1876 he was chosen, after competition, organist of Ealing Parish Church, and,

STILLIE.

in 1880 of Christ Church, Ealing. In this place he started a series of popular concerts. In 1884 he went to Cape Town, and after holding various appointments, settled in Johannesburgh, where he was organist of St. Augustine's, Doomfontein. Now resident at Wynberg, Cape Town. In 1887, he toured Cape Colony with Remenyi, and has conducted performances of opera. He composed a national part-song, "Around the Throne of England"; also church music, and songs. He has contributed to the local press, and is known as a writer of verse. A Colonial national anthem, and lyric tributes to visiting artists, being successful efforts of his muse.

Stillie, Thomas Logan, amateur musician and writer, born at Maybole in 1832. He was engaged in business in Glasgow, and acted for many years as musical critic for the *Glasgow Herald*. He died at Glasgow, June 6, 1883. He left a valuable library to the University of Glasgow.

Stillingfleet, Benjamin, poet, musician, and naturalist, was born in 1702, and died in 1771. Author of the words of five oratorios, and of a "Treatise on the principles and power of harmony," London, 1771, a commentary on Tartini's "Trattato di Musica."

Stillingfleet, Rev. Henry Anthony, author of "The antiquity and advantages of church music, a sermon," 1803.

Stimpson, James, organist and composer, born at Lincoln, February 29, 1820. His father was a lay-vicar of Lincoln Cathedral, but removed to Durham in 1822. He was a chorister in Durham Cathedral in 1827, and in 1834, he was articled to Mr. Ingham, the organist of Carlisle Cathedral. In 1836, he became organist of St. Andrew's, Newcastle; and in 1841, he succeeded as organist of Carlisle Cathedral. He was appointed organist of the Town Hall, Birmingham in 1842, and in the same year took a similar appointment at St. Paul's Church; organist of St. Martin's Church, 1852; Francis Road Chapel, Edgbaston, from 1869. He founded the Birmingham Festival Choral Society in 1843, and was its conductor till 1855. Professor of Music at the Birmingham Institution for the Blind. He gave many important organ recitals in Birmingham, and superintended the production of Mendelssohn's "Elijah." He died at Birmingham, October 4, 1886. Editor of "Services of the Church: being those portions of the Book of Common Prayer, which are appointed to be chanted, arranged for the use of congregations and choirs," Newcastle, Richardson, 1840; "The Organist's Standard Library," etc.; and composed songs and pf. music. Author of a "Manual of the theory of Music."

Stimpson, Orlando John, organist and teacher, born at Durham, June 21, 1835,

STOCKLEY.

brother of the preceding. Received his musical training at Durham Cathedral. Graduated Mus. Bac., Oxford, 1871; Mus. Bac. *ad eundem*, Durham, 1871. Music master, Durham Diocesan Training College, 1871. Now resident at Tunbridge Wells. Author of "Singing Class Book for use in Elementary Schools, Glasgow, 1877.

Stirling, Elizabeth, MRS. F. A. BRIDGE, organist and composer, born at Greenwich, February 26, 1819. Studied under W. B. Wilson, Edward Holmes, J. A. Hamilton, and G. A. Macfarren. In 1839, she was appointed organist of All Saint's, Poplar, an office she retained until 1858. In 1856, she presented an Exercise, Psalm 130, for 5 voices, and orchestra, for the degree of Mus. Bac. at Oxford; but though it passed the examiners, there was no power to confer the degree. She was organist of St. Andrew's, Undershaft, from 1858 to 1880, when she resigned. An expert organist, she was one of the earliest to play Bach's fugues, and gave performances at the Apollonicon, in different London Churches, and at the International Exhibition of 1862. As a composer she will be known by her Six Pedal fugues, and slow movements for the organ, but more for her part-songs of which "All among the barley" achieved remarkable popularity. Her marriage with Mr. F. A. Bridge took place May 16, 1863. She died in London, March 25, 1895.

Stockley, William Cole, organist and conductor, born at Farningham, Kent, February 1, 1830. Studied locally, and appeared at concerts. In 1849 went to Birmingham, and entered the house of Sabin, music-sellers, etc. Became organist of St. Stephen's; St. Mary's; and St. Luke's churches; and up to 1889, was organist at Carr's Lane Chapel. He formed a Choral Society while at St. Stephen's; and in 1855 was invited to become conductor of the Festival Choral Society. He gave up business in accepting the offer; and his first work was to conduct a performance of the "Messiah," on Boxing Night, 1855. On December 26, 1894, he conducted the 40th consecutive annual performance of the same. He severed his connection with the Society in 1895. He was also conductor of Societies at Wolverhampton, conducting the Festivals there to 1880; and at Walsall and elsewhere. Gave his first Orchestral Concert in Birmingham Town Hall, December 11, 1873, and his last, March 11, 1897. During this period he introduced many works and composers to the city, and made the nearest approach to a permanent orchestra that Birmingham has witnessed. As choirmaster to the Birmingham Festival, 1858-94, his work and experience have been unique. In 1873 he resumed business, and resigned his teaching connection and many appointments.

STOCKS.

He has received many tokens of the appreciation in which his public work has been held.

Stocks, William Henry, organist born at Chatteris, Isle of Ely, August 13, 1860. Received his earliest musical training from his father, and at the age of thirteen was appointed music-reader at the Royal Normal College for the Blind, Norwood. Among those he assisted in this capacity was Prince Alexander, now Landgrave of Hesse. He also accompanied the pupils of the College to Windsor, when performances were given before Her Majesty. While at the College he studied pf. with Oscar Beringer, and Fritz Hartvigson, and organ playing and choir-training under Dr. E. J. Hopkins. Harmony and composition was studied with H. C. Banister, and further pf. study pursued with Dr. von Bülow, at Berlin. A.R.C.O., 1885, and L.R.A.M. (organ), 1887. In 1879, was appointed private organist to Sir Robert Menzies. After holding other positions, was appointed assistant music-master at Dulwich College, in 1885, and organist of the College Chapel, 1887. Author of A short History of the Organ, Organists, and Services of the Chapel of Alleyn's College of God's Gift at Dulwich (W. Reeves, 1891), a most interesting book.

Stokes, Charles, organist and composer, born in 1784. Chorister S. Paul's Cathedral, London. Organist at Croyden, etc. He died at London, April 14, 1839. Composer of anthems, glees, songs, and organ music. Also " The Banquet, a selection from the music performed at the Caledonian Asylum," 1817.

Stokes, Walter, composer, born at Shipston-upon-Stour, Worcester, June 28, 1847. His parents were parochial school teachers, and his father, a good baritone singer, acted as choirmaster, and his mother as organist, of the parish church. The son was intended for the scholastic profession, and after being a pupil teacher, he obtained a Scholarship at Saltley College, Birmingham, and held positions in schools in London and Birmingham. From his childhood he was devoted to music. He received his first lessons from Mr. J. Bourne, of Stourbridge ; then had organ lessons from Dr. Roland Rogers ; and later studied under Dr. Belcher, and composition under Dr. C. S. Heap. Graduated Mus. Bac., 1878 ; Mus. Doc., 1882, Cambridge. Now resident in Worcester. His compositions include a Cantata, "The Idol Bel," for soli, eight-part chorus and orchestra (in MS.) ; and he has published a large number of songs and part-songs. Also a sonata for violin and pf., prize composition, performed at the I.S.M. Conference at Bristol, January, 1890 ; Sonata for pf. ; pieces and studies for pf. ; pieces for violin, organ, etc.

Stonard, William, organist and composer. He was organist of Christ Church,

STORACE.

Oxford, and graduated Mus. Bac., Oxon., in 1608. He died in 1630. Composer of anthems in Clifford's Collection, and in MS. in the Music School of Oxford.

Stone, Alfred, musician, born at Bristol in 1841 ; died there January 3, 1878. Organist successively of St. Paul's, Clifton ; Arley Chapel and Highbury Chapel, Bristol. He was conductor of the Orpheus Glee Society, teacher of music in several Bristol schools, and organised and was chorus-master of the Bristol musical festivals of 1873 and 1876. He edited " The Bristol Tune Book," revised edition, 1876. Stone did much to popularize music in Bristol.

Stone, William Henry, physician, and amateur musician, born July 8, 1830. Only son of the late Rev. William Stone, sometime canon of Canterbury Cathedral. Educated at Balliol College, Oxford, graduating B.A. 1852 ; M.A. Entered the medical profession, taking degree of M.B. 1856. Among his appointments was that of consulting physician and lecturer on Physics at St. Thomas's Hospital, London. In 1881 he accepted the office of lecturer on musical acoustics at Trinity College, London. An enthusiastic amateur, he played the double-bassoon, and also the oboe di caccia, the latter in Bach's Christmas Oratorio in Westminster Abbey, and at the Hereford Festival of 1879. He was an authority on wind instruments, especially those of ancient date, and had a fine collection of them. His articles in Grove's " Dictionary " display his knowledge in this direction. Author of Sound as Music, 1876 ; Elementary Lessons on Sound, 1879 ; and The Scientific Basis of Music, Novello.

Stonex, Henry, organist and conductor, born at Norwich, 1823. Studied first under James Harcourt, and afterwards was apprenticed to Dr. Buck. In June, 1850, he was appointed organist of Great Yarmouth Parish Church, an office he held till the close of 1894, when he resigned through ill-health. He gave the first recital on the fine new organ in the church, January 22, 1883. The Yarmouth Musical Society was under his direction for many years up to 1894. A public presentation was made him in May, 1893, for his services to music in Yarmouth. He died in that town, January 10, 1897, aged 73.

Storace, Anna Selina, soprano vocalist, born at London in 1766. She was the daughter of Stefano Storace, an Italian double-bass player, and sister of Stephen Storace. She studied under her father and Rauzzini, and appeared as a concert vocalist in London, 1774-1778. Afterwards she studied at Venice under Sacchini, and sang at Florence, 1780 ; Parma, 1781 ; Milan, 1782 ; and Vienna,

STORACE.

1784. Married to J. A. Fisher, 1784, but separated from him soon afterwards. She appeared in Mozart's "Figaro," at Vienna, 1786. Returned to London and appeared in English and Italian opera from 1787. Sang at Handel Festival, 1791. Retired in 1808, and died at Dulwich, London, August 24, 1817.

Storace, Stephen, composer, born at London in 1763. Son of Stefano Storace, an Italian double-bass player. He studied under his father, and at Naples in the Conservatorio of St. Onofrio. Resided in London as composer to the principal theatres. He died at London, March 19, 1796.

Works.—*Musical Dramas:* Gli sposi malcontenti, 1785; Gli Equivoci, Vienna, 1786; Doctor and Apothecary, London, 1788; Haunted Tower, 1789; La Cameriera astuta, 1790; No song no supper, by Prince Hoare, 1790; Siege of Belgrade, 1791; Cave of Trophonius, 1791; Pirates, 1792; Dido, 1792; The Prize, 1793; My Grandmother, 1793; Venus and Adonis, 1794; Glorious First of June, entertainment for the benefit of the widows, etc., of the men who fell in the late engagement under Lord Howe, 1794; Lodoiska, 1794; Cherokee, 1794; Le Nozze di Dorina, 1795; Iron Chest (Colman), 1796; Mahmoud, 1796; Three and the Deuce, 1795. Lamentation of Marie Antoinette; Captivity, a ballad (1793); Shepherds, I have lost my love, song. Collection of original harpsichord music, London, 1790, 2 vols. Six easy and progressive sonatinas for pf. or harpsichord. Three sonatas for harpsichord or pf. [1785].

Storer, John, composer, organist, and critic, born at Hulland, near Derby, May 18, 1858. Choirboy, Ashbourne Parish Church, to 1869, when his parents removed to Scarborough. He then entered the choir of All Saints', Scarborough; was solo boy, and afterwards articled pupil of Dr. John Naylor. Graduated Mus. Bac., Oxford, 1878; and in 1886 took the Mus. Doc. degree, Trinity College, Toronto. Organist and choirmaster, St. Michael's, Whitby, 1879-81, when he left to study composition in London. Returned to Scarborough, 1882, as organist of the parish church, and conductor of the Scarborough Philharmonic Society. Organist of the Parish Church, Folkestone, 1885-7, when he joined the Roman Communion. He then undertook similar duties at the Church of the Redemptorist Fathers, Clapham, London. Resigned in 1891 to devote more time to composition, for which he was attracting notice. Has been musical director at the Globe, Royalty, Strand, Olympic, and other theatres at different times. Musical critic to *The Morning*, 1894, *St. Paul's*, and *Court Circular*, and contributor to other papers. At present time he is director of the musical studies at St. Gregory's College,

STRATTON.

Downside, Bath, and takes Sunday duty as organist at the new Benedictine Church attached to Downside Monastery.

Works.—Festival Mass in F, 1888; Mass of Our Lady of Ransom, for soli, chorus, and orchestra, op. 50, 1891; Grand Solemn Mass in F minor, 1895. Anthems, etc. Comic opera, The Punchbowl, Novelty Theatre 1887; Comedy opera, Gretna Green, Comedy Theatre, 1890; Operettas, various. Part-songs. Six vocal impromptus, songs, etc Dramatic cantata, The Tournament, 1885; Concert overture, composed for the opening of the Folkestone Fine Art Treasures Exhibition, May 22, 1886. Organ and pf. pieces, etc.

Strachan, James Kelt, organist, born at Errol, Perthshire, October 1, 1860. Choirboy at St. Paul's Episcopal Church, Dundee, and pupil of W. H. Richmond and John Kinross. At sixteen he was appointed organist at St. Enoch's, Dundee; and two years later at Kelvingrove United Presbyterian Church, Glasgow. At this time he studied under Dr. Armes, and went to Paris for some months, studying under Alexandre Guilmant, the two henceforth becoming fast friends. Returning to Glasgow, he was appointed organist of Claremont United Presbyterian Church; and in 1892, of the Free College Church, where he still officiates. It is as a concert organist that he is most widely known; and his recitals at St. Andrew's Hall, Glasgow; the Royal Albert Hall, Kensington; the Bow and Bromley Institute, etc., have established his reputation as one of the finest executants of the day.

Strang, Walter, composer and teacher, was born at Edinburgh on December 26, 1825. He was choirmaster of Free St. George's Church, Edinburgh, from 1848 till 1885, and from 1867 to 1889 he was precentor to the General Assembly of the Free Church. He was music master at the Free Church Normal and other schools in Edinburgh for many years. His compositions include hymn tunes and school songs, some of which latter appear in his "School Music," Edinburgh, 1853.

Stratton, Alexander, musician of the early part of the present century, who was a teacher of music in Banff. He published a "Collection of Waltzes, Opera Dances, Strathspeys and Reels, arranged for the pf., violin, and German flute," n.d.

Stratton, Stephen Samuel, composer, writer, and lecturer, born at London, December 19, 1840. He first studied the pf. under Miss Elizabeth Chamberlaine (Mrs. H. von Höff), and subsequently the organ under Charles Gardner, and composition under Charles Lucas. Assistant organist, St. Michael's, Paddington, 1862; organist, St. Mary the Virgin, Crown Street, Soho, 1863. From 1864 to 1866 he was professor of music

STREATFEILD.

at Totteridge Park School, Herts., and organist of St. James's, Friern Barnet. Was an original member of the College of Organists, 1864, resigning in 1894. In 1866 he settled in Birmingham as a teacher, and was organist of St. Barnabas Church, 1866-7; Edgbaston Parish Church, 1867-75; St. John's, Harborne, 1876-7; and Church of the Saviour, Birmingham, 1878-82. He is an Associate of the Philharmonic Society, 1882; and musical critic of the *Birmingham Daily Post*. He has published some church music, songs, and part-songs, and pf. pieces.

Streatfeild, R. A., is the author of " Masters of Italian Music," London, Osgood, 1895; and " The Opera : a history of the development of opera, with full descriptions of all works in the modern repertory," London, Nimmo, 1896. The first-named work treats only of modern composers like Verdi, Boito, Mascagni, etc.

Street, Josiah, musician of the 18th century, compiler of " A Book containing great variety of Anthems in 2, 3, 4, and 6 parts, likewise a set of Psalm-tunes in 4 parts,.." London, n.d. [1729]; 2nd edition, 1746; 3rd edition, 1785.

Strelezki, Anton. The *nom de plume* of an English composer, whose real name is understood to be BURNAND. Born at Croydon, December 5, 1859 (Pauer's Dictionary of Pianists). Pupil of the Leipzig Conservatorium, and later of Madame Schumann. Has given recitals in America. He is a most voluminous writer for the pianoforte, his principal compositions being Eight pieces, op. 47; Three pieces, op. 146; Three books of pieces, op. 191, 197, 204; Leichte Klavierstücke, op. 220; besides Polonaises, a grand Tarantella, Barcarolle, and many detached pieces. Also a Minuet for pf. and violin, and some songs.

Stretton, A. J., bandmaster. Received his early education in the Royal Artillery Band Is an excellent violinist, and has a general knowledge of every instrument. Appointed bandmaster, 2nd Battalion Cheshire Regiment, 1893 ; Musical Director, Kneller Hall, February, 1896, with honorary rank of Lieutenant.

Strong, David, tenor vocalist, born in London, March 9, 1852. He has given concerts, and has appeared with success as a vocalist ; and is well known as a teacher. In 1886, he was appointed a Gentleman of Her Majesty's Chapel Royal, St. James', and also a Professor at the Guildhall School of Music.

Stroud, Charles, composer, who was born in 1710. He was a pupil of Dr. Blow. Died at London, April 26, 1726, in his 16th year. He composed anthems which possessed merit, and was a musician of promise.

Stroud, Henry Charles, *see* HENRY, CHAPLIN.

SUCH.

Stuart, Ralph, pianist, born at Dartmouth, Devon. His father was an army staff-surgeon. He studied at Leipzig and Heidelberg, and in 1880, went to New Zealand for the benefit of his health. He was heard in concerts at the principal towns there, and in Australia; and was the pianist of the Melba Concert Party. In July, 1888, he gave a Chopin recital at the Princes' Hall, London; and has since given recitals at various times, making a speciality of his interpretation of the music of Chopin.

Stubley, Simon, was organist of St. John's Church, Clerkenwell, from about 1740 to 1754. He died at London in 1754. He composed some vocal music, chiefly songs, a few of which appear in the " Gentleman's Magazine " for 1744, 1746, 1749, 1753, etc. He was succeeded at St. John's, by PHILIP MARKHAM, elected July, 1754—died 1764; and he in his turn was succeeded by JOHN BACON, appointed April 10, 1764—died May 16, 1816, who held the post for the long period of 52 years.

Sturges, Edward, organist and composer, born at London, February 25, 1808. Organist of the Foundling Hospital. He died at London, February 15, 1848. Composer of " I know their sorrows," anthem; Selection of choruses by Handel, 1846 ; Organ gems, 1845 ; Arrangements of Boyce's anthems, Haydn's " Creation," etc.

Sturges, Richard Yates, flutist, violinist, and poet, born at Birmingham, April 10, 1843. Studied under W. Tilly and Webbe, local teachers. Made his *début* at Mr. James Stimpson's Monday Popular Concerts, Town Hall, Birmingham, September, 1861. In 1864 he played at Mr. Rea's Concerts, Town Hall, Newcastle-on-Tyne ; was for some months in the orchestra at the Theatre Royal there ; and has toured in the provinces on several occasions. He visited Italy, 1884, and took up the study of the violin. As a flute player he has given much attention to the works of Adolph Terschak, and has been complimented by having a piece written expressly for him— " The Fire Worshippers of the Caspian Sea." This he played at Southport, December 9, 1895. He has published " The Solitary, and other Poems," Edinburgh, Nichol, 1868; " The Angel of Love, and other Poems," London, Provost, 1875; Summer-day Secrets; " The Black Philosopher, or Scipio Africanus;" and other poetical works.

Such, Edwin Charles, composer and teacher, born in London, August 11, 1840. Educated at Merchant Taylors' School, and London University College, graduating B.A. Studied music under Hiller and Molique at Cologne Conservatorium, 1861. Conductor of the Barnet and Ibis Choral Society, 1884-93; professor of harmony at Portman Academy.

SUDLOW.

His compositions include Ps. 46, for solo, chorus, and orchestra; Dramatic cantata, "Narcissus and Echo," produced at a concert at R.A.M., July 6, 1881; Cantata, The Watersprite; Anthems, part-songs, songs, pf. pieces, etc. His son, HENRY SUCH, violinist, pupil of Joachim and Wilhelmj, made his first appearance at a Berlin Philharmonic concert in 1893. After a tour in Germany he returned to London, and gave his first recital at St. James' Hall, October 24, 1896. PERCY SUCH, another son, is a violoncellist, pupil of Robert Hausmann, and of the High School, Berlin.

Sudlow, William, composer, organist, and violoncellist, born in 1772. He was an organist in Manchester, and died there in 1848, Composer of anthems, songs, and other vocal music. His brother, EDWARD, born 1786, died at Manchester, September 16, 1845, was a viola player.

Suett, Richard, composer, actor, and singer, born at Chelsea, London in 1755. He was a singer and actor chiefly in London. Died at London, July 6, 1805. Composer of Corin and Joan, pastoral [1800]; Six canzonets, with an accompaniment for a harpsichord or pf., London, 1803. Six glees [1794]. Songs: Kiss; Oh cruel absence; Signs of faithful love; Soft music; Sylvia again is true, etc.

Sullivan, Sir Arthur Seymour, Kt., composer and conductor, born in London, May 13, 1842. His father, THOMAS SULLIVAN, was connected with Kneller Hall almost from the commencement of that institution, as professor of bass brass instruments, and was also a clarinet player. He had a high reputation throughout the army as an instructor. He died suddenly, of heart disease, September, 23, 1866. · The son entered the Chapel Royal in 1854 as a chorister, under the Rev. Thomas Helmore. He made rapid progress in music, and his first song was published in 1855. In July, 1856, he was elected the first Mendelssohn Scholar, but did not leave the Chapel Royal until 1857. He studied at the R.A.M., under Goss and Sterndale Bennett, and in 1858 proceeded to Leipzig Conservatorium, where his teachers were Plaidy, Hauptmann, E. F. Richter, Moscheles, and others. At the Hauptprüfung, May 26, 1860, he conducted a performance of his overture, "Lalla Rookh;" and while there he also wrote some string quartets, and the "Tempest" music, which he brought with him to London in April, 1861. This was produced at the Crystal Palace, April 5, 1862. For a time he was organist of St. Michael's, Chester Square; and St. Peter's, Onslow Gardens, 1867-72. He soon rose into notice as a composer; and from the production of his cantata, "Kenilworth," at the

SULLIVAN.

Birmingham Festival, 1864, his career has been one of continued success. His light operas have attained a popularity without a parallel. He was appointed musical director of the Royal Aquarium, Westminster, and conducted a concert of English music at its opening, January 23, 1876; Principal of National Training School for Music, and professor of composition, 1876, resigning in 1881. Conducted the orchestral concerts of the Glasgow Choral Union, 1875-7; Promenade concerts, Covent Garden, 1878-9. British Commissioner for Music, Paris Exhibition, 1878. Appointed conductor of Leeds Festivals, 1880, to present time; Philharmonic Society, 1885-7. Visited America in 1885, and conducted "The Mikado" in New York. Conducted concerts at Crystal Palace, Manchester, Buckingham Palace, etc. F.R.A.M.; Mus. Doc., Cambridge, 1876, Oxford, 1879, both *honoris causâ;* Chevalier, Legion of Honour of France, 1878; corresponding member of the Royal Musical Institute, Florence, 1888; instituted grand organist of the Freemasons, April 27, 1887; elected president of the Birmingham and Midland Institute, 1888, on October 19, giving his address in the Town Hall; received the honour of knighthood from the Queen, 1883; knight of the Order of the House of Coburg, and recipient of the Order of the Medjidieh from the Sultan of Turkey, 1888.

WORKS.—*Oratorios and Cantatas:* Kenilworth, Birmingham Festival, 1864; The Prodigal Son, Worcester, 1869; On Shore and Sea, composed for the opening of Royal Albert Hall, Kensington, May 1, 1871; Festival Te Deum, Crystal Palace, 1872, to commemorate the recovery of H.R.H. the Prince of Wales; The Light of the World, oratorio, Birmingham Festival, 1873; The Martyr of Antioch, Leeds Festival, 1880; The Golden Legend, the same, 1886; ode, I wish to tune my quiv'ring lyre, baritone solo and orchestra, Gloucester Festival, 1880. *Operas and Plays:* Cox and Box, Adelphi, May 11, 1867; The Cantrabandista, St. George's Hall, December 18, 1867; Thespis, Gaiety, December 26, 1871; Trial by Jury, Royalty, March 25, 1875; The Zoo, St. James's, June 5, 1875; The Sorcerer, Opera Comique, November 17, 1877; H.M.S. Pinafore, the same, May 25, 1878; Pirates of Penzance, the same, April 3, 1880; Patience, the same, April 25, 1881. And at the Savoy Theatre, Iolanthe, November 25, 1882; Princess Ida, January 5, 1884; The Mikado, March 14, 1885; Ruddigore, January 22, 1887; Yeomen of the Guard, October 3, 1888; Gondoliers, December 7, 1889; Haddon Hall (Sydney Grundy), September 24, 1892; Utopia, October 7, 1893; and The Grand Duke, May 7, 1896. Grand opera, Ivanhoe

SUMMERS.

(Julian Sturgis), produced Royal English Opera House, January 31, 1891. These works have also, for the most part, been performed in Germany, America, etc. Incidental music to The Tempest, op. 1, Crystal Palace, 1862; Merchant of Venice, Manchester, September 18, 1871; Merry Wives of Windsor, Gaiety, December 19, 1874; Henry VIII., Manchester, August 29, 1877; Macbeth, Lyceum, December 29, 1888; King Arthur, completed 1894. *Orchestral:* Procession march, composed in celebration of the marriage of the Prince of Wales, and performed Crystal Palace, March 14, 1863; symphony in E, Crystal Palace, March, 1866; overture, In Memoriam (his father), Norwich Festival, 1886; Marmion, Philharmonic Society, June 3, 1867; Di Ballo, Birmingham Festival, 1870. Concerto, 'cello and orchestra, Crystal Palace (Piatti), 1866. Ballets, L'Isle Enchantée, 1864; Victorian and Merrie England, Alhambra, May 25, 1897. Six Day Dreams, and other pieces for pf. Te Deum, Jubilate, and Kyrie in D; Hearken unto Me; O, love the Lord; Who is like unto Thee? and other anthems. Hymn tunes in various collections. Musical editor of Church Hymns with tunes, S.P.C.K., 1874. The last night of the year; O, hush thee, my babie; Joy to the victors; and other part-songs, 1871. *Songs:* The Window, or the loves of the wrens (Tennyson), 1871; Bride from the North; Arabian love song; Orpheus with his lute; O, mistress mine; Sweethearts; Will he come? The lost chord; Edward Gray; Thou'rt passing hence; Snow lies white; Let me dream again; O fair dove, O fond dove; A weary lot is thine; Looking back; St. Agnes' Eve; The Sisters, duet; and many others.

His brother, FREDERICK SULLIVAN, whose talent for humour was so conspicuous, was by profession an architect. He turned to the stage, and his impersonation of *The Judge* in "Trial by Jury" had much to do with the success of the piece. While on a provincial tour he caught cold from damp sheets at Newcastle, and died, January 18, 1878, at the age of 39.

Summers, James Lea, composer and pianist, born at London, 1837. Son of William Summers, a musician. He was blind from his birth, but became a pupil of Miss Kate Loder and of (Sir) G. A. Macfarren. He appeared as a pianist at the Crystal Palace about 1850-60. Died at London, July 8, 1881.

WORKS.—Quintet for strings; Quartet in E flat for strings; Quartet in A, pf. and strings; Andante and rondo brillante, pf.; Two musical sketches, pf.; Valses. etc., pf. Anthems, duets, and songs.

Summers, Joseph, organist and com-

SURENNE.

poser, born in Somerset, 1843. Received his early training at Wells Cathedral, under C. W. Lavington, afterwards studying with Sterndale Bennett, and Dr. Gauntlett. Took degree of Mus. Bac. at Oxford, 1887, and in 1890 was made Mus. Doc., Cantuar. Has been organist successively at St. Andrew's College, Bradfield, 1861; Holy Trinity, Weston-super-Mare, 1864; St. Peter's, Notting Hill, 1865. On going to Australia in 1865 he was appointed to St. Peter's, Melbourne, and now holds a similar position at All Saints', St. Kilda, near Melbourne. Is Government inspector of music for public schools, Victoria, and holds other appointments of a similar nature.

WORKS.—*Oratorios:* Deborah; St. Sebastian. Cantata, A Song of Triumph. *Odes:* "Galatea Secunda;" "Thanksgiving;" Psalm 31, soli, chorus, and orchestra; Anthems, Services, etc. The Australian National Anthem, "Maker of Earth and Sea." Hymn Tunes contributed to The Bristol Tune Book; Psalmody, British Empire; Parish Tune Book. "In Memoriam," for orchestra; marches; songs, part-songs, etc.

Sunderland, Susan, *born* SYKES, soprano vocalist, born at Brighouse, Yorkshire, April 30, 1819. Was instructed chiefly by local teachers, and first sang in concerts at Deighton, near Huddersfield, about 1834. She married Mr. Henry Sunderland, June 7, 1838. Made her *début* at the Sacred Harmonic Concerts, London, April 1, 1846, singing as *Achsah* in Handel's "Joshua." Sang at the Birmingham Festival Choral Concert on the 10th of the same month; and at intervals up to 1859; at the Free Trade Hall, Manchester, 1849. So famous in the North as to receive the title of the "Yorkshire Queen of Song," she was a special favourite at the Bradford Festivals; she also sang at the first Leeds Festival in 1858. Her last public appearance was at Huddersfield, June 2 and 3, 1864, in the "Messiah," and a miscellaneous concert. Her golden wedding was celebrated by a "Jubilee" concert, June 7, 1888, the proceeds of which went to founding the Sunderland Vocal Prize, for natives of the West Riding of Yorkshire. At the meeting in December, 1888, when the Jubilee committee completed the work, Mrs. Sunderland sang "Home, sweet home," greatly delighting and affecting her old friends and admirers.

Surenne, John Thomas, organist and composer, born at London, March 4, 1814. His father, GABRIEL SURENNE, was a French musician and teacher, who settled in London, and afterwards in Edinburgh, about 1817, where he taught French and edited a well-known French-English dictionary. In 1831, J. T. Surenne, who studied under his father

Z

SURMAN.

and Henri Herz, became organist of St. Mark's Episcopal Church, Portobello, and he also held, for many years, the appointment of organist of St. George's Episcopal Chapel, Edinburgh. He died at Edinburgh, February 3, 1878. Composer of an Overture for orchestra in D; a Rondo de concert for pf. and strings; many other pf. pieces, and some part-songs and songs. He compiled "The Dance Music of Scotland, a Collection of all the best Reels and Strathspeys, both of the Highlands and Lowlands, for the Pianoforte." Edinburgh [1851], 5 editions. "Songs of Scotland without Words," 1852 and 1854. "Songs of Ireland," 1855. A Collection of Church Music, consisting of chants, psalms, and hymn-tunes, principally original (with H. E. Dibdin), 1843-44, 2 vols. The Scottish Episcopal Church Music Book, Edinburgh, n.d. Students' Manual of Classical Extracts for Pf., and other instrumental compositions. Surenne wrote most of the accompaniments for the original edition of Graham and Wood's "Songs of Scotland."

Surman, Joseph, conductor and writer, born at Chesham, November 14, 1804. He was conductor of the Sacred Harmonic Society, 1832-48. First conductor of the London Harmonic Society, which he started in November, 1848, with the "Messiah." Music publisher in London. Conductor of the Worcester Festival. He died at London, January 20, 1871. He wrote "Statement submitted to the consideration of the members of the Society, in reply to charges preferred against the Conductor of the Society," London, 1848; also a supplement. He had been removed from the conductorship of the Sacred Harmonic Society on certain charges against his management being made. Editor of "The London Psalmist. Psalms and Hymns adapted to the services of the Church of England," London [1850].

Sutcliffe, Alfred Lister, organist and composer, born at Leckhampstead, Bucks. November 13, 1859. Studied music under the Rev. L. G. Hayne, and was by him appointed organist of Bradfield, 1875; and of Mistley with Bradfield, 1878. Composer of a few hymn tunes.

Sutcliffe, Charles Thomas, organist, born at Manchester, April 12, 1853. Chorister at Manchester Cathedral, and assistant-organist there later. Organist successively at Salford; Longsight; Parish Church, Eccles; and now of St. Catherine's, Barton, near Manchester. He is the composer of some pf. pieces, songs, etc.

Sutcliffe, Jasper, violinist. Scholar R.C.M. Made a successful appearance at Mr. De Jong's Manchester concerts, February 2, 1889, when he played Max Bruch's concerto in G minor. He has been associated with

SWEPSTONE.

the British Chamber Music concerts, 1894, and other artistic undertakings.

Sutherland, G., musician and composer, author of "A Manual of the theory of Music," London, 2 editions to 1871; and composer of a few songs.

Sutherland, John, musician. Published "The Edinburgh Repository of Music: containing the most select English, Scottish, and Irish airs, reels, strathspeys, etc," Edinburgh, n.d., 3 vols.

Sutton, Alfred James, organist, composer, and conductor, born at Droitwich, May 1, 1827, Resident in Birmingham, where he was appointed conductor of the Amateur Harmonic Association, on its formation in 1855, an office he held until 1877. Was chorusmaster, with W. C. Stockley, at the Birmingham Festival, 1858-76; and has held other appointments. Sometime organist of St. Thomas's, Birmingham; St. Mary's, Warwick, and other churches. Composer of an oratorio, "Ruth"; and an opera, "Put to the test," both in MS. His published works include a Serenade for soli, chorus, and orchestra, composed in celebration of the marriage of the Prince of Wales; a cantata, "Sage Advice," composed for Madame Sainton-Dolby's Choir; songs, part-songs, and pieces for organ. Mrs. SUTTON, his wife, is a soprano vocalist, and for many years held a prominent position in the Midlands as an oratorio singer. She also took part in concerted pieces at the Birmingham Festivals, 1861-73, and has been heard with favour in London.

Sutton, Rev. Frederick Heathcote, author of "Some account of the mèdiæval organ case still existing at Old Radnor, South Wales," London, 1866; "Church Organs, their position and construction," London, 1872; also 1883. The Appendix to this contains the Old Radnor tract.

Sutton, Richard, musician, compiled "Book of musical varieties," London [1835].

Sutton, Robert, musician, author of "Elements of the theory of music," London, Cocks [1870]; 3rd edition, 1874.

Sutton, William Walter, composer, pianist, and teacher, born at Dover, 1793; died there, in March, 1874. He published a number of arrangements for the Pf., etc.

Swaine, N., author of "The Young Musician, or the science of music familiarly explained, with a glossary of musical terms," Stourport, 1818.

Swan, William David, pianist and composer, born Glasgow, November 30, 1856; died Burslem, May 27, 1889. He composed a few pieces for the piano and was a good pianist, acting in this capacity for a time as accompanist to the Glasgow Select Choir.

Swepstone, Edith, composer. Studied at the Guildhall School of Music. One of her

SWIFT.

earliest works to be performed was a symphony, part of which was given under her direction at Leyton, March 10, 1887. Other compositions are : Elegiac Overture, " Les Ténèbres," performed in the Queen's Hall, February 9, 1897 ; Quintet in F minor, pf. and strings ; Quartet in G minor, strings ; pieces for 'cello and pf. ; and for pf. solo. Two cantatas for female voices—The Ice Queen ; and Idylls of the Morn ; songs, etc. Miss Swepstone has lectured on music at the City of London School, 1895, etc.

Swift, George Henry, organist and composer, born at Lambourn, Berkshire, 1856. Organist of Lambourn Church, and conductor of a choral society there till 1884, when he went to Hungerford. He has composed an Evening Service in E; O sing unto the Lord ; Show us Thy mercy ; and other anthems. Part-songs. A Sonata in C, for pf., etc.

Swift, James Frederick, composer and bass vocalist. For many years resident at Liverpool, and now at Liscard. Under the name of GODFREY MARKS, he has published a number of songs, Sailing ; A brave heart, etc., some of which have enjoyed great popularity. He has conducted various musical societies at Liverpool, and given concerts.

Sydenham, Edwin Augustus, organist and composer, was a choirboy at the Parish Church, Stratford-on-Avon. Studied at Leipzig Conservatorium, and became organist of St. Martin's, Dorking ; St. Andrew's, Farnham, 1873 ; St. James's, Bury St. Edmund's, 1879 ; and All Saints', Scarborough, 1882. There he worthily maintained the musical reputation of the church. He gave concerts, was busy as a teacher and composer, and was the inventor of a patent touch regulator for the pianoforte. He died suddenly at Scarborough, February 18, 1891. His compositions embraced a number of anthems : Christ is risen; O give thanks ; Great is the Lord ; Sing unto God ; and others. An Evening Service. A battle song; The maiden of the Fleur-de-Lys; The parting kiss; and other part-songs. Duet, pf. and harmonium ; pieces for violin and pf.; 'Cello and pf.; and various compositions for pf. solo.

Symmers, James, amateur musician, who was rector of Alloa Academy. He wrote " Outlines of the Sol-fa method of singing," Glasgow, 1849. " The Sol-fa method of singing at sight from the common musical notation," Glasgow, 1858-59, 2 parts.

Symmes, Thomas, amateur musician and clergyman, born in 1678, died in 1725. He wrote " Utile dulci, or a joco-serious dialogue concerning regular singing," Boston, 1723.

Symonds, Henry, composer and organist. He was one of the King's Band of Music. Organist of St. Martin's, Ludgate, and of the

TAGORE.

Church of St. John, London. He died in 1730. Composer of Six sets of lessons for the harpsichord, etc.

Synge, Mary Helena, pianist, born at Parsonstown, Ireland. Daughter of the late Sir Edward Synge, Bart., and descended from Archbishop Synge, of the 17th century. After some private study, she went to Brussels for further instruction in pf. playing and singing. On her return she gave a recital in London, July 10, 1883, which brought her into favourable notice. She played at the exhibition in Cork the same year, and has since been heard at concerts in many places in England and Ireland. As a composer she is known by a vocal trio, " Spring " ; Songs, Time and Eternity ; Fate, and others ; and a number of pf. pieces. Of the same family was the Rev. EDWARD SYNGE, born at Lockeen Glebe, Parsonstown, June 30, 1829. He graduated Mus. Bac., Oxford, 1865, and Mus. Doc., Dublin, 1869. His compositions included an unfinished oratorio, " Hezekiah " ; settings of Psalm 127, and Psalm 150, for soli, chorus, and organ; Milton's Ode to May, soli and chorus ; and some songs. He published a Te Deum, and other church music ; Morning song ; Evening song ; Spring song ; Winter song, etc. Died, 1895.

Synyer, Henry, violinist and conductor, born at Nottingham, June 7, 1818 ; died at King's Heath, near Birmingham, July 17, 1892. He went to Birmingham as a young man, and as the junior in the firm of Harvey and Synyer ; was well-known in the Midlands as an *entrepreneur.* For thirty years he was a member of the Birmingham Festival orchestra, and for a long period was bandmaster of the 1st Warwickshire Rifle Volunteers. In conjunction with Alfred W. Gilmer, Henry Synyer formed a military band which had a high reputation, and was in great request in many parts of the country.

Sympson, *see* SIMPSON, C.

Taas, William, musician of latter part of last century. He was an itinerating teacher of psalmody in Banffshire, etc. Author of the " Elements of Music, wherein the fundamental principles of that science are explained and illustrated. To which is annexed a collection of the best church tunes generally in use, and fitted to various measures of poetry. With several anthems, chants, and canons. The whole selected from the best authors with a view to the improvement of church music in Scotland," Aberdeen, 1787.

Tagore, Rajah Sourindro Mohun, Hindu amateur musician, was president of the Calcutta Music School. Compiler of " Hindu music, from various authors,"..Calcutta, privately printed, 1875. This contains all the treatises on the subject of any import-

TAILOUR.

TATE.

ance, by Willard, Sir Wm. Jones, Sir W. Ouseley, Nathan, etc. Six original Râgas ; The Musical Scales of the Hindus. Some specimens of Indian Songs.

Tailour, Robert, musician of the latter part of 16th and early part of 17th centuries. He issued " Sacred Hymns consisting of fifte select Psalms of David and others, paraphrastically turned into English verse, and by R. Tailour set to be sung in five parts, as also to the vicle and lute, or orpharion. Published for the use of such as delight in the exercise of music in her original honour," London, 1615.

Tait, Andrew, musician of the first half of the 18th century, issued " A New and correct Set of Church Tunes," Aberdeen, 1753, 3rd edition. We have not been able to trace an earlier edition.

Tait, Annie, pianist and composer, who studied at R.A.M. under Sir G. A. Macfarren. She died at Eastbourne, Febuary 24, 1886, at an early age, after a career of much promise. Among her works are a Trio for pf. and strings; Sonata in F for pf. : and other pieces for pf. and songs.

Tait, Patrick Macnaghten, F.S.S., F.R.G.S., son of the late William Tait, Esq., was born in Edinburgh. In 1851 proceeded to India, and was there through the Mutiny, when he raised the Rifle Company of the Calcutta Volunteer Guards. Contributor to various magazines, chiefly on subjects of Mortality and Insurance. The work claiming notice here is " Vital and other Statistics applicable to Musicians," 1880.

Tallis or **Tallys, Thomas,** composer and organist, born about 1520-1529. He is supposed to have been a chorister in the Chapel Royal. Organist of Waltham Abbey till 1540. Gentleman of the Chapel Royal during reigns of Henry VIII., Edward VI., Mary, and Elizabeth. Joint organist with Byrd, of the Chapel Royal, and joint patentee with him in the exclusive right to print music. He died on November 23, 1585, and was buried in Parish Church of Greenwich.

WORKS. — Cantiones quæ ab argumento Sacræ vocantur, quinque et sex partium, London, 1575. The Preces, Chants, Te Deum, Benedictus, Responses, Litany, Kyrie, Creed, Sanctus, Gloria, Magnificat, and Nunc Dimittis (Church of England Service), first printed in Barnard's Collection, 1641, and since reprinted many times by Novello, Rimbault, Jebb, etc. Song of Forty Parts, for eight choirs of five voices each, "Spem in alium non habui." The Order of the Daily Service of the United Church of England and Ireland, edited by John Bishop, London, 1843. *Anthems*: All people that on earth do dwell; Come, Holy Ghost; Hear the voice and prayer; I call and cry; If ye love Me; Hear my prayer;

Blessed are those ; Salvator Mundi (motet) ; and many others in MS. contained in the British Museum, Music School of Oxford, Fitzwilliam Museum, Cambridge, and elsewhere.

In 1876 a brass memorial tablet was placed in Greenwich Parish Church, which was provided by subscriptions gathered on the suggestion of Henry Walter Miller (*q.v.*).

Tamplin, Augustus Lechmere, organist and composer, born in London, 1837; died Fulham, London, May 8, 1889. He was organist of St. James' Church, Marylebone, and was a performer of great ability. In 1883 he lectured in London on the history, construction and technicalites of the pianoforte. He introduced the double touch in harmonium playing. Composer of an operetta, "Fleurette," performed, Crystal Palace, 1874 ; Pf. music ; Songs : Daybreak ; Love, and other pieces.

Tans'ur, William, composer and collector, born at Dunchurch, Warwickshire, in 1699 or 1700. He was a teacher of music at different times in Barnes (Surrey), Ewell near Epsom, Cambridge, Stamford, Boston, Leicester, and other parts of England where he worked along with his son, but lately he settled in St. Neots as a bookseller and teacher of music, and died there, October 7, 1783.

WORKS.—A Compleat Melody, or the Harmony of Sion . . London [1724 ?], other editions 1730, 1736, 1738, 1764-66, etc. [The titles and contents of the various editions of this work vary greatly]. Heaven on earth or the beauty of holiness . . London, 1738. Sacred mirth or the pious soul's daily delight . . 1789. The Universal harmony containing the whole book of psalms . . 1743, 1746, etc. The Psalmsinger's jewel, or useful companion to the book of Psalms . . London, 1760, 1766, etc. Melodia Sacra, or the devout psalmist's new musical companion, a choice selection of psalm tunes in 4 parts . . 1771, 1772. A new musical grammar, or the harmonical spectator . . Leicester, 1746 ; 2nd edition, London, 1753 ; 3rd edition, 1756 ; 7th edition, 1829. The elements of musick displayed . . London, 1772. Poetical meditations . . 1740. .

Tanymarian, see STEPHEN, EDWARD.

Tapley, Joseph, tenor vocalist, was a scholar of the National Training School, South Kensington, to 1882. Sang at Mr. De Jong's concerts, Manchester, 1888 ; toured in the "Old Guard," and other comic opera companies, 1887 ; and sang in comic opera for three years in Australia, his *Rev. Henry Sandford*, in "The Vicar of Bray," being a pronounced success. He appeared in a round of characters in the Gilbert-Sullivan operas. Returned to England in 1896.

Tate, Nahum, poet and musician, born at Dublin in 1652. He succeeded Shadwell as poet laureate in 1692. Died at London in 1715. Author of " An Essay for promoting

TATTET.

psalmody," London, 1710, but is best known for his metrical version of the psalms, which he executed along with Nicholas Brady.

Tattet, J. A., organist and composer of first half of the present century. He edited MacMurdie's "Sacred Music," 1827, and composed a large number of songs and ballads, such as "The Blind boy" [1825], "Forget me not when beauty smiles," "May Day," etc.

Tattersall, Rev. William DeChair, clergyman and musician, was born in 1752. Rector of Westbourne, Sussex, 1778, and of Wootten-under-Edge, 1779, where he died on May 26, 1829. Compiler of "Psalms selected from Merrick's version, the music new and partly chosen from the works of the most eminent composers," London, 1791. "Improved Psalmody, with new music," London, 1794; also 1795, 3 vols., and "Improved Psalmody, the words selected from a poetical version of the Psalms by J. Merrick, the music adapted from the sacred compositions of Handel," London, 1802.

Taverner, John, organist and composer of the 16th century. He was organist of Boston, Lincolnshire, and of Christ Church, Oxford. He was involved in the Reformation struggle, and narrowly escaped martyrdom. He composed masses, motets, and anthems, now existing in MS.

Taverner, John, musician, born 1584. Professor of music at Gresham College, 1610. Was vicar of Stoke Newington. Died there, 1638.

Taylor, Amram, musician of first part of present century. Composer of "The Sacred Harp, a new set of original psalm and hymn tunes, composed and harmonized for four voices," London [1842].

Taylor, Brook, mathematician and musician, born at Edmonton in 1685. He distinguished himself at Cambridge, and became Secretary of the Royal Society in 1714. He died in 1731. Celebrated for his theorem, which Lagrange adopted as the basis of the differential calculus. He was the first to publish analytical researches into the vibrations of strings, and contributed to the Philosophical Transactions of 1713 a paper on the "Motion of a tense string."

Taylor, Ebenezer William, organist and composer, born at Stafford, November 26, 1851. Began to study music when six years old, afterwards articled to G. Townshend Smith, of Hereford Cathedral, and subsequently studied with Dr. C. W. Corfe, at Oxford. Graduated Mus. Bac., 1876; Mus. Doc., 1883, Oxford; F.R.C.O., 1879. Appointed organist of St. Thomas', Stafford, 1872; and of St. Mary's, 1880. Hon. local examiner for R.C.M. His compositions comprise an oratorio, "St. Stephen"; a cantata,

TAYLOR.

"God our Refuge"; service for Holy Communion; songs, pf. pieces, etc. Author of Vocal score reading exercises; Figured bass and melody exercises; Pedal and manual scales, arpeggios, etc., for organ. Contributor to National Book of Hymn tunes, etc.

Taylor, Edward, writer and musician, born at Norwich, January 22, 1784. Son of John Taylor, a Unitarian preacher there. He studied music under Charles Smyth and Dr. Beckwith. Bass singer at the Norwich Concerts. Established, with others, the Norwich Musical Festival, 1824. Settled in London, 1825, and became bass singer, teacher, and musical critic of the *Spectator*, and a writer in the *Harmonicon*. Professor of music, Gresham College, in succession to Stevens, 1837. Conducted Norwich Festivals of 1839 and 1842. Founded the Purcell Club, and with Rimbault and Chappell, the Musical Antiquarian Society. Secretary of the Vocal Society. He died at Brentwood, March 12, 1863.

WORKS.—Three inaugural lectures (Gresham College), London, 1838; An address from the Gresham Professor of Music to the patrons and lovers of art,...London, 1838; The Vocal School of Italy in the sixteenth century, madrigals, full anthems, motets, and villanellas, adapted to English words, London [1839], A collection of Psalm tunes in various metres.. London, 1812; The People's Music Book (with J. Turle), London, 1844; The English Cathedral Service: its glory, its decline, and its destined extinction, London, 1845 (reprinted from the *British and Foreign Review*); The art of singing at sight (with Turle), London, 1846, 2nd edition, 1855; Airs of the Rhine, edited. Edited Purcell's "King Arthur" for the Musical Antiquarian Society. Translated librettos of Mozart's Requiem, Haydn's Seasons, Graun's Death of Jesus, Spohr's Last Judgment and Fall of Babylon. Songs: Guarda che bianca luna; I'll be a fairy; Rover's farewell, etc. He also edited Major's collection of Sacred Music [1820].

Taylor, Franklin, pianist and teacher, born at Birmingham, February 5, 1843. Studied under C. Flavell, pf., and T. Bedsmore, organ, taking the services for the latter at Lichfield Cathedral when eleven. Went to Leipzig in 1859, and studied at the Conservatorium under Plaidy, Moscheles, Hauptmann, and others. Left for Paris in 1861, and studied further with Madame Schumann. In 1862 he returned to London, and was engaged in teaching. He played at the Crystal Palace, February 18, 1865, Hiller's Concerto in F sharp minor; and made his first appearance at the Monday Popular Concerts, June 15, 1866, in a Beethoven programme. He has also played in Liverpool (Philharmonic), Birmingham—where he was a great favourite—and other places. Of

TAYLOR.

late years he has devoted himself chiefly to teaching, writing, and editing. He was sometime organist of Twickenham Parish Church, and St. Michael's, Chester Square. Was professor at the National Training School, 1876-82; at the R.C.M., 1883; now Member of the Board of Professors, and Member of the Associated Board. Examiner for South Africa, 1894. Member, and sometime Director, Philharmonic Society; and President of the Academy for the higher development of pf. playing. Author of Primer of Pianoforte Playing, Macmillan, 1877; Technique and Expression in Pianoforte Playing, Novello, 1897. Translator of Richter's Harmony, Cramer, 1864; Counterpoint, 1874; Canon and Fugue, 1878. Compiler of a Pianoforte Tutor, London, Enoch. Editor of Beethoven's Sonatas, 1-12, Boosey; Progressive Studies for pf. 52 books, Novello; Scales and Arpeggios, Novello's Primers, No. 53. Arrangement of Sullivan's Tempest Music, pf., four hands, etc. Contributor of some valuable articles to Grove's Dictionary of Music and Musicians.

Taylor, Harry James, organist and composer, born at Cheltenham, August 1, 1866. Articled pupil of J. A. Matthews. Gained National Prize, Trinity College, London, 1884. F.R.C.O., 1888. For several years organist to the Cheltenham Festival Society; in 1886 appointed organist and choirmaster, Parish Church, Cullompton, Devon; and from 1888 has held a similar position at Christ Church, Dover, and is also conductor of the Dover Choral Union. Hon. local examiner, R.C.M. His works include Two overtures, orchestra; Serenade, for strings and harps, Cheltenham Festival, 1896; String quartet; Trio in D minor, pf. and strings; Serenata; Gavotte, pf. and two violins. Pianoforte sonatas; Organ pieces, etc. Author of The Choralists' Handbook, and Historical facts relating to music (London, Weekes, 1894), which has gone through several editions.

Taylor, James, musician and writer, born at Norwich, October 7, 1781; died there June 7, 1855. Author of "A Course of Preceptive Lessons for the Spanish Guitar, designed for the assistance of master and pupil," London [1827]; and composer of Twelve easy preludes for the harp [1820]. He contributed essays on music to the *Quarterly Magazine* and *Review of Music,* 1818-29.

Taylor, James, Scottish musician of present century, issued "A Collection of Psalms, etc., with a familiar introduction to the theory and practice of vocal music," Aberdeen; Cornwall, n.d.

Another JAMES TAYLOR, who was a violinist at Elgin, issued "A Collection of Strathspeys and Reels, dedicated to Lady Dunbar, of Northfield," Elgin, n.d.

TAYLOR.

Taylor, John organist and writer, organist to the Queen at Kensington Palace'; Professor of Sight Singing, G.S.M., 1897. Author of "A Manual of Vocal Music," London, 1872; "Music and the Sol-fa Systems in Elementary Schools," London, 1873; Mutation Singing Method, London, 1873. "A few words on the Anglican Chant," London, n.d.; "Student's Text Book on the Science of Music," London, 1876; Music sheet Stave Modulator [1882]. The Stave Sight-Singing Method for use in army schools. How to sing at sight from the Staff, London, Philip & Son, 1897.

Taylor, Rev. John, clergyman and writer, born at Lancaster in 1694; died at Warrington in 1761. Author of "The Music Speech at the Public Commencement at Cambridge," London, 1730; "A Collection of Tunes in various Airs, with a scheme for supporting the spirit and practice of Psalmody in congregations," London, 1750.

Taylor, John Bianchi, composer and conductor, born at Bath in 1801. He was a distinguished teacher of singing. Died at Bath, April, 1876. Composed "A set of seven glees," Bath [1840]. Duets; Green leaves, part-song. Songs: Convent bell, Flowers, I ask thee not, I never can forget, Mariner's life, Moonlight, Oh peaceful lake, Slave wife, When I leave thee, etc.

Taylor, Richard, composer and writer, born at Chester in 1758. He died at Chester, February, 1813. Author of "The principles of music at one view," London, 1791; "Beauties of sacred verse," London, 1795, 3 vols. National songs. Composer of Buxom Joan, a burletta, 1778; A collection of favourite songs and an overture, London [1780]. *Glees:* Now Winter with her hoary train; The gloomy season's past; Summer now upholds her scenes; Clad in her brown vesture; Gently as the breathing gale. Songs, etc. His son, THOMAS, born at Chester in 1787, was organist of St. John's, Liverpool. He published "A Book of Original Chants," songs, etc.

Taylor, Robert, conductor and organist. While a child was organist at Badsey, Worcester, and Child's Wickham, Gloucester. Thence he entered Worcester Cathedral as a chorister, and was afterwards acticled to W. Done, and became his assistant organist. Appointed organist of St. Patrick's, Hove, Brighton, he established the Brighton Sacred Harmonic Society, of which he has been conductor since 1870, doing excellent work in the cause of music. In 1869 he was appointed organist of Brighton College, an office he held for nineteen years. With Dr. Alfred King he established the Brighton School of Music. He is choirmaster at the Church of St. Michael and All Angels, Brighton.

Taylor, Samuel Priestley, organist,

TAYLOR.

born in London in 1779. Son of Rev. James Taylor, Rector of Cumberland Street Chapel. When seven the boy played the organ for the choir of that Chapel, having previously sung in the choir of Surrey Chapel. He was taught music by John Whittaker, and Dr. Russell of Oxford. Went to New York in 1806, and was organist of Christ Church, when he introduced chanting. Played the clarinet and kettle-drums in the band of the American garrison, New York, in the war of 1812, and received a pension up to his death. Was president, 1812, of a musical organisation, now become the New York Philharmonic Society. His last public appearance was at Holy Trinity, Brooklyn, in 1865, when he played Luther's "Judgement Hymn" for a chorus of 100. In 1874 the Handel and Haydn Society of Brooklyn gave him a testimonial concert. Known as the oldest organist in the world, he died at New York, in the summer of 1875, at the age of 96.

Taylor, Sedley, M.A., author of "Sound and Music," a non-mathematical Treatise on the physical constitution of musical sounds and harmony.." London, 1873, 2nd edition, Macmillan, 1883.

He has lectured at the Birmingham and Midland Institute, on the "Physical basis of sound"; at the Musical Association on "Improved Notation"; on Bach's Church Cantatas, Cambridge, 1893; and elsewhere. Composer of part-songs, songs, and author of contributions to musical journals.

Taylor, Silas, composer, born at Harley, Shropshire, July 16, 1624; died November 4, 1678. Published "Court Ayres, or Pavins, Almaines, Corants, and Sarabands," London, 1655.

His brother, SYLVANUS, who died at Dublin in 1672, was a violinist.

Taylor, Mrs. Tom, born LAURA W. BARKER. Third daughter of the Rev. Thomas Barker, vicar of Thirkleby, Yorks. Married Mr. Tom Taylor, the dramatist, in June, 1855. Composed Sonata for pf. and violin, the Country Walk, 1860. "Ballads and Songs of Brittany..Translated by Tom Taylor, with some of the Original Melodies harmonized by Mrs. Tom Taylor," London, 1865. "Enone," cantata, 1850; Glees; Six Songs, London [1847]; Six Songs for voice and pf. [1852]; Music to "As You Like It," London, April 14, 1880; Songs of Youth, 1883, etc.

Taylor, William, organist and composer, born at Kidderminster, December 8, 1832. Studied under Dr. William Marshall. Graduated Mus. Bac., Oxford, 1854. Organist and choirmaster, St. John the Baptist, Kidderminster, 1849-68; and of the Parish Church from 1868. Honorary Borough organist. Compositions: Psalm 104, for soli, chorus, and orchestra; oratorio, St. John the Baptist

TEMPLETON.

(composed 1862; published 1879); Te Deum, Benedicite, Evening Service in F. Songs, etc.

Taylor, William Frederick, pianist and composer, born at Bristol in 1835; died in February, 1887. Composer of Diana, operetta, 1884; quartet for pf. and strings. Fantasias, galops, marches, gavottes, and numerous transcriptions for pf. Part-songs and songs. He gave concerts at which five of his own family took part.

Temple, Hope, composer, born in Dublin, of English parents. At the age of thirteen came to England to complete her education. Studied under J. F. Barnett and E. Silas; and in Paris with André Messager. Gave concerts, Steinway Hall, 1890, etc. Composer of an operetta, "The Wooden Spoon," and of a number of songs, among which may be named 'Tis all that I can say, An Old Garden, Were we lovers then? Mary Grey, A Mother's love, Queen of Roses, etc.

Temple, Richard, see COBB, Richard Barker.

Templeton, John, tenor vocalist, born at Riccarton, near Kilmarnock, July 30, 1802. One of a family of which other members were singers. He was precentor in Dr. Brown's Secession Church, Edinburgh, about 1822, but went to London, and studied under Blewitt, Welsh, and T. Cooke. Début on stage at Worthing, 1828 First appeared in London as *Belville* in Shield's "Rosina," October 13, 1831. Became associated with Malibran in 1833, and sang with her in opera in London with great success. Sang in Scotland, 1836. Appeared in the United States as lecturer and vocalist, 1845-6, and published his lecture as "A Musical Entertainment," Boston, 1845. He retired from public life in 1852. He sang in operas of Meyerbeer, Spohr, Mozart, Auber, Barnett, Balfe, Benedict, and Rossini, and was one of the most popular and refined ballad vocalists of his time. He died at New Hampton, near London, July 1, 1886. See Templeton and Malibran, reminiscences of these renowned singers, with original letters and anecdotes, by W. H. H., London, 1880, 3 portraits. He composed a few songs, "Put off! put off!" (Queen Mary's escape from Lochleven), etc.

His brother JAMES (born in 1784; died January 4, 1868), was an alto singer, and acted as precentor of St. Andrew's Parish Church, Edinburgh, for many years. ROBERT (born in 1790; died 1853), was a tenor, and held a precentor's appointment in a church in Kilmarnock. MATTHEW (born in 1792; died April 16, 1870), was a bass singer, and a teacher of music. ANDREW (born in 1796; died in June, 1841), was a precentor in Kirkwood's Relief Church at Edinburgh, and possessed a fine alto voice.

TENCH.

THOMAS.

Tench, Mrs. Albert, see CULLEN, Rose.

Thicknesse, Mrs. Philip, see FORD, Ann.

Thackeray, Duncan, organist, tenor vocalist and composer. Graduated Mus. Bac., Oxford, 1870; Mus. Doc., Dublin, 1871. Sometime organist of St. John's Church, Perth; later at Southgate, Middlesex. Since 1860 tenor in choir of Armagh Cathedral. He has composed two sacred cantatas for soli, chorus (8 part), and orchestra; Church Service; Songs, etc.

Thillon, Anna, born HUNT, soprano vocalist, born in London in 1819. Left England at the age of ten, and studied at Havre, marrying, when fifteen, M. Thillon, who was at one time principal first violin in Jullien's band. She made her *début* at the Théâtre de la Renaissance, Paris, November 17, 1838, in Grisar's "Lady Melvil"; and after singing in opera in Paris for some years, returned to England, and appeared first at the Princess's Theatre, May 2, 1844, as the Queen in Auber's "Crown Diamonds." She sang at the Philharmonic Concert on June 24 following, and later, in the provinces. Visited the Continent, and was in America, 1850-4. Returning to England, sang at Jullien's Concerts, 1854. Made her last appearance in opera at the Lyceum Theatre, May, 1855, in the "Crown Diamonds," and retiring from public life some years later, went to reside at Torquay.

Thirlwall, John Wade, composer and violinist, born at Shilbottle, Northumberland, January 11, 1809; died at London, June 15, 1876. He was leader of the band at Covent Garden Theatre, etc. Composer of a "Book of Ballads," 1843; Songs, violin music, etc.

His daughter ANNIE (born 1830; died, London, October 19, 1881), who married E. Dussek Corri (*q.v.*), was a soprano vocalist.

Thom, Rev. Robert Riach, clergyman, poet, and musician, born at Montrose, December 16, 1831. Educated at Edinburgh University, etc. Minister of Free St. David's, Glasgow, and afterwards of the Free High Church, Kilmarnock. He has composed a number of hymns and other music for the church, and in 1868 he edited a "Manual of Praise," containing music for the service of the church.

Thomas, see also APTOMMAS.

Thomas, Adelaide Louisa, pianist, born at Clapham, London. Scholar of the National Training School, Kensington; A.R.C.M. Gave pf. recitals in London, 1883, etc. In 1892 passed the examination for Mus. Bac., Oxford, but was not allowed to take the degree. Author of "A Royal Road to Pianoforte Playing," Williams; and composer of Festival Setting of Magnificat and Nunc Dimittis. Principal of the Scientific Training School for Music, 1894.

Thomas, Arthur Goring, composer, born at Ralton Park, near Eastbourne, Sussex, November 21, 1851. Intended for another profession, he did not enter upon the serious study of music until he was over twenty years of age. Studied at Paris, under Emile Durand, 1874-6; and subsequently at R.A.M., London, under Sullivan and Prout. Lucas Prizeholder, 1879-80. F.R.A.M. He resided in London, and devoted himself entirely to composition. His death was melancholy. Suffering from mental depression, he threw himself in front of a train at West Hampstead Station, March 20, 1892, and was instantly killed. A Goring Thomas Scholarship was founded, 1892, at the R.A.M.

WORKS.—*Operas :* The light of the Harem (R.A.M. composition, 1880); Esmeralda, produced by Carl Rosa, Drury Lane, March 26, 1883; Nadeschda (Julian Sturgis), the same, April 16, 1885; The Golden Web (left unfinished, scoring completed by S. P. Waddington), produced, Court Theatre, Liverpool, February 15, 1893. Choral Ode, The Sun-worshippers, Norwich Festival, 1881; Cantata, The Swan and the Skylark (orchestral score by C. V. Stanford), Birmingham Festival, 1894. Four vocal scenas, Hero and Leander (Lucas Prize), 1880, etc. Psalm for soprano solo, chorus and orchestra, R.A.M. concert, St. James's Hall, June 19, 1878. *Songs :* Twelve Lyrics; Lullaby; Breeze from shore; Song of Spain; Chanson de Mai; Know'st thou the land; A Summer land; The Kiss; Album of ten songs (selected from a number found among his MSS.), six are settings of French words by Victor Hugo, and others. Duet, The Dawn, Birmingham Festival, 1891; Duet, Sunset. Suite de Ballet, orchestra, composed for Cambridge University Musical Society, and produced, June 9, 1887; Sonata, pf. and violin, etc.

Thomas, C. N., amateur organist. For twenty-five years he was organist of St. George's Cathedral, Cape Town, resigning in 1888. A good baritone vocalist, he has taken an active part in musical doings in the colony, by his work at concerts as well as in the church.

Thomas, Cadwallader, bandmaster, born on November 15, 1838. Joined the band of the Coldstream Guards in 1853, and became serjeant in 1866, at that time being solo clarinet player. Bandmaster to the Duke of York's School, 1870-80; and on the retirement of Frederick Godfrey, 1880, was appointed bandmaster of the Coldstream Guards. This he held until early in 1896, when he retired.

Thomas, Dudley, tenor vocalist. Won the prize for tenors at the Crystal Palace Competitions, June 27, 1872. Was a member of Sidney Leslie's Royal English Opera Company, 1885; and also sang in Italian opera at

THOMAS.

Covent Garden in 1887. Later details are wanting.

Thomas, Evan William, violinist and composer, pupil of Spagnoletti. He played in the orchestra at the production of Weber's "Oberon," 1826. Most of his professional life was passed in Liverpool, where he was appointed leader of the Philharmonic band, 1850. He gave successful shilling Saturday Concerts in Liverpool, 1854; also classical chamber concerts in Manchester, 1853, etc. He composed a concerto in A minor, for violin and orchestra, 1863, and other pieces. Retired many years ago, and resided at Dinas Dinlle, North Wales, where he died October 4, 1892, in his 79th year.

Thomas, Florence A., see sub. MAR- SHALL, JULIAN.

Thomas, Frances, clarinet player of present time. She has been heard at concerts in London, Birmingham, etc., from 1878, and has gained a reputation for tone and execution.

Thomas, John, PENCERDD GWALIA, harpist and composer, born at Bridgend, Glamorganshire, March 1 (St. David's Day), 1826. When a child he played the piccolo, and then the harp, winning the prize of a triple harp at Abergavenny Eisteddfod when eleven years old. Through the influence of the Countess of Lovelace he was placed in the R.A.M. in 1840, where he studied the harp under J. B. Chatterton, and composition under Charles Lucas and Cipriani Potter. Many compositions, including an opera, "Alfred the Great," were written during his student days, and produced at the R.A.M. concerts. In succession he was elected Associate, Fellow, and Professor, R.A.M. In 1851 he was harpist at the Royal Italian Opera; and 1852-62, undertook annual tours on the continent, playing at Vienna, Berlin, Moscow, St. Petersburg, etc. Played at the Leipzig Gewandhaus Concerts, October 3, 1852, and again in January, 1861. In 1861 the title of *Pencerdd Gwalia* (Chief Bard of Wales), was conferred upon him at the Aberdare Eisteddfod. He gave his first concert of Welsh music at St. James's Hall, July 4, 1862, with a chorus of four-hundred voices, and a band of twenty harps, creating a great sensation. Some of his harp compositions were introduced. These concerts have been continued annually. In 1871 he was appointed Harpist to the Queen, in succession to the late J. B. Chatterton. That year he also was conductor of the Welsh Choral Union. By his efforts a Welsh Scholarship was founded at the R.A.M. in 1883, and which bears his name. He acted as adjudicator at the Eisteddfod at Chicago Exhibition, 1893; his cantata, "Llewelyn," was performed September 6, and gave a harp concert there, September 18. Public recog-

THOMAS.

nition of his services to music has not been wanting, and he has been elected Member of the Academy of St. Cecilia, and Philharmonic, Rome; Philharmonic, and Royal Musical Academy, Florence; Philharmonic Society, London. He is professor of the harp at R.C.M., and a Member of the Royal Society of Musicians, and of the I.S.M. At the Cardiff Conference, 1896-7, he gave a lecture on the Music of Wales.

WORKS.—Llewelyn, dramatic cantata, produced, Swansea Eisteddfod, 1863; The Bride of Neath Valley, a Welsh scene, Chester, 1866. The memory of love; The Minstrel; There be none of Beauty's daughters; and many other songs. Welsh patriotic songs, arranged for chorus and harp. Edited and arranged a Collection of Welsh Melodies, for voice, with harp or pf. accompaniment, 2 vols., 1862; later, 4 vols. *Harp:* Concerto in E flat, produced, Philharmonic Concert, May 3, 1852; Concerto in B flat. Duets for two harps; for harp and pf.; Two sets of six studies, and many pieces for harp solo. Romance and rondo piacevole, harp and violin. Transcription of Mendelssohn's Lieder ohne Worte, 8 books; Schubert's songs; Welsh melodies; Beethoven's Sonata, op. 27, No. 2; Handel's variations in E, etc.

Thomas, John. Born at Blaenanerch, Cardiganshire, December 11, 1839. Composer of many anthems, glees, and part-songs, of a popular type. Adjudicator and conductor of Psalmody Festivals.

Thomas, John L., IEUAN DDU, musician and editor, born near Carmarthen in 1795; died at Treforest, Glamorgan, June 30, 1871. He compiled "Y Caniedydd Cymreig: the Cambrian minstrel, being a collection of the melodies of Cambria, with original words in English and Welsh," Merthyr Tydvill, 1845. Thomas was a schoolmaster by profession.

Thomas, John Rogers, composer, and baritone vocalist, born at Newport, Monmouth, March 26, 1830. He went to the United States, and became a teacher and editor. He published "Church Music, a selection of Gems from the best masters," New York, 1863; Thomas' Sacred Music, a collection of psalm and hymn tunes, New York, 1863. Composed "The Pic-nic" cantata; "Diamond cut Diamond," operetta, 1876. *Songs:* After long years; Beautiful isle of the sea (1865), Bonnie Eloise; Cottage by the sea; Evangeline; Pretty Nelly; Thine alone; 'Tis but a little faded flower.

Thomas, Lewis William, bass vocalist, born at Bath. of Welsh parentage, April, 1826. He was brought up as a wood-carver, but developing a fine bass voice, he studied singing under Bianchi Taylor. In 1850 he was appointed lay-clerk in Worcester Cathedral, and, in 1852, master of the choristers,

THOMAS.

For some years he assisted at the Three Choirs' and Birmingham Festivals. He was a great favourite in Birmingham, and sang at the Festival Choral and other concerts for many years. He first appeared in London at St. Martin's Hall, December 20, 1854, in "The Messiah," at Mr. Hullah's concerts, and sang at the Sacred Harmonic concerts for the first time, November 23, 1855. The next year he settled in London, and was in the choir of St. Paul's Cathedral. This appointment he left in 1857 for the Temple Church, and about the same time was appointed a Gentleman of the Chapel Royal. He sang at the Temple Church until 1885, and resigned his position at the Chapel Royal in 1887. For a short time, about 1857, he sang in opera. During Mr. Joseph Bennett's visit to America, 1884-5, Lewis Thomas undertook his musical duties on the *Daily Telegraph*, and later was placed on the staff of that paper. From 1886 he edited *The Lute* for some time. He died, after a lingering illness, in London, June 13, 1896.

Thomas, Llewelyn, physician, born in 1848. M.D., Brussels. He was surgeon to the Central London Throat and Ear Hospital; Hon. physician to the R.A.M. and G.S.M. ; lecturer on Vocal Physiology, T.C.L., resigning in 1882. A Llewelyn Thomas Prize was instituted at the R.A.M., 1877, and continued in memory of him. It is a Gold Medal for declamatory English singing. Dr. Thomas died in London, November 26, 1884.

Thomas, Robert Harold, pianist and composer, born at Cheltenham, July 8, 1834. He studied at the R.A.M. under Bennett, Potter, and Blagrove, and played at concerts in London from about 1850. He was a professor of the pf. at the R.A.M. and the Guildhall School of Music. He died at London, July 29, 1885.

WORKS.—*Overtures :* Mountain, lake, and moorland, Philharmonic Society, February 19, 1880; "As you like it"..1864. Nocturnes, fantasias, and numerous transcriptions for the pf. Songs, etc.

Thomas, T. D., musician, compiled "Sacred Harmony : a selection of church music....for the use of country choirs...." Winchester [1815].

Thomas, Thomas, see APTOMMAS.

Thomas, William Edwin, organist and composer, born at Oxford in 1867. Chorister at Christ Church at age of seven, and pupil of Dr. Corfe; at the same time playing (Gregorian) services at St. Nicholas' Chapel, Oxford. Graduated Mus. Bac., 1888; Mus. Doc., 1894, Oxford. While still a chorister he was selected four successive years by Sir F. Ouseley to sing at his Festivals, St. Michael's, Tenbury. After acting as deputy at St. Paul's, Oxford, for some time, he was

THOMAS.

appointed to a church at Ellesboro', near Tring; but in a few months he returned to Oxford as organist and choirmaster of St. Mary and St. John, under Father Benson. In 1886 he was appointed organist and music master at All Saints', Bloxham, Banbury. There he founded a Choral Society which did good work. In 1894 he went to Bournemouth, obtaining the conductorship of the Boscombe Philharmonic Society there, and in 1895 was appointed to St. Clement's Church, which posts he still holds. His compositions comprise Psalm 71, for eight-part chorus and orchestra (1893) ; Communion Service in F ; Magnificat and Nunc Dimittis in D ; A prize madrigal (Brighton Philharmonic), "And wilt thou weep? " ; The School Song of All Saints', Bloxham (words by J. H. T. Goodwin, B.A.) ; serenade ; song, "The Holy Child," etc.

Thomas, William Henry, pianist, organist, and conductor, born at Bath, May 8, 1848. Son of Lewis W. Thomas. Removed with the family to Worcester, 1850, and frequently sang with the choir boys in the Cathedral, though not an enrolled member of the choir. Went to London in 1856. His studies were continued under his father for singing, J. B. Zerbini for pf., J. H. B. Dando violin, and E. J. Hopkins organ and harmony. Has been organist successively at St. Andrew's, Lambeth ; St. Martin's, Ludgate Hill ; St. George's, Tufnell Park from 1871 to present time. Has deputised at Crystal Palace for Jas. Coward, and at Chapel Royal for G. Cooper ; was formerly much engaged as accompanist at the Novello Concerts at the Albert Hall, etc. Conductor of Tufnell Park Choral Society from 1879 ; Popular Ballad Concerts ; Oratorios at the People's Palace ; and an earnest worker in the cause of musical education. Professor of singing at the Guildhall School from its foundation ; also at R.A.M. Examiner for Associated Board, R.A.M. and R.C.M. Editor of "Major and Minor Scales in various forms and rhythms." His younger brother, FRANK LEWIS THOMAS, studied at R.A.M. under W. G. Cusins and F. Ralph, and, after leaving there, studied with A. H. Thouless and C. S. Jekyll. His first appointment was as organist of Christ Church, Lancaster Gate, while the late W. H. Monk was choirmaster. From 1880 to present time he has been organist and C.M. of St. Mary's, Bromley, Kent. He founded the Bromley Musical Society, in 1880, and has conducted many important concerts each year since ; and has been frequently engaged as accompanist at the Covent Garden Promenade and Queen's Hall Concerts. He has composed a number of pieces for pf., and "I saw thee weep," "The impress of the Creator," "Love's wherefore," and other songs.

THOMPSON.

Thompson, Lady Henry, see LODER, Kate.

Thompson, General Thos. Perronet, political writer and musician, born at Hull, in 1783 ; died at London, September 6, 1869. Author of "Instructions to my Daughter for playing on the enharmonic guitar, being an attempt to effect the execution of correct harmony, on principles analogous to those of the ancient euharmonic," London, 1829. "Enharmonic theory of Music," London, 1829 ; Second edition issued as "Theory and practice of just intonation," London, 1850 ; Third ed.: "Principles and practice of just intonation, with a view of embodying the results of the Sol-fa Associations, as illustrated on the enharmonic organ . . ," London, 1859. Exercises . . , London, 1842, 6 vols. ; containing Enharmonic of the ancients, Harmonics of the violin, Musical periodicals, Jews harps, etc.

Thomson, Alexandra, composer of present time. Daughter of the Most Rev. W. Thomson, Archbishop of York (1819-1890). Studied under Dr. Naylor. Her setting of Campbell's "Battle of the Baltic," for chorus and orchestra, was produced October, 1890, at the Festival at Hovingham, Yorkshire. She has also composed some madrigals, "The shepherd's elegy," "Holiday in Arcadia," op. 12, etc.

Thomson, Rev. Andrew Mitchell, clergyman and musician, born at Sanquhar, Dumfriesshire, in June, 1778, baptized July 11, 1778. He was successively minister of Sprouston, Roxburgh, 1805-08 ; East Church, Perth, 1808-10 ; New Greyfriars' Church, Edinburgh, 1810-14 ; and St. George's Church, Edinburgh, 1814-31. He died at Edinburgh, February 9, 1831. Famous for his patronage of R. A. Smith, and for his efforts to promote good psalmody in the Church of Scotland. Edited "Sacred harmony for the use of St. George's Church, Edinburgh," 1820. He composed "St. George's, Edinburgh," "Redemption," and other well-known psalm tunes and some other pieces for the musical service of the church.

Thomson, Andrew, musician and violinist, was born about 1792. Teacher and violinist in Glasgow, where he died May 24, 1860. Author of a "New and improved Violin instructor," London, 1840. Compiler of "Evenings in Scotland, a collection of Scottish melodies," Glasgow [1845] ; "Selections from the melodies of Scotland, with characteristic words by W. H. Bellamy," London, 1851, 2 vols.

Another ANDREW THOMSON has published the "Dance Music of Scotland, arranged as sets, for dancing," Glasgow [1883], and dance music for flute, pf. music, etc.

Thomson, Andrew D., composer and

THOMSON.

teacher, who resided in Glasgow, and was teacher in the Free Church Normal School, 1846 till 1854. He held other appointments. Author of "Training-School Song Book," Glasgow, 1848-49, compiled with W. Sugden ; "Union Sacred Music Chap-Book," Glasgow [1853] ; Contributions to Mitchison's Psalm books, etc.

Thomson, George, collector and editor, born at Limekilns, Fife, March 4, 1757. Secretary to the Board of Trustees for the Encouragement of Arts and Manufactures in Scotland, 1780. He died at Leith, February 18, 1851. Published "A Select Collection of original Scottish airs for the voice, to each of which are added introductory and concluding Symphonies and accompanyments for the pianoforte, violin, and violoncello [by Pleyel, Kozeluch, Haydn, and Beethoven, vol. titles differ], with select and characteristic verses by the most admired Scottish Poets...." London [1793-1841], 6 vols: v. 1, 1793 ; 2, 1798 ; 3, 1799 ; 4, 1802 ; 5, 1818-1826 ; 6, 1841. Collection of the Songs of Burns, Sir Walter Scott, and other eminent lyric poets, ancient and modern, united to the select melodies of Scotland, and of Ireland and Wales, with symphonies and accompaniments for the pianoforte, by Pleyel, Haydn, and Beethoven, etc.....London, 1822, 6 vols. Select Collection of original Welsh airs, adapted for the voice, united to characteristic English poetry, with introductory and concluding symphonies [by Haydn, Beethoven, etc.], London, 1809, 3 vols. Select collection of original Irish airs, united to characteristic English poetry, with symphonies and accompaniments for the pianoforte, violin, and violoncello, composed by Beethoven, London, 1814-16, 2 vols. Twenty Scottish melodies, added in 1838-39 to G. Thomson's new edition of the Melodies, Edinburgh, 1839.

Thomson was an enthusiastic musician, and frequently gave musical parties and dances in his house His neighbours objected to the *noise*, and under cover of a new police act, Thomson was proceeded against and an injunction was obtained against him in the police courts. This case gave rise to a controversy to which Thomson contributed two pamphlets—"Statement and review of the recent decision of the judge of police in Edinburgh, authorizing his officers to make domiciliary visits in private families, and to stop dancing," Edinburgh, 1807 ; and a four-page "Postscript" on the same subject.

Thomson, James, musician, was precentor of Lady Yester's Church, Edinburgh, from 1800 to 1830. He was also a teacher of music at Leith. Author of "Rudiments of Music, to which is added a Collection of the best church tunes, hymns, canons, and anthems." Edinburgh, 1778, 3rd edition, 1793.

THOMSON.

Thomson, James, organist, composer and teacher, born at Kendal, November 15, 1832. Studied at R.A.M. under Sterndale Bennett and others. F.R.A.M. Has held organ appointments at King's Lynn, Torquay, Liverpool, and Belfast. Resident at Saffron Walden, and Professor at the Training College there, and at Cavendish College, Cambridge. Of his compositions a symphony in A was heard at Liverpool in 1869; and an Ode to Hope (1880), and a cantata "The Lady of the Lake, have been performed in public.

Thomson, John, composer, conductor, and professor, born at Sprouston, Roxburgh, October 28, 1805. Son of the Rev. Andrew M. Thomson. Became acquainted with Mendelssohn in Edinburgh, and renewed his acquaintance at Leipzig, where he studied under Schnyder von Wartensee. Returned to Edinburgh, and in 1839 became first Reid Professor of Music at the University. Conducted the first Reid Concert, February 12, 1841, at which for the first time analytical programmes were used. He died at Edinburgh, May 6, 1841.

WORKS.—*Operas:* Hermann, or the Broken Spear, London, 1834; The House of Aspen, London, 1834; The Shadow on the Wall, London, 1835. Vocal Melodies of Scotland, with symphonies and accompaniments by John Thomson and Finlay Dun, Edinburgh [1836], n.d.; New Edition, London, 1880. Minuetto for pf. and flute; Capriccio for pf. and violin. Bagatelle, 1831; Divertimento (duet); Polonaises; and waltzes for pf. *Songs:* Arab to his steed; Blow light, thou balmy air; Cleveland's farewell to Minna; Die tanti mei tormenti; Farewell, my love; If here still I linger; Lady! awake; Love, art thou waking or sleeping?; Love wakes and weeps; The merry moonlight hour; Midnight Dream; O, cauld to me; O! sweet be your slumbers; The pirate's serenade; Poor Camille; Song of Harold Harfager; Song of the Rhenish peasant; Song of the Spanish maid; The Savoyard's return; Where art thou?; Zara! art thou sleeping?; etc.

Thomson, Mrs., *see* LAIDLAW, ANNA ROBENA.

Thomson, William, Scottish musician, son of Daniel Thomson, King's Trumpeter in Edinburgh. He went to London, and became known as a singer. Published "Orpheus Caledonius, or a collection of the best Scotch songs set to Musick by W. Thomson," London [1725]; Second edition, London, 1733, 2 vols. This is the earliest printed collection of Scots songs with music and contains 50 melodies. The selection issued by John Playford in 1700 as "Collection of original Scotch tunes," is without the lyrics, which in Thomson's case, were pilfered from Ramsay's "Tea table miscellany" without acknowledgment.

THORNE.

Thorley, Thomas, English composer and vocalist, who flourished at the end of the 18th and beginning of the present centuries. He composed a large amount of vocal and instrumental music, among which may be mentioned an extraordinary piece of discriptive music called "The Siege of Algiers, a characteristic divertimento for the pf."..1820, containing passages respecting rockets and bombs bursting; ships on fire. Briton's triumph, christian slavery abolished for ever! etc. His other works include, "Ten voluntaries for the organ or harpsichord [1775]; Epitaph hymn on the death of the Princess Charlotte of Wales [1817]; Sacred cabinet, or divine repository, containing original hymns, etc., London [1818].

Thorndike, Herbert Elliot, baritone vocalist, born at Liverpool, April 7, 1851. Educated at Cambridge University, and while an undergraduate won the prize for baritone at the National Music Meetings, Crystal Palace, July 5, 1873. Studied at Milan under Francesco Lamperti, and on his return to England continued his studies with H. C. Deacon and Alberto Randegger. Sang at various concerts in London, and appeared at the Norwich Festival, and the Monday Popular Concerts in 1884; Crystal Palace, etc. In July, 1886, he sang at Drury Lane Theatre in Hervé's "Frivoli."

Thorne, Edward Henry, organist, pianist, and composer, born at Cranborne, Dorset, May 9, 1834. Musically educated at St. George's Chapel, Windsor, under (Sir) George Elvey. Organist successively at Henley-on-Thames, 1853; Chichester Cathedral, 1863; St. Patrick's, Brighton, 1870; St. Peter's, Cranley Gardens, London, 1873; St. Michael's, Cornhill, 1875; and St. Anne's, Soho, 1891 to present time. He has given concerts and pf. recitals in London, Brighton, and other places, for a number of years; recitals at Queen's Hall, 1895-6; and is conductor of St. Anne's Choral and Orchestral Society; and societies at Clapham and Worthing.

WORKS.—Psalm 57, for tenor solo, chorus, and orchestra, St. James's Hall (Willing's choir), February 26, 1884; Psalm 125; Magnificat and Nunc Dimittis, for soli, chorus, orchestra, and organ, composed for the Festival of the Sons of the Clergy; Church Services. *Anthems:* All Thy works praise Thee; Behold, the Lord, the Ruler, is come; In sweet consent; Let us now praise famous men (men's voices); The Lord that brought us; and others. Sacred Music for the home circle, 1859. Edited A Selection of single and double chants (1860?), London, Hamilton. Songs, various. Overture, Peveril of the Peak (prize), Promenade Concerts, Covent Garden, October 29, 1885. Two trios, pf. and strings; Sonatas for pf. and violin, and pf.

THORNE.

and 'cello; Sonata Elegia, pf. Romance, pf. and 'cello; Suite, pf. and clarinet, etc. Original compositions for organ, seven books; Organ pieces, various.

His son, HERBERT EDWARD, born at Henley-on-Thames, October 11, 1861, is a pianist and organist. Appointed to All Souls', South Hampstead; St. Saviour's, Brixton, 1884; and to Clapham Parish Church, 1891. He has appeared as pianist at his father's concerts at Brighton, 1882, etc. His daughter BEATRICE, born in London, April 14, 1878, made her *début* as a pianist at Princes' Hall in 1888; played at Jersey the same year; Brighton, 1890; and at her father's recitals, Queen's Hall, November, 1895; and 1896. She has composed some pieces for pf., of which a gavotte is published.

Thorne, George, comedian, son of the late Richard Samuel Thorne, dramatic manager. He has been associated with the D'Oyly Carte travelling companies for many years; and his impersonations of the characters of *Ko Ko, Jack Point*, the *Chancellor*, and others in the Gilbert-Sullivan operas, have been extremely popular.

Thouless, A. H., pianist and composer. Studied under James Harcourt at Norwich, and at R.A.M. Was appointed a professor of pf. at R.A.M. in 1867, and was also an Associate. He produced his pf. concerto in E flat, at the concerts of the International Exhibition, Kensington, 1873, himself playing the solo part. As accompanist to various concert parties, he toured in the provinces, 1877-80, etc. He composed a *Tantum Ergo*, and *O Salutaris*, that were performed at St. John's (R.C.) Church, Norwich, 1883; and a "Hymn to Diana," for soprano solo, and chorus, 1884. He died about the year 1893. H. THOULESS, tenor vocalist, was for years a member of Norwich Cathedral Choir.

Thudichum, Charlotte, soprano vocalist, born at Kensington, London. Her father, German by birth, is a physician of repute, F.R.C.O., and her mother is descended from a French Huguenot family. Miss Thudichum studied under Manuel Garcia at the R.A.M., and won the Parepa-Rosa Scholarship, 1880, and the Westmorland, 1882. In Paris she studied opera with Madame Viardot. Sang at the Monday Popular and Crystal Palace Concerts in 1883; for the Birmingham Festival Choral Society, November 1884; and elsewhere, early arriving at success. Took the part (with Miss Macintyre) of *Rebecca* in Sullivan's "Ivanhoe," 1891. Undertook a long tour, with success, in Australia, 1896-7.

Thumoth, Burk, Irish musician and flute player, of the latter part of last century. He issued "Six Solos for a German flute, violin, or harpsichord" [1740]; "Twelve Scotch and twelve Irish airs," London [1775]; "Forty-

TINNEY.

eight English, Irish, and Scotch airs with variations," London [1785].

Thunder, Henry G., pianist and composer, born near Dublin, February 10, 1832. He studied under Thalberg, and settled as a teacher and pianist in New York, where he also held appointments as organist of St. Augustine's, St. Clement's, and St. Stephen's Roman Catholic Churches. He died at New York, December 14, 1881. Composer of church music, songs, etc.

Thurnam, Edward, organist and composer, born at Warwick, September 24, 1825. Organist of Reigate Parish Church, 1849-1880; and conductor of Reigate Choral Society. He died at Reigate, November 25, 1880. Composer of music for the church. Songs, and pf. music.

Tiagya Raj, composer, born at Trivadi, Tanjore, in the Presidency of Madras, India. He was the composer of many sacred songs, called Kruthis, and other pieces. He flourished from about 1820-1840.

Tiley, Joseph Crispin, composer, was born in 1843. He graduated Mus. Bac., Oxford, in 1866, and Mus. Doc., in 1874. Organist of Christ Church, Rotherhithe; St. Matthew's Episcopal Chapel, Westminster, 1862; St. Michael, Bassishaw, 1864. Gave recitals, 1866. Being possessed of private means he devoted himself chiefly to musical composition, but only a few of his pieces were published, and these chiefly in the *Organists' Quarterly Journal*, 1882-84. He died at London, July 1, 1879.

Tilleard, James, editor and composer, born in 1827; died, January 17, 1876. He edited "Collection of sacred music, for the use of schools," London, 1849; "Secular music for schools," 1851; "The People's Chant Book," 1853; "Patriotic Part-songs," London [1864], 19 Nos. Composer of Te Deums, anthems, part-songs and songs.

Timbrell, Francis, musician of the 18th century, issued "The Divine Musick Scholar's Guide, with the famous Mr. Tho: Ravenscroft's Psalm tunes in four parts, corrected and revised. To which is added a choice collection of new psalm tunes, hymns and anthems. Also rules and directions for playing on the spinnet, harpsichord, or organ," London [1715].

Tinney, Charles Ernest, bass vocalist, born at Pimlico, London, March 15, 1851. Chorister at Westminster Abbey, under J. Turle. Sang at Alexandra Palace, April 1, 1876, in revival of Handel's "Susanna," and at various concerts. In 1877 he was appointed to the choir of St. Paul's Cathedral, and professor at the Guildhall School, 1883. These he gave up for a professorship at the New England Conservatory, Boston, U.S.A., remaining in America four years. Returning to England in 1890, he was appointed professor

TINBUTT.

of singing at the Royal Normal College for the Blind, Trinity College, London, and other institutions. He is choirmaster of All Saints', Blackheath; and conductor of the Blackheath Glee and Madrigal Club. He is the composer of an Evening Service in D, several anthems, songs, etc.

Tirbutt, John Charles Brettel, organist and conductor, born at Bromsgrove, Worcestershire, March 30, 1857. Studied under private teachers. Graduated Mus. Bac., Durham, 1891. Has been organist of All Saints', Reading, from 1879; organist to the Reading Philharmonic, 1884; Conductor of Berkshire Amateur Musical Society, and lecturer in music University Extension College, Reading, 1892. His compositions are Psalm 130, for soli, chorus and strings; "The Phantom Ship," for chorus and orchestra, produced, Reading, May 8, 1890; "The Vale of Pearls," cantata for female voices; anthems, songs, part-songs, etc.

Tofts, Catherine, English soprano vocalist, of the 18th century. She was the first English vocalist who attempted Italian opera, and appeared in "Arsinoe," "Camilla," "Rosamond," and "Love's Triumph." She is said to have been very avaricious, and was continually mixed up in the broils and rivalry which early beset the Italian opera in England. Latterly she married Mr. Joseph Smith, British Consul at Venice. She was living in Venice in 1735, and is supposed to have become insane, but is said to have died in 1760.

Tolhurst, George, composer and organist, was born in 1827. He was a teacher in London, and for some time acted as organist of Melbourne Cathedral. He died at Barnstaple, January 18, 1877.

WORKS.—Ruth, oratorio, Melbourne, 1867. Christmas, song and chorus, 1846. Songs: England the land of the free; Fear thou not, for I am with thee; Little brown jug; Pray without ceasing; There's sunshine in the sky; Where there's a will. His father, WILLIAM HENRY TOLHURST, who was born on October 23, 1798, conducted the first performance of "Ruth" in Melbourne. He died there in 1873. HENRY TOLHURST, brother of W. H. and uncle of George, was born on April 19, 1778. Died after 1820. Composer of "Six Anthems and six Psalms, for use of country choirs"; Chart Sutton [1810]; Glee, "As I saw fair Clora," etc.

HENRY TOLHURST, violinist and composer, born London, September 24, 1854, son of HENRY TOLHURST, brother of GEORGE [born September 6, 1825; died at Maidstone, May 28, 1864] is conductor of the Lee (Kent) Philharmonic Society. Author of Cramer's Rudimentary Tutor for the violin [1891]; Gavottes, Berceuse, Andante, Allegretto, etc. for violin; also songs, etc.

TOMS.

Tollet, Thomas, author of "Directions to play the French Flageolet"; and composer, with John Lenton, of "A Consort of Musick in three parts," 1694; also of "Tollet's Ground" [1720].

Tomkins, Thomas, organist and composer, was born at Gloucester in 1586. He became a chorister in Gloucester Cathedral. Educated at Magdalen College, Oxford. Mus. Bac., Oxon., 1607. He studied under Byrd, and became a Gentleman of the Chapel Royal in 1621, and organist in 1621. Organist of Worcester Cathedral. He died at Worcester, in June, 1656. He composed "Songs of 3, 4, 5 and 6 parts," 1622; "Musica Deo Sacra et Ecclesiæ Anglicanæ, or Musick dedicated to the Honor and Service of God..," London, 1664 (issued in 10 parts).

His father, the Rev. THOMAS, who was a minor canon in Gloucester Cathedral, composed "The Faunes and Satirs tripping," madrigal in the "Triumphs of Oriana."

His brother JOHN (died, London, September 27, 1638), was organist of King's College, Cambridge, 1606, and afterwards of St. Paul's Cathedral, London.

Another brother, GILES, was organist successively of King's College, Cambridge, and Salisbury Cathedral, till his death in 1668.

Tomlins, William Lawrence, conductor and teacher of singing, born in London, February 4, 1844. Studied under G. A. Macfarren and E. Silas. Settled in America, 1869. Conductor of Apollo Glee Club, Chicago, from 1875; Choral Director, Chicago Exhibition, 1893. Member of American College of Musicians. Author of a work on Elementary vocal tuition, "Children's Songs, and how to sing them," Boston, Ditson, 1885 (?) A paper on "Music and Education," delivered at Indianapolis, February, 1897, etc.

Tomlinson, Henrietta, see MIDGLEY, SAMUEL.

Tomlinson, Richard, composer and conductor, born at Sheffield, August 22, 1822. Self-taught in music. Choirmaster since about 1860 of the Primitive Methodist Chapel, Heeley, near Sheffield. Composer of "Original Tunes, Anthems, etc.," 1879, etc., and of various hymns, etc.

Toms, Charles James, pianist, born at Devonport, July, 1824. Son of JAMES TOMS, professor of music at Plymouth. Entered R.A.M. about 1839, studying harp and pf. under J. B. Chatterton, F. B. Jewson, and Cipriani Potter. King's Scholar, 1841. Settled in Liverpool, 1844, on leaving the Academy, when he was made an Associate, and later, elected a Fellow. Was pianist to the Liverpool Philharmonic Society, and a successful teacher. Died about 1880.

JOHN R. TOMS, organist of St. John's, Wellington, Somerset, has been many years

TONKING.

engaged in that town as teacher and concert giver. His son, EDWARD JOHN KELWAY TOMS, born January 25, 1863, studied at R.A.M. He was a skilful organist; gave recitals at the Fisheries Exhibition, Kensington, 1883; concerts at Wellington, etc. A promising career was cut short by his death, of typhoid fever, August 24, 1890, at the age of 27.

Tonking, Henry Charles, violinist, organist, and composer, born at Camborne, Cornwall, January 17, 1863. He was taught the violin by his father, a very clever amateur, and when quite a child appeared at concerts in different parts of Cornwall. He then studied under J. H. Nunn, of Penzance, and in 1876 was appointed organist of Illogan Parish Church, Cornwall. In 1881 he entered the R.A.M., studying under Sainton, Steggall, Prout, G. A. Macfarren, and others. He was organist of Westminster Chapel, 1883; the Royal Aquarium, 1886; Covent Garden Opera, 1888; and at different churches, the last being St. Lawrence, Jewry. As a recitalist he has been heard at the different exhibitions at South Kensington; and has played at the Earl's Court Exhibitions, 1892-5; Edinburgh, Glasgow, and St. George's Hall, Liverpool; and was one of those selected to compete for the Birmingham Town Hall appointment in 1888. He has been violinist in the orchestras of the Royal Italian Opera; Leeds and Norwich Festivals; and, with Bernard Carrodus, has given organ and violin recitals in various parts with much success. He is now devoting himself to composition, and has published All the world to me; Do you love me? and other songs; organ pieces, etc.

Topliff, Robert, organist and composer, was born in 1793. He was organist of Holy Trinity, Southwark, London. Died at London in 1868. He was blind. Editor of " Selection of the most popular melodies of the Tyne and Wear, harmonised, with appropriate words, symphonies. etc.," London [1820]; " Scripture Melodies, the words from Holy Writ," London, 2 vols, n.d.; Six Sabbath Melodies, 1844; Original Sabbath Melodies, issued in parts. *Songs:* Consider the lilies, Heaven our home, How blest were I in yonder cot, Let the night darken in, Look from thy lattice, Spirit's call, etc.

Torrance, Rev. George William, composer, born at Rathmines, Dublin, 1835. Chorister, Christ Church Cathedral, and later, organist of St. Andrew's and St. Anne's, Dublin. In 1856 visited Leipzig for further study in music. Graduated B.A., 1864; M.A., 1867, Dublin. Ordained Deacon, 1865; Priest, 1866. In 1869 he emigrated to Australia, settling in Melbourne. Ten years later the degrees of Mus. Bac. and Mus. Doc. were conferred upon him by Trinity College, Dublin, on the recommendation of Sir

TORRINGTON.

Robert P. Stewart, professor of music at the University. Member of the Board of Examiners in Music under the Education Department of Victoria; Mus. Doc., *ad eundem,* Melbourne University; Incumbent of Holy Trinity, Balaclava until 1895, when he was preferred to St. John's, Melbourne. Author of several papers on music.

WORKS.—*Oratorios :* Abraham, produced in Dublin, 1855; The Captivity, Dublin, 1864; The Revelation, Melbourne, June, 1882. Te Deum and Jubilate. Anthems and services. Opera, William of Normandy. Part-songs. *Songs :* Angel of Light, with 'cello obligato; The Land beyond the Sea, etc.

Torrington, Frederick Herbert, conductor, organist, violinist, and pianist, born at Dudley, Worcestershire, October 20, 1837. His early studies were under local teachers, and he was afterwards articled to Mr. James Fitzgerald, of Kidderminster. In 1853, he was appointed organist and choirmaster at St. Anne's, Bewdley; and in 1856 he left England for Montreal, Canada, where he became organist of Great St. James's Church, an office he held for twelve years. While there he was solo violinist, leader of orchestras, conductor, and for a time bandmaster of the 25th Regiment, King's Own Borderers, organ recitalist, etc. He was invited to furnish an orchestral contingent to represent Canada at the Peace Jubilee, Boston, in 1872; and was offered and accepted the position of organist and music director at King's Chapel, Boston, remaining there four years, teaching at the New England Conservatory of Music, and being one of the first violins in the Harvard Symphony, Handel and Haydn, and other societies. Gave recitals at Plymouth Church, Brooklyn (Ward Beecher's). In 1873 he accepted the post of organist and choir-master at the Metropolitan Church, Toronto, Canada, and conductor of the Toronto Philharmonic Society, holding both appointments to the present time. By his energy and skill the musical resources of the district were developed and in 1886 the first Toronto Festival was held under his direction. Since that time he has introduced many important compositions. He founded the Toronto College of Music in 1888, of which he has been musical director to the present time, doing much for the cause of musical education. In 1891, he made a tour of Europe, visiting the great music schools and studying their organizations. He conducted the festival at the inauguration of the new Massey Music Hall, Toronto, June, 1894; the Jubilee performance of "Elijah," Massey Hall, November 28, 1896, and is actively engaged in promoting the cause of music in Canada. He has composed church services, hymn-tunes, choruses and songs; organ voluntaries, etc.

TOSH.

Tosh, James Westwood, teacher and conductor, born at Dundee, January 16, 1849, Has been chiefly engaged in music teaching in connection with the School Boards of Jarrow, Sunderland, and London. Author of " The Musical Inspection, and how to prepare for it," London (Curwen), 1888 ; "Sight-singing, voice and ear training for Schools," 1889, etc.

Towers, John, organist and writer on music, born at Salford, Lancashire, February 18, 1836. Chorister in Manchester Cathedral and afterwards studied at R.A.M., 1856, and with Adolph Marx, Berlin, 1857. Organist of Wilmslow Parish Church, 1863 ; St. Stephen's Conell, Manchester, and conductor of glee societies at Rochdale and neighbourhood for some years. Went to America, and in 1890 was appointed director of the vocal department in the School of Music, Indianapolis ; and in 1892, to Utica Conservatorium. Author of " Beethoven, a Centenary Memoir ;" "The Mortality of Musicians ;" a lecture ; "Some Lancashire-born Musical Worthies" (1888), etc.

Towerson, Rev. Gabriel, D.D., clergyman and writer, born in 1635. Rector of St. Andrew Undershaft. He died in 1697. Author of " A Sermon concerning Vocal and Instrumental Musick in the Church," London, 1696.

Townsend, Horace, author of "An Account of the visit of Handel to Dublin." Dublin, 1852. "The moral uses of music, a lecture." Dublin, 1862.

Townsend, John, flute player and author, born in Yorkshire about 1795. He studied under Müller and Ware, and was a teacher and performer in Manchester. He died at Lytham on April 2, 1864. Author of " New and complete Flute preceptor." London, n.d.

Townsend, Mrs., author of a "Floral music book for young learners." London, 1862.

Townsend, Pauline D., author of " Haydn." London, 1884. Published in the Great Musicians Series, and translator of Otto Jahn's " Mozart," 3 vols. London, Novello, 1882.

Townsend, William, pianist and teacher, was born at Edinburgh, November 26, 1849, He studied at the Royal Academy of Music, London (1865-68), under Bennett, Goss, Holmes, etc., and afterwards at Leipzig (1871-72), under E. F. Richter and Reinecke. In 1870 he became an Associate of the R.A.M., and has acted as an examiner for the Royal College of Music since 1883. He has given many recitals of high-class music in Edinburgh.

Towsey, Arthur, conductor and organist, was musically educated at St. Michael's College, Tenbury. He went to New Zealand, and is now conductor of the Auckland Orchestral Union. He has given some excellent

TRAVERS.

concerts, and done good work. At the Wellington Industrial Exhibition, 1896-7, he gave a series of organ recitals.

Tozer, Augustus Edmonds, organist and composer, born at Sutton, Cheshire, January 13, 1857. Studied at R.A.M., and was City of London Scholar, National Training School, Kensington. F.R.C.O., 1876 ; L.R.A.M. (pf. performer), 1882 ; A.R.C.M. (theory and composition), 1887. Mus. Bac., Durham, 1893 ; Mus. Bac., Oxford, 1895, and qualified for Mus. Doc., November of the same year. Appointed organist and choirmaster, St. Mary Magdalene, St. Leonards-on-Sea, and choirmaster, Holy Trinity, Hastings, 1876 ; Hon. organist, St. Mary, Star-of-the-Sea, Hastings, 1884 ; St. Gregory's Priory Church, Cheltenham, 1885 ; Church of the Sacred Heart, West Brighton, 1888. In 1890 he received from Pope Leo XIII., the order of Chevalier of the Pontifical Order of St. Sylvester, for his services to Roman Catholic Church Music. He has composed six Masses ; Te Deum ; Motets ; Magnificats ; Antiphons, etc. Editor of Catholic hymns, with accompanying tunes ; Complete Benediction Manual ; and Modern Church Music for Catholic Choirs.

Tozer, Ferris, organist, tenor vocalist, and composer, born at Exeter, November 8, 1857. Chorister, Exeter Cathedral, and pupil of Alfred Angel and D. J. Wood. Graduated Mus. Bac., 1891 ; Mus. Doc., 1896, Oxford. At eighteen he was appointed organist of St. David's, Exeter ; and in 1882, of St. Michael's, Heavitree, Exeter. Well-known in the Western and Southern Counties as a tenor vocalist. He holds a position in the Devon and Cornwall Bank, Exeter.

WORKS.—Psalm 3, for soli, chorus, and strings ; oratorio, Baalam and Barak, produced at the Western Counties' Musical Association Festival, Exeter, April 22, 1897 ; cantata, King Neptune's Daughter, female voices. Morning and evening service in F ; Benedicite ; Kyries, etc. Postlude in D minor, organ. Songs, of which Lead Kindly Light has acquired much popularity. Pieces for pf., etc. The flight of Summer, prize, Exeter Madrigal Society. Edited and arranged a book of Sailors' songs or chanties (collected by Capt. F. J. Davis, of the P. & O. Service), London, Boosey, 1887.

Traubner, Eliza, see KINLOCK, ELIZA.

Travers, John, composer and organist, born about 1703. Chorister in St. George's Chapel, Windsor. He studied under Greene and Pepusch, and became organist of St. Paul's, Covent Garden, 1725, and afterwards organist at Fulham. Organist of Chapel Royal May 10, 1737. He died in 1758. Published " The Whole Book of Psalms for one, two, three, four, and five voices, with a Thorough Bass for the Harpsichord," London, 1746, 2

TRAVIS.

TROMAN.

vols. " Eighteen Canzonets for two and three Voices, the words chiefly by Matthew Prior," London [1745]. " Twelve Canzonets for two and three Voices." *Anthems:* Ascribe unto the Lord; Ponder my words; Keep, we beseech Thee, O Lord. XII. Voluntaries for the organ or harpsichord [1760]. *Songs:* Bibs, Bright author of my present flame; Haste my Nanette ; When vernal airs, etc.

Travis, Deborah, *see* KNVYETT, DEBORAH.

Tree, Anna Maria, mezzo-soprano vocalist and actress, born at London in 1802. Sister of Mrs. Charles Kean. She studied under Lanza and Tom Cooke, making her first appearance at Bath, as Polly, in the Beggar's Opera, 1818. Afterwards she appeared at Covent Garden as Rosina, in the Barber of Seville, 1819, and from that time till her marriage in 1825 to Mr. James Bradshaw, a rich tea merchant and member of parliament, she was a popular singer and actress. In May, 1823, she sang in Payne and Bishop's " Clari, the Maid of Milan," being the first to sing " Home, sweet home," and her other parts were chiefly in minor English opera. She died at London, February 17, 1862. Her sister, ELLEN TREE (1805-1880), was the celebrated actress who was married to Charles Kean. She also had a voice of some sweetness and power.—This cancels the notice under Bradshaw on page 57.

Tregarthen, William Coulson, organist, born at Penzance, September 17, 1856. Articled pupil of George Riseley, and pupil of Dr. S. S. Wesley. Mus. Bac., Trinity College, Toronto, 1892. Went to South Africa, where he has held organ appointments at the Collegiate Church of St. Mary's, Port Elizabeth; Queenstown, and other places; and is now organist of St. George's Church, Johannesburg. He has given organ recitals and concerts, and done good work in the cause of musical education in the country where he has made his home.

Treherne, Georgina, *see* WELDON GEORGINA.

Tremain, T., organist and composer of latter part of the 18th century. Composed " Thirteen Canzonets for two voices, op, 5 " [1786] ; Brown Jugg, canzonet for two voices [1780] ; Do not ask me, charming Phyllis (3 voices) 1780; Six Sonatas for the Harpsichord or Pf., op. 4 ; Six Concertos for strings, oboes, and horns [1790].

Trembath, Henry Gough, organist and composer, born at Penzance, Cornwall, July 29, 1844. Studied at R.A.M. Graduated Mus. Bac., Oxford, 1869; hon. fellow, College of Organists, 1875 ; organist at Truro : and from 1874 at St. John Baptist, Woodlands, Isleworth. Composer of a Sonata in D minor, Impromptu, and other pf. pieces ; Songs, One Day, The Miner and his boy, etc. ;

also an anthem, Let not your hearts be troubled.

Trew, Charles A., pianist and composer of present time. Sometime organist of St. Paul's, Rusthall, Tunbridge Wells. Resident in London, where for some time he has given annual concerts. His compositions embrace a trio for pf. and strings, Musical Artists' Society, 1884 ; Sonata in D minor; Romance ; and other pieces for violin and pf. Author of Harmony Lessons, adapted for classes, London, Schott, 1888. His wife, SUSAN TREW, is also a pianist and composer, and among her works a sonata for violin and pf. was produced by the Musical Artists' Society, June 26, 1893.

Trickett, Arthur, organist, pianist, and composer, born at Coventry. F.R.C.O. Held organ appointments at Coventry ; Holy Trinity, Birmingham ; and Hackney Parish Church. Conductor of Coventry Musical Society to 1883 ; societies in Birmingham and London. Appeared as pianist at concerts in Birmingham, etc. Composer of musical sketches for pf. and orchestra ; Notturno, Capriccietto, and other pieces for pf., Songs, etc.

Trimnell, —., the oldest lay clerk of Bristol Cathedral. Died at Clifton, January 23, 1865, having retired on a pension several years previously. He was a sound and enthusiastic musician, and much respected.

THOMAS TALLIS TRIMNELL, his son, was born at Bristol, and at the age of eight became a chorister in the cathedral, afterwards being articled to J. D. Corfe, cathedral organist. Graduated Mus. Bac., Oxford, 1875. He held organ appointments at Clifton, Chesterfield, Sheffield Parish Church, 1875-86. Director of Derby Choral Union, 1882. In 1886 he went to New Zealand, and was organist at St. Mary's, Parnell, Auckland ; and later of St. Peter's, Wellington. He was well known as an executant, giving recitals at the Bow and Bromley Institute, Albert Hall, Sheffield, etc. In New Zealand he has given recitals in different places. He has composed church services and anthems, "The Earth is the Lord's " was performed at the opening of the Wellington Exhibition, November 18, 1896. His brother, WILLIAM FREDERICK, was also a chorister in Bristol Cathedral. Organist and Musical Director, Clifton College, to 1896, when he resigned.

Trinks, C., organist of St. John's Church, Calcutta, edited " Hindoostanee Songs," Calcutta, n.d.

Troman, Thomas, organist and composer, born at Old Hill, Cradley, Worcester, March 21, 1839. Studied under local teachers, and was organist of Cradley Parish Church in 1848. Then appointed to Rowley Regis, 1855 ; Halesowen, 1862 ; Smethwick Old Church,

TROTTER.

1869; St. John's, Ladywood, Birmingham, 1880; Handsworth Parish Church, 1882. Graduated Mus. Bac., Oxford, 1875. Conducted the first Festival of Choirs of Handsworth Rural Deanery, 1885. Invested as Grand Organist, Grand Lodge of Mark Masons, 1889. Went to Boulogne, 1889, as organist of St. John's Church; and in 1892 was appointed to St. George the Martyr, Deal. Conductor of Deal and Walmer Choral Society. His compositions include Psalm 137, for soli, chorus, and orchestra; services, anthems, etc. Pieces for organ, Melodie for pf. organ, viola, 'cello, and bassoon; Romance, 'cello, and pf., etc.

Trotter or **Trotère, Henry,** composer, born in London, December 24, 1855. Composer of a number of songs: Once for all; Toreador, Hola! Léonore; The Deathless Army; Asthore; Ever dear; Love can wait, etc.

Trotter, Thomas Henry Yorke, organist and composer, was born at Great Stainton, Durham, November 6, 1854. Educated at Durham School, and at Oxford. Graduated B.A., 1878; M.A., 1887; Mus. Bac., 1887; Mus. Doc., 1892, Oxford. He is Director of Studies at the London Organ School, and is the composer of a number of works, which mostly remain in MS.

Troup, Emily Josephine, composer of present time. Of her songs may be named Spring showers; On a faded violet; Portuguese love song, etc. She has also written Song by the river; Hark! the lark; Trios for ladies' voices; Two sketches, violin and pf., etc.

Troutbeck, Rev. John, clergyman and musician, born at Blencowe, Cumberland, November 12, 1832. He was educated at Oxford, and graduated B.A., 1856; M.A., 1858. From 1865 to 1869 he was precentor of Manchester Cathedral, and in 1869 he became canon of Westminster. He has published "The Manchester Psalter," 1868; Manchester Chant Book, 1871; "The Cathedral Paragraph Psalter," Novello, n.d.; "Hymn Book for use in Westminster Abbey"; "Music Primer for Schools," London, 1873 (with Reginald F. Dale), other editions; "Church Choir Training," London [1879]. English words for Beethoven's "Mount of Olives," Gade's "Crusaders," Wagner's "Flying Dutchman," etc.

Trowbridge, Leslie, soprano vocalist, studied at R.A.M. Gave her first concert in the R.A.M. concert room, May 16, 1883; and has given concerts at the Portland Rooms, etc. She is the composer of a Mass in D; My rose; Our love; and other songs.

Troyte, Arthur Henry Dyke, *born* ACLAND, amateur musician, was born at Killerton, near Exeter, May 3, 1811. He was

TUDWAY.

second son of Sir Thomas Dyke Acland of Killerton, and was educated at Harrow and Oxford. He studied for the bar, and also was much engaged in scientific pursuits. In 1852 he changed his name to Troyte. He died at Bridehead, near Dorchester, Dorset, June 19, 1857. He composed the well-known chants bearing his name which were composed at the request of Bishop Hamilton of Salisbury, and first appeared in the "Salisbury Hymn Book," 1857. He also composed a number of hymns, and wrote "Liturgia Domestica," a book of family prayers; "The Hours"; "Daily steps towards heaven"; and "Letters on Musical Notation," London, 1841.

Trust, Helen Mary, *born* STARK, soprano vocalist, born at Norwich. Great-niece of the artist James Stark. Educated at Norwich and Paris. Sang for some time as an amateur. Studied chiefly in London under Signor Tramezzani, of Naples. One of her earliest professional appearances was in the Town Hall, Birmingham, in October, 1887. In the season 1891-2, she frequently sang at the Monday Popular Concerts; at the Leeds Festival, 1892; and at the production of Barnett's "Wishing Bell," and Gaul's "Una," at the Norwich Festival, 1893. She formed one of the party in Madame Patey's farewell tour, and was with that artist when she died. Mrs. Trust now holds a high position among vocalists of the time.

Trydell, Rev. John, author of "Two Essays on the theory and practice of Music," Dublin, 1766.

Tubbs, Mrs. F. Cecilia, translator of Dr. Joseph Schlüter's "General History of Music," London, 1865.

Tucker, Isaac, composer, of Westbury Leigh, Wilts; born in 1761; died in 1825. Composer of "Sacred Music, consisting of melodies composed for three and four voices," London [1800]; "Sacred Music, consisting of Psalm and Hymn tunes," London [1810].

Tucker, Rev. William, composer of the 17th century. He was a gentleman of the Chapel Royal, and a minor canon and precentor of Westminster Abbey, 1660. He died at London, February 28, 1678, and was buried in Westminster Abbey. Composer of anthems and other Church music.

Tudway, Thomas, composer and organist of the 17th century, was born about 1650. He was a chorister in the Chapel Royal under Dr. Blow, from 1660. Layvicar St. George's Chapel, Windsor, 1664. Organist of King's College, Cambridge, 1670. Instructor of choristers, King's College, 1679-80. Organist of Pembroke College. Mus. Bac., Cantab., 1681. Professor of music in Cambridge University, 1704. Mus. Doc., Cantab, 1705. Suspended from his University offices, 1706-7. Resigned his organ at

TULLY.

TURNER.

King's College in 1726, and retired to London, where he employed himself in forming a collection of music for Edward (Lord Harley) Earl of Oxford. He died in 1730.

WORKS.—A Collection of the most celebrated Services and Anthems used in the Church of England, from the Reformation to the Restoration of K. Charles II., composed by the best masters and collected by Thomas Tudway...," 6 vols [1715-1720], now preserved in MS. in the British Museum, London. Of this collection a list will be found in the British Museum Catalogue of MS. Music. From it a number of services and anthems have been printed at various times. Tudway composed various anthems, motets, services, and songs.

Tully, James Howard, composer and conductor, born in 1814. He was conductor of the opera at Drury Lane Theatre and elsewhere. He died at London, January 28, 1868.

WORKS.—*Operas:* The Desert, 1847; Forest maiden, 1847; Island Jewels, 1850; King Charming, 1851; Loan of a Lover, 1834; Rape of the Lock, 1837; William and Susan, 1859. *Songs:* Happy muleteer, I'm a light bright water sprite, Katty Moyle, Lovely May, Noreen, Summer hours, etc. Dance music for pf., etc.

Tunsted, Simon, English Franciscan monk and Doctor of Theology, born at Norwich early in the 14th century. He died at Bruzard, Suffolk, 1369. Author of "De Musica Continua et Discreta cum Diagrammatibus," and "De Quatuor Principalibus in quibus totius Musicæ Radices Consistunt," two works preserved in MS. in the Bodleian Library, Oxford.

Turges, Edmund, musician and composer of the 15th century. One of the contributors to the Fayrfax MSS. in the British museum. An anthem: "Enforce yourself as God's own knight," was published by Novello in 1894.

Turle, James, organist, composer, and writer, born at Somerton, Somerset, March 5, 1802. Chorister in Wells Cathedral, 1810-13. Organist of Christ Church, Southwark, 1819-1829, and of St. James', Bermondsey, 1829-31. Assistant organist to Greatorex at Westminster Abbey till 1831, and succeeded him as organist and master of the choristers, 1831. Music-master at the School for the Indigent Blind, 1829-56. He died at London, June 28, 1882.

WORKS.—Art of Singing at Sight (with E. Taylor), London, 1846. Psalms and Hymns, 1855. Psalms and Hymns for public worship, with appropriate tunes, London, 1863, 1864, 1869. Hymns for public worship, revised, 1863. Psalter and Canticles, with Chants, London, 1865. Child's own Tune Book, 1865. The People's Music Book (with E. Taylor),

London, n.d. Edited Wilbye's First Set of Madrigals, for the Musical Antiquarian Society, 1841. Single and Double Chants, composed for the use of the Choral Service of Westminster Abbey. The Westminster Abbey Chant Book, with Dr. J. F. Bridge, n.d. Church Services in D, E flat, etc. *Anthems:* Almighty and most merciful God; Hear my crying, O God; The Lord that made heaven and earth; This is the day which the Lord hath made; Arise and help, etc. Hymn tunes and chants.

His cousin, WILLIAM TURLE, born at Taunton in 1795, was organist of St. Mary's, Taunton, and composed glees, a number of dances for pf., and issued arrangements from Beethoven. ROBERT TURLE, brother of James, born at Taunton, March 19, 1804, was organist of Armagh Cathedral from 1823 to 1872. He died at Salisbury, March 26, 1877. HENRY FREDERICK TURLE, son of James, was born in Lambeth, London, July 23, 1835; died, London, June 28, 1883. He was a journalist and writer.

Turnbull, John, composer and writer, born at Paisley, January 12, 1804. He was precentor of New Church, Ayr, 1827, and afterwards precentor of St. George's Church, Glasgow, 1833. He died at Glasgow, November 1, 1844. Published "A selection of original Sacred Music, in vocal parts..adapted to the various metres used in Presbyterian churches and chapels..Glasgow, 1833 (forming vol. 6 of Steven's Sacred Music). "The Sacred Harp, a selection of the most approved sacred melodies, ancient and modern....by Robert Burns. Edited with a complete course of initiatory lessons and practical examples in the art of Singing, by John Turnbull," Glasgow [1840], 2 editions. The Garland of Scotia, a musical wreath of Scottish Songs, with descriptive and historical notes, Glasgow, 1841 (with Patrick Buchan). Easy and progressive exercises in Singing and in reading music, Glasgow, n.d. Six Glees, for three and four voices, Glasgow, n.d. He issued an edition of R. A. Smith's Devotional Music, and composed a number of anthems, psalms, and songs, of which "Jeannie Lee" and "Thistle and the Briar" are the best.

Turnbull, Thomas, musician of early part of the present century. Compiler of "The British Musical Miscellany, being a collection of Scotch, English, and Irish songs, set to music with proper keys for the voice, violin, German flute, and military fife," Edinburgh, 1805.

Turner, Austin T., organist, composer, and conductor, born at Bristol, 1823. Was a chorister there, and for some time a vicar choral at Lincoln Cathedral. In 1854 he went to Australia, and settled at Ballarat, which has since been his home. As singing master to the Government School, and conductor of the Philharmonic Society, he did much to promote the study of music. He conducted the Harmonic Society, formed in 1864, and apparently the successor to the Philharmonic, which in some seasons gave as many as six concerts. At the last concert we find any record of, Good Friday, 1875, he conducted a performance of his cantata, "Adoration," produced at Melbourne, in November, 1874. His compositions include two Masses (performed in Melbourne); two Marches for orchestra (Ballarat, 1868); choral pieces, etc. He has held the office of organist at Christ Church, Ballarat, for many years.

Turner, Rev. J. Egbert, O.S.B., organist and composer, born at Preston, Lancashire, 1853. Sometime organist and choirmaster, St. Ann's R.C. Church, Edge Hill, Liverpool. Composer of Masses, St. John the Baptist, St. Cecilia, and St. Mary Magdalene; Ascendit, Deus, for bass solo, and orchestra, etc.

Turner, James William, tenor vocalist, born at Sutton Ashfield, Nottingham, June 5, 1845. Sang as a treble at local concerts. Toured in China, India, etc., with a concert party, 1864, and made his *début* at Foo Choo, China; and his first stage appearance at Melbourne the same year, as *Elvino*, in "La Sonnambula." Some time later he sang in an opera company at San Francisco. Returning to England he studied with Schira at the London Academy of Music; appeared in opera at the Crystal Palace, 1872; with the Carl Rosa Company, London, 1873; and in 1875 took an opera company to South Africa. In 1876 he rejoined the Carl Rosa Company. Formed a company of his own in 1885, opened at Nottingham in February. He has toured the provinces every year since; given seasons of opera at the Princess's, Standard, and other London Theatres; and became proprietor of the Grand Theatre, Birmingham, 1893. His Fra Diavolo, and Don Cæsar de Bazan, are among the most popular of his assumptions. He has revived operas of Balfe and Macfarren.

Turner, John, author of "Manual of Instruction in Vocal Music, chiefly with a view to Psalmody.." London, 1833, 2nd edition 1835, Boston edition 1836; "Class Singing Book for Schools," 1844, 2 parts. Te Deum, songs, and other vocal music.

Turner, John Bradbury, pianist, composer, and teacher, born at Stockport. Was taught the violoncello by Lieut.-Col. S. W. Wilkinson, an amateur of repute, and played in local orchestras as a lad. Entered R.A.M., 1852, as a resident pupil, and studied under Sterndale Bennett, G. A. Macfarren, C. Steggall, and others, remaining there till 1861. F.R.A.M. Graduated Mus. Bac., Cambridge, 1865. He was one of the founders of

Trinity College, London, and has for years been Director of Studies there. In his younger days he composed a great deal of music, but his onerous duties at the College have precluded his engaging of late in that pursuit. His compositions include a cantata, "Thy Kingdom come"; Ps. 13, for soli, chorus, and orchestra. An Overture and a Symphony for orchestra; Trio in C minor, pf. and strings; various pieces for pf.; songs, etc. Technical studies for pf.

Turner, Robert Henry, organist, born at Scarborough, in 1859. Received his first training from his father (who was for twenty-five years organist of Christ Church, Scarborough), and afterwards studied under Dr. Creser, and while a student at Cambridge, with Dr. Garrett. Graduated M.A., 1886; Mus. Bac., 1891, Cambridge. His first appointment, organist and choirmaster, St. Paul's Cathedral Church, Dundee, he still retains. Conducted for some years the Dundee and Kingskettle Choral Societies. Among his compositions is an Evening Service, composed for the eighth Festival of Associated Choirs, Dundee, 1883. He has published "Abide with me," and other anthems, hymns, etc.

Turner, William, composer, was born at Oxford in 1651. He became a chorister of Christ Church, Oxford, under Lowe, and afterwards chorister in Chapel Royal under Cooke. Chorister in Lincoln Cathedral, and Gentleman of the Chapel Royal, 1669. Vicar-choral of St. Paul's, and lay-vicar Westminster Abbey. Mus. Doc., Cantab., 1696. He died at Westminster, January 13, 1739-40.

WORKS.—*Operas:* Presumptious Lover, 1716; Woman's a riddle, 1717; Generous choice, 1720; Virgin Sacrifice, 1725. Twenty new songs of humour, London [1716]. Two catches for three voices. Anthems in the collections of Boyce and Tudway. Select Lessons...extracted from the works of Turner, etc. [1740]. *Songs:* Betty's panegyrick, Fair Susan, On decanting a flask of Florence, Wanton Cupid, When Phœbus did the skies adorn, etc. Edited Ravenscroft's Psalm Tunes, 1728.

Turner, William, musician and author, published "A Philosophical Essay on Musick, directed to a friend," London [1677]; 3rd edition, 1740; afterwards issued as "Sound Anatomiz'd in a philosophical essay on musick, to which is added a discourse concerning the abuse of musick," London, 1724.

Turpin, Edmund Hart, organist, composer, and writer, born at Nottingham, May 4, 1835. Son of James Turpin, a lace manufacturer and enthusiastic musical amateur. Studied under C. Noble, and local teachers, and later in London under Hullah and Pauer. Was appointed organist of St. Barnabas Church, Nottingham, 1850; and in 1851 gave

TURPIN.

his first recital at the Great Exhibition, Hyde Park. He settled in London in 1857, but retained some appointments in Nottingham. In 1869 he became organist of St. George's, Bloomsbury; and from 1888 has held a similar appointment at St. Bride's, Fleet Street, Since 1875 he has been Hon. Sec. of the College of Organists; was presented by the Council with the diploma of Fellowship, 1869; and he has frequently acted as Examiner for the College. Licentiate, Trinity College, London, 1874; and Warden from 1892. He was elected an Hon. Member of the Tonic Sol-fa College, 1885; and of the R.A.M., 1890. In 1889 the Archbishop of Canterbury conferred upon him the degree of Mus. Doc. He edited the *Musical Standard* at different periods; was joint editor, 1891, of *Musical News*; and has contributed many articles to periodical literature, besides lectures at R.C.O., Musical Association, and other societies. He is widely known as a concert organist, and has opened organs in all parts of the kingdom; he is also a pianist, and plays nearly every instrument in the orchestra.

WORKS.—Mass in A flat, voices alone; Mass in D, for soli, chorus, brass, drums, and organ; Motet, Jubilate Deo, for the same, except drums; Stabat Mater, voices alone. Oratorios, St. John the Baptist, and Hezekiah (MS.); Cantatas, A Song of Faith, and Jerusalem. Services and anthems. Symphony for orchestra, The Monastery; Overtures, As you like it; Talisman; Richard II.; Concert overture in C. Quartet for strings; for pf. and strings; pf. Trio; pieces for pf. Overtura Pastorale; Musette; Andante, and other organ pieces. Editor of Students' Edition of Classical Compositions for pf.; Collection of Hymn Tunes, 1872.

Turpin, James, organist, brother of the foregoing, born at Nottingham, December 15, 1840. F.R.C.O.; Mus. Bac., Cambridge, 1880. Organist of Roman Catholic Cathedral, Nottingham; Londonderry Cathedral; Parish Church, St. Leonards; Parish Church, Berkhampstead; St. Andrew's, Watford. Music master at Berkhampstead School; Professor of harmony and counterpoint, Trinity College, London. As an organ player he was well known, and he gave recitals at the Royal Albert Hall (Inventions Exhibition, 1885), and in many provincial towns. He was also a good pianist. He gave lectures before the College of Organists, the Musical Association, etc. He composed a church service, songs, a sonata, and other pieces for pf. He suffered from paralysis for some years, and died, July 29, 1896.

Turton, Rev. Thomas, BISHOP OF ELY, was born in Yorkshire in 1780. He was educated at Cambridge, and after holding various ecclesiastical offices, became, in 1830,

TYE.

dean of Peterborough, and of Westminster in 1842. In 1845 he was consecrated Bishop of Ely. He died January 7, 1864. Bishop Turton was a composer of some ability, and wrote the hymn tunes, "Ely," "St. Ethelreda," and other music for the church.

Tutt, William Henry, organist, conductor, and composer of present time. Graduated Mus. Bac., Cambridge, 1882; L.R.A.M. (composer), 1883. Organist of Okeover Church, Staffordshire, and conductor of Ashborne (Derby) Amateur Orchestral Society, and Choral Society. Has given many excellent concerts, and conducted a performance of Handel's "Messiah" in Bentley Church, Staffordshire, the first Festival of the Fenny Bentley Church Choral Society, December 1, 1893. Has composed a setting of Psalm 104, for voices and orchestra; Pieces for orchestra, etc.

Tutton, James Rufus, bandmaster and composer, was one of the founders of the Society of British Musicians, 1834. Composed a dramatic overture (1834), and has published a large amount of dance music for pf. and band; Overtures arranged for pf.; March of the Men of Kent, pf. [1850]. Songs, etc.

Twining, Rev. Thomas, clergyman and musician, born at London, in 1734. Rector of St. Mary, Colchester, 1770. He died at Colchester, August 6, 1804. Published "Aristotle's Treatise on Poetry, translated with Notes..and Two Dissertations on poetical and musical imitation," Oxford, 1789; London, 1812, 2 vols., 2nd edition. In 1882, was published a selection from his correspondence, entitled "Recreations and studies of a Country Clergyman of the Eighteenth Century," London, Murray.

Tye, Christopher, organist, composer, and verse-writer, born at Westminster, early in the 16th century. He was a chorister and Gentleman of the Chapel Royal, 1545. Mus. Bac., Cantab., 1536. Organist of Ely Cathedral, 1541-1561. Mus. Doc., Cantab., 1545, and Oxon. (*ad eundem*), 1548. He was a clergyman, and was successively minister of Little Wilbraham, 1564; Newton, 1567-70; and Doddington-cum-March, 1570-72, all in Cambridgeshire. He died in March, 1572.

WORKS.—The Actes of the Apostles, translated into Englyshe meter, and dedicated to the Kynge's moste excellaunte Maiestye.. with notes to eche chapter, to synge and also to play upon the lute....London, 1553; A notable historye of Nastagio and Traversari, no less pitiefull than plesaunt, out of Italian, London, 1569; Service in G minor. *Anthems:* I will exalt Thee; Sing unto the Lord; This is the day which the Lord hath made; Arise, and help us. Masses, anthems, and other works in MS. A number of psalm tunes have been adapted from Tye's compositions.

TYLEE.

Tylee, Henry Dixon, musician, published "Eight Indian Airs..adapted for the pf. or harpsichord," London [1805].

Tyndall, John, scientific author, born at Leighlin Bridge, near Carlow, in 1820; died, December 4, 1893. Author of "Sound: a course of eight lectures delivered at the Royal Institution of Great Britain." London, 1867, various later editions.

Tyson, A. G., author of "An Essay on the poetic and musical customs of the Ancients, etc.," 1852.

Tyler, Sarah, see Keddie, Henrietta.

Tyler, William, of Woodhouselee, antiquary and author, was born at Edinburgh, October 12, 1711. He was educated for the law and became a writer to the Signet in Edinburgh. He died at Woodhouselee, near Edinburgh, September 12, 1792. Author of "A Dissertation on the Scottish music," which was printed in Arnot's "History of Edinburgh," 1779, and also in Napier's "Selection of favourite Scotch songs," and in "The Poetical remains of James I. of Scotland." He also published in the "Transactions of the Society of Antiquaries of Scotland." "An account of fashionable amusements and entertainments of Edinburgh in the last century, with the plan of a grand concert of music performed there on St. Cecilia's Day, 1695." His other works were "A Historical and Critical Inquiry into the evidence produced against Mary Queen of Scots," 1750, etc.

Uglow, John, organist, violinist, and conductor, born at Gloucester, 1814? When six years old was admitted a chorister at Gloucester Cathedral, by Mr. Mutlow, then organist. In 1824 he sang at the Assembly Rooms, Cheltenham, at a concert given by Mr. Thomas Woodward, organist of the parish church, to whom he was afterwards articled. Later he studied under Crotch and Neukomm; violin with N. Mori; and violoncello with William Lindley. He was organist, at different times, of Trinity, St. James's, and St. John's churches, Cheltenham. In 1842 he went to Ireland, but the climate compelled his return to Cheltenham. He was the founder of the first Choral Society in Cheltenham, and had a high reputation as an organist, violinist, and violoncellist. .In his later years he was a great invalid. In May, 1893, a grand concert was given for his benefit, a number of eminent artists assisting, with Mr. J. A. Matthews as conductor. Uglow died May 6, 1894, and was buried in Cheltenham Cemetery.

Upton, Emily, pianist, born in London, September 5, 1864. Showed musical ability at a very early age, and was placed under some of the best masters. She afterwards went to Dresden, as a pupil of J. L. Nicodé.

VALENTINE.

Returning to England in 1890, she made her *début* as a pianist, and has given a series of recitals and concerts at Steinway Hall since that time. In 1892 she succeeded to the principalship of the Anglo-German School of Music at Norwood, which she successfully directs at the present time.

Urich, John, amateur composer, born, of German parentage, at Trinidad, West Indies, in 1850. Studied at Stuttgart and Paris. Composer of several operas: Flora Macdonald, produced at Bologna, December? 1882; Le Serment, one act opera, Brussels, 1883; Le Pilotte, Monte Carlo, 1890; cantata, Nourmahal, London, 1882; song, The Angel and the Sunshine, etc.

Valentine, John, musician of 18th century. Resided at Leicester, where he died in 1791. Composer of "Thirty Psalm tunes in four parts with symphonies, interludes and instrumental bass, being set part to the old and part to the new version, op. 7," London [1787]. Ode on the birthday of the Marquess of Granby [1768]. Eight easy Symphonies for two violins, 2 hautboys, 2 horns a tenor and bass, op. 6 [1785]; Sixteen marches and minuetts, op. 8.

ANN VALENTINE, probably a relative of the above, composed "Ten Sonatas for harpsichord and violin," op. 1 [1798]; waltzes, marches, etc., for pf.

Valentine, John, composer and pianist, author of "Elements of Practical Harmony, or what is generally called thorough base." London [1834]. Songs: All round my hat, Medical student, Soldier's last dream. Pf. music, etc.

Valentine, Robert, composer and violinist, who flourished during the first part of the 18th century.

WORKS.—Six setts of aires and a chacoon for 2 flutes and a bass, London [1720]. Op. 2, Twelve Sonatas or solos for a flute; Op. 3, Twelve Sonatas for a flute [1701]; Op. 4, Six sonatas for 2 violins, 2 hoboys, or German flutes [1720]; Op. 6, Six sonatas for 2 violins and a bass; Op. 7, Six sonatas of 2 parts for 2 violins; Op. 13, Sonatas for flute and harpsichord [1706].

Valentine, Thomas, composer and writer, born in 1790. He was a teacher, and at one time popular as a composer. He resided for many years at King's Heath, near Birmingham, and died there, February 11, 1878. As a tribute to his memory, a road at King's Heath has been named Valentine Road.

WORKS.—Rondos for pf.; Flowers of English melody for pf.; Scotch and Irish Quadrilles [1845]; Early lessons for the pf.; Numerous arrangements for pf.; songs, etc. Instructions for the pianoforte, to which is added a selection of favourite airs .. London [1826];

VANCE.

Dictionary of terms used in music, London, 1833, various editions. He edited choruses from Handel, etc.

Vance, Alfred Glenville, see STEVENS, ALFRED PECK.

Vandernan, Thomas, musician, of 18th century, was a Gentleman of the Chapel Royal, and died October 2, 1778. He compiled " Divine Harmony, being a collection of two hundred and seven double and single chants in score .. sung at His Majesty's Chapels Royal.." 1770.

Vaughan, Thomas, tenor vocalist, was born at Norwich in 1782. Chorister in Norwich Cathedral under Beckwith. Lay-clerk St. George's Chapel, Windsor, 1799. Gentleman of the Chapel Royal, 1803. Vicar-choral St. Paul's London, and lay-vicar Westminster Abbey. Married Miss Tennant, a soprano singer. He sang at the Concert of Ancient Music, and at the principal London and provincial concerts. He died at Birmingham, January 9, 1843.

Vautor, Thomas, composer of late 16th and early 17th centuries He issued " The first Set : being songs of divers ayres and natures, of five and six parts ; apt for vyols and voyces," London, 1619.

Venables, George I., choir trainer, born at St. John's Wood, London, May 16, 1845. Studied music through the classes of the Tonic Sol-fa College. Was deputy conductor of the South London Choral Association, of which he was also hon. sec. from its foundation in 1869. He was founder of the South London Institute of Music, an outcome of the society previously named, which began its educational work in 1880, and of which he was the hon. sec. A tenor vocalist of repute, he was a zealous worker for popular musical education ; but in the midst of his varied avocations he was seized with congestion of the lungs, and died on December 23, 1887.

Venables, Leonard Charles, brother of the preceding, conductor and bass vocalist, born at St. John's Wood, London, November 5, 1847. He was a choir boy at St. Stephen's, Avenue Road, St. John's Wood, and studied under various masters. Is a Graduate and Professor of the Tonic Sol-fa College. Has conducted the South London Choral Association since its formation in 1869, raising it from small beginnings to an important position among metropolitan organisations, its concerts being of high excellence. The Upper Choir sang in the "Romeo and Juliet" of Berlioz, at the Philharmonic Society's Concert, March 10, 1881. Mr. Venables conducted the concert by certificated adult singers at the Tonic Sol-fa Festival, Crystal Palace, July 13, 1895. He has been principal of the South London Institute of Music since its

VERTUE.

commencement in 1880. Author of "The Choral Society, practical hints and experiences," London, Curwen ; also, of several vocal instruction books ; and has composed part-songs, etc. The work of the two brothers and their colleagues is told in the History of the South London Choral Association, and Institute of Music, by Eben. Lock, London, 1892.

Verne, see sub. WURM, MARIE.

Vernham, John Edward, organist, born at Lewes, Sussex, April 17, 1856. Studied under Dr. Steggall and George Cooper. Appointed organist of All Saints', Lambeth, when fifteen ; All Saints', Surrey Square, London, 1872 ; and at the present time is organist of St. Paul's Knightsbridge. Succeeded the late W. H. Monk as Professor of Music at King's College, London, 1889. Author of fifty three-part studies, Novello's Primers (1896). His wife is the composer of "Twilight," "Sleep," and other songs.

Vernon, Joseph, tenor vocalist, born at Coventry [1738]. He studied under W. Savage, and appeared at Drury Lane Theatre, London, 1751, and from 1756 sang at Vauxhall and other London concerts, and appeared on the stage in various musical dramas. He died at Lambeth, London, March 19, 1782. Composer of an epilogue to the Irish Widow, 1780 ; music for The Witches, a pantomime, 1771 ; Strawberry Hill, a song, and other vocal works.

Vernon, M., author of "Analogy of the laws of musical temperament to the natural dissonance of creation," London, 1867.

Verrinder, Charles Garland, organist and composer, born at Blakeney, Gloucestershire. Studied under Sir G. J Elvey. Graduated Mus. Bac., Oxford, 1862 ; Mus. Doc., Cantuar, 1873 ; F.R.C.O. Organist successively at Holy Trinity, Windsor ; St. Giles' in the Fields, London ; Christ Church, Lancaster Gate ; St. Michael's, Chester Square ; and St. Mary's, West Kensington. Also organist of the Reformed Synagogue, London. Conductor of the Hebrew Choral Association, and of St. Mary's and Ealing Choral Societies. Composer of a cantata, "Israel " ; Church Service in E ; Seek ye the Lord ; The Light hath shined upon us ; Hear my cry, O God (Jubilee) ; and other anthems, kyries, etc. Hebrew music and psalms, 7 vols. Out of the deep, ancient Hebrew melody, "Kol Nidrai." Songs and part-songs, organ music, etc. Assisted Lady Elvey in the preparation of the memoir of the late Sir George J. Elvey.

Vertue, Matthew, organist and composer, born about 1770. He was an organist at Weymouth, where he died, October 8, 1849. Composer of a Collection of Psalms (R. Rooke), 1845 ; Bards have sung ; How blest is the

VESTRIS.

friendship; If thou canst live on humble fare ; duets, songs, and other vocal music.

Vestris, Lucia Elizabeth, *born* BARTO-LOZZI, contralto vocalist and actress, born in London, of Italian parents, in 1797. She studied under Corri, and in 1813 married Armand Vestris, a ballet-master. Appeared in opera in 1815. Appeared in Paris, 1816, and again sang in London from 1820, appearing in operas and numerous theatrical pieces. She became manager successively of the Olympic, Covent Garden, and Lyceum Theatres, and produced a large succession of dramatic pieces, in many of which she appeared. Married to Charles Mathews the younger, 1838. She died at Fulham, London, August 8, 1856. Famous for her beauty, and her charming style of acting and singing. *See* Madame Vestris : Memoirs of her public and private life and adventures, with anecdotes of celebrated characters of the fashionable world, with amorous confessions of Madame Vestris, from a series of letters written to Handsome Jack. London, 1839.

Vicary, Walter, organist and composer, was born in 1770. He was organist of Magdalen College, Oxford, from 1797 to 1845 ; in 1805 he graduated Mus. Bac., Oxford; and he also held the appointments of Lay-chaplain of New College, Oxford, 1812-44 ; Singing man of St. John's College, Oxford, 1816-28 ; and organist of St. Mary's Church, Oxford, 1830. He died at Oxford, January 5, 1845. Composer of Church music, songs, etc.

Vincent, Charles John, organist and composer, born at Houghton-le-Spring, Durham, September 19, 1852. His father, CHARLES JOHN VINCENT, was organist of St. Michael's Church in that place, a good musician, and composer of organ music, now head of a music business at Sunderland. The son entered Durham Cathedral as a chorister in 1864, studying under Dr. Armes, having received his first lessons from his parents. In 1869 he was appointed organist of Monkwearmouth Parish Church. Studied at Leipzig Conservatorium, 1876-8 ; graduated Mus. Bac., 1878 ; Mus. Doc., 1885, Oxford. Organist of Tavistock Parish Church, and Kelly College, 1878 ; and of Christ Church, Hampstead, London, 1883-91. Hon. Sec. of the London Section of the I.S.M., and Divisional (Oxford) Hon. Sec. Union of Graduates in Music. Examiner for Trinity College, in which capacity he has been to South Africa, 1893, and Australia, 1897. He is a voluminous composer, and is joint editor of the *Organist and Choirmaster.*

WORKS.—Oratorio, Ruth, produced, Hampstead, December, 1886 ; Cantatas, Psalm 68, and The day of rest (both in MS.) ; The Crowning of the wheat, harvest cantata ; Church services and anthems. Cantatas for

VINEN.

treble voices : Village Queen ; Little mermaid ; A night in fairyland ; Spanish gipsies ; Persian princess ; The two queens. Operetta, Count Carlo. Honour and Praise to Music, choral fugue in 8 parts. Two-part songs ; upwards of a hundred songs. The Storm overture, orchestra, produced, Bradford, February 24, 1894. Other orchestral pieces in MS. Pieces for 'cello and pf. ; violin and pf. ; and for pf. solo. Organ pieces, various. Author of A Year's Study in the Piano ; First Principles of Music ; Choral Instructor for treble voices ; On scoring for an orchestra (*British Musician,* 1897). Editor (with Sir John Stainer and Dr. D. J. Wood) of Hymnal Companion to the Book of Common Prayer (1890 edition) ; Chant Book Companion ; Anglican organist ; Anglican choir ; Bach's 48 Fugues in score ; and Bach's organ Fugues, miniature edition.

Vincent, George Frederick, organist and composer, brother of the preceding, born at Houghton-le-Spring, March 27, 1855. Received private instruction in music to 1874 ; studied at Leipzig Conservatorium, 1874-6. Organist and choirmaster, Sunderland Parish Church, 1872-4 ; St. Mary's, Whitburn, Durham, 1877 ; and from 1882 to present time of St. Thomas's, Sunderland. Conductor of Choral Society, Ladies' Orchestral Society, and Amateur Opera Society, Sunderland. Examiner in practical music, I.S.M., from 1889. Has given organ recitals in Sunderland, etc., and orchestral concerts at Newcastle Exhibition, 1887. He has composed several operettas: Peter's pledge, 1878 ; Romany Lore, St. George's Hall, London, 1889 ; Jedediah the Scarecrow, Nottingham, 1895. Cantata, Sir Humphrey Gilbert, for baritone solo, chorus, and orchestra, 1895. Two choral fantasias on national airs. Volume of 20 songs ; Songs, various. Anthems. Two Fantasias and Fugues for two pianos ; pf. pieces, various. Offertoire and Fugue, etc., for organ. Original organ compositions, 2 vols. Overtures, galop, valse, for orchestra. Pieces for violin and pf., etc.

Vincent, Rev. William, D.D., author of " Considerations on Parochial Music," London, 1790.

Vinen, Ernest Edward, organist and composer, born in London, October 12, 1865. Pupil of the Guildhall School of Music. F.R.C.O., 1890. Was appointed organist and choirmaster, St. John's, Horsleydown, 1881 (when sixteen years old) ; St. Augustine's, Bermondsey, 1886 ; and, in 1888, to his present position at St. Augustine's, Honor Oak Park. WORKS. — Cantata, The Legend of the Faithful Soul, for soli, chorus, and orchestra (Honor Oak, 1890) ; " Into the Silent Land," chorus and orchestra (1894) ; Festival Te Deum, soli, double chorus, and orchestra ;

VINER.

WADDELL.

Evening Service in C; hymn-tunes, chants, etc.; Songs. Two concert overtures, in E minor, and A minor; Romance in E flat, orchestra, etc.

Viner, William Letton, organist and composer, born at Bath, May 14, 1790. He studied under Charles Wesley, and in 1820 became organist of St. Michael's, Bath. In 1838 he was appointed organist of St. Mary's, Penzance, and remained there till 1859, when he went to the United States. He died at Westfield, Mass, U.S., July 24, 1867. Editor of "A useful selection from the most approved psalms," London [1846]. "One hundred psalm and hymn-tunes in score," London, 1838. "The Chanter's companion" [1857]. He composed church music, organ music and songs, and wrote the well-known hymn-tune, "Helston" or "Kingston," sometimes described as an ancient Cornish melody.

Vinning, Louisa, soprano vocalist, born at Kingsbridge, Devon, November 10, 1836. Her father, JOHN VINNING, was a musician, and at twelve years of age was organist of Torquay Chapel, and held other similar appointments later, being also a composer. Louisa Vinning showed an extraordinary passion for music even in infancy. She sang at the Plymouth Theatre when only two-and-a-half years old, and a year later was taken by the Duke of Wellington to sing to the Queen, who gave her a diamond ring. As the "Infant Sappho," she sang in various country towns, and at the Adelaide Gallery, London, 1840-2; gave concerts up to 1847. Then studied under F. Mori, and others. Sang in 1856, on tour with Alfred Mellon; in the "Messiah," Sacred Harmonic Society, December 12; at the Worcester Festival, and Crystal Palace, 1857; Hereford, 1858; and gave annual matinées in London up to 1860, on July 5 of that year introducing the pianist, Mlle. Remaury, to an English audience. Sang at the Monday Popular Concerts, January 21, 1861. On her marriage with Mr. J. S. C. Heywood soon after that time, she retired from the concert platform. She had many offers to go to America, and elsewhere, but declined them all.

Vinning, Rosetta, see O'LEARY, Mrs. ARTHUR.

Vinning, William Skinner, organist and composer, is a native of Devonshire. Pupil of Charles Fowler, Torquay, in which town he held organ appointments at the Parish Church, and St. Luke's. Organist of St. Peter's, Bayswater, London, since 1884. Mus. Bac., Cambridge, 1880. Composer of two sacred cantatas, "Song of the Passion," and "Song of the Nativity"; a setting of Psalm 84, for soli, chorus, and strings; church services, etc. Also an operetta. "Equality Jack," produced at Ladbroke Hall, Feb-

ruary 28, 1891. Author of Papers on Choir Management, and other subjects.

Vitton, Arthur, see CROWEST, F. J.

Vokes, Henry, musician, compiler of "Psalms and hymns, with select sentences of scripture, sung at the Parish Church of St. Botolph, Aldersgate," London [1820].

Von Hoff, Henry, tenor vocalist and teacher, was educated at R.A.M., singing at the Academy concerts in 1842, and in public, 1846. Studied under Mazzucato, in Milan, 1851, and sang there. Returning to London, he acquired an excellent teaching connection. He wrote many songs: Could I but call a heart my own; Sing me a song, love, etc., most of them of high quality. He died in London, December, 1862. His wife, *born* ELIZABETH CHAMBERLAINE, a pianist, was also a pupil of the R.A.M., where she studied under W. S. Bennett, and others, and was a King's scholar, 1843. From 1857 she was, for a number of years, organist of the Rectory Church, Marylebone. She published a few pieces for pf., but was better known as a teacher. She died some time before 1890.

Waddel, William, violinist and conductor, born at Edinburgh in 1842. Studied under Carmichael and Howard, and in London under Henry Blagrove. When twenty he went to Leipzig and studied under Ferdinand David. Returning to Edinburgh he became organist of Dublin Street Baptist Church, an office he held for many years. From the choir of this church sprang the organisation known as "Mr. Waddel's Choir," which he conducted for twenty-five years, introducing all Schumann's choral works, and many other compositions to the city of Edinburgh. He founded a Violin School, and formed a Ladies' Orchestra chiefly of his pupils; established chamber concerts, and gave Free Musical Evenings for the People. Has been choirmaster for some years at St. Cuthbert's Established Church. He married the daughter of the late Sir Daniel McNee, president of the Royal Scottish Academy, and is himself a painter of reputation, for many years an exhibitor at the Royal Scottish Academy and other places.

Waddell, James, bandmaster, born at Banff, January 20, 1797. He was appointed bandmaster of the 80th regiment in 1817, but was compelled to resign on account of ill health. He settled in Perthshire as a teacher of music, but in 1832 was asked to re-organise the band of the 1st Life Guards, and remained as bandmaster in that regiment for 27 years, resigning in 1863. He died at Kensington, London, April 10, 1879. Composer of "Fair Maid of Perth," overture; Polkas, Galops, Quadrilles, and arrangements for band, between 1843 and 1860.

WADDINGTON.

Waddington, Sidney P., composer of present time. Studied at R.C.M., and was elected Mendelssohn Scholar in 1891. Resident in London, and conductor of an amateur opera society which gave its first performance, "Dorothy," at St. George's Hall, May 27, 1896. To him was allotted the task of completing the score of the late Goring Thomas's opera, "The Golden Web." His compositions consist of a Ballad, "John Gilpin," for chorus and orchestra, produced at R.C.M. concert, November 14, 1894; a concerto for pf. and orchestra; Trio, pf. and strings, Queen's Hall, December 11, 1894; Sonata, pf. and 'cello, etc.

Wade, James Clifft, organist and composer, was born at Coven, Staffordshire, on January 26, 1847. He studied music under Drs. Winn and Bradford, and became organist at Coven, 1860-65. Afterwards he studied in Birmingham during 1865-66, and then held the appointments of organist at the Parish Church, Iver, near Uxbridge, 1867-69; private organist to W. S. Dugdale, Esq., Merevale, Warwickshire; and organist of St. Mary's Church, Maidenhead, from 1880. Conductor of the Maidenhead Orchestral Society, and composer of church music, hymns, action songs for children, and other vocal music.

Wade, Joseph Augustine, composer and writer, born in Dublin, [1796]. He married a Miss Kelly of Garnavilla. For a time he was a surgeon, but afterwards he went to London, and worked for the theatres and publishers. He died at London, July 15, 1845.

WORKS.—Two Houses of Granada, opera, 1826; Pupil of Da Vinci, operetta; Prophecy, oratorio, 1824. Polish Melodies, London, 1831. Songs of the Flowers [1827-28], 2 books. Many duets, "I've wandered in dreams,". etc. *Songs:* The Bridge; Meet me by moonlight alone; Love was once a little boy; A Woodland life; and others. Fantasias for pf. and a large number of arrangements. Child's first Quadrilles, Waltzes, etc., for pf. His son, JOSEPH AUGUSTINE WADE, has composed a very large number of pieces for pf. and other instruments, songs, etc.

Wade, Mrs., *see* GREY, ANNIE.

Wade, Richard, pianist and writer, who flourished in London about the middle of the 18th century. Author of "The Harpsichord illustrated and improved, wherein is shewn the Italian manner of Fingering..." London, n.d., anon.

Wade, W. J., musician, author of "Complete Instructions for the cornopean and saxhorn." London [1860], 1864, etc.

Wadham, Walter T., a native of Tasmania, is the composer of a number of songs, among which may be mentioned: Who will be my love? and My heart's Queen.

WAINWRIGHT.

Wadmore, John Lofting, baritone vocalist, born in 1849. He studied at the R.A.M., gaining the Parepa-Rosa prize in 1875. A.R.A.M. He sang at concerts of the Philharmonic Society in London, and at important concerts in the provinces, and achieved a high reputation, particularly in oratorio. He died at London, November 4, 1878, from the effects of a cold, aged 29.

Wadsworth, Joseph, musician, compiled "Selection of Psalm and Hymn tunes, adapted to the most useful measures," Halifax, 1852.

Wagstaff, William, organist and composer; born 1784; died in London, March 11, 1852. He was organist at Battersea Church for about 30 years. Compiled "Sacred Music, a hymn and chorus for Easter day and Kyrie Eleison, as sung at St. Mary's Church, Battersea," London [1827]. Composer of pf. rondos and other music.

Wainwright, Harriet, afterwards MRS. COLONEL STEWART, composer, who was probably related to the Wainwrights noted below. She flourished between 1780 and 1840. Composer of "Collection of Songs, duetts, trios, and choruses," London [1810]; "Comāla, a dramatic poem from Ossian," 1803; Merrily, merrily passes the day, glee; songs, etc. Author of "Critical remarks on the art of Singing," London, 1836.

Wainwright, John, composer and organist, born at Stockport about 1723. He became organist of Manchester Cathedral in 1767. He died in January, 1768, and is buried at Stockport. He composed anthems, hymns, etc., and issued a "Collection of psalm tunes, anthems, hymns, and chants, for 1, 2, 3 and 4 voices," London [1766], in which is contained the well-known hymn or carol usually sung to Byrom's words, "Christians, awake, salute the happy morn."

His son ROBERT, born in 1748, succeeded him as organist of Manchester Collegiate Church in 1768. In 1774 he accumulated the degrees of Bac. and Doc. Mus., Oxford, and in 1775 he became organist of St. Peter's, Liverpool. He died on July 15, 1782, aged 34. He composed an oratorio entitled "The Fall of Egypt"; a Te Deum (degree exercise), 1774; The Psalm Tunes, "St. Gregory," "Manchester," and "Liverpool," etc.

Another son, RICHARD, was born in 1758. He was organist of the Collegiate Church, and St. Ann's, Manchester, and succeeded his brother in 1782 as organist of St. Peter's, Liverpool. He also held the appointment of organist of St. James', Toxteth Park, Liverpool, for a time, but returned again to St. Peter's. He died at Liverpool, August 20, 1825. He composed "Life's a bumper," a well-known glee [1800]; the hymn tune,.

WAINWRIGHT.

"Wainwright," and other pieces of vocal music. Also editor of "A Collection of Hymns with appropriate symphonies," Liverpool [1809]. The Rev. J. J. Waite edited "Hallelujah, a selection of tunes from Wainwright." Both brothers were celebrated as organists. WILLIAM WAINWRIGHT, another brother (died at Manchester, 1797), was a vocalist.

Wainwright, Rev. Jonathan Mayhew, composer, born at Liverpool in 1792, and died at New York, September 21, 1854. Composer of chants, psalms, and other church music in collections such as "Music of the Church, a collection of psalm, hymn, and chant tunes," Boston [1852].

Wait, William M., organist and composer, born at Chester, December 4, 1854. His parents were church singers in that city, and his uncle, William Wait (died November 10, 1888), was for 33 years tenor lay-clerk at the cathedral. As a chorister at Chester Cathedral he received pianoforte lessons from the late John Munns, sub-organist; he afterwards studied at Liverpool, and later, had organ lessons from J. F. Bridge, and J. Kendrick Pyne, at Manchester, and studied harmony and counterpoint with R. H. Wilson. From 1870 he held various organ appointments in Manchester and London, being from 1895 organist and choirmaster (for the second time) at St. Margaret Pattens. He has given organ recitals at the Bow and Bromley Institute, the Agricultural Hall, Earl's Court Exhibition, etc., etc. His compositions consist of the cantatas, "St. Andrew" (1888); "The Good Samaritan" (1892); "God with us," Christmas cantata (1893); an Evening Service in C; Part-songs, etc.

Waite, Rev. J. J., amateur musician and clergyman, was a busy worker, though blind, in the cause of musical education in Gloucester and Hereford. He died at Hereford in October, 1868. Among other works he edited "Hallelujah....being a selection of tunes from the works of Wainwright."

Wakefield, Augusta Mary, amateur contralto vocalist and composer, born at Kendal, August 19, 1853. Studied singing under Randegger, Henschel, and Blumenthal, also at Rome. Has sung in various parts of the country, and took part in the Gloucester Festival of 1880. Established an annual series of vocal competitions about 1885, which have culminated in the Wakefield Festivals, held at Kendal every spring, and which are intended to encourage the study of music. Miss Wakefield conducts the performances, and appears as vocalist. She is the composer of several songs, No, sir! Yes sir!; Bunch of Cowslips; May time in mid-winter; More and more, etc. Her chorus, Queen of sixty years, was sung at Kendal, April 29, 1897. She has

WALENN.

given lectures on music, and has edited Ruskin on Music, 1894, and contributed to various periodicals.

Walch, James, organist and composer, was born at Egerton, near Bolton, June 21, 1837. His father was a musician, and he studied under him, and afterwards under Henry Smart. Organist successively of Duke's Alley Congregational Church, Bolton, 1851; Walmsley Church, 1857; Bridge Street Wesleyan Church, 1858; St. George's Parish Church, Bolton, 1863. He was conductor of Bolton Philharmonic Society in 1870, and in 1874 he retired. Composer of hymn tunes and other church music, of which the best known is "Sawley," a popular hymn, composed in 1857, and printed for private circulation in 1860.

Walenn. Family of musicians. JAMES FARQUHARSON WALENN, the eldest, was born in London, January, 1860. A chorister, All Saints', Margaret Street, and afterwards pupil of W. S. Hoyte. In December, 1877, he won the Novello Scholarship at the National Training School for Music, and two years later was appointed organist and choirmaster of St. Alban's, Holborn, and was also conductor of the St. Alban's Choral Society. He composed some church music; two pf. trios; many songs, and left an opera unfinished. He died at Hornsey, February 10, 1884, a loss to the art he gave such promise to adorn. ARTHUR WALENN, his brother, born in London, was educated at All Saints' Choir School, and at the R.A.M. He began as a viola player, and was soon engaged in the orchestras of the opera and concert rooms. With his sister and two younger brothers he formed the Walenn quartet of strings, and gave concerts; but an excellent baritone voice developing, he, by the advice of Sir A. C. Mackenzie, devoted himself to singing, and the combination was broken up. After a course of study under G. Henschel, he made his *début* at the morning concerts at the Queen's Hall, in November, 1895, afterwards being engaged for the London Symphony Concerts. He has since been heard in many provincial centres, and has fairly established a reputation. CHARLES WALENN, the next brother, born in London, 1869, is also a baritone singer, and has for some years been a member of the D'Oyly Carte No. 1 Company. HERBERT WALENN, violoncellist, born in London, June 25, 1870, studied under Hugo Becker, at Frankfort, and has appeared with success in Germany, and at the Queen's Hall, 1897. GERALD WALENN, the youngest brother, born in London, 1872, studied the violin at the R.A.M., under Sainton and Sauret. At the age of fourteen he played before the Queen, at Windsor, and soon afterwards was heard at various concerts. He was in Germany, 1896,

WALEY.

where he was very successful, and has since played at chamber concerts, Queen's Hall. DOROTHEA WALENN, born in London, is also a violinist; pupil of Sainton, Sauret, and Hugo Heermann. After playing in the quartet mentioned, she devoted her attention to teaching, in London.

Waley, Simon Waley, pianist and amateur composer, born at London, in 1827. He was engaged in commercial life in London, being a member of the Stock Exchange, and he was also an active member of the Jewish community in London, He studied music, the pf. under Moscheles, Bennett, and G. A. Osborne, and theory under W. Horsley, and Molique. As a pianist he displayed ability, and performed at the concerts of the Amateur Musical Society. He died at London, December 30, 1875.

WORKS.—Music for the services of the Jewish Church ; Duets. Songs : Angel's voices; Dream of home ; I'll rest ; Lost chord ; Sing on, sing on, ye little birds; Fairies song, etc. Concerto for pf. and orchestra ; Romance for oboe, or violin and pf. (1861) ; Romance for violin and pf. (1878) ; Marches, caprices, and other works for pf.

Walkeley, Antony, organist and composer, was born in 1672. He was trained as a chorister in Wells Cathedral, where he afterwards became vicar-choral. Organist of Salisbury Cathedral, in succession to D. Rosingrave, 1698. Died at Salisbury, January 16, 1717. Composer of a Morning service in E flat, in Tudway's collection, and of anthems in MS.

Walker, Alexander, violinist and composer, of latter part of the 18th century. Composer of "A Collection of Strathspeys, reels, marches, etc....dedicated to Sir Charles Forbes, Bart., of Newe." Aberdeen, n.d.

Walker, Augustus Hayter, teacher of composition and ' musical science, born in London, February 8, 1855. Studied under Dr. F. J. Sawyer. Graduated Mus. Bac., 1883 ; Mus. Doc., 1886, London, being with Dr. W. H. Hunt (q.v.), the first to receive the degree of Mus. Doc. at London University. Sometime resident in Brighton, and professor of harmony and composition at Brighton College, and Conservatoire of Music. Lecturer in musical acoustics, T.C.E., and tutor in music, University Correspondence College. His compositions are; Psalm 95, for soli, chorus, and strings ; Requiem, for soli, eight-part chorus and orchestra, performed, London, February 20, 1886 ; songs, part-songs, and organ pieces, etc.

Walker, Bettina, pianist and writer, born at Dublin. Not originally intended for the musical profession. Studied under Adolphe Henselt chiefly, and settled in London about 1890 as an exponant of his method

WALKER.

of teaching. Author of " My Musical Experiences," London, Bentley, 1890. ·She died at Fulham, February 4, 1893.

Walker, Francis, baritone vocalist of present time. Sang at various concerts in London up to 1885, when he went to Italy for further study. On his return he gave a concert at Burlington Hall, London, April 7, 1886. His experiences he embodied in a book; "Letters of a Baritone," London, Heinemann, 1895.

Walker, Frederick Edward, tenor vocalist, born at Marylebone, London, January 17, 1835. Entered the choir of the Chapel Royal, St. James's, when nine. Studied under private teachers, and became a vicar-choral of St. Paul's Cathedral in 1858. In 1867 he succeeded Henry Buckland as Master of the Boys. Sang in the quartets in "Elijah," Sacred Harmonic Concerts, June 15, 1855, and in the same work at Madam Goldschmidt's farewell performance, December 17, at Exeter Hall. For many years a familiar figure on the concert platform. Conductor of the London Vocal Union, which assisted at the first performance in England of Brahms' "Rinaldo," Crystal Palace, April 15, 1876. He was also appointed conductor of the Brixton Philharmonic Society, 1883. Professor of singing, and Hon. member (1887), of R.A.M. ; professor, G.S.M. He is an organist, pianist, violinist, and performer on the ophicleide ; and accompanied the recitatives on the pf. at the performance of Bach's "Matthew Passion," St. Paul's, April 8, 1873.

Walker, James, violinist and composer, was born at Dysart, Fife, in the latter half of last century, and died there on April 8, 1840. He published " A Collection of new Scots reels, strathspeys, jigs, etc.†with a bass for the violoncello or harpsichord," Dysart, n.d. [1797]. "Second collection of reels, strathspeys, jigs, etc., with bass for the violincello or harpsichord, also defferent marches for volunteer corps," Dysart, n.d. [1800].

Walker, James, amateur musician, born at Aberdeen, July 6, 1827. A tea merchant in Aberdeen, and prominent in city and town council affairs. Author of "On Just Intonation in Song and Speech," Aberdeen, 1876, privately printed. " Some notes regarding the proposed Municipal Band," Aberdeen, 1878. He collected a valuable musical library, which he presented to the Public Library of Aberdeen in 1891. For some years he was president of the Aberdeen Musical Association.

Walker, Joseph, tenor vocalist and writer. Son of Thomas Walker (q.v.) He was one of the founders of the Sacred Harmonic Society. Author of " Walker's Chro-

WALKER.

matic Solmization," London [1825]; "Pocket Memorial for the musical tyro," London, 1835.

Walker, Joseph Cooper, writer and musician, born at Dublin, November, 1760; died at St. Valery, near Bray, April 12, 1810. Author of Historical Memoirs of the Irish Bards, interspersed with anecdotes and occasional observations on the Music of Ireland...." Dublin, 1786. "An Historical account and critical essay on the Opera, and on the revival of the drama in Italy," Edinburgh, 1805. "Memoirs of Alessandro Tassoni, edited by S. Walker," 1815. Other works, chiefly on Irish antiquities.

Walker, Lawrence, organist and pianist. Studied at Armagh Cathedral, and at the Raff Conservatorium, at Frankfort, and gained high praise for a pf. trio performed at a concert there, July 9, 1889. Graduated Mus. Bac. Cambridge, 1891; is also B.A., Dublin. Organist of St. James's Church, Belfast, in which place he is resident as a teacher. He has composed a setting of Psalm 137, for soli-chorus, strings, and organ.

Walker, Reginald, H., musician, was born in 1839. He was the youngest son of J. H. Walker, music master of Rugby School. Died at Kingstown, Ireland, in October, 1876. Composer of "Jerusalem," a cantata, and other vocal music.

Walker, Thomas, composer and alto vocalist, was born at London in 1764. Teacher in London. Died at Queenhithe, July 5, 1827. Composer of "Anthems and set pieces for 2, 3, 4, and 5, voices," London [1808]; "Walker's Companion to Dr. Rippon's Tune Book," London, 1811, 2 vols.; also 1815. Songs and other vocal music.

Wallace, Frank M., violinist, son of Paul Wallace, was a pupil of A. C. Mackenzie, and studied later at Leipzig Conservatorium under F. David and others. For some years he was a member of the principal London orchestras; but failing health caused him to leave England in 1886, and take up his abode in New Zealand. He has given concerts at Christchurch; is the conductor of a musical society there; and holds a good position as a violinist.

Wallace, Lady Maxwell, born GRACE STEIN, born at Edinburgh about 1815. Married in 1836 to Sir James Maxwell Wallace. She died in 1878. Translated "Letters from Italy and Switzerland, by Felix Mendelssohn-Bartholdy," London, 1862 (2 editions); "Letters of Felix Mendelssohn-Bartholdy, from 1833 to 1847 . . ." 1863; "Letter of Wolfgang Amadeus Mozart, 1769-1791 . . ." London, 1865; "Beethoven's Letters, 1790-1826," London, 1866, 2 vols.; "Letters of Distinguished Musicians, Gluck, Haydn, P. E. Bach, Weber, Mendelssohn,"

WALLACE.

London, 1867; "Reminiscences of Felix Mendelssohn-Bartholdy, by Elise Polko," London, 1869.

Wallace, William, composer, born at Greenock in 1860. Educated at Fettes College, Edinburgh, and afterwards entered upon a course of medical study, which was continued at Vienna. He had already commenced to compose music, and on going to London he entered the R.A.M., and decided his career. In 1890 a scena of his was performed at the Academy concerts.

WORKS.—*Orchestral:* Suite in A (based on Ibsen's The Lady of the Sea), produced by the Stock Exchange Orchestral Society, February 18, 1892; Symphonic Poem, The Passing of Beatrice, Crystal Palace, November 26, 1892; Prelude to the Eumenides of Æschylus, the same, October 21, 1893; Concert overture, In Praise of Scottis Poesie, the same, November 17, 1894; Symphonic prelude, Amboss oder Hammer (on Goethe's Kophtisches Lied), the same, October 17, 1896. Trio in A, pf. and strings; Suite in Olden Style, pf. The Rhapsody of Mary Magdelene, Queen's Hall, December 15, 1896; Lyric from Prometheus Unbound, with accompaniment for violin and pf.; Six Songs (Heine); Cycle of Spanish Songs for 4 voices; Madrigal, In a glorious garden green, etc.

Wallace, William Vincent, composer, pianist, and violinist, was born at Waterford, June 1, 1814. Son of Scottish parents, his father being an army bandmaster and bassoon player. On the removal of the family to Dublin, young Wallace frequently appeared at concerts as a violinist from 1829, and in 1834 he played a concerto of his own composition at a concert. He married, first, Miss Kelly, from whom he soon separated, and about 1836 went to Australia, and travelled about there, in New Zealand, India, and South America. He appeared in London in 1845, and produced his operas, but soon after resumed his wanderings, this time visiting the United States as well as South America. In 1850 he married Helène Stoepel, who had some vogue as a pianist. He died at the Chateau de Bagen, Haute Garonne, France, October 12, 1865.

WORKS.—*Operas:* Maritana, London (Drury Lane), November 15, 1845; Matilda of Hungary, London, 1847; Lurline, London (Covent Garden), February, 1860; The Amber Witch, London, February, 1861; Love's Triumph, London, November, 1862; The Desert Flower, London, October, 1863; The Maid of Zurich (never performed); Estrella (unfinished); Gulnare, operetta; Olga, operetta. *Cantata:* May Pole (E. Oxenford). Four Hymns by J. Keble. Corin for Cleora dying, four-part song. *Pianoforte:* Air Russe; Barcarolle; Caprice heroïque; Chant d'Amour,

WALLBRIDGE.

op. 26; Chant des Pelerines, op. 19; Danse Cossaque; Fairy march; Gondellied [1859]; La Gondola, op. 18; Mazurka-étude; Grand mazurka guerrier; Premier nocturne [1856]; Three nocturnes, op. 20; Nocturnes, op. 32; Polka de concert; Le Rêve, romance, op. 21; Romances. op. 25, 36; Six valses; Tarantellas; Village Festival; Woodland murmurs; Le Zephyr, op. 47; numerous transcriptions of popular airs and arrangements from operas. *Songs*: Alice; Autumn (1853); If doughty deeds; Hope in absence; Katie Strang; Winds that waft my sighs to thee; Silent love; Bellringer (1860); Coming of the flowers; Gipsy maid; Star of love; Wood-nymph; etc. His life, which was full of adventure and somewhat romantic, was written by Arthur Pougin under the title of "William Vincent Wallace, étude biographique et critique," Paris, 1866. In 1896 a concert was given in London for the benefit of Wallace's son.

His sister ELIZA was a distinguished violinist and vocalist; who toured in Europe and America as a concert giver. She was married to John Bushelle. Settled latterly in Australia as a teacher, and died at Sydney in August, 1878.

Wallbridge, Arthur, *see* LUNN, Wm. A. B.

Wallis, Ebenezer John, amateur composer, born in London, May 9, 1831; died at Sutton-at-Hone, Kent, October 26, 1879. Composer of "Barossa," a popular hymn tune, which was issued in "Anthems, canticles, and hymns," 1869.

Wallis, John, mathematician and writer, born at Ashford, Kent, November 23, 1616; died at London, October 28, 1703. Author of "Observations concerning the swiftness of sound," London, 1672; "Claudii Ptolemæi Harmonicorum. ." Oxford, 1680. Also numerous papers on musical subjects in the Philosophical Transactions.

Wallworth, Thomas Adlington, composer, teacher, and writer, born at Liverpool, January 18, 1831. The family removed to Huddersfield when he was two years old. He was taught the Lancashire sol-fa by Jackman. of Huddersfield; sang as a baritone at Liverpool. Entered the R.A.M. in 1848, studying chiefly under Crivelli. Sang in the first performance of Bach's Passion (St. Matthew), given by the Bach Society at the Hanover Square Rooms, April 6, 1854. Toured with the Pyne and Harrison opera company, and for many years was actively engaged in concert work. He was appointed professor of singing at the G.S.M. from its opening; also professor, R.A.M., to 1890, and F.R.A.M., and Associate of the Philharmonic Society. His health failing he left England in October, 1886, to reside at Cape Town. Among his

WALSH.

pupils were Madame Valleria, Mr. Iver McKay, and others who have made a reputation. He composed an operetta, "Kevin's Choice," produced at the Adelphi Theatre, March 25, 1882; a prize glee, Up, Sailor boy (1865); and other vocal pieces. Author of A Course of Study and Practice for the Voice; Art of Voice Training and Vocalisation.

Walmisley, Thomas Forbes, composer and organist, born at London in 1783. He was a chorister in Westminster Abbey, and studied under Attwood. Married eldest daughter of Wm. Capon, 1810. Organist of St. Martin-in-the-Fields, London, 1812. He died at London, July 23, 1866.

WORKS.—Six Glees for 3, 4, 5, and 6 voices, London, 1814; A Collection of Glees, Trios, Rounds, and Canons, London, 1826; Six Glees, dedicated to the Catch Club, London, 1830; Six Glees for 4 voices, 3rd collection, London, 1830, ; Six Glees, 4th collection, London; many single glees, including prize glees, etc. Six Anthems and a short Morning and Evening Service, London, n.d. Sacred Songs, London, 1841. Songs.

Walmisley, Thomas Attwood, organist and composer, born at London, January 21, 1814. Son of above. He studied under Attwood, who was his godfather. Organist of Croydon Church, 1830, and of Trinity and St. John's Colleges, Cambridge, 1833. Mus. Bac. Cantab., 1833. Professor of Music at Cambridge, 1836. B.A., 1838; M.A., 1841. Mus. Doc. Cantab., 1848. He died at Hastings, January 17, 1856.

WORKS.—Cathedral Music, a collection of services and anthems, London, 1857, edited by T. F. Walmisley. Odes on installation of Duke of Northumberland (1842) and Prince Albert (1849) as chancellors of Cambridge University. Collection of Chants with the responses in use at the chapels of King's, Trinity, and St. John's Colleges, Cambridge, London [1845]. Choral hymn in four parts. Cambria, trio. Four songs by Mrs. Elliott (1854); Chatelar to Mary, Queen of Scots, and other songs.

Walond, William, organist and composer of the 18th century, was a member of Christ Church, Oxford, and in or about 1757 graduated as Mus. Bac. He composed an ode "St. Cecilia's Day" (1790), by Pope, and other works. Another WILLIAM WALOND, probably the son of the above, was born about 1750. He was organist of Chichester Cathedral, and died at Chichester, February 9, 1836. He composed some music for the church.

Walsh, George, organist, who succeeded Rosingrave at Christ Church Cathedral, Dublin. He died in 1765.

Walsh, Thomas, teacher of singing, was born in the latter part of the 18th century. He was proprietor of the Argyle Rooms, Lon-

WALSH.

don, when the Philharmonic Society gave its concerts there. Best known as a successful voice trainer. Kitty Stephens was one of many distinguished vocalists trained by him. He died at Brighton, January 24, 1848.

Walsh, William J., musician, issued " Grammar of Gregorian Music, with numerous exercises and examples," Dublin, 1885.

Walshe, Walter Hayle, physician and writer, born at Dublin in 1816. Author of "Dramatic Singing Physiologically estimated" London, 1881.

Walter, Ida, composer of the present time. Niece of chief proprietor of the *Times*. Studied at R.A.M. Composer of an opera, "Florian," produced, Novelty Theatre, July 14, 1886 ; also of The Sea hath its pearls ; O let the solid ground ; and other songs.

Walter, John, composer and organist, of latter part of 17th and beginning of the 18th centuries. He was organist of Eton College early in the 18th century. Composer of music for the church. Was teacher of John Weldon.

Walters, Dr. Allan, conductor of the Musical Union, Brisbane, Queensland, Australia, is the composer of a Jubilee Ode, for chorus and orchestra, produced, Brisbane, June, 1887. He is said to be doing good service to music in his district.

Walthew, Richard H., pianist and composer. Pupil of Dr. Hubert Parry, at R.C.M. First came into notice by playing a pf. concerto of his own at a concert of the Strolling Players, Queen's Hall, May 3, 1894. An orchestral suite, and a Festival overture, have been performed by the Stock Exchange Society, 1895-6 ; and the Highbury Philharmonic Society produced his setting of Browning's Pied Piper of Hamelin (for soli, chorus, and orchestra), in 1893. He has also composed a Festival March for orchestra ; Trio, pf. and strings ; pieces for clarinet and pf. ; Snowdrops, cantata for female voices ; songs, etc.

Walton, Rev. C. B., amateur musician. Sometime vicar (or curate ?) of St. James's, Ogley Hay, compiled " A selection of original chants, hymn tunes, kyries, etc.," Birmingham, Harrison [1880].

Walton, Emanuel, composer and organist, of first half of present century. Composer of " An original set of psalm and hymn tunes, arranged for four voices," Leeds [1810]; " Church psalmody, selected and arranged for four voices," London [1830]; Walton's psalmody, 2nd edition [1835]. *Songs:* How sleep the brave ; Radiant queen ; When the sun is fast declining, and other vocal music.

Wanless, Thomas, organist and composer of the latter part of the 17th and early part of the 18th centuries. He graduated Mus. Bac. Cambridge in 1698, and afterwards

WARD.

became organist of York Minster. He died in 1721. Composer of the " York Litany" and some anthems.

Ward, Adelaide, see NEWTON, MRS. ALEX.

Ward, Cornelius, organist, composer, and writer, born at Speen, Buckinghamshire, June 29, 1814. Organist and teacher at Speen. WORKS.—Prodigal Son, oratorio ; Nativity, cantata ; Seraphic tidings, ode. Buckinghamshire Melodist, a new set of psalm and hymn tunes, London, 1844. Wesleyan Minstrel, comprising a set of tunes adapted to all the varieties of metre in the Rev. J. Wesley's hymn book [1854]. The Choristor, 5 vols. ; Choral Beauties, 2 vols. The Flute explained being an examination of the principles of its structure and action, London, 1844. Anthems, songs, etc. He also edited a reprint of Nicholds' oratorio, "Babylon."

Ward, Francis Marshall, bass vocalist, organist, and conductor, born at Lincoln, December 26, 1830. Educated as a chorister at Lincoln Cathedral, and in 1845 was appointed organist of St. Peter in Eastgate, Lincoln. Was elected principal bass at Hereford Cathedral, 1851, and during the next twenty years sang a good deal in oratorio and general concert work. Organist and choirmaster Abergavenny Parish Church, 1856 ; St. Mary's, Lincoln, 1857. Was bandmaster of the 1st Lincolnshire Volunteers when the movement started, and won several prizes at brass band contests. Removed to Nottingham about 1867, and was organist of Lenton Parish Church, and after holding similar appointments at other churches, was appointed in 1894 to Broad Street Wesley Chapel, where an orchestra is employed on Sunday Evenings. Was organist and music master at the Blind Institution, Nottinghom, for ten years ; and has conducted societies at Lincoln and other places. The Nottingham Philharmonic Society, under his direction, won the prize of £100 at the Liverpool Exhibition, 1886. He is also musical director of the Nottingham Glee Club. His compositions include a Minuet for orchestra, church services, anthems, songs, and part-songs, only a few of which are published. His daughters, LILY, a soprano, and JESSIE a contralto vocalist, have sung in the Midlands and the North with success since 1885.

Ward, Frederick, violinist and composer, born in Birmingham, December 26, 1845. Principal violinist in orchestral concerts, Birmingham, and in great request in the Midlands as a soloist. Member of the Birmingham Festival Orchestra. Has composed a concert overture for orchestra ; two concertos for clarinet and orchestra ; a sextet, and ten quartets for strings ; pieces for violin ; songs, part-songs, etc.

Ward, John, composer of the 16th and

WARD.

17th centuries. He died about 1640. Composed "The First Set of English Madrigals, to 3, 4, 5, and 6 parts, apt both for viols and voyces ; with a Mourning Song in memory of Prince Henry.." London, 1613. Songs in Leighton's "Teares," and service and anthem in Barnard's collection.

Ward, John, English writer, author of " Lives of the Professors of Gresham College, to which is perfixed the life of the founder, Sir Thomas Gresham, with an appendix consisting of orations, etc..." London, 1740. Contains lives of Bull, Clayton, Taverner, and other professors of music.

Ward, John Charles, organist and composer, born at Upper Clapton, London, March 27, 1835. Entered the choir of the Temple Church with his brother, R. J. Ward (noticed below), in 1842, remaining there until 1848. Studied pf. under his father, violin under Howard Glover, and concertina with George Case. Played a concertina solo at Crosby Hall, December 2, 1846, and for a long time was known as a *virtuoso* on the instrument. He has been organist successively at Bridewell Hospital Chapel, 1852 ; St. John's Chapel, Hampstead, 1853 ; Eaton Chapel, Eaton Square, 1856 ; Christ Church, Hampstead, 1863 ; Quebec Chapel, 1868 ; Holy Trinity, Haverstock Hill, 1884 ; Christ Church, Streatham Hill, 1886 ; and St. Mary the Virgin, Primrose Hill, from 1890. Member of the Leslie Choir from its foundation in 1855, and organist and assistant-conductor from 1856 to 1885. For his services as organist when the choir visited Paris in 1878, he was awarded a medal. He has given organ recitals in various places.

WORKS.—Motet, Thy Word is a Lantern, double choir ; Sanctus, double choir (sung by Leslie's Choir) ; Cantata, The Wood ; Testimonial Ode ; A Psalm of Life, men's chorus and orchestra ; Church services ; anthem, I am the Resurrection, *In Memoriam,* Henry Leslie. Collection of hymn tunes and chants. Lives of great men ; Rove not to the Rhine ; and other part-songs. Trios, Faith, Hope, for soprano, mezzo-soprano, and tenor. Cantata, The Swedish Singers, female voices. Fugue on the Sailor's Hornpipe, orchestra, written for the Bradford Permanent Orchestra. *Organ:* Nautical Symphony in four movements ; Prelude and Fugue, Westminster Chimes ; Prelude and March, Wedding Chimes ; Fugue on London New, etc. Fugues and other pieces for pf. Trio, for Æola, 'cello, and bass concertina ; Minuet for 3 concertinas ; Polonaise in E flat, pf. and concertina, etc. Mr. Ward invented a new form of piano, and the Harmonic Angelute.

His two sisters and brother were musicians. The elder sister EMILY (Mrs. Alexander Newton) is separately noticed. The second, ELIZA

WARE.

A. WARD, is a pianist and vocalist. Was the pianist of the concert party on tour with Jenny Lind, when Sims Reeves, Mrs. A. Newton, F. Lablache, and other singers were included ; and was one of the original members of Leslie's Choir. Resident in London as teacher. His brother, R. J. WARD, born in 1813, was a chorister at the Temple Church, 1842-6. Afterwards he studied the slide-trumpet, and became eminent as a performer. He belonged to the Royal Italian Opera, and other leading orchestras. While officiating at a concert at Brighton he had an apoplectic stroke which closed his professional career ; but he survived for fifteen years, and so far recovered as to be able to walk from ten to fourteen miles a day without fatigue. His remaining years were devoted to the amelioration of the sufferings of others, by remedial appliances so successful in his own case. He died at East Dulwich, January 22, 1884, aged 53. CLEMENTINE, daughter of J. C. Ward, is resident organist of St. Saviour's Hospital, Osnaburg Street, London. She has sung at her father's organ recitals, and is the composer of a March, Gavotte, and "Dickens Series " of little pieces, etc., for pf. EVELYN, another daughter, born at Hampstead, January 9, 1865, is a soprano vocalist. She studied under her father, and took leading parts in various comic operas in England and the United States of America, from 1884 to 1893, when she retired from the stage. She married Mr. Hamilton Tetley.

Ware, Alfred, musician, issued "Sacred Melodies, containing Psalm, Hymn, and Anthems, arranged for the Violin," London [1852].

Ware, George, composer and writer, was born in 1762 ; died at Liverpool in 1850. Son of George Ware (1723 : London, March 7, 1814), a teacher and composer of vocal music. George, the younger, composed glees, songs, and rondos, and other music for the pf., and wrote "A Dictionary of musical chords, arranged so as to find any modulation by various methods, through the twelve half-tones," London, n.d.

Ware, William Henry, composer and violinist, was another son of George Ware, the elder. For some years he was leader at Covent Garden Theatre, but no further trace of his career seems to have been preserved.

WORKS.—*Music to Plays, Pantomimes, etc. :* Aladdin, 1813 ; Bonifacio and Bridgetina, 1808 ; Cariolanus, 1806 ; Cymbeline, 1806 ; Don John, 1821 ; Grand tour, 1820 ; Harlequin and Mother Bunch, 1821 ; Harlequin and Mother Goose, 1806 ; Harlequin and the sylph of the oak, 1816 ; Macbeth, 1806 ; Montrose, 1822 ; Ogre, 1807 ; Two galley slaves, 1822 ; Undine, 1821 ; Vision of the sun, 1823 ; Zembuca, 1815. Six ballads and songs, [1835].

WAREHAM.

Three duets for two violins, op. 2; Trio for two violins and 'cello, etc.

Wareham, Edwin James, tenor vocalist and organist, born at Wimborne, Dorset, September 16, 1864. Having a good soprano voice he was a successful concert singer at eight years of age, and when twelve was appointed at one of the churches in Wimborne. In 1881, he was appointed organist of Woodbridge Parish Church, and conductor of the East Suffolk Church Choir Union; moving, in 1884, to Glasgow, as organist of Claremont Church. A year later he succeeded the late Channon Cornwall, as organist and accompanist to the Glasgow Choral Union. He also frequently conducted the rehearsals; and played the organ at the great Jubilee service in the Cathedral, 1887, and at the opening of the Exhibition, 1888. His next appointment was to St. George's, Albemarle Street, London, 1890, where he greatly improved the musical services. He now resumed the study of singing at the Guildhall School, under T. A. Wallworth, and at the R.A.M., under W. H. Cummings. Made his *début* in opera at the Olympic Theatre, October, 1892, as the poet in "Eugene Onegin"; created the part of Geoffrey Norreys in Thomas's "Golden Web," produced at Liverpool, February, 1893. Appeared in Grand Opera, Covent Garden, 1895; at Richter Concerts, 1893; Crystal Palace, 1894, etc. Sang in South Africa, 1896-7, and at first Festival in Johannesburg, 1897.

Wareing, Herbert Walter, composer and organist, born in Birmingham, April 5, 1857. Studied under Dr. C. Swinnerton Heap, and at Leipzig Conservatorium, under Reinecke, Jadassohn, E. F. Richter, and others. Graduated Mus. Bac., Cambridge, 1882; Mus. Doc., 1886. Has held organ appointments at St. John's, Wolverhampton, 1876-9; Edgbaston Parish Church, 1881-8; and since 1891, at King's Norton Parish Church. Resident at King's Norton, engaged in composition, and teaching. He is professor of the pf. at Malvern College, and has other important engagements.

WORKS.—Cantatas, Prayer and Praise (Mus. Bac. Exercise); New Year's Eve (Exercise for Mus. Doc.); The Wreck of the Hesperus, for tenor and bass soli, chorus and orchestra, 1895. Church service in G; Anthems, part-songs, songs, etc. Concert overture in F (Birmingham, 1879); String quartet in F (performed at the Hauptprüfung, Leipzig, 1876); Ten concert pieces for violin and pf.; Two pieces for violoncello and pf.; Pieces for organ and pf.

Waring, William, musician of latter part of 18th century. Translator of Rousseau's "Dictionnaire de Musique" as complete Dictionary of Music, consisting of a

WARNER.

copious explanation of all words necessary to a true knowledge and understanding of music, translated from the original French of J. J. Rousseau," London, 1770; 2nd edition [1779].

Warman, John Watson, organist and writer, born at Canterbury, August 12, 1842. Son of a private schoolmaster, and descended from a family of French Huguenot refugees. Received a few lessons from Dr. Longhurst, and E. H. Thorne, otherwise self-educated in music. Articled to organ building about 1858. Was assistant organist at Ashford Church, Kent, 1862; organist at Hunton Bridge, near Watford, 1865; afterwards at Faringdon, Berks., and Hove, Sussex. Went to Quebec in 1872 as organist of the Anglican Cathedral there, but returned at the end of a year. He then, for the purpose of acquiring practical knowledge, worked for some months as an ordinary journeyman at Hill's organ factory, London. Returned to Canterbury in 1877, and was sometime local examiner for R.C.M. In 1887 he removed to Thornton Heath, Croydon, where he is giving himself up entirely to literary work. Author of a series of papers on Counterpoint, published in *Musical Opinion,* vols. v. and vi., and other contributions to various periodicals. The Organ, its compass, etc., London, Wm. Reeves, 1884. Now engaged on a large bibliography of organ, structural, musical, and mechanical works allied. He has composed a few hymn tunes, chants, etc.

Warne, George, composer and organist, was born in 1792. He was blind, but for a number of years held the appointment of organist at the Temple Church, London. Died at Bath, October 29, 1868.

WORKS.—Set of psalm tunes, as sung at the Temple Church, London [1838]. Songs: Broken gold; Come away to the grot; Evening song; O bring me my harp; We meet again in heaven. Quadrilles, galops, and other music for the pf.

Warner, Daniel, musician, who was a singing master at the end of the 17th and beginning of the 18th centuries. Compiler of the "Devout Singer's Guide, containing all the common tunes now in use, with select portions of the psalms adapted to each tune," London, 1711. "Singing Master's Guide," 1719. The "Devout Singer's Guide" is *recommended* by Warner, so he may not have actually compiled it.

Warner, Harry Ernest, organist, pianist and composer, born at Isleworth, Middlesex, July 1, 1859. Received his first lesson from the organist of the Parish Church, whose deputy he became at the age of fourteen. Later, he studied with the Rev. Dr. Hayden, M.A., and when eighteen was appointed organist and choirmaster of Brentford Parish Church, which he left seven years later for the

WARREN.

Royal Church, Kew, where he is still in office. Honorary local examiner for R.C.M. Though busily engaged in concerts and teaching, he has found time for composition, and his works include two Cantatas for female voices, "Merry May" (1891), and "The Golden Valley" (1893). Also anthems, O God have mercy; If ye love me; hymn tunes, part-songs, seventeen part-songs for female voices, etc.—"La Felicite," orchestra; Air de ballet, string quartet; Romance in D, pf. and strings; Royal Bridal March, military band; Reverie, for violin, harp, pf., and organ; pieces for violin and pf., and pf. solo, etc., etc.

Warren, Ambrose, author of "The Tonometer, explaining and demonstrating by an easy method in numbers and proportions, all the 32 distinct and different notes, adjuncts, or supplements contained in each of four octives inclusive of the gamut.." London, 1725.

Warren, Edmund Thomas, music-publisher and collector, was born about 1730. He was engaged in business in London and acted as Secretary of the Catch Club. He died in 1794. Editor of "Reliques of ancient music," and "Vocal Harmony," a collection of catches and glees, issued in parts.

Warren, Joseph, organist and composer, born at London, March 20, 1804. He studied music under J. Stone, and from 1843 was organist and choirmaster of St. Mary's Roman Catholic Chapel, Chelsea. He died at Bexley, Kent, March 8, 1881.

WORKS.—Selection of Cathedral Chants [1840]. Selection of one hundred chants, London, 1845. Repertorium Musicæ Antiquæ, London, 1848 (with John Bishop). Collection of psalm and hymn tunes, 1850-54, 4 vols. Hymns and canticles, 1852. The burial service as performed at the funeral of the Duke of Wellington..London, 1853. Hymns of Joh. Sebastian Bach, London, n.d. *Theoretical, etc.:* Hints to young organists, London, 1844. Biographical dictionary of deceased musicians, London, 1845 and later editions. Chanter's hand-guide, London, 1845. Hints to young composers, London, 1846. Writing for the orchestra, 1846. Instruction book for the organ, London, n.d. Instructions for the harmonium, London, 1852. Complete instructions for the concertina [1855]. Introduction and observations on the mode of singing catches, rounds, canons, glees, and madrigals, London, n.d. Most of these works were published in various editions, chiefly by R. Cocks and Co.

Warren, Samuel P., organist and pianist, born at Montreal, Canada, February 18, 1841. Son of S. R. Warren, organ builder (died, Toronto, 1882). Studied locally, and was organist at a church in Montreal, 1853-61. Then went to Berlin and studied under

WARWICK.

Haupt, G. Schumann, Wieprecht, and others, 1861-4. Returned to America in 1864, and the next year became organist of All Souls' Church, New York. From 1874 he was organist of Holy Trinity, New York, for two years, his latest appointment being at Grace Church in that city. For a number of years he has given a series of organ recitals, embracing the entire literature for the instrument. He is also known as an excellent pianist. His compositions consist of church services, anthems, and songs.

Warren, William, organist and composer, was born in the latter part of the 18th century. He was organist of Christ Church Cathedral, Dublin, 1814, and graduated Mus. Doc., Dublin. Died at Dublin in July, 1841. Composer of a prize glee, "Shepherds, hither come," 1802, and others.

Warriner, John, organist, pianist, and writer, born at Bourton, Shropshire, May 12, 1858. Pupil of Chevalier de Val (Brussels), and G. Riseley. Organist of Dunster Parish Church, 1880, and concurrently, 1884-7, of St. Andrew's, and the Parish Church, Minehead. Conductor of Dunster Philharmonic Society, which gave some excellent concerts with orchestra; and organ recitalist. Graduated Mus. Bac., 1887; Mus. Doc., 1892, Dublin. In 1887 he was appointed to St. Matthew's, Denmark Hill, London, where he introduced oratorio serivces as he had done at Dunster. Conductor of Walthamstow Musical Society, 1893. Professor of pf., T.C.L., 1890, and examiner there, 1894. His compositions are, Psalm 30, for soli, five-part chorus, organ, and strings; Psalm 13, for soli, eight-part chorus and orchestra; and orchestral works in MS. He has published some church music, and pieces for organ, pf., etc. Author of a primer on Transposition, Novello; Editor of National Portrait Gallery of British Musicians, Sampson Low, 1896. Editor for two years of *The Minim.*

Warrington, Frederick, bass vocalist, of Toronto, Canada, has sung at the leading concerts in the Dominion. He took part in the first festival held at Toronto, in June, 1886; sang in the Jubilee performance of "Elijah," Toronto, November 28, 1896; and has a good reputation as a vocalist, and choir trainer.

Warwick, Giulia, soprano vocalist, pupil of Madame Sainton-Dolby. Sang at concerts in London, and on tour with Wilhelmj, in 1877. Was a member of the Carl Rosa Opera Company, 1879-82; and later, sang in comic opera. Formed a company of her own, and produced, for the first time, an English version of Vasseur's "Madame Cartouche," at Leicester, September, 1891. In 1894 she was appointed professor of deportment, etc., at the Guildhall School of Music; and in 1896, professor of singing, succeeding her sister, ALEXANDRA EHRENBERG, who died September 2, 1896. She was a contralto singer, educated at the R.A.M., of which she was an Associate. For some years she sang in oratorio and other concerts in London, and the provinces, appearing at the Crystal Palace in 1883. In 1891 she was appointed a professor of singing at the Guildhall School. She died at the early age of thirty-three.

Warwick, Thomas, organist and composer of 17th century. In 1625 he was lutenist to Charles I., and in the same year succeeded Orlando Gibbons as organist of the Chapel Royal. He died sometime after 1641. His son, Sir Philip Warwick, was secretary to the Treasury in the time of Charles II. Composer of a song in 40 parts, said to have been performed in 1635.

Wass, John, composer, born in 1800; died at London, in July, 1865. He was a teacher of singing in London. Composer of "The Foresters' Roundelay," a cantata, 1863; Part-songs. *Songs :* Flower spirit ; Good night to thee, etc. Pf. music. British Navy quadrilles, etc. Finger exercises for the pf., 1843. Author of "Boosey's Universal Singing Method," London [1855].

Waterhouse, George, organist and composer of the latter half of the 16th century. He was organist of Lincoln Cathedral, and afterwards of Queen Elizabeth's private chapel. In 1592 he graduated Mus. Bac., Oxford. He died in 1601. Composer of canons, etc., none of which are known to be extant.

Waterson, James, bandmaster, was a pupil of James Waddell, and succeeded him as bandmaster of the 1st Life Guards in 1876. After his retirement from that post he was appointed conductor of the band of the Viceroy of India. He arranged a great deal of music for military bands ; was the composer of a dramatic overture, founded upon the "Tale of Two Cities," by Charles Dickens, produced, Alexandra Palace, February 19, 1876 ; a quintet for wind instruments, etc. He was one of the joint editors of the *British Bandsman* when it started, October, 1887. He died, October, 1893, and was buried in Windsor Cemetery on the 13th.

Waterworth, Robert, musician, who published "Original selection of Psalm and Hymn tunes, chants, and responses," Halifax [1852].

Watlen, John, musician of the latter part of last and early part of the present century. He seems to have been originally in the navy, but afterwards became an assistant to Corri and Co., music-sellers, Edinburgh, previous to 1788. He next commenced business as a tuner, teacher, and music-seller, on his own account in the North Bridge, Edin-

burgh, but failed in 1798, and subsequently went to London and started business in Leicester Place, Leicester Square. He was the first secretary of the Edinburgh Musical Fund, established in 1790. Compiler of "Celebrated circus tunes, performed at Edinburgh..with the addition of some new reels and strathspeys, set for the pianoforte or violin and bass," Edinburgh, n.d. [1791]. He also issued a "Collection of old Scots songs," 1793, published in 12 parts ; "Watlen's Complete collection of Scots songs, plain and simple, without being Italianized in the least ..," 1796. Watlen altered a reel of Robert Petrie's to form the melody usually sung to Burns' song, "Comin' thro' the Rye." His compositions include Lord's Prayer, anthem ; Anna, song ; Sonata for pf. or harpsichord and violin, Edinburgh [1798] ; Grand sonata for pf. and violin, op. 9, London [1800] ; Edinburgh, grand march for pf. ; Glorious battle of Trafalgar, pf. (1805), etc.

Watson, Alfred Reuben, violinist, composer, and conductor, born at Nottingham, July 22, 1845. Studied under T. Leeson Selby, and the late Henry Farmer. Joined the orchestra of the Theatre Royal, Nottingham, in 1871, and in 1876 succeeded Mr. Leverton as musical director, a position he retained until 1888. During that period he composed and arranged the whole of the music for the pantomimes produced there. He conducted the first fortnight's performances of Byron's "Sardanapalus," when it was produced at the Old Duke's Theatre, London, 1878, and conducted the concerts at Woodhall Spa, Lincolnshire, 1891-2-3. His principal composition is a comic opera, "Geraldine" (libretto by Edgar Wyatt), which was produced at Nottingham, September 5, 1887, and which met with much success at Brighton, Birmingham, Dublin, and elsewhere during the following year. He has also written music to various plays; for the Manchester Theatre Royal Pantomime, 1889 ; a great number of pieces for violin and pf., and some church music.

Watson, Henry, organist, pianist, composer, and conductor, born at Burnley, Lancashire, April 30, 1846. Studied music privately. Graduated Mus. Bac., 1882; Mus. Doc., 1887, Cambridge. Has held several organ appointments, the last being at the Congregational Church, Withington, Manchester. Established in 1867 (with Henry Wilson), the Manchester Vocal Union, and on the death of Mr. Wilson in 1885, became conductor. He is also conductor of the Manchester Athenæum Musical Society ; Gentlemen's Glee Club ; and societies at Stretford and Stockport ; and conductor of the Choral class at the Manchester Royal College of Music.

His works include Psalm 103, for soli, chorus, and strings ; cantata, The deliverance of Israel, for soli, chorus, and orchestra. Also an opera, Fair Rosine, Manchester, 1882 ; A Shakesperian cantata, 1890 ; Music to Antony and Cleopatra (for Louis Calvert, Manchester, 1897) ; Part-songs, songs, etc.

Watson, James, amateur composer, born at Glasgow, June 10, 1816. He identified himself with the Free Church movement in Scotland, and in 1845 he entered the firm of Nisbet and Co., publishers, London, as a partner. He died at London, September 1, 1880. He aided in the compilation of "Psalms and Hymns for Divine worship," 1867 ; and composed the hymn tune "Holyrood," generally included in Scottish collections.

Watson, John, composer and pianist of latter part of 18th and beginning of 19th centuries. He was composer to Covent Garden Theatre, London.

WORKS.—Pride shall have a fall, musical comedy by G. Croly, Covent Garden, 1824. Musical Moralist, containing a collection of songs and hymns..London [1805]. Royal Psalmist, or sacred melodies..London [1825]. Six favourite dances, pf. Songs and instrumental music.

Watson, Thomas, poet and musician of the 16th century. He died in 1592. Composer of "The first sett of Italian madrigals Englished, not to the sense of the original dittie, but after the affection of the noate," London, 1590.

Watson, William Michael, composer and poet, born at Newcastle-on-Tyne, July 31, 1840. He originally studied painting at Leigh's School, London, along with Fred. Walker, H. S. Marks, and others, but in 1860 he adopted music as his profession. In 1883 he established the West End School of Music at London. He died at East Dulwich, London, October 3, 1889.

WORKS.—Aladdin, cantata, 1885. *Songs :* Afloat ; Anchored ; Blush rose ; My country calls me ; Powder monkey (1881) ; Quaker's daughter ; Somebody's pride ; Talisman ; Winter story, etc. Part-songs and pf. music. He composed under the pseudonym of *Jules Favre.*

Watts, John, organist and composer, was born in 1780. Teacher and arranger of music in London. Died in Lambeth, London, October 16, 1854. He arranged Handel's 48 overtures for pf. or organ [1824] ; Mozart's quartets for pf., and edited much instrumental music of various kinds.

Watts, Joseph Virgo, organist and composer, born at Wotton-under-Edge, Gloucester, June 27, 1822. He studied music under Hullah, Mainzer, and G. W. Martin. Subsequently he became organist at Chromhall, Lydney, and Berkeley, all in Gloucestershire ; then held

appointments successively at Midsomernorton (Somerset) ; Box Parish Church (Wilts.) ; All Saints' Chapel, Bath ; Kensington, etc. Afterwards he became choir-master of the Abbey Church, Bath, from which he retired in 1885. He composed some church music, and published " Original Hymn-Tunes, chants, kyries, and chant services," 1876.

Watts, Thomas Isaac, organist and composer. Studied at R.A.M. Graduated Mus. Bac., 1886 ; B.A., 1887 ; M.A., 1891, Cambridge. F.R.C.O. He was Choral Scholar of Queen's College, Cambridge, 1884-7 ; and in 1887 was appointed organist, choir-master, and assistant master, Trinity College, Glenalmond, N.B., where he still remains. His compositions are : Ps. 19, for tenor solo, chorus, and strings ; Ode, The Ages of Almond, written for the 50th anniversary of the foundation of Trinity College, Glenalmond, 1892 ; an evening service, hymn tunes, etc.

Waud, John Haydn, contrabassist and violoncellist, born in London, March 9, 1848 ; Principal double-bass at the Alexandra Palace, 1876 ; of the Glasgow Choral Union orchestra for many years ; and member of the Philharmonic and Provincial Festival orchestras ; principal double-bass, Birmingham Festival, from 1891. Musical director at the Garrick Theatre, and professor at G.S.M. Author of a Progressive Tutor for the Double-Bass, London, Augener, 1895.

Waylett, Mrs. Harriett, *born* COOKE, soprano vocalist, was born at Bath, February 7, 1800. She studied under Loder, and first appeared at Bath in 1816. In 1819 she married a Mr. Waylett, but separated from him in 1822. She afterwards married Geo. Alex. Lee, the composer. She first appeared in London in 1820 ; at Dublin in 1826 ; and she afterwards sang at all the principal London and provincial concerts. She died at London, April 26, 1851.

Weale, William, or **Wheall,** organist and composer, was organist of St. Paul's, Bedford, from about 1715. Mus. Bac. Cantab., 1719. He died at Bedford in August or September, 1727. Composer of the psalm tune "Bedford," etc.

Weatherly, Frederic E., poet and composer, born at Portishead in 1848. Educated at Oxford and graduated B.A., 1871 ; M.A., 1874. Tutor in Oxford. Best known as author of many of the most popular songs, cantatas, etc. of the present day. He has himself composed a number of songs, chiefly to his own words.

Webb, Daniel, author and musician, born at Taunton in 1735. Died at Bath, August 2, 1815. Author of " Observations on the Correspondence between Poetry and Music," London, 1769 (Anon). Reprinted in his " Miscellanies," 1802.

WEBB.

Webb, F. Gilbert, organist, composer, and critic. Studied under H. F. Frost. Has been for some years organist of St. Luke's, Brompton, London. Is chiefly devoted to musical literature, and has read papers before the Musical Association, etc., contributed to the *Musical World* and other periodicals; and is much associated with musical criticism. He has composed church music, songs, pieces for violin and pf., etc.

Webb, Francis, author of "Panharmonicon, an illustration of an engraved plate, in which is attempted to be proved that the principles of Harmony more or less prevail throughout the whole system of nature, but more especially in the human frame," London [1815].

Webb, George James, organist and composer, born at Rushmore Lodge, near Salisbury, June 24, 1803. He was taught music by Alex. Lucas, of Salisbury, and afterwards became organist at Falmouth, but resigned in 1830, when he went to the United States. He was appointed organist of the Old South Church, Boston, Mass., and took an active part in the musical life of that city, being president of the Handel and Haydn Society in 1840. In 1870, he went to Orange, New Jersey, and from 1876, resided in New York as a teacher. He returned to Orange in 1885, and died there, October 7, 1887. Author of "Vocal Technics," Boston, n.d., and "Voice Culture," with C. G. Allen; and editor of "Young Ladies' Vocal Class Book," Boston, 1853; "Glee Hive" (with L. Mason); "The Odeon,"1840; "New Odeon" (with L. Mason); "Cantica Laudis" (with Mason), New York, 1850. He composed a number of anthems, the well-known hymn, "Morning Light," etc.

Webb, Rev. Richard, M.A., clergyman and musician, was a minor canon of St. Paul's, London. He died near Windsor, April 13, 1829. Published "A Collection of Madrigals for 3, 4, 5, and 6 voices, selected from the works of the most eminent composers of the 15th and 16th centuries," London, 1808. Collection of Madrigals for 3, 4, and 5 voices, London, 1814. Composer of a Set of four Glees for 3 voices, London, n.d.

Webb, William, organist and composer of 18th century, who was choirmaster and organist of St. George's Chapel, Windsor. He died in 1788, from loss of blood, after undergoing an operation for removal of a wen in the nostril. He was nearly seventy years of age.

Webbe, Samuel, composer and organist, was born at Minorca, in the Balearic Islands, in 1740. His father was a government official there. He was principally self-taught in music, but he had some lessons from Charles Barbandt. He married in 1763. Chapelmaster in Portuguese Chapel, London, 1776.

WEBSTER.

Secretary to Noblemen and Gentlemen's Catch Club, 1794. He died in London, May 25, 1816, and is buried in the Roman Catholic part of old St. Pancras churchyard.

WORKS.—A Collection of Sacred Music, as used in the Chapel of the King of Sardinia in London, London, n.d. A Collection of Masses, with an accompaniment for the organ.... London, 1792. A Collection of Motetts or Antiphons, for 1, 2, 3, and 4 voices, London, 1792. Eight Anthems by Samuel Webbe, the organ parts by V. Novello, London, n.d. A Collection of original Psalm Tunes for 3 and 4 voices, by S. Webbe, Senior and Junior, London. *Glees:* A Selection of Glees, Duets, Canzonets, etc., published at different periods from the year 1764, to which are added many new glees and canzonets never before published, London, 3 vols. A Collection of Catches, Canons, and Glees, London, 9 vols. Six original Glees, London, 1840. *Single Glees:* Breathe soft, ye winds; Cecilia, more than all the muses skilled; Come live with me; Come, rosy health; Discord, dire sister, 1771; Glorious Apollo; Great Apollo, strike the lyre; Great Bacchus, O aid us; Hence, all ye vain delights; Hail, star of Brunswick; Mighty conqueror of hearts, 1775; Swiftly from the mountain's brow, 1788; Thy voice, O harmony; When winds breathe soft. Those dated are prize glees. Duets, songs. Concerto for harpsichord. Pf. music, and other works. The well-known hymn tunes, "Melcombe," and "Benevento," are by him.

Webbe, Samuel, Junr., composer, writer, and organist, son of the above, born at London in 1770. He studied under his father and Clementi. Organist successively of the Unitarian Church, Paradise Street, Liverpool; Spanish Ambassador's Chapel, London; St. Nicholas' Church, and St. Patrick's R. C. Chapel, Liverpool. He died at Hammersmith, London, November 25, 1843.

WORKS.—Collection of Psalm Tunes, intermixed with airs adapted as such, for four voices, London, 1808. Glees, duets, etc. Convito Armonico, a collection of madrigals, elegies, glees, canons, catches, and duets, selected from the works of the most eminent composers, London, 4 vols., n.d. L'Amico del Principiante, being 28 short sol-faing exercises for a single voice, London, n.d.; 2nd edition edited by J. B. Sale. 42 Vocal Exercises..n.d. Short exercises for young singers ..n.d. Harmony epitomised, or elements of the thoroughbass, London, n.d.

His son, EGERTON WEBBE (born Liverpool, 1810; died there June 24, 1840), wrote many valuable papers on music for the early numbers of the *Musical World*.

Webster, Clarinda Augusta, pianist, born in London. Daughter of the late Robert Thomson, M.R.C.S., L.D.S., of London. She

WEBSTER.

was musically educated in London, and went to reside in Scotland after her marriage. In 1860 she established the Aberdeen Music School, and gave herself up to the work of musical education. As the outcome of her theoretical teaching she published the "Groundwork of Music," two books; and the "Child's Primer of the Theory of Music," Novello. Author of "Handel: an outline of his Life," and lecturer on Piano Technic. Mrs. Webster is now resident in London, but is still Principal of the Aberdeen School, which she frequently visits. She is a Licentiate of the R.A.M. for pf., as professor and teacher.

Webster, Richard, composer and teacher, was born at Huntley, Gloucestershire, in 1783. He was a teacher and pianist in Glasgow, where he died, on December 26, 1848. Composer of various glees, songs, etc., some of which are contained in "Lyric gems of Scotland." His best known song is "Bonnie Jeanie Gray." "Oh, not upon so cold a shrine," another song, is contained in "The Western Garland," 1832. He composed some instrumental music. Introduction and polonaise rondo, for pf., op. 1, etc.

Weekes, Samuel, organist, pianist, and teacher. Studied at R.A.M., and elected an Associate. Graduated Mus. Bac., Cambridge, 1873; Mus. Doc., Dublin, 1896. F.R.C.O. Organist of St. Peter's, Hammersmith, 1861-2; Baptist Church, Plymouth, 1876, to present time. Conductor of Plymouth Choral and Orchestral Society; Principal of Music School, Stoke, Devonport. Author of a Choral primer, and Questions on Acoustics. Compositions: Cantata, Bless the Lord, for soli, chorus, and orchestra; Hymn tunes, songs, pf. pieces, etc.

Weelkes, Thomas, organist and composer of latter part of the 16th and early part of the 17th centuries. Very little is known about his biography. In 1600 he was organist of Winchester College; in 1602 he graduated Mus. Bac. at Oxford, and in 1608 he was organist of Chichester Cathedral. Neither his birth or death dates seem to have been preserved.

WORKS.—Madrigals to 3, 4, 5, and 6 voyces, London, 1597; also edited by E. J. Hopkins for the Musical Antiquarian Society, London, 1843. Ballets and madrigals to five voyces, with one to six voyces, 1598. Madrigals of five and six parts, apt for viols and voices, 1600. Madrigals of six parts, apt for the viols and voices, London, 1600. Ayres or phantasticke spirites for 3 voices, with a song, a remembrance of my friend Mr. Thomas Morley, for 6 voices, London, 1608, 3 parts. Contributions in Leighton's "Teares"; Anthems, etc., in the collections of Clifford and Rimbault; MS. Music in British Museum, etc.

WELDON.

Weichsell, Elizabeth, see BILLINGTON, ELIZABETH.

Weir, John, musician of first part of present century, who was a teacher of music in Glasgow. Compiler of "A Collection of Psalm tunes and Anthems," Glasgow, n.d.

Weiss, Willoughby Hunter, bass singer and composer, born at Liverpool, April 2, 1820. He gave his first concert at Liverpool, May 5, 1842. His first stage appearance was as Count Rodolfo, in "La Sonnambula," at the Princess' Theatre, 1843; and he was for years a member of the Pyne and Harrison company. He was heard in the title part, in "Elijah," at the Birmingham Festival, 1867. As a vocalist he had a great reputation. He died at London, October 24, 1867. Composer of many songs, among which may be named :— Autumn leaves; Bowmen of old England; Chimes of England; Crossing the moor; Fisherman's cottage; Gleaner; The ice, the ice!; Knight's vigil; Let me be near thee; Mid watch; Mower; O salutaris hostia; Rolling home across the sea; Shipwreck; Twenty years ago; Village blacksmith (Longfellow) [1858]; Watcher by the sea; Wreck of the Hesperus; Wreck of the homeward bound, etc. He was married to GEORGINA ANSELL BARRETT, a soprano vocalist, who was born at Gloucester in 1826, and died at Brighton, November 6, 1880.

Welch, John Bacon, teacher of singing, born at Pattishill Vicarage, Northampton, December 26, 1839. Studied in London, and in 1861 went to Milan, where he placed himself under Gaetano Nava. His voice was a baritone, and he sang in public for a short time. It was as a teacher, however, that he excelled. He was a professor at the G.S.M., and had many private pupils, among the most distinguised being Miss Anna Williams, Miss Annie Marriott, Messrs. Bridson, Brereton, and others. He gave concerts at Princes' Hall, 1887, etc. He died in London, July 1, 1887, and was buried in Highgate Cemetery.

Weldon, Georgina, *born* TREHERNE, soprano vocalist and writer, born in London, May 24, 1837. She studied under her mother and Jules de Glimes, and gave concerts in Canada, and afterwards in London. She organized a training school for vocalists in 1871, and lectured and sang in Birmingham and elsewhere, 1882-1886; but for a number of years past she has not been professionally connected with music. Author of "Musical reform," London, 1872; "Hints for pronunciation in singing, with proposals for a self-supporting academy." London, 1872. "Autobiographie de Ch. Gounod.." London, n.d.

Weldon, John, composer and organist, born at Chichester, January 19, 1676. He studied under John Walton, of Eton College,

WELLINGS.

WESCHÉ.

and H. Purcell. Organist of New College, Oxford, 1694. Gentleman extraordinary of Chapel Royal, June 6, 1701. Organist of Chapel Royal, 1708. Second composer to Chapel Royal, 1715. Organist of St. Bride's, Fleet Street, and St. Martin-in-the-Fields, London, 1726. He died at London, May 7, 1736.

WORKS.—*Operas :* Agreeable disappointment, 1715 ; Fair Unfortunate, 1710 ; Judgment of Paris (masque), 1702 ; Orpheus and Eurydice, 1710 ; She would and She would not, 1703. Divine Harmony, six select anthems for a voice alone, with a thorowbass for the organ, harpsichord, or arch lute.... performed by the late famous Mr. Richard Elford, London, n.d. Hear my crying ; In Thee, O Lord ; O God, Thou hast cast us out ; Who can tell how oft he offendeth, anthems. Collection of New Songs performed at his concert in York Buildings ; Collection of new Songs [1707] ; Collection of Aires for 2 flutes and a bass, London, 1710. *Songs :* An amorous swain to Juno pray'd ; As the snow in valley lying ; Clarinda ; Let ambition fire thy mind ; Wakeful nightingale.

Wellings, Joseph Milton, composer, born at Handsworth, near Birmingham, December 4, 1850. Of his larger works, a sketch, "The Dancing Master," was produced at the Criterion Theatre, London, February, 1894. His songs include Golden Love, At the ferry, I wait no more, Some day, My bonnie boy, Only a rose, You sang to me, Be mine again, You know best, Old fashions, and many others, most of which have had a wide circulation.

Wells, Alfred, flutist, pupil of William Card, made his *début* at a concert of the Societa Armonica, June 3, 1844, he then being eleven years old. For many years he was a member of the Crystal Palace orchestra, and distinguished as a soloist, especially in the concertas and suites of J. S. Bach. His death, January 1, 1892, was the result of a fall down stairs, at his house, in London.

Wells, Benjamin, flutist, born at Cambridge in 1826. Studied at R.A.M., under Richardson and Clinton, and appeared with great success at an academy concert in April, 1845. He was elected A.R.A.M., and was for years a professor at the Academy. In later years he has been more widely known as a lecturer on music.

Wells, Madame Thaddeus, contralto vocalist, born early in the present century. She sang at many important concerts in her time, but latterly had dropped out of notice. She died at London in March, 1885.

Wells, Wallace, tenor vocalist, born at Dilham, Norfolk, 1842. Educated at R.A.M. Sang at the Sacred Harmonic, and other London concerts ; Birmingham Festival, 1879, in Rossini's "Moses in Egypt," etc. Principal tenor at Marylebone Rectory Church, and for thirteen years at St. Andrew's, Wells Street. Professor of Singing at G.S.M., and other educational institutions.

Welsh, John, musician of latter part of last century, issued "Sacred Harmony..consisting of psalm and hymn tunes," London [1800].

Welsh, Thomas, bass vocalist, teacher and composer, born at Wells, Somersetshire, 1770. He was a chorister in Wells Cathedral, and also studied under J. B. Cramer and Baumgarten. First appeared in opera in Attwood's "Prisoner," 1792. Engaged by Linley to sing in oratorio at Haymarket Theatre, London, 1796. Gentleman of Chapel Royal. Celebrated as a vocal teacher in London, and numbered among his pupils John Sinclair, Charles Horn, Miss Stephens, and Miss Mary Anne Wilson, who became his second wife. He died at Brighton, January 31, 1848.

WORKS.—*Music to* "The Green Eyed Monster"; Twenty years ago, 1810 ; Kamschatka, and other dramatic pieces. Sonatas for pf. [1819]. Part-songs, glees, and duets : Hark, 'tis the whistling wind ; Come, jovial friends; Fairy feast ; Hence, away ! ye sirens ; Merry gipsies ; Shed not your sweets. Songs : Harry Bluff, etc. Vocal Instructor, or the art of singing exemplified in fifteen lessons leading to forty progressive exercises, London [1825].

His wife, *born* MARY ANNE WILSON, was a native of London, born in 1802. She studied under her husband and first appeared as *Mandane* in Arne's "Artaxerxes" at Drury Lane, January 18, 1821. She sang in many important concerts in her day as a soprano, and died in 1867.

Wensley, Frances Foster, pianist and composer, who studied under Kalkbrenner. She married Alderman Garrett. Composer of "Four Songs" [1823] ; variations on "God save the Queen," etc.

Wesché, Walter, composer, pianist, and organist, born at Colombo, Ceylon, August 26, 1857. Studied under Oscar Beringer and Berthold Tours, and orchestration under F. H. Cowen. In 1879 he was appointed organist and choirmaster at the Lock Chapel, Paddington ; then to St. Thomas's, Westbourne Grove ; and, 1891, to St. Stephen's, South Hampstead. He is professor of harmony and composition at the Academy for the higher development of pf. playing (Oscar Beringer) ; and professor of pf. at the Royal Normal College for the Blind, Norwood. He has given organ recitals at Gresham Hall, 1882 ; the Bow and Bromley Institute, 1883, etc., but is now chiefly engaged in teaching.

WORKS.—*Orchestral :* Symphony in C minor ; Rhapsodies in F and G ; Suite op. 18,

WESLEY.

prize, Westminster Orchestral Society, performed, March 16, 1892; Ballad, The Legend of Excalibur, Crystal Palace, March 3, 1894; Romance, Melbourne (Cowen), December 10, 1888. Concerto in A, 1886; Andante and Allegro; both for pf. and orchestra. Overture, Dagmar, organ and orchestra, 1881. Idyll, organ and strings. Quintet in E minor; Trios in E flat and E minor for pf. and strings; sonata in B flat, pf. and violin; in E flat, pf. and 'cello. Canzonetta for 'cello. Three Dances, pf. 4 hands. Three Rhapsodies, pf. solo, etc.

Wesley, Charles, organist and composer, born at Bristol, December 11, 1757. Son of the Rev. Charles Wesley, and nephew of John Wesley, the Methodist leader. He studied under Rooke, Kelway, and Boyce, and became a teacher in London, and organist of St. George's, Hanover Square. Organist in ordinary to George IV. He gave subscription concerts at his house in London. He died at London, May 23, 1834. Composed "A Set of Eight Songs," 1784; "A Set of Six Concertos for the Organ or Harpsichord"; Anthems in Page's "Harmonia Sacra," hymns, etc.

Wesley, Rev. John, clergyman and amateur musician, born in 1703, died in 1791. The celebrated founder of the Wesleyan Methodist body. He issued "A Collection of Tunes, set to music as they are commonly sung at the Foundery," 1742, and belonged to the same family as the Wesleys, Charles, Samuel, etc., so celebrated in music.

Wesley, Samuel, organist and composer, born at Bristol, February 24, 1766. Brother of Charles. He gave very early indications of a disposition for music, and was a pupil of his brother Charles. From an early age he excited great interest among musicians by his extraordinary genius for music. He became the greatest organist of his time, and was the first Englishman to make known the music of Bach. He was deputy organist for a time of the Abbey Church, Bath, and on coming to London as a teacher, he became organist of Camden Chapel, in 1824. He died at London, October 11, 1837.

WORKS.—Church Service in F. *Anthems and Motets:* My soul hath patiently; Thou, O God, art praised in Zion; I said, I will take heed to my ways; Dixit Dominus; Exultate Deo; In exitu Israel; and other church music. Original Hymn Tunes adapted to every metre in the collection of the Rev. J. Wesley, London, n.d. Sonatas for pf. Organ voluntaries, fugues, etc. "O, synge unto my roundelaie," madrigal, etc. The Misanthrope, opera (MS.). Letters of Samuel Wesley to Mr. Jacobs, relating to the introduction into this country of the works of Bach, edited by E. Wesley, London, 1878.

See also "An account of the remarkable

WEST.

musical talents of several members of the Wesley family, collected from original MSS. with memorial introduction and notes by W. Winters," London, 1874.

Wesley, Samuel Sebastian, organist and composer, born at London, August 14, 1810. Son of the preceding. He was a chorister in the Chapel Royal, and held in London the appointments of organist of St. James', Hampstead Road, 1827; St. Giles', Camberwell, 1829; and St. John's, Waterloo Road, and Hampton-on-Thames. He was afterwards successively organist of Hereford Cathedral, 1832; Exeter Cathedral, 1835; Leeds Parish Church, 1842; Winchester Cathedral, 1849; Gloucester Cathedral, 1865. He graduated Mus. Bac., and Mus. Doc., Oxon., 1839. He died at Gloucester, April 19, 1876, and is buried in the Old Cemetery, Exeter, and a tablet in the Cathedral there notes his connection with the town.

WORKS.—Church services in E (1845), F, F (chant), and G. *Anthems:* Ascribe unto the Lord; All go unto one place; Blessed be the Lord; Blessed be the God and Father; Cast me not away; Give the King thy judgments; Glory be to God on high; God be merciful; I am Thine; I will arise; Let us lift up our heart; Man that is born of a woman; O give thanks; O God, whose nature; O Lord, my God; O Lord, Thou art my God; Praise the Lord; The face of the Lord; The wilderness; Thou wilt keep him in perfect peace; Wash me thoroughly; etc. The Psalter, with Chants, arranged for Daily Morning and Evening Service, Leeds, 1843. *Glees and Part-songs:* At that dread hour; I wish to tune my quiv'ring lyre; Shall I tell you whom I love?; When fierce conflicting passions; etc. *Songs:* The butterfly; Orphan hours the year is dead; There be none of beauty's daughters; Wert thou like me; etc. *Organ:* A Studio for the Organ, exemplified in a series of exercises; Air composed for the Holsworthy Church Bells; Andantes in G, A, E minor, etc. Two sets (6 pieces) of Organ Pieces, etc. Melodia Sacra, Handel's airs arranged for pf. The English Cathedral Service, its glory, its decline, and its designed extinction, London, 1845. A few words on Cathedral Music and the musical system of the church, with a plan of reform, London, 1849. Selection of Psalms and Hymns, arranged for the public service of the Church of England, by the Rev. Charles Kemble, rector of Bath, London, 1864, *edited.* The hymn-tunes "Aurelia," "St. Sebastian," "Radford," "Wimbledon," etc., were also composed by Wesley.

West, Benjamin, organist and composer, of 18th century. Composer of "Sacra concerto, or the voice of melody, containing an introduction to the grounds of music, also

forty-one psalm tunes and twelve anthems."
London, 1769. 2nd edition.

West, George Frederick, organist, composer, and writer, born at Bath. In 1844 he was organist of St. George the Martyr, Southwark, in which year he published "The National Church Service" (R. Cocks). Author of "Questions relating to the theory of music" (London, 1864); Hints to young teachers of the pianoforte" (R. Cocks), and other works. He has written and arranged an immense amount of music for pf., chiefly of an educational type.

West, Henry, composer and writer. Author of "Singing Preceptor," London, 1846; "Accordian Preceptor," London, 1846; Preceptor for the accordion or flutina, London [1855]. Composer of Pretty little songs for pretty little singers, a collection of nursery rhymes. Pf. music, songs, etc.

West, John Ebenezer, organist, composer, and conductor, born at South Hackney, London, December 7, 1863. Son of William and Clara West (noticed below). Received his early instruction from his parents, later studying organ under Dr. J. F. Bridge, and composition at R.A.M. under E. Prout, F.R.C.O. In 1884 he was appointed organist and C.M. of St. Mary's, Berkeley Square; and since 1891 has held similar positions at South Hackney Parish Church. He has given organ recitals in various places, and is also known as a pianist. He is one of the musical advisers to the firm of Novello, Ewer and Co. WORKS.—*Cantatas:* The Healing of the Canaanite's Daughter, Hackney, December 20, 1882; Seed-Time and Harvest, Choral Festival, St. Mary's, Newington, October 12, 1892; Psalm 130, N.E. London Choral Society, January 31, 1891. *Anthems:* The Lord is exalted, St. Paul's Cathedral, May 24, 1883; Lord, I call upon Thee; and others. Festival Evening Service in E flat, composed for Festival of London Church Choir Association, St. Paul's, 1890; Evening Service in A; Te Deum in B flat, etc. Songs, part-songs, incidental music to Longfellow's King Robert of Sicily (for declamation), Queen's Hall, October 8, 1896. Overture in E minor, 1881; Victoria, our Queen, 1897, march, both for orchestra. Sonata in D minor, 1895; Fugue in E minor; March in G; Postlude in B flat, etc., for organ.

West, Rev. Lewis Renatus, clergyman and amateur composer, born at London, May 3, 1753. He belonged to the Moravian brethren, and was in charge of the congregation at Dublin in 1784. He subsequently held other charges in Ireland and England in connection with the Moravian body. He died at Tytherton, Wiltshire, August 4, 1826. He composed some hymns and other music for the Church Service.

West, William, composer, teacher of singing, and lyric author, born at Hackney, London, September 17, 1830. He comes of an old Wiltshire family. His father was a musician, and his mother's father was the Samuel Hayter mentioned in the notice of Aaron Upjohn Hayter (*q.v.*) His early studies were devoted to singing, but his delicate organ gave way through over exertion, and he then gave himself up to teaching. In 1863 he founded the North-East London Academy of Music, which has been a successful and useful institution. For fifteen years he was organist of the Congregational Church, Bethnal Green Road, resigning in 1885, and holding for a time a similar appointment at Hackney. He has composed hymn tunes, chants, Sanctuses, etc. *Songs:* Speak gently of the erring; Casabianca; Were I a little bird; The Christian's song; Life in Love; The Rivals (a proverb song); and others. His first pf. pieces, Welsh air, Cotillon, Fall of Paris, duets, were written at the age of seven. Others are Le Garçon Volage, Sophie, valse, mazurka brillant, and various operatic transcriptions. He is the author of a number of lyrics, set by his son and other composers. His sister is the wife of Professor Prout.

MADAME CLARA WEST, his wife, is a soprano vocalist, born at Chatham, September 9, 1844. Her maiden name was Ainsworth. She studied under her husband, and Madame Rudersdorff. An excellent musician, she first came into notice about 1876, through her ability to fill the place of other vocalists in important works at a moment's notice. She was long associated with the concerts of the Borough of Hackney Choral Association, and has sung throughout Great Britain. Invitations to visit America have been declined.

LOTTIE WEST, daughter of the preceding, was born at South Hackney, November 5, 1865. She is a contralto vocalist, pianist, and teacher. Received her musical education chiefly at home, but became a student for a time at the R.A.M., studying singing with Edwin Holland. She sang at concerts in London and the provinces with success from 1882, but since her marriage to Mr. Millard she has practically retired from the concert platform. She is the composer of some songs, and a sketch for violin and pf.

Westbrook, William Joseph, composer, organist and writer, was born at London, January 1, 1831. He was organist successively of St. Bartholomew, Bethnal Green, 1849; St. Bartholomew, Sydenham, 1851-84; and Crystal Palace (co-organist), 1860. From 1865 to 1878 he was conductor of the South Norwood Musical Society, and he was also musical examiner to the College of Preceptors.

WESTLAKE.

Mus. Bac., 1876, and Mus. Doc., 1878, Cambridge. With A. W. Hammond and John Crowdy he established the *Musical Standard* in 1862. He died at Sydenham, London, on March 24, 1894.

WORKS.—Jesus, oratorio, 1877; also Goldsmith's Institute, London, 1892. The Lord is my Shepherd, cantata, 1875. Services in G, D, etc. Anthems. Part-songs and trios; Songs, and other vocal music. Sonatas for organ in E flat, G, etc. Voluntaries. The Organist, 1876, etc.; Young Organist; Practical Organist; Organ Journal; Ancient and Modern Fugues, 1865-80; New organ arrangements, and many similar collections for organ and harmonium. Elementary Music, a primer, London, 1879. Practical Organ Tutor, London, 1872, etc. Alphabet of Musical Notation, London [1873]. Translations of De Beriot's, Dancla's, and Alard's Violin Schools, and many other works.

Westlake, Frederick, composer and pianist, born at Romsey, Hants, February 25, 1840. Studied at R.A.M., 1855-9; elected Associate, then Fellow. Professsor of pf., R.A M., and Member of the Philharmonic Society. He has played in public with success, and at one of H. Holmes's "Musical Evenings" (St. George's Hall, October 22, 1873), performed, with Miss Channel, Chopin's Rondo, op. 73, for two pianos, probably for the first time in London. Teaching now chiefly occupies his time.

WORKS.—Mass in E flat; Mass of the Holy Name, produced, Brompton Oratory, November 26, 1893 (for voices, orchestra, and organ). O Salutaris; Kyrie and Gloria (with orchestra); the first named sung by Leslie's Choir, February 22, 1883. Tunes contributed to Hymns Ancient and Modern. She 'dwelt among the untrodden ways; Evangela; and other songs. Part-songs, Lyra Studentium, etc. Duo Concertante, pf. and 'cello. Allegro con forza; Fugue in octaves; a set of nine episodes for pf. Completed Sterndale Bennett's edition of Bach's 48 Preludes and Fugues.

Westmoreland, John Fane, Earl of, *known as* LORD BURGHERSH, amateur composer, born at London, February 3, 1784. He entered the army in 1803, and became envoy at the Court of Florence in 1814. He studied music under Hague, Mayseder, Portogallo, and Bianchi. He succeeded to the title in 1841. In 1841-51 he was the British Minister at Berlin. He established the Royal Academy of Music in 1822, and in 1861 a Scholarship was founded in his memory. He died at Apthorpe House. October 16, 1859.

WORKS.—*Operas:* Bajazet, Florence, 1821, London, 1822; L'Eroe di Lancastre, R.A.M. pupils, 1826; Lo Scompiglio teatrale, Florence, 1836, published 1846; Catarina, London, 1830,

WESTROP.

also in English as Catherine, the Austrian captive; Fedra, Florence, 1828, published at Berlin in 1848; Il Torneo, Florence, 1826, London, 1838; Il Ratto di Proserpina, 1845. Three symphonies for orchestra; Quartets for strings; Pf. music, etc. Cathedral Service, 1841; Messa Solenne. 1858; Requiem to the memory of Samuel Webbe; Six cantatas of Metastasio for solo voice and pf., 1831. Madrigals, glees, single songs.

Westrop, East John, composer and editor, born at Lavenham, Suffolk, in 1804. He was a teacher and editor in London. He died at London, in 1856.

WORKS.—Domestic Psalmody, a selection of modern tunes for 1, 2, or 3 voices, 1851. Carmina Sacra, London, 1857. 100 Little Songs for little singers, London, 1857. Normal Singer, 1857. 200 Psalms and hymns, 1859 (with Wade). Universal Psalmodist. London, 1856. Musical Services of the Church of England. for 4 voices, London [1845], 4 vols. The Antiphonal, a collection of anthems, 1856, etc. Composer of quadrilles, miscellaneous pf. music and songs.

Westrop, Henry John, composer, violinist, organist and conductor, born at Lavenham, Suffolk, July 22, 1812. He was organist successively of St. Stephen's Norwich; Little Stanmore, 1831; Fitzroy Chapel, London, 1833; St. Edmund the King and Martyr, Lombard Street, 1834. He was also violinist at the Italian opera and Philharmonic Society; conductor of the Choral Harmonist's Society; and a member of the Philharmonic Society and Royal Society of Musicians. He died at London, September 23, 1879.

WORKS.—Maid of Bremen, opera, in MS. Symphony for orchestra, 1838; Quintets for pf. and strings in E flat, 1843, and C minor, 1844; Quartetto concertante, for pf. and strings, in A flat, op. 2 [1850]; Sonata for pf. and flute in F, op. 6 (1846); Sonata for pf. and viola in E flat; Quartets for strings in A and E flat (op. 1, 1835, etc.) Allegro in E flat for pf. Anthem, O taste and see; Winter, descriptive cantata for bass voice and orchestra, etc.

His daughter KATE, who is a pianist and organist of much ability, succeeded him as organist of St. Edmund, Lombard Street, a position she resigned in 1887. Composer of "Four short voluntaries for organ " (1885); Songs, and other works.

Westrop, Thomas, composer and writer, brother of the above, was born at Lavenham in 1816. Died at London, December 17, 1881. He edited "120 selected short anthems," London, 1861; Psalms, hymns, etc., 1862; Eighteen selected vocal duets, London, 1863; Sacred songs, 1863. Universal violin tutor, 1862. Complete organ tutor, 1863. Composer of a large number of comic and other songs, hymns, pf. pieces, etc.

WETTON.

Wetton, Henry Davan, organist and composer, born at Brighton, July 18, 1862. Received his musical training at Westminster Abbey, and from private teachers. F.R.C.O.; Mus. Bac., Durham, 1891. Organist of All Saints', Stoke Newington, 1877; Christ Church, Woburn Square, 1884; St. Gabriel's, Pimlico, 1886-9 and 1890-3; sub-organist, Wells Cathedral, 1890; organist of Finchley Parish Church, 1892. In 1892, succeeded M. B. Foster as organist and musical director at the Foundling Hospital. He is head of the musical department of the Northampton Institute, Clerkenwell. Has given lectures at T.C.L., etc. His compositions are Psalm 9, for soli, chorus, strings and pf.; Te Deum and Benedictus; Evening service for men's vioces; anthems, carols, songs, pf. pieces, etc.

Weyman, David, Irish collector, was vicar-choral of St. Patrick's, Dublin, 1819. He died at Dublin in August, 1822. Published "Melodia Sacra, or the Psalms of David, arranged for 1, 2, 3, or 4 voices," Dublin, 1812-14. Sequel in 3 vols., 1840-52. New edition edited by J. Smith. Hymns and psalms as sung in the Magdalen Asylum, Leeson Street..Dublin [1822]; Hymns and anthems as sung in Protestant Churches and Chapels throughout Ireland..Dublin. Fifty of the psalms of David, Dublin.

Wharton, Edward, bass vocalist, and teacher of singing, born in Birmingham. Educated at Dulwich College, and solo choir boy. Sometime choirmaster and assistant organist to Sir A. S. Sullivan at St. Peter's, South Kensington. Organ pupil of George Cooper. Gained the first prize for bass vocalists at the National Music Meetings, Crystal Palace, July 3, 1875. Appeared at different concerts, and took part in the performance of Liszt's "St. Elisabeth," given by Walter Bache, February 24, 1876. Joined the staff of the Guildhall School of Music in 1881, and has been successfully conducting large classes there since that time.

Whatmoor, Freeman, pianist, organist, and composer, born at Bradford, Yorkshire, 1856. Studied under Dr. Spark, F. W. Hird, and, also, at the National Training School, Kensington, where he won a scholarship. Has held organ appointments at Leeds and Gateshead; sometime assistant to Henry Farmer, at Harrow, now resident at Watford, as conductor and teacher, etc. In 1887, he won the *Musical World* prize for an organ postlude. Graduated Mus. B., Cambridge, 1892. He has published some school songs, part-songs, pieces for pf., organ, etc. He has given chamber concerts and lectures, at Hemel-Hempstead, 1887. etc.

HERBERT W. WHATMOOR (a brother?) is organist of Christ Church, Roxeth; he is also

WHITAKER.

a pianist, and has given chamber concerts, Harrow, 1888, etc.

Wheall, *see* Weale.

Wheeler, Richard, composer and organist, who was a teacher in Cambridge. He issued "Six Glees for three and four voices," Cambridge [1800]. These were originally published in the collections of Dr. Charles Hague.

Whelan, Rev. Ernest Hamilton, organist and composer, graduated Mus. B., 1887; M.A., Dublin. Was organist successively of Malahide Church, near Dublin, 1868; Swords Parish Church, 1869; St. Andrew's, Dublin, 1875-6. Conductor of Dublin Diocesan Choral Festival, 1875. Curate of Powerscourt, 1876-83; Rector of Kilbride, Bray, 1883. He has composed a setting of Ps. 100 for five voices and organ; Hymn tunes in Irish Church Hymnal, and Children's Hymnal; sacred songs, etc.

Whichello, or **Wichello, Abiell,** organist and composer, of the 18th century, was deputy organist to Philip Hart. He afterwards became organist of Church of St. Edmund the King. Played at Britton's concerts. He died about 1745.

WORKS.—Apollo and Daphne, cantata, 1730; Vertumnus and Pomona, cantata. *Songs:* Charms of beauty; Haste, haste dear youth; Heart that's bleeding; So many charms; Ye virgin powers. Lessons for the Harpsichord or Spinett [1720].

Whishaw, Frederick J., tenor vocalist and composer, born in 1854. Received his musical training in St. Petersburg and London. He has published an Album of Seven Songs (Reid); an Album of Russian Songs (Lucas); and two Albums of Russian Songs (Boosey). He has sung at concerts in different parts of the country; but devotes himself chiefly to literature, and is author of a number of lyrics, tales for juvenile readers, novels, etc.

Whitaker, John, composer and organist, was born in 1776. He was organist of St. Clement, Eastcheap, London; and in 1808 succeeded to C. H. Purday's business as a music-seller in St. Paul's Churchyard. He died at London, December 4, 1847.

WORKS.—*Music for plays, etc.:* Boarding school miss, burletta, 1800; Guy Mannering (with Bishop), 1816; Heir of Vironi, 1817; Iwanowna, 1815; Sweethearts and wives, 1812; Up to town, 1811; Who's to have her? 1813. An "Epicedium" to the memory of Princess Charlotte (1817). Odes of Anacreon. *Songs:* Emigrant's farewell; Fly away dove; Indian maid; Let the epicure boast; Lily that blooms; Mary's love; My poor dog Tray; Oh rest thee babe; Oh say not woman's heart is bought; Remember me; Thine am I my faithful fair; Wandering harper; Young Lochinvar. *Glees:* Winds, gently whisper;

WHITE.

Sailor's return; etc. Edited "Gems of English harmony," with E. J. Loder, 5 vols; " The Seraph : a collection of sacred music, consisting of celebrated psalm and hymn tunes.... arranged for 4 voices, pf. or organ, and violoncello," London, 1818, 2 vols.

White, Adolphus Charles, contrabassist, born in Canterbury, October 10, 1830. Chorister at the Cathedral there, and studied organ, violin, and other subjects under Dr. Longhurst, and later in Ireland. Returning to Canterbury he took up the study of the double-bass, and, proceeding to London, received lessons from James Howell, for whom he soon deputised with marked success. In 1853 he went with Jullian to America. After his return he was engaged at Her Majesty's opera, the Philharmonic and other concerts ; and when Howell died, in 1879, he succeeded him at the Handel, Leeds, Birmingham (1876-1888), and Three Choirs Festivals; and was also principal double-bass at the Royal Italian opera to 1897. He is professor of his instrument at R.A.M., and R.C.M.; Hon. R.A.M., 1877; and, in 1890, was appointed Musician in Ordinary to Her Majesty the Queen. Was for 22 years organist of St. Philip's, Waterloo Place. Served in the Volunteer force, retiring in 1887 with the rank of Major, receiving a silver sword in acknowledgment of his services. His compositions include church music, carols, songs, pf. pieces, and solos for the double-bass His Primer for that instrument (Novello), with appendix for the four stringed bass, is of great merit.

White, Hamilton, organist and conductor, born at Maryport, Cumberland, October 1, 1834. Has held various organ appointments, and was for some time at Holy Trinity, Whitehaven, in 1872 removing to East Retford, Notts., where he has since resided, as organist of the Parish Church. He is also conductor of a Choral Society, and for many years has given concerts at Retford, Worksop, etc., as well as organ recitals. He is an active worker for music in the district.

White, Mrs. Harrison, see BABER, MISS COLBOURNE

White, John Jesse, violinist, organist, and composer, born at Bermondsey, London, but at the age of eighteen months was taken by his parents to Birmingham. Pupil of James Stimpson, for organ and theory. Became musical director at Theatre Royal, Birmingham, when twenty. Went to Paris, and studied under Halévy. Was first violin in the orchestra of the Théâtre Lyrique, Paris, 1856-7. At the same time there was another violinist of the name in Paris (mentioned below), and they were distinguished as M. White *le Blanc*, and M. White *le Noir*. In later years the two were together at Rio de

WHITE.

Janeiro, Brazil, and the compositions of the one have at times been taken as the work of the other. As musical director, composer, and organist, J. J. White spent many years in Chili, Peru, La Plata, and South America generally, and his experiences have been far out of the common. He had played in early Masses on the day of the great Festival at Lo Compania, Santiago, when 3000 persons were burned to death, December 8, 1863, and but for a previous engagement, would have been in the orchestra in the evening. His deputy, a Spaniard, perished in the fire. A Spanish opera of his was performed in La Plata, and a Portuguese opera in Rio de Janeiro. In 1881 he was back again in Europe, and appeared, for the first time as a soloist, at Bayreuth, May 13; was for a time a member of the Meiningen orchestra, under Hans von Bülow, and played at the production of " Parsifal," in 1882. Soon after this he returned to England, but the change of climate caused a long and dangerous illness. He gave recitals and lectures in Birmingham and neighbourhood, in 1885, and the next year was appointed music director, Southport Winter Gardens. There he remained nine years, and some of his compositions were introduced. In 1895, he removed to Sydenham, where he still resides.

WORKS.—Two Masses, of large dimensions, one produced, Rio de Janeiro, 1873; four smaller ones. Italian opera, La Figlia della Dora, produced, Lima, Peru, 1868; a French opera. Ode, Queen of the North, composed for the Centenary celebration, Southport, and performed, June 18, 1892. Two symphonies; Concert overture, Titania, Southport, November 12, 1887; Descriptive pieces, Judah, the same, 1891. Concerto, Hedwig, violin and orchestra, performed at Munich. Six string quartets; pieces for violin, Delires de Sapho, etc.

The JOSEPH WHITE referred to was born at Cuba. His grandfather was English. He was appointed professor to the Imperial Family of Brazil. He gave chamber concerts at Rio de Janeiro, as late as 1884, and has published violin pieces, etc.

White, Joseph, organist of St. Sidwell's Church, Exeter, is the composer of a sacred cantata, " The Magi," produced, Exeter, November 26, 1888 ; and a setting of Southey's " Inchcape Rock," produced, Exeter, 1891.

White, Matthew, organist and composer, of early part of the 17th century. He was a bass singer of Wells Cathedral; organist of Christ Church, Oxford, 1611-1613; and a gentleman of the Chapel Royal till 1614. In 1629 he accumulated the degrees of Bac. and Mus. Doc., Oxford. Composer of anthems and other church music.

White, Maude Valerie, composer, born

WHITE.

at Dieppe, of English parents, June 23, 1855. Studied under Oliver May and W. S. Rockstro. Entered R.A.M., 1876, and was elected Mendelssohn scholar, 1879, completing her studies in Vienna. Resident in London, and Broadway, Worcestershire,

WORKS. — Mass (R.A.M. concert, 1881). Songs: To Blossom; Montrose's Love Song; My soul is an enchanted boat; When passion's trance; Ye Cupid's drop; The devout lover; Absent, yet present; I prithee send me back my heart; Four songs from Tennyson's *In Memoriam*; Album of German Songs; Chantez, chantez (Hugo); and others. Pictures from Abroad, 14 pf. pieces; Scherzetto, etc., for pf. Naissance d'amour, pf. and 'cello, etc. Translator from the Swedish of Letters from a Mourning City, Naples during the autumn of 1884, by Axel Munthe, London, Murray, 1887.

White, Mrs. Meadows, *see* SMITH, ALICE MARY.

White, Nathaniel Chandler, organist, was a son of S. Phillips White, solicitor. He was organist of Tewkesbury Abbey Church, and of Bipple Church. He died at Tewkesbury, February 10, 1869. Remarkable for his organ playing, and his memory, which enabled him to play entire oratorios by Handel, Spohr and Mendelssohn.

White, Robert, composer and organist of the 16th century. He was organist of Westminster Abbey? and of Ely Cathedral in 1562, in succession to Tye. He was also master of the choristers in Westminster Abbey. Mus. Bac. Cambridge in 1561. He died in 1574. The Library of Christ Church College, Oxford, contains a number of his compositions in MS.

White, Tench James, teacher and dealer in musical instruments, born at Canterbury in 1830. Chorister in Canterbury Cathedral, 1839, and pupil of T. E. Jones, and Dr. Longhurst. After leaving the Cathedral he became organist of St. Mildred's Church, Canterbury. Conductor, for many years, of the St. Lawrence Musical Society, Canterbury. Song composer and editor of "Tench White's organ, harmonium, and American organ library." Many of his songs were published under the *nom de plume* of Arthur Hare. He died at Canterbury, March 14, 1891.

White, W. J., composer and editor, issued "Sacred Melodies suitable for public and private devotion," London [1820]. "New sacred melodies,".. London [1825], 7th edition. "The Bury melodies, adapted for public and family worship.." London [1830].

Whitehouse, Henry, bass vocalist, born at Worcester, January 15, 1823. Studied for a short time under Sir George Smart, but was chiefly self-instructed. About 1849, he was appointed a Lay Vicar of Worcester Cathedral,

WHITTEN.

and a year later to St. George's Chapel,. Windsor, and Eton College. He held these appointments till about the year 1857, when he was made Lay Vicar of Westminster Abbey, and Gentleman of the Chapels Royal. He was. for many years a member of the Choir Benevolent Fund, and for some time served on the Committee. His voice was a true bass, but of extraordinary compass; and by long practice, he united the chest and head registers so that he could sing purely tenor songs like "The Message," with as fine effect as those appertaining to the bass voice proper. An advocate for general culture on the part of singers, his own work exemplified his individual acquirements. He died in London, May 11, 1892. Three of his sons have attained more or less distinction in the musical profession :—WILLIAM EDWARD WHITEHOUSE, violoncellist, born in London, May 20, 1859. As a boy he studied the violin under Adolphus Griesbach; but later on, turning to the violoncello, he took lessons from Walter Pettit, ultimately entering the R.A.M., 1877. There he had for instructors Piatti and Pezze for violoncello, and H. C. Banister for harmony. He was first to take the Bonamy Dobree Prize for violoncello playing, 1878; and after carrying off academic honours, was appointed Professor and A.R.A.M., 1883, and elected F.R.A.M., 1895. In 1891 he was made Professor at the R.C.M., and later at the Royal College of Music, Manchester. He is a member of the Royal Society of Musicians Distinguished as a solo and quartet player, he has appeared at the Popular Concerts St. James' Hall (from 1891), and many high-class concerts in London and the provinces; whilst as a teacher he counts Paul Ludwig, Kate Ould, and other performers of repute, anong his pupils. JAMES FREDERICK WHITEHOUSE, bass vocalist, born at Windsor, 1860. Chorister, St. George's Chapel; solo and head boy; now Vicar choral, and of Her Majesty's Private Chapel, Windsor Castle. Known as a finished exponent of Bach's vocal music, and as an able teacher of singing, also as violinist and pianist. ALFRED JOHN WHITEHOUSE, studied at R.A.M. Since 1878, organist and choirmaster, St. John's, Pimlico, and resident in London as teacher of pf., organ, and violin.

Whitfeld, *see* CLARKE-WHITFELD.

Whitmore, Charles Shapland, amateur composer, born at Colchester in 1805; died in 1877. He was a major in the army. Composer of the celebrated cavatina, Isle of Beauty ("Shades of evening") first issued about 1830, arranged by T. A. Rawlings. This appears to be the only published song of any importance written by Whitmore.

Whitten, A., author of "The Music of the Ancients, a lecture delivered in the Normal School, Calcutta, May 12, 1866." Calcutta, 1866.

WHITTINGHAM.

Whittingham, Alfred, organist and writer, was formerly in business as a dealer in old music, etc. Organist of St. Michael's, Bassishaw, London, from about 1878 until the closing of the church. He translated several works from Fèlis, Basevi, and others, which were published in the *Orchestra,* new series, from 1882. Author of Life and Works of Mozart, 1880; Life and Works of Handel, 1881, both published by W. Reeves. Composed First Studies for the pf.; Musical Time, 20 easy studies in C, R. Cocks. Editor and arranger of music by various composers, and writer on general musical subjects. He died suddenly in May, 1895.

Whomes, Joseph, member of a noteworthy family of organists. His father was organist of Eltham Church, Kent; he died in 1838. JOSEPH WHOMES, the eldest son, was born in 1817, and in 1833 was appointed organist at Charlton-next-Woolwich, and afterwards to Eltham Church; Woolwich Parish Church; and lastly, St. George's Garrison Church, Woolwich, a post he still holds. His brother, HENRY WHOMES, born in 1829, was appointed to St. Mary's, Cray, Kent, at the age of nine, and four years later, to Eltham, to which he twice returned after holding office for a time at Sidcup and North Cray. He was an organist for just fifty years, his last services being on Christmas Day, 1888. Two days later he had a paralytic seizure, but partly recovered; on the 9th of April following, he was stricken a second time, and died April 11. He was a sound musician, but his retiring disposition caused him to be but little known. JOSEPH WHOMES had two sons, organists: JOSEPH, who died in 1876; and FREDERICK, organist of the Dockyard Church, Woolwich, who was one of the unfortunate victims of the collision between the Bywell Castle, and the saloon boat, Princess Alice, September 3, 1878, when the latter went down off Woolwich, more than 600 lives being lost. He was a thorough musician and able teacher, and only thirty years of age at the time of the sad disaster. A sister, CLARA, was an excellent pianist, educated at the R.A.M. Settled in Sydney, Australia, she died there in 1884, at the age of thirty-one. EMMA, another daughter of Joseph Whomes, is at the present time organist of St. Mary's Parish Church, Woolwich; and EDMUND, nephew of Joseph Whomes, is an organist and conductor at Bexley Heath.

Whyte, James, tenor vocalist and teacher, born at Strathmiglo, Fife, September 20, 1857. Studied under Oakey, McNaught, and others, and is a Fellow of the Tonic Sol-fa College. Precentor successively at Kilmany, 1877; Brechin, 1881; Free St. Bernard's, Edinburgh, 1888; and from 1892 at Dunoon, and conductor at the Curwen

WILD.

Institute of Music. He has translated into Tonic Sol-fa notation Loder's Violin Tutor, and other works; and is editor of Köhler's Sol-fa violin music, etc.

Whythorne or **Whithorne Thomas,** composer of the 16th century, was born in 1531. He composed " Songes of three, fower, and five voyces . . . ," London, Day, 1571. " Bassavo, Duos, or Songs for Two Voices," 1590.

Whytock, Janet M., *see* Patey.

Wichello, *see* Whichello.

Wigan, Arthur Cleveland, musician and author, was born at London in 1815. He composed songs, canzonets, and other vocal music, and issued a " Modulating dictionary, consisting of 552 modulations with the returns," London, 1852; also Miscellaneous Music, vocal and instrumental, London, [1839].

Wight, Arthur Norton, pianist and composer, born at Düsseldorf, on the Rhine, in 1858, his parents being English, and at the time travelling on the Continent. Studied under Otto Lessmann and Oscar Raif, Berlin. Settled in London, and since 1884, pianoforte master at Dulwich College. His compositions consist of a symphony in G minor, written for the Symphony Orchestra, Washington, U.S.A., 1896; two overtures—" The village fair " (London, 1893) and " The Merry Month of May " (1894). Sonata in C, " Kirmess," duet, pf.; Berceuse, pf. and oboe; Six miniatures, pf. Part-songs and songs. Longfellow's " Norman Baron," for recitation, with pf. accompaniment, etc., etc. Several of his works have been produced with success on the Continent and in America.

Wilbye, John, composer of the 16th century. His biography is very obscure. In 1598 he was a teacher of music in Austin Friars, London. He composed " Madrigals to 3, 4, 5, and 6 Voices...." London, Este, 1598. Reprinted by Musical Antiquarian Society, edited by James Turle, 1841. " The Second Set of Madrigals, to 3, 4, 5, and 6 parts, apt both for Voyals and Voyces," London, 1609. Reprinted by Musical Antiquarian Society, edited by G. W. Budd, 1846. " The Lady Oriana," madrigal, is in the " 'Triumphs of Oriana." Among his best-known madrigals are " Flora gave me fairest flowers," " Sweet honey-sucking bee," " Die, hapless man," " When Chloris heard," " Stay, Corydon," " Lady, when I behold," " Why dost thou shoot," etc. These madrigals are among the sweetest, most appropriate, and fanciful pieces of pastoral music ever composed.

Wild, Margaret, pianist. Studied at the Leipzig Conservatorium, and played at the Hauptprüfung in 1882. Gave concerts in London, 1885, and also played in the provinces.

WILKES.

Studied under Madame Schumann, 1886-8. Returned to London, and appeared at the Monday Popular Concerts, November 28, 1888. Has given concerts at Princes' and St. James's Halls, annually, and has gained a good position among the younger pianists of the day

Wilkes, John, organist and composer, was organist at Monkland Church, near Leominster, about 1860. He studied at the R.A.M., and composed the well-known hymn tune, "Lyte," first contributed to "Hymns Ancient and Modern," 1861.

Wilkins, Matthew, organist and composer, who was born at Great Milton, Oxford, about July, 1704, and died there in August, 1772. He was a butcher, but also taught music. Compiler of "Book of Psalmody, containing some easy instructions for young beginners, to which is added a select number of psalm tunes, hymns, and anthems" [1730].

Wilkinson, Sarah, see MOUNTAIN, SARAH.

Willard, N. Augustus, author, was a captain in the army in India. Author of "Treatise on the Music of Hindoostan, in ancient and modern practice," Calcutta, 1834.

Willems, Miss, see ADDISON, JOHN.

Williams, Aaron, teacher and publisher of psalmody, was born in 1731. He was a music engraver in West Smithfield, as well as a teacher, and acted as clerk to the Scotch Church in London Wall, London. He died at London in 1776. He compiled and published "The Universal Psalmodist, containing 1. A complete introduction to psalmody.... 2. A choice and valuable collection of tunes.." London, n.d., 3rd edition, 1765 ; 4th edition, 1770. "New Universal Psalmodist," 1770. "Harmonia Coelestis, or the harmony of heaven imitated, a collection of scarce and much esteemed anthems...." London, n.d., 6th edition [1775]. "Psalmody in miniature, in 3 books, containing the tenor and bass of all the tunes generally used in churches, chapels, or dissenting congregations, London. 1778. Royal Harmony, or the beauties of church music.. , London [1780].

Williams, Albert, bandmaster and composer, born at Newport, Monmouthshire, March 14, 1863. Joined the Depôt of the 61st Regiment, at Bristol, about 1878 ; went to India in 1880 as euphonium player in the band. Received instruction from Barthmann, the bandmaster, and at the Military Exhibition held at Poona, 1884, carried off first and second prizes for composition and arrangement. Left India in December, 1885, for Kneller Hall ; and in February, 1888, was appointed bandmaster of the 10th Hussars. Graduated Mus. Bac., Oxford, 1891, and received his degree wearing the uniform of the 10th Hussars. In 1892 he succeeded John Winterbottom as bandmaster of the Royal Marine Artillery, and did good work at Portsmouth, where he remained

WILLIAMS.

until 1896, when he was appointed bandmaster of the Grenadier Guards in succession to Dan Godfrey. His compositions include Psalm 30, for soli, chorus, and orchestra. Overtures, Heloise and Abelard, Proserpine, and Plutus, for orchestra. Grand marches, Processional and Ecclesiastical ; waltzes, etc. Arrangements for military bands.

Williams, Anna, soprano vocalist, born at Campden Hill, London. Daughter of W. Smith Williams, literary adviser to Smith, Elder, and Co., publishers. She received lessons from H. C. Deacon and J. B. Welch, and took the first soprano prize at the National Music Meetings, Crystal Palace, June 27, 1872. Studied at Naples under Domenico Scafati, and made her first appearance on her return at the Crystal Palace, January 27, 1874. She was soon engaged in concert work ; sang in the revival of Handel's "Susannah," Alexandra Palace, April 1, 1876, etc. Her first festival engagement was at Worcester, 1878, then at Birmingham, 1879, and Leeds, 1880. As an oratorio singer especially she gained a high position. At the Birmingham Festival of 1891, she received a handsome present from the Committee, in acknowledgment of her readiness in taking extra work—Stanford's "Eden," etc.—on account of the illness of Madame Albani. She has appeared in opera, but her reputation has been greatest in the concert room. In 1896 she joined the teaching staff of the R.C.M. and G.S.M.

Williams, Anne and Martha, known as the Misses Williams, soprano and contralto vocalists, born at Bitterley, Salop, in 1818 and 1821, respectively. Studied under T. S. Cooke and Luigi Negri. Sang at Stafford, Shrewsbury. and other places, 1839-40 ; at the Hereford Festivals, 1840-43 ; Gloucester, 1844 ; Worcester, 1845 ; and Birmingham, 1846, taking part in the first performance of "Elijah." The sisters were engaged for the Wednesday concerts, Exeter Hall, from the commencement, November 22, 1848. Though of repute in oratorio, they were more celebrated for their finished duet singing. Anne married, May 13, 1850, Mr. Alfred Price, of Gloucester, and retired ; Martha sang at the Hereford Festival, 1852 ; was married to Charles Lockey, tenor vocalist (q.v.), May 24, 1853, but continued her professional career to 1865. She is now resident at Brighton, with her husband.

Williams, Annie, Welsh contralto vocalist, who appeared successfully as a concert singer. For some time she was organist of the Welsh Chapel, Jewin Street, London. She died at London, October 16, 1890.

Williams, Charles Francis Abdy, composer and organist, born at Dawlish, Devon, July 16, 1855. Educated for the Church, at

WILLIAMS.

Cambridge, studying music as an amateur. Was on the committee of University Musical Society, 1876-8, and played violin in its concerts. In 1879 he went to New Zealand, and was organist of St. Mary's Church, Auckland. On his return he became music master of Dover College, 1881. Graduated B.A., 1879; M.A., 1882, Cambridge. In 1882 he went to Leipzig, and remained three years at the Conservatorium, besides taking private lessons from Reinecke, Papperitz, Grell, and others. Organist and choirmaster of St. Mary Boltons, South Kensington, 1885-91. Graduated Mus. Bac., Oxford, 1889; Mus. Bac., Cambridge, 1891. Since 1895 he has been organist and music master at Bradfield College.

WORKS.—Psalm 24, and 29, for soli, chorus and strings; Communion service in E flat; Evening service in F; Chants for Benedicite, etc. Music to Euripides' Alcestis, written in Greek modes, and for Greek flutes and cithara produced at Bradfield College, June, 1895. Love's philosophy; My true love hath my heart, and other songs. Quartet in D minor (1887); Sonata in F, pf. and 'cello (1888); Four canons, pf., violin, and clarinet (1889), Musical Artists' Society. Author of A short historical account of the Degrees in Music at Oxford and Cambridge, with a Chronological List of Graduates in that Faculty, from the year 1463, London, Novello, 1893. Contributions on Greek Music to the *Classical Review ; Musical Times ;* and *Musical Quarterly Review ;* on Rhythm, to *Musical News,* 1891. Papers on various subjects, Musical Association, 1891, and '93; on Elements of Plain Song, Plain Song and Mediæval Music Society, 1895, etc.

Williams, Charles Lee, organist, composer, and conductor, born May 1, 1852, fourth son of Rev. David Williams, rector of Barnes, Wiltshire. Chorister of New College, Oxford, 1861-5. Pupil of Dr. G. B. Arnold, and assistant organist Winchester Cathedral, 1865-70; organist of Upton Church, Torquay, 1870; tutor and organist, St. Columba College, Dublin, 1873. Graduated Mus. Bac., Oxford, 1876. F.R.C.O. Acting organist for a time (in 1876) at Winchester Cathedral, during an illness of Dr. Arnold; then appointed to Llandaff Cathedral the same year; and in 1882, became organist of Gloucester Cathedral, in succession to C. Harford Lloyd. He also took the conductorship of the Gloucester Choral Society, the first concert under his direction taking place, December 12, 1882. The next year he conducted the Gloucester Festival, showing great ability; and continued in that until his resignation, owing to failing health, in November, 1896. He also conducted the Worcester Festival of 1890. From 1886 he gave annual series of organ recitals in Gloucester Cathedral, with the addition of

WILLIAMS.

choral music, and large congregations attended. Various societies in Gloucester were improved through his help. He is an Hon. R.A.M., and Associate of the Philharmonic Society.

WORKS.—Church cantatas, Bethany, Gloucester Festival, 1889 ; Gethsemane, the same, 1892 ; and A Dedication, the same, 1895. A Harvest Song of Praise, Tewkesbury Festival, 1895. Te Deum, composed for South Shropshire Choral Association Festival, 1895 ; Morning and evening services; Thou wilt keep him; To Thee, O Lord; and other anthems. Music, a choral song, Cheltenham Festival, 1893 ; Twilight ; Kindred hearts; If doughty deeds; The song of the Pedlar; and other part-songs, some of which are extensively popular ; Songs, carols, etc. ; Gavotte and minuet ; the Gloucester minuet, both for strings. Chimes of Gloucester Cathedral, arranged for pf., etc.

Williams, Evan, Welsh musician and harpist of first half of the 18th century. He edited "Antient British Music," 1772, in association with Parry of Ruabon.

Williams, Frederick Williams, author, vocalist and conductor, born in London (?), 1860. Studied at G.S.M. and R.C.M. Took the Toronto degree of Mus. Bac., 1889. F.S.A. of Scotland. Gave frequent lectures on musical subjects, 1886-7. Contributed to the musical press, and was the composer of some pf. pieces. Author of a History of Music for Students ; and the Five Great Schools of Composition, Stanley Lucas, 1889. He died at Hastings, February 7, 1891, at the early age of 31.

Williams, George Ebenezer, composer and organist, was born in 1783. He was a chorister of St. Paul's Cathedral under R. Bellamy, and in 1814 he became deputy-organist of Westminster Abbey. He died at London, April 17, 1819. He composed "Sixty Chants, single and double," and some church and secular vocal music. Author of "An Introduction to the art of playing on the pf." London [1810] ; 2nd edition, 1815. Exercises for the pf. and examining questions for school classes. London [1815].

Williams, Hamerton John, musician and composer. Edited "Musæ Sacræ, consisting of Hymns, Psalms, and Sacred Songs for one, two, or three voices." London [1838].

Williams, Joseph, clarinet player and composer, born in 1795. He was a director of the Philharmonic Society, and a member of the Queen's private band. Died at London in April, 1875. He composed a concerto for the clarinet, produced at a Hereford Festival, some dance music, and wrote an instruction book for the clarinet. Edited "Christmas minstrelsy of carols, anthems, and chants. revised by Gauntlett." London [1865].

WILLIAMS.

Williams, Joseph (FLORIAN PASCAL), composer, born in London, 1850. Son of the late Joseph Williams, music publisher. Studied at Zurich and Stuttgart.

WORKS.—*Comic Operas:* Cymbia, or the Magic Thimble, Strand Theatre, March 24, 1883; Gipsy Gabriel, Theatre Royal, Bradford, November 3, 1887. The Sirens of the Sea, soprano solo, female chorus and orchestra; cantata, The Dream Ship; Six sacred songs. *Songs:* For children of all ages; May Morn; Captain's Daughter; More than all, etc. Songs of the Upper Thames (William Mackay), 1896. Six vocal duets; Masque of Flowers, little suite for treble voices; overtures; suites for orchestra; trios, pf. and strings; pieces for 'cello and pf., etc.; Six Scandinavian Sketches, pf.

Williams, Lucas, bass vocalist, born at Treforest, Glamorganshire, February 17, 1852. In his eleventh year he removed to Stockton-on-Tees, where for some time he was a roller in the ironworks. As a boy he had a good contralto voice, and was taught by John Thomas (*q.v.*); learned the Tonic Sol-Fa from William Harris, at Stockton; took the elementary and intermediate certificates from John Roberts (*q.v.*); and learnt harmony analysis through the postal classes of the Tonic Sol-Fa College. While engaged as a workman he conducted a choir, and was the winner of prizes in local Eisteddfodau. In 1875 he won the baritone prize at the Pwllheli National Eisteddfod, and entered the R.A.M. the next year. After a few months at the Academy he went under Georg Henschel, and, later, studied under Randegger. He soon gained a reputation as an oratorio singer, and his popularity in the North of England is very great. He has been on tour with Sims Reeves, and has sung at the Royal Albert Hall Concerts the part of Sennacherib in Mancinelli's "Isaias" (February 20, 1889), and appeared in many important works; he has also acted as adjudicator at Eisteddfodau.

Williams (Maria Jane), *Llinos,* soprano singer and editor, born in Glamorgan, October 9, 1793; died November 10, 1873. Compiler of "Ancient national airs of Gwent and Morganwg: being a collection of original Welsh melodies hitherto unpublished......" Llandovery, 1844. This work, in a less perfect state, was awarded a prize at the Abergavenny Eisteddfod of 1838.

Williams, Owen, composer and editor, was a native of Anglesey. Issued "Brenhinal Ganiadau Sion, neu Gynghanedd newydd gymraeg yn cynwys...." London [1830], arranged by S. Wesley and V. Novello.

Williams, Owen Jones, musician, who published in parts a work entitled, "Psal-

WILLIAMS.

modia Cambro Britannica, or the original English and Welsh psalmody," London [1826].

Williams, Sidney, violinist and composer, born at Newport, Monmouthshire, in 1844. Appeared as soloist when eleven years of age. Was sometime leader of the band at Sadler's Wells, and afterwards at the Surrey Theatre. Occupied the position of musical director of the Cheltenham Theatre for many years, and composed the music for a number of pantomimes. Organist of the Unitarian Church, Cheltenham, and teacher of the violin. He has composed a number of pieces for violin, Swing song, Eventide, Lelia, and others.

Williams, Thomas, musician of 18th century, compiled "Psalmodia Evangelica, a complete set of psalm and hymn tunes for public worship," 1789.

Another THOMAS WILLIAMS, or perhaps the same, who lived on Clerkenwell Green, London, issued "Instructions in miniature for learning Psalmody," London [1800].

Williams, Thomas, HAFRENYDD, born at Llanidloes, Montgomery, December 7, 1807. Published a number of collections of tunes, anthems (1845, 1852, 1860, etc.), and the choruses of the Great Masters arranged to Welsh words, and which were of much service. He also published a Musical Grammar and Dictionary. He died at Llanidloes, December 16, 1894.

Williams, Thomas E., composer, who was born in latter part of last century, and died at London in November, 1854, at an advanced age. He composed the Larboard Watch, duet, and a large number of songs: Army and navy; Bright sword no more in anger drawn; Call to battle; Devil and St. Anthony; First vid de grace; Kiss, dear maid; Lord Ullin's daughter; Not a drum was heard; Pride of the ocean, etc. He also wrote quadrilles, and other music for the pf.

Williams, Warwick, composer and bandmaster, born at Holborn, London, in 1846. His father was in the East India Company's service, and the boy went with him to India in 1856, remaining there four years, during the period of the mutiny. He learned to play the cornet, and after being in several orchestras, became bandmaster of the 3rd West Yorkshire Volunteer Regiment in 1869. He joined the Mohawk Minstrels, for which association he composed more than a hundred songs and ballads. Was co-conductor of the London Military Band, 1891, while D. Godfrey, Junior, was in South Africa; and in 1893 was appointed professional musical adviser to the London County Council regarding bands in parks, etc. Editor of the *Eclipse Journal* for bands, since its establishment. He has composed the overtures, On

D2

WILLIAMS.

the mountains, Eclipse, Morimo, and others; and much dance music of a popular kind, besides songs, etc.

Williams, W. Langton, composer and didactic writer, born about 1832. Author of Æsop's Fables, versified and arranged for pf. Composer of pf. album, Home pictures, twelve pieces; numerous songs, etc. He died of apoplexy, December 23, 1896, aged 64.

Williams, William Aubrey, GWILYM GWENT. Born at Tredegar, Monmouth, July 28, 1834. A working miner who gained the reputation of being the best Glee writer Wales has produced. Lacking in musical culture and scholarship, he had a rich fund of melody, and an intuitive grasp of the characteristics of various forms. He was a prolific writer, and probably competed more, and won more prizes, than any other Welsh composer. His compositions included several cantatas, to one of which, "The Prodigal Son," was awarded a prize at the National Eisteddfod, Aberystwith, 1865. He also produced anthems, choruses, trios, duets, hymn tunes, glees, and part-songs. In 1872 he emigrated to America, and died at Plymouth, Pennsylvania, July 3, 1891. In 1895, by public subscription, a monument was erected over his grave in Hollenback Cemetery, Wilkesbarre, Pa.

Williamson, T. G., musician, published "Twelve original Hindoostanee airs" op. 4. London [1797]; and a "Second collection of twelve original Hindoostanee airs," op. 9. London, 1798. Composer of Six favourite sonatinas for the pf., op. 1; Six grand troops with six quicksteps, op. 6. Thirty little airs for two flutes or violins, op. 7. Ten easy lessons for the pf., op. 8. Songs: Bird's nest, Gipsey, Lubin's return, Pretty Nell, Wooden leg.

Willing, Christopher Edwin, organist and conductor, born in Devon, February 28, 1830. Son of CHRISTOPHER WILLING, alto vocalist and Assistant-Gentleman of the Chapel Royal (born 1804; died May 12, 1840). Chorister of Westminster Abbey, under Jas. Turle, 1839. Organist of Blackheath Park Church; and assistant-organist, Westminster Abbey. Organist of Foundling Hospital, May 11, 1848, and musical director shortly after, resigning in November, 1879; also organist concurrently at St. Paul's, Covent Garden, 1857, and All Saints', Margaret Street, 1860-1868. Organist, Her Majesty's Theatre, 1848-57, and chorus-master at Covent Garden Opera. In 1883 Sir Michael Costa presented him with a collection of bâtons as a souvenir of their official connection. In 1882 he formed, from the old Sacred Harmonic, a choir bearing his name, and gave concerts, 1882-5. Later he was conductor of the St. Alban's Choral Union, and its triennial

WILSON.

festivals. He has composed some songs, the well-known hymn tune "Alstone" ("We are but little children"), and other works.

Willis, Mary, mezzo-soprano vocalist, pupil of Madam Sainton-Dolby. Made her first public appearance at a concert of Madame Dolby's Vocal Academy, December 14, 1882. Sang at various concerts, and took the part of Gipsy in Macfarren's "Jessy Lea," 1890. Has given concerts in Steinway Hall, 1891, etc.

Willman, Thomas Lindsay, clarinet player, son of a German, who in the latter half of the 18th century came to England as a military bandmaster. Neither date nor place of the son's birth are known. He became principal clarinet of the Opera and other orchestras about 1816, and was master of the Grenadier Guards' band. From 1817 to 1839 he played solos at the Philharmonic Concerts, and was considered the most delicate and finished player of his time. He died in London, November 28, 1840, at the stated age of 56, but he was supposed to have been much older.

Willmore, Walter Graham, organist, born in London, May 24, 1851, son of the late Arthur Willmore, the eminent line engraver. Chorister at Chapel Royal, Whitehall, 1860-3, and pupil, for organ, of George Cooper. Went to United States of America, and was organist of St. Mark's, Philadelphia, 1874-6, and of the Roosevelt organ built for the Centennial Exhibition of 1876. Two years later he was established as organist of All Saints' Brisbane, Australia, a position he retained till 1893. He visited England in 1883, and, as a member of the College of Organists, keeps up relation with the mother country.

Willoughby, Robert, musician of latter part of last and beginning of the present centuries. Edited "Social Harmony, being a choice collection of catches, glees, etc., for two, three, and four voices . . ," London, [1810], 2 vols. "Sacred Harmony, consisting of a collection of Anthems," London [1800]. A short and easy introduction to vocal music, London [1802].

Willy, John Thomas, violinist, was born at London, July 24, 1812. He established an orchestra in London, which gave concerts for some years. With T. Cooke he was principal violin at the Birmingham Festival of 1846, and played also at the Three Choir Festivals. Composed music for the "Young Widow," 1843. Died at Clapham, London, August 8, 1885. His son, J. H. WILLY, who was an organist, died at Madras, October 12, 1869.

Wilson, Mrs. Cornwall Baron, composer and lyric poet of the present century. In 1837 she gained the prize of the Melodist's Club, and also medals at Bardic Festivals in Wales. She died at London, January 12,

WILSON.

1846. Composer of Songs of the ship ; Water music, a collection of national melodies.. arranged with a guitar accompaniment, London [1835]. The Lyrist's Offering. She also wrote many detached songs to her own words ; wrote the poetry for Parry's Welsh Melodies, vol, 3 ; and edited Memoirs of the Duchess of St. Albans.

Wilson, Daniel Ferguson, organist and composer, born at Kilmarnock, October 6, 1859. Studied under A. L. Peace and others. Graduated Mus. Bac., 1886; Mus. Doc., 1894. Oxford. Organist of St. Marnock's Parish Church, 1874 ; Parish Church, Ayr, 1878 ; and of Ayr Town Hall, 1880. His compositions are Psalm 30, for soli, chorus and strings ; Cantata. Legend of the Drachenfels. He has arranged as part-songs, John Anderson, my Jo ; My heart is sair, etc.

Wilson, Haydn, organist and composer of the first half of the present century. He was organist of St. Mary's, Newington, London. Composer of Six Overtures for pf., with accompaniment for flute, violin and violoncello [1828]. Six Waltzes for pf. [1850]. Other instrumental and vocal pieces.

Wilson, Hilda (Matilda Ellen), contralto vocalist, born at Monmouth, April 7, 1860. The daughter of a musician (her father, JAMES WILSON, was bandmaster of the Monmouth Volunteer Corps, and afterwards held important posts at Gloucester), her earliest childhood was devoted to the art. Her parents removing to Gloucester, she became a member of the choir of St. Michael's Church, and appeared as a solo vocalist at concerts of the Gloucester Choral Society, 1874-5. In 1879 she entered the R.A.M., and was Westmorland Scholar, 1880-1 ; and Parepa-Rosa Prizeholder, 1882. Elected A.R.A.M. She sung in the quartets, etc., in " Elijah," and in Palestrina's *Stabat Mater,* at the Gloucester Festival of 1880 ; was second contralto at Worcester, 1881 ; at Hereford, 1882 ; added to her reputation at the Leeds Festival, 1883 ; and was first contralto at Norwich Festival, 1887. She had by that time acquired a leading position, and at the Philharmonic concerts, Birmingham Festival, 1891, and the chief concerts in the Kingdom, worthily sustained it. In 1890 she began a series of vocal recitals, assisted by her sister and two brothers, at Steinway Hall.

AGNES WILSON, her sister, also a contralto vocalist, was born at Gloucester, October 8, 1864. She studied at the G.S.M. under Visetti, and at R.A.M under W. Shakespeare. Appeared at concerts in 1887 ; has sung with success at the Lincoln and Hovingham Festivals ; and took part in the Hereford Festival of 1894. She has also sung at the principal London and provincial concerts. She is a professor of singing at the Blackheath

WILSON.

Conservatoire, and, with her brother W. S. Wilson, director and professor of the West London Conservatoire of Music.

H. J. LANE WILSON, pianist, organist, and composer, was born at Gloucester. Removed to London in 1882, and studied under F. G. Cole. Later he studied at R.A.M., singing under A. Oswald, and composition under F. Corder. In 1888 he was engaged as accompanist on Madame Minnie Hauk's tour, and has had much work of that kind, besides touring with Madame Albani in America, 1895-6. He has composed a Meditation for strings, performed at Cheltenham Festival, 1893, etc. ; an *Ave Maria* for soprano, with pf., violin, and organ, sung by Madame Albani, Queen's Hall, April 20, 1895 ; A mother's vigil ; Voices of the Angels ; Annette ; and other songs.

W. STROUD WILSON, violinist, and baritone vocalist was born at Gloucester, May 20, 1868. Studied the violin under his father, and later at the Guildhall School and R.A.M. under the late Francis Ralph. He was engaged by Mr. Cowen for the orchestral concerts at Melbourne Exhibition, 1888-9 ; has also toured in America. Was leader in Madame Marie Roze's " Carmen " tour, and is a member of the orchestras of the Royal Italian opera, Crystal Palace, Queen's Hall Promenade concerts, and the provincial festivals. He is solo baritone in the choir of Holy Trinity, Sloane Square, and director and professor of the West London Conservatoire of Music.

Wilson, Hugh, shoemaker and amateur composer, was born at Fenwick, Ayrshire, in 1764. He was originally a shoemaker with his father in Fenwick, and occasionally acted as precentor in the Secession Church there. He afterwards went to Pollokshaws, near Glasgow, and subsequently resided at Duntocher in Dumbartonshire as manager in a mill. He died at Duntocher, August 14, 1824, and is buried in the churchyard of Old Kilpatrick. He composed a number of psalm tunes, but his chief claim to remembrance lies in his well-known tune " Martyrdom," which for many years has been a favourite with congregations in Scotland.

Wilson, James W., musician and editor, issued " Musical Cyclopædia, being a collection of songs with appropriate music. To which is added an essay on the first principles of Music," London [1835]. New edition, 1852. The essay is by W. Grier (*q.v.*).

Wilson, John, composer and lute player, born at Faversham, Kent, April 5, 1594. He was made Mus. Doc., Oxon., 1644. Afterwards he resided with the family of Sir Wm. Walter of Sarsden, Oxfordshire, as music master, from 1646. He was professor of music at Oxford University, 1656-1662. Gen-

WILSON.

tleman of the Chapel Royal, and chamber musician to Charles II., 1662. He died at Westminster, February 22, 1673. Supposed by Rimbault to have been the Jack Wilson who sang in Shakespeare's plays. He composed " Psalterium Carolium, the devotions of his Sacred Majestie in his solitude and sufferings, rendered in verse, set to musick for three voices, and an organ or theorbo," London, 1657; "Cheerful Airs or Ballads, first composed for one single voice, and since set for three voices," Oxford, 1660; "Aires for a voice alone to a theorbo or bass viol. Divine services and anthems," 1663; "Fantasias for viols."

Wilson, John, tenor vocalist and composer, was born in the Canongate, Edinburgh, December 25, 1800. He was apprenticed to the printing trade in 1810, and afterwards became reader for the press in Ballantyne's printing office, Edinburgh. He studied music under John Mather and B. Gleadhill, and was a choir-singer in Duddingston Parish Church, where the Rev. John Thomson was pastor. He was married about 1820, and became precentor of the Relief Church, Roxburgh Place, Edinburgh, and of St. Mary's, 1825. He sang at concerts in Edinburgh, and studied for a time under Finlay Dun, and singing in London, under Lanza, 1827, and Crivelli, 1830; also harmony under Aspull. First appeared in opera, as Harry Bertram in " Guy Mannering," Edinburgh, March, 1830. Sang in opera in London, from 1830, and became highly successful in English opera at Covent Garden, Drury Lane, and other theatres. He afterwards travelled in Britain giving his Songs of Scotland entertainment, and appeared as a concert and opera singer till 1838. Appeared in the United States, 1838, and visited Canada in 1849. He died at Quebec, July 8, 1849.

One of the most successful Scottish singers. His entertainments consisted of Nights with Burns; Jacobite songs; Lady of the Lake, 1848; Mary, Queen of Scots, 1847, etc.; and were very well patronised wherever he appeared. He published " Wilson's edition of the Songs of Scotland, as sung by him at his entertainments on Scottish Music and Song," London, 1842, 3 books. A Selection of Psalm tunes, sanctuses, doxologies, etc., for the use of the congregation of St. Mary's Church, Edinburgh, 1825. The songs Love wakes and weeps, Hail to the Chief, Bonnie Bessie Lee, Auld Joe Nicolson's bonny Nannie, etc., were introduced by him, and by many are believed to be his own compositions.

Wilson, Joseph William, composer of the present time. He has written a church oratorio, " The Earthly and Heavenly Harvest," produced at St. Mary's Church, Wandsworth, April 10, 1888; also an opera, " Donna Theresa," performed, Wandsworth, 1885.

WINDSOR.

Wilson, Leigh, professional name of WILLIAM EDWARD COCKRAM, a tenor vocalist, who was born at Bristol in 1836. He was son of John Cockram, music-seller there. He was a singer of great promise and made a very good impression when he first appeared. Died in London, of brain fever, in February, 1870, aged 34.

Wilson, Marmaduke Charles, composer and pianist, was born at London in 1796. Teacher and pianist in London. He died after 1870. Composer of Sonata for pf. op. 10; Duet for harp and pf. op. 15; Rondoletto for pf. op. 7; Polonaise for pf. op. 12; Les plaisirs de Printemps, pf. Duets, songs, etc.

Wilson, Mary Ann, see sub. WELSH THOMAS.

Wilson, Matthew, Scottish amateur composer, who flourished in Glasgow in the first half of the present century. He studied music under John Turnbull and appears to have been an accompanist at free and easy concerts in Glasgow. To the "Lyric Gems of Scotland " and other collections he contributed a number of songs, among which may be named "Meet me on the gowan lea," "Sweet Jessie o' the dell," " Mary and me," "Morag's Faery Glen," "O far may ye roam." He also wrote several hymn tunes, among which may be named "Drumclog."

Wilson W., author of a " New Dictionary of Music," London [1830].

Wilton, Fanny W., see LABLACHE, FANNY W.

Wilton, Thomas Egerton, 2nd Earl of, composer, born December 30, 1799; died March 7, 1882. Composer of "Hymn to Eros;" " O, praise the Lord;" anthem, chants, and other vocal music.

Winchester, Ernest Charles, organist and composer, born at Osborne, May 22, 1854. Organist and C.M., Christ Church, Southwark. Compositions : If ye love Me ; The Lord is my Shepherd ; I will give thanks ; and other anthems. Te Deum and Benedictus ; Eight settings of the Te Deum ; Jubilate ; Preces and responses ; Communion Service, Kyries, Offertory sentences, etc. Six original hymn tunes; Litanies, etc.; Crowning the May Queen, trio.

Windle, Walter Wardle, organist, born at Chesterfield. Chorister when eight at Chesterfield Parish Church, and pupil of Thomas Tallis Trimnell, and later of Dr. Spark. Organist of Parish Church, Brimington, when sixteen; and since 1882 of Belper Parish Church. In 1886 he was appointed conductor of Ripley (Derby) Choral Union. He has given organ recitals in many places Composer of Supplemental Hymn tunes, Kyries, doxologies, and chants ; Six Kyries, etc.

Windsor, James W., composer and

WINGHAM.

pianist, was born at London in 1776. He was a teacher in Bath, and died there on January 28, 1853. He harmonized a number of popular songs and composed some vocal music.

Wingham, Thomas, pianist and composer, born in London, January 5, 1846. When ten years old he became organist of St. Michael's Mission Church, Southwark. Studied at London Academy of Music, 1863 ; entered R.A.M., 1867, studying under W. S. Bennett and Harold Thomas. In 1871 he was appointed a professor of the pf. there, and afterwards elected a Fellow. He was also a professor at the G.S.M. In 1864 he was appointed organist of All Saints', Paddington ; and he was musical director at the Oratory, Brompton, from 1882 until the time of his death, which took place in London, March 24, 1893.

WORKS.—Mass in D, produced, Antwerp Cathedral, 1876 ; Mass, Brompton, 1887 ; Te Deum, for voices, orchestra and organ, Brompton, 1884 ; Motets, offertories (composed for Antwerp Cathedral), and other church music. Songs. *Orchestral :* Symphony, No. 1, in D minor (composed at R.A.M., 1869) ; No. 2, in B flat, Crystal Palace, March 23, 1872 ; No. 3, in E minor, with choral finale, 1873 ; No. 4, Crystal Palace, April 28, 1883. Concert overture, No. 1, in C, composed for the Jubilee of the R.A.M., 1872 ; No. 2, in E, Eros, Crystal Palace, November 27, 1875 ; No. 3. in D, choral, Alexandra Palace, May 10, 1877 ; No. 4, in F, Fair laughs the morn, Crystal Palace, February 16, 1878 ; No. 5, in A, Brighton Festival, 1879 ; No. 6, in D, Mors Janua Vitæ, Leeds Festival, 1880. Elegy on the death of Sterndale Bennett, Crystal Palace, March 6, 1875 ; Serenade in E flat Philharmonic Society, March 26, 1885. Concert Capriccio, pf. and orchestra ; String quartets, in B flat and G minor. Septet for pf., strings, and wind, and an opera Nala and Damayanti, left unfinished. Only a Barcarolle for pf., and one or two songs by this composer have been published.

Winn, Rowland Mellor, pianist, organist and composer, born in Birmingham, April 24, 1856. Descended from musical families, by both parents, his mother's maiden name being Mellor. Articled pupil of A. R. Gaul. Graduated Mus. B., 1876 ; Mus. D., 1883, Oxford. F.R.C.O. Organist and choirmaster, Harborne Parish Church, from 1874. Has appeared as solo pianist at Mr. Stockley's Orchestral, and other concerts, and is widely known as an able accompanist. He has composed an oratorio, "The Sea of Galilee," and has published part-songs and pf. pieces ; also "Sixty-one Melodies and unfigured basses" (Novello), 1891.

Winn, William, baritone vocalist and composer, born at Bramham, Yorkshire, May 8,

WINTERBOTTOM.

1828. Gentleman of Chapel Royal, 1864. Vicar choral of St. Paul's London, 1867. He died at Willesden, near London, June 4, 1888, aged 60. Well-known as a baritone singer of great ability, and for his connection with various Glee and Quartet parties in London and elsewhere. Composer of Glees : Autumn (1868) ; Go rose, prize glee, 1870. Life : Who falls in fight, etc. Songs : England's gallant defenders, Evening thoughts, Gipsy charms, Her pathway strewn with flowers, Nothing more, Old ice king, Quite by chance, Who wins the bride, Wild old woods, etc.

His daughter, FLORENCE WINN, made her *début* as a contralto singer at a concert of her father's in St. James' Hall, London, May 31, 1881.

Winny, H., organist and conductor, for many years an active musical worker in South Africa. As pianist he assisted in concerts at Grahams Town from 1883 ; and conducted the Handel Bicentenary Festival in the Town Hall there, when "Israel in Egypt" was performed for the first time in South Africa, June 3, 1885. In 1886 he was elected organist of St. George's Cathedral, Grahams Town ; and after some years removed to a similar post at St. Winian's Cathedral, Pretoria. He died at Grahams Town, from heart disease, July, 1895.

Winter, Pattie, soprano vocalist. Pupil of William Carter. Made her *début* at the Royal Albert Hall, Kensington, April 22, 1882. Sang at the Alexandra Palace the same year, and at various concerts up to 1888, when she went to Milan and studied under Sangiovanni. On her return she sang at St. James' Hall, April 3, 1889, and has established herself among the accepted vocalists of the time.

Winterbottom, a remarkable family of military musicians, consisting of five brothers, sons of JOHN Winterbottom, of the 1st Life Guards, who fought at Waterloo, and was, on his retirement from the service, appointed one of the wardens of the Tower of London. He died in 1855. THOMAS WINTERBOTTOM, the eldest son, was in the band of the Royal Horse Guards nine years, and afterwards bandmaster of the Royal Marine Light Infantry, Plymouth Division, for seventeen years. He died at Plymouth in 1869. WILLIAM WINTERBOTTOM, born about 1822, was a trombone player in the band of the 1st Life Guards. Then he was bandmaster of the Woolwich Division, and succeeded his brother at Plymouth, thence exchanging to the 2nd Life Guards. He died at Boulogne-sur-Mer, September 29, 1889. JOHN WINTERBOTTOM, the celebrated bassoon-player, was born about 1817. He was a member of the famous Jullien orchestra when a young man. From about 1852 he was in Australia, giving

WINTERBOTTOM.

promenade concerts at Melbourne, Sydney, and elsewhere. On his return to England he was appointed to organize the band of the Royal Marine Artillery. This was in 1870, as he completed twenty-one years' service November, 1891, and retired March 31, 1892. He then became bandmaster of the Artists' Rifle Corps, London. He died at Putney, May 18, 1897. HENRY WINTER-BOTTOM was bandmaster of the 7th Royal Fusiliers, the 18th Royal Irish, and the Royal Marines, Woolwich. AMMON WINTER-BOTTOM was a double-bass player, member of the Queen's private band, Philharmonic orchestra, etc. He died in 1891.

FRANK WINTERBOTTOM, son of the last named, was born in London in 1861. Educated at Bruce Castle, Tottenham. Studied music under his father and his uncle William. Held appointments as professor of music at Dulwich College, and conductor of orchestral societies at Croydon, Clapham, etc. In 1890 was appointed bandmaster Plymouth Division Royal Marine Light Infantry, a position he still holds. He gives symphony concerts in the Town Hall, Stonehouse, during the winter months, also entertainments in the divisional theatre, etc. His compositions include: Overture and ballet music, "Jorinda;" interlude, "Phaulos;" Illustration of Shakespeare's "Seven Ages," Portsmouth, 1892; a descriptive fantasia, "V.R." Also string quartets; pieces for violoncello, upon which instrument he is a skilled performer; selections, arrangements, etc.

Winterbottom, James, musician, born at Glossop, in 1816. He was sexton of All Saints' Church, Glossop, an office his family had held for 200 years. In addition he was organist of the church for 20 years. He died at Glossop, in January, 1889.

Wise, Charles Stanley, organist and composer. Studied under private teachers, and graduated Mus. B., Cambridge, 1890. Was appointed organist of Petworth Church, 1876; Godalming, 1878; St. Michael's, Alnwick, 1881. He is conductor of a choral Society at Wooler, Northumberland, and gave the first performance of an oratorio ("Creation") in that place, February 21, 1896. He has composed orchestral pieces, string quartet, songs; anthems, church services, etc.

Wise, Michael, composer and organist, born at Salisbury in 1638. He was a chorister in the Chapel Royal under Cook. In 1668 he was appointed organist and choirmaster of Salisbury Cathedral, and in 1675 he became Gentleman of the Chapel Royal. He was made almoner and master of the choristers of St. Paul's Cathedral, London, 1686-87. He was killed at Salisbury, in a midnight brawl with the watch, on August 24, 1687. Composer of a magnificat in E flat. Anthems—

WOOD.

Prepare ye the way of the Lord; Awake, put on thy strength; Blessed is He; Awake up, my glory; The ways of Zion do mourn; Thy beauty, O Israel, etc.

Woakes, W. H., organist and author, was organist at Hereford early in the present century. He wrote "A Catechism of Music," Hereford, 1817; "A Catechism of Thoroughbass, catechism on music and dictionary," Hereford, 1820. He also wrote "Ten glees for three and four voices," [1830]; Songs and anthems, and dance music for the pf.

Woffington, Margaret or **Peg,** a celebrated actress and singer, was born at Dublin, in 1718. First appeared in London, in 1738. She died in 1760. Her life is given at large in Reade's novel, "Peg Woffington," in Molloy's biographical work, the "Thespian Dictionary," etc. Best known as an actress.

Wolstenholme, William, organist and composer, born at Blackburn, February 24, 1865. Showed remarkable powers when quite young; and the late Henry Smart promised to take him as a pupil, but he died just at the period agreed upon. Blind from his birth, he was educated at the Worcester College for the Blind Sons of Gentlemen, and was musically trained by Dr. Done. He appeared in public while at Worcester, giving organ recitals, and he played Mendelssohn's Concerto in G minor at a concert of the Worcester Philharmonic Society, December 4, 1885. Graduated Mus. B., Oxford, 1887, and in his preparatory work committed to memory and transcribed into Braille the score of Beethoven's "Fidelio." In 1888 he was appointed organist and choirmaster of St. Paul's Church, Blackburn, in which town he is settled as teacher, etc.

WORKS.—Cantata, Lord Ullin's Daughter, for soli, chorus, and strings; Anthem for Easter; To take the air, madrigal, 5 voices; Part-song; The voice of love; Thou art high above me, lady; and other songs. Organ: Sonata in D, in the style of Handel; Canzona; Minuet; Cantilena in F minor; Finale in B flat; Die Frage und die Antwort; Volkslied, etc. Pianoforte: A Collection of pieces in 3 books; Minuet in D; Allegro alla burla in F; Wedding march; Nocturne; Scherzo in F; and others. Also detached pieces for harp, violin, oboe, viola, and for mandolin and guitar.

Wood, Anthony à, antiquary and writer, born at Oxford, December 17, 1632; died there, November 29, 1695. From his writings many biographies of the older musicians have been taken. His "Athenæ Oxoniensis....," London, 1691-92, 2 vols., contains notices of musicians who were educated at Oxford, and there exists in MS. in the Ashmolean Museum a work entitled "Some Materials towards a History of the Lives and Compositions of all

WOOD.

English Musicians." "A Wood," as he styles himself, was a great amateur musician.

Wood, Charles, composer and organist, born at Armagh, Ireland, June 15, 1866, son of Charles Wood, a lay vicar in the Cathedral. Obtained the Morley Scholarship for composition, R.C.M., 1883, and was appointed professor of harmony, etc., 1888. In 1889, he won the Organist Scholarship, Caius College, Cambridge; and graduated Mus. B. and B.A., 1890; Mus. D. and M.A., 1894, in which last year he was made Fellow of Gonville and Caius College. A.R.C.M. While a student at the R.C.M. he wrote a pf. concerto, string quartet, and other works. He won the Musical World Prize, 1887, by a setting of Alex. Grant's "Through the Twilight"; the Madrigal Society's prize and gold medal, 1888, with five-part madrigal, "Slow, slow, fresh fount"; and, in 1889, the prize offered by the Wind Instrument Chamber Music Society for a Quintet for wind. He has written incidental music to Euripides' "Ion," and "Iphigenia in Tauris," produced, at Theatre Royal, Cambridge, 1890 and 1894; also set Shelley's "Ode to the West Wind," for tenor solo, chorus and orchestra (op. 3, Cambridge, 1889); and Swinburne's "Ode to Music," for soprano solo, chorus and orchestra, written for. and performed at the opening of the New Building, R.C.M., May 2, 1894. He has further published church music, songs, part-songs, and edited a collection of Irish folk-songs, Boosey, 1897.

His elder brother, WILLIAM G. WOOD, was a distinguished organist. He was born at Armagh, January 16, 1859, and received his early musical training at the Cathedral, where he was deputy organist, 1873-7. He afterwards entered the R.A.M., and won the Lucas Prize for composition, 1882. Was professor of the organ, and F.R.A.M., F.R.C.O. While a student, he was appointed organist of Christ Church, Woburn Square (1880): gave frequent organ recitals, appearing at Bow and Bromley Institute (1883), and elsewhere; played the organ at the first concert held in the Queen's Hall, December 2, 1893. In 1886 he was appointed organist and music master of Highgate Grammar School, a post he retained until his death, September 25, 1895. He composed an operetta, The Bride of Cambus (1883), and published three settings of the Magnificat and Nunc dimittis. He wrote a concert overture for orchestra, and much music for the organ: Fantasia and Fugue in C minor; Sonata in D minor; Three Canons, etc., etc., by which he will be long remembered.

Wood, Daniel Joseph, organist, conductor and composer, born at Brompton, near Chatham, Kent, August 25, 1849. Chorister at Rochester Cathedral, and pupil of J. Hopkins, 1859-64. Appointed organist of Holy

WOOD.

Trinity, Brompton, Kent, 1864; Parish Church, Cranbrook, 1866; Lee, Kent, 1868; Boston, Lincolnshire, 1869; Chichester Cathedral, 1875; and of Exeter Cathedral, 1876. This appointment he holds to the present time. F.C.O., 1873; Mus. B., Oxford, 1874; and in 1896 received the Mus. D., Cantuar. He has been instrumental in procuring a fine new organ for the Cathedral, and one in Victoria Hall, to which he was appointed organist in 1882. He is also teacher of harmony at Exeter University Extension College, and has done much for music in Exeter. Was one of the promoters of the Western Counties' Musical Association, and has been conductor of its Annual Festivals since its formation in 1880. His compositions are confined to church and organ music, with tunes contributed to the Hymnal Companion (joint editor of the new edition), and chants for the Chant Book Companion.

Wood, Ernest, organist, was elected to the post of organist and precentor of St. Paul's Cathedral, Melbourne, Australia, 1888. Previously he was known in England as a clever performer on the organ. He gave recitals with much success at Melbourne, 1891; in 1893 was appointed conductor of the Royal Metropolitan Liedertafel, Melbourne; and in 1894 introduced the performance of oratorios in Melbourne Cathedral. He gave the first performance of Bach's Matthew "Passion Music" at Melbourne, in April, 1897, and has done good work in the cause of musical education there.

Wood, Henry Joseph, composer and conductor, born in London. Received his early training from his father, and was deputy organist of St. Mary's, Aldermanbury, when ten years old. Gave organ recitals at the "Fisheries," and other exhibitions, South Kensington, 1883-5. Entered the R.A.M. in 1886, studying under E. Prout, Dr. Steggall, W. Macfarren, Manuel Garcia, and others. On leaving the Academy he became conductor of various societies; also of the Rousbey Opera Company, 1890; the Carl Rosa provincial tour, 1891-2; the Georgina Burns "Cinderella" tour, 1892; and Lago's season at the New Olympic, 1892. In 1894 he was conductor during Madame Marie Roze's farewell tour. His career at the Queen's Hall began with the promenade concert season of 1895, the programmes of which were of the highest class. He has since conducted the Symphony Concerts there, and his work has been characterised by enterprise and distinguished ability. All this time he has also been occupied as a teacher of singing, especially for the stage, whilst as a composer he has done a considerable amount of work.

WORKS.—Mass, performed, St. Mary's, Bayswater, December, 1892; Mass in E flat,

WOOD.

op. 55, St. Joseph's Retreat, Highgate, June, 1896. Anthems. Dramatic oratorio, Dorothea, Grosvenor Hall, February 15, 1889; Dramatic cantata, Nacoochee, 1890. *Operettas :* Daisy, 1890; Returning the compliment; Comic opera, Zuleika, the Turkish slave, 1890; One hundred years ago, Royalty Theatre, June 16, 1892. Romance, violin and. pf., 1887. *Songs :* The sea hath its pearls; Six songs, op. 15 ; The king and the miller ; To one I love ; Will her heart to me incline ? and others. Author of a work on his method of vocal teaching, Breathing, Tones, and their qualities, London, 1896.

Wood, John Muir, writer and music-publisher, was born at Edinburgh, July 31, 1805. He established music-publishing businesses in Edinburgh and Glasgow, and was associated with Chopin and other great artists who visited Scotland on concert-giving enterprises. His firm published for a time the *Scottish Monthly Musical Times,* a journal which lived only for a short time 1876-78. He edited a new edition of Graham's "Songs of Scotland" (1884), and contributed important Scottish matter to Grove's "Dictionary of Music." He died at Cove, Dumbartonshire, June 25, 1892.

Wood, Joseph, tenor vocalist, was born at Crigglestone, Yorkshire, on March 1, 1801. He appeared in opera and at concerts, and in 1831 married Mary Ann Paton (*q.v.*); and some time after her death Sarah Dobson, a singer. He died at Harrogate, in September, 1890.

Wood, Mrs. Joseph, *see* Paton, Mary Anne.

Wood, Mary Louisa, organist and teacher. Appointed to St. Thomas's Church, Douglas, Isle of Man, 1877 ; now of St. German's Parish Church in that town. Sometime conductor of Castletown Choral Society. Has done much for the promotion of music in the island, and given frequent organ recitals. Is an Associate of the Royal College of Organists. She read a paper on the "Liturgy of the Church from the musical point of view," at the Sodor and Man Diocesan Conference, December, 1896. In August 1895, she was presented with an address and testimonial in acknowledgment of her work in the cause of music and charity.

Woodcock, Robert, English composer of the 18th century. He composed "XII. Concertos in eight parts . . ," n.d., chiefly for strings and flutes and oboe.

Woodcock, R. J., musician and teacher, author of "Progressive system of Class-singing. etc," London [1843].

Woodcock, William, organist and composer, born in 1754. He was organist and singing man of new College, Oxford, from 1799 to 1825; Graduated Mus. B., Oxford,

WOODWARD.

1806 ; and was clerk of Magdalen College from 1784 to 1818. Died at Oxford in 1825.

Woodd, Rev. Basil, clergyman and musician, born at Richmond, Surrey, August 5, 1760. He was educated at Oxford, and after acting as morning preacher at Bentinck Chapel, Lisson Grove, London, 1785, was minister of Drayton, Beauchamp, Bucks., from 1808 to 1830. He died at London, April 12, 1831. He wrote "A new metrical version of the Psalms of David," etc., and composed "Paddington," a psalm tune, contained in the "Bentinck Chapel Collection," 1800.

Woodham, Joseph, double-bass player, was born in 1768. He was a member of the Royal Society of Musicians for 45 years, and played the double-bass in the orchestra of Covent Garden Theatre, for over 40 years. Died at London, January 25, 1841.

Woodman, Rev. W., author of "Singing at sight made easy, a complete course of instruction," London, 1860.

Woods, Francis Cunningham, organist and composer, born in London, August 29, 1862. Studied at National Training School, Kensington, 1877-80, under Sullivan, Stainer, Prout, and others. Organist, Brasenose College, Oxford, 1883-6 ; appointed organ scholar, Exeter College, 1887. Graduated M.A., 1890 ; Mus. B., 1891, Oxford. F.R.C.O. In 1891 was appointed private organist to the Duke of Marlborough, at Blenheim; and. from 1895, organist and music master, Highgate School. Recitalist and teacher. Conductor of Oxford Choral and Philharmonic (1893) ; Bicester Choral ; and Lincoln and Exeter College Musical Societies. Lecturer for Sir John Stainer ; to the British Association (Oxford, 1894); Oxford University Extensionists (1895). Associate of the Philharmonic Society.

Published Compositions. — Cantata, King Harold, produced, Crystal Palace, June 6, 1896 ; A Greyport Legend, men's chorus, with solo bass, and orchestra ; anthems; madrigal, Lie down, poor heart ; Carmen Exoniense (Exeter College song); six songs, op. 1, in MS. Incidental music to Two Gentlemen of Verona (Oxford, 1893); to The Tempest (Oxford, January, 1894). Suite in D, for string orchestra ; in C minor, for military band ; Minuet, for small orchestra ; Romance in F, violin and orchestra ; in G, for violin, organ, and pf. Morning and evening service. Anthems, songs, etc.

Woodward, Edwin George, violinist, organist, and conductor, born at Bath, December 10, 1835. Was a chorister of Gloucester Cathedral, and studied the violin under G. Martin of that city, and harmony with J. Uglow, of Cheltenham. Resided in Gloucester many years as teacher, and organist of St. Mary's, St. John's, and All Saints', resigning the last in 1889. He still conducts the

WOODWARD.

Gloucester Orchestral Society, and has had other societies under his direction. Succeeded Henry Blagrove as leader of the old Cheltenham Philharmonic, an office he retained until the dissolution of the society. He has been a member of the Birmingham Festival Orchestra; is still member of the Three Choirs' Festival Orchestra; and leader of the Cheltenham Festival, Cardiff, Swansea, Newport, and other societies. He is a Mason, P.M., and organist, and has composed some music for Masonic service, church hymn-tunes, etc. Resident in Cheltenham.

Woodward, Rev. H. H., clergyman and composer, born at The Friars, near Liverpool, in 1847. Educated at Radley College, and Corpus Christi College, Oxford. Studied music under Rev. Dr. Hayne, Oxford. Spent a year and a half at Cuddesdon Theological College, and was ordained in the Diocese of Oxford, becoming curate and precentor of Wantage. Remained there eleven years, working as assistant priest under Dr. Butler, afterwards Dean of Lincoln. In 1881 he was appointed a minor canon of Worcester Cathedral, and in 1890 succeeded the Rev. E. V. Hall (*q.v.*), as precentor. From 1869 to the present time he has published a complete Morning, Evening, and Communion Service in E flat; a second in D; Communion Service (unison) in A; Te Deum in B flat. The Radiant Morn; The Sun shall be no more thy light; Behold, the days come; The souls of the righteous; Rejoice greatly; and other anthems, most of which have been much in use.

Woodward, Richard, organist and composer, born at Dublin, about 1744. He was made Bac. Mus., Dublin in 1768, and Doc. Mus. in 1771. Vicar-choral, St. Patrick's Cathedral, 1772. Organist of Christ Church Cathedral, 1765. Master of choristers, St. Patrick's and Christ Church Cathedrals. He died at Dublin, November 22, 1777. Composed "Cathedral Music in Score," op. 3. Anthems. "Songs, Catches, and Canons," n.d., etc.

Woodward, William Wolfgang, organist and conductor, born in 1822. He was organist of the Catholic Church, and conductor of the Choral Union, Derby. Died at Derby, August 4, 1882.

Woodyatt, Emily, soprano vocalist, who was born at Hereford in 1814. She appeared at many of the principal concerts of her time, in London and the provinces. Married Mr. William Loder, and retired.

Woolf, Sophia Julia, pianist and composer, born in London, 1831. Commenced learning music when five years old, and afterwards, upon the advice of Cipriani Potter, entered the R.A.M., 1846, becoming his pupil. Elected King's Scholar that year, and again in 1848, and on leaving was made

WORGAN.

an Associate, and later, elected a Fellow. Married a Mr. Isaacson. She composed pieces for pf., and songs; also a comic opera, "Carina," produced at the Opéra Comique, London, September 27, 1888. She died at West Hampstead, November 20, 1893. Potter's last letter was written to her.

Woolhouse, Wesley S. B., mathematician and writer on music, born at North Shields, May 6, 1809. He became Head Assistant on the Nautical Almanac Establishment, and while in that position published his "Essay on Musical Intervals, Harmonics, and the Temperament of the Musical Scale," London, Souter, 1835. Second edition, Charles Woolhouse, 1888, issued as "Treatise on musical intervals, temperament, and the elementary principles of music." Also author of "A Catechism of music," London, 1843; "Treatise on Singing," London, n.d. He also composed some instrumental music, and edited works by Spohr, Raff, etc. He was elected F.R.A.S. He made a fine collection of violins, and was a man of great scientific attainments. Died at Canonbury, London, August 12, 1893. His daughter, EMMA MAY, was a pianist, and married Dr. William Rea (*q.v.*); his son EDMUND is a violoncellist, of the Philharmonic and festival orchestras; and CHARLES is the well-known London music publisher.

Woolnoth, Charles Hall, pianist and composer, born at Glasgow, April 13, 1860. Son of Charles N. Woolnoth, a distinguished landscape painter. He studied under Reinecke and E. F. Richter in Germany, and John Farrar Howden (born, Leeds, 1818; died at Glasgow, December 25, 1875), in Glasgow, whose daughter he married. He was for many years an active figure in the musical life of Glasgow, but about 1891 he went to London, where he is a teacher and pianist. Composer of a cantata, "Il Penseroso"; "The skeleton in armour," choral ballad, Glasgow, 1889. Part-songs. Music for pf., etc.

Wordsworth, W. A., musician and teacher. He contributed papers to the Dramatic and Musical Review, 1842. Lectured in London on English composers, 1844-5. Died, January 25, 1846. Author of "Treatise on Singing, embodying with a course of initiatory exercises, a critical analysis of the principles of the art," London, 1837. Composer of some ballads, etc.

Worgan, George, musician, who was a grandson of Dr. John Worgan, was born in 1802. He went to New Zealand, and died at Wellington on April 2, 1888. He issued "Gems of sacred melody: a choice collection of psalm and hymn tunes," London, 1841. Songs and other works.

Worgan, John, organist and composer,

WORGAN.

born at London, 1724. He studied under Rosingrave and Geminiani. Organist and composer to Vauxhall Gardens, 1751-74. Organist of St. Andrew's, Undershaft, with St. Mary Axe, 1749; St. Botolph's, Aldgate, London, 1758; and St. John's Chapel, Great James Street, Bedford Row, 1760. Mus. Bac., Cantab., 1748. Mus, Doc., 1775. He died at London, August 24, 1790, and is buried in St. Andrew's, Undershaft.

WORKS.—*Oratorios :* Hannah, op. 1, 1764; Manasseh. Anthems. Hymns in Riley's collection. Agreeable Choice, a collection of songs, London [1760]; A collection of new songs and ballads, sung at Vauxhall, London, 1752, 1754, 1771, etc. Six canzonets for 2 and 3 voices, London [1785]; Three new English cantatas, 1750. *Songs and Duets :* Bright Phœbus, Cordelia, Hark! the loud drums, I fill not the glass, Jockey and Jenny, Neptune's resignation, Nun and Friar, Port and Sherry, The thief, To the nightingale, etc. Pieces for the harpsichord [1780]; Six sonatas for the harpsichord, London, 1769. Organ and other pieces.

His brother, JAMES WORGAN, born at London in 1715; died there in 1753, was also a composer. He wrote Sappho's Hymn to Venus, 1750; With beauteous Araminta ranging, and other songs, etc.

Worgan, Thomas Danvers, son of John Worgan, was born at London in 1774. He was a teacher and author in London. Brother-in-law of Sir William Parsons. Died at Croydon, in 1832. Author of "Rouge et noire de musique, or harmonic pastimes, being games of cards constructed on the principles of music," London, 1807; The Musical Reformer, comprising an apology for intellectual music, London, 1829; The composer or contrapuntist, with explanatory notes, London [1826]. Composer of Vocal Sonatinas, forming a coalition of vocal and instrumental harmony, 1820, issued in parts. The Heroe's welcome, a motet, comprising 45 parts, 1824. Songs, etc.

His brother, JOHN WORGAN, jun., composed marches for the pf., and Absence, Emma [1799], Soft downy sleep, and other songs. Other members of the family were MARY WORGAN, who composed a number of songs about 1750-60, and RICHARD WORGAN, who published a "Set of Sonnets, etc," in 1810.

Worrell, Marie, born DUVAL, soprano vocalist, born in London(?), March 3, 1856. Studied at R.A.M. Westmorland Scholar, 1875. A.R.A.M. Sang at concerts in Birmingham and elsewhere while still a student, and both in London and the provinces achieved much success as a concert vocalist. She died at Tulse Hill, London, February 12, 1895.

Wotton, William Bale, bassoonist, born at Torquay, September 6, 1832. Son of a

WRIGHT.

Corporal-major in the 1st Life Guards, he entered the band of the regiment when he was thirteen. Studied at R.A.M. under Chas. Lucas. Remained in the band of the Life Guards until 1866, when he joined the orchestra of the Crystal Palace. He is principal bassoon of the Philharmonic, and festival orchestras, and has played in chamber concerts in many places. He is professor of the bassoon at the R.A.M. and R.C.M. His sons, L. V. WOTTON and T. E. WOTTON, are both bassoon players of repute.

Woycke, Emmy Drechsler, violinist, daughter of Adam Hamilton (*q.v.*), was born at Edinburgh. Appeared at concerts as soloist from her eleventh year. Played at the Gewandhaus concerts, Leipzig (with her sister BERTHA, also a violinist), October 21, 1869. Is now an artist of repute in Edinburgh. In 1871 she was married to Herr EUGEN WOYCKE, a German composer and pianist, settled in Edinburgh. Their son, VICTOR WOYCKE, born in Edinburgh, in 1872, is a violinist. He was taught at home, and made his first appearance at a concert given by his parents, November 30, 1889. In 1892 he went to New York, where he is established as a soloist of the first rank; and where he was also professor of the violin at the National Conservatory of Music.

Wragg, J., flute player, composer, and writer, of end of last and early part of present century. Author of The Flute preceptor, or the whole art of playing the German flute. London [1790]; Improved Flute preceptor, or the whole art of playing the German Flute rendered perfectly easy without the aid of a master, op. 6. London, 1806. Oboe preceptor, 1792. These works went through several editions. He composed duets, solos, and other pieces for the flute; songs; arrangements and other works.

Wrenshall, C. L., pianist and composer. Studied under Henri Herz. For many years resided at Birkenhead as teacher. Died at Rock Ferry, near Birkenhead, at a great age, in November (?), 1892. He wrote a good deal of music for the pf., but it is now forgotten.

Wrenshall, William, an organist at Liverpool, was the composer of some anthems. He died in 1854.

Wright, Adam, organist and composer, born at Birmingham, August 5, 1810. Was for more than 40 years organist of Carr's Lane Chapel, Birmingham; now living in retirement at Erdington. He edited "The Congregational Tune-Book, a comprehensive collection of psalm and hymn tunes.." London, 1847. Sacred melodies for 4 voices [1855]. "Church Music"..1861. Hymns for Home [1868]. He composed many pf. pieces, marches, polkas, gavottes, up to op. 124; some part-songs; The Sanctus, harmonized;

WRIGHT.

and a cantata, "Phyllis," produced at Erdington Public Hall, May 29, 1888. Author of "Pianoforte Students' Daily Practice," London [1876].

Wright, Elizabeth, see ARNE, MICHAEL.

Wright, Ellen, song composer, born in London, daughter of an American engineer, George Riley. Married to Mr. Wright, solicitor, London. At first guided only by her natural talent, she began to compose, and her first songs were published in 1891. Afterwards she studied harmony with Henry Gadsby, and instrumentation under F. W. Davenport. Among the songs she has composed are: She walks in beauty; Queen of my days; Had I but known; Love's entreaty; set of six songs (poetry by Prior, Burns, etc.), sung by Mr. Santley at the Saturday Popular Concerts, March 10, 1894; Three songs, the same, December 1; The dawn of life (with orchestral accompaniment), and others.

Wright, Henry Smith, author of "An Introduction to the Study of Music, with historical and other references," London [1872], 3rd edition, 1882. Composer of part-songs, etc.

Wright, Thomas, organist and composer, born at Stockton-on-Tees, September 18, 1763. Assistant organist to Garth and Ebdon of Durham. Organist at Sedgefield, 1785-97: afterwards organist at Stockton in succession to his father, Robert Wright, an organist of some repute, 1797-1818. He died at Wycliffe Rectory, near Barnard Castle, November 24, 1829. Composer of "Rusticity," an operetta, 1800; Anthems, songs, and psalm tunes, "Stockton," etc. Fifth ode of the first book of Horace [1796]. Concerto for harpsichord or pf. and 2 violins, 2 obes, 2 horns, a tenor and bass [1795].

Wright, Thomas Henry, author of "New Preceptor for the Harp, including a series of exercises . . . and succeeded by preludes, and progressive lessons . . London, 1825; also 1835. Instructions for the harp, London [1866]. Composer of Fantasias and arrangements for the harp.

Wrighton, W. T., English composer, born in 1816. Died at Tunbridge Wells, July 13, 1880. He composed numerous popular songs, among which may be named Her bright smile haunts me still [1856]; Approach of Spring; A wish; April showers; Days gone by; Ever with thee; Faded Rose; My mother's name; Norah; Our English rose; Postman's knock [1855]; She sang among the flowers [1863]; You need na' come courting o' me; Shylie Bawn [1863], etc. With Henry Wolfgang Amadeus Beale he edited "Congregational Psalmody, a collection of ancient and modern tunes, chants and sentences . . " London [1858].

Wrigley, James Grimwood, organist, pianist, and conductor, born at Rochdale,

WRIGLEY.

April 16, 1849. Studied pf. under Thomas Ashworth, T. Mekin, and Ed. Dannreuther; organ and harmony under Henry Stevens and Dr. J. F. Bridge. F.R.C.O., 1873; Mus. B., Cambridge, 1878. Was the first organist of St. Mary's Balderstone (1871-3); then of Christ Church, Blackpool (1873-5); and for twenty years, from 1875, organist and choirmaster of the Parish Church, High Wycombe. Was conductor of the Blackpool Vocal Society, 1874-5; and is now conductor of the High Wycombe Choral Association, an appointment held since 1875, and of the Maidenhead Philharmonic Society, from 1879. The concerts given under his direction have been noted for the production of works by British composers. Mr. Wrigley has given organ recitals in many parts of the country, and appeared at the Bow and Bromley Institute in 1882; he is also known as a solo pianist. He has composed a setting of Ps. 23, for soli, chorus and orchestra; and published church music, songs, and part-songs.

His brother, WILLIAM ALFRED WRIGLEY, graduated Mus. B., Oxford, 1883. Has held the office of organist at St. Mary's Rochdale (1871); Christ Church, Manchester (1879); Holy Innocents', Fallowfield (1882); and of Todmorden Parish Church since 1884. His compositions include Ps. 46, for soli, chorus, and orchestra; part-songs, etc.

Wrigley, John, pianist, organist, composer, and vocalist, born at Ashton-under-Lyne, Lancashire, September 29, 1830. Received his first instruction in music from his father, who was organist of Ashton Parish Church. After some study under Richard H. Andrews and others, he entered the R.A.M. in 1849, studying composition under Cipriani Potter. In 1853 he was elected an Associate and in 1887 a fellow of R.A.M. Many years of his life were spent in Manchester, as a teacher and lecturer; he was also sometime organist of St. Saviour's Church, Chorlton-on-Medlock. He began his career as a composer in 1848, and gave a concert in 1849, before proceeding to the R.A.M.. Since 1876 he has been local examiner for R.A.M., and also R.C.M. since its foundation. He has been President of the Victoria Glee Club, and in 1890 was elected a Vice-President of the Manchester Vocal Union, which Society has performed his larger choral works. His pf. compositions have been played by F. Dawson and other distinguished pianists. He gave pf. recitals up to 1885, but of late years he has relinquished active work, remaining hon. local representative of R.A.M.

WORKS.—*Anthems:* Make a joyful noise; Holy, Holy, Holy; He brought down my strength (all for soli, quartet, and chorus, and performed in the Gentlemens' Concert Room, Manchester). Spring time, part-song;

WURM.

O, merry lark, glee; The lover's choice; O, give me music ; Ave Maria, and other songs. Jubilee march (performed at opening of Manchester Exhibition, 1887). Introduction and variations, Go bury thy sorrow, organ. *Pianoforte:* Sonata No. 1, in A (1870) ; No. 2, in G (1892) ; Grand waltz ; Sprites' Frolic ; Tarantella in A minor ; Allegretto grazioso in C ; Allegro de concert ; and other pieces.

Wurm, Marie J. A., pianist and composer, born at Southampton, May 18, 1860. Her father, J. E. Wurm, was a pianist and concert giver in that town. He died, 1892. Marie Wurm studied at the Stuttgart Conservatorium, and also with F. Taylor, Madame Schumann, J. Raff, and others. In 1884 she won the Mendelssohn Scholarship, and studied under Sir Arthur Sullivan, Drs. Stanford and J. F. Bridge. She played Schumann's pianoforte concerto at the Crystal Palace, November 11, 1882, and appeared at the Monday Popular Concerts in 1884. In this year she appeared at her father's concert, Southampton, with her sister Alice, also a pianist. She has given recitals in London, and played in Leipzig, Berlin, Meiningen, and other places with great success. Her compositions comprise a pf. concerto in B minor, and an overture (Berlin, 1887); String quartet in B flat, op. 40 (London, 1894) ; Sonata, pf. and violoncello ; Four pf. duets, op. 24 ; Pf. pieces, part-songs, and duets, etc. Her sister, MATHILDE WURM, is also a pianist of repute. She has given recitals in Steinway Hall, London ; Chamber concerts in Princes' Hall ; and played at the Saturday Popular Concerts (January, 1887), and elsewhere. In 1893 she adopted the name of Verne.

Wydow, or **Wedow, Robert,** clergyman and musician of the 15th century, was a native of Thaxted, in Essex. He was educated at Oxford, and became Mus. B. there, and at Cambridge in 1502. He was presented to the living of Thaxted by Edward IV. in 1481, and held it till 1489. In 1497 he succeeded Abyngdon as succentor of Wells Cathedral. He died in 1505.

Wylde, Henry, composer and writer, born at Bushey, Hertfordshire, in 1822. Son of Henry Wylde, gentleman in ordinary to George IV. He was organist of St. Ann's, Aldersgate Street, London, in 1844, and in 1852 he founded the New Philharmonic Society, at which he produced Liszt's " St. Elizabeth " in 1870, and other modern works. In 1871 he established the London Academy of Music. Mus. D., Cantab., 1851 (accumulated degrees). Gresham Professor of music in succession to Professor E. Taylor, 1863. Associate of R.A.M., etc. He died at London, March 13, 1890. Author of " Harmony, and the Science of Music," London, 1865 and 1872 ; " Music in its Art Mysteries," London,

WYNNE.

1867 ; "Modern Counterpoint in major keys," London, 1873 ; "Occult Principles of Music," 1881 ; " Music as an Educator..," 1882. Evolution of the Beautiful in Sound, Manchester, 1887. Composer of Praise and prayer, op. 14, and Paradise Lost (selections), 1850, cantatas ; a Pianoforte Concerto in F minor ; Sonatas for pf., op. 1 and 7 ; Rhapsody for pf., op. 2. Selection of Chants.., London [1864].

His brother, JAMES WYLDE, was a harpist in London.

Wynne, John, vocal composer, of the 18th century, composed, among other works, " Twelve English Songs," London [1750].

Wynne, Kate, contralto vocalist, sister of undernoted, was born at Holywell, Flintshire. Her countrymen gave her the title of *Llinos Gwynedd*—The Linnet of Wales. With her sister she has appeared at many concerts in London and the provinces. At St. George's Hall, the sisters introduced to a London audience John Thomas's cantata, " The Bride of Neath Valley," February 12, 1867. After her marriage with Mr. Henry Matthison, of Birmingham, she still sang a good deal in public, and was a great favourite in the Principality, receiving compliments from Lord Penrhyn and others. She retired from the profession about the year 1877.

Wynne, Sarah Edith, Eos CYMRU PENCERDDES, The Nightingale of Wales. Soprano vocalist, born at Holywell, Flintshire, March 11, 1842. Sang, at the age of nine, at a concert of the Holywell Philharmonic Society, and a few years later was placed under Mrs. Scarisbrick, of Liverpool. In 1862 (July 4), she made her first appearance in London, at a concert of Welsh music, given by Mr. John Thomas. About this time she entered the R.A.M., and in 1863 won the Westmorland Scholarship. Her reputation rapidly spread, and she was engaged for the principal concerts. In 1869 she studied for a short time under Romani, of Florence. She sang at the Birmingham Musical Festival of 1870, and afterwards at other like celebrations, and in 1871, visited America. From this time her career was an unbroken success. In 1872 she sang at a State concert, and, two years later, was the recipient of a flattering testimonial at the Hanover Square Rooms. A marble bust of herself was presented to her by Sir Watkin W. Wynn, and a diamond bracelet by Mr. Osborne Morgan. She was married to Mr. Aviet Agabeg at the Savoy Chapel Royal, November 16, 1875, since when her time has been chiefly devoted to tuition in singing, but she occasionally appeared in public, singing at St. James's Hall so late as July, 1894, and at Aberystwith in the summer of 1896. She had some little stage experience, singing in the first per-

WYVILL.

formance of Macfarren's "Jessie Lea," at the Gallery of Illustration, November 2, 1863; in "Maritana," and other English operas, at the Crystal Palace, from 1869, for a season or two. She also took part in the performance of the second part of King Henry IV, at Drury Lane in 1864, when she interpolated the Welsh song, "The Bells of Aberdovey." It was, however, in the simple ballad that her greatest charm was exercised. This eminent artist died suddenly in London, January 23, 1897.

Wyvill, Zerubbabel, composer and organist, born at Maidenhead, Berks., in 1763. He was a teacher of music at Maidenhead, and organist of the Chapel of St. Mary Magdalene and Andrew there. Resided at Inwood House, Hounslow, and was twice married. In 1828 he was involved in Chancery proceedings concerning the estate of his father-in-law. He died at Hounslow Middlesex, May 14, 1837.

Works.—A collection of psalms and hymns for four voices, London, n.d. A collection of catches and glees for 3 and 4 voices, London, n.d. Anthem, two hymns, and two dismissions, selected and composed for the General Thanksgiving, June 1, 1802. In this appears the well-known hymn tune "Eaton." Berkshire March, in 8 parts, London, 1793. Armed Yeoman, song [1795], etc.

His son Robert, born 1789; died at Maidenhead in August, 1869, was organist of St. Mary's Chapel there, and published a Collection of hymn tunes and chants; and "A second set of Hymns arranged for the pf. or organ," London, 1840.

Another musician of the name of J. Wyvill, composed "Friar John in his cell," an epigram, London [1780], and other vocal music.

Wyse, John, musician, issued "Music of the hymns, anthems, and litanies, intended for the use of the co-fraternities of La Salette, established in England," London, 1855.

Xiniwe, Paul, bass vocalist, and member of the South African Choir that visited Great Britain in 1891. He was educated at the Lovedale Institution, Cape Colony, has a fine bass voice, is remarkably intelligent, and acted as the spokesman of the choir, which sang by command before the Queen. While in England he obtained the Elementary and Intermediate Certificate of the Tonic Sol-fa College, and is now exercising his skill in his native district.

Yarwood, Joseph, composer and bass singer, born at Manchester, May 6, 1829. Composer of anthems Glees : Our jolly tars ; Merry boys at sea ; Town and trade ; Fill the goblet ; Hail to the woods ; Welcome brothers ; etc. Also polkas and other pf. music.

YOUNG.

Yates, William, composer, who flourished in the latter half of the 18th century. He wrote among other works a "Collection of moral songs or hymns, by I. Watts," London, 1769. "New musical address to the town on the opening of Marylebone Gardens," London [1763]; "Collection of songs sung at Vauxhall and Marylebone Gardens," London [1764]. *Songs :* Colin's address : Haughty Delia ; Tell-tale, etc. Six easy sonatas for harpsichord, op. 3 [1770].

Yonge, Nicholas, musician of the 16th and 17th centuries. Published "Musica Transalpina, madrigales translated, of 4, 5, and 6 parts, chosen out of divers excellent authors...." London, 1588. "Musica Transalpina, the second book of madrigales to 5 and 6 voices, translated out of sundry Italian authors....." London, 1597.

Youll, Henry, a composer of madrigals and other vocal music, who flourished at the end of the 16th and beginning of the 17th centuries. He issued "Canzonets to three voyces," London, 1608.

Young, Anne, *see* Gunn, Anne.

Young, Cecilia, *see sub.* Arne, Thomas A.

Young, Rev. Edward, author of "The Harp of God," twelve lectures on liturgical music, its import, history, present state and reformation," London, 1861. Composer of A morning and evening service, Te deum, jubilate, magnificat, and nunc dimittis, hymn tunes, etc.

Young, Harriet Maitland, composer, of the present time, who has written several operettas : "An Artist's Proof, produced Brighton, February 4, 1882 ; "The Queen of Hearts," Dartford, February 6, 1888.; "The Holly Branch," and "When one door shuts, another opens," produced at Bradford, November 28, 1896. Also composer of Tell me so ; A passing cloud, and other songs.

Young, Isabella (Mrs. Lampe), soprano vocalist, sister of Mrs. T. A. Arne, and daughter of Charles Young, organist of All Hallows, Barking. She sang at concerts, and after her marriage to Johann Friederich Lampe (1703-1751) she sang on the stage in works by her husband and others.

Young, John Matthew Wilson, organist and composer, born at Durham, December 17, 1822. Was principal solo boy in the cathedral choir; pupil of Dr. Henshaw, and afterwards his assistant. For six years he was music-master at the York and Ripon Training College. In 1850 he was appointed organist of Lincoln Cathedral. When the Peterborough and Lincoln "Oratorio Festival" was established, in 1888, Mr. Young was joint conductor with the organist of Peterborough Cathedral, the first Lincoln Festival occurring June 19, 1889. After holding his appointment at Lincoln Cathedral for 45 years, he retired in

YOUNG.

1895, and removed to London. He died at West Norwood, March 4, 1897. His works include a sacred cantata, "The Return of Israel to Palestine," produced at the Lincoln Festival, June 15, 1892 ; "I will extol my God," and other anthems ; a Festival Service in C : Morning Service in D ; several settings of the Te Deum, and other Church music.

Young, Mary, MRS. BARTHELEMON, soprano vocalist, was born about 1745. She was taught singing in London, and appeared at Drury Lane in "The Spring," pastoral, in 1762. In 1766 she married F. H. Barthelemon, the French violinist and composer. She was the original Nysa in O'Hara's "Midas." Died September 20, 1799.

Young, Rev. Matthew, clergyman and musician, born at Roscommon, 1750. Died in 1800. Author of "Inquiry into the principal phenomena of sounds and musical strings," London, 1784.

Young, William James, organist and composer, brother of J. M. W. Young, born at Durham, April 18, 1835. Chorister, Durham Cathedral, 1843. From 1852 studied under his brother at Lincoln ; assistant organist, Lincoln Cathedral, 1857-8. Organist of St. John's, Longsight, Manchester, 1858-71 ; St. Peter's, Levenshulme, 1871-80; St. James', Birch-in-Rusholme, 1880 ; and St. Elizabeth's, Reddish Green, near Stockport, 1895. Composer of a large number of part-songs, Gaily thro' the greenwood ; I love the merry springtime; Hail! merry christmas ; O, welcome, merry May, etc., most of which have been widely popular. He has also composed some songs, "The Winter King" (with orchestra) ; and marches for orchestra which have been performed at Manchester, Scarborough Spa, etc.

ZUCCHELLI.

Younger, Montague, organist, born at Sydney, New South Wales. Pupil of C. S. Packer. Has been organist of St. Andrew's Anglican Cathedral, Sydney, since 1868. Conducted a performance of Benedict's "St. Peter" (the first in Australia), at the Sydney International Exhibition, April 10, 1880.

Zerbini, John Baptist, violinist and pianist, son of an Italian musician (J. B. Zerbini, member of the London Philharmonic orchestra, died December 27, 1889), was born in London in 1839. He began his career in the band at Drury Lane when he was seventeen, and in 1867 joined Mr. Chappell's string quartet at the Popular Concerts as viola player, and also as pianoforte accompanist. He married Anna Patey, who was for a long time amanuensis and secretary to the eminent geologist, Sir Charles Lyell. His wife died in June, 1884, and Zerbini, in failing health, went to Australia. He soon established himself as a teacher of repute; directed Chamber concerts at Victoria, in 1887; and died at Melbourne, November 28, 1891. He was a man of quiet, unassuming manners, an excellent accompanist, and a good all-round musician.

His brother, LEANDER, a native of London, was a vocalist and composer.

Zotti, Carlo, see CROAL, GEORGE.

Zucchelli, Carlo, bass singer, born at London, of Italian parents, January 28, 1793. In 1814 he sang at Novara, and afterwards sang in other Italian towns till 1818. He made his *début* at the King's Theatre in April, 1822, and also appeared at the Ancient Concerts. He sang in Paris in 1825, and other continental towns. He died at Bologna, in February, 1879.

APPENDIX.

ADDITIONS AND CORRECTIONS.

Albertazzi, Emma, page 5. *Correct to—*
Died September 25, 1847.

Allon, Henry Erskine, page 8. *Add—*
Cantata, "Oak of Geismar" was produced
by the Highbury Philharmonic, January 26,
1897. After undergoing an operation for
abscess, Allon died suddenly at London, April
3, 1897, aged 32.

Alquin, F. C. d', page 9. *Should be—*
ALQUEN.

Anne, Susanna Maria, page 13, *should
be* ARNE.

Beale, Thurley, page 36. *Add—*Died in
London, May 5, 1897.

Bennett, Sir W. S., page 42. *Correct
from line* 7 *of notice to—*He resided at Leipzig,
1836-7, at the suggestion and expense of the
firm of Broadwood and Sons, in order that he
might gain experience, and profit by the
influence and companionship of Mendelssohn
and other great artists.

Best, W. T., page 44. *Add date of
death—*May 10, 1897.

Bowling, page 55. *Correct year of birth—*
John Bowling, to 1817. *Date of death—*
J. O. Bowling, to July 10, 1886.

Bridge, J. F., page 60. *Add—*Knighted
by Queen Victoria, in June, 1897. *Additional
Works—*"The Flag of England" (Rudyard
Kipling), for soprano solo, chorus, and orchestra, produced, Royal Albert Hall, May 6,
1897.

Buswell, John, page 72. *Add—*He was
a Gentleman of the Chapel Royal, and died
November 14, 1763.

Carr, Frank O., page 79. *Add—*Born
near Bradford, April 23, 1858.

Corfe, John Davis, organist, born at
Salisbury, in 1804. Son of Arthur Thomas
Corfe. He was for more than half a century
organist of Bristol Cathedral, and conductor
of the Bristol Madrigal Society for many
years. He died at Bristol, January 23, 1876.

Culwick, James C., p. 111. *Add to
Works—*Overture for orchestra, prize, "Feis
Ceoil," Dublin, May, 1897.

Flower, Sara, contralto, p. 148. The
date of birth, February 22, 1805, is that of
the Sarah Flower of the preceding paragraph.
The singer made her *début*, when a young
girl, at Drury Lane, January 7, 1843, in an
English version of "La Gazza Ladra." She
had been a student at the R.A.M.

Gadsby, H. R., p. 154. *Add to Works—*
Concerto for organ and orchestra, produced,
Crystal Palace, January 24, 1874.

Garrett, G. M., p. 156. *Add—*After a
long illness, he died at Cambridge in the night
of April 8, 1897.

McGuckin, Barton, p. 262. After Theatre
Royal, *add* Birmingham.

Mann, Arthur H., p. 269. *Add—*He
was appointed organist to the University of
Cambridge, May, 1897, in succession to the
late Dr. Garrett.

Martin, Dr. C. G., p. 273. *Add—*Knighted
by Queen Victoria in 1897.

Parry, C. H. H., p. 310. *Add to Works—*
Theme and variations, orchestra, produced
Philharmonic Society, June 3, 1879.

Stanford, Charles V., p. 389. *Add—*
Appointed Conductor of Leeds Philharmonic
Society, June, 1897.

DERBY:
PRINTED BY CHADFIELD & SON, LTD., "FRIARY WORKS."
1897.